ΕΑRLY CHRISTIAN MISSION

VOLUME ONE

JESUS AND THE TWELVE

ECKHARD J. SCHNABEL

InterVarsity Press
Downers Grove, Illinois

Apollos
Leicester, England

InterVarsity Press, USA
P.O. Box 1400, Downers Grove, IL 60515-1426, USA
World Wide Web: www.ivpress.com
E-mail: mail@ivpress.com

APOLLOS (an imprint of Inter-Varsity Press, England)
38 De Montfort Street, Leicester LE1 7GP, England
Website: www.ivpbooks.com
E-mail: ivp@uccf.org.uk

English translation, revision and expansion ©2004 by Eckhard J. Schnabel. Original German edition published as Urchristliche Mission *by Eckhard J. Schnabel, ©2002 R. Brockhaus Verlag, Wuppertal.*

InterVarsity Press®*, U.S.A., is the book-publishing division of InterVarsity Christian Fellowship/USA*®*, a student movement active on campus at hundreds of universities, colleges and schools of nursing in the United States of America, and a member movement of the International Fellowship of Evangelical Students. For information about local and regional activities, write Public Relations Dept., InterVarsity Christian Fellowship/USA, 6400 Schroeder Rd., P.O. Box 7895, Madison, WI 53707-7895, or visit the IVCF website at* <www.intervarsity.org>.

Design: Cindy Kiple

Images: Monastery Icons

USA ISBN 0-8308-2791-9
UK ISBN 1-84474-045-3

Printed in the United States of America ∞

Library of Congress Cataloging-in-Publication Data

Schnabel, Eckhard J.
  Early Christian mission/Eckhard J. Schnabel.
     p. cm.
  Includes bibliographical references and index.
  ISBN 0-8308-2791-9 (v. 1: hardcover: alk. paper)
  1. Missions—History—Early church, ca. 30-600. I. Title.
  BR165.S3585 2004
  266'.009'015—dc22

                                                                    2004017281

British Library Cataloguing in Publication Data

A catalogue record for this book is available from the British Library.

| **P** | 18 | 17 | 16 | 15 | 14 | 13 | 12 | 11 | 10 | 9 | 8 | 7 | 6 | 5 | 4 | 3 | 2 | 1 |
| **Y** | 18 | 17 | 16 | 15 | 14 | 13 | 12 | 11 | 10 | 09 | 08 | 07 | 06 | 05 | 04 | | | |

For

Barbara,

Mirjam and Benjamin

CONTENTS OF VOLUME 1

PART III: BEGINNINGS
The Mission of the Apostles in Jerusalem

PART IV: EXODUS
The Mission of the Twelve from Jerusalem to the Ends of the Earth

OUTLINE OF VOLUMES 1 & 2

Volume 1: Jesus and the Twelve

INTRODUCTION

1. THE HISTORY OF EARLY CHRISTIANITY AS HISTORY OF MISSIONS

2. QUESTIONS AND ISSUES OF METHOD

    2.1. Historical and Theological Questions

    2.2. Methodological Considerations

        Relevant and Extraneous Statements of the Questions

        Hermeneutical Presuppositions

        The Sources

    2.3. The Semantic Field of "Mission"

3. CHRONOLOGY AND EVENTS

PART I: PROMISE
Israel's Eschatological Expectations and Jewish Expansion in the Second Temple Period

4. THE REALITY AND THE WORK OF YAHWEH THE CREATOR

    4.1. Creation and History

    4.2. Particularism and Internationalism

    4.3. The Promise of Genesis 12:3

5. THE RELATIONSHIP BETWEEN ISRAEL, ISRAELITES AND GENTILES

    5.1. The Evidence in the Mosaic Law

    5.2. The Evidence in Historical Texts

    5.3. The Evidence in the Psalms

    5.4. The Evidence in Prophetic Texts

        Isaiah

        Joel

        Jonah

        Micah

        Malachi

    5.5. Conclusions

Oral Communication
Public Speech
Synagogues
Associations
Schools
Mystery Cults

19. THE HELLENISTIC JEWISH CHRISTIANS IN JERUSALEM

19.1. Stephen and His Friends
19.2. Theological Insights
19.3. Implications for Missionary Work

20. THE FIRST TRANSREGIONAL MISSION OF JEWISH CHRISTIANS FROM JERUSALEM

20.1. The Death of Stephen and Its Consequences
20.2. Missionary Work in Samaria by Philip
20.3. The Conversion of the Royal Official from Ethiopia
20.4. Missionary Work in the Cities of the Coastal Plain
20.5. Christians in Damascus

21. THE MISSIONARY WORK OF PETER

21.1. The Missionary Work in Judea, Galilee and the Cities of the Coastal Plain
        Sermon in Solomon's Portico
        Speech Before the Sanhedrin I
        Speech Before the Sanhedrin II
        Missionary Travels
21.2. The Vision of Peter in Joppa
21.3. Missionary Work in Caesarea
21.4. Missionary Work After A.D. 41

22. THE JEWISH-CHRISTIAN MISSIONARY WORK FROM JERUSALEM TO ROME

22.1. Missionary Work in Jerusalem and Judea
        Jerusalem
        The Successors of James
        Judea
22.2. Missionary Work in Galilee and in Gaulanitis
        Missionary Churches
        Capernaum
        Bethsaida
        Cana

Volume 2: Paul and the Early Church

PART VI: GROWTH

Consolidation and Challenges of the Early Christian Churches

PREFACE

The road from Jerusalem to Europe is a long one, and the journey to North America is even longer. The distance increases when we think of Jerusalem as the capital of Judea in the first century A.D., called *Hierosolyma* by the Romans, controlled by a Roman governor in Caesarea Maritima. Jerusalem was the city where the first Christian community came into existence, the "mother church" of all Christian churches and denominations. Jerusalem was the city where the early Christian missionary movement arose that led to the international expansion of faith in Jesus of Nazareth as Messiah and Lord.

Missiologists, missionaries and representatives of missionary societies seek to promote interest in crosscultural dialogue and witness and to encourage and develop the involvement of Christians, young and old, in active outreach to non-Christians. As laudable as these endeavors are, their proponents have not always sought to provide exegetical explanations or to engage in theological discussion when presenting models for missionary work and paradigms for effective evangelism. Tite Tiénou, missionary theologian and dean of Trinity Evangelical Divinity School, has deplored such a lack of exegetical foundation and theological sophistication in regard to the widely popular writings of Don Richardson. This is but one example. Typically, understanding among evangelicals about the early Christian period and about the endeavors of the earliest Christians is, more often than not, unconsidered, and sometimes naive or romanticized.

Views that fail to take into account the historical and social conditions of life in the first century are potentially problematic. For example, the view that the early Christians recognized the significance of "small groups" or of "house churches" fails to recognize the fact that outside of local synagogues Christians had no other option but to meet in private homes whose largest rooms could accommodate about forty people. Another example is the view, naive despite the notice in Acts 4:32, that the early Christians were a united group of activists, uniform in their theology and thick as thieves in their relationships, who were willing and eager to subordinate differences of opinion and behavior to the missionary mandate. This view fails to recognize, for example, that the conflict whose solution is recorded in Acts 15 evidently was not supported by all missionaries based in Jerusalem, or that Paul was willing to separate from missionary coworkers as a result of differences of opinion, or that churches recently established by Paul were visited by Jewish-Christian missionaries whose goal was to influence them theologically and institutionally. Or note the romantic view that the organization of the early Christian missionary work among non-Jews corresponds, at least in general terms, to the foreign missions endeavors of one's denomination or missionary society. Before we can develop "lessons" for Christians today, we need to heed the facts as they present themselves in the New Testament. As far as mission and evangelism are concerned, this has not always happened.

The last full study of the early Christian missionary movement was published just over a century ago. Adolf von Harnack's classic work *The Mission and Expansion of Christianity in the First Three Centuries* was first published in Germany in 1902 and translated into English in 1904. Compared with Harnack's thousand-page study, Ferdinand Hahn's *Habilitationsschrift* with the title *Mission in the New Testament* (German edition 1963, English translation 1965) is a slim volume that seeks to show "the basic problems as well as the connecting links in the New Testament view of the Christian mission." A more popular study by Michael Green, *Evangelism in the Early Church* (1970), focuses on the processes of preaching the gospel. Due to Green's thematic approach it is next to impossible to trace historical developments in the early church. Moreover, like Harnack, he does not focus on earliest Christianity in the first century but includes facts and factors until the time of Constantine in the fourth century. The recent work by Wolfgang Reinbold entitled *Propaganda und Mission im ältesten Christentum* (2000) discusses the modalities of the expansion of the early church; geographical and theological questions are largely ignored. Reinbold's view that missionaries played no major role in the first or second century is as misguided as his opinion that Paul did not try to win Jews to faith in the gospel of Jesus Christ. A new study by Peter O'Brien and Andreas Köstenberger, *Salvation to the Ends of the Earth* (2001), provides a very helpful exegetical and literary survey of the missionary theology of the New Testament authors but hardly touches on historical or geographical issues.

There is an obvious need for an exhaustive study that integrates old and new insights and both historical-geographical and exegetical-theological material into a comprehensive description of the missionary movement of the first Christians. Theological studies in general and New Testament studies in particular witness constantly increasing specialization and immense growth in the production of secondary literature. I am convinced that consistent reflection upon the basic convictions and upon the praxis of the earliest Christians is more important than ever. The question is, of course, whether it is possible for one individual to write a history of the early Christian missionary movement. The increasing number of integrated studies on early Christian history, on the history of early Christian theology and on the theology of the New Testament demonstrates that such an endeavor should be possible. In view of the disagreements concerning numerous exegetical and historical questions, one might be tempted to wait until there is a broader consensus on more issues relevant for a description of the history of the early church and its expansion. However, scholarly consensus is never a criterion for historical truth in and of itself. And in light of the continuing flood of critical studies, the ongoing hermeneutical discussion about exegetical methods, and the perpetual disputes over the proper evaluation of relevant historical and theological questions, waiting for a larger consensus may simply indicate a lack of courage to attempt a synthesis. Anyone who presents and comments on numerous and diverse historical, exegetical and theological subjects that in many cases deserve comprehensive scholarly treatment risks the danger of neglecting this or that perspective, point or proposition. But there is also the danger of too much awe of specialists, which makes syntheses impossible—syntheses that we need if we want to understand historical developments, theological convictions and individual behavior. Scholars need to attempt comprehensive descriptions of the history and proclamation of Jesus and of the early church so that the church that carries the name of Jesus Christ and accepts the witness of the apostles as normative criterion of faith and practice may render an account of its identity, purpose and goals. In order to accomplish this task in a somewhat satisfactory manner, we need to engage in the detailed and painstaking presentation that characterizes academic discussion and demands patience from the reader. For those readers who look for easy and quick answers, such patience amounts to long-suffering.

One reason for the length of this book is that I do not want simply to offer the results of my research or my own opinions. Rather, I seek to document primary source material and present both sides of controversial discussions, allowing the reader to come to his or her own informed conclusions. I fully appreciate the apprehension of Eduard Norden when he wrote in the preface of his monumental study *Die antike Kunstprosa* (2 vols.; Stuttgart, 1909, 1:vii), "The only troublesome factor that accompanied the joy of searching and finding was the fear of the μέγα βιβλίον [large book]." (This allusion to Callimachus's well-known aphorism "A great book is like great evil," μέγα βιβλίον μέγα κακόν [R. Pfeiffer, *Callimachus: Fragmenta*, frg. 465], must be understood in proper context. The poet from Cyrene criticizes his student Apollonius of Rhodos, who wanted to revive the classical Greek epic with his work *Argonautika*. In other words, Callimachus did not issue a blanket criticism of every large book.) I have written this book with the conviction that the last century of scholarly investigation of the faith and the history of the first Christians, the discovery of new primary sources, and contemporary explorations of old sources have yielded insights that make a new comprehensive study of the history of the missionary work of the early church a worthwhile endeavor. Whether this study is in fact what it is meant to be remains for the reader to determine—ἡμεῖς δὲ οὐκ εἰς τὰ ἄμετρα καυχησόμεθα (2 Cor 10:13).

It is my hope this study will be read not only by scholars and students but also by pastors, missionaries and evangelists and by everyone who looks for detailed and reliable information about the geographical expansion of the early church. This explains why primary sources are not simply cited but are quoted verbatim. Gerd Theissen perceptively emphasizes that one should not "succumb to the academic tendency to confuse profundity with a lack of clarity" if one seeks to reach readers beyond scholarly circles (Gerd Theissen and Annette Merz, *The Historical Jesus: A Comprehensive Guide* [Minneapolis: Fortress, 1998], viii).

In regard to technical details, four remarks are pertinent. First, when quoting secondary literature listed in the general bibliography, I follow the format of citing the name of the author and the date of publication. This helps to keep the footnotes brief. When I cite literature for very specialized matters not listed in the general bibliography, I give full bibliographical details in the footnotes. Commentaries are referred to by citing the name of the author and the title (sometimes abbreviated) of the biblical book (e.g., Jervell, *Apg,* for Jacob Jervell, *Die Apostelgeschichte*); full bibliographical details can be found in the commentary bibliography. Bibliographical details for primary sources and general resources are also listed in a separate bibliography; they are cited by name of the author and short title. Second, in regard to ancient cities that are mentioned, one should consult the *Barrington Atlas of the Greek and Roman World;* in its map-by-map directory one can find the identifications with modern place names. In regard to Judea, Samaria and Galilee, one should consult, in the Tabula Imperii Romani, *Iudaea-Palaestina* with its accompanying gazetteer. The *Tübinger Atlas des Vorderen Orients* provides excellent maps relevant for biblical studies, now readily available in the *Tübingen Bible Atlas.* The spelling of ancient names is a notorious problem; even the venerable *Oxford Classical Dictionary* is not consistent in the preference of Latin forms. I have attempted to preserve the Greek form of Greek personal and geographical names and the Latin form of Roman names and cities, although in both cases I often have retained traditionally familiar forms (e.g., Corinth not Korinthos, Colossae not Kolossai; one exception is the use of Antiocheia for [Pisidian] Antioch in Phrygia, while Antioch is used for [Syrian] Antiocheia on the Orontes). Consistency has not been routinely achieved; for example, the Greek kings of Egypt are called Ptolemy, while the Greek geographer is referred to as Ptolemaios. Third, the transliteration of Hebrew and Greek terms follows, with some exceptions, the *SBL Handbook of Style* (Peabody, Mass., 1999). For the uninitiated, the following information on Hebrew transliteration may be helpful: ' stands for *alef,* ' for *ayin; ḥ* is pronounced similarly to Spanish *j* (or as in German *doch*), ṣ as in *tsar,* ś as in *son,* š as in *shift;* a circumflex (e.g., *ê*) over a vowel indicates the presence of *yod* or *nun* or final *he;* a macron (e.g., *ā*) indicates a long vowel, while a breve (e.g., *ă*) indicates a short vowel. Fourth, unless otherwise noted, biblical quotations are from the New Revised Standard Version.

The original version of this book was published in October 2002 by R. Brockhaus Verlag under the title *Urchristliche Mission*. This English edition corrects mistakes, revises some arguments and expands the information at several points. The origins of the present study date back to lectures on aspects of the missionary work of the early church held in 1990 at the Freie Theologische Akademie in Giessen, Germany. Since 1998 I have discussed the history of the expansion of the early church in apostolic times regularly in doctoral seminars at Trinity Evangelical Divinity School in Deerfield, Illinois. I thank all the students who challenged my thinking through their engagement, critical interaction and response papers. I thank my colleagues in the New Testament department at Trinity Evangelical Divinity School for their interest and encouragement: Don Carson, Grant Osborne, David Pao and Robert Yarbrough. I express my sincere thanks to the student assistants who helped with bibliography, proofreading and compiling the indexes, especially Patrick Egan. I thank Zachry Kincaid, Robert G. Maccini and especially Daniel G. Reid from InterVarsity Press for very competent editorial help. I thank the staff of Rolfing Library for their aid in procuring literature from other libraries. The Vaughn Foundation and Trinity Evangelical Divinity School helped finance a research trip to Turkey and Greece in the summer of 2000; I thank Gregory L. Waybright and W. Bingham Hunter for their assistance, and I thank Roy Christians, my doctoral student, for his help and support between Adana and Athens. This large manuscript was written with Nota Bene Lingua Workstation, a superb word-processing and research tool whose power and flexibility continue to amaze; I thank Steve Siebert and his staff in technical support in New York for advice and assistance. And I will always be grateful to Dave Bucknam for introducing me to the joys of marathon running which allows for the heightened experience of the interplay of body, soul and spirit on trails in the countryside and on roads in cities. Most importantly, I thank my wife, Barbara, for her unfailing love and cheerful dedication and fellowship; her life in the years after her severe stroke was at least as difficult and challenging as the circumstances in which the early Christian missionaries proved themselves to be faithful and courageous. Her life is an example of Christian fortitude, consistent discipline and tenacious joy. I dedicate this book to her and our children, who moved with us "from place to place"—from Aberdeen in Scotland, to Manila in the Philippines, to Bergneustadt and Giessen in Germany and to Chicago in the United States—and who found that believers in Jesus Christ are "at home" no matter where they live, as there are Christians in all nations, even to the ends of the earth.

ABBREVIATIONS

AA	*Archäologischer Anzeiger*
AAA	*Athens Annals of Archaeology*
AASF	Annales academiae scientiarum fennicae
AASFDHL	Annales academiae scientiarum fennicae: Dissertationes humanarum litterarum
AAWGPHK	Abhandlungen der Akademie der Wissenschaften in Göttingen: Philologisch-historische Klasse
ABD	*Anchor Bible Dictionary*. Edited by D. N. Freedman
AE	*L'Année épigraphique*
AGAJU	Arbeiten zur Geschichte des antiken Judentums und des Urchristentums
AGSU	Arbeiten zur Geschichte des Spätjudentums und Urchristentums
AJA	*American Journal of Archaeology*
AJP	*American Journal of Philology*
AJT	*Asia Journal of Theology*
ALGHJ	Arbeiten zur Literatur und Geschichte des hellenistischen Judentums
AMSt	Asia Minor Studien
AnBib	Analecta Biblica
AncB	Anchor Bible
AncBRL	Anchor Bible Reference Library
ANET	*Ancient Near Eastern Texts Relating to the Old Testament*. Edited by J. B. Pritchard
ANRW	*Aufstieg und Niedergang der römischen Welt*. Edited by W. Haase and H. Temporini
AnSt	*Anatolian Studies*
ANTJ	Arbeiten zum Neuen Testament und Judentum
ANTZ	Arbeiten zur neutestamentlichen Theologie und Zeitgeschichte
APAT	*Die Apokryphen und Pseudepigraphen des Alten Testaments*. Edited by E. Kautzsch
APF	*Archiv für Papyrusforschung*
APOT	*The Apocrypha and Pseudepigrapha of the Old Testament*. Edited by R. H. Charles
AramBib	The Aramaic Bible
ASNU	Acta seminarii neotestamentici upsaliensis
ATD	Das Alte Testament Deutsch
AThANT	Abhandlungen zur Theologie des Alten und Neuen Testaments
AThJ	*Africa Theological Journal*
AThR	*Anglican Theological Review*

AThRSup	Anglican Theological Review Supplements
AzTh	Arbeiten zur Theologie
BA	*Biblical Archaeologist*
BAA	W. Bauer, *Griechisch-deutsches Wörterbuch zu den Schriften des Neuen Testaments und der frühchristlichen Literatur.* Edited by Kurt Aland and Barbara Aland
BAGD	W. Bauer, W. F. Arndt, F. W. Gingrich, F. W. Danker, *A Greek-English Lexicon of the New Testament and Other Early Christian Literature*
BAGRW	*Barrington Atlas of the Greek and Roman World.* Edited by R. J. A. Talbert
BAR	*Biblical Archaeology Review*
BASOR	*Bulletin of the American Schools of Oriental Research*
BBB	Bonner biblische Beiträge
BBR	*Bulletin for Biblical Research*
BCH	*Bulletin de correspondance hellénique*
BDAG	W. Bauer, F. W. Danker, W. F. Arndt and F. W. Gingrich, *A Greek-English Lexicon of the New Testament and Other Early Christian Literature.* 3rd ed.
BDR	*Grammatik des neutestamentlichen Griechisch.* Edited by F. Blass, A. Debrunner and F. Rehkopf
BECNT	Baker Exegetical Commentary on the New Testament
BEFEO	*Bulletin de l'École Française d'extreme d'Orient*
Begs.	*The Beginnings of Christianity: Part 1, The Acts of the Apostles.* Edited by F. J. Foakes-Jackson and K. Lake
BeO	*Bibbia e oriente*
BETL	Bibliotheca Ephemeridum Theologicarum Lovaniensium
BevTh	Beiträge zur evangelischen Theologie
BFChTh	Beiträge zur Förderung christlicher Theologie
BGL	Bibliothek der griechischen Literatur
BHG	*Bibliotheca hagiographica Graece*
BHH	*Biblisch-historisches Handwörterbuch: Landeskunde, Geschichte, Religion, Kultur.* Edited by B. Reicke and L. Rost.
BHTh	Beiträge zur historischen Theologie
Bib	*Biblica*
BJRL	*Bulletin of the John Rylands Library*
BJS	Brown Judaic Studies
BKAT	Biblischer Kommentar, Altes Testament
BNot	*Biblische Notizen*
BNTC	Black's New Testament Commentaries
BRev	*Bible Review*
BSac	*Bibliotheca sacra*

BTAVO	Beihefte zum Tübinger Atlas des Vorderen Orients
BTB	*Biblical Theology Bulletin*
BThS	Biblisch-theologische Schwerpunkte
BThSt	Biblisch-theologische Studien
BU	Biblische Untersuchungen
BWANT	Beiträge zur Wissenschaft vom Alten und Neuen Testament
BZ	*Biblische Zeitschrift*
BZAW	Beihefte zur Zeitschrift für die alttestamentliche Wissenschaft
BZNW	Beihefte zur Zeitschrift für die neutestamentliche Wissenschaft
CaE	*Cahiers évangile*
CAH	*Cambridge Ancient History*
CBET	Contributions to Biblical Exegesis and Theology
CBQ	*Catholic Biblical Quarterly*
CCIS	*Corpus Cultus Iovis Sabazii.* Edited by M. J. Vermaseren and E. N. Lane
CCSA	Corpus Christianorum: Series apocryphorum
CCSG	Corpus Christianorum: Series graeca
CCSL	Corpus Christianorum: Series latina
CGTC	Cambridge Greek Testament Commentary
CHI	*Cambridge History of Iran,* vol. 3. Edited by E. Yarshater
CHJ	*The Cambridge History of Judaism.* Edited by W. D. Davies et al.
CIG	*Corpus inscriptionum graecarum.* Edited by A. Böckh
CIJ	*Corpus inscriptionum judaicarum.* Edited by J. B. Frey
CIL	*Corpus inscriptionum latinarum*
CIRB	*Corpus Inscriptionum Regni Bosporani.* Edited by V. V. Struve
CIS	*Corpus inscriptionum semiticarum*
CJ	*Classical Journal*
CJT	*Canadian Journal of Theology*
CMRDM	*Corpus Monumentorum Religionis Dei Menis.* Edited by E. N. Lane
ConBNT	Coniectanea biblica: New Testament Series
ConBOT	Coniectanea biblica: Old Testament Series
CPJ	*Corpus papyrorum judaicarum.* Edited by V. Tcherikover and A. Fuks
CRAI	*Comptes rendus de l'Académie des inscriptions et belles-lettres*
CRINT	Compendium rerum iudaicarum ad Novum Testamentum
CSCO	Corpus scriptorum christianorum orientalium.
CSEL	Corpus scriptorum ecclesiasticorum latinorum
CSHJ	Chicago Studies in the History of Judaism
CTQ	*Concordia Theological Quarterly*
CurTM	*Currents in Theology and Mission*
DBSup	*Dictionnaire de la Bible: Supplément.* Edited by L. Pirot and A. Robert

DCPP	*Dictionnaire de la civilisation phénicienne et punique.* Edited by E. Lipinski
DDD	*Dictionary of Deities and Demons in the Bible.* Edited by K. van der Toorn et al.
DF	*Donateurs et fondateurs dans les synagogues juives.* Edited by B. Lifshitz
DJD	*Discoveries in the Judaean Desert [of Jordan]*
DJG	*Dictionary of Jesus and the Gospels.* Edited by J. B. Green, S. McKnight and I. H. Marshall
DLNTD	*Dictionary of the Later New Testament and Its Developments.* Edited by P. H. Davids and R. P. Martin
DNP	*Der Neue Pauly: Enzyklopädie der Antike.* Edited by H. Cancik and H. Schneider
DNTB	*Dictionary of New Testament Background.* Edited by C. A. Evans and S. E. Porter
DPL	*Dictionary of Paul and His Letters.* Edited by G. F. Hawthorne, R. P. Martin and D. G. Reid
DSSSE	*The Dead Sea Scrolls Study Edition.* Edited by F. García Martínez and J. C. E. Tigchelaar
EA	*Epigraphica Anatolica*
EAEHL	*Encyclopedia of Archaeological Excavations in the Holy Land.* Edited by M. Avi-Yonah and E. Stern
EBC	Expositor's Bible Commentary
EdF	Erträge der Forschung
EDNT	*Exegetical Dictionary of the New Testament.* Edited by H. Balz and G. Schneider
EDSS	*Encyclopedia of the Dead Sea Scrolls.* Edited by L. H. Schiffman and J. C. VanderKam
EHS	Europäische Hochschulschriften
EKK	Evangelisch-Katholischer Kommentar
EKL	*Evangelisches Kirchenlexikon.* Edited by E. Fahlbusch et al.
EMZ	*Evangelische Missionszeitschrift*
EncJud	*Encyclopaedia Judaica*
EPRO	Études préliminaires aux religions orientales dans l'empire romain
ESV	English Standard Version
ET	English translation
ETAM	Ergänzungsbände zu den Tituli Asiae Minoris
ETL	*Ephemerides theologicae lovanienses*
EÜ	Einheitsübersetzung
EvJ	*Evangelical Journal*
EvQ	*Evangelical Quarterly*

EvRT	*Evangelical Review of Theology*
EvTh	*Evangelische Theologie*
EWNT	*Exegetisches Wörterbuch zum Neuen Testament*. Edited by H. Balz and G. Schneider
ExpTim	*Expository Times*
FB	Forschung zur Bibel
FGrH	*Die Fragmente der griechischen Historiker*. Edited by F. Jacoby
FKDG	Forschungen zur Kirchen- und Dogmengeschichte
FRLANT	Forschungen zur Religion und Literatur des Alten und Neuen Testaments
FS	Festschrift
GBL	*Das Große Bibellexikon*. Edited by H. Burkhardt
GCS	Die griechischen christlichen Schriftsteller der ersten [drei] Jahrhunderte
GGM	*Geographi Graeci Minores*. Edited by K. Müller
GLAJJ	*Greek and Latin Authors on Jews and Judaism*. Edited by M. Stern
GLM	*Geographi Latini Minores*. Edited by A. Riese
GN	Gute Nachricht Bibel; Mit den Spätschriften des Alten Testaments. Revidierte Fassung 1997
GNS	Good News Studies
GNT	Grundrisse zum Neuen Testament
GRBS	*Greek, Roman, and Byzantine Studies*
GThA	Göttinger Theologische Arbeiten
Guarducci	M. Guarducci, *Epigrafia greca*
HAL	*Hebräisches und Aramäisches Lexikon zum Alten Testament*. Edited by W. Baumgartner, L. Koehler and J. J. Stamm
HALOT	*The Hebrew and Aramaic Lexicon of the Old Testament in English*. Edited by L. Koehler, W. Baumgartner and J. J. Stamm
HAT	Handbuch zum Alten Testament
HGIÜ	*Historische griechische Inschriften in Übersetzung*. Edited by K. Brodersen, W. Günther and H. Schmitt
HNT	Handbuch zum Neuen Testament
HRG	*Handbuch religionswissenschaftlicher Grundbegriffe*. Edited by H. Cancik
HS	E. G. Hoffmann and H. von Siebenthal, *Griechische Grammatik zum Neuen Testament*
HSCP	*Harvard Studies in Classical Philology*
HThKAT	Herders Theologischer Kommentar zum Alten Testament
HThKNT	Herders Theologischer Kommentar zum Neuen Testament
HThKNTSup	Herders Theologischer Kommentar zum Neuen Testament Supplementbände
HTR	*Harvard Theological Review*

HTS	Harvard Theological Studies
HUCA	*Hebrew Union College Annual*
I. AlexTroas	*The Inscriptions of Alexandreia Troas.* Edited by Marijana Ricl
I. Anazarbos	*Die Inschriften von Anazarbos und Umgebung.* Edited by M. H. Sayar
I. Asoka	*The Moral Edicts of King Asoka.* Edited by P. H. L. Eggermont and J. Hoftijzer
I. Assos	*Die Inschriften von Assos.* Edited by R. Merkelbach
I. CosPH	*The Inscriptions of Cos.* Edited by W. R. Paton and E. L. Hicks.
I. Délos	*Inscriptions de Délos.* Edited by A. Plassart et al.
I. EgJud	*Jewish Inscriptions of Graeco-Roman Egypt.* Edited by W. Horbury and D. Noy
I. Ephesos	*Die Inschriften von Ephesos.* Edited by H. Wankel et al.
I. Erythrai	*Die Inschriften von Erythrai und Klazomenai.* Edited by H. Engelmann and R. Merkelbach
I. GBulg	*Inscriptiones Graecae in Bulgaria repertae.* Edited by G. Mihailov
I. GRIAsia	*Greeks and Romans in Imperial Asia.* Edited by R. A. Kearsley
I. KilikiaDF	*Inscriptions de Cilicie. Edited by G. Dagron and D. Feissel*
I. Knidos	*Die Inschriften von Knidos.* Edited by W. Blümel
I. KorinthKent	*Corinth: Results of Excavations Conducted by the American School of Classical Studies at Athens,* vol. 8.3, *The Inscriptions 1926-1950.* Edited by J. H. Kent
I. KyrenJud	*Corpus jüdischer Zeugnisse aus der Cyrenaika.* Edited by G. Lüderitz
I. Kyzikos	*Die Inschriften von Kyzikos und Umgebung.* Edited by Elmar Schwertheim
I. Laodikeia	*Die Inschriften von Laodikeia am Lykos.* Edited by T. Corsten
I. Lykaonien	*Die kaiserzeitlichen Inschriften Lykaoniens.* Edited by G. Laminger-Pascher
I. MagnSip	*Die Inschriften von Magnesia am Sipylos.* Edited by T. Ihnken
I. MakedChr	*Recueil des inscriptions chrétiennes de Macédonie au IIIe au VIe siècle.* Edited by D. Feissel.
I. ManMus	*Greek and Latin Inscriptions in the Manisa Museum.* Edited by H. Malay
I. Pergamon	*Die Inschriften von Pergamon.* Edited by M. Fränkel
I. Perge	*Die Inschriften von Perge.* Edited by S. Şahin
I. Pisidia	*The Inscriptions of Central Pisidia.* Edited by G. H. R. Horsley and S. Mitchell
I. PontEux	*Inscriptiones antiquae orae septentrionalis Pontis Euxini Graecae et Latine.* Edited by V. Latyshev
I. Priene	*Inschriften von Priene.* Edited by F. Hiller von Gaertringen

I. Prusa	*Die Inschriften von Prusa ad Olympum.* Edited by Thomas Corsten
I. Smyrna	*Die Inschriften von Smyrna.* Edited by G. Petzl
I. Stratonikeia	*Die Inschriften von Stratonikeia.* Edited by S. Şahin
I. Tyana	*Tyana.* Edited by D. Berges, J. Nollé
I. WEuropeJud	*Jewish Inscriptions of Western Europe.* Edited by D. Noy
IBD	*The Illustrated Bible Dictionary.* Edited by J. D. Douglas
IBM	*Ancient Greek Inscriptions in the British Museum.* Edited by E. L. Hicks et al.
IBS	*Irish Biblical Studies*
ICC	International Critical Commentary
IEJ	*Israel Exploration Journal*
IG	*Inscriptiones graecae.* Edited by O. Kern
IGLSyria	*Inscriptions grecques et latines de la Syrie.* Edited by L. Jalabert et al.
IGR	*Inscriptiones Graecae ad res Romanas pertinentes.* Edited by E. Leroux
IGUR	*Inscriptiones Graecae Urbis Romanae.* Edited by L. Moretti
IJudO	*Inscriptiones Judaicae Orientis.* Edited by D. Noy et al.
IK	*Inschriften griechischer Städte aus Kleinasien*
ILS	*Inscriptiones Latinae Selectae.* Edited by H. Dessau
Int	*Interpretation*
Inv	*Inventaire des inscriptions de Palmyre.* Edited by J. Starcky
ISBE	*International Standard Bible Encyclopedia.* Edited by G. W. Bromiley
IThS	Innsbrucker theologische Studien
ITQ	*Irish Theological Quarterly*
ITS	*Indian Theological Studies*
JA	*Journal Asiatique*
JAC	*Jahrbuch für Antike und Christentum*
JAOS	*Journal of the American Oriental Society*
JB	Jerusalem Bible
JBL	*Journal of Biblical Literature*
JBTh	*Jahrbuch für biblische Theologie*
JEH	*Journal of Ecclesiastical History*
JETh	*Jahrbuch für evangelikale Theologie*
JETS	*Journal of the Evangelical Theological Society*
JGRChJ	*Journal of Greco-Roman Christianity and Judaism*
JHC	*Journal of Higher Criticism*
JHS	*Journal of Hellenic Studies*
JJS	*Journal of Jewish Studies*
JÖAI	*Jahreshefte des Österreichischen archäologischen Instituts*

JPTSS	Journal of Pentecostal Theology Supplement Series
JQR	*Jewish Quarterly Review*
JR	*Journal of Religion*
JRA	*Journal of Roman Archaeology*
JRASup	Journal of Roman Archaeology Supplement Series
JRS	*Journal of Roman Studies*
JSHRZ	*Jüdische Schriften aus hellenistisch-römischer Zeit.* Edited by W. G. Kümmel and H. Lichtenberger
JSJ	*Journal for the Study of Judaism in the Persian, Hellenistic, and Roman Periods*
JSJSup	Journal for the Study of Judaism Supplements
JSNT	*Journal for the Study of the New Testament*
JSNTSup	Journal for the Study of the New Testament Supplement Series
JSOT	*Journal for the Study of the Old Testament*
JSOTSup	Journal for the Study of the Old Testament Supplement Series
JSP	*Journal for the Study of the Pseudepigrapha*
JSPSup	Journal for the Study of the Pseudepigrapha Supplement Series
JSQ	*Jewish Studies Quarterly*
JSS	*Journal of Semitic Studies*
JTS	*Journal of Theological Studies*
KAT	Kommentar zum Alten Testament
KD	*Kerygma und Dogma*
KEK	Kritisch-exegetischer Kommentar über das Neue Testament
KJV	King James Version
KP	*Der Kleine Pauly.* Edited by K. Ziegler, W. Sontheimer and H. Gärtner
LBW	P. Le Bas and W. H. Waddington, eds., *Inscriptions grecques et latines*
LCL	Loeb Classical Library
LD	Lectio divina
LSJ	H. G. Liddell, R. Scott and H. S. Jones, *A Greek-English Lexicon*
LThJ	*Lutheran Theological Journal*
LThK	*Lexikon für Theologie und Kirche.* Edited by W. Kasper
LÜ	Luther-Übersetzung
MAAR	Memoirs of the American Academy in Rome
MAMA	*Monumenta Asiae Minoris Antiqua.* Edited by W. M. Calder et al.
MM	J. H. Moulton, G. Milligan, *The Vocabulary of the Greek Testament Illustrated from the Papyri and Other Non-Literary Sources*
NA[27]	*Novum Testamentum Graece.* 27th rev. ed. Edited by B. and K. Aland et al.
NAMZ	*Neue allgemeine Missionszeitschrift*

NASB	New American Standard Bible
NBL	*Neues Bibel-Lexikon.* Edited by M. Görg and B. Lang
NCBC	New Century Bible Commentary
NDBT	*New Dictionary of Biblical Theology.* Edited by T. D. Alexander and B. S. Rosner
NEAEHL	*The New Encyclopedia of Archaeological Excavations in the Holy Land.* Edited by E. Stern
NEASB	*Near East Archaeological Society Bulletin*
NEB	Neue Echter-Bibel
Neot	*Neotestamentica*
NewDocs	*New Documents Illustrating Early Christianity.* Edited by G. H. R. Horsley and S. R. Llewelyn
NHC	Nag Hammadi Codices
NIBC	New International Biblical Commentary
NICNT	New International Commentary on the New Testament
NICOT	New International Commentary on the Old Testament
NIDNTT	*The New International Dictionary of New Testament Theology.* Edited by C. Brown
NIGTC	New International Greek Testament Commentary
NIV	New International Version
NKZ	*Neue kirchliche Zeitschrift*
NLT	New Living Translation
NovT	*Novum Testamentum*
NRSV	New Revised Standard Version
NSBT	New Studies in Biblical Theology
NSS	W. Haubeck and H. von Siebenthal, *Neuer sprachlicher Schlüssel zum Griechischen Neuen Testament*
NTA	Neutestamentliche Abhandlungen
NTD	Das Neue Testament Deutsch
NTDH	Neukirchener Theologische Dissertationen und Habilitationen
NTOA	Novum Testamentum et Orbis Antiquus
NTS	*New Testament Studies*
NovTSup	Novum Testamentum Supplements
NTTS	New Testament Tools and Studies
OBO	Orbis biblicus et orientalis
OCD	*The Oxford Classical Dictionary.* Edited by S. Hornblower and A. Spawforth
OEANE	*Oxford Encyclopedia of Archaeology in the Near East.* Edited by E. M. Meyers
OED	*Oxford English Dictionary.* 2nd ed. (online)
OGIS	*Orientis graeci inscriptiones selectae.* Edited by W. Dittenberger
ÖTKNT	Ökumenischer Taschenbuchkommentar zum Neuen Testament

OTL	Old Testament Library
OTP	*The Old Testament Pseudepigrapha.* Edited by J. H. Charles-worth
P.Coll.Youtie	*Collectanea Papyrologica: Texts Published in Honor of H. C. Youtie.* Edited by A. E. Hanson
P.Köln	*Kölner Papyri.* Edited by B. Kramer and R. Hübner
P.Lond.	*Greek Papyri in the British Museum.* Edited by F. Kenyon et al.
P.Oxy.	*Oxyrhynchus Papyri.* Edited by B. P. Grenfell et al.
P.Ryl.	*Catalogue of the Greek Papyri in the John Rylands Library at Manchester.* Edited by A. S. Hunt et al.
PAAJR	*Proceedings of the American Academy for Jewish Research*
PCPS	*Proceedings of the Cambridge Philosophical Society*
PECS	*The Princeton Encyclopedia of Classical Sites.* Edited by R. Still-well
PEQ	*Palestine Exploration Quarterly*
PG	Patrologia graeca. Edited by J.-P. Migne
PGM	*Papyri graecae magicae: Die griechischen Zauberpapyri.* Edited by K. Preisendanz
PL	Patrologia latina. Edited by J.-P. Migne.
PNTC	Pillar New Testament Commentary
PO	Patrologia orientalis
Pre. Pet.	*Preaching of Peter (Kerygina Petri)*
PTMS	Princeton Theological Manuscript Series
PTS	Patristische Texte und Studien
PTSDSSP	*Princeton Theological Seminary Dead Sea Scrolls Project.* Edited by J. H. Charlesworth
PVTG	Pseudepigrapha Veteris Testamenti Graece
PW	A. F. Pauly and G. Wissowa, *Paulys Realencyclopädie der classischen Altertumswissenschaft*
PWSup	Supplement to PW
QD	Quaestiones disputatae
QDAP	*Quarterly of the Department of Antiquities in Palestine*
RAC	*Reallexicon für Antike und Christentum.* Edited by T. Kluser et al.
RB	*Revue biblique*
RECAM	*Regional Epigraphic Catalogues of Asia Minor II: The Ankara District; The Inscriptions of North Galatia.* Edited by S. Mitchell.
REG	*Revue des études grecques*
REI	*Revue des études islamiques*
REJ	*Revue des études juives*
RestQ	*Restoration Quarterly*
RevExp	*Review and Expositor*
RevQ	*Revue de Qumran*

RGG	*Religion in Geschichte und Gegenwart.* Edited by K. Galling
RHPR	*Revue d'histoire et de philosophie religieuses*
RHR	*Revue de l'histoire des religions*
RivB	*Rivista biblica italiana*
RNT	Regensburger Neues Testament
RSR	*Recherches de science religieuse*
RSV	Revised Standard Version
RTP	*Revue de théologie et de philosophie*
SBB	Stuttgarter biblische Beiträge
SBEC	Studies in the Bible and Early Christianity
SBFLA	*Studii biblici Franciscani liber annuus*
SBLDS	Society of Biblical Literature Dissertation Series
SBLMS	Society of Biblical Literature Monograph Series
SBLSBS	Society of Biblical Literature Sources for Biblical Study
SBLSP	*Society of Biblical Literature Seminar Papers*
SBLTT	Society of Biblical Literature Texts and Translations
SBS	Stuttgarter Bibelstudien
SBT	Studies in Biblical Theology
SC	Sources chrétiennes
Schürer	*The History of the Jewish People in the Age of Jesus Christ (175 B.C.–A.D. 135).* Edited by G. Vermès, F. Millar and M. Black
SE	*Studia evangelica I, II, III*
SEÅ	*Svensk Exegetisk Årsbok*
SEG	*Supplementum epigraphicum graecum*
SFSHJ	South Florida Studies in the History of Judaism
SH	*Studia Hierosolymitana*
SIG³	*Sylloge inscriptionum graecarum.* 3rd ed. Edited by W. Dittenberger
SIHC	Studies in the Intercultural History of Christianity
SJLA	Studies in Judaism in Late Antiquity
SJT	*Scottish Journal of Theology*
SNT	Schriften des Neuen Testaments
SNTSMS	Society of New Testament Studies Monograph Series
SNTU	*Studien zum Neuen Testament und seiner Umwelt*
SÖAI	Sonderschriften des Österreichischen archäologischen Instituts
SRHEC	Studies in the Religion and History of Early Christianity
StANT	Studien zum Alten und Neuen Testaments
StBL	Studies in Biblical Literature
STDJ	Studies on the Texts of the Desert of Judah
StNT	Studien zum Neuen Testament
StPB	Studia post-biblica
Str-B	Hermann L. Strack and Paul Billerbeck, *Kommentar zum Neuen*

	Testament aus Talmud und Midrasch
StTh	*Studia Theologica*
StUNT	Studien zur Umwelt des Neuen Testaments
SVTP	Studia in Veteris Testamenti pseudepigraphica
SwJT	*Southwestern Journal of Theology*
TAM	*Tituli Asiae Minoris*
TANZ	Texte und Arbeiten zum neutestamentlichen Zeitalter
TAPA	*Transactions of the American Philological Association*
TAVO	*Tübinger Atlas des Vorderen Orients*
TB	Theologische Bücherei: Neudrucke und Berichte aus dem 20. Jahrhundert
TDNT	*Theological Dictionary of the New Testament.* Edited by G. Kittel and G. Friedrich.
TDOT	*Theological Dictionary of the Old Testament.* Edited by G. J. Botterweck, H. Ringgren and H.- J. Fabry
TEV	Today's English Version (Good News Bible)
THAT	*Theologisches Handwörterbuch zum Alten Testament.* Edited by E. Jenni and C. Westermann
ThBeitr	*Theologische Beiträge*
ThBLNT	*Theologisches Begriffslexikon zum Neuen Testament, Neubearbeitete Ausgabe.* Edited by L. Coenen and K. Haacker
ThF	Theologische Forschung
ThGl	*Theologie und Glaube*
ThHK	Theologischer Handkommentar zum Neuen Testament
ThLZ	*Theologische Literaturzeitung*
ThQ	*Theologische Quartalschrift*
ThR	*Theologische Rundschau*
ThSt	Theologische Studien
ThWAT	*Theologisches Wörterbuch zum Alten Testament*
ThWNT	*Theologisches Wörterbuch zum Neuen Testament*
ThZ	*Theologische Zeitschrift*
TIB	Tabula Imperii Byzantini. Edited by H. Hunger
TIR	Tabula Imperii Romani. Edited by Union Académique Internationale
TJ	*Trinity Journal*
TJT	*Toronto Journal of Theology*
TLNT	*Theological Lexicon of the New Testament.* Edited by C. Spicq
TLOT	*Theological Lexicon of the Old Testament.* Edited by E. Jenni and C. Westermann
TNIV	Today's New International Version
TNTC	Tyndale New Testament Commentaries
TRE	*Theologische Realenzyklopädie*

TSAJ	Texte und Studien zum antiken Judentum
TUGAL	Texte und Untersuchungen zur Geschichte der altchristlichen Literatur
TynBul	*Tyndale Bulletin*
UBS⁴	*The Greek New Testament.* 4th rev. ed. Edited by K. Aland et al.
USQR	*Union Seminary Quarterly Review*
UTB	Uni-Taschenbücher
VE	*Vox evangelica*
VigChr	*Vigiliae christianae*
VT	*Vetus Testamentum*
WBC	Word Biblical Commentary
WBEH	Wissenschaftliche Beiträge aus Europäischen Hochschulen
WE	*The Wolfe-Expedition to Asia Minor.* Edited by J. R. S. Sterrett
WF	Wege der Forschung
WMANT	Wissenschaftliche Monographien zum Alten und Neuen Testament
WTJ	*Westminster Theological Journal*
WUNT	Wissenschaftliche Untersuchungen zum Neuen Testament
ZAW	*Zeitschrift für die alttestamentliche Wissenschaft*
ZBK	Zürcher Bibelkommentare
ZDPV	*Zeitschrift des deutschen Palästina-Vereins*
ZKG	*Zeitschrift für Kirchengeschichte*
ZKTh	*Zeitschrift für katholische Theologie*
ZMR	*Zeitschrift für Missionskunde und Religionswissenschaft*
ZN	*Zeitschrift für Numismatik*
ZNW	*Zeitschrift für die neutestamentliche Wissenschaft*
ZPE	*Zeitschrift für Papyrologie und Epigraphik*
ZThK	*Zeitschrift für Theologie und Kirche*

ILLUSTRATIONS

Fig. 1: The Roman Empire in the First Century
Fig. 2: Palestine Between 37 B.C. and A.D. 33
Fig. 3: Peter's House in Capernaum
Fig. 4: The Fisherman's House in Bethsaida
Fig. 5: Galilee in the First Century
Fig. 6: Jerusalem
Fig. 7: World Map of Hekataios
Fig. 8: World Map of Eratosthenes
Fig. 9: World Map According to *Jubilees*
Fig. 10: Samaria in the First Century
Fig. 11: Caesarea
Fig. 12: Damascus
Fig. 13: Judea in the First Century
Fig. 14: The House of the Vintner in Bethsaida
Fig. 15: The Syrian Mediterranean Coast
Fig. 16: Antioch
Fig. 17: Rome
Fig. 18: Asia Minor I (Provinces and Territories)
Fig. 19: Pergamon (Lower City)
Fig. 20: Alexandria
Fig. 21: India
Fig. 22: India: Travel Routes
Fig. 23: The Nabataean Kingdom (Arabia)
Fig. 24: The Province of Syria (North)
Fig. 24: The Province of Syria (South)
Fig. 25: Cilicia
Fig. 26: Roads in Pamphylia
Fig. 27: Cyprus
Fig. 28: South Galatia
Fig. 29: Phrygia and Galatia
Fig. 30: Antiochia
Fig. 31: Asia Minor II (Cities and Roads)
Fig. 32: Greece
Fig. 33: Macedonia
Fig. 34: Thessalonike
Fig. 35: Athens
Fig. 36: Corinth

Fig. 37: Illyricum
Fig. 38: Ephesus
Fig. 39: Ephesus, Terrace House 2
Fig. 39: Ephesus, Terrace House 2, Unit 6
Fig. 40: Spain
Fig. 41: Travel Times
Fig. 42: Communication Model (modified from Westley and MacLean)

Figs. 2, 5, 10, 13, 15 are modifications of Y. Tsafrir, L. di Segni and J. Green, *Tabula Imperii Romani* (Jerusalem, 1994); fig. 3 of B. B. Blue, "Acts and the House Church," in *The Book of Acts in Its Graeco-Roman Setting* (ed. D. W. J. Gill and C. Gempf; Exeter, 1994), 193, fig. 1, and V. C. Corbo, *Cafarnao I* (Jerusalem, 1972), fig. 9; fig. 4 of R. Arav and R. A. Freund, eds., *Bethsaida* (Kirksville, Mo., 1995-1999), 2:380; fig. 6 of R. Riesner, "Das Jerusalemer Essenerviertel und die Urgemeinde," *ANRW* II.26.2 (1995): 1792; fig. 1 of H. Geva. *NEAEHL* 2:718; figs. 7, 8 of E. Olshausen, *Einführung in die Historische Geographie der Alten Welt* (Darmstadt, 1991), 236; fig. 9 of P. S. Alexander, "Geography," *ABD* 2:982; fig. 11 of K. G. Holum et al., eds., *Caesarea Papers 2* (JRASup 35; Portsmouth, R.I., 1999), 8; fig. 12 of D. Sack, *Damaskus* (Mainz, 1989), 13; fig. 14 of R. Arav and R. A. Freund, eds., *Bethsaida* (Kirksville, Mo., 1995-1999), map 9; fig. 16 of G. Downey, *A History of Antioch in Syria* (Princeton. N.J., 1961), fig. 11, and F. Kolb, "Antiochia in der früheren Kaiserzeit," in *Geschichte, Tradition, Reflexion II* (FS M. Hengel; ed. H. Cancik; Tübingen, 1996), 107; fig. 17 of M. Beard, J. North and S. Price, *Religions of Rome* (Cambridge, 1998), vol. 1, maps 1-3, and R. Gross, *KP* 4:1445; fig. 18 of S. Mitchell, *Anatolia* (Oxford, 1995), 2:156; fig. 19 of W. Rad, *Pergamon* (Cologne, 1988), 104; fig. 20 of B. A. Pearson, in *The Roots of Egyptian Christianity* (ed. B. A. Pearson and J. E. Goehring; Philadelphia, 1986), 189, and E. Schwertheim, *DNP* 1:463-66; fig. 21 of W. Watson, "Iran and China," in *Cambridge History of Iran* (Cambridge, 1983), 3:544-45, and Joseph E. Schwartzberg, ed., *A Historical Atlas of South Asia* (Chicago, 1978), 24, plate III.C.5a; fig. 23 of A. Negev, "The Nabataeans and the Provincia Arabia," *ANRW* II.8 (1978): 550; fig. 24 of F. Millar, *The Roman Near East, 31 BC–AD 337* (Cambridge, 1993), 566-76, and J.-M. Dentzer and W. Orthmann, eds., *Archéologie et histoire de la Syrie II: La Syrie de l'époque achéménide à l'avènement de l'Islam* (Saarbrücken, 1989), 582, 586-87; fig. 25 of R. Ziegler, *Kaiser, Heer und städtisches Geld* (ETAM 16; Vienna, 1993), 161; fig. 26 of D. French, "Roads in Pisidia," in *Forschungen in Pisidien* (ed. E. Schwertheim; AMS 6; Bonn, 1992), 174-75; fig. 27 of T. B. Mitford, "Roman Cyprus," *ANRW* II.7.2 (1980): 1286-1384, E. Herscher, "Archaeology in Cyprus," *AJA* 99 (1999): 258, and D. Rupp, in *BAGRW,* map 72; fig. 28 of D. French, *Studies in the History and Topography of Lycia and Pisidia* (London, 1994), x; fig. 29 of D. French, *Roman Roads and Milestones of Asia Minor* (Oxford, 1981), part 1, appendix;

fig. 30 of S. Mitchell and M. Waelkens, *Pisidian Antioch* (London, 1998), 2.92; fig. 31 of A. D. Macro, "The Cities of Asia Minor under the Roman Imperium," *ANRW* II.7.2 (1980): 659-97, and D. H. French, "The Roman Road-System of Asia Minor," *ANRW* II.7.2 (1980): 698-729; fig. 32 of G. Stählin et al., in *Biblisch-historisches Handwörterbuch* (eds. B. Reicke and L. Rost; Göttingen, 1979); fig. 33 of I. Touratsoglou, *Makedonien* (Athens, 1997), 31; fig. 34 of I. Touratsoglou, *Makedonien* (Athens 1997, 62), and C. vom Brocke, *Thessaloniki* (Tübingen, 2001), 23; fig. 35 of W. Zschietzschmann, "Athenai," PWSup 13 (1973): 55-140, fig. 9 (J. Travlos); fig. 36 of C. K. Williams, "Roman Corinth as a Commercial Center," in *The Corinthia in the Roman Period* (ed. T. E. Gregory; JRASup 8, Ann Arbor, Mich., 1993), 32; and D. G. Romano, <http://ccat.sas.upenn.edu/~dromano/cplanfr.html>; fig. 37 of J. Wilkes, *The Illyrians* (Oxford, 1992), xxiii; fig. 38 of P. Scherrer, "Die historische Topographie von Ephesos," *Forum Archaeologiae* 4.8 (1997): 2; fig. 39 of K. Koller, <http://www.oeaw.ac.at/antike/homepage/ephesos/hh/hh2/hh2befund/ hh2befund.html>; fig. 40 of G. Winkler, *C. Plinius Secundus d. Ä. Naturkunde,* books 3-4 (Munich, 1988), 208-9; fig. 41 of M. B. Thompson, "The Holy Internet: Communication Between Churches in the First Christian Generation," in *The Gospels for All Christians* (ed. R. Bauckham; Grand Rapids, 1998), 61; fig. 42 of M. Burgoon et al., *Human Communication* (3rd ed.; London, 1994), 26, 31.

INTRODUCTION

1

THE HISTORY OF EARLY CHRISTIANITY
AS HISTORY OF MISSIONS

In the beginning was Jesus. Without the person of Jesus of Nazareth, the messianic Son of Man, there would be no Christians. Without the ministry of Jesus there would be no Christian missions. Without Christian missions there would have been no Christian Occident. The first Christian missionary was not Paul, but Peter, and Peter would not have preached a "missionary" sermon at Pentecost if he had not been a student of Jesus for three years.

On the morning of May 27 in A.D. 30, the day of the Jewish Feast of Pentecost, a sabbath, 120 men and women were gathered in Jerusalem—people who were convinced, after having met the risen Jesus, that the eschatological kingdom of God had dawned with Jesus, who had been crucified seven weeks earlier, and that it was a tangible reality in the presence of the risen and exalted Jesus Christ. And they were convinced that the kingdom of God, inaugurated by Jesus, would be carried from Jerusalem to the ends of the earth through their ministry as witnesses empowered by the Holy Spirit (Acts 1:3-15). In the course of this day, after the first public speech given by Peter, about three thousand Jews received forgiveness of their sins as they pledged faith in and allegiance to the crucified and risen Jesus as Messiah. They soon formed a new community in which believers in Jesus the Messiah worshiped and lived together (Acts 2:37-41). Within a few weeks the community of Jews believing in Jesus had grown to five thousand people (Acts 4:4). There were followers of Jesus during these first weeks and months after the resurrection in cities and villages in Judea outside Jerusalem as well as in Galilee (cf. 1 Cor 15:6), but we have no information about their number.

Nineteen years after the founding of the first Christian community in Jerusalem, Christians in Rome, the capital of the empire, attracted public attention in the context of events that forced the emperor to take action. In A.D. 49 Claudius ordered the expulsion of all Jews from the city of Rome after the missionary activity of Christians in the local synagogues had caused turmoil (Suetonius, *Claud.* 25.4). Fifteen years later, in A.D. 64, we read of a "large crowd" (*multi-*

tudo ingens) of Christians that was indicted in the burning of Rome, many of whom were executed in the persecution instigated by Nero (Tacitus, *Ann.* 15.44; cf. *1 Clem.* 6:1). Suetonius refers to the *Christiani* who had been condemned to death in this persecution as "a class of men given to a new and mischievous superstition" (*genus hominum superstitionis novae ac maleficae* [Suetonius, *Nero* 16.2]). In A.D. 111/112 Pliny the Younger, the governor of the province of Bithynia-Pontus, complained in a letter to Emperor Trajan about the aggressive expansion of the "wretched" cult (*superstitionem pravam, immodicam*), initiated by the crucifixion of Jesus, a superstition that now reached a "great number of persons of every age and class," both men and women, and infected "not only the towns, but villages and rural districts too" (Pliny, *Ep.* 10.96.8-10). Thus four emperors became aware of the Christians and of their faith before the end of the apostolic period (taking negative action against them): Claudius, Nero, Domitian and Trajan.

We have no statistical figures for the Christians in the Roman Empire, neither for the mid-60s, when Peter and Paul died as martyrs in Rome, nor for the close of the apostolic period at the end of the first century, when John sent his Revelation to the churches in Asia Minor. Some historians estimate that there were 40,000 Christians in the Roman Empire around A.D. 66; this would be about 0.07 percent of a total population of some 60 million people.[1] Estimates for the number of Christians around A.D. 100 are 320,000,[2] representing about 0.5 percent of the population. For the time around A.D. 300, the time of Emperor Constantine, some estimates reach 5 million Christians,[3] which would amount to 8.4 percent of the total population.

The first Christians were characterized first and foremost by their convictions, centered on faith in Jesus of Nazareth as the crucified and risen Messiah, who inaugurated the kingdom of God that the prophets had promised, and who put into effect forgiveness of sins, salvation from death, and eternal life—this for both Jews and non-Jews because it is Jesus Christ, and "no one else," who makes salvation possible for all people (Acts 4:12). No other religious community, with the exception of the Jews, made such exclusive claims concerning salvation. No other religious community, including the Jews, accorded a historical person such a central place as the Christians did. No other religious community or cult was engaged in deliberate and active "missionary" expansion, not even the Jews (see §6), and no other religious group had such clear strategic goals with result-oriented tactical implemen-

---

[1]Reicke 1982, 302.

[2]Reicke 1982, 303. Stark (1997, 6) estimates that there were about 7,530 Christians in A.D. 100. However, his assumption of a growth rate of 40 percent per decade is not only purely hypothetical, but also much too schematic.

[3]MacMullen (1984, 32, 135): 5 million; Stark (1997, 6-7): 6.3 million; Congar (1970, 3): 15 percent of 60 million people, thus 9 million Christians; Hertling (1934, 245-64): 15 million.

tation as the first Christians had. Jesus had called his disciples to be "fishers of people" (Mt 4:19; Mk 1:17). No scholar doubts that the first Christians actively spread their faith, doing "missionary work"—Stephen and Philip, Peter and Paul as well as other apostles, and in the first decades after the decisive year A.D. 30 many unnamed Christians. The question of *how* they operated as "fishers of people" is often ignored but is highly interesting. Did they operate as a strategically cooperating "fleet," or were they solitary "anglers" who essentially reacted to circumstances without much planning? Ferdinand Hahn certainly was correct when he wrote, "The early church was a missionary church. The proclamation, the teaching, all activities of the early Christians had a missionary dimension. The fact that it is not possible to find a defined concept of 'missions' in the New Testament does not alter the fact that early Christianity was controlled by the missionary task in their entire existence and in all their activities."[4]

A flood of literature, both scholarly and popular, discusses the foundation and the faith of the early Christians, including books and articles about the historical Jesus and the focus of his preaching,[5] biographies of Paul and studies on his theology,[6] and descriptions of the theology of the New Testament and of the history of the early church.[7] In the last category the missionary activity of the early church is more narrated than analyzed and is usually secondary to a broad description of the origins of the church, of the development of the christological creeds, of the conflicts between Jewish Christians and Gentile Christians, and of the dispute over orthodox doctrine.[8] In a new monograph on early Palestinian Christianity in the first century, César Vidal Manzanares describes the missionary

---

[4]Hahn 1972, 95; see also Pesch 1982, 11.

[5]See Bornkamm 1995 [1956]; Vermes 1983; Stanton 1974; Riesner 1988; E. P. Sanders 1985, 1993; G. Beasley-Murray 1986; Riches 1980; Horsley 1987; Freyne 1988; Gnilka 1990; Crossan 1991; Meier 1991-2001; *DJG;* Schnackenburg 1993; Vermes 1993; Borg 1994; Witherington 1994a, 1995; Becker 1995; J. Sanders 1996; Theissen and Merz 1996; N. T. Wright 1996; Chilton and Evans 1997.

[6]See Bornkamm 1993 [1969]; Eichholz 1972; Ridderbos 1975; Bruce 1977; E. P. Sanders 1977, 1991; Beker 1987; Becker 1992; A. F. Segal 1990; *DPL;* Barrett 1994a; Witherington 1994b; D. Wenham 1995; Murphy-O'Connor 1996; Gnilka 1996; Hengel and Schwemer 1998; Lohse 1996; Dunn 1998.

[7]On the last topic see Conzelmann 1969 [1989] and now Schenke 1990; Dassmann 1991; Vouga 1994; Winkelmann 1996; Barnett 1999; Witherington 2001. Guthrie (1975) combines a presentation of the history of the early church with a description of early Christian literature and theology.

[8]Conzelmann (1969 [1989]) describes the "outward course of the mission" of Paul on five pages (79-84 [ET, 95-100]); Vouga (1994) writes just over one page on Paul's missionary work (94-96) and three pages about "the Pauline mission and its co-workers" (101-3). More comprehensive is Schenke (1990), who discusses on twelve pages the "mission of the 'Hellenists'" (186-97) in his discussion of earliest Christianity before the apostolic council, as is Dassmann (1991), who devotes twenty pages to a description of the "Gentile mission" (34-53). Less analytical are the "narrative" presentations by Barnett (1999) and Witherington (2001).

activity of the first Christians in two brief sections on five pages.[9] The body of
literature on the early Christian mission is not large.[10] This is true even for Paul's
missionary activity—a fact that may be traced back to the conviction that "Paul
is important for us today as a theologian" while being "primarily a missionary"
for the early church.[11] The missionary activity of the early church is banished to
incidental remarks even in commentaries on the Acts of the Apostles or in studies on Luke's theology.[12] It is thus hardly surprising that Paul's missionary work
is almost completely ignored in popular descriptions of Paul's life.[13] A noteworthy exception is the recently published monograph on Paul's theology by
Thomas Schreiner, who discusses "The Pauline Mission" in the second chapter.[14]
In studies on the literary character of the New Testament and on New Testament
rhetoric, the reality of missions is basically ignored as well.[15] Since Ferdinand
Hahn's monograph on mission in the New Testament, written forty years ago,
several books on the topic have been published,[16] especially on the mission of
Paul[17] and on the missiological conceptions of Matthew, Mark, Luke and John,[18]
but no comprehensive synthesis describes all relevant historical developments
and geographical data and presents the significant exegetical evidence combined with theological analyses.

The portrait of early Christian missions often is painted with broad brush-
strokes. Even classical scholars pass simple and sweeping verdicts, as in the case
of Frank Trombley, who writes in the second volume of the *New Paul* on the

---

[9]Vidal Manzanares 1995; in part 3, which deals with the theology of early Palestinian Christianity, missions is completely ignored.

[10]Older works include Harnack 1924 (ET 1908; 1962); Oepke 1920; E. Meyer 1921-1923; Liecht-
enhan 1946; Lerle 1960; Goppelt 1962. On Harnack and Meyer see Jantsch 1990. Note also
the complaint by Senior (1984, 64 with n. 3).

[11]Hübner (1996, 133), who, however, does not attempt to make a virtue of necessity (cf. ibid.,
148); see already Wernle 1909, iii.

[12]See Jervell, *Apg,* 90-105; Pokorný 1998.

[13]See E. P. Sanders 1991, 1, 6-7, 19-21; see also the history of research presented in Witherington
1998a, and Jeffrey L. Sheler, "Reassessing an Apostle: The Quest for the Historical St. Paul,"
U.S. News & World Report, April 5, 1999, 52-55.

[14]Schreiner 2001, 37-72 ("Proclaiming a Magnificent God: The Pauline Mission"). See also Kittel
1990, 91; R. P. Martin 1993, 93-94.

[15]An exception is Murphy 1993.

[16]See Hahn 1963 (ET 1965); Bieder 1964; Schille 1966, 1967; Kasting 1969; M. Green 1970; Hengel 1979, 1983a; Kertelge 1982; Legrand 1988 (ET 1990); Minnerath 1994; Ådna and Kvalbein
2000; Reinbold 2000; Köstenberger and O'Brien 2001.

[17]See Allen 1977; Grassi 1965; Bussmann 1971; Haas 1971; Bowers 1976; Dahl 1977; Elliger
1987; Buss 1980; Hultgren 1985; Pak 1991; Reck 1991; Riesner 1994; Wander 1994; cf. Ndya-
bahika 1992; see now Lietaert Peerbolte 2003.

[18]On the Synoptic Gospels see Bosch 1959; Wilk 2002; on Matthew see Cerfaux 1957; Uro 1987;
Weaver 1990; Grilli 1992; Tisera 1993; LaGrand 1995; on Mark see Böttger 1981; Kato 1986;
on Luke-Acts see Wilckens 1974; Burchard 1970; S. Wilson 1973; Kee 1990a; Stenschke 1999a;
T. Lane 1996; on John see W. Oehler 1936; 1941; Ruiz 1987; Okure 1988; Köstenberger 1998a.

expansion of early Christianity that the Christian faith was first established in the Greek cities of the eastern Mediterranean world—that is, in Ephesus, Corinth and Thessalonike—and that missionaries such as Paul first preached in synagogues and turned to non-Jewish audiences only after having no success among the Jews.[19] Trombley's survey ignores the first Christian churches in Jerusalem, in Judea and in Damascus and Antioch in Syria and overlooks the fact that neither the missionary work of Peter in Caesarea before a pagan audience (Acts 10—11), nor the early missionary activity of the Jewish Christians from Jerusalem in Antioch (Acts 11:19-20), nor Paul's focus on non-Jews (Gal 1:16; 2:2, 7-9) was motivated by a lack of success among Jews. A frequently repeated misjudgment is that the path to missionary work among Gentiles was opened up by Paul of Tarsus, who was converted to the Christian faith somewhat late, who gained acceptance for a Gentile mission during the apostolic council in A.D. 48, and who made sure with great consistency that the "Jewish sect" of believers in Jesus became a worldwide movement.[20] Even a classics specialist such as Reinhold Merkelbach writes that Paul was the first to preach the gospel before non-Jewish audiences; Peter sought to "reserve" the new message for the circumcised during a fierce clash in Antioch; in view of the missionary successes of Paul and on account of the large amounts of financial gifts that Paul collected and sent to Jerusalem, the "authorities in Jerusalem" allowed Paul to do missionary work among the uncircumcised as well.[21] It is perhaps easy to excuse missiologists and official representatives of missionary societies who focus more on contemporary plans and challenges when they occasionally paint an undifferentiated picture of the early Christian mission. However, before we draw conclusions and formulate "lessons" from the missionary work of the early church, we must first present and analyze the facts from which such lessons are drawn. This has not always happened.

Martin Hengel wrote recently in his introduction to a volume on Jews, Christians and pagans that the question of how the early Christians turned to pagans—a mission that opened the Jewish commonwealth within two generations and achieved a significance that impacted world history—is one of the most important questions in the study of earliest Christianity, a question "which we still cannot answer in a satisfactory manner and which, from a historical perspective, will always remain an open question."[22]

This assessment is perhaps overly pessimistic. We will see that the road to

---

[19]F. R. Trombley, "Christentum. D. Ausbreitung," *DNP* 2:1158.

[20]Lipsius 1897, 182; Bleicken 1978, 2:141; cf. Breytenbach (1996, 142), who writes, "The Christian mission to Gentiles originates with Paul and with the Hellenists who fled from Jerusalem to Antioch."

[21]Merkelbach 1997a, 124.

[22]Hengel 1994, xv-xvi; similarly Frank Trombley ("Christentum," 2:1158), who comments that there is still no conclusive study on the expansion of early Christianity.

Gentile missions was not easy. Roads frequently are branched connections be-tween two obligatory transition points (in contrast to the Roman roads that were straight as an arrow, finding the shortest and most direct connection between two points). The road that the early Christians traveled to fulfill the task of mis-sionary work was not a triumphal one. Many details of their missionary activ-ity—the proclamation of faith in Israel's God as faith in Jesus Christ, as climax of God's revelation that alone can bring salvation—were contested, including strategies, tactical procedures and personnel. The outcome was uncertain. This is one of the main reasons why we need a study that describes all facts that were relevant for the missionary strategy and tactics of the early church and that ex-plains the significant exegetical aspects and theological dimensions of the early Christian mission, integrating the views of numerous studies published in the last decades into an overall picture.

2

QUESTIONS AND ISSUES OF METHOD

The first Christians initially were but one of many groups in Second Temple Judaism. This quickly changed. The new identity of the Jews was intimately linked with the "nations."[1] They believed that Jesus of Nazareth was the Messiah and were convinced that his person, his ministry and particularly his death and resurrection signified the arrival of the eschatological revelation of YHWH with the promised messianic salvation. The exclusively Jewish movement quickly became multiethnic as non-Jews joined the communities of believers in Jesus.

If we accept the thesis of historians that every society seems to have aspirations, if not a blueprint, a specific goal (Jacques Le Goff), and if we understand the first Christian communities as a unique "society," several questions arise: What did the first Christians want? What did the first Christian communities want? What did the leaders of the Christian movement want? What were their central motivations? Which goal, or goals, did they aspire to achieve? Did they seek to cultivate, as the silent minority in the land, their private piety, waiting for the end of the world? Did they hope, as social reformers, to change society? Without doubt, many of the first Christians were actively involved in missionary work, often with immense personal sacrifice. Did these Christians simply fulfill a task given to them, perhaps grudgingly? Or were they willing and eager to reach other people with the gospel of Jesus Christ?

The drive to expansion is not an intrinsic, necessary element of the nature of a community of faith.[2] From the time of the first public sermon of Peter after Easter, followers of Jesus actively and energetically publicized their faith in Jesus Christ and invited people to join their communities.

The early Christian church is, from the beginning, a *movement*. The leading representatives endeavored, with fearless commitment and sacrificial courage, to win other people to their convictions, as even a casual reading of the first chapters of the book of Acts shows. This "mission" was carried out, perhaps already at a very early stage, with deliberate planning, eventually working toward

---

[1]See Walter 1995, 341.
[2]Conzelmann 1969, 3 (ET, 14).

the goal of converting non-Jews to faith in YHWH and in Jesus Christ.

The following discussion describes the early Christian mission. I take the term *early Christianity* to refer to the time of the apostles, tangible in the apostolic writings. The preaching and teaching of Jesus cannot and must not be excluded or relegated to a mere presupposition of the early Christian faith. It is a self-evident part of the history of early Christianity.[3] Jesus' preaching and healing ministry triggered an enormous messianic movement that was designed for continuity. The calling of the disciples as "fishers of people" and their practical training in missionary activity clearly demonstrates this. This movement that was set in motion by Jesus impacted history in a significant way after his death and resurrection. Its effects, though controversial, could not be ignored. Since Jesus and his followers, and all the early Jewish Christians, regarded the sacred Scriptures of Israel—what most Christians call the "Old Testament"—as divine revelation, and since Jesus and his followers cannot be separated from the world and the convictions of their Jewish contemporaries, the Old Testament and the texts of Second Temple Judaism also need to be investigated.

The notion of an "apostolic period" was not devised around A.D. 100—that is, in the time of the third generation, which stood at some distance from the time of the foundation of the church—as is often assumed in historical-critical reconstructions. This dating implies that there was no longer direct contact with the earliest traditions and thus paints an idealized picture of the early church.[4] If the book of Acts was not written by an anonymous author in A.D. 80/100, but by Luke, Paul's companion,[5] and if we take into account the fact that Paul defended his apostolic authority, it becomes evident that the notion of "apostolicity" played an important role at a very early stage.

In regard to the term *mission* or *missions,* I distinguish (1) a missionary dimension that is not directly missionary activity but implies universal or universalistic aspects, and (2) missionary intention that is linked with specific actions[6] and proceeds from a "center" from which envoys or "missionaries" are "sent" (Lat. *mittere*) to other people.[7] The term "mission," understood from a history-of-religion perspective, thus has a theoretical and a practical dimension. There is the conviction of being in possession of a message that is universally signifi-

---

[3]Contra the famous dictum of Rudolf Bultmann that "the message of Jesus is a presupposition for the theology of the New Testament rather than a part of that theology itself" (1984, 1-2 [ET, 1:3]).

[4]See, for example, Conzelmann 1969, 6-8; Vouga 1994, 4-5.

[5]See C.-J. Thornton 1991, with comprehensive discussion of all relevant external (patristic) and internal evidence; see also Riesner 1994, 366; 1997, 391-94; Botermann 1996, 15-28; Jervell, *Apg,* 79-86.

[6]This distinction was introduced by Lesslie Newbigin and developed by Hans-Werner Gensichen; see Beyerhaus 1996, 386.

[7]Cf. the definition of "mission" and the missiological conception of DuBose (1983).

cant for all people, and there are conscious (intentional) activities that aim at convincing nonmembers of the truth of this message and integrating them into the new community of believers.[8] Many exegetical studies on missions fail to indicate which notion of mission is used or presupposed. Some authors operate with a vague concept of mission, sometimes linked with the term "mission," used in official declarations (e.g., that of the World Council of Churches), that describes comprehensively all aims, efforts and activities of the church, including care for creation but excluding "proselytism." It is not uncommon to encounter the view that mission "has nothing to do with inducing people of non-Christian faiths or of other Christian denominations to convert to one's own church."[9] The abandonment of a clear definition is not helpful, and to take into consideration current ecclesial discussions would be both historically anachronistic and, in a study on realities in the first century, irresponsible.

When I use the term "mission" or "missions," I refer to the activity of a community of faith that distinguishes itself from its environment in terms of both religious belief (theology) and social behavior (ethics), that is convinced of the truth claims of its faith, and that actively works to win other people to the content of faith and to the way of life of whose truth and necessity the members of that community are convinced. This definition of "mission" involves a threefold reality: (1) people communicate to people of different faiths a new interpretation of reality—a different, new view of God, humankind and salvation; (2) people communicate a new way of life that replaces, at least partially, the former way of life; (3) people integrate those whom they win over to their faith and way of life into their community. This definition may imply geographical movement. As far as the ancient world is concerned, this definition always implies the oral communication of convictions. The communication of beliefs and behavior happens through active, expansive proclamation (the centrifugal dimension of mission) or through winsome, attractive presence (the centripetal dimension of mission). Thus, the significant elements of mission are "establishing contact, attempt at understanding, representation of Christ and of what it means to be a Christian, ministry of the word (proclamation, preaching, teaching, sermons, catechesis, witness), ministry of grace, of moral life, of social realities, charity."[10]

The people who are active in mission are *missionaries,* in the original sense of the word "apostle"; they are envoys sent by the risen Jesus Christ to proclaim

---

[8]See E. J. Sharpe, "Mission," in *A Dictionary of Comparative Religion* (London: Weidenfeld & Nicolson, 1970), 444; McKnight 1991, 4-5; M. Goodman 1994, 2-7; Hvalvik 1996, 270-71. On the history of the use of the term "mission" see Ohm 1962, 33-57.

[9]Reinbold 2000, 7, in a survey of the discussion, with quotations from J. Wietzke, J. Moltmann and V. Fedorov; for a critique of this reinterpretation of "mission" see ibid., 9-10.

[10]Thomas Ohm, "Mission," *LThK* 7:453. The word "propaganda" generally is understood in a negative way and is therefore not helpful in describing aspects of the early Christian mission; contra Reinbold 2000, 12-14.

the good news.[11] The result of mission is conversion: people accept and adopt the message proclaimed by the missionaries, they are integrated into the new community of faith, and they start to practice a new way of life with new behavioral patterns.[12] Definitions of "conversion" often narrowly focus only on interior, "private" processes, on spiritual-religious reorientation.[13] From a history-of-religion point of view, the question is important whether the people that are the target of a mission belong to the same ethnic group as the missionaries or whether they have a different ethnic identity—that is, the question of whether the missionary activity is "ethnically open" or "nonethnic."[14] This question provoked vehement discussions among Jewish Christians in the early Christian mission. Mission in this specific sense of concrete missionary praxis should be distinguished from theological convictions that imply or express a universal horizon and could be labeled as "potentially missionary" but are not necessarily linked with a specific, concrete missionary praxis.

2.1 Historical and Theological Questions

Historical change happens in phases that can be analyzed. If history is studied as a unified whole, the questions of continuity and discontinuity are particularly important. A contemporary theology of missions that seeks to learn from the *actio missionis* of the early church must not limit itself to the history of individual events. Rather, it needs to integrate structural history, including social history that investigates the everyday life of people, the history of mentalities that describes the convictions, attitudes, dispositions and certainties, and the history of religion that examines the religious beliefs and practices.[15] My description of the history of the early Christian mission, therefore, seeks to integrate relevant positions and developments in Jewish and in Greco-Roman society and culture. I will concentrate on historical matters as much as on theological motivations and positions.

Here several questions arise that also need to be considered in the following discussion: Do the person, ministry and summons of Jesus signify a new phase in the history of God's people? Does Jesus' commission to an international mission initiate a new phase in the history of God's people? Did Jesus "plan" the

---

[11]The term "missionary" has not been attested before A.D. 1610; see J. Glazik, "Missionar," *LThK* 7:457.
[12]See Frankemölle 1982, 99; Schnabel 1994, 47-48.
[13]Thus, for example, the influential definition by Nock (1933, 7): "The reorientation of the soul of an individual, his deliberate turning from indifference or from an earlier form of piety to another, a turning which implies a consciousness that the old was wrong and the new is right." See the critique in Gallagher 1993, 1-2.
[14]On this terminology see Runesson 1999, 62-63; cf. the discussion concerning the term "Jewish Christian" by Paget (1999, 733-42), who, however, complicates the subject matter unnecessarily.
[15]See Padberg 1991, 111-12.

later international mission of his followers, an unprecedented phenomenon in the history of religions, perhaps with his call extended to some of his followers to be trained as "fishers of people"? Are the origins of the Gentile mission of the early church to be seen in the old stipulations that Abraham or Moses received from God, decrees that amounted to a responsibility that Israel is guilty of having neglected? Should the normative precursor of the early Christian mission be seen in the Jewish expansion during the Second Temple period? Is the interpretation of Jesus' activity in terms of "missionary existence" par excellence, as envisioned in the Gospel of John, adequate? Does the mission of the early, "pre-Pauline" Jewish-Christian church in Jerusalem mark a new beginning as unprecedented outreach to adherents of other faiths? What was the role of Peter's vision in Caesarea, recounted three times in Acts 10:1-11, 18, which he received in connection with his contact with Cornelius, a Roman officer? What was the role of the Greek-speaking Jewish Christians who fled from Jerusalem to Antioch, where they proclaimed the good news of Jesus the Kyrios "to Greeks also" (Acts 11:19-21)? What do we know about the activities of the Twelve, beyond what we know about Peter? Should we connect the occasion of the great "take-off" of the early Christian mission, with its communities that soon were distinct from the Jewish synagogues, with the conversion of the Pharisee and scribe Saul/Paul of Tarsus, who understood his ministry as a missionary to non-Jews, perhaps as no other follower of Jesus in the first century? Which continuities and which discontinuities existed between the activity of the apostle Paul and the activities of the Jerusalem apostles?

Historical-critical scholarship would assert that there is a consensus concerning some of these questions—for example, the view that the summons to missionary work among non-Jews in Mt 28:18-20 cannot be an authentic saying of Jesus (a "consensus" that will be questioned in a later chapter). Differing answers to these questions provide different foundations for an account of the history of the early Christian church. Critics who view evangelical scholarship with skepticism are reminded that it is part of the "self-understanding of every scientific discipline, New Testament studies included," that opinions that have been elevated to a *consensus plurium* "need to be constantly examined, more precisely formulated and often enough revised."[16]

A central process of missionary intention is winning people for specific convictions and ways of behavior—that is, their "conversion." Here, another set of questions arises. How does the expansion of the Christian faith take place? How did the number of Christian churches grow and multiply? Hans Conzelmann correctly pointed out that this expansion and growth cannot be compared with ideas or fashions that arise and become popular because they are "in the air" as a certain group of people or an entire era identifies with the trend. He com-

---

[16]Sänger 1995, 75-76.

ments, "The Christian faith was not 'in the air.' The Christians indeed believed that God sent his Son 'in the fullness of time' (Gal 4:4). But by this they meant neither that the world in and of itself was ripe to receive the redeemer nor that at that time the world situation was especially favorable for the success of Christianity. Rather, they meant that God determines the times and the fulfillment. The new teaching does not spread by, so to speak, contagion. It is borne through the world by witnesses of the faith because the Lord of the church wills to be recognized as Lord of the *world*. Therein the church knows that the success is not the result of human cleverness; it is the Lord himself who 'adds' believers (Acts 2:47)."[17]

Again, several important questions arise that need to be taken up in this discussion. Which preparatory factors made the early Christian missionary movement possible? Were the methods of the missionaries confrontative or accommodating? Is it even possible to speak of "methods" of the early Christian mission? What was the content of the early Christian preaching? What role did rhetorical considerations play in missionary proclamation? What convinced Jews and pagans to adopt the convictions of the Christians and join their churches? What was the role of baptism? Did the political climate in Judea, Syria, Asia Minor, Achaia and Macedonia, in Antioch, Alexandria and Rome, and in targeted regions such as Spain influence the missionary work of the apostles? Did the social status of the early missionaries play any role?

These questions imply both historical and theological aspects. In regard to the *origins* of the early Christian mission, in which Jewish Christians seek to win pagans for their beliefs and practices, important issues need to be clarified on the *historical level:* the attitude of Israelites and of Jews over against non-Israelites and non-Jews; the significance of Jesus and his proclamation for the activity of his followers; the role of the disciples (i.e., the Twelve) after Jesus' death and resurrection. On a *theological level* the following questions are significant: What is the relationship between missionary activity of the early Christians and the resulting conversions of pagans to YHWH, the one true God, the God of Abraham, Isaac and Jacob, who revealed himself in Jesus Christ for the salvation of the world, and the "last days" that the prophets had announced and that both Jews and Christians expected? Which factors, which thought processes, prompted the first Christians to turn to pagan polytheists? How did they manage the necessity of living with "unclean" pagans in the Christian communities? Which specific aspects of the traditional biblical faith and life of pious Israelites/ Jews changed or needed to change? If the Gentile mission was indeed a new, unprecedented historical "innovation," if Jews who had been taught and trained to maintain their ritual purity and ethnic identity regarded the Gentile mission as revolutionary, as indeed they must have, then it is of foundational importance

---

[17]Conzelmann 1969, 3 (ET, 14).

to address these questions that imply historical and theological perspectives.

In regard to the *progress* of the early Christian mission, I will describe, first, *events:* the growth of the church in Jerusalem; the preaching activities in towns outside Judea; the conversion of the first Gentile who already feared God, of the first proselyte, of the first "total" pagan; the foundation of the first church; the manner of expansion. Second, *towns and regions:* the missionary activity in Jerusalem and in Judea, in Galilee and in the neighboring regions, in Damascus and in Antioch, in Asia Minor, in Greece, in Italy and in Spain, and the question of Gaul and of northern Africa as potential or actual targets of missionary outreach in the first century. Third, *chronological issues:* the sequence of the first missionary contacts with Gentiles; the time between Paul's conversion and the beginning of his missionary activity; the time line of the apostolic mission. Fourth, *persons:* Peter and the other apostles who had been disciples of Jesus, Stephen and Philip, James and Barnabas, Paul, Timothy and Titus, Aquila and Prisca, Epaphras and Apollos.

We will see that several factors were responsible for the origins and the development of the early Christian mission. These factors impacted the missionary movement of the early church not in an isolated fashion; rather, they functioned together in an interlocking system, enhancing each other and intensifying the effect and the dynamics of sometimes simple symptoms.

If we apply our definition of mission consistently to this goal of a comprehensive description of the early Christian mission, we would also need to discuss the new formulations of faith and the new social forms and practices that were characteristic for the early church; that is, we would need to investigate, using later systematizing terminology, the theology, christology, soteriology and anthropology of the apostles, as well as the ecclesiology and ethics of the new converts and their congregations. In other words, we could, indeed should, describe in a comprehensive manner early Christian theology and ethics. Peter Stuhlmacher is correct when he writes, in his *Biblical Theology of the New Testament,* in the first sentence of his long chapter about Paul, "Besides a description of the proclamation and of the ministry of Jesus, a description of the missionary theology of the Apostle Paul is a focal point of every and thus of our own (Biblical) Theology of the New Testament"; he further comments, "The theology of Paul that we can describe on the basis of these epistles, of course, is not a systematically consistent blueprint, but is a *missionary theology with a universal horizon* drafted, often rather hastily, as a result of practical needs."[18] It goes without saying that it is not possible to present such a comprehensive description of the theology of the early church as "missionary theology" in the present work. We need to make do with summarizing individual theological, christological, soteriological, ethical and ecclesiological aspects and elements of the early church when necessary.

2.2 Methodological Considerations

Every historical account of events and developments in antiquity has the twofold problem of fragmentary sources and of ignorance or uncertainty concern-

---

[18]Stuhlmacher 1992-1999, 1:221, 232.

ing the connection between individual specific facts and events and general realities and developments.[19] What Ramsay MacMullen wrote in his description of
the expansion of the Christian faith in the period A.D. 100-400 applies for the
period A.D. 30-100: because the information that we have for the time period is
unsatisfactory both in terms of quantity and quality, it is impossible to arrange
the material in a simple linear narrative.[20] François Vouga expresses this state of
affairs with a graphic image: "The historian stretches his net between several
pinheads and thus on elegant bridges traverses the places that remain dark."[21]
However, the historian needs to take care that the "pinheads" are indeed fixed
points and not hypothetically reconstructed possibilities. If conservative exegetes sometimes appear overly confident because they think they are standing
on secure foundations, not realizing that there is only a high wire or net, their
liberal counterparts often seem rather self-confident because they mistake the
pinheads for broad Greek columns. Still others may seem subdued, fearing
earthquakes beneath every pinhead.[22]

The fact that we do not possess unequivocal, direct archaeological evidence for the first
Christians is well known. New archaeological discoveries have not substantially altered
this fact. This is true with regard to the stone plaque engraved with the name and title of
Pilate ("Pontius Pilate, Prefect of Judea") discovered in Caesarea in 1961, the Caiaphas inscription on an ossuary discovered in 1990 ("Joseph, son of Caiaphas"), and the recent
discovery, announced in the November 2002 issue of *Biblical Archaeology Review,* of the
ossuary with the inscription "James, son of Joseph, brother of Jesus," verified as authentic
by André Lemaire, who dates the inscription to approximately A.D. 63 (there are, however,
increasing doubts about the inscription's authenticity). Another important discovery is the
private dwelling, excavated after 1968, belonging to a fisherman in Capernaum, dated to
the first century and identified with the house of Peter. However, the majority of the 118
synagogues and all of the 390 churches that Yoram Tsafrir, Leah di Segni and Judith Green
list in the TIR for western Palestine (1994) date to the third century at the earliest.

Relevant and Extraneous Statements of the Questions
As we seek to understand the Jewish and Greco-Roman world of the early imperial period and to properly evaluate the early Christian sources in the context
of relevant historical, social and religious data, we need to be careful not to introduce questions that fail to take into account in an adequate manner the nature of the ancient sources. Lutz von Padberg warns that "the endeavor to adequately understand the missionary period faces the danger of distortion caused
by inadequate methodological presuppositions such as monocausal explana-

---

[19]Lane Fox 1986, 7.
[20]MacMullen 1984, vii.
[21]Vouga 1994, 1.
[22]It is not possible to discuss basic hermeneutical questions here. For a comprehensive descrip-
    tion of a hermeneutically adequate investigation of the history, theology and literature of the
    New Testament see N. T. Wright 1992, 29-144.

tions or evaluations that are based on fixed perspectives. The modern observer may not notice it, but his description of history is usually the result of a subsequent process of rationalization, as his desire for objectivity encounters the subjective experience of a reality of life that is distant both chronologically and emotionally."[23] The world of the early Roman Empire, which included Palestine, Asia Minor and Greece, was far more complex and diverse than the interpretations based on research can grasp or the sources themselves suggest.

The approach of the "history of mentalities" that was developed in France in connection with historical anthropology seeks to describe the entire historical reality: "the sum of reaction mechanisms and basic convictions of specific social groups within a definite timeframe and their chronological comparison"; historical mentality is "the ensemble of the modes and the contents of the thought and the perceptions that are formative for a specific collective in a specific time. Mentality manifests itself in actions."[24] Modes of thought pertain to the manner of dealing consciously with information—for example, primarily causal-logical or more associative thinking. The contents of cultural thought include the fundamental convictions in ideological, political, religious, ethical and aesthetic areas that are generally valid for the culture and society that is being described, but also notions that exist only in images, such as representations of deities or religious myths. Modes of perception and sentiment include automatic value judgments that belong to a specific everyday view of the world. The contents of such perceptions include unreflected stereotypes—for example, the basic attitudes of Torah-observant Jews over against pagans. If the "collective" is described in terms of the inhabitants of Judea or Asia Minor, for example, or indeed of the entire Roman Empire, historians speak of a fundamental reality within which specific mentalities can be described that characterize a particular group, such as the inhabitants of Corinth, a new Roman colony, or even people of a certain age group.

Mentalities can be recognized in actions that are prompted by specific situations, as they channel the reactions of people. František Graus argues, significantly, that there are few specific sources for mentalities; what we have are specific questions.[25] What Lutz von Padberg has argued with regard to the Christian mission in the early medieval period applies even more to the Christian mission in the first century, for which we have far fewer sources than for the missionaries of the seventh and eighth centuries: the history of mentalities can be particularly helpful for a description of the history of missions "because it shifts the

---

[23]Padberg 1995, 18; for the Middle Ages see ibid., 18-19.
[24]Dinzelbacher 1993, xxi; for the second observation see ibid., xxii-xxvi. See also P. H. Hutton, "The History of Mentalities: The New Map of Cultural History," *History and Theory* 20 (1981): 239-59; V. Sellin 1985; Dressel 1996, 263-70.
[25]Graus 1987, 47.

focus from an ecclesiastical history of events to the content of their faith."[26] The
early Christian missionaries did not live and work in a secular world. If we want
to give an adequate account of their missionary work, we need to take their own
faith and beliefs seriously, but also the religious convictions of the pagans with
whom they had contact. We note, however, that there are only a few descriptions of mentalities in the Greco-Roman world that we can use for our description of the first century.

The biblical scholar who investigates historical events and developments
thus needs to make skillful use of the available historical, social and religious
data in their complex diversity as he or she seeks to explain the connection of
some data with other data as objectively and as carefully as possible. Before describing the ministry of Jesus, I thus will outline relevant social and cultural realities in Palestine (§8), and before describing the international missionary ministry of the apostles beyond Jerusalem, I will survey significant realities of the
Roman Empire (§18). As we describe events and developments, persons and activities of the early Christian missionary enterprise, we seek to pay proper attention to historical contexts in their specific totality and in their individual uniqueness. Therefore I describe with some detail the cities and towns in which the
early Christian missionaries preached or might have preached when I outline
the geographical expansion of the church (§§10.5; 15.2; 20.2-5; 22.1-12; 26.1-3;
27.1-8).

Historical reconstructions will more closely reflect the realities that historians
seek to describe if and when they avoid generalizations, which are always a
danger, particularly in the rich "first world"—the poor "third world," or "two-
thirds world," is in many respects closer to the social realities of the "ancient
world." Some aspects of this problem are difficult to avoid. For example, there
is the notion that "religion" is "doctrine," which is an assumption that we hardly
discuss but is not necessarily correct, particularly when applied to the specific
realities of the ancient world in the first century whereby every individual "pagan" could choose to "believe" in any deity, as long as people did not aggressively act against other variants of religious belief.[27] Another example that
should prompt the historian to be careful is the fact that an account of the process of conversion of people in antiquity is not self-evident. Lutz von Padberg
comments, "A change of faith (or religion), however thoroughgoing it may be,
is initiated by people in the context of a communication process, but is then
perceived by the new believer, in terms of the individual impact and the exis-

[26]Padberg 1995, 18.
[27]MacMullen 1981, 99-108; 1984, 8. Richard Strelan (1996, 13-14) deduces from the fact that the
veneration of a particular deity could have many diverse forms that research into the religious
situation in Ephesus needs to be careful not to identify *Artemis Ephesia* with *Artemis Soteria*
or with other variants of Artemis worship in Ephesus or in other cities.

tential affect, as intervention of divine activity in his life. The modern claim to explain even metaphysical realities encounters here the thinking of the authors of that period, which is completely different."[28]

Hermeneutical Presuppositions

No history is written without presuppositions. The notion that there was no "apostolic period" is as much a *theory* of history dependent on certain presuppositions as is the conviction that the apostles could claim an authority given to them by Jesus the Messiah, and that an investigation of their writings, as collected in what we call the New Testament, has priority over other Christian writings as Christians give an account of the nature of the church and its mission. François Vouga, in the preface to his history of the early church, emphasized that we can speak of a certain objectivity regarding a process of interpretation and reconstruction as represented by the historiography of early Christianity only insofar as "the description gives an account of presuppositions and methods," and that the one-sidedness that may result might be counterbalanced by references to diverging interpretation.[29] I agree with this assessment but cannot resist pointing out that evangelical scholars often do a better job in this respect than exegetes who follow traditional historical-critical consensus positions.[30]

Following Ernst Dassman, I summarize my fundamental presupposition as follows: the following description of the early Christian mission should be understood as both a historical and a theological discourse "that traces how God's salvation was realized in history. If Jesus' death and resurrection brought salvation and forgiveness of sins, the effects should be visible in history. Of course this demonstration cannot be objectified, and it is not easy. However, when some historians argue with history against the church and with the reality of contemporary Christianity against the Christian message, a history of the church written from a theological perspective has to achieve more than the gratification of historical curiosity. Such a history has to deal with faith itself, because faith is made insecure, or strengthened, but never left in peace by history, at least subjectively and for the individual observer."[31] As we reflect on the missionary work of the first Christians, we need to remind ourselves constantly that each epoch of history needs to be understood in the context and on the basis of its thought and its possibilities. The spirituality of the early Christian missionaries can hardly be grasped with the "enlightened" pathos of agnostic academics.

Presuppositions are damaging when they are not recognized as being oper-

---

[28]Padberg 1995, 21-22. For an investigation of conversion in the Gospels in light of contemporary conversion stories see McKnight 2002.
[29]Vouga 1994, vii.
[30]Vouga himself is an example, as he ignores evangelical (and nonevangelical) arguments supporting the historical reliability of the Acts of the Apostles.
[31]Dassmann 1991, 5.

ative in the hermeneutical approach of the scholar, and they are particularly problematic if they are turned into instruments for the discriminating exclusion of alternative interpretations and suggestions. The latter has become an acute problem since Hermann Reimarus (1694-1768) in the historical-critical investigation of the New Testament and its origins and in the investigation of the history of Jesus of Nazareth, of the early church and of the apostle Paul. Biblical scholars face the pressure of the historical-critical guild to prove that their research is "critical" and that they thus belong to the company of academic *Neutestamentler* who bask in the sun of critical rationality.[32]

This pressure "guarantees" that a scholar is not a biblicist in disguise or, *horribile dictu*, a fundamentalist. If specific historical or exegetical suggestions are eliminated from the start as "unscientific" in such a context, then the legitimate desire for serious and consistent historical discussion and evaluation of sources is perverted. Such "critical" scholars ignore the basic condition of historical investigation: the evaluation and interpretation of all available data.[33] If, for example, some scholars eliminate certain sayings of the "historical Jesus" as secondary (redactional) creations of the church that resulted from specific needs of diverging and sometimes competing early Christian churches, then the counter-question must be permitted whether this hypothesis explains *the data* better than the "simple" assumption that Jesus indeed said in any given instance what the Gospel writers narrate. Helga Botermann, a classical scholar, comments, "Scholars who reject the 'most obvious' understanding, as it arises for the ancient or the modern reader—and presumably in accordance with the intention of the author—and argue for a different understanding must, on principle, have the better arguments."[34] On the other hand, the criterion of the "simple explanation" is, of course, not a panacea for solving historical questions; events and developments in history seldom emerge in clean and orderly ways, and more often than not their particulars are strange, unrepeatable and improbable. The experience that the individual exegete has with the data of the early Christian sources prompts diverse and differently accentuated evaluations of their authenticity and usefulness. This leads us to the next point.

The Sources

The following account of the early Christian mission details the missionary activity of the apostles, meaning Jesus' disciples, Paul and his coworkers and other missionaries of the first century. This means that we describe a specific epoch of the history of missions: the era in which the missionaries of the first and second generation of the church were active. The sources for this account

---

[32]Cf. Botermann 1996, 18 n. 10, in a similar context.
[33]N. T. Wright 1992, 105-6; for the remarks that follow above see ibid.
[34]Botermann 1996, 25.

are therefore the following: (1) the narrative of the earliest missionary work written by Luke, who was not only an eyewitness but also evidently a missionary himself; (2) the letters written by individual missionaries, besides the letters of Peter and John primarily the letters of Paul; (3) the Gospels as presentations of the life of Jesus, probably written by Christians who were active as missionaries themselves and who reveal interests and convictions relevant for the missionary task. A second group of texts are the "acts" of individual apostles written in the second, third and fourth centuries, several generations after the events narrated; their information is therefore of doubtful value.

These sources will be described more fully in the following remarks. Historical accounts rely on direct and indirect sources: literary, inscriptional (epigraphical) and archaeological sources that "speak" directly to the events and developments in question, and also on literary, inscriptional and archaeological sources that date to the same period and illuminate the circumstances in which the events took place. The only direct sources that we possess for a description of the early Christian mission are the writings of the New Testament, in most cases written (in my opinion) before A.D. 70, in many cases written by authors who were directly involved in the missionary outreach of the early church. The Christians of the first and second generations generally did not produce inscriptions—at least none have been found, with the possible exceptions of the inscription on the ossuary of James and the inscription in Lystra mentioning Philtatos (see §27.1). Apart from the "house of Peter" in Capernaum and the discovery of what may have been a house church in Bethsaida (see §9.2), there are no archaeological primary sources for the early Christian movement.[35]

When all available sources are exhausted, scholars may arrive at different hypotheses that explain the extant data, for a variety of reasons. If we allow the hypotheses of some scholars who analyze the Gospels and Acts as a matter of principle with skepticism regarding their historical reliability, then intellectual integrity demands that other scholars be permitted to explore these same sources with advance confidence that they convey reliable information. Advance confidence means not simply a confidence resulting from dogmatic loyalties (as if traditional historical-critical skepticism is not tied to dogmatic condi-

---

[35]In regard to epigraphical sources (inscriptions), even specialists deplore the fact that they are published in a diverse and uncoordinated manner that approximates the scattered places in which they have been discovered. New electronic media promise to open up new avenues of presentation. Since 1993 the Deutsche Forschungsgemeinschaft has financed the program Historische Grundlagenforschung im antiken Kleinasien—Epigraphik, Numismatik und Geographie (Basic Historical Research in Asia Minor in Antiquity: Epigraphics, Numismatics and Geography), which aims at presenting an epigraphical database for Asia Minor, to be made available on CD-ROM. See H. Halfmann and C. Schäfer, "Epigraphische Datenbank zum antiken Kleinasien," in *Datenbanken in der Alten Geschichte* (ed. M. Fell et al.; Computer und Antike Band 2; St. Katharinen: Scripta Mercaturae, 1994), 17-25.

tions!), but one grounded in the experience that the data that the Gospels and Acts recount can be explained adequately and perhaps even better without some other hypothesis. Biblical scholars should finally abandon their skepticism concerning New Testament authors, who write with pronounced theological interests. Recent studies have shown that Luke should be understood as both a historian and a theologian.[36] Critics who think that an author must be interpreted as either a theologian or a historian project a dualism into first-century sources informed by the philosophical-hermeneutical demands of the Enlightenment. This dualism is incapable of truly understanding early Christian (and many early Jewish) texts[37] and is rejected by classical scholars.[38]

An unprejudiced reader who surveys the New Testament's table of contents will assume that the most important source for a description of the history of the early Christian mission is the Acts of the Apostles, especially when he or she notices that the author of that document has also written an account of the life of Jesus Christ—Luke thus being an author who described the history of Jesus and his followers from the earliest beginnings to approximately A.D. 62. Biblical scholars at German-speaking universities remain doubtful, at times even contemptuous, of the historical reliability of the information provided by Luke, following the positions of Ferdinand Christian Baur and his students. This skepticism results in the methodological decision to treat Acts as a source of only secondary value, "inferior" to the letters of Paul as true primary sources for earliest Christianity. Baur compared Acts with the undisputed letters of Paul in the same way critics compare the Gospel of John with the Synoptic Gospels and concluded that "the huge difference of the respective presentations means that historical truth can be found only on one side or the other."[39] This means, in plain language, that we cannot trust Luke as a historian. Heinz Schürmann is not prepared to characterize Luke as a historian, "despite his historiographical expertise," but neither does he want to describe Luke as an artist or a theologian. Rather, Luke was an "inspired man of the church who was concerned about the practical questions of the life of the church during the final years of the apostolic period and who put pen to paper in a responsible manner."[40] Jürgen Wehnert is convinced that "the outline of Acts is unsuitable as framework for a history of early Christianity"; Günter Wasserberg warns that it is methodologically important "not to switch immediately from the narrated level to the world of history. The Acts of the Apostles cannot directly be interpreted in terms of providing his-

---

[36]I. H. Marshall 1970; see R. Strelan 1996, 22.
[37]See N. T. Wright 1992, 384.
[38]See Botermann (1996, 30-31), who refers to Herodotus and Seneca.
[39]Baur 1866, 1:7; similarly Dibelius 1968; Haenchen, *Apg;* Conzelmann, *Apg;* Schille, *Apg;* Zmijewski, *Apg;* see also Lüdemann 1980, 45-49; Murphy-O'Connor 1996, vi. On Baur's view of the history of early Christianity see Alkier 1993, 200-253.
[40]Schürmann, *Lk,* 1:16-17.

torical information"; Wolfgang Reinbold is prepared to admit that Luke "may be basically right about one or another notice of success" of the apostles' ministry, but he believes that the narration of events shows "the hand of the author of Acts to such a degree that we cannot arrive at conclusions concerning the successes of the apostles."[41] Critics sometimes make curious misjudgments in the context of such fundamental skepticism—for example, Martin Dibelius, who suggests that "the author of the Book of Acts in the New Testament wanted to describe the first Christian mission but really only presented Paul's journeys."[42]

Among German-speaking scholars there were few exceptions to this critique of Luke after Adolf von Harnack, who defended a conservative position.[43] The situation has changed in more recent years, particularly as a result of the work of Martin Hengel.[44] English-speaking biblical scholars more often are prepared to acknowledge the historical value of Acts, perhaps because they frequently have been involved in interdisciplinary dialogue with classical scholarship.[45] Classical scholars such as Robin Lane Fox and Helga Botermann repeatedly have defended information provided by Acts against critical *Neutestamentler.*[46]

Helga Botermann, a classical scholar who teaches in Göttingen, writes, "I have been shocked for many years concerning the manner in which New Testament scholars treat their sources. They have managed to question everything to such a degree that both the historical Jesus and the historical Paul are hardly discernible any longer. If classical scholars were to adopt their methods, they could take their leave immediately. They would not have much left to work with. . . . If classical scholars analyzed their sources as 'critically' as most New Testament theologians do, they would have to close the files on Herodotus and Tacitus."[47] Martin Hengel has voiced similar criticism. Jürgen Becker protests against this dressing-down of his guild. In Becker's opinion, Hengel's critique of research into Acts in Germany is a sweeping dismissal that amounts to a methodological regression to the time before Martin Dibelius, and it is dressed in the cloak of a "materialism of facts"

---

[41]Wehnert 1997, 273; Wasserberg 1998, 236; Reinbold 2000, 103.

[42]Dibelius, "Paulus in Athen," in Dibelius 1968, 71 (ET, 78).

[43]Harnack 1906-1911; see also Wikenhauser 1921, as well as E. Meyer (1921-1923), who has largely been ignored by New Testament scholars. On Harnack and Meyer see Jantsch 1990, esp. 32-81 for their respective concepts of history.

[44]Hengel 1979, 11-61; 1983b; 1991, 178-79; see also C.-J. Thornton 1991; Stuhlmacher 1992-1999, 1:227-28; Riesner 1994, 282-90; Breytenbach 1996; Stenschke 1999a; Reiser 2001.

[45]See the survey in Gasque 1989a, 251-66, and more recently Breytenbach 1996, 5-10. Important contributions come from William Ramsay, William Calder and more recently F. F. Bruce (1985a; *Acts*), I. H. Marshall (1970, 21-76), Colin Hemer (1989) and the six-volume series edited by Bruce Winter, *The Book of Acts in Its First-Century Setting* (1993-1997). See also Balch 1995; R. Strelan 1996, 20-23. Bock (*Lk,* 1:13) characterizes Luke as "first-class ancient historian." See further Witherington, *Acts,* 1-102; 2001, 174-78, 383-86. Barrett (*Acts;* 1999) is more critical than Bruce, Hemer or Marshall but generally evaluates the historical reliability of Acts in a positive manner.

[46]Lane Fox 1988, 99-100, 293; Botermann 1991; 1993; 1996, 17-49.

[47]Botermann 1993, 64, 73; cf. idem 1996, 24 n. 39.

that operates with a preconceived view of history—a critique that cannot answer the question of *how* the New Testament texts should be read.[48] This response is not only unfair; it also fails to interact with the critical issues raised by Hengel, Botermann and others, abiding instead by the old, cherished literary-critical positions.

A recent example of an irresponsible handling of the book of Acts is found in Ludger Schenke's study of the historical and theological development of the early church. He acknowledges that several passages of Luke's narrative have "some historical value."[49] But when he surveys the account of the origins of the church in Antioch (Acts 11:19-26), he asserts that any data that reflect "typical elements of Lukan style" or correspond with "Luke's view of the church"—as, for example, the missionary pattern in 11:19: first to the Jews, then to the Gentiles—can be explained in terms of redaction and thus cannot be used for a historical account; on the other hand, data that contradict the "Lukan conception of history"—as, for example, the initiation of the Gentile mission by the Hellenists—contain "primitive information."[50] The methodological problems of such a position and procedure are immense. How can we recognize typical elements of Luke's style in connection with their dissimilarity regarding stylistic characteristics of "primitive information"? How can we know Luke's view of the church or of the missionary work of the church if not from Luke's book of Acts? What if Luke agrees in terms of both substance and "style" with "primitive information" that he introduces? How can we separate tradition and redaction if we do not want to cross the line into speculative hypotheses? Is the premise really convincing that the only early Christian historian whose work has survived—perhaps the only Christian author in the first century who wrote an account of the development of early church—and acquired canonical dignity is historically reliable only when he contradicts his own view of history? Ron Cameron believes that it is problematic for a reconstruction of the beginnings of Christianity to rely, like Eusebius, on the book of Acts, as the latter is characterized by legendary and idealizing tendencies, and as Luke's starting point is the dramatic event of the death and resurrection of Jesus, a myth—only to suggest the apocryphal *Gospel of Thomas* as an alternative source for the early history of the Christian movement![51]

The skepticism regarding information in the book of Acts seems, at least occasionally, to find an explanation in the fact that university theologians are not familiar with missionary realities from personal experience; they have not seen antagonistic or indifferent people being converted to the Christian faith, or they have not been part of a team that planted a new local church. And it seems that often they have not attempted to at least gather relevant information on such matters. When Luke speaks of three thousand new converts (Acts 2:41), Ernst Haenchen deems it necessary to eliminate this information as unhistorical, pointing out that people do not realize how difficult it is to speak to so many people "without a microphone." He follows Martin Dibelius, who thought it far more likely that the small band of Christians lived "a quiet and, in the Jewish sense, 'pious' existence in Jerusalem. It was a modest existence, and nothing but the victorious conviction of the believers betrayed the fact that from this company a movement would go out which was to change the world."[52] This explanation by Haenchen is somewhat embarrassing when we read that in the eighteenth century George Whitefield preached, of course with-

---

[48]Becker 1997, 983-85.
[49]Schenke 1990, 322.
[50]Schenke 1990, 318 with n. 2.
[51]Cameron 1994, esp. 515, 517, 518-25.
[52]Haenchen, *Apg,* 190 (ET, 188-89), quoting Dibelius 1968, 109 (ET, 124).

out a microphone, at least on one occasion to forty thousand people,[53] and that Greek or Roman generals evidently were able to speak in front of thousands of soldiers.

Even conservative scholars sometimes are influenced more by reconstructed trajectories of development or style than by specific statements of the text. For example, James Dunn thinks that the astonishing confidence of Peter and John in Acts 3:8-12 is a stylistic device, although he discusses the possibility that the Lukan narrative may reflect "the burgeoning boldness" of the apostles, who are "still swept along on a wave of spiritual enthusiasm."[54] When Peter, at the end of his first defense before the Sanhedrin, describes Jesus as the divinely provided cornerstone, and when he emphasizes that "there is salvation in no one else" but Jesus (Acts 4:11-12), then this has, according to Dunn, "the ring of enthusiastic hyperbole," while at the same time these claims "seem to express the product of a longer period of reflection than the narrative has allowed." When Dunn concludes by pointing out that "we may assume that Luke is providing what would have been regarded in his own time as a highly responsible historical account," he seems to imply that modern methods of historical research help us to understand developments in the early church better than Luke did. It is therefore hardly surprising that Acts 4:11-12 plays no role in his description of the historical developments in Jerusalem.[55] However, what is the evidence for any assumption concerning the time frame in which Jesus' disciples recognized the significance of Jesus in terms of redemptive exclusiveness? How much time did the disciples need to grasp the significance of Jesus: after their encounter with the crucified Jesus after the resurrection, after receiving a call to embark on a worldwide mission to Jews and Gentiles, after the reception of the Holy Spirit? That the disciples remained in Jerusalem after Jesus' crucifixion despite the fact that Galilee was their home and despite the potential and soon acute danger of living and preaching in Jerusalem as followers of Jesus demonstrates that they understood at least that much about the significance of Jesus, that they were willing not only to invest their efforts in Jesus' cause but also to risk their very lives. The confidence of some critics in their own reconstructions and verdicts on what was historically possible or impossible two thousand years ago in Jerusalem is much more astonishing than the confidence that the apostles had in Jesus as crucified and risen messianic Savior.

The search for written sources that the author of Acts used has not been successful. We must not forget that Luke's informants were at the same time his (potential) critics. Helga Botermann comments, "This fact renders the assumption that he [Luke] would have been able to impose, arbitrarily, his prejudices and his intentions upon the historical narrative implausible from the start."[56]

An important indicator of the historical reliability of Luke's account and of his sources is the often remarkable precision of detail. For example, he traces the founding of the church in Antioch, a major metropolis in the Roman Empire, and the conversion of non-Jewish citizens to faith in Jesus Christ not in terms of an idealized geography of salvation history, nor does he continue the trajectory of Peter's preaching ministry from Jerusalem via Lod, Jaffa and Caesarea to include Antioch, but he affirms that Jewish Christians from Jerusalem, whose origins

---

[53]Arnold Dallimore, *George Whitefield: The Life and Times of the Great Evangelist of the Eighteenth-Century Revival* (2 vols.; Edinburgh: Banner of Truth Trust, 1970-1980), 1:292, 296.

[54]Dunn, *Acts,* 51; for the remarks that follow above see ibid., 51-52.

[55]Dunn 1991, 117-39.

[56]Botermann 1993, 72, giving examples from Acts.

were in Cyprus and Cyrene, worked as missionaries in Antioch (Acts 11:19-20).[57]
A comprehensive analysis of several areas clearly indicates that Luke's account
is both conscientious and reliable: (1) the chronological links of detailed information in Acts with the historical milieu of the middle of the first century; (2) the
geographical information on matters of secondary, negligible importance; (3) information on political, local and cultural matters that cannot be assumed to have
been general knowledge; (4) the internal correlation of minor details that otherwise assume no leading role in Luke's account; (5) items that are not significant
for Luke's theological intentions but are important enough to be mentioned.[58]
Thus it must be seen as a calculated decision when biblical scholars refuse to
investigate Acts with positive expectations or at least with a neutral attitude.

Hans Conzelmann counters such arguments, not without a polemical undertone, with reference to the "rule" of Karl May (1842-1912), a German author of fictional accounts of the
exploits of European, particularly German, heroes among Native Americans: "A precise description of milieu or extensive reports of direct speech proves nothing regarding the historicity or the 'correctness' of the narrated event," since such a conclusion could be used
to prove the historicity of May's fictional stories.[59] This argument, as applied to an evaluation of the historical reliability of the book of Acts, works only if May maintained that the
actors of the plots in his books are historical personalities (rather than fictitious figures in
novels), or if it could be shown that Luke's Acts does not claim historical reliability and
that the persons whom he describes are, apart from historical figures such as emperors,
kings and governors, purely imaginary and fictional. Both assumptions are patently false.
Karl May never wanted his readers to believe that Old Shatterhand and Winnetou actually
lived, their exploits proving to be a blessing for the good people among Native Americans
and whites alike. If wide-eyed youths believed such things, carried away by the author's
gripping tales, May could not care less; he simply wants to entertain, and he writes neither
a work of history nor historical biographies. Luke, on the other hand, clearly portrays Peter
and John, Stephen and Philip, James and Barnabas and Paul as historical persons whose
ministry influences the history of the church and of the world. Finally, Conzelmann's argument is anachronistic: Greek and Roman authors of novels did not write historical fiction, providing specific details to give the appearance of historical verisimilitude.

The book of Acts is not a work of fiction, nor does it belong to the category of
historical fiction.[60] We must not forget that Acts is the second volume of a larger
work that begins with a prologue (Lk 1:1-4) in which Luke outlines his historiographical principles, whose criteria clearly apply also to Acts as the second volume of Luke's project (Acts 1:1-2).[61]

---

[57]Löning 1987, 93.
[58]See Bruce 1985a, 2576-79; Hemer 1989, 101-243 (cf. H. Bayer in *JETh* 4 [1990]: 158-62).
[59]H. Conzelmann, *Erasmus* 28 (1976): 68, in a review of Gasque 1989a [1975]; see also Conzel-
    mann and Lindemann 1995, 48. Today Conzelmann could "substantiate" his argument by
    pointing to the recent publication of *Karl-May-Atlas* (ed. H. H. Gerlach; Bamberg and Rade-
    beul: Karl-May-Verlag, 1997): imaginative adventures are indeed possible in "grid squares."
[60]Thus Pervo 1987; see the critique in Witherington, *Acts,* 2-39.
[61]See Dunn, *Acts,* x; I. H. Marshall 1993, 177.

In the prologue to his Gospel (Lk 1:1-4) Luke comments on the choice of his subject matter, the nature of the material that he has carefully (ἀκριβῶς) researched, the organization (καθεξῆς) of the material, and on the purposes of his account, not least of which is objective reliability (ἀσφάλεια). This program stands in the tradition of Greek historiography, linked with the names of Herodotus and Thucydides. Both content and presentation of material in the two-volume work of Luke-Acts display distinct affinities with Greek and Roman historical monographs[62] and biographies.[63] Luke published his material in the form of the ancient "treatise," with similarities in scientific treatises,[64] that gives an account of the "beginnings" of Christianity.[65] Naymond Keathley describes Luke's intentions in connection with Acts 15—28 in terms of the "triumph of Gentile Christianity,"[66] which is, however, anachronistic: at the end of Acts Paul is indeed in Rome but he is in prison; also, Luke gives no indication whether there were more Gentile Christians than Jewish Christians by A.D. 60 or 62. And in general the promulgation of the Christian faith certainly was not an "unhindered triumph" in the last decades of the first century.

If we could not trust the narrative literary sources of a certain period in history, if we were completely dependent on "remains"—archaeological finds such as foundation walls of buildings, pottery, coins and official documents—it would be "practically impossible to reconstruct a coherence of events [*Ereigniszusammenhang*]".[67] For example, classical scholars are unable to present a historical description of the history of the republic of Rome between 167 B.C., when the historiography of the Roman historian Livius ends (or has been lost), and 133 B.C., when literary historical descriptions become available again. The book of Acts is the only "narrative" source describing the origins of early Christianity. If scholars adopt the critical view that the book of Acts is a theological work, a political tractate or Christian *belles lettres,* and that it therefore must be regarded as lacking historical authenticity and reliability, then they should be consistent enough to admit that we are not, and never will be, able to provide a coherent account of the history of the earliest Christian churches and their missionary work. As important as Paul's letters are as primary sources for the life and work of this apostle, they do not allow us to evaluate which data provided in the book of Acts are historically authentic and which are spurious; they belong to the "genre" of historical "remains" and thus cannot be understood in and by themselves in terms of their place in and significance for the history of the early Christians.[68] To accept the Pauline letters as primary sources and evaluate the book of Acts as a secondary source is neither serviceable nor appropriate for a

---

[62]See Hemer 1989, 66-70; C.-J. Thornton 1991, 161-63; Botermann 1993, 67-69; D. Palmer 1993.
[63]See Talbert 1974.
[64]See L. Alexander 1993a; see also Bruce 1985a, 2570-71.
[65]I. H. Marshall 1993, 179-80; see also Eckey, *Apg,* 1:28-30; on the purpose of Acts see Gasque 1989a; Maddox 1982, 19-23; and the commentaries.
[66]Keathley 1999, 49-62.
[67]Botermann 1993, 65.
[68]Botermann 1993, 66; 1996, 29 n. 53.

description of the history of early Christianity. Despite the difficulties just mentioned, many historical-critical scholars work with this distinction. For example, Jürgen Becker recently asserted yet again that the "secure Pauline data" are often irreconcilable with "the narrated world of Acts."[69] On the other hand, the great classical scholar Eduard Meyer, whose view of the Christian faith was not uncritical, contended, "As regards the history of Christianity . . . we have the extraordinary, invaluable advantage, very rare for the great intellectual movements, that an account of the initial stages of its development has been preserved that has been written directly by one of the persons involved. This fact alone secures for the author an eminent place among the most significant historians of world history."[70] Gerd Lüdemann emphasized in regard to the historical reliability of the book of Acts and its use for a reconstruction of the history of early Christianity that the question of the eyewitness is of great importance.[71] Since the second century the tradition of the early church is unanimous in identifying the author of the book of Acts as Luke, the companion of Paul. The historical-critical consensus holds that this identification of the author is deduced on the basis of both the book of Acts and personal references in Paul's letters.[72] This argument is not necessarily cogent: (1) the early Christian tradition does not name any other candidate for the author of the book of Acts; (2) if the tradition concerning the authorship of Luke is but a deduction, other companions of Paul might have been candidates as well—for example, we know more about Timothy than about Luke, and Timothy had important functions in the leadership of churches comparable to other apostolic authors.[73] The tradition of the church, however, mentions only Luke as author of the book of Acts.

A main reason for rejecting the early Christian tradition concerning the authorship of the book of Acts is the argument that its portrait of Paul cannot be reconciled with the historical Paul as we know him from his letters.[74] However, this argument has been refuted successfully by many exegetes:[75] (1) The alleged theological differences between Paul and Luke's portrait in the book of Acts are

---

[69]Becker, *Gal,* 14. Since Volkmar (1887), Clemen (1893), Barnikol (1929) and Knox (1950), many historical-critical scholars have abandoned the framework of the book of Acts in their discussions of the chronology of the life of the apostle Paul; cf. Riesner 1994, 9-23; on Knox see the critique in T. Campbell, 1955.

[70]E. Meyer 1921-1923, 1:2-3; followed by Riesner 1994, 290 (ET, 326).

[71]Lüdemann 1987, 12 (ET, 4).

[72]See Pesch, *Apg,* 1:26.

[73]Marshall, *Acts,* 45.

[74]The article by Philipp Vielhauer, written in 1950, continues to be quoted in support of this argument: see "Zum Paulinismus der Apostelgeschichte," in Vielhauer 1965, 9-27; see also Haenchen, *Apg,* 120-24 (*Acts,* 112-16); Plümacher 1978a, 519; more recently Lentz 1993.

[75]See Ellis, *Lk,* 45-47; F. F. Bruce, "Is the Paul of Acts the Real Paul?" *BJRL* 86 (1976): 282-305; Marshall, *Acts,* 42-44; 1992, 96-98; Carson, Moo and Morris 1992, 187-90; Bruce 1993, 680-81; D. Wenham 1993; Porter 1999, esp. 187-206.

often exaggerated. For example, Acts 14:4, 14 show that Luke knew that Paul was an apostle, even though he generally focuses on the Twelve when he uses the term *apostolos*. (2) We know that the contemporaries of Paul—conservative Jewish-Christian opponents, for example—interpreted Paul's theology in various ways, which may hold true for Luke as well.[76] (3) The argument that Luke concealed basic conflicts that we encounter in Paul's letters does not hold water: the book of Acts repeatedly provides the reader with hints that the author knew much more than he reports—for example, concerning the collection during Paul's last visit in Jerusalem (cf. Acts 20:4). (4) The suggestion that a companion of Paul would have used the apostle's letters in composing the book of Acts is in keeping with procedures of modern historians who work with documents. However, an author in antiquity who personally knew Paul, a charismatic and fascinating person, would hardly have thought of searching for written documents in archives.[77]

Gerd Lüdemann suggests that we accept only those arguments against Luke as Paul's companion that can demonstrate for historical statements that the author of the book of Acts could not possibly have known Paul personally. He submits that the question of the number of visits that Paul paid to Jerusalem is such a proof: whereas Paul says that he visited Jerusalem three times after his conversion (cf. Gal 1:15-24; 2:10; and the story of the collection for the Jerusalem church), Luke reports five visits to Jerusalem (Acts 9:26; 11:30; 15:2-4; 18:22; 21:15-18).[78] Against Lüdemann, numerous (and not only evangelical) scholars accept all five visits by Paul reported in the book of Acts as historical.[79] If the visit to Jerusalem mentioned in Gal 2:1-10 is not identical with the visit on the occasion of the apostolic council (Acts 15) but rather coincides with the Antiochene collection visit mentioned in Acts 11:30—and there are good arguments for this identification[80]—then the historical reliability of Luke's report is further confirmed.

The "We-Passages" are evidence that Luke was a contemporary of Paul and an eyewitness to many incidents that he reports:[81] (1) The abruptness of the We-Passages can be explained by the unpretentiousness that characterizes both Luke's reference to his legitimacy for writing a reliable historical account (Lk 1:1-

---

[76]For this point and the next see Lüdemann 1987, 12-13 (ET, 4-6).
[77]Botermann 1996, 36.
[78]Lüdemann 1987, 13-14 (ET, 5-6).
[79]Riesner (1994, 6) refers for the period after 1970 to J. J. Gunther, J. van Bruggen, D. Moody and Hemer 1989, 251-70 and accepts this position; see his chronological synthesis in ibid., 286 (the collection visit from Antioch in A.D. 44/45 takes Paul for the second time to Jerusalem, after the visit in A.D. 33/34, a fact that should be listed in his table).
[80]Several scholars argue for this solution, more recently Longenecker, *Gal,* lxxiii-lxxxiii; D. Wenham 1993, 226-43. See §25.1 in the present work.
[81]See E. Meyer 1921-1923, 1:17-19; more recently Fitzmyer 1989a, 1-26; Hemer 1989, 312-64; C. J. Thornton 1991; F. Spencer 1992, 246-50; Botermann 1993, 74; Kurz 1993, 123; Pao 2000, 20-25. Porter (1994a; 1999, 10-46) suggests that the We-Passages derive from a source that was written by an author other than Luke; the meticulous manner with which Luke uses this source may demonstrate, in the light of the prologue in Lk 1:1-4, that the We-Passages derive from an eyewitness (which is, according to Porter, not certain). Differently D. Koch 1999.

4) and his role and participation in the missionary movement that he describes.[82] (2) Since the book of Acts is an account written in the first person singular (*Ich-Erzählung*), it cannot have appeared anonymously but must have been linked with the name of an author right from the beginning; in the tradition no alternatives to Luke are ever mentioned.[83] A historical account in the first person plural (*Wir-Erzählung*) that does not allow the reader to identify the narrator is a literary absurdity. Again, when we add up all available evidence from the apostolic and patristic periods, there is no alternative to Luke. (3) It is implausible to interpret the We-Passages as a stylistic device of Greco-Roman historiography that seeks to feign *autopsia* ("seeing with one's own eyes"), an eyewitness account; Luke does not include a self-presentation of the author, which was the standard device for this purpose. When ancient historians emphasize, in addition to being eyewitnesses, their active participation in the events, they do this in a self-reference (usually formulated in the third person singular). Luke writes (part of) his report in the first person, which is very rare for Greek and Roman authors (in contrast to Jewish tradition). Of course, it is theoretically possible that the We-Passages are an indication that the author of the book of Acts copied mechanically from available source documents that were written in the first person plural. This assumption is implausible, however, in light of the customs of Greek and Roman historiography and the literary capabilities of the author of the book of Acts, and in light of the fact that there was no literary model that would have allowed readers in the first century to understand the We-Passages in this sense. "This means that the We-Passages of the Book of Acts must be understood in terms of the author aspiring to mark his personal part in the event."[84]

The dating of Luke-Acts does not automatically prejudice the historical reliability of the book of Acts. With careful historical research it is possible to provide an accurate account from a distance of forty years or so. However, since critical scholars who treat the book of Acts as a literary source of the third generation of Christians generally have a low view of its historical value, the date of composition of Luke-Acts needs to be addressed. The (predominantly German) historical-critical consensus can be summarized as follows:[85] (1) the book of Acts was written as the second volume of Luke-Acts; (2) the Gospel of Luke is dependent upon the Gospel of Mark and must have been written after A.D. 70, as the eschatological discourse in Lk 12, which depends on Mk 13, looks back *ex eventu* on the destruction of Jerusalem and of the temple at the end of the First Jewish Revolt; (3) since the book of Acts contains no reference to the

---

[82]Hemer 1989, 328.
[83]C.-J. Thornton 1991, 84-98, 122, 147, 199.
[84]C.-J. Thornton 1991, 199; see 84-197.
[85]See Weiser, *Apg,* 1:40-41; Pesch, *Apg,* 1:28; Zmijewski, *Apg,* 14-15.

persecution of Christians in Rome and in Asia Minor at the end of Domitian's reign (A.D. 81-96) and betrays no knowledge of a collection of Paul's letters (often dated to about A.D. 100), the work should be dated to about A.D. 80-90; (4) thus the most plausible date for the composition of the book of Acts is A.D. 90.

This argumentation has not convinced all exegetes:[86] (1) The book of Acts contains no references to the persecution of Christians in Rome under Nero, to the death of Paul or James around A.D. 62 or to the destruction of Jerusalem and of the temple in A.D. 70.[87] (2) Roman authorities often are portrayed in a positive light in the book of Acts; they are not yet certain about how to evaluate the (Jewish? Greco-Roman?) movement of people who believe in Jesus. After the persecution of Christians under Nero, such a portrayal becomes more unlikely. (3) The fulfillment of Agabus's prophecy is explicitly mentioned (Acts 11:28), while a similar notice is not linked with the announcement of the destruction of Jerusalem by Jesus (Lk 21:20). (4) If Luke wrote the book of Acts after A.D. 70, we would expect a reference to the destruction of Jerusalem, perhaps as an editorial aside, in, for example, Stephen's speech (Acts 7) or the account of the arrest and imprisonment of Paul (Acts 21—23). (5) The portrayal of tensions between Jewish Christians and Gentile Christians in the book of Acts corresponds to similar references in Paul's letters (Galatians; 1 Cor 8—10; Romans) and supports a rather early date for the composition of Acts, as does the detailed report on questions related to the interpretation of the Torah and table fellowship (Acts 6:1-6; 10-11; 15). (6) The premise that Mk 13:2, 14-20 and Lk 19:41-44; 21:20-24 presuppose the destruction of Jerusalem and the temple in A.D. 70 is not conclusive: (a) We cannot and should not exclude the possibility that Jesus was able to prophecy future events. (b) The fall of Jerusalem is not explicitly mentioned in these texts, which contain no detail that presupposes knowledge of the historical events of the years A.D. 66-70. On the contrary, many elements cannot be closely correlated with events during the First Jewish Revolt: the notice that many will come in the name of Jesus; the reports of wars (*polemoi* [plural]) and national uprisings on an international scale; the notice that kingdom will rise "against kingdom" (Mk 13:8), which can hardly refer to Judea since the Jewish commonwealth in Palestine was not organized as a kingdom at the time. And the New Testament texts fail to mention remarkable events during the siege of Jerusalem after A.D. 66, such as cannibalism, plagues and massacres committed by Jews against Jews, as reported by Josephus.[88] (c) If Mark or Luke "created" an eschatological discourse after A.D. 70, the disparity between the disciples' question

---

[86]In addition to the authors mentioned by Schneider, *Apg,* 1:119 n. 88, see Marshall, *Acts,* 46-48; Hemer 1989, 365-410; Moessner 1989, 308-15; Carson, Moo and Morris 1992, 116-17, 190-94; Bock, *Lk,* 1:16-8; see also H.-J. Schulz 1995, 243-90.

[87]Robert Moberly 1993, who thus concludes that the book of Acts must have been written between A.D. 60 and 62.

[88]Gundry, *Mk,* 754-55; for the argument that follows above see ibid.

and Jesus' answer is difficult to explain: the disciples inquire about the destruction of the temple, while Jesus speaks about the profanation of the temple. If the texts represent a *post factum* construction of a dominical eschatological discourse, we would expect the prophecy *ex eventu* to deal first with the prophesied destruction and then explain the chronology and the sign that the disciples asked about. A historian who pretends to be a prophet would have at his disposal the chronology of events (of A.D. 66-70) and preceding "signs." (d) References to a siege of Jerusalem by a hostile army (Lk 21:20) and the occupation of Jerusalem by foreign rulers who send Jewish prisoners into exile (Lk 21:24) are conceivable before A.D. 70 even in nonprophetic speech: a Jewish teacher who wants to threaten God's people, whom he perceives to be living in unrepentant rebellion against YHWH's revealed will, with divine judgment would only need to remember the biblical description of the destruction of Solomon's temple in 586 B.C. and contemporary reports about military operations against cities. (7) On the assumption that Luke wrote his Gospel after Mark wrote and that Mark's Gospel was composed before A.D. 70, Luke could have seen and used the Gospel of Mark even at such an early period: both Luke and Mark belonged to the circle of Paul's co-workers. (8) The notice in Lk 1:1 that many attempted to write the history of Jesus allows a date as early as A.D. 62, or even earlier, for the composition of Luke-Acts: more than thirty years had already passed since Jesus' crucifixion and resurrection. For these reasons many exegetes date the composition of the book of Acts to A.D. 62-65.

To sum up, if the book of Acts was indeed written by an eyewitness (at least of Paul's travels) not long after the events narrated in the account, it must be treated as a primary source in any description of earliest Christianity. "Since Luke was the first author to conceptionally compose his subject, he is according to Droysen 'the first source' that controls the tradition."[89] This means for the description of the early Christian mission that the book of Acts, together with Paul's letters and the Gospels, is a primary source for the period A.D. 30-70. Since I limit my description of the early Christian mission to the apostolic period (without excluding evidence for this period in the patristic sources), and since the late dates assigned by historical-critical scholars to some (allegedly inauthentic) letters of Paul and to the Gospels have been contested on the basis of good arguments for early dates, we may group the literary sources for this study into two groups: (1) sources written between A.D. 30 and 70: the letters of Paul,[90]

---

[89]Botermann 1993, 66; cf. idem 1996, 34-37. Botermann (1996, 41-42) dates the book of Acts to the Flavian period, after A.D. 80.

[90]For an early dating (before A.D. 64) of Paul's letters to the Ephesians, to Timothy and to Titus, whose authenticity is contested by scholars, see J. Robinson 1976; Carson, Moo and Morris 1992; *DPL;* and the following commentaries: Barth, *Eph,* 36-50; O'Brien, *Col,* xli-xlix; Dunn, *Col,* 35-39; Barth and Blanke, *Col,* 114-26; Marshall, *Thess,* 28-45; Wannamaker, *Thess,* 17-28; Fee, *1-2 Tim,* 23-26; Knight, *PastEp,* 21-52; Spicq, *ÉpPast,* 1:157-214.

the letters of Peter,[91] the letter of James, the Gospel of Mark,[92] the Gospel of Luke and the book of Acts, the Gospel of Matthew,[93] the letter to the Hebrews (?); (2) sources written between A.D. 70 and 100: the letter of Jude, the Gospel of John, the letters of John, the book of Revelation.

François Vouga groups the available sources that are relevant for a description of the history of early Christianity into the following periods: (1) A.D. 30-60: the authentic letters of Paul, the collection of Jesus logia (Q), the first version of the *Gospel of Thomas;* (2) A.D. 60-80: the first letter of Peter, the letters to the Colossians and to the Ephesians, the Gospel of Mark; (3) A.D. 80-100: the Gospel of Matthew, the letter to the Hebrews, the letter of James, the first letter of Clement, the Gospel of Luke, the book of Acts, the Gospel of John, the book of Revelation; (4) A.D. 100-150: the *Apocryphon of James,* the letters of John, the Pastoral Epistles (to Timothy and Titus), the letters of Ignatius, the letter of Jude, the second letter of Peter.

The decision to use the accounts in the book of Acts and the Gospels with the "prejudice" of confidence in their historical reliability[94] does not relieve us from the obligation to discuss in detail arguments that suggest that texts or textual elements in these sources were redactionally altered or created *de novo.* Arguments for historical facts or events are meaningless if the assumed evidence—sources that are merely postulated, or assumed redactional interests—is based on wrong information. These discussions must allow the attempt to harmonize ostensible discrepancies between specific statements within the biblical sources or between the biblical sources and extrabiblical evidence. Such attempts at harmonization of conflicting evidence in different literary sources regularly occur among classical scholars. However, since I want to maximize the readability of this study, I cannot discuss in detail every single exegetical or historical decision.[95]

A good example for legitimate harmonization is the following argument by Eduard Lohse, who generally is not reluctant to accuse a biblical author of error. Herodotus (7.30) states that the river Lycus disappears near Colossae in a crevice

---

[91]For arguments for a date before A.D. 64 see J. Robinson 1976; Carson, Moo and Morris 1992; Davids, *1 Pet,* 3-7.

[92]A date at the end of the 50s is suggested by Carson, Moo and Morris 1992, 96-99; Gundry, *Mk,* 1026-45; cf. Schulz 1995, 186-217. A date in the late 60s is supported by W. Marxsen (A.D. 67-69), M. Hengel (A.D. 68-69), E. Lohse, L. Schenke, R. A. Guelich (A.D. 67-70). Schnelle (1994, 239) dates Mk to the early 70s.

[93]A date between A.D. 50 and 60 is suggested by J. Robinson 1976, a date between A.D. 60 and 70 by F. Godet, W. Michaelis, B. Reicke, G. Maier, R. H. Gundry, D. A. Carson, C. F. D. Moule, E. E. Ellis, D. A. Hagner; cf. Carson, Moo and Morris 1992, 76-79; Schulz 1995, 218-42; see the list in Davies and Allison, *Mt,* 1:127-28. Many scholars date Mt after A.D. 80: see Luz, *Mt,* 1:75-76 (not long after A.D. 80); Davies and Allison, *Mt,* 1:138 (between A.D. 80 and 95).

[94]For the Gospels see France et al. 1980-1986; Riesner 1988; Blomberg 1987; *DJG;* see more recently Theissen and Merz 1996, 96-124 (ET, 90-124) for arguments against the traditional historical-critical skepticism concerning the historical evaluation of the Jesus tradition.

[95]See Becker 1995, 19.

and reappears in a distance of five stadia. Lohse remarks that today this statement can no longer be verified on the ground, but he goes on to explain, "Either Herodotus mistakenly made an incorrect report or the bed of the river was altered by one of the severe earthquakes which have continuously plagued this region for centuries."[96] The second sentence "harmonizes" and is hypothetical but constitutes a justifiable assumption, as Lohse presupposes that Herodotus did not simply invent his comment but reported information on the course of the river Lycus that presumably is reliable.

Finally, a comment on apocryphal books of Acts. Research into these texts has made much progress since the studies of Richard Lipsius, particularly as a result of newly discovered manuscripts.[97] The main focus of current research is on the literary sources themselves, on their theological and historical *Sitz im Leben,* on the literary genre and on the theological emphases of the individual Acts. The historical value of these texts rarely is addressed, usually in the context of a discussion of their genre. If we follow E. Rohde and interpret the apocryphal Acts as Christian versions of the Hellenistic novel,[98] we will hardly investigate the historical value of specific comments in these texts. Wilhelm Schneemelcher, quoting Rosa Söder in the third edition of his edition of the New Testament apocrypha, characterized the Acts as "evidence of ancient popular narratives of the adventures, exploits and love affairs of great men, as now fixed in literary form and in a Christian spirit."[99] Jean-Daniel Kaestli and Eric Junod, the editors of a new edition, argue that the apocryphal Acts should not be understood against the background of the Greek novel, nor should they be interpreted as popular literature: the apocryphal Acts do not correspond to any genre of ancient literature; they are independent Christian texts that have been influenced by various genres and that incorporated various ecclesiastical traditions.[100] This approach does not exclude the possibility that the apocryphal Acts incorporate old traditions that include reliable information on the activity of the respective apostles. Theodor Zahn maintained with regard to the *Acts of John* that the text contains not only fictitious elements but also some information on the historical John, as the majority of the characters mentioned in the text are

---

[96]Lohse, *Kol,* 37 (ET, 8).

[97]Lipsius 1883-1890. See the reports on recent research in Jean-Daniel Kaestli, "Les principales orientations de la recherche sur les actes apocryphes des Apôtres," in Bovon 1981, 49-67; the essays in *ANRW* II.25.6 (1988); the introductions to the individual Acts of Apostles in the second volume of Hennecke and Schneemelcher 1990-1997 (6th ed.; rev. repr. of 5th ed. [1987-1989]); the series Corpus Christianorum: Series apocryphorum (since 1983); the series Studies on the Apocryphal Acts of the Apostles (since 1995; ed. Jan Bremmer; Kampen: Kok Pharos).

[98]Erwin Rohde, *Der griechische Roman und seine Vorläufer* (Leipzig: Breitkopf & Härtel, 1876 [5th ed., 1974]). See, for example, Vielhauer 1981, 693-718; Plümacher 1978b, esp. 12, 63-64.

[99]In Hennecke and Schneemelcher 1959-1964, 2:116 (ET, 2:176), following the genre analysis of Söder 1932, 187.

[100]Kaestli, "Principales orientations," 57-66; Junod 1983, 271-85.

historical personalities.[101] Richard Bauckham suggests that the genre of the apocryphal Acts is not totally dissimilar from the genre of the canonical book of Acts: the apocryphal Acts are best understood as novelistic biographies.[102] Clearly the apocryphal Acts are not "Christian fiction" seeking to entertain readers with tales of wondrous adventures of great men and women. For example, the *Acts of Peter* emphasizes God's provision for his people as God cares for the church through miracles and other supernatural events; the miracles serve to strengthen the faith of the believers and to bring Christians who have fallen into sin back to God's flock, and they have a missionary function as they seek to lead outsiders to faith in God.[103]

The *Acts of John* is dated around A.D. 125-150[104] or 150-200,[105] the *Acts of Andrew* around A.D. 150-200,[106] the *Acts of Peter* around A.D. 180-190,[107] the *Acts of Paul* around A.D. 150[108] or 180-200,[109] the *Acts of Thomas* around A.D. 200-240.[110] Younger apocryphal Acts, such as the *Acts of Philip*,[111] date to the fourth century at the earliest.[112]

2.3 The Semantic Field of "Mission"

The missionary activity of the early church is reflected in the terms with which the authors of the books of the New Testament described the existence and self-understanding, the activity and the expansion of the church. Since we will sur-

---

[101]Zahn 1880, clii-cliv. Lipsius (1883-1890, 1:516-19) argued against Zahn.

[102]Bauckham 1993b, 150-52; more recently Lalleman 1998, 41-42, 99-110.

[103]See Misset-van de Weg 1998, 110.

[104]Lalleman 1998, 268-70.

[105]Junod and Kaestli 1983, 694-700; Bovon and Geoltrain 1997, 983; J. K. Elliott 1993, 306; J. Bremmer, in Bremmer 1995, 16. Schäferdiek, in Hennecke and Schneemelcher 1959-1964, 2:155 (cf. ET, 2:214-15), dates the book to A.D. 200-250, Plümacher (1978b, 18-19) to A.D. 250-300.

[106]Prieur 1989, 413-14; idem, in Hennecke and Schneemelcher 1990-1997, 2:107; idem, in Bovon and Geoltrain 1997, 881; Plümacher 1978b, 34; cf. A. Hilhorst and P. J. Lalleman, in Bremmer 2000, 12. J. K. Elliott (1993, 236) suggests the early third century.

[107]See Stoops 1994, 390-404; W. Schneemelcher, in Hennecke and Schneemelcher 1959-1964, 2:255 (ET, 2:275); Plümacher 1978b, 23; J. Bremmer, in Bremmer 1998, 16-17. Gérard Poupon dates the Latin translation (*Actus Vercellenses*) to the first half of the third century and thus dates the *Acts of Peter* earlier, see Poupon 1989, 4381; idem, in Bovon and Geoltrain 1997, 1043.

[108]W. Rordorf, in Bovon and Geoltrain 1997, 1122.

[109]W. Schneemelcher, in Hennecke and Schneemelcher 1959-1964, 2:214 (ET, 2:351); Plümacher 1978b, 30; J. K. Elliott 1993, 357; J. Bremmer, in Bremmer 1996, 56-57.

[110]G. Bornkamm, in Hennecke and Schneemelcher 1959-1964, 2:308 (ET, 2:441); H. J. W. Drijvers, in Hennecke and Schneemelcher 1990-1997, 2:290; Plümacher 1978b, 42; J. K. Elliott 1993, 442 (third century); P.-H. Poirier and Y. Tissot, in Bovon and Geoltrain 1997, 1323.

[111]Bovon, Bouvier and Amsler 1999 (text and translation); Amsler 1999 (commentary).

[112]A. de Santos Otero, in Hennecke Schneemelcher 1959-1964, 2:381-438 (cf. ET, 2:577); Amsler, in Bovon and Geoltrain 1997, 1184.

vey the full scope of the missionary activity of the early Christians, a list of relevant terms in the New Testament demonstrates the range of missionary concepts and activities (see table 2.1).[113] The terms, grouped according to subject matter, are not "technical terms" for "mission" but describe missionary activity. Some terms will be described in greater detail later (e.g., ἁλιεύς, with the meaning "fisher [of people]," will be explained in the course of a discussion of Mk 1:17 in §10.1).

Table 2.1. Terms for Missionary Activity

(1) Subjects of missionary work:
ἁλιεύς	fisher
ἀπόστολος	apostle
ἐργάτης	worker, laborer
εὐαγγελιστής	evangelist
κῆρυξ	herald, proclaimer
κοινωνός	companion, partner
μάρτυς	witness
συνεργός	fellow worker
ὑπηρέτης	helper, assistant

(2) Addressees of missionary work:
ἀκροβυστία	the uncircumcised
ἀλλόφυλος	alien, foreigner
ἁμαρτωλοί	sinners
ἄνθρωποι	people
βάρβαρος	non-Hellene
γένος	nation, people
τὰ ἔθνη	nations, Gentiles, polytheists
Ἕλληνες	Greeks
Ἰσραήλ	Israel
Ἰουδαῖοι	Jews
λαός	people
περιτομή	the circumcised

(3) Place of missionary work:
ἀγρός	countryside, farm
γῆ	earth
ἐπαρχεία	province
κλίμα	region, district
κολωνία	colony
κόσμος	world, humanity
κώμη	village, small town
τὰ μέρη	region, district

οἰκουμένη	inhabited earth, humanity
τὰ ὅρια	region, district
πατρίς	homeland, hometown
περίχωρος	neighborhood
πόλις	city, town
χώρα	district, region, place

(4) Sending and position of the missionaries:
ἀποστέλλειν	send away/out
ἀποστολή	office of an apostle
ἀπόστολος	apostle, envoy
διακονία	service
κλῆσις	call, calling
μάρτυς	witness

(5) Proclamation by word:
ἀναπείθειν	persuade, induce
ἀπαγγέλλειν	report, announce
ἀποφθέγγομαι	speak out, declare
γνωρίζειν	make known, reveal
διαμαρτύρομαι	bear witness to
διδάσκειν	teach
διηγέομαι	relate, describe
εὐαγγελίζομαι	announce good news
καταγγέλλειν	make known in public
κατηχεῖν	inform, instruct
κηρύσσειν	announce, proclaim
λαλεῖν	talk, speak
λέγειν	say, tell
μαθητεύειν	make disciples, teach
ὁμολογεῖν	acknowledge, profess
παραδίδωμι	hand down, pass on, teach
παρακαλεῖν	appeal to, exhort, implore
πείθειν	convince, persuade
φυτεύειν	plant

[113]The following list develops Pesch 1982, 14-15.

(6) Content of the proclamation:

ἀλήθεια	truth
διδασκαλία	teaching
εὐαγγέλιον	good news
καταλλαγή	reconciliation
κήρυγμα	proclamation
ὁμολογία	confession
παράδοσις	tradition
ῥῆμα	word, statement
λόγος	word
μαρτύριον	testimony, proof
μαρτυρία	testimony, witness
ὁδός	the way, teaching

(7) Goal of the proclamation:

ἀκοή	hearing
ἀκολουθεῖν	follow, obey
ἀκούειν	hear, listen
βαπτίζειν	wash, purify, baptize
βάπτισμα	baptism
βεβαιοῦν	confirm, establish
δέχομαι	take, receive
εἴσοδος	entrance, acceptance
ἐκκλησία	assembly, church
ἔμφυτος	implanted
θερίζειν	reap, harvest
θερισμός	harvest
καταλλάσσειν	reconcile
κερδαίνειν	gain
μαθητεύειν	make disciples
μετανοεῖν	feel remorse, repent
μετάνοια	repentance, conversion
πιστεύειν	belief, be convinced of
πίστις	faith, trust, confidence
συνάγειν	gather, bring together
σῴζειν	save, keep from harm, rescue
σωτηρία	salvation, deliverance
φυτεύειν	plant

(8) Proclamation by deed:

ἀναστροφή	way of life, behavior
ἐκβάλλειν	
δαιμόνια	drive out demons

ἐνεργεῖν	work, be effective
ἐργάζομαι	work, accomplish
θεραπεύειν	heal, restore
θερίζειν	reap, harvest
θερισμός	harvest
ἰάομαι	heal, cure
κοπιᾶν	work hard, toil
οἰκοδομεῖν	build

(9) Execution of the missionary task:

ἀπέρχομαι	go out, go, depart
διέρχομαι	go through, penetrate
ἐξέρχομαι	go out
θριαμβεύειν	lead in triumph
σπόρος	seed

(10) Interpretation of missionary work:

ἁλιεύς	
ἀνθρώπων	fisher of people
ἔμφυτος	implanted
θερίζειν	reap, harvest
θερισμός	harvest
θριαμβεύειν	lead in triumph
πρόβατον	sheep
συνάγειν	gather, bring together
οἰκοδομεῖν	build
σπείρειν	sow seed
σπόρος	seed
φυτεύειν	plant

(11) The effort of missionary work:

ἀναπαύειν	rest from toil
διώκειν	run, press on
δρόμος	course of life, mission
ἐργάζομαι	work
κοπιᾶν	work hard, toil
κόπος	work, labor

(12) Misunderstandings:

ἀναστατοῦν	disturb, upset
ἐπιστολαὶ	
συστατικαί	letters of recommendation
καπηλεύειν	peddle, huckster
πείθειν	cajole, mislead

I conclude with some remarks on the term "Gentiles." In the following discussion I use this word not as an abstract category of definition but as a term corresponding to Judaism ("Gentiles" as non-Jews) and to Christianity ("Gentiles" as non-Christians),[114] as a general designation for all people who are neither Jews nor Christians.[115]

The term "Gentile" is derived from Latin *gentilis,* "belonging to the same family or clan (*gens*), stock, or race," which came to be used in ecclesial language for "heathen" and "pagan" and is defined as "of or pertaining to any or all of the nations other than the Jewish."[116] When Jerome translated the Bible into Latin in the fourth century, the Latin adjective *gentilis* received the negative meaning "belonging to a non-Roman, barbaric people." Jerome translated the Greek terms *hellēn* and *hellēnisthēs* fourteen times with *gentiles,* only three times with *Graeci;* twice *gentilis* is the translation of *ethnē* (Acts 14:5; Rom 15:27), marking the origin of the later polemical meaning of the term in the sense of "Gentile," which had come close in meaning to Latin *paganus.*[117] The term "heathen" is perhaps etymologically linked with the Celtic-Germanic root **kaito-,* meaning "forest, uncultivated tract of land," reconstructed as the Proto-Germanic cardinal form **haithanas,* from which are derived Old English (Anglo-Saxon) *hœðen,* Old Frisian *hêthin,* Old High German *heidan,* Middle High German *heiden,* English *heathen,* German *heide.*[118] The terms "Gentile" and "heathen" were used as a translation of Latin *paganus,* from *pagus,* for "district, countryside," hence used for "country people"; the *paganus* is the nonmilitant or civilian, the nonspecialist or layperson, the person dwelling in the countryside, the villager. The older explanation of "pagan" as an adapation of Latin *paganus,* "villager, rustic," indicating the fact that "the ancient idolatry lingered on in the rural villages and hamlets after Christianity had been generally accepted in the towns and cities of the Roman Empire"[119]—"pagan" thus designating the unbeliever who lives in the countryside, in wild, uncultivated regions[120]—is chronologically and historically untenable, as the usage of *paganus* for non-Christians goes back to Tertullian around A.D. 202, a time when non-Christian religions still comprised the public and dominant religion. Tertullian used *paganus* for the non-Christian: "Apud hunc [Christum] tam miles est paganus fidelis quam paganus est miles infidelis" (*Cor.* 11) ("With Him the faithful citizen is a soldier, just as the faithful

---

[114]See Rosenkranz 1980; Gensichen 1985; Fredouille 1986.

[115]See L. von Padberg, "Christen und Heiden: Zur Sicht des Heidentums in ausgewählter angelsächsischer und fränkischer Überlieferung des 7. und 8. Jahrhunderts," in *Iconologia Sacra* (FS K. Hauck; ed. H. Keller et al.; Berlin: de Gruyter, 1994), 291-312, esp. 297 n. 26.

[116]For the following discussion see Dabelstein 1981, 37-38; U. Heckel 1994, 270-72; Colpe 1990; J. M. Scott 1995, 57-134; *Oxford English Dictionary* (2nd ed.; 1989), s.v. "gentile."

[117]Colpe 1990, 103-4, 114.

[118]See *Oxford English Dictionary* (2nd. ed.; 1989), s.v. "heathen"; Moritz Heyne, "Heide," in *Deutsches Wörterbuch* (ed. J. Grimm and W. Grimm; Leipzig: Hirzel, 1877), 799-801; F. Kluge, *Etymologisches Wörterbuch der deutschen Sprache* (Berlin: de Gruyter, 1975), 297.

[119]*Oxford English Dictionary* (1st ed.; 1933 [= 1961]), s.v. "pagan," referring to Orosius I Præf.; Richard C. Trench, *On the Study of Words* (22nd ed.; London: Macmillan, 1906), 102.

[120]Colpe 1990, 113.

soldier is a citizen"). Thus, as the Christians understood themselves as *mīlitēs* ("enrolled soldiers") of Christ, as members of his militant church, they applied to non-Christians the term *paganus,* which was applied by soldiers to all who were "not enrolled in the army."[121] In the Vulgate, the term *paganus* is not used. As the term "heathen" is used in all the Germanic languages in the sense "non-Christian, pagan," a meaning that could have arisen only after the introduction of Christianity, many scholars think that the term probably was first used in Gothic, from where it was passed on to other Germanic tribes. This is supported by Bishop Ulfilas's translation in Mk 7:26, where he translates Latin *mulier gentilis* (Gk., *hē gynē ēn Hellēnis* ["the woman was a Greek"]) with *haithnô;* this word probably is adapted from Gothic *haithi* ("hearth"), thus "dweller on the heath" as a loose translation of Latin *paganus* ("villager"); others suggest Armenian influence on the language of Ulfilas, with *haithnô* indicating the masculine form *haithans,* which could adapt Armenian *het'anos* ("heathen"), a term adapted from the Greek ἔθνος (*ethnos*), meaning "nation" or "non-Jewish people."[122]

In the Septuagint and in the postexilic Jewish literature the expression τὰ ἔθνη (*ta ethnē*) no longer simply designated "peoples, nations" (as Hebrew גוים) but (1) the "nations" of the world, including the nation of Israel; (2) "(all) nations," in distinction from Israel; (3) the individual "pagans," meaning non-Israelites and non-Jews. Paul likewise uses the term τὰ ἔθνη to designate (1) the "nations" of the world, including Israel;[123] (2) "(all) nations," in distinction from the people of Israel;[124] (3) individual "pagans," meaning non-Jews,[125] and "non-Jews" also in the sense of non-Jewish ("Gentile") Christians.[126] If the term "Gentile Christian" designates followers of Jesus who were converted to faith in Jesus as Savior as polytheists (or as "God-fearers"), the term "Jewish Christian" designates Jews (and proselytes) who accepted Jesus as Messiah, without implying a certain degree of adherence to "Jewish praxis" such as circumcision or dietary laws.[127]

When Paul uses the term *ta ethnē* (τὰ ἔθνη) in contrast to Jews, to Israel, to his own (Jewish) people or to circumcised people, the ethnic-religious meaning of the term dominates: "Gentiles" are the people who do not worship and serve YHWH. It is questionable whether, as Ulrich Heckel claims, this usage is polemical or pejorative, because a missionary whose life and ministry is dominated by

---

[121] *Oxford English Dictionary* (2nd ed.; 1989), s.v. "pagan."
[122] Elmar Seebold, "Das germanische Wort für den Heiden," in *Beiträge zur Geschichte der deutschen Sprache und Literatur* 93 (1971): 29-45; F. Kluge, *Etymologisches Wörterbuch der deutschen Sprache* (22nd ed.; Berlin: de Gruyter, 1989), 300; *Oxford English Dictionary* (2nd ed.; 1989), s.v. "heathen." On the influence of the Armenian language see Sophus Bugge, *Indogermanische Forschungen* 5 (1895): 178.
[123] Rom 4:17, 18; Gal 3:8.
[124] Rom 1:5, 13-14; 15:10-11; Gal 2:15.
[125] Rom 11:13; 1 Cor 12:2; Eph 2:11.
[126] Rom 11:13; 15:27; 16:4; Gal 2:12, 14; Eph 3:1; Acts 15:19, 23.
[127] Contra J. E. Taylor 1990, 314.

the love of Jesus Christ and who calls people to accept the atoning reconciliation made possible through Jesus Christ's death for sinners (2 Cor 5:14-21) will
not despise the people to whom he preaches. The implication of a religious
contrast is not automatically pejorative. The term *ta ethnē* does not necessarily
imply a polemical, disparaging sense. The context must determine whether pos-
itive/neutral or negative connotations are present. Does this hold true for the
English words "Gentile," "heathen" and "pagan"? Some have suggested that
these terms clearly are pejorative today and should be avoided; alternative terms
that one may use are "non-Jews," "nations" and "polytheists."[128] But these terms
are problematic as well: the term "non-Jew" is a coined word of modern technical language that is hardly conceivable as a self-designation of Greeks or Romans; the term "nations" refers to large ethnic entities but cannot be used for
individuals, while *ethnē* as "Gentiles" can refer both to groups of people and to
individuals; in regard to "polytheists," the so-called God-fearers who had not
been integrated into the Jewish community through circumcision and obedience
to the Torah surely would not deserve the label "polytheists," for they worshiped, probably in an exclusive manner, Israel's God. Thus I will use in differing contexts the terms "Gentiles," "pagans," "nations," "non-Jews" and "polytheists" without ever implying pejorative connotations.

---

[128]For "non-Jew" see Dabelstein 1981, 11, 37-38; for "nations" see U. Heckel 1994, 291-92
("Völker"), ibid. for a critique of Dabelstein; for "polytheist" see F. W. Danker, BDAG, s.v.
"ἔθνος (2.a)." This statement by Ernst Strasser ("Der Begriff des Heidentums," *Neue Kirchliche
Zeitschrift* 39 [1928]: 859) clearly is problematic: "Der Begriff des Heidentums ist unentbehr-
lich. In ihm kommt zum Ausdruck, daß die christliche Religion die Norm aller Religionen ist"
("The concept of heathenism is indispensable. It expresses the truth that the Christian religion
is the norm of all religions").

3

CHRONOLOGY AND EVENTS

The first Christians understood their mission as being sent by the risen Christ "into the world" to all nations. It therefore is appropriate to conclude the introductory section of this study with a chronological survey of the most important political events in the first century. I begin with the principate of Emperor Tiberius. Luke, the only New Testament author who reports on the missionary activity of the early Christians, provides the following notice, the only exact date in his two-volume work:

Lk 3:1-2: "In the fifteenth year of the reign of Emperor Tiberius, when Pontius Pilate was governor of Judea, and Herod was ruler of Galilee, and his brother Philip ruler of the region of Ituraea and Trachonitis, and Lysanias ruler of Abilene, [2]during the high priesthood of Annas and Caiaphas, the word of God came to John son of Zechariah in the wilderness."

Some of the dates in tables 3.1 and 3.2, particularly dates that concern early Christian history, are contested. It is not possible to justify dates in a chronological table, which is also the reason why I have refrained from providing bibliographical details for the individual dates.[1]

Table 3.1. Chronology of Political Events, 4 B.C. to A.D. 111

(R) = Rome, **(P)** = provinces, **(J)** = Judea, **(JD)** = Jewish Diaspora.

From the beginnings to the persecution under Herod Agrippa I

4 B.C.	**(J)** Death of Herod I (the Great).
	Archelaos becomes king in Judea, Idumea and Samaria (until A.D. 6).
	Herod Antipas becomes tetrarch in Galilee and Perea (until A.D. 39).
	Herod Philip becomes tetrarch in Gaulanitis, Trachonitis, Batanea, Paneas (until A.D. 33).

---

[1]For Roman history see M. Deissmann 1990; Kienast 1990; Christ 1992; Gill and Gempf, 1994; Millar 1996; for Jewish history see Schürer, vols. 1-2; Smallwood 1976; Millar 1993; Gill 1995a; on individual questions see D. Schwartz 1992a; on Paul see Riesner 1994 (ET, 1998); Murphy-O'Connor 1982; 1996; L. Alexander 1993b.

A.D. 6	**(J)** Archelaos deposed by Augustus and exiled to Vienne (Gaul).
	Judea (with Samaria and Idumea) becomes Roman province under a *praefectus*.
14	**(R)** Death of Augustus on August 19; consecration on September 17 as *Divus Augustus*.
14-37	**(R)** Principate of Tiberius (Tiberius Caesar Augustus), after September 17.
18-19	**(P)** Germanicus is commander-in-chief in the East, proconsul of the "overseas" (Eastern) provinces with *maius imperium*.
19	**(P)** Death of Germanicus in Daphne near Antioch in Syria.
	Unrest in Cilicia.
	Second edition of Strabo's *Geography* (before his death in A.D. 21).
	(JD) Expulsion of Jews from Rome on orders from Tiberius.
23	**(R)** The province of Asia decides to erect a temple dedicated to Tiberius, Livia and the senate.
26	**(J)** Pontius Pilate is prefect of Judea (26-36).
	Herod Antipas divorces the daughter of the Nabatean king Aretas IV (9 B.C.-A.D. 40) and marries Herodias.
26/27	Ministry of John the Baptist.
27	Beginning of the ministry of Jesus of Nazareth.
30	**(J)** Earthquake in Jerusalem, with minor damages.
	Crucifixion (Friday, April 7) and resurrection (Sunday, April 9) of Jesus.
	Pentecost, coming of the Holy Spirit (Saturday, May 27).
	Mission of the disciples in Jerusalem and in Judea.
31/32	**(R)** Execution of L. Aelius Seianus, powerful prefect of the guard.
	Martyrdom of Stephen in Jerusalem.
	Mission of Philip in Samaria.
	Mission of Peter in Samaria.
	Conversion of Saul/Paul near Damascus, call to be a missionary.
32	**(P)** Pomponius Flaccus is prefect of Syria (32-35?).
	Mission of Jewish Christians in Antioch (32? or 35?).
	Mission of Paul in Arabia (32-33 [Auranitis? Decapolis?]) and Damascus.
33	**(J)** Death of Herod Philip, annexation of his territory (Batanea, Trachonitis, Auranitis, Gaulanitis) into the Roman Province of Syria.
	(P) Disturbances caused by the Parthian king Artabanos in Armenia.
	Titus Helvius Basila (33-39) is governor of the province of Galatia.
	Paul leaves Damascus, as the Nabatean ethnarch seeks his arrest.
33/34	Paul in Jerusalem (first visit).
34	Mission of Peter in Judea, Galilee, Samaria, cities of the coastal plain.
	Mission of Paul in Syria and Cilicia (until 42).
35	**(P)** Lucius Vitellius is prefect of Syria (35-39).
	Establishment of a church in Antioch, the capital of the province of Syria.
	Mission of Josef-Barnabas in Antioch.
36	**(R)** Fire in Rome (November 1).
	(P) Mithradates is king of Armenia (36-51).
	(J) Jonathan b. Ananus is high priest (36-37) (appointed by L. Vitellius).
	Accusations against Pontius Pilate because of problems in his administration of Judea; Vitellius dismisses Pilate as prefect of Judea (after Passover in 36, or early 37?); Marcellus is new prefect of Judea (36-37).
	Vitellius dismisses Caiaphas as high priest and appoints Jonathan b. Ananus.
	Herod Agrippa I visits Emperor Tiberius on Capri (spring) and maintains contacts with Gaius Caligula.
	War between Herod Antipas and the Nabatean king Aretas IV; defeat of Antipas.
37	**(R)** Death of Tiberius (March 16); Gaius Caligula becomes emperor.

(P) Commagene becomes vassal kingdom of Rome.

Earthquake in Antioch (Syria).

(J) During the period between prefects in Judea, Jonathan the high priest is deposed (as reaction of the Romans against illegal actions during the machinations against Stephen?); L. Vitellius visits Jerusalem (during Passover) to organize Judea after the deposition of Pilate; Marullus is new prefect (37-41); Theophilus is appointed high priest.

> The followers of Jesus are called *christianoi* in Antioch (by Roman authorities in the Syrian capital?) (or in 39?).

L. Vitellius visits Jerusalem again (during Pentecost); he plans a military move against Aretas IV with Herod Antipas.

37-41	**(R)** Principate of Gaius Caligula (C. Caesar Augustus Germanicus).
37	**(R)** Dedication of the temple of Augustus in Rome (August 30).

(P) Gaius Iulius Antiochos IV Epiphanes is king in Commagene (annexation of some Cilician territories).

(J) Herod Agrippa I (37-44) receives the tetrarchy of Herod Philip and the title of king; he stays in Rome for one and a half years.

Marullus is prefect of Judea (37-41).

Birth of Josephus in Jerusalem.

> Mission of Peter in Joppa and Caesarea.
> Conversion of Cornelius, a Roman centurion in Caesarea (date uncertain).

38	**(P)** Installation of Polemon II as king of Pontus.

Installation of Kotys as king of Armenia Minor.

(J) Herod Agrippa I returns from Rome to Palestine via Alexandria in Egypt.

(JD) Anti-Jewish pogroms in Alexandria during Agrippa's visit, provoked by Caligula; destruction and profanation of synagogues; flogging of the members of the gerousia.

(P) Deposition of Avillius Flaccus as prefect of Egypt.

(J) Agrippa I promotes pro-Torah policies.

Herod Antipas participates in negotiations between L. Vitellius and the Parthian king Artabanus on the river Euphrates.

39	**(P)** C. Vitrasius Pollio is prefect of Egypt (39-41).

P. Petronius is prefect of Syria (39-41).

39/40	**(R)** Caligula is in Lugdunum (Lyon) during the winter; Petronius is commanded to set up a statue of Caligula in the Jerusalem temple (winter).

(J) Unrest in Jamnia between the Jewish population and non-Jews who erected an altar honoring the emperor; Petronius moves two legions to Judea and is confronted with large demonstrations in Ptolemais and Tiberias.

(P) Unrest in Antioch (Syria) between Jews and Gentiles.

> Followers of Jesus are called *christianoi* in Antioch (Syria) (or in 37?).

40	**(R)** Caligula marches to the English Channel; *ovatio* in Rome on August 31.

(P) Malichus II is king of the Nabateans after the death of Aretas IV (40-70).

(JD) Jewish embassy from f active in Rome (with Philo).

(J) Herod Antipas (or his wife Herodias) seeks to obtain the royal title from Caligula (like Herod Agrippa I), but is sent into exile in Lugdunum in Gaul; his territory (Galilee and Perea) is given to Herod Agrippa I.

Unrest in Judea against Caligula; Herod Agrippa I visits Caligula in Rome (or in Puteoli) at the end of September and intervenes in the matter of the statue; negotiations by Petronius in Tiberias with the request expressed to Caligula that the emperor refrain from forcing the statue on the Jews.

40/41	**(JD)** Anti-Jewish unrest in Alexandria.
41	**(R)** Caligula commands Petronius to commit suicide (beginning of January).

(J) Unrest among the Jewish populations in Caesarea, Jerusalem, Seleucia and Scythopolis.

(JD) Unrest in Antioch.

(R) Caligula is murdered in Rome (January 24); Petronius hears of Caligula's death in March.

41-54 (R) Principate of Claudius (Tiberius Claudius Caesar Augustus Germanicus), beginning January 24; restoration of the traditional religion of Rome; Claudius was generally tolerant as far as religious questions were concerned.

(P) Large-scale local famines in the Roman Empire.

L. Aemilius Rectus is prefect of Egypt.

41 (R) Famine in Rome.

(P) Cornelius Lentulus Scipio is proconsul of the province of Asia (41/42); Rome recognizes the sovereignty of the Bosporan kingdom under Mithradates; Polemon II is made king of Cilicia; Seneca lives in exile on Corsica.

(J) Herod Agrippa I rules in Galilee, Perea, Gaulanitis, Trachonitis, Batanea, Paneas, receives Judea and Samaria; Simon Cantheras b. Boethus, Matthias b. Ananus and Elionaeus b. Cantheras are high priests.

(JD) Claudius, prompted by Herod Agrippa I, sends an edict to Alexandria that confirms the privileges of the Jews in Egypt (CPJ II 153).

(J) Herod (grandson of Herod I and brother of Herod Agrippa I) is made king of Chalkis (41-48); appointment of Joseph b. Camydus and Ananias b. Nebedaios as high priests.

(JD) Trial of the anti-Jewish agitators Isidor and Lampon in Alexandria; the pro-Jewish actions of the emperor result in the allegation by Alexandrian Jews that he is the illegitimate son of a Jewish woman named Salome (presumably the sister of Herod I).

(J) Herod Agrippa I returns from Rome (March), where he had been appointed king by the new emperor Claudius.

(R)/(JD) Claudius's first edict concerning the Jews, prompted by unrest in Rome (apud Cassius Dio): prohibition of holding meetings and order to adhere to the ancestral Jewish way of life.

Persecution of the Jerusalem church by Herod Agrippa I (during Passover, April 5?).

James b. Zebedee, the apostle, is executed in Jerusalem.

Departure of Peter from Jerusalem (goes to Rome in 41/42?).

Departure of the Twelve for international missionary work (?).

From the beginnings of the worldwide mission to the deaths of Peter and Paul

42 (P) Defeat of a Mauretanian rebellion; Mauretania Caesariensis and Mauretania Tingitana become new provinces.

Gaius Vibius Marsus is prefect of Syria (42-45).

(J) Herod Agrippa I is forced to abandon the building of a third (northern) wall of Jerusalem.

James, the brother of Jesus, is leader of the Jerusalem church.

Peter is active in the northeastern regions of Asia Minor (?).

Thomas is active in India (?).

Andrew is active in Skythia (?).

Matthew is active in Ethiopia (?).

Mark is active in Alexandria (?).

Thaddaeus (and/or Addai) is active in Edessa (?).

Paul is active in Antioch in Syria (42-44), with Barnabas.

43	**(P)** Invasion of Britain by Aulus Plautius.

Lycia-Pamphylia (with southern Pisidia) becomes imperial province; Q. Veranius II is the first procurator (43/44-47/48).

(J) Herod Agrippa I invites five Roman vassal kings to Tiberias: Antiochos of Commagene, Sampsigeramus of Emesa, Cotys of Armenia Minor, Polemon of Pontus, and his brother Herod of Chalkis; the emperor orders the premature end of the conference.

44   **(P)** Triumph of Claudius over Britain; Achaia and Macedonia become senatorial provinces; Vardanes, king of the Parthian Empire, attempts to recruit Izates of Adiabene for a coalition against Rome.

C. Cassius Longinus is prefect of Syria (44-50).

(J) Sudden death of Herod Agrippa I; reversing a previous decision, Claudius organizes Judea again as a Roman province under a procurator.

Cuspius Fadus is procurator of Judea (44-46), claims authority over the high priestly garments.

Herod Agrippa II, who at first stays in Rome (king of Judea, 50-93), is given, together with Herod of Chalkis, by Claurius the right to supervise the temple and its treasury; Claudius restores the high priestly garments to Jewish control.

Tensions between Jews and Romans increase; revolt of Theudas; famine in Judea (44-46).

(P) Conversion to Judaism of Helena, queen of Adiabene, of her son Izates and his brother Monobazus; Helena distributes food in Jerusalem during the famine; Helena and Monobazus have palaces in Jerusalem.

    Letter of James (early or mid-40s? or around 55?).

44   Church in Antioch organizes famine relief for the Jerusalem Christians.

    Paul in Jerusalem (second visit), consultation with Peter.

45-47   Mission of Paul and Barnabas, with John Mark, on Cyprus and southern Galatia (45-47 [so-called first missionary journey]).

45   Establishment of churches (?) in Salamis, Paphos on Cyprus.

46   **(P)** The command of the influential C. Poppaeus Sabinus in the Balkan territories is dissolved; Moesia and Thrace are separated from Macedonia and organized as separate imperial provinces.

Lucius Sergius Paullus is proconsul of Cyprus (46-48).

(J) Tiberius Iulius Alexander is procurator of Judea (46-48), a Jewish renegade; during the famine there are only private relief operations; heightening of apocalyptic expectations; increase of armed attacks against Romans; execution of the Jewish rebels James and Simon (sons of Jude of Galilee).

    Establishment of the church in southern Galatia: Antiocheia, Iconium, Lystra, Derbe.

47   **(R)** Claudius celebrates the eight hundreth anniversary of the founding of Rome (April 21) with *ludi saeculares;* programmatic speech promoting the renewal of the old Roman oracles; census by Claudius and L. Vitellius (47/48).

(P) C. Cadius Rufus (47/48) is governor of Pontus-Bithynia.

(J) Ananias b. Nebedaios is high priest (47-59), appointed by Herod of Chalkis.

48   **(P)** M. Calpurnius Rufus is procurator of Lycia-Pamphylia (48-53).

(J) Ventidius Cumanus is procurator of Judea (48-49); situation deteriorates decisively; unrest in Jerusalem as a result of provocative behavior of Roman soldiers; 20,000 Jewish citizens killed.

Earthquake in Palestine, with some damage in Jerusalem.

(JD) Unrest among the Jews in Antioch (Syria).

    Persecution of Jewish Christians in Judea and Jerusalem (48/49 [*apud* Malalas]).

        Paul returns from his mission in Galatia; stays in Antioch (Syria) in spring.
        Peter visits Antioch (Syria).
        Clash of Paul and Peter in Antioch.
        Letter to the Galatians (?).
        Apostlolic council in Jerusalem; Paul in Jerusalem (third visit).

49   **(R)/(JD)** Claudius's second edict concerning the Jews (between January 25 of 49 and January 1 of 50 [*apud* Suetonius]): expulsion of the Jews from Rome as a result of continued disturbances caused by Jewish Christians and their missionary preaching about Jesus as Messiah.

(R) Seneca returns from exile and is appointed educator of Nero in Rome. Claudius intensifies his program to restore the old religion of Rome; expansion of the *pomerium* in Rome (where only Roman gods were allowed to be worshiped) to include the Aventine and a part of Campus Martius; denunciation of political enemies on account of contacts with oriental astrologers.

(P) L. Pedanius Secundus (49/50 or 50/51) is governor of the province of Asia. M. Annius Afrinus is procurator of Galatia (49-54).

(J) Bloody incident between Jews and Samaritans. Procurator Cumanus is deposed by Claudius on the initiative of Herod Agrippa II. Antonius Felix is procurator of Judea (49-59, or 52-59?); he was a brother of Pallas, whose lover Julia Agrippina had married Claudius in 49 and who had attained a powerful position in Rome. Situation in Judea continues to deteriorate; military actions against Eleazar b. Dinaeus, the leader of the Zealot movement.

        Mission of Barnabas and John Mark on Cyprus.
        Mission of Paul in Macedonia and Achaia (49-51 [so-called second missionary journey]).
        Mission in Philippi (August-October?) and Thessalonike (October-December).

50   **(R)** Adoption of Nero by Claudius, and installation as guardian for Ti. Claudius Britannicus; Pomponius Secundus is victorious against the Germanic tribe of the Chatti.

(P) Birth of the philosopher Epictetus in Hierapolis (ca. 50-100). C. Ummidius Durmius Quadratus is prefect of Syria (50-60).

(JD) Death of Philo of Alexandria.

        Mission of Paul in Beroea (December/January?).
        Mission of Paul in Athens.
        Mission of Paul in Corinth (from February/March 50 to September 51).
        Letter to the Galatians (?) and the letters to the Thessalonians.

51   **(R)** Famine in various regions of the Roman Empire.

(P) Vologaeses I is king of Parthia (51-76/79); Radamistos is king of Armenia. Cn. Domitius Corbulo (between 51 and 54) is governor of the province of Asia. L. Iunius Annaeus Gallio is proconsul of Achaia (51-52).

        Paul before Gallio in Corinth.
        Paul in Syria and in Jerusalem (51/52 [fouth visit]).

52-55   Mission of Paul in Ephesus (52-55 [so-called third missionary journey]). Mission of Epaphras in the Lycus valley, in Colossae, Laodikeia and Hierapolis.

53   **(P)** The procurators of the imperial provinces are given the right of jurisdiction. Armenia is occupied again by the Parthians and Tiridates I of Armenia (53-60).

(J) Herod Agrippa II receives, in place of Chalkis, the tetrarchies of Philip (Batanea, Trachonitis, Gaulanitis) and Lysanias (Abilene) as well as the territory of Varus (50-92/3); he vigorously promotes Jewish interests.

54	**(R)** Claudius is poisoned by Agrippina, Nero's mother (October 13); deification of Claudius; the powerful proconsul Silanus is murdered at the instigation of Agrippina (December 54 or January 55).
	(J) Antonius Felix, procurator of Judea, is permitted by Claudius to marry Drusilla, the sister of Herod Agrippa I (who had been married since 53 to Aziz, king of Emesa, who had converted to Judaism).
	Letter to the Corinthians (1 Corinthians).
54-68	**(R)** Principate of Nero (Nero Claudius Caesar Augustus Germanicus), beginning on October 13.
	Creation of the province Galatia-Cappadocia (until 64 or 66/67); Pamphylia and eastern Pontus are annexed to Galatia.
	(J) Herod Agrippa II receives further territories in Galilee and Perea (Tiberias, Tariachea, Julias).
55	**(R)** Nero is granted an *ovatio* for his diplomatic success in negotiations with the Parthians; he accepts the title *pater patriae*.
	(P) Marius Cordus (?) is governor of the province of Asia.
	Titus Claudius Hiero is one of the Asiarchs in Ephesus.
	(J) Jubilee year of the Jewish people (55/56).
	Paul visits Corinth (May/June?) and returns to Ephesus.
	Paul travels from Ephesus to Alexandria Troas.
	Paul travels to Macedonia (August?).
	Letter to the Corinthians (2 Corinthians [written in Philippi?]).
	Paul stays in Macedonia over the winter.
56	**(P)** M. Vettius Niger is governor of the province of Asia (between 56 and 58).
	Birth of the historian Tacitus in Gaul.
	(JD) Revolt of an Egyptian Jew (during the month of Nisan?) who leads 4,000 Sicarii into the desert.
	Mission of Paul in Illyricum (summer 56).
	Paul visits Achaia/Corinth (winter 56/57, until March 57).
	Letter to the Romans.
57	**(R)** Nero forces senators and *equites* to attend games.
	Paul travels from Corinth to Philippi.
	Paul leaves Philippi and travels to Jerusalem (April 15).
	Pentecost in Jerusalem (May 29).
	Paul in Jerusalem (fifth visit), hands over the collection from the churches.
	Arrest of Paul (during Pentecost?), imprisonment in Caesarea (57-59).
	Letters to the Philippians, to Philemon, to the Ephesians (?).
	(P) Plautius Silvanus is imperial legate in Moesia; he is victorious in battles against tribes from the North, and settles 100,000 people, including their tribal chiefs, in Moesia.
58	**(P)** Armenia is conquered by Cn. Domitius Corbulo and vassal kings of Rome.
	(R) Unrest in Rome resulting from high taxation; Nero suggests abolishing the indirect taxes.
59	**(R)** Nero has his mother, Agrippina, murdered (March).
	(J) Porcius Festus is procurator of Judea (59-62).
	Unrest in Caesarea between Jews and Syrians over citizenship rights; Felix sends representatives of both parties to Nero, who decides in favor of the Syrians.
	Ishmael b. Phiabi is high priest (59-61), appointed by Herod Agrippa II.
	Gospel of Mark (end of the 50s? or 68/69?).
	Paul is taken to Rome as prisoner (59/60).
60	**(P)** Cn. Domitius Corbulo is prefect of Syria (60-63).
	Tigranes VI of Cappadocia is king of Armenia (60-62).

(R) Nero introduces Greek games in Rome (*Neronia*); birth of satirist Juvenal.
Paul as prisoner in Rome (60-62).
Paul writes to the Philippians, the Colossians, Philemon, the Ephesians.
(R)/(J) A Jewish delegation petitions Nero to be allowed to retain the wall that prevents people from seeing the interior sections of the temple in Jerusalem; Nero grants the request for the benefit of his lover Poppaea Sabina, who is a sympathizer of the Jews.

61   (P) Tigranes V attacks Adiabene; Syria is threatened by the Parthians; truce between the Parthian king Vologaeses I and Cn. Domitius Corbulo.
(J) Joseph Cabi b. Simon is high priest, appointed by Herod Agrippa II.
Peter in Rome (?).

62   (R) Nero divorces Octavia and marries Poppaea Sabina; Octavia is sent into exile and eventually murdered.
(P) Caesennius Paetus arrives in Cappadocia with the task of annexing Armenia; Vologaeses I capitulates near Rhandeia; P. Volasenna is governor of the province of Asia (62/63).
(J) Lucceius Albinus is procurator of Judea (62-64).
Ananus b. Ananus is high priest, appointed by Herod Agrippa II.
James the brother of Jesus and other Christians are murdered, at the instigation of Ananus, as Albinus is on his way to Judea.
Ananus is deposed; appointment of Jesus b. Dammaios as high priest.
Luke writes his two-volume work, Luke-Acts (60-65?).
Paul is released from imprisonment in Rome.

63   (R) Earthquake in Campania.
(P) C. Cestius Gallus is prefect of Syria (63-66).
Tiridates I is king of Armenia (63-75).
(J) Jesus b. Gamaliel is high priest (63-64), appointed by Herod Agrippa II.
Mission of Paul in Spain (63/64?).

64   (R) Rome sends a research delegation to Ethiopia.
Fire in Rome, July 18/19-27.
Beginnings of a general discrimination against Christians.
Persecution of Christians in Rome.
(J) Gessius Florus is procurator in Judea (64-66), the last procurator before the revolt.
Temple rebuilding program, begun by Herod I and financed by the temple treasury, is finished, leaving over 18,000 Jewish workers unemployed; Herod Agrippa II has them pave the streets of Jerusalem "with white stones."
Peter writes to Christians in Asia Minor (1 Peter) (?).
Mission of Paul with Titus on Crete (64-65?).

65   (R) Rome is rebuilt; second celebration of the *Neronia* (April/May).
Pisonian intrigue against Nero; suicide of Seneca; the philosophers Musonius Rufus and Annaeus Cornutus are sent into exile.
(J) Matthias b. Theophilus is high priest, appointed by Herod Agrippa II.
Paul writes to Timothy (1 Timothy) and Titus (?).
Paul visits Nikopolis in Epirus (winter 65/66).

66   (R)/(P) Nero marries Statilia Messalina; crowns Tiridates king of Armenia; closes the gates of the temple of Janus (late summer); Nero is in Greece after September 25, proclaims "freedom" for Corinth (November 28).
(J) Revolt of the Jews against Rome in Galilee and in Judea (May).
(JD) The Jews in the Diaspora do not participate in the revolt against Rome.
(P) A. Caesennius Gallus, legate of Legio XII Fulminata, conquers Galilee.
Gospel of Matthew (late 60s, before 70?).

Letter to the Hebrew Christians (late 60s, before 70?).
Paul travels to Macedonia and to Troas/Ephesus (?).
Arrest of Paul (in Ephesus? in Rome?).

67   **(R)** Nero initiates a canal project at the isthmus of Corinth; forces Corbulo to
commit suicide; Vespasian is appointed as legate for the war in Judea.
(J) In Galilee, Jotapata is conquered by the Roman army; Josephus is a prisoner.
(P) C. Licinius Mucianus is prefect of Syria (67-69).
(J) Phannias b. Samuel is high priest (67/68), appointed by the people.
Paul writes to Timothy (2 Timothy) (?).
Paul martyred in Rome (October ?).
Peter martyred in Rome (?).

68   **(R)** Senate decrees Nero a public enemy; Nero returns to Italy, commits suicide
on June 9; *damnatio memoriae.*

The last decades of the apostolic period

68-69 **(R)** Principate of Galba (Servius Sulpicius Galba), beginning on June 8.
Gospel of Mark (or at the end of the 50s?).

68   **(R)** Galba marches on Rome and takes over power; Verginius Rufus crushes the
rebellion of C. Iulius Vindex in Gaul.
(J) Vespasian suspends the siege of Jerusalem after learning of Nero's death.

69   **(P)** Two Roman legions in Mainz (Germania) renounce their allegiance to Galba,
who is murdered on January 15; *damnatio memoriae.*
L. Caesennius Paetus is prefect of Syria; is victorious in 71/72 against Antiochos
of Commagene.

69   **(P)** Otho (Marcus Salvius Otho) is proclaimed emperor by the Praetorians on
January 15.
Aulus Vitellius is proclaimed emperor in Cologne (Germania) on January 2.
Otho is defeated near Bedriacum, commits suicide on April 16; *damnatio
memoriae.*
Vitellius is in Lugdunum (April) and Rome (since July); rebellion of Iulius Civilis
with the help of German tribes in Vetera (Xanten) and Novaesium (Neuss) on the
river Rhine.
(R) On the Capitol, the temple of Jupiter is burned down (December 19); Vitellius
is tortured and murdered (December 20); *damnatio memoriae.*

69-79 **(R)** Principate of Vespasian (Titus Flavius Vespasianus); proclaimed emperor by
the senate of Rome on December 21.

69   **(P)** Vespasian is proclaimed emperor by Roman legions in Egypt, Judea and Syria
(July 1-11).
(R) The legionary legate M. Antonius Primus enters Rome on behalf of Vespasian.

70   **(R)** Vespasian arrives in Rome (October); plots by Iulius Classicus, Iulius Tutor
and Iulius Sabinus, who attempt to create an Imperium Galliarum; on the Capitol,
the temple of Jupiter is rebuilt (finished in 71); birth of the historian Suetonius.
(P) Rabbel II is king of the Nabateans (70-106).
(J) Five-month siege and destruction of Jerusalem and the temple (Tuesday,
August 28) by Titus Flavius Vespasianus, the elder son of Vespasian; about
220,000 Jews are killed in the siege, over 19,000 are taken prisoner, of whom
many are executed or enslaved; Judea is organized as an imperial province under
a *legatus Augusti pro praetore* who controlled a Roman legion; 800 veterans are
stationed in Emmaus; the land is leased; levy of a yearly tax of two drachmas
(*didrachmon* tax) that all Jews have to pay to the temple of Jupiter in Rome (*fiscus
Iudaicus*).

Establishment of the *collegium quod est in domo Sergiae Paullinae,* possibly a Christian house church, by the consul L. Sergius L. f. Paullus.

Baptism of Polycarp in Smyrna between 70 and 80 (martyred in 156? 166?).

71   **(JD)** Rebellion of the Jews in Antioch (Syria) because of false accusations of arson; Titus, during a visit to the city, refuses to curtail the rights of the Antiochene Jews.

(R) Titus returns from Judea and Syria to Rome; participation in Vespasian's *tribunicia potestas;* closure of the doors of the temple of Janus.

(R)/(J) Triumph of both Vespasian and Titus on the occasion of their victory over the Jews (June), with Jewish prisoners and objects from the temple paraded through the streets of Rome.

(J) The fortress Machaerus falls to the Romans.

72   **(P)** Antiochos IV of Commagene is deposed as king; Armenia Minor and Commagene are annexed to Cappadocia-Galatia; the new Province of Cilicia is created.

73   **(J)** The fortress Masada (Judea) falls to the Romans.

(JD) Closure of the Jewish temple of Onias in Egypt, as Vespasian is afraid that Jewish Sicarii might exploit disturbances in Alexandria to form a new resistance movement.

73/74   **(R)** Census by Vespasian and Titus.

(P) Military actions of Roman legions in Upper Germany.

(JD) Disturbances in the Cyrenaica caused by Jewish Sicarii; the prefect Catullus kills 1,000 rich Jews; accusations against the Jews of Alexandria and Rome, which are, however, cleared up by Vespasian and Titus.

74   **(R)** Expulsion of astrologers and Stoic philosophers from Rome.

75   **(R)** Building of a *templum pacis* (temple of peace) to commemorate the victory in Judea, in which treasures from the Jerusalem temple are stored.

(R)/(JD) M. Iulius Agrippa II and Berenike, the Jewish lover of Titus, visit Rome. Expansion of the *pomerium* of Rome.

(P) Invasion of the Alans, pastoral tribes in northern Pontus, in Media and Armenia.

76   **(J)** Josephus finishes the original Aramaic version of *Bellum judaicum.*

79   **(R)** Vespasian dies (June 23); consecration as *Divus Vespasianus.*

79-81   **(R)** Principate of Titus (Titus Flavius Vespasianus), beginning June 24.

79   Eruption of Vesuvius on August 24; destruction of Pompeii and Herculaneum.

80   **(R)** Fire in Rome, destruction of the Jupiter temple on the Capitol; inauguration of the Colosseum (Amphitheatrum Flavium).

(J) Publication of the Greek version of Josephus's *Bellum judaicum* (77-81).

81-96   **(R)** Principate of Domitian (Titus Flavius Domitianus), beginning September 14. Promotion of the imperial cult; use of the salutation *dominus et deus;* has his own bust inserted on the statue of Jupiter on the Capitol.

(J)/(JD) Rigorous collection of the Jewish tax; Domitian declares conversion to the Jewish religion a capital crime, the charge being atheism.

Persecution of Christians.

82   **(R)** Consecration of the temple of Jupiter on the Capitol that had been rebuilt.

(P) Malaca and Salpensa in Spain receive municipal status.

83   **(P)** Domitian triumphs over the Chatti; expansion of the limes in Germania.

85   **(R)** Domitian declares himself *censor perpetuus.*

86   **(R)** Institution of the Capitolian games; first war against the Dacians.

87   **(R)** Discovery of a plot against Domitian on September 22.

88   **(R)** Celebration of the *ludi saeculares* on June 1-3.

(P) Second war against the Dacians; Roman victory near Tapae.

89	**(R)** Edict against astrologers and philosophers.
92	**(R)** Completion of the imperial palace on the Palatine.
	(P) Domitian fights in wars against the Marcomanni, Iazyges and Quadi.
	Letters of John (early 90s?).
92/93	**(J)** Herodes Agrippa II dies, (probably) resulting in disturbances.
94	**(J)** Josephus publishes *Antiquitates judaicae* (written 82-94).
95	**(R)** Expulsion of the philosophers from Italy.
	John writes the book of Revelation (last years of Domitian's rule?).
96-98	**(R)** Principate of Nerva (Marcus Cocceius Nerva), beginning in September 18. Pressure on the Jews reduced; prohibition of denunciations for "atheism" or "Jewish way of life."
	First letter of Clement
98-117	**(R)** Principate of Trajan (Marcus Ulpius Traianus), beginning January 28.
98	**(R)** Tacitus writes *Germania*.
	(J) Josephus writes his autobiography (*Vita*).
99	**(R)** Trajan returns to Rome.
100	**(J)** Josephus writes *Contra Apionem* (98-100).
106	**(P)** Dacia becomes a Roman province; annexation of Arabia by Rome.
111	**(P)** Pliny the Younger is prefect of Bithynia; exchange of letters with Trajan. Persecution of Christians in Pontus.
	Letters of Ignatius of Antioch (late summer 113 or earlier).

Table 3.2. Important Events of Early Christian History

From the beginnings to the persecution under Herod Agrippa I

26/27	Ministry of John the Baptist
27	Beginning of the ministry of Jesus of Nazareth
30	Crucifixion and resurrection of Jesus
	Mission of the disciples in Jerusalem and in Judea
31/32	Martyrdom of Stephen in Jerusalem
	Mission of Philip in Samaria
	Mission of Peter in Samaria
	Mission of Christians from Jerusalem in Antioch (Syria)
	Conversion of Saul/Paul near Damascus, call to be a missionary
32/33	Mission of Paul in Arabia and Damascus
34-	Mission of Peter in Judea, Galilee, Samaria and in the coastal plain
	Mission of Paul in Syria and Cilicia
37	Followers of Jesus called *christianoi* in Antioch
	Mission of Peter in Joppa and Caesarea
	Conversion of Cornelius, a Roman centurion, in Caesarea
41	Persecution of the Jerusalem church by Herod Agrippa I
	James b. Zebedee, the apostle, executed in Jerusalem
	Departure of Peter from Jerusalem (goes to Rome in 41/42?)
41/42	Change of leadership in the Jerusalem church
	Departure of the Twelve for international missionary work (?)

From the beginnings of international missionary work to the deaths of Peter and Paul

| 42- | James the brother of Jesus, leader of the Jerusalem church |

PART I

PROMISE

*Israel's Eschatological Expectations
and Jewish Expansion
in the Second Temple Period*

4

THE REALITY AND THE WORK
OF YAHWEH THE CREATOR

The question of missionary work in the Old Testament is seldom posed by Old Testament scholars. Most textbooks on the theology of the Old Testament rarely if ever mention the term "mission" or the subject matter designated as "mission."[1] Gerhard von Rad lists the term "mission" just once in the index of his two-volume *Theology of the Old Testament*.[2] In the section "Deutero-Isaiah: The New Saving Event" von Rad refers to the fact that the prophet portrays the salvational activity of Yahweh (YHWH) always with references to the pagan nations, thus introducing a new perspective into Israel's outlook. The prophet is convinced that YHWH's acts of salvation for Israel will have consequences for the political environment of Israel: the nations will recognize the impotence of their gods, they will be put to shame, they will turn to YHWH, they will bring the scattered Israelites to Zion, they will worship YHWH.[3] On one occasion YHWH speaks, through the prophet, directly to the nations: "Turn to me and be saved, all the ends of the earth! For I am God, and there is no other" (Is 45:22). The prophet designates Israel as a "witness" for the nations (Is 43:10; 44:8; 55:4). Gerhard von Rad comments that the term "witness" does not imply that Israel is meant to send out messengers: "In the prophet's mind Israel is thought of rather as a sign of which the Gentiles are to become aware, and to which, in the course of the eschatological events, they will resort of their own accord."[4] This is all that von Rad has to say on the subject of missionary activity or missionary concepts. Walther Zimmerli, in his *Old Testament Theology in Outline,* avoids the term "mission" entirely, even in his discussion of Is 44:8; 43:10; 55:4, even though he refers there to Israel as "witness for the nations."[5] Claus Westermann,

---

[1] See Schultz 1996, 34.
[2] Rad 1960, 2:454 (ET, 2:461); for the discussion that follows above see ibid., 2:254-60 (ET, 2:243-60).
[3] Is 41:11; 42:17; 45:24; 49:22-23; 49:7.
[4] Rad 1960, 2:259 (ET, 2:249).
[5] Zimmerli 1972, 196 (ET, 220).

in his *Elements of Old Testament Theology,* uses only three sentences when he discusses those passages that speak of the last days, which will bring salvation to the nations (Is 19; 45:20-25) and which display the universalism that relates God's activity to all of humanity.[6] Brevard Childs, in his book *Old Testament Theology in a Canonical Context,* does not use the term "mission" either but he extensively discusses "the nations as recipients of God's revelation."[7] Another exception is Horst Dietrich Preuss, who discusses in the last chapter of his *Theologie des Alten Testaments,* entitled "The People of God and the Nations," the Old Testament statements about the relationship between YHWH and Israel with the nations.[8] In the last paragraph Preuss discusses those (few) passages that more than merely allude to the nations as receiving YHWH's salvation. "But these are mostly statements on the promised state of consummation that Israel hopes for and thus part of eschatology. Israel always remains the real recipient of salvation, whereas the nations are allowed to place themselves as something like a second circle around Israel and Zion. . . . The author however[9] . . . does not refer to an active missionary activity among the nations, carried out by Israel or the Servant; rather, Israel's existence and fate, YHWH's glory in Zion and the light that emanates from there radiate effectively outward, and the nations who see these events and who as a result acknowledge YHWH are taken into and drawn into these events." Previous generations of Old Testament scholars were not so reluctant. Emil Kautzsch spoke explicitly of "Israel's missionary vocation," as Is 40—66 emphasizes "the missionary vocation of the Servant [i.e., of Israel] with regard to the pagan world. He occupies center stage in the entire world of thought of our prophet: he alone provides the explanation for the enigma of Israel's election and abandonment in God's plan for the world. Israel's intense suffering was the indispensable condition for the salvation of the entire world."[10]

Israel's relationship to foreigners[11] and to the nations[12] has been discussed often. Occasionally scholars have treated the question of the concept of missions in the Old Testament[13] or, more generally, the international and universal perspective of Old Testament traditions.[14] The latter can readily be observed in Israel's literature in the numerous points of contact with the cultures of Egypt

---

[6]Westermann 1978, 130 (ET, 148).
[7]Childs 1985, 103-7.
[8]Preuss 1991-1992, 2:305-27; the quotations that follow above, ibid., 2:321, 323.
[9]Analogous to Gen 12:3; 26:4; 28:14; Ex 19:6.
[10]Kautzsch 1911, 304; cf. Kautzsch's subject index with references to ibid., 302ff., 351, 360.
[11]See Bertholet 1896; K. Schmidt 1945; Houten 1991; C. Bultmann 1992.
[12]See Schmökel 1934; H. Wolff 1951; Lutz 1968; H. Schmidt 1968.
[13]See Riehm 1880; M. Löhr 1896; Heinisch 1916; E. Sellin 1925; Stärk 1925; Brunner 1934; Raguin 1947; Rowley 1955 [1944]; Liagre-Böhl 1950; Hempel 1954; Martin-Achard 1959; G. Wright 1961; Hahn 1963, 10-12; Bosch 1956; Lauha 1977; Bovati 1990; Koenen 1990; Sundermeier 1990; Oswalt 1993; Bosch 1993b; Widbin 1993; Neufeld 1994; C. Wright 1996; McDaniel 1998.
[14]See Eissfeldt 1954; Altmann 1964; Reventlow 1977; Smick 1989; Sundermeier 1990.

and Mesopotamia. On the linguistic level there are links with ancient Near Eastern languages, particularly the languages of Canaan, such as Ugaritic. This "international horizon" of the material and social culture of the people of Israel cannot, however, be identified with "mission." Contacts with people in an international context are not the same thing as using these contacts with the awareness of being responsible for convincing people who worship other gods that there is only one true God, YHWH, the God of Israel. Erich Scheurer concludes his survey of the history of research on the question of "mission" in the Old Testament by pointing out that we need to distinguish between missionary praxis and missionary ideas: whereas missionary ideas are clearly present in the Old Testament, particularly in the emphasis that YHWH is the only true God, missionary praxis—Israelites or Jews, acting on behalf of YHWH, sent by God's people to pagans—is unknown in the Old Testament.[15]

4.1 Creation and History

The Old Testament begins with this sentence: "In the beginning God created the heavens and the earth" (Gen 1:1). God created the cosmos, created the world, created man and woman; when the book of Genesis speaks of the Creator, it speaks of total reality, the totality of the world (Gen 1) and the totality of humankind (Gen 2). The book of Genesis is the very first text of the sacred Scriptures of God's people. This means that Gen 1—11 emphasizes right from the beginning in a fundamental way that the existence and the activity of YHWH are not limited by the borders of the people of Israel: they concern the entire cosmos and all of humankind. YHWH is the Lord of world history and the Lord of human history. "Everything that happens between Israel and its God, everything that happens between an individual and God stands in this broad context."[16]

The revelation of God the Creator is the revelation of God who blesses people. The blessing of Adam and Eve implied in the command "Be fruitful and multiply" (Gen 1:28) has consequences for all following generations—for the depth of time (Gen 5: genealogy from Adam to Noah) and for the width of space (Gen 10: genealogy of Noah's descendants). As the creation of light is mentioned first, the temporal category has precedent over the spatial category.[17] The explicit reference to the goal of creation in Gen 2:1-4 emphasizes the fact that as the days of the week move toward a goal, so does the history of humankind: human beings are intended to serve YHWH, who created the world. Man and woman, created in the image of God, are to live their lives with reference to

---

[15]Scheurer 1996, 416; similarly Köstenberger and O'Brien 2001, 25-53.

[16]Westermann 1978, 72-74 (ET, 88); for the observations that follow above see ibid., 75-80 (ET, 90-102).

[17]Gen 1:3-5 (time) comes before Gen 1:6-10 (space); then vegetation (Gen 1:11-13); sun, moon and stars (Gen 1:14-19); animals (Gen 1:20-25); humanity (Gen 1:26-31).

YHWH, who created them. They are to hear and listen to God's voice and respond to what God says. "If God is the creator of the world and of humanity, then world events and human history are in his hands from beginning to end. What began with the creation of heaven and earth must reach its destination with all that belongs to it: the history of the cosmos and this history of nature, the history of humanity and the history of God with his people."[18]

The conviction that YHWH is the Creator is thus linked, from the very first pages of the Scriptures, with a universal perspective that surfaces repeatedly in central passages: (1) in the patriarchal narratives that speak of God's blessing for all families of the earth; (2) in the psalms, in which nations and kings, indeed all creation (Ps 148), are called to praise YHWH; (3) in prophecies addressed to foreign peoples, as God uses other nations as his instrument—for example, to bring judgment upon Israel;[19] (4) in the prophecies of Isaiah that promise salvation to the nations; (5) in the promises of a new heaven and a new earth (Is 65:17; 66:22).

Some authors link the Old Testament emphasis that God, as the Creator of the universe and of the earth, possesses universal sovereignty, with a reference to non-Israelites who worship the true God.[20] Well-known examples are Melchizedek, who worshiped, as did Abraham, El Elyon (Gen 14) and Jethro, who worshiped YHWH (Ex 18); Abimelech (Gen 20) and Job (Job 1:8) are also mentioned. Bryan Widbin does not want to exclude the possibility that Melchizedek and Jethro received the names of God, which God revealed to Israel (Ex 6:1-3), by an independent divine revelation.[21] His opinion that Israel was convinced that YHWH was active independently of Israel and outside of his covenant with Israel, and that Israel accepted this divine activity for practical and theological reasons, remains hypothetical. It is anachronistic, however, when he labels such non-Israelites who worship the true God as "God-fearers."[22]

Many authors, with good reason, accept this universalistic dimension of Israel's faith as the origin of missionary concepts in the Old Testament. Because YHWH, the God of Israel, is the only true God,[23] because YHWH is the Creator of all things and the Lord of all creatures,[24] because it is therefore only YHWH who deserves to be served and worshiped, he will reveal his divine reality and sovereignty as Creator and as Lord outside of Israel as well when he establishes his future universal rule (Is 40—55).

---

[18]Westermann 1978, 87 (ET, 102).

[19]See Amos 1—2; Is 13—23; Jer 45—51; Ezek 25—32; Obadiah; Nahum; Habakkuk; Zeph 2:4-15. Westermann (1978, 143 [ET, 136]) writes, "Yahweh as the savior of his people is the Lord of history. He is able to carry out his plan with Israel by means of other nations."

[20]See Schultz 1996, 41.

[21]Widbin 1993, 82.

[22]With reference to Job 1:8; Gen 20:11; Ex 1:17; 18:21; Deut 25:18; Gen 22:12; Lev 19:13, 32; Ps 15:4; 22:23.

[23]See Deut 4:35, 39; 32:39; 1 Sam 2:2; 2 Sam 7:22; Is 43:11; 44:6; 45:5, 6, 14, 18, 21, 22; 46:9; Hos 13:4. For the observations that follow above see Bauckham 1999, 9-15.

[24]See Is 40:26, 28; 42:5; 44:24; 45:12, 18; 48:13; 51:16; Neh 9:6; Hos 13:4 LXX.

Israel, of course, not only asserts God's universality but also confesses YHWH as the one and only God. Central passages that Israelites recite in the Shema twice every day speak of the uniqueness of YHWH: "Hear, O Israel: YHWH is our God, YHWH alone" (Deut 6:4). This confession is followed immediately by a fundamental reference to the Israelites' obligation to be totally dedicated to this one God: "You shall love YHWH your God with all your heart, and with all your soul, and with all your might" (Deut 6:5). In the Decalogue the first two commandments demand the exclusive worship of YHWH, who allows no other gods before him (Ex 20:2-6; Deut 5:6-10). The confession that YHWH is one implies and emphasizes (1) the unity and thus the continuity of the history between YHWH and Israel, his people;[25] (2) the *one* worship to be offered to the *one* God, who dwells in the midst of Israel (in Zion); (3) the nothingness of other gods (Is 43:10; 44:6); (4) the universality of YHWH's salvation beyond Israel's boundaries (Is 40—66). It is particularly Isaiah who goes beyond the Mosaic demand of worshiping YHWH and no other god, as he emphasizes the conviction that there are no gods besides YHWH.[26]

Is 43:10: "You are my witnesses, says YHWH, and my servant whom I have chosen, so that you may know and believe me and understand that I am he. Before me no god was formed, nor shall there be any after me."

Is 44:6: "Thus says YHWH, the King of Israel, and his Redeemer, YHWH of hosts: I am the first and I am the last; besides me there is no god."

If there is only one God, and if this God is YHWH, the God of Israel, and if YHWH is the Creator of the world and the Lord of history, then there can be salvation only in Zion or emerging from Zion. Thus Israel's confession of the uniqueness of YHWH is the foundation for missionary concepts. However, concepts of mission do not automatically lead to missionary praxis.

Old Testament scholars give varying dates for the origins of "missionary concepts" in Israel. Ernst Sellin traced missionary concepts in the Old Testament to Moses, who taught Israel obedience concerning the God of Sinai.[27] Otto Eissfeldt dated the beginning of universalistic tendencies in the "Israelite-Jewish history of religion" to the time of the conquest.[28] Hans Walter Wolff emphasizes the interest of the prophets for the history of the world, acknowledging Israel's God as the one and only Lord of reality, who will come in the future; already Amos implies that the reality of the world as history is fully understood only when it is placed in the context of the history of the nations.[29]

---

[25]Westermann 1978, 25 (ET, 32)
[26]Lauha (1977, 257) believes that this was a theological development in the sixth century B.C.
[27]Sellin 1925, 37.
[28]Eissfeldt 1954, 284.
[29]H. Wolff 1960, 229, 227.

The universalistic content of Israel's faith cannot, however, be identified with mission in the sense of an active endeavor of Israelite or Jewish messengers who seek to win non-Israelites or non-Jews to faith in YHWH and for integration into Israel. Still, the universalistic dimension of Israel's faith provides the salvation-historical foundation of the early Christian mission and illuminates its structure. The missionary activity of the early (Jewish) Christians is ultimately a ramification of the fact that YHWH, Israel's God, is the Creator of the world and the Lord of humankind. God controls the history of humankind, he guides history from beginning to end, he directs history to the goal that he stipulated, and he leads history and cares for humankind as the Creator who blesses and who holds people responsible.

4.2 Particularism and Internationalism

Many historical-critical scholars used to believe that "the Old Testament, as far as its oldest traditions are concerned, attests a particularistic religion that understands the relationship between Yahweh and his people as an exclusive relationship founded upon special election, which leaves foreign nations only the role of applauding spectators or, at best, of recipients of bread crumbs from the tables of the privileged (Gen 12:3; cf. further Mk 7:28). They maintain that it is only in Deutero-Isaiah and a few other late passages within the Old Testament canon that we find a genuine universalism that incorporates the salvation of the nations."[30] Such statements often leave the terms "universalism" and "particularism" undefined. The definitions of Gerardus van der Leeuw are helpful: particularism is "the restriction of the religious assets to a specific group, family, tribe and lineage, state, people, race"; universalism is "the rejection of this restriction."[31]

This one-sided emphasis on Israelite particularism is abandoned by many scholars in recent research. Many noted Old Testament scholars suggest that Israel's faith in Yahweh already had a universalistic horizon by the time of the conquest and the contacts with the peoples and the culture of Canaan, especially since the time of the integration of the Canaanite city-states into the Davidic kingdom. Scholars assume that the Canaanite cult of El, with its universalistic conceptions, was influential, particularly in Jerusalem as the "place of transmission of manifold traditional elements."[32] Claus Westermann emphasizes, in his commentary on Genesis, the universal dissemination of the motifs of the narratives about the creation of the world and about primeval history, with their significance for the traditions that circulated in Israel, traditions that probably had a long prehistory—a fact that makes the search for direct historical depen-

---

[30]Reventlow 1977, 354, with reference to Liagre-Böhl 1950, 2; Altmann 1964, 5, 25-32.
[31]Cited in Huber 1976, 193-94.
[32]Reventlow (1977, 354-55), who refers to "Jahwe und die Kulttradition von Jerusalem," *ZAW* 67 (1955): 168-197; Lutz 1968; Stolz 1970.

dence methodologically impossible.[33] Westermann believes that the traditional element of the genealogies is particularly important for a proper understanding of the primeval traditions, as their nomadic *Sitz im Leben* points to pre-state and thus nonparticularistic modes of thinking and living. Henning Graf Reventlow attempts to extend these observations to the patriarchal narratives and delineates traditions in which "international" customs are significant—that is, traditions that lead beyond the narrow national boundaries.[34] He concludes,

"The time of the patriarchs presents itself . . . as a period in which the various clans and tribes that belonged to semi-nomadic culture were not sharply differentiated from each other. The earliest period in which the anonymous primeval stories first circulated cannot be described in terms of ethnic identity; all we have are widespread stories that transpose common experiences of life of families that lived at the periphery of civilization into typical situations and events, often exhibiting traits of folk tales. . . . It was the Yahwist who poured the stream of these traditions into the narrow bed of the national patriarchal narrative, without, however, eliminating their genuine international character with regard to the genealogies or suppressing it consistently in the context of the stories. He pays a final tribute to this international horizon in his comment in 12:3b, as he understands the blessing for Abraham as a source from which all other clans of the earth can draw, if they only understand his meaning properly."

Even if we do not share the presupposed critical analysis of the pentateuchal sources and of Israel's history and identity, it is evident that the horizons of Israel's thought and life were not particularistic in an exclusive sense, but indeed international. This international dimension presented Israel again and again with the potential danger of syncretism, of adapting to and integrating beliefs and practices of pagan cults, a problem with which the prophets regularly had to grapple.

Before I discuss Israel's contacts with non-Israelites, we need to consider the foundational passage Gen 12:3.

4.3 The Promise of Genesis 12:3

The universal horizon of Israel's faith is expressed in Gen 12:1-3, a foundational passage in the book of Genesis.[35]

1a:	Now the LORD said to Abram:	וַיֹּאמֶר יְהוָה אֶל־אַבְרָם
1b:	Go from your country	לֶךְ־לְךָ מֵאַרְצְךָ
1c:	and your kindred	וּמִמּוֹלַדְתְּךָ
1d:	and your father's house	וּמִבֵּית אָבִיךָ

---

[33]Reventlow 1977, 355, with reference to Westermann, *Gen*, 1:1-97 (ET, 1:1-68).

[34]Reventlow 1977, 354; the quotation that follows above, ibid., 369-70.

[35]Repeated in Gen 18:18 (Abraham); Gen 22:18 (Abraham); Gen 26:4 (Isaac); Gen 28:14 (Jacob).

1e:	to the land that I will show you	אֶל־הָאָרֶץ אֲשֶׁר אַרְאֶךָּ
2a:	and I will make of you a great nation	וְאֶעֶשְׂךָ לְגוֹי גָּדוֹל
2b:	and I will bless you	וַאֲבָרֶכְךָ
2c:	and make your name great	וַאֲגַדְּלָה שְׁמֶךָ
2d:	And you will be a blessing	וֶהְיֵה בְּרָכָה
3a:	and I will bless those who bless you	וַאֲבָרֲכָה מְבָרֲכֶיךָ
3b:	and the one who curses you I will curse	וּמְקַלֶּלְךָ אָאֹר
3c:	and in you all the families of the earth shall be blessed	וְנִבְרְכוּ בְךָ כֹּל מִשְׁפְּחֹת הָאֲדָמָה

The first section (Gen 12:1b-2c)[36] involves just two parties: YHWH and Abraham. In the second section (Gen 12:2d-3c) others are mentioned, including the "families of the earth." The first section focuses on the blessing promised to Abraham; the second section places other people in the center, people who are described in terms of their relationship with Abraham. The blessing promised to Abraham's descendants and to the nations of the earth is not unconditional; it depends on Abraham being obedient to God's call to "go" from his country. In other words, the divine blessing promised in the second section depends on the realization of YHWH's blessing for Abraham.

The Niphal construction נִבְרְכוּ (*nibr^ekhû*), often discussed by scholars, occurs apart from Gen 12:3c only two other times in the Old Testament[37] and is best understood as expressing a middle force, designating "an action completed on the subj[ect], without viewing the subj. itself (hitp.) or another person (pu.) as the author of the action."[38] The Hebrew formulation thus should be translated "to obtain blessing, to find blessing, to participate in the blessing."

Interpretations that assume a passive meaning ("will be blessed") understand Gen 12:3 in terms of an articulation of "the final goal in a divine plan for universal salvation" in which "Abraham is the divinely chosen *instrument* in the implementation of that plan."[39] A reflexive interpretation ("shall bless themselves") asserts that the nations wish to be blessed, analogous to the blessing that Abraham received[40]—that is, Abraham is the *measure* of blessing.[41] This reflexive meaning is theoretically possible but not necessary; the promises are linked with Abraham personally and directly, not simply with his name. The interpretation in terms of a middle force is to be preferred, since the passive voice of the verb usually is construed with the Pual or Qal (passive participle). The context of Gen 12:3

---

[36]For the analysis that follows above see P. Williamson 2000, 229-30.

[37]In the parallel passages Gen 18:18; 28:14.

[38]C. A. Keller, "ברך *brk* 3," *THAT* 1:364 (*TDOT* 1:274), referring to the Hitpael and the Pual forms of the verb; see also Wenham, *Gen*, 1:266 nn. 3-4, 277-78; C. Mitchell 1987, 31-33; P. Williamson 2000, 223-28 (and the list of other authors, 227 n. 33).

[39]Hamilton, *Gen*, 1:374 (italics added).

[40]B. Albrektson, *History and the Gods* (ConBOT 1; Lund: Gleerup, 1967), 79.

[41]See N. Sarna, *Genesis* (Philadelphia: Jewish Publication Society, 1989), 89.

supports the middle force as well.[42] Gordon Wenham translates, "and all the families of the earth will find blessing in you."

Does Gen 12:3 speak of Abraham and his descendants as active *mediators* of blessing? Does Abraham and thus Israel receive from YHWH God the assignment to lead other nations to the worship of the one true God? Some authors answer these questions in the affirmative,[43] while others are skeptical. Wolfgang Kraus correctly points out that Gen 12:1-3 speaks of the prominent position that YHWH has given to Abraham (and Israel): "The promise of blessing for the clans of the earth first of all relates to Abraham and to his descendants. The blessing of Abraham is meant to come true in the blessing for the nations—thus underlining his unique position."[44] Kraus suggests that the parallel passages Gen 18:18 and Gen 28:14 take back in part the meaning of Gen 12:3 or focus it more consistently on Israel. It is the translation by the Septuagint that transformed Abraham into the mediator of salvation for all nations.[45] Horst Dietrich Preuss asserts that Gen 12:3 speaks of an existence or being that blesses, rather than of an activity, of a continued effectiveness of the power of the blessing by participation in Israel and the gifts and the nature of Israel's God, rather than of an active mediation of blessing in the sense of an imperative and an assignment.[46]

The blessing for the nations is a promise, not a command. Abraham does not receive an assignment to carry YHWH's blessing to the nations; rather, the nations are promised divine blessing if and when they see Abraham's faith in YHWH and if and when they establish contact with his descendants (cf. Gen 22:16-18). The meaning of the statement in Gen 12:3c supplements the other assertions in Gen 12:1-3: (1) Abraham will be blessed by God (Gen 12:2b); (2) Abraham will be a blessing: when people bless each other, they will do so by using Abraham's name (Gen 12:2d);[47] (3) all people who bless Abraham will in turn be blessed (Gen 12:3a); (4) all families will find blessing in Abraham (Gen 12:3c)—that is, Abraham will become a source of blessing for all people who seek the blessing of YHWH. The ensuing chapters of the book of Genesis illustrate Gen 12:1-3: people who are well disposed toward Abraham and his descendants fare well (Melchizedek, Abimelech), whereas people who oppose Abraham or his descendants are punished (Hagar). Thomas Mann asserts in this context that the promise of blessing for the "families of the earth" es-

---

[42]See Wenham, *Gen,* 1:277; for the translation that follows above see ibid., 1:265. On "blessing" see C. Mitchell 1987.

[43]See, for example, L. Perlitt, "Israel und die Völker," in *Frieden, Bibel, Kirche* (ed. G. Liedke; Stuttgart: Klett, 1972), 17-64; Schultz 1996, 39; Kaiser 2000, 20.

[44]Kraus 1996, 37-38; for the remarks that follow above see ibid., 41-42.

[45]Gen 12:3 LXX: καὶ ἐνευλογηθήσονται ἐν σοὶ πᾶσαι αἱ φυλαὶ τῆς γῆς.

[46]Preuss 1991-1992, 1:307-8.

[47]Cf. Zech 8:13; see Wenham, *Gen,* 1:276.

tablishes the theological unity of the book of Genesis.[48]

Abraham's story tells Israel that obedience to God's will, with the goal of worshiping YHWH in the promised land, brings blessing—for God's people themselves, but then also for the entire world. Israel's identity as the people of YHWH, being descended from Abraham, the father of the fathers, rests upon the effectiveness of YHWH's blessing. Odil Hannes Steck comments, "And what Israel is in the present, it is for the fulfillment of a single task: to be a sign of Yahweh's blessing that is able to overcome the nations, so that all may leave the primeval realm of depreciation and enter the realm of blessing. The foundational promise to Abraham indissolubly binds together primeval history and salvation history."[49] Gerhard von Rad described Abraham's calling, with its references to Yahweh's plan of history that aims at blessing all nations through Abraham, as "the beginning of saving history. . . . An indication of the final universal goal to what Jahweh intends to bring this history is already given in the beginning of the story of this particular election."[50] Claus Westermann comments on Gen 12:3, "This promise places the history of God with his people Israel from the very beginning into the wider horizon of the history of God with all humankind. It will resound repeatedly in the history of the people of God until at the end of the nation's history it again acquires determinative significance in the songs of the suffering servant, which then extend into apocalyptic."[51]

Yahweh's covenants with Abraham in Gen 15 and 17 take up various aspects of the promise of Gen 12:1-3 and thus interpret this foundational text.[52]

Gen 15:18: "On that day the LORD made a covenant with Abram, saying, 'To your descendants I give this land, from the river of Egypt to the great river, the river Euphrates.'"

Gen 17:4, 8: "As for me, this is my covenant with you: You shall be the ancestor of a multitude of nations. . . . [8]And I will give to you, and to your offspring after you, the land where you are now an alien, all the land of Canaan, for a perpetual holding; and I will be their God."

Gen 17:5-6, 16: "No longer shall your name be Abram, but your name shall be Abraham; for I have made you the ancestor of a multitude of nations. [6]I will make you exceedingly fruitful; and I will make nations of you, and kings shall come from you. . . . [16]I will bless her [Sarah], and moreover I will give you a son by her. I will bless her, and she shall give rise to nations; kings of peoples shall come from her."

Several observations are important. (1) The covenant in Gen 15 takes up the

---

[48]T. Mann 1991; cf. Wisdom 2001, 30.

[49]Steck 1971, 553-54; see also Rendtorff 1994, 130.

[50]Rad 1960, 1:178 (ET, 1:164).

[51]Westermann 1978, 53 (ET, 63).

[52]For the interpretation that follows above see P. Williamson 2000, 78-120; on Gen 15 see ibid., 121-44; on Gen 17, ibid., 145-216; on the literary context in the book of Genesis, ibid., 217-59.

promise of descendants and of land and thus, in the context of the canon of the Hebrew Bible, focuses on Israel as a nation (Gen 15:18). (2) The covenant in Gen 17 takes up the promise of descendants and land (Gen 17:4, 8) but emphasizes, first, the increase of descendants in an international framework (Gen 17:5-6, 16), and second, the establishment of an eternal relationship between the people and God (Gen 17:7). (3) In the literary context of the Abraham narrative, which begins with the divine promise in Gen 12:1-3 and ends with Abraham's temptation on Mount Moriah, where Abraham is willing not to spare his own son (Gen 22:1-19), it becomes manifest that Gen 15 and Gen 17 depict two different, albeit related, covenants. The combined stipulations of the two covenants guarantee that YHWH's blessings for Abraham in Gen 12:1-3 are being fulfilled. The first covenant confirms the divine promise that Abraham will become the "father," the ancestor, of a nation. The second covenant confirms the promise that Abraham will become the "father," the benefactor, of an international community. The second message of the angel that follows upon the sacrifice of the ram that YHWH provided (Gen 22:16-18) is best understood as ratification of the eternal covenant of Gen 17:

Gen 22:16-18: "By myself I have sworn, says the LORD: Because you have done this, and have not withheld your son, your only son, [17]I will indeed bless you, and I will make your offspring [זַרְעֲךָ; LXX: τὸ σπέρμα σου] as numerous as the stars of heaven and as the sand that is on the seashore. And your offspring [זַרְעֲךָ; LXX: τὸ σπέρμα σου] shall possess the gate of their enemies, [18]and by your offspring [בְזַרְעֲךָ; LXX: ἐν τῷ σπέρματί σου] shall all the nations of the earth gain blessing for themselves, because you have obeyed my voice."

The first element of the promise—Abraham will have numerous offspring—is emphasized through the comparison with the stars of heaven and the sand on the seashore. The second element of the promise—the offspring will be victorious over their enemies—is new. The "offspring" or "seed" mentioned in Gen 22:18 could collectively refer to all of Abraham's descendants. In view of the singular suffix of the noun "enemies" (אֹיְבָיו; lit., "his enemies") in Gen 22:17, however, it is more likely that "seed" in Gen 22:18 is to be interpreted as an individual. If this interpretation is correct, then the promise of Gen 22:17b-18 possibly speaks of an individual. The only passage outside of the book of Genesis that refers to Gen 22:17-18 is Ps 72:17, where the heir of this patriarchal promise is a royal figure.[53] The third element in the promise—Abraham's influence will have an international dimension—repeats Gen 12:3 (and Gen 18:18) but replaces Abraham's role with the role of the "seed." Thus in Gen 22:1-19 Abraham's willingness to sacrifice Isaac, the son of the promise, is linked with Yahweh's blessing that is transferred from Abraham to the promised offspring.

---

[53]P. Williamson 2000, 249-50, with reference to T. D. Alexander 1997; for the interpretation that follows above see ibid., 250-51; quotation, 251.

Paul Williamson comments, "It was by obediently surrendering his promised heir that Abraham secured the blessing of his promised 'seed.' The blessing promised here will find fulfilment not in Abraham himself, but rather in his 'seed.'" Since Gen 22 constitutes the conclusion of the Abraham narrative, this means for the promise of divine blessing for Abraham, for his descendants and for the "families of the earth" in Gen 12:1-3, that the international dimension of Abraham's influence is fulfilled when the one "seed" of Abraham bestows Yahweh's blessings upon the nations of the earth.

5

THE RELATIONSHIP BETWEEN ISRAEL, ISRAELITES AND GENTILES

There are essentially three options for understanding the relationship between Israel and other nations: (1) individual non-Israelites or non-Jews are accepted into God's people, as the promises of the covenant are applied to them (Zech 2:11); (2) God gives to a nation other than Israel the predicate "people of YHWH" (Is 19:16-25), or particular nations are equated with the people of God (Is 25:6-8); (3) the concept of "the people of God" is redefined: in the last chapters of the book of Isaiah membership in the people of God is no longer dependent on ethnic origin (Is 56:3-8); pagans receive a position formerly reserved for Israelites (Is 66:18-24).[1]

5.1 The Evidence in the Mosaic Law

The universal horizon of the patriarchal narratives is not a decisive element of the Mosaic law; it is not even a secondary criterion for the behavior of Israelites that the law demands. Non-Israelites are called נָכְרִי (nokrî), זָר (zār) and most frequently גֵּר (gēr). The term גֵּר (gēr) designates the non-Israelite resident alien who lives within the borders of Israel—that is, the non-Israelite "who is almost or (with the exception of circumcision) wholly accepted into the religious constitution of the Jewish people. Religiously, then, the term comes very close to the 'proselyte' of later Judaism."[2] The Septuagint translates the Hebrew term גֵּר seventy-seven times with προσήλυτος (prosēlytos).

The LXX translates גֵּר in fourteen cases with other Greek terms: eleven times with πάροικος, twice with γ[ε]ιώρας, and once with ξένος. The term πάροικος is usually the translation for the Hebrew term נָכְרִי (nokrî). This diverse usage is largely explained by the fact that προσήλυτος was used in religious contexts and thus was not appropriate in all passages. At the same time the Israelites in Egypt are several times designated as προσήλυτοι.[3]

---

[1]Kraus 1996, 37-38. For the discussion that follows above see also Schnabel 2002c.
[2]K. Kuhn 1959, 730 (*TDNT* 6:729).
[3]Ex 22:20; 23:9; Lev 19:34; Deut 10:19.

It must be noticed, however, that the Hebrew term *gēr* is not used for every foreigner who joins the worship of Yahweh, but only the non-Israelite foreigner
who lives in the land of Israel. The Mosaic law stipulated that the Israelites must
take care of the foreigner who lives within Israel.[4] Besides the גֵּר (*gēr*) we find
the תּוֹשָׁב (*tôšāb,* "sojourner, foreigner"). The difference in meaning between the
two terms often is difficult to establish. The following stipulations are most relevant:[5] (1) The alien must not be oppressed (Ex 22:20; 23:9). (2) The alien must
be treated justly in legal respects (Deut 1:16; 24:17; 27:19) and like any Israelite
in economic matters (Deut 24:14). (3) The sabbath laws apply also to the alien
(Ex 23:12; 20:10; Deut 5:14). (4) The alien, provided that he is circumcised, may
and indeed should participate in the Passover without any difference between
him and the indigenous Israelites (Ex 12:19; 12:48-49; Num 9:14). He can also
participate in the Day of Atonement (Lev 16:29). (5) Some cultic stipulations apply explicitly to the alien.[6] The reason for the generally equal treatment of aliens
and Israelites[7] is the history of the people of Israel and their status as aliens in
Egypt:

Lev 19:34: "The alien who resides with you shall be to you as the citizen among you; you
shall love the alien as yourself, for you were aliens in the land of Egypt: I am the LORD
your God" (cf. Deut 10:17-19).

In this context we even find the statement that YHWH loves the alien (Deut
10:18).[8] These passages indicate that the *gēr,* when he was circumcised, normally was regarded as an integrated "proselyte." But these passages neither state
nor imply that "proselytism" was expected in Israel, and proselytism was not
regulated in the law.[9]

Christiana van Houten, who presupposes an exilic/postexilic date for these passages,
thinks that this possibility was a late development.[10] After an extensive discussion of the
Deuteronomic laws concerning the *gēr,* she concludes that "aliens" were treated consistently as non-Israelites during the time of the kings, with no possibility for aliens to become Israelites. The radical demarcation from foreigners in postexilic Judea (Neh 9:2;

---

[4]In contrast to the "foreigner" (*nokrî*) who stays only temporarily in Israel as, for example,
traveler; see Deut 14:21; 15:3; 23:21; 29:21.

[5]See R. Martin-Achard, *THAT* 1:409-12 (*TLOT* 1:307-10); D. Kellermann, *ThWAT* 1:979-91
(*TDOT* 2:439-49); J. R. Spencer, *ABD* 6:103-4; see also K. Schmidt 1945; Klinghardt 1988;
C. Bultmann 1992.

[6]Lev 17:10, 12, 13: eating of blood; Lev 18:6-17, 18-23: sexual sins; Lev 22:17-33: the quality of
a sacrifice; Num 15: additional regulations for sacrifices—for example, regarding the atoning
efficacy of the sin-offering; Num 19: purification with the ashes of the red heifer.

[7]A few passages differentiate between the Israelite and the *gēr;* for example, according to Deut
14:21, an Israelite may not eat carrion, while an alien (*gēr*) or a foreigner (*nokrî*) may eat it.

[8]On the motivation in regard to the treatment of the alien see Houten 1991, 166-72.

[9]Against Smick 1989, 3.

[10]Houten 1991, 132-35; for the remarks that follow above see ibid., 68-108, 160.

13:30), as in the prohibition of mixed marriages (Ezra 10; Neh 13:23-31), renders this reconstruction of the development of the laws concerning the *gēr* implausible.

The stipulation of Num 15:15-16 demonstrates that the *gēr* was largely regarded as proselyte:

Num 15:15-16: "As for the assembly, there shall be for both you and the resident alien a single statute, a perpetual statute throughout your generations; you and the alien shall be alike before the LORD. [16]You and the alien who resides with you shall have the same law and the same ordinance."

At the same time we observe that the alien had a lower social status compared with the Israelite. This is obvious in that the alien is specifically mentioned in the Mosaic law. Also, the listing of the *gēr* in the Decalogue after the sons, daughters, slaves and cattle, in last place, indicates this low social status.[11]

Ex 20:10: "But the seventh day is a sabbath to the LORD your God; you shall not do any work—you, your son or your daughter, your male or female slave, your livestock, or the alien resident in your towns."

The possessive pronoun "your" (alien resident) designates, in the context of the enumeration of persons and animals that customarily belonged to the household of an Israelite whose livelihood was agriculture, probably the non-Israelite slave who was dependent on the master of the house economically; thus this was a person for whom the master had a certain responsibility. The low social status of the *gēr* is further seen in the fact that passages that most frequently mention the *gēr* refer to orphans, widows and the poor.[12] Also, the *gēr* does not possess hereditary real estate and thus has no legal status.

Christoph Bultmann interprets the term *gēr* as a social type designation. He suggests that *gēr* designates the stranger ("der Fremde") with respect to residence within Israel or across the borders of the nation, that person in a certain locality who is free but economically dependent with regard to work, wages and food, in contrast to the free owner of house, farmland, cattle and slaves. Bultmann claims that the inclusion of the *gēr* in the sabbath stipulation of the Decalogue in Deut 5:12-15 does not imply the integration ("Einbeziehung") of an alien or "sojourner" who originally did not worship YHWH but rather relates to the needy person whom the Judean landowner should allow to participate in the sabbath rest that obtained for himself and his household.[13] This analysis fails, in my view, because of the reason given for the equal treatment, namely, the reference to Israel's "sojourn" in Egypt: the Israelites certainly were not "non-Egyptian aliens with resident permits"; economic and social factors that also apply do not alter this fact.

---

[11]Houten 1991, 62-66.
[12]Lev 23:22; Deut 10:18; 14:29; 16:11, 14; 24:17, 20, 21; 26:13; 27:19; Jer 7:6; 22:3; Ezek 22:7, 29; Zech 7:10; Ps 94:6; 146:9.
[13]C. Bultmann 1992, 73.

An important theological point is the assertion that YHWH himself cares for the aliens who live in Israel, which is the reason for the stipulation that the alien must not be oppressed but should be positively loved. It is this love and care for the aliens in Israel that is motivated by Israel's experience in Egypt.[14]

The נָכְרִי (*nokrî*)[15] and the זָר (*zār*)[16] is generally the "alien" in an ethnic or political sense, meaning the non-Israelite, the foreigner—for example, the trader from abroad who stays only temporarily in the land of Israel or (thus in most occurrences of *zār*) the foreign soldier. Most passages use these terms in negative contexts. The prophets use *nokrî* and *zār* for other nations with whom Israel has contact, nations that actually or potentially destroy or exploit Israel,[17] perhaps as instruments of YHWH's judgment.[18] Contacts with these foreign nations is condemned[19] because they may lead Israel to apostasy. Ezra and Nehemiah exhort Israel to keep as far away from foreign nations as possible.[20] The prophets hope for a future when Israel can cast off the domination of foreign nations and instead be their ruler.[21]

Joel 3:17: "So you shall know that I, the LORD your God, dwell in Zion, my holy mountain. And Jerusalem shall be holy, and strangers shall never again pass through it."

Is 60:10: "Foreigners shall build up your walls, and their kings shall minister to you; for in my wrath I struck you down, but in my favor I have had mercy on you."

Is 61:5: "Strangers shall stand and feed your flocks, foreigners shall till your land and dress your vines."

The aliens who reside in Israel are denied political, economic and cultural rights.[22] B. Lang comments, "Of all those with whom Jews came into social contact, the *nŏkrî* was treated worst."[23]

There is no doubt that non-Israelites could join Israel. However, in this context there is never a reference to Gen 12:3 as a "commission" that is fulfilled when non-Israelites join Israel. No passage mentions a missionary activity of Is-

---

[14]See Martin-Achard, *THAT* 1:412 (*TLOT* 1:309).

[15]See Lang, *ThWAT* 5:454-62 (*TDOT* 9:423-32); Martin-Achard, *THAT* 2:66-68 (*TLOT* 2:739-41); Begg, *ABD* 2:829-30.

[16]See Martin-Achard, *THAT* 1:520-21 (*TLOT* 1:390-92); Snijders, *ThWAT* 2:556-64 (*TDOT* 4:52-58); Begg, *ABD* 2:829-30.

[17]Is 1:7; 62:8; Jer 5:19; Lam 5:2; Hos 7:9; 8:7; Obad 11.

[18]Ezek 7:21; 11:9.

[19]Is 2:6; Jer 2:25; 3:13; Ezek 16:3; 44:7.

[20]Ezra 6:21; 9:1; 10:11; Neh 9:2; 10:29. On the use of בדל as a technical term for the separation of Israel see E. Schwarz 1982, 63-74.

[21]Is 25:2, 5; 60:10; 61:5; Jer 30:18; Joel 3:17.

[22]On political rights see Deut 17:15; on economic privileges, Deut 15:3; 23:21; on cultural rights, Ex 12:43; Lev 22:25; Ezek 44:9.

[23]Lang, *ThWAT* 5:457 (*TDOT* 9:426).

raelites. And there is no legal stipulation that addresses the acceptance of non-Israelites into Israel. Passages that report the entry of aliens into Israel therefore should not be read as indicating how Israel specifically conceived its role as being a blessing for the nations in Gen 12:1-3.[24] The aliens approach Israel of their own accord, as a result of very diverse motivations, not least because of expulsion by military action. It is hardly plausible to speak of "missionary praxis."

Some authors interpret the statement in Ex 19:6, which belongs to the context of the inauguration of the Sinaitic covenant and formulates in a fundamental manner that the chosen people of Israel is to be "a kingdom of priests" (מַמְלֶכֶת כֹּהֲנִים, *mamleket kohănîm*), in the sense of Israel being a mediator between God and the nations: as a priest serves YHWH among his people, so Israel is to serve as priest among the nations.[25]

Since Theodoret (*Quaest. in Ex.* 35) many Christian authors have interpreted the reason for the election of Israel according to Ex 19 in terms of Israel possessing a unique mission among the nations: Israel has been given a universal "great commission" to mediate YHWH's salvation to the world. Often linked with this interpretation is the view that Israel has failed to carry out this divine assignment.

A more plausible interpretation of the theophany narrative in Ex 19 focuses on the emphasis on the relationship between the chosen people and YHWH: the entire people of Israel "is being dedicated to YHWH and is thus so close to him as only priests can be close to Yahweh."[26] Thus the NRSV translates *mamleket kohănîm* as "priestly kingdom."

Georg Beer suggests that Ex 19:6-7 marks the origin of the "idea of the priesthood of all believers which has provoked immense religious upheavals in early Christianity and in church history."[27] J. Philip Hyatt links the two ideas: "As a 'kingdom of priests' the Israelites were all to have access to Yahweh, and the nation was to serve as priest for the rest of the nations."[28] Hyatt does not explain, however, what the task alluded to in the second part of the sentence might entail.

Several reasons make this interpretation more plausible. (1) If Ex 19:6 formulates a missionary task for Israel among non-Israelites, this task, formulated in the context of the inauguration of the Sinaitic covenant, would be a fundamental obligation, and we would be justified to expect that this task is specified and elaborated in the Sinaitic law. However, the Sinaitic law contains neither individual stipulations for a "missionary" activity of Israel, which would be indis-

---

[24]Differently Bosch 1959, 111; Kaiser 2000, 40-50.
[25]See Schultz 1996, 40, with reference to Martin-Achard 1962 [1959], 39, and Kaiser 1981, 29-30; see also Schultz 2000; Childs, *Exod*, 367; C. Wright 1996.
[26]Preuss 1991-1992, 1:73.
[27]Georg Beer, *Exodus* (HAT 1.3; Tübingen: Mohr-Siebeck, 1939), 97.
[28]J. Philip Hyatt, *Exodus* (NCBC; Grand Rapids: Eerdmans, 1980 [1971]), 200.

pensable in the context of the Holiness Code, nor stipulations that regulate the entry of pagans into God's people. The visions of the prophets who speak of YHWH's law, light and righteousness going out to the nations and of the nations' coming to YHWH, Israel and Zion are no proof for the hypothesis[29] that Ex 19:6 establishes the historical (!) task of YHWH's people as a "missionary" task. Not insignificant is that the phrase *mamleket kohănîm* ("kingdom of priests") is singular in the Old Testament. (2) Pagan nations are the objects of warfare or at least kept at a distance; they are not "neutralized" in regard to their potential danger or won over by missionary takeover. The stipulations of the law concerning the *gēr* speak of equal treatment, not of priestly care for the *gēr*. (3) The prophets never accuse Israel or Judah of neglecting or abandoning a missionary task concerning the nations as a covenant obligation. (4) When the prophets speak of the nations coming to Zion, this clearly is an event of the "last days," an event that is not prompted by an active mission organized by Israel or Judah. The nations come to Zion without Israelites or Jews having gone out to them to invite them to convert to YHWH. The only exception is Is 66:19 (see below). (5) The passages that speak of the conversion of the nations to YHWH and of pagans joining God's people in the eschaton are not central passages in the Old Testament canon but climactic expectations. (6) The texts that speak of the nations' future worship of YHWH do not have a fixed literary form and do not used technical terms or fixed formulations,[30] which makes the assumption of a missionary commission of Israel to convert the nations, in the context of the Sinaitic covenant, unlikely as well.

5.2 The Evidence in Historical Texts

Israel's confession of the uniqueness of YHWH causes judgment over the nations of Canaan in the context of the conquest of the promised land after the exodus from Egypt.

Deut 7:1-2: "When the LORD your God brings you into the land you are entering to possess and drives out before you many nations—the Hittites, Girgashites, Amorites, Canaanites, Perizzites, Hivites and Jebusites, seven nations larger and stronger than you—[2]and when the LORD your God has delivered them over to you and you have defeated them, then you must destroy them totally. Make no treaty with them, and show them no mercy." (NIV)

The book of Joshua relates the execution of this command (Josh 11:1-11). In the history of Israel the exodus and the conquest were the most significant events in God's intervention since creation. The author of the book of Joshua clarifies

---

[29]Differently C. Wright (1996, 39), who asserts, "As the people of Yahweh they would have the historical task of bringing the knowledge of God to the nations, and bringing the nations to the means of atonement with God. This dual movement is reflected in prophetic visions."
[30]Rendtorff 1994, 133.

that the eradication of the Canaanite peoples was not the typical behavior of the Israelites vis-à-vis pagans.[31] There are two examples for aliens who join the nation and the community of Israel: Rahab the prostitute, who asks for mercy (Josh 2:8-13), and the Gibeonites who want to escape the fate of the inhabitants of Jericho and of Ai and thus seek to be joined with Israel (Josh 9). The author of the book of Samuel relates to people who, at the beginning of King David's rule, evidently seek full membership in the Israelite community while at the same time retaining their non-Israelite ethnic identity: Uriah the Hittite fought in David's army and followed the purity laws during times of war (2 Sam 11:6-13).

Solomon mentions foreigners in his prayer on the occasion of the dedication of the temple: they come to the temple in Jerusalem because they have heard of the mighty acts of YHWH. Solomon expresses his hope that as foreigners come to the temple, all nations of the earth may see that YHWH is God and that there is no other besides him:

1 Kings 8:41-43: "As for the foreigner who does not belong to your people Israel but has come from a distant land because of your name—[42]for men will hear of your great name and your mighty hand and your outstretched arm—when he comes and prays toward this temple, [43]then hear from heaven, your dwelling place, and do whatever the foreigner asks of you, so that all the peoples of the earth may know your name and fear you, as do your own people Israel, and may know that this house I have built bears your Name." (NIV)

At the same time Solomon made the non-Israelites who still lived within the borders of the land into slaves of the king (1 Kings 9:15-22). It is not certain, however, whether we can identify these pagan slaves as "aliens," since they are designated as slaves.[32]

The narratives of the prophets Elijah and Elisha relate four visits to regions beyond Israel where they were active in the name of YHWH as well (1 Kings 17—19; 2 Kings 8). However, the narrator does not report that either of these prophets was sent to pagans with the assignment to preach repentance and conversion to YHWH. A special case is the story of the Aramean general Naaman, who is healed through the mediation of Elisha and who comes to faith in YHWH (2 Kings 5):

2 Kings 5:15: "Then Naaman and all his attendants went back to the man of God. He stood before him and said, 'Now I know that there is no God in all the world except in Israel. Please accept now a gift from your servant.'" (NIV)

The subsequent narrative highlights the relation between YHWH and the land (of Israel). Since Naaman believes that he cannot serve YHWH in his own

---

[31]The interpretation of Malchow (1990), that Israel's "intolerance" can be explained by the intolerance of the peoples of the ancient Near East, remains at the surface.
[32]Houten 1991, 160.

country, he asks to be given Israelite earth to be carried back to Aram by two mules so that he "will never again make burnt offerings and sacrifices to any other god," as he will worship only YHWH (2 Kings 5:17). At the same time he asks, in advance, for forgiveness, as he will not be able to avoid visits to the temple of Rimmon (2 Kings 5:18). This incident may be interpreted as an early form of proselytism "that is less concerned with acceptance into a community of people (Israel) largely defined along territorial and ethnic lines, rather than with the admission to the group of people who legitimately worship the God of this community (Yahweh as God of Israel) and who are thus allowed to view themselves as part of the people of God"; Naaman becomes "the prototype of the worshiper of Yahweh outside of Israel who cannot fall back on membership in the people of Israel secured by genealogical lineage but whose participation in the worship of Yahweh is nevertheless regarded as legitimate."[33]

Two Old Testament books deal with the subject of the admission of pagans into the people of God and the positive reaction of pagans to a message from Yahweh: the book of Ruth and the book of Jonah. These short texts illustrate the conviction that Yahweh's salvation and mercy are not limited to Israel.[34] Some scholars interpret these books in terms of an effort by the authors to compensate a "constriction" of the people of Israel "by tracing an ancestor of David to Moab (Ruth 4:17), generally viewing this Moabite woman in a very positive light, by portraying pagan sailors as better praying men compared with an Israelite prophet, and by depicting the evil city of Nineveh as open for the proclamation of this prophet."[35]

Some scholars interpret Ruth 4:13-22 in terms of a protest against the legislation of Deut 23:3, which stipulates that descendants of Moabites to the tenth generation may not be admitted to Israel; according to this stipulation, King David would have been excluded (on account of the ancestry of his father).[36]

The foreign origins of Ruth are explicitly emphasized (Ruth 2:6, 10). This emphasis is striking. She is designated a Moabite several times, even in contexts where the subject matter does not demand it (Ruth 1:22; 2:2; 4:5, 10). Morton Smith suggests that the main aim of the book of Ruth is the portrayal of the "ideal proselyte."[37]

In the context of the constitution of Judea after the Babylonian exile, foreigners are excluded for the sake of the purity of "true Israel." Mixed marriages are

---

[33]Marinković 1994, 6, 12.
[34]Sellin 1925, 33.
[35]Preuss 1991-1992, 2:314.
[36]See Scobie 1992, 288.
[37]R. M. Smith 1984, 251.

forbidden (Ezra 10; Neh 13:23-31).[38] The book of Nehemiah formulates segregation from foreigners as a principle, as the following examples demonstrate:

Neh 9:2: "Those of Israelite descent had separated themselves from all foreigners. They stood in their places and confessed their sins and the wickedness of their fathers." (NIV)

Neh 13:30: "So I purified the priests and the Levites of everything foreign, and assigned them duties, each to his own task." (NIV)

5.3 The Evidence in the Psalms

Several psalms contain statements that have been linked with the concept of missions: (1) the nations are called upon to praise, serve and fear YHWH;[39] (2) the worship of YHWH by the nations is expected for the present and promised for the future;[40] (3) the Israelite worshiper "plans" to worship YHWH among the nations;[41] (4) Israel is challenged to proclaim the acts and the royal rule of YHWH among the nations;[42] (5) the nations are described as belonging to Israel in the future;[43] (6) at the same time the psalms speak of YHWH's judgment of the nations.[44]

The interpretation of Ps 47:9 is disputed: "The nobles of the nations assemble as the people of the God of Abraham, for the kings of the earth belong to God; he is greatly exalted" (NIV). Most scholars suggest that this statement alludes to the "universalism" of the blessing of Abraham of Gen 12:3b or Gen 17:4-6, linked with the assumption that the Masoretic Text and the Septuagint have been used to form a mixed quotation: "The nobles of the nations assemble *with the people* of the God of Abraham." On the other hand, Erich Zenger argues that the notion of Abraham as mediator of salvation for the nations, which is central for Gen 12:3, is not echoed in Ps 47, neither on the literary level nor in terms of subject matter. He concludes, "The events mentioned in V. 10ab mean, therefore, that 'one people' arises out of the many peoples, as they assemble at the throne of Abraham's God and accept him as their God-King. . . . Their assembly is an acknowledgement 'of the *God* of Abraham.' They abandon their previous gods and acknowledge the God of Abraham as their God."[45] H.-J. Kraus comments, "One may certainly imagine that at the great annual festivals in Jerusalem there were emissaries of foreign nations present. The psalm singer sees this as

---

[38]Blank (1936, 159-65), whose reconstruction is dependent on the his assumption of a late date for several texts.

[39]See Ps 47:2; 66:8; 96:7; 117:1; cf. 72:11; 102:23; cf. 102:16.

[40]See Ps 67:2-7; also 72:17; 86:9; 102:16, 23.

[41]See Ps 18:50; 57:10; 108:4.

[42]See Ps 9:12; 96:3; 105:1; also 96:10.

[43]See Ps 2:8; 111:6.

[44]See Ps 2:9; 7:9; 9:20; 96:10.

[45]Zenger 1989, 428-29; cf. Preuss 1991-1992, 2:313; Kraus, *Ps*, 1:353 (ET, 1:470).

a sign for a realization of the universal rule of God."[46] The text refers to Abraham because YHWH removed him from the worship of alien gods—that is, because Abraham renounced his gods and decided to worship YHWH, the one and only true God. Some scholars regard it as an open question whether Ps 47:9 wants to comment further on the relationship between Israel as the people of God and other peoples. In view of the fact that texts such as Is 60:3-14; 66:23; Zech 14:16; Ps 102:23 keep the nations and Israel separate, even though they speak of the nations as worshiping YHWH, the answer to this question seems to be negative.

Lucien Legrand argues that statements such as these that mention the nations merely express a "cultural universalism" and thus should be understood as proclamation of the universal sovereignty of YHWH. As fields, trees and mountains are called upon to acknowledge the greatness of Israel's God, so are the nations.[47]

Richard Schultz argues that this interpretation is a depreciation, considering the eschatological visions of the prophets; if Israel acknowledges, for example, the statements in Ps 96 and Ps 98, it should be expected that Israel is a witness to God's redemptive acts among the nations, inviting them to join in praise and thanksgiving addressed to YHWH.[48] However, it is questionable whether these psalms indeed constitute the beginnings of "centrifugal missions": the only true parallels are the prophets' promises for the eschaton, for the future, and we do not know how Israel or the psalmist would have envisioned the specific historical realization of such witness among other nations. Schultz is right if he refers to "missionary ideas," but there is good reason to doubt that these psalms are evidence of "missionary praxis" in terms of deliberately organized and actively pursued efforts to convert non-Israelites to the worship of YHWH.

5.4 The Evidence in Prophetic Texts

It is not likely that the oracles against foreign nations[49] are evidence for missionary ideas or missionary praxis in Israel. Some scholars argue that these messages demonstrate YHWH's claims upon the nations. This view is implausible, however. (1) There is no evidence that these prophetic oracles were ever "sent" to foreign nations. Thus it is not clear that these oracles are "messages." (2) The behavior of these surrounding nations that these oracles address characterized Israel or Judah as well. This means that these oracles could well have been written with the people of Israel or Judah as the sole intended audience. (3) The oracles against foreign nations generally contain the threat of judgment rather than promises of salvation. They can hardly be said to attempt to "win" the foreign nations.[50]

---

[46]Kraus, *Ps,* 1:353 (ET, 1:470).
[47]Legrand 1990, 16-18.
[48]Schultz 1996, 46-47.
[49]Cf. Is 13—23; Jer 46—51; Ezek 25—32; Amos 1—2; Zeph 2.
[50]Thus Schultz 1996, 45.

Friedrich Huber analyzed Isaiah's words for foreign nations and concludes that the prophet portrays YHWH's interventions in the history of other nations in terms of sovereign divine decrees, emphasizing particularly the sovereignty of YHWH. The prophet expresses neither the idea of YHWH's universal control of the affairs of the world nor the idea of a true universalism: "The center of his proclamation is Judah and her relationship to Yahweh."[51] This analysis appears convincing, but Huber omits, on the basis of complex issues concerning authorship, the announcements of salvation for foreign nations in Is 2:2-4; 9:1-6; 11:1-9; he further defends this omission with the argument that he discusses primarily the question of "prophecy and foreign politics" rather than "prophetic eschatology."

The missionary theology and praxis that we find in the New Testament is, in the Old Testament, the subject of the eschatology of the prophets. Hans Jochen Margull comments, "The promise concerns the gathering of the nations and their integration into God's people on account of Yahweh's intervention in the history of mankind, in which the Lord of the nations who controls history achieves his goals, and their goals, in judgment and in gathering them."[52] Johannes Hempel asserts in this context that "mission is the beginning of the end times."[53]

John Oswalt suggests that the vision of the prophets concerning Israel's mission to the nations did not change over the course of the four hundred years of "classical prophecy" and summarizes this vision as follows:[54] (1) Israel was conscious of the fact that its "commission" included the nations as well: the prophets repeatedly envision a time when the nations will come to Jerusalem to worship YHWH as Israel worships YHWH. (2) Israel has the function of a witness: the people of God are called to testify to YHWH's being and to YHWH's acts through life and deed. However, the conversion of pagans is not Israel's responsibility: God himself will cause the nations to come to Zion. (3) Even though Israel does not have the task of converting the nations, its testimony is still normative: God is not one of many gods, but he reveals himself in and through Israel. (4) Israel's testimony has a universal scope: since YHWH is the only God of creation, the truth that Israel lives and proclaims concerns "all flesh" (i.e., all nations). (5) Israel's universal witness is not at the center of the prophets' proclamation or ministry: their focus is on calling Israelites and Jews to be obedient to YHWH, the God of the covenant, and they remind Israel of the dire consequences that result from continuous disobedience.

John Oswalt does not seem to notice that a "universal commission" of Israel is not the same as the future pilgrimage to Zion that the prophets speak about. He gives a negative answer to the basic question of whether Israel is responsible for making sure that the nations hear about YHWH and his salvation, which can be acquired only in Zion. This interpretation of the evidence is convincing but

---

[51]Huber 1976, 202.
[52]Margull 1960, 974.
[53]Hempel 1954, 270.
[54]Oswalt 1993.

seems to render impossible the view that Israel had a universal commission or assignment. The *mission* of Israel, focused on following joyously and obediently the injunctions of the covenant that YHWH had granted Israel, was local. What is universal is the *future consequences* of this obedience.

Isaiah

Oracles of salvation for the nations are concentrated in Is 40—66. The second part of the Isaianic prophecies contains visions on the subject of the relationship between Israel and the nations that are climactic within the Old Testament.[55] The new era of salvation that the prophet envisions for the time when YHWH finally and visibly establishes his rule illustrates the responsibility of Israel's election. Paul Volz writes, in an excursus on the history of missionary ideas in Israel, "In this historical movement, the poet of the Ebed songs looms as the founder of missions."[56] According to Aarre Lauha, the origins of the notion that one should propagate faith in YHWH among foreign nations are intimately linked with the fact that the prophet interprets his own time in terms of an eschatological perspective: the concept of missionary work was made possible on account of a new interpretation of the traditional Israelite notion of election, prompted by the experience of the exile.[57] The evidence of the book of Isaiah concerning a universal vision for Israel's mission can be summarized as follows:[58]

1. YHWH is the Creator of the world, and he will return to Zion as Israel's God (Is 52:7-10).

Is 52:7-10: "How beautiful upon the mountains are the feet of the messenger who announces peace, who brings good news, who announces salvation, who says to Zion, 'Your God reigns.' [8]Listen! Your sentinels lift up their voices, together they sing for joy; for in plain sight they see the return of the LORD to Zion. [9]Break forth together into singing, you ruins of Jerusalem; for the LORD has comforted his people, he has redeemed Jerusalem. [10]The LORD has bared his holy arm before the eyes of all the nations; and all the ends of the earth shall see the salvation of our God."

2. YHWH is the Creator of humankind, and as the Lord of the nations he one day will remove the darkness that covers the nations, so that they will see the splendor of YHWH's glory over Jerusalem (Is 60:1-5) and serve Israel (Is 60:10-14).

---

[55]See Wodecki 1982; Van Winkle 1985; Westermann 1987; Blenkinsopp 1988; G. Davies 1989; Franke 1999; Gelston 1992; Pao 2000, 37-69; Köstenberger and O'Brien 2001, 45-50.
[56]Volz, *Jes,* 169; cf. H. Wolff 1951, 1-2.
[57]Lauha 1977, 257, presupposing a postexilic date for Is 40—55.
[58]The amount of literature is immense; see Margull 1960; Hermisson 1982; Wodecki 1981; G. Davies 1989, 93-106; Preuss 1991-1992, 2:324-26; Schultz 1996, 49-53. Questions of date and literary and redaction-critical issues will not be discussed; see Dion 1970; G. Davies 1989, 107-20.

Is 60:1-5: "Arise, shine; for your light has come, and the glory of the LORD has risen upon you. [2]For darkness shall cover the earth, and thick darkness the peoples; but the LORD will arise upon you, and his glory will appear over you. [3]Nations shall come to your light, and kings to the brightness of your dawn. [4]Lift up your eyes and look around; they all gather together, they come to you; your sons shall come from far away, and your daughters shall be carried on their nurses' arms. [5]Then you shall see and be radiant; your heart shall thrill and rejoice, because the abundance of the sea shall be brought to you, the wealth of the nations shall come to you.

Is 60:10-14: "Foreigners shall build up your walls, and their kings shall minister to you; for in my wrath I struck you down, but in my favor I have had mercy on you. [11]Your gates shall always be open; day and night they shall not be shut, so that nations shall bring you their wealth, with their kings led in procession. [12]For the nation and kingdom that will not serve you shall perish; those nations shall be utterly laid waste. [13]The glory of Lebanon shall come to you, the cypress, the plane, and the pine, to beautify the place of my sanctuary; and I will glorify where my feet rest. [14]The descendants of those who oppressed you shall come bending low to you, and all who despised you shall bow down at your feet; they shall call you the City of the LORD, the Zion of the Holy One of Israel."

3. The coming Davidic king will judge the godless; he will reestablish righteousness (Is 11:3-5), create peace (Is 11:6-9), fill the world with the knowledge of YHWH (Is 11:9) and draw the pagan nations to himself (Is 11:10).

Is 11:3-5: "His delight shall be in the fear of the LORD. He shall not judge by what his eyes see, or decide by what his ears hear; [4]but with righteousness he shall judge the poor, and decide with equity for the meek of the earth; he shall strike the earth with the rod of his mouth, and with the breath of his lips he shall kill the wicked. [5]Righteousness shall be the belt around his waist, and faithfulness the belt around his loins."

Is 11:6-10: "The wolf shall live with the lamb, the leopard shall lie down with the kid, the calf and the lion and the fatling together, and a little child shall lead them. [7]The cow and the bear shall graze, their young shall lie down together; and the lion shall eat straw like the ox. [8]The nursing child shall play over the hole of the asp, and the weaned child shall put its hand on the adder's den. [9]They will not hurt or destroy on all my holy mountain; for the earth will be full of the knowledge of the LORD as the waters cover the sea. [10]On that day the root of Jesse shall stand as a signal to the peoples; the nations shall inquire of him, and his dwelling shall be glorious."

4. The Servant of YHWH, mentioned repeatedly in Is 42—53, can be identified with this coming king, but he has been given a different task.[59] On the one hand, he serves Israel "as a covenant to the people" (Is 42:6)—that is, he effects the restoration of God's people (Is 49:6a) by replacing the original "servant Israel" (Is 49:3), who is deaf and blind (Is 42:18-20). On the other hand, he serves the world as a "light to the nations" (Is 42:6) as he takes the justice of God to them with the result that even "the coastlands," meaning the nations of the Mediter-

---

[59]Cf. Schultz 1996, 49-53.

ranean, wait for his instruction (Is 42:1, 4; 49:1) so that his salvation reaches "to the end of the earth" (Is 49:6b). The Servant will affect many nations with his suffering (Is 52:15), atoning their sins.

Hans-Jürgen Hermisson thinks that the traditional alternatives of an "individual" and a "collective" interpretation of the Servant Songs are problematic. "The various links between the servant of the Songs and the servant Israel indicate, rather, that the prophetic servant occupies a substitutionary and representative role for Israel."[60] Hermisson describes the basic idea of the Servant Songs: "Yahweh will liberate Israel by Cyrus from the Babylonian exile, and he will lead Israel through a transformed desert, accompanied by signs and wonders, back to an exalted Zion. Israel will rejoice with praise and thanksgiving; the nations will be overwhelmed by the only God who saves and they will join him. Thus the entire earth will share salvation." But the servant Israel is a despondent people. In order to convince the world that Israel's God is the only God, one needs to prove "that YHWH has already revealed his creative word audibly and in an articulated manner and that this word is active in the world." For this reason there is a second servant, the prophet, who has the task of setting Israel on course with the task of being YHWH's witness before the world. The prophet proclaims YHWH's creative and saving word in advance. The prophetic servant achieves what Israel withholds: he is "the ideal Israel and a model for Israel" as he trusts in YHWH. If the messianic interpretation of the Servant Songs is not just a late "continuation" but implied in the Isaianic texts themselves, the Songs speak not simply of Israel or of an anonymous prophet in the exile but of Israel, of the prophet and of the redeemer that Israel expected for the "last days."

A centrally significant passage is Is 42:6:

"I am the LORD,   אֲנִי יְהוָה

I have called you in righteousness,   קְרָאתִיךָ בְצֶדֶק

I have taken you by the hand   וְאַחְזֵק בְּיָדֶךָ

and kept you;   וְאֶצָּרְךָ

I have given you as a covenant to the people,   וְאֶתֶּנְךָ לִבְרִית עָם

a light to the nations."   לְאוֹר גּוֹיִם

The term עָם (ʿām) in Is 40—55 always designates the people of YHWH, in contrast to גּוֹיִם (gōyîm)—Israel in contrast to the pagans.[61] This means that the phrases בְּרִית עָם (bĕrît ʿām) and אוֹר גּוֹיִם (ʾôr gōyîm) form not a parallelism but an apposition. Karl Elliger interprets the phrases differently as completely parallel in terms of subject matter.[62] He believes that the passage was part of a Cyrus song and suggests the following interpretation: "Yahweh, the creator and sustainer of the world, has summoned the Persian king to bring to the entire world, and thus to Israel as well, the order that he intended." Thus Elliger speaks only of a "world historical task" that Cyrus has been given; he does not discuss a universal commission that

---

[60]Hermisson 1996b, 61; the quotations that follow above, ibid., 44-45.

[61]Whereas some scholars relate the term ʿām to "the people" of Israel, other scholars interpret the word in terms of humanity in general; see Elliger, DtJes, 233-35.

[62]Elliger, DtJes, 235; for the remarks that follow above see ibid., 230-31, 228, 239.

Israel may have. He sees two ideas expressed in Is 42:5-9 that go beyond the contemporary conditionality of the prophetic word and have eternal validity: "First is
the notion that reoccurs again and again in Deutero-Isaiah that the only true God,
the creator and sustainer of the world, is at the same time the Lord of the history
of the world and thus of the history of each individual nation. The second notion
is that God desires salvation, the salvation of humanity. For Deutero-Isaiah, 'the
light of the nations' here is Cyrus. This means that he understands salvation in political terms, as he interprets it as opportunity to live one's own life in freedom."
However, the interpretation of *bĕrît ʿām* and *ʾôr gōyîm* as appositional phrases is
more plausible: the prophet asserts that the pagan nations will have the opportunity in the future new era of salvation to enter into the same *bĕrît* (covenant) relationship that Israel, the people of God, enjoys at present. Access to the *ʿām*-cove-
nant, to fellowship with YHWH, the one true God, means light for the pagan
nations,[63] as it puts into effect the salvation of God's new redemptive activity.[64]

5. There will come the day when the pagan nations will come to Mount Zion
and inquire after the instructions of YHWH.[65] As the nations come to Jerusalem,
the promised royal rule of YHWH is realized. The main impetus for the nations'
coming to Zion is God's redemptive acts (Is 55:3-5; 56:6-8).

Is 55:3-5: "Incline your ear, and come to me; listen, so that you may live. I will make with
you an everlasting covenant, my steadfast, sure love for David. [4]See, I made him a witness
to the peoples, a leader and commander for the peoples. [5]See, you shall call nations that
you do not know, and nations that do not know you shall run to you, because of the LORD
your God, the Holy One of Israel, for he has glorified you."

Is 56:6-8: "And the foreigners who join themselves to the LORD, to minister to him, to love
the name of the LORD, and to be his servants, all who keep the sabbath, and do not profane it, and hold fast my covenant—[7]these I will bring to my holy mountain, and make
them joyful in my house of prayer; their burnt offerings and their sacrifices will be accepted on my altar; for my house shall be called a house of prayer for all peoples. [8]Thus
says the Lord GOD, who gathers the outcasts of Israel, I will gather others to them besides
those already gathered."

Isaiah prophesies for the time when God will reveal his justice and righteousness that the alien who joins YHWH will come to the temple as the "house of
prayer for all peoples." Jostein Ådna comments, "Is 56:7 promises to the Gentiles, in a unique manner, participation, on equal terms with Israel, in eschatological salvation in the sanctuary on Zion."[66]

David Bosch suggests that the missionary activity of the Servant of the Lord

---

[63]Lauha 1977, 259-60.
[64]M. Saebo, "*ʾôr*," *THAT* 1:89 (*TLOT* 1:66). See also Is 49:6.
[65]On the "pilgrimage" of the nations to Zion see Is 2:1-4 (Mic 4:1-4); Jer 3:17; Is 25:6-9; 56:6-7;
   60:1-5; Zeph 3:8-10; Hag 2:6-9; Zech 8:20-23.
[66]Ådna 2000a, 282; cf. Fredriksen 1991, 545-47.

among the nations is "not proclamation but the reality of God's actions in connection with him. He does not proclaim; rather, he *is* proclaimed, specifically in *Israel*. . . . Israel's task consists in remaining faithful to Yahweh. Insofar as Israel is faithful to Yahweh, it is also faithful to the nations. Because if Israel is obedient to Yahweh in all respects, it does not even need to go out to the nations in order to proclaim YHWH's message. Rather, the nations will come to Israel, attracted by the light that emanates from it. Israel simply needs to be truly Israel, needs only to fulfill the task for which God has called it. Israel itself *is* proclamation, both in its history and in its fate."[67] This interpretation is hardly plausible in view of texts such as Is 43:9; 45:21; 48:20; 52:7; 55:3-4; 61:1-2; 66:19. In Isaiah's visions of the eschaton Israel and the Servant clearly have a more active role.

Hugh Williamson shows how the tension may be resolved that exists between the "universalistic" visions of the salvation of the pagan nations integrated in a future new people of God and the "nationalistic" statements according to which the nations will be subservient to Israel. The mediating role of the king between YHWH and Israel (God ⇒ king ⇒ people) is transformed by Isaiah into a mediating role for the people of God between God and the nations (God ⇒ people ⇒ nations): God will bless the nations through Israel.[68] When Gentiles will have become servants of the Lord together with the gathered of Israel, when they love YHWH and worship him in the temple, the distinction between faithful Israelites and believing foreigners is removed, as the criteria for membership in the new community of God have been changed fundamentally.[69]

6. The admission of the nations to the salvation of Israel does not happen in a wholesale arrangement: Isaiah's visions do not remove the necessity for individuals to acknowledge YHWH and his salvation. The prophet expects the conversion of individuals.[70]

Is 44:3-5: "For I will pour water on the thirsty land, and streams on the dry ground; I will pour my spirit upon your descendants, and my blessing on your offspring. [4]They shall spring up like a green tamarisk, like willows by flowing streams. [5]This one will say, 'I am the LORD's,' another will be called by the name of Jacob, yet another will write on the hand, 'The LORD's,' and adopt the name of Israel."

This promise is not limited to Jews or Gentiles; in the context of Is 43:22-28 the prophet speaks of God's future acts of salvation that result in people, whether Jews or Gentiles, regarding it as an honor to belong to Israel and to its God.[71]

7. The process that leads to the participation of the nations in YHWH's salva-

---

[67]Bosch 1959, 21, with reference to H. Wolff 1951, 11.
[68]H. Williamson 1998, 113-66.
[69]H. Williamson 1998, 197.
[70]H. Wolff 1951, 10-11.
[71]Oswalt, *Is,* 2:167-68.

tion seems to be understood as primarily a "centripetal" process.[72] The prophet does not speak of Israel or individual Israelites being sent to the nations; rather, the nations congregate in Jerusalem as a result of YHWH's epiphany and as a result of the redemptive ministry of the Servant. The main task of Israel seems mainly to be the calling to be truly and consistently "Israel" (Is 40:1-5). In view of its blindness and deafness, Israel seems to be a rather reluctant witness: Israel and its history represent the acts of YHWH and thus refer to YHWH's holy absoluteness (Is 42:18-25; 43:1-7, 8-13).

Is 40:1-5: "Comfort, O comfort my people, says your God. [2]Speak tenderly to Jerusalem, and cry to her that she has served her term, that her penalty is paid, that she has received from the LORD's hand double for all her sins. [3]A voice cries out: 'In the wilderness prepare the way of the LORD, make straight in the desert a highway for our God. [4]Every valley shall be lifted up, and every mountain and hill be made low; the uneven ground shall become level, and the rough places a plain. [5]Then the glory of the LORD shall be revealed, and all people shall see it together, for the mouth of the LORD has spoken.'"

Is 42:18-21: "Listen, you that are deaf; and you that are blind, look up and see! [19]Who is blind but my servant, or deaf like my messenger whom I send? Who is blind like my dedicated one, or blind like the servant of the LORD? [20]He sees many things, but does not observe them; his ears are open, but he does not hear. [21]The LORD was pleased, for the sake of his righteousness, to magnify his teaching and make it glorious."

Is 43:1-7: "But now thus says the LORD, he who created you, O Jacob, he who formed you, O Israel: Do not fear, for I have redeemed you; I have called you by name, you are mine. [2]When you pass through the waters, I will be with you; and through the rivers, they shall not overwhelm you; when you walk through fire you shall not be burned, and the flame shall not consume you. [3]For I am the LORD your God, the Holy One of Israel, your Savior. I give Egypt as your ransom, Ethiopia [Cush] and Seba in exchange for you. [4]Because you are precious in my sight, and honored, and I love you, I give people in return for you, nations in exchange for your life. [5]Do not fear, for I am with you; I will bring your offspring from the east, and from the west I will gather you; [6]I will say to the north, 'Give them up,' and to the south, 'Do not withhold; bring my sons from far away and my daughters from the end of the earth—[7]everyone who is called by my name, whom I created for my glory, whom I formed and made.'"

8. However, there is a twofold "centrifugal" movement originating in Israel. The first movement emanates from the Servant of the Lord, who, as light of the nations, carries YHWH's will to the nations (Is 42:1, 6-7; 49:6; cf. 51:4-5). The second movement emanates from the survivors of Israel whom YHWH sends to the na-

---

[72]Preuss 1991-1992, 2:323; similarly Schultz 1996, 51-52. It sometimes is difficult to decide whether a passage should be interpreted in a centripetal or a centrifugal sense (cf. Is 61:9; 62:2). The terms "centripetal" and "centrifugal," as they related to missionary activity, were first used by Sundkler (1936). Cf. Hermisson (1996a, 23), who speaks of an indirect effect of the Servant of the Lord on the nations: "The process gets started only through the gathering of Israel to Yahweh."

tions so that foreigners may become priests and Levites (Is 66:19-21).[73]

Is 42:1: "Here is my servant, whom I uphold, my chosen one in whom I delight; I will put my Spirit on him and he will bring justice to the nations" (NIV). [Karl Elliger translates the last sentence, "Ich habe meinen Geist auf ihn gelegt, den Entscheid bringt er den Völkern hinaus" ("I have put my Spirit on him, and he will take the decree out to the nations").]

Is 42:6-7: "I am the LORD, I have called you in righteousness, I have taken you by the hand and kept you; I have given you as a covenant to the people, a light to the nations, [7] to open the eyes that are blind, to bring out the prisoners from the dungeon, from the prison those who sit in darkness."

Is 49:6: "It is too light a thing that you should be my servant to raise up the tribes of Jacob and to restore the survivors of Israel; I will give you as a light to the nations, that my salvation may reach to the end of the earth."

Is 66:19: "And I will set a sign among them. From them I will send survivors to the nations, to Tarshish, Put [Pul], and Lud—which draw the bow—to Tubal and Javan, to the coastlands far away that have not heard of my fame or seen my glory; and they shall declare my glory among the nations."

The "survivors" (פְּלֵיטִים, *pĕlēṭîm*) in Is 66:19 are either Jews who have survived God's judgment on his people[74] or converted Gentiles from the neighboring nations who are sent to the more remote nations as "missionaries."[75] They are sent to the remote regions of the earth in order to make known YHWH and his salvation.

Tarsis (*Taršîš* [cf. Gen 10:4]) refers perhaps to Tartessus in Spain at the western end of the Mediterranean area.[76] More recently scholars have suggested identifications with Tunis, with cities on Sardinia or on Rhodos, or even with western Anatolia. Others identify *Taršîš* with Carthage.[77] Rainer Riesner points out that Josephus, who is the only ancient author who provides an extensive geographical explanation of the Greek name Θαρσις, identifies the *Taršîš* of Gen 10:4 with Tarsus in Cilicia; he also has the prophet Jonah flee to Tarsus in Cilicia (Jon 1:3; 4:2).[78] Eusebius mentions this interpretation of Josephus but goes on to point out that the relevant passages in the Greek translation of Ezekiel (Ezek 27:12, 25; 38:13) identify the city with Carthage; he also points out that "others think it is in India" (Eusebius, *Onom.* 102).[79]

Put (cf. Gen 10:6) is usually located in North Africa, often in Libya. The Septuagint translates the Hebrew *Pût* mostly with Λίβυες, "Libya" (cf. Jer 46:9; Ezek 27:10; 30:5; 38:5);

---

[73]Núñez Regodón (1984, 67-76) sees only a decentralized universalism: the salvation of the nations happens through Israel's mediation. Cf. Haag 1985, 186.

[74]Oswalt, *Is,* 2:688-89.

[75]Ådna 2000a, 281.

[76]A. Schulten, PW 2.8 (1932): 2446-47; cf. Oswalt, *Is,* 1:429, 2:689.

[77]See Wenham, *Gen,* 1:218.

[78]Riesner 1994, 222-23, with reference to Josephus, *A.J.* 1.127; 9.208.

[79]See Riesner 1994, 223; J. M. Scott 1995, 142 n. 34.

many scholars suggest an identification with Cyrene.[80] The Hebrew text has פוּל (*Pûl*), which is usually amended with the LXX (Φουδ) to *Pût*. John Oswalt rejects this emendation:[81] the Septuagint translates all passages where the Masoretic Text has *Pût* with Λίβυες, which is what we would also expect for Is 66:19 if the Hebrew text originally read *Pût*. Oswalt wants to retain *Pûl*, even though this place is not mentioned again in the Old Testament and cannot be located.

Lud (cf. Gen 10:22) refers perhaps to the Lydians in Asia Minor (Josephus, *A.J.* 1.144), whom the Assyrians called *Luddu*.[82] However, the Lydians/Luddu were not Semites, which Gen 10:22 presupposes. Lud needs to be distinguished from the Ludim (Gen 10:13), who are localized in North Africa, often in Libya (in Ezek 27:10 they are linked with the Persians). Gordon Wenham mentions the Lubdu at the upper Tigris River as another possibility.

(Meshech) "which draw the bow" (מֹשְׁכֵי קֶשֶׁת) is translated in the Septuagint with *Mosoch* (with omission of "bow"), which corresponds with the Hebrew *Mešek* (מֶשֶׁךְ). Many interpreters change the Hebrew text according to the Septuagint and read a fourth geographical name, Meshech (cf. Gen 10:2),[83] which is identified with a people living in central Anatolia. This emendation is not required, however, as the Masoretic Text makes good sense as it is. Lud is described as an expert in archery in Jer 46:9 as well. The term קֶשֶׁת ("bow") is awkward;[84] only once מֹשְׁכֵי has been changed to *Mešek,* which would force the interpreter to look for a fifth geographical term in the next word. Instead of changing מֹשְׁכֵי and eliminating קֶשֶׁת it is quite possible to simply accept the Masoretic Text as it stands; the phrase makes good sense and agrees with Jer 46:9 (וְלוּדִים תֹּפְשֵׂי דֹרְכֵי קָשֶׁת): both passages provide a closer characterization of "Lud" as a people adept at using the bow.[85]

Tubal (cf. Gen 10:2) is found in eastern Anatolia, north of Cilicia. The rabbis identified Tubal with Bithynia.

Javan (cf. Gen 10:2) refers in Is 66 to the Greeks who live on the Ionian coast—that is, in Asia Minor. The term was used later for all Greeks; the Septuagint translates with Ἕλλας.

The "distant islands" (NRSV translates with "the coastlands far away") represent the "ends" of the earth, which often were linked with islands (cf. Sir 47:17).[86]

The statement in Is 66:19 is the only passage in the Old Testament, excepting the Servant Songs, that refers to a proclamation to Gentiles by human emissaries. "This is the first unambiguous passage that speaks of missions in our sense of the word: individual people are sent to distant nations in order to proclaim to them the glory of God. It corresponds exactly with the apostolic mission at the beginning of the Christian church. We can only acknowledge with astonishment that here, at the periphery of the Old Testament, the prophet already envisions God's path from the small realm of the chosen people into the vast

---

[80]W. S. LaSor, *ISBE* 3:1059; Baker, *ABD* 5:560; Wenham, *Gen,* 1:221; Riesner 1994, 222-23.

[81]Oswalt, *Is,* 2:681-82 n. 62.

[82]Wenham, *Gen,* 1:230; Riesner 1994, 223.

[83]See Westermann, *Jes,* 336; Riesner 1994, 223. Cuneiform sources refer to the Mushki; Greek authors speak of the Μόσχοι.

[84]Riesner 1994, 223.

[85]See Oswalt, *Is,* 2:682 n. 63.

[86]Riesner 1994, 224; Oswalt, *Is,* 2:689.

world."[87] The converted Gentiles participate rightfully in the worship of YHWH in the "house of prayer for all nations," not as "lay people" but as people involved in priestly service.[88]

9. When the nations are gathered on Zion, they will proclaim the mighty deeds of YHWH (Is 60:4-7).

Is 60:4-7: "Lift up your eyes and look around; they all gather together, they come to you; your sons shall come from far away, and your daughters shall be carried on their nurses' arms. [5]Then you shall see and be radiant; your heart shall thrill and rejoice, because the abundance of the sea shall be brought to you, the wealth of the nations shall come to you. [6]A multitude of camels shall cover you, the young camels of Midian and Ephah; all those from Sheba shall come. They shall bring gold and frankincense, and shall proclaim the praise of the LORD [MT: וּתְהִלֹּת יְהוָה יְבַשֵּׂרוּ; LXX: τὸ σωτήριον κυρίου εὐαγγελιοῦνται]. [7]All the flocks of Kedar shall be gathered to you, the rams of Nebaioth shall minister to you; they shall be acceptable on my altar, and I will glorify my glorious house."

Joel

The prophet Joel speaks of the nations coming to Zion, where they will be judged by YHWH.

Joel 3:9-16: "Proclaim this among the nations: Prepare war, stir up the warriors. Let all the soldiers draw near, let them come up. [10]Beat your plowshares into swords, and your pruning hooks into spears; let the weakling say, 'I am a warrior.' [11]Come quickly, all you nations all around, gather yourselves there. Bring down your warriors, O LORD. [12]Let the nations rouse themselves, and come up to the valley of Jehoshaphat; for there I will sit to judge all the neighboring nations. [13]Put in the sickle, for the harvest is ripe. Go in, tread, for the wine press is full. The vats overflow, for their wickedness is great. [14]Multitudes, multitudes, in the valley of decision! For the day of the LORD is near in the valley of decision. [15]The sun and the moon are darkened, and the stars withdraw their shining. [16]The LORD roars from Zion, and utters his voice from Jerusalem, and the heavens and the earth shake. But the LORD is a refuge for his people, a stronghold for the people of Israel."

Jonah

The book of Jonah talks about the possibility that foreign nations repent after listening to the proclamation of divine judgment and thus are spared.

Jon 3:4-5, 10: "Jonah began to go into the city, going a day's walk. And he cried out, 'Forty days more, and Nineveh shall be overthrown!' [5]And the people of Nineveh believed God; they proclaimed a fast, and everyone, great and small, put on sackcloth. . . . [10]When God saw what they did, how they turned from their evil ways, God changed his mind about the calamity that he had said he would bring upon them; and he did not do it."

Jonah is the only prophet sent by God to pagans with the assignment to

---

[87]Westermann, *Jes*, 337; quoted also in Riesner 1994, 219.
[88]Ådna 2000a, 281.

preach repentance from sins. Evidently the notion that he should go to Nineveh and preach to its people was not incompatible with Israel's faith. He rejected God's commission, however, because he begrudged the pagans in Nineveh God's mercy.

Gerhard von Rad suggests that the book of Jonah warns "those who know covenant and community . . . against the temptation of using their peculiar position in God's sight to raise claims which compromise Jahweh's freedom in his plans for other nations."[89] God achieves his goals of salvation in any case, even when his emissaries are guilty of refusing to cooperate. However, since the book of Jonah does not mention the subsequent behavior of the Ninevites, we should be cautious in regard to assumptions about the "state of salvation" of the Ninevites.

In view of the evidence of the narratives and the stipulations in the Torah it is more than doubtful whether Jonah should be regarded as a "missionary" book.[90] Jonah does not want to convert the inhabitants of Nineveh to the Jewish faith.[91] The interpretation of the story of Jonah in rabbinic literature is instructive. The rabbis' comments on the repentance of the Ninevites are generally positive;[92] they emphasize and comment on the exemplary character of their repentance. However, their interpretation is fundamentally linked with the self-definition and the establishment of the identity of the Jewish commonwealth: "The personal aspect of the motif of repentance, the success of Jonah the preacher or the momentous penitential efforts of the Ninevites do not carry any particular weight in the rabbinic tradition. The actions of the nations receive attention because of their Jewish domestic relevance. The repentance of the Ninevites becomes a signpost for Israel." Jonah the prophet is not presented as a "missionary" whose proclamation in Nineveh should serve as a paradigm for Israel's relationships with the nations.[93]

Micah

The prophet Micah, like Joel before him, speaks of an attack against Zion by foreign nations who will be vanquished by YHWH. Israel will be victorious and the nations will perish (Mic 4:11-13).

Mic 4:11-13: "Now many nations are assembled against you, saying, 'Let her be profaned, and let our eyes gaze upon Zion.' [12]But they do not know the thoughts of the LORD; they do not understand his plan, that he has gathered them as sheaves to the threshing floor.

---

[89]Rad 1960, 2:302-3 (ET, 2:292).
[90]Thus Hahn 1963, 11-12, against Bousset (1926, 82), who believed that the book of Jonah was written in the context of the interests of a Jewish mission to Gentiles; similarly Nordheim 1994; Kaiser 2000, 69-70.
[91]See Runesson (1999, 69), who speaks of a "religious-ethical" mission of Jonah.
[92]See *m. Ta'an.* 2:1; *b. Ta'an.* 16a; *b. Roš. Haš.* 16b; *Mek. R. Yishm.* Piska 1; *y. Sanh.* 11:7 (30b); *Gen. Rab.* 44:12. On this subject see Ego 1994; the quotation that follows above, ibid., 174-75.
[93]See most recently Köstenberger and O'Brien 2001, 45.

[13]Arise and thresh, O daughter Zion, for I will make your horn iron and your hoofs bronze; you shall beat in pieces many peoples, and shall devote their gain to the LORD, their wealth to the Lord of the whole earth."

At the same time Micah speaks of the nations coming to Zion, where they will learn from YHWH: "many nations" in "far away" lands will be instructed by YHWH (Mic 4:1-3):

Mic 4:1-3: "In days to come the mountain of the LORD's house shall be established as the highest of the mountains, and shall be raised up above the hills. Peoples shall stream to it, [2]and many nations shall come and say: 'Come, let us go up to the mountain of the LORD, to the house of the God of Jacob; that he may teach us his ways and that we may walk in his paths.' For out of Zion shall go forth instruction, and the word of the LORD from Jerusalem. [3]He shall judge between many peoples, and shall arbitrate between strong nations far away [עַמִּים רַבִּים . . . . לְגוֹיִם עֲצֻמִים עַד־רָחוֹק]; they shall beat their swords into plowshares, and their spears into pruning hooks; nation shall not lift up sword against nation, neither shall they learn war any more."

Some scholars seek to solve the tension between the prophecy of judgment and the prophecy of redemption for the nation with redaction-critical explanations:[94] a redactor of the Minor Prophets used the tradition of the nations' pilgrimage to Mount Zion in order to answer the question posed by Joel 3 in terms of the possibilities suggested by the book of Jonah; the redactor linked the attack of the nations against Mount Zion with the near future (Mic 4:11: וְעַתָּה) while postponing the pilgrimage of the nations to Mount Zion to the "last days" (Mic 4:1: וְהָיָה בְּאַחֲרִית הַיָּמִים). However, a different solution may be more plausible: the nations who come to Zion and turn to YHWH for instruction are the people, or peoples, who marched to Zion without bellicose intentions.[95]

The texts that speak about the nations' pilgrimage to Zion are not uniform: (1) the nations travel to Zion, without Israel being mentioned as mediator or as goal of these events;[96] (2) the nations bring their riches to Jerusalem, with the texts silent concerning worship of YHWH;[97] (3) the nations that come to Zion worship YHWH and have a positive relationship with Israel.[98]

Malachi

An isolated, climactic statement even for the prophetic tradition is found in Malachi (Mal 1:5).[99]

---

[94]See recently Zapff 1999, 614-15.
[95]See I. Fischer 1996, 208-16.
[96]Is 2:2-5/Mic 4:1-4; Jer 16:19-21; Zech 8:20-22; 14:16-19; cf. Tob 13:13. See Gross 1989, 39.
[97]Is 14:2; 49:22-23.
[98]Is 45:14; 55:5; 66:20; Zeph 3:9-10; Zech 8:23.
[99]Verhoef, *Mal,* 222-32; Preuss 1991-1992, 2:314; Viberg 1994; Schultz 1996, 41.

Mal 1:5: "Your own eyes shall see this, and you shall say, 'Great is the LORD beyond the borders of Israel!'"

Mal 1:11: "For from the rising of the sun to its setting my name is great among the nations, and in every place incense is offered to my name, and a pure offering; for my name is great among the nations, says the LORD of hosts."

These prophecies seem to eliminate the dividing wall between Israel and the nations and the fundamental differentiation between the promised land and the whole earth. Israel's designation as "kingdom of priests" (Ex 19:6) is correlated with the nations "from the rising of the sun to its setting"—that is, with the nations from the East to the West, from Persia and India to Spain. And the central location of worship, the temple in Jerusalem (cf. Deut 12), is expanded to include all locales of the earth. Many scholars interpret the "nations in every place" that worship YHWH in terms of all the pagans who worship in their idols, unknowingly, the one true God—a notion that is called "absorptive monotheism." Friedrich Horst observes, "The author asserts . . . a universal monotheism, similar to the veneration of the 'god of heaven' which became popular during the Persian period. This worship is claimed as worship of Yahweh, the only true God (cf. Zeph 2:11; Ps 65:3, 6; Jon 1:16)."[100] This interpretation is hardly plausible, since the sacrifices that Malachi refers to are offered to the name of YHWH (Mal 1:11: לִשְׁמִי, *lišmî*).

Also, Malachi's prophecy does not erode in any noticeable manner the separation between the covenant people and the pagan peoples. Thus many scholars understand the Gentiles who offer sacrifices in Mal 1:11 to be proselytes or, as does the Targum of the prophets, Diaspora Jews,[101] or they interpret the statement as a purely eschatological promise. Richard Schultz comments, "Because the prophet primarily contrasts the pure worship outside of Israel 'among the nations' with the objectionable worship in Jerusalem (1:6—2:9), we should at least see here a hint that worship of 'the great king' without temple and without involvement of the Jews is conceivable (and partially a reality), even though a future fulfillment may be in view simultaneously."[102] Åke Viberg suggests a consistent metaphorical meaning of Mal 1:11: Malachi, who criticizes in his first chapter the priests who neglect their duties, emphasizes in Mal 1:11 that YHWH is the great king, who must be worshiped as such; the nations are mentioned in order to highlight the image of YHWH as ruling king, who is the highest God in cultic respects as well.[103]

---

[100]Horst, *KlProph*, 259-60; similarly Elliger, *KlProph*, 199.
[101]See Blenkinsopp 1983, 240-41, 272-73; Utzschneider 1989, 84-86.
[102]Schultz 1996, 41; cf. Preuss 1991-1992, 2:314; Gross 1989, 37; Verhoef, *Mal*, 229-31.
[103]Viberg 1994, esp. 308-19.

5.5 Conclusions

Four emphases of the Old Testament are particularly significant for the concept of "missions" in the New Testament:[104] (1) God is the Creator of the world and therefore the Lord of nations and of their history; (2) the nations will be admitted to God's salvation in the eschaton, in Israel or in connection with Israel; (3) Israel is a (passive) witness of God's acts of salvation; (4) in the "last days" the Servant of the Lord will have an active role, and "survivors of Israel" will be sent by YHWH to the nations.

Missionary ideas need to be distinguished from missionary praxis. From an early time onwards there were "proselytes" in Israel, even though the pagans who were admitted to the people of God were not designated with this technical term. The most explicit statements about the Gentiles and their admission to YHWH's salvation are found in the prophets: the future will bring not only the fulfillment of YHWH's promises for Israel but also salvation for the nations. "Here we see the universalism which has God's activity in all humanity in view."[105] Fundamentally, however, the Old Testament does not envisage a practical, specific sending of the community of Israel to convert other nations to the worship of YHWH.[106] The blessing for the nations that YHWH promised to Abraham plays essentially no role outside of the patriarchal narratives.[107]

It is in Isaiah's prophecies concerning the Servant of the Lord that we find the breakthrough of missionary concepts. Isaiah unequivocally expresses a divine commission to "go" and to "witness." The prophet and the Servant is not only a witness but also YHWH's messenger for the nations. Erich Scheurer states that "the experience of YHWH and his redemptive intervention and his faithfulness to his Servant needs to be proclaimed to the whole earth so that Yahweh is worshiped in all areas of his creation."[108] Many scholars believe that his "missionary" emphasis is linked with the origins of Israel's monotheistic faith.

Walter Gross observes, in the context of texts such as Zech 8:20-22 and Is 2:2-5/Mic 4:1-4, which speak of nations that will come to Zion and worship YHWH, "The more that monotheism became formulated in a clear and self-assured manner, the more clear it became that the religion of YHWH, which was limited to Israel, restricted YHWH, the Lord of the world, to such a degree that it was impossible to conceive of a redemptive relationship between YHWH and the nations within this framework. Thus the boundaries regarding cult, priesthood and the people of YHWH were forced open without sufficient consideration of the consequences for Israel. Does Israel give itself up or does Israel permit YHWH to lead the nation to a more perfect realization of their relationship? Israel was never

---

[104]For the first three points that follow above see Hahn 1963, 11-12.
[105]Westermann 1978, 130 (ET, 148).
[106]Scheurer 1996, 417; cf. Bosch 1959, 11; Hahn 1963, 1; Gensichen 1971, 57; cf. Lohse (1960, 971), who asserts, "Ancient Israel did not know of a mission among Gentiles."
[107]Wisdom 2001, 42, 221.
[108]Scheurer 1996, 240.

forced to put these risky theological statements to the test of reality, as the nations never opened up. Because these words were promises of YHWH, they were not suppressed; they continued to be part of the tradition. But they were defused through reinterpretations and thus remained without effect."[109]

However, if Israel's monotheism was not a late (postexilic) development but an integral part of Israel's faith since Abraham, Isaac and Jacob, such historical reconstructions need to be revised. Still, the observation remains valid that the claims of YHWH, the Creator of the world and Lord of history, upon all nations did not lead to an active propagation of faith in YHWH among the neighboring nations, who worshiped other gods. The universalistic elements of Israel's faith and the general flexibility in contacts with non-Israelites and non-Jews cannot be compiled into an offensive, centrifugal missionary program in Israel that would have aimed at converting pagan nations, or at least individual polytheists, to faith in YHWH. The conversion of the nations is expected for the messianic "last days." The Old Testament gave a twofold answer to the question of Israel's relationship with the pagan nations: (1) individual pagans could be integrated historically as proselytes; (2) the gathering of the nations to Zion is eschatologically expected to happen on account of the activity of YHWH's Servant or the "survivors" of Israel.[110] These eschatological promises integrate God's concern for his people Israel in its historical dimension and his concern for humankind in its creational dimension.

In the next chapter I will discuss the question of whether we find missionary ideas and missionary praxis in Second Temple Judaism. We can expect that Jews developed, or perhaps reinterpreted, the "missionary ideas" of the Old Testament. If there was a missionary praxis in Second Temple Judaism, then we need to investigate the reasons for this new development. If we find that there was no organized, practical missionary work purposefully carried out by Jews among polytheists, then we will not be surprised, considering the Old Testament evidence.

---

[109]Gross 1989, 40.
[110]Scobie 1992; Köstenberger and O'Brien 2001, 35.

6

THE EXPANSION OF GOD'S PEOPLE
IN EARLY JEWISH TEXTS

Beginning in the second half of the second century B.C., Judaism became slowly but surely a "world religion," a religion practiced and well known in many cities of the Mediterranean world. Martin Hengel points to three factors that were decisive for the expansion of Judaism beyond Judea and Galilee. First, there was an enhanced self-confidence of Palestinian Judaism resulting from the successes of the Maccabean period. After being ruled by foreign powers for four hundred years, the Jews were able to establish a national state, after forcefully preserving their Jewish identity in the face of infiltration by Hellenistic elements. Second, there was a rapid expansion of a Jewish presence in all major cities of the Roman Empire, including the provinces.[1] The third factor highlighted by Hengel will be studied more closely in what follows. Wilhelm Bousset, in his influential study *Die Religion des Judentums im späthellenistischen Zeitalter* (*The Religion of Judaism in the Late Hellenistic Period*), wrote, "One cannot overrate the significance of the missionary activity of Judaism. It valiantly prepared the way for Christianity. The curious successes of the Pauline mission in *one* generation can be understood only when we remind ourselves of how Judaism loosened up and prepared the ground."[2] Adolf von Harnack argued similarly, as is shown by the first chapter of his monumental work *The Mission and Expansion of Christianity in the First Three Centuries,* entitled "Judaism: Its Diffusion and Limits."[3] Karl Georg Kuhn suggested that the first century A.D. was "the great missionary century of Judaism," and Joachim Jeremias begins his study *Jesus'*

---

[1]Hengel 1969, 568 (ET, 1:313).
[2]Bousset 1926, 80. Siegfried (1890, 443), spoke disparagingly of the "zeal of making proselytes in the Diaspora."
[3]Harnack 1924, 1:5-23 (ET, 1:1-18). In the German title, "Das Judentum, seine Verbreitung und Entschränkung," the term "Entschränkung" does not mean "limits" but "removal of barriers." For a discussion of Harnack's study see S. Cohen 1991. Gottlieb Klein (1909, 137-43) suggested a "scheme of a catechism for proselytes." For a position similar to Harnack's see Rosen, Rosen and Bertram 1929; G. Moore 1927, 323-53; Derwacter 1930, 62; Bamberger 1939, 3.

Promise to the Nations with this sentence: "At the time of Jesus' appearance an unparalleled period of missionary activity was in progress in Israel."[4] Eduard Lohse could simply presuppose a Jewish mission to Gentiles in an article written forty years ago, while more recently, and in an influential handbook of New Testament studies, Hans Conzelmann and Andreas Lindemann still described missionary activity among Gentiles as "typical for Judaism."[5] Some scholars have suggested that Paul was a "Jewish missionary" among Gentiles before his conversion.[6] Whereas in years past only a few scholars voiced doubts about the existence of a Jewish mission to Gentiles,[7] more recently an increasing number of scholars—Martin Goodman, Scot McKnight, Edmund Will, Claude Orrieux, Bernd Wander—argue that there was clearly no organized missionary activity of Jews among pagans.[8]

An inquiry into the attitude of Jews concerning non-Jews must take into account that Greeks and Romans respected the Jews but also that anti-Jewish remarks appear as early as the second century B.C.[9]

Greeks and Romans generally respected the Jews and treated them well. "The Hellenistic cities welcomed Jews as new citizens; they granted them certain privileges that the Romans maintained and defended; their religious regulations—sanctification of the sabbath, prohibition of the worship of idols—were respected."[10] On the other hand, we find a hos-

---

[4]K. Kuhn 1954, 161; Jeremias 1956, 9 (ET, 11); similarly Goppelt 1954, 80 (ET, 110).

[5]Lohse 1960, 972; Conzelmann and Lindemann 1995, 192; similarly, but with different emphasis, Georgi 1964, 83-187; Rappaport 1965; Bussmann 1971, 26-38; J. Thompson 1971, 19; Stuhlmacher 1981, 107-8; Ker 1986; Pak 1991; Niebuhr 1992, 95; Perelmutter 1994, 20-21; Siegert 1994a, 53; LaGrand 1995, 149-54; Lapide 1995; Lang 1996, 419; Donaldson 1997a, 51-74; Georgi 2001, 539. Recently Hvalvik (1996, 268-318) wanted to prove the existence of an active Jewish mission among Gentiles, without discussing new sources, however; similarly Dickson 2003, 11-85.

[6]See Wanamaker, *Thess,* 85; Dalton 1991; for a critical discussion see Murphy-O'Connor 1992a. This suggestion is made also by Donaldson (1997a, 78, 275-84), whose criticism of the allegedly "Christian" definition of "missions" in studies by Scot McKnight and Martin Goodman, who argue against the assumption of a Jewish mission among pagans, is unwarranted.

[7]See, for example, Kirsopp Lake, "Proselytes and God-fearers" (note viii), in *Begs.* 5:74-96; Munck 1954, 259.

[8]S. Cohen 1991; M. Goodman 1992; 1994, 60-90, 109-53; McKnight 1991; Murphy-O'Connor 1992a; Will and Orrieux 1992; Wander 1998, esp. 218-27; see also O. Betz 1994, 24; S. Stern 1994, 88-89; Fredriksen 1991, 537-43; C. Hezser, *JRS* 85 (1995): 316-17 (review of M. Goodman 1994); Reiser 1995, 85; Breytenbach 1996, 140-43; Botermann 1996, 162; Ware 1996, 104-64; Bedell 1998; Hengel and Schwemer 1998, 129 (ET, 75); Ridgway 1999, 14-16; Barnett 2000; J. J. Collins 2000, 262-64; Riesner 2000; Köstenberger and O'Brien 2001, 55-71. Fergus Millar lamented as late as 1986 that there is no competent study on the question of missionary activity in Second Temple Judaism. The studies of Braude 1940 and Lerle 1960 are dated and unsatisfactory; see Hengel 1983a, 166 n. 1.

[9]On the politics concerning Jews in the Roman Empire see §18.1.

[10]Lange and Thoma 1978, 115; see further Noethlichs 1996.

tile or at least cool attitude on the part of pagan contemporaries.[11] The anti-Semitism of antiquity, fueled by religious motifs, seems to have arisen in the second century B.C. in Egypt.[12] With regard to terminology used in this context, we should note that not all utterances of contempt and hostility concerning Jews are to be identified automatically with anti-Semitism. Anti-Semitism differs from other group prejudices, as group prejudices normally are linked with contemporary phenomena (i.e., real events), whereas anti-Semitism essentially has no relationship with actual events but arises out of a web of fantasies that continues to grow stronger and stronger.[13]

According to the most recent estimates, between 150,000 and 200,000 Jews lived in Egypt at the beginning of Roman rule (on August 1 in 30 B.C. the troops of Octavian occupied Alexandria). This corresponds to about 3 percent of the total population of some 6 million. About 100,000 Jews lived in Alexandria.[14] The Jews of Alexandria lived in all five districts of the city, with a high concentration in the fourth district in the eastern part of the city, called "Delta." Hostile attitudes concerning the Jews resulted repeatedly in bloody attacks, despite the fact that the Jews of Alexandria long ago had accepted the Greek language and Greek culture.[15] The anti-Semitic ideology of Alexandrian citizens may be illustrated with Josephus's apologetic text *Contra Apionem,* in which he quotes anti-Jewish pagan authors. The polemic against the Jews focused on a "revised version" of the exodus from Egypt: it is alleged that the Jews originally were Egyptians who had contracted leprosy and other illnesses, which resulted in their expulsion from the country; as they left Egypt under the leadership of Moses, they established their own nation, with Jerusalem as capital. A sad climax of Alexandrian anti-Semitism occurred in A.D. 38 (about five years after Paul's conversion to faith in Jesus Christ), when citizens instigated a pogrom, indirectly tolerated by the Roman prefect, destroyed synagogues and tortured and killed many Jews in Alexandria (Philo, *Flacc.* 62-70; Josephus, *A.J.* 18.257-260).

Sentiments hostile to Jews were influential outside of Egypt as well. Cicero, Seneca, Quintilian, Juvenal, Tacitus and Marcus Aurelius make derisive comments about Jews. Cicero calls Judaism a *barbara superstitio* (*Flac.* 28.67). Juvenal pokes fun at the country "where a long-established clemency suffers pigs to attain old age" and where the meat of pigs is regarded to be as valuable as the flesh of human beings, and explains the sabbath rest of the Jews as laziness (*Sat.* 6.160; 14.96-106). Tacitus calls the Jews "the meanest of subjects" (*despectissima pars servientium*) and "this basest of peoples" (*taeterrima gens*) (*Hist.* 5.8).[16]

The origins of anti-Jewish propaganda and persecution have several factors.

---

[11]See Schürer 3:150-58 (with sources); Menachem Stern, "The Jews in Greek and Latin Literature," in Safrai and Stern 1987, 1101-59; Lange and Thoma 1978; Emilio Gabba, "The Growth of Anti-Judaism or the Greek Attitude Towards Jews," in *CHJ* 2:614-56; now especially Feldman 1993a, chs. 3-5.

[12]See Petersen 1992, 116-17; see also Goodman 1994, 57, who refers to the earliest report of hostility toward the Jews, written by Manetho (third century B.C.) and characterized by nationalistic Egyptian features; cf. *FGrH* 609 F 10 = Josephus, *C. Ap.* 1.223-253.

[13]James W. Parkes, *Antisemitism* (Chicago: Quadrangle, 1964), 57-73; cf. Lange and Thoma 1978, 115.

[14]*NewDocs* 5:37, with reference to J. Mélèze-Modrzejewski, in Hassoun 1981, 15-49, esp. 20-21; see also Mélèze-Modrzejewski 1991; Bernand 1998, 262-64.

[15]See Hengel 1976b, 126-44; Kasher 1985; on the rights of the Jews of Alexandria, ibid., 233-326; on anti-Semitic literature, ibid., 327-45.

[16]On Marcus Aurelius see Ammianus Marcellinus 22.5; *GLAJJ* I 68; II 281, 298, 301, 506.

(1) The inhabitants of the Hellenistic cities, who reputedly were cosmopolitan, progressive, transnational and tolerant, repeatedly took offense at Judaism, which was nonconformist and yet sympathetic. Particularly offensive was the Jews' refusal to eat with, to marry or to worship with non-Jews. If a Jewish father permitted his daughter to marry a pagan, he accepted pagan grandchildren. Thus Jews did not only tolerate a conversion of the future husband to Judaism but demanded it (in pre-Tannaitic times the patrilinear principle was in force).[17] (2) The political expansion of the Hasmoneans in Palestine and the political and military power of the Jews during the late Ptolemaic period caused Jews to have greater self-confidence but also could cause non-Jews, depending on the local situation, to feel threatened.[18] (3) Rulers threatened by crisis situations could manipulate events and provide cover for attacks against the Jews in order to secure the sympathies of the local population.[19]

6.1 Palestinian Judaism Between Exclusiveness and Universalistic Expectation

The Maccabean Revolt in the middle of the second century B.C. was foundational for Jewish self-understanding. The revolt was caused in part by the attempts of certain Jewish circles to achieve the assimilation of the Jewish commonwealth to Hellenistic civilization.[20] The convictions of the Jewish-Palestinian Hellenists is succinctly summarized in 1 Macc 1:11-15.

1 Macc 1:11-15: "In those days certain renegades came out from Israel and misled many, saying, 'Let us go and make a covenant with the Gentiles around us, for since we separated from them many disasters have come upon us' [πορευθῶμεν καὶ διαθώμεθα διαθήκην μετὰ τῶν ἐθνῶν τῶν κύκλῳ ἡμῶν, ὅτι ἀφ’ ἧς ἐχωρίσθημεν ἀπ’ αὐτῶν, εὗρεν ἡμᾶς κακὰ πολλά]. [12]This proposal pleased them, [13]and some of the people eagerly went to the king, who authorized them to observe the ordinances of the Gentiles [τὰ δικαιώματα τῶν ἐθνῶν]. [14]So they built a gymnasium (γυμνάσιον) in Jerusalem, according to Gentile custom, [15]and removed the marks of circumcision, and abandoned the holy covenant [ἀπέστησαν ἀπὸ διαθήκης ἁγίας]. They joined with the Gentiles and sold themselves to do evil."

It is unnecessary to analyze more fully this text and the convictions that surface in the activities of these Hellenists. It is clear, however, that the proponents of this "project" did not intend to expand the concept of the people of God, much less make an attempt to win pagans for faith in Israel's God. On the contrary, these Hellenistic Jews sought to abolish, or at least to bypass, the biblical and

---

[17]See Mireille Hadas-Lebel, "Les mariages mixtes dans la famille d'Hérode et la *halakha* prétalmudique sur la patrilinéarité," *REJ* 152 (1993): 397-404.
[18]R. M. Smith 1999, 192-95.
[19]Lange and Thoma 1978, 115-16; Hengel 1969, 559 (ET, 1:306-7). On ancient anti-Semitism see further Yavetz 1993.
[20]See Hengel 1969, 464-564 (ET, 1:255-309); cf. Schunck, *JSHRZ* 1.4:287-373, esp. 299-300.

traditional conviction that the Jewish people are the chosen people of God.[21] The so-called Hellenistic reform attempt effectively influenced the development of Judaism, even though it failed. Martin Hengel points to several factors: (1) the extreme sensitivity of the Jews in Palestine toward any (even only apparent) attacks on the law and on the temple; (2) a more intense tendency toward segregation from non-Jews—a pattern that encouraged the anti-Semitism of antiquity; (3) the strengthening of the national self-consciousness of the Jews; (4) the prevention of syncretistic tendencies in Palestine, in contrast to the situation in the Jewish Diaspora; (5) the fixation of the intellectual development on the Torah; (6) the prevention of any criticism directed against the law or the cult, and of criticism directed against the exclusive self-understanding of the Jewish commonwealth; (7) the promotion of the unique vitality and dynamism of the Jewish people and of the Jewish faith (which, according to Hengel, developed most strongly in the worldwide mission of the early Christians).

In regard to the attitudes of Palestinian Judaism concerning pagans, we find both the tendency toward brusque segregation and moderate positions. However, the tendency toward segregation outweighed the other options. In the following discussion I will survey and analyze the evidence of Second Temple texts concerning the relationship between Jews and Gentiles in general, and Jewish views of Gentiles and their (potential) conversion to Israel's God in particular.[22]

1 Maccabees

The first book of Maccabees repeatedly describes the purification of the land from pagan cult objects and from pagan inhabitants as the most significant result of the Hasmonean wars (1 Macc 4:42-45; 5:68; 13:47-48, 50; 14:36).

1 Macc 5:68:[23] "But Judas turned aside to Azotus in the land of the Philistines; he tore down their altars, and the graven images of their gods he burned with fire; he plundered the cities and returned to the land of Judah."

1 Macc 13:47-48: "So Simon reached an agreement with them and stopped fighting against them. But he expelled them from the city and cleansed the houses in which the idols were, and then entered it with hymns and praise. [48]He cast out of it all uncleanness [ἐξέβαλεν ἐξ αὐτῆς πᾶσαν ἀκαθαρσίαν], and settled in it men who observed the law [οἵτινες τὸν νόμον ποιήσωσιν]."

1 Macc 14:36: "And in his [Simon's] days things prospered in his hands, so that the Gentiles were put out of the country [ἐξαρθῆναι τὰ ἔθνη ἐκ τῆς χώρας αὐτῶν], as were also the men in the city of David in Jerusalem, who had built themselves a citadel from which they used to sally forth and defile the environs of the sanctuary and do great damage to its purity

---

[21]See Kraus 1996, 45; for the remarks that follow above see Hengel 1969, 558-64 (ET, 1:306-9).
[22]See Novak 1983, 107-65; M. Goodman 1994, 38-59, 109-28; also Colpe 1990.
[23]Translation follows the RSV.

[ἐμίαινον κύκλῳ τῶν ἁγίων καὶ ἐποίουν πληγὴν μεγάλην ἐν τῇ ἀγνείᾳ]."

The political expansion of Judea at the time of the Hasmoneans accentuated the contrasts between the Jewish and the Gentile population in Syria-Palestine.[24] Neighboring peoples that the Hasmonean kings conquered were forced to be circumcised: the Idumeans in the south by Hyrcanus I (135-104 B.C.), the Itureans in Galilee by Aristobulus I (104-103 B.C.) and the peoples living east of the Jordan River, particularly the people of Pella, by Alexander Jannaeus (104-76 B.C.).[25] These forced circumcisions at least demonstrate the possibility that non-Jews could be absorbed through circumcision.[26]

1 Enoch

The only Jewish text of the Second Temple period that clearly speaks of an equal status of Israel and pagan nations, albeit in the eschaton, is a passage in the so-called Animal Apocalypse (*1 En.* 85—90), written between 250 and 160 B.C., a text that divides world history into four epochs.[27] The first epoch (primeval period) extends from Adam to Isaac and is symbolized by white cows (*1 En.* 85:3—89:11). The second epoch comprises the history of Israel and extends from Jacob to the surrender of the nation; the people of God are symbolized by sheep (Israel's leaders appear as rams), the foreign nations by wild donkeys, boars and wolves (*1 En.* 89:42-77). This epoch ends with the surrender of the sheep (Israel) to seventy shepherds (foreign rulers). The third epoch begins after the judgment, when the old sanctuary is "wrapped" by God and a new sanctuary is "unwrapped" (*1 En.* 90:28-29). The animals of the field and the birds of the sky (the pagan nations) submit to the sheep (*1 En.* 90:30). The sword of hostility is sealed in the sanctuary, and all people worship God in the new sanctuary (*1 En.* 90:33-34). The fourth epoch begins with the arrival of a messianic figure, symbolized by a white cow with large horns (*1 En.* 90:37). Finally all generations are transformed into white cows, as the patriarchs in the first epoch were white cows (*1 En.* 90:38).

1 En. 90:33-38:[28] "All those which have been destroyed and dispersed, and all the beasts of the field and the birds of the sky were gathered together in that house; and the Lord of the sheep rejoiced with great joy because they had all become gentle and returned to his house. [34]I went on seeing until they had laid down that sword which was given to the sheep; they returned it to the house and sealed it in the presence of the Lord. All the sheep were invited to that house but it could not contain them (all). [35]The eyes of all of them were opened, and they saw the beautiful things; not a single one existed among them that could not see. [36]Also I noticed that the house was large, wide, and exceedingly full. [37]Then

---

[24]See Sievers 1985, 602, with references to Additions to Esther, Judith and Apollonios Molon.
[25]See Schürer 2:3, 9-10, 11-12; Hengel 1976a, 202, with sources.
[26]See Kraus 1996, 71.
[27]For the description that follows above see Kraus 1996, 53-57.
[28]Translation from E. Isaac, *OTP* 1:13-89.

I saw that a snow-white cow was born, with huge horns; all the beasts of the field and all the birds of the sky feared him and made petition to him all the time. [38]I went on seeing until all their kindred were transformed, and became snow-white cows; and the first among them became something, and that something became a great beast with huge black horns on its head. The Lord of the sheep rejoiced over it and over all the cows."

In *1 En.* 90:38 we have "a portrait of salvation for all mankind which breaks the bounds of all national limitations."[29] The difference between Jews and Gentiles is abolished in connection with the coming of a messianic figure. In the words of Wolfgang Kraus, "There will be a return to the time before the segregation since Jacob. . . . Jacob and his descendants live, for a limited time, in the form of white sheep, until they are transformed back, after the judgment, into white cows, being again equal to the other nations."[30] The new sanctuary is linked with a new people of God.

Testaments of the Twelve Patriarchs

Several passages in *Testaments of the Twelve Patriarchs,* a text written probably in the second century B.C., convey a universal outlook.[31] Even though some of the universalistic statements may be the work of a Christian interpolator,[32] the view of Jacob Jervell that all universalistic passages are due to Christian influence[33] is exaggerated. Wolfgang Kraus is convinced that critical analysis proves that the following passages clearly are early Jewish texts.[34]

T. Levi 18:9[35] describes the priesthood of the eternal messiah-priest, whom God will establish.

---

[29]Hengel 1969, 344 (ET, 1:188).

[30]Kraus 1996, 55, 57.

[31]On the literary history of *Testaments of the Twelve Patriarchs* see Marinus de Jonge, ed., *Studies on the Testaments of the Twelve Patriarchs: Text and Interpretation* (SVTP 3; Leiden: Brill, 1975); see Hollander and de Jonge 1985, 64-67, for a summary on "Israel and the Gentiles"; see Ulrichsen 1991, who dates the (Hebrew or Aramaic) *Grundschrift* to around 200 B.C. and reckons with two Jewish revisions and with a translation into Greek in the first century A.D. as well as with Christian interpolations at the end of the first century A.D.

[32]Thus probably *T. Levi* 2:11 and *T. Zeb.* 9:8; on these passages see Becker, *JSHRZ* 3.1.

[33]J. Jervell, "Ein Interpolator interpretiert: Zu der christlichen Bearbeitung der Testamente der zwölf Patriarchen," in *Studien zu den Testamenten der Zwölf Patriarchen* (ed. W. Eltester; BZNW 36; Berlin: de Gruyter, 1969), 42.

[34]For the discussion that follows above see Kraus 1996, 73-76; translation above from H. C. Kee, *OTP* 1:782-828.

[35]Fragments of *Testament of Levi* were found in Qumran: 1Q21; 4Q213-214, 540-541; see Beyer, *Aramäischen Texte,* 1:193-209; 2:72-82; *DJD* 1:87-90 (J. T. Milik); *DJD* 22:1-72 (M. E. Stone and J. C. Greenfield). According to Hollander (1985, 64, 181), the passage *T. Levi* 18 did not belong to the *Grundschrift* of *Testaments of the Twelve Patriarchs.* Ulrichsen (1991, 204-5) describes *T. Levi* 18 as one of the most complicated and contested texts in that book: "Most scholars advocate their own interpretation, even though they share some similarities." He maintains that *T. Levi* 18 has "without doubt a Jewish background. However, the Christian revision is so extensive that the chapter, in its present form, may be considered to be a Christian composition" (205).

T. Levi 18:9: "And in his priesthood the nations shall be multiplied in knowledge on the earth, and they shall be illuminated by the grace of the Lord, [but Israel shall be diminished by her ignorance and darkened by her grief.][36] In his priesthood sin shall cease and lawless men shall rest from their evil deeds, and righteous men shall find rest in him."

The Gentiles' attainment of the knowledge of God is equivalent to participation in salvation.[37] This is particularly true if the verses that follow, *T. Levi* 18:10-14, are not seen as a separate section[38] but as a continuation of the statements in *T. Levi* 18:1-9 on the priestly messiah:[39] the priestly messiah opens the doors of paradise (*T. Levi* 18:10), grants to "the saints" to eat from the tree of life (*T. Levi* 18:11), and rejoices in "his children" and is well-pleased "by his beloved ones" (*T. Levi* 18:13); then Abraham, Isaac and Jacob will rejoice (*T. Levi* 18:14). If the epithets "saints," "children" and "beloved ones" are to be linked, in the context of *T. Levi* 18:9, with the nations that are filled with the knowledge of God, then the text implies an integration of Gentiles into the people of God. The modalities of this integration are not spelled out, however. Still, we may assume that the author does not envisage an equal status of Jews and Gentiles but rather the admission of the Gentiles into Israel as provided in the law: (1) When the "lawless men" stop doing evil (*T. Levi* 18:9), they evidently begin to keep the law. (2) The light that illuminates the nations and conveys to them the knowledge of God (*T. Levi* 18:9) illuminates Israel as well as the coming priest-messiah (*T. Levi* 18:4); this light is identified in the final paranesis (*T. Levi* 19:1) with the "law of the Lord." (3) Several passages closely link priesthood and sacrifice (*T. Levi* 9:7, 11-14; 16:1). We may conclude, therefore, that the statements of *T. Levi* 18:9-14 do not go beyond the Old Testament expectation that the nations will acknowledge the God of Israel in the eschaton. The text does not speak of an active mission of Jews among Gentiles.

T. Jud. 24:5-6[40] contains a promise for the time after Israel's return from captivity among the nations (*T. Jud.* 23:5).

T. Jud. 24:5-6: "Then he will illumine the scepter of my kingdom, [6]and from your root will

---

[36]The bracketed words are regarded as a Christian gloss critical of Israel; see the discussions in Charles, *APOT* 2:282-367, and Becker, *JSHRZ* 3.1:15-163.

[37]*Pace* Kraus (1996, 73), who seems to assume a wrong alternative. Hollander and de Jonge (1985, 179, 181) translate, "And during his priesthood the Gentiles will be multiplied in knowledge upon the earth," and they interpret the "multiplication" in terms of a numerical growth of the Gentiles (in comparison with Israel) as a sign of divine blessing.

[38]According to Becker (*JSHRZ* 3.1:61 n. 10a), *T. Levi* 18:10-14 is an independent Jewish apocalypse that speaks of God rather than of the Messiah.

[39]Hollander and de Jonge 1985, 181-82; not considered by Kraus.

[40]For Ulrichsen (1991, 174) *T. Jud.* 24 is among the most contested chapters of *Testaments of the Twelve Patriarchs;* he suggests that the text is a Christian composition, which, however, does not exclude the (remote) possibility that it is based on a revised original, particularly in *T. Jud.* 24:5-6.

arise the Shoot, and through it will arise the rod of righteousness for the nations, to judge and to save all that call on the Lord."

The section immediately following, *T. Jud.* 25:1-5, deals with the resurrection of Abraham, Isaac and Jacob (*T. Jud.* 25:1a) and with the establishment of Jacob's twelve sons as "chiefs (wielding) our scepter in Israel" (*T. Jud.* 25:1b-2). The following passage also provides implicit evidence for the equal status of the nations and Israel in the eschaton (*T. Jud.* 25:3-5).

T. Jud. 25:3-5: "And you shall be one people of the Lord, with one language. There shall no more be Beliar's spirit of error, because he will be thrown into eternal fire. [4]And those who died in sorrow shall be raised in joy; and those who died in poverty for the Lord's sake shall be made rich; those who died on account of the Lord shall be wakened to life. [5]And the deer of Jacob shall run with gladness; the eagles of Jacob shall fly with joy; [the impious shall mourn and sinners shall weep,][41] but all peoples shall glorify the Lord forever."

T. Naph. 8:3-4 also refers to the glorification of Israel's God among the nations in the end times.

T. Naph. 8:3-4: "Through his kingly power God will appear [dwelling among men on the earth],[42] to save the race of Israel, and to assemble the righteous from among the nations. [4]If you achieve the good, my children, men and angels will bless you; and God will be glorified through you among the gentiles. The devil will flee from you; wild animals will be afraid of you, and the angels will stand by you."[43]

T. Ash. 7:2-3 mentions the salvation of Israel and of the nations in the end times.

"For I know that you will sin and be delivered into the hands of your enemies; your land shall be made desolate and your sanctuary wholly polluted. [3]You will be scattered to the four corners of the earth; in the dispersion you shall be regarded as worthless, like useless water, until such time as the Most High visits the earth. [He shall come as a man eating and drinking with human beings,][44] crushing the dragon's head in the water. He will save Israel and all the nations."

T. Benj. 9:2 expects for the end times the worship of God by all people.

"But in your allotted place will be the temple of God, [and the latter temple will exceed the former in glory.][45] The twelve tribes shall be gathered there and all the nations, [until

---

[41]The bracketed words are omitted in MS A; Charles and Becker regard them as extraneous elements in the context and eliminate them as secondary.
[42]The bracketed words are regarded as a Christian interpolation; see Becker, *JSHRZ* 3.1:104 n. 3c.
[43]According to R. H. Charles, *T. Naph.* 8:4, 6 originally was an independent poem with two stanzas; see Becker, *JSHRZ* 3.1:105 n. 4a.
[44]The bracketed words are regarded as a Christian interpolation; see Becker, *JSHRZ* 3.1:117 n. 3a.
[45]The bracketed words possibly are secondary (see Ulrichsen 1991, 141) but may be original in view of the parallel notion of an eschatological sanctuary in *Jub.* 1:17, 29 and *1 En.* 90:29; see Becker, *JSHRZ* 3.1:136 n. 2a.

such time as the Most High shall send forth his salvation through the ministration of the unique prophet.]"[46]

T. Benj. 10:6-11 follows references to the future resurrection of the patriarchs and of all Israelites (*T. Benj.* 10:6-7) after the judgment on Israel and on the nations (*T. Benj.* 10:8-9). Then the author compares Esau's rebuke by the Midianites with the rebuke of Israel by "the chosen Gentiles" (*T. Benj.* 10:10): when the Midianites become "children" and share the "lot" of "those who fear the Lord," the author evidently believes that "the chosen Gentiles" belong to this "lot"—that is, that individual Gentiles will be integrated into the people of God. In this case the term "all Israel" in 10:11 includes "the chosen Gentiles."[47]

T. Benj. 10:6-11: "And then you will see Enoch and Seth and Abraham and Isaac and Jacob being raised up at the right hand in great joy. [7]Then shall we also be raised, each of us over our tribe, and we shall prostrate ourselves before the heavenly king. [8]Then all shall be changed, some destined for glory, others for dishonor, for the Lord first judges Israel for the wrong she has committed[9] and then he shall do the same for all the nations. [10]Then he shall judge Israel by the chosen gentiles as he tested Esau by the Midianites who loved their brothers. You, therefore, my children, may your lot come to be with those who fear the Lord. [11]Therefore, my children, if you live in holiness, in accord with the Lord's commands, you shall again dwell with me in hope; all Israel will be gathered to the Lord."

Thus several passages in *Testaments of the Twelve Patriarchs* refer to a future participation of Gentiles in the salvation of the people of God in the end times, when God will judge the world and fulfill his promises.

Ben Sira

The priest and scribe Ben Sira, who lived and wrote around 200 B.C. in Jerusalem,[48] is hardly interested in non-Jews. Israel is, nearly alone, at the center of Ben Sira's world.[49] In Sir 8:18 he warns against betraying secrets to strangers: "In the presence of a stranger do nothing that is to be kept secret, for you do not know what he will divulge." In Sir 9:3 he warns against contacts with a foreign woman, and in Sir 11:34 against taking into one's house a stranger who will alienate people from the Jewish way of life: "Receive a stranger into your home and he will upset you with commotion, and will estrange you from your family." In the prayer for the restoration of Israel in Sir 36:1-19, which includes the gath-

---

[46]The bracketed words are regarded as Christian interpolation; see Becker, *JSHRZ* 3.1:136 n. 2b; Hollander and de Jonge 1985, 435-36; Ulrichsen 1991, 140.
[47]Thus Kraus 1996, 75. This formulation brings to mind Paul's statement in Rom 11:26. Text-critical issues of the passage cannot be discussed here.
[48]See Schürer 3:198-212. Paul McKechnie ("The Career of Joshua Ben Sira," *JTS* 51 [2000]: 3-26) suggests that Ben Sira was evacuated as a member of the pro-Ptolemaic elite around 200 B.C. to Alexandria, where he wrote his work.
[49]Kraus 1996, 47; for the remarks that follow above see ibid.

ering of the tribes of Jacob (Sir 36:13), he asks God to frighten (Sir 36:2) and to lift up his hand against all foreign nations (Sir 36:3), to pour out his wrath against them (Sir 36:8, 11) and to crush the heads of hostile rulers (Sir 36:12). The nations should see the mighty acts of God (Sir 36:3) and thus come to the recognition that there is no God but YHWH (Sir 36:5 [Heb., 36:17]). But the focus on Israel is not abandoned: as Wolfgang Kraus points out, "The nations are but spectators of the glorification."[50] This emphasis is not altered by the fact that Ben Sira views the fear of the Lord as a notion that pushes other differences into the background (cf. Sir 10:19-25). In his review of salvation history in Sir 44:1—50:21 Ben Sira refers in Sir 44:19, 23 to the nations in the context of God's promise of blessing to Abraham in Gen 12:1-3.

Sir 44:19-23:[51] "Abraham was the great father of a multitude of nations, and no one has been found like him in glory. [20]He kept the law of the Most High, and entered into a covenant with him; he certified the covenant in his flesh, and when he was tested he proved faithful. [21]Therefore the Lord assured him with an oath that the nations would be blessed through his offspring; that he would make him as numerous as the dust of the earth, and exalt his offspring like the stars, and give them an inheritance from sea to sea and from the Euphrates to the ends of the earth. [22]To Isaac also he gave the same assurance for the sake of his father Abraham. The blessing of all people and the covenant [23]he made to rest on the head of Jacob; he acknowledged him with his blessings, and gave him his inheritance; he divided his portions, and distributed them among twelve tribes."

The continuation of the passage shows clearly that Ben Sira relates the promise of blessing only with the twelve tribes, i.e., Israel's descendants.[52] Wolfgang Kraus concludes, "Ben Sira does not envisage the Gentiles' participation in salvation."[53]

The conservative, somewhat quietistic wisdom teacher from Jerusalem propagated a culture that was too complicated to find a real audience. Oda Wischmeyer comments, "Sirach wanted to continue to work on a peaceful culture in Israel on the ground of Israel's religion in Hebrew, the only successful literary language of the ancient Near East, in the broad political framework of Hellenistic states."[54] For Ben Sira the representative of the Jewish elite was "a person thoroughly educated, active as a literary author in the tradition of his national literature, even active as political adviser of the Hellenistic rulers, engaged in theological and ethical research and teaching under the terms of his national religion, and focused on shaping his life in *pietas, religio* and *cultura animi*."

---

[50]Kraus 1996, 48. The Septuagint intensified this emphasis: Sir 36:14 (Heb.) refers to the glorification of the temple (היכל), LXX (Sir 36:13) to the glorification of the people (λαός).

[51]Translation follows the NRSV; German translation in Sauer, *JSHRZ* 3.5.

[52]See Hahn 1971b, 99 n. 42.

[53]Kraus 1996, 50; this is missed by Wisdom (2001, 65-67), who emphasizes the significance of Gen 12:3 for Ben Sira.

[54]O. Wischmeyer 1995, 300; the quotation that follows above, ibid.

Psalms of Solomon

Psalms of Solomon, written probably around 50 B.C. in Pharisaic circles, portrays the Gentiles as those who profane the temple.[55] The author announces that when the Messiah comes, he will purge Jerusalem from Gentiles (*Pss. Sol.* 17:22-23). The "unlawful nations" will be destroyed by the word of his mouth (cf. Is 11:4); the nations will flee while the holy people of God will be gathered (*Pss. Sol.* 17:24-26). There will no longer be any aliens or foreigners (ἀλλογενής) in Jerusalem: the Messiah will distribute the land among the tribes of Israel and he will judge the nations with justice (*Pss. Sol.* 17:28-29). The Gentiles will be forced into compulsory labor in Israel; at the most they will be allowed to admire the glory of Jerusalem (*Pss. Sol.* 17:30-31). The coming of the Messiah does not bring about the salvation of the nations. Foreigners and foreign nations are portrayed consistently in a negative manner.[56]

Pss. Sol. 17:21-31:[57] "See, Lord, and raise up for them their king, the son of David, to rule over your servant Israel in the time known to you, O God. [22]Undergird him with the strength to destroy the unrighteous rulers, to purge Jerusalem from gentiles who trample her to destruction; [23]in wisdom and in righteousness to drive out the sinners from the inheritance; to smash the arrogance of sinners like a potter's jar; [24]to shatter all their substance with an iron rod; to destroy the unlawful nations with the word of his mouth. [25]At his warning the nations will flee from his presence; and he will condemn sinners by the thoughts of their hearts. [26]He will gather a holy people whom he will lead in righteousness; and he will judge the tribes of the people that have been made holy by the Lord their God. [27]He will not tolerate unrighteousness (even) to pause among them, and any person who knows wickedness shall not live with them. For he shall know them that they are all children of their God. [28]He will distribute them upon the land according to their tribes; the alien and the foreigner will no longer live near them. [29]He will judge peoples and nations in the wisdom of his righteousness. . . . [30]And he will have gentile nations serving him under his yoke, and he will glorify the Lord in (a place) prominent (above) the whole earth. And he will purge Jerusalem (and make it) holy as it was even from the beginning, [31](for) nations to come from the ends of the earth to see his glory, to bring as gifts her children who had been driven out, and to see the glory of the Lord with which God has glorified her."

2 Baruch

Apocalypse of Baruch, written around A.D. 100, conveys similar notions (*2 Bar.* 68:5-7; 70:7-10; 72:2-6).

2 Bar. 68:1-8:[58] "And the twelfth bright waters which you have seen; this is the word. [2]For there will come a time after these things, and your people will fall into such a distress so

---

[55]*Pss. Sol.* 2:2-3, 19, 23-24.
[56]See Kraus 1996, 52.
[57]Translation from R. B. Wright, *OTP* 2:639-70; cf. Holm-Nielsen, *JSHRZ* 4.2.
[58]Translation from A. F. J. Klijn, *OTP* 1:615-52; cf. Klijn, *JSHRZ* 5.2; P.-M. Bogaert, *Apocalypse de Baruch.*

that they are all together in danger of perishing. ³They, however, will be saved, and their enemies will fall before them. ⁴And to them will fall much joy one day. ⁵And at that time, after a short time, Zion will be rebuilt again, and the offerings will be restored, and the priests will again return to their ministry. And the nations will again come to honor it. ⁶But not as fully as before. ⁷But it will happen after these things that there will be a fall of many nations. ⁸These are the bright waters you have seen."

2 Bar. 70:7-10:[59] "The Most High will then give a sign to those nations which he has prepared before, and they will come and wage war with the rulers who will then remain. ⁸And it will happen that everyone who saves himself from the war will die in an earthquake, and he who saves himself from the earthquake will be burned by fire, and he who saves himself from the fire will perish by famine. ⁹And it will happen that everyone who will save himself and escape from all things which have been said before—both those who have won and those who have been overcome—that all will be delivered into the hands of my Servant, the Anointed One. ¹⁰For the whole earth will devour its inhabitants."

2 Bar. 72:2-6: "After the signs have come of which I have spoken to you before, when the nations are moved and the time of my Anointed One comes, he will call all nations, and some of them he will spare, and others he will kill. ³These things will befall the nations which will be spared by him. ⁴Every nation which has not known Israel and which has not trodden down the seed of Jacob will live. ⁵And this is because some from all the nations have been subjected to your people. ⁶All those, now, who have ruled over you or have known you, will be delivered up to the sword."

4 Ezra

Apocalypse of Ezra, written around A.D. 100 and extant only in translations, makes similar statements.

4 Ezra 13:5, 9-11:[60] "After this I looked, and behold, an innumerable multitude of men were gathered together from the four winds of heaven to make war against the man who came up out of the sea. . . . ⁹And behold, when he saw the onrush of the approaching multitude, he neither lifted his hand nor held a spear or any weapon of war; ¹⁰but I saw only how he sent forth from his mouth as it were a stream of fire, and from his lips a flaming breath, and from his tongue he shot forth a storm of sparks. ¹¹All these were mingled together, the stream of fire and the flaming breath and the great storm, and fell on the onrushing multitude which was prepared to fight, and burned them all up, so that suddenly nothing was seen of the innumerable multitude but only the dust of ashes and the smell of smoke."

The nations that wage war against Israel are destroyed by the Messiah. They are contrasted with the peaceful multitude of the ten (northern) tribes, which God had led away into captivity, to be protected miraculously (*4 Ezra* 13:33-50).

---

[59] *2 Bar.* 69 interprets the "last waters" that came after the twelfth water and "apply to the whole world" (*2 Bar.* 69:1); *2 Bar.* 70 interprets "the last black waters which will come after the black waters."

[60] Translation from B. M. Metzger, *OTP* 1:517-60; cf. Schreiner, *JSHRZ* 5.4; A. F. J. Klijn, *Esra-Apokalypse.*

4 Ezra 13:33-40, 49-50: "And when all the nations hear his voice, every man shall leave his own land and the warfare that they have against one another; [34]and an innumerable multitude shall be gathered together, as you saw, desiring to come and conquer him. [35]But he will stand on the top of Mount Zion. [36]And Zion will come and be made manifest to all people, prepared and built, as you saw the mountain carved out without hands. [37]And he, my Son, will reprove the assembled nations for their ungodliness (this was symbolized by the storm), [38]and will reproach them to their face with their evil thoughts and with the torments with which they are to be tortured (which were symbolized by the flames). [39]And as for your seeing him gather to himself another multitude that was peaceable, [40]these are the ten tribes which were led away from their own land into captivity in the days of King Hoshea, whom Shalmaneser the king of the Assyrians led captive; he took them across the river, and they were taken into another land. . . . [49] Therefore when he destroys the multitude of the nations that are gathered together, he will defend the people who remain. [50]And then he will show them very many wonders."

The Essenes (Qumran Community)

The tendencies toward antagonism and segregation are preeminent in the texts written in the sphere of influence of the Essenes and the Qumran community. The latter emerges as an independent group around 152 B.C. when the Maccabean ruler Jonathan became high priest in Jerusalem despite the fact that he was not a descendant of Zadok.[61] Since the Essenes also collected texts in the library that came from "outside," it is not always easy to ascertain what was typical for the Qumran Essenes. At any rate, there are texts that project a friendlier attitude toward Gentiles. Passages relevant for our subject can be found in 4QDibHam, CD, 4QMMT, 1QM, 11QT, 4QFlor, 4QOrNab and 4Q246.

Jubilees. This text was written in the second century B.C., not by members of the Qumran community but by circles close to the Essene movement. This is the reason why I treat *Jubilees* at this point. The book is meant to be understood as an account of the revelation at Mount Sinai. The author seeks to impress upon the reader "the certainty of the promises that have not yet been fulfilled and to teach the commandments free of error in such a manner that the expected time of salvation can come together with the righteousness of those who repent and pursue the commandments."[62] Israel's identity as the people of God needs to be continuously secured and implies segregation and separation from the Gentiles.[63] Keeping the sabbath and practicing circumcision are of central significance. The author laments that "the sinners of the nations" oppress the people of God (*Jub.* 23:23-24). Israel is exhorted to avoid contact with pagans, as they will fall under God's judgment (*Jub.* 22:20-22).

Jub. 22:20-22:[64] "Be careful, my son, Jacob, that you do not take a wife from any of the

---

[61]See Deines 1994; Kraus 1996, 57-71; see also Piattelli 1990.
[62]Berger, *JSHRZ* 2.3:279.
[63]See E. Schwarz 1982, esp. 85-98.
[64]Translation from O. S. Wintermute, *OTP* 2:35-142; cf. Berger, *JSHRZ* 2.3.

seed of the daughters of Canaan, because all of his seed is (destined) for uprooting from the earth; [21]because through the sin of Ham, Canaan sinned, and all of his seed will be blotted out from the earth, and all his remnant, and there is none of his who will be saved. [22]And for all of those who worship idols and for the hated ones, there is no hope in the land of the living; because they will go down into Sheol. And in the place of judgment they will walk, and they will have no memory upon the earth. Just as the sons of Sodom were taken from the earth, so (too) all of those who worship idols shall be taken away."

Similar statements are found in *Jub.* 24:28-30 with reference to the Philistines, in *Jub.* 25:1-10 with regard to advice that Rebecca gives to Jacob concerning his choice of a bride, and in *Jub.* 30:5-23 in the context of the episode of Dina and Shechem. The author clearly wants to warn fellow Jews against the dangers of mixed marriages that evidently (often?) occurred prompted by the *Zeitgeist* of Hellenism.[65] The warning that there is no atonement for this sin (*Jub.* 30:16) highlights the seriousness of this lapse. The marriage to a Gentile leads to (sexual) impurity, as does sharing a meal with a Gentile.[66] Admission of Gentiles into the people of God is discussed only in the context of Abraham's circumcision: integration of non-Jews presupposes, as a matter of course and in agreement with Old Testament laws, circumcision (*Jub.* 15:24).

Jub. 15:24: "And that very same day Abraham was circumcised and every man of his house and the servant of his house. And all of those who were purchased for money from the sons of aliens were also circumcised with him."

The description of God's blessing for Abraham includes the nations of the earth: "all the nations of the earth will bless themselves by you [Abraham]" (*Jub.* 12:23).[67] On the other hand, God's blessing is accentuated and limited to Jacob and his descendants: Jacob will take the place of Abraham "upon the earth and for a blessing in the midst of the sons of men" (*Jub.* 19:17);[68] the text leaves open the question of the identity of these "sons of men."[69] Jacob's descendants are the heirs of the earth; the nations will serve Jacob.

4QPrNab ar. This early Aramaic text[70] is a prayer of thanksgiving of the pagan ruler Nabonidus to the God of Israel, as "God Most High" restored his health.

---

[65]See M. Elliott 2000, 169-71.
[66]*Jub.* 20:4; 22:20; 25:1-9; 27:10; 30:1-15 (marriage); 22:17 (food). See Milgrom 1993, 281-82.
[67]Cf. *Jub.* 15:6-8; 20:10; 24:11; 27:23.
[68]Cf. *Jub.* 19:20-24; 27:11.
[69]Wisdom (2001, 73) surmises that the nations are in view.
[70]On 4QPrNab ar (= 4Q242) see *DJD* 22:83-93 (J. Collins); Beyer, *Aramäischen Texte,* 1:223-24; 2:104; *PTSDSSP* 5; *DSSSE* 1:486-89; Maier, *Qumran-Essener,* 2:185-86. Hengel (1969, 205 [ET, 111-12]) dates 4QPrNab ar to the Persian period; see also A. S. van der Woude, "Fünfzehn Jahre Qumranforschung (1974-1988) IV," *ThR* 57 (1992): 33-35; Deines 1994, 61 n. 6. Maier (*Qumran-Essener,* 2:185) describes the text as late Hasmonean/Herodian; see also Schürer 3:440.

The liberty with which this pagan prays to the God of Israel recalls 2 Kings 5, Jon 1, Zeph 2 and Mal 1—a fact that does not, however, automatically lead to further implications. It is striking that the author of the text deliberately avoids addressing God in the first person singular.[71]

4QDibHam[a-c] *(4Q504-506)*. These early Essene prayers, written in the second century B.C., known as "Words of the Lights" (דברי המארות),[72] emphasize Israel's election, which is highlighted in contrast to the insignificance of the nations.

4QDibHam[a] 1-2 III, 3-5:[73] "Behold, all the nations (are) [as no]thing before you; as nothingness and emptiness th[ey] are considered before you. [4]Only your name have we [acknow]ledged, and for your glory you have created us and (as) sons [5]you have established us for yourself before the eyes of all the nations."

4QDibHam[a] 1-2 IV, 8-13 refers to the nations that bring offerings. This is, however, not a reference to a future time of salvation for Gentiles but a historical review of the time of King David.

4QDibHam[a] 1-2 IV, 4-13: "For you loved [5]Israel more than all the peoples, so you chose the tribe of [6]Judah, and your covenant you established with David (so he would) be [7]as a shepherd, a prince over your people. He was seated upon the throne of Israel before you [8]all the days, and all the nations saw your glory [9](by) which you were honored as holy in the midst of your people Israel; and to your great [10]name they brought their offering: silver and gold and precious stone(s) [11]with all the treasure(s) of their land in order to glorify your people and [12]Zion, your holy city, and your marvelous house. There is no adversary [13]or evil occurrence, but peace and blessing."

Even though this liturgical text provides a positive picture of the relationship between Israel and the nations, it does not speak of an integration of the nations into Israel or of an equal status of Jews and non-Jews.[74]

Roland Deines has suggested that "the eschatology of the Qumran Community, which evidently had two stages, can be cleared with the ambivalent Old Testament attitude concerning the Gentiles in the eschaton."[75] The first stage is characterized by a total segregation from everything that is alien or foreign and aims at the restoration of the cov-

---

[71]See Beyer, *Aramäischen Texte,* 1:223; Kraus 1996, 69.

[72]See *DJD* 7:137-70 (M. Baillet); for an assessment of the historical context of the text see ibid., 7:143-45; also Deines 1994, 70; translation above from *PTSDSSP* 4A:107-53 (D. T. Olson); *DSSSE* 2:1008-1121.

[73]Translation from *PTSDSSP* 4A:129 (D. T. Olson); cf. *DSSSE* 2:1015; Maier, *Qumran-Essener,* 2:607.

[74]See Kraus 1996, 68. D. Schwartz (1992b, 107-8, 111-12) emphasizes that the offerings that the nations bring to Zion must be understood in the sense of ἀναθήματα ("things devoted to destruction"), not in the sense of θυσίαι ("sacrifices").

[75]Deines 1994, 64.

enant people and of a perfect temple cult on Mount Zion. This first stage witnesses (1) the establishment of the Qumran community as the nucleus of the new covenant people; (2) the repossession and the purification of Jerusalem and the temple by the members of the Qumran community followed by the complete liberation of the land from the last pagan bastions and by the restoration of Israel; (3) the war of eschatological Israel against the remaining inhabitants and then against all the rest of the descendants of the three sons of Noah. The second stage is the time of universal salvation, when the nations will come to Zion and bring their riches.

Deines suggests that the second stage makes possible the salvation of the nations.[76] The texts that he quotes do not seem to warrant this conclusion, however. 1QM XII, 13-16 and 1QM XIX, 4-7 indeed talk about the nations that bring their riches to Zion. However, the author continues by asserting that the kings of the nations who oppressed Israel will serve Israel and lick the dust of its feet. Again, 1QSb III, 27-28 states that the nations will bring to Israel "the first fruits of all delights," and in 1QSb IV, 27-28 the people of Israel are described as light that illuminates the earth with knowledge. However, 1QSb III, 18-21 speaks of God's judgment of the nations, and 1QSb V, 24-29 announces that God will defeat the nations, devastate the earth, kill the wicked and crush the nations like the mud of the streets, so that all the nations will serve Israel. Deines particularly emphasizes the text 4QpJes[a] (= 4Q161) 7 II 22-29:[77] this passage may reflect the eschatological scenario as outlined by Deines with this interpretation of Is 10:22—11:5. However, I fail to see that the subjugation of the Kittim as Israel's last enemy (4QpJes[a] 7 III 7-13) "establishes a universal kingdom of peace in Zion, ruled by a descendant of David."[78] Wolfgang Kraus comments on Deines's hypothesis that the segregation from the Gentiles is portrayed much more specifically than their participation in eschatological salvation, and for the Essenes the earthly Jerusalem remained the central place of salvation: "In view of the particular concept of the land as Israel's inheritance, which is the premise of the assertions in 4QMMT, 11QT and 4QFlor, an admission into the people of God is out of the question precisely for the eschaton."[79] Kraus thus puts Deines's suggestion more precisely: "The salvation of the nations is (1) not of primary interest to the pious in Qumran; their participation in salvation is (2) limited to the function of spectators or servants of Israel."

4Q246 (4QApocalypse ar). In this pre-Qumran or non-Qumran Aramaic apocalyptic text, published in 1992,[80] a figure is mentioned who is designated in II, 1 as "son of God" (ברה די אל) and "son of the Most High" (בר עליון).

---

[76]Deines 1994, 66, with reference to texts in n. 24.

[77]Translations in *DJD* 5:11-15 (J. M. Allegro); *PTSDSSP* 6B:83-97 (M. P. Horgan); *DSSSE* 1:313-17; Maier, *Qumran-Essener,* 2:68-70.

[78]Deines 1994, 66 n. 24.

[79]Kraus 1996, 71; the quotation that follows above, ibid.

[80]See Émile Puech, "Fragment d'une Apocalypse en araméen (4Q246 = pseudo-Dan[d]) et le 'Royaume de Dieu,'" *RB* 99 (1992): 98-131; cf. *DJD* 22:165-84 (É. Puech); Beyer, *Aramäischen Texte,* 2:109-13; *DSSSE* 1:492-95; García Martínez, *Dead Sea Scrolls,* 138; Vermes, *Dead Sea Scrolls,* 331-32; Maier, *Qumran-Essener,* 2:189-191; see also J. A. Fitzmyer, "4Q246: The 'Son of God' Document from Qumran," *Bib* 74 (1993): 153-174, esp. 155-56; J. J. Collins 1995, 154-72; and especially J. Zimmermann 1998, 128-70 (text, German translation, comments, form, interpretation).

The debate over whether this figure should be interpreted negatively[81] or positively now can be decided in terms of the second option. What is still debated, however, is the question of whether the "son of God" should be understood as a future Jewish ruler (J. T. Fitzmyer), as an angelic being in terms of a celestial liberator analogous to Dan 7 (F. García Martínez),[82] as a collective entity analogous to Dan 7:13 (M. Hengel), or as the Messiah (J. J. Collins). The analysis of 4Q246 by Johannes Zimmermann has shown that the Son of Man from Dan 7 could be designated "son of God" in pre-Christian Judaism.

After a description of the transitory kingdoms in 4Q246 II, 1-3, the author focuses in II, 4-9 on God's eternal rule as king.

4Q246 II, 1-III, 1:[83] "He will be called son of God, and they will call him son of the Most High. Like the sparks ²that you saw, so will their kingdom be; they will rule several year[s] over ³the earth and crush everything; a people will crush another people, and a province another provi[n]ce. ⁴ *Blank* Until the people of God [עם אל] arises and makes everyone rest from the sword. *Blank* ⁵His kingdom [מלכותה] will be an eternal kingdom, and all his paths in truth. He will jud[ge] ⁶the earth in truth and will make peace. The sword will cease from the earth, ⁷and all the provinces will pay him homage [lit., 'fall down before him']. The great God is his strength, ⁸he will wage war for him; he will place the peoples in his hand and ⁹cast them all away before him. His rule will be an eternal rule, and all the abysses ^{III, 1} [of the earth will be subject to him . . .]"

Following the structural analysis of Johannes Zimmermann in terms of a concentric structure,[84] we may interpret 4Q246 as an "apocalyptic description of history" that portrays in the central middle section God's universal, eternal rule of peace, which restores a creation that has fallen into disorder. The text does not speak in this context of an integration of the nations into the people of God. In connection with the future time of salvation, the reference to the nations falling down might be an allusion to the Old Testament passages about the pilgrimage of the nations to Zion and about the universal acknowledgment of YHWH. The peace in II, 6-7 is "no peace dictated by the victor or maintained by force of arms."[85] However, since the falling down of the nations "stands in deliberate antithesis to the rising up of the people of God, no worship of God is necessarily in view; it may refer to the state of submission and the servitude of the nations."[86]

---

[81]J. T. Milik suggested an allusion to Alexander Balas, and H. Stegemann (1993, 341) to Antiochos IV Epiphanes.
[82]García Martínez 1993.
[83]Translation from *DSSSE* 1:495; cf. J. Zimmermann 1998, 130-31; for III, 1 in the translation above see ibid.
[84]J. Zimmermann 1998, 134-37, on the genre of the text see ibid., 137-38.
[85]J. Zimmermann 1998, 151.
[86]J. Zimmermann 1998, 151; thus also Kraus 1996, 70.

lines 1-2	transience of the rule of the nations
lines 2-3	destructive rule of the nations
lines 3-4	wars of the cities and provinces
line 4a	*rising up* of the people of God
line 4b	rest of the sword
line 5a	eternal rule
line 5b	God's paths in truth
line 5c	God's judgment in truth
line 6a	conclusion of peace
line 6b	removal of the sword
line 7a	*falling down* of all provinces
lines 7-8	war of God
lines 8-9	subjugation of the nations
line 9	eternity of the rule of God

Damascus Document (CD). This comprehensive presentation of Essene regulations, written or redacted perhaps around 100 B.C.,[87] presupposes two boundaries that are important for the community: (1) the inherited, traditional boundary between Israel and the Gentiles (i.e., non-Jews); (2) the boundary between the "true Israel" and the "false Israel," meaning between the Damascus community and the rest of Israel.[88] This means that the difference between "false Israel" and the non-Jews is somewhat irrelevant: the "false Israelites" are outside the scope of the true people of God just as the non-Jews are.

The predestinarian, dualistic description of the origins of humankind in CD II, 2-13 differentiates between the "elect" and the "evil ones," without the difference between Israel and non-Israel being in any way relevant. The Damascus Document never refers to a confrontation with non-Jews: the world outside of "false Israel" is of no interest to the authors.[89]

The Essene community regulated the contacts with non-Jews. As did all Jews, the Essenes emphasized segregation from the Gentiles (CD XI, 14-15; XII, 8-11).

CD XI, 14-15:[90] "Let no man rest in a place near [15]gentiles on the Sabbath."

CD XII, 8-11: "Let no man sell clean animals or [9]birds to gentiles in order that they may not sacrifice them. And from his granary [10]and his vat he shall not sell to them from whatever he possesses; and his slave and his maidservant he shall not sell [11]to them, because they entered with him into the covenant of Abraham."

---

[87]See H. Stegemann 1993, 165-66. Philip R. Davies (*The Damascus Covenant: An Interpretation of the "Damascus Document"* [JSOTSup 25; Sheffield: JSOT Press, 1983]) suggests that CD is a pre-Essene writing adopted by the Essenes. J. M. Baumgarten and D. Schwartz ("Damascus Document [CD]," in *PTSDSSP* 2:6-7) describe CD as being "definitely a Qumran text."
[88]P. Davies 1995, 134-35; for the remarks that follow above see ibid.
[89]On this passage see also Murphy-O'Connor 1970.
[90]Translation from *PTSDSSP* 2:4-79 (J. M. Baumgarten and D. Schwartz); cf. *DSSSE* 1:551-81; Maier, *Qumran-Essener,* 1:1-43.

According to CD XI, 2, one should forgo services of a "foreigner" if they are prohibited for the Jews by the Torah. Contacts with Gentiles generally were not prohibited; even in Palestine such a precept could hardly have been followed. But segregation from non-Jews was the ideal of "pure doctrine."[91] According to the "rule for the settlement of all the camps," the non-Jews, if they are proselytes, came in fourth (and last) place (CD XIV, 4).

A fragment of the Damascus Document found in Qumran (4QD^a = 4Q266) contains a prayer that the priest, who is responsible for the full members, is to speak over a member who has to be sent away. Part of the text reads as follows:

4QD^a 18 V, 9-12:[92] "Blessed are you, who are everything, in your hands is everything, you do everything, you have founded [10]the [na]tions according to their families, and according to their languages, and according to their tribes, and you have led them astray in a trackless [11]wilderness. You chose our fathers and gave their descendants your truthful regulations [12]and your holy precepts, so that man could carry them out and live."

Here the authors apply consistently the doctrine of election to the foreign nations: their lawlessness is as much due to God's decrees as is his revelation of the law to his people.

The boundary between the Damascus community and outsiders can be overcome: by marriage and by birth as the child of a member (CD VII, 6-9), as a new member (i.e., as proselyte) or as the slave of a member (CD XIV, 3-6). The last passage mentions four categories of members: priests, Levites, Israelites and the גר (gēr), a term that refers here either to the "proselyte" or to the "non-Jew." Philip Davies argues on the basis of Ezek 14:7; 22:7, 29; 47:23 for the meaning "proselyte": nonmembers had the same status as non-Jews who lived in Israel. This means that when Jews decide to live in "Israel"—that is, to become members of the Essene community, a process that turns them into "proselytes"— they must be regarded as "Israelites" and accepted as members of the community.[93] John Lübbe argues in the context of a discussion on the meaning of גר (gēr) in CD that the meaning "non-Jew" is to be preferred, as CD XIV, 4, 6 permit the admission of non-Jews who have become slaves of members of the Damascus community.[94]

CD XI, 2 contains perhaps a reference to non-Jews in the Essene community. This passage stipulates that nobody should send a בן הנכר (ben ha-nekar) "to do his business on the sabbath day." This term, translated as "foreigner" by J. M. Baumgarten and D. Schwartz (J. Maier translates as "Fremdling"), occurs in the Old Testament only in Is 56:3, 6, a prophecy concerning "foreigners"[95] who will join Israel's God. If the authors of CD XI, 2 allude to this passage, they describe at least the possibility that non-Jews can be admitted.

---

[91]Deines 1994, 84-85.

[92]See *DJD* 18:23-94 (J. M. Baumgarten); translation from *DSSSE* 1:597; Maier, *Qumran-Essener,* 2:230.

[93]P. Davies 1995, 136.

[94]Lübbe 1996.

[95]*HAL* 661, s.v. "נכר 2"; for the translation of CD XI, 2 see J. M. Baumgarten and D. Schwartz (*PTSDSSP* 2:47 with n. 162), who identify the subject of the stipulation to be "non-Jews."

We do not know, however, whether the Essene community actually admitted non-Jews, assuming that the latter were willing to join.[96]

4QMMT (4Q394-399). The early Essene text 4QMMT,[97] presumably a letter from the Teacher of Righteousness to the Maccabean high priest Jonathan in which he provides the reason for his and his followers' separation, lists the following stipulations among the halakot that are in dispute:

4Q394 3 I, 4-16 + 4:[98] "These are some of our regulations [. . .] which [. . .] [5][the] works which we [. . .] they [a]ll concern [. . .] [6]and purity of [. . .] . . . [And concerning the offering of the wh]eat of the [Gentiles which they . . .] [7]and let their [. . .] touch it [. . .] and they de[file it: you shall not eat] [8]of the wheat of [the Gen]tiles, [and it shall not] be brought into the temple. [And concerning the sacrifice of the sin-offering] [9]which they cook in vessels [of bronze . . .] [10]the flesh of their sacrifices and [. . .] in the courtyard [. . .] [11]with the broth of their sacrifices. And concerning the sacrifice of the Gentiles: [. . . they sacrifice] [12]to the [. . .] it is [li]ke who whored with him. [And also concerning the cereal-offering of the sacrifice of] [13]the pea[ce-offerings], which they leave over from one day to another, and also [. . .] [14]that the cere[al-offering should be eaten] with the fats and the meat on the day of [their] sacri[fice, for] [15]the priest[s] should oversee in this matter in such a way that [they] d[o] not [16]lead the people into sin."

The Teacher of Righteousness demands that the priests refuse to accept cereal-offerings from Gentiles; they must not eat of these offerings or permit them to be brought to the temple.

We encounter the position that 4QMMT attests to again during the First Jewish Revolt (A.D. 66-70) when the Zealots refused to accept dedicatory offerings and sacrifices from non-Jews (Josephus, *B.J.* 2.409-416).[99] When Eleazar stopped the sacrifices for the emperor, this set the war in motion.[100]

The Temple Scroll (11QT). The Temple Scroll, written at the latest during the late Hasmonean period,[101] offers a reconceptualization of the temple cult. In the first preserved lines of the second column the author cites Ex 34:11-13 and warns against entering into a covenant with the peoples of the land, lest Israel be seduced to idolatry (11QTemple II, 1-13). The citation of Deut 7:25-26 emphasizes that Israel must not bring any pagan items into the tem-

---

[96]See P. Davies 1995, 139-40.
[97]4QMMT has now been fully edited: Elisha Qimron and John Strugnell, *Miqsat Ma'ase Ha-Torah 4Q 394-399: Qumran Cave 4.V (DJD* 10; Oxford: Clarendon, 1994).
[98]Translation from *DSSSE* 2:790-805; cf. García Martínez, *Dead Sea Scrolls*, 77-85; Maier, *Qumran-Essener,* 2:361-76.
[99]See D. Schwartz 1992b, 111-13; Kraus 1996, 71.
[100]See Hengel 1976a, 210.
[101]See *DJD* 23:347-451; cf. *DSSSE* 2:1228-1305; Maier, *Qumran-Essener,* 1:371. H. Stegemann (1993, 137) dates 11QT to the first half of the fourth century B.C. Michael O. Wise ("The Temple Scroll: Its Composition, Date, Purpose and Provenance" [Ph.D. diss.; University of Chicago, 1988], 260, 269, 290-93) interprets 11QTemple as the eschatological programmatic writing of the Teacher of Righteousness; cf. Kraus 1996, 64 n. 116.

ple.[102] In 11QTemple III, 5-6 the text evidently warns against using foreign building materials. Even more significant is the fact that in the three court-yards that surround in concentric circles the eschatological temple there is no court of the Gentiles. Roland Deines comments that "the outermost court-yard in 11QT corresponds functionally to the court of the women in the Herodian temple; it is accessible only to the ritually clean Israelite women and children under twenty years of age, as well as to the descendants of the proselytes beginning with the third generation (Col. 40)."[103]

4QFlorilegium (4Q174). The exclusion of the foreigners from the future sanc-tuary is found also in the eschatological writing 4QFlor, a midrash on 2 Sam 7:10-11 and Ps 1—2.

4QFlor I, 1-6:[104] *"[And no] enemy [will oppress him an]ymore, [and no] son of deceit [shall afflict] him [agai]n, as formerly, from the day that* [2]*[I appointed judges] over my people Is-rael.* This is the house which [he will build] for [him] in the latter days, as it is written in the book of [3]*[Moses, 'The Sanctuary,] O Yahweh, which your hands have fashioned. Yah-weh will reign for ever and ever.'* This (is) the house which these will not enter [4][an un-circumcised person in the heart or an uncircumcised person in the flesh][105] [for]ever, nor an Ammonite, a Moabite, a bastard, a foreigner [נכר נכר], or a proselyte [גר] forever, for his holy ones (are) there. [5][His glory shall] be revealed for[ev]er; it shall appear over it perpetually. And strangers shall lay it waste no more, as they formerly laid waste [6]the sanctua[ry of I]srael because of their sin."

Interpretations of the term גר in other than the "technical" sense of "proselyte"[106] may be seen as resulting from the attempt to harmonize the statement with rab-binic sources that, like the Old Testament, do not exclude proselytes from the temple cult.[107] According to 4QFlor I, 4, the Gentiles and even the proselytes are excluded from admission to the eschatological temple that God will establish in the last days.

It is debated whether 4QFlor speaks of two or three temples, and there is no clear con-sensus concerning the question of the relationship of the Qumran community and the es-

---

[102]Cf. the interpretation by Deines (1994, 75).

[103]Deines 1994, 81-92; cf. Kraus 1996, 64-65.

[104]See *DJD* 5:53-57; translation from *PTSDSSP* 6B:248-64 (J. Milgrom); cf. *DSSSE* 1:352-55; Maier, *Qumran-Essener,* 2:102-7; see also A. Steudel, *Der Midrasch zur Eschatologie aus der Qum-rangemeinde (4QMidrEschat*[a.b]*)* (STDJ 13; Leiden: Brill, 1994).

[105]Thus the reconstruction of the fragmentary line by Deines (1994, 78), who follows J. Strugnell ("Notes en marge du volume V des 'Discoveries in the Judaean Desert of Jordan,'" *RevQ* 7 [1969-1971]: 163-276), who follows the list in Ezek 44:9. Brooke (1985, 86, 92) reconstructs on the basis of Deut 23:3-4, where in addition to the Ammonites and the Moabites, eunuchs and bastards are excluded from admission to the community (for a discussion of the passage see ibid., 101-7).

[106]See Kuhn and Stegemann 1962, 1268.

[107]Thus Deines 1994, 82 n. 67; see also Kraus 1996, 67; J. Baumgarten 1972.

chatological temple. Devorah Dimant, who discusses 4QFlor I, 1-13 in detail,[108] reckons with three temples: (1) the existing temple in Jerusalem (4QFlor I, 6; described in 11QT as the "ideal" temple), (2) the "human temple" (4QFlor I, 6), (3) the future eschatological temple (4QFlor I, 2-5; cf. 11QT XXIX, 8-9). The "human temple" (מקדש אדם; translated by Dimant as "Temple of Men") represents an interim temple between Israel's temple of the past (and the present?) and the eschatological temple in the future. The latter is to be linked with the Qumran group, which, as a community resembling the temple, aims at restoring the ministry of the "assembly of the priests" in the holy precinct of the tabernacle or of the temple city. In regard to the self-understanding of the Qumran community, an important conviction was that the pure eschatological worship takes place in the interim temple already in the present, including participation of the angels.[109]

The War Scroll (1QM). In 1QM XII, 11-16 and XIX, 3-7 the motif of the pilgrimage of the nations is taken up, at the same time the nations appear as peoples who have been vanquished and serve Israel.

1QM XII, 11-16:[110] "Put your hand upon the neck of your enemies and your foot upon the piles of the slain! Smite the nations, your foes, and let your sword [12]devour the guilty flesh. Fill your land (with) glory and your inheritance (with) blessing; a multitude of cattle in your fields, silver, gold, and precious [13]stones in your palac[e]s. Zion, rejoice greatly! Shine forth in jubilation, Jerusalem! Be glad, all you cities of Judah! Open [14][your] gate[s] continually, that through them may be brought the wealth of the nations! Their kings shall serve you; all your oppressors shall bow down before you and [15][lick] the dust [from your feet. Daughter]s of my people, shout with a voice of jubilation! Deck yourselves with glorious ornaments! Have dominion over [the ki]n[gdoms . . .] [16][. . . I]srael shall reign forever."

1QM XIV, 5-7:[111] "He has called the stumbling to wonderful [mighty deed]s. He has gathered an assembly of nations for destruction without any remnant. He has raised in judgment [6]the melted heart, opened the mouth of the mute to sing the might [of . . .], taught war to the weak [. . .] He gives to the staggering knees strength to stand [7]and steadiness of loins to the smitten back. Through the humble spirit [. . .] the stubborn heart, and through the perfect of Way shall all the wicked nations be destroyed."

1QM XIX, 3-7:[112] "Put your hand upon the neck of your enemies and your fo[ot . . .] [4]yo[ur foes,] and let your sword devour flesh. Fill your land (with) glory and your inheritance (with) blessing; a mu[ltitude . . .] [5][. . .] in your palaces. Zion, rejoice greatly! Be glad all you, cities of Ju[dah! . . .]. [6][. . .] the wealth of the nations! Their kings shall serve you and

---

[108]Devorah Dimant, "4Q Florilegium and the Idea of the Community as Temple," in *Hellenica et Judaica* (FS V. Nikiprowetzky; ed. A. Caquot et al.; Leuven: Peeters, 1986), 165-89.

[109]See A. M. Schwemer, "Gott als König und seine Königsherrschaft in den Sabbatliedern aus Qumran," in Hengel and Schwemer 1991, 45-118. A. S. van der Woude ("Fünfzehn Jahre Qumranforschung [1974-1988] IV," *ThR* 57 [1992]: 30-32) accepts this interpretation; see also Deines 1994, 79-80; Kraus (1996, 66 with n. 126) remains undecided.

[110]Translation from *PTSDSSP* 2:121 (J. Duhaime); cf. *DSSSE* 1:112-45; Maier, *Qumran-Essener*, 1:143-44.

[111]Translation from *PTSDSSP* 2:125 (J. Duhaime).

[112]Translation from *PTSDSSP* 2:139 (J. Duhaime); for the reconstruction of fragmentary lines see ibid., 2:138 (notes).

[al]l [your oppressors] shall bow down before you, [7][. . .] Daughters of my people, burst into a voice of jubilation! Deck yourselves with glorious ornaments!"

On the one hand, the nations appear in the vicinity of Zion; on the other hand, they obviously are excluded from YHWH's blessing that will be poured out on the "inheritance" of Israel (i.e., the promised land); they are devoured by God's judgment.

4Q381. The last lines of 4Q381, the fragment of an early Jewish psalm, describe the divine election of the people (of Israel) from among the nations, over whom Israel one day will rule.

4Q381 76-77, 14-16:[113] "He chose yo[u] [15][from m]any [peoples] and from great nations to be his people, to rule over all [. . .][114] [16][. . . hea]vens and earth, and as most high over every nation of the earth."

11QPs[a] XVIII (11Q5 XVIII, 1-16 = Ps 154). This sapiential psalm extends an invitation to join the holy and pure community in which God's law forms the center.[115] The text includes universalistic motifs similar to some Old Testament psalms. Clearly, however, Zion remains the central focus.

11QPs[a] XVIII, 15-16:[116] "[Bless] Yahweh who redeems the poor ones from the hand of [16]enemies [and delive]rs [the perfect ones from the hand of the wicked,] [who raises up the horn of Ja]cob, and judges [the peoples of Israel;] [(so that) he may prolong] his sojourn in Zion, ch[oosing Jerusalem forever.]"[117]

11QPs[a] XXIV (11Q5 XXIV, 3-17 = Ps 155). This individual prayer of thanksgiving also combines an exclusive particularism with a universalistic hope that remains, however, general and vague.

11QPs[a] XXIV, 8-9: "Grant me discernment, O Yahweh, in your Torah and from your precepts teach me, [9]that many may hear of your works, and peoples may honor your glory."

11QPs[a] XXII (11Q5 XXII, 1-15; Apostrophe to Zion). This text, evidently a hymn on Zion, refers to the great hope that Zion has been promised, a hope that will be fulfilled "on the day of your salvation" (XXII, 4): the righteous and the pious

---

[113]Translation from *PTSDSSP* 4A:11-39 (E. M. Schuller); cf. *DJD* 11:87-171 (E. Shuller); *DSSSE* 2:754-63; Maier, *Qumran-Essener,* 2:332-46.

[114]Probably גוים or עמים should be supplied; see Deines 1994, 68, with reference to 4Q503 24-25, 4.

[115]See Deines 1994, 69.

[116]Translation from *PTSDSSP* 4A:171-77, esp. 177 (J. A. Sanders); cf. *DJD* 23:29-37; *DSSSE* 2:1172-79; Deines 1994, 69; also J. A. Sanders, *The Psalms Scroll of Qumran Cave II (11QPs[a])* (DJD IV; Oxford: Clarendon, 1965), 64, 67; Woude, *JSHRZ* 4.1:45.

[117]Vermes (*Dead Sea Scrolls,* 239) translates, "He desires his tabernacle in Zion, and chooses Jerusalem for ever."

will inhabit Zion, whose glory will fill the earth, after the enemies have been destroyed.

11QPs[a] XXII, 10-12:[118] "All about are your enemies [11]cut off, O Zion, and all your foes have been scattered. Laud of you is pleasing, O Zion, [12]cherished through all the world."

4QpNah 3-4 II, 1 (4Q169). The commentary on Nah 2:14 in the Nahum pesher[119] is interpreted by Roland Deines as a possible critique of the missionary praxis of the Pharisees.[120]

4QpNah 3-4 II, 1: "And 'his messengers' are his envoys, whose voice will no longer be heard by the nations."

In 4QpNah 3-4 I, 2; II, 4; III, 3, 7 the Pharisees are described as people who advise "smooth things." In the commentary on Nah 2:12 (4QpNah 3-4 I, 2) they are accused of having invited to Jerusalem "Demetrius, King of Greece"—probably Demetrius III Eukairos (95-88 B.C.)[121]—who, however, did not come. Since the text discusses political events that took place in Judea and included the role of the Pharisees, it seems rather unlikely that the text quoted above comments on a Pharisaic (religious) mission among Gentiles.[122]

Rabbinic Literature

The Mishnah tractate *'Abodah Zarah* ("Idolatry"), in the fourth division, *Neziqin* ("Damages"), provides the most extensive discussions on Gentiles.[123] It deals primarily with the practical question of what one should do in order to avoid giving the impression of sanctioning or promoting pagan customs. The rabbis stipulate that personal contacts with Gentiles should be limited as much as possible, mainly because of the danger of pagan immorality.

m. 'Abod. Zar. 2:1-2:[124] "They do not leave cattle in gentiles' [גוים] inns, because they are suspect in regard to bestiality. And a woman should not be alone with them, because they are suspect in regard to fornication. And a man should not be alone with them, because they are suspect in regard to bloodshed. An Israelite girl should not serve as a midwife

---

[118]Translation from *PTSDSSP* 4A:201-5 (J. A. Sanders, with J. H. Charlesworth and H. W. L. Rietz); cf. *DJD* 4:85-89; *DSSSE* 2:1177; Maier, *Qumran-Essener*, 1:337-38.

[119]4QpNah (= 4Q169) is a late Hasmonean/early Herodian text; see J. M. Allegro in *DJD* 5:37-42. Translation above from *PTSDSSP* 6B:144-55 (M. P. Horgan); cf. *DSSSE* 1:334-41; García Martínez, *Dead Sea Scrolls,* 195-97; Vermes *Dead Sea Scrolls,* 336-39; Maier, *Qumran-Essener,* 2:88-92.

[120]Deines 1994, 83 n. 69.

[121]See Schürer 3:432; Saldarini 1988, 278.

[122]Saldarini (1988, 278-79) discusses 4QpNah but does not discuss the issue of a Pharisaic mission. McKnight (1991) does not discuss 4QpNah.

[123]See Sievers 1985, 603-4.

[124]Translation from Neusner, *Mishnah.*

to a gentile woman, because she serves to bring forth a child for the service of idolatry.[125] But a gentile woman may serve as a midwife to an Israelite girl. An Israelite girl should not give suck to the child of a gentile woman. But a gentile woman may give suck to the child of an Israelite girl, when it is by permission. [2]They accept from them healing for property, but not healing for a person. 'And they do not allow them to cut hair under any circumstances,' the words of R. Meir. And sages say, 'In the public domain it is permitted, but not if they are alone.'"

Rabbi Eliezer ben Hyrcanus argued according to *t. Sanh.* 13:2 that no Gentile will share the world to come.

t. Sanh. 13:2:[126] "And the children of the wicked among the heathen will not live [in the world to come] nor be judged.[127] R. Eliezer says, 'None of the gentiles has a portion in the world to come, as it is said, *The wicked shall return to Sheol, all the gentiles who forget God* (Ps. 9:17). *The wicked shall return to Sheol*—these are the wicked Israelites.' [Supply: *And all the gentiles who forget God*—these are the nations.] Said to him R. Joshua, 'If it had been written, *The wicked shall return to Sheol*—*all the gentiles* and then said nothing further, I should have maintained as you do. Now that it is in fact written, *All the gentiles who forget God,* it indicates that there also are righteous people among the nations of the world, who do have a portion in the world to come.'"

This view presumably was shared only by a minority of rabbis.[128] Another view that was popular in a later period emphasized that Gentiles who keep at least the seven Noahic commandments will share the world to come (*b. Sanh.* 105a).

The so-called Noahic commandments have been attested, at the earliest, for the second part of the second century A.D.[129] They are perhaps the result of a development that integrated local customs, suggestions and agreements into something like "fundamental ethics" for Gentiles who came close to Judaism without becoming full proselytes.[130] According to the fully developed rabbinic view,[131] the Noahites must keep the following seven commandments and prohibitions: (1) prohibition of idolatry (ʿabodah zarah); (2) prohibition of blasphemy (qillelat ha-shem); (3) prohibition of shedding blood (shefikut damim)— that is, illegally killing a person; (4) prohibition of immorality (gilluy ʿarayōt)—that is, sexual perversions, particularly sodomy; (5) prohibition of robbing people and of possessions that belong to others (ha-gezel); (6) commandment to institute an orderly adminis-

---

[125]The second clause is missing in MS München.

[126]Translation from Neusner, *Mishnah;* cf. Rengstorf et al., *Tosefta, Seder Neziḳin: Sanhedrin,* 203-4; Str-B 4.2:1180.

[127]Rengstorf comments in a note to his translation, "They will then not be punished after their death; rather, their dying is equivalent to their final destruction. This view corresponds with the Christian doctrine of *annihilatio.*"

[128]See Sievers 1985, 604; Herweg and Herweg 2001, 50; differently Donaldson 1990, 4.

[129]See Novak 1983, 3-41; M. Goodman 1994, 53-54; Flusser, 1994; see also Urbach 1981, 275-78.

[130]Flusser 1994, 582-83; cf. J. J. Collins 2000, 155-85, on the "common ethic" of Second Temple Judaism; M. Goodman (1994, 54 n. 26) remains skeptical.

[131]Cf. *t. ʿAbod. Zar.* 8:4-6; *y. ʿAbod. Zar.* 2:1 (40c); *b. ʿAbod. Zar.* 64b; *b. Sanh.* 56b-57a; *Gen. Rab.* 16 on Gen 2:17.

tration of justice (*ha-dinim*); (7) prohibition of eating parts of a living animal (*'eber min ha-hay*). In the proto-Essene book of *Jubilees* three different, though related, commandments are mentioned:[132] the sons of Noah shall protect themselves against immorality, impurity and injustice. According to the midrash on Deut 4:41 in *Deut. Rab.* 2.25, Adam followed the first six Noahic commandments, while the seventh commandment became relevant only at the time of Noah. With this interpretation the Noahic commandments are seen as "expanded primitive law of humanity."[133]

It is debated whether the Noahic laws were imposed on the "aliens" (*gerim*) living in Palestine or on the "God-fearers,"[134] or whether they remained merely theoretical statements;[135] the latter is rather unlikely, however. It is further debated whether the Noahic laws provide the tradition-historical background of the stipulations of the apostolic decree in Acts 15:20 (29), where the converted Gentiles are told to abstain "from the pollutions of idols and from unchastity and from what is strangled and from blood" (RSV).[136] Martin Goodman warns against reading the (later) rabbinic conception of the Noahic laws back into early Christian literature written before A.D. 100.[137] Moreover, this suggestion is valid only if we follow the Western text of the apostolic decree. Since the Western text omits "what is strangled," the three remaining prohibitions of idolatry, immorality and blood (interpreted by David Flusser as shedding blood) may be compared with the three cardinal sins that a Jew may not commit at all costs (according to the decision of an assembly in Lydda dated to around A.D. 120): idolatry, immorality and shedding blood.[138] However, since the priority of the Western text for the apostolic decree is rather unlikely,[139] many scholars interpret the stipulations of Acts 15:20 in terms of a reference to the stipulations for the "aliens" (גרים) in Lev 17—18[140]—that is, as a (cultic-ritual) compromise formula that sought to facilitate the communal living together of Jewish Christians and Gentile Christians,[141] or as a minimal requirement that was binding for Jews even at the risk of their own life.[142] Richard Bauckham argues that the pragmatic desire to facilitate table fellowship between Jewish and Gentile Christians cannot fully explain the selection of the four stipulations in Acts 15:20, as, for example, stipulations for the *gēr* such as the sabbath commandment (Ex 20:10; Deut 5:14) are missing. He suggests that the term בתוך (*betôk*), which links Jer 12:16 and Zech 2:11 (via the quotation Amos 9:11-12) with Lev 17—18 explains the selection.[143]

The rabbinic texts reveal that proselytes did not have the same status in all matters compared with "natural" Jews. According to *m. Qidd.* 4.1, members of priestly families were prohibited from marrying proselytes or their daugh-

---

[132]*Jub.* 7:20-21; 20:5-6; 23:14.

[133]Strecker 1960, 1501 ("erweitertes Urrecht der Menschheit")

[134]Thus Lohse 1960, 972.

[135]Strecker 1960, 1501.

[136]Thus Flusser 1994, 583; Flusser and Safrai 1986, 173-92; and many others.

[137]M. Goodman 1994, 53.

[138]Cf. *Sipre Deut.* 41:85; *b. Qidd.* 40b; *b. Sanh.* 74a; *y. Sanh.* 3:21b; 4:35a.

[139]See the discussions in W. Strange 1992, 87-105; Head 1993, 438-42; Bauckham 1995b, 459.

[140]See Heiligenthal 1994, 585-87; Dunn, *Acts,* 204; Bauckham 1995b, 459-60.

[141]See Dunn, *Acts,* 202, 206-7; N. Taylor 1992, 140-42.

[142]See Nägele 1995, 105-7.

[143]Bauckham 1995b, 460-61; on the apostolic decree see more extensively §25.3 in the present work.

ters.[144] An anonymous mishnah stipulates that proselytes were not allowed to utter certain confessional formulae; for example, instead of mentioning "God of our fathers" in prayers, they were to say, "God of the fathers of Israel," and in the synagogue service, "God of your fathers" (*m. Bik.* 1.4). Some rabbis believed that no proselytes would be admitted to the people of God in the last days (*b. Yebam.* 24b; *b. 'Abod. Zar.* 3b).[145]

b. Yebam. 24b: "Our rabbis have taught on Tannaite authority: Converts will not be accepted in the days of Messiah, just as they did not accept proselytes either in the time of David or in the time of Solomon. Said R. Eleazar, What verse of Scripture supports that claim? 'Behold, he shall be a convert who is converted for my own sake; he who lives with you shall be settled among you' (Is 54:14)—only he who lives with you in your misery will be settled among you, and no other." (Neusner, *Talmud*)

b. 'Abod. Zar. 3b: "Said R. Isaac, 'Laughter before the Holy One, blessed be He, takes place only on that day alone.' *There are those who repeat as a Tannaite version this statement of R. Isaac in respect to that which has been taught on Tannaite authority:* R. Yosé says, 'In the coming age gentiles will come and convert.' *But will they be accepted? Has it not been taught on Tannaite authority:* Converts will not be accepted in the days of the Messiah, just as they did not accept proselytes either in the time of David or in the time of Solomon? Rather, 'they will make themselves converts, and they will put on phylacteries on their heads and arms and fringes on their garments and a mezuzah on their doors.'" (Neusner, *Talmud*)

Rabbinic interpretations of Is 49:6 assert that the Jews have been given the task of promoting a world that is free from idolatry.[146] Several statements in the halakic midrashim probably should be interpreted in this context when they assert that the Torah was offered to all nations at Mount Sinai. In *Sipre Deut.* 343 we read that the Torah was also revealed in the "language of Rome." A classical passage is found in the *Mekilta de Rabbi Yishmael*, a text compiled in the third century A.D.:

Mek. R. Yishm. Baḥodesch 1 on Ex 19:2:[147] "The Torah was given in public, openly in a free place. For had the Torah been given in the land of Israel, the Israelites could have said to the nations of the world: You have no share in it. But now that it was given in the

---

[144]See also *m. Bik.* 1:4; *b. Qidd.* 70b; *'Abod. R. Nat.* A 12; *t. Qidd.* 5:4 [Zuckermandel, *Tosefta,* 342]; *y. Qidd.* 64d; for more references see Feldman 1993a, 338-41; cf. Kraus 1996, 67; for the observations that follow above see Herweg and Herweg 2001, 49.

[145]There are no exact parallels in rabbinic literature for the exclusion of proselytes from the eschatological temple, as is found in 11QTemple and in 4QFlor. See Gerald Blidstein, "4Q Florilegium and Rabbinic Sources on Bastard and Proselyte," *RevQ* 8 (1972-1975): 401-36.

[146]See Pawlikowski 1988, 387.

[147]Translation from Lauterbach, *Mekilta,* 2:198; cf. Horovitz and Rabin, *Mechilta,* 205; Neusner, *Mekhilta,* 2:44; Lichtenberger 1990, 200; E. P. Sanders 1985, 83. See also *Mek. R. Yishm. Baḥodesch* 5 on Ex 20:2 (Horovitz and Rabin, *Mechilta,* 221); *Sipre Deut.* 343 (Finkelstein, *Sifre on Deuteronomy,* 396).

wilderness publicly and openly in a place that is free for all, everyone wishing to accept
it could come and accept it."

This interpretation argues from the fact that God revealed the Torah in the desert
and not in the land of Israel that the Torah is not the possession of Israel alone
but had all nations in view.[148] A similar statement is found in *Sipre Num*. 119, a
commentary on Num 18:20, following an interpretation by Rabbi Yishmael:

Sipre Num. 119: "There are three crowns: the crown of the Torah, the crown of priesthood, and the crown of royalty. Aaron was worthy of the crown of priesthood and took
it. David was worthy of the crown of royalty and took it. As to the crown of the Torah,
lo, it still lies undisposed of, in order that those who come into the world should not have
any occasion to grumble, and say: 'If the crown of priesthood and the crown of royalty
were still available, I might be worthy of them, and take them!' Lo, here is the crown of
the Torah for all those who come into the world! For whosoever is worthy of it, I (God)
consider it, as though all three are still available and he is not worthy of any of them!"
(Levertoff, *Sifre on Numbers;* cf. Str-B 3:116).

In *Mek. R. Yishm.* Amaleq/Yitro 2 (on Ex 18:27) Rabbi Nathan argues that the
covenant that was made with Yehonadab ben Rechab—that is, with the Rechabites, the descendants of Jethro—"was greater than the one made with
David" because the covenant with Yehonadab ben Rechab "was made without
any condition" (cf. Jer 35:19a).[149] Marc Hirshman concludes from these passages that at least the school of Rabbi Yishmael attempted in the second century A.D. to define the Jewish faith "universalistically," allowing non-Jews to
join. He argues that this universalism was not messianic or eschatological but
based on a "historical" perspective that probably reflected a "missionary" position.[150] This conclusion is hypothetical: these texts do not refer to an active
endeavor to convert pagans to the Jewish faith. The attempt "to define Judaism
as available to the non-Jew"[151] is not identical with an active missionary activity. The question is not whether non-Jews can join Israel, but whether Jews
believe that they have been given the assignment to prompt non-Jews,
through active propaganda for their faith and for the way of life, to join the
Jewish commonwealth. Friedrich Avemarie points out that in such texts Edom
(or Rome) is always only one among many nations that have rejected the Torah from the start all together.[152]

The noncanonical tractates that did not find their way into the Mishnah or

---

[148]See Hirshman 2000, 103. Philo interprets the location of the revelation of the Torah differ-
    ently: with reference to the negative effects of life in the city (*Decal.* 1.4-7); see Rajak 1996,
    305.
[149]See E. P. Sanders 1977, 94-95; Avemarie 1996, 166, 177-78; Hirshman 2000, 110-11.
[150]Hirshman 2000, 111-15.
[151]Hirshman 2000, 112.
[152]Avemarie 1994, 201 n. 153.

the Talmud[153] include in the thematic collection of the "seven minor tractates" the writing ("Proselytes").[154] This tractate discusses details of the conversion to Judaism, including immersion ("proselyte baptism") and the obligations of the new convert and the legal consequences of conversion. It never speaks of an active propaganda of Jews seeking to lead pagans to join the Jewish faith and community.

Conclusions

Jews faithful to the Torah may have regarded the expulsion of pagans from Palestinian cities by military force (1 Macc 13:47-48; 14:36; 2 Macc 10:17) and the forced conversion of Idumeans and Itureans as a necessity prompted by a crisis situation and thus not as normally the rule.[155] But the physical removal of pagans was clearly *one* possibility for abolishing pagan idol worship. Such a program is, of course, the opposite of "missionary work." Jewish texts generally emphasize that Jews should be careful when they have contacts with Gentiles.[156] Several texts expect that the Gentiles will be purged from Jerusalem,[157] even that proselytes be excluded from the eschatological temple,[158] and that the nations will be subject to Israel in the eschaton.[159] In regard to the "positive" statements or expectations concerning the Gentiles, the evidence can be summarized as follows:

1. Several texts show that the admission of Gentiles into the people of God was possible only by circumcision (for the males).[160] Other passages show that Jews were friendly to Gentiles and that some Gentiles participated in Jewish religious activities.[161] The Gentiles were regarded as unclean and therefore were

---

[153]Since the Romm-Wilna edition of the Babylonian Talmud (1886) they are printed at the end of the division *Neziqin*. On the noncanonical tractates see Strack and Stemberger 1982, 215-21; M. B. Lerner, "The External Tractates," in S. Safrai 1987, 367-403. The fact that some of the smaller tractates, including *Gerim,* are mentioned in early midrashim (*Lev. Rab.* 22:1; *Ruth Rab.* 2:22), the classical mishnaic Hebrew, and the fact that the rabbis that are quoted are all Tannaim suggest that they were written during the Tannaitic period. M. B. Lerner (ibid., 401) classifies them as baraita or "extraneous Mishna"—that is, mishnah outside of the Mishnah.

[154]See M. Higger, ed., *Seven Minor Treatises: Sefer Torah, Mazuzah, Tefillin, Zizit, 'Abadim, Kutim, Gerim, and Treatise Soferim II* (New York: Bloch, 1930); for a German translation see Polster, "Der kleine Talmudtraktat über die Proselyten," *Anggelos* 2 (1926): 1-38.

[155]Feldman (1993a, 324-26) accepts the reports of forced conversions of Idumeans and Itureans under Hasmonean rule as historically reliable.

[156]Sir 8:18; 9:3; 11:32; *Jub.* 22:20-22; CD XI, 14-15; XII, 8-11; 4Q394 3 I, 4-16 + 4; *m. 'Abod. Zar.* 2:1-2.

[157]*Pss. Sol.* 17:22-26, 28-29.

[158]4QFlor I, 4; cf. *t. Sanh.* 13:2.

[159]*Pss. Sol.* 17:30-31; 4QDibHam[a] 1-2 IV, 8-13 [?]; 4Q246 II, 4—III, 1; 1QM XII, 12-16; XIV, 5-7; XIX, 3-7; 4Q381 76-77, 14-16; cf. 11QPs[a] XXII, 10-12; *2 Bar.* 72:2-6.

[160]*Jub.* 15:24.

[161]Josephus, *A.J.* 7.330; 13.85; 16.43-44; cf. Philo, *Flacc.* 94; *Virt.* 105-108.

denied access to the temple proper (i.e., the inner court). But the priests accepted their thanksgiving offerings; however, the Gentiles were not allowed to participate in the eating of the sacrificial meat.[162]

2. Some texts reflect the Old Testament tradition of the arrival of the nations on Mount Zion in the last days.[163] Some authors assume that, analogous to Old Testament passages,[164] in the future the nations will worship Yahweh.[165] In *T. Levi* 18:9-14 we find the expectation that the nations will acknowledge Israel's God in the days of the Messiah.

3. Some texts expect a participation of the nations in the salvation of the eschaton.[166] Ben Sira does not mention this expectation, even though he refers to the nations in the context of God's promise of salvation to Abraham. In rabbinic Judaism the participation of the Gentiles in the world to come is linked, in some texts, to their obedience to the Noahic laws.[167]

4. The only Jewish Palestinian text that clearly speaks of an equal status of Israel and the pagan nations is eschatological: *1 En.* 90:33-38 anticipates a messianic figure who will abolish the difference between Israel and the nations, between Jews and Gentiles. Perhaps *T. Jud.* 24:5-6; 25:3-5 imply the assimilation in status of the nations and the people of God in the coming era of salvation as well. In *T. Benj.* 9:2; 10:9-11 is expected, perhaps, for the future the abolition of the ritual boundary between Israel and the nations and the integration of Gentiles into the people of God.

6.2 Diaspora Judaism Between Demarcation and Openness

It is estimated that the small, preexilic Jewish population of perhaps 150,000 grew to around 8 million in the first century A.D. Of these, only 700,000 to 2.5 million lived in Palestine. This means that between 2 million and 7 million Jews lived outside Palestine in the Diaspora.[168]

Salo Baron suggested in his social history of Judaism that the number of inhabitants in Palestine had grown considerably since the eighth and seventh centuries B.C. (Jerusalem

---

[162]Schürer (2:309-13) refers to the following texts: *m. Šeqal.* 1:5; 7:6; *m. Zebaḥ.* 4:5; *m. Menaḥ* 5:3-6; 6:1; 9:8; Josephus, *B.J.* 2.408-421; *A.J.* 11.329-330; 13.242-243; 15.422; 16.14; 18.122; *C. Ap.* 2.48; Philo, *Legat.* 45 (356); *Sib. Or.* 3:576, 626. See also S. Safrai 1981, 105-11, 287; D. Schwartz 1992b; Deines 1994, 72-73 n. 36.

[163]*T. Naph.* 8:3-4; cf. 1QM XII, 13; XIX, 6.

[164]Zech 2:11; Is 19:16-25; 25:6-8; 56:3-8; 66:18-24; Ps 25:12-15; 47:9; 87:4-6.

[165]Tob 14:6-7; *1 En.* 10:20-21; 90:30; *T. Benj.* 9:2; *T. Naph.* 8:3; 1QM XII, 13-15; 1QH VI, 12; 11QPsᵃ XXIV, 8-9.

[166]Tob 14:6-7; *1 En.* 10:21; 48:4-5; 51:1-5; 90:33-36; 105:1; *4 Ezra* 3:36; *Pss. Sol.* 17:30-31; *T. Levi* 18:9; *T. Jud.* 24:6; 25:3-5; *T. Benj.* 9:2; 10:9-10; *T. Ash.* 7:2-3.

[167]*t. Sanh.* 13:2; *b. Sanh.* 105a.

[168]Feldman 1993a, 293. L. Levine (2001, 501) reckons 3-5 million Diaspora Jews. Other scholars assume only 4-5 million Jews worldwide in the first century A.D.; see Lohse 1960, 111. Hengel and Deines (1995, 33 n. 85) estimate that 800,000 Jews lived in Palestine.

was destroyed in 586 B.C.), when Judah had at least 250,000 inhabitants,[169] to roughly 2.5 million people, including 500,000 Samaritans, Greeks and Nabateans. He argued that if we add the 4 million Jews who lived in the Roman Empire outside Palestine and the at least 1 million Jews in Babylonia, the total number of Jews in the first century was around 8 million.[170] Baron relied on the account of Bar-Hebraeus, a Jewish-Christian author from Syria in the thirteenth century, who mentions, in connection with the Jewish census of Emperor Claudius, the number 6,944,000.[171] Magen Broshi, an expert on the question of the demography of the Jewish population in antiquity, is convinced, however, that there were never more than 1 million people living in Palestine at any time.[172] Recent demographic studies show that the population numbers given by Josephus are inflated: the decimal point of his figures should be moved one position to the left.[173]

Strabo of Emesa writes in the first century B.C., "The habitable world was filled with Jews. . . . This people has already made its way into every city, and it is not easy to find any place in the habitable world which has not received this nation and in which it has not made its power felt" (*Historica Hypomnemata*, in Josephus, *A.J.* 14.114-118). And Philo of Alexandria writes (after A.D. 41), "For so populous are the Jews that no one country can hold them,[46] and therefore they settle in very many of the most prosperous countries in Europe and Asia both in the islands and on the mainland, and while they hold the Holy City where stands the sacred Temple of the most high God to be their mother city [*metropolis*], yet those which are theirs by inheritance from their fathers, grandfathers, and ancestors even farther back, are in each case accounted by them to be their fatherland in which they were born and reared, while to some of them they have come at the time of their foundation as immigrants to the satisfaction of the founders" (*Flacc.* 45-46). Philo mentions a letter by King Agrippa I written to Caligula: "As for the holy city [Jerusalem], I must say what befits me to say. While she, as I have said, is my native city, she is also the mother city [*metropolis*] not of the one country, Judaea, but of most of the others in virtue of the colonies sent out at divers times to the neighboring lands—Egypt, Phoenicia, the part of Syria called the Hollow [Coele Syria] and the rest as well and the lands lying far apart, Pamphylia, Cilicia, most of Asia up to Bithynia and the corners of Pontus, similarly also into Europe, Thessaly, Boeotia, Macedonia, Aetolia, Attica, Argus, Corinth and most of the best parts of Peloponnese. And not only are the mainlands full of Jewish colonies, but also the most highly esteemed of the islands—Euboea, Cyprus, Crete. I say nothing of the countries beyond the Euphrates, for except for a small part they all, Babylon and of the other satrapies those where the land within their confines is highly fertile, have Jewish inhabitants." (*Legat.* 281-282).

Since Salo Baron's study the large number of Jews is regarded as indication of the quantitative successes of the missionary activity of Jews among Gentiles. For example, Ferdinand Dexinger comments on statistics concerning Jews in the first century, "Due to the nearly complete lack of useful sources, these figures are uncertain, but they must be explained at any rate by the addition of proselytes"; and Louis Feldman states that "the most likely explanation of this increase is prose-

---

[169]See John Bright, *A History of Israel* (3rd ed.; Philadelphia: Westminster, 1981), 344.
[170]Baron 1952, 1:168-70 with n. 7 (see ibid., 1:370-72).
[171]Juster (1914, 209-12) referred to Bar-Hebraeus as well; see Rabello 1980, 690.
[172]Broshi 1980, 1-10.
[173]See J. Strange 1997, 47.

lytism."[174] Fergus Millar believes that Jewish missionaries had considerable success. He is convinced that the dissemination of Judaism in the Roman Empire can hardly be explained solely by biological increases.[175] However, demographic statistics as such, which always are estimates, can hardly serve as proof of the existence or the effectiveness of a Jewish missionary activity among Gentiles. If the figures of Salo Baron are correct, that there were approximately 8 million Jews in the first century, then we have a doubling of the Jewish population every one hundred years since about 600 B.C., which is not impossible given the conditions of antiquity.[176] Walter Ameling explains the growth of the Jewish population with the Jews' rejection of birth control, abortion and the exposure of infants, leading to continuous "demographic pressure" for which "emigration was the most obvious solution."[177]

Proselytes

Some non-Jews (pagans, polytheists) turned to the Jewish faith and were circumcised, thus becoming "proselytes."[178] This is undisputed. However, it is not possible "even to guess"[179] the numerical percentage of proselytes in the Jewish communities in the Diaspora. Several Jewish ossuaries were found in the necropolis Dominus Flevit in Jerusalem with inscriptions that mention proselytes—for example, "Shalom [or Salome] the proselyte" (CIJ I 1), "Judah the proselyte of Tyre" (CIJ I 4), "prosēlytos [προσήλυτος] Diogenes son of Zenon," the latter being an inscription dating to the late first or early second century A.D.[180] These clearly were pagans who had converted to Judaism, not members of the Jewish-Christian church, as some scholars had surmised.[181] The Talmud mentions proselytes repeatedly.[182] A classic passage is the statement of Josephus, who was proud that many Greeks had adopted Jewish customs (C. Ap. 2.282-284).

C. Ap. 2.282-284: "The masses have long since shown a keen desire to adopt our religious observances; and there is not one city, Greek or barbarian, nor a single nation, to which

---

[174]Dexinger 1988, 343; Feldman 1986, 59; cf. idem 1993a, 293, where Feldman acknowledges, however, that "aggressive proselytism is only one possible explanation for the numerous conversions."

[175]Millar, in Schürer 3:171; see also Urbach 1981, 273-74; 1975, 541-54.

[176]See the review of Feldman 1993a by Joseph Sievers, Bib 76 (1995): 280.

[177]Ameling 1996, 33, with reference to Tacitus, Hist. 5.5. Wander (1998, 139-40) is skeptical with regard to the argument of demographic development.

[178]The inscriptions were collected by Figueras 1990; see also Levinskaya 1996, 19-33.

[179]Delling 1987, 83.

[180]Guarducci 4:441-44 (fig. 131); cf. NewDocs 6:1 (no. 136a). The lower part of the text displays the letter P superimposed on the letter X, which means that Diogenes may have been a proselyte who had become a Christian; this is not entirely clear, however.

[181]See Guarducci 4:440-44; see the critique in Paul Figueras, Decorated Jewish Ossuaries (Documenta et monumenta Orientis antiqui 20; Leiden: Brill, 1983), 82-86.

[182]For references see Bamberger 1939, 111; McKnight 1991, 32.

our custom of abstaining from work on the seventh day has not spread, and where the fasts and the lighting of lamps and many of our prohibitions in the matter of food are not observed. [283]Moreover, they attempt to imitate our unanimity, our liberal charities, our devoted labor in the crafts, our endurance under persecution on behalf of our laws. [284]The greatest miracle of all is that our Law holds out no seductive bait of sensual pleasure, but has exercised this indulgence through its own inherent merits; and, as God permeates the universe, so the Law has found its way among all mankind. Let each man reflect for himself on his own country and his own household, and he will not disbelieve what I say."

There is evidence that pagan women in particular found the Jewish faith attractive. Josephus claims that almost the entire female population of Damascus was devoted to the Jewish faith; this fact prevented the pagan inhabitants of Damascus from taking action against the Jews with death penalties: "Their only fear was of their own wives who, with few exceptions, had all become converts to the Jewish religion" (*B.J.* 2.560). Since this comment does not appear in an apologetic context but in an "unsuspicious historical narrative," many scholars regard this information as generally credible.[183]

Traditionally scholars assumed that Diaspora Jews, notably, were engaged in an energetic campaign to win proselytes. The Jewish missionary activity, it is believed, evidently was not directed by a central organization or institution but was the result of the personal initiative of individual Jews, but also profited from the potent attractiveness of the synagogues.[184]

David Bosch differentiated in an early study between "propaganda" and "missionary activity," which, at least today, seems polemical. He writes, "It is an accepted fact in contemporary research that the Jews were engaged in vigorous propaganda in the time of Jesus. Indeed: propaganda and not missionary work. However indefatigable the Jews may have been in their advertising attempts, and whatever zeal they may have displayed in the literary propaganda, the fact remains that this literature is not much more than 'speeches on religion to its cultured despisers' and that the Jews were more interested in the glory and dignity of the Jewish name than in the selfless devotion to serving Yahweh. . . . [Their activity] was propaganda and not missionary work because it lacked the awareness of being sent and because it grew out of zeal for Yahweh and his cause rather than out of obedience to him. Here, 'mission' is never a task but an incidental attribute. As their activity was not born of obedience to God, it is the master of something that really belongs to God."[185]

In view of the recurring hostility against Jews, it surely is striking that any Gentile wanted to join the Jewish community. At least four factors are regarded as being responsible for such decisions of individual Gentiles to convert to Judaism.[186] (1) The Jewish propaganda managed to accommodate the religious needs of Greeks

[183]Wander 1998, 146. S. Cohen (1987, 417) interprets the women as "adherents."
[184]For example, Lohse 1960, 971.
[185]Bosch 1959, 31-32, 40-41, with reference to Friedrich Schleiermacher's speeches *On Religion,* published in 1789 in Berlin (initially anonymously).
[186]See Schürer 3:151; Solin 1983, 599-600.

and Romans through an acceptable interpretation of the Torah. Unusual or potentially repulsive statements or events in Scripture were pushed into the background
as something insignificant or reinterpreted allegorically. The unity and uniqueness
of Israel's God was particularly attractive: Jews did not worship a multitude of
gods, each of them limited to a personal sphere, but the one Lord and Creator of
the cosmos, who is almighty and just and repays each person according to his or
her moral behavior. (2) The practical orientation of the Jewish faith was attractive,
focusing consistently on behavior in everyday life. The economic solidarity of the
Jewish community was attractive as well. (3) Greeks and Romans were open to
new ideas, which facilitated the rise of new ways of worship and faith that originated in the East. (4) The civic privileges of the Jews (in the East) that the Seleucids
and the Romans had granted "prompted a large number of non-Jewish orientals
and half-Greeks in many cities to join this privileged category of non-citizens."[187]

Louis Feldman lists thirty-one factors that contributed to the attractiveness of Judaism for
non-Jews in the third century:[188] the influence of Jewish Christians, the Hellenization of the
Jews (e.g., in their adoption of the Greek language), the Jews' loyalty to the state, their
regard for law and order, opportunistic political attempts to court the favor of influential
Jewish communities, the synagogues as shelters against persecution, the antiquity of Judaism, the reputation of Jews for ethical behavior, their reputation for incorruptible judges,
admiration for the Jews' philanthropy and lack of materialism, mutual protection and self-
help, close social contacts, the lending of money by Jews, economic advantages for non-
Jewish businessmen, commercial reasons, religious factors, political-religious expectations
linked with Jerusalem and the temple, opportunity for relaxation as a result of the observance of the sabbath, performing certain tasks on the sabbath that were prohibited to Jews,
the celebration of Jewish festivals, the reading of sacred Scriptures in the synagogues, ancient oaths taken before Torah scrolls, the relics of Jewish martyrs, the theatricality of synagogue services, the Mishnah as exposition of the Bible, the ritual baths, admiration for
Jewish astronomers, the Jews' reputed skill in astrology, the reputation for magic and the
occult, the role of some Jews in alchemy, and the Jewish skill in effecting cures.

The conversion of Gentiles to Judaism always had political implications, as the
Jewish nation and the Jewish faith were intimately linked.[189] Philo defines in
Spec. 1.52 the term προσήλυτος (*prosēlytos*), on the basis of Gen 12:1-2, as the
non-Jew who abandons homeland, friendships, relatives and ancestral customs
and submits to the Jewish constitution. Philo goes on to say,

Spec. 1.51: "All of like sort to him, all who spurn idle fables and embrace truth in its purity,
whether they have been such from the first or through conversion to the better side have
reached that higher state, obtain His approval, the former because they were not false to

---

[187]See Norris 1978, 101; also Solin 1983, 599 with n. 7. For evidence, scholars point to Josephus,
   B.J. 7.43-45; *A.J.* 19.287-291.
[188]Feldman 1993a, 369-82; cf. idem 1989, 282-97.
[189]Cf. Solin 1983, 616: "It was the nexus of nation and religion, unique in antiquity, that gave
   Judaism in the dispersion its extraordinary stability."

the nobility of their birth, the latter because their judgment led them to make the passage to piety. These last he called 'proselytes,' or newly-joined, because they have joined the new and godly commonwealth (καινῇ καὶ φιλοθέῳ πολιτείᾳ)."[190]

As a result of conversion to Jewish monotheism, Gentiles become members of the Jewish ethnos.[191]

Christian Noack disputes this, referring to Philo (*Virt.* 219), who does not refer specifically to the Jewish people: "It is not ethnic affiliation with the unique Jewish people that possesses theological dignity, but participation in God's universal commonwealth."[192] However, Philo refers in *Spec.* 1.51 to historical possibilities and realities; he does not make a merely philosophical or hermeneutical observation.

It was this connection between faith and people or nation that guaranteed the immense strength of the Jewish Diaspora. At the same time this connection prevented, with few exceptions, "really extensive missionary success, although in the more open, Greek-speaking Diaspora attempts were made to rob this element of its force."[193] A Gentile who opted to become a Jew made not only a religious but also a political decision.[194]

Thus there is a grain of truth in Tacitus's comment, despite its polemical one-sidedness, that Jewish proselytes quickly learn how to despise the gods, to disown their homeland and to despise their parents.[195] The full proselyte was "in every respect an Israelite" (*b. Yebam.* 47b).[196] It was but consistent when the emperor imposed the *fiscus Iudaicus* after A.D. 70 upon all circumcised Jews, including the proselytes. Martin Hengel comments, "Intrinsically a punitive tax for the rebellious 'ethnos' of the Jews (see Suetonius, *Domitian* 12.2: *posita genti tributa*), it also affected the Jews as a 'religious association.'. . . The two could not be separated."[197]

The conversion of the Ammonite leader Achior, narrated in the book of Judith,[198] is an example of the close connection between faith and national affili-

---

[190]See Noack 2000, 102; also K. Kuhn 1959, 732.

[191]Hengel 1969, 560 (ET, 1:307); Birnbaum 1993, 65.

[192]Noack 2000, 102 with n. 310.

[193]Hengel 1969, 560 (ET, 1:307).

[194]This remains true today. Israel's supreme court decided in December 1989 that a "messianic Jew," meaning a Jew who believes that Jesus of Nazareth is the Messiah, does not automatically have the right to naturalization, as provided in Israel's constitution for Jews who live abroad.

[195]Tacitus, *Hist.* 5.5: "Contemnere deos, exuere patriam, parentes liberos fratres vilia habere."

[196]S. Cohen (1990) dates the ceremony of conversion (*b. Yebam.* 47a-b; *Gerim* 1:1) to the second century A.D.; cf. idem 1989, 26-30.

[197]Hengel 1969, 561 n. 282 (ET, 2:204 n. 303). On Suetonius, *Dom.* 12.2 (*GLAJJ* II 320) see M. Goodman 1989b.

[198]The book of Judith, a novel, was written between 150 and 76 B.C.; see Eissfeldt 1964, 795-96; Zenger, *JSHRZ* 1.6:431; Moore, *Jdt*, 50-52, 70; deSilva 2002, 91-92; Nickelsburg (1984, esp. 50-51) reckons with a Hebrew *Grundschrift* written in the Persian period and revised under Hasmonean rule.

ation. Achior had provided a faithful summary of Israel's history, including the argument that the Jews are invincible as long as they are faithful to the law of God, before Holofernes, Nebuchadnezzar's general (Jdt 5:5-19). Expelled by the Assyrians, he experienced persecution and hatred (as elements of conversion?) from his surroundings, and he received sympathy from the "sons of Israel" (Jdt 6:10-16) and was invited by Uzziah to stay in his house (Jdt 6:21; 14:6). When Achior heard of Judith's act of liberation and saw the head of Holofernes (Jdt 14:6-8), he came to faith in Israel's God and was circumcised (Jdt 14:10).

Jdt 14:10:[199] "And when Achior saw all that the God of Israel had done, he believed firmly in God [ἐπίστευσεν τῷ θεῷ σφόδρα], and was circumcised [περιετέμετο τὴν σάρκα τῆς ἀκροβυστίας αὐτοῦ], and joined the house of Israel [προσετέθη εἰς τὸν οἶκον Ἰσραηλ], remaining so to this day."

This account is the first extant reference to the manner in which a Gentile was admitted to the people of God, emphasizing faith in Yahweh and circumcision.[200] The "contradiction" to the stipulation of Deut 23:4, according to which Ammonites and Moabites were not to be admitted into the congregation of Israel, evidently was not regarded as a problem. This indicates that passages such as Is 19:24-25; 25:6-8; Zech 2:11; Mal 1:11; Zeph 2:11 provided the theological justification for the account in Jdt 14:10.[201] However, this text does not allow inferences for an active "Gentile mission" of Jews. Achior finds faith in the God of Israel by his own initiative. Even circumcision is not suggested by one of the "sons of Israel" (Jdt 6:10) as something he could or should do. It is doubtful, therefore, that the phrase "he believed in God" (ἐπίστευσεν τῷ θεῷ), used in connection with Achior's circumcision and acceptance into the house of Israel, should be regarded as a "technical term."[202]

The demographic analyses of Heikki Solin show that the number of proselytes in Rome (as in the other Hellenistic cities) probably was not very high. Of the approximately five hundred Roman inscriptions, only six clearly refer to proselytes.[203]

Heikki Solin points to several reasons for the small number of people willing to become Jews: (1) the close connection between nation and religion; (2) aversion to circumcision; (3) the hostility of many contemporaries toward Jews; (4) the exclusivity of the Jews;

---

[199]Translation follows the RSV.

[200]McEleney (1974) and Gilbert (1991) dispute the necessity of circumcision for being accepted as a proselyte. For a discussion of the process of conversion and associated rites such as circumcision, immersion ("proselyte baptism") and sacrifices see Schiffman 1985; also Nolland 1981; Delville 1995; S. Cohen 1989, 26-31; 1990; McKnight 1991, 78-89; S. Stern 1994, 88-95. The most extensive rabbinic discussion is found in b. Yebam. 47a-b and Gerim; see S. Cohen 1990.

[201]See Zenger, JSHRZ 1.6:512 n. 10a.

[202]Thus Brandenburger 1988, 181-82. On the conversion of Achior see further Priotto 1990, 46-54.

[203]Solin 1983.

(5) the exclusion from privileges granted to the Jews but not granted, in the case of Rome, to non-Jews who had converted to Judaism: if the converts refused to participate in the public cult, they would be punished in accordance with the law; (6) the *didrachmon* tax introduced by Vespasian, forcing proselytes to make economic sacrifices; (7) the prohibition of circumcision by Hadrian, still enforced by Antonius Pius for non-Jews.

Proselytes could be found not only in the Diaspora but also in Palestine. A rabbinic discussion indicates that descendants of proselytes were members of the Sanhedrin: the tradition of Jethro, who "merited that his descendants should sit in the Chamber of Hewn Stone."[204] These descendants are the Kenites and the Rechabites. According to *b. Sanh.* 41a, "the Chamber of Hewn Stone" was a room in the temple precinct that was used by the Sanhedrin until forty years before the destruction of the temple. This rabbinic tradition possibly reflects the attempts of members of the Sanhedrin who were the descendants of proselytes to justify their status (evidently before A.D. 30). They claimed to be descendants of Jethro, who provided for Moses in the desert, who taught him the law (Ex 18) and thus received the right to sit in the Chamber of Hewn Stone.

Whereas the Temple Scroll of the Essenes excluded proselytes from visiting the temple (11QT XL, 6), rabbinic literature does not discuss such halakic restrictions. The Latin and Greek inscriptions on the stone barrier surrounding the temple building proper prohibited, under penalty of death, non-Jews from access to the inner forecourt, but they did not apply to proselytes. The text of the warning inscriptions, extant in two exemplars discovered in 1871 and 1935, reads,

"No one of another nation may enter [μηθενὰ ἀλλογενῆ εἰς πορεύεσθαι] within the fence and enclosure round the temple [τὸ ἱερόν]! Whoever is caught shall have himself to blame that his death ensues [τὸ ἐξακολουθεῖν θάνατον]!"[205]

God-fearers

In Caesarea, Peter met Cornelius, "a devout man who feared God with all his household."[206] Paul preached in the synagogue of Antiocheia in Pisidia before "Israelites" and "those who fear God"; the latter are also called "devout proselytes" or "those who are devout."[207] In Philippi, Paul met a certain Lydia of

---

[204]*b. Soṭah* 11a; *b. Sanh.* 106a; *Exod. Rab.* 1.15-16; *Pesiq. Rab Kah.* Piska 3d; cf. Knights 1990.

[205]Translation from Fitzmyer, *Acts,* 698 (on Acts 21:28). See C. Clermont-Ganneau, "Une Stèle du Temple de Jérusalem," *Revue archéologique* 23 (1872): 213-34, 290-96, pl. X after p. 280; J. H. Iliffe, "The ΘΑΝΑΤΟΣ Inscription from Herod's Temple," *QDAP* 6 (1938): 1-3; for the Greek text see *OGIS* II 598; *SEG* VIII 169; *CIJ* II 1400; *CIJ* II 329 (photograph); Schürer 2:285 n. 57; German translation in Schwier 1989, 57. Cf. J. Baumgarten 1982; *GBL* 3:1540; *IBD* 3:1529 (photograph).

[206]Acts 10:2: εὐσεβὴς καὶ φοβούμενος τὸν θεόν.

[207]Acts 13:16: οἱ φοβούμενοι τὸν θεόν; Acts 13:43: τῶν σεβομένων προσηλύτων; Acts 13:50: τὰς σεβομένας γυναῖκας.

Thyatira, a "God-fearer"; in Thessalonike he met "devout Greeks"; in Beroea the "Greek women and men of high standing" also seem to have been "God-fearers," and in the synagogue of Athens he meets "devout persons."[208] These "God-fearers" that Luke mentions in the book of Acts,[209] as do Josephus and Juvenal,[210] are usually identified with the "God-fearers" (θεοσεβεῖς, *theosebeis*) known from about a dozen inscriptions from Aphrodisias, Rhodos, Cos, Prusa, Miletus, Pantikapaion, Tralleis, Philadelphia (Lydia), Phaina (Syria) and Lorium (Latium).[211]

Scholars usually agree that the term "God-fearers" (θεοσεβεῖς, *theosebeis;* σεβόμενοι τὸν θεόν, *sebomenoi ton theon;* φοβούμενοι τὸν θεόν, *phoboumenoi ton theon;* Latin *metuens*) should be regarded as a technical term for a fourth group between Gentiles, Jews and proselytes. They are Gentiles who were attracted by the Jewish faith and who visited the synagogue services but did not follow all stipulations of the Torah nor were (yet) circumcised. Besides the Gentiles who converted to Judaism through circumcision and full obedience to the Torah, some Gentiles in the synagogues became sympathetic to the Jewish faith but had not formally converted.

This interpretation was questioned by Louis Feldman (in an early article) and particularly by Thomas Kraabel.[212] According to Feldman, the Greek adjectives describe in a nontechnical sense the qualities of all Jews without distinction; it was only in the heyday of Jewish proselytism that a designation was needed for people who were not full proselytes. Thus the term "God-fearers" was used (e.g., by Josephus and by Luke) in the sense of "Gentiles sympathizing with Judaism." Kraabel questioned the existence of "God-fearers" entirely: the term does not occur in synagogue inscriptions of the Diaspora; it is an artificial device used by Luke in the book of Acts to show how the Christian faith became a Gentile (i.e., non-Jewish) religion without losing its roots in Israel's traditions. Feldman, who in the meantime had changed his opinion, argued against Kraabel that there is indeed indirect as well as literary and epigraphical evidence for the existence of Gentile sympathizers in the context of the synagogues.[213] Günter Wasserberg recently defended a mediating position: the term "God-fearer" is neither a technical term nor the designation of a group, and it is not a literary invention of Luke, but a "piety label" (*Frömmigkeitsprädikat*).[214] Wasserberg does not seem to know the inscription of Aphrodisias in which the "technical" meaning of the term is clearly present.

---

[208]Acts 16:14: σεβομένη τὸν θεόν; Acts 17:4: τῶν σεβομένων Ἑλλήνων; Acts 17:12: τῶν Ἑλληνίδων γυναικῶν τῶν εὐσχημόνων καὶ ἀνδρῶν; Acts 17:17: τοῖς σεβομένοις.

[209]Acts 10:2, 22, 35; 13:16, 26, 43, 50; 17:4, 17; 18:7.

[210]Josephus, *B.J.* 2.560; 7.45; *A.J.* 14.110; Juvenal, *Sat.* 14.96-106.

[211]Aphrodisias: *SEG* XXXVI 970 (*IJudO* II 14); Rhodos: *IG* XII 1 893 (*IJudO* II 8 n.72); Cos: see S. Mitchell 1998, 57 (*IJudO* II 6); Prusa: *I. Prusa* 115; Miletus: *SEG* IV 441 (*IJudO* II 37); Pantikapaion: *CIJ* I² 683a (*IJudO* I BS7); Tralleis: *CIG* 2924 (*IJudO* II 27); Philadelphia: *CIJ* 754 (*IJudO* II 49); Phaina: *CIJ* 500; Lorium: *I. EgJud* I 12.

[212]See Feldman 1950; A. T. Kraabel, "The Disappearance of the 'God-fearers,'" *Numen* 28 (1981): 113-26; idem 1982; MacLennan and Kraabel, 1986; see also Robert 1964, 41-45; Wilcox 1981, 102-122; Solin 1983, 618-21 with n. 49; Finn 1985.

[213]Feldman 1986; 1989, esp. 274-82; 1992, 389-93; 1993a, 370-81.

[214]Wasserberg 1998, 53, referring to Stegemann and Stegemann 1995, 223.

Most scholars today agree that there is sufficient evidence, outside of the book of Acts, for the existence of "God-fearers" as an identifiable group of Gentile sympathizers with Judaism.[215] Folker Siegert studied all relevant passages in rabbinic literature, Josephus and the New Testament and concluded that in the book of Acts the phrases σεβόμενοι [τὸν] θεόν (*sebomenoi [ton] theon*) and φοβούμενοι [τὸν] θεόν (*phoboumenoi [ton] theon*) clearly designate in several passages adherents to Judaism who were not proselytes, whom he distinguishes from more loosely connected sympathizers.[216] Bernd Wander has surveyed all relevant literary and epigraphical source material. He concludes that no fixed term for "God-fearers" existed and that the various terms are "partial designations of groups within a particular literary genre" presupposing certain criteria for the identification of the people. He identifies God-fearers as (1) Jews who are prominent in their obedience to the Torah; (2) uncircumcised Gentiles who have certain functions in the synagogue, such as assistance with the study of Torah or in prayer; (3) Gentiles who are honored because they participated in charitable activities. "Sympathizers" are "in the broadest sense people attracted by Judaism" and who demonstrate their sympathy in some way. Sometimes we encounter "interested persons," Gentiles who simply attend synagogue services. "Imitators" are Gentiles who adopt certain Jewish views and ways of behavior but have no social contact with Jewish communities. The boundaries between these groups are fluid, both in terms of terminology and identification. At any rate, however, the "God-fearers" in the book of Acts are not historical fiction but "a formidable historical entity on which he [Luke] reports authentically."[217]

A new suggestion has been made by Stephen Mitchell: the God-fearers (θε–οσεβεῖς, *theosebeis*) are people who worship "Most High God" (Θεὸς Ὕψιστος, *Theos Hypsistos*), a god whose similarities with the Jewish (or Christian) God inspired an impressive syncretism by Jews, Christians and the pagan worshipers of *Theos Hypsistos*.[218] This suggestion does not appear helpful as an analysis of clearly Jewish texts (including the book of Acts) that mention God-fearers: Jews (!) designate pagans as "god-fearing" surely because they worship the God of Israel.[219]

The following two inscriptions illustrate the possible connections between Gentile sympathizers to the Jewish faith and the local synagogue. In an inscrip-

---

[215]See Schürer 3:165-69; M. Simon, *RAC* 11:1061-64; Gager 1986; Hemer 1989, 444-47; McKnight 1991, 110-14; Trebilco 1991, 146-66; Hvalvik 1996, 249-67; Levinskaya 1996, 51-126; Hengel and Schwemer 1998, 101-32 (ET, 61-76); Collins 2000, 264-70.

[216]Siegert 1974.

[217]Wander 1998, 200, 232-33 ("eine ernstzunehmende historische Größe, von der er wahrheitsgemäß berichtet"); cf. S. Mitchell 1998, 56; on the spectrum between interest and conversion see S. Cohen 1989.

[218]S. Mitchell 1998; 1999.

[219]On Mitchell's suggestion see the extensive discussion in §18.4 in the present work.

tion found in Akmonia (Phrygia), dated to A.D. 60-80, we read,

"This building, constructed by Julia Severa, was restored by Gaius Tyrronius Clades, head of the synagogue for life [ὁ διὰ βίου ἀρχισυνάγωγος]; and Lucius son of Lucius, head of the synagogue [ἀρχισυνάγωγος], and Popilius Rufus, archon [ἄρχων], from their own funds and from money contributed the walls and the roof, and they made safe the little doors and all the remaining decorations. These men the synagogue honored with a golden shield on account of their virtuous life and their goodwill and zeal for the synagogue [διά τε τὴν ἐνάρετον αὐτῶν δ(ι)άθ(ε)σιν καὶ τὴν πρὸς τὴν συναγωγὴν εὔνοιαν τε καὶ σ(που)δήν]."[220]

Julia Severa was active around A.D. 60-80, as attested by coins that mention her. The numismatic and epigraphical evidence shows that she was a high priestess (ἀρχιέρεια, *archiereia*) of the imperial cult in Akmonia and that she belonged through marriage to an influential family. The claim that she was Jewish or that she was married to one of the men mentioned in the inscription cannot be substantiated. Julia Severa had positive connections with the local synagogue. She was "a benefactor who helped the Jewish community. She did this as the highest representative of another cult, which might have happened more often than not."[221] The inscription does not inform us about the specific ways in which she supported the synagogue. Perhaps she helped finance the building of the synagogue, as did the Herodian centurion in Capernaum in Lk 7:5.

The second inscription was discovered in 1977 (published in 1987) in Aphrodisias, a city some thirty miles west of Colossae in Caria. The long text is inscribed on a stele (2.8 by 0.45 m) dated to A.D. 210 or later.[222] The inscription mentions three proselytes and fifty-four God-fearers (θεοσεβεῖς, *theosebeis*).

Face *a* documents the endowment of a charity[223] by the presidents of an association[224] who are described as "disciples of the law." Three proselytes (lines 13, 17, 22) and two

[220] *CIJ* 766 (= *MAMA* VI 264; *IJudO* II 168). Translation by M. Reinhold, in Feldman and Reinhold 1996, 69-70 (no. 3.23); for a German translation see Wander 1998, 133 n. 163; Ameling in *IJudO* II 168.
[221] Wander 1998, 134; see also Trebilco 1991, 58-60, 83-84.
[222] Reynolds and Tannenbaum 1987 = *SEG* XXXVI 970 = *NewDocs* 9:73-80 (no. 25) = *IJudO* II 14; for an English translation see also L. H. Feldman, in Feldman and Reinhold 1996, 142-43 (nos. 7, 12); for a German translation see Barrett and Thornton, *Texte zur Umwelt des Neuen Testaments,* 66-67 (no. 64); Wander 1998, 235-39 (with discussion 121-27); Ameling, in *IJudO* II 14. See further Feldman 1989; Horst 1989b; idem, "Das Neue Testament und die jüdischen Grabinschriften aus hellenistisch-römischer Zeit," *BZ* 36 (1992): 161-78, esp. 170; Murphy-O'Connor 1992c; Levinskaya 1996, 70-80. H. Botermann ("Griechisch-jüdische Epigraphik: Zur Datierung der Aphrodisias-Inschriften," *ZPE* 98 [1993]: 184-94) dates the inscription to the fourth century.
[223] Reynolds and Tannenbaum (1987) suggest a "soup kitchen for the poor"; cf. R. F. Tannenbaum, "Jews and God-fearers in the Holy City of Aphrodisias," *BAR* 12 (1986): 54-57; others suggest a "burial society," see McKnight 1991, 158 n. 64. See Ameling, in *IJudO* II 14, 83-86.
[224] The association evidently promoted the study of the Torah and communal prayer.

"God-fearers" (lines 19, 20) were members of the board of the association. Face *b* presents two lists: first a list with the names of fifty-five Jews, then, visibly separated from the first list, a list of fifty-two persons who are introduced with the words "and as many as are God-fearers."

The discussion of this inscription contributed to our understanding of the God-fearers: the term *theosebeis* (1) intends to accentuate certain Jewish persons within the synagogue community; (2) describes Gentiles who have taken over certain tasks in the synagogue community; (3) describes Gentiles who demonstrate their sympathies for the Jewish faith by financial contributions to the synagogue community.[225] The late date of the Aphrodisias inscription shows that the terminological uncertainties that we encounter in the time before A.D. 70 persisted in the subsequent centuries.

Suetonius's account of Domitian's measures relating to the tax for Jupiter Capitolinus provides evidence for the existence of Gentile sympathizers for the Jewish faith (*Dom.* 12.2). Citizens of Rome inform against two groups: people who practice a Jewish way of life out of the eyes of the public, and people who seek to keep their ancestry secret in order to avoid paying these taxes.[226] The first group clearly consists of "sympathizers of Judaism who came under pressure in times of obligatory taxes and who could continue to live in this manner only in secret."[227]

The God-fearers, the third group beside the Jews and the proselytes, must have not only worshiped Yahweh as the one true God but also, as they lived in the social context of the synagogues, kept the sabbath, the food laws and, depending on personal choice, further stipulations of the Torah.[228] It is less important whether this group was designated in all synagogues with a fixed term. It is plausible to assume that such Gentile "sympathizers" needed to be, and were, instructed in Jewish faith and practice. We have no information, however, about the manner in which Gentiles became interested in Judaism. This means that the "God-fearers" cannot be used as proof for the existence of an active Jewish mission among Gentiles.

Joseph Tyson argues, aided by literary-critical inquiry about the "implied reader," that the "reader" whom the text of the book of Acts presupposes should be understood in terms of the "God-fearers" or that Theophilus (Lk 1:3; Acts 1:1) belonged to the "God-fearers."[229]

---

[225]See Wander 1998, 121-28.

[226]Suetonius, *Dom.* 12.2: *"qui uel[ut] inprofessi Iudaicam uiuerent uiitam . . . uel dissimulata origine imposita genti tributa non pependissent."*

[227]Wander 1998, 172.

[228]See Schürer 3:169, with reference to Josephus, Juvenal and Tertullian.

[229]Tyson 1992, 19-41.

The Septuagint

The Greek translation of the Hebrew Bible, the foundational document of Hellenistic Judaism,[230] consistently distinguishes between λαός (*laos*) and ἔθνη (*ethnē*), whereby the term ἔθνος, which occurs 1003 times, stereotypically translates גּוֹי (*gôy*), designating primarily the "countergroup" to the people of God. In the Pentateuch,[231] the Septuagint translates גֵּר (*gēr*) nearly always with προσήλυτος (*prosēlytos* [63 times]), only occasionally with πάροικος (*paroikos* [6 times]) or with γειώρας (*geiōras* [once]). The translators of the Pentateuch evidently interpreted the *gēr* as *prosēlytos*. They used *paroikos* only when the context made it clear that a proselyte could not have been in view. The exact meaning of the term *prosēlytos* at this time (the third century B.C.) is uncertain because it seems to have been the Septuagint that coined the word as a designation for non-Jews who "came to" the community of Israel (formation from προσέρχομαι, *proserchomai*).[232] No convincing explanation for this neologism has been given.[233] As we have seen, it was Philo who first defined the term *prosēlytos*. Even so, the word only started to become a technical term for Gentiles who had converted to Judaism: in the Greek translation of Ex 22:20 the term *prosēlytos* refers to the Israelites in Egypt; that is, it designates the "resident alien." In his commentary on this passage in *QE* 2.2, Philo does not replace the word *prosēlytos* with another Greek term for the Hebrew *gēr*, which shows that in the first century A.D. the term *prosēlytos* had both technical and (still) nontechnical meanings.[234]

Several Greek terms designate "guests," "strangers" and "foreigners," particularly ξένος (*xenos*)—terms that the translators of the Septuagint did *not* use. The fact that they used προσήλυτος (*prosēlytos*) to translate the Hebrew גֵּר (*gēr*) leads to the conclusion that they knew the phenomenon of Gentile conversions to Judaism and that Alexandrian Jews at this time accommodated proselytes.

Christiana von Houten thinks that the reformatory legislation of the exilic/postexilic period (i.e., in her view the priestly law and other Pentateuch texts that she assigns to a late redactional stage), where the autochthonous population was permitted to join Israel's cultic community, started a process that was taken up several centuries later in Alexandria when pagans who had converted to the Jewish faith were permitted to join the Jewish community.[235]

---

[230]See C. H. Dodd, *The Bible and the Greeks* (London: Hodder & Stoughton, 1935), xi.

[231]For the following observations see W. C. Allen, "On the Meaning of προσήλυτος in the Septuagint," *The Expositor* 4.10 (1894): 264-75, whose analysis was confirmed by Houten (1991, 179-83).

[232]See Allen, "Meaning of προσήλυτος," 265; K. Kuhn 1959; Houten 1991, 182; Hengel 1994a, xiv-xv.

[233]Houten 1991, 182.

[234]M. Goodman 1994, 73.

[235]Houten 1991, 182.

The Septuagint presumably was used in the instruction of God-fearers and pros-elytes. The suggestion, however, that peculiarities of the translation indicate that the Septuagint as a whole should be regarded as a "missionary document"[236] cannot be proven. The characteristics of this Greek translation would serve a relevant, and perhaps necessary, purpose for Greek-speaking Jews and newly converted proselytes who lived in a metropolis such as Alexandria.

Jewish Apologetic Literature

A relatively large number of Jewish writings written in Greek has been labeled "missionary literature."[237] Besides writings of Aristobulus, Philo and Josephus, these include Wisdom of Solomon, *Sibylline Oracles, Letter of Aristeas, Joseph and Aseneth* and the works of Demetrius and Eupolemos. Scholars suggest that these texts should be understood as a Jewish reaction to the anti-Semitism of the Greco-Roman world, characterized by the optimistic view that a crucial fac-tor in the discussion with non-Jews is clarification through enlightenment, per-suasion through argumentation.[238] In other words, these writings served "mis-sionary" purposes. Advocates of this hypothesis argue that the Jewish Diaspora literature pushes the doctrine of election into the background—a strategic fea-ture of apologetic argumentation.[239] Abraham appears as the head of a philo-sophical school and as the father of many nations,[240] and as ideal ruler who has all the qualities that the Hellenistic codes for kings and princes (*Fürstenspiegel*) demand.[241] Whereas the rabbis, with the significant exception of Hillel,[242] em-phasized the exclusive revelation of the Torah in Israel, the Diaspora literature emphasized the universal validity of the Mosaic law, which was interpreted eth-ically. Martin Hengel argues that this reflects "its more exposed position and consequent missionary tendency."[243] The apologetic argumentation of the Jew-ish Diaspora literature usually is linked with the upper segments of Jewish so-ciety in the cities of the Diaspora. Scholars suggest that the educated and cul-tured Greek-speaking Jews of Alexandria and other cities "made their Jewish faith competitive and highlighted its superiority by taking over Stoic concep-

---

[236]See Feldman 1993a, 310-16.
[237]Note the programmatic title of the 1954 study by Dalbert, who presupposed the existence of "Hellenistic-Jewish missionary literature." On Philo in this context see Noack 2000, 18-20, 27-31.
[238]Lange and Thoma 1978, 121.
[239]See Lange and Thoma 1978, 121.
[240]Josephus, *A.J.* 1.161, 200; 12.226; 14.255.
[241]Thus Eupolemos; Josephus, *A.J.* 1.178; Philo, *Abr.* 208-216; *Let. Arist.* 208-211.
[242]See *m. 'Abot* 1:12b; *b. Šabb.* 31a [bar.].
[243]Hengel 1969, 317 (ET, 1:174). Several scholars assumed a deliberate missionary utilization of literature by Diaspora Jews; see Axenfeld 1904; Hegermann 1966, 314-42; Dalbert 1954, 27-123; Bosch 1959, 31-35; Munck 1954, 262-63; F. Millar, in Schürer 3:160; Feldman 1993a; Noack 2000, 18-31.

tions."[244] Hans Dieter Betz suggests that the Jewish Hellenistic wisdom tradition sympathized primarily with the Socratic tradition and with Stoic and Middle Platonic philosophy, while rejecting the views of the Epicureans.

Christian Noack wants to defend the hypothesis of Dieter Georgi that Philo's interpretation of the Mosaic law[245] was composed for both the Jewish and the non-Jewish public. He writes,

"These writings clearly have not only a defensive and apologetic character; they have primarily an *offensive missionary character.* They want to bring Judaism into the conversation of the Hellenistic world, in an *intelligible* manner, as the true philosophy and the true worship of God that sustain the world. They appeal to the reason of the educated reader of the Hellenistic world, propagating the monotheism of the Bible in the language of Hellenistic culture and education. Peculiarities of Jewish piety are made plausible with the help of generally accepted notions. Large sections of the *Expositio Legis* [i.e., the interpretation of the law] presumably build on the *interpretation of the Bible in the public sermons and instructions of the synagogues,* which was informed by reason and thus had a missionary purpose. They may be based on sermons and lectures that Philo delivered in the synagogue, revised for literary publication. In terms of form and content they have a *protreptic character,* as they advertise the Torah in the public arena of the Hellenistic and Roman world."[246]

Noack designates Philo's interpretation of the law, together with the philosophical treatises *Quod omnis probus liber sit, De aeternitate mundi, De vita contemplativa, De providentia* and *De animalibus,* as well as the historical-political writings *Hypothetica, Legatio ad Gaium* and *In Flaccum,* as "mission-theological writings" ("missions-theologische Schriften") that should be interpreted as "witnesses to the offensive mission-theological branch of the Jewish wisdom tradition with a tendency informed by reason."[247] The "soteriological profile" of these writings consists, according to Noack, in the argument for the reasonableness of Old Testament and Jewish belief in God, which Noack interprets as "monotheistic perception of truth": "They articulate the truth claims of the Jewish belief in God in the context of the truth consciousness of their contemporaries, so that the compatibility and the noncompatibility with other truth claims becomes apparent."[248] Noack is convinced that this "mission theology" was politically motivated.

Karl-Wilhelm Niebuhr suggests that *Contra Apionem,* written by Josephus

---

[244]Lange and Thoma 1978, 121. For the observation that follows above see H. D. Betz, "Hellenismus III," *TRE* 15 (1986): 27.

[245]In his writings *De opificio mundi; De Abrahamo; De Iosepho; De vita Mosis; De decalogo; De specialibus legibus; De virtutibus; De praemiis et poenis.*

[246]Noack 2000, 19-20; on the connection with Dieter Georgi see ibid., 19-20, 219 n. 668, and passim.

[247]Noack 2000, 20; similarly Koen Goudriaan, "Ethnical Strategies in Graeco-Roman Egypt," in Bilde et al. 1992, 74-99, esp. 84.

[248]Noack 2000, 216-17, 249; quotations, ibid., 245.

after A.D. 94, is "the only extant definite witness, at least in terms of its claims, to an apology of Judaism directed to outsiders."[249] He points out that Josephus discusses in this writing the arguments of pagan opponents of Jews. First, Josephus attempts to demonstrate the antiquity of Judaism by pointing to evidence in pagan authors and by arguing with Israel's tradition inspired by God (*C. Ap.* 1.69-218). Second, he refutes pagan calumnies (*C. Ap.* 1.219—2.144). The Jewish faith is not godless: the Torah does not teach godlessness but piety in its fullest and purest form. The Jewish faith does not promote the hate of strangers: the Torah demands neighborly love concerning all people; every stranger who wants to join Judaism is welcomed gladly (*C. Ap.* 2.261). The Jewish faith is not hostile toward culture: the Greek philosophers were disciples of Moses; and with regard to animal sacrifices, circumcision, the sabbath and the rejection of pork, one should note that other nations have the same or similar customs.

It is theoretically possible that these arguments were used by Jewish missionaries trying to win Gentiles,[250] but there is no historical proof for this assumption. *Contra Apionem* represents Jewish apologetic and may be derived from sources that were used by Alexandrian Jews to defend themselves in the disturbances of the 30s and 40s in the first century A.D.[251] *Contra Apionem* as such is no proof for the existence of a Jewish mission among Gentiles. We should note that Josephus tells us that Abraham, when he went to Egypt, taught arithmetic and astronomy (*A.J.* 1.161, 166-167)—there is no reference to instruction in the Jewish faith.[252]

David Rokéah points to the discussions between Abraham and the Egyptian priests: according to Josephus, Abraham sought to demonstrate the lack of substance of their customs, with the result that they admired him "as a man of extreme sagacity, gifted not only with high intelligence but with power to convince his hearers on any subject which he understood to teach" (*A.J.* 1.167).[253] It is rather ambitious to infer from this comment a "theological-missionary work" on the part of Abraham reported by Josephus.

Josephus did not describe Abraham as a missionary among Gentiles, nor did Philo.[254]

We find different, and at times opposing, apologetic emphases in 3 Maccabees, in the Greek translation of the book of Esther and in most Jewish apoca-

---

[249]Niebuhr 1987, 67. For the discussion that follows above see Lange and Thoma 1978, 119-20.
[250]See Feldman 1993a, 321.
[251]See Samuel Belkin, "The Alexandrian Source for Contra Apionem II," *JQR* 27 (1936): 1-32; S. Cohen 1987, 425.
[252]See Will and Orrieux 1992, 145; M. Goodman 1994, 89.
[253]See Rokéah 1996, 214, with a discussion of the interpretations by M. Goodman and L. H. Feldman.
[254]See Hayward 1998, 24, 29-30, 36.

lyptic writings.[255] These texts react to anti-Jewish attacks with a massive theology of history "in which election and retribution play a major role. They prominently highlight the absolute superiority of God over all pagan kings. The entire history of the world moves, in total correspondence with the divine plan, towards the judgment and the destruction of the empires of the world and towards the victory and the salvation of the Jews who faithfully keep the Torah."[256] Three lines of argumentation are repeatedly used: (1) the pagan empires, together with apostate Jews, constitute the old aeon hostile to God that will soon come to an end in the messianic woes; (2) the pagan gods are angels of the nations[257] or angels of Satan;[258] (3) table fellowship with non-Jews and mixed marriages are prohibited. There is no bridge between Jews and Gentiles.[259]

In light of this evidence, the traditional assumption of a missionary purpose behind the Jewish Hellenistic apologetic literature becomes increasingly problematic.[260] There are two options regarding the addressees of the Jewish Diaspora literature: the authors may have sought to win pagans for the faith of Israel, as scholars suggest, or they may have intended to safeguard Diaspora Jews against the dangers of assimilation by demonstrating the dignity of the Jewish faith. The following survey of the most relevant texts provides insight into the attitudes concerning Gentiles in the Jewish Diaspora literature.

Aristobulus. A good examplar of the Jewish debate with the Hellenistic *Zeitgeist* is Aristobulus, an Alexandrian Jew who probably belonged to a high priestly family (2 Macc. 1:10). He wrote, around 175-170 B.C., for the young king Ptolemy VI Philometor a didactic work, fragments of which have been preserved. Aristobulus presents a doctrine of wisdom and creation that combines Israel's traditions with ideas from Greek philosophy.[261] He has to be considered an eclectic, as he was not influenced by one particular school of thought. The goal of his work is to demonstrate that the Jewish faith represented the true "philosophy" and does not contradict reason as informed by philosophical inquiry.

Aristobulus presupposes two notions: (1) If one seeks to understand the true

---

[255]Lange and Thoma (1978, 121) and others regard the latter as a "reaction of the lower classes."

[256]Lange and Thoma 1978, 121, with reference to Dan 7—12; *Jub.* 24; 28ff.; 36:10; *1 En.* 1:9; 5:4ff.; 38:2ff.; 48:8ff.; *Sib. Or.* 3:57ff.; 4:171ff.; *Apoc. Ab.* 29:14ff.; 31:3ff.; 3 Macc. 2:2ff.; 6:12ff.

[257]*Jub.* 15:30ff.; *1 En.* 56:5-6; *T. Naph.* (Heb.) 8:4ff.

[258]*1 En.* 89:59-60; 99:7; *Jub.* 1:11; 11:4; 19:28.

[259]*Jub.* 22:16; 30:7ff.; *Jos. Asen.* 8:47; 19:10-11.

[260]See Tcherikover, 1956; Schürer 3:609; Fredriksen 1991; McKnight 1991, 57-62; M. Goodman 1992.

[261]Translation above from A. Yarbro Collins, *OTP* 2:831-42; for a German translation see Walter, *JSHRZ* 3.2. For the fragments preserved in Eusebius—*Praep. ev.* 8.10.1-17 (frg. 2); 13.12.1-2 (frg. 3); 12.3-8 (frg. 4); 13.12.9-16 (frg. 5)—see K. Mras, ed., *Eusebius VIII.1-2: Praeparatio evangelica* (GCS 43.1-2; Berlin: Hinrichs, 1954-1956), 8.1:451-54, 8.2:190-97. Cf. Nikolaus Walter, *Der Toraausleger Aristobulos* (TU 86; Berlin: Akademie-Verlag, 1964), and particularly Hengel 1969, 295-307 (ET, 1:163-69).

"philosophical" (φυσικῶς, *physikōs*) meaning of the Pentateuch, one must not "fall into the mythical and human way of thinking about God." Passages often considered offensive due to their anthropomorphic form need to be interpreted allegorically in order "to grasp the fitting conception of God."[262] Aristobulus provides the earliest extant form of Alexandrian allegorical exegesis. He is more cautious in the application of the allegorical method than are Aristeas and Philo. Some scholars therefore describe his exegetical method as "Hellenistic midrash."[263] (2) The Torah, rightly interpreted, is for "those who are able to think well" a clear proof of the "wisdom" and "the divine spirit" of its author.[264] Aristobulus understands God as not limited to space or time, as omnipresent and metatemporal. On the basis of his fusion of the Bible's wisdom tradition and doctrine of creation with the cosmology and epistemology of Greek philosophy, he seeks "to demonstrate a unitary divine ordering of the cosmos embracing both the world and men."[265] Connected with the significance of the number "seven," biblical wisdom and the Stoic logos become the spiritual principle of the order of the cosmos and simultaneously the foundation of knowledge and morality.

Aristobulus identified the seventh and the first day of creation: "God's rest" on the seventh day did not signal the end of the divine activity but the "fixing of the order of things," and the work of the six days is to be understood, according to Martin Hengel, "as the establishing of the course of time (ἵνα τοὺς χρόνους δηλώσῃ) and of gradations within the created world (13.12.11f.). In this way Aristobulus attempted to bring the Old Testament conception of the creation of God in time in accord with the Greek idea of the timeless activity of God. Not God himself, but only his creation is subject to the course of time."[266] Aristobulus takes up Pythagorean and Platonic number speculation in his interpretation of the "seventh day" as the principle of the cosmic order in the number "seven."

This position can be understood as an attempt to engage in a "missionary counterattack" in a dominant civilization. Martin Hengel comments, "What Ben Sira only hinted at was not made plain: 'wisdom' was comparable with the Stoic Logos, the law of the world or the world-soul. It was the spiritual principle of order and knowledge of the cosmos, recognized in the number seven and created by the supra-temporal and transcendent God. The individual man shared in this principle by right thinking (8.10.4 καλῶς νοεῖν) and the resultant right action; he had to direct his life by it if he was to be happy. It is understandable that in this approach the cosmological-psychological ori-

---

[262]Aristobulus, see Eusebius, *Praep. ev.* 8.10.2: καὶ μὴ ἐκπίπτειν εἰς τὸ μυθῶδες καὶ ἀνθρώπινον κατάστημα . . . τὴν ἁρμόζουσαν ἔννοιαν περὶ θεοῦ.

[263]See Walter, *Toraausleger Aristobulos;* Hengel 1969, 298 n. 371 (ET, 2:107 n. 382).

[264]Aristobulus, see Eusebius, *Praep. ev.* 8.10.4: οἷς μὲν οὖν πάρεστι τὸ καλῶς νοεῖν . . . τὴν περὶ αὐτὸν σοφίαν καὶ τὸ θεῖον πνεῦμα.

[265]Hengel 1969, 304; for the exposition that follows above see ibid. (ET, 1:167-68).

[266]Hengel 1969, 301; the quotation that follows above, ibid., 304-5 (ET, 1:166, 168).

entation came to overshadow that of salvation history, but as in pre-Christian Jewish understanding 'salvation history' predominantly implied the exclusive limitation of salvation to Israel and its separation from the 'peoples,' in the more open circles of the Diaspora a certain reorientation was necessary in the face of the missionary task which went beyond the narrow boundaries of the people."

The philosophical-theological position of Aristobulus might indeed be suitable as an argumentative basis for missionary activity of Jews among Gentiles, but it cannot prove the latter's existence. The writings of Aristobulus that are extant in the fragments do not specifically betray missionary interests, as his goals are more philosophical than religious.[267]

Letter of Aristeas. In this literary "letter" written in the second century B.C. by an Alexandrian Jew to his brother Philocrates,[268] the author, Aristeas, presents himself as a (non-Jewish) court official of King Ptolemy II Philadelphos (285-246 B.C.). He recounts how pagan authorities such as King Ptolemy and his envoy Aristeas highly valued the Jewish law and more generally the Jewish religion. This focus does not mean, however, that this "novel in epistolary form" was written for a pagan audience.[269] The author writes for a Jewish audience. This is seen precisely in those sections in which he describes and defends Jewish practices: he passes over such well-known customs as circumcision, the refusal to work on the sabbath and the prohibition of eating pork, Jewish practices that pagans regularly ridiculed and attacked, but he discusses the much more detailed and complex stipulations concerning the ruminating and the cloven-footed animals (*Let. Arist.* 150-54).[270]

Aristeas clearly shows his admiration for the superior Greek culture and erudition, not only in his Greek style but also in his report about the translation of the Torah into Greek, the central feature of his letter, which he presents as an act that bridged the divide that separated Jews and Gentiles.[271] At the same time he emphasizes forcefully the separation that the Torah demands of the Jews concerning contacts with other people as the crucial characteristic of Jew-

---

[267]Thus C. Holladay 1992, 150.

[268]See Schürer 3:679; Shutt (*OTP* 2:8-9) dates the work to around 170 B.C., Meisner (*JSHRZ* 2.1:42-43) to 127-118 B.C. (on Meisner's arguments see the critique in Schürer 3:683 n. 287). A date in the second half of the second century B.C. is also assumed by Hadas, *Aristeas to Philocrates*, 18-54; Nickelsburg 1984, esp. 77-78; Feldmeier 1994b, 20. Translation above from Shutt, *OTP* 2:7-34.

[269]Thus Schürer 3:679. Feldmeier (1994b, 20) uses the phrase "novel in epistolary form."

[270]See Hadas, *Aristeas to Philocrates*, 65-66; Nickelsburg 1984, 78; V. Tcherikover, "The Ideology of the Letter of Aristeas," in *Studies in the Septuagint: Origins, Recensions, and Interpretations* (ed. S. Jellicoe; New York: Ktav 1974), 181-207, esp. 182. Feldmeier (1994b, 33-34) thinks that a Greek audience is possible but that Jews were the primary addressees.

[271]On Torah as the quintessence of justice and wisdom in *Letter of Aristeas* see Feldmeier 1994b, 33-34.

ish identity. This conviction finds expression in two well-known passages (*Let. Arist.* 139, 142).

Let. Arist. 139: "In his wisdom the legislator, in a comprehensive survey of each particular part, and being endowed by God for the knowledge of universal truths, surrounded us with unbroken palisades and iron walls to prevent our mixing with any of the other peoples in any matter [μηδενὶ τῶν ἄλλων ἐθνῶν], being thus kept pure in body and soul, preserved from false beliefs, and worshiping the only God omnipotent over all creation."

Let. Arist. 142: "So, to prevent our being perverted by contact with others or by mixing with bad influences, he hedged us in on all sides with strict observances connected with meat and drink and touch and hearing and sight, after the manner of the Law."

Aristeas declares that all people worship God the Most High (16), but he asserts at the same time that only the Jews worship the one true God (132-33) while all other people worship many gods and the work of their hands or, in the case of exceedingly stupid people, deify living and dead animals (134-38). The consequences of false worship can be seen in the fact that non-Jews are interested only in food, drink and clothes. Such things "are of no account" for Jews, as they are mainly concerned "with the sovereignty of God" (140-41). Aristeas sharply distinguishes between the Jewish faith and pagan religiosity.[272]

This is a good example of the manner in which Aristeas manages to connect basic Jewish convictions with ideals of the Hellenistic world: the contemplation of divine sovereignty corresponds to the ultimate purpose of life in Cynic and Stoic philosophy. As Aristeas distinguishes with regard to the world of the Gentiles between the things that are valuable and good, and the people who serve many gods and their own belly, he is able to explain the cultic separation of the Jews from the Gentiles that the Torah demands "as expression or result of their religious and ethical superiority. In a certain sense Judaism is identified with the ideal of the Hellenistic world. In the description of the *Letter of Aristeas* the Jews represent, in spiritual-religious as well as in ethical terms, the aspirations of their contemporaries."[273]

The attempt to interpret the Jewish purity and food laws as an expression of ethical and religious superiority over non-Jewish religiosity and way of life presumably was not very convincing for Aristeas's Greek contemporaries. Educated Greeks, the target of potential proselytizing efforts, would hardly have concurred with the Jewish claim of possessing the monopoly on truth in basic ethical and religious questions. They would have rejected such claims as antisocial arrogance.

---

[272]See C. Holladay 1992, 147.

[273]Feldmeier 1994b, 32, with reference to the "Zeus Hymn" of Cleanthes (frg. 537; *Stoicorum veterum fragmenta* [ed. H. von Arnim; 4 vols.; Leipzig: Teubner, 1903-1924], 1:537; English translation in Long and Sedley 1987, vol. 1, no. 54; German translation in Barrett and Thornton, *Texte zur Umwelt des Neuen Testaments,* 82, no. 77); Epictetus, *Diatr.* 1.9.26; cf. C. Holladay 1992, 149.

This leads us to the conclusion that Aristeas wants to achieve a twofold goal with regard to the primary Jewish audience. First, he desires to defend the attempts of the Jewish upper class in Alexandria who wanted to engage Hellenistic culture on a positive note. Second, he wants to reformulate, in the context of the changed conditions of the Diaspora, the conviction of Israel's election and the consciousness of being separated by God. Thus *Letter of Aristeas* is "an apology directed to the insiders, his goal is to ascertain their identity by a modern interpretation of the Torah."[274] Aristeas's comments on other ethnic groups reveal a "rhetoric of moral superiority" derived from a well-developed ethnic self-confidence.[275]

Despite his high regard for Hellenistic culture, Aristeas does not remove the barriers that surround the Jews as the people of God. He links the purity laws explicitly and directly with the worship of the true God and thus presents cultic purity as prerequisite for permanent membership in the people of God.[276] If potential Greek readers of Aristeas's work were convinced by his treatise and were willing to draw consequences for themselves, Aristeas left them little room with his insistence on the purity laws: they would have had to become proselytes.

Sibylline Oracles. The third book of *Sibylline Oracles,* presumably written largely before 150 B.C.,[277] provides a panorama of the end times, beginning in *Sib. Or.* 3:702, which also addresses the relationship between Israel and the nations.[278] The author expects in *Sib. Or.* 3:615-17 that all people will bend their knees before God after the defeat of Egypt, in *Sib. Or.* 3:710-23 that all islands and cities will be converted to God, and in *Sib. Or.* 3:719 that the Greeks will "ponder the Law of the Most High God." The Gentiles come to Jerusalem (*Sib. Or.* 3:716-23) in order to contemplate God's righteous law. Then God will raise up his eternal kingdom for all ages and people (*Sib. Or.* 3:767-95).

Sib. Or. 3:757-59, 772-76: "The Immortal in the starry heaven will put in effect [758]a common law for men throughout the whole earth [759]for all that is done among wretched mortals. . . . [772]From every land they will bring incense and gifts [773]to the house of the great God. There will be no other [774]house among men, even for future generations to know, [775]except the one which God gave to faithful men to honor [776](for mortals will invoke the son of the great God)."[279]

Whereas the Old Testament passages that mention the nations' pilgrimage to

---

[274]Feldmeier 1994b, 32; see also Kraus 1996, 79.

[275]C. Holladay 1992, 156.

[276]See Kraus (1996, 79, following Siegert [1980-1992, vol. 1]), who emphasizes the precision of Aristeas's description of the Jews' obedience to the purity laws; see further Delling 1987, 92-93.

[277]See J. J. Collins, *OTP* 1:355-56; Schürer 3:618-54; translation above from Collins, *OTP* 1:362-80.

[278]For the exposition that follows above see Kraus 1996, 94-96.

[279]The last phrase in *Sib Or.* 3:776 usually is regarded as a Christian interpolation; see Johannes Geffcken, *Die Oracula Sibyllina* (GCS 8; Leipzig: Hinrichs, 1902 [repr., Amsterdam: Hakkert, 1970]), 87; Collins, *OTP* 1:379 n. b4; differently Blass (*APAT* 2:183), who sees a textual corruption and wants to change "son" into "temple"; see also Kraus 1996, 94-96 n. 252.

Zion do not clearly specify the path by which they arrive, *Sib. Or.* 3 specifically states that the nations will be moved by insight into the control of history by the God of Israel (*Sib. Or.* 3:710-14, 718-19) and that they will recognize and accept the Torah as the most righteous law. "As the Torah will be accepted as 'common law for men throughout the whole earth' (*Sib. Or.* 3:758), the question of Israel's relationship to the nations has been answered."[280] It is difficult to decide whether the text speaks of the Gentiles joining Israel as proselytes in the eschaton or of the Gentiles worshiping Israel's God without becoming members of God's people:[281] the text does not mention a circumcision of the non-Jewish peoples, and the "Law of the Most High God" that the nations ponder (*Sib. Or.* 3:719) is not identical with the Torah but is linked with a general moral code.[282] However, as *Sib. Or.* 3:773-75 refers to a single "house" in which God is worshiped by all people, the Gentiles have de facto the same status as the Jewish people. Still, it is obvious that the entry of Gentiles into the people of God does not need to be initiated or organized by an active missionary work of Jews among Gentiles, as this event will take place in the messianic period.

Tobit. This text, written in pre-Maccabean times, draws "the ideal picture of a devout and righteous Jew."[283] Tobit had to live in captivity in Assyria but he did not abandon the word of God (Tob 1:3-8). Because he feared Yahweh with all his heart, he was careful not to eat "the food of the Gentiles" (ἄρτων τῶν ἐθνῶν [Tob 1:10]). We see the same tendency toward separation from the Gentiles as in the texts of Palestinian Judaism. Two passages have a universalistic horizon (Tob 13:11; 14:5-6).

Tob 13:11: "A bright light will shine to all the ends of the earth [φῶς λαμπρὸν λάμψει εἰς πάντα τὰ πέρατα τῆς γῆς]; many nations will come to you from far away [ἔθνη πολλὰ μακρόθεν], the inhabitants of the remotest parts of the earth to your holy name, bearing gifts in their hands for the King of heaven. Generation after generation [γενεαὶ γενεῶν] will give joyful praise in you, the name of the chosen city will endure forever."

The pagan nations that arrive in the holy city evidently bring gifts and live in Israel. The text does not anticipate an integration of the foreigners into God's people.[284]

Tob 14:5-7a: "But God will again have mercy on them, and God will bring them back into the land of Israel; and they will rebuild the temple of God, but not like the first one until the period when the times of fulfillment shall come [πληρωθῇ ὁ χρόνος τῶν καιρῶν]. After

---

[280]Kraus 1996, 94-95.

[281]The first position is that of Kraus 1996, 94-96; the second, that of Delling 1987, 89.

[282]See Donaldson 1990, 17-18.

[283]Niebuhr 1987, 91. Translation above follows the NRSV.

[284]Kraus 1996, 77, referring to P. Deselaers, *Das Buch Tobit* (Geistliche Schriftlesung 11; Düsseldorf: Patmos, 1990), ad loc.

this they all will return from their exile and will rebuild Jerusalem in splendor; and in it the temple of God will be rebuilt, just as the prophets of Israel have said concerning it. ⁶Then the nations in the whole world will all be converted [πάντα τὰ ἔθνη τὰ ἐν ὅλῃ τῇ γῇ, πάντες ἐπιστρέψουσιν] and worship God in truth [φοβηθήσονται τὸν θεὸν ἀληθινῶς]. They will all abandon [ἀφήσουσιν] their idols, which deceitfully have led them into their error; ⁷ᵃand in righteousness they will praise the eternal God [εὐλογήσουσιν τὸν θεόν]."

The expectation that both texts express corresponds with the Old Testament and Jewish Palestinian tradition of the nations' pilgrimage to Zion and of the nations' worship of Yahweh. Wolfgang Kraus comments, "Again, these texts hardly speak of the Gentiles' integration into the people of God or of an attainment of equal status with Israel."[285] A missionary activity among Gentiles is not envisioned either. Nor does Tob 13:3-4 speak of a Jewish Gentile mission.

Tob 13:3-4: "Acknowledge him before the nations, O children of Israel (ἐξομολογεῖσθε αὐτῷ, οἱ υἱοὶ Ἰσραήλ, ἐνώπιον τῶν ἐθνῶν); for he has scattered you among them. ⁴He has shown you his greatness even there. Exalt him in the presence of every living being (ὑψοῦτε αὐτὸν ἐνώπιον παντὸς ζῶντος), because he is our Lord and he is our God; he is our Father and he is God forever."

In regard to the exhortation that the Jews praise Yahweh before the nations, the genre of praise is to be taken seriously as providing the hermeneutical horizon of the statements connected with this appeal. The exhortation of Tob 13:3-4 does not correspond to Mt 28:19-20—it is not a command to active missionary work; rather, it corresponds to those passages in the Old Testament psalms in which the nations are exhorted to praise the God of Israel. The end of Tob 13:4 demonstrates that in the final analysis this passage has a nationalistic focus. The sons of Israel praise God "in the presence of every living being" with emphasis on "our" Lord, "our" God and "our" Father.[286]

Joseph and Aseneth. This writing, composed probably toward the end of the first century B.C.,[287] on first reading wants to clarify what the Hebrew Bible did not address: the problem of how the devout and chaste Joseph could marry a pagan Egyptian woman. The author writes this novel from the perspective of Aseneth, the daughter of an Egyptian priest, who becomes a proselyte before marrying Joseph. The writing is hardly a romance in the narrow sense of the

---

[285]Kraus 1996, 78; cf. Donaldson 1990, 19-20; less helpful is Wisdom 2001, 67-68.
[286]Tob 13:4: αὐτὸς ἡμῶν κύριός ἐστιν καὶ αὐτὸς θεὸς ἡμῶν καὶ αὐτὸς πατὴρ ἡμῶν.
[287]Translation above from C. Burchard, *OTP* 2:177-247. On introductory questions see C. Burchard, *Untersuchungen zu Joseph und Aseneth: Überlieferung, Ortsbestimmung* (WUNT 8; Tübingen: Mohr-Siebeck, 1965), 91ff., 133ff. Though in this study Burchard dated *Joseph and Aseneth* to the end of the first century B.C., he now is more cautious, suggesting a date between 100 B.C. and A.D 100, cf. idem, *JSHRZ* 2.4:613-14; *OTP* 2:187-88; see also Chesnutt 1995, 80-85. Marc Philonenko (*Joseph et Aséneth* [SPB 13; Leiden: Brill, 1968]) dates the book to the second century A.D., while D. Sänger ("Erwägungen zur historischen Einordnung und zur Datierung von 'Joseph und Aseneth,'" *ZNW* 76 [1985]: 86-106) suggests A.D. 38 as the date of composition.

genre, as the story of Aseneth's conversion dominates.[288] Aseneth is a proselyte par excellence: she destroys idols and turns in prayer to the only true God, the God of the Hebrews, as her new "father" (*Jos. Asen.* 12:8-15). A missionary is unnecessary: Joseph, the "(firstborn) son of God"[289] shakes Aseneth with his appearance and petitions God for her (*Jos. Asen.* 8:9); then he departs. Aseneth is converted because she heard many people talk about the mercy of the God of the Hebrews (*Jos. Asen.* 11:10-11).

Jos. Asen. 11:10-11: "But I have heard many saying that the God of the Hebrews is a true God, and a living God, and a merciful God, and compassionate and long-suffering and pitiful and gentle, and does not count the sin of a humble person, nor expose the lawless deeds of an afflicted person at the time of his affliction. [11]Therefore I will take courage too and turn to him, and take refuge with him, and confess all my sins to him, and pour out my supplication before him."

Aseneth is accepted by God on account of her repentance and the intercession of the princely angel who appears to her from heaven. Her prayer to the true God (*Jos. Asen.* 12:1—13:15) includes a parable (*Jos. Asen.* 12:8): a child flees to its father, and likewise God is a loving and merciful father and therefore the refuge for the sinners whom he rescues from persecution by the devil.[290] It is only after this experience that Joseph conveys to Aseneth, through kisses, life, wisdom and truth (*Jos. Asen.* 19:11). Christoph Burchard comments, "Many conversions to Judaism presumably took place in this manner, minus the supernatural events."[291] This assessment may well be correct, perhaps with the exception of the last clause if we do not preclude the possibility of visions and other "supernatural events."[292]

Joseph and Aseneth is not "missionary literature."[293] The author does indeed assert that Gentiles who convert to faith in the one true God should be accepted into the fellowship of God's people. But he does not even indirectly refer to missionaries or to ceremonies that proselytes have to submit to.[294] Christoph Burchard considers it unlikely that *Joseph and Aseneth* was intended

---

[288]See C. Burchard, "Joseph und Aseneth," *TRE* 17 (1988): 246-49, esp. 247; idem, *OTP* 2:186-87.

[289]*Jos. Asen.* 6:3, 5; 13:13; 18:11; 21:4; 23:10.

[290]See Peter Dschulnigg, "Gleichnis vom Kind, das zum Vater flieht (JosAs 12,8)," *ZNW* 80 (1989): 269-71.

[291]Burchard, *JSHRZ* 2.4:609. On the conversion of Aseneth see also Gallagher 1993, 7-11.

[292]Note the reports of visions that are frequently linked with conversions of Moslems to the Christian faith. According to missiologist J. Dudley Woodberry, 25 percent of all converted Moslems report visions; cf. J. D. Woodberry, "Missiological Issues in the Encounter with Emerging Islam," in *The World of Islam CD-ROM* (Colorado Springs, Colo.: Global Mapping International, 2000).

[293]Contra Nickelsburg 1981, 262; Philonenko, *Joseph et Aséneth*, 106-7.

[294]Thus Chesnutt (1995, 118-50, 155-65), who emphasizes after extensive religion-historical comparisons that the conversion of Aseneth is without any analogies both in Jewish or non-Jewish groups; cf. idem, "The Social Setting and Purpose of Joseph and Aseneth," *JSP* 2 (1988): 21-48.

to attract outsiders, arguing that "it is more likely that the author wanted to inform Jewish readers/listeners about the benefits of Judaism rather than instruct them to make or appreciate proselytes," and he concludes that "there is no hint in Joseph and Aseneth that Jewish missionaries or zealous individuals spread the good news of salvation and called for conversion."[295] Idolatry is condemned (*Jos. Asen.* 10:12-13), but Aseneth's pagan parents are portrayed in a positive manner (*Jos. Asen.* 3:1-8). Burchard observes that "*Joseph and Aseneth* does not portray a missionary Judaism. Proselytes are welcomed, not made, as conversion is not easy. Nor is *Joseph and Aseneth* a book for beginners. . . . Even if we grant that a missionary writing does not need to emphasize the difficult parts of the law, as an introduction to Judaism *Joseph and Aseneth* would be a failure. At best the book might encourage advanced God-fearers to make the final decision. But they would have been better served by something more robust than a novel."[296] Burchard interprets *Joseph and Aseneth* as an "expression of internal Jewish self-communication" ("Ausdruck innerjüdischer Selbstverständigung"), perhaps with a particular concern for new converts. "*Joseph and Aseneth* does not betray any knowledge of missionaries, if they ever existed in a Jewish context, nor does it know of individuals who advertise Judaism with a particular message. The encounter with a Jew can and will, if it is genuine, set into motion a conversion, but the latter takes its course by itself. Joseph does surprisingly little for Aseneth." Some scholars even refuse to see Aseneth as a prototypical proselyte. For example, J. C. O'Neill interprets her as a metaphor for Israel, having abandoned the true faith and the proper way of life, being won back for God by Joseph—that is, by the Messiah, the Son of God, Israel's bride.[297]

Pseudo-Phocylides. The didactic text Pseudo-Phocylides was written probably at the end of the first century B.C. or the beginning of the first century A.D. in Alexandria.[298] Rabbi Gottlieb Klein described Pseudo-Phocylides as "catechism

---

[295]Burchard, *TRE* 17 (1988): 247, cf. idem, *OTP* 2:192. Similarly Sänger (1980, 209-15), who points out that only Jews or people conversant with the Jewish faith would have understood the numerous allusions to Old Testament material and traditions. See further McKnight 1991, 60-62; Chesnutt 1995, 257-62; Terry Griffith, "'Little Children, Keep Yourselves from Idols' (1 John 5.21): The Form and Function of the Ending of the First Epistle of John" (Ph.D. diss., University of London, 1996), ch. 3 (cf. idem, "Little Children, Keep Yourselves from Idols," *TynBul* 48 [1997]: 188). Feldman (1993a, 316) comments on *Joseph and Aseneth* only briefly.

[296]Burchard, *JSHRZ* 2.4:615; the quotation that follows above, ibid., 2.4:608.

[297]J. C. O'Neill, "What Is *Joseph and Aseneth* About?" *Henoch* 16 (1994): 189-98.

[298]On the text of Pseudo-Phocylides see Albert-Marie Denis, ed., *Fragmenta Pseudepigraphorum quae supersunt graeca, una cum historicorum et auctorum Judaeorum Hellenistarum fragmentis* (PVTG 3b; Leiden: Brill, 1970), 149-56; translation above from P. W. van der Horst, *OTP* 2:565-82; for a German translation see Walter, *JSHRZ* 4.3:182-216. Walter dates the book between 100 B.C. and A.D. 100; van der Horst, between 30 B.C. and A.D. 40. See further P. W. van der Horst, *The Sentences of Pseudo-Phocylides: With Introduction and Commentary* (SVTP 4; Leiden: Brill, 1978) (text: 88-102).

for the Gentiles."[299] James Crouch argued similarly when he suggests that the general missionary tendency of Pseudo-Phocylides is controlled by the proclamation of an ethical monotheism that eliminated everything exclusively Jewish.[300] The only positive argument that Crouch advances for his claim that the Jewish ethical material was intended for Gentiles is a reference to the Noahic laws. This argument is not cogent, however, as such a use of the Noahic laws cannot be proven: of the seven commandments listed by Crouch, two are not mentioned in Pseudo-Phocylides (blasphemy, idolatry), and one occurs in Pseudo-Phocylides (nonkosher meat [147-48]) but in no other source. The other four commandments (immorality, murder, robbery, just legislation) can, of course, be derived from traditions other than missionary outreach among Gentiles.[301]

Several characteristic of Pseudo-Phocylides seem to suggest, at first sight, a pagan Hellenistic audience as the intended readership: the linguistic form, the genre, the lack of typical Jewish features, the connection with a pagan authority. On the other hand, both the content and the traditional background of the text clearly point to a Jewish author: the central message is the proclamation of the basic claims of the Jewish law on the life of Jews. Karl-Wilhelm Niebuhr comments, "Because he never explicitly characterizes his proclamation as Jewish, and because he publishes it even under the name of a pagan authority, he inevitably would have been misunderstood by pagan addressees, an audience that did not already know the essential content of his message. In such a context, his intention to win Gentiles for the high ideals of Judaism was bound to come to nothing. Thus Ps.-Phoc. becomes intelligible as a writing addressed to Jewish addressees."[302] The use of "Phocylides" as a pseudonym—the Ionian poet Phocylides lived in Miletus in the sixth century B.C.—can be understood as an expression of the apologetic and devotional tendency of the text: "Phocylides, the Greek sage *par excellence*, is in a certain sense a witness to the perfection of the Mosaic Law, as he marvelously confirms its moral precepts."

Nikolaus Walter is convinced that a missionary purpose of Pseudo-Phocylides is impossible: "If someone wanted to engage in missionary activity for Judaism, he would not appear in the mask of a pagan wisdom teacher and attempt to fade out as much as possible everything specifically Jewish. And if someone wanted to engage in hidden proselytization, he would use the pagan mask to sound the praise of Judaism even more sonorously. . . . And it can hardly be a 'catechism' for God-fearers or perhaps proselytes, that is, more generally for non-Jews who are interested in Judaism through their own initiative, since even then the specifically Jewish concerns would have to be more clearly

---

[299]Gottlieb Klein 1909, 143.

[300]Crouch 1972, 90-95.

[301]See Niebuhr 1987, 68. n. 243.

[302]Niebuhr 1987, 68; the quotation that follows above, ibid., 70.

emphasized or explained, for example the characteristics of Judaism that were
known in antiquity to outsiders but certainly not always understood: the keeping of the Sabbath and circumcision."[303] The anonymous Jewish author probably
wanted to demonstrate to his Jewish Hellenistic readers that Greek and biblical
moralities are close, and thereby "counteract the unwarranted fascination of
some Hellenistic Jews with the world of Hellenistic culture and the deviation
from the Jewish 'way of righteousness' (cf. vv. 229-230) for a Greek way of life
thought to be more highly developed."[304]

   Wisdom of Solomon. This sapiential text, written perhaps during the principate of Caligula (A.D. 37-41) in Alexandria,[305] clearly expresses the views of Diaspora Jews concerning Gentiles. Note the description in Wis 14:22-31:

Wis 14:22-31:[306] "Then it was not enough for them to err about the knowledge of God,
but though living in great strife due to ignorance, they call such great evils peace. [23]For
whether they kill children in their initiations, or celebrate secret mysteries, or hold fren-
zied revels with strange customs, [24]they no longer keep either their lives or their marriages
pure, but they either treacherously kill one another, or grieve one another by adultery,
[25]and all is a raging riot of blood and murder, theft and deceit, corruption, faithlessness,
tumult, perjury, [26]confusion over what is good, forgetfulness of favors, defiling of souls,
sexual perversion, disorder in marriages, adultery, and debauchery. [27]For the worship of
idols not to be named is the beginning and cause and end of every evil. [28]For their worshipers [Gk., 'they'] either rave in exultation, or prophesy lies, or live unrighteously, or
readily commit perjury; [29]for because they trust in lifeless idols they swear wicked oaths
and expect to suffer no harm. [30]But just penalties will overtake them on two counts: because they thought wrongly about God in devoting themselves to idols, and because in
deceit they swore unrighteously through contempt for holiness. [31]For it is not the power
of the things by which people swear, but the just penalty for those who sin, that always
pursues the transgression of the unrighteous." .

Non-Jewish people are sinners pure and simple. Their idolatry results in all conceivable evils; they practice any perversion. If the Jewish author intends such a
general verdict to motivate his Jewish readers to engage in missionary encounters with their pagan neighbors, which is implausible but theoretically possible,
he never indicates that this is his intention. The statement in Wis 12:2 sometimes
has been construed as a reference to the conversion of Gentiles:

Wis 12:2: "Therefore you [God] correct little by little those who trespass, and you remind

---

[303]Walter, *JSHRZ* 4.3:191-92. Folker Siegert (1974, esp. 124-25) interprets Pseudo-Phocylides as
   a writing addressed to God-fearers. Walter (*JSHRZ* 4.3:185 n. 27) calls it misleading when Gottlieb Klein (1909, 39) asserts that Pseudo-Phocylides seeks to convert pagans. A missionary
   intention of Psedo-Phocylides is rejected also by Schürer (3:690) and van der Horst (*OTP*
   2:568-69).
[304]Walter, *JSHRZ* 4.3:192.
[305]See Winston, *Wisdom of Solomon;* Schürer 3:572-73.
[306]Translation follows the NRSV; for a German translation see D. Georgi, *JSHRZ* 3.4.

and warn them of the things through which they sin, so that they may be freed from wickedness and put their trust in you, O Lord."

This text may state the stages of a conversion process: (1) demonstration of sin; (2) warning with regard to God's judgment; (3) turning away from past behavior, which was a failure; (4) turning to God as the Creator and Lord of the earth.[307] It is not impossible that the Jewish author, living in Egypt, remembered Gentiles who experienced their conversion to the God of Israel in this manner. It remains hypothetical, however, to suggest that the tradition behind the praise in Wis 11:20—12:17 was characterized by a missionary consciousness—that is, that the text provides evidence that Jews were engaged in missionary work among pagans. It is striking that in Wis 12:2 it is not missionaries but God himself who convicts the "trespassers" of their sin.[308]

The suggestion that the description of the law as "imperishable light" for the world (Wis 18:4) finds agreement "with the rationalistic missionary ideology of Jewish Hellenistic apologetics"[309] is unlikely. Equally implausible is the suggestion that the entire writing was addressed primarily to Gentiles who were wealthy and thirsty for education and were interested in Jewish traditions.[310]

Pseudo-Philo (Liber antiquitatum biblicarum). This text, written probably after A.D. 70,[311] leaves little hope for the non-Jewish nations. God's covenant was given only to Israel; the law serves to preserve Israel and punish the nations (*L.A.B.* 11:1-5). The mediator of the light for the world is not Abraham but the Torah.[312] The barrier between Israel and the nations is bridged only once, in the song of Hannah: surprised by God's amazing action, Hannah, a woman who was infertile but now gives birth to a child, describes her son as "the light to the peoples" (*L.A.B.* 51:6) through which all people will find truth (*L.A.B.* 51:4). The end of the hymn is dispassionate: Hannah prays that her son may be "a light for this nation" (*L.A.B.* 51:6), meaning for the people of Israel (cf. *L.A.B.* 51:7).[313]

Philo of Alexandria

Philo does not use the term τὰ ἔθνη (*ta ethnē*), in contrast to the Septuagint, as

---

[307]Brandenburger 1988, 183; for the critical observation that follows above see ibid., 182.
[308]Thus correctly Brandenburger 1988, 185.
[309]D. Georgi, *JSHRZ* 3.4:464-65; taken up by Garlington 1991, 87 n. 116.
[310]David Volgger, "Die Adressaten des Weisheitsbuches," *Bib* 82 (2001): 153-77.
[311]See P.-M. Bogaert et al., *Les Antiquités Bibliques/Pseudo-Philon.* (2 vols.; SC 229-230; Paris: Cerf, 1976); for an English translation see D. J. Harrington, *OTP* 2:297-377; for a German translation see C. Dietzfelbinger, *JSHRZ* 2.2.
[312]Wisdom (2001, 75), who still wants to see a connection with Gen 12:3.
[313]See John R. Levison, "Torah and Covenant in Pseudo-Philo's Liber Antiquitatum Biblicarum," in Avemarie and Lichtenberger 1996, 111-27, esp. 124-26.

a technical term for "the Gentiles" or non-Jews.[314] Philo evidently had little interest in the subject "Jews and Gentiles."

In his recently published dissertation Christian Noack does not discuss the studies of Naoto Umemoto and others who question the existence of a Jewish mission among Gentiles. He simply presupposes such a mission, following Dieter Georgi. He asserts "with certainty" that "Philo, as author, produced his mission-theological writings ['missionstheologische Schriften'] for both the Jewish and the non-Jewish book market" but provides no hard evidence whatsoever that would make this statement plausible. He maintains that Philo "utilizes mission-theological traditions, i.e., exegetical material that had already been formed in the public missionary proclamation."[315] Even though Noack attests for Philo's *Quaestiones et solutiones* and *Legum allegoriae* a "radical dehistoricizing of soteriology," a feature that he believes is missing in the "mission-theological writings,"[316] he fails to draw the proper conclusions. If the latter indeed provide a historical structure for reality and emphasize the "salvation-historical relevance" (!) of the historical future (!) in terms of an immanent eschatology, one would assume that these texts are much less appropriate for proactively winning pagans to the Jewish faith than is the contemplative mysticism of *Quaestiones et solutiones* or *Legum allegoriae*, which aim at coaching readers or listeners in a nonecstatic consciousness of God. Noack asserts that Philo wrote *Quaestiones et solutiones*, in which he emphasizes the need to distance oneself from the passions and from the world as well as the necessity of contemplation, in order to "exert influence over the larger camp of the Jewish interpretation of Scripture." And he concludes that Philo's *Legum allegoriae* emphasizes more strongly the contemplative consciousness "which positively integrates the immanent perspective and reflects, in the company of the initiated, the dangers (the consciousness that absolutizes itself) and also expanded possibilities of mystical existence (to experience God in things)." It was not written with the goal to convince academically but to "strengthen dogmatically the consciousness of the students who are already initiated" and to communicate to this "circle of the initiated" his understanding of mystical exegetical theology.

Thus the question arises why the "mission-theological writings," as Noack calls them, were not also written for this "circle of the initiated." Why should a "historicizing soteriology" be attractive for Alexandrian pagans in contrast to the integrating and spiritual *Quaestiones et solutiones*, a text that communicates, according to Noack, the certainty (!) of identity? Why should the salvation-historical meaning of biblical eschatology that can be found in the "mission-theological writings" be better suited for a pagan audience and the "cultural competition" than the dualism of consciousness that we find in the *Legum allegoriae*, a text that accentuates the critique of the existing conditions? Pagan philosophers engage again and again in precisely such a critique as well, and a historicizing salvation-history appears to be much more relevant for Jews than for Gentiles. When Noack dismisses the analysis of Philo by Gerhard Sellin as "strangely detached"

---

[314]See Umemoto 1994, 23: of 280 occurrences of (τὸ) ἔθνος, only 141 designate the Jewish people; and only 30 occurrences of τὰ ἔθνη (10 times), ἔθνη without definite article (17 times) and τὸ ἔθνος (3 times) designate the "pagan" nations. For the observations that follow above see Delling 1987, 111; Will and Orrieux 1992, 111; Umemoto 1994, 23; Kraus 1996, 90; Wander 1998, 140-43.
[315]Noack 2000, 27, 245.
[316]Noack 2000, 221, 226, 234-35; the quotation that follows above, ibid., 221.

because he allegedly fails to take into account the *Sitz im Leben* of Philo's writings,[317] the same objection could be made concerning his own interpretation of Philo in regard to the *Sitz im Leben* of actual missionaries and their proclamation. A "mission-theological speaker" exists only if there is a missionary intention, which has not been demonstrated for Philo. It may be telling that Noack mentions only the synagogue and private homes when he lists the specific social places where Philo taught, omitting the agora—a place mentioned by Philo as the location where philosophical teachings are publicly communicated (*Spec.* 1.319-323).[318] On a different note, the argument of Neil McEleney and others that Philo knew uncircumcised proselytes cannot be maintained.[319]

Philo's works allow us to reconstruct an impressive description of life in Alexandria in the first century A.D. He speaks of law courts, lawyers and jurors, of the great Caesareum, of King Ptolemy II Philadelphos, of the theater and the gymnasium, of barracks, of imposing houses with colonnades and stables for the horses, of slaves, of ships and their captains, of medical doctors and operations, of thugs and homosexuals in the marketplace, of prostitutes, beggars, Sophists, Cynics, tax collectors, banquets, the worship of animals, and of Jewish life in the numerous synagogues and private homes.[320] He knows Jewish peasants, ship owners, traders and artisans.[321] He complains about the secret activities of the mystery cults and suggests that they should recruit new members publicly in the market (*Spec.* 1.319-320). He never alludes to missionary attempts by Jews to convert their Gentile neighbors.[322]

In *Spec.* 4.179 Philo discusses the segregation of the Jews from all other people, explaining this fact as something inevitable.

Spec. 4.179: "One may say that the whole Jewish race is in the position of an orphan compared with all the nations on every side. They when misfortunes fall upon them which are not by the direct intervention of heaven are never, owing to international intercourse, unprovided with helpers who join sides with them. But the Jewish nation has none to take its part, as it lives under exceptional laws which are necessarily grave and severe, because they inculcate the highest standard of virtue. But gravity is austere, and austerity is held in aversion by the great mass of men because they favor pleasure."

In his treatise *De virtutibus,* the section "On Nobility" (*Virt.* 187-227) serves to demonstrate that all virtuous people are noble, irrespective of their lineage. The arguments in *Virt.* 211-219 show that proselytes are virtuous Gentiles and thus

---

[317]Noack 2000, 5 n. 11 (with regard to G. Sellin 1986, 92-171); for the comment that follows above see ibid., 27.

[318]Noack (2000, 27-29), who relates *Spec.* 1.319-323 to the ideal or typical places for teaching activity in antiquity.

[319]McEleney 1974, 328-29. Nolland (1981, 173-79) disagrees.

[320]See Sly 1996.

[321]Delling 1987, 58, with reference to *Flacc.* 57.

[322]Cf. Sly 1996, 95: "There is no indication from anywhere in his writings that Philo engaged in give-and-take in the agora." See recently also Riesner 2000, 239-41.

can claim the same "nobility" as Abraham, who himself was not of aristocratic birth.

Virt. 219: "He [Abraham] is the standard of nobility for all proselytes [ἅπασιν ἐπηλύταις ἐν γενείας ἐστικανών], who, abandoning the ignobility of strange laws and monstrous customs which assigned divine honors to stocks and stones and soulless things in general, have come to settle in a better land, in a commonwealth full of true life and vitality, with truth as its director and president."

Proselytes and Jews therefore possess equal status and the same civic rights (*Virt.* 102-103; *Spec.* 1.52):

Virt. 102-103: "Having laid down laws for members of the same nation, he holds that the incomers [proselytes] too should be accorded every favor and consideration [προνομία][323] as their due, because abandoning [ἀπολελοιπότας] their kinsfolk by blood, their country, their customs and the temples and images of their gods, and the tributes and honors paid to them, they have taken the journey to a better home [καλὴν ἀποικίαν], from idle fables to the clear vision of truth and the worship of the one and truly existing God. [103]He commands all members of the nation to love the incomers [τοῖς ἀπὸ τοῦ ἔθνους ἀγαπᾶν τοὺς ἐπηλύτας], not only as friends and kinsfolk but as themselves [ὡς ἑαυτούς] both in body and soul: in bodily matters, by acting as far as may be for their common interest; in mental by having the same griefs and joys, so that they may seem to be the separate parts of a single living being which is compacted and unified by their fellowship in it."

Spec. 1.52: "Thus, while giving equal rank [ἰσοτιμίαν] to all incomers with all the privileges which he gives to the native-born, he exhorts the old nobility to honor them not only with marks of respect but with special friendship and with more than ordinary goodwill (φιλία καὶ εὐνοία). And surely there is good reason for this; they have left, he says, their country, their kinsfolk and their friends for the sake of virtue and religion. Let them not be denied another citizenship of other ties of family and friendship, and let them find places of shelter standing ready for refugees to the camp of piety. For the most effectual love-charm, the chain which binds indissolubly the goodwill which makes us one is to honor the one God."

The beginning of the treatise *De specialibus legibus* shows, however, that circumcision is prerequisite for joining those who see God (*Spec.* 1.1-11).[324] The philanthropy taught among Jews is not only the basic principle that controls the life of the Jews; it is at the same time the key to the reconciliation of the nations, which, Philo confidently asserts, will become "true reality" if the Jews consistently practice their Jewish way of life—that is, if they are always kind to other people (*Virt.* 118-120). The statement that the Jewish nation represents for the

---

[323]The term προνομία means "privilege" (LSJ).
[324]Thus Kraus 1996, following Feldman 1993a. Yet we should note that *Spec.* 1.1-11 mentions neither Gentiles nor proselytes, and circumcision is not explicitly described as prerequisite for the vision of God; in *Spec.* 1.2 Philo merely asserts that there are other people, particularly the Egyptians, who also value circumcision.

entire inhabited world what the priest is for the state (*Spec.* 2.163) is to be understood in this general political context.[325]

In *De vita Mosis* Philo describes Moses as the "greatest and most perfect of men" (*Mos.* 1.1, 48, 59, 148). Despite his power, he was not arrogant and remained reasonable (*Mos.* 1.150-154). He shares God's possessions (1.155-156) and is thus a cosmopolitan (κοσμοπολίτης), a world citizen: he is "not on the roll of any city of men's habitation, rightly so because he has received no mere piece of land but the whole world as his portion" (*Mos.* 1.157). He is a lawgiver superior to any that the Greeks ever had (*Mos.* 2.12-25). The practice of keeping the sabbath and fasting on special days has been adopted by many cities, as many people have been attracted by the Jewish laws (*Mos.* 2.20-24). Philo relates that many non-Jewish inhabitants of Alexandria participated in the anniversaries celebrating the Greek translation of the Hebrew Bible, which took place on the island Pharos (*Mos.* 2.41-44). This description has been taken by some scholars as evidence for active Jewish attempts to win sympathizers.[326]

However, even the future victory of the Jewish people over the nations, which Philo expects, "becomes primarily visible when the nations abandon their own customs and laws and are converted to the Jewish faith by adopting the Jewish laws."[327]

Mos. 2.43-44: "Thus the laws are shown to be desirable and precious in the eyes of all, ordinary citizens and rulers alike, and this too though our nation has not prospered for many a year. It is but natural that when people are not flourishing their belonging to some degree are under a cloud. [44]But, if a fresh start should be made to brighter prospects, how great a change for the better might we expect to see! I believe that each nation would abandon its peculiar ways, and, throwing overboard [καταλιπόντας] their ancestral customs, turn [μεταβαλεῖν] to honoring our laws alone. For, when the brightness of their shining is accompanied by national prosperity, it will darken the light of the others as the risen sun darkens the stars."

The passages that demonstrate, according to Dieter Georgi, that the synagogue services and the interpretation of the law presented therein were the decisive "medium of Jewish propaganda"[328] do not prove what is proposed.[329] An analysis of these passages and a survey of Philo's writings show that there are no specific references to Jews directly "addressing" Gentiles. Peder Borgen inter-

---

[325]Hvalvik (1996, 271) wants to interpret this passage as evidence for a Jewish missionary consciousness.

[326]But see Donaldson 1990, 13-14.

[327]Umemoto (1994), who refers further to *QE* 2.22. Unfortunately, Noack (2000) does not discuss this text. Schwemer (1996, 69) speaks in this context of Philo's "completely unrestricted praise for the proselytes."

[328]Georgi 1964, 87-91; quotation, 87 (ET, 84-87; quotation, 84): Philo, *Mos.* 2.17-27, 209-16; *Spec.* 2.62-63; *Hypoth.* 7.13.

[329]McKnight 1991, 65.

prets the passages in which Philo speaks of a future universal role of the Jews in terms of a political vision according to which the Jews one day will replace the Romans as the leading nation; this goal is achieved through peaceful means. The militaristic undercurrent of some passages became continuously stronger, until it provoked in A.D. 117 the violent reaction of the Roman army to the Jewish rebellion, leading to the destruction of Egyptian and Alexandrian Judaism.[330] The conclusion of Wolfgang Kraus is straightforward: "According to Philo there is thus no admission of Gentiles into the existing people of God; he rather expects a de-nationalization of the Torah and its universal dissemination and acceptance."[331] The basic aim of Philo's writing was the defense and preservation of the Jewish identity.[332]

Josephus

Josephus reports that the Jews in Antioch were granted considerable freedoms that led to considerable numerical growth of the Jewish colony, particularly since "they were constantly attracting [προσαγόμενοι] to their religious ceremonies multitudes of Greeks, and these they had in some measure incorporated with themselves" (*B.J.* 7.45)[333] This passage indicates at least that Gentiles regularly attended Jewish services and practiced Jewish customs because they found them attractive. Bernd Wander deduces from the middle participle προσ—αγόμενοι (*prosagomenoi*) that "the Jewish communities actively summoned and invited the Greek population to attend their meetings."[334] It remains unclear whether this is a necessary or valid interpretation. The passage does not mention a full integration of Antiochene Greeks into the people of God, which would have required circumcision. Perhaps Josephus paints in *B.J.* 7.45 too rosy a picture of the Jewish community in Antioch. In the preceding sentence in 7.44 he maintains that the Jews of Antioch possessed the same rights as the Greek citizens—a comment that generally is regarded as incorrect.[335]

Josephus repeatedly reports forced circumcisions that were politically motivated: John Hyrcanus circumcised the Idumeans (the ancestors of Herod's family [*A.J.* 13.257-258]). Aristobulus circumcised the Itureans (*A.J.* 13.318-319). Al-

---

[330]Peder Borgen, "Philo and the Jews in Alexandria," in Bilde et al. 1992, 122-38, esp. 136-37, with reference to Philo, *Mos.* 1.149, 155-157, 217, 289-291; 2.12-65, 66-186, 187-291; *Praem.* 93-97.

[331]Kraus 1996, 89.

[332]Thus McKnight 1991, 69-70; differently Feldman 1993a, 318-19.

[333]*B.J.* 7.45: προσαγόμενοι ταῖς θρησκείαις πολὺ πλῆθος Ἑλλήνων... μοῖραν αὐτῶν πεποίηντο.

[334]Wander 1998, 148; cf. Georgi 1964, 88-89. McKnight (1991, 65) suggests that the passage does not speak of a missionary intention of the members of the synagogue in Antioch. In his summary of the evidence in Josephus, Wander (1998, 153-54) is ambivalent: on the one hand, he speaks of a "partial sense of mission" of Judaism; on the other hand, he describes the forced conversions as important background information for the investigation of these questions.

[335]Acknowledged by Wander (1998, 148 n. 18).

exander Jannaeus destroyed Pella because its citizens refused to convert to Judaism (*A.J.* 13.397). A similar case is the story of Galilee's rebellious Jews who wanted to forcibly circumcise two Gentile subjects of the king of Trachonitis, who had brought weapons and money, which Josephus prevented with his authority as military commander (*Vita* 112-113). These forced circumcisions were motivated by military concerns. While it is possible here to attest to "zeal for their religion," clearly these were not "gradually missionary measures."[336] This is equally true for two further cases: Azizos, the king of Emesa, submitted to circumcision on account of his marriage to Drusilla; and Polemo, king of Cilicia, was circumcised before his wedding to Berenike (*A.J.* 20.139, 145-146). These events imply neither exclusive loyalty to the God of Israel nor integration into the local Jewish community—both Azizos and Polemo evidently had no difficulties in remaining the rulers of their territories.[337]

Josephus reports in both of his two main works the conversion to the Jewish faith of the royal family of Adiabene, extensively in *A.J.* 20.17-96,[338] an event dated to around A.D. 35.[339]

Ananias, a Jewish merchant, visited Charax Spasini (now Jebel Khayabir, in the delta of the rivers Tigris and Euphrates), where Izates, the son of King Monobazus of Adiabene, was living at the time. The region of Adiabene was a small kingdom in northeastern Mesopotamia (see §22.12 in the present work). Ananias taught the wives of Monobazus to worship God according to the manner of Jewish tradition (ἐδίδασκεν αὐτὰς τὸν θεὸν σέβειν, ὡς 'Ιουδαίοις πάτριον ἦν [*A.J.* 20.34]). Ananias becomes acquainted with Izates through these women, and eventually he is won to the Jewish faith as well. In Adiabene, Helena, the mother of the king, had adopted the Jewish laws as a result of the instruction of another Jew (μετακεκομίσθαι νόμους 'Ιουδαίων ἔωεσιν [20.35, 38]). Izates returns to Adiabene after Monobazus's death. When he learns of the conversion of his mother, he wants to be circumcised. Helena suggests that this may be too dangerous in view of the possible reaction of his subjects (20.39-40). Even Ananias the Jew attempts to talk him out of this course of action: matters might get out of hand if the king has himself circumcised (20.41). He argues that he can worship God without circumcision (χωρὶς τῆς περιτομῆς τὸ θεῖον σέβειν [20.41]): to be a devoted adherent of Judaism counted more than circumcision.[340] God would pardon him when he relinquishes the rite of circumcision on account of political necessity. The king initially was convinced by these arguments. Some time later a Galilean Jew named Eleazar, who had "a reputation for being extremely strict when it came to the ancestral laws" (περὶ τὰ πάτρια δοκῶν ἀκριβὴς εἶναι [20.43]), meets Izates and

---

[336]Contra Wander (1998, 144), who, however, rejects generalizations based on these measures. See also Rappaport 1965 and the critique in R. M. Smith 1999.

[337]S. Cohen 1987, 421.

[338]See S. Cohen 1987, 417-18, 424-25; Schiffman 1987; Gilbert 1991; Broer 1994; M. Goodman 1994, 63-65; D. Schwartz 1996; Hengel and Schwemer 1998, 108 (ET, 64); Wander 1998, 62-64, 224.

[339]D. Schwartz 1992a, 195-96.

[340]Contra McEleney (1974, 328), who interprets the passage as evidence for uncircumcised proselytes; cf. Nolland 1981, 192-94.

is aghast when he learns that Izates is not circumcised. He challenges him not just to read the law but to obey it and to be circumcised. Izates accepts this teaching of Eleazar (a strict Pharisee?), who argues that the renunciation of circumcision is a particularly grave infringement of the law and a serious "impiety" (20.44-46). The previous fears of Helena and of Ananias prove to be unfounded. Izates is circumcised and retains his throne: God preserved Izates and his children in the face of all dangers and "thus demonstrated that those who fix their eyes on Him and trust in Him alone do not lose the reward of their piety" (20.48). Helena and Monobazus, Izates' son, later built palaces in Jerusalem (*B.J.* 5.252), and Helena was buried in Jerusalem (*A.J.* 20.95; *B.J.* 5.55). Members of the royal house of Adiabene later fought against the Romans on the side of the Jews defending Jerusalem (*A.J.* 20.17-96; *B.J.* 2.388, 520; 5.356).

Izates II (A.D. 30-54) probably should not be regarded as prototypical for proselytes. After all, he was king. One therefore should refrain from far-reaching conclusions regarding a general missionary praxis of Diaspora Judaism based on this passage. We also must not forget that Ananias is described as a merchant, not as a Jewish envoy, scribe or Pharisee, nor as a traveling preacher of the Jewish faith. Josephus does not report a "missionary" initiative of Ananias. He is to be understood "as a Jew who did not want to rebuff the interest shown to his 'religion'. . . . The 'religious' dimension should not be overtaxed in this case either."[341] The "mission" of Eleazar may even have had a political background: he visited Adiabene at a time when the Jewish resistance movement against Rome became more radical in Judea and especially in Galilee. His insistence that King Izates be circumcised may be linked with the attempt to secure a more committed form of solidarity of the royal house of Adiabene, whose members sympathized with the Jewish faith and were God-fearers, so that the Jews in Palestine would gain support for the political conflict that was brewing.[342] The story of the conversion of the royal house of Adiabene to the worship of Yahweh provides no proof for the existence of an active, organized mission by Jews among Gentiles. The story demonstrates, however, how normal contacts, even contacts that a merchant maintained with a foreign royal court, could lead to conversations about faith in God, which at times prompted Gentiles to convert to Judaism.

In regard to the viewpoint of Josephus himself, Shaye Cohen concludes that the positive evaluation of the conversion of the royal family of Adiabene in *Antiquitates judaicae* is a special case.[343] In *B.J.* 2.520; 6.356; 5.474, Josephus notes simply that the royal house of Adiabene supported the Jewish rebels in the war against Rome, without ever mentioning the fact that they had converted to Judaism. In *A.J.* 20.17-96, the conversion of Izates and members of his family is nar-

---

[341]Wander 1998, 224. Hvalvik (1996, 295-96) regards Ananias as a Jewish missionary but is not able to ascertain whether "mission" was the intention of Ananias's journey; intentionality seems to be part of Hvalvik's definition of "mission" (see ibid., 270).

[342]Wander 1998, 226-27.

[343]S. Cohen 1987, esp. 417, 424-25, 427-30.

rated in detail, perhaps because the kingdom of Adiabene was situated beyond the borders of the Roman Empire and resisted the Parthians, the enemies of Rome. In other passages in *Antiquitates judaicae,* Gentiles who convert to Judaism are neither a model for others nor examples for the view that Gentiles fared better after their conversion. If groups of people submit to circumcision, then fear (*A.J.* 11.285) or force are factors.[344] Individuals who are circumcised do not enjoy a happy life: Fulvia, a converted aristocratic woman in Rome, is robbed by Jewish criminals (*A.J.* 18.81-84); King Azizos, who had himself circumcised because of his wife, Drusilla, is abandoned when Drusilla marries Felix (*A.J.* 20.141-443); King Polemo, circumcised because of Berenike, is also deserted by his wife: "He was relieved simultaneously of his marriage and of further adherence to the Jewish way of life" (*A.J.* 20.146). Josephus omits, presumably for apologetic reasons, a comment in the Septuagint according to which "proselytes" fought in Asa's army next to men from the tribes of Judah and Benjamin.[345] The positive assessment of Gentile adherents of Judaism in *Contra Apionem* is a special case, although even here Josephus neither praises converted Gentiles nor lists advantages that accrued to them as a result of their conversion.

Still, the story of the conversion of the royal house of Adiabene demonstrates four facts: (1) some Jews believed that Gentiles could join the Jewish way of life only through circumcision (Eleazar); (2) some Jews took the interest that some Gentiles showed in the Jewish faith seriously and provided instruction with the hope that they might believe in Israel's God, without insisting on an "official" conversion through circumcision (Ananias); (3) some Gentiles who were in contact with Jews were willing, after further instruction, to worship the God of the Jews and to adopt Jewish laws and customs (Izates, Helena); (4) family circumstances played an important role in the expansion of circles of "sympathizers" with Judaism (Monobazus son of Izates).

Roman Historians

Comments by Valerius Maximus, Tacitus, Suetonius and Cassius Dio, who report proceedings of Roman officials against Jewish activities, often are cited as evidence for the existence of a Jewish mission among Gentiles.[346] Heikki Solin, the author of an important ethno-demographic study on the Jews in the Roman world, suggests on the basis of these reports of the Roman historians "that individual congregations and individual Jews spontaneously engaged in religious propaganda. And this propaganda must have been at times rather fervent."[347]

---

[344]Josephus, *A.J.* 13.257-258, 318-319, 397.

[345]2 Chron 15:9 LXX; see L. H. Feldman, "Josephus' Portrait of Asa," *BBR* 4 (1994): 41-59, esp. 56.

[346]See Schürer 3:73-81; Schniewind, *Mt,* 229; M. Stern 1987, 161, 164; M. Whittaker 1984, 85-91; Hengel and Schwemer 1998, 105-106 (ET, 62-63).

[347]Solin 1983, 111 n. 45. Solin points out, however, that it may not be possible to assume "a missionary activity in the Christian sense of the word" (ibid.).

Valerius Maximus reports in *Facta et dicta memorabilia,* written after A.D. 27 (extant in the *Epitome* of Iulius Paris, compiled in the fourth century), that Cn. Cornelius Scipio Hispalus[348] expelled Jews from Rome who wanted to introduce the cult of Jupiter Sabazius.[349]

Valerius Maximus, *Facta* 1.3.3: "Cn. Cornelius Hispalus, Foreign Praetor [*praetor peregrinus*],[350] in the Consulship of M. Popillius Laenas and L. Calpurnius, ordered the astrologers by edict to leave Rome and Italy within ten days [*edicto Chaldaeos citra decimum diem abire ex urbe atque Italia iussit*]. For they spread profitable darkness with their lies over frivolous and foolish minds by fallacious interpretation of the stars [*levibus et ineptis ingeniis fallaci siderum interpretatione quaestuosam mendaciis suis caliginem inicientes*]. The same Hispalus made the Jews go home, who had tried to infect Roman manners with the cult of Jupiter Sabazius [*Idem Iudaeos, qui Sabazi Iovis cultu Romanos inficere mores conati erant, repetere domos suas coegit*]."

Many scholars have interpreted this note in terms of Jews who engaged in religious propaganda—that is, who attempted to win others for the Jewish faith—and were expelled as a result.[351]

The suggestion that these may have been syncretistic Jews from Phrygia who propagated their mixed cult from Judea and Asia Minor in Rome is not very plausible.[352] Sabazios was a Phrygian-Thracian god whose syncretistic cult spread in the Mediterranean world. A close analysis of the manuscript tradition leads E. N. Lane to the conclusion that the original text of Valerius Maximus mentions three deportations ordered by Cornelius Hispalus: one of astrologers, one of worshipers of Sabazios, and one of Jews.[353] The expression *Sabazios Iovis* probably represents an identification with *Iao Sabaoth,* representing the Jewish designation Yahweh Zebaoth, formulated by Gentiles on etymological grounds.

Some scholars link the deportation mentioned by Valerius Maximus with the Jewish delegation sent to Rome by Simon (the third of the Maccabean brothers) and led by Numenius. They negotiated in 140/139 B.C. with the Roman senate concerning the renewal of an alliance and ultimately were successful (1 Macc 14:24;

---

[348]Cornelius Scipio Hispalus was praetor in Rome in 139 B.C. See H. G. Gundel, "Cornelius 78," *KP* 1:1313.

[349]Valerius Maximus, *Factorum et doctorum memorabilium libri novem; cum Iiulii Paridis et Ianuarii Nepotiani epitomis* (ed. C. Kempf; 2nd ed.; Leipzig: Teubner, 1888 [repr., Stuttgart: Reclam, 1982]), 17; cf. E. N. Lane, *CCIS* 2:47 (no. 12); David R. Shackleton Bailey, *Valerius Maximus: Memorable Doings and Sayings* (LCL; Cambridge, Mass.: Harvard University Press, 2000), 46-47.

[350]This office corresponded to the juridical office for noncitizens in Rome.

[351]M. Stern 1987, 160-61; McKnight 1991, 73; Rokéah 1996, 209-10; Wander 1998, 163-65; Hvalvik 1996, 297-99; differently M. Goodman 1992.

[352]See Hengel (1969, 479 [ET, 1:263]), who tends to agree with this hypothesis proposed by F. Cumont, R. Reitzenstein and A. D. Nock.

[353]E. N. Lane, "Sabazius and the Jews in Valerius Maximus: A Re-examination," *JRS* 69 (1979): 35-38; see also Schürer 3:111; S. E. Johnson, "The Present State of Sabazios Research," *ANRW* II.17.3 (1984): 1583-1613, esp. 1602-3; Trebilco 1991, 38.

15:15-24). The account in 1 Maccabees suggests that members of the Jewish delegation attempted to convince Roman citizens to convert to the Jewish faith. They evidently behaved in such a peculiar and offensive manner that the praetor saw no other recourse than to deport the Jews from Rome.[354] It is doubtful, however, that this scenario is plausible, since 1 Macc 15 states that the delegation returned successfully after attaining a *senatus consultum* that guaranteed for the Jews uncontested ownership of their territory. It is more plausible to assume that there were attempts by Jews to influence Roman citizens to become sympathizers of Judaism. It remains unclear whether these attempts were politically or religiously motivated, whether they should be regarded as the typical behavior of a particular group in Rome, or whether they were caused by specific circumstances.

The *Facta et dicta memorabilia* of Valerius Maximus were written for use in the rhetorical schools; even though they are based on good sources, many classical scholars think that their historical value is often doubtful. Besides other authors whom he uses as sources, Valerius imitates and modifies especially Cicero and Livius, abbreviating or expanding them according to rhetorical patterns, willing to include entirely fictional material. G. Maslakov comments, "Valerius was not a careful or a systematic writer. The 'pictures' or 'images' that emerge through collation are most probably the incidental product of much haphazard accumulation of material."[355] Since Valerius does not write as a historian, he should not be accused of an uncritical use of his sources or of adopting historical errors: the mistakes usually are the result of carelessness, lack of knowledge or errors in the sources. It has not been proven that Valerius is guilty of deliberate falsifications.[356] This does not mean, however, that the note in 1.3.3 is fictitious.

Since both the content and the historical value of the notice in Valerius Maximus, *Facta* 1.3.3 are contested, it should at least not be overrated in the debate about the existence of an active Jewish missionary outreach to Gentiles.[357]

Suetonius (ca. A.D. 70-150), who was able to utilize his familiarity with the imperial archives,[358] reports how the emperor Tiberius (A.D. 14-37) "abolished

---

[354]See Ludwig Friedländer, *Darstellungen aus der Sittengeschichte Roms in der Zeit von August bis zum Ausgang der Antonine* (10th ed.; 4 vols.; Aalen: Scientia, 1964 [1921-1923]), 3:209.

[355]See G. Maslakov, "Valerius Maximus and Roman Historiography: A Study of the *exempla* Tradition," *ANRW* II.32.1 (1984): 437-96, esp. 461; quotation, 489. The verdict of Buchwald (*Tusculum-Lexikon,* 821) is less sympathetic: the *Facta* were written "without criticism and without a sense for historical truth."

[356]Thus Ursula Blank-Sangmeister, ed., in Valerius Maximus, *Facta et dicta memorabilia,* 342, with reference to Michael Fleck, "Untersuchungen zu den Exempla des Valerius Maximus" (diss., University of Marburg, 1974), 122.

[357]See Feldman 1993a, 303-4.

[358]See L. de Coninck, "Les sources documentaires de Suétone, 'Les XII Césars': 1900-1990," *ANRW* II.33.5 (1991): 3675-3700. On the discussion about Suetonius's historigraphical reliability see also Riesner 1994, 142-43 (ET, 160-61). Suetonius's comments on Judaism have been collected in *GLAJJ* II 108-31. Although Suetonius's view of Christianity clearly was negative, as was that of Tacitus, he did not seek opportunities to include information hostile to the Jews; see Malitz 1996, esp. 376 with n. 27.

foreign cults, especially the Egyptian and the Jewish rites [*Aegyptios Iudaicosque ritus*]" (*Tib.* 36.1). He goes on to describe Tiberius's measures:

Tiberius compelled "all who were addicted to such superstitions to burn their religious vestments and all their paraphernalia. Those of the Jews who were of military age he assigned to provinces of less healthy climates, ostensibly to serve in the army; the others of that same race or of similar beliefs he banished from the city [*reliquos gentis eiusdem vel similia sectantes urbe summovit*], on pain of slavery for life if they did not obey" (*Tib.* 36.1).

This expulsion of the Jews from Rome in A.D. 19 by Tiberius is mentioned also by Tacitus, Josephus and Cassius Dio. Tacitus reports of hearings in the senate on "the proscription of the Egyptian and Jewish rites [*de sacris Aegyptiis Iudaicisque pellendis*]" (Tacitus, *Ann.* 2.85.5).

Ann. 2.85.5: "A senatorial edict [*patrum consultum*] directed that four thousand descendants of enfranchised slaves, tainted with that superstition [*quattuor milia libertini generis ea superstitione infecta*] and suitable in point of age, were to be shipped to Sardinia and there employed in suppressing brigandage: 'if they succumbed to the pestilential climate, it was a cheap loss.' The rest had orders to leave Italy, unless they had renounced their impious ceremonial by a given date [*nisi certam ante diem profanos ritus exuissent*]."

Josephus reports that "a certain Jew, a complete scoundrel" (*A.J.* 18.81) who had moved from Palestine to Rome, together with three friends, cheated Fulvia, an aristocratic woman "who had become a Jewish proselyte" and met with them regularly, presumably for instruction, out of purple and gold. Saturninus, Fulvia's husband, reported this incident to his friend the emperor Tiberius, who "ordered the whole Jewish community to leave Rome," banishing four thousand Jews to Sardinia as soldiers (*A.J.* 18.83-84).[359] Cassius Dio later reports that Tiberius deported most of the Jews from Rome "as the Jews flocked to Rome in great numbers and were converting many of the natives to their ways."[360] Tiberius seems to have eased or repealed this edict soon after the fall of Sejanus in A.D. 31 (Philo, *Legat.* 160-161).

Suetonius reports that Domitian had one of his cousins executed, the consul Flavius Clemens (*Dom.* 15.1). Cassius Dio provides further details on this episode: Flavius Clemens and his wife, Domitilla, were accused of atheism, "a charge on which many others who drifted into Jewish ways [ἄλλοι εἰς τὰ τῶν Ἰουδαίων ἤθη ἐξοκέλλοντες] were condemned." Clemens was executed, while Domitilla was sent into exile (Cassius Dio, 67.14.1-3). It is possible, but not certain, that Flavius Clemens and Domitilla were Christians (thus Eusebius, *Hist. eccl.* 3.18.4): the "Jewish ways" may imply a reference to the Christian faith, since official authorities in the first century regarded Christianity as a form of Judaism. It therefore must remain an open question whether the verb ἐξοκέλλειν (*exokellein*) refers to

---

[359]On this episode see Smallwood 1976, 201-10; more recently Wander 1998, 150-53, 223.
[360]Cassius Dio 57.18.5a: καὶ συχνοὺς τῶν ἐπιχωρίων ἐς τὰ σφέτερα ἔθη μεθιστάντων.

Gentiles who "drifted" into Jewish circles; the verb, which can mean "run aground" (referring to a ship) or "drift into" (metaphorically), implies no reference to missionary activity of Jews.

Do these brief passages provide evidence for a Jewish mission among Gentiles, or at least for a Jewish mission among the inhabitants of Rome? Heikki Solin thinks that the repetition of protective measures by Roman authorities shows that they proved to be weak "regarding the unwanted proselytizing successes"; that is, he evaluates these notices in terms of an active Jewish missionary endeavor.[361] We should note, however, that the remark by Valerius Maximus is the only explicit reference to Jewish proselytism. Neither Suetonius nor Tacitus explicitly refers to organized attempts by Jews to actively win citizens of Rome to their faith. The "infection" that Valerius Maximus refers to could have been "caught" by Roman citizens themselves as they sympathized with the synagogues or converted to Judaism; that is, the God-fearers and the later proselytes themselves could have taken the initiative to develop an interest in the Jewish faith. The men whom Josephus describes in *A.J.* 18.81-84 are not "recruiters" for the Jewish faith but people who use the interest of Gentiles and the attractiveness of the Jewish faith for their own (criminal) activities.[362] Josephus never indicates that Jews were punished because they converted a member of the ruling classes to Judaism.[363] And we should not forget that the number of proselytes in Rome (as in the other Hellenistic cities) probably was low.

Scot McKnight explains the sparse references to a Jewish missionary activity in Rome in terms of an extraordinary and sporadic situation. He points out that the relevant comments are made by antagonistic authors who may have exaggerated the behavior of the Jews in order to justify the actions of the emperors.[364]

Roman Satirists

In the satires of Horace (65-8 B.C.) and Juvenal (b. A.D. 60) we find three passages that often are quoted as evidence for a Jewish mission among pagans.[365]

Horace, *Sat.* 1.4.138-143: "Thus, with lips shut tight, I debate with myself; and when I find a bit of leisure, I trifle with my papers. This is one of those lesser frailties I spoke of, and

---

[361]Solin (1983, 618), who believes, somewhat problematically, that the Jews were "a constant ferment of disturbance" ("ständiges Ferment der Unruhe") (ibid., 686; similarly 690 n. 224). See further Smallwood 1976, 205-8. For an explanation similar to Solin's see Margaret H. Williams, "The Expulsion of the Jews from Rome in A.D. 19," *Latomus* 48 (1989): 765-84.

[362]Thus Wander 1998, 223; on these questions see also M. Goodman 1994, 82-83.

[363]Rutgers 1989, 102.

[364]McKnight 1991, 74.

[365]Georgi 1964, 105-6 (ET, 96-98); similarly Wander (1998, 163, 168-70), who is more cautious, however.

if you should make no allowance for it, then would a big band of poets come to my aid—for we are the big majority—and we, like the Jews, will compel [*cogemus*] you to make one of our throng."

Juvenal, *Sat.* 6.542-544: "No sooner has that fellow departed than a palsied Jewess, leaving her basket and her truss of hay, comes begging to her secret ear; she is an interpreter of the laws of Jerusalem, a high priestess of the tree, a trusty go-between of highest heaven [*interpres legum Solymarum et magna sacerdos arboris ac summi fida internuntia caeli*]. She, too, fills her palm, but more sparingly, for a Jew will tell you dreams of any kind you please for the minutest of coins."

Juvenal, *Sat.* 14.96-106: "Some who have had a father who reveres the Sabbath [*metuentem sabbata*] worship nothing but the clouds, and the divinity of the heavens, and see no difference between eating swine's flesh, from which their father abstained, and that of man; and in time they take to circumcision [*praeputia ponunt*]. Having been wont to flout the laws of Rome, they learn and practice and revere the Jewish law, and all that Moses handed down in his secret tome, forbidding to point out the way to any not worshiping the same rites, and conducting none but the circumcised to the desired fountain [*non monstrare vias eadem nisi sacra colenti, quaesitum ad fontem solos deducere verpos*]. For all which the father was to blame, who gave up every seventh day to idleness, keeping it apart from all the concerns of life."

John Nolland demonstrates that Horace refers not to the Jews' ability to convert people forcibly by aggressive missionary work but to their aptitude for gaining political or personal advantages through public assemblies.[366]

Nor does the Juvenal passage constitute evidence for the suggestion that Diaspora synagogues and the interpretation of the law presented therein were a means for a Jewish mission among Gentiles. There is no reference to a synagogue, a female Jewish beggar is hardly the prototype of a Jewish missionary who teaches Torah, and the reference to the sons of a sabbath-keeping pagan[367] who eventually renounce pork and ultimately have themselves circumcised can be interpreted in terms of Gentiles growing slowly into the Jewish identity. The comment that what Moses handed down was to forbid "to point out the way to any not worshiping the same rites" and to conduct "none but the circumcised to the desired fountain" (14.103-104) refers to pagan converts who display secretive behavior; it is the pagan who takes the initiative, not a Jewish missionary.[368] Still, this passage indicates that there were circles of pagan sympathizers with Judaism that were somewhat significant so that pagan authors took offense.[369]

New Testament Evidence

Several items in the New Testament are cited as evidence for the existence of a

---

[366]See Nolland 1979; followed by Kraabel 1982, 455; McKnight 1991, 64.
[367]See Goldenberg, 1979, esp. 430-32.
[368]McKnight 1991, 64, 113.
[369]Wander 1998, 169.

Jewish mission among Gentiles.

1. Two parallel texts from Matthew and Luke are not very telling (Mt 15:14/ Lk 6:39; Mt 23:13/Lk 11:52).

Mt 15:14/Lk 6:39: "Let them alone; they are blind guides of the blind. And if one blind person guides another, both will fall into a pit."

Mt 23:13/Lk 11:52: "But woe to you, scribes and Pharisees, hypocrites! For you lock people out of the kingdom of heaven. For you do not go in yourselves, and when others are going in, you stop them."

In regard to the first text, it is unclear whether the "blind" are Gentiles who are to be converted. In the second text, it is equally impossible to demonstrate that the scribes and Pharisees prevent Gentiles from entering the kingdom of God.

2. A more significant text is Mt 23:15. Many New Testament scholars regard this verse as clear evidence for the existence of a Jewish mission among Gentiles.[370]

Mt 23:15: "Woe to you, scribes and Pharisees, hypocrites! For you cross sea and land [περιάγετε τὴν θάλασσαν καὶ τὴν ξηράν] to make a single convert [ποιῆσαι ἕνα προσήλυτον], and you make the new convert twice as much a child of hell as yourselves."

Does this text presuppose the existence of missionary activity of Pharisees among Gentiles? The main argument for this interpretation is the usage of the term *prosēlytos* in the New Testament: in Acts 2:11; 6:5; 13:43 this term designates non-Jews who converted to Judaism through circumcision and obedience to the Torah. Eduard Schweizer contends that Mt 23:15 constitutes "evidence of intense Jewish missionary activity," since a proselyte is a full convert to Judaism, a circumcised Gentile who follows the law.[371]

However, the polemical tone of Mt 23 and the hyperbolic formulation— scribes and Pharisees travel across "sea and land" to win "a single convert"— suggest that Mt 23:15 cannot be easily or directly evaluated in terms of the extent or the intensity of a Pharisaic proselytizing propaganda.[372] Nothing in this comment forces us to interpret in terms of a "burning zeal of the Pharisaic mission,"[373] since no Jewish, Greek or Roman texts unambiguously prove the exis-

---

[370]Besides the commentaries see, for example, Lerle 1960, 63-66; more recently Hvalvik 1996, 291-95.

[371]Schweizer, *Mt,* 287 (ET, 440); cf. Zahn, *Mt,* 653; Schlatter, *Mt,* 674-76; Grundmann, *Mt,* 490-91; Gnilka, *Mt,* 2:286.

[372]Thus H. Kuhli, "προσήλυτος," *EWNT* 3:410-13, esp. 412-13 (*EDNT* 3:170-71), who believes that "this passage presupposes the Pharisaic movement's generally positive posture regarding missionary activity."

[373]Thus Schlatter, *Mt,* 674. For a critique of this traditional interpretation see Will and Orrieux 1992, 115-36; M. Goodman 1994, 69-72; McKnight 1991.

tence of Jewish missionary work among Gentiles. Assertions such as that of
Walter Grundmann, who states that Jewish missionary activity "reached its climax at the time of Jesus and the apostles,"[374] are sheer inventions.

The προσήλυτοι (*prosēlytoi*) in Mt 23:15 are, in the context of Mt 23, not
Gentiles who are converted to Judaism per se, but rather Gentiles who are
converted to *Pharisaic* Judaism. The zeal of the scribes and Pharisees that
makes the newly won *prosēlytos* "twice as much a child of hell as yourselves"
must be understood in the context of Jesus' indictment of the scribes and Pharisees as zeal for the minute details of the Torah.[375] Why would Jesus criticize
missionary endeavors of Pharisees who wanted to win pagans for faith in Israel's God and for a way of life consistent with this faith? In Mt 23 Jesus con-
demns the results of the piety and way of life of the Pharisees, who concentrated on the most minute details of the Torah while refusing to accept him
with his messianic claims as prerequisite for entrance into God's kingdom.
Jesus evidently criticizes in Mt 23:15 the results of the Pharisees' preaching
ministry in the Diaspora synagogues: the interpretations and precepts that they
derive from the law and teach to the God-fearing Gentiles leave no room for
faith in Jesus the Messiah. More than that, their new converts who surpass the
Pharisaic missionaries in their zeal and rigor[376] are thereby barred from the
possibility of entering into the messianic kingdom of God.

If Martin Goodman is correct, we should not exclude the possibility that *prosēlytos* in this
passage retains its general sense of "adherent" and refers to Jews: Jesus attacks Pharisees
who attempt to convince other Jews to become Pharisees and to follow the Pharisaic halakah.[377] The term *prosēlytos* could still be used in the second century, in diverse contexts,
for "converts" to Judaism or to Christianity.[378]

Mt 23:15 probably refers to the efforts of (scribal) Pharisees to convince pagan sympathizers with Judaism and "God-fearers" who attended the Diaspora
synagogues that they should accept circumcision and thus to win them fully
and completely to the Jewish faith (and at the same time to the Pharisaic understanding of Torah-righteousness).[379] Since no Second Temple writing attests an active mission of Jews among Gentiles, and since devout Pharisees
would not have been forced to derive such an assignment from the Hebrew

---

[374]Grundmann, *Mt,* 490.
[375]Thus D. E. Garland, *The Intention of Matthew 23* (NovTSup 52; Leiden: Brill, 1979) 130-31.
[376]Carson, *Mt,* 478, referring to psychological plausibility, suspects that "they 'out-Pharisee' the
    Pharisees."
[377]M. Goodman 1992a, 60-63; 1994, 70-75; thus already Munck 1954, 262; now also Levinskaya
    1996, 36-39; note, however, the critique in Feldman 1993a, 298-300; Hvalvik 1996, 294.
[378]See Justin, *Dial.* 23.3; 28.2; 80.1; 122.1; 122.3-4.5; 123.1-2.
[379]Thus McKnight 1991, 106-8; Carson, *Mt,* 478; Hagner, *Mt,* 669; Wander 1998, 227. Not very
    convincing is the hypothesis of Will and Orrieux (1992, 111), who interpret Mt 23:15 in terms
    of late Matthean redaction as a reaction against Jewish-Christian "Judaizers."

Bible, this is a plausible explanation. If this interpretation is valid, we may speak of a synagogue mission by Pharisees: the God-fearers and other pagan sympathizers with the Jewish faith belonged to the "environment" of the Diaspora synagogues on the sabbath and might be won over to become proselytes by sermons preached in the Jewish houses of worship and study. The proselytes won by Pharisees would have been Pharisaic proselytes—that is, proselytes who adopted the Pharisees' halakah. In conclusion, Mt 23:15 cannot be used as clear evidence for an organized Jewish missionary activity among pagans.

3. Another text cited as evidence for Jewish missionary activity among Gentiles is Rom 2:19-20.[380]

Rom 2:19-20: "and if you are sure that you are a guide to the blind [ὁδηγὸν εἶναι τυφλῶν], a light to those who are in darkness [φῶς τῶν ἐν σκότει], [20]a corrector of the foolish [παιδευτὴν ἀφρόνων], a teacher of children [διδάσκαλον νηπίων], having in the law the embodiment of knowledge and truth."

None of the formulations in Rom 2:19-20 that remind the reader in part of Is 42:6-7 and of several Jewish texts force us to assume an active Jewish mission. Rather, the passage implies the kind of Jewish self-confidence that is certain of possessing superior privileges, willing to accept Gentiles who acknowledge their blindness and who therefore turn to Jews in order to receive instruction.[381]

As there is no direct evidence for Jewish missionary activity among Gentiles, the description in Rom 2:19-20 need not be interpreted in that sense: the terms "corrector" and "teacher" can be understood in terms of everyday Jews in the context of their contacts with Gentiles or as a reference to those Jews who teach converted pagans who had become proselytes.[382]

4. There are the "Torah missionaries" who caused difficulties for Paul in Galatia. These probably were Jewish Christians who wanted to convince newly converted Christians in the churches established by Paul that they needed to be circumcised and to obey the law.[383] Since they were Jewish *Christians,* their activity hardly serves as proof for a general Jewish missionary activity.

Rabbinic Sources

In the rabbinic texts compiled and redacted after A.D. 100—Mishnah, Tosefta, Palestinian and Babylonian Talmuds, midrashim—[384]we find both positive and

---

[380]See Althaus, *Röm,* 24; Michel, *Röm,* 129; Käsemann, *Röm,* 66; Zeller, *Röm,* 71-72; Stuhlmacher (*Röm,* 47) speaks of a "missionary Judaism in the time of Paul." More cautious are Wilckens, *Röm,* 1:148-49; Moo, *Rom,* 162.
[381]See Dunn, *Rom,* 1:112, 116-17.
[382]See Cranfield, *Rom,* 1:167.
[383]See the commentaries; recently Longenecker, *Gal,* xciv-xcv; cf. Dunn 1993, 10-11.
[384]On questions of date see Strack and Stemberger 1982 (ET, 1992); S. Safrai 1987.

negative positions concerning proselytes.[385] These two options are reflected in the story of the three proselytes whom Hillel admitted to the Jewish faith; the proselytes commented, "Shammai's impatience sought to drive us from the world, but Hillel's gentleness brought us under the wings of the Shechinah" (*b. Šabb.* 31a). One proselyte had the following experience:

b. Šabb. 31a: "On another occasion it happened that a certain heathen came before Shammai and said to him, 'Make me a proselyte, on condition that you teach me the whole Torah while I stand on one foot.' Thereupon he repulsed him with the builder's cubit which was in his hand. When he went before Hillel, he said to him, 'What is hateful to you, do not to your neighbor: that is the whole Torah, while the rest is the commentary thereof; go and learn it'" (cf. *'Abot R. Nat.* 15:3 [24a-b]). Perhaps Hillel indeed stood on one foot (Heb., *'al regel*) when he converted the Gentile and made him a proselyte; perhaps we have a play on the Latin word *regula,* which would have Hillel referring to the Golden Rule.[386]

Even though this is a late tradition, it shows that at least in the Amoraic period the view that proselytes are welcome was linked with the name of Hillel. We should note, however, that Hillel is not presented as a teacher who approaches pagans, trying to convince them of the possibility or the necessity of converting to faith in Yahweh. These Gentiles approached the rabbis on their own accord.

In a discussion with Rabban Gamaliel, Rabbi Joshua b. Hananiah (A.D. 90) argues that the restrictions that applied, according to Deut 23:3, to the Ammonites should be lifted so that they can become proselytes (*b. Ber.* 28a). Rabbi Simeon b. Yohai (A.D. 150) argues the same position (*m. Yebam.* 8:3). It is doubtful, however, that this permits the conclusion that rabbinic halakah generally permitted converted Ammonite, Moabite, Edomite and Egyptian girls to promptly marry Jewish men. These two texts do not provide enough evidence for the conclusion that the rabbis of the first century wanted to encourage Gentiles, at least Gentile women, to convert to Judaism, softening some of the strict rulings of the Torah.[387]

Rabbi Simeon b. Eleazar (A.D. 190) argued that prayers should be offered for all people who live outside of Palestine because in the future all people would become proselytes (*b. Ber.* 57b). The Amoraic rabbis (A.D. 200-500) make posi-

---

[385]For the positive statements see Bamberger 1939; Braude 1940; E. Grünebaum, "Die Fremden (Gerim) nach rabbinischen Gesetzen," *Jüdische Zeitschrift für Wissenschaft und Leben* 1870: 43-57; Schürer 2:455-63; McKnight 1991, 40-43. For the negative statements see Bertholet 1896, 339-48; Bamberger 1939, 161-69; McKnight 1991, 40-43. See also Kern-Ulmer 1994; Hvalvik 1996, 273-83.

[386]See Raphael Jospe, "Hillel's Rule," *JQR* 81 (1990): 45-57; Lichtenberger, 1990, esp. 201-2. On the Golden Rule as summary of the Torah see A. Nissen 1974, 389-415; more recently E. P. Sanders 1992, 257-60.

[387]Contra Rokéah 1996, 220-21.

tive statements concerning proselytes more frequently.[388] According to Rabbi Eleazar b. Pedath (A.D. 270), God "did not exile Israel among the nations save in order that proselytes might join them" (*b. Pesaḥ* 87b). The rites that Gentiles who converted had to submit to is explained in *b. Ker.* 9a as follows: "As your forefathers entered the covenant only by circumcision, immersion and the sprinkling of blood, so shall they [proselytes] enter the covenant only by circumcision, immersion and the sprinkling of the blood."[389] Gentiles continued to convert to Judaism in the post-Constantine period, as the measures of state and church against Jews and against proselytes demonstrate.[390] We note again that the conversion of proselytes is described in *b. Pesaḥ.* 87b in passive formulations, not in terms of an active Jewish missionary activity among Gentiles.

Negative statements evidently are less numerous, but they can be rather drastic. Rabbi Helbo (A.D. 300) is reported to have said, "As bad as leprosy are the proselytes for Israel" (*b. Qidd.* 70b; *b. Yebam.* 47a). Amoraic rabbis sometimes make similarly negative statements.[391] We should further note that the rabbis ascribed to God's covenant with the descendants of Noah only limited significance: the covenant with Noah is surpassed by the covenant with Abraham.

Gen. Rab. 44:5 (428-429): "*After these things* [Gen 15:1]: There were some second thoughts. Who had second thoughts? Abraham did. He said before the Holy One, blessed be he, 'Lord of the ages, you made a covenant with Noah that you would not wipe out his children. I went and acquired a treasure of religious deeds and good deeds greater than his, so the covenant made with me has set aside the covenant made with him. Now is it possible that someone else will come along and accumulate religious deeds and good deeds greater than mine and so set aside the covenant that was made with me on account of the covenant to be made with him.' Said the Holy One, blessed be he, 'Out of Noah I did not raise up shields for the righteous, but from you I shall raise up shields for the righteous.'" The phrase "shields for the righteous" is an allusion to Gen 15:1b; as *Gen. Rab.* 44 further explains, they are to be identified with those descendants of Abraham, "by whose righteousness atonement is made when in Israel sin increases."[392]

A story by Rabbi Tanhuma (A.D. 380) illustrates the relationship between Jews and Gentiles.

---

[388]See *b. Ber.* 17b; *b. Pesaḥ.* 91b; *b. Menaḥ* 44a-b; *b. 'Abod. Zar.* 11a; 13b; *b. Šeb.* 39a; *b. Ned.* 32a; *t. Sanh.* 13:2. Hvalvik (1996, 276-83), unfortunately, does not provide chronological differentiations.

[389]See Avemarie 1996, 198. On the discussion of *b. Pesaḥ* 92a; 96a; *m. Ḥul.* 1:1; *b. Yebam.* 46b, passages that McEleney (1974, 329-30) interprets in terms of uncircumcised Gentiles who may celebrate the Passover, see Nolland 1981, 182-92.

[390]See Solin 1983, 623 with n. 56; Noethlichs 1971; E. L. Abel, "Jewish-Christian Controversy in the Second and Third Centuries A.D.," *Judaica* 22 (1972): 112-25.

[391]See *b. Qidd.* 62a-b; *b. Yebam.* 76a; 109b; *b. Sanh.* 96b; 99b; *b. Menaḥ* 44a; *b. Giṭ* 56b; *b. Ned.* 13b.

[392]See Avemarie 1996, 207. Avemarie observes that this limited view of the covenant with Noah is explained by the fact of Israel being God's elect people, which prevents Israel from granting other peoples a similar relationship with God (ibid., 209).

y. Ber. 9 [13b]: "Once a boat load of gentiles was sailing the Mediterranean. There was one Jewish child on the boat. A great storm came upon them in the sea. Each person took his idol in his hand and cried out. But it did not help them. Once they saw that their cries were of no avail, they turned to the Jewish child and said, 'Child, rise up and call out to your God. For we have heard that he answers you when you cry out to him, and that he is heroic.' The child immediately rose up and cried out with all his heart. The Holy One, blessed be He, accepted his prayer and quieted the seas. When the ship reached dry land [at the port], everyone disembarked to purchase his needed staples. They said to the child, 'Don't you wish to buy anything?' He said to them, 'What do you want of me? I am just a poor traveler.' They said to him, 'You are just a poor traveler? They are the poor travelers. Some of them are here, and their idols are in Babylonia. Some of them are here, and their idols are in Rome. Some of them are here and their idols are with them, but they do them no good. But wherever you go, your God is with you'" (see Str-B 1:452).

This story describes the existence of the Jews as strangers in the midst of a pagan world.[393] The Jewish youngster is alone on the ship, surrounded by Gentiles who own the ship. The "strangeness" of the Jew becomes dramatically obvious in the storm: the calamity of the storm hits everybody without exception, but as the Gentiles "take" their idols—small statues of their gods that they carry with them—and pray for help, the Jew does not pray. He cannot pray at the same time that Gentiles pray. When he prays, he hopes that he will be heard, and if Yahweh makes the storm cease, his pagan co-travelers would believe that their gods made the storm go away. "The ugly ditch between the Jew and the non-Jew cannot be bridged, not even in the hour of a common calamity. Thus the Jew prays (naturally holding nothing in his hands) only at the moment when the non-Jews despair of their gods." When the ship arrives in port, the foreignness of the Jew is evident again: while the Gentiles disembark and shop at the market, he stays on board the ship because he knows himself to be a "stranger," a guest, even in a port city. "A Jew among Gentiles is always but a guest." The end of the story notes the thankfulness of the Gentiles who were saved through the prayer of the Jew: they invite him to accompany them on a shopping spree in the city; they are concerned for him. They express the decisive difference between their religiosity and the faith of the Jew by pointing out that their gods are bound to their far-away temples, and even the images of their gods that they carried with them were impotent[394] because ultimately they remain bound to their temples in Babylon, in Rome or wherever they are located. The God of the Jews, on the other hand, has no house and thus accompanies each Jew everywhere. This observation ends the story. The narrator knows "that the non-Jews will not understand what to say concerning their 'geographical theology.'" The Gentiles are everywhere "at home," both on the ship and in the city, even though their gods are

---

[393]For the interpretation that follows above see Fraenkel 1993, 67-69 (quotations, 68, 69).
[394]Fraenkel omits this sentence from the story and from his interpretation.

far away in Rome and in Babylon, being of no help in times of need. The Jew knows that his God is close to him no matter where he is, and he knows that his God will hear when he prays, but he understands himself to be a stranger everywhere. This difference is to be explained as follows: people who know that their god is far away feel free and at home everywhere because their god cannot see them; people who know that Yahweh is omnipresent realize that he is, as Creator, the Lord of the world, in which a person can only be a guest. Rabbi Tanhuma does not relate a conversation of the Jewish youngster with the sailors in which he explains to the friendly and thankful Gentiles that they can join the faith in Yahweh, the powerful God of the universe, and become Jews.

Martin Goodman assumes that the impetus for the conversion of Gentiles to Judaism was expected to come from the Gentiles themselves. He states that "it was extremely unusual for any Jew in the first century A.D. to view the encouragement of gentiles to convert to Judaism as a praiseworthy act."[395] In regard to later rabbinic Judaism, Goodman concludes from the (sparse) extant evidence that no Amoraic text refers to a Tanna of the second century who had a positive opinion of a proselytizing mission. He notes that "although they accepted proselytes, they refrained from missionary activity."[396] Positive opinions surface in the statements of rabbis of the third and early fourth century. Goodman explains the rising interest in missionary activity in the third century as a result of the influence of the missionary successes of the Christian churches.[397]

Louis Feldman accepts Martin Goodman's hypothesis for the period after the third century but rejects it concerning the Hellenistic and early Roman period.[398] David Rokéah agrees with Feldman with regard to the first and second century but rejects both Goodman's and Feldman's evaluations of the evidence for the third century. He believes that there was a vigorous Jewish missionary activity among Gentiles in the first and the early second centuries.[399] However, he offers no new evidence from Second Temple Judaism or Roman authors, nor does he offer a convincing interpretation of the known sources. His discussion of rabbinic texts suffers from the difficulty that we cannot unambiguously determine the historical reliability of information on rabbis before A.D. 200. As scholars draw conclusions from the fact that the sources never explicitly mention a Jewish missionary activity in pagan territories, and from the fact that neither Jewish nor pagan sources ever mention the name of a Jewish missionary, Feldman counters with the charge of indulging in an *argumentum e silentio*. This overlooks, first, that sometimes silence can indeed speak loud and clear, and, second, that his explanation that Josephus did not want to offend his benefactors and that Philo had to counter the charge of Jewish aggressiveness in a sensitive manner[400] is derived from "silence" as well.

---

[395]M. Goodman 1989a, 175; cf. S. Stern 1994, 88-89.
[396]Cf. S. Cohen 1999, 944.
[397]M. Goodman 1989a, 185.
[398]Feldman 1993a, 288-341.
[399]Rokéah 1996.
[400]Feldman 1993a, 323, arguing against Martin Goodman.

Three reasons explain why the notion of a universal missionary assignment that needed to be carried out actively and purposefully was not developed in Second Temple Judaism: (1) Jewish faith and Jewish society and culture were fused in a nearly absolute manner; (2) the pressure toward national self-preservation was immense; (3) rabbis and synagogues actively sought to prevent assimilation of Jews to pagan society.

The Targumim

Robert Hayward demonstrates in a recent interpretation of Gen 21:33 that Abraham is portrayed in *Targum Pseudo-Jonathan* as a preacher who proclaims to passersby that they should repent and believe in the God of the Jews. The author of this Targum, written in the second or third century, reminds his Jewish readers that Abraham is not a passive, timeless example of faith in Yahweh, but rather that he actively proclaimed the universal God. The Targum aims at educating its readers and is perhaps even apologetic, but it makes no statements about winning proselytes.[401] In *Targum Neofiti* on Gen 21:33[402] Abraham is a missionary who seeks to win proselytes for the Jewish faith. This interpretation depends on traditions that surface for the first time in the Talmud and in the midrashim. This Targum dates in its present form to the fourth century A.D. This shows that the synagogues of the fourth century in which the Palestinian Targumim were in use were willing and presumably eager to convert Gentiles to the Jewish faith and win them as proselytes. This evidence agrees with my reading of the rabbinic texts.

6.3 Conclusions

The universal dimension of the Jewish faith can be observed in texts of Diaspora Judaism more frequently and more explicitly than in Palestinian texts. The greater openness toward Hellenistic culture did not lead to the abolition of the cultural and ritual barriers that the Mosaic law erected between Israel, the people of God, and the Gentiles. The repugnance of pagan idol worship and its ethical and social consequences are not infrequently described in blunt words. It seems that Jews in the Diaspora agreed that cultic purity was prerequisite if Gentiles wanted to join the people of God. Conversion and adoption of the Jewish faith as a proselyte resulted even in the Diaspora in a fundamental "rehabilitation," the entry into a new society. If God chose Israel as his people, then conversion to Israel's God and to Israel's faith is, at the same time, a turning to Israel as a nation. This means that proselytes who converted from paganism to Judaism lived according to the same laws and observed the same customs that Jews held to. The conversion of Gentiles on

---

[401]Hayward 1998, 31-33, 37; for the observation that follows above see ibid., 33-35, 37.
[402]And the glosses in frg. Paris MS 110, and in frg. Vat. MS 440.

a massive scale was expected for the eschaton, both in the Diaspora syna-gogues and in Palestine.[403]

We find positive statements about Gentiles as well as evidence for tolerant dealings with non-Jews, accepting them as God-fearers in the synagogues or as proselytes in the Jewish communities. Gentiles could participate in the Jewish way of worship and in the Jewish way of life if they fully converted to Judaism. The resistance to proselytes had no racist foundation but was due rather to re-ligious and ethical reasons.[404] However, this fundamentally positive stance is not synonymous with an active endeavor to convince Gentiles who worship other gods and who practice different customs that their religious convictions are wrong, that their behavior is improper, that they must believe in the God of Is-rael and that they need to be integrated into the Jewish community. An interest for Judaism on the part of Gentiles is not synonymous with an interest for "lost" Gentiles who need to be converted. The Mishnah and the Tosefta constantly re-mind Jews that they are "different" with respect to the Gentiles.[405] Discussions about Gentiles in Jewish texts (and sermons) served to maintain the Jewish self-definition; they were not meant to be understood as precise ethnographical analyses. Most Jews were indeed willing to accept Gentiles into their community if they converted to worshiping Yahweh, submitted to circumcision and adopted the Mosaic law. It is a different matter whether this was regarded as desirable and whether it should be actively encouraged through attractive preaching in the synagogues (or in the market!) and through cogent argumentation. A list of the attractive features of Judaism tells us little about the reality of conversions as social fact at any given time or in any given place.[406]

It is important to remember in this context that the promise of blessing for the nations in the Abrahamic blessing in Gen 12:3 is rarely commented on. This is true even for the interpretation of Gen 22:17-18 in Philo, *Leg.* 3.203-204, and in Jose-phus, *A.J.* 1.236, as well as for the interpretation of Gen 28:14 in the Tannaitic mid-rashim.[407] Gerhard Sass comments, "Their interest focuses on other matters. One interpretation substantiates the blessing for the nations in Abraham's behavior, in his intercession or in his righteousness. Another interpretation relates the blessing back to Israel itself. . . . Yet another interpretation identifies the blessing with the advice that the nations can, and do, obtain in Israel when they have difficulties."[408]

---

[403]Tob 13:11; *b. Ber.* 57b; cf. Philo, *Praem.* 164-172; *Mos.* 2.43-44.

[404]A. F. Segal 1988, 358-59; Schiffman 1985, 21; McKnight 1991, 46.

[405]See Porton 1985; 1988, 2; 1993.

[406]Thus Rajak 1994, 24, with regard to Feldman 1993a, 177-287.

[407]See Sass 1995, 209 n. 152, with reference to *Mek. R. Yishm. Bešalaḥ* 2 (185; II 157); 3 (98-99; I 218ff.); *Exod. Rab.* 38:6; 44:6; *Num. Rab.* 2:12.

[408]Sass 1995, 209; cf., on the one hand, *Jub.* 18:16; 24:11; Philo, *Migr.* 121-122, and on the other hand, Is 51:2; Ps 46:4-5 LXX; Sir 44:21; Josephus, *A.J.* 1.235-236, as well as *Gen. Rab.* 39:12. See Barrett 1962, 1.

The texts that have been described as "Jewish Hellenistic missionary literature" should be understood as apology directed at the synagogue communities themselves—that is, as texts that seek to ascertain for the readers and listeners their Jewish identity.[409] The statements of neither New Testament authors nor Roman authors assume the existence of a Jewish missionary activity among Gentiles to be inevitable.

If we abandon the demographic argument—a main reason for the assumption of a Jewish mission among Gentiles[410]—then the literary sources that often are adduced lose their force. This means that the evidence for Jewish missionary activity on a larger scale is rather slim, if not decidedly doubtful.[411] There was no missionary activity by Jews in the centuries before and in the first centuries after Jesus' and his followers' ministry, no organized Jewish attempts to convert Gentiles to faith in Yahweh.

The majority of rabbis today understand Judaism to be a nonmissionary religion. Ben-Zion Bokser distinguishes sharply between the Jewish concept of "religious witness" and Christian concepts and practices that aim at winning people of other faiths to the Christian faith, for which claims of exclusive and absolute validity are made. In Judaism "religious witness" signifies the general enlightenment of people and the recognition of the universal sovereignty of God and of the primacy of the moral order of the world. Bokser comments, "It does not call for the disappearance of diverse forms of religious expression but for the recognition that, transcending all these diversities, is the common reverence for a universal God in whom all life, including all manifestations of the religious disposition, can find its harmonious coexistence. The effort of any religion to supersede all others, with the claim that it alone offers the means of salvation, is from the perspective of Judaism a form of religious particularism due to be transcended as we grow toward true universality."[412] And when Jews such as Lawrence Epstein demand a missionary Judaism, we read statements to the effect that plans and strategies for the admittance of converted non-Jews should renounce the active solicitation of people who are not interested, as the initiative to learn more about Judaism should come from non-Jews themselves.[413] Martin Goodman comments, "The illogicalities of today reflect the confused formation of rabbinic attitudes in the second to fifth centuries CE."[414]

---

[409]Sänger (1980, 210-11) asks "whether the literature that we attach this label to ever actually reached, ever could reach, the non-Jewish population as allegedly intended."
[410]See the extensive study by Feldman (1993a).
[411]See P. van Minnen, *ZPE* 100 (1994): 254; J. Sievers, *Bib* 76 (1995): 280. Ameling (1996, 33) remarks, "There was no missionary activity that would have secured a numerically significant growth."
[412]Bokser 1979, 89-107; quotation, 102-3.
[413]Epstein 1992, esp. 140.
[414]M. Goodman 1994, 153.

7

SUMMARY

From the beginning, Israel's faith included universalistic elements. The Israelites lived in close contact with non-Israelites, an arrangement that certainly was characterized by flexibility. Early on there were "proselytes" in Israel. However, the Israelites did not conceptualize an "offensive" mission with the goal of converting all Gentiles to YHWH. The conversion of the Gentiles is expected for the "last days." The most explicit statements regarding the Gentiles and their conversion and admission to God's salvation is found in prophecy, especially in the statements regarding the Servant of the Lord in Isaiah: the last days provide salvation for the nations; YHWH's Servant is not only a witness but also his messenger to the nations. In regard to the Old Testament, we must distinguish consistently between missionary ideas and missionary praxis, the latter being the subject of prophecies concerning the "last days."

In regard to early Judaism, the once universally accepted assumption of a Jewish mission to Gentiles is increasingly questioned. The universal horizon of faith in YHWH the Creator is more frequently and more explicitly expressed in the Jewish Diaspora than in Palestinian Judaism. However, the traditional cultic and ritualistic barriers are not lifted. On the contrary, the loathing for idolatry and its consequences for pagan society is sometimes described with blunt words. Even for the Jewish Diaspora, the cultic purity of Gentiles is a prerequisite for their admission into the people of God. A major revival among the Gentiles continues to be expected for the "last days." The positive attitude toward proselytes is not synonymous with missionary activity among Gentiles. Rabbinical writings always point out that Jews are different from Gentiles.

The writings that used to be designated as "Jewish-Hellenistic missionary literature" were written as an apology for internal use in the Jewish community, as texts that sought to affirm for the members of the synagogues their Jewish identity. There are no statements by Jewish or Roman authors that force us to conclude that there was an active Jewish mission among Gentiles. Judaism had neither a missionary theory nor organized missionary activity before the first century A.D. The missionary work of the first Christians cannot be explained with prototypes in the Old Testament or with models of an early Jewish mission.

PART II

FULFILLMENT

The Mission of Jesus

8

HISTORICAL AND SOCIAL REALITIES
IN PALESTINE

The missionary activity of the early Christians began in Palestine, in terms of both geography and personnel: the first center of the movement set in motion by the followers of Jesus of Nazareth was the church in Jerusalem, and the first missionaries were Jewish Christians residing in Jerusalem. The early Christian mission is closely linked with the person and the ministry of Jesus of Nazareth. Before I analyze the role that the ministry of Jesus in Galilee and in Judea, in Samaria and in the Decapolis played for the beginnings of the missionary activity of the early church, I will survey the basic historical, social and cultural factors of Jewish life in these territories. A major mistake of traditional historical-critical scholarship is to isolate the sayings of Jesus from their literary context, whose underlying historical authenticity often is denied. Since it is precisely the literary framework of the sayings of Jesus that provides the context for the proclamation of Jesus, together with the narrative material in the Gospels, that provides much information on geographical, historical, cultural and social facts and factors of the first-century world, an isolated examination of the sayings of Jesus favors the subjectivity of the individual exegete who seeks to reconstruct with form-critical analyses a *Sitz im Leben* in the life of the early church. Such reconstructions remain, by necessity, hypothetical, and they are not conducive for an integrated interpretation of the ministry of Jesus that fuses literary, historical, social and theological perspectives. Many scholars today acknowledge this basic problem of the historical-critical method as traditionally practiced.[1]

A good example of the disregard of social and cultural data contained not only in the literary texts of the New Testament but also in archaeological finds is the treatment of the word "house," which is of basic importance both for the ministry of Jesus (cf. Lk 5:29; 7:36; 8:41) and his disciples (cf. Mt 10:11-14; Lk 9:3-4; 10:5-9) and the life and missionary activity of the early church (cf. Acts 2:46; 5:42; 20:20). The Greek terms οἶκος (*oikos*) and οἰκία (*oikia*) occur in the New Testament 208 times (36 times in Mt, 31 times in Mk, 57

---

[1]See Horsley 1994, 91-135, esp. 93.

times in Lk, 10 times in Jn, 37 times in Acts).[2] Peter Weigandt lists in an article on οἰκία and οἶκος several titles on the question of infant baptism but never refers to the archaeological evidence for private houses in the Jewish and Greco-Roman world or to cultural and social factors linked with "house."[3] The same applies to an article by Otto Michel that informs extensively on the concept of the "house of God" but fails to provide information on the size and the architecture of private houses in the first century or on the significance of private houses for the missionary activity of the early church.[4] The same disregard can be observed in most commentaries on passages such as Mt 10:11-14; Lk 9:3-4; 10:5-9. Fuller information is provided in an article on "house" by J. S. Holladay.[5]

The following survey of relevant historical, geographical, cultural and social data prepares the way for the description of the missionary activity of the early church.[6] A survey of relevant dates is provided in §3.

8.1 Geography and Population

Jesus and his disciples lived and worked in Galilee, but we find them also in the Decapolis, Judea and Samaria. As pointed out previously (§6.2), between 700,000 and 2.5 million people lived in Palestine: at least 800,000 Jews and 500,000 Samaritans, Greeks and Nabateans. Judea had roughly 500,000 Jewish inhabitants. Some scholars estimate that only 1 million people lived in Palestine.

Geography

Josephus divides the "territory of the Jews" (τῆς Ἰουδαίων χώρας [A.J. 14.250]) into the regions of Galilee, Samaria, Judea to the west of the Jordan River, and

---

[2]Thus occurring more frequently than the terms "church/congregation" (ἐκκλησία, 114 times), "kingdom (of God)" (βασιλεία, 162 times), "work/works" (ἔργον/ἔργα, 169 times), "law" (νόμος, 195 times) or "Jew/Jews" (Ἰουδαῖος/Ἰουδαῖοι, 195 times).

[3]P. Weigandt, "οἰκία," EWNT 2:1210-11 (EDNT 2:495); idem, "οἶκος," EWNT 2:1222-29 (EDNT 2:500-503).

[4]O. Michel, "οἶκος, οἰκία," ThWNT 5:122-36 (TDNT 5:119-34).

[5]J. S. Holladay, ABD 3:308-18; see also M. J. Selman, IBD 2:668-72 (GBL 2:529-33). Not very helpful is the TRE article by Bieritz and Kähler (1985). On "house" see §§10.3; 18.3; 28.1 in the present work.

[6]See M. Avi-Yonah, "Palaestina," PWSup 13 (1973): 322-454; C. N. Raphael, ABD 2:964-77; Leipoldt and Grundmann 1990; Lohse 1994; Dommershausen 1987; Smallwood 1976, esp. 144-80, 256-92; Safrai and Stern 1987; Schürer 1973-1987; Davies and Finkelstein, CHJ 2:1990; Kasher 1990, esp. 192-312; Otzen 1990; E. P. Sanders 1992; Bauckham 1995a; Stegemann and Stegemann 1995, 95-216 (ET, 97-220); Kokkinos 1997 (cf. D. J. Bryan, TynBul 53 [2002]: 223-38); Gabba 1999. On Judea see A. Offer, NEAEHL 3:814-16; Sullivan 1977; Gill 1995a. On Samaria see A. Zertal et al., NEAEHL 4:1311-18; J. D. Purvis, ABD 5:914-21; Egger 1986; Zangenberg 1998, 12-27; Böhm 1999, 37-44. On Galilee see W. S. LaSor, ISBE 2:386-91; R. Riesner, GBL 1:406-7; M. Aviam, NEAEHL 2:453-58; Rafael Frankel, ABD 2:879-95; Freyne 1980; M. Goodman 1983; Bösen 1985; Freyne 1988; Edwards 1992; Freyne 1992a; 1992b; 1994; L. Levine 1992; Hengel 1995, 67-78; Horsley 1995; Edwards and McCollough 1997; Reed 2000; Sawicki 2000. On the Decapolis see R. Riesner, GBL 1:263-64; Jean-Paul Rey-Coquais, ABD 2:116-21; S. Thomas Parker, OEANE 2:127-30; R. E. Ciampa, DNTB 267-68; Schürer 2:130-60; Bietenhard 1977; Moors 1992; Millar 1993, 38-40, 408-14, and passim; Ball 2000, 181-97.

Perea to the east of the Jordan River (*B.J.* 3.35-58 [fig. 2]). Josephus begins with a description of Judea (fig. 13): it extends from Anuathu Borkaios (Kh. Berqit) in the north to Iardan (Arad?) in the south; Josephus includes Idumea in Judea.

According to Yoram Tsafrir, the cities of Gophna and Apharaema, situated 22 and 24 km south of Anuathu Borkaios, were each the seat of a toparchy in southern Samaria, and both Rimmon and Deir Shabab as well as Adasa are included in the territory of Samaria as well.[7]

The eastern boundary of Judea was the Jordan River; the western boundary was the city of Joppa, situated on the Mediterranean 17 km northwest of Lod. Herod I had organized the towns and villages of Judea into thirteen toparchies, supervised by an administrator. We can only guess how many towns and villages existed in Judea. Cassius Dio claims to know that Iulius Severus, a general of Emperor Hadrian, destroyed as many as 985 Jewish villages in A.D. 132 (69.14.1).[8]

North of Judea was Samaria (fig. 10), extending from Anuathu Borkaios or Gophna and Apharaema to Ginae on the southern end of the Jezreel Valley. The latter is treated as a separate entity, presumably on account of the Herodian estates in the fertile valley. After Archelaos, the oldest son of Herod I, had been deposed in A.D. 6, Samaria was governed by Roman procurators with equestrian rank who resided in Caesarea and had (inter alia) the authority to appoint the high priest. In A.D. 41 Judea and Samaria were combined under King Agrippa I, and in A.D. 44 the area again became a Roman province, governed by a procurator.

Galilee (fig. 5) extended from Ptolemais, Mount Carmel and Gaba (at the entrance to the Jezreel Valley) in the south to Gischala in the north; the eastern boundary was the Jordan River as far as Lake Hule; in the west, Galilee extended as far as Chabulon. Josephus describes Galilee in the first century as follows (*B.J.* 3.35-43):

"Galilee, with its two divisions known as Upper and Lower Galilee, is enveloped by Phoenicia and Syria. Its western frontiers are the outlying territory of Ptolemais and Carmel, a mountain once belonging to Galilee, and now to Tyre; adjacent to Carmel is Gabba, the 'city of cavalry,' so called from the cavalry who, on their discharge by King Herod, settled in this town. On the south the country is bounded by Samaria and the territory of Scythopolis up to the waters of Jordan; on the east by the territory of Hippos, Gadara, and Gaulanitis, the frontier-line of Agrippa's kingdom; on the north Tyre and its dependent district mark its limits. Lower Galilee extends in length from Tiberias to Chabulon, which is not far from Ptolemais on the coast; in breadth, from a village in the Great Plain called Xaloth to Bersabe. At this point begins Upper Galilee, which extends in breadth to the village of

---

[7]Tsafrir, di Segni and Green, *Iudaea-Palaestina,* 57, 64, 111, 137, 215. On Josephus's knowledge of and experience in Galilee see S. Cohen 1979.

[8]This information is one of the very few quantitative data concerning villages given by ancient historians. See Dennis G. Glew, "400 Villages? A Note on Appian, *Mith.* 65, 271," *EA* 32 (2000): 155-61, esp. 155 with n. 5.

Baca, the frontier of Tyrian territory; in length it reaches from the village of Thella, near the Jordan, to Meroth. With this limited area, and although surrounded by such powerful foreign nations [ἔθνεσιν ἀλλόφυλοις], the two Galilees have always resisted any hostile invasion, for the inhabitants are from infancy inured to war, and have at all times been numerous; never did the men lack courage nor the country men. For the land is everywhere so rich in soil and pasturage and produces such variety of trees, that even the most indolent are tempted by these facilities to devote themselves to agriculture. In fact, every inch of the soil has been cultivated by the inhabitants; there is not a parcel of waste land. The towns [πόλεις], too, are thickly distributed, and even the villages [κωμῶν], thanks to the fertility of the soil, are also densely populated that the smallest of them contains above fifteen thousand inhabitants."

From north to south, Galilee measured 50 km (32 mi.) long, from west to east about 40 km (25 mi. [a distance that a well-trained amateur marathoner can run in less than three and a half hours]). Any Galilean town or village could be reached in two days of walking at the most; according to Josephus (*Vita* 52), a traveler on foot needed three days to cover the approximately 100 km (62 mi.) from Galilee to Jerusalem, which means that it was possible to cover 30 km (18 mi.) per day. Galilee covered an area of about 2,000 km^2 (770 sq. mi.).

For comparison: New York City covers 322 sq. mi. (826 km^2), Los Angeles 467 sq. mi. (1,210 km^2), greater London 659 sq. mi. (1,706 km^2), the greater Paris region 890 sq. mi. (2,305 km^2), the State of Rhode Island 1,045 sq. mi. (2,706 km^2). Willibald Bösen observes that "the Galilee at the time of Herod in which Jesus lived and ministered was a small country."[9]

Lower Galilee, with hills that reach 588 m, extended from the Jezreel Valley to the rise up to Upper Galilee near Kefar Chanania. Lower Galilee was densely populated: on the Judea map in the TIR we find for this area, with dimensions of 40 by 35 km, approximately 120 towns and villages for the Roman period; for Upper Galilee, add 55 towns.[10] The only cities (*poleis*) in Galilee were Sepphoris and Tiberias, the latter situated on the Sea of Galilee.[11] All other settlements were small towns and villages. Upper Galilee had not a single Greek polis, but it did have close trade connections with Tyrus to the north.[12] Coins from Tyre circulated in Lower Galilee also.

---

[9]Bösen 1985, 28.

[10]The map in *BHH* 2:1293-94 has 48 places in a region measuring 23 by 29 km. See M. Aviam, (*NEAEHL* 2:455), who lists 138 towns and villages for the Roman period; he points out that 93 villages dating to the Hellenistic period were discovered in Upper Galilee, which were largely inhabited by Gentiles and abandoned at the end of the Seleucid period (ibid., 2:453). See also Freyne 1997a, 60. H. Lapin ("Rabbis and Cities in Later Roman Palestine," *JJS* 50 [1999]: 187-207) provides a "historical geography" for the second and third centuries on the basis of rabbinic literature.

[11]M. Goodman 1983, 129-30.

[12]R. Hanson, *Tyrian Influence in the Upper Galilee* (Meiron Excavation Project 2; Cambridge, Mass.: ASOR, 1980), 67-69. On the observation that follows above see D. Barag, "Tyrian Currency in Galilee," *Israel Numismatic Journal* 6-7 (1982-1983): 7-13; Freyne 2000, 168.

The figure of 175 towns and villages includes ruins whose ancient name is unknown (omitted in fig. 5). Examples: in Khirbet Kur, 3 km west of Capernaum, ruins of buildings, including a synagogue, have been found. In Chorvat Veradim (Khirbet Wadi el Chammam), 2.5 km west of Magdala, ruins of a synagogue and of a public building were found. In Reina, 2.5 km northeast of Nazareth, graves and a Roman water reservoir were found. In ʿIlut, 3.8 km northwest of Nazareth, again traces of occupation were discovered, including ruins of a synagogue and graves (perhaps to be identified with Aithelu, mentioned in rabbinic sources [see *t. Nid.* 1:9; *y. Nid.* 48d]). In Khirbet Maluf (Chorvat Sahar), about 3 km southeast of Nain, ruins of buildings (including perhaps a synagogue), rock graves, sarcophagi, an olive press, coins and bronze weights were found.[13]

At the time of Jesus, Galilee was governed by Herod Antipas, the second son of Herod I. In A.D. 40 Galilee came under the rule of Herod Agrippa I (A.D. 41-44), after whose short rule Galilee was placed under direct Roman administration again, governed from Judea.

Perea, a strip of land east of the Jordan River 16 km wide, extended from the Jordan to the territory of Philadelphia and the eastern region of Nabatea (Arabia); the southern boundary was Machairos, and the northern boundary was Pella. At the time of Jesus, Perea was ruled by Herod Antipas, and after A.D. 40 by Herod Agrippa I.

The cities of the coastal plain between Gaza and Askalon in the south and Jamnia in the north, and the Decapolis (Δεκάπολις) east of the Sea of Galilee extending from Damascus in the north to Philadelphia in the south, were situated outside of the territory described by Josephus. The list of cities belonging to the Decapolis varied.[14] The following cities are mentioned in the sources: Abila (el-Qwēlbeh), Dion (?), Gadara (Umm Qeis), Gerasa (Jerash), Hippos (Qalʾat el-Hosn, near En Gev), Kanatha (Qanawat), Pella (Tabaqat Fachl), Philadelphia (Amman), Raphana (?), Scythopolis (Beth Shean). According to Pliny, Damascus also belonged (at a later date?) to the cities of the Decapolis.

Claudius Ptolemaios, writing under the name Antoninus Pius (*Geogr.* 5.7.14-17), also lists Abida (identical with Abila?); there is epigraphical evidence that this city belonged to the Decapolis. If this is correct, then the "Decapolis" ("Ten Cities") included eleven cities. With the exception of Scythopolis, all the cities of the Decapolis were situated east of the Jordan River. The reason for belonging to the Decapolis was, for most of the cities, having been liberated from Jewish or Semitic rule in 63 B.C. by the Roman general Pompey. Gerasa had been under Jewish control since the conquest of Alexander Jannaeus, and Kanatha was ruled by the Nabatean tyrant Ptolemy; only Philadelphia was not under Jewish control in 63 B.C. Scholars assume that Pompey integrated the "liberated" cities into a (Greek) confederation of cities (cf. Josephus, *B.J.* 1.155-156; *A.J.* 14.74-75). The eras of the cities thus began in 64 B.C. (Hippos, Scythopolis, Gadara) or in 63 B.C. (Pella, Gerasa).[15] The designation "Decapolis" was used for hundreds of years. It is unclear whether the ten

---

[13]Tsafrir, di Segni and Green, *Iudaea-Palaestina,* 152, 169, 177, 214, 256.
[14]See Pliny, *Nat.* 5.16.74; Ptolemaios, *Geogr.* 5.7.14-17. Cf. Moors 1992, 2-16.
[15]See Moors 1992, 159-254, with much detail.

cities had a common *koinon* (assembly) for the Roman province of Syria. And it is debated whether Pompey integrated Damascus into the Decapolis in the first century B.C.; this may have happened only at the time of Nero. The reference to a prefect of the Decapolis in epigraphical sources[16] demonstrates that politically the Decapolis belonged to Syria.

The cities of the Decapolis owed their prosperity to the caravan routes. They were islands of Greek culture in the midst of the Semitic rural population. Excavations have demonstrated that there were sizable Jewish communities not only in the villages but also in the cities, as in Gerasa, Gadara, Abila and likewise in Capitolias (Beth Ras).[17] The excavations in Gadara show that the cities of the Decapolis had the usual institutions of a Greek polis: Gadara had two theaters, a hippodrome, baths and a magnificent colonnaded street. Famous poets, rhetors (Menippos, Meleager, Apsines) and philosophers (the Cynic Oinomaios, the Epicurean Philodemos) hailed from Gadara. Some scholars have estimated that over 1 million people lived in the cities and villages of the Decapolis—a figure that probably is too high.

Cities and Villages

The literary sources use the term "city" (Heb., עִיר, *ʿir;* Gk., πόλις, *polis*), which designates in the Old Testament a "permanent settlement without any reference to its size."[18] Accordingly, New Testament authors and Josephus can use the term *polis* for a village, which is otherwise designated as כְּפַר (*kĕfar*) or κώμη (*kōmē*).[19] The term χώρα (*chōra*) generally can designate "settlements" or the "territory" that belongs to a city. Josephus refers to "towns and villages" that were plundered by bandits (*A.J.* 16.278). In 1 Macc 5:65 we read of "daughter villages" (θυγατέρες, *thygateres*), "strongholds" (ὀχυρώματα, *ochyrōmata*) and "towers" (πύργοι, *pyrgoi*) of Hebron.

Galilee was known as a densely populated territory. Josephus comments that even the smallest of the 204 Galilean towns and villages (πόλεις καὶ κῶμαι) had over 15,000 inhabitants (*Vita* 235)—an exaggerated estimate.[20] Many scholars assume with regard to Josephus's statistics of population figures that the decimal point needs to be moved one position to the left. Still, it can be regarded as certain that Galilee was more densely populated than the rest of Palestine because of its fertile soil. The population of Galilee is estimated for the first century A.D. at 200,000.

---

[16]B. Isaac, "The Decapolis in Syria: A Neglected Inscription," *ZPE* 44 (1981): 67-74.
[17]See Meyers 1997, 62.
[18]*HALOT* 2:821, "עִיר A.1" (*HAL* 776); A. R. Hulst, *THAT* 2:268-72 (*TLOT* 2:880-83); cf. Z. Safrai 1994, 17-20.
[19]See Schürer 2:196-97; Hirschfeld 1997, esp. 80.
[20]See Byatt 1973, 51; Z. Safrai 1994, 40-41; for the observation that follows above see J. Strange 1997, 47.

Some scholars suggest a higher figure of 300,000 for the Galilean population, while others assume 150,000.[21] The attempt to provide precise demographic figures for regions or cities in the Greco-Roman world is notoriously difficult.[22] Neither inscriptions nor ancient literary texts are interested in statistical data on the population of cities, regions or provinces. Most sources do not distinguish between the city (*polis*) and the territory (*chōra*) belonging to the city. If authors do provide figures, they usually include only the free citizens, omitting women, children, slaves and the poor. The reason for this limitation is that the few available statistical data are based on the determination of the tax rate in a particular administrative area. We also know that the data of ancient historians are often stereotypical and exaggerated and thus not always reliable. They often state multiples of a "myriad," with the Greek μυριάς (*myrias*) designating not only the number 10,000 but also "a large number that cannot be exactly determined," or "countless numbers." Josephus's work is a good example of this practice.[23]

Contemporary estimates are based on archaeological data such as land areas of the town, population density and soil fertility. Archaeologists assume 400 to 500 inhabitants per hectare or one person per 10 m^2 of enclosed living space.[24] The reliability of such numbers depends, of course, on the number of stories of the houses.[25] And it is not known how many poor people and slaves lived in the open, outside proper buildings. The geographical location of a city and the existence of city walls can have a marked influence on the population density of the city.

For most towns in Galilee we need to assume a population coefficient of approximately 100 people per hectare. The ruins of Julias, built by Herod Philip at the location of Bethsaida, occupy 10 ha; the ruins of Gaba, built by Herod I for his retired cavalry, occupy 14 ha; the ruins of Gath Hepher occupy 5 ha; the ruins of many Galilean villages occupy 1 ha or less.[26] This means that the villages had 400 to 600 inhabitants on average, "rural towns" ("Landstädte," as A. Ben-David calls them) between 600 and 7,500 inhabitants, larger cities—in first-century Galilee only Magdala, Sepphoris and Tiberias—between 10,000 and 20,000 inhabitants.[27]

Josephus mentions the following of the approximately 200 Galilean towns and villages (cf. fig. 5): Gischala, Asor Iamneith, Meroth, Baka, Sepph, Akchabare, Bersabe, Saah, Selame, Kepharnomos (Kafarnaum, Capernaum), Chabolon, Sogane, Gabara, Gennesar

---

[21]Meyers (1997, 59) estimates between 150,000 and 175,000 people of Sepphoris, Tiberias, Tarichaeae and Gaba, living in 200 villages with about 500 inhabitants each.

[22]For the discussion that follows above see Reed 1994, 203-19; Z. Safrai 1994, 436-58. The assumptions by Habbe (1996, 46-47) concerning Palestine are not up to date; cf. R. Riesner, "Das Lokalkolorit des Lukas-Sonderguts: Italisch oder palästinisch-judenchristlich?" *SBFLA* 49 (1999): 51-64.

[23]See Byatt 1973, 51; Reed 1994, 205-6. See LSJ 1153, "μυριάς I"; BDAG, s.v. "μυριάς 1-2"; BAA 1072.

[24]See Broshi 1980, 1; also R. Naroll, "Floor Area and Settlement Population," *American Antiquity* 27 (1962): 587-89; also, more generally, J. R. Sallares and M. H. Crawford, "Population, Greek/Roman," *OCD* 1221-23. One hectare equals 2.4711 acres; 1 m^2 equals 1,549.9 sq. in.

[25]In Ostia 30,000 inhabitants lived on 59 ha (ca. 500 per hectare); in Pompeii about 10,000 inhabitants lived on 64 ha (ca. 150 per hectare). The reason for this difference is that the houses in Ostia, located between the Tiber River and a swamp, had three stories on average, while the houses in Pompeii had one or two stories.

[26]See Reed 1994, 213-14; on the observation that follows above see Ben-David 1974, 48-57.

[27]Reed 1994, 214; 2000, 80 (Sepphoris: 8,000 to 12,000 inhabitants in the first century). Meyers (1997, 59) estimates 18,000 inhabitants for Sepphoris and 24,000 for Tiberias.

chora, Iotapata, Kana, Tarichaia (Tarichea), Arbela, Rhouma, Asochis, Bethmaous, Tiberias, Ammathous, Sepphoris, Garis, Domai, Simonias, Iapha, Exaloth, Debariththa, Sennabris.[28]

The Gospels mention only eight Galilean towns: Capernaum (Kafarnaum), Nazareth, Chorazin, Bethsaida, Cana, Gennesaret (Kinneret), Magdala, Nain.

Capernaum had been regarded as a small fishing village with less than 1,000 inhabitants.[29] Today, some scholars estimate the population to have reached 12,000 or 15,000[30] or even 25,000[31] inhabitants by the first century. The town covered at the most 17 ha in the early Roman period; due to the type of buildings and their distribution, the population density could not have exceeded 150 people per hectare. This means that Capernaum, with an area of 6 ha of enclosed living space, had between 600 and 1,500 inhabitants, if we assume a realistic population coefficient of 100 persons per hectare.[32]

Nazareth occupied an area of 4 ha at the most and thus had fewer than 400 inhabitants.[33] The lower limit can be deduced from the existence of a synagogue, which required at least ten adult men (i.e., five to ten families, thus fifty to eighty people). The upper limit is set by the available arable land in the valley and on the hill slopes in the vicinity, as well as by the fact that evidently there was only one source of water.[34]

A past generation of archaeologists concentrated on known cities of antiquity, usually on their monumental architecture—palaces, temples and public buildings such as baths, council halls, theaters and stadia. This focus was understandable for two reasons: these cities were already known from literary texts, and discoveries and results came more quickly. It was only in more recent times that private houses became the focus. The investigation of ancient villages has only begun, sometimes with dramatic new insights. A recently conducted archaeological survey in central and southern Moab led to the discovery of 443 ancient settlements, 291 of which belong to the Nabatean period, and 146 to the early Roman period.[35] Scholars reckon with more than 800 villages in the limestone

---

[28]See *TAVO* B V 19 (1980), listing the identified places from north to south. See also Christa Möller and Götz Schmitt, *Siedlungen Palästinas nach Flavius Josephus* (BTAVO B 14; Wiesbaden: Reichert, 1976).

[29]S. Loffreda, *A Visit to Capernaum* (Jerusalem: Franciscan Press, 1972), 20.

[30]Meyers and Strange 1981, 58.

[31]Saldarini 1992, 27 n. 9.

[32]Reed 2000, 149-52; cf. idem 1994, 211-12. Vasileios Tzaferis (*Excavations at Capernaum, 1978-1982* [Winona Lake, Ind.: Eisenbrauns, 1989], 216) estimates between 1,500 and 2,000 inhabitants.

[33]Ben-David 1974, 49; Strange, *ABD* 4:1050-51; Reed 2000, 82, 131. Riesner (*DJG* 36) assumes 200 inhabitants.

[34]Bösen 1985, 105.

[35]James M. Miller, ed., *Archaeological Survey of the Kerak Plateau* (ASOR Archaeological Reports 1; Atlanta: Scholars Press, 1991), 307-319; D. Kennedy, "Greek, Roman and Native Cultures in the Roman Near East," in Humphrey 1995-2002, 2:77-106, esp. 93. The Nabatean period is dated from 300 B.C. to A.D. 106, the early Roman period from 64 B.C. to A.D. 135.

massif of northwestern Syria.[36] In Samaria, we now know of 146 villages from the early Roman period, besides 140 settlements from Hellenistic times.[37] For Judea, Galilee and Samaria an increasing number of farmsteads are being discovered.

Population

Due to its geographical location Galilee can be regarded as a Jewish enclave surrounded by centers of Hellenistic culture: in the northwest with the Mediterranean coast it bordered on Syria with Sidon, Tyre and Ptolemais; in the east it bordered on the Decapolis with Philadelphia and Gadara; in the south it bordered on Samaria with Sebaste. The population of Galilee was mixed: the majority of people were Jews, while many pagans lived in the larger towns. The relationship between Jews and Gentiles was never without tension. Interaction could not be avoided, especially in the markets and in trade, but they were restricted by the existing cultural barriers (cf. §6). Jesus' encounters with a Syrophoenician woman (Mk 7:24-30/Mt 15:21-28) and with a Roman officer in Capernaum (Mt 8:5-13/Lk 7:1-10) demonstrate that there was always a distance between Jews and Gentiles that needed to be bridged. And, of course, there were thoroughgoing Hellenistic influences in Jewish society.

In the early part of the first century A.D. pagans in Galilee were in the minority. Even though some Judeans did not trust the Galileans in religious matters,[38] the rural population in Galilee must be regarded as having remained faithful to the Torah. The view that Galilee was "half pagan"[39] is clearly wrong.

This does not exclude the possibility that some settlements had a majority of pagan inhabitants, especially settlements on the borders of Galilee. For example, Tel Anafa (ancient name unknown; mod. Kibbutz Shamir), a town 2.7 km east of the Jordan River and 10 km northeast of Lake Hula that the Canaanites had already settled, subsequently settled by the Israelites, had a mostly pagan population, despite the fact that the inhabitants in the first century during the time of Herod Philip were very little oriented toward Tyre (as the inhabitants around 100 B.C.) but bought their pottery wares from Jewish settlements in Galilee. The non-Jewish identity in the first century A.D. is demonstrated by the discovery of pig bones and by the lack of ritual baths (*miqvaot*). Only 37 percent of the pigs in Roman Tel Anafa were older than one year, which indicates that pork was on the menu of the population.[40]

---

[36]Georges Tate, "The Syrian Countryside During the Roman Era," in Alcock 1997, 55-71; Kennedy, "Greek, Roman and Native Cultures," 98.

[37]Adam Zertal, "Mount Manasseh Survey," *NEAEHL* 4:1312; Böhm 1999, 102; for the observation that follows above see Hirschfeld 1997.

[38]Cf. Jn 7:52; see Str-B 1:156-59.

[39]See Rostovtzeff [1929] 1957, 147.

[40]See Sharon C. Herbert, in *Tel Anafa I: Final Report on Ten Years of Excavation at a Hellenistic and Roman Settlement in Northern Israel* (ed. S. C. Herbert et al.; JRASup 10; Ann Arbor, Mich.: Kelsey Museum, 1994), 21-22. On the 195 pig bones (*sus scrofa*) found in Tel Anafa see Richard W. Redding, "The Vertebrate Fauna," in Herbert et al., *Tel Anafa I*, 279-322, esp.

Samaria had been depopulated after the conquest by Sargon II in 721 B.C. It
was resettled by colonists from other regions of the Assyrian Empire (2 Kings
17:24). Asarhaddon and Assurbanipal relocated people from Elam and Babylonia to Samaria (Ezra 4:2, 9-10). Some Israelites continued to live in the old capital Samaria; they are called "Samaritans" (ha-Šomronîm) in 2 Kings 17:29. Alexander the Great conquered Samaria in 331 B.C.,[41] and Macedonian colonists
settled in the city. The Maccabean John Hyrcanus completely destroyed Samaria in 108/107 B.C., and in 63 B.C. the Roman general Pompey detached the
territory of the old city from Judea. Under Aulus Gabinius, the Roman prefect
in Syria, the city of Samaria was rebuilt in 56 B.C. It was only when Herod I
refounded the city in 25 B.C. that Samaria received a fresh impetus. He settled
6,000 colonists in the city, among them non-Jewish soldiers, and renamed it
Sebaste. In the first century A.D. Samaria-Sebaste was a predominantly pagan
city, with a large Augustus temple and a sanctuary dedicated to Persephone-
Kore. A second Hellenistic city in Samaritan territory was Scythopolis[42] (the
former Beth Shean), which appears in 2 Macc 12:29-31 as a non-Jewish city.
Scythopolis was independent since Gabinius and belonged to the Decapolis
(Pliny, Nat. 5.16.74; Josephus, B.J. 3.446).

The inhabitants of the Hellenistic city of Samaria-Sebaste are not be confused with the Samaritans,[43] whose religious center was on Mount Garizim.
The most important city of the Samaritans was Sychar (mod. ʾAskar), only
about 1 km northeast of the ruins of former Shechem.[44] The Samaritans probably derive from a group of religious purists, descendants of the people who
had been allowed to stay when the Assyrians drove parts of the Israelite population of the northern kingdom into exile. In the fourth century B.C. they built
a temple on Mount Garizim. In the third century the relationship with the
priestly aristocracy in Jerusalem deteriorated, partly because of the political
tension arising from the fact that Jerusalem belonged to Ptolemaic Egypt,
whereas Samaria belonged to Seleucid Syria. As a result of the strong Hellenistic influence in Samaria and the Samaritans' refusal to participate in the rebellion against Antiochos IV Epiphanes, Jewish resentments grew. The exis-

---

288-29 (for comparison: 354 cattle bones and 477 sheep and goat bones were found; in the
late Hellenistic period the domestic pig evidently was as important as sheeps and goats).
[41]See Schürer 2:160-64; now Böhm 1999, 48-55.
[42]See Freyne 1980, 108-13; Schürer 2:142-45. The name often was linked with the "Scythians"
and thus the (re)founding of the city with (hypothetical) Scythian units in Ptolemy's army (see
M. Avi-Yonah, "Scythopolis," IEJ 12 [1962]: 127); this theory cannot be proven, however.
[43]On the Samaritans see H. G. M. Williamson, DJG 724-28; Robert T. Anderson, ABD 5:940-47;
Schürer 2:16-20; James D. Purvis, "The Samaritans," in CHJ 2:591-613; Egger 1986; Crown
1989; Dexinger and Pummer 1992; Zangenberg 1998, 10-57; Böhm 1999, 37-203; Stenschke
1999a, 64-69; S. Isser, "The Samaritans and Their Sects," in CHJ 3:569-95.
[44]On Sychar see Z. Stephanovic, ABD 3:608 ("Jacob's Well"); Böhm 1999, 90-92. See §22.3 in
the present work.

tence of separate Jewish and Samaritan communities in the Diaspora increased the tensions further. The politics of expansion by the Hasmonean rulers caused the definitive break, with a first climax in the destruction of the Samaritan sanctuary on Mount Garizim by John Hyrcanus in 128 B.C. In A.D. 6/7 the Samaritans provoked the Jews when they scattered bones in the temple in Jerusalem during Passover (Josephus, *A.J.* 18.29-30); in A.D. 52 Samaritans massacred Galilean pilgrims near En-Gannim (*A.J.* 20.118). The Samaritan "syncretism" probably is an invention of Jewish polemics, however. Samaritan sources indicate that the Samaritans were not more syncretistic than their Jewish contemporaries in Judea.[45] The religious practice of the Samaritans can be compared with the Torah observance of the Jewish Sadducees (cf. *m. Nid.* 4:2). During the first century A.D. the prophet Dositheus was active in Samaria. He evidently belonged to a Samaritan group similar to the Jewish Pharisees and attracted followers who continued to be loyal for a long time.[46]

Josephus mentions the following (identified) towns and villages for Judea:[47] Koreai, Akrabeta, Gerasa, Alexandreion (fortress), Anouath Borkaios, Ain, Phasaelis, Ioudaia, Rhamatain, Thamna, Isana, Adida, Lydda, Berzetho, Gophna, Ephraim, Archelais, Modein, Bethela, Sappho, Gittha, Baithoron, Kapharsalama, Machma, Neara, Dagon (fortress), Gazara, Ammaous, Gabaon, Adasa, Parathon, Kypros (fortress), Ierichous (Jericho), Gabath Saoul, Bethgala, Ammaous, Jerusalem (Hierosolyma), Bethleptepha, Hyrkania (fortress), Bethzacharia, Herodeion (fortress), Thekoe, Bethsoura.

8.2 The Economic and Social Situation

The most important aspect of the national economy of Judea and Galilee was agriculture. The main products included fruit (olive, grape, fig, date), vegetables (onion, garlic, leek, squash, cabbage, radish, beet), legumes (lentil, bean), spices (salt, pepper, ginger) and meat (fish, cow, ox, lamb, goat). Wool was produced and dyed and clothing was manufactured. In the Jordan Valley date palms were cultivated and balsam was produced. Many people worked in trade and crafts, as in, for example, the production and sale of pottery wares. Since the rebuilding of the temple by Herod I, Jerusalem was the most visited city in the entire Roman Empire. A large proportion of the population was economically dependent on the temple and the pilgrims who traveled from the Diaspora communities to Jerusalem. As a result the inhabitants of Jerusalem were more open toward a friendly coexistence with strangers. The dependence upon the local aristocracy probably was more pronounced than in the countryside. These factors all played a role not only in the trial of Jesus in A.D.

---

[45]Hengel 1995, 72.

[46]See Stanley Isser, *The Dositheans: A Samaritan Sect in Late Antiquity* (SJLA 17; Leiden: Brill, 1976).

[47]See *TAVO* B V 19 (1980); listed from north to south.

30 but also in the prehistory and the first phase of the Jewish revolt against Rome in A.D. 66-70.[48]

Jesus ministered mainly among the rural population in Galilee, preaching to and healing people who lived and worked in the numerous small settlements. The valleys of Galilee were the granary of Palestine.[49] Rabbinic texts mention several Galilean centers of wheat production: Arbela (2.5 km west of the Sea of Galilee), Kfar Chittaya (5 km southwest of Arbela), Hukkok (10 km west of Capernaum) and Chorazin (3 km northwest of Capernaum).[50] According to *m. Menaḥ*. 8.1, Hafarajim in the Jezreel Valley produced the second-best wheat in the country. Galilean wine was exported into the Phoenician cities since Hellenistic times. Vineyards were cultivated in several regions. Date palms and other fruit trees were cultivated near Gennesaret. The main production was olive oil: the northern Galilean town of Teqoa (Ḥirbet Šāmʿ) evidently produced the best oil in the entire country; second was Gischala (*m. Menaḥ*. 8.2). Another important Galilean product was flax. Industrial products were textiles and pottery wares; glass was produced in Tiberias (and on Mount Carmel).[51] The fishing operations in the Sea of Galilee produced not only for local needs but also for export, particularly the salted fish from Tarichea (Magdala; Aram., Migdal Nunya, "tower of the fishermen") (see Strabo 16.2.45).

Capernaum, with some 17,000 inhabitants, required an area of 9 km² (3.5 sq. mi.) to produce sufficient wheat. We assume that the inhabitants of Capernaum worked the land themselves. A harbor town on the Sea of Galilee, Capernaum attracted people from the surrounding villages who bought and sold various commodities and offered various services. Ramsay McMullen estimates that three-fourths of the entire trade in the Roman Empire took place within 24 km of a town.[52] Capernaum had few structures typical of urban life in the Greco-Roman world: no city walls, aqueduct, theater, colonnaded streets, administrative complex, temples. Places with a "public" character were the synagogue and the harbor facilities. Capernaum was a town that invested only a small part of its (limited) income in public buildings.

The rural population was not engaged in agriculture exclusively. New discoveries from the surrounding region of Sepphoris show that local industries flour-

---

[48]See Hengel and Deines 1995, 64. On the economy of Palestine see Ben-David 1974; M. Goodman 1983; Oakman 1986; Fiensy 1991; Z. Safrai 1994; see also Philip A. Harland, "The Economy of First-Century Palestine: State of the Scholarly Discussion," in Blasi, Duhaime and Turcotte 2002, 511-27.

[49]On Galilean agriculture see Z. Safrai 1994, 104-88, 322-39; Habbe 1996, 75-94; M. Har-El, "Agriculture," *EDSS* 1:13-16. On the production of wine and oil cf. Rafael Frankel, *Wine and Oil Production in Antiquity in Israel and Other Mediterranean Countries* (JSOT/ASOR Monograph Series 10; Sheffield: Sheffield Academic Press, 1999).

[50]See *y. Pe'ah* 20a; *y. Pesaḥ.* 27c; *b. Menaḥ.* 85a.

[51]On the Syrian-Palestinian glass industry see E. M. Stern, "Roman Glassblowing in a Cultural Context," *AJA* 103 (1999): 441-84.

[52]R. McMullen, "Market Days in the Roman Empire," *Phoenix* 24 (1970): 333.

ished in many villages that maintained trade contacts even with more remote regions.[53] The towns and the rural regions of Upper and Lower Galilee were connected with one another as well as with Judea in the south and with the Golan Heights in the northeast by a highly developed network of local trade routes on which goods and services were transported. This network of local routes made it possible for some villages to concentrate on a single product. Artisans in Kfar Chanania produced pottery wares for everyday use that were transported to Upper Galilee—for example, to Sepphoris, at a distance of 24 km, and to the western Golan.[54] Studies of Galilean pottery show that 75 percent of the early Roman pottery wares found in private houses in Sepphoris was produced in Kfar Chanania. A further 15 percent of the pottery found in Sepphoris came from Shikhin (mod. Asochis), a village 1.5 km away. For Sepphoris itself, the production of oil lamps has been ascertained for the fourth century.[55]

It can be assumed that similar centers existed for olives, barley, wine and flax as well as for finished products such as fabric, clothes, baskets, accessories made of metal and perfume. Future archaeological research may yet discover such centers. Literary texts and archaeological evidence demonstrate that at least seven Galilean villages and towns played a major role in the wine industry: Sepphoris, Tiberias, Kfar Sogane, Sallamin, Akchabaron (9 km northwest of Capernaum), Beth-Shearim and Gennesaret.

Within Galilee goods evidently could be transported without any problems, as well as to areas outside of Galilee, even though the Galilean roads were not paved in the first century. Capernaum was located on the old trade route traditionally called the Via Maris, running from Egypt along the Mediterranean coast via Caesarea, the residence of the Roman governor, and via Acco-Ptolemais along the northern shore of the Sea of Galilee to Damascus in Syria. The suggestion that Galilee was an isolated territory is untenable, and it does not even apply to Upper Galilee.[56] Excavations in Galilee discovered pottery wares from Italy dating to the first century. Excavations on the Golan and in the Decapolis show that Galilean pottery was transported to these regions.

In regard to the economy of Samaria, we know that the population produced oil that was exported as far as Egypt (Jerome, *Comm. Os.* 1.2), raised cattle and cultivated wine, nuts, pomegranates and vegetables. In the coastal plain we find

---

[53]For the discussion that follows above see David Adan-Bayewitz and Isadore Perlman, "The Local Trade of Sepphoris in the Roman Period," *IEJ* 40 (1990): 152-72, esp. 171-72; Edwards 1992; D. Adan-Bayewitz, *Common Pottery in Roman Galilee: A Study in Local Trade* (Ramat Gan: Bar-Ilan University Press, 1993); Overman 1993, 42-43; Z. Safrai 1994, 64; J. Strange 1994.

[54]For example, Tel Anafa; see S. C. Herbert, in Herbert et al., *Tel Anafa I*, 21. Habbe (1996, 50) asserts that trade with goods for everyday use was not widespread, and that trade was limited to rare luxury and export goods. This view needs to be revised.

[55]See D. Adan-Bayewitz, in Humphrey 1995-2002, 1:177-82.

[56]Meyers 1997, 58; J. Strange 1997, 42.

salt production; Neapolis and Caesarea had a dyeing industry. The economy of the Decapolis was similar to that of Galilee and Samaria.

Since Roman rule, the area that could be cultivated by the population became increasingly rare, one reason being the economic concentration that resulted from the politics of the Herodian dynasty. Josephus, the New Testament and inscriptions from the second century mention wealthy landowners who often controlled several villages and whose land was cultivated by local peasants.[57] An increasing number of small landowners were forced to cultivate ever more limited land. Surface surveys have prompted the suggestion that the land that the small landowners cultivated could hardly have supported them. On average, about 25 ha (62 acres) were sufficient to feed a family of six people—in Galilee and in Samaria the average size of a family farm was only 10 ha (25 acres).[58] When Herod Antipas rebuilt Sepphoris, which had been destroyed in 4 B.C., and when he founded Tiberias in A.D. 19 as his new capital instead of Sepphoris, the economic impact of these projects for the Galilean population was pronounced.[59] The existing trade structures changed. Lower Galilee, with its villages, hamlets and farmsteads, now had to feed the two large cities of Sepphoris and Tiberias, each having 10,000 to 24,000 inhabitants. The agricultural production of the Beit Netofa Valley and the area around Nahal Sippori (Wadi el-Muscherife and Wadi el-Malik) had to support Sepphoris. Traditionally, the small landowners cultivated their own land, the tenant farmers worked the land of wealthy landowners and paid rent, the landless peasants worked as wage laborers on estates, and the shepherds herded flocks of sheep and goats—all working for the subsistence of their families. Now, people were needed who could increase and guarantee farm production as entrepreneurs, producing crops for the granaries of Sepphoris. This meant that the small landowner had to work for wages part of the time or develop a specialization that could be marketed. This "class" of people, not simply peasants, worked at the same time as artisans and as merchants. As a result of the size and the significance of Sepphoris and Tiberias, the demand for goods of all kinds grew, and thus production increased in the two cities themselves as well as in the settlements in the surrounding area. This view of the economic development in Galilee in the first century A.D. is closely connected with the hypothesis of Moses Finley, who argued that ancient cities were "consumer cities" and exerted a parasitic influence on the surrounding regions.[60] Some scholars see a process of pauperization at

---

[57] See Yehuda Landau, "A Greek Inscription Found Near Hefzibah," *IEJ* 11 (1961): 54-70; J. Strange 1997, 46. Hefzibah is located in the Beth-Schan Valley, the eastern extension of the Jezreel Valley.

[58] Berl Golomb and Yehuda Kedar, "Ancient Agriculture in the Galilee Mountains," *IEJ* 21 (1971): 136-40; cf. J. Strange 1997, 46-47.

[59] See Schürer 2:172-82; Fiensy 1991; Freyne 1994, 114-21; 1996.

[60] Finley 1977; cf. Freyne 1992a; 2000, 172; Reed 2000, 67-68.

work, arguing that the decline from free peasant (small landowner) to dependent tenant farmer to day laborer to beggar was common.[61] However, James Strange and Douglas Edwards question this view, arguing for a more symbiotic relationship between both Sepphoris and Tiberias and the Galilean "hinterland."[62] More research is needed to clarify the tensions that existed between these two Hellenistic cities and the Jewish countryside.

The taxes that the Jewish population had to pay included religious duties (temple tax, tithes, duties such as first fruits and first births), tributes and direct taxes (land tax, head tax, trade tax, property tax), indirect taxes (salt tax, sales tax, etc.), customs duties (import and export duties, harbor duties, road taxes or toll) and other duties, as well as compulsory labor.[63] The duties imposed by the state alone were an unbearable burden for many people working at the subsistence level.[64] Tacitus writes with regard to A.D. 17 that "the provinces of Syria and Judaea, exhausted by their burdens [*fessae oneribus*], were pressing for a diminution of the tribute" (Tacitus, *Ann.* 2.42).[65] Herod I was repeatedly forced to grant tax reductions.

In regard to the villages of Palestine, we can assume that each one had a spokesperson. Larger villages and smaller towns may have had councils or elders, identical with or closely connected to the leaders of the local synagogues.[66]

Some scholars have doubted the existence of synagogues in Judea and Galilee before A.D. 70.[67] The archaeological evidence for synagogues in Palestine in the first century is sparse but indisputable. Seven synagogues can be dated before A.D. 70: the synagogues in Gamla

---

[61]Stegemann and Stegemann 1995, 107-8 (ET, 111-13).

[62]Edwards 1992, esp. 56-57; J. Strange 1994; 1997.

[63]Stenger 1988; cf. Freyne 1980, 183-94; Stegemann and Stegemann 1995, 108-17 (ET, 113-23); D. C. Snell, *ABD* 6:338-40.

[64]According to Habbe (1996, 61-62), the free Galilean landowner had 40 percent of his produce available for himself, and the Judean dependant upon a tenant farmer only 10 percent. The 60 to 90 percent tax rate that these figures imply is much too high. Horsley (1989) estimates that as much as 40 percent of produce went for taxation and religious dues, while E. P. Sanders (1992, 146-69) estimates the total burden on the average peasant at no more than 28 percent in most years, increasing to 33 percent in bad years, and Oakman (1986, 68-72) estimates that 20 to 35 percent of total produce was needed for rents and taxes. See also Harland, "Economy of First-Century Palestine," 521-22.

[65]For the observation that follows see Josephus, *A.J.* 15.303, 365; 16.64.

[66]See G. McLean Harper, "Village Administration in the Roman Province of Syria," *Yale Classical Studies* 1 (1928): 105-68; Habbe 1996, 47-48; on the situation after A.D. 70 see Z. Safrai 1994, 17-103. On synagogues see Hüttenmeister 1977; Eric M. Meyers, *ABD* 6:251-60; Urman and Flesher 1995; Binder 1999; Hanswulf Bloedhorn and Gil Hüttenmeister, *CHJ* 3:267-97; B. Chilton and E. Yamauchi, *DNTB* 1145-53; L. Levine 2000; idem, *TRE* 32 (2001): 499-508. On the functions of the synagogue before A.D. 70 see now L. Levine 2000, 124-59; on synagogal architecture, ibid., 291-356; on the synagogue leadership, ibid., 387-428.

[67]Kee 1990b; 1995; Horsley 1995, 223-26.

(25.5 by 17 m, four tiers of benches, late first century B.C.),[68] Masada (15 by 12 m, four tiers of benches, first century A.D.),[69] Herodion (15.5 by 10.6 m, three tiers of benches, first century),[70] Jerusalem,[71] Migdal-Magdala (8.2 by 7.2 m),[72] Qiryat Sefer near Modein (8 by 8 m),[73] and Jericho (16.2 by 11.1 m, 75-50 B.C.).[74] The date of the synagogue in Capernaum (24.5 by 18.7 m) is contested (see §9.2); some date the earliest level to the first century A.D.[75] The historical reliability of references to a synagogue in Capernaum in the New Testament should not be doubted, nor should corresponding literary references to synagogues in Nazareth, Tiberias, Dor and Caesarea in Josephus and in the New Testament.[76]

Some scholars have suggested that the leading priests in Jerusalem disapproved of the synagogues that were beginning to be established.[77] Others assume that Jews conducted religious services in private homes in the first century A.D., with synagogal buildings being built in Palestine in the third century and later. According to Lee Levine, one of the leading experts on ancient synagogues, the Jews in Palestine (in contrast to the Jews in the Diaspora) gathered in synagogues not for religious activities, which were characteristic of the Diaspora synagogues (usually called *proseuchē*, "prayer house") and which developed in Judea only after the destruction of the temple in A.D. 70. He argues that before A.D. 70 the synagogues served social and political purposes, particularly in Judea, as the architecture of the synagogues in Gamla, Masada, Herodion and Qiryat Sefer demonstrates: these synagogues consisted of a square or rectangular room lined by columns and benches, which facilitated the participation of those present, as

---

[68]S. Gutman, *NEAEHL* 2:460-62; Flesher 1995, esp. 34, 38; Groh 1995, 59-60; Binder 1999, 197, 162-71; L. Levine 2000, 34-35, 51-52; idem, *TRE* 32 (2001): 500-501; Runesson 2001, 357-60, and passim.

[69]Yigael Yadin, *Masada: Herod's Fortress and the Zealots' Last Stand* (London: Weidenfeld & Nicolson, 1966), 181-91; Ehud Netzer, *Masada—The Yigael Yadin Excavations, 1963-1965, Final Reports, III* (Jerusalem: Israel Exploration Society, 1991), 402-13; Flesher 1995, 35-36; Binder 1999, 172-79; L. Levine 2000, 58-60, 69-72, 582-83; idem, *TRE* 32 (2001): 500-501; Runesson 2001, 177-78, 357-58, and passim.

[70]Flesher 1995, 37; Binder 1999, 180-85; L. Levine 2000, 43, 60, 70-72; idem, *TRE* 32 (2001): 500-501; Runesson 2001, 132; 177-78; 357-60, and passim.

[71]R. Weill, *La Cité de David* (Paris: Geuthner, 1920), 186-90; A. Deissmann 1923, 378-80; Flesher 1995, 33-34 (uncertain); L. Levine 2000, 52-58, and passim; Riesner 1995b; on the Theodotos inscription see ibid., 192-200; on the latter see also Binder 1999, 104-8; John S. Kloppenborg Verbin, "Dating Theodotos (CIJ II 1404)," *JJS* 51 (2000): 243-80 (who defends a first-century date against H. C. Kee's dating of the inscriptions into the second and third centuries); Runesson 2001, 174-75, 226-31, 314-16, and passim.

[72]Flesher 1995, 34, 38; Groh, "Stratigraphic Chronology," 57-59; cf. L. Levine 2000, 43, 67; Runesson 2001, 175, 177.

[73]Y. Magen et al., *Qadmoniot* 32 (1999): 25-32; Binder 1999, 197; L. Levine 2000, 43, 45, 65-66; idem, *TRE* 32 (2001): 500-501; Runesson 2001, 175, 357-58, 360-63, and passim.

[74]E. Netzer, "A Synagogue from the Hasmonean Period Recently Exposed in the Western Plain of Jericho," *IEJ* 49 (1999): 203-21; E. Netzer et al., *Qadmoniot* 32 (1999): 17-24; L. Levine 2000, 68-69; Runesson 2001, 175, 357-59, and passim; cf. Y. Rapuano, "The Hasmonean Period 'Synagogue' at Jericho and the 'Council Chamber' Building at Qumran," *IEJ* 51 (2001): 48-56.

[75]S. Loffreda, "Le sinagoghe di Cafarnao," *BeO* 26 (1984): 103-14; Riesner 1995b, 203; Binder 1999, 186-96.

[76]Nazareth: Mt 13:53-58/Mk 6:1-6/Lk 4:16, 30; Tiberias: Josephus, *Vita* 277, 279; Dor: Josephus, *A.J.* 19.300-311; Caesarea: Josephus, *B.J.* 2.266-270, 284-292; *A.J.* 20.173-178, 182-184.

[77]See Flesher 1995, 27-39. For the observation that follows above see Meyers, "Synagogue," *ABD* 6:255.

in a Hellenistic *bouleuterion*.[78] Donald Binder argues that the synagogues, including those that existed in Palestine before A.D. 70, should be understood as "extensions" of the Jerusalem temple: they expand the holiness of the sanctuary in Jerusalem spatially and thus allow Jews outside of Jerusalem and outside of the Holy Land to participate in the central temple cult. Anders Runesson evaluated the discussion about the origins of the synagogue and concluded that synagogues developed in two distinct forms: the synagogues in the land of Israel developed from village or town or city assemblies, while the synagogues in the Diaspora developed from voluntary associations. The interior features of the synagogues derived from features of the city gate, not from temple stoas, indicating that the synagogue was not an extension of the temple in Jerusalem. The major common characteristic of the Holy Land synagogues and the Diaspora synagogues was "the public reading and teaching of torah."[79]

In regard to the leadership of the synagogues, Donald Binder distinguishes between the *archōn* (*prostatēs, archiprostatēs*), who was responsible for the legislative and legal concerns of the village and town community, and the *archisynagōgos,* who led the religious services; both *archōn* and *archisynagōgos* were members of a council of elders (*presbyteroi, gerontes, dynatoi*) who functioned as advisers and representatives of the synagogue members.[80] This differentiation can be demonstrated only for a few synagogues, however, and it is too "neat" to be a valid description for all local situations. Lee Levine distinguishes for the period before A.D. 70, particularly for Judea and for Galilee, the priest and the *archisynagōgos* as leaders of the synagogue.[81] The sources focus mostly on one of the two functions, the *archisynagōgos* (for Heb., *rosh knesset*) is mentioned most frequently. The *archisynagōgos* usually was a wealthy person, a leading member of the town community who, with others, looked after the ritual, administrative and financial aspects of the synagogues. In the Diaspora the *archisynagōgos* also appears as patron of the Jewish communities who donated or renovated the synagogue building, or who financed, for example, a mosaic floor.[82] The function of the "elders" (*presbyteroi*) cannot be determined with certainty: the priest Samuel ben Yedaya is the *archōn* of the synagogue in Dura-Europos, but at the same time (in a Greek inscription) he is *presbyteros*. The function of the "elders" presumably was different, depending on local circumstances: they probably carried out administrative and financial, and perhaps also religious-liturgical, tasks. Small communities probably managed without a council of elders.[83] The practice of a Torah reading (*seder*) was firmly established by the first century A.D., at least in the synagogues in Palestine. The Torah was read in a three-year cycle; the one-year cycle of the Babylonian synagogues probably has Palestinian roots as well.[84] The reading of the Torah was accompanied by a reading from the Prophets (*haftarah*), at the very latest by the first

---

[78]L. Levine, "Synagogues," *NEAEHL* 4:1421; idem 2000, 69-72, 127-28, 357-428. For the comment that follows next above see Binder 1999; see also S. J. D. Cohen, "The Temple and the Synagogue," in *CHJ* 3:298-325.

[79]Runesson 2001; quotation, 478; for a survey of research on the origins of the synagogue see ibid., 67-168; on the first-century synagogue see ibid., 169-235; for a critique of Binder see ibid., 353.

[80]Binder 1999, 343-71.

[81]L. Levine 2000, 125-26, referring to Jerusalem (Theodotos inscription) and Dura-Europos. For the the observation that follows above see ibid., 126-27, 390-404; see also *NewDocs* 4:214-17; Rajak and Noy 1993 (ibid., 89-93: "Appendix I. Jewish Texts Mentioning Archisynagogoi").

[82]See Rajak and Noy 1993, 87-89, 90-91 (nos. 17-25).

[83]L. Levine 2000, 407-8, with reference to *DF* 58; Kraeling 1957, 263-68, 277.

[84]L. Levine 2000, 140-41; S. C. Reif, "The Early Liturgy of the Synagogue," in *CHJ* 3:326-57.

century A.D.; Lk 4:17-21 indicates that the reading from the Prophets determined the content of the sermon.[85] The readings from the Hebrew text were accompanied by translations into Aramaic (*targum*).[86]

The income of the communities in the villages and small towns from dues on water and leases of public land usually would have sufficed just to maintain the water supply by building cisterns or laying water pipes.

Jewish society could be divided into the upper class, the retainers of the upper class, and the lower class. The criteria for membership in the upper class was power by office, role, property or influence, as well on account of privileges and prestige.[87] In the first century A.D. the upper class consisted of the Herodian court and the aristocratic priestly families, from which the high priests were appointed. It should be noted, however, that no Jew belonged to the Roman senate, not even to the equestrian order. The retainers of the members of the upper class included the administrators of the courts of Herod I and his sons, the members of the Sanhedrin in Jerusalem, local magistrates; the lower echelons of the retainer group consisted of secretaries, administrators and managers of estates, the tax collectors (*publicani*), military officers, property managers, accountants, treasurers of cities, local judges, priests, wholesalers, traveling tradespeople. Since this social group was numerically very small in Judea and in Galilee, we may ask whether it is appropriate at all to speak of a "class." The lower class included everyone who did not participate in the privileges of, and was not employed by, the elites: peasants and fishers, farm workers and tenant farmers, day laborers and wage laborers, serfs and slaves, artisans and traders, small tradespeople and peddlers. The lowest rung of the lower class included beggars, prostitutes, shepherds and bandits. A major cause for disturbances resulted from egocentric politics: the Herodian dynasty and retainers dependent upon the royal courts were unable to secure some or any prestige among the general population.[88]

Since the work of Michael Rostovtzeff, New Testament scholars have argued that there was tension between cities and villages because the urban elites oppressed and expropriated the peasants. Dennis Groh and J. Andrew Overman argue that this hypothesis should be abandoned for Palestine. First, even anti-Marxist historians such as Rostovtzeff applied

---

[85]See L. Levine 2000, 142-43.

[86]See P. S. Alexander, "Targum, Targumim," *ABD* 6:320-31; idem, "Jewish Aramaic Translations of Hebrew Scriptures," in Mulder 1988, 217-54; see now L. Levine 2000, 147-51; M. McNamara, "Some Targum Themes," in Carson et al. 2001, 303-56. Written Targumim, extant only in fragmentary form, dating before A.D. 70 include 4QtgLev and 11QtgJob. The large Palestinian Targumim date to the third century but could have roots in the first century.

[87]Groh (1997, 29, 32) provides a critique of the model of "power elites," which has been established in other provinces of the Roman Empire and applied, in an inadmissible manner according to Groh, to the situation in Palestine.

[88]See M. Goodman 1987; Stegemann and Stegemann 1995, 124 (ET, 132-33).

the dynamic of Russian society before the revolution in 1917 to the Roman Empire—a methodological decision that is somewhat problematic.[89] Second, several studies have shown that the theory of a dichotomy between the urban upper class and the rural lower class does not apply, for example, for ancient northern Africa.[90] Third, the archaeological investigation of Judea and Galilee of the last twenty years has shown that there was no tension between rich urban centers and an impoverished rural population.[91] Scholars suggest that Jewish life in the towns and villages of Galilee was largely egalitarian, at least toward the outside; even the writings of Josephus do not point to tensions between Jews living in Judea and in Galilee. The attempts by rich urbanites to drive out small landowners and tenant farmers from the lands they cultivated date to the second half of the fourth century.[92] The views of Groh and Overman probably are somewhat overstated, but they counterbalance popular analyses of Galilean and Judean society in a significant way. We should further note that Lower Galilee was not "urban," as Sepphoris and Tiberias did not constitute classical Greek *poleis* in the early first century A.D.: Sepphoris did not mint coins before A.D. 66, and Tiberias not until A.D. 100.

We must not forget, however, that Herod Antipas respected the religious sensibilities of the Galilean population—for example, by issuing coins not bearing images. In neither Sepphoris nor Tiberias have statues of Augustus or Tiberius been discovered (as of yet). James Strange suggested in this connection that since the encounter with Hellenistic culture had been in progress for well over a hundred years, the Galilean population was prepared for Herod Antipas's program of "romanization," with the result that there was no real confrontation between traditional and important values; this can be seen in the material remains of Sepphoris but also in the proclamation of Jesus of Nazareth, who used urban as well as rural metaphors.[93]

Richard Horsley and John Dominic Crossan maintain that Jesus must be understood in the context of a Galilean agricultural society that had come under pressure as a result of Roman imperialism and the politics of the leading circles in Judea, facing the danger of losing the social structures that provided security. It is in this historical and social context that Jesus proposed a reform program that sought to push back the destructive influences of the colonial power and its local representatives.[94] This hypothesis lacks the methodological meticulousness that analyses of agricultural societies demand as well, nor is it supported by archaeological evidence[95] or by the New Testament texts. The theoretical models of G. Lenski and J. Kautsky that Horsley applies to the society of Galilee focus in a rather one-sided manner on social conflicts that cause historical change, disregarding the close connection that the Galilean Jews had with the Jewish institutions in Jerusalem. And Crossan operates with stereotypical categories of values and tendencies in "the Mediterranean world" in terms of anthropological rather than historical categories, with the

---

[89]On Rostovtzeff [1929] 1957 see Groh 1997, 30-31.
[90]See Brisson 1958; cf. Groh 1997, 32.
[91]See Groh 1997, 32; Overman 1997.
[92]See Sperber 1978, 96-118.
[93]J. Strange 1992. On this discussion see Freyne 1997a; 2000, 173-74.
[94]Horsley 1987; 1995; Horsley and Hanson 1999; Crossan 1991.
[95]See Overman 1997; Brece 1990.

result that the specific Galilean reality as we know it from archaeological discoveries and literary analyses of texts appears to be largely faded out.[96] The "urban context" that Crossan stipulates for his understanding of Jesus as proclaimer of Cynic ideas who wanted to ameliorate the injustices under which the rural population had to suffer cannot be demonstrated for Galilee. That is, at any rate, the verdict of Eric Meyers, who has conducted excavations in Galilee for more than thirty years; he comments, "Crossan in my opinion has confused the ethos of Galilee with the ethos of the autonomous cities, or even with the culture of the hellenistic cities of the west."[97]

An important issue in scholarly discussion is the ʿam ha-ʾareṣ, a designation that cannot be clearly identified with a particular social group. Adolf Büchler identified the ʿam ha-ʾareṣ with the Galilean population of the second century, Solomon Zeitlin with the peasants, Gedalyahu Alon with heretics, Aharon Oppenheimer with all Jews who, in the view of the rabbis, did not obey the law faithfully.[98]

8.3 Religious and Political Developments

Stories play a central role in the self-understanding of cultures. Stories determine how people think, feel and act.[99] The story that shaped Second Temple Judaism and thus Jesus' contemporaries is the story that the Old Testament recounts: the story of the one God who created the world, the story of the relationship between this God and this world, the story of the place of the people of Israel as the covenant people of this God in this world and its history.

The story of Israel begins with Abraham, and it is told against the background of the creation of the world and the fall of humankind into sin. The story of Abraham and his descendants thus is narrated as God's answer to the problem that humankind had to deal with since Adam: separation from God, which men and women experienced as a peril to their personal lives. The first climax of Israel's history was the deliverance from slavery in Egypt under the leadership of Moses. The theme of liberation is an important subject in Israel's subsequent history, the subject of Israel's political and religious leaders. The central question was this: why, when YHWH had rescued his people from Egypt and had brought Israel into the promised land, were conditions still far from perfect? The conquest, the period of the judges and even the Davidic monarchy were a mystery: the kingdom was divided, most kings were corrupt, very few people listened to God's messengers the prophets, the northern kingdom was dissolved, and eventually even Jerusalem was conquered by a pagan army and

---

[96]See the critique in Freyne 2000, 18-20, 184.
[97]See Meyers 1997, 59; quotation, ibid., 64; see similarly Freyne 1996, 184-85, 197-98; 2000, 175.
[98]Büchler 1906; S. Zeitlin, "The Am Ha-arez," *JQR* 23 (1932): 45-61; Alon 1980-1984, 2:677-79; Oppenheimer 1977, 18-22, 170-88.
[99]See Frei 1974; Alter 1981; Schnabel 1996a, 151-71, with reference to N. T. Wright 1992, 38-80.

destroyed and the people forced into exile in Babylonia. The promises of a new exodus and the ambitious new beginning under Zerubbabel, Ezra and Nehemiah did not initiate the end of Israel's history and the restoration of paradise. Rather, the old promises still were not fulfilled; Israel's hopes had not yet become reality. The Jews of the Second Temple period, Jesus' contemporaries, thus read the story of the sacred Scriptures as a story whose ending was still pending. The end that Israel expected was to bring the full liberation and redemption of Israel, arising from the beginnings and the climactic events of Israel's past in accordance with God's promises. These hopes for an intervention of Israel's covenant God were kept alive after the death of Herod I in 4 B.C., after the removal of Herod Archelaos, who was sent into exile in Gaul in A.D. 6, and in connection with the domination of Judea by Roman prefects since A.D. 6 and by lower-ranking Roman procurators since A.D. 44 (death of Herod Agrippa I), through sporadic rebellions and through increasing military resistance by Jewish groups.[100]

The piety of the Jews in Judea, Samaria and Galilee had little to do with theological discussions about life after death; it focused on the maintenance of the traditional Jewish identity in the midst of a reality characterized by political humiliation and economic crisis situations. The large majority of the Jews was and remained ready to accept inconveniences on account of their faith in YHWH, their loyalty to the Torah and their Jewish heritage. The Jews prayed, participated in synagogue activities and traveled to festivals in Jerusalem. They circumcised their children, rested on the sabbath, fasted and abstained from eating unclean food. They believed in YHWH as the only true God and in Israel's election as God's covenant people, and they were convinced that the fate of the nations was dependent upon the fate of Israel. They hoped for the full restoration of Israel, for the realization of the promised new covenant, for the coming of the Messiah, for the renewal of the world, and for the coming of God and of his visible kingdom. The scribes' theological perception of the world and the praxis of the ordinary Jews becomes tangible in the four traditional symbols of Israel: in the temple as place of God's presence, effecting holiness and forgiving sin; in the Torah as God's revelation, making life possible in a fallen world; in the land given to Israel by God as a gift; and in circumcision and the purity laws as boundary markers of the ethnic identity of God's people.

The self-understanding of the Jews, governed by the faith of Israel's forebears, had not been abandoned, despite 150 years of Hellenistic influence. New studies have shown, at least for the first century A.D., that the Jews did not frequent the Greco-Roman centers of entertainment that Herod I built in Jerusalem, Caesarea and Jericho,[101] and that his successors built in several

---

[100]On Jewish nationalism see Mendels 1992.
[101]See Josephus, *A.J.* 15.268-273, 341; 15.339-341; 16.137; 17.161-162, 175-178, 254-255.

cities in Galilee and in the Decapolis, and that existed in the cities of the coastal plain: the theaters, amphitheaters and hippodromes. It is rabbis of the second century who discuss plays and games in the theaters and amphitheaters.[102]

Herod I built the first theaters of Palestine in Jerusalem, Caesarea and Jericho. Other theaters existed in Scythopolis, Neapolis, Sepphoris, Sebaste, Shuni, Hammat Gader and in the Nabatean cities of Philadelphia, Gadara, Gerasa and Bostra. Herod I also built the first hippodromes (stadia) for chariot races and athletic games in Jerusalem, Jericho and Caesarea; more stadia were built later in Tarichea, Tiberias and Sebaste (and in the second and third centuries in Neapolis, Bostra, Gadara, Gerasa, Gaza, Scythopolis and Philadelphia). And Herod I built the first amphitheaters in Jerusalem, Caesarea and Jericho for gladiator contests and animal fights (in the first century the terms *amphitheatron* and *hippodromos* perhaps were interchangeable).[103] Other amphitheaters were built later in Neapolis, Scythopolis, Gerasa, Bostra, and Eleutheropolis.

Generalizations often are difficult, especially with regard to cultural factors and developments. Literary texts and inscriptions are nearly always connected with the local elites in the cities, who were more thoroughly Hellenized than the rural population in the numerous villages. Societies are multicultural in often surprising ways, not only today but already in antiquity. David Kennedy emphasizes this reality with regard to the ancient Near East: in the first century we find not only Semitic families who gave their children Greek names (e.g., the architect "Diodorus son of Zebsaos") but also parents with Greek names who gave their children Semitic names (e.g., "Zabdion son of Aristomachus," who was the priest of Tiberius Caesar in Gerasa in A.D. 22/23.)[104] In view of such facts it is only with caution that we may speak of an increasing, or a more thoroughgoing, Hellenization in Judea, Galilee or Syria. On the use of the Greek language see §8.4.

Some scholars like to use the term "Judaisms" to characterize the Second Temple period, particularly with regard to the first century, highlighting the pluralism of convictions and ways of life. This view is as exaggerated as it is unnecessary. Of course there were differences in viewpoint regarding convictions, opinions, ways of behavior and even the national symbols. The three traditional religious "parties"—the Sadducees, Pharisees and Essenes—certainly played a

---

[102]See Zeev Weiss, "Adopting a Novelty: The Jews and the Roman Games in Palestine," in Humphrey 1995-2002, 2:23-49; cf. his (Hebrew) dissertation, "Games and Spectacles in Roman Palestine and Their Reflection in Talmudic Literature" (Hebrew University, 1994).

[103]See Yosef Porath, "Herod's 'Ampitheatre' at Caesarea: A Multipurpose Entertainment Building," in Humphrey 1995-2002, 1:15-27; John H. Humphrey, "Amphitheatrical 'Hippo-Stadia,'" in Raban and Holum 1996, 121-29.

[104]D. Kennedy, "Greek, Roman and Native Cultures in the Roman Near East," in Humphrey 1995-2002, 2:77-106, esp. 103. The inscriptions date from A.D. 27/28 and 22/23 and were found in Gerasa. See also Millar 1993, 411-12.

decisive role in these connections.[105] It cannot be shown unequivocally from the primary sources that it is justified to speak of an "unprecedented factionalism" of the Jewish majority society.[106]

Some scholars seek to explain these Jewish groups or "sects" with the help of deviance theory: the formation of groups or parties is regarded as a result not just of nonconformism but of fundamental crisis situations in societies.[107] This explanation is unconvincing. Although the "deviance" of the Qumran Essenes perhaps is a plausible assumption, the social structure of the Pharisees is not clearly recognizable, and the "deviance" of the Sadducees is only "indirect," as Ekkehard Stegemann and Wolfgang Stegemann admit. In a newer study, Albert Baumgarten suggests that there was a close connection between literacy and the Jewish "sects" that needed to justify their specific interpretations with the help of scriptural exegesis. They recruited their members from the educated classes, especially in the cities, and regarded themselves as an elite that stood above the uncultured "people of the land." As a result it is possible to compare the Jewish sects with the members of the Greco-Roman philosophical schools.[108]

The religious practices in everyday life were determined by the Pharisees, at least according to Josephus: "Because of these views they [the Pharisees] are, as a matter of fact, extremely influential among the townsfolk; and all prayers and sacred rites of divine worship are performed according to their exposition. This is the great tribute that the inhabitants of the cities, by practicing the highest ideals both in their way of living and in their discourse, have paid to the excellence of the Pharisees" (*A.J.* 18.15).[109] The polemic of some Qumran texts against the Pharisees illustrates the widespread adherence to Pharisaic halakah as well as their influence on broad sections of the population.[110] At the time of Jesus the Pharisaic movement had been a piety and holiness move-

---

[105]See Schürer 2:381-415, 555-90; Saldarini 1988; Stemberger 1991; N. T. Wright 1992, 167-214; Stegemann and Stegemann 1995, 138-48 (ET, 149-62); E. P. Sanders 1992, 315-451 (cf. the critique in Hengel 1994b); Meier 1991-2001, 3:289-613. On the Pharisees see A. J. Saldarini, *ABD* 5:289-303; A. I. Baumgarten, *EDSS* 2:657-63; McKnight 1986, 30-71; Mason 1990; Peter Schäfer, "Der vorrabbinische Pharisäismus," in Hengel and Heckel 1991, 125-75; Deines 1997; J. Schaper, "The Pharisees," in *CHJ* 3:358-401; R. Deines, "Pharisäer," *ThBLNT* 2:1455-68; idem, "The Pharisees Between 'Judaisms' and 'Common Judaism,'" in Carson et al. 2001, 443-504. On the Sadducees see C. Burchard, "Sadduzäer," PWSup 15 (1978): 466-78; G. G. Porton, *ABD* 5:892-95; E. Main, *EDSS* 2:812-16; LeMoyne 1972; G. Stemberger, *CHJ* 3:402-27. On the Essenes and on Qumran see J. J. Collins, *ABD* 2:619-26; T. S. Beall, *EDSS* 1:262-69; C. Hempel, *EDSS* 2:746-51; H. Stegemann 1993; O. Betz, "The Essenes," in *CHJ* 3:444-70.

[106]Contra Stegemann and Stegemann 1995, 129 (ET, 138).

[107]Stegemann and Stegemann 1995, 138-44 (ET, 149-56), for the caveats that follow above see ibid., 140 (ET, 151-52).

[108]A. Baumgarten 1997, esp. 49-51; now also Hezser 2001, 199-200.

[109]See Josephus, *A.J.* 18.17. This evaluation is disputed by scholars.

[110]See CD IV, 19; VIII, 12, 19; XIX, 24, 31. See L. H. Schiffman, "New Light on the Pharisees," in *Understanding the Dead Sea Scrolls* (ed. H. Shanks; New York: Bantam, 1992), 217-24. On the translations of the psalms in the Septuagint as "proto-Pharisaic document" see Schaper 1995, 160-64.

ment for over a hundred years with a strong focus on personal righteousness. "Here righteousness concerns the relationship with the fellow-creatures, while piety concerns the relationship with God."[111] The Pharisees' struggle for a thoroughgoing sanctification of everyday life and their striving for ritual purity in accordance with God's laws is explained, first, by their piety and way of life, which were oriented by the Torah and its interpretation in the tradition of the sages, and, second, by a messianic expectation of the imminent end that increased, at least in some circles, the readiness to take action. The connection between God's activity and human activity is characteristic for the Pharisees, who occupied a middle position between the Sadducees, who, according to Josephus, denied the power of "fate" and the Essenes, who explained everything with fate. The Pharisees were convinced that "certain events are the work of Fate, but not all; as to other events, it depends upon ourselves whether they shall take place or not."[112] As a result, the Pharisees practiced and taught an ethic that emphasized the responsibility of the individual, "since his position before God was also determined in a decisive way by his own volition. . . . They demanded the study of the Torah emphatically because everybody must and can know his part in the covenant obligation to God." The Pharisees were organized in habûrôt ("communities, associations"), a committed nucleus of members, but they attracted a large following of adherents and sympathizers. The Pharisees were a "people's party."

The Sadducees[113] emphasized the personal responsibility of the people, more so than did the Pharisees, from whom they also differed with regard to a doctrine of immanent retribution: people experience reward and punishment in exact correspondence with their actions. They rejected belief in the resurrection of the dead as well as the last judgment. And they rejected the tradition of the oral law. Günther Baumbach comments, "Because of their rigid adherence to the written Torah they were on the one hand 'more heartless in judgment than any other Jews' (Ant. xx.199), yet on the other hand more generous and open regarding the cultural achievements of Hellenism." The Sadducees understood themselves as successors of the legitimate high priestly line of the Zadokites, which explains their name. At least by the first century A.D. they were the "party of the Jerusalem priestly nobility." They championed a national temple-state ideology, presumably inherited from the Hasmoneans. The increasing difficulties of the political situation under the Roman prefects and procurators forced the prominent priestly families and the leading Pharisaic scribes to cooperate. Both

---

[111]Deines, ThBLNT 2:1461; for the summary that follows above see ibid., 2:1460-61.

[112]Josephus, A.J. 13.172; cf. B.J. 2.162-163. The quotation that follows above is from Deines, ThBLNT 2:1460.

[113]See LeMoyne 1972; R. Meyer, ThWNT 7:35-54 (TDNT 7:23-26); G. Baumbach, EWNT 3:530-31 (EDNT 3:222-33); the quotations that follow above, G. Baumbach, EDNT, 3:223.

groups sought to avoid as much as possible an open confrontation with the Roman overlords. The frequent changes in the office of the high priest, enforced by the Romans, compelled the priestly aristocracy to be careful.

8.4 Communication Structures

The communication structures of Judea and Galilee are largely similar, but there are significant differences as well. Because language, written and spoken, is the central medium of human communication,[114] I first will discuss the languages spoken by Jesus and his disciples. There were two linguae francae in first-century Palestine: Aramaic and Greek; Hebrew still played an important role; Latin was not widely used.[115]

1. The vernacular of Judea and Galilee was Aramaic, which was spoken in the first century from the Mediterranean to India, from Asia Minor to Egypt. When Jesus spoke with Galilean peasants, he had to use Aramaic, which must be considered his native language.

2. The Greek language increasingly took the place of Aramaic as lingua franca in the eastern regions of the Roman Empire during the Hellenistic period. By the first century A.D. many Jews spoke Greek, as illustrated by hundreds of coins, inscriptions and papyri from Judea and Galilee. A third of the approximately 250 inscriptions found in or near Jerusalem dating to the Second Temple period are written in Greek; about 7 percent are bilingual. This fact supports the conclusion that between 10 and 15 percent of Jerusalem's population spoke Greek as their native language in the first century—that is, as many as 15,000 of some 100,000 inhabitants.[116] A certain Soumaios, a Gentile member of the commando structure of the "revolutionary administration" of Bar Kokhba, wrote a letter in Greek, apologizing that he did not write in Hebrew or in Aramaic but reckons quite naturally with the fact that the addressees will be able to read the letter or find somebody who can translate it.[117] Many Jews in Lower Galilee spoke Greek as well, particularly among the population that lived in the regions around the Sea of Galilee.[118] Jesus very probably was able to speak Greek; he used it presumably in contacts with Gentiles, perhaps also during his trial before Pilate.[119]

---

[114]Reck 1991, 68; for a discussion of ancient communication structures see ibid., 68-157. Habbe (1996, 50) is fixated in a one-sided manner on a "system of mail and envoys," a "structure resembling the press" and traveling artisans.

[115]See Schürer 2:20-28, 74-80; Rosen 1980; Meyers and Strange 1981, 62-91; Riesner 1988, 382-92; Porter 1994b; idem, *DNTB* 433-34; see also M. O. Wise, *DJG* 434-44; Fitzmyer 1979, 29-56; G. Mussies, in Safrai and Stern 1987, 1040-64; Meier 1991-2001, 1:255-67.

[116]Hengel 1991, 258.

[117]Hayim Lapin, "Palm Fronds and Citrons: Notes on Two Letters from Bar Kosiba's Administration," *HUCA* 64 (1993): 111-35, esp. 125-26; for text and translation see ibid., 114-15. Editio princeps by B. Lifshitz, "Papyrus grecs du désert de Judea," *Aegyptus* 42 (1962): 241-48.

[118]See Meyers 1976, 97; Edwards 1992, 70-71.

[119]See Meier 1991-2001, 1:266-67.

3. The role of the Hebrew language in the first century is debated. Some scholars believe that Hebrew was spoken only in the synagogues and in the learned disputations of the scribes and priests. Other scholars are convinced that Hebrew continued as the colloquial language of Palestinian Jews, perhaps in particular in Jerusalem, possibly even as the language of the common people in Galilee. Yet other scholars think that Hebrew was used by specific groups defined by particular social or geographical contexts. Undisputed is that Hebrew was heard in the synagogues and taught in the schools: the Torah was the "textbook" of the elementary students as well as of the scribes. Jesus probably spoke Hebrew in his discussions with Pharisees and scribes.[120]

4. The Latin language played only a minor role. The Romans did not engage in a systematic "language imperialism," and the administration of the provinces in the East was carried out in Greek. It is unlikely that Jesus or his disciples knew Latin.

5. It is debated what percentage of the population in Judea and Galilee was able to read and write. Catherine Hezser concludes in a recent study of the relevant data that literacy was not very common in Roman Palestine.[121] She argues that during the first and second centuries people wrote primarily for pragmatic reasons: to identify the grave of the family, to protect property, to collect debts, to record accounts, to identify crops and to declare ownership of vessels. If Meir Bar-Ilan is correct,[122] only about 2 to 15 percent of the population (women included) in cities such as Tiberias could read and write, in other towns only 1 percent, and in some villages complete illiteracy was the case. Not everybody who could read was also able to write: in the schools it was primarily (or exclusively) reading that was taught. This analysis applies perhaps more particularly to the situation after A.D. 70: according to Albert Baumgarten, the period after the destruction of Jerusalem witnessed a partial return to orality.[123] Rainer Riesner arrives at a different conclusion: he argues that a pious Jew at the time of Jesus had a solid education based on a knowledge of the Torah, had mastered reading and writing, and could memorize large amounts of data due to the use of simple mnemonic aids.[124] Palestinian Jews who learned to speak, read and write Greek would have been dependent upon private schools, such as, for example, at the court of King Herod I.

There was no production of literary texts on a large scale in Judea, probably out of deference to the Torah[125] and presumably also because of the cost in-

---

[120]See Meier 1991-2001, 1:267.
[121]Hezser 2001; see her conclusions, 496-504.
[122]Bar-Ilan 1992; cf. Hezser 2001, 35.
[123]A. Baumgarten 1997, 134; cf. Hezser (2001, 35-36), who bases her study primarily on rabbinic and early Byzantine sources.
[124]Riesner 1988, 199; on the elementary school see ibid., 153-206; see also Hezser 2001, 39-109.
[125]See Hezser 2001, 146; for the observation that follows above see ibid.

volved. A short text on papyrus cost between five and six drachmas, which was the average weekly wage of a laborer. Emperor Diocletian restricted the prices that could be demanded for copied books to 25 denarii for 100 lines in *scriptura optima* (i.e., written in calligraphy).[126]

Perhaps not even the library of the Qumran community is an exception, as the approximately 850 texts found in Kh. Qumran were not all written there. Some texts were brought into the community from outside. And the analysis of the scripts of these texts establish that they were written by several hundred authors and/or copyists.[127] A few rich Jews may have owned a private library. The synagogues probably functioned as the Jewish equivalent of Greek and Roman libraries.[128] In the Greek cities of Palestine libraries presumably existed in the gymnasia and the rhetorical schools. In Jerusalem before the year A.D. 70 there were public archives; otherwise an archive is attested only at Sepphoris.[129] The archives contained official correspondence, tax and census lists, private contracts, legal documents, genealogies.[130]

A second key factor in human communication is the bridging of spatial distance, which was possible in antiquity only by travel.[131] The itineraries included the large trade routes, which were paved roads, and the network of local routes, which were unpaved tracks that people traveled to nearby towns and villages. Older maps of Galilee record primarily the roads of the second century, with the result that Galilee appears nearly isolated, with no west-east routes.[132] The research of David Dorsey has shown that Galilee had a dense network of roads and paths in pre-Roman times that the Romans expanded in the second century. The close trade contacts between production centers in Galilean villages and towns in the vicinity and in more remote areas, illuminated by the research of David Adan-Bayewitz, provide evidence for the existence of an elaborate network of roads that connected towns and villages.[133] If we take the new map of Palestine that Yoram Tsafrir published for the Hellenistic and Roman period and trace the regional and the supraregional roads and paths documented by these trade contacts, it can be ascertained that it was easily possible to reach any of about forty villages from Sepphoris within a single day's journey.[134]

In the second and third centuries Judea had a network of roads that encom-

---

[126] *CIL* III 831; Hezser 2001, 145.

[127] D. Dimant, "Qumran: Written Material," *EDSS* 2:739-40.

[128] See recently L. Levine 2000, 380-81. Hezser (2001, 165-66) is cautious.

[129] Josephus, *B.J.* 2.426-427; 6.354; 7.61; *C. Ap.* 1.31; for Sepphoris see Josephus, *Vita* 38; *m. Qidd.* 4:5.

[130] On archives and libraries see Hezser 2001, 150-68, 498.

[131] See Casson 1994; Reck 1991, 81-91.

[132] For example, Avi-Yonah, *Map of Roman Palestine;* idem, *The Holy Land.* For the observation that follows above see Dorsey 1991.

[133] See J. Strange 1997, 39-42.

[134] See J. Strange 1997, 42.

passed some 1,500 km (over 900 mi.). These roads followed the old routes that sometimes dated back to the Bronze Age and presumably were in use during the first century.[135]

An average traveler could walk about 25 km (15 mi.) per day. In regard to accommodations, a traveler in antiquity (as today) had two options: to lodge in the private home of friends, acquaintances or friends' acquaintances, or to rent accommodations in a public guest house. Traveling Jews might find a place to stay overnight in synagogues, especially in the Diaspora's larger cities. In the poorer regions of Galilee, where we have to reckon with humble synagogues in private homes, this would not have been possible. A traveler in Galilee was dependent upon the hospitality of local people. The communicative potential of hospitable homes was just as important as that of public guest houses as relay stations for news—presumably an important factor in the preaching and healing ministry of Jesus and of his disciples.

The trade activities in Galilee with Sepphoris and Tiberias as important centers, and in Judea with Jerusalem as the main center, served not only the exchange of goods but also the dissemination of information. We should note in this context that Judea and Galilee maintained trade relations not only in terms of regional trade within Judea and Galilee and supraregional trade with areas such as Perea, the Decapolis and Syrophoenicia, but also with other regions such as Egypt and Syria and, indirectly, even India.

Close trade relations between India and the Mediterranean world existed since the first century B.C., and they were intensified since the principate of Augustus. At least in the larger Palestinian towns one could find Indian goods—not only luxury goods but also cotton and spices.[136] A well-known comment in Second Temple sources is the information in 1 Macc 6:37 that Antiochos V Eupator (164-162 B.C.) used war elephants (ἐλέφαντες) in his campaign against the Jews, driven by Indians (ὁ Ἰνδὸς αὐτοῦ). No regular connections between Israel and India existed, but Jews could buy Indian products in some markets: ivory, ebony, sandalwood and exotic animals.[137]

The significance of pilgrimages to Jerusalem and the temple must not be underestimated for communication among Jews.[138] Jerusalem had become a world city, not least on account of the reign and the building activities of Herod I. The capital of the Jewish commonwealth could compete with the leading cities of the

---

[135]See Fischer et al., 1996, 328-29; I. Roll in Tsafrir, di Segni and Green, *Iudaea-Palaestina,* 21-24 (with map). A recent study of the road network in Upper Galilee established, not surprisingly, that the Roman roads followed the natural migration routes, which depended on topographical factors; see April L. Whitten, "Roman Roads in the Upper Galilee and Lower Golan Regions: Relationships to Natural Migratory Routes" (M.A. thesis, University of Nebraska, 1997).

[136]See Rostovtzeff [1929] 1957, 147.

[137]See J. K. Lott, *ABD* 3:410.

[138]See S. Safrai 1981, 262; Schürer 3:148-49; S. Safrai, "Relations between the Diaspora and the Land of Israel," in Safrai and Stern 1987, 117-83.

Roman Empire in terms of its magnificence and prestige (not with regard to its size). Jerusalem was the city of perpetual temple services and of grand pilgrim festivals attended by hundreds of thousands of visitors. The transfer of the yearly *didrachmon* tax and the offerings and gifts of the pilgrims who came from Mesopotamia and northern Africa, from the coastlands of the Black Sea and from Armenia, from Macedonia and from Achaia, from Asia Minor and from Syria, from Rome and from Alexandria, from Antioch and from Damascus brought substantial wealth into Judea. According to Josephus, about 2.5 million pilgrims congregated in Jerusalem for the large festivals (*B.J.* 6.425).[139] Jerusalem was an international city. Jewish pilgrims, traveling in groups and meeting other pilgrims en route, had ample opportunity to exchange information during the journey and also in Jerusalem, where they met pilgrims from all parts of the Roman Empire.

A further, rather plausible, means of communication in Judea and Galilee in the first century was the public speech in front of larger groups of people.[140] The most common means of communication was, of course, personal conversation in the (extended) family in private homes, in the neighborhood and in the workplace (if the latter was spatially separated from the home). The importance of private homes for Jews and Christians can be seen in the fact that the majority of synagogues in Galilee, in rural Judea and in the Diaspora were small house synagogues.[141] The meeting places of the early Christian communities were private homes as well.

In regard to the domestic culture of Galilee,[142] I noted earlier that the architecture of Galilean private houses and of public buildings did not differ from the architectural traditions of Syria, Asia Minor or Egypt during the Greco-Roman period. The only features that would have struck non-Jewish travelers to Galilee as foreign were "objects" in the private realm—for example, in the synagogues the columns between the benches along the walls and the central place of worship (in Greco-Roman buildings the columns stood behind the backs of the worshipers),[143] and the handmade stone vessels for the purification rites stipulated by the law.

---

[139]On the geographical dimensions of the Jewish Diaspora see Schürer 3:3-86; M. Stern, "The Jewish Diaspora," in Safrai and Stern 1987, 117-83; P. Trebilco, "Diaspora Judaism," *DLNTD* 287-91.

[140]See Josephus, *C. Ap.* 1.177-181; *A.J.* 8.46-48; 18.81-84; 20.24-26, 43-46, 142; Mt 23:15; Jn 7:35; Acts 13:6; 19:13-14; *m. 'Abot* 1:4. Cf. Riesner 1988, 355-57; Reck 1991, 99-100. On the Stoic-Cynic philosophers see §§10.2; 18.5 in the present work. It is not clear whether Oinomaos, a Cynic philosopher from Gadara (second century A.D. [cf. *Gen. Rab.* 65:20; *Ruth Rab.* 2:12]) should be regarded as an itinerant philosopher (contra Reck 1991, 99 n. 222).

[141]See Klauck 1981; Riesner 1988, 136.

[142]See John S. Holladay, "House, Israelite," *ABD* 3:308-18; Shmuel Safrai, "Home and Family," in Safrai and Stern 1987, 728-92; Blue 1994, 138-44; Pieter J. J. Botha, "Houses in the World of Jesus," *Neot* 32 (1998): 37-74; now Gehring 2000, 51-127.

[143]This architectural peculiarity probably is to be explained by the architecture of Solomon's temple, whose "courts" were surrounded by columns: the worshipers who watched the actions of the priests faced columns.

The size and the layout of the private houses of the "common people" are illustrated by the house dating to the first century A.D. that Virgilio Corbo discovered in Capernaum underneath the octagonal Byzantine church that had been built in the fifth century as a memorial at an important Christian site. The original private house from the first century evidently was the house of Peter (fig. 3).[144] Following Hellenistic models, the house consisted of a complex of several buildings grouped around an inner courtyard (Lat., *insula,* "island"). The house of Peter had northern and southern courtyards, where everyday life took place, as is evident from the ovens and the mills discovered there. The courtyards, in other words, corresponded to our "living rooms." The buildings, made of unhewn basalt stone, served as sleeping quarters and store rooms. The *insulae* were used by extended families; thus, for example, according to Mk 1:29-31, Simon Peter's mother-in-law lived in his house.s

The house of Peter (25 by 20 m) had nine rooms. The largest room (7 by 6.5 m [45.5 m² or 54.4 sq. yd.]) occupied the central space between the northern and the southern courtyards. There is clear evidence that this room was used as a Christian meeting place by the second half of the first century at the latest: during this period the floor of this central room was renovated at least six times, and the walls were plastered white. No remains of household items or fishing hooks were found here, unlike the other rooms; instead, lnumerous clay lamps from the Herodian period were found. In the fourth century this room was provided with a stable roof, at a time when the house was transformed into a house church (Lat., *domus ecclesiae*).[145]

---

[144]See Virgilio C. Corbo et al., *Cafarnao* (4 vols.; Publications of the Studium Biblicum Franciscanum 19; Jerusalem: Franciscan Printing Press, 1972-1975); Corbo 1972; idem, *ABD* 1:866-69; Meyers and Strange 1981, 114-16, 128-30; V. Tzaferis, "New Archaeological Evidence on Ancient Capernaum," *BA* 46 (1983): 198-204; Bösen 1985, 75-82; Riesner, *GBL* 2:764-68; S. Loffreda, in Manns and Alliata 1993; Blue 1994, 138-40; Perkins 1994, 38.

[145]Egeria, the pilgrim from Spain, saw this house church during her visit to Capernaum in A.D. 383; see Baldi 1955, 299.

9

JESUS' MISSION TO ISRAEL

In the beginning was Jesus. Without Jesus, there would have been no messianic Jewish community in Jerusalem whose leaders proclaimed that God had revealed himself in the crucified and resurrected Jesus of Nazareth, procuring the salvation of the world. Without Jesus, no messianic community would have existed in Damascus, in Antioch, in Ephesus, in Pergamon, in Rome, or in any of the provinces of the Roman Empire. Jesus stands at the beginning of the missionary activity of the early Christians.[1]

Jesus' ministry defined a missionary ministry in the proper sense: he understood himself as "sent" by God (Lk 4:43) to gather "the lost sheep of the house of Israel" (Mt 15:24).[2] Jesus traveled through Galilee, visiting villages and towns, proclaiming the good news of the dawn of God's kingdom, calling Israel to repent and to believe in the present fulfillment of God's covenant promises. Jesus saw himself as anointed by God's Spirit (Lk 4:18), who set off the liberating power of the turning point of God's history with his people and with the world through his teaching activity, through healing the sick and through liberating people from demons, thus making visible the eschatological power of God (Mt 12:28-29).[3] It was precisely in this sense that his message was *euangelion,* "good news" (Mt 4:23; 11:5, following Is 61:1), the proclamation that God's kingdom had arrived (Mk 1:14-15; cf. *Tg. Isa.* 52:7). At the same time he gathered students to train them as "fishers of people," coworkers in his own missionary activity.

Jesus preached and healed primarily in Galilee, but also in Judea and on occasion in the regions east of the Jordan River. Jesus was known to be a teacher: he was addressed by his contemporaries as "rabbi" (Heb., *rabbi;* Gk., *didaskalos*

---

[1]See Burchard 1980, contra Gensichen (1971, 68) and the view of the Bultmann school that Gensichen supports at this point. However, Burchard sees Jesus not as the person who caused and established the early Christian mission, but rather as "cause and grounds of mission . . . because people felt prompted to do missionary work on account of him and substantiated their missionary work with reference to him" (ibid., 20).

[2]Cf. Mk 12:6; Lk 4:18. See O. Betz 1994, 24; J. Harvey 1998a, 36-38.

[3]See O. Betz 1994, 24; for the observation that follows above see ibid.

and *epistatēs*).[4] His mode of teaching differed from that of the rabbis of his time: he walked from settlement to settlement and taught men and women, large crowds and small groups, in synagogues and in the open fields, in small marketplaces and in private houses. This programmatic statement by Jesus is reported in Mk 1:38/Lk 4:43:

Mk 1:38: "Let us go on to the neighboring towns [*kōmopoleis*], so that I may proclaim the message there also; for that is what I came out to do."

Jesus evidently followed a plan, seeking to visit all towns and settlements in Galilee to preach his message of the dawn of God's kingdom, with no particular town really being his "hometown."[5]

The ministry of John the Baptist is the historical precondition for the missionary activity of the early church.[6] The Baptist is presented as God's envoy (Jn 1:6: ἄνθρωπος ἀπεσταλμένος παρὰ θεοῦ). Preaching as a prophet, he confronted all his listeners, without exception, with his message of necessary repentance and thus invalidated the salvational automatism that was postulated, at least on occasion, with respect to Israel as the people of God in Jewish theology. If the immersion in water that he demanded of all Israelites who repented is indeed linked with the concept of proselyte baptism,[7] he asserts that in view of God's impending intervention all Israelites need to become "proselytes" if they want to belong to the eschatological people of God and escape God's judgment. The effect of John's preaching, if not his activity, had "centripetal" character. His disciples probably were not simply assistants who helped with the immersion ceremony, but rather were "multipliers of his message of repentance."[8] This is also seen in the fact that his disciples evidently continued to be active in preaching and establishing communities after John's death.[9]

Since the missionary activity of the early church is intimately linked with Jesus' ministry, I will describe the teaching and preaching activity of Jesus in the following section before investigating the geographical dimension of his ministry.

9.1 The Message of the Arrival of the Kingdom of God
Jesus' Self-understanding
The question of who Jesus was and what his intentions were receives rather different answers in the academic discussion of the historical Jesus. For some,

---

[4]See particularly Riesner 1988; also Theissen and Merz 1996, 311-21 (ET, 347-58).
[5]Burchard 1987, 39; Michaels 1999, 188-89; on πατρίς with the meaning "hometown" see U. Hutter, *EWNT* 3:137-38 (*EDNT* 3:58).
[6]See Pesch 1982, 22-24.
[7]Thus Böcher 1978, 51; Pesch 1982, 23.
[8]Pesch 1982, 24.
[9]Hengel (1968, 40) sees a messianic movement that competed with early Christianity.

Jesus was a Cynic wisdom teacher,[10] for others a prophet,[11] for others both a Cynic teacher and a Jewish prophet.[12] Some scholars argue that Jesus was non-political,[13] while others believe that he pursued primarily political goals.[14] The picture that scholars paint of Jesus and his goals invariably informs their understanding of the Gospel accounts.[15] If Jesus was a Cynic teacher, one appreciates his ethical challenges, exhortations and encouragements but has difficulties with his death—the post-Easter church, with its missionary proclamation of Jesus' messianic identity, his atoning death on the cross and his resurrection as fundamental convictions and central subject matter, becomes an aberration. If Jesus was an apocalyptic prophet, scholars will regard all Gospel sayings that imply continuity (e.g., references to a future community of followers and their missionary activity) as redactional and secondary—with the conclusion that Jesus failed in his mission, since he was executed at the cross without the kingdom of God having become a reality in Galilee or in Judea. If Jesus was a visionary with political goals, scholars will reinterpret his interest for individuals and his reference to the forgiveness of sins in terms of concerns of the early church or in terms of the restoration of Israel—his "alternative vision" will be regarded as utopian, his solidarity with the poor as idealistic, and his mission as a failure, since neither he nor his followers were able to replace the Herodian dynasty.[16]

If, on the other hand, Jesus was indeed the messianic Son of Man, aware of his divine dignity and divine authority, and if he wanted to bring the fulfillment of the old promises and of Israel's hopes for a conclusive solution for the problem of sin and alienation from God, and if he therefore advanced purposefully toward his death and the resurrection, then one would not doubt as a matter of principle the historicity of the miracle accounts nor hypercritically determine what Jesus could and could not have said. Scholars who accept as authentic only a minority of the Gospel narratives are forced to reconstruct the goals of Jesus independently of the Gospel texts, in a more or less interested "dialogue" with the Gospel writers, if they do not abstain entirely from asking historical questions, as scholars did following the lead of Rudolf Bultmann. The diversity of opinions is large; the confusion is enormous. There is no doubt, of course, that the Gospels were first written in Greek, which means that the early church translated the words of Jesus from Aramaic or Hebrew into Greek. There is also no doubt that the Gospel writers selected from an abundance of material as they

---

[10]Crossan 1991; Mack 1988, 53-77; Vaage 1994; Downing 1988; 1992. For a critique see H. Betz 1994; Freyne 1996, 184-85, 197-98; N. T. Wright, in Chilton and Evans 1999b, esp. 98-111.
[11]E. P. Sanders 1985.
[12]Horsley 1987.
[13]Mack 1993.
[14]Borg 1984; Overman 1997; Rhoads 1995a; 1995b; Freyne 1996; 1997b.
[15]See Freyne 2000, 170.
[16]Explicitly acknowledged by Freyne 1996, 205-6.

wrote their accounts of Jesus' life, and that they did this in correspondence with their individual perspectives, despite the fact that the first three Gospels "synoptically" included much parallel material. And finally, there is no doubt that the Gospel writers did not simply string together events and sayings of Jesus but rather recorded the meaning of his words and actions in a process of interpretation, as they sought to write books for the early Christian churches that were meant to help them in their faith in Jesus as Messiah.

The criteria used to evaluate the historical reliability of the Gospels cannot comprehensively be discussed here.[17] The traditional criteria of double dissimilarity (criterion of difference), of multiple attestation, of Palestinian milieu and of coherence have proved, in part, their value for the historical investigation of the historical Jesus. However, many of their presuppositions and some of their approaches have been strongly criticized, especially the criterion of difference, according to which only such sayings of Jesus are authentic that cannot be derived either from Judaism or from early Christianity. Gerd Theissen replaces this highly problematic criterion with the criterion of historical plausibility: "Jesus traditions reflect plausible historical influence when they can be explained by the influence of the life of Jesus—partly because independent sources correspond, and partly because elements in these sources go against the *Tendenz*. Coherence and opposition to the *Tendenz* are complementary criteria for the plausibility of historical influence. . . . Traditions of Jesus have a plausible historical context when they fit into the Jewish context of the activity of Jesus and are recognizable as individual phenomena within this context. Contextual correspondence and contextual individuality are complementary criteria for the plausibility of the historical context."[18] The elimination of the Gospel of John as a source for a description of the ministry and proclamation of Jesus is a hermeneutical prejudice against which scholars have, for good reasons, begun to protest.[19]

Since Jesus' mission is inseparably linked with his self-understanding, and his ministry with his message, the following section summarizes Jesus' intentions and goals and the content of his preaching, teaching and healing activity.

1. Jesus' proclamation focused on the "kingdom of God."[20] The summaries that describe Jesus' ministry,[21] the frequency of this term[22] and the central role that it has in many texts indicate that the kingdom of God is the *cantus firmus*, the heart, of Jesus' proclamation. The scholarly discussion of the last 150 years often focused on the question of whether the kingdom of God should be re-

---

[17]See Riesner 1988, 80-96; Dunn 1985; Blomberg 1987; Theissen and Merz 1996, 96-122 (ET, 90-124); Theissen and Winter 1997; Chilton and Evans 1999a; 1999b; A. Baum 2000; Porter 2000.
[18]Theissen and Merz 1996, 118-19 (ET, 116-17).
[19]J. Robinson 1985, 1-122; Ensor 1996, esp. 48-84. Note the new program unit of the Society of Biblical Literature called "John, Jesus and History"; at the annual meeting in Toronto in 2002, Robert Kysar, Paula Fredriksen and others protested against the "de-historicizing" of the Gospel of John.
[20]Gk., βασιλεία τοῦ θεοῦ (*basileia tou theou*); Aram., מלכותא דאלהא (*malkuta' delaha'*).
[21]Mt 4:17/Mk 1:14-15 (beginning of Jesus' ministry); Mt 4:23; 9:35; Lk 4:43; 8:1 (Jesus' ministry); Mt 10:7; Lk 9:1-2 (mission of the Twelve).
[22]Matthew has 55 occurrences, Mark 20, Luke 46, John 3.

garded as a purely future entity or as a present reality, ignoring the fact that a more important question for Jesus was that of *who belongs* to the kingdom of God. If Jesus' answer to this latter question is those people who accept his message as revelation from God and his miracles as demonstrations of God's power, then it becomes obvious that the present dimension of the kingdom of God stands in the foreground: the eschatological kingdom of God has become a present reality in the words and deeds of Jesus of Nazareth; the coming reign of God is now present in the person of Jesus. An important saying of Jesus asserts, "Blessed are the eyes that see what you see! For I tell you that many prophets and kings desired to see what you see, but did not see it, and to hear what you hear, but did not hear it" (Lk 10:23b-24/Mt 13:16-17). This means that the establishment of God's rule on earth has become a present reality in the ministry of Jesus.[23] Jesus changes the messianic age that the Jews hoped would bring the visible and uncontested establishment of God's rule. He takes up the "seeing" from this tradition and also the "hearing": the members of the kingdom of God have a true understanding, they recognize Jesus' mighty deeds as signs pointing to the presence of the kingdom of God, and they hear the proclamation of Jesus as the word of the kingdom of God. In the Beelzebul controversy (Mt 12:22-30/Mk 3:22-27/Lk 11:14-26) Jewish scribes raise the question of the origins of Jesus' power. Jesus rejects the charge that his actions can or should be explained with reference to the power of the prince of the demons.

The charge that Jesus acts in the authority of Beelzebul ("lord of sublimity," "lord of the [heavenly] dwelling") possibly should be interpreted against the background of the Jewish polemic against the Semitic "god of heaven" (Baal-shamem). If this suggestion is correct, then the scribes' charge against Jesus has to be understood as an accusation that he is an exorcist in league with the highest god of the Phoenicians, the Itureans and the Arameans.[24]

Jesus argues that his opponents' suggestion is illogical because Satan's kingdom would collapse if he started to fight against himself; if, therefore, his exorcisms are indeed caused by Yahweh's power, they are evidence that God's kingdom has arrived: "If it is by the finger of God that I cast out the demons, then the kingdom of God has come to you" (Lk 11:20).[25] Jesus argues with compelling logic: if he drives out the demons not by the power of Beelzebul, then there is only one alternative, the power of Yahweh; and if this is indeed the case, then they should

---

[23]On the historicity of Lk 10:23-24 see Dunn 1988, 29-49; Evans 1995, 307. Other scholars interpret the saying as an interpretation of the Christian community; see, for example, Bovon, *Lk*, 2:74.
[24]Feldtkeller 1993, 104-9, 119; Hengel and Schwemer 1998, 135 (ET, 77). This accusation is not linked with a law-free Gentile mission of the Q community, as Feldtkeller proposes; cf. Hengel and Schwemer 1998, 135 n. 557 (ET, 372 n. 418).
[25]Mt 12:28 has "by the Spirit of God"; both phrases designate God's activity.

draw the proper conclusion, that the kingdom of God has arrived.[26] Jesus speaks of the presence of God in his actions, particularly in the miracles, the healings and the exorcisms that he performs: the presence of the Spirit of God signifies the presence of the *basileia*.[27] Two paragraphs further on, Jesus says, "See, something greater than Solomon is here!" (Lk 11:31/Mt 12:42)—that is, a "Son of David" who has greater significance, the Messiah. Jesus was asked in at least one case to perform a miracle as the "Son of David" (Mk 10:47-48), an address that has messianic overtones.[28] Jesus' claim to be Israel's messianic king is highlighted in his triumphal entry into Jerusalem (Mk 11:1-10), not least in the exclamation of the crowd: "Blessed is the coming kingdom of our ancestor David! Hosanna in the highest heaven!" (Mk 11:10).[29] Jesus exercised God's rule and proclaimed the arrival of God's kingdom. It is in this sense that he represented the kingdom of God: "No one stood beside him, and no one would come after him."[30]

At the same time Jesus repeatedly spoke of a future arrival of the kingdom of God: in the prayer that he taught his disciples (Mt 6:10/Lk 11:2); in the beatitudes (Mt 5:3-12/Lk 6:20-23); in the saying about the kingdom of heaven in which "many" will come from east and west and eat with Abraham, Isaac and Jacob (Mt 8:11-12/Lk 13:28-29); in the saying about the wine that he will drink again in the kingdom of God (Mk 14:25). Jesus clearly spoke both of a present arrival of the kingdom of God that takes place in his person and in his message and deeds and of a final arrival of the kingdom of God that will take place in the future.[31]

2. Jesus' self-designation "Son of Man" communicates in many contexts particularly the universal dimension of his ministry. Florian Wilk describes this perspective with regard to the evidence in the Gospel of Mark: "The Jesus who demonstrates his authority in Galilee (2:10, 28), who travels according to the will of God (8:31; cf. 12:6) to Jerusalem (10:33), in order to suffer and die (8:31; 9:12, 31; 10:33-32, 45; 14:21, 41; cf. 14:36, 48-49) and be raised from the dead after three days (8:31; 9:9, 31; 10:34; cf. 16:6) according to the Scriptures (9:12; 14:21) is the same Jesus who will come 'with the clouds of heaven' (14:62) and 'in the glory of his Father with the holy angels' (8:38) in order to gather his elect from the four corners of the earth 'from the ends of the earth to the ends of heaven' (13:26-27)."[32]

3. In the Gospel of John, Jesus often describes himself as the Son who has

---

[26]See Marshall, *Lk*, 475. On the historicity of this passage see also Davies and Allison, *Mt*, 2:339.
[27]See M. Wolter, "'Reich Gottes' bei Lukas," *NTS* 41 (1995): 541-63, esp. 550. The literature on Jesus' miracles is immense; see now particularly Meier 1991-2001, 2:509-1038.
[28]See O. Betz, "Die Frage nach dem messianischen Bewußtsein Jesu," *NovT* 6 (1963): 20-48, esp. 41.
[29]On the historicity of this incident see Gundry (*Mk*, 631-34), who points out that Zech 9:9 is *not* being quoted.
[30]Burchard 1987, 30.
[31]See now with much detail Meier 1991-2001, 2:289-506; cf. the summary in Schnabel 1993, 115-31.
[32]Wilk 2002, 71.

been sent by the Father (or he is thus described by the evangelist). The sending of Jesus usually is described with the (practically synonymous) verbs *apostellein* (ἀποστέλλειν) and *pempein* (πέμπειν).[33] The classic text is Jn 3:16-17:

Jn 3:16-17: "For God so loved the world that he gave his only Son, so that everyone who believes in him may not perish but may have eternal life. [17]Indeed, God did not send the Son into the world to condemn the world, but in order that the world might be saved through him."

An analysis of the relevant passages[34] shows that they highlight the obedience and the dependence of the Son on the Father: the Son was obedient to the Father in the execution of his mission. Passages that speak of his "coming into the world" (e.g., Jn 3:19) underline that Jesus is not a passive instrument of the Father: he was actively involved in his own sending. The statements of the Gospel of John can be summarized as follows: (a) Jesus brings glory to the Father (Jn 7:18; 8:50, 54; 11:4, 40), just as envoys honor their senders or patrons (in antiquity often a city that sends an envoy to another city). Jesus often points to the difference between himself and others who seek their own glory (Jn 5:41-44; 7:18; 8:50, 54; 12:43). Jesus emphasizes that the glory of God, his Father, is the ultimate goal of his mission (Jn 11:4, 40; 12:28; 13:31; 14:13; 17:1, 4, 5). (b) As envoys do not implement their own wishes but rather the wishes of the people or city who sent them, being responsible to the latter in terms of what they say and do, so Jesus fulfills in his mission the will of God: "My food is to do the will of him who sent me and to complete his work" (Jn 4:34). He refers to his works as evidence that God has sent him (Jn 5:36): they are an expression of his obedience to the Father. Jesus knows himself to be totally dependent upon his Father during his mission: "Very truly, I tell you, the Son can do nothing on his own, but only what he sees the Father doing; for whatever the Father does, the Son does likewise" (Jn 5:19). (c) As do envoys who pass on the message that they received from their sender, Jesus says what God has told him to say: "My teaching is not mine but his who sent me" (Jn 7:16; cf. 12:48-50; 14:24). (d) As envoys represent their sender, so Jesus represents the Father: "Very truly, I tell you, whoever receives one whom I send receives me; and whoever receives me receives him who sent me" (Jn 13:20; cf. 12:44-45; 14:9). This representation is linked with the awareness and the determination not to know or do anything on the basis of his own authority: "Very truly, I tell you, the Son can do nothing on his own, but only what he sees the Father doing; for whatever the Father does, the Son does likewise" (Jn 5:19). (e) The representation of the Father is linked with the task of giving testimony of him. Jesus summarizes the goal of

---

[33]See Köstenberger 1998a, 97-106; also Marco 1992; Kuhl 1967, esp. 53-57.
[34]Bühner 1977, 191-267; G. Beasley-Murray 1991, 15-33; 1992; and particularly Köstenberger 1998a, 107-21, which I follow in the summary above.

his mission before Pilate as follows: "You say that I am a king. For this I was born, and for this I came into the world, to testify to the truth. Everyone who belongs to the truth listens to my voice" (Jn 18:37). (f) The representation of the Father is linked with Jesus exercising (delegated) authority. Jesus asserts that he has been given, by the Father who sent him, authority "over all people, to give eternal life to all whom you have given him" (Jn 17:2). The fact that Jesus possesses authority to give life (Jn 5:21-22) is seen in the resurrection (Jn 11:1-44). The authority to forgive sins (Jn 1:29) is part of this authority. (g) As envoys know their sender, so Jesus knows the Father who has sent him: "I know him, because I am from him, and he sent me" (Jn 7:29). However, it is at this point that it becomes apparent that Jesus is more than an envoy: only the Son, the only Son, whom the Father loves, could have his complete confidence to represent the interests of the Father and to implement the will of the Father.[35] For this reason Jesus also transcends the "prophetic model" of sending: Jesus is more than an eschatological prophet (promised by Moses); he is not merely an envoy commissioned by God, but the one who has been sent from heaven, who reveals the Father and who accomplishes the salvation of the world with the authority given to him by the Father.[36] Since the Son knows the Father as no one else knows him, since the Father is always with him, even in the hour of death in which all others desert him (Jn 16:32), he can fulfill the Father's will as nobody else could: he saves the "world" and restores life that had been lost on account of sin (Jn 3:16-17).

4. Jesus offers to the sick and to sinners healing and salvation (Mt 9:12-13/ Mk 2:17/Lk 5:31-32). The offer of salvation for sinners is demonstrated vividly when Jesus dines with "tax collectors and sinners." Levi, the tax collector whom Jesus called as a disciple, invites Jesus into his house, where "tax collectors and sinners" had gathered (Mt 9:10/Mk 2:15/Lk 5:29). Pious Jews such as the Pharisees avoided contact with "sinners," who lived in "conscious or witting opposition to the divine will."[37] They react negatively to Jesus' table fellowship with these "sinners."

In Jewish tradition various occupations and people are designated as "sinners" because there was reason to suspect that they did not fully keep the Torah or the halakah—a suspicion that led to social sanctions: donkey drivers, camel drivers, coachmen, bargees, shepherds, shopkeepers, doctors, butchers, goldsmiths, flax hecklers, sharpeners of stones of hand mills, peddlers, weavers, hair cutters, cleaners, bath attendants, tanners, gatherers of dog droppings, copper smelters, dice players, usurers, organizers of pigeon flights, merchants dealing with the produce of the sabbatical year, leviers of taxes, tax collectors.[38] The people who were present at the table responded to the blessing recited

---

[35]Köstenberger 1998a, 110-11, 120-21, with reference to A. Harvey 1987.
[36]See G. Beasley-Murray 1992, 1865.
[37]K. H. Rengstorf, "ἁμαρτωλός," ThWNT 1:331 (TDNT 1:327).
[38]m. Qidd. 4:14; b. Qidd. 82a; m. Ketub. 7:10; m. Sanh. 3:3; b. Sanh. 25b. See Landmesser 2001, 89 n. 90.

by the master of the house with "Amen," invoking God's blessing for all who were present.[39] The subject of Jesus' table fellowship[40] occurs in diverse genres: in sayings,[41] in parables,[42] in controversy dialogues and in instructional settings,[43] in miracles stories,[44] in biographical accounts,[45] in the passion narrative,[46] in the context of the appearances of the risen Christ.[47] Jesus had table fellowship with his disciples,[48] with sympathizers and interested people,[49] with sinners,[50] with the poor,[51] with Gentiles.[52] János Bolyki argues that the inclusive nature and the openness of the table fellowship that Jesus had with others "stood in complete contrast to the Jewish and Gentile table fellowship meals of the time. Jesus accepted any invitation, no matter who extended it, and included everybody at his own table. Some people, however, kept a distance from his table because they despised some of the people sitting there, actually or metaphorically (tax collectors, prostitutes, sick people, poor people, Gentiles). Jesus rejected such self-chosen separation and therefore accepted the stigma of irritating the pious." The second characteristic of Jesus' communal meals is joy, "the joy that comes from deep within, a joy shared with the eschatological God, the joy to sit at Jesus' table. This is the joy of having been found and accepted. It is closely connected with the forgiveness of sins that Jesus sometimes announced as personal truth, sometimes as truth that affects everybody sitting at the table. Jesus linked the proclamation of the forgiveness of sins with his own mission." The third characteristic of Jesus' table fellowship is the decision and the transformation that it effected among the participants. "Confession of sin, restitution, acceptance of the others, faith, sacrifice or at least thankfulness for repletion were the consequences of the communal meals in the lives of the participants."

When the Pharisees and scribes criticize Jesus' table fellowship with tax collectors and sinners, Jesus responds by emphasizing his divine commission to save the lost sinners and to heal the sick (Mt 9:13; Mk 2:17). When Jesus describes himself as "physician," he probably alludes to Ezek 34:1-6:[53] here the prophet accuses the "shepherds," Israel's leaders, of feeding themselves while neglecting the flock entrusted to their care, of not strengthening the weak, of not healing the sick, of not bandaging the wounded, of not bringing back

---

[39]Landmesser 2001, 90. This does not mean, however, that table fellowship was an "act of worship" ("gottesdienstliche Handlung").
[40]For what follows above see Bolyki 1998, 64-67; quotations from the summary, ibid., 228-29.
[41]Mt 8:11-12; 11:18-19; Lk 7:33-35; 13:23-30.
[42]Mt 22:1-14; Lk 12:35-38; 14:16-24; 15:1-2, 11-32.
[43]Mt 9:14-17/Mk 2:18-22/Lk 5:33-39; Mt 15:21-28/Mk 7:24-30; Lk 14:7-14.
[44]Mt 14:13-21/Mk 6:30-44/Lk 9:10-17/Jn 6:1-15; Mt 15:32-38/Mk 8:1-10; Jn 2:1-11.
[45]Mt 9:9-13/Mk 2:15-17/Lk 5:27-32; Lk 7:36-50; 10:38-42; 19:1-10.
[46]Mt 26:26-30/Mk 14:17-26/Lk 22:14-23, 28-30; Jn 13:1-20.
[47]Lk 24:13-35, 36-43; Jn 21:1-14.
[48]Mt 9:14-17/Mk 2:18-22/Lk 5:33-39; Mt 26:26-30/Mk 14:17-26/Lk 22:14-23, 28-30; Mk 8:14-21; Lk 12:35-38; 24:13-35, 36-43; Jn 6:26-63; 13:1-20; 21:1-14.
[49]Lk 7:36-50; 10:38-42; 14:7-24; Jn 2:1-11.
[50]Mt 9:9-13/Mk 2:13-17/Lk 5:27-32; Mt 11:18-19; 22:1-14; Lk 15:1-2, 11-32; 19:1-10.
[51]Mt 14:13-21/Mk 6:30-44/Lk 9:10-17; Mt 15:32-39/Mk 8:1-10; Lk 16:19-31; Jn 6:1-15; 6:26-63.
[52]Mt 15:21-28/Mk 7:24-30; Mt 8:11-12; 22:1-14; Mk 8:1-10.
[53]Landmesser 2001, 104-5.

those who have gone astray, of not seeking the lost, of not inquiring after the sheep of God that wander over all the mountains and on every high hill and are scattered over all the face of the earth. The "word of Yahweh" in Ezek 34:7-31 removes them from their office as shepherds: God rescues the sheep from the mouths of the evil shepherds. The shepherds face the acute danger of being cast out from the fellowship of God's covenant people. Yahweh himself will now take care of his flock; he will seek out the lost and those who have gone astray and "rescue them from all the places to which they have been scattered on a day of clouds and thick darkness" (Ezek 34:12). Indeed, he will lead them out from all nations and gather them from all countries and bring them back into the promised land, where he will graze them on the best pastures: "I will seek the lost, and I will bring back the strayed, and I will bind up the injured, and I will strengthen the weak" (Ezek 34:16). And he will destroy those who rejected the weak and scattered them (Ezek 34:21). God will do all this by sending a new shepherd, "one shepherd, my servant David" (Ezek 34:23)—that is, the promised Davidic prince of the coming time of salvation in which God will make a covenant of peace (Ezek 34:24-25). This shepherd will carry out the tasks of Israel's shepherds who had failed. In those days God will bless Israel, he will eradicate evil animals, he will send showers of blessing and good crops, he will guarantee security in the land as he breaks the yoke of the Gentile nations that oppress Israel (Ezek 34:26-29). In those days Israel will experience the reality of God being "with them" (Ezek 34:30), caring for his people as the "sheep of my pasture" (Ezek 34:31). Jesus identifies himself in Mt 9:12-13/Mk 2:17/Lk 5:31-32 with this prince of salvation: he is the physician sent by God to heal the sick and to save the lost, the sinners.[54] The goal of his mission, visibly expressed as table fellowship with the tax collectors and sinners, is the invitation to the sinner to come to the table of the festival of God's kingdom. The righteous are not excluded, but God's activity in the ministry of Jesus aims primarily at the sinners. "His invitation does not exclude anybody, but it includes especially those who have been excluded by others."[55] If the "righteous" rejected John the Baptist's call to repentance, and if the "righteous" now reject Jesus and his message, then they reject the kingdom of God.[56]

5. Jesus claims to have authority to forgive sins. In the Gospel of Mark this claim leads to the first controversy with the scribes in the context of the healing of a lame man in Capernaum (Mk 2:1-12; Mt 9:1-8/Lk 5:17-26). This claim to be able to forgive sins goes beyond a fundamental conviction of Jewish thought

---

[54]For arguments in support of the historicity of this passage see Pesch, *Mk,* 1:166-68; Davies and Allison, *Mt,* 2:103, 106. The connection with Ezek 34 is missed by many commentators.
[55]Pesch, *Mk,* 1:168.
[56]Burchard 1987, 27.

and practice: "As Jesus claims in 2:10 for himself the authority to forgive sins on earth, he disconnects the process of forgiveness from the temple as a matter of principle and places it in a universal horizon."[57] In the Gospel of Mark the term γῆ (*gē,* "earth"), when it does not designate the surface of the earth ("soil"), is always related to a universal perspective. Jesus' fellowship with the sinner (Mk 2:17) indicates that he provides for "the many" participation in God's salvation on account of his substitutionary death (Mk 10:45; 14:24). The early Christians acknowledged this claim. Especially Matthew emphasizes the forgiveness of sins as a fundamental aspect of Jesus' ministry, already seen in his designation as "Emmanuel" (Mt 1:23): forgiveness of sins signifies the redemptive presence of God among his people.[58]

6. Jesus' lifestyle, which can be described as "missionary," was an important factor in the controversies with the scribes, Pharisees and Sadducees. An important aspect in these conflicts was the fact that "God's claim on human beings is released in new ways beyond its traditional scope."[59] The itinerant ministry of teaching, not tied to one particular place, and the replacement of familial bonds by the new "relatives" of his followers as God's children (Mt 12:48-50/Mk 3:33-35/Lk 8:20-21) illustrate how Jesus moved beyond the boundaries of the traditional social milieu of Judeans and Galileans.

7. An important event for Jesus' self-understanding is his action in the temple in Jerusalem, specifically in the court of the Gentiles.[60] Some interpret the so-called cleansing of the temple as a protest against a corrupt temple establishment,[61] others as an enacted parable that prophesies the imminent destruction of the temple.[62] The meaning of Jesus' action needs to be established from his own interpretation, which the Gospel writers indicate with two quotations from Scripture. Referring to Is 56:7, Jesus, standing in the court of the Gentiles, advocates "the holiness of the entire temple precinct, the possibility that Yahweh may be worshiped by the Gentiles also who were allowed to stand here. Jesus does not demonstrate for a cult without sacrifices, he does not disturb the sacrifices in the interior temple courts, whose execution did not depend upon the sale of sacrificial offerings and sacrificial animals in the court of the Gentiles; the visitors to the temple could bring their own sacrifices, and the pilgrims could buy them on the Mount of Olives, where four markets for temple sacrifices existed, managed by

---

[57]Wilk 2002, 78; for the observation that follows above see ibid. with n. 350; cf. Mk 4:31; 9:3; 13:27, 31. On the authenticity as saying of Jesus see Gundry, *Mk,* 121-22; see also Guelich, *Mk,* 93.

[58]See Landmesser 2001, 15.

[59]Bürkle 1979, 34; for the observation that follows above see ibid., 35.

[60]Mt 21:12-13/Mk 11:15-17/Lk 19:45-46. See W. T. Herzog, "Temple Cleansing," DJG 817-21; more recently Ådna 2000a.

[61]See Evans 1995, 319-44.

[62]See E. P. Sanders 1985, 61-76.

the Bene Harman."[63] The expression "den of robbers" (Mt 21:12) refers to Jeremiah 7—8: like the prophet Jeremiah, Jesus announces the destruction of the temple because the people and their leaders do not obey God. Jesus' action expresses symbolically his conviction that the arrival of the kingdom of God and thus the arrival of Yahweh do not need the temple any longer. N. T. Wright comments, "Jesus' action symbolized his belief that, in returning to Zion, YHWH would not after all take up residence in the Temple, legitimating its present administration and its place and function within the first-century Jewish symbolic world."[64]

8. Jesus linked his mission as Son of Man with his death. Passages such as Mt 17:22-23/Mk 9:31/Lk 9:44 and Mt 20:28/Mk 10:45 clearly show, in the words of Peter Stuhlmacher, that "Jesus went to his death knowingly and willingly. He understood his death as a substitutionary death of atonement for 'the many' (i.e., for Israel and for the nations). Jesus' atoning death . . . is the substitutionary act of salvation of the messianic Son of Man in the name and by request of God, who, according to Is 43:3-4, seeks to procure righteousness and salvation for the many burdened with guilt by the self-sacrifice of his servant, out of love for his chosen people. . . . Jesus took upon himself suffering and death out of love for God and for the people. It is because he was the messianic mediator and reconciler that the apostolic missionary gospel became the 'message of reconciliation' (λόγος τῆς καταλλαγῆς, 2 Cor 5:19)."[65]

9. In Jesus' suffering and death Scripture is fulfilled (Mk 14:49). As Florian Wilk observes, "Jesus' suffering and death correspond not only to the statements of Scripture on the Son of Man (9:12; 14:21); it leads to a sequence of further events that are also foretold in Scripture: the flight of the disciples (14:27), the resurrection of Jesus as establishment of the eschatological house of prayer for all nations, replacing the Jerusalem temple, which has become a den of robbers (12:10-11; cf. 11:17), and the exaltation of Jesus at the right hand of God as completion of his status as Son of David (12:36). Thus the Scriptures show God's history with Israel is transferred by the death and the resurrection of Jesus into a new history of God with all nations."[66]

10. Jesus claimed to bring the final salvation that the prophets had promised for the last days.

The terms "salvation" and "redemption" stand for several Hebrew, Greek and Latin terms. They are key terms of the Old and New Testament traditions but also play a role in the Hellenistic and the Egyptian religions.[67] The basic meaning of the Latin *red-*

---

[63]Pesch, *Mk*, 2:199.
[64]N. T. Wright 1996, 423.
[65]Stuhlmacher 1992-1999, 1:142-43, with extensive discussion, ibid., 1:125-42.
[66]Wilk 2002, 73.
[67]For the observations that follow above see C. Colpe, "Erlösungsreligion," *HRG* 2:323-29; quotation, 2:325.

imere, "to buy again/back, ransom," is linked with the use of the term in trade and in commercial law. It presupposes "a legal relationship in which one person owes something to another person and wants something from another person and is coerced by this other person until the first person, or a third person, furnishes a payment that cancels the debt or procures the possession of what was desired." The terms "salvation" and "redemption" are used, with divers nuances of meaning, with regard to the following areas: (a) politics, war, criminal law: to ransom prisoners, to rescue from exile or servanthood, to make peace, to rescue from danger, to rescue from death; (b) law, morality, ethics: satisfaction, repentance, pardon, reconciliation, justification, forensic exoneration; (c) family law: release of things and persons; (d) psychology: victory over fear; (e) work and everyday life: liberation from toil and trouble, tranquility, cleansing; (f) medicine: healing of illness.

The Call to Repentance

Jesus called people to repentance (Mk 1:15). Repentance consists of a twofold movement: away from the old and toward the new. The New Testament uses the verb *metanoein* ("to repent, change one's mind, feel remorse, be converted") for the first part of the movement, and sometimes *epistrephein* ("to turn around, turn"). The verb *pisteuein* ("to be convinced of something, believe, trust") is used for the second part of the movement.[68]

The repentance of Jews can be called an "insider conversion": when Jesus calls his Jewish listeners to repent, he calls them to correspond fully to the already existing covenant relationship with the one true God, which means in the context of his message of the kingdom of God to accept the dawn of God's return to Israel that takes place in his ministry of teaching and healing. Jesus' preaching included distinct references to the fact that something new is happening that the listeners dare not miss or disregard. The parables of the treasure in the field and of the pearl (Mt 13:44-46) illustrate this dramatically: what was invisible and hidden has now become visible and public. In the parables of the two sons (Mt 21:28-32), of the tenants of the vineyard (Mt 21:33-46), and of the royal wedding banquet (Mt 22:1-14) Jesus emphasizes that the rejection of his message has consequences: "Therefore I tell you, the kingdom of God will be taken away from you and given to a people that produces the fruits of the kingdom" (Mt 21:43).

Jewish ancestors and Jewish identity are no longer sufficient criteria for membership in the true people of God in the messianic period that has arrived. In the speech in Jn 8:31-59 Jesus emphasizes that the Jews, who appeal to their status as children of Abraham, do not automatically have salvation. In the parable of Lazarus, the rich man who calls to "father Abraham" is informed that the mere status of being a descendant of Abraham no longer rescues a person from Hades (Lk 16:26). Similarly, the parable of the fig tree (Lk 13:6-9) emphasizes

---

[68]France 1993, 295-96; for what follows above see ibid., 292, 294, 298-99. Cf. BDAG, s.v. "μετ–ανοέω, πιστεύω."

that belonging to Israel does not provide protection against God's judgment.[69] Repentance is the movement away from reliance upon membership in Israel, away from reliance upon the fulfillment of the commandments of the Torah, away from reliance upon the election of Israel as God's blessing of Abraham's descendants.

Luke grouped together three parables in Lk 15 that elucidate the subject of repentance. (1) Jesus tells the parable of the lost sheep (Lk 15:3-7) to illustrate his acceptance of sinners who listen (Lk 15:1), repent and have table fellowship with him, which is promptly criticized by the Pharisees and scribes (Lk 15:2). One of the tasks of a shepherd is to look for a sheep that has gone astray, unable to find the way back by itself, and to bring the sheep back to the flock. (2) The parable of the lost drachma (Lk 15:8-10) illustrates and underlines the element of passive helplessness of the lost. A lost coin cannot find itself; it needs to be found, and this requires the total effort of the owner, who (in the parable) lights a lamp, cleans the entire house and searches tirelessly (ἐπιμελῶς, *epimelōs*) until she has found the coin. (3) The parable of the lost son (Lk 15:11-32) does not emphasize the effort of the father to find the son, nor does it highlight the initiative of the son who sets out to return to the father. Somebody who is about to die of hunger and who returns to the one person he knows can and will rescue him from perdition (Lk 15:17), somebody who offers himself to the father as an object in order not to have to die (Lk 15:18-19), surely does not display an admirable effort. Jesus tells the parable in order to emphasize that every sinner can turn back, no matter how shocking the rebellion against the father was and no matter how low the rebel has sunk. Jesus emphasizes the mercy of the father, the haste with which he reconciles himself with his son, and the embraces, kisses and festivities that accompany the reception of the lost son back into the family. At the end of the parable, however, in the reference to the uncharitable attitude of the older son, who never left the father, Jesus also warns his listeners that if the righteous in Israel refuse to acknowledge the repentance and readmission of the lost into the father's family, they risk being "lost" themselves.

John Drane suggests that the three parables constitute a "methodology of finding," illustrating the twofold dynamic of the "model of evangelization" of Jesus and later of Paul: the two dynamics of "going" and "waiting."[70] It is correct that these parables comment on Jesus' specific behavior: he takes the initiative to go to the sinner, he calls them to repentance, he accepts people who find their way back to him. However, it is doubtful that the parable of the lost son wants to teach the "dynamic of waiting" to the Christian community that reads the Gospel of Luke: in Lk 15:20 the parable comments that the father saw the

---

[69]Besides the commentaries see, for example, Jeremias 1956, 42; Bock 1990, 507.
[70]Drane 1994, 293; for the observation that follows on repentance and personal freedom see ibid., 294.

son "from far away" (μακράν, *makran*) and ran toward him (δραμών, *dramōn*). Drane further suggests that Jesus accepted people as they were, that he called them to follow him
without talking about conditions, so much so that repentance was often but the second
act: Jesus gave his followers "space" to determine for themselves how to understand discipleship with regard to their own thinking and their own personality. This understanding
of Jesus' notion of repentance and personal freedom seems equally problematic. The
prominent emphasis on repentance in the summaries of Jesus' proclamation renders this
suggestion rather unlikely, and the foundational emphasis on the will of God—Jesus proclaims *God's* kingdom!—exposes it as a modern construct that owes more to Rudolf Bultmann's existential interpretation (which Drane quotes in this connection repeatedly) than
to Jesus' program.

The parables in Lk 15 teach several aspects of repentance: the lost must repent
if they want to escape perdition, destruction, death; it is always possible to turn
back, as God is merciful; repentance requires the acknowledgment of one's personal failure, of one's sin, the return to God in one's own heart; repentance is
not tied to or dependent upon achievements, since God forgives all offenses
and transgressions without condition and "in a hurry"; repentance results in joy,
both with God and among people; repentance leads to the reunion and the an-
imated unity of the complete flock, of the full treasure, of the reunited family.[71]

The Call to Faith

The call to repentance corresponds with the call to "faith in the good news"
(πιστεύετε ἐν τῷ εὐαγγελίῳ, *pisteuete en tō euangeliō* [Mk 1:15]).

The tradition-historical origin of the term for "faith" and the conceptual context in which
the early Christians used this term are debated.[72] The history-of-religions school and especially Rudolf Bultmann believed that the Greek noun πίστις (*pistis*, "faith"; verb, πιστεύειν, *pisteuein*) was a catchword of the Hellenistic religions and their proselytizing propaganda. This explanation was successfully refuted by Dieter Lührmann.[73] Lührmann
suggested that the usage and meaning of *pistis* can be traced back to the salvation oracles
that people sought in the temple in crisis situations. He asserts, "To believe means to link
the confession for God as creator of the world with the concrete experience of this world
that seems to contradict this confession."[74] Scholars have pointed out, however, that the
derivation from the Old Testament salvation oracle, the definition in terms of theological
reflection and experience of the world, and the application of this definition to all occurrences of *pistis* in the New Testament is problematic.[75] Egon Brandenburger derives the
usage of *pistis* in the earliest stages of early Christianity from Jewish Hellenistic passages
such as Jdt 14:10: Gentiles are converted to faith in Israel's God, they are circumcised and
accepted into the people of God. This model, according to Brandenburger, was adopted

---

[71]On the last point see Bovon, *Lk,* 3:17.
[72]For the observations that follow above see Haacker 1984; Brandenburger 1988.
[73]Dieter Lührmann, "Pistis im Judentum," *ZNW* 64 (1973): 19-38; cf. G. Barth, *EWNT* 3:217
(*EDNT* 3:91-97); Haacker 1984, 290.
[74]Lührmann 1976, 34; cf. idem, "Glaube," *RAC* 11:48-122.
[75]See the critique in Brandenburger 1988, 171-77.

in the missionary praxis of the Hellenistic Jewish Christians who led Gentiles to faith in the one true God, who baptized them and accepted them into the church as the true Israel. The beginnings of this practice are to be seen in the ministry of John the Baptist, who pointed to the impending wrath of God as the reason why their appeal to their status as Abraham's children is no longer valid and why all Jews are thus called upon to repent and be baptized. In the linguistic context of the Palestinian mission to Jews, the Christians spoke of "faith" only seldom. The application of *pisteuein* (in the aorist) probably can be traced to Paul.[76] Brandenburger briefly refers to Mk 1:14-15, a text that he, following the majority of historical-critical scholars, does not acknowledge as an authentic saying of Jesus.[77] Against such tradition-historical hypotheses, the following arguments support the authenticity of the call to faith in the proclamation of Jesus.[78] (1) The construction *pisteuein* + *en* ("believe in") in Mk 1:15 does not, with the exception of Jn 16:30 (cf. Jn 3:15; Eph 1:13) occur in the New Testament again and also is not attested in extrabiblical Greek literature. Thus it is implausible that this formulation was borrowed from early Christian preaching. (2) There is no parallel in the New Testament for the formulation "believe in the good news." The phrase can be explained only against a Semitic background. On the basis of the criterion of double dissimilarity and Semitic background one cannot deny that Jesus could have used this phrase. (3) The parallelism of the double statements in Mk 1:15 also supports authenticity. (4) The absolute *to euangelion* ("the good news") belongs in Mk 14:9 to the authentic Jesus tradition. (5) The "technical" usage of *pisteuein* (in the aorist) with the meaning "to come to faith" may have been related in the Old Testament and in Hellenistic Judaism to the conversion of Gentiles,[79] but we must not forget that we have only a handful of passages as evidence, which makes it difficult to speak of a "technical" usage of the formulation.

Jesus' call to believe in the good news, in the context of his proclamation of the arrival of the kingdom of God, can be explained, at least, in the following terms.[80]

1. Faith in the "good news" is the answer to God's coming for the salvation of humankind. The indicative of salvation, announcing that the time is fulfilled and the kingdom of God is arriving, is followed by the imperative to believe and to follow Jesus (Mk 1:15). The time of salvation that Jesus announces makes faith in the good news of God's arrival possible, and at the same time it demands this faith with great earnestness. Jesus not only talked about the royal presence of God but also demonstrated that presence in the miracles he performed. As a result, a close connection exists between faith and miracles in the ministry of Jesus.[81] The account of the healing of the epileptic boy is a good illustration.

---

[76]Brandenburger 1988; summary, 193-98; for the observation that follows above see ibid., 191-92.

[77]See Haacker 1984, 292; Haacker and Michel, "Glaube," *ThBLNT* 1:792.

[78]See Pesch, *Mk,* 1:103; Gundry, *Mk,* 70.

[79]Brandenburger 1988, 197, referring to Jon 3:5; Jdt 14:10.

[80]For the discussion that follows above see Schnabel 1991, 66-69; cf. Söding 1985, 133-97, 290-313, and passim.

[81]On Jesus' miracles see Betz and Grimm 1977; Theissen and Merz 1996, 256-83 (ET, 281-315); Twelftree 1999; with great detail Meier 1991-2001, 2:509-1038; on the healing miracles see

Jesus tells the father of the boy that "everything is possible" for the person who believes (Mk 9:23). The disciples, who were unable to help the demon-tormented boy while Jesus was away, are rebuked for their unbelief (Mk 9:19). We find the expression "your faith has healed/saved you" in three healing accounts.[82] The woman who touches Jesus' garment (Mt 9:19-22/Mk 5:24-34/Lk 8:42-48), the Samaritan leper (Lk 17:11-19) and the blind man Bartimaeus (Mt 20:29-34/Mk 10:46-52/Lk 18:35-43) all expect the healing from God, but they trustingly expect at the same time that the healing will happen on account of Jesus' presence and word. Their faith in God is faith in Jesus, and thus they experience healing in their current physical need, and they experience rescue in the situation as social outsiders.

2. The faith that Jesus demands is trust in God's gracious rule and at the same time trust in Jesus as mediator of God's rule (Mk 1:1; 8:35; 13:10; 14:9). Those who confess Jesus as Son of God (Mk 15:39) can do so properly only when the entire "beginning of the good news" (Mk 1:1)—from the ministry of John the Baptist (Mk 1:2) to the announcement in the empty tomb of Jesus' resurrection (Mk 16:6)—is the foundation of the confession of faith that Jesus demands. This confession for Jesus corresponds to his demand and call if and when it is the expression of following after Jesus after having taken up one's cross—that is, the result of the fundamental renunciation of all personal possibilities, even of one's life, and of a reorientation under the horizon of the rule of God that has dawned (Mk 8:27-38; 15:39-41).

3. The call to faith, related to the message of the kingdom of God, corresponds to the entrance requirements in Mk 10:14-15, 17-25: the kingdom of God that Jesus proclaims must be accepted "as a child" accepts, meaning with unreserved trust, with unconditional receptiveness. If a person seeks to enter the kingdom of God, he or she must become so "small" as to fit through the "eye of a needle": only God can make possible what is impossible for human beings, only God can enable people to enter the eschatological kingdom. Those who want to attain the salvation of the messianic days must depend totally on God's mercy. In this context of the entrance requirements for the kingdom of God, Jesus' call to faith assumes a programmatic character and summarizes all other demands of Jesus.

4. The faith demanded by Jesus is faith in the sense of confidence and trust.[83] The unusual formulation πιστεύειν εἰς (*pisteuein eis*, "believe in" [Mk 1:15]), not only finds its explanation probably in Semitic usage[84] but also shows that faith

Meier 1991-2001, 2:679-772; on the authenticity of Jesus' healing miracles see Nielsen 1987, 8-20; on the relationship between faith and miracles see recently Yeung 2002.
[82]On the authenticity of the expression ἡ πίστις σου σέσωκέν σε see Yeung 2002, 53-63; for the observations that follow above, ibid., 170-95.
[83]See Söding 1985, 301-2, 305-8.
[84]Pesch, *Mk,* 1:103; for the observation that follows above see Gnilka, *Mk,* 1:68.

is confident reliance upon the redemptive power of the message that Jesus proclaims. Faith as trust grows out of the good news of Jesus and is intimately
linked with the good news.[85] For Mark, the term "good news" (*euangelion*, "gospel") repeatedly designates the manifestation of God's power to bring about salvation (Mk 1:9-11, 15; 8:35; 10:29). As in the cases of Abraham, Moses and the
prophets, faith is the result of God speaking to people, a word on which one
can rely: God is speaking to Israel in the person and in the ministry of Jesus, in
whom God's saving power is present.

5. Jesus' call to believe in the good news is therefore an expression of his
unique authority.[86] The announcement of the new saving activity of Yahweh,
present in the kingdom of God that Jesus proclaims and mediates, entails the
necessity of faith as obedient trust in Jesus. If the ministry of Jesus "fulfills" the
time, if the kingdom of God has come near, if the members of the people of
God are thus called to trust unconditionally God's messianic engagement by believing the message of Jesus and by trusting in Jesus, then no one who has eyes
to see and ears to hear (Mk 8:18) will spurn this call.

The Call to Follow Jesus

The purpose of Jesus' gathering of God's people is exemplified in the fact that
Jesus called twelve followers to form the inner circle of his disciples.[87] Jesus
called them to become "fishers of people,"[88] an assignment for which Jesus
trained them during his ministry.[89] After his death and resurrection Jesus repeated this call to mission.[90] Seen in the context of Jesus' proclamation of the
dawn of God's kingdom, the number "twelve" speaks of the eschatological gathering of Israel.

Otto Betz suggests that Jesus hoped "that the people of Israel, won over for the kingdom
of God, could become salt of the earth, light of the world and city on a hill (Mt 5:13-14):
as Mount Zion, wonderfully elevated in the last days, will attract the nations and lead them
to the justice of God (Is 2:2-3), thus Israel was to move the people in the entire world to
worshiping God by proclamation and by good deeds (Mt 5:16)."[91] If this indeed was Jesus'
intention, we would have to agree with Betz's conclusion: "The expectations concerning
a missionary role of Israel were not fulfilled in this manner. *For this reason* Jesus adopted
the ministry of the Servant of God of Is 53 and made salvation and the new covenant possible through his self-sacrifice 'for the many' (inclusive, i.e., for all people)." This reconstruction seems implausible for two reasons: (1) Jesus experienced rather early on the opposition of leading representatives of Israel, not only in Galilee but also in Jerusalem. In

---

[85]Adolf Schlatter, *Der Glaube im Neuen Testament* (Stuttgart: Calwer, 1885 [6th ed., 1982]), 591.
[86]Söding 1985, 290-91, referring to Mk 2:2, 10; 6:2; 9:7; 11:27-33.
[87]Mk 3:14; Mt 19:28; cf. 1 Cor 15:5.
[88]Mk 1:17. See §10.1.
[89]Mk 3:15-16; Mt 10:1-42; Lk 9:1-6. See §10.4.
[90]Mt 28:19-20; Jn 20:21-23; Acts 1:8. See §12.3.
[91]Betz 1994, 25; the quotation that follows above, ibid. (italics added).

the parable of the sower, which Jesus used in this teaching perhaps at an early stage, he speaks clearly of manifold rejection, a motif that reoccurs in many of Jesus' statements and parables. (2) If my earlier analysis is correct, Jesus' claim to forgive Israel's sins, linked with the awareness of "giving" his life, literally, as a ransom for "the many," belonged to Jesus' self-understanding and was not the result of rejection during the latter part of his ministry. Jesus' first announcement of his death[92] was not the last such announcement[93] before his last week in Jerusalem, during which he repeatedly spoke of his death.[94] The dating of Jesus' first announcement of his death is difficult; Mark places it in the middle part of his Gospel, which may have literary or theological reasons. At any rate, Jesus' announcement of his death is formulated as a conscious, actively accepted fate, motivated by the mission that Jesus was given as the messianic Son of Man, not by the rejection in Israel.

Since the studies by Gerd Theissen, many New Testament scholars believe that Jesus' sayings express an ethic of homelessness. The missionary activity of the movement set in motion by Jesus, as described by Mark, for example, did not want to establish (stationary) congregations with members, admission procedures and confessions of faith; rather, they argue, Jesus and his movement wanted to renew interpersonal relationships that find expression in mutual care and hospitality, in preparation for the imminent arrival of the kingdom of God.[95] Such theories are dependent on a problematic understanding of Jesus as (merely) an apocalyptic prophet, and they fail to see both the fundamental Old Testament and Jewish tradition of the righteous "remnant" and the "training aspect" of the ministry of the Twelve before Easter.

In his first public sermon, according to Luke, preached in Nazareth, Jesus explains his mission with the words of Is 42:7 (and Lev 25:10):

Lk 4:18-19: "The Spirit of the Lord is upon me, because he has anointed me to bring good news to the poor. He has sent me to proclaim release to the captives and recovery of sight to the blind, to let the oppressed go free, [19]to proclaim the year of the Lord's favor."

The meaning of "the poor" must be seen in the context of Jesus' mission: sayings that speak of the purpose of his coming specify that he came to call sinners (Mt 9:13), to serve and to give his life as a ransom for "the many" (Mk 10:45), to seek and to save the lost (Lk 19:10), to give life to the "sheep" (Jn 10:10), to lead those who believe out of darkness (Jn 12:46), to open the eyes of the blind (Jn 9:39). Those who answer Jesus' call, those who accept the sacrifice of his life, those who acknowledge him as the messianic Son of Man belong to the new flock, to the new people whose leadership the Twelve are appointed to take over.

New Testament scholars such as E. P. Sanders and many others following his lead have argued that Jewish theology and praxis in the Second Temple period were characterized

---

[92]Mt 16:21/Mk 8:31/Lk 9:22; cf. the earlier hints in Mt 9:15/Mk 2:20/Lk 5:35.

[93]Mt 17:12b/Mk 9:12; cf. Lk 17:25; again Mt 17:22-23/Mk 9:31/Lk 9:44; again Lk 13:33; again Lk 17:25; again Mt 20:18-19/Mk 10:33-34/Lk 18:31b-33; again Mt 20:22/Mk 10:38; cf. Lk 12:50; again Mt 20:28/Mk 10:45; again Mt 21:38-39/Mk 12:7-8/Lk 20:14-15.

[94]Mt 26:2; Mt 26:12/Mk 14:8; Mt 26:24/Mk 14:21/Lk 22:22; Mt 26:26-28/Mk 14:22-24/Lk 22:15-20; Mt 26:31-32/Mk 14:27-28.

[95]Rhoads 1995a; summary, 1727-29; 1995b, esp. 350-51; cf. Theissen 1989, 83.

by a nationalistic notion of election that included the expectation of an eschatological restoration of *all* Israel. Mark Elliott has shown in a recent major study that this interpretation has no basis in the Second Temple primary sources.[96] He argues as follows. (1) Numerous early Jewish texts emphasize that Israel lives in a time of apostasy and that very many Jews are in danger of falling under God's judgment.[97] (2) Many Jewish authors do not envision the rescue of all Israelites, or of all Jews, in the last judgment. Rather, they speak of a mercy of God that is qualified: God is merciful to the righteous,[98] to those who repent,[99] to all Israelites who love God,[100] to the elect,[101] to the Jews who belong to the Essene "sons of light" as a result of their repentance, knowledge and divine election.[102] (3) Evidently there were purist conservative voices in Judea who protested, on the basis of religious motivations, against both the masses and the establishment. These groups understood themselves theologically as the "remnant" in Israel that the prophets had talked about. (4) The claim of E. P. Sanders and others that the Jewish covenant theology was unilateral, irrevocable and nationalistic, postulating the salvation of Israel in the eschaton on the basis of God's election, is misleading. The apocalyptic and the Essene literature shows that many Jewish groups had an individual and dualistic understanding of God's covenant with Israel, taking their cue from important aspects of the Old Testament concept of the covenant: present salvation and future salvation both depend on each individual Israelite or Jew obeying God's will, which is the only way in which he or she genuinely belongs to the righteous and to the elect. The fact that there are various covenants, the modification of earlier covenant stipulations, the listing of conditions for membership in God's covenant people, dualistic covenant formulas (righteous/unrighteous, life/death), the role of the "witness" of heaven and earth for the curses of the covenant formula, woes and the visionary journeys through the cosmos during which the seer spots the (Jewish) sinners in Hades all provide crucial evidence.[103] (5) Essene texts as well as the apocalyptic books of *Ezra* and *Baruch* display a distinct soteriological dualism, following important biblical texts: there are two camps, not just generally in the world but specifically in Israel: the righteous and the unrighteous, the sons of light and the sons of darkness, "the few" and "the many." This dualism corresponds to the gradual abandonment of the corporate identity of Israel—the notion of the entire ethnic or national people of Israel being the "people of God"—and the establishment of new communities, as, for example, the Essene community in Qumran.[104] (6) The understanding and description of the last days in Essene and apocalyptic texts present the reader with a host of heavenly revealer figures and messianic figures, the common denominator being the concentration of the future redeemer figure on the specific group of the righteous or the elect. The most important contrast is not between an earthly, national messiah and a heavenly, apocalyp-

---

[96]M. Elliott 2000, 52-56, and passim; contra E. P. Sanders 1977; 1992; J. M. Scott 1993.

[97]See *1 En.* 93:9; 94:1, 5; 102:5; 108:2-3; *Jub.* 1:7-14; 30:13-17; *Pss. Sol.* 17:14-15; *4 Ezra* 8:55-57; CD II, 22-23 [B]; 1QH IV, 6-22; 1QM I, 2-3; 4Q266; 4Q386. See M. Elliott 2000, 57-113.

[98]See *1 En.* 1:8; 5:5; 27:3-4; *Pss. Sol.* 2:35; 9:7.

[99]See *Jub.* 1:15, 22-23; *Pss. Sol.* 9:6-7.

[100]See *Jub.* 23:31; *Pss. Sol.* 4:25; 6:6; cf. 2:33, 36; 6:1-6; 13:12.

[101]See 1QH XV, 14-16; *4 Ezra* 7:50-61; 8:2-3.

[102]See 1QS II, 1-3; XI, 13-15; 1QH IV, 35-37; V, 5-6; XV, 14-16; *Pss. Sol.* 2:33; 16:1-5. See M. Elliott 2000, 115-85; for the point that follows above see ibid., 187-243.

[103]For details and references see M. Elliott 2000, 245-307.

[104]1QS I, 1-5; 1QH II, 8-18; VI, 14-19; CD II, 16-21 [B]; *1 En.* 83:3-10; 84:5-6; *Jub.* 16:7-9, 16-30; 22:10-15; 36:9-11; *Pss. Sol.* 18:3-5; *2 Bar* 39:2—43:4. See M. Elliott 2000, 309-54; 434-514; for the point that follows above see ibid.

tic Son of Man, but between a nationalistic understanding of the Messiah and a view that understands the Messiah as "messiah for the elect."

Rudolf Pesch sees it as a serious problem that Jesus' mission focused primarily on the gathering of Israel but that he threatened his Jewish contemporaries and thus Israel with definitive exclusion from salvation and judgment from God as he was about to be rejected by the people and their leaders. Pesch raises the question of why the disciples did not shake the dust of Eretz Israel off their feet after Jesus' crucifixion, leaving Israel for the Gentiles: "How did it happen that the post-Easter missionary activity of Jesus' disciples offered them a new opportunity for conversion?"[105] Pesch finds the answer to this question in the confession of the apostolic kerygma that "Christ died for our sins in accordance with the Scriptures" (1 Cor 15:3, cf. Rom 3:25-26). In other words, when the apostles interpreted the death of Jesus as a death of atonement, an interpretation that can be traced back to Jesus and the last Passover before his death, they were empowered to grant Israel another chance for repentance. In my view, another explanation is more likely: Jesus did not make the Gentile mission of his disciples dependent upon his rejection by Israel.[106] Instead, he commissioned the disciples to go to the Gentiles. It needs to be acknowledged, however, that the Gospels do not provide an extensive salvation-historical explanation for the Gentile mission (see §12).

9.2 Ministry in Galilee

Cities and Villages

The Gospels report that Jesus visited "all the cities and villages" of Galilee (Mt 9:35/Lk 8:1). Mark distinguishes "villages or cities or farms" that Jesus visited (Mk 6:56). According to Luke, Jesus and his disciples walked "through the villages" (Lk 9:6). Crowds followed Jesus "on foot from the towns" (Mt 14:13; Lk 8:4; Mk 6:33: "from all the towns").

Mt 9:35: "Then Jesus went about all the cities [τὰς πόλεις πάσας] and villages [τὰς κώμας] teaching in their synagogues, and proclaiming the good news of the kingdom, and curing every disease and every sickness."

Mt 11:1: "Now when Jesus had finished instructing his twelve disciples, he went on from there to teach and proclaim his message in their cities [ἐν ταῖς πόλεσιν αὐτῶν]."

Mt 14:13: "Now when Jesus heard this, he withdrew from there in a boat to a deserted place by himself. But when the crowds heard it, they followed him on foot from the towns [ἀπὸ τῶν πόλεων]."

---

[105]Pesch 1982, 28-29.

[106]Schlier (1942, 90) argues a position similar to Pesch's: "The Gentile mission is possible only on the basis of the presupposition that Israel rejected Jesus the Messiah and thus itself has been rejected as the chosen people."

Mk 1:38: "Let us go on to the neighboring towns [εἰς τὰς ἐχομένας κωμοπόλεις], so that I may proclaim the message there also; for that is what I came out to do."

Mk 6:56: "And wherever he went, into villages [εἰς κώμας] or cities [εἰς πόλεις] or farms [εἰς ἀγρούς], they laid the sick in the marketplaces [ἐν ταῖς ἀγοραῖς], and begged him that they might touch even the fringe of his cloak; and all who touched it were healed."

Lk 4:43: "But he said to them, 'I must proclaim the good news of the kingdom of God to the other cities [ταῖς ἑτέραις πόλεσιν] also; for I was sent for this purpose.'"

Lk 9:6: "They departed and went through the villages [διήρχοντο κατὰ τὰς κώμας], bringing the good news and curing diseases everywhere [πανταχοῦ]."

The meaning of the word "city" or "town" (πόλις, *polis*) in the Gospels follows the usage of the Septuagint, where every fortified settlement was called "town,"[107] not just the political center that controlled a specific territory. The "village" (κώμη, *kōmē*) is the smaller, unfortified settlement. However, the distinction between "town" and "village" is not always clear, a fact that is seen in the combined term κωμόπολις (*kōmopolis* [Mk 1:38; replaced by *polis* in Lk 4:43]). According to U. Hutter, the remark in Mk 1:38 refers to "a small market town that legally occupied the position of κώμη."

The Gospels mention the following Galilean towns: Nazareth,[108] Capernaum,[109] Chorazin, Nain and Cana.[110] It is striking that Sepphoris and Tiberias, the large towns, in fact the only "cities" in Galilee, are not mentioned.

1. Nazareth was the home town of Mary the mother of Jesus (Lk 1:26). Joseph, her husband, hailed from Bethlehem (Mt 2:1-11; Lk 2:4-5) and settled after the return from Egypt in Nazareth (Mt 2:19-23). Nazareth therefore was Jesus' hometown. Luke reports that Jesus preached in the first months of his public ministry in the synagogue of Nazareth, explaining his mission (Lk 4:16-27).[111] Matthew and Mark also report on Jesus' preaching activity in Nazareth (Mt 13:54-57/Mk 6:1-6).

Nazareth (Ναζαρέτ, Ναζαρά; mod. Nazareth)[112] was situated in a high-lying valley in the

---

[107]See U. Hutter, *EWNT* 3:308 (*EDNT* 3:129); on Mk 1:38 see ibid.

[108]Mt 2:23; 21:11; Mk 1:9; Lk 1:26; 2:4, 39, 51; Jn 1:45-46.

[109]Mt 4:13; 8:5; 11:23; 17:24 cf. 9:1; Mk 1:21; 2:1; 9:33; Lk 4:23, 31; 7:1; 10:15; Jn 2:12; 4:46; 6:17, 24, 59.

[110]Chorazin: Mt 11:21; Lk 10:13; Nain: Lk 7:11; Cana: Jn 2:1, 11; 4:46; 21:2.

[111]The literature on this passage is immense; besides the commentaries see Eltester 1972; L. Levine 2000, 45-48; Pao 2000, 70-84.

[112]G. Hölscher, PW 16 (1935): 2096-97; J. W. Charley, *IBD* 2:1061-62; H. Kuhli, *EWNT* 2:1114-17 (*EDNT* 2:453-54); R. Riesner, *GBL* 2:1031-37; J. F. Strange, *OEANE* 4:113-14; idem, *ABD* 4:1050-51; V. Tzaferis and B. Bagatti, *NEAEHL* 3:1103-6; J. Pahlitzsch, *DNP* 7:769; Hüttenmeister 1977, 339-42; Meyers and Strange 1981, 56-57, 130-37; Bösen 1985, 97-132; Riesner 1988, 222-37; Pixner 1994, 47-50, 336-39, 378; Reed 2000, 82, 105-6, 115-17, 131-32. Excavations: Bellarmino Bagatti, *Excavations in Nazareth* (vol. 1; Jerusalem: Franciscan Printing Press, 1969).

hills in western Lower Galilee that fall away steeply toward the Jezreel Valley, only 5 km (3 mi.) south of Sepphoris, the most significant market center in Galilee and the capital of Herod Antipas (in which he had engaged in lavish building activities until he established Tiberias as his new capital in A.D. 18-20). The international route from Egypt via Caesarea to Damascus ran only 3 km east of Nazareth at the edge of the Jezreel Valley; the junction leading to Sepphoris must have been very close to Nazareth. The town was situated about 500 m above sea level; the slope to the Jezreel Valley below the town (150 m above sea level) is steep. Sepphoris could be reached more easily, after a 200 m steep descent, through the valley of Naḥal Zippori. Nazareth thus was oriented toward Sepphoris, not least because the fertile Jezreel Valley was controlled by royal estates or by the cities of Beth Shean (Scythopolis) and Megiddo and evidently did not belong to the Galilee of Herod Antipas.[113] Nazareth is mentioned in the New Testament for the first time as the town in which Mary and Joseph lived (Lk 1:26; 2:4) and in which Jesus grew up (Mt 2:23; Lk 2:39; 2:51). According to later Jewish sources, priests lived in Nazareth (*Eccl. Rab.* 2:8). Excavations have shown that there was a settlement already in the Bronze Age. From the Roman period only a few remains have been discovered. In the first century the village of Nazareth covered about 4 ha (9.9 acres) and thus presumably had fewer than 400 inhabitants.[114]

Luke presupposes that another person in the synagogue service had read the Torah reading (*seder*).[115] Jesus speaks in the second part of the service, which was more didactic, after he had volunteered for the reading from the prophets (*haftarah*), where either he could choose the text himself or he had to read a given text. Jesus explained in his homily that the prophecy in Is 61:1-2 (and Is 58:6) was being fulfilled in his ministry (Lk 4:21). The "year of the Lord's favor" (Lk 4:19) is not only the jubilee year stipulated in the Torah as a year of forgiveness and blessing but also the eschatological turn of the ages, the time of the Messiah when God establishes his kingdom. The poor, the captives, the blind, the oppressed that are mentioned in the text of Isaiah are not simply the literally poor, or the people who sit in real prisons, or the physically blind and oppressed: Jesus' offer of good news (*euangelion*) for the poor, release (*aphesis*) of the captives and of the oppressed, new sight (*anablepsis*) to the blind is a description of Yahweh's messianic salvation. The initial reaction of the listeners is affirmative. They applaud Jesus and admire him (Lk 4:22). In his response to the reaction of the people of Nazareth he clarifies that one cannot comprehend him or his message if he is viewed simply as "son of Joseph." If they reject him, they join a broad tradition in Israel that rejected prophets in their hometowns again and again. Their rejection thus confirms him as prophet, validated on account of his wisdom and his mighty deeds (Lk 4:23-27).[116] The indignant reaction of the villagers leads to an attempt on Jesus'

---

[113]Reed 2000, 115-16.
[114]Ben-David 1974, 49; Strange, *ABD* 4:1050-51; Reed 2000, 82, 131.
[115]Bovon, *Lk*, 1:211.
[116]Pesch, *Mk*, 1:321 (on the parallel in Mk 6:4).

life. They push him to the steep slope outside of Nazareth with the intention of throwing him down (Lk 4:28-29). Matthew comments that Jesus' rejection by the inhabitants of Nazareth was the grounds for why he performed only a few miracles in his hometown (Mt 13:58).

During the persecution under Emperor Decius, around A.D. 250/251, a certain Konon died as a martyr in Magydos in Pamphylia, a gardener working on an imperial estate who, according to *Acts of the Martyrs,* hailed from Nazareth and was a relative of Jesus.[117] The "Acts of Konon the Martyr" probably are largely fictitious; however, the surprising identification of a relative of Jesus in Pamphylia in the third century, a time in which the church seems to have lost interest in Jesus' relatives, probably is historical.[118] The grotto in Nazareth dedicated to his memory existed already in the third century[119] and confirms that Jewish Christians lived in Nazareth by the third century at the latest. In connection with the archaeological work of the Franciscans in Nazareth, Rainer Riesner comments that this cave may originally have been a storage facility in the vicinity of Mary's house.[120] Joseph of Tiberias, a Jewish Christian who lived in the early fourth century, received permission from Emperor Constantine to build a church in Nazareth. Piacenza the Pilgrim, around A.D. 570, is the first to report churches in Nazareth; he visited the basilica that had been built at the site of Mary's house, the source where Mary had drawn water, and the synagogue, in which he was shown the bench on which Jesus had sat to study Torah with other children.[121]

2. Capernaum was the center of Jesus' public ministry in Galilee (Mt 4:13-17; Jn 2:12). Capernaum was "his own town" (ἡ ἰδία πόλις [Mt 9:1]), his base when he was visiting the towns and villages of Galilee. Capernaum thus became his "hometown," where he had an extensive teaching ministry and performed many miracles. Peter and his family lived in Capernaum as well.

Capernaum (Καφαρναούμ; Kĕfar Naḥum in rabbinic literature; Arab., Talḥum)[122] was situated at the northwestern shore of the Sea of Galilee, at a distance of about 5 km (3 mi.) from the upper Jordan River. Capernaum was one of at least sixteen harbors of the Sea of Galilee, besides Tiberias, Tabgha, Kursi (Gergesa), Hippos (Sussita), Magdala and Gadara.[123] Excavations have confirmed a settlement in the early Bronze Age; after a gap in the history of the settlement during the Israelite kingdom, the site was occupied again during the Persian pe-

---

[117]*Martyrium Canonis* 4.2; see the edition by Musurillo 1972, 186-92.

[118]Bauckham 1990, 122; cf. Riesner, *GBL* 2:1036.

[119]Bagatti, *Excavations in Nazareth,* 185-213; on the Jewish-Christian traditions in Nazareth see Emmanuele Testa, *Nazaret Giudeo-Christiana: Riti, iscrizioni, simboli* (Jerusalem: Franciscan Printing Press, 1969).

[120]Riesner, *GBL* 2:1036, with reference to S. Loffreda, *SBFLA* 36 (1986): 211-34.

[121]Antoninus Placentinus, *Itinerarium* 5; CCSL 175, 130-131.

[122]G. Beer, PW 10 (1919): 1889-91; J. P. Kane, *IBD* 1:245-48; Balz, *EWNT* 2:690-91 (*EDNT* 2:279-80); Riesner, *GBL* 2:764-68; Loffreda and Tzaferis, *NEAEHL* 1:291-96; Loffreda, *OEANE* 1:416-19; Corbo, *ABD* 1:866-69; Pahlitzsch, *DNP* 6:257-58; Hüttenmeister 1977, 260-70; Pixner 1994, 114-26; Reed 2000, 139-69, 183-84, and passim; Freeman-Grenville 2003, 139. Excavations: Corbo et al., *Cafarnao;* Tzaferis, *Excavations at Capernaum.*

[123]On the harbors of the Sea of Galilee see Nun 1999; 2001.

riod. The earliest written evidence for the existence of Capernaum is the Gospels; the silence of other Jewish sources can be explained by the size and significance of the neighboring towns of Magdala (Taricheae) and Bethsaida. In the first century Capernaum was a small village, without walls, extending for about 300 m along the shore of the Sea of Galilee, with some 600 to 1,500 inhabitants (see §8.1). Josephus was taken to Capernaum after being wounded in a battle near the Jordan River (*Vita* 403). The monumental synagogue (24.5 by 18.7 m)[124] stood in the center of the east-west axis. Archaeologists Virgilio Corbo and Stanislaus Loffreda, who excavated the synagogue, date the structure after A.D. 360, while Yoram Tsafrir and others argue for an earlier date in the third century.[125] The synagogue of the first century, built (or financed) by a Roman officer, according to Lk 7:5, probably stood at the same site. Corbo and Loffreda found a floor made of basalt stones beneath the central nave that probably belonged to a public building; this floor is interpreted by some scholars as the remains of the synagogue of the first century.[126] Capernaum's inhabitants subsisted on fishing, agriculture and trade. The road, paved during the time of Hadrian, that ran along the Jordan River via the western shore of the Sea of Galilee to the north passed through the town. Capernaum was situated near the border between the tetrarchy of Herod Antipas and the Transjordanian tetrarchy of Herod Philip, and thus had a customs post—Levi-Matthew, the tax collector, one of Jesus' disciples, lived in Capernaum (Mt 9:9)—and a Roman garrison (Mk 8:15 mentions a *centurio*). The private houses of Capernaum were built with basalt stones; public buildings like the synagogue were constructed from white limestone.

3. The Gospels presume a teaching ministry of Jesus in Chorazin (Mt 11:20-24; Lk 10:12-15), although they provide no details. Chorazin and Bethsaida, a town in the vicinity in the region of Batanea, were among the towns in which Jesus performed "most of his deeds of power" (αἱ πλεῖσται δυνάμεις [Mt 11:20]). Like Capernaum (3 km to the south), Chorazin was situated on the northwestern shore of the Sea of Galilee.

Chorazin (Χόραζιν; mod. Khirbet Karazeh)[127] was located on the road from the Mediterranean (Acco-Ptolemais) via Bethsaida to Damascus. Josephus does not mention Chorazin; in rabbinic texts Chorazin is mentioned as a village of medium size (*t. Mak.* 3:8). With a size of less than 10 ha, Chorazin probably had about 1,000 inhabitants. The earliest remains that have been discovered date to the first and second centuries A.D. Chorazin flourished around A.D. 300; remains of a synagogue (20.7 by 15.3 m) dating to the third century have been found.[128] The synagogue that J. Ory identified in 1926 can no

---

[124]See V. C. Corbo and S. Loffreda, *Cafarnao*, vols. 1-2; Y. Tsafrir, "The Synagogues at Capernaum and Meroth and the Dating of the Galilean Synagogue," in Humphrey 1995-2002, 1:151-61; Binder 1999, 186-93; L. Levine 2000, 195-98, and passim.

[125]Zvi Uri Ma'oz ("The Synagogue at Capernaum: A Radical Solution," in Humphrey 1995-2002, 2:137-48) argues that this building never served as the synagogue of a Jewish community; rather, it should be interpreted as a Christian building erected in the late fifth century, from spoils of several older Jewish synagogues, as a place where Christian pilgrims could see the site where Jesus preached. It is fair to say that this radical solution will not convince many.

[126]S. Loffreda, *NEAEHL* 1:294; Binder 1999, 190-93; L. Levine 2000, 66-67.

[127]A. Negev, *PECS* 223; Z. Yeivin, *NEAEHL* 1:301-4; R. Riesner, *GBL* 1:227-28; Robert W. Smith, *ABD* 1:911-12; Hüttenmeister 1977, 275-81; Pixner 1994, 62-63; Reed 2000, 183; Freeman-Grenville 2003, 124.

[128]Binder 1999, 198.

longer be verified.[129] Chorazin, along with Bethsaida and Capernaum, is mentioned in the New Testament as one of the three cities that Jesus rebuked for the lack of faith of their inhabitants (Mt 11:21-24; Lk 10:13-16). According to Eusebius, Chorazin was destroyed at the beginning of the fourth century (*Onom.* 174).

4. The village of Nain witnessed, according to Lk 7:11-17, one of the most dramatic miracles that Jesus performed: the resurrection of the son of a widow. News of this miracle spread not only in the "surrounding country" (πάσῃ τῇ περιχώρῳ) of Galilee and Samaria but also "throughout Judea" (ἐν ὅλῃ τῇ Ἰουδαίᾳ [Lk 7:17]), presumably as far as Jerusalem. Even John the Baptist, at that time a prisoner in the fortress of Machaerus, heard of it (Lk 7:18).

Nain (Ναΐν; mod. Nein),[130] located about 8 km southeast of Nazareth and 35 km southwest of Capernaum on a plateau at the eastern edge of the Jezreel Valley on the northern side of Mount Moreh (Arab., Jebel Ed-Dahī; [515 m high]), probably belonged to Galilee rather than to Samaria, although this is not certain. The international route from Egypt via Caesarea to Damascus passed just north of Nain. About 5 km northeast of Nain was Endor (En-Dor), where King Saul had consulted a medium (1 Sam 28:7), and 5 km south of Nain, on the south side of Mount Moreh, was Sunem, where Elisha had brought a boy back to life (2 Kings 4:18-37). The text of Lk 7:11 refers to Nain as a *polis* ("city"), which seems to correspond to the meaning of the Hebrew *ʿir*, which could be used for both a town and a village. When Lk 7:12 mentions the "gate" (*pylē*) of the town, this may simply refer to the exit of the village road from the closely grouped houses.[131] The site of Nain has not been investigated; graves dating to the first century have been discovered southeast of the site.

5. Cana was the site of Jesus' first miracle, according to Jn 2:1-12. Jesus, along with his disciples and his mother, had been invited to a wedding organized by a family that evidently was wealthy: the house owned "six stone water jars for the Jewish rites of purification" (Jn 2:6). On a later visit to Cana, Jesus was asked by a royal official (or a member of the military) from Capernaum to heal his son (Jn 4:46). According to Jn 1:45-51, Nathanael hailed from Cana (Jn 21:2) and was one of the first Galileans to react positively to Jesus.

Cana (Κανά; mod. Khirbet Qana)[132] was situated 14 km north of Nazareth on the northern end of the Asochis Valley on the important east-west road from Acco-Ptolemais to Taricheae (Magdala); connecting roads led to Asochis, Sepphoris and, according to Jn 2:1, evidently also directly to Capernaum. The site had been settled since 1200 B.C. and flourished from the first to the sixth centuries A.D. Coins and pottery from the early Roman to the Byzantine periods have been discovered at the site. Since Cana guarded the ascent to

---

[129]See L. Levine 2000, 68, 162, 179-80, 321-26.
[130]R. Riesner, *GBL* 2:1022-23; Schürmann, *Lk,* 1:399; Fitzmyer, *Lk,* 1:658; Pixner 1994, 378.
[131]See Riesner, *GBL* 2:1023.
[132]Riesner, *GBL* 2:751-53; idem, *DJG* 36-37; J. F. Strange, *ABD* 1:827; B. Bagatti and S. Loffreda, "Le Antichità de Khirbet Qana e di Kegar Kanna in Galilea," *SBFLA* 15 (1969): 251-92; cf. Schnackenburg, *Joh,* 1:331 (ET, 1:326).

the fortress of Jotapata (Jotba), Josephus temporarily had his headquarters in Cana at the beginning of the First Jewish Revolt in A.D. 66 (*Vita* 86). After the Bar Kokhba Revolt, the priestly family of Eliaschib lived in Cana, a fact that establishes the Jewish identity of the settlement in the early second century. Cana evidently was built along a north-south axis; in the northwestern part of town there was a large building whose function has not yet been identified. On the southern and southeastern slopes of the hill on which Cana was situated rock graves have been found. On the hill itself numerous large and small cisterns that guaranteed the water supply were discovered. In the western part of town a wall has been identified. The village was situated 100 m above the valley floor at an ideal geographical location, which explains why a "royal official" (Jn 4:46) would be in Cana to manage the royal estates in the Asochis Valley.

Jesus evidently knew a wealthy family in Cana that could provide hospitality for him and his disciples. That he recruited his disciple Nathanael from this family must remain a hypothesis. The fact that Cana is mentioned several times in the Gospel of John suggests the possibility that Jesus visited this town and this region repeatedly, and may imply the existence of a Christian community at the time of the composition of the Fourth Gospel.

6. Jesus probably visited Magdala, about 10 km south of Capernaum, on the western shore of the Sea of Galilee, but the Gospels do not explicitly describe a ministry there. Mary Magdalene is mentioned numerous times in the Gospels,[133] and presumably she hailed from Magdala.

Magdala (Μαγδαλά)[134] is identified by most scholars with the town of Taricheae (or Tarecheae) mentioned by Josephus,[135] situated about 5 km north of Tiberias. The Hebrew name means "tower," the Greek term *taricheiai* means "factories for salting fish," which corresponds to the designation *migdal nunaja*', "fish tower" (*b. Pesah* 46a). In Magdala a road that branched off the Via Maris led through Wadi El-Hamam to western Galilee. During the Maccabean revolt important battles took place near Magdala (1 Macc 9:2). In 52 B.C. the Romans occupied the city and forced a large part of the population into slavery. In A.D. 44 Magdala, together with the rest of Galilee, was annexed to the Roman province of Judea. During the Jewish revolt Magdala was an important center of the Zealot resistance against the Romans (Josephus, *B.J.* 3.462-502). Suetonius mentions the capture of Magdala by Titus (*Tit.* 4.3), and Josephus reports that Vespasian ordered 12,000 prisoners from the city to be killed in the stadium of Tiberias, and had 6,000 prisoners transported to Corinth to build Nero's canal through the Isthmus; 30,400 prisoners were sold as slaves (*B.J.* 3.539-540). Magdala itself did not have 40,000 inhabitants, however, as Josephus maintains (*B.J.* 2.608). Strabo knows the salted fish and the fertile territory of Magdala (16.2.45). According to *b. Ketub.* 106a, the curtains for the Jerusalem temple were manufactured in Magdala. The presence of a hippodrome (Josephus, *B.J.* 2.599) shows Hellenistic influence in the town, which was confirmed during the excavations of 1971.[136]

---

[133]Mt 27:56, 61; Mk 15:40, 47; 16:1, 9; Lk 8:2; 24:10; Jn 20:1, 18.

[134]Riesner, *GBL* 2:909-10; J. F. Strange, *ABD* 4:463-64; F. Manns, "Magdala dans les sources littéraires," *SH* 1 (1976): 307-37; Sawicki 2000, 143-44.

[135]Josephus, *B.J.* 1.635; 2.599, 608, 634; 3.445, 457, 462-502; *Vita* 403-404.

[136]V. Corbo, "Scavi archeologici a Magdala (1971-1973)," *SBFLA* 24 (1974): 5-37; idem, "La città

Magdala/Taricheae had a highly developed water supply, with baths in private houses, a paved main road in north-south orientation, houses of affluent citizens, shops and expansive harbor facilities. A mosaic depicting a fishing boat dates to the first century, as does a small building (8.1 by 7.2 m) with columns and five benches at the northern wall, identified as a synagogue (before A.D. 70?). The date of a large quadrangular plaza surrounded by four stoas or colonnaded halls has not yet been established with certainty. According to Josephus, Magdala had a fishing fleet with 230 boats (*B.J.* 1.635).

7. Sepphoris and Tiberias, the largest cities in Galilee, are not mentioned in the Gospels. This is striking for several reasons. First, even though these were Hellenistic cities, archaeological investigations have established that they were Jewish centers with a largely Jewish population. Second, Sepphoris is only 5 km (ca. 3 mi.) north of Nazareth, and Tiberias is about 15 km (ca. 9 mi.) south of Capernaum. Third, the Gospel writers mention the fact that Jesus visited the territory of Gadara, Tyre, Sidon and Caesarea Philippi, which indicates that he would not fear visiting Sepphoris or Tiberias.

Sepphoris (Σέπφωρις; later Diocaesarea; Arab., Ṣafuriyye; mod. Moshav Zippori),[137] situated on a hill above the Bet Netopha Valley in central Lower Galilee about 5 km north of Nazareth, was settled already in the Iron Age. At the time of Alexander Jannaeus it probably functioned as the administrative center of Galilee (Josephus, *A.J.* 13.338). Between 57 and 55 B.C. the Roman proconsul Gabinius made Sepphoris the administrative center of the district of Galilee, with its own regional sanhedrin (*A.J.* 14.91; *B.J.* 1.170). When Herod I attacked the city during a snow storm, it capitulated (*A.J.* 14.414; *B.J.* 1.304). After Herod's death the Romans occupied the city and sold the citizens into slavery (*A.J.* 17.289; *B.J.* 2.68). When the kingdom of Herod I was divided among his sons, Herod Antipas resided in Sepphoris as the capital of Galilee before he built Tiberias as the new capital. Antipas fortified Sepphoris and called it "Autokratoris" to honor Augustus (*A.J.* 18.27). Josephus calls Sepphoris "the ornament of all Galilee" (*A.J.* 18.27). Sepphoris was the dominant market town in central Galilee, a fact confirmed by the presence of large subterranean silos and the newly discovered evidence for the fish trade.[138] The city had at least 10,000 citizens.[139] The water supply was guaranteed by two aqueducts. Sepphoris had an

---

romana di Magdala," *SH* 1 (1976): 355-78; S. Loffreda, "Alcune osservazioni sulla ceramica di Magdala," *SH* 1 (1976): 338-54.

[137]Honigmann, PW 2.A (1922): 1546-49; Negev, *PECS* 827-28; Strange, *ABD* 5:1090-93; Z. Weiss, *NEAEHL* 4:1324-28; Schürer 2:172-76; Hüttenmeister 1977, 400-18; S. Cohen 1979, 215-16; Stuart S. Miller, *Studies in the History and Traditions of Sepphoris* (SJLA 37; Leiden: Brill, 1984); E. M. Meyers, "Sepphoris, Ornament of All Galilee," *BA* 49 (1986): 4-19; P. T. Crocker, "Sepphoris: Past History and Present Discoveries," *Buried History* 23 (1987): 64-76; Meyers et al. 1992; Stuart S. Miller, "Sepphoris, the Well Remembered City," *BA* 55 (1992): 74-83; J. Strange 1992; E. M. Meyers, "Aspects of Roman Sepphoris in the Light of Recent Archaeology," in Manns and Alliata 1993, 29-36; Horsley 1995, 163-69; Nagy 1996; Meyers 1997, 63-64; Reed 2000, 100-38; Mark Chancey, "The Cultural Milieu of Ancient Sepphoris," *NTS* 47 (2001): 127-45. For the reports of the South Florida Expedition and the Joint Sepphoris Project see *IEJ* since 1983.

[138]Arlene Fradkin, "Long-Distance Trade in the Lower Galilee: New Evidence from Sepphoris," in Edwards and McCollough 1997, 107-15.

[139]Reed 2000, 94. Meyers (1997, 59) assumes 18,000 inhabitants.

upper and a lower market, at least by the rabbinic period, with its own standard for weights and measures; a recently found lead weight mentions a market inspector (*agoranomos*) and depicts a colonnaded hall.[140] The theater (73 m in diameter, with a capacity for 4,500 spectators) is dated by archaeologists Ehud Netzer and Zeev Weiss to the late first century A.D. at the earliest, and by James Strange to the early first century.[141] During the Jewish revolt Sepphoris remained loyal to the Romans and capitulated to Vespasian, issuing coins with the caption "peacemaker" (εἰρηνοποίος), calling itself "city of peace" ("Eirenopolis Neronias"). Under Emperor Hadrian the city, now called Diocaesarea ("City of Zeus and of the Emperor") was ruled by a non-Jewish magistrate. At the end of the second century Rabbi Judah ha-Nasi resided in Sepphoris and compiled the Mishnah, the first document of rabbinic Judaism; the sanhedrin met in the city for seventeen years (*y. Kil.* 9:4 [32b]). Rabbinic sources mention eighteen synagogues of Sepphoris in connection with the funeral of Rabbi Judah ha-Nasi, none of which has been located so far. The site of ancient Sepphoris has been excavated since 1983. The synagogue (20.7 by 8 m) discovered in 1993, with a beautiful mosaic floor (16 by 16.6 m) is dated to the fifth century.[142] The cultural milieu of Sepphoris in the first century was Jewish; "pagan" finds have been discovered only for the second century, and Greek seems to have been used more widely only in the second century as well.[143]

Tiberias (Τιβεριάς; mod. Khirbet Qunaytirah; Arab., et-Ṭabarije)[144] was established in A.D. 20 by Herod Antipas as his new capital, named after the emperor Tiberius. Ancient Tiberias was located north of modern Tiberias between Magdala-Taricheae to the north and Hammath to the south; west of the city rose the hill Berenike (200 m), to the east was the Sea of Galilee. The hot springs that Pliny mentions (*Nat.* 5.15) were so hot that they could cause injuries (*m. Neg.* 9:1). Since the city was built over graves and thus had to be regarded as unclean (cf. Num 19:16), Antipas forced Galileans to settle in the city and gave houses and land to people "from any and all places of origin" (Josephus, *A.J.* 18.36-37). Tiberias was governed as a Greek polis by a council with six hundred members, led by an elected *archōn;* the administration was controlled by an *hyparchos* ("officer") and an *agoranomos* ("overseer of markets"). Antipas built a stadium, a market, baths and, on the hill overlooking the city, a palace. Josephus reports that the royal palace was decorated with depictions of animals and that the ceilings were made partially of gold (*Vita* 65-66). Until at least A.D. 61 the palace housed the royal treasury and the archives (*Vita* 38); after A.D. 61 Caesarea Philippi became the capital under Agrippa II, and Sepphoris became a banking center under Nero, when the archives were returned to Sepphoris (*Vita* 38, 346). Josephus calls the synagogue (*proseuchē*) of Tiberias "a very large building" (*Vita* 277).[145] Later rabbinic sources mention thirteen synagogues (*b. Ber.* 8a; 30b). The *cardo maximus*

---

[140]See *b. Yoma* 11a; *b. 'Erub.* 54b; 83a-b; *y. Šabb.* 8:1 [11a]; *SEG* XXXVI 1342.

[141]Z. Weiss and E. Netzer, "Hellenistic and Roman Sepphoris," in Nagy 1996, 32.

[142]See Z. Weiss and E. Netzer, *Promise and Redemption: A Synagogue Mosaic from Sepphoris* (Jerusalem: The Israel Museum, 1996); Z. Weiss, "The Sepphoris Synagogue Mosaic and the Rôle of Talmudic Literature in Its Iconographical Study," in Levine and Weiss 2000, 15-30.

[143]Chancey, "The Cultural Milieu," 133-37, 144.

[144]F. Münzer, PW 6.1 (1936): 779-81; H. Kippenberg, *KP* 5:812; A. Negev, *PECS* 920-21; J. F. Strange, *ABD* 6:547-49; Y. Foerster, G. Foerster and F. Vitto, *NEAEHL* 5:1464-73; Tsafrir, di Segni and Green, *Iudaea-Palaestina,* 249-50; Schürer 2:178-82; Hüttenmeister 1977, 437-61; S. Cohen 1979, 216-21; H. Dudman and E. Ballhorn, *Tiberias* (Jerusalem: Carta, 1988); Horsley 1995, 169-74.

[145]See L. Levine 2000, 49-51, and passim.

that ran parallel to the Sea of Galilee was 12 m wide and was lined by colonnaded halls that were 5 m wide and had shops (ca. 3.6 by 3 m). The city gates, presumably built by Antipas, were flanked by round towers (7 m in diameter). Tiberias had between 10,000 and 20,000 inhabitants.[146] The city capitulated at the beginning of the Jewish revolt and thus was spared destruction; in the stadium 12,000 Jewish refugees from Magdala were massacred (*B.J.* 3.539-540). Under Hadrian a temple honoring the emperor (Hadrianeum) was built in the city. After Tiberias was cleansed by Rabbi Simeon Bar Yoḥai, the famous Rabbi Yoḥanan lived in the city (around A.D. 235). In the third and fourth centuries Tiberias was the seat of the rabbinic patriarchate (until A.D. 429). The Palestinian Talmud was compiled in Tiberias.

It is difficult to imagine that Jesus made no contact with the citizens of these Herodian cities during his Galilean ministry between A.D. 27 and 30. Several explanations for the silence of the Gospels concerning Sepphoris and Tiberias have been offered.[147]

a. Jesus visited Sepphoris and Tiberias, and the silence of the Gospels is purely accidental. Some scholars hypothesize that Jesus probably visited Sepphoris during his teenage years with his father, who, as a "construction worker" (*tektōn* [Mt 13:55]) living in nearby Nazareth, may have found work when Sepphoris was developed by Herod Antipas.[148] Until Tiberias replaced Sepphoris, Jesus lived in close proximity to the capital of Galilee for twenty years; a reflection of the proximity to this urban center may be seen in the parables that speak of a royal palace, a merchant bank or the seat of jurisdiction.[149] The fact that the Gospels do not mention characteristic buildings or institutions of a Greco-Roman polis, such as imperial and pagan temples, gymnasia, hippodromes or monumental fountains, may be explained by the fact that as far as we know, the two Herodian cities did not have such buildings in the early first century. If Jesus frequented Sepphoris as a youngster, there is no reason why he could not have visited the city as an adult.[150] However plausible such considerations may be with respect to Jesus' education and worldview, they do not explain why the authors of the Gospels do not mention a preaching or healing activity of Jesus in these two Galilean centers.

b. Jesus preached in these cities but had no success.[151] This explanation is hardly convincing. According to Mt 11:20-24/Lk 10:13-15, Jesus had no "success" in Chorazin, Capernaum and Bethsaida, and still these towns are mentioned repeatedly. If the citizens of Sepphoris or Tiberias had rejected Jesus, we would expect a rebuke similar to the one directed against those other three towns.[152]

---

[146]Reed 2000, 94. Meyers (1997, 59) estimates 24,000 inhabitants.
[147]On this discussion see now Reed 2000, 100-138.
[148]See Batey 1984; 1991; on Batey see Reed 2000, 107-8.
[149]Riesner 1988, 219, 237; mentioned by Reed (2000, 132-33) as possibility.
[150]Mack 1993, 57-62.
[151]See Bösen 1985, 74-75.
[152]Thus Freyne 1996, 190; Meyers 1997, 60.

c. Jesus avoided Sepphoris for ethnic reasons: he ministered only to the Jewish population and avoided contact with Gentiles.[153] This explanation is implausible for two reasons. First, Sepphoris was not a Gentile city: the only pagan objects that have been discovered (so far) are several small household items; the Dionysos mosaic that has been discovered in a villa dates to the second century. Second, Jesus did not avoid contact with Gentiles at all costs (see §9.3).

d. Jesus avoided Sepphoris for cultural reasons: the former capital of Herod Antipas was a city whose Hellenistic culture had strained relations with the surrounding Jewish countryside. Gerd Theissen speaks of "differences of mentality" and thinks that "it is quite improbable that in his youth Jesus was decisively stamped by influences from Hellenistic culture through Sepphoris."[154] He suggests that these differences of mentality explain why the Gospel writers never mention the two Herodian cities: "Jesus above all addressed the country population, which lived in the many smaller places."[155] However, such differences of mentality, which may well have existed, are not easy to document from the sources; they cannot be derived solely from the difference between city and countryside. Also, this explanation exaggerates the differences between Sepphoris and Tiberias and the Jewish peasantry, as the two cities, particularly Sepphoris, were not Greek *poleis* in the technical sense of the word but rather Jewish centers with a Jewish population. Further, this hypothesis does not take into account the fact that Jesus visited the territories and cities of Caesarea Philippi and Bethsaida, the two Hellenistic centers in the tetrarchy of Herod Philip.[156] And we should not forget that Jesus did have contacts with Gentiles. Finally, the sayings of Jesus do not address specifically Hellenistic matters, such as pictorial representations of human beings or animals or bathing in the nude.[157]

e. Jesus avoided the Herodian cities for socioeconomic reasons: he expressed solidarity with the economic victims of the politics of the urban centers (i.e., the poor of the peasantry), and he developed and proclaimed a prophetic critique of the existing unjust social structures that was at the same time a critique of the urban elite.[158] This explanation is more plausible than the suggestions surveyed so far: presumably there were tensions between the urban centers Sepphoris and Tiberias and the Jewish peasantry (see §8.2). Furthermore, Jesus repeatedly pronounced critical verdicts on the rich (Mt 19:23; Mk 10:25, 41-45; Lk 6:24). Nevertheless, this explanation is unconvincing. First, Jesus' teaching can hardly be interpreted in terms of a social reform program or a revolutionary social

---

[153]Alt 1949; on Alt see Reed 2000, 105-6, 135.
[154]Theissen and Merz 1996, 163 (ET, 170-71).
[155]Theissen and Merz 1996, 163; see also Meier 1991-2001, 1:283-84, 350-53; E. P. Sanders 1993, 104.
[156]Strickert 1995, 168.
[157]See Reed 2000, 135.
[158]Freyne 1988, 139-40; 1996, 196-206.

agenda. Jesus focused on the relationships of people with one another and particularly with God, not on social classes and their differences.[159] Second, the Gospels contain ample evidence that Jesus not only knew the large cities of Galilee but also claimed that his proclamation must be heard there as well:[160] According to Luke, Jesus mentions royal palaces (Lk 7:25), marketplaces (Lk 7:32; 11:43), roads and streets (Lk 10:10; 13:26; 14:21), law courts and prisons (Lk 12:57-59; 18:2), city gates (Lk 13:24) and banks (Lk 19:23); he meets prostitutes (Lk 7:37) and accepts the invitation to a banquet in the house of a leading Pharisee (Lk 11:37; cf. 14:16-24); in the parable of the talents he speaks of the control of five or ten cities (Lk 19:17, 19); and according to Lk 12:11, Jesus expects that his disciples will visit large cities where they will be brought to trial before "rulers and authorities." Third, even though Jesus spent most of his time among the poor peasants in the villages of Galilee, his eating habits provoked the charge that he was "a friend of tax collectors and sinners" (Lk 7:34), and tax collectors and "sinners" would have been much more common in Sepphoris and Tiberias than in the countryside. Fourth, we do encounter rich people among Jesus' sympathizers. Note the episode of the rich young man (Mk 10:17-22), Jesus' stay in the house of Levi the tax collector (Mk 2:13), and the social status of some of the women who followed him, among them Joanna, the wife of Chuza, an administrator (*epitropos*) of Herod Antipas (Lk 8:3).[161] And we should keep in mind that neither Sepphoris nor Tiberias is explicitly condemned by Jesus.

f. Jesus avoided Sepphoris and Tiberias for political reasons: he wanted to avoid a direct confrontation with Herod Antipas.[162] John the Baptist, an enormously successful prophet whom the Sadducees and scribes dared not touch, was executed in A.D. 28 at the fortress of Machaerus because he castigated Herod Antipas for having committed adultery.[163] Herod Antipas was alarmed that John's powerful effect on the populace might lead to some form of sedition (Josephus, *A.J.* 18.118). Jesus' influence on the population in Galilee was no less significant. Presumably, Jesus wanted to avoid an open confrontation with Herod at this point.

If Gerd Theissen's interpretation of Mt 11:7/Lk 7:24 is correct, Jesus did in fact criticize Herod Antipas, although in an indirect manner. The rhetorical question "What did you go out into the wilderness to look at? A reed shaken by the wind?" may be a reference to Herod Antipas, who, on the occasion of the foundation of his new capital Tiberias in A.D. 19, minted a series of coins that depicted on the obverse a reed (*canna communis*). The tetrarch of Galilee was a clever politician who always managed to adapt to changing political constellations: he survived the intrigues at the court of his father, Herod I, the down-

---

[159]See Reed 2000, 136.
[160]See Bösen 1985, 69-75; J. L. Reed, "The Social Map of Q," in Kloppenborg 1996, 17-36.
[161]Reed 2000, 137. On Joanna see Bauckham 2002, 109-202.
[162]Meyers 1997, 64; Reed 2000, 137-38. On Herod Antipas see Stenschke 1999a, 126-36.
[163]Mt 14:3-12; Mk 6:17-29; Lk 3:19-20; Josephus, *A.J.* 18.116-119.

fall of his brother Archelaos in A.D. 6, the downfall of his good and powerful friend Sejanus in Rome in A.D. 31, and the military conflict with the Nabatean king Aretas IV in A.D.
36/37. He was "shaken" between two capitals, Sepphoris and Tiberias; between two
wives, the daughter of Aretas and Herodias (Josephus, *A.J.* 18.111); and between a positive and a negative view of John the Baptist (Mk 6:17-29). When Jesus speaks of a "shak-
ing reed," he may be alluding to Herod Antipas; the answer that Jesus seeks to elicit from
his listeners is evident from the context: "Of course not: we wanted to see not Herod Antipas but his prophetic antagonist!"[164]

Luke reports that Herod Antipas plotted Jesus' elimination: sympathizers among
the Pharisees warned Jesus, prompting him to leave the area and move to another region in order not to fall into the hands of "that fox." Jesus informs the
king in a "communiqué"[165] sent through the Pharisees who are present that he
plans to continue his activity, that he will not be intimidated, and that a prophet
can die only in Jerusalem (Lk 13:31-33). Jesus encounters Herod Antipas only
during his trial, when Pilate has Jesus taken to the Galilean ruler (Lk 23:6-12).
Herod wants to see his compatriot perform a miracle and asks him "many questions"; since Jesus remains silent and since the high priests and the scribes bring
strong accusations against Jesus, Herod demonstrates his contempt for Jesus by
having his soldiers dress him in royal robe. When Jesus designates Herod Antipas as "that fox" (Lk 13:32), and when he refers to his capital Sepphoris (Heb.,
zippori, "little bird") in the saying "Foxes have holes, and birds of the air have
nests; but the Son of Man has nowhere to lay his head" (Lk 9:58), he underlines
the contrast between Herod and himself. Since Capernaum was larger than Nazareth and was located at the border of the territory that Herod controlled, it was
ideally suited to be the center of his ministry.[166]

Since the studies by Gerd Theissen, many scholars describe the lifestyle of Jesus during his
public ministry as *Wanderradikalismus,* as a radical charismatic itinerant. Theissen explained the "ethical radicalism of the sayings transmitted to us" as "the radicalism of itinerants." "It can be practiced and passed on only under extreme living conditions. It is only
the person who has severed his everyday ties with the world—the person who has left
home and possessions, wife and child, who lets the dead bury their dead, and takes the
birds and the lilies of the field as his model—it is only a person like this who can consistently preach renunciation of a settled home, a family, possessions, the protection of the
law, and his own defense. It is only in this context that the ethical precepts which match
this way of life can be passed on without being unconvincing. This ethic only has a chance
on the fringes of society; this is the only real-life situation it can have. Or to be more exact:
it does not have a situation *in* real life at all. It has to put up with an existence *on the fringes*
of normal life, an existence that from the outsider's point of view is undoubtedly questionable. It is only here that Jesus' words were saved from being reduced to allegory, from
reinterpretation, from softening or repression—simply because they were taken seriously

---

[164]Theissen 1992a, 26-44, quotation, 38; cf. Theissen and Merz 1996, 105 (ET, 101).
[165]Chappuis 1982, 9-10. On the localization of this event see Fitzmyer, *Lk,* 2:1029.
[166]Reed 2000, 138.

and put into practice. And that was possible only for homeless charismatics."[167]

Massimo Grilli presents an important critique of this interpretation: Matthew (and, we might add, Mark and Luke as well) does *not* present Jesus as the model for a radical charismatic itinerant ministry. (1) In Mt 4:23; 9:35 Matthew does not describe Jesus' travels but rather tells about his activities in proclaiming the good news. The verbs that control the syntax of these verses are *didaskein* ("teach"), *kēryssein* ("proclaim") and *therapeuein* ("heal"). (2) In Mt 2:13-15; 8:20 the focus is not on homelessness and travels but on obedience to the plan of God.[168] (3) Another objection develops from the fact that Jesus concentrated his ministry largely on Galilee, which means that he could reach dozens of small towns and villages from Capernaum within one or two days. In other words, the "itinerant travels" generally would have been quite short: Jesus and his disciples were not really "homeless."

The Crowds

Jesus preached before large crowds of people: "great crowds" (ὄχλοι πολλοί [Mt 4:25]) followed Jesus and heard him preach (Mt 5:1). The Gospel writers often mention crowds of people when they describe Jesus' ministry.[169] The term ὄχλος (*ochlos*) designates in Greek literature "crowd, throng, mass, multitude," in the sense of "the public, in contrast to individual people, and particularly in contrast to the nobility or people of rank,"[170] in other words, "the 'leaderless and rudderless mob,' the 'politically and culturally insignificant mass.'"

The crowds mentioned in the Gospels are not a peripheral entity. They are a crucial group of people who often are portrayed in a positive light and who have a particular relationship with Jesus. The "transvaluation of the term" that this implies highlights, on the linguistic level, the significance that the Gospel writers ascribe to this group of people.[171] Scholars have differing views of the meaning of the "crowds" in the Gospels. Studies on the Gospel of Matthew, for example, interpret *ochlos* as an anonymous background to Jesus' ministry, as an applauding background, as a responding choir, as potential disciples, as representatives of the many people who accepted Jesus, as lay members of the Matthean community.[172] Robert Cousland recently argued that in Matthew "the

---

[167]Theissen 1973, 79-105; quotation, 86 (ET, 40).

[168]Grilli 1992, 237-41; cf. 241: "Matteo non intende presentare ai destinatari del suo scritto un modello di 'itineranza,' ma piuttosto un esempio di 'obbedienza' al piano di Dio, unito allo scandalo del rifiuto degli uomini."

[169]The terms *ochlos* ("crowd") or *ochloi* ("crowds") occur 50 times in Matthew, 38 times in Mark, 41 times in Luke, 20 times in John.

[170]H. Bietenhard, *ThBLNT* 2:1819 (*NIDNTT* 2:800); the quotation that follows above, R. Meyer, *ThWNT* 5:582-83 (*TDNT* 5:583).

[171]Thus Küster 1996, 59; for an investigation of the semantic field see ibid., 37-53. See also R. Meyer, *ThWNT* 5:582-90 (*TDNT* 5:582-90); H. Balz, *EWNT* 2:1354-55 (*EDNT* 2:553-54); Zingg 1974, 61-63; Meier 1991-2001, 3:21-39; Meiser 1998.

[172]See R. Meyer, *ThWNT* 5:586 (*TDNT* 5:586); Strecker 1971, 86-122, esp. 107; Sand, *Mt*, 194, 205; Luz, *Mt*, 1:416; Tilborg 1972, 142-65; Minear 1974, 28-44; also Gundry, *Mt*, 65, 139, 290; Cousland 2002, 35-51 ("definite choric function"); the quotation that follows above, ibid., 302.

crowds recapitulate and epitomize the chequered history of Israel's involvement with Yahweh. . . . They do not represent members of Matthew's community, but the Jewish people—as distinguished from their leaders—of Matthew's own day. They have not yet accepted the Christian proclamation, but their doing so remains a possibility that is deliberately courted by the evangelist." Such one-dimensional attempts at interpretation fail to do justice to the complex picture that the Gospel writers present.[173]

A closer investigation of the role of the *ochlos/ochloi* in the Gospel of Matthew shows the following: (1) The crowds follow Jesus literally in a geographical sense: they go where Jesus goes, they accompany him from village to village. Matthew thus describes Jesus as a charismatic figure, as a sensation in first-century Galilee.[174] (2) The people in the crowds readily listen to Jesus' preaching and react to his message and to the healing miracles with astonishment and awe.[175] (3) The crowd believes that Jesus is a prophet (Mt 21:11, 46), as impressive as John the Baptist (Mt 14:5; 21:26). (4) On one occasion several people in a crowd raise the question of whether Jesus is the Son of David—that is, the Messiah.[176] (5) The crowd is the object of Jesus' missionary activity: the crowds receive his mercy[177] because they are "sheep without a shepherd" (Mt 9:36; cf. 10:6) and because they react differently than the Pharisees do.[178] (6) The people in the crowds are not identical with disciples of Jesus,[179] as they are "sheep without a shepherd." Thus the crowds hardly represent the post-Easter church. (7) The crowds are involved in the sentencing and death of Jesus.[180]

The crowds that wanted to hear Jesus preach and see him heal do not appear as monochromatic. Rather, the presentation of the crowds reflects the historical reality that would surround any charismatic and popular itinerant preacher who is also controversial. Because crowds of people wanted to hear Jesus preach again and again, and because they brought their sick trusting that he would heal them (while ignoring the negative verdicts of priests, Pharisees, Sadducees and scribes), they appear in an essentially positive light. The people of these *ochloi*

---

[173]Carter 1993, 54-55; for the discussion that follows above see ibid., 57-64; Davies and Allison, *Mt,* 1:419-20.

[174]Mt 4:25; 8:1, 18; 11:7; 12:46; 15:30; 17:14; 19:2. On the crowds "following" (*akolouthein*) Jesus see Cousland (2002, 145-73), who highlights ecclesiological, christological and salvation-historical concerns of the author.

[175]Mt 9:8, 33; 12:23; 15:31; 22:23. See generally Cousland 2002, 125-35.

[176]Mt 12:23. Thus Davies and Allison, *Mt,* 2:335; differently Carter 1993, 61. See the discussion in Cousland 2002, 175-99.

[177]Mt 9:36; 14:14; 15:32. Emphasized in Citron 1954.

[178]Mt 9:33-34; 15:1-10; 23:1. On the crowds as sheep see Cousland 2002, 86-94, 120-22, 169-71; on Jesus as the messianic shepherd in the Gospel of John see Köstenberger 2002.

[179]Mt 5:1; 8:23; 12:46; 13:11-15, 36; 14:22-23. On the crowds and demands of Jesus see Cousland 2002, 148-52.

[180]Mt 26:47, 55; 27:20, 24. Besides the commentaries see Cousland 2002, 227-39.

are not true followers of Jesus who are committed to being his disciples, but neither are they like the Pharisees and scribes who reject him. They know that he is a prophet, and they ask themselves, at least on one occasion, whether he might be the Messiah. In Jerusalem they watch as Jesus is put on trial, manipulated by their leaders. The crowds stand between agreement and mistrust, between acceptance and rejection—they are the "lost sheep of the house of Israel" (Mt 10:6). This is the reason why Jesus has compassion on them.

The Christian communities that read the Gospel in a post-Easter situation learn from the evangelists' presentation of the crowds at least two lessons.[181] First, as Jesus extended his compassion to the crowds, Christians should receive all the curious, the neutral and the skeptical people whom they encounter in their everyday lives with similar compassion. It was Jesus who sent the disciples to the crowds that pressed around (Mt 9:35-38) in order to preach and heal people (Mt 10:1, 7-8). Second, just as the crowds reacted negatively to Jesus' ministry, so also Christians will experience rejection (Mt 5:10-12; 10:16-25; 13:3-9; 24:9-14), which is the reason why their own ministry must be faithful and steadfast (Mt 24:36—25:46). The people in the crowds often reacted positively, however, which means that the churches and their missionaries may also expect and hope for positive reactions.

The Gospel writers do not mention specific names of persons in the crowds, but nevertheless the "crowds" are not simply a foil for Jesus' ministry. The crowds are the target of Jesus' preaching. Hans Bietenhard observes that "it is especially to these people, who have nothing particular to offer, that Jesus directs his teaching and his compassion (Matt. 9:33)," in contrast to the Pharisees and the scribes "who despise the *ochlos* as the ignorant masses who did not keep the law" (Jn 7:48-49).[182]

Conversations with Individuals

Whereas Matthew, Mark and Luke depict Jesus, nearly exclusively, speaking to groups of people, John relates several conversations of Jesus with individuals. The conversations with Nicodemus in Jerusalem (Jn 3:1-21) and with the Samaritan women at Jacob's well (Jn 4:1-26) are prime examples.

Not many scholars see the narrative of Jn 4 having any historical value. If Jürgen Zangenberg is correct in his assumption that the Gospel of John cannot be read as a direct source about the Samaritans in the first century, then the narrative in Jn 4, of course, does not inform the reader about a conversation that Jesus had with a Samaritan woman. Zangenberg suggests that the author wanted to convince his readers "that a particular group of Samaritans near Sychar, with whom the Johannine community had come into contact," had become committed Christians and that "their independent missionary activity after their conversion to the Christian faith among their countrymen was a legitimate mission."[183] He believes that the evangelist portrays "the plea for accepting the Samaritan

---

[181]Carter 1993, 65-66; see also Cousland 2002, esp. 302.
[182]H. Bietenhard, *ThBLNT* 2:1819-20 (*NIDNTT* 2:800).

Christian church at Sychar as an event in Jesus' life," but he does not want to exclude the possibility that the narrative is based on "knowledge about actual contacts that Jesus had with Samaritans." Scholars who think it impossible that Jesus could have had a conversation such as John narrates in Jn 4 have to postulate an anonymous missionary at the end of the first century who was capable of brilliant, rhetorically flexible and theologically creative conversations with unbelievers.

Several scholars apply the categories of communication theory to the conversation in Jn 4.

Jean-Marc Chappuis[184] finds in Jn 4:1-26 eight types of communication: (1) everyday communication ("Give me a drink!"); (2) impossible communication ("How is it that you, a Jew, ask a drink of me, a woman of Samaria?"); (3) verbal communication ("If you knew the gift of God"), (4) dialogical communication ("Jesus answered . . . the woman said to him"); (5) poetic communication ("living water"), (6) existential communication ("Go, call your husband, and come back"); (7) theological communication ("Salvation is from the Jews. . . . I am he, the one who is speaking to you"); (8) narrative communication ("Come and see a man who told me everything I have ever done").

An interpretation of Jn 4:1-26 using insights of conversation research, a branch of communication theory, helps to identify the following strategies in the conversation.[185]

1. Jesus begins the conversation despite major obstacles. When Jesus met the woman at the well, he faced a fivefold challenge that required ignoring social taboos and personal barriers if a conversation was to ensue. (a) The conversation partner was a woman. It was much easier for a Jewish male in the first century to speak with a man than to speak with a woman, particularly a woman who was a stranger. (b) The woman presumably was uneducated. It was more attractive for a rabbi to converse with a Torah expert, such as Nicodemus, than to speak with an illiterate woman. (c) The woman had a questionable reputation, which could well have been deduced from the fact that she came to the well alone at the hottest time of the day. Pious Jewish men were well advised to speak only with people who were not morally suspect. (d) The woman was a Samaritan. It was much easier for a Jew to talk with a fellow Jew than to speak with a Samaritan. (e) The woman appeared at the well at the hottest time of day, and Jesus was tired. It would have been understandable for a tired man not to speak with a woman about questions of faith and practice at all in this situation. If Jesus wanted to begin a conversation, he would have to break cultural norms. And if he wanted to talk with this Samaritan woman about his mission, and thus about himself, he would have to overcome theological barriers.

---

[183]Zangenberg 1998, 193; the quotation that follows above, ibid., 195.
[184]Chappuis 1982; cf. Ritt 1989, 288 n. 5.
[185]For the discussion that follows above see the helpful analyses in Okure 1988; Cotterell and Turner 1989, 276-78.

2. The primary missionary characteristic of the conversation between Jesus and the Samaritan woman is Jesus' dependence upon the woman. Jesus brings God's revelation, but he allows the woman to determine the course of the conversation.

4:8   Jesus: asks the woman to give him a drink from the well
         Subject: water
4:9   Woman: speaks about Jesus' Jewish identity; her own Samaritan identity
         New subject: historical and social problems; Jesus as Jew
4:10   Jesus: gift of God; "who it is that is saying to you"; living water
         Subject: Jesus' identity; Jesus accepts her intervention: if she knew who
         he was!
4:11-12 Woman: bucket to draw water; well; living water; ancestor Jacob
         New subject: the well and its tradition
4:13-14 Jesus: water from this well
         Subject: well; water; Jesus accepts the change of subject, speaks of the
         well's water
4:15   Woman: physical thirst
         New subject: her thirst; the advantage of not having to come to the well
         any more
4:16-18 Jesus: "Go, call your husband"
         Subject: personal situation of the woman; Jesus accepts the turn to per-
         sonal issues unwittingly prompted by the woman
4:19-20 Woman: prophet; ancestors; worship on Mount Gerizim; worship in
         Jerusalem
         New subject: Jesus' identity as prophet; dispute between Jews and Sa-
         maritans
4:21-24 Jesus: Jerusalem is the legitimate place of worship; the new worship of
         the future; Jesus again accepts the change of subject
4:25   Woman: the messiah who will reveal the full truth
         Subject: the woman introduces the subject "messiah"
4:26   Jesus: "I am he, the one who is speaking to you"
         Self-revelation as the Messiah

The woman determines the form in which Jesus conveys the good news. The woman, in other words, determines not only the course of the conversation but also the linguistic categories by which Jesus expresses his message. Jesus takes her interventions seriously and uses them as opportunities to convey his message in the context of her particular situation and against the background of her interests and concerns. He uses "her" language to formulate his message.

4:7-10   draw water   ⇒ the gift of God as living water
4:11-14 Jacob's well   ⇒ water that can quench thirst once
                                and for all

4:15	drudgery of fetching water	⇒ basic problem of the woman
4:16	problem of isolation	⇒ basic problem of the woman
4:17-18	marriage situation	⇒ full truth about the situation
4:19-20	Gerizim/Jerusalem	⇒ irrelevant distinction in the messianic age
4:25	the coming messiah	⇒ self-revelation of Jesus

3. Jesus takes the "linguistic incompetence" of the woman into consideration: he is willing to risk misunderstanding. When he speaks of "living water" (Jn 4:10), the women speaks of a bucket that Jesus does not have. When Jesus speaks of "water" that can quench any thirst forever (Jn 4:14), she responds, sarcastically, by speaking of magic water. Jesus considers it more important, for the time being, to interact with the concerns of the woman than to clarify misunderstandings.

The misunderstandings of the woman demonstrate the formidable difficulties in the communication of divine revelation in words intelligible to human beings. The question of which topics are addressed depends on the linguistic competence of the dialogue partner(s). Some topics are treated with the help of paraphrases and analogies, as a concession to the assumed linguistic lack of competence. With Nicodemus, Jesus could discuss "the new birth from water and the spirit," the promised messianic-eschatological transformation of humankind (Jer 31; Ezek 36—37), the difference between flesh and spirit, the Son of Man descending from heaven (Dan 7:13), the "lifting up" of the bronze serpent by Moses (Num 21:8-9). Even though Nicodemus did not understand what Jesus was talking about, Jesus insisted that he should be able to understand (Jn 3:10).

4. Jesus interacts with the woman as an individual. The woman thinks and speaks in general categories: she talks about Jews and Samaritans (Jn 4:9), about Jacob and his sons (Jn 4:12), about the ancestors (Jn 4:20), about the messiah who will proclaim all things to "us" (Jn 4:25). Jesus is personal, willing to address the woman's core problem: "If you knew the gift of God" (Jn 4:10a), "Go, call your husband, and come back" (Jn 4:16), "You are right in saying, 'I have no husband'" (Jn 4:17b), "You have had five husbands, and the one you have now is not your husband" (Jn 4:18a), "What you have said is true!" (Jn 4:18b), "Woman, believe me" (Jn 4:21), "I am he, the one who is speaking to you" (Jn 4:26). Jesus does not use the woman as a foil for his teaching. His message is "universal," but he patiently accepts the interventions of the women, the abrupt changes of subject; he is willing to speak about the personal situation of the woman. He accepts the risk of misunderstandings because the conversation partner is, as a person, important to him. This explains, for example, why he does not clarify right from the beginning the misunderstanding on the part of the woman that he, being a Jew, should be afraid of contracting ritual uncleanness as a result of his contact with her, a Samaritan woman. He could have pointed out that he has no reason to fear uncleanness, and he could have told her that everybody who comes into contact with him,

believing his message, becomes clean.

5. Jesus leads the woman through a process of recognition and perception. (a) He eventually shows the woman her real needs. Even here Jesus uses formulations that the woman is familiar with in order to lead her to the knowledge of spiritual truth. He speaks of living water (Jn 4:10), of eternal life (Jn 4:14), of the true place of worship (Jn 4:21), of the fact that salvation is from the Jews (Jn 4:22), of true worship (Jn 4:23). (b) Jesus reminds the woman of the sad reality of her life. He does not gloss over her failures, but he does address the subject in a cautious and restrained manner. The fact that the woman came to the well alone, at the hottest time of the day, is abnormal. The woman must have expected that the man sitting at the well would comment on this (if he, obviously a Jew, would even address her, a Samaritan). Jesus, however, does not refer to her strange behavior at all. He asks for water, which in the context of the encounter at the well is an entirely normal opening. But the subject of her personal situation that causes her abnormal behavior during the noon hour of a hot day is present in the background. The introduction of the subject "husband" (Jn 4:16) is therefore not as abrupt as it may seem: her personal situation was a possible topic of conversation right from the beginning because her unusual behavior signaled social isolation. Jesus displays supernatural knowledge (Jn 4:17b-18), but he does not place himself in the center: he seeks to help the woman understand the character of the gift that he has to offer her. The introduction of the subject "worship" (Jn 4:21-22) also is not as abrupt as it may seem: it is implied in the description of Jesus as a prophet who has special knowledge (Jn 4:19-20). (c) Jesus shows the woman who he is. However, he does not blurt out that he is the messianic Son of Man who brings the kingdom of God. He reveals himself in categories that she can understand: he speaks of Jacob's well as a source of water (Jn 4:6-7), of himself as a gift of God (Jn 4:10), of a spring of water in terms of eternal life (Jn 4:14); he reveals himself as a prophet (Jn 4:19), he speaks of the new worship of God in spirit and in truth (Jn 4:23). It is only when the woman speaks of the messiah who is to come that he reveals himself as the Messiah (Jn 4:26). Both the well and Jacob the ancestor are important to the woman, and this is what Jesus utilizes in the conversation. When necessary he "commands" ("Go, call your husband, and come back"), but then he allows the woman to "lead" again, with the goal of helping her to discover the knowledge that will provide true life (Jn 4:10, 26).

6. Jesus provokes curiosity. (a) He makes the woman curious. The process of self-knowledge is supported by the growing curiosity of the woman, who, at the end of the conversation, must have stood open-mouthed at the well (Jn 4:9, 11, 15, 19, 25). (b) Jesus violates the "principle of contextuality": he makes himself dependent upon the woman (as a male), and he accepts her interventions (as a rabbi). He does not behave in conformity with the woman's expectations (Jn 4:16, 18, 26). (c) Dialogue (Jn 4:7-25) precedes "dogma" (Jn 4:26). Jesus does

not suppress the "dogmatic" assertion of Jn 4:26, but he does wait for the optimal time to make it. (d) Jesus has patience; he waits with his self-revelation (Jn 4:26). He does not simply deliver theological truth to the woman, expecting her to somehow deal with it. The process of finding faith is not cheap: even after the woman asks for eternal (magic) water (Jn 4:15), Jesus does not yet explain what he meant when he spoke of "living water" (Jn 4:10, 13-14) and in what sense this is "the gift of God" (Jn 4:10). He first engages the basic problem of the woman (Jn 4:16-18).

The Focus on Galilee

Jesus concentrated his ministry of preaching, teaching and healing in Galilee. The authors of the first three Gospels state this focus unequivocally, and John implies it as well.

Mt 4:23: "Jesus went throughout Galilee, teaching in their synagogues and proclaiming the good news of the kingdom and curing every disease and every sickness among the people."

Mk 1:39: "And he went throughout Galilee, proclaiming the message in their synagogues and casting out demons."

Lk 4:14-15: "Then Jesus, filled with the power of the Spirit, returned to Galilee, and a report about him spread through all the surrounding country. [15] He began to teach in their synagogues and was praised by everyone."

For John see Jn 1:43; 2:1, 11; 4:3, 43, 45-47, 54; 7:1, 9, 41, 52.

Referring to Mt 11:21-24/Lk 10:13-15, scholars often point to three towns on the northwestern shore of the Sea of Galilee as the crucial centers of Jesus' preaching ministry: Chorazin, Bethsaida and Capernaum. However, the summary statements in Mt 4:23; Mk 1:39; Lk 4:14-15 demonstrate that Jesus preached "throughout Galilee." The comment that Jesus traveled "to the district/region of Tyre and Sidon" (Mt 15:21; Mk 7:24 [RSV]) indicates that Jesus not only visited towns and villages in Lower Galilee but also that he preached in Upper Galilee.[186] If Jesus spent two days in each of the 138 settlements of Galilee that Mordechai Aviam mentions,[187] he would have needed 276 days, or 46 weeks (not counting the sabbath days), to reach every single Galilean town and village—not an impossible task in view of the three years of Jesus' public ministry.

Jesus' concentration on Galilee can be interpreted as symbolic messianic action Matthew refers to Is 9:1-2 to explain Jesus' ministry in Galilee (Mt 4:14-16).

Is 9:1-2 (Heb. and LXX, 8:23—9:1): "Nevertheless, there will be no more gloom for those

---

[186]See Meyers 1997, 59.
[187]M. Aviam, *NEAEHL* 2:455.

who were in distress. In the past he humbled the land of Zebulun and the land of Naphtali, but in the future he will honor Galilee of the Gentiles [גְּלִיל הַגּוֹיִם; LXX: Γαλιλαία τῶν ἐθνῶν], by the way of the sea, along the Jordan]. ²The people walking in darkness [בַּחֹשֶׁךְ הָעָם הַהֹלְכִים; LXX: ὁ λαὸς ὁ πορευόμενος ἐν σκότει] have seen a great light; on those living in the land of the shadow of death [יֹשְׁבֵי בְּאֶרֶץ צַלְמָוֶת; LXX: οἱ κατοικοῦντες ἐν χώρᾳ καὶ σκιᾷ θανάτου] a light has dawned." (NIV)

Matthew's quotation corresponds exactly to neither the Greek nor the Hebrew text but is closest to the Hebrew (Masoretic) text. The condensation of the Isaiah passage in the original wording focuses the attention on the geographical references to Zebulun, Naphtali, the area beyond the Jordan River and Galilee, as well as on the second part of the quotation in Is 9:2.[188] The southern borders of the tribal area of Zebulun (Josh 19:10-16) were marked by the river Kishon (in the Jezreel Valley), the eastern borders were marked by the heights of Mount Tabor, and in the north Zebulun reached probably as far as the extension of the northern end of the Sea of Galilee; in other words, Zebulun encompassed southwestern Galilee, including the town of Nazareth. Naphtali occupied the territory of the northern regions of Israel to the west of the Sea of Galilee, from Mount Tabor in the south far to the north (Josh 19:32-39), thus encompassing eastern and northern (Upper) Galilee, including Capernaum.

We do not know whether Is 9:1-2 was interpreted in a messianic sense by the scribes of the Second Temple period. Scholars agree, however, that many Jewish circles expected the dawn of the eschaton from "Hermon"—that is, from the north, where the fateful devastation of Israel had begun. Zebulun and Naphtali were among the first tribes forced into exile and deported after the Assyrian king Tiglath-Pileser had conquered the cities of this region as well as "Gilead and Galilee, including all the land of Naphtali" (2 Kings 15:29). In the larger context of Is 7:1—9:7 the prophet addresses the rejection of God's promise by the royal house of David and the devastation of the people of God in the Syro-Ephraimite crisis that resulted from the obstinacy of the people; he addresses the hopes for a faithful remnant, the hopes for the prophetic sign of the child, the son Emmanuel (Is 7:14), who would come in the hour of Israel's deepest humiliation to establish the eternal and righteous rule of Yahweh, and he addresses the hopes for the beginning of Yahweh's messianic rule in Israel.[189]

Matthew interprets Jesus' public ministry in Galilee as fulfillment of this Isaianic prophecy. It was Jesus himself, however, who implied, albeit indirectly, a messianic claim by concentrating his ministry on Galilee.[190] The "Galilee of the Gentiles"—the Galilee surrounded by Gentile peoples, the Galilee in which Gentiles live,[191] the Galilee of Isaiah's promise—becomes, paradoxically, the

---

[188]See Luz, *Mt*, 1:69; Davies and Allison, *Mt*, 1:380-86.
[189]See Childs, *Is*, 60-81.
[190]See Riesner 1987; 2002, 83-132; idem, "Galiläa," *GBL* 1:407; idem, "Galilee," *DJG* 253.
[191]See Judg 18:7, 28 (period of the judges); 2 Kings 15:29; 17:24-27 (period after the deportation of the population of the northern kingdom); 1 Macc 5 (second century B.C.); see also Strabo

land of fulfillment: the "great light" of Yahweh's messianic revelation shines not on Mount Zion in Jerusalem but in the villages and towns of Galilee.

The Success

The Gospel writers use summaries to note the supraregional fame and reputation of Jesus, who was known not only in Galilee and Judea but also in all the surrounding regions of the Near East, including Idumea in the south, Perea, Batanea and the Decapolis in the east, as well as Syria with Tyre and Sidon in the north.

Mt 4:24-25: "So his fame spread throughout all Syria, and they brought to him all the sick, those who were afflicted with various diseases and pains, demoniacs, epileptics, and paralytics, and he cured them. [25]And great crowds followed him from Galilee, the Decapolis, Jerusalem, Judea, and from beyond the Jordan."

Mk 3:7-8: "Jesus departed with his disciples to the sea, and a great multitude from Galilee followed him; [8]hearing all that he was doing, they came to him in great numbers from Judea, Jerusalem, Idumea, beyond the Jordan, and the region around Tyre and Sidon."

Lk 6:17-19: "He came down with them and stood on a level place, with a great crowd of his disciples and a great multitude of people from all Judea, Jerusalem, and the coast of Tyre and Sidon. [18]They had come to hear him and to be healed of their diseases; and those who were troubled with unclean spirits were cured. [19]And all in the crowd were trying to touch him, for power came out from him and healed all of them."

The region "beyond the Jordan" (πέραν τοῦ Ἰορδάνου [Mk 3:8]) refers to the territory east of the Jordan River, to Perea or to Batanea.[192] In the first century Perea was Jewish[193] and belonged to the territory of Herod Antipas. The other geographical terms will be explained later (§12.1).

The So-called Galilean Crisis

Some scholars assume a crisis in Jesus' ministry caused by the fact that Jesus realized after some time that his preaching did not lead to the conversion of the populace on a large scale. The initial "spring" of his early successes was soon replaced with disillusionment. As a result, supposedly, Jesus announced God's judgment on the main centers of his missionary activity: Capernaum, Chorazin, Bethsaida (Mt 11:21-24; Lk 10:13-15).

(16.2.34), who speaks of Egyptians, Arabs, Phoenicians and Greeks living in Galilee. Cf. Davies and Allison, *Mt,* 1:383.

[192]The tribal areas of Gad and Reuben (Gilead); see G. Schneider, *EWNT* 2:467 (*EDNT* 2:191). See, however, Riesner 2002, 65-70; idem, *GBL* 2:736; idem, "Betanien II," *GBL* 1:193; Riesner interprets in terms of Batanea: he takes the second καί in Mt 19:1 as explicative (cf. BDAG 495, s.v. "καί 1c"): "Jesus came to Judea, *viz.* (the area) beyond the Jordan" (see Riesner 2002, 66).

[193]See Schürer 2:12-13.

Mt 11:21-24: "Woe to you, Chorazin! Woe to you, Bethsaida! For if the deeds of power done in you had been done in Tyre and Sidon, they would have repented long ago in sackcloth and ashes. [22]But I tell you, on the day of judgment it will be more tolerable for Tyre and Sidon than for you. [23]And you, Capernaum, will you be exalted to heaven? No, you will be brought down to Hades. For if the deeds of power done in you had been done in Sodom, it would have remained until this day. [24]But I tell you that on the day of judgment it will be more tolerable for the land of Sodom than for you."

Jesus sensed toward the end of his ministry, some scholars argue, that the crowds that had followed him increasingly rejected him. For this reason, and in order to evade Herod Antipas, who plotted his arrest, Jesus left Galilee and moved to the border regions of Gaulanitis, Batanea and the Decapolis.[194] The statement in Jn 6:66 plays an important role in this scenario: "Because of this many of his disciples turned back and no longer went about with him."

The hypothesis of a Galilean crisis has few advocates today,[195] not least because it cannot explain the efforts of the high priests and the scribes to eliminate Jesus on account of the accusation that he puts the peace of the nation at risk and that he seduces the people.[196]

9.3 Ministry in Batanea and Gaulanitis

Jesus traveled repeatedly in the regions of Batanea and Gaulanitis, the areas east of the Jordan River that belonged to the tetrarchy of Herod Philip.[197] The Gospel writers mention two towns for this area in which Jesus spent time: Bethsaida and Caesarea Philippi. The comment in Jn 10:40-42 that Jesus preached and healed in Bethany "across the Jordan" seems to understand "Bethany" to refer to Batanea.[198]

Jesus in Bethsaida

John (Jn 12:21) and Pliny (*Nat.* 5.15.71) locate Bethsaida (Julias) in Galilee, which is a somewhat informal localization because Galilee ended at the Jordan River; Bethsaida actually was situated in the region of Batanea. The town of Bethsaida is mentioned, without geographical comment, in Mt 11:20-21; Mk 8:22; Lk 9:10; Jn 1:44. The ministry in Batanea followed a tense situation in Galilee, where Jesus was threatened with arrest. It appears that he stayed in this region "beyond the Jordan" for a longer period: he "remained there" (ἔμεινεν ἐκεῖ

---

[194]See Dodd 1963, 222; Mussner 1973, 238-52; Riesner 1988, 476; idem, *GBL* 1:407; idem, *DJG* 253.
[195]See the critique in Bornkamm 1995; Meier 1991-2001, 3:25-26, 36-37; cf. McKnight 2001, 224 n. 63.
[196]See Mt 27:11-14; Mk 15:2-5; Lk 23:2-3; Jn 18:29-31.
[197]On Gaulanitis see T. Longstaff, *ABD* 2:911; Urman 1995, 379-85; idem, *EAEHL* 2:456-67.
[198]See Riesner 1987; accepted by Pixner (1994, 159-79); Appold 1995b, 395 n. 33; cf. now Riesner 2002, esp. 57-82.

[Jn 10:40]). Although an older generation of scholars believed that Bethsaida was a small village at Jesus' time, excavations have confirmed that it was an up-and-coming town whose infrastructure continued to be developed. In A.D. 30 Herod Philip officially granted Bethsaida the status of a city.

Bethsaida (Βηθσαϊδά; et-Tell; near mod. el-Amiriyye)[199] was situated in Gaulanitis at the northern end of the Sea of Galilee, about 250 m east of the Jordan River. Since a landslide in A.D. 363, the site is about 2 km removed from the lake. New geomorphological studies have shown that Bethsaida had a direct link to the lake in the first century.[200] Bethsaida, possibly the capital of the Geshurites,[201] dates back to 1500 B.C. In the Hellenistic and early Roman periods Bethsaida was a rather modest settlement whose population subsisted from fishing the lake. A house dating to this period that was discovered in the northern part of town is known as "the house of the fisherman."[202] The house (18 by 27 m [see fig. 4]) was built around an open courtyard, with three rooms on the northern end, one room at the western end (probably with a stairway) and a sizable kitchen at the eastern end of the courtyard. About one hundred fishing implements were found in the house, including lead and basalt weights for nets, fishing hooks, bronze and iron needles for repair work, and anchors.[203] Herod Philip, who resided in the neighboring town of Caesarea Philippi, granted Bethsaida city rights, probably on September 1, A.D. 30 (six months after Jesus' crucifixion) and named it Julias in honor of Livia Julia, the wife of Caesar Augustus.[204] This measure probably should be seen in connection with the support for the imperial cult in the region. It is uncertain whether the large building in the southern part of the city represented a Roman (imperial) temple.[205] The fact that Bethsaida is called a city (πόλις) in Mt 11:20-21; Lk 9:10; Jn 1:44, and a village (κώμη) in Mk 8:23, 26, can thus be explained on the basis of the history of the place. It is a plausible assumption that the infrastructure of Bethsaida was expanded and developed in the years before this turning point in its history. Josephus informs us that Bethsaida had a large population as well as fortifications, with military posted in the city (δύναμις [*A.J.* 18.28]). Both Pliny (*Nat.* 5.15.71) and Ptolemaios (*Geogr.* 5.15.3) know Bethsaida. The comment in Mk 8:22 seems to imply that Bethsaida was linked with Caesarea Philippi by a road. Possibly, Herod Philip minted coins not only in Caesarea Philippi but also in Bethsaida.[206] When Herod Philip died in A.D. 33, he was buried in Bethsaida (Josephus, *A.J.* 18.108).

---

[199]Benzinger, PW 3 (1899): 365-66; R. Riesner, *GBL* 1:197-98; R. H. Mounce, *ISBE* 1:475; J. F. Strange, *ABD* 1:692-93; C. Colpe, *DNP* 2:596-97; Urman 1995, 519-27; Pixner 1994, 127-41; especially Arav and Freund 1995-1999 (with reports of the excavations since 1988); R. Arav, "Bethsaida" [Hebrew] *Qadmoniot* 32 (1999): 78-91. See the website of the Bethsaida Excavations Project: <http://lisa.unomaha.edu/ips/bethsaida/bethsaida.html>.

[200]J. F. Shroder et al., in Arav and Freund 1995-1999, 1:65-98; 2:115-73.

[201]Thus J. T. Greene, in Arav and Freund 1995-1999, 1:223; R. Arav, in ibid., 2:107.

[202]R. Arav, in Arav and Freund 1995-1999, 1:3-63, esp. 22-23, 26-28.

[203]See Sandra Fortner, "Fishing Implements and Maritime Activities," in Arav and Freund 1995-1999, 2:269-80.

[204]The name "Julias" does not refer to Julia, Augustus's daughter, as Josephus assumes (*A.J.* 18.28); see Strickert, 1995, esp. 183-84; J. T. Greene, "The Honorific Naming of Bethsaida-Julias," in Arav and Freund 1995-1999, 2:307-31; M. D. Smith, "A Tale of Two Julias: Julia, Julias, and Josephus," in ibid., 2:333-46.

[205]See Arav, in Arav and Freund 1995-1999, 1:21; idem, in ibid., 2:18-24.

[206]So Strickert 1995, 185.

Bethany "beyond the Jordan" (Jn 1:28) possibly refers to the region of Batanea, the Bashan of Old Testament times.[207] This was the area "beyond the Jordan" in which John the Baptist had preached and baptized, and in which Jesus called his first disciples from the followers of John and his revival movement began (Jn 1:35-51).

Bethsaida was the hometown of three of Jesus' disciples: Philip, Andrew and Peter (Jn 1:44; cf. 12:21). According to Mk 1:29, Andrew and Peter lived in Capernaum. There is no reason to doubt the geographical comment in Jn 1:44 that "shows precise knowledge" concerning the background of these three disciples,[208] who evidently moved to Capernaum at the western shore of the lake at some point.

Jesus healed a blind man in Bethsaida (Mk 8:22-26). Jesus' charge to the healed man not to go into the town (Mk 8:26) is not a command to keep the miracle secret:[209] Jesus expects the man to go back to his house (εἰς οἶκον αὐτοῦ) and that he will no longer beg in the marketplace of the town.[210] The parallel statement in Mk 2:11-12 helps us to understand Mk 8:26: the lame man who was healed in Capernaum is also sent home by Jesus (ὕπαγε εἰς τὸν οἶκόν σου); he took his stretcher and walked out "in full view of them all" (TNIV), thus demonstrating publicly that a miracle had taken place, which prompted everyone present to be amazed and to praise God. Similarly, the healed blind man in Mk 8:26 can walk home alone: he no longer needs the people who brought him from the marketplace to Jesus.

The miraculous feeding of five thousand people took place, according to Lk 9:10, in the vicinity of Bethsaida. Jesus is said to have withdrawn, with his disciples, "privately to a city called Bethsaida."[211] This formulation may simply refer to the surrounding territory of Bethsaida: in Lk 8:26, 34 Luke also describes a city as the center of a larger region.[212] In Mk 6:31-32 and Mt 14:13 the miracle is located at a "deserted place" (*erēmos topos*).

Since the parallel accounts in Mk 6:32-44, Mt 14:13-21 and Jn 6:1-13 do not mention Bethsaida, many scholars regard the localization in Lk 9:10 as redactional.[213] The information provided by Mk 6:45—Jesus directs the disciples after the feeding miracle to get

---

[207]R. Riesner 2002, 57-82, idem, *GBL* 1:193-94.

[208]Schnackenburg, *Joh,* 1:313 (ET, 1:314). Later tradition claims that John and James, the sons of Zebedee, also hailed from Bethsaida. See Baldi 1955, 266.

[209]Cf. the strongly worded commands in Mk 5:43; 7:36.

[210]Gundry, *Mk,* 419; for the observation that follows above see ibid. Differently Pesch (*Mk,* 1:419-20), who suggests that the "strangely specific" formulation of the command to keep silent makes sense only if the blind man did not live in the village (Bethsaida) but was brought to Jesus at Bethsaida from another town.

[211]Lk 9:10: ὑπεχώρησεν κατ᾽ ἰδίαν εἰς πόλιν καλουμένην Βηθσαϊδά. The preposition εἰς indicates perhaps "the direction, not the place of destination" (Bovon, *Lk,* 1:468).

[212]Green, *Lk,* 363 n. 30; cf. Marshall, *Lk,* 359.

[213]See Nolland, *Lk,* 1:440; Bovon, *Lk,* 1:468.

into the boat and go ahead of him to Bethsaida—already prompted early copyists to change the text, as the omission in P[45] shows. A localization of the miracle in the vicinity of Bethsaida, rather than in the city itself, solves the problem. The account in Jn 6:1-13 does not mention Bethsaida but assumes for Philip, who hails from Bethsaida (Jn 1:44), local geographical knowledge: Jesus asks Philip, "Where are we to buy bread for these people to eat?" (Jn 6:5). The comment that Jesus traveled from Capernaum with a boat "to the other side of the Sea of Galilee" (Jn 6:1), followed by a large crowd of people who evidently walked (Jn 6:2), fits the topographical situation at the northern part of the lake in the vicinity of Bethsaida.[214]

Jesus' activity in Batanea prompted many (πολλοί) who had heard John the Baptist preach and who had waited for the arrival of the messiah to come to faith in Jesus (Jn 10:41-42). His preaching in Bethsaida itself, however, evidently encountered strong opposition: Jesus announced judgment of Bethsaida for lack of faith (Mt 11:21; Lk 10:31). This pronouncement and the history behind it were perhaps linked with the development of Bethsaida toward becoming a polis: the "secular" progress of the town stands in contrast to Jesus' message of a kingdom that is "not of this world" (Jn 18:36).[215]

Jesus in Caesarea Philippi

Caesarea Philippi also was situated east of the Jordan River. It is mentioned in Mt 16:13/Mk 8:27 as a city in whose territory Jesus preached—that is, he visited villages that were controlled by Caesarea Philippi.

Caesarea Philippi (Καισαρεῖα ἡ Φιλίππου; Kaisareia Paneas; Banias)[216] was located 40 km north of the Sea of Galilee at the southwestern foot of Mount Hermon. In the Hellenistic period the town was called Panion, named after a source and grotto dedicated to Pan, the god of nature. The cult of Pan was part of the dynastic Dionysos cult of the Ptolemies. The site is first mentioned in connection with the battle around 200 B.C. in which the Seleucid king Antiochos III was victorious against the Egyptian general Scopas, thus establishing Seleucid rule in Palestine (Polybius 16.18.2; 28.1.3). After the death of Lysanias, the king of Iturea, the area came under the control of Herod I around 20 B.C. (Strabo 16.2.10). Josephus knew that Herod built a temple dedicated to Caesar Augustus (11.5 by 18 m) in Paneas on the occasion of Augustus's visit to the region when he gave this area to Herod (A.J. 15.363; B.J. 1.404). The coins of Herod Philip that depict the Herodian Augusteum indicate that it was a tetrastyle temple with four Ionian columns standing on a raised platform. Herod Philip, tetrarch since 4 B.C. in northeast-

---

[214]H-W. Kuhn (1995, 246-48) is not convinced, however; he argues that the localization in Lk 9:10 is due to Luke's omission of Mk 6:45—8:26 (note that Mk 6:45 and 8:22 mention Bethsaida). Other scholars are not so skeptical, see Bock, *Lk,* 1:828-29.

[215]M. D. Smith, in Arav and Freund 1995-1999, 2:342.

[216]Benzinger, "Caesarea Nr. 9," PW 3 (1899): 1291-92; G. Hölscher, PW 13.3 (1949): 594-600; C. Colpe, "Caesarea 2," *KP* 1:1004; J.-P. Rey-Coquais, "Paneas," *PECS* 670; John Kutsko, *ABD* 1:803; Z. U. Maoz, "Banias," *NEAEHL* 1:136-43; Moors 1992, 211-17; Strickert 1995, 167; Urman 1995, 389-90. See <http://www.pepperdine.edu/seaver/religion/isar/Banias/baniasgallery.htm>.

ern Palestine in Gaulanitis, Trachonitis, Hauran and Batanea, recognized the significance of this temple; in 2 B.C. he erected south of the sources of the Jordan River the
polis Caesarea, named in honor of Caesar Augustus; in order to distinguish the city from
Caesarea on the Mediterranean, the city was named Caesarea Philippi. Later, the city
was called Caesarea Panias (Ptolemaios, *Geogr.* 5.15.21). The Roman road from Tyre to
Damascus ran right through the Roman city center (300 by 300 m). East of the Augusteum was a temple dedicated to Pan and the nymphs (18 by 15 m), whose beginnings
date back to the first century A.D. The marble of the twenty-eight sculptures that can be
reconstructed, dating to A.D. 50-400, was imported from marble quarries in Asia Minor.[217] West of the temple of Pan, on a large terrace (20 by 120 m), presumably stood
the royal palace that evidently was built by Italian stone masons whom Marcus Agrippa
had provided for Herod Philip. After the latter's death in A.D. 34, the city came under
direct Roman control within the province of Syria. The territory of Caesarea Philippi bordered in the west on the territories of Sidon and Tyre, and in the east probably on the
territory of Damascus; several villages on the Golan belonged to Panias-Caesarea. After
the brief interregnum of Herod Agrippa I in A.D. 37-44, the city was ruled after A.D. 53
by Agrippa II, who refounded the city as Neronias in A.D. 61; he controlled the city until
his death in A.D. 92/93. During the Jewish revolt against Rome both Vespasian and Titus
visited the city; after A.D. 70 numerous Jewish prisoners died in animal fights and gladiator games (Josephus, *B.J.* 7.23-24). In the first century A.D. Caesarea Philippi was
largely a pagan city, with Itureans and Phoenicians as the major ethnic groups among
the population. Varus, the local strategos at the beginning of the Jewish revolt, had the
Jewish population massacred (Josephus, *Vita* 51-61, 74). Some scholars[218] conclude
from Mt 16:13/Mk 8:27 that Jews lived in the villages that belonged to the territory of
Caesarea Philippi. Pagan traditions were alive and well in the city for a long time: in the
second century another temple (11 by 13 m) was built east of the temple of Pan, and
an inscription of A.D. 221 identifies a *cheresterion* (dream oracle) in the city. Since 1988
systematic excavations have been carried out.

According to an old tradition, the first bishop of the church in Caesarea Philippi was
a contemporary of the apostle Paul. In A.D. 325 the bishop Philokalos represented the
church of the city at the Council of Nicea.

The Gospel writers do not comment on the success of Jesus' ministry in Caesarea Philippi with regard to his preaching either in the villages of the city (Mk
8:27: κῶμαι) or in the district (Mt 16:13: τὰ μέρη). They refer to Caesarea Philippi in order to locate the messianic confession of Peter in this region.[219]

Jesus in the Decapolis

In the Decapolis, Jews lived not only in the villages but also in the towns. Studies in the manufacture of and trade in oil lamps in the Roman period have
shown that Jewish lamps (e.g., the Darom lamp) were found in all cities of the
Decapolis as far as Pella. This confirms a brisk trade between Galilee and the

---

[217]See Elise A. Friedland, "Graeco-Roman Sculpture in the Levant: The Marbles from the Sanctuary of Pan at Casearea Philippi (Banias)," in Humphrey 1995-2002, 2:7-22.
[218]See Maoz, "Banias," *NEAEHL* 1:138.
[219]Mt 16:13-20/Mk 8:27-30; cf. Lk 9:18-21.

Decapolis.[220] Mark's comment that Jesus traveled to the Decapolis (Mk 7:31) thus reflects not simply a "Markan perspective" but the historical reality in the first century.[221] According to Mt 4:25, many people from the Decapolis flocked to Jesus, who healed a demon-possessed man in the region of Hippos on the eastern shore of the Sea of Galilee.[222]

The localization of this healing miracle is uncertain, as the tradition of the various readings in the Greek manuscript tradition is difficult to interpret. The Greek manuscripts mention, in all three parallel accounts, three places: Gadara, Gerasa, Gergesa. The cities Gadara and Gerasa belong to the Decapolis: Gadara is located 10 km southeast of the Sea of Galilee, Gerasa 60 km southeast of the Sea of Galilee. Most scholars assume that Mk 5:1 and Lk 8:26 originally had "Gerasa," whereas Mt 8:26 located the healing in Gadara.[223]

Gadara (mod. Umm Qeis),[224] the capital of a toparchy, possibly extended as far as the Sea of Galilee: coins minted in the city depict ships. Alternately, Mt 8:26 may simply refer in a general sense to the area on the eastern side of the lake populated by Gentiles.

Gerasa, a city of the Decapolis, is too far away from the Sea of Galilee to be a possibility. Some scholars therefore assume that there was a settlement with the name "Gerasa" near the lake.[225] The existence of such a place has not been confirmed, however.

Another plausible possibility is the assumption that the original reading in the Greek manuscripts was "Gergesa," rather than "Gerasa," at least in Mk 5:1 and possibly in Mt 8:26.[226] Many scholars believe that the reading "Gergesa" can be traced back to Origen, while others accept it as the original reading.[227] Gergesa is identified with ancient Chorsia and located at the ruins of modern Tel el-Kursi (Kersa),[228] situated on Wadi Sermakh on the shore of the Sea of Galilee, an area that belonged to the Decapolis. Near Tel el-Kursi there is a steep slope toward to the lake. This localization can be traced back as early as a Christian tradition in the third century.[229] A localization in Gergesa, a small and insignificant settlement, could well have been changed by a copyist in the

---

[220]Eric C. Lapp, "The Archaeology of Light: The Cultural Significance of the Oil Lamp from Roman Palestine" (Ph.D. diss., Duke University, 1997); cf. Meyers 1997, 62.

[221]Lang (1978, 145-60) wants to combine both perspectives.

[222]Mt 8:28-34; Mk 5:1-17; Lk 8:26-37. See R. Riesner, "Dekapolis," *GBL* 1:264-65.

[223]Besides the commentaries, especially Guelich, *Mk,* 1:274-77, see Annen 1976, 201-2.

[224]S. Holm-Nielsen and U. Wagner-Lux, *ABD* 2:865-67; Ute Lux, "Umm Qeis (Gadara)," *RB* 73 (1980): 581-82; 89 (1982): 247-50; U. Wagner-Lux et al., "Bericht über die Oberflächenforschung in Gadara (Umm Qeis) in Jordanien im Jahre 1974," *ZDPV* 94 (1978): 135-44; Thomas Weber and Rami G. Khouri, *Umm Qais: Gadara of the Decapolis* (Amman: Al Kutba, 1989); Urman 1995, 595-605; Yitzhar Hirschfeld, *The Roman Baths of Hammat Gader* (Jerusalem: Israel Exploration Society, 1997); Ball 2000, 196-97.

[225]See Carson, *Mt,* 219; Bock, *Lk,* 1:782.

[226]For the discussion that follows above see Gundry (*Mk,* 255-56), who refers to F. G. Lang, *ZDPV* 94 (1978): 145-46; see also Davies and Allison, *Mt,* 1:78-79; Gnilka, *Mk,* 1:201; Witherington, *Mk,* 180; Fitzmyer, *Lk,* 1:736-37; R. Riesner, "Gerasener," *GBL* 1:442; Annen 1976, 201-6; Ådna 1999b, 294-95.

[227]See Gundry, *Mk,* 255-56.

[228]V. Tzaferis, *The Excavations of Kursi-Gergesa* (Atiqot 16; Jerusalem: Israel Antiquities Authority, 1983); idem, "Kursi," *NEAEHL* 3:893-96; Nun 1999.

[229]See R. Riesner, "Gerasener," *GBL* 1:442; V. Tzaferis, "A Pilgrimage to the Site of the Swine Miracle," *BAR* 15 (1989): 44-51; Pixner 1994, 142-48.

West to the well-known city "Gerasa," which copyists in the East would have "corrected" to "Gadara." The fact that Gergesa is totally insignificant and little known leads Robert Gundry to the assumption that the reading "Gergesa," which is relatively early (Codex Sinaiticus, fourth century) and generally well attested, should be regarded as original; a change from "Gergesa" to "Gerasa" and then to "Gadara" is easier to explain than a change from "Gadara" and "Gerasa" to "Gergesa."

Hippos (ἡ ἵππος; Susita; mod. Qalʾat el-Ḥosn, near ʿEn Gev)[230] probably was founded as a polis at the eastern shore of the Sea of Galilee in the Seleucid period. The city belonged to the Decapolis and is mentioned by Pliny (*Nat.* 5.15.71; 5.16.74) and frequently by Josephus. The villages el-ʾAl (9 km northeast of Hippos) and Khisfin[231] (17 km northeast of Hippos) belonged to the territory of the city; the southern border must have been north of the Yarmuk River.

Mark reports that on one occasion Jesus "went through Sidon, down to the Sea of Galilee" and "into the region of the Decapolis" (TNIV; ἀνὰ μέσον τῶν ὁρίων Δεκαπόλεως), where he healed a deaf-mute (Mk 7:31). Mendel Nun identifies the southeastern coast of the Sea of Galilee as the "coast of the Decapolis," with Tel Samra as the ancient harbor of the city of Gadara, as the area to which Mark refers.[232]

East of the Jordan River was Dabbura, a town that had a synagogue and a school, according to inscriptions found on the site.

Dabbura (Arab., Dabūra),[233] situated on the northern river banks of Naḥal Gilbon, about 17 km north of the Sea of Galilee, had at least thirty buildings and is at the moment the largest ancient Jewish settlement on the Golan. In the western part of town six olive presses were found. Several Jewish inscriptions belong probably to a synagogue and a school (third century). A bilingual inscription confirms that the population spoke both Aramaic and Greek. A Hebrew inscription mentions Rabbi Eliezer ha-Qappar and his Torah school: "This is the *bet / midrash /* of rabbi / Eliezer ha-Qappar."[234] Rabbi Eliezer ha-Qappar is repeatedly mentioned in rabbinic texts,[235] a Tanna of the fifth generation who taught around A.D. 200, an opponent of Rabbi Judah ha-Nasi. It can be assumed that the Jewish community in Dabbura existed already in the first century. Perhaps Dabbura was one of the towns that Jesus visited when he was active in the region of the Decapolis (Mk 7:31).

The information that Jesus was "in the region" (εἰς τὰ ὅρια) of Tyre and Sidon (Mk 7:24, 31)[236] does not indicate that he went there in order to preach to Gen-

---

[230]Beer-Hepding, "Hippos Nr. 4," PW 8 (1913): 1913-14; C. Burchard, *KP* 2:1177-78; idem, *DNP* 5:608; Jones 1937, 252, 259-61, 271-72; Schürer 2:130-32; Riesner, *GBL* 2:581; Moors 1992, 217-19; Urman 1995, 575-78; Nun 1999; 2001; Ball 2000, 197.
[231]Urman 1995, 556-61, 569-74.
[232]Nun 1996; he also locates the healing of the demon-possessed man in Mk 5:1-20 in this area.
[233]Hüttenmeister 1977, 91-95; Z. U. Maoz, *NEAEHL* 2:544-45; Urman 1995, 427-33; L. Levine 2000, 313, 362-63.
[234]Dan Urman, "Jewish Inscriptions from Dabbura in the Golan," *IEJ* 32 (1982):16-23; Hüttenmeister 1977, 91-95; Urman 1995, 432-33 (no. 6).
[235]See *m. ʾAbot* 4:21; *t. Beṣah* 1:7; *y. B. Qam.* 1:3; *y. Hor.* 3:48c.

tiles, nor that he wanted to reach Jewish communities in these areas with his message of the dawn of God's kingdom. In view of the lively trade contacts between Upper Galilee and Tyre (see §8.2), and in view of the Jewish community in Tyre (and Sidon), we should not identify Tyre too quickly with "pagan territory."[237] The Gospel texts never refer to a preaching activity of Jesus in this area. Jesus evidently wanted to withdraw with his disciples for a time of rest (cf. Mk 7:24). The house that he enters (Mk 7:24b) may have belonged to a Jewish sympathizer, presumably a wealthy owner of a villa who could provide hospitality for thirteen men: according to Mt 15:23, the disciples accompanied Jesus on this trip.

9.4 Ministry in Judea

Matthew and Mark report that Jesus was active in "the region of Judea beyond the Jordan," where large crowds followed him (Mt 19:1/Mk 10:1).[238] This notice usually is interpreted as the beginning of the Synoptic passion narrative.[239] Scholars assume that Jesus left Galilee toward the end of his public ministry and that he traveled via Perea to Judea, avoiding Samaria. It is argued that Mark, especially, emphasizes Jesus' journey to Jerusalem. Luke is said to have a different agenda: according to Lk 9:51-56, Jesus travels to Jerusalem via Samaria. The central section of Luke (9:51—18:14) is a "travel narrative" that has been interpreted by some scholars in terms of a ministry of Jesus in Perea.[240]

It is doubtful that the impression that the accounts of Matthew and Mark might create—Jesus came to Judea for the first time at the end of his public ministry—is historically correct.

Howard Marshall suggests that the original form of Luke's source may have included the motif of a journey but that this does not have to have been the final journey to Jerusalem.[241] He suggests further that Luke probably placed his entire middle section under the subject "Jerusalem" as a kind of motto: since the individual events are not bound to specific localities, Luke could not have intended to describe the geographical progression from Galilee to Jerusalem. The motifs of the journey and of Jerusalem are used by Luke to emphasize that from now on (Lk 9:51) Jerusalem is the goal of Jesus' ministry. In other words, the entire central section is under the shadow of the cross and the resurrection. Donald Carson argues that it is impossible to interpret the references to Jerusalem in Lk 9:51-53; 13:22; 17:11 in terms of the goal of Jesus, in the sense of a direct travel route: the chronology and the topography do not permit such an interpretation.[242] He suggests that these three references to Jerusalem can be coordinated with the refer-

---

[236]Mk 7:24: ἀπῆλθεν εἰς τὰ ὅρια Τύρου; 7:31: ἐκ τῶν ὁρίων Τύρου; Mt 15:21: εἰς τὰ μέρη.
[237]Thus many commentators; however, see Pesch, *Mk*, 1:387.
[238]Some manuscripts add καί ("and") after "Judea" in Mk 10:1 (‭א‬ B C D L Δ Ψ 892 1241 *pc*).
[239]See Gnilka, *Mt*, 2:151, Pesch, *Mk*, 2:121. For the following see Marxsen 1959, 34.
[240]See Moessner (1989, 293), who argues against this position.
[241]Marshall, *Lk*, 152.
[242]For the points that follow above see Carson, *Mt*, 408-9.

ences to Jerusalem in the Gospel of John: (1) Jesus' journey to Jerusalem on the occasion of the Feast of Tabernacles (Jn 7:2-10); (2) Jesus' journey to Judea in connection with the death and resurrection of Lazarus (Jn 11:17-18); (3) Jesus' final journey to Jerusalem with the climax of the crucifixion. This solution creates other problems, however. Note, for example, the argument that the apparent parallels between Luke (central section) and Matthew/Mark could refer to the same historical events—a position that could be defended, even though this seems rather unlikely. The assumption remains possible that Luke's central section is bracketed by historical journeys to Jerusalem, which Luke uses theologically as references to the last journey.

Luke's central section, known as the "travel narrative," has generated a diverse number of scholarly interpretations.

Eduard Lohse suggested in an older contribution that the travel narrative should be interpreted in terms of the subject of salvation-historical fulfillment, a subject that dominated Jesus' missionary activity: the move from Galilee to Samaria indicates a new period in salvation history, as Jesus shows his disciples that "the messengers of their Lord must not stop at the borders of Israel."[243] Helmuth Egelkraut interprets the travel narrative in terms of redactional interest whereby Luke wanted to show how Israel rejected Jesus.[244] Joseph Fitzmyer follows Hans Conzelmann in retaining the concept of travel as an important Lukan motif: Luke places the sayings, parables, dialogues, controversies and speeches of Jesus in this long section deliberately in the framework of a journey to Jerusalem. Jesus goes to Jerusalem, where his ministry will come to an end; he journeys with his disciples, however, who will be the witnesses of his teaching and of his actions. Luke uses the travel narrative as a stylistic device to depict the continued training of Jesus' witnesses: Jesus goes to Jerusalem and thus to his foreordained fate, while equipping his successors for their task of proclaiming, after his death and resurrection, him and his message of salvation "to the ends of the earth" (Acts 1:8). Fitzmyer concludes that "the travel account becomes, then, a collection of teachings for the young missionary church, in which instruction of disciples alternates with debates with opponents."[245]

Some scholars have interpreted Luke's travel narrative in terms of a realistic picture of Jesus' travels.[246] In Lk 4:43-44 Luke hints at a previous ministry of Jesus in Judea.

Lk 4:43-44: "But he said to them, 'I must proclaim the good news of the kingdom of God to the other cities also; for I was sent for this purpose.' [44]So he continued proclaiming the message in the synagogues of Judea."[247]

Many commentators interpret the remark in Lk 4:44 in terms of a broader meaning of *Ioudaia*, that is, as a reference to Galilee belonging politically to the prov-

---

[243]Lohse 1954, 12-13.
[244]Egelkraut 1976; summary, 222-23.
[245]Fitzmyer, *Lk*, 1:826.
[246]Moessner 1989, 294. For the observations that follow above see R. Riesner, "Judäa," *GBL* 2:735-36, esp. 736; J. Robinson 1985, 125-26.
[247]Older versions (e.g., KJV) that follow the Textus Receptus have "Galilee" instead of "Judea"; several manuscripts read "Galilee" (A D Θ Ψ f¹³ 𝔐 latt sy^{p.hmg} bo^{pt}).

ince of Judea.[248] It is more likely, however, that Luke, who speaks of Judeans and citizens of Jerusalem who come to hear Jesus in Lk 5:17; 6:17; 7:17, indicates in the comment in Lk 4:44 that Jesus left Galilee in order to proclaim his message of the dawn of God's kingdom in other areas, including Judea.[249]

Mt 23:37/Lk 13:34: "O Jerusalem, Jerusalem, killing the prophets and stoning those who are sent to you! How often would I have gathered your children together as a hen gathers her brood under her wings, and you would not!"

It seems rather artificial when commentators interpret these words—the last words Jesus utters in public in the Gospel of Matthew and of Luke—as a redactional creation of the early church. The reason for this interpretation usually is the implicit christological claims or an alleged reference to the "Israel-mission" of the early church.[250] The term ποσάκις (*posakis,* "how many times? how often?") refers not (primarily) to God's history with Israel with which Jesus identifies but to Jesus' own activity.[251] The statement makes sense if we understand it as a reminder of the fact that Jesus had been in Jerusalem several times. The word of judgment expressed in Jer 22:5 ("this house shall become a desolation"), and quoted by Jesus in Mt 23:38, makes no sense if Jesus had never visited Jerusalem before.[252]

There are further hints in the Synoptic Gospels that Jesus had been active in Judea.[253] (1) Jesus knows people in Bethany who provide hospitality for him and his disciples, people who love him and assist him in times of danger: Mary and Martha (Lk 10:38-42), Simon the leper (Mt 26:6-13/Mk 14:3-9/Jn 12:1-8; cf. Mt 21:17; Mk 11:11). (2) Jesus knows someone in the vicinity of Jerusalem who willingly provides a donkey for "the Lord" (Mk 11:3). (3) Jesus knows someone who owns a house in Jerusalem and is loyal to him, so much so that he provides the upper room of his house so that Jesus and his disciples can celebrate (prematurely?) Passover (Mk 14:13-15).

The summaries quoted above (Mt 4:25; Mk 3:7; Lk 6:17) indicate that Jesus regularly had listeners from Judea. In John's Gospel, Judea, and more specifically Jerusalem, is the most significant location of Jesus' ministry.[254]

---

[248]See Marshall, *Lk,* 198-99. Bovon (*Lk,* 1:220) argues that the "striking reference to Judea" makes specific "the salvation-historical will of God and of Jesus to go somewhere else."
[249]See Fitzmyer, *Lk,* 2:558, as possibility.
[250]See Gnilka, *Mt,* 2:303: "From Matthew's standpoint, the Christian missionaries to Israel are to be included as well; among them would have been those who were stoned."
[251]Thus Carson (*Mt,* 487), who does not proceed to comment on a missionary activity of Jesus in Judea. Marshall (*Lk,* 575) sees this as the literal interpretation but does not comment further.
[252]J. Robinson 1985, 126, referring to H. S. Holland, *The Fourth Gospel* (London: Murray, 1923), 131, 133.
[253]See J. Robinson 1985, 125-26.
[254]Jn 3:22; 4:3, 47, 54; 7:1, 3; 11:7. See Riesner, *GBL* 2:736.

9.5 Ministry in Samaria

The account in Lk 9:51-56 does not speak of missionary activity in Samaria but of a rejection of Jesus and of his disciples.[255] Jesus is on the way from Galilee to Jerusalem; he does not travel via Perea but takes the direct route via Samaria, which allows travelers to reach the Jewish capital in three days. Jesus sends envoys ahead[256] who evidently were to make sure that Jesus and his companions, probably a larger circle than only the Twelve, find accommodation in one of the villages. The comment on the envoys indicates that Jesus planned the process of his travels and took care of matters such as adequate accommodations. The perennial hostility between Samaritans and Jews made a positive contact in this particular (unknown) village impossible. The story of the good Samaritan (Lk 10:30-37) perhaps reflects a certain interest of Jesus (or Luke) in the Samaritans, but clearly it does not speak of a Samaritan mission.

The exemplum of the story of the good Samaritan who helps a Jew, told as a response to a "test" by a scribe (Lk 10: 25, 29), explains Jesus' reaction to the Samaritan insult of Lk 9:52-56. Whereas the disciples wanted to follow Elisha's example and see fire fall from heaven, Jesus thinks and acts differently. People who are sinners are not rejected by Jesus, even if they display a hostile attitude.[257]

Eduard Lohse concludes his study of Lk 9:51-56 with the contention that "Luke's so-called travel narrative needs to be seen with regard to the subject of salvation-historical fulfillment, which governs Jesus' missionary activity. Luke emphasizes the significance of this second phase of Jesus' ministry by characterizing the point at which Jesus moves from Galilee to Samaria as the beginning of a new stage in salvation-history. By entering Samaritan territory and by continuing on his way despite the rejection that he experienced, Jesus showed that the messengers of the Lord must not stop at the borders of Israel."[258]

Luke relates a ministry of Jesus among Samaritans in Lk 17:11-19: while traveling "through the region between Samaria and Galilee" (Lk 17:11),[259] he heals ten lepers, one of whom is a Samaritan. It is the Samaritan who alone returns to thank Jesus for the healing. The passage does not indicate, however, whether Jesus preached to Samaritans (note that most of the healed lepers were Jews).

This leaves Jn 4:1-42 as the only, though rather extensive, passage that describes a missionary activity of Jesus in Samaria. The introductory remarks in Jn 4:1-4 allow specific chronological and historical conclusions.[260] (1) The reason for

---

[255]Enslin (1980) argues that Lk 9:51—18:14 is the redactional construction of a mission in Samaria.

[256]Lk 9:52: ἀπέστειλεν ἀγγέλους πρὸ προσώπου αὐτοῦ.

[257]J. J. Kilgallen, "The Plan of the 'ΝΟΜΙΚΟΣ' (Luke 10.25-37)," NTS 42 (1996): 615-19.

[258]Lohse 1954, 12-13.

[259]Lk 17:11: διὰ μέσον Σαμαρείας καὶ Γαλιλαίας. Samaria is mentioned first probably because the account will concern a Samaritan; see Bovon, Lk, 3:149; on the difficulties of the passages see also Bock, Lk, 2:1400-401.

[260]For the observations that follow above see J. Robinson 1985, 137.

the shift of Jesus' early ministry from Judea to Galilee is the opposition of the Pharisees, which increased as a result of his activity (Jn 3:26-30). (2) The journey via Samaria to Galilee took place in May (A.D. 28): the necessity (ἔδει [Jn 4:4]) to travel through Samaria rather than to take the route through the Jordan Valley existed only when it was extremely hot in the Jordan depression;[261] this agrees with the comment in Jn 4:35 on the wheat fields that are ready for harvest.[262] (3) Sychar, the place that Jesus visited, presumably is the village Askar, located about 1 km north of Shechem, approximately 1.5 km (ca. 1 mi.) from Jacob's well.

Shechem (Tell Balâtah, near mod. Nablus),[263] situated between Mount Ebal and Mount Gerizim, is already attested in Egyptian sources as a city-state. In the Old Testament, Shechem is linked with Abraham and his sons (Gen 12:6; 33:18-20; 34; 37:12-17). Situated on the border between Ephraim and Manasseh (Josh 17:7), Shechem was an important political and cultic center during the Israelite period (see Josh 20:7; 21:21; Judg 9; 1 Kings 4:8) and the first capital of the northern kingdom after the division of the monarchy (1 Kings 12:25). After the Assyrian conquest in 721 B.C., the population was deported, at least in part, and replaced by colonists from other regions of the Assyrian empire (2 Kings 17:24; Ezra 4:2, 9-10). Some Israelites were allowed to remain in the old capital Samaria; they are called "the people of Samaria" (or "Samaritans") in 2 Kings 17:29. During the Second Temple period Shechem was the most important city of the Samaritans (Josephus, *A.J.* 11.340-347). Alexander the Great conquered Shechem in 331 B.C. and settled Macedonian colonists in the city. After the Seleucid king Antiochos III defeated the Ptolemies of Egypt in 198 B.C., Samaria came under Seleucid control. In the course of the expansionist policies of the Maccabean John Hyrcanus, Jewish forces destroyed Shechem completely in 108/107 B.C. The Roman general Pompey detached the territory of Shechem from Judea in 63 B.C. In A.D. 72 the emperor Vespasian built the city of Flavius Neapolis (mod. Nablus) about 1.5 km west of ancient Shechem.

Samaria-Sebaste (Heb., Šomrôn; mod. Sebastiya [see §8.1]),[264] about 13 km (8 mi.) northwest of Shechem, was strategically located near the crossroads of the major north-south and east-west routes to Shechem and the Jordan Valley on the east, the coastal plain on the west, the Jezreel Valley on the north and Jerusalem on the south. Omri (887-876 B.C.), the sixth king of the northern kingdom, relocated his capital from Tirzah to the "hill of Samaria" (1 Kings 16:24), where he built a new city. His son Ahab built a temple dedicated to Baal in the city (1 Kings 16:32). Excavations have uncovered a royal quarter with a palace and two defense walls from this period. In 722/721 B.C. the city was destroyed

---

[261]Jn 4:4: διέρχεσθαι διὰ τῆς Σαμαρείας. See Josephus, *B.J.* 4.471.

[262]J. Robinson 1985, 132-35.

[263]L. E. Toombs, *ABD* 5:1174-86; E. F. Campbell, *NEAEHL* 4:1345-54; Schürer 2:160-64; Böhm 1999, 48-55. Excavations: Dan P. Cole and Edward F. Campbell, *Shechem* (3 vols.; Ann Arbor, Mich.: American Schools of Oriental Research, 1984-2002).

[264]J. D. Purvis, *ABD* 5:914-21; R. Tappy, *NEAEHL* 4:463-67; Shimon Dar, *Landscape and Pattern: An Archaeological Survey of Samaria 800 B.C.E.-636 C.E.* (BAR International Series 308; Oxford: British Institute of Archaeology, 1986); J. Magness, "The Cults of Isis and Kore at Samaria-Sebaste in the Hellenistic and Roman Periods," *HTR* 94: 157-77. Excavations: John W. Crowfoot and Kathleen M. Kenyon, *The Objects from Samaria* (London: Palestine Exploration Fund, 1957); idem, *The Buildings at Samaria* (repr., London: Dawsons, 1966 [London: Palestine Exploration Fund, 1942]).

by the Assyrian king Shalmaneser V or Sargon II, who deported nearly thirty thousand inhabitants and forced them into exile. Sargon claims to have rebuilt the city. Sanballat, the governor of Samaria around 445 B.C., resisted Nehemiah's efforts to rebuild the walls of Jerusalem (Neh 4). After the conquest by Alexander the Great, a rebellion against Macedonian rule was crushed by Perdikkas, a general of Alexander. Many citizens fled to nearby Shechem, which was rebuilt at the time. After Antiochos III conquered Samaria in 198 B.C., a new city wall was built, which was destroyed when John Hyrcanus destroyed Samaria in 108/107 B.C. Aulus Gabinius, the Roman prefect in Syria, rebuilt Samaria in 56 B.C. Herod I refounded Samaria in 25 B.C., renaming it Sebaste in honor of his patron Augustus (Gk., *sebastos* = Lat., *augustus*), and settled six thousand colonists in the city, among them non-Jewish soldiers. He rebuilt the city on a grand scale. In the city center stood a large temple dedicated to Augustus (24 by 35 m), which stood on a raised platform (83 by 72 m) reached by a monumental staircase. There was also a sanctuary dedicated to Persephone-Kore (84 by 45 m; the temple measured 36 by 15.5 m; the octagonal temple had a dedicatory inscription). Statues of Augustus, Kore, Apollo, Dionysos and Hercules have been found. In the first century Samaria-Sebaste was a predominantly pagan city. The city of Samaria is not mentioned in the New Testament.

Mount Gerizim (Jebel eṭ -Ṭur)[265] rises 500 m above the plain south of Shechem. Josephus links the beginning of the strife between Jews and Samaritans with the time of Alexander the Great, when Sanballat, the governor in Samaria, went with his army to Tyre, capitulated and asked for permission to built a temple on Mount Gerizim. When Ptolemy I Soter (305-283 B.C.) conquered Palestine, he resettled Samaritans in Egypt: these Samaritan colonists started to quarrel with the Jews who lived in Egypt over the question of whether offerings should be sent to Jerusalem or to Mount Gerizim (Josephus, *A.J.* 12.7-10). According to 2 Macc 6:2, the temple on Mount Gerizim was named after Zeus Xenios. Josephus mentions a temple dedicated to Zeus Hellennios (*A.J.* 12.257-264). Thus far it has not been possible to locate a temple from the Ptolemaic period. At the time of Antiochos III a town with four living quarters was built on the mountain. On the summit there was a temple, whose layout followed the model of the Jerusalem temple. The inhabitants of the city on Mount Garizim reached the temple by a western staircase (10 m wide). The temple was destroyed in 107 B.C. by John Hyrcanus. The Roman temple that has been located on one of the foothills (Tell er-Râs) of Mount Garizim was built around A.D. 150.[266]

The conversation that Jesus initiated with a Samaritan woman, leading to a longer visit with Samaritans, underlines the character of Jesus' mission as a gift.[267] (1) Jesus' mission excludes no one (Jn 4:13-14, 21-24, 42). (2) His mission is a gift in every respect: salvation is obtained not as an inheritance from the patriarchal ancestor (Jn 4:11-12, 20a), nor is it forced upon people as superior theology (Jn 4:20b, 22); it can be received only as a gift. (3) Since the missionary activity of the disciples is not something that they engineered but is something received as a gift on the basis of Jesus' previous activity, the "glory" of their mission cannot be credited to their own efforts (Jn 4:38).

---

[265]See I. Magen, *NEAEHL* 2:484-87.
[266]I. Magen, *NEAEHL* 2:488-90.
[267]Okure 1988, 184.

10

THE MISSION OF THE TWELVE

J esus marks the beginning of the missionary activity of the early church. Soon after the start of his public ministry, he chose twelve disciples from a larger group of followers: they were to leave their fishing nets—actually give up their profession—and join him as students with the goal of being trained as "fishers of people." The call of Simon and Andrew, James and John is Jesus' first public action in the Gospels of Matthew, Mark and John.

10.1 The Twelve

Jesus called twelve followers into permanent discipleship. The term "the twelve" (οἱ δώδεκα, *hoi dōdeka*) occurs in all four Gospels,[1] and Paul and Luke in the book of Acts know the Twelve as a fixed group of disciples.[2] The four New Testament texts that list the twelve disciples provide the following names:

Mt 10:2-4	Mk 3:16-19	Lk 6:13-16	Acts 1:13
Simon Peter	Simon Peter	Simon Peter	Simon Peter
Andrew	James	Andrew	John
James	John	James	James
John	Andrew	John	Andrew
Philip	Philip	Philip	Philip
Bartholomew	Bartholomew	Bartholomew	Thomas
Thomas	Matthew	Matthew	Bartholomew
Matthew	Thomas	Thomas	Matthew
James b. Alphaeus	James b. Alphaeus	James b. Alphaeus	James b. Alphaeus
Thaddaeus	Thaddaeus	Simon the Zealot	Simon the Zealot
Simon Cananaeus	Simon Cananaeus	Judas b. James	Judas b. James
Judas Iscariot	Judas Iscariot	Judas Iscariot	[vacancy]

---

[1]Mt 10:1-2, 5; 11:1; 20:17; 26:14, 20, 47; Mk 3:14, 16; 4:10; 6:7; 9:35; 10:32; 11:11; 14:10, 17, 20, 43; Lk 6:13; 8:1; 9:1, 12; 18:31; 22:3, 47; Jn 6:67, 70-71; 20:24.
[2]1 Cor 15:5; Acts 6:2.

Continental historical-critical scholarship usually argues that the real historical background of the circle of the Twelve cannot be established with any degree of certainty because, among other problems, the lists present tradition critical problems that can hardly be solved.[3] Some argue that the Twelve were not appointed by Jesus himself; rather, this group was created by Luke as a theologically relevant topic,[4] or it grew out of the vision of Peter, who concluded from "his" Easter appearance that God's eschatological people should be constituted, which he did by forming the Twelve, who, as representatives of the church, represent God's people.[5]

The group of the Twelve is not a creation of the early church: Jesus himself called twelve of his followers to be his permanent disciples. The following arguments are relevant.[6] (1) The main argument for rejecting the Twelve as a historical group called by Jesus is unconvincing.[7] Some scholars point out that the list of witnesses for the resurrection in 1 Cor 15:5 mentions "the Twelve," which, they argue, is anomalous because Judas Iscariot was not a witness of the resurrection. However, the statement in 1 Cor 15:5 is a formula that Paul takes from a tradition that evidently was widely known. In Acts 6:2 the expression "the Twelve" (οἱ δώδεκα) is a fixed term for an entity that functions as a specific group as well. (2) A pre-Easter origin is made likely by the uncertainty concerning some of the names in the list of disciples[8] and by the "complete insignificance of the majority of the names and of 'the Twelve' after Easter."[9] (3) All four Gospel writers include Judas Iscariot, the traitor, as a member of the original Twelve.[10] After Easter, Judas Iscariot would hardly have been included in a newly created list of twelve disciples. The group of the Twelve, with Judas Iscariot, can hardly be a post-Easter creation.[11] John Meier applies the "criterion of embarrassment" to argue for authenticity at this point.[12] (4) The Twelve disappear as a group from the New Testament tradition after Acts 6:2, with the ex-

---

[3]Roloff (1978, 434), who, however, accepts the historicity of the circle of the Twelve; cf. idem 1993, 36-37. Since Julius Wellhausen, it mainly has been German scholars who have doubted the existence of the Twelve; see Schmithals 1961, 58-65; Günter Klein 1961, 34-38; Kasting 1969, 89, 124-26; W. A. Bienert, in Hennecke and Schneemelcher 1987-1989, 2:11; also H. Braun, G. Schille, S. Schulz, H. Conzelmann, and J. D. Crossan.

[4]See Günter Klein 1961, esp. 202-16.

[5]Conzelmann and Lindemann 1995, 419.

[6]See Meier 1997; 1991-2001, 3:125-97; McKnight 2001, 205-11; also Gerhardsson 1961, 221; E. P. Sanders 1985, 98-106.

[7]K. H. Rengstorf, *ThWNT* 1:424-25 (*TDNT* 1:424-27); Roloff 1965, 138-40; T. Holtz, *EWNT* 1:874-80 (*EDNT* 1:361-63).

[8]The position of Andrew, Thomas and Simon Cananaeus is uncertain, and Matthew and Mark have Thaddaeus (Lebbaeus), whereas Luke and Acts have Judas son of James. See the commentaries.

[9]Holtz, *EWNT* 1:878 (*EDNT* 1:362).

[10]Cf. Mk 14:10, 20, 43; Mt 26:14; Lk 22:3; Jn 6:71.

[11]See Trilling 1978, 201-22; Lang 1996, 420.

[12]Meier 1997, 663-70; 1991-2001, 3:141-46.

ception of the brief reference of Paul in 1 Cor 15:5. If the circle of the Twelve was an early Christian creation, we would expect repeated references in more New Testament texts to this group of people and their significance for the early church.[13] (5) The criterion of multiple attestation also supports authenticity: the Twelve are mentioned in the Synoptic Gospels (sometimes with different names), in the Gospel of John, in the book of Acts and in a letter of Paul. (6) Since Jesus' disciples began to engage in missionary activity in Jerusalem immediately after Easter, according to the testimony of Acts, first among Jews but soon among Gentiles as well, the creation of the group of the Twelve by Peter is an assumption that is not only entirely hypothetical and speculative but also at least as "naive" as the willingness to trust the testimony of the New Testament sources. It seems impossible to assume that Paul distilled from a private vision of the crucified Jesus, "experienced" as Easter faith, an integrated theology of "people of God/new covenant/last days/Gentiles/mission," combined with an action program in which twelve men symbolize the eschatological restoration of Israel. There was no Israelite Gentile mission, no missionary activity of Second Temple Judaism, no Greek or Roman model for an actively organized expansion of religious associations across ethnic and political borders. Given the choice either to credit a hypothetical vision of Peter with the creation of the Twelve along with the mission to Jews and Gentiles, or to credit Jesus with the calling of the Twelve and with their commissioning to engage in missionary work among Jews and Gentiles, the latter alternative being supported by the sources, it should not be difficult to come to a decision (unless we are unwilling to abandon a picture of Jesus, reconstructed on the basis of various literary-critical and tradition-critical presuppositions and conclusions, according to which he waited for the apocalyptic inbreaking of God's kingdom—a reconstruction that excludes both the vision of communities of Jesus' followers and a missionary movement.)

The Disciples

Simon (Σιμών, *Simōn;* also Συμεών, *Symeōn*),[14] whom Jesus later called Cephas-Peter, may have been the same age as Jesus.[15] His brother was Andrew; the name of their father was Jonah (Mt 16:17) or John (Jn 1:42; 21:15-17). The family came from Bethsaida (Jn 1:44), on the northern shore of the Sea of Galilee. Peter

---

[13]See Meier 1997, 670; McKnight 2001, 209.

[14]Simon: Mk 1:16/Mt 4:18; Mk 1:29/Lk 4:38; etc.; Jn 1:41; 6:8, 68, 71; etc.; Acts 10:5, 18, 32; 11:13. Symeon: Acts 15:14; 2 Pet 1:1. Critical of Luke is Perkins 1994, 40.

[15]Böcher 1996, 267; for the survey that follows above see ibid., 268. For bibliography on Peter see §21 n. 2 in the present work. For the names "Simon" and "Peter" see also BDAG 544 (Κηφᾶς), 809-10 (Πέτρος), 924 (Σίμων), 957 (Συμεών); cf. recently Gnilka 2002, 19-20. On Galilean Aramaic see Caspar Levias, *A Grammar of Galilean Aramaic* (New York: Jewish Theological Seminary of America, 1986).

spoke Galilean Aramaic: he could be recognized in Jerusalem from his manner of speech (Mk 14:70/Lk 22:59). Both "Simon/Symeon" and "Andrew" are frequently used Greek names (a similar-sounding Semitic name is the Hebrew שִׁמְעוֹן, *Šimʿōn*), which may indicate that their family was open to Hellenistic culture, and may perhaps even hint at an early knowledge of the Greek language. The brothers worked as fishermen on the Sea of Galilee. They owned a house in Capernaum.[16] Simon was married. Jesus called him Peter (Πέτρος, *Petros*), the Greek equivalent of the Aramaic surname Cephas (Κηφᾶς, *Kēphas*): the Aramaic כֵּיפָא (*kepāʾ*) means "rock," while the Greek πέτρος (*petros*) means "stone," and πετρά (*petra*) "rock" in the sense of "bedrock." As a personal name, *Petros* can scarcely be pre-Christian. The conferring of the name Cephas-Peter upon Simon focuses on his task and responsibility that he was to assume as the leader and spokesman of the Twelve and as the foundation of the new "house" of the messianic community.[17] Despite the skepticism of many scholars,[18] I see no reason to doubt the Gospel writers. There is no need to assume a post-Easter development on the basis of, for example, the argument that Peter's behavior before Easter was hardly a model of rocklike firmness: the difficulty disappears if we allow that Jesus, as the prophet that he *also* was, could speak reliably about both future historical events and future character developments of people. On Peter's role and ministry see §§14.3-5; 15; 21.

Andrew (᾿Ανδρέας, *Andreas*),[19] the brother of Simon, is listed among the Twelve in the disciple lists and also in Mk 13:3; Jn 1:35-44; 6:8; 12:22. Like Simon Peter, he was a disciple of John the Baptist. Andrew is the first follower of Jesus who is identified by name, when he brought Simon Peter to Jesus (Jn 1:35-42). Later he brought to Jesus the boy with the bread and the fishes (Jn 6:8), and also, together with Philip, the Greeks who wanted to see Jesus (Jn 12:22). Whereas the brothers James and John are regularly mentioned together (as sons of Zebedee), it is striking that Andrew, with the exception of a few passages in Mark,[20] does not appear next to Peter. Luke does not mention him in the book of Acts after the disciple list in Acts 1:13.

James (᾿Ιάκωβος, *Iakōbos*) and John (᾿Ιωάννης, *Iōannēs*) were the sons of a certain Zebedee (Ζεβεδαίος, *Zebedaios;* Heb., זַבְדִּי, *Zabday*). They hailed from Bethsaida, as did Simon and Andrew, and belonged with these two brothers to

---

[16]Mk 1:21, 29; Mt 8:14; Lk 4:38; for Peter's marital status see Mk 1:29-31; 1 Cor 9:5. See Gnilka 2002, 26.

[17]Böcher (1996, 268) suggests that the basic meaning in view is "precious stone," as the meaning "foundation" is a post-Easter development, but he accepts the conferring of the name as historical.

[18]See Perkins 1994, 28-29, and passim; Dschnulnigg 1996, 65-66; Gnilka, *Mt,* 2:48-50; idem 2002, 159; but see Minnerath 1994, 22-36.

[19]Peterson 1958, esp. 1-5; Dennis R. MacDonald, *ABD* 2:242-43.

[20]Mk 1:16-18/Mt 4:18-20; Mk 1:29. See Meier 1991-2001, 3:203.

the more intimate circle of disciples. If their family was not wealthy, they certainly were not poor: they owned a boat and employed wage laborers (Mk 1:20). The wife of Zebedee supported Jesus during his ministry (Mt 27:55-56; cf. Lk 8:3), and she accompanied Jesus during his last journey to Jerusalem (Mt 20:20); it has been suggested that she is identical with the Salome mentioned in Mk 15:40 or with the sister of Mary, Jesus' mother, mentioned in Jn 19:25, but this is unlikely.[21] Jesus called the brothers James and John Βοανηργές (*Boanērges*), Greek for the Aramaic בְּנֵי רְגֵשׁ (*běnê regeš*), a term that Mark translates as υἱοὶ βροντῆς ("sons of thunder" [Mk 3:17]), presumably because of their fiery temperament (cf. Lk 9:54; Mk 9:38; 10:35-40). James[22] is the first of the Twelve to be killed on account of his allegiance to Jesus: Herod Agrippa I ordered his execution by sword in A.D. 41 (Acts 12:2). John[23] is to be identified with "the disciple whom Jesus loved"; this identification is suggested by hints in the Fourth Gospel and explicitly supported in the early Christian tradition, whose reliability should not be doubted.[24] There is good evidence for the traditional identification of the author of the Fourth Gospel with John the disciple of Jesus.[25] John was the only disciple from the group of the Twelve who directly witnessed Jesus' crucifixion (Jn 19:25-26), and he was the first disciple to see the empty tomb (Jn 20:2-5). He belonged to the leadership of the Jerusalem church, at least in the first years of its existence. Paul describes him as one of the "pillar apostles" (Gal 2:9). According to reliable early Christian tradition, John was active in Ephesus during the last decades of the first century.

Philip (Φίλιππος, *Philippos*)[26] also came from Bethsaida (Jn 1:44; 12:21) and was also a disciple of John the Baptist. In the disciple lists he stands at the head of the second group of four disciples. He brought Nathanael (Jn 1:45-46) and the Greeks who wanted to see Jesus (Jn 20:21-22) to Jesus, and he played an important role in the miracle of the multiplication of the bread (Jn 6:5-7) and during the conversation on Jesus' statement "I am the way, and the truth, and the life. No one comes to the Father except through me" (Jn 14:6, cf. 14:8-14). This Philip is not identical with the Jewish-Christian Philip in Jerusalem, mentioned in the book of Acts, who later preached the gospel in Samaria and in Caesarea.

---

[21]Contra Zahn 1900, 341; J. Wenham 1975, 10-11; Carson, *Mt*, 238, 583. See the critique of this position in Bauckham 1990, 12-13.

[22]On James see D. A. Hagner, "James 1," *ABD* 3:616-17; Meier 1991-2001, 3:212-13.

[23]See R. F. Collins, *ABD* 3:883-85; Culpepper 1994; Meier 1991-2001, 3:213-21. On the "beloved disciple" and the question of the authorship of the Gospel and the Epistles of John see Smalley 1978; J. Robinson 1985; Kügler 1988; Hengel 1993; Charlesworth 1995, with differing approaches and conclusions.

[24]Jn 13:23; 19:26-27; 20:2; 21:7, 20; 21:4; cf. 1:40; 18:15; 19:35.

[25]See Eusebius (*Hist. eccl.* 3.1.1; 3.31.3; 5.24.2-3), who refers to Irenaeus and Polycrates.

[26]JoAnn F. Watson, "Philip 6," *ABD* 5:311; Meier 1991-2001, 3:201-2. On Philip in the Gospels see recently Matthews 2002, 95-128.

Bartholomew (Βαρθολομαῖος, *Bartholomaios*) is mentioned in all disciple lists; otherwise the New Testament authors are silent. His Aramaic name may have been Nathanael Bar-Talmai (בַּר תַּלְמַי, *bar talmay,* "son of Talmay"). He often is identified with Nathanael, mentioned in Jn 1:43-46; 21:2, although this is uncertain.[27]

Thomas (Θωμᾶς, *Thōmas*),[28] called "the twin" (Gk., δίδυμος, *didymos;* Heb., תְּאֹם, *tě'om* [Jn 11:16; 20:24; 21:2]), is mentioned in the disciple lists of the Synoptic Gospels and Acts and several times in the Gospel of John, where he is described as a courageous disciple of Jesus (Jn 11:16; cf. 14:5), as a disciple who doubted the reports of the resurrection (Jn 20:24-29), displaying the same skepticism as did the other disciples earlier, and as a disciple who confessed Jesus as the divine Messiah (Jn 20:28). On the tradition that he was a missionary in India see §22.12.

Matthew (Μαθθαῖος, *Maththaios*) is mentioned in all four disciple lists, in the second group of four disciples in the last (Mt 10:3; Acts 1:13) or penultimate (Mk 3:18; Lk 6:15) position. In the First Gospel Matthew is explicitly identified with Levi the tax collector (*telōnēs* [Mt 9:9; 10:3]), whose call is described more extensively than that of any other disciple in the Synoptic Gospels.[29] I see no reason to doubt this identification.[30] Early church tradition credits Matthew-Levi with the authorship of the First Gospel.

James (Ἰάκωβος, *Iakōbos*), son of Alphaeus,[31] is mentioned only in the disciple lists, where he is placed in the third group of disciples. He often is identified with "James the younger" (Mk 15:40), the brother of a certain Joses, whose mother was a certain Mary; the appellation "younger" probably is meant to distinguish him from James the disciple and from James the brother of Jesus, but it is highly unlikely that he is identical with either of those two.[32] Levi is also described as "son of Alphaeus" (Mk 2:14), which suggests the possibility that James and Matthew-Levi were brothers. Since the disciple lists mention the brothers in pairs, which is not the case here, this possibility is an unlikely one. The identification of this James with James the brother of Jesus, found in Jerome and Augustine, is false. Late traditions mention a missionary activity by James

---

[27]Michael J. Wilkins, *ABD* 1:615; idem, *DJG* 180; Meier 1991-2001, 3:199-200. The identification with Nathanael can be found since the ninth century.

[28]R. F. Collins, *ABD* 6:528-29; Meier 1991-2001, 3:203-5, 255-56.

[29]Mt 9:9-13/Mk 2:13-17/Lk 5:27-32; see the extensive discussion of Landmesser 2001, esp. 65-132.

[30]Contra the majority of liberal historical-critical scholars; see Meier 1991-2001, 3:201.

[31]Ἰάκωβος is the Grecized form of Ἰάκωβ, *Iakōb;* Heb., יַעֲקֹב; Alphaeus (Ἁλφαῖος, *Halphaios*) also is a Hebrew name (חַלְפִּי, *Halpî*); see the dictionaries. The English form "James" is derived from the Old French *James* (*Gemmes, Jaimes*), which derives from popular Latin *Jacomus* for *Jacobus*, altered from Latin *Iacobus* (from Greek *Iakobōs*); see *OED.* On James the disciple see W. Haubeck, *GBL* 2:646; D. A. Hagner, "James 2," *ABD* 3:617-18.

[32]See Bauckham 1990, 12-15; Meier 1991-2001, 3:201.

Alphaeus in southwestern Palestine and in Egypt, where supposedly he was crucified in the town of Ostrakine.[33]

Thaddaeus (Θαδδαῖος, *Thaddaios;* Heb., חַדַּי, *Tadday* [Mt 10:3/Mk 3:18]) probably is identical with "Judas (brother) of James" mentioned in Lk 6:16 and Acts 1:13.[34] Apart from the disciple lists he is mentioned only in connection with Jesus' last Passover, during which "Judas, not Iscariot" asks, "Lord, how is it that you will reveal yourself to us, and not to the world?" (Jn 14:22). The identification of Thaddaeus Judas with Judas the brother of Jesus, the author of the Epistle of Jude, is unlikely.[35] According to the apocryphal *Acts of Thaddaeus,* this disciple later did missionary work in Edessa. Eusebius records this tradition as well (*Hist. eccl.* 1.13; 2.1.6-8) but reckons Thaddaeus to have been one of the Seventy(-Two) (*Hist. eccl.* 1.13.4, 11).

Simon (Σίμων)[36] is mentioned in the last group of disciples; he has the surname ὁ Καναναῖος (*ho Kananaios,* "the Cananean" [Mk 3:18/Mt 10:4]), which is derived from the Aramaic קַנְאָנָא (*qan'ānā,* "the enthusiast, zealot"), as he is explicitly called ὁ ζηλωτής (*ho zēlōtēs* [Lk 6:15; Acts 1:13]). In the first century A.D. the terms *qan'ānā'* and *zēlōtēs* had a broad spectrum of meaning: everyone who stood for a committed fulfillment of the law could be so designated. Whether this second Simon among the Twelve formerly belonged to the party of the Zealots—that is, he had been a Jewish nationalist prepared to engage in active resistance against the Romans—must remain an open question.

Judas Iscariot (Ἰούδας Ἰσκαριώθ, *Ioudas Iskariōth*) probably came from a place called Kariot (Tell Qirioth in the Negev? or Askaroth near Shechem?).[37] He was the treasurer of the Twelve, which means that evidently he was regarded as reliable and competent in money matters. In the end he proved to be dishonest (Jn 12:4-6; 13:19). Luke and John emphasize that Judas was under the influence of Satan when he betrayed Jesus (Lk 22:3; Jn 13:2). William Klassen's suggestion that Judas was not a failure, since he handed Jesus over to the Jewish authorities with Jesus' full knowledge and consent, contributing to the final fulfillment and realization of Jesus' mission, is neither exegetically nor historically plausible.[38]

---

[33]Nicephorus Callistus, *Historia ecclesiastica* 2.40; according to the *Martyrologium Hieronymi,* he died in Persia (PL 30:478).

[34]See JoAnn F. Watson, *ABD* 6:435. Meier (1991-2001, 3:200) rejects this identification.

[35]Bauckham 1990, 67-68, contra John J. Gunther, "The Meaning and Origin of the Name 'Judas Thomas,'" *Museion* 93 (1980): 113-48. Carson (*Mt,* 239) identifies Thaddaeus with "Judas son of James"—that is, with a son of James the brother of Jesus.

[36]See Meier 1991-2001, 3:205-8.

[37]G. Schwarz (1988, 6-12) reports nine identifications. On Judas Iscariot see R. P. Martin, *GBL* 2:738-39; Klassen, *ABD* 3:1091-96; Kurt Lüthi, *TRE* 17 (1988): 296-304; Vogler 1983; H. Wagner 1985; G. Schwarz 1988; Klauck 1987; 1992b; Klassen 1996; Meier 1991-2001, 3:141-45, 208-12.

[38]Klassen (1996; summary, 202-4), who finds it deplorable that Judas Isacriot has been "demonized" in the Christian tradition.

The Symbolism of the Number "Twelve"

The fact that Jesus chose twelve disciples was "a programmatic action."[39] Since the disciples were not physical descendants of the twelve Israelite tribes, and since "Israel" consisted only of two or two and a half tribes (Judah, Benjamin, the priests from Levi), the Twelve are to be seen as a symbol of Israel: they represent the hope for Israel's eschatological restoration. Jesus' twelve disciples are, in the words of Joachim Gnilka, "the spiritual ancestors of the people of God that awaits restoration . . . the number twelve is a sign of hope."[40] In the Qumran community twelve lay leaders symbolized, in a similar manner, the claim of the Essenes to be the eschatological covenant community.[41] The twelve disciples correspond to the twelve tribes of Israel (Mt 19:28/Lk 22:29-30);[42] they represent symbolically the restoration of the people of God in the last days.[43] "Symbolically" refers here, in the context of the symbolic actions of some of Israel's prophets, not simply to a symbolic gesture that is well meant but remains in the final analysis without consequences. Rather, it designates here an action of Jesus that pertains to the future and at the same time is inspired by the reality of which the symbol speaks: Jesus' calling of twelve disciples sets into motion the expected eschatological restoration of Israel.[44]

Ched Myers characterizes the Twelve as a revolutionary committee, as a government in exile, as resistance group.[45] This view is supported neither by the text nor by the activities of Jesus or of the disciples. Scot McKnight suggests that Jesus' intention in calling twelve disciples was eschatological-political: he wanted to train the twelve disciples as the new leaders of Israel who were to control the country after a coup d'état and who were to lead a radically obedient Israel in connection with a cleansed temple.[46] This view cannot be defended, it seems to me, with Jesus' baptism in the Jordan River, interpreted as allusion to the covenant renewal in Josh 4 with the erection of twelve stones, and it hardly har-

---

[39]Jeremias 1988, 225-26 (ET, 234-35) (J. Bowden translates "war eine programmatische Tat" with "had a particular programme in mind," which does not quite capture Jeremias's meaning); cf. T. Holtz, *EWNT* 1:879 (*EDNT* 1:363); Trautmann 1980, 168-233; Roloff 1993, 36-37; Theissen and Merz 1996, 200-201 (ET, 216-17); Hooker 1997.

[40]Gnilka, *Mt,* 1:355.

[41]1QS VIII, 1; 1QSa 11-22; 4Q159 frg. 2-4, 3-4; 1QM II, 1-3. Cf. 1QT LVII, 11-14, referring to twelve princes, twelve priests and twelve Levites. See J. M. Baumgarten, *EDSS* 1:456.

[42]Cf. Gen 35:22-26; 42:13, 32; 49:28; Ex 24:4; Num 1:5-16; Deut 1:22-23; Josh 4:2-3, 8-9, 20; 18:24; 19:15; 21:7, 40; Ezra 6:17.

[43]Cf. Is 11:11-12; 49:6; Jer 3:18; 29:14; 30:3; 31:7-10; 32:36-41; Ezek 36:8-11; 37:19; 47:13; Amos 9:14; Mic 2:12; 4:6-7; Zeph 3:19-20; Zech 10:8-10; cf. Sir 36:18-21; Tob 14:7; 2 Macc 1:27-28; 2:18; *T. Levi* 16:6; *T. Ash.* 7:7; *T. Benj.* 9:2; *Jub.* 1:15; *Pss. Sol.* 11; 17:26-34; *2 Bar.* 77:5-6; 78:7; *Jos. Asen.* 5.6; 4Q508 frg. 2, 2.

[44]Meier 1991-2001, 3:152-54.

[45]Myers 1988; see the critique in France, *Mk,* 159 n. 14.

[46]McKnight 2001, esp. 220-31; cf. earlier idem 1986, 381. McKnight explicitly disagrees, however, with the political interpretations of Jesus by George W. Buchanan and Richard A. Horsley; see McKnight 2001, 230.

monizes with the prediction of his death and of his resurrection as salvation events that are an integral part of Jesus' divine mission, nor with the general character of his ministry. The calling of a disciple with the surname *zēlōtēs* (Lk 6:15) is not linked with political implications. The transformation of religious zeal (Gk., *zēlos*) into a political, anti-Roman party seems to have taken place in the 50s of the first century A.D. Whether Simon was a "patriot" or an "ultranationalist"[47] is debated; possibly his surname simply identifies him as a religious enthusiast, passionately committed to the Torah.

That the number twelve was important is illustrated by two facts. First, it was preserved in the early Christian tradition, despite some uncertainties about the precise composition of the group of the Twelve, reflected in the Greek manuscript tradition where different names appear for some disciples. Second, the necessity of having twelve disciples of Jesus as a unified group prompted the election of Matthias after Judas Iscariot had eliminated himself (Acts 1:15-26).[48] The fact that Jesus himself did not belong to the Twelve, that only his disciples symbolized the restoration of God's people, implies a reference to his self-understanding: his relationship with Israel corresponds to the mission that God has given him, whose rule (kingdom) over Israel he proclaims in his preaching, demonstrates in his miracles and incarnates in his person.

The symbolism of the number "twelve" shows that Jesus intended right from the beginning a necessary missionary activity: the twelve disciples are called to contribute in both a fundamental and a climactic manner to the restoration of God's people promised by the prophets, and it implies at the same time the success of their mission. The statement in Mk 3:14a "and he appointed twelve"[49] describes the Twelve as Jesus' creation. Rudolf Pesch interprets the verb ποιεῖν (*poiein*) as implying the authority of the apostolic office ("amtstheologischer Gebrauch") and compares the statement with Ex 18:25-26 (Moses) and 1 Kings 12:6 (Moses and Aaron), as well as with statements in which Yahweh appears as the creator of his people (Is 43:1; 44:2).[50] The disciples are witnesses of Jesus' claims on the entire people of Israel, "the nucleus of the eschatological community," a claim that the missionary activity of the Twelve is to realize and will realize. The number "twelve" indicates that Jesus pursued a program of gathering the entire people of Israel, taking up the hope of the prophets who had prophesied the return of Israel's dispersion in the messianic last days.

---

[47]A political interpretation is supported by Hengel 1976a, 384-86; H. Merkel, *EWNT* 2:250-51 (*EDNT* 2:101); Schürer 2:605 n. 51; BDAG 507, s.v. "Καναναῖος"; Bock, *Lk,* 1:545-46. For arguments against this connection see B. Salomonsen, *NTS* 12 (1966): 164-76; Morton Smith, "Zealots and Sicarii: Their Origins and Relation," *HTR* 64 (1971): 1-19; Meier 1991-2001, 3:205; Christophe Mézange, "Simon le Zélote, était-il un révolutionnaire?" *Bib* 81 (2000): 489-506.

[48]See France, *Mk,* 159; for the remark that follows above see ibid., 13, with reference to M. D. Hooker.

[49]Mk 3:14: καὶ ἐποίησεν δώδεκα; Rudolf Pesch translates "he created."

[50]Pesch, *Mk,* 1:204 n. 4; the quotation that follows above, ibid., 1:204.

10.2 The Call to Be Fishers of People

The calling of the disciples is narrated in the Gospels in connection with the beginning of Jesus' ministry. It is possible, even probable, that Jesus had started to preach his message of the dawn of God's kingdom before calling the first disciples. The sequence of Mt 4:12-17 (preaching repentance and the good news of the kingdom in Galilee) and Mt 4:18-22 (calling of the first disciples) seems to suggest this possibility. However, the calling at the shore of the Sea of Galilee could have taken place on the occasion of Jesus' journey from Judea to Galilee (Mt 4:12-13). The accounts of the calling of the disciples are Mk 3:13-19/Mt 10:1-4/Lk 6:12-16.

Mt 10:1-4: "Then Jesus summoned his twelve disciples and gave them authority over unclean spirits, to cast them out, and to cure every disease and every sickness. [2]These are the names of the twelve apostles: first, Simon, also known as Peter, and his brother Andrew; James son of Zebedee, and his brother John; [3]Philip and Bartholomew; Thomas and Matthew the tax collector; James son of Alphaeus, and Thaddaeus; [4]Simon the Cananean, and Judas Iscariot, the one who betrayed him."

Martin Dibelius and Rudolf Bultmann interpreted Mk 3:13-19/Mt 10:1-4 as biographical apophthegms, as "ideal scenes," on the basis of supposed Old Testament models, the lack of interest in biographical details of the narrative, and the paraenetic motifs.[51] Such skepticism concerning the historical authenticity of the account is unnecessary.[52] (1) The brothers who are mentioned belonged indeed to Jesus' followers in Galilee. (2) Jesus' authoritative call to leave the nets, abandon working for one's livelihood and follow him is historical, as the rabbis did not call their students: rabbinical students chose their own teachers (criterion of dissimilarity). (3) Jesus' authoritative call corresponds with Jesus' activity as a prophet. (4) Jesus' call produced not just followers, students, but "fishers of people," missionaries—a *novum* that was unheard of in both the Jewish and the Greek world, a project that hardly could have been invented by the early church: note that the term "fishers of people" does not occur in the New Testament outside the Gospels. (5) The term "fishers of people" (Mk 1:17) can easily be translated back into Hebrew or Aramaic.[53] Authenticity is also supported by the fact that there are no rabbinic or Hellenistic parallels for this expression. (6) The listing of the Twelve in pairs corresponds with the historical situation of the missionary activity of the disciples before and after Easter. And the sequence of the names—Simon, Andrew, James, John—reflects correctly the historical significance of these disciples.

The Disciples as Followers of Jesus

Mk 1:16-20 is closely connected with the saying about the disciples as "fishers of people" and thus would have had no vitality as a mere "discipleship narrative." The text is not just a "paradigm of discipleship" but is a narrative about the disciples providing the foundation, and justification, for their "profession" as

---

[51]See R. Bultmann 1995, 26-27, 58-60, 65 (ET, 28-29, 61-64).
[52]See Pesch 1969, 18-25; for some points of the discussion that follows above see idem 1989.
[53]See Hengel 1968, 85 (ET, 76-78).

missionaries.[54] The following aspects of Jesus' calling of the Twelve are particularly important.

1. Jesus calls the disciples by his own authority, not with reference to a divine commission as Elijah did when he called Elisha (1 Kings 19:15-21).[55] Jesus' call is "spoken without presuppositions and without preconditions and is thus characterized as a call with divine authority."[56] The present-tense formulation of the call may indicate that the call to be "fishers of people" can be, and is, repeated at any time.

2. Jesus calls at least Simon and Andrew and James and John in a situation where they had experienced their own personal helplessness. Luke reports their call in connection with the story of a huge catch of fish that follows an unsuccessful night's work (Lk 5:1-11). Before Peter is called to become a "fisher of people," he has to acknowledge his helplessness in the normal affairs of life that he is well versed in as a Galilean fisherman but that he cannot control: he had fished throughout the entire night and had caught nothing. As a result of the miracle that Jesus caused to happen, Peter recognizes the presence of God in the word and in the person of Jesus. He falls at Jesus' feet and confesses his unworthiness and his sin. This reaction is reminiscent of the call narratives of the Old Testament prophets who recognized their unworthiness in view of God's revelation and commission.[57] Peter is called to be a different kind of fisherman "who will no longer catch fish for his everyday needs but who will lead people out of their impotence and helplessness to a life of freedom."[58] Because Peter experienced his helplessness and because he recognized the presence of God in the words of Jesus, he left his fishing boat and his business partners (Lk 5:7) and followed Jesus immediately and unconditionally (Lk 5:11).

The interpretation of the comment in Lk 5:6, that the net was in danger of rupturing because of the size of the catch, in terms of a symbolic description of the endangered unity of the church on account of the huge missionary successes[59] has no basis in the text. Very large missionary successes happened, as far as we know, in the first century only in the period A.D. 30-60 in Jerusalem, a place that generally is not connected by scholars with the composition of the Gospel of Luke. The similarities with Jn 21:1-14 do not prove that both texts belong to a common (post-Easter) tradition;[60] we should note that Lk 5:1-11 includes no elements that remind us of a resurrection narrative.[61] If the readers of the Gospel of Luke detected parabolic elements in the text, then surely it was in the connection between catching fish and the proclamation of the gospel: the success of this fishing

---

[54]Pesch 1969, 8-13. Cf. M. J. Wilkins, *DJG* 182-89; Best 1981.

[55]Hengel 1968, 19 (ET, 17); cf. recently Landmesser 2001, 84.

[56]Pesch 1969, 15-16. For the remark that follows above see Gnilka, *Mt*, 1:101, on Mt 4:19.

[57]Cf. 1 Kings 19:19-21; Is 6:1-10; Jer 1:4-10.

[58]Busse 1989, 72.

[59]T. Heckel 1999, 163.

[60]Marshall, *Lk*, 200; Bock, *Lk*, 1:449.

[61]Schürmann, *Lk*, 1:273; Fitzmyer, *Lk*, 1:561.

trip, which results from the presence of Jesus and his authority, is a prophetic symbol
for the mission for which Peter and the other disciples will be, and indeed have been,
commissioned.[62]

3. The commissioning call of Jesus is an action of God. This is seen in the fact
that Simon and Andrew, James and John, and Matthew obeyed Jesus' call immediately and unconditionally. Only God has the authority to extend such an
unconditional call as Jesus issued. The focus of the call narratives is not on the
obedience of the would-be disciples but rather "the immediate effect of Jesus'
call, which can be understood as a creational call."[63] Obedience then assumes
definite importance when discipleship is lived out in real life. The fact that these
men accept Jesus' call to follow him and to be trained by him instantly highlights
Jesus' authority as divine.

4. Jesus summons the disciples to "come away" (δεῦτε, deute) from their
work. Simon and Andrew leave their nets, James and John leave their boat, Matthew-Levi leaves his tax station. The trade or profession of the disciples is formulated in durative (or iterative) present tense[64] and in durative imperfect;[65]
Jesus' imperative is also formulated in the present tense.[66] This means, as
Christof Landmesser observes, that "the actions that are described and the actions that are demanded form a sharp opposition,"[67] hinting at the life-changing
consequences of Jesus' call. Father Zebedee is left behind in the boat (Mk 1:20):
the sons whom Jesus called to become fishers of people leave their trade behind
but indeed their family as well.

5. Jesus calls these Galileans to follow after him (ὀπίσω μου, opisō mou). Following Jesus comes before the commission. The missionary activity of the disciples as fishers of people is based upon following Jesus. The disciples are the
constant companions and co-workers of Jesus. As followers of Jesus (Mk 1:18;
6:1; 10:28) they leave their families (Mk 1:20; 10:29), even risk their hostility (Mk
13:12), but they gain a new home and a new family: the group of Jesus' disciples
is characterized by a family-like structure (Mk 10:30). The inner circle of the
Twelve is surrounded by another group of supporters who also follow Jesus,[68]
whom Jesus describes as his "family" in which the will of God is being fulfilled
(Mk 3:33-35). The contrast that is explicitly emphasized in this context with re-

---

[62]See Green, Lk, 233.

[63]Landmesser 2001, 79 n. 60.

[64]Simon and Andrew: βάλλοντας ἀμφίβληστρον/ἀμφιβάλλοντας (Mt 4:18/Mk 1:16); James
and John: καταρτίζοντας τὰ δίκτυα αὐτῶν (Mt 4:21/Mk 1:19); Matthew: καθήμενον ἐπὶ τὸ
τελώνιον: (Mt 9:9/Mk 2:14/Lk 5:27). See HS §197a-b.

[65]Mt 4:18/Mk 1:16: ἦσαν γὰρ ἁλιεῖς. See HS §198a.

[66]Mt 4:19/Mk 1:17: δεῦτε ὀπίσω μου; Mt 9:9/Mk 2:14/Lk 5:27: ἀκολούθει μοι.

[67]Landmesser 2001, 71. His suggestion that the active "following" to which the "sitting" tax collector is called (ibid., 72) is an overinterpretation.

[68]See Mk 2:15; 10:32, 52; 15:41; and parallels.

spect to Jesus' relatives (Mk 3:21, 31-32) shows that doing God's will (Mk 3:35) is synonymous with acknowledging Jesus, which later becomes synonymous with taking up one's cross (Mk 8:34).[69] Florian Wilk comments, "This group of adherents thus prefigures the large number of non-Jews who allow themselves to be introduced into an existence as followers of Jesus in the universal proclamation of the gospel after Easter. The fact that the group of Jesus' disciples is embedded in the circle of adherents and the fact that the proclamation of the Twelve that Jesus entrusted them with is carried into the entire world after Easter (14:9) shows: the goal of Jesus' ministry is the fellowship of faith and life of people from *all* nations (13:10)."

6. On a later occasion Peter said to Jesus, "Look, we have left everything and followed you. What then will we have?" (Mt 19:27/Mk 10:28/Lk 18:28). Following Jesus indeed means renouncing status and prestige, possessions and security guaranteed by human beings. However, Jesus does not create a program of social revolution: he does not attack possessions, professional success, house and family as such. The loss of status, the suffering of deprivation, opposition and hostility is *not* the full answer to the question "What then will we have?" When the twelve disciples "left everything," then, this was not a sacrifice of fellowship, security, acknowledgment:[70] Jesus promises the Twelve that they will sit on thrones and judge Israel when he returns, and that they will receive "in this age" a hundredfold houses, brothers, sisters, mothers, children and fields (Mk 10:30).

Fishers of People

Jesus formulates the goal of the call that he extends to the potential disciples: "Follow me and I will make you become fishers of men" (Mk 1:17 RSV; NRSV: "Follow me and I will make you fish for people").[71] Jesus calls them not just for their own sake but rather "through his fellowship with them into cooperation with him."[72] He calls them to be involved in his ministry of gathering the "lost sheep of the house of Israel," which eventually will be extended to gathering the nations from the corners of the world.

The term "fishers of people"(ἁλιεῖς ἀνθρώπων, *halieis anthrōpōn*) occurs only in Mt 4:19 and Mk 1:17. There are no genuine parallels in the Old Testament or in rabbinic or Hellenistic texts, nor is it used in early Christian literature.[73] Rather striking is the fact that

---

[69]Wilk 2002, 80; the quotation that follows above, ibid.

[70]Gittins (1994, 172) has not noticed the continuation of Mt 19:27/Mk 10:28/Lk 18:27.

[71]Mk 1:17/Mt 4:19: ποιήσω ὑμᾶς ἁλιεῖς ἀνθρώπων; cf. Lk 5:10: "From now on you [Peter] will be catching [ζωγρῶν] people."

[72]Schlatter, *Mt,* 118; cf. Gnilka, *Mt,* 1:101.

[73]For the discussion that follows above see, besides the commentaries, Mánek 1958; C. W. F. Smith 1959; O. Betz 1961, 53-61; Bieder 1961, 7-15; H. Betz 1967; Wuellner 1967 (see the critique in H. C. Kee, *JBL* 87 [1968]: 220-21); Best 1981, 166-74; Meier 1991-2001, 3:159-61.

Luke does not use the term at all, neither in the Gospel nor in the book of Acts, in which he reports rather intensive and extensive "fishing." The symbolic term "fishers of people" is first of all linked with the fact that these are fishermen who used to fish in the Sea of Galilee to earn their livelihood.[74] It is noteworthy that Jesus, who uses the metaphor, is not a fisherman himself. At least five possible connotations for the term "fishers of people" have been suggested. (1) Jesus perhaps alludes to Jer 16:16: "I am now sending for many fishermen [ἐγὼ ἀποστέλλω τοὺς ἁλεεῖς τοὺς πολλούς], says the Lord, and they shall catch them; and afterward I will send for many hunters, and they shall hunt them from every mountain and every hill, and out of the clefts of the rocks." The context of Jer 16 refers to the gathering of the children of Israel; the focus, however, is the dominating topic of God's judgment. Rudolf Pesch suggests that Jesus used the metaphor of the fishers of people against the original sense of the word of judgment: "As fishers of people the disciples are to gather Israel from the dispersion, after Easter 'all the dispersed children of God' (Jn 11:52)."[75] It is not necessary, however, to assume a modification of the original meaning of the Old Testament passage (which is not quoted, we should note): Jesus could have used the term "fishers of people" with regard to the final judgment, which John the Baptist had announced as imminent and which provides the background for Jesus' announcement of the dawn of the kingdom of God—Jesus chooses, calls and sends the disciples in view of the approaching judgment so that they will proclaim his message of the kingdom of God and gather Israel for a new "exodus."[76] In the parable of the dragnet, the metaphor of fishing is related to the salvation that is confirmed and vindicated in the final judgment (Mt 13:47-50). (2) Other scholars interpret the metaphor against the background of passages that refer to the activity of fishing or to hooks (Ezek 29:4-5; Amos 4:2; Hab 1:14-17; 1QH III, 26; V, 7-8)[77] and could be linked with warfare, also in the context of judgment: Jesus may have called the disciples to participate in God's holy war in the last days.[78] This interpretation is implausible, considering the structure and content of Jesus' preaching and in light of passages in which his followers are challenged to love their enemies and be willing to be cheated. (3) Some scholars refer to Greco-Roman and Jewish-Hellenistic texts in which the metaphor of fishing has positive connotations, as, for example, the meaning "teacher":[79] the call to "fish people" is a commission to teach.[80] This usage is not a valid parallel either, however: Jesus does not call the disciples to study and teach (Torah).

It is probable that Jesus, who used many metaphors from everyday Galilean life, coined the metaphor "fishers of people."[81] The disciples were called for the purpose of assisting Jesus, who gathers the "lost sheep of the house of Israel" in view of the dawn of the kingdom of God. They are to recruit more people who accept Jesus' message and become members of the movement that he has set

---

[74]See Davies and Allison, *Mt,* 1:398. On fishing in the Sea of Galilee see Nun 1993.
[75]Pesch, *Mk,* 1:111.
[76]C. W. F. Smith 1959; cf. Marcus, *Mk,* 184; Davies and Allison, *Mt,* 1:398.
[77]Wuellner 1967, 88-133.
[78]Marcus, *Mk,* 184, as a possibility.
[79]Diogenes Laertius 2.67; *Let. Arist.* 2.23; on the connotation "teacher" see Plato, *Soph.* 218d-222d; *'Abot R. Nat.* Rec A 40; cf. Wuellner 1967, 67-75; Guelich, *Mk,* 1:51.
[80]Mánek 1958; Marcus, *Mk,* 184.
[81]Guelich, *Mk,* 1:51; Meier 1991-2001, 3:160-61.

in motion.[82] The men who have spent their days fishing the Sea of Galilee now are to "catch" people: they will win people for Jesus' message of the arrival of God's kingdom. The disciples called by Jesus are disciples who are sent: as they follow Jesus, they will be trained for missionary activity.[83] Their discipleship serves to intensify and to extend Jesus' proclamation of the kingdom of God.[84] Discipleship and mission are inseparably linked, at least in the case of the Twelve. Their mission is founded upon their commitment to Jesus. When Jesus called the Twelve with the purpose of training them to "catch people," they presumably thought of Israelites, or Jews.[85] Matthew, who writes his Gospel after Easter and in the context of the reality of missionary work that fulfills Mt 28:16-20, probably also thinks of Gentiles.[86]

In early Christian spirituality and art the symbol of the fish (Gk., ἰχθύς, *ichthys*) stands for Jesus, as an acronym for the confession "Jesus Christ, Son of God, Savior" (Ἰησοῦς Χριστὸς Θεοῦ Υἱὸς Σωτήρ, ΙΧΘΥΣ; *Iēsous Christos Theou Huios Sōtēr*), and for Christians themselves. On Christian sarcophagi the fisherman appears as a symbol for baptism.

It is important to note in this context that the disciples, unlike students at that time who chose their rabbi, did not choose Jesus as teacher and master.[87] The discipleship of the Twelve is linked not with their own initiative but rather exclusively with Jesus' initiative. In the three instances in which people approach Jesus with the request of being accepted as disciples, Jesus safeguards his sovereignty: in the first case he flatly refuses the request, in the second case he gives an answer that amounts to a refusal, and in the third case he dismisses the reservations that accompany the request.[88]

The calling of the twelve disciples in Galilee must not be burdened with the view that Jesus called uneducated Galileans to the task of preaching and teaching.[89] It is rather probable that Jesus' disciples, including the fishermen Simon and Andrew, were educated.

According to Jn 1:44, Peter, Andrew and Philip came from Bethsaida, an up-and-coming town that was granted the status of a polis in A.D. 30 and was located in the vicinity of the Greek city Caesarea Philippi. Rainer Riesner argues that people "who grew up in such close proximity to a Hellenistic city must have spoken more than a few scraps of Greek. Thus

---

[82]See Davies and Allison, *Mt,* 1:398; Meier 1991-2001, 3:161.
[83]Pesch 1982, 27.
[84]Pesch *Mk,* 1:113; cf. ibid., 1:205, on Mk 3:14-16.
[85]Best 1984, 1.
[86]Davies and Allison, *Mt,* 1:398-99, with reference to Mt 5:16; 10:22; 12:41.
[87]Note this statement by Jehoshua b. Perachja: "Provide yourself with a teacher and get yourself a fellow-[disciple]" (*m. 'Abot* 1:6).
[88]Mk 5:18/Lk 8:38-39; Mt 8:19-20/Lk 9:57-58; Lk 9:61-62; cf. Jn 15:16a. See Riesner 1988, 416; Meier 1991-2001, 3:50-54.
[89]The same point is made in Riesner 1988, 413; Luz, *Mt,* 1:177.

Jn 12:21 presupposes that Philip could speak Greek."[90] Andrew, Philip and Simon had Greek names, which may not be coincidental. Riesner observes, "The Galilean fishermen in Jesus' group of disciples belonged not to the rural lower class but to the vocational middle class. As the latter had religious interests, we may assume a certain degree of education in the case of disciples such as Peter and John. . . . We may assume that several disciples came from that segment of the Jewish people who displayed religious interests and that they had received, like Jesus, a good elementary education in the parental home, in the synagogue and in elementary school."[91] A Jew who came from a pious background "had a solid, albeit one-sided, education. He could read and write and he could retain large quantities of material in his memory by applying simple mnemonic devices. . . . Whether a boy of the lower classes received an elementary education depended on two preconditions: the piety of the father and the existence of a synagogue in the village."

The view that Jesus had untutored disciples is a romantic and entirely unwarranted one. Note, for example, the calling of Matthew-Levi, a tax collector (*telōnēs* [Mt 9:9]).[92]

A Syrian *telōnēs* was a "collector of tolls" (Heb., *mōkes*) who collected direct and indirect taxes as well as dues in kind from the population that he had to pay in advance to the authorities.[93] A tax collector belonged to the higher levels of society. His position presupposed not only that he was wealthy but also that he had some degree of education—for example, that he could read and write. The calling of Matthew has prompted some scholars to assert that it is not impossible that there were those among Jesus' followers who were able to take (written) notes during his teaching and preaching ministry.[94]

If we link Jesus' saying about asking, seeking and knocking (Mt 7:7/Lk 11:9) to the missionary task of the disciples, several provocative perspectives regarding social conventions ensue. Jesus' directive is direct, clear and perhaps somewhat embarrassing.[95] Jesus himself sought help: he asked the Samaritan woman at a well for a drink of water (Jn 4:7); he asked the tax official Zacchaeus for lodging (Lk 19:5). Also, Jesus praises the man who asks his friend, around midnight, for three loaves of bread (Lk 11:5); he praises the widow who unabashedly puts a judge under so much pressure that he grants her request (Lk 18:1-8); he praises the blind man who keeps calling out until bystanders take him to Jesus (Lk 18:35). In Mt 7:7 Jesus teaches his disciples that they can fully depend on God, on the basis of the trusting knowledge that God will grant them everything they need.

The fact that in the call narratives and disciple lists the names of some of the disciples are mentioned in pairs reflects, according to some scholars, their later

---

[90]Riesner 1988, 412.

[91]Riesner 1988, 413, on popular education in Second Temple Judaism in these three areas see ibid., 97-199; the quotation that follows above, 199.

[92]On the calling of Matthew see Landmesser 2001, esp. 65-132.

[93]Herrenbrück 1990, 291-92; cf. idem, "Wer waren die 'Zöllner'?" *ZNW* 72 (1981): 178-94; followed by Landmesser 2001, 66-67.

[94]See Riesner 1988, 497-98.

[95]See Gittins 1994, 173.

sending in pairs.[96] However, the diverse forms of the disciple lists, which are not readily harmonized, make this assumption unlikely.

The Disciples in the Fourth Gospel

In John's Gospel the term "disciple" (*mathētēs*) occurs seventy-eight times.[97] John does not report a direct, personal call of a follower as in the Synoptic Gospels. Instead, John emphasizes "the alien witness for the true essence and the salvation-historical significance of the person of Jesus: Jn 1:36, 41, 45. The affiliation of the very first followers with Jesus is thus presented explicitly as an act of faith." John describes the task that Jesus gave to the disciples with five "words of sending":

Jn 4:38: "I sent you to reap that for which you did not labor. Others have labored, and you have entered into their labor."

Jn 13:16, 20: "Very truly, I tell you, servants [slaves] are not greater than their master, nor are messengers greater than the one who sent them. . . . [20]Very truly, I tell you, whoever receives one whom I send receives me; and whoever receives me receives him who sent me."

Jn 15:16: "You did not choose me but I chose you. And I appointed you to go and bear fruit, fruit that will last, so that the Father will give you whatever you ask him in my name."

Jn 17:18: "As you have sent me into the world, so I have sent them into the world."

Jn 20:21: "Peace be with you. As the Father has sent me, so I send you."

The significance of these words of sending for the disciples' mission to the world in John's Gospel can be summarized as follows. (1) Jesus' own sending happened in total dependence upon the Father. He was absolutely faithful to the will of the Father who had sent him; he was utterly dedicated to do the work that he had been given.[98] If this is true for Jesus as an envoy of the Father, it is even more true for the mission of the apostles as "servants" (*douloi*) of God (Jn 13:16). (2) The work of the disciples is not a new work that they have initiated but rather the "continuation of the work of others,"[99] namely, the prophets and Jesus (Jn 4:38). (3) The sending of the disciples into the world is based on the relationship between the Son and the Father, between Jesus and God (Jn 13:20). The mission of the disciples is the consequence and the result of the mission of Jesus. (4) The fruit that Jesus refers to (Jn 15:16) is the mutual love of his followers, which cor-

---

[96]See Pesch, *Mk,* 1:114.
[97]For the survey that follows above see Kuhl 1967, 135-49; quotation, 139; Köstenberger 1998, 141-98.
[98]See Kuhl 1967, 141.
[99]See Kuhl 1967, 142; for the observation that follows above see Köstenberger 1998a, 180-84.

responds to the love of Jesus (Jn 15:4, 7-8), and it is at the same time, in the context of "going," a reference to the missionary success, to the conversion of people to faith in Jesus Christ. Such fruit exists only as a gift from God, for which the disciples can only pray. (5) The sending of the disciples that happens according to the example of the sending of the Son by the Father (Jn 17:18) is based upon mutual love and unity, characteristics of the relationship between the Father and the Son.[100] The internal relationships of the disciples among themselves are not more important, however, than their external relationship with the world. Their mission is not simply a "mission by attraction": the disciples are to "go" and bring fruit (Jn 15:16), to "bear witness" with the help of the Spirit (Jn 15:26-27), to proclaim a message that helps people come to faith in Jesus (Jn 17:20), to offer forgiveness to people (Jn 20:23). (6) The sending of the disciples by Jesus corresponds to the sending of Jesus by the Father: this entails that they should know Jesus as intimately as Jesus knows the Father (Jn 15:15; 17:7, 8, 25), be utterly dependent upon Jesus as the Son is dependent upon the Father (Jn 4:13-14; 15:7-8, 16), bring glory to Jesus and do his will as Jesus did the will of the Father (Jn 4:3; 5:30, 38), be obedient to Jesus and keep his word (Jn 14:21, 23-24; 15:14, 20; 17:6), make Jesus known and testify of him as Jesus made known the Father and bore witness of him (Jn 12:44, 45; 13:20).[101]

Apostles

The term ἀπόστολος (*apostolos*) has foundational significance for the missionary theology and praxis of the early church. This term, particularly in Luke's writings, refers in several central texts to the group of the Twelve. Mark describes the calling of the Twelve as calling to be apostles (Mk 3:13-15):

Mk 3:13-15: "He went up the mountain and called to him those whom he wanted, and they came to him. [14]And he appointed twelve, whom he also named apostles, to be with him, and to be sent out to proclaim the message, [15]and to have authority to cast out demons."

The phrase "whom he also named apostles" (οὓς καὶ ἀποστόλους ὠνόμασεν) is found in the important MSS ℵ B (C') Θ f[13] 28 *pc* sy[hmg] co, but it is missing in MSS A C[2] (D) L 0133 f[1] 𝔐 latt sy sa[ms]. Many scholars think that the phrase was taken from Mt 10:1 or Lk 6:13 and is therefore not original.[102] This argument is not conclusive, however:[103] (1) The external evidence clearly supports the first reading. (2) The internal evidence is not as clear. One could argue that the omission of the word "apostle" is more difficult to explain than its addition. On the other hand, the reading that includes the term "apostle" could be regarded as the more difficult reading (*lectio difficilior*) because *apostolos* is extremely rare in the Gospel of Mark (only one other occurrence, Mk 6:30). (3) The suggestion that the

---

[100]Popkes 1978, 66; Köstenberger 1998a, 189; for the critique of Popkes that follows above see ibid., 189-90.
[101]Köstenberger 1998a, 194-95.
[102]Pesch, *Mk,* 1:203; Gnilka, *Mk,* 1:139 n. 18; Marcus, *Mk,* 263; France, *Mk,* 157; Reinbold 2000, 32-33.
[103]See Metzger, *Textual Commentary,* 69; Guelich, *Mk,* 154; especially Gundry, *Mk,* 168.

phrase "whom he also named apostles" is the product of Lukan redaction[104] is not very
plausible: Luke employs this formulation only once (Lk 6:13); thus, it is equally possible
that Luke borrowed the phrase from Mark.[105] (4) The statements in Mk 6:7, 30 confirm
that Mark identified the Twelve with the "disciples" and the "apostles," even though he
prefers the term "the Twelve."[106] Matthew also refers once to "the twelve apostles" (Mt
10:2) but otherwise prefers the term "disciples" (Mt 10:1; 11:1).

Some scholars have argued that the Twelve were declared to be apostles only after the
end of the Pauline period.[107] This view has been harshly criticized,[108] often with the argument that the term *apostolos* in Mk 6:30/Lk 9:10 and in Mt 10:2 cannot simply be declared
redactional. In Lk 17:5 the term *apostolos* is used instead of "disciple," which appears in
the parallel texts Mt 17:19/Mk 9:28; the *apostoloi* in Lk 24:10 are the Twelve (minus Judas)
and other followers of Jesus. The fact that the term "apostle" is not limited to the Twelve
in the Synoptic Gospels, but may refer to a wider circle of disciples, renders the assumption
of post-Pauline origin very unlikely, as does the fact that the term "apostle" occurs very
rarely in the Gospels.[109] In the three passages in which the term is used for the Twelve,
the usage fits the context and makes sense: Mk 3:14 speaks of their sending by Jesus and
their commission as preachers, and both Mt 10:2 and Mk 6:30/Lk 9:10 talk about the sending of the disciples on a preaching tour through Galilee and about their return. Surely, *apostolos* was not a "title" that Jesus or the disciples used for a fixed group of people, but it
should not be doubted that Jesus called the disciples *apostoloi* (Aram., *šeluḥim*).[110]

Mk 3:13-15 clarifies what "apostle" (*apostolos*) means. (1) The twelve disciples are going to be "sent" (*apostellein*): they will literally go to people, like envoys who cover some specific distance in order to transport an object or some
piece of information.[111] (2) They are given the assignment to "proclaim"
(*kēryssein*): they will convey a message, the message that Jesus himself proclaims. (3) They receive "authority" (*exousia*) over demons: they will liberate
people, as does Jesus, from the power of the evil one; thus they will participate
in the authority of Jesus.

The semantic field of "sending" contains primarily, in the Gospels and in the book of Acts,
the verbs *apostellein* (Lat., *mittere,* "send") and *pempein* ("dispatch, send"): of 132 occurrences of *apostellein* and 79 occurrences of *pempein,* 120 and 58 occurrences, respectively,
are found in the Gospels and in Acts. The noun *apostolos* occurs 80 times: 28 times in Acts
and 29 times in Paul's letters. The verb *presbeuein* ("be an ambassador/envoy, travel/work
as an ambassador") occurs twice in Paul (2 Cor 5:20; Eph 6:20); the noun *presbeia* ("am-

---

[104]Pesch, *Mk,* 1:203; Reinbold 2000, 33.
[105]See Gundry, *Mk,* 168; Schramm 1971, 113-14.
[106]Mk 3:14, 16; 4:10; 6:7; 9:35; 10:32; 11:11; 14:10, 17, 20, 43.
[107]Günter Klein 1961; Schmithals 1961; Campenhausen 1963, 15-16 (ET, 14-15); Conzelmann
   1969, 23-24, 129 (ET, 36, 148); recently, again, Reinbold 2000, 34-35; cf. Meier 1991-2001,
   3:165-66 n. 6.
[108]See Gundry, *Mk,* 168; K. Lake, in *Begs.* 5:37-59; K.-H. Rengstorf, *ThWNT* 1:431-32 (*TDNT*
   1:431-32); Roloff 1978, 433; Riesner 1988, 460.
[109]John never calls Jesus' disciples "apostles" (but see Jn 13:16).
[110]See Meier 1991-2001, 3:126.
[111]See J.-A. Bühner, *EWNT* 1:340 (*EDNT* 1:141-42).

bassador") occurs twice in parables in Luke's Gospel (Lk 14:32; 19:14).

The Septuagint uses ἀποστέλλειν (*apostellein*) in over 700 passages for the Hebrew verb שׁלח (*šalaḥ*), which designates in over 450 passages the sending of a person ("to send/ dispatch somebody [with a specific assignment/as envoy]"). God sends specific people as his instruments (e.g., Joseph [Gen 45:5, 7]) or as savior of the people (e.g., Gideon [Judg 6:14]). The prophets are called "envoys" of God (e.g., Moses [Ex 3:14-15]; Samuel [1 Sam 15:1]; Isaiah [Is 6:8]; Jeremiah [Jer 19:14]; Ezekiel [Ezek 2:3-4]). In the New Testament, subjects of the verb *apostellein* are God or people; the verb indicates with respect to the one doing the sending "that such a one has messengers at his disposal and either wishes to convey a piece of information or an object or to make a claim on a third party."[112] The verb *pempein* as a term designating human communication describes the "sending of persons to communicate (usually) important messages"; sometimes objects are "sent" as well.[113] Paul uses the verb for the sending of co-workers; John uses it for the sending of the Son by the Father (32 times).

Karl Heinrich Rengstorf, in an influential article in the first volume of the *Theological Dictionary of the New Testament* (German original, 1933), explains the early Christian usage of *apostolos* in connection with the Jewish legal institution of the שׁליח (*šaliaḥ*, "one who is sent, agent, envoy"), who represents the one who sent him with authority, according to the principle "a man's agent [*šālûaḥ*] is like to himself" (*m. Ber.* 5:5).[114] Rengstorf assumes that the term *šaliaḥ* was fixed legally and institutionally, and he argues that the term and concept of *šaliaḥ* must be distinguished from the sending of the prophets. This view has been rightly criticized.[115] (1) The Jewish legal institution of the *šaliaḥ* arose only after A.D. 70 as an expression for persons with an official function, in the sense of "official commissioners of the great Sanhedrin who collected dues in the Diaspora for the central agency, who undertook inspection journeys, who gathered collections for the Palestinian sages and who introduced Bible and Mishnah teachers."[116] Before A.D. 70 the term *šaliaḥ* designated authorization, with the specific details dependent upon the context and the situation—that is, upon the sender and on the commission or assignment. (2) The rabbinic *šaliaḥ* usually had a commission that was clearly limited in scope and duration by the sender of the agent. He possessed no divine commission for proclamation. The rabbinic *šaliaḥ* does not represent a religious term, as, for example, a designation for Jewish missionaries. (3) The sending of envoys was a well-known phenomenon in both the Jewish and the Greco-Roman worlds. It is therefore not useful to derive terms of sending, such as *apostolos,* from a single tradition.[117] Margaret Mitchell suggests that the early Christian "envoys" should be understood in the context of contemporary diplomacy and its conventions. This attempt is attractive with regard to several substantial parallels but is hindered by the fact that the terms *presbeuein* and *presbeia,* standard terms in Greek diplomacy, occur only four times in the New Testament; this makes Mitchell's suggestion difficult despite the important text 2 Cor 5:20 (see §24.3).

Structural similarities between the rabbinic *šaliaḥ* and the early Christian *apostolos* are

---

[112]J.-A. Bühner, *EWNT* 1:341 (*EDNT* 1:142).

[113]H. Ritt, *EWNT* 3:160 (*EDNT* 3:68)

[114]K. H. Rengstorf, "ἀπόστολος," *ThWNT* 1:406-46 (*TDNT* 1:407-45).

[115]For the discussion that follows above see Roloff 1978; J.-A. Bühner, *EWNT* 1:342-51 (*EDNT* 1:142-46); W. A. Bienert, in Hennecke and Schneemelcher 1987-1989, 2:6-28 (cf. ET, 2:25-31); K. Haacker, *ThBLNT* 2:1654-67.

[116]Roloff 1978, 432.

[117]M. Mitchell 1992, 645 with n. 13.

significant despite recent corrections of K. H. Rengstorf's interpretation, especially with regard to authorization (delegation of power) and personal representation. Jürgen Roloff comments, "The authorized person is the representative of his principle both legally and personally. As a result of his commission (sending) he has the right, and the duty, to safeguard his interests in independent decisions. The commission is valid only when he is gone; it ceases as soon as the envoy returns to him."[118] The New Testament usage of *apostolos* does not represent a conscious introduction of a clearly defined term, and it should be understood as "a semantic 'gap' in the available vocabulary" with narrower and broader meanings.[119]

The following nuances of meaning of *apostolos* can be distinguished in the New Testament: (1) "envoy," as a courier sent by a church;[120] (2) "messenger of Christ (Jesus)," as designation of a task;[121] (3) "apostle," as designation of an office (without subsequent genitive);[122] (4) "apostle," as a class of early Christian leaders;[123] (5) "apostle," as a numerically limited group, sometimes identified with the Twelve.[124] The evidence from the Synoptic Gospels shows that the term "apostle" is sometimes limited to the group of Jesus' twelve disciples,[125] but on occasion it designates the wider group of Jesus' followers.[126] Several passages connect *apostolos* or *apostellein* with a specific process of sending.[127]

Wolfgang Bienert believes that there was no uniform "concept" of apostle or apostleship in early Christianity. He suggests that there was a charismatic-pneumatic tradition, represented by Paul and other itinerant apostles who traced their apostolic authority to a direct commission by Christ, and there was the tradition of the first witnesses of the resurrection—that is, the disciples who had lived with Jesus, the "guarantors of the tradition that established the church" and the "prototypes of church officials."[128] This hypothesis is unconvincing for four reasons. (1) These two "traditions" or "lines of tradition" are a modern construct that owes more to the history of interpretation than to a dispassionate evaluation of early Christian history. The differentiation between a "charismatic apostolate" that appeals to the Spirit and an apostolate of "church officials" that is anchored in history operates with an understanding of church office that dominated New Testament studies (especially in Germany) in the nineteenth century, an understanding that would have been alien to the early Christian communities. In his letter to the Galatians and in his second

---

[118]Roloff 1978, 432, with reference to *m. Ber.* 5:5: *šĕluhô šel ʾādām kĕmôtô* ("a man's agent is like to himself").
[119]Haacker, *ThBLNT* 2:1661-62; for the observations that follow above see ibid., 2:1662.
[120]2 Cor 8:23; Phil 2:25.
[121]1 Cor 1:1; 2 Cor 1:1; Eph 1:1; Col 1:1; 1 Thess 2:7; 1 Tim 1:1.
[122]Rom 1:1; Gal 1:1; 1 Tim 2:7.
[123]1 Cor 12:28-29.
[124]Mt 10:2; Lk 9:1 (v.l.); 22:14; Rev 21:14; cf. 1 Cor 15:7 (not in 1 Cor 15:5, 7).
[125]Mt 10:2; Mk 3:14; 6:30; Lk 6:13; 9:10; 17:5; 22:14.
[126]Lk 11:49; 24:10.
[127]Mt 10:2, 5; Mk 3:14; 6:7, 30; Lk 9:2, 10; 11:49.
[128]See W. A. Bienert, in Hennecke and Schneemelcher 1987-1989, 2:6-28; quotation, 2:14; cf. Roloff 1978.

letter to the Corinthians Paul vehemently defended his apostleship, but he used the term "apostle" not only for James, the brother of Jesus and the leader of the Jerusalem church (cf. Gal 1:19 with 2:9, 12), but also for Barnabas (1 Cor 9:5-6) and for Andronicus and Junia (Rom 16:7). The decisive criterion for the use of the term "apostle" was, at least for Paul, not an "office" but the fact that somebody was a follower of the crucified Christ (1 Cor 4:9-13) and had been called to missionary service (Rom 1:1, 5). (2) The term "witness" (μάρτυς, *martys*) is an equivalent for the term "apostle" in the book of Acts, explaining and sometimes replacing "apostle."[129] Although Luke, with the exception of Acts 14:4, 14, designates only the Twelve as "apostles" (Acts 1:13, 26; 2:14; 6:6), he calls both them and, with emphasis, Paul "witnesses" (Acts 22:15; 26:16; cf. 22:1, 8; 23:11). This implies an assimilation in status with regard to the Twelve, which fits the fact that Luke calls Paul an "apostle" in Acts 14:4, 14.[130] (3) The designation of Barnabas and Paul as "apostles" in Acts 14:4, 14 does not describe them in general terms simply as missionaries, nor does Luke only grudgingly acknowledge that Paul was recognized as an apostle: Luke regarded both Paul and Barnabas as apostles who had a role similar to that of the Twelve.[131] Two points show this clearly: first, Luke describes in the preceding context (Acts 13:47) the task of Paul with words from Is 49:6, while the phrase "ends of the earth" reminds the reader of the commissioning of the Twelve by Jesus in Acts 1:8; second, the reference to "signs and wonders" that happened through the "hands" of Paul and Barnabas in Acts 14:3 reminds the reader of the parallel formulation in Acts 5:12, where it is used for the ministry of the Twelve. (4) If the Twelve were indeed "guarantors of the tradition that established the church," they clearly would have this role not simply as "prototypes of church officials" but also in the "charismatic" sense as preachers and teachers who have been sent and commissioned by Jesus Christ. And Paul was not the only "itinerant apostle," as the Twelve, at least some of them, were involved in missionary travels as well (see §16). And we should note that while Luke affirms the apostleship of the Twelve in terms of historical eyewitnesses, he emphasizes the same for Paul, who encountered the risen Christ on the road to Damascus.

Ernst Dassmann described Paul the apostle as a "thorn in the flesh" of early Christianity.[132] Whether Paul occupies a special position as apostle depends on the answer to two questions: (1) did Jesus give the Twelve a commission to worldwide missionary work? and (2) if he did, did the Twelve respond positively and were they engaged in missionary work outside of Judea and Galilee, reaching Jews and Gentiles with the gospel? If the answer to these questions is affirmative, then Paul has a "special position" only because we have much more information about his missionary activity and his theology, whereas the activities of the other apostles remain largely unknown, and also because the discussion about the significance of Paul's theology has never ceased in the history of the church. However, his historical "accident" hardly establishes a special or privileged position.

Women

Luke mentions, in the context of a comment about Jesus' ministry in Galilee, several women who accompanied Jesus.[133]

---

[129]Acts 1:8, 22; 2:32; 3:15; 5:32; 10:34, 41; 13:31.
[130]K. Haacker, *ThBLNT* 2:1664; see also Burchard 1970. The contrary position was argued by Günter Klein 1961; not very convincing is Maddox 1982, 70-79.
[131]See Clark 1998, 182-85.
[132]Dassmann 1979; cf. W. A. Bienert, in Hennecke and Schneemelcher 1987-1989, 2:17.
[133]On women in the Gospels see G. Osborne 1989.

Lk 8:1-3: "Soon afterwards he went on through cities and villages, proclaiming and bringing the good news of the kingdom of God. The twelve were with him, [2]as well as some women who had been cured of evil spirits and infirmities: Mary, called Magdalene, from whom seven demons had gone out, [3]and Joanna, the wife of Herod's steward Chuza, and Susanna, and many others, who provided for them out of their resources."

Luke emphasizes the following points.

1. The women are "with Jesus" as the Twelve are "with him" (σὺν αὐτῷ, *syn autō* [Lk 8:1]). The women are disciples of Jesus as the Twelve are Jesus' disciples. Does that mean that the women are on the same "level" as the Twelve[134] or that they preached as the Twelve did?[135] In Lk 8:1 only Jesus is described as one who preaches; neither the disciples nor the women have such a role in Luke's comment.[136] Nor does the text assert that the women had the same "rights" or tasks as the Twelve did: Luke does not report that the women were called by Jesus as disciples (*mathētai*) or to be fishers of people; rather, they joined Jesus after they were healed by him (8:2a). The text does not say that they preached. However, it is plausible that they spoke to others about their liberation from demon possession and about the healing from illness, thus confirming Jesus' message of the coming of God's kingdom.

2. The women traveled with Jesus and the Twelve from town to town and from village to village. They witnessed Jesus' miracles, they heard his preaching, and surely they must have played a role similar to that of the Twelve, as large numbers of people who crowded around Jesus needed to be "organized," perhaps particularly with regard to women who came to Jesus.

Joel Green wonders whether they were single women who were independent and thus free to accompany Jesus: In Lk 7:11-17, 36-50 Luke mentions widows and prostitutes.[137]
It is true that Luke does not mention husbands for Mary from Magdala or for Susanna. And it is true that women who were demon-possessed or stricken with some other chronic illness probably were isolated in various ways and discriminated against. It remains hypothetical, however, whether this explains why they accompanied Jesus and joined the new community that was forming. Also, it is questionable how isolated women could have been wealthy in first-century society (cf. Lk 8:3b). And, of course, Luke does mention Joanna's husband.

3. The role of the women is described with the verb "serve" (διακονεῖν, *diakonein*), which in Lk 8:3 should be translated "provide for" (NRSV) or "support" (TNIV): these women supported them with the resources that they had (Lk 8:3b). This means that at least the three women were well-to-do: as they traveled with Jesus, they supported him and his disciples not with natural produce but with

---

[134]See Grundmann, *Lk*, 174; Marshall, *Lk*, 316.
[135]See Quesnell 1983, 68.
[136]Thus correctly Green, *Lk*, 317 with n. 4.
[137]Green, *Lk*, 318.

financial resources. Luke provides us here with an insight into the way Jesus operated: when he arrived with his followers—men and women—in a town or village, he evidently did not expect free room and board,[138] but he needed financial means that were provided, at least in part, by these women.[139]

The later information that women supported rabbis and their students from their private resources are not relevant: the rabbinic sources point out that the women were instructed by their husbands to act in this manner, while the women mentioned in Lk 8:2-3 acted independently, apart from the fact that they were directly, personally and permanently connected with Jesus' ministry of teaching and preaching. The suggestion that the list of three women was meant to remind the reader of the "inner group of the Twelve"[140] is purely hypothetical.

4. These women later will play an important role: they belong to the few witnesses who had experienced all four stages of the traditional early Christian confession in 1 Cor 15:3-5 (Jesus' death, burial, resurrection, appearances): they were present at Jesus' crucifixion (Lk 23:49), they were present at Jesus' burial (Lk 23:55), they were first at the empty tomb (Lk 23:3; 24:22), and they received the news that Jesus was alive again (Lk 24:4-8).[141]

5. Mary Magdalene (Μαρία Μαγδαληνή; i.e., "the Mary from Magdala") came from the important city of Magdala at the Sea of Galilee. We do not know whether she encountered Jesus during a ministry in Magdala that the Gospel writers do not specifically report, but such a ministry there is plausible.[142] Mary had been cured from possession by "seven" demons (Lk 8:2; Mk 16:9), and thus from "the worst possible state of demonic disorder."[143] She was one of the most faithful of Jesus' disciples: she was present at Jesus' crucifixion and burial, and she probably was the first person at the empty tomb.

Marianne Sawicki suggests that Mary must have been engaged regularly in travel; otherwise she would not have been known as "Mary from Magdala." Sawicki surmises that Mary may have been active in the export of fish.[144] The latter assumption is possible on principle: at Masada jars for storing food have been found bearing the names of three businesswomen who were active in trade activities.[145] In general, however, Sawicki's suggestion is implausible: the evangelists use the term *Magdalēnē* ("from Magdala") to distin-

---

[138]As later the Twelve; see §10.5.

[139]Marshall, *Lk,* 317; cf. Witherington 1979, 244-45; for the observations that follows above see ibid., n. 9.

[140]Bovon, *Lk,* 1:398.

[141]Nolland, *Lk,* 1:366; cf. Bovon, *Lk,* 1:398.

[142]Riesner, *GBL* 2:910; Bauckham 2002, 117-19, 186-89.

[143]Marshall, *Lk,* 316. She is mentioned repeatedly in the Gospel tradition: Mt 27:55-56/Mk 15:40/ Jn 19:25; Mt 27:61/Mk 15:47/Lk 23:55; Mt 28:1/Mk 16:1/Lk 24:10.

[144]Sawicki 2000, 144.

[145]See H. M. Cotton and J. Geiger, "The Economic Importance of Herod's Masada: The Evidence of the Jar Inscriptions," in Fittschen and Foerster 1996, 163-70.

guish this Mary from other women with the same name who are mentioned in the Gospels; and it is unlikely that a woman totally controlled by demons had a profession that required travel and involved important responsibilities.

6. Joanna is "the wife of Chuza" (Lk 8:3), a steward of Herod Antipas. The term ἐπίτροπος (*epitropos*) can be used for the supervisor of a vineyard (Mt 20:8), but here it is used for one of the managers at the royal court. Perhaps he was the manager of an estate of Herod.[146] The name "Chuza" occurs in Nabatean and Syrian inscriptions,[147] which means that Joanna's husband probably was a Nabatean whom Herod had appointed to high office at his palace. Some have linked this Chuza with the royal official of Jn 4:46 and with Manaen, the companion of the young Herod Antipas (Acts 13:1)—a suggestion that must remain hypothetical. The suggestion that the news that Luke possesses about Herod Antipas and his court came from Chuza or Joanna is plausible.[148] In Lk 8:3 Luke informs his readers that there were followers of Jesus among members of the Herodian aristocracy.[149] Joanna was, however, not simply the "prominent aristocrat," as her social status was mixed: the Herodian dynasty, being the interface of the Romans in Galilee, was not loved, as is seen in the negative comments by Luke on Herod.[150] Jesus thus was not afraid to include among his disciples Galileans who were potentially problematic. Joanna belongs to the many who found a new identity in the community of people forming around Jesus, free of social discrimination or isolation. And she was willing, as an aristocrat, to "serve." Luke does not tell us how Joanna was able to accompany Jesus during his travels. She was among the women who visited Jesus' grave on Easter morning (Lk 24:10). Joanna (and possible Chuza) evidently played an important role in the early church.[151]

Some have suggested that the sequence of the women's names reflects competing claims in the early church.[152] We should note, however, that according to Lk 8:3b, "many other" women traveled with Jesus and had similar or identical experiences (cf. Lk 24:10). The imaginative description that Marianne Sawicki provides for Joanna, suggesting that Joanna and Mary Magdalene were the only disciples who had international economic and political connections and were thus responsible for the expansion of the Jesus movement beyond the borders of Galilee and Judea,[153] is not very plausible, considering Luke's account of the missionary activity of the Hellenistic Jewish Christians of Jerusalem and of the missionary advances of Peter and of Paul.

---

[146]Fitzmyer, *Lk*, 1:698; cf. Hoehner 1972, 120, 303-305; H. Balz, *EWNT* 3:1129 (*EDNT* 3:471).

[147]See Bauckham 2002, 151-56; cf. BDAG 1087, s.v. "Χουζᾶς."

[148]Marshall, *Lk*, 317; Bauckham (2002, 189), who also refers to Manaen (Acts 13:1).

[149]Marshall, *Lk*, 317; Nolland, *Lk*, 1:366

[150]Green, *Lk*, 321, with reference to Lk 3:1, 19-20; cf. 1:46-55; for the observation that follows above see ibid.

[151]Marshall, *Lk*, 317. Bauckham (2002, 165-98) thinks that Joanna is identical with the Junia of Rom 16:7.

[152]Hengel 1963, 248-51; see the critique in Nolland, *Lk*, 1:366-67.

[153]Sawicki 2000, 134-35, 146-53, esp. 147-48.

Religious-Historical Parallels

For the Twelve, following Jesus meant leaving their social environment: Peter and Andrew are called to leave their fishing nets, Matthew-Levi leaves his tax station. For the Twelve, at least, following Jesus often meant not knowing where they would stay overnight (Mt 8:20/Lk 9:58) as they traveled with Jesus from town to town, from village to village.[154] Scholars attempt to explain this phenomenon with the help of two parallels.

1. Cynic itinerant philosophers often are cited as a cultural background for the discipleship of the Twelve, in view of descriptions and specifications of Cynic philosophers that seem to parallel the calling and lifestyle of the twelve disciples who followed Jesus during his travels in Galilee.[155] The following elements of the Cynic wandering philosophers are important: (a) their equipment, consisting of threadbare cloak (τριβώνιον, *tribōnion*),[156] bag or pouch (πηρίδιον, *pēridion*) and club (ξύλον, *xylon*); (b) a divine calling;[157] (c) homelessness; (d) a commission to teach; (e) sober reflection before abandoning the old way of life. The Cynic hypothesis often is linked with the people responsible for the sayings source Q: scholars suggest that the Q-people, like the Cynic philosophers, criticized society, refused to follow cultural norms, and protested the disjunction between word and deed, between theory and practice (e.g., in the critique of the Pharisees).[158] A central characteristic of the assumed parallel with the Cynic philosophers is the notion that social relationships with other people, including marital relationships, represent obligations that hinder a person from carrying out a divinely given task, as one is diverted from one's σχολή (*scholē,* "learned discussion, disputation") and encumbered with an existence that is no longer unattached and free.[159]

The hypothesis of the Cynic philosophers providing the background for the calling and lifestyle of Jesus and his disciples is implausible for at least four reasons (see §§16.5; 18.5).[160] (a) The parallels that scholars refer to are not extant in original sources, but only in literary texts written by Stoic philosophers. Also, the Cynic and Stoic texts would have to be analyzed and evaluated historically; they

---

[154]See Klinghardt 1988, 60-65; cf. Theissen 1973; 1977; Meier 1991-2001, 3:54-55.

[155]Georgi 1964, 32-34, 110-12, 193-96 (ET, 28-29, 99-100, 156-57); Hoffmann 1972, 318; Theissen 1973; Klinghardt 1988, 62-63; Crossan 1991; Downing 1992, 1998; Mack 1993; Vaage 1994. For a description of this view and a (mild) critique see Kloppenborg Verbin 2000, 184-93, 420-44 (see ibid., 423-24, with a list of Cynic philosophers in the first century). Meier (1991-2001, 3:47) is much more cautious.

[156]The term *tribōnion* is a diminutive of *tribōn;* the term *pēridion* is a diminutive of *pēra.*

[157]Epictetus, *Diatr.* 3.22.2: "The man who lays his hand to so great a matter as this without God, is hateful to Him."

[158]See Downing 1992, 136; Mack 1993, 46; Vaage 1994, 56.

[159]See Klinghardt 1988, 62-63.

[160]See Horsley 1989; H. Betz 1994; Eddy 1996; Tuckett 1996, 369-73; for a critique from an evangelical perspective see Boyd 1995.

cannot safely be used for describing a popular philosophical movement, especially since the Cynic movement was characterized by substantial diversity.[161] (b) The influence of Cynic philosophers in the first century needs further clarification;[162] the assumption that they existed in Galilee might not be more than a vivid fantasy.[163] (c) Some parallels that scholars point to are not exclusively Cynic or not Cynic at all.[164] (d) The presuppositions and motivations of Cynic philosophy and the presuppositions and motivations of followers of Jesus who were responsible for the traditions in the Synoptic Gospels display considerable differences, especially with regard to the significance of prophetic traditions for understanding Jesus.[165] This means that noticeable parallels explain little.

2. Some scholars suggest that the activities of Levitical Torah preachers may explain the itinerant ministry and lifestyle of Jesus and the Twelve.[166] Two texts are particularly relevant for this suggestion. First, in *4 Ezra* 13:54-56 Ezra is the type of the wise man who forsakes everything for the law and receives in his new way of life a new mother and heavenly compensation.[167]

4 Ezra 13:54-56: "You have forsaken your own ways and have applied yourself to mine, and have searched out my law; [55]for you have devoted your life to wisdom, and called understanding your mother. [56]Therefore I have shown you this, for there is a reward laid up with the Most High."

Second, Philo relates the same connection between Levites and "forsaking everything," concentrated on the abandonment of social, mostly familial, relationships. Interestingly, Philo speaks in this connection about the conversion of Gentiles to Judaism.

Philo describes the Levite as a countermodel to forsaking father and mother in marriage, where the union of man and woman transforms the better part (the man as spirit) into the inferior part (the sensuousness of the woman): Levites forsake their family relationships and thus gain a share in God.[168]

Matthias Klinghardt suggests that the description of the early Christian itinerant preachers might have been influenced by the description of the Levitical Torah

---

[161]H. Betz 1994, 473; Eddy 1996, 459; Tuckett 1996, 351-52. But see Seeley 1996; 1997; Kloppenborg Verbin 2000, 422-42.
[162]H. Betz 1994, 471-74; Eddy 1996, 466-47; Tuckett 1996, 373; cf. Kloppenborg Verbin 2000, 422-26.
[163]H. Betz 1994, 471; Boyd 1995, 153-58; Witherington 1995, 61; Eddy 1996, 467; on the question of Cynics in Galilee see Kloppenborg Verbin 2000, 426-29.
[164]H. Betz 1994, 473; Tuckett 1996, 351-52; cf. Kloppenborg Verbin 2000, 430-31.
[165]See Sato 1988; R. H. Horsley, "Logoi Prophētôn: Reflections on the Genre of Q," in Pearson 1991, 195-209; idem 1995, 268-71; Tuckett 1996, 376, 391-92.
[166]See Klinghardt 1988, 63.
[167]Klinghardt 1988, 63; for the observation that follows above see ibid.
[168]Philo, *Leg.* 2.49-52 (§50); cf. *Sacr.* 128-129.

teachers.[169] However, the primary evidence for the existence of organized Levitical Torah teachers is quite limited, making conclusions tenuous. Furthermore, it is not possible to elucidate all details of the disciples' way of life and ministry. This is also true with regard to the rabbinical students, from whom the disciples differed in their exclusive commitment to the person of Jesus. Rabbinical students lived with their rabbis in a community experience that was indispensable, but they received the advice to change teachers. For example, Rabbi Chisda (b. A.D. 309) said, "He who studies the law only from one teacher will never see in his life a sign of victory" (*b. 'Abod. Zar.* 19a).[170]

10.3 The Commission to Preach and Heal in the Galilean Towns and Villages

Jesus called the twelve disciples with the specific goal that they would be active as "missionaries" in the future, as Mk 3:14 shows: "And he appointed twelve, whom he also named apostles, to be with him, and to be sent out to proclaim the message" (ἵνα ἀποστέλλη αὐτοὺς κηρύσσειν, *hina apostellē autous kēryssein*). Some scholars interpret this statement in terms of the "establishment of a missionary body."[171]

The Missionary Discourse

After preparing the disciples for their task—it is impossible to reconstruct or even speculate about the length of this training period—Jesus sent the Twelve in six teams of two disciples each to preach and heal in the towns and villages of Galilee (Mk 6:7-13/Mt 10:5-16/Lk 9:1-6). They were to proclaim the good news of the dawn of the kingdom of God in regions that Jesus had not visited or wanted to visit later.[172]

Luke reports a second sending out of (seventy-two) disciples in Lk 10:1-24, after his account of the sending out of the Twelve in Lk 9:1-6. Many scholars regard the account of a second sending of disciples as a doublet (see §11 for arguments against this view). The explanations for this second mission charge range from two missionary assignments (Mk 6:7-13/Mt 10:5-16/Lk 9:1-6 and Lk 10:1-24), one missionary assignment (Mt 10:5-16/Mk 6:7-13, divided into two parts by Luke) and no missionary assignment at all.[173] Many critical scholars dispute that Mt 10:5-16/Lk 9:1-6 represents authentic words of Jesus; they argue that the rules of Mt 10 and Lk 9 are the result of clarifications of problems and situations that arose after Easter.[174] Scot McKnight argues in his study of Mt 9:35—11:1 that Matthew was a creative interpreter who sought to interpret the traditions available to him for the benefit of itinerant Christian

---

[169]Klinghardt 1988, 64.
[170]Riesner 1988, 417.
[171]T. W. Manson 1967, 241.
[172]See Pesch 1982, 27. For a history of research on Mt 10:1-15 see Ridgway 1999, 17-83.
[173]The last position is defended by Beare 1970.
[174]R. Bultmann (1995, 156) regards both Mt 10:5-6 and Mt 28:19-20 as inauthentic: he and many others allege that the two passages reflect various stages of the missionary history of the early church; cf. Beare 1970; recently Cousland 2002, 89 n. 68.

missionaries of his time who were persecuted by Pharisees, adding and absorbing traditions and explicating them within the framework of his theology.[175] Other scholars doubt that Mt 10:17-23 belonged to a mission charge of the disciples before Easter, since the text speaks of persecution by synagogues and of giving testimony before pagan audiences.[176] Some argue on the basis of the second mission charge in Lk 10:1-24 that it is unclear how often the disciples were sent out by Jesus before Easter. The numerous source-, tradition- and redaction-critical suggestions for Mt 10 (and for the parallels in Lk 9 and 10) cannot be discussed in detail here.[177] A study by Risto Uro may serve as one example of the imaginative and hypothetical reconstructions that scholars have presented. Uro believes that the earliest collections of missionary instructions were put together in order to justify the rights and the lifestyle of the itinerant ascetic preachers who were the charismatic authorities of the early Christian communities in Palestine in the first decades after Jesus' crucifixion. These preachers proclaimed the imminent arrival of the kingdom of God and sought to gather the "sons of peace." As a result of their rejection by their Jewish contemporaries, their proclamation increasingly became a proclamation of divine judgment. Uro suggests that the final redactor of Q used these polemical and missionary traditions and edited them for the benefit of his church.[178]

There is no cogent reason for such skepticism. The position taken by William Manson is still valid: the sending out of the disciples by Jesus belongs to the most solidly authenticated facts of Jesus' life.[179] The following seven observations support the historicity of the sending out of the disciples. (1) All three Synoptic Gospels provide an account of a least one mission of the disciples. (2) Paul refers to a saying of Jesus from the mission charge to the disciples in his explanation of his own missionary praxis (1 Cor 9:14; cf. Lk 10:17). Paul evidently knew the tradition of the mission charge to the disciples. (3) Several "radical" instructions (e.g., the directive not to take provisions) were not characteristic for the early Christian missionary activity after Easter. The directive "Eat what is set before you" (Lk 10:8) hardly fits the later Palestinian church, and evaluated in its entire context it cannot be derived from the mission of the Greek-speaking churches free of the demands of the law, but it "accords with Jesus' sovereign attitude towards the ritual law" (cf. Mk 7:15).[180] (4) The description of the proclamation of the disciples who are sent out by Jesus does not include any material that would hint at a fictitiously reconstructed situation after Easter. The mission charge lacks christological content, which was central in the preaching of the early church. The Twelve are said to have been instructed to proclaim Jesus' message of the dawn of God's kingdom. (5) The fact that sayings of Jesus that are part of the mission charge occur in other Gospels in different contexts (cf. Mt 10:17-23 with Mk 13:9-13) is no automatic proof for later traditions of the Christian communities. The statements in Mt 10:17-23 clearly transcend a short-term mission of the disciples in Galilee before Easter, but the themes are not new: Jesus already had spoken about persecution (Mt 5:10-12), about the time of a more permanent

---

[175]McKnight 1986; see the conclusions, 367-84.

[176]See Beare 1970, 4; S. Brown 1978; further Fusco 1990.

[177]See Carson, *Mt,* 240-42; Bartnicki 1988; Fuchs 1992; 1994, 73-77.

[178]Uro 1987; see the summary, 241-42.

[179]T. W. Manson 1949, 73; cf. Riesner 1988, 453; Pesch, *Mk,* 1:330-31. For the arguments that follow above see Riesner 1988, 453-54. See also Catchpole (1991), who accepts as authentic at least the saying about the sheep and the wolves and also the instructions concerning the equipment and the behavior of the envoys. The historicity of the mission charge is now defended also by Gehring 2000, 93-103; Meier 1991-2001, 3:154-63.

[180]See Hengel 1971-72, 36 (ET, 62); followed by Pesch 1982, 27. For the observation that follows above see Hengel, ibid.

witness before the "world" (Mt 5:13-14; 7:13-14) after his death (Mt 9:15), and he had spoken about the future when Gentiles participate in the messianic banquet (Mt 8:11-12). And we should not exclude the possibility that Jesus used instructions for a short-term mission of his disciples as a paradigm for their later missionary work that would last longer and would take place in a different context.[181] (6) If Jesus never sent his disciples on a mission or gave instructions concerning such a mission, then the calling of the disciples to follow him—who himself was engaged in a "mission" as he traveled from place to place and preached and healed—ultimately loses its significance. (7) The way in which Jesus reminds the Twelve shortly before his arrest of an earlier sending (Lk 22:35: "When I sent you out without a purse, bag, or sandals, did you lack anything?") alludes more clearly to Lk 10:4 ("Carry no purse, no bag, no sandals; and greet no one on the road") than to Lk 9:3 ("Take nothing for your journey, no staff, nor bag, nor bread, nor money—not even an extra tunic.") This fact may refer exactly to a second mission in which the Twelve were active besides the seventy-two followers.[182]

Rudolf Pesch thinks that the Synoptic missionary discourses suggest a single mission and probably conceal the fact "that the disciples were repeatedly employed in short-term missionary work by Jesus," which would best explain the formation of rules for envoys (*Botenregel*) and their later compilation: "rules" usually are the result of experiences, of unsolved problems, of repeated and repeatable situations.[183] It is possible that Matthew, who omits the sending of the seventy-two disciples, included elements of the instructions for the Seventy-Two, of whom the Twelve were a part, in his missionary discourse in Mt 10.

Some scholars argue that the restriction of the disciples' mission in Mt 10 to Israel contradicts the universal scope of the disciples' mission in Mt 28, implying that one of these charges therefore must be inauthentic. This argument is unconvincing. Equally unconvincing is the suggestion by Schuyler Brown that Matthew could not ignore the particularistic trends of his community and thus included Mt 10:5-6 in his missionary discourse, which, however, presupposed the Gentile mission.[184] Roman Bartnicki thinks that Matthew directed the missionary discourse to all members of his Christian community, with the mission of the earthly Jesus as a model that they should follow; the emphasis on Jesus' mission to Israel may have served the apologetic goal of highlighting the messianic dignity of Jesus; the restriction of a historical mission of the Twelve to Jews was no longer binding for the later Christians.[185] Adolf Schlatter resolved this tension with the argument of the historical sequence of the mission to Israel followed by the beginnings of the mission among Gentiles: Mt 10 and Mt 28 represent different stages of the ministry of Jesus and the ministry of the disciples.[186] The sending of the disciples to Israel was a "preparatory exercise" for the real missionary task.[187] Axel von Dobbeler argues on literary- and redaction-critical grounds that this solution is impossible: the missionary discourse points beyond the specific historical situation, since it lacks any direct function in the narrative flow of the evangelist; the discourse has a foundational ecclesiological significance for the Matthean community.[188] This position

---

[181]See Carson, *Mt,* 242.

[182]Thus Bock, *Lk,* 2:987.

[183]Pesch 1982, 27. For the observation that follows above see Carson, *Mt,* 241.

[184]S. Brown 1977, 32.

[185]Bartnicki 1988, 48-53.

[186]Schlatter, *Mt,* 798.

[187]Zahn, *Mt,* 712.

[188]Dobbeler 2000b, 22-23, with reference to Luz, *Mt,* 2:75.

argues from the silence of the Gospel writers. It clearly is not the only possible explanation: Schlatter argues that Matthew would not have regarded his account as having gaps, as the Gospel portrays Jesus, not the disciples; David Hill suggests that the reader has to assume that the disciples were sent out, since they are not mentioned in Mt 11; Ernst Bammel thinks that the success of the mission of the disciples may have been the basis for the question by John the Baptist and for Jesus' answer in Mt 11:2-6; Davies and Allison surmise that the reason why the return of the disciples who had been sent out on a missionary tour is not mentioned is that such comments would have rendered the statement in Mt 10:23 as unfulfilled prophecy and the mission among Jews as complete.[189] The instructions concerning a persecution by synagogue representatives (Mt 10:16-25) often are taken as indicative of a post-Easter redaction. This conclusion, too, is not necessary: Jesus may well have spoken about persecution, either as a result of his evaluation of Jewish messengers (and prophets) or as a result of prophetic inspiration.

In the first part of the missionary discourse (Mt 10:5-16) Jesus instructs the disciples concerning a proclamation activity that they will be responsible for in Galilean villages, the duration of which is not specified. The instructions contain five elements:[190]

I. Target audience (10:5b, 6)
II. Task (10:7-8)
    A. Proclaim the dawn of the kingdom of God (10:7)
    B. Heal the sick (10:8a)
    C. Drive out demons (10:8b)
III. Prohibition of provisions (10:9-10)
IV. Room and board: reception and rejection (10:11-15)
V. Behavior in dangerous situations (10:16)

These instructions concerning the missionary activity of the twelve disciples in Galilean villages are to be explained as follows.

    1. Jesus instructs the Twelve in terms of a short-term missionary tour through Galilean villages. At the same time he describes their imminent mission as a paradigm of a permanent mission in the future. The short-term mission is training for their later missionary activity.[191] This twofold perspective explains the following phenomena: (a) The Twelve are instructed to restrict their preaching to the "lost sheep of the house of Israel" (i.e., Jews) and to avoid Samaria (Mt 10:5b-6).[192] They will be dragged, as a result of their preaching of Jesus' message, before rulers and kings "as a testimony to them and the Gentiles" (Mt

---

[189]Schlatter, *Mt,* 355; Hill, *Mt,* 196; Bammel, *ThWNT* 6:903 (*TDNT* 6:903-4); Davies and Allison, *Mt,* 2:239.

[190]See Riesner 1978, 181-82; cf. Gnilka (*Mt,* 1:359-60), who analyzes the first section as including 10:5-15. Other scholars divide the section as 10:5b-16/17-25; see Grilli 1992, 31-48.

[191]Carson, *Mt,* 242.

[192]A.-J. Levine (1988, 13-58) believes that Mt 10:5b-6 is redaction. The passage does not constitute evidence for a tendency in early Christianity that was hostile to Samaritans (contra Lindemann 1993, 67, 76).

10:18). (b) The Twelve should reckon with the possibility that they will not be welcomed (Mt 10:14), and they must know that they will be flogged in synagogues, that they will be hated and persecuted (Mt 10:17-25).

Heinrich Kasting suggested that there was no immediate continuity between the sending out of the disciples during Jesus' earthly ministry and the early Christian missionary activity.[193] Jesus' mission charge to the Twelve was indeed limited in terms of duration. However, the reference to a witness before rulers and kings and the announcement of persecution indicate that the commissioning of the Twelve was not just an "incident" but rather training for the proclamation of the kingdom of God and exemplary preparation for future missionary activity. The argument that the early Christian mission began only after Easter, that there would have been no early Christian missionary activity without Easter, is not cogent: there would have also been no Pentecost without Easter, and there would have been no church without both Easter and Pentecost. Kasting, following Willi Marxsen, separates Easter from Jesus' earthly ministry too sharply. The main problem with Kasting's description is that he locates the historical origins of the early Christian apostolic ministry and mission in the Easter events,[194] not in Jesus' ministry and his calling and commissioning the twelve disciples. In order to prove that the Easter events constitute *the* key function for the origins of the early Christian mission, he has to argue that the early church engaged in extensive missionary work "practically from the first day." This hypothesis, however, is not supported by the evidence of the first chapters of the book of Acts.

2. The Twelve are instructed to go (πορεύεσθε, *poreuesthe* [Mt 10:6]) in pairs (δύο δύο, *dyo dyo* [Mk 6:7]),[195] thus in six groups of two disciples each. This pairing provides mutual encouragement and support, attests the veracity of the testimony of two witnesses,[196] and represents the new community that is being established.[197]

Detlev Dormeyer remarks that Jesus preferred the number "two" both in the calling and in the sending out of the Twelve "in order, on the one hand, to trace the call and the commission to each individual; on the other hand, he wishes to avoid the individualization of the processes. . . . Duality, as the smallest plural, guards against having to standardize and schematize calling, sending, and community with Jesus as a mass movement. Community with Jesus lives from the common actions between *two,* which are open to being isolated (one) or being enlarged (three)."

3. The Twelve are instructed to remain within the borders of Galilee. In Mt 10:5 Jesus directs them to "go nowhere among the Gentiles" (εἰς ὁδὸν ἐθνῶν, *eis*

---

[193]Kasting 1969, 126.

[194]Kasting 1969, 61-81; the comment that follows above, ibid., 81.

[195]The instruction to go in pairs is omitted in Mt 10 and Lk 9; but see the mission charge to the seventy-two disciples in Lk 10.

[196]Cf. Deut 19:15; Num 35:30. See Fitzmyer, *Lk,* 2:846; earlier Jeremias 1959, 139.

[197]Thus D. Dormeyer, *EWNT* 1:872-73 (*EDNT* 1:360): "Discipleship to Jesus occurs first when at least *two* are gathered in his name"; the quotation that follows above, ibid.

hodon ethnōn), meaning that they should not enter the territory of Tyre and Sidon in the north, and to "enter no town of the Samaritans" (εἰς πόλιν Σαμαριτῶν, *eis polin Samaritōn*), meaning that they should not preach in Samaria in the south. Most scholars interpret the latter restriction as a general statement because Jesus does not mention a specific town (e.g., Samaria-Sebaste). If the καί (*kai*) in Mt 10:5 is additive, then the Samaritans are deliberately distinguished from the Gentiles but still classified as "non-Israel."[198] If the *kai* is epexegetical, then the prohibition to enter Gentile territory represents a theological verdict on the Samaritans: they are described as *ethnē,* Gentiles.[199] The fact that Jesus specifically mentions Samaria perhaps presupposes the events of Jn 4:39-42: now, while traveling from Jerusalem to Galilee, the disciples might have been tempted by the success of an earlier mission in Samaria to return and proclaim the good news where they were already known. The experience of Lk 9:52-56 shows that due to their temperament, the disciples did not possess the maturity required to do missionary work among Samaritans.[200] The real reason for the restriction of the mission to Galilee was not pragmatic, however, but rather theological and salvation-historical: salvation is offered first to Israel, then to the Gentiles. This also explains why the number "twelve" is emphasized in Mt 10:1, 2, 5: the Twelve represent Israel and therefore are sent to the Jews.[201] The acceptance of Gentiles into the people of God, hinted at already in Jesus' ministry (see §12.2), was not to be a stumbling block for the Jews right from the beginning; the resistance of the Jewish people was not to be provoked even more by an active missionary activity among Gentiles.[202] Since Jesus and his disciples had visited the towns and villages in Galilee for many months, it can be assumed that the Twelve had already visited many of the Galilean settlements and were known to their inhabitants.

4. The Twelve were instructed to proclaim (κηρύσσειν, *kēryssein*) the dawn of the kingdom of God, following the lead of Jesus' own proclamation (Mt 10:7). Joachim Gnilka comments that their proclamation "concerned, as in Jesus' preaching, the universal, worldwide liberating and saving reign that comes from God to us, a rule that is in its essence and in its completion a reality of the future, indeed the future itself, but a reign that can already be experienced in the present as it is proclaimed and pronounced."[203] The proclamation of the dawn of the kingdom of God is teaching (διδάσκειν, *didaskein* [Mk 6:30]), in continuation of Jesus' teaching. This suggests that the sending out and the missionary activity of the disciples before Easter were already an occasion and cause for

---

[198]Egger 1986, 193.
[199]Zangenberg 1998, 188; cf. Böhm 1999, 97-100.
[200]Carson, *Mt,* 244.
[201]Grilli (1992, 105) speaks of a "relazione fondamentale tra 'questi Dodici' e la 'casa d'Israele.'"
[202]Carson, *Mt,* 244-45; Gnilka, *Mt,* 1:362-63; cf. Grilli 1992, 222-33.
[203]Gnilka, *Mt,* 1:364.

the forming of tradition about Jesus' words and message.[204]

5. Along with with the assignment to proclaim the good news of the kingdom of God, the disciples are instructed to heal the sick and to free people from demons (Mt 10:8). They will be able to heal and exorcise on account of Jesus' "transfer of authority" (Mt 10:1): the disciples are to continue Jesus' messianic ministry in these areas as well. The reference to healing the sick and driving out demons generally summarizes the miracle-working activity of the disciples, while the reference to raising the dead and cleansing lepers (Mt 10:8) is specific. "It is the liberation from these bonds, particularly, that documents the possibility of experiencing the reign of the heavens that has come close. . . . It is meant to show that God ultimately wants this liberation which can happen at the moment only in singular cases."[205]

6. Jesus directs the disciples not to accept money (Mt 10:9): they have experienced the free grace of God's reign themselves, and therefore they should pass on the reality of the kingdom of God as a gift. They must carry out their work free of charge: the disciple who has been sent out by Jesus must make no personal demands or charge others, but may expect to receive needed provisions.[206] Rabbi Hillel said similarly that the Torah is not a "spade"; that is, expertise in the law must not be used for one's own advantage.[207] The disciples could assume that most people whom they would encounter on their missionary tour had already heard of Jesus and his message, because Jesus had already visited their town or village, or because they had visited Jesus when he was in the vicinity, or because they had heard of Jesus.

7. Jesus directs the disciples to take no provisions on the missionary tour: Matthew mentions gold, silver, copper, bag, extra tunic, sandals and staff (Mt 10:9-10).

In Mk 6:8-9 Jesus orders them "to take nothing for their journey except a staff; no bread, no bag, no money in their belts; but to wear sandals and not to put on two tunics." In other words, whereas Mt 10:9-10 prohibits sandals and a staff, Mk 6:8-9 allows them. This discrepancy with regard to the staff (ῥάβδος, *rhabdos*) and sandals (ὑποδήματα, *hypodēmata*) is best explained by the different verbs that are used. Matthew has κτάομαι (*ktaomai*), which means "to gain possession of, procure for oneself, acquire"; Mark uses αἴρειν (*airein*), which means "to take/carry along." Mark probably describes what the disciples were allowed to take along, while Matthew presupposes that the disciples already

---

[204]Riesner 1988, 454-55, with reference to B. S. Easton, *Christ in the Gospels* (New York: Scribner, 1930), 41; V. Taylor, *The Formation of the Gospel Tradition* (2nd ed.; London: Macmillan, 1935), 94; Schürmann 1968, 56-61.

[205]Gnilka, *Mt,* 1:364. On the role of miracles in the disciples' mission see also Kelhoffer 2000, 249-61; he claims that Mt 10:8; 11:2-6, 20-21; 17:14-20 reveal a "competition" among rival missionaries who perform miracles and fight for acknowledgment in the Christian communities (ibid., 261). There is no evidence in the text to support this claim.

[206]Gnilka, *Mt,* 1:365; for the observation that follows above see ibid.

[207]Carson (*Mt,* 245) remarks, "The danger of profiteering is still among us."

possessed various items (tunic, sandals, staff) and points out that Jesus directed them not to buy additional equipment that they already own.[208] Joachim Gnilka rejects an interpretation that emphasizes the grammatical dependence of the prohibitions on μὴ κτήσησθε (*mē ktēsesthe*) as an alleviation of the harsh directives: "The radical nature of the instruction consists in the fact that obvious necessities were not allowed. . . . The disciple who is sent out must begin his journey without any material provisions."[209] Although this evaluation may explain the text of Mark and Matthew, it cannot explain the text of Luke, who prohibits with the verb αἴρειν a staff (Lk 9:3) and sandals (Lk 10:4).[210] Several other solutions have been suggested that are not fully convincing, however. Donald Carson suggests the following as the most straightforward solution:[211] Luke has not changed the text of Mark but depends in both texts (Lk 9:3; 10:4), as does Matthew, on the sayings source Q; in Lk 9:3 Luke changes the verb κτάομαι to αἴρειν, whose semantic range can include κτάομαι, and in Lk 10:4 he changes κτάομαι to βαστάζειν in order to describe the carrying of provisions and luggage—"no purse" means no money, "no bag" means no luggage, "no sandals" means no extra pair of sandals.

The empowerment to perform miracles (Mt 10:8) stands in stark contrast to the lack of financial means and provisions (Mt 10:9-10; cf. Mk 6:8-9; Lk 10:4; 22:35). Some scholars compare Jesus' directives to carry no provisions with the frugality of the Essenes:

"They carry nothing whatsoever with them on their journeys, except arms as a protection against brigands. In every city there is one of the order expressly appointed to attend to strangers, who provides them with raiment and other necessaries. In their dress and deportment they resemble children under rigorous discipline. They do not change their garments or shoes until they are torn to shreds or worn threadbare with age" (Josephus, *B.J.* 2.125).

Even though the Essenes did not engage in missionary work, which reduces the value of the parallel, Josephus's description shows that, depending on the particular circumstances, travel with minimal equipment was possible, especially if the traveler could expect room and board from acquaintances or sympathizers with the religious movement to which he belonged. The Cynic itinerant philosophers had a frugal lifestyle as well. Their provisions consisted of a wallet and an oil flask (Epictetus Diss 1.24.11); their frugality sought to demonstrate their sovereignty over all earthly matters, a motif that is irrelevant for Jesus and for his disciples.

Many interpreters understand the behavior of the disciples that Jesus expects as a sign of the kingdom of God, which they proclaim: the reality and the requirements of God's kingdom claimed their full attention. "As they perform miracles they help others experience the salvation of God's reign. They are helpless

---

[208]Thus the *Mt* commentaries of Zahn, Schlatter and Carson, ad loc.
[209]Gnilka, *Mt*, 1:365-66.
[210]Marshall (*Lk*, 352-53), who suggests a source-critical explanation: Matthew and Luke depend on Q against Mark.
[211]Carson, *Mt*, 247.

and defenseless in their poverty, but they are fully occupied with the imminent
basileia. They let no unnecessary concern distract them. The frugality is thus an
element of the credibility of their message."[212] Such an interpretation must demonstrate the credibility of the message of the gospel of Jesus Christ in the frugality of the missionaries of the early church.[213] However, the evidence of the
early Christian texts does not easily support this interpretation. It is preferable
to interpret Jesus' directives concerning the provisions of the Twelve in the context of a missionary activity that was limited in time and that took place in a
region where he was already known and where he had sympathizers if not followers (cf. Lk 22:35-38).[214] The Twelve are directed not to engage in extensive
preparations and not to carry unnecessary provisions during their short-term
missionary tour through the Galilean towns and villages. They were to travel
unencumbered with material possessions and to rely on people's hospitality and
God's providential care.

8. The disciples are directed to look for accommodations after they arrive
in a town or village. Some scholars interpret the instruction in Mt 10:11-15 in
terms of a "house mission." Some argue that "perhaps Matthew's wording has
been influenced by the thought that house churches are the bases for Christian
mission."[215] The consequences of the reception or the rejection of the greeting
of peace that Jesus describes at some length (Mt 10:12-13) indicate that the
"peace" that he refers to should be understood as a summary of his message
of salvation and thus as an offer of messianic salvation.[216] A more "minimalist"
interpretation in terms of the social convention of the *šalôm* greeting cannot
be ruled out completely, however, especially if we accept the authenticity of
the instructions of Jesus in Mt 10:5-15 and refrain from interpreting the passage
as reflecting an "early stage of the early Christian missionary praxis."[217] It is
undisputed that private houses played a major role in the missionary activity
of the early church. It is uncertain, however, whether Jesus' instructions must
be interpreted in terms of "mission tactics" with houses as the starting point
and the base of the disciples' preaching ministry, followed by a "city mission"
as a second phase.[218] The suggestion that Mt 10:11-14 refers to a "house mission" as the first, and foundational, stage of the missionary work of the disciples presupposes that the greeting of peace is understood as a proclamation

[212]Gnilka, *Mt,* 1:167.
[213]Gnilka (*Mt,* 1:371) attempts to do this when he writes, "The church can have a convincing
ministry only as a poor church. Poverty is the characteristic of apostolicity."
[214]Thus earlier Zahn 1886, 109; recently Carson, *Mt,* 245-47.
[215]Davies and Allison, *Mt,* 2:175-76; cf. Gundry, *Mt,* 189; Gnilka, *Mt,* 1:368; Klauck 1981, 56-57;
see recently Gehring 2000, 103-13.
[216]On "peace" in Mt 10:12-13 see Ridgway 1999, 85-301, esp. 268-99.
[217]See Gnilka, *Mt,* 1:367, 370.
[218]Thus Gehring 2000, 106; for the observations that follow above see ibid., 108-13.

of the dawn of the kingdom of God, and the acceptance of the preaching disciples who extend this "greeting" is understood as an acceptance of Jesus' message of salvation, particularly by the head of the family. The text, however, does not state this clearly. The Gospel writers do not speak explicitly of a missionary activity in houses, nor do they speak of a "conquest of the village or town" from houses as headquarters in which the disciples stayed.[219] A related view that also has no basis in the text is the interpretation that the mission of the disciples was focused on towns and villages because Jesus sought "corporate" reactions rather than individual conversions.[220] As Jesus stays in houses and enjoys the hospitality of people who welcome him,[221] so the disciples may expect the welcome and hospitality of people in the Galilean villages that they visit during their preaching tour.

The typical Israelite house had four rooms, with a ground plan of 8 by 10 m (ca. 9 by 11 yd.). The "living room" in which the family ate, slept and did indoor work, ranged in size from 10 to 40 m^2 (ca. 12 to 48 sq. yd.). During summer the cooking usually was done in the courtyard, out in the open. A family that had two living rooms may be regarded as wealthy.[222] I have already referred to the "house of the fisherman" in Bethsaida (fig. 4), with a size of 18 by 27 m, consisting of four rooms grouped around an open courtyard.[223] The "house of the vintner" in Bethsaida (fig. 14) measured 16 by 18 m (17.5 by 19.7 yd.), including the central courtyard, and also belonged to a family that was fairly wealthy: the house had a large courtyard (12 by 12.8 m), a kitchen (10 by 4.5 m), a large room (4.5 by 5.4 m) and a smaller room (3.5 by 2.1 m).[224] Houses were built of stone or mud-brick; the mud-bricks were coated on the inner faces of the walls with waterproof plaster, chalked white; cracks in the walls and the flat, mud-plastered roof needed to be repaired annually.

In the ancient world the house was not only the most important material element of human culture but also the most elementary social reality, as it constituted the domains of life, residence and work.[225] The house was a hierarchal entity, as the father was the master of the family (*pater familias*), the head of the social relations in the house (husband/wife, parents/children, master/servants-slaves). The economic basis of the family was, with the exception of the larger cities, agriculture, cattle breeding and, in many families, crafts and trade. It appears that no alternative modes of existence and ways of life existed in Israel: "An existence without a house signified the loss of the absolutely vital solidarity that was inseparably linked with the house."

Alfons Weiser points out that Jesus' proclamation of the kingdom of God entailed a relativizing, indeed in part a reversal, of the ways of life and of the orders of the house:[226] Jesus calls some individuals to leave their "house" and profession, their par-

---

[219]Contra Klauck (1981, 57), who refers to Mt 10:11/Lk 10:8.
[220]See Egelkraut 1976, 148.
[221]Cf. Mk 1:29; 14:14; Lk 7:36; 19:5, also Mk 14:3; Lk 7:36; 10:38; 14:1.
[222]J. S. Holladay, *ABD* 3:313-16; cf. M. J. Selman, *IBD* 2:668-72.
[223]R. Arav, in Arav and Freund 1995-1999, 1:22-23, 26-28.
[224]R. Arav, in Arav and Freund 1995-1999, 2:97-98.
[225]Bieritz and Kähler 1985, 478, cf. ibid., 479-80; the quotation that follows above, 480.
[226]Weiser 1990, 71-72; cf. Bieritz and Kähler 1985, 483; Schnackenburg 1986-1988, 1:125-55.

ents and their relatives, and to follow him.[227] Jesus himself was a itinerant preacher, without a fixed residence (Mt 8:20/Lk 9:58); his own relatives did not understand his way of life (Mk 3:21), and he pointed out that one result of people's reaction to his person and message is the division of families: "They will be divided: father against son and son against father, mother against daughter and daughter against mother, mother-in-law against her daughter-in-law and daughter-in-law against mother-in-law" (Lk 12:53/Mt 10:35). This relativizing dimension corresponds, positively, to Jesus' critique of Jewish divorce law, which placed women at a disadvantage,[228] his "liberal" association with women (cf. Lk 8:1-3; Jn 4), and his demand that the disciples be willing to serve one another and others without establishing hierarchies of importance and control.[229] "This clear and at the same time non-fundamental break with the hierarchical structures of the house derives its justification from the claims of the kingdom of God which liberates people from old bonds and which enables people to be committed to the one who alone should be called 'Father' (Mt 23:9)."

The instructions in Mt 10:11-15 are most naturally understood in a specific and practical manner: "The disciples were not to shop around for the most comfortable quarters."[230]

Jesus informs the disciples of the possibility that they will not be welcomed and accepted in any given house or town. This announcement reflects his own experience: the proclamation of the message of the dawn of God's kingdom provokes divisions.

Jesus states concerning such towns, "Truly I tell you, it will be more tolerable for the land of Sodom and Gomorrah on the day of judgment than for that town" (Mt 10:15). Some scholars have suggested that this assertion is not a prophecy or a commentary on the fate of these cities in the final judgment but rather emphasizes that greater privileges carry greater responsibilities: "It is an unprecedented honour to hear the disciples' proclamation, and incomparable failure to reject it. To whom much is given, from them will much be required."[231]

9. At the end of his instructions Jesus speaks about dangerous situations that the Twelve will experience (Mt 10:16). Sheep who encounter hungry wolves have no chance: a miracle is required in order for them to survive. The introductory phrase "See, I am sending you" (ἰδοὺ ἐγὼ ἀποστέλλω, *idou egō apostellō*) emphasizes the divine protection that Jesus promises his disciples for their upcoming missionary tour through Galilee. The promised divine protection does not exclude, however, the obligation on the part of the disciples to take dangerous situations into account: they should be "wise as serpents"; that is, they should

---

[227]Mt 8:22; 10:37; Mk 1:16-20; 10:29-31; Lk 9:57-62; 14:26.
[228]Mt 5:31-32; 19:3-9; Mk 10:2-12; Lk 16:18.
[229]Mk 10:43-45/Lk 22:25-27. The quotation that follows above is from Bieritz and Kähler 1985, 483.
[230]Carson, *Mt*, 245.
[231]Davies and Allison, *Mt*, 2:179.

behave circumspectly, prudently, carefully considering the dangers, so that their reliance on God's protection becomes evident.[232] They must neither seek martyrdom nor play evasive or tactical games: they must be "innocent as doves"—that is, not cunning, overcautious, suspicious of everybody and everything. Jesus warns them against both foolhardy confidence and calculating furtiveness.[233] The disciples are instructed to avoid conflicts and attacks as far as possible, and at the same time to make sure that their caution does not degenerate into fear or elusiveness.

In the second part of the missionary discourse (Mt 10:17-42) Jesus looks ahead to a more permanent time of missionary service of his disciples. He emphasizes again that there will be opposition and persecution. At the end of the discourse Jesus summarizes again the characteristics of discipleship. This section can be divided as follows:[234]

VI. Warning of future suffering: list of hardships (10:17-25)
      A. Arrest by local councils and flogging in synagogues (10:17b-18)
         Promise of the support of God's Spirit (10:19-20)
      B. Rejection and hate in families and "by all" (10:21-22)
         Promise of the coming of the Son of Man (10:23)
      C. Inspiration: correspondence of the disciples' and Jesus' ministry (10:24-25)
VII. Encouragement: there is no need to have fear (10:26-31)
      A. The truth will become manifest (10:26-27)
      B. Death is not final (10:28)
      C. The heavenly Father continuously cares for them (10:29-31)
VIII. Characteristics of discipleship (10:32-39)
      A. Confessing Jesus before people (10:32-33)
      B. Accepting tribulation as the mark of the messianic era (10:34-36)
      C. Following Jesus whatever the earthly cost (10:37-39)
IX. Encouragement: the welcome of the missionaries (10:40-42)

Jesus encourages the disciples that they should not be afraid. As Florian Wilk comments, "He who fears God does not *need* to be afraid of human adversaries, since God takes care of the disciples; he who fears God *must* not be afraid of those adversaries, since in that case the disciple fails to fulfill his task to proclaim and to confess."[235]

Similar statements in Jesus' discourse about the end of this age in Mt 24 help us to understand Mt 10:17-42: Jesus instructs his disciples that the missionary task that is accompanied by persecution must be understood as an event and process that takes place in the time before the return of the Son of Man.[236] Scholars who accept

---

[232]Gnilka, *Mt*, 1:375; for the remark that follows above see Schweizer, *Mt*, 155.

[233]See Schlatter, *Mt*, 338. For the discussion that follows above see Carson, *Mt*, 247.

[234]See Gnilka, *Mt*, 1:373; Davies and Allison, *Mt*, 2:160-62.

[235]Wilk 2002, 127.

[236]Gnilka, *Mt*, 1:381. For the observation that follows above see Schweizer, *Mk*, 158.

Mt 10 as a literary and thematic unity emphasize that the disciples are directed by Jesus to regard tribulation, resistance and persecution as something normal, precisely in the context of their missionary activity. The tribulation that the disciples will experience as missionaries will bring to light the fact that the effective testimony that is needed in the mission of the followers of Jesus comes not from human beings but from God's Spirit, who works in them (cf. Mt 10:19-20).[237]

In the Gospel of John the promise of the Spirit of God for the mission of the disciples plays a crucial role.[238]

Jn 16:7-11: "Nevertheless I tell you the truth: it is to your advantage that I go away, for if I do not go away, the Advocate will not come to you; but if I go, I will send him to you. [8]And when he comes, he will prove the world wrong about [convict the world of] sin and righteousness and judgment: [9]about sin, because they do not believe in me; [10]about righteousness, because I am going to the Father and you will see me no longer; [11]about judgment, because the ruler of this world has been condemned."

The mission of the disciples, corresponding to the mission of Jesus (Jn 20:21), is characterized by the convicting work of the Holy Spirit, the "helper" or "advocate" (παράκλητος, *paraklētos*) of the disciples in the legal battle between God or Jesus and the world. The Spirit uncovers sin, righteousness and judgment. He establishes for the world the nature of sin as disobedience against God. Because it was God who sent Jesus into the world in order to give life to all who believe (Jn 3:16), "every definitive No against Jesus is a definitive No against God."[239] Sin is the refusal to believe in Jesus as the one Son whom God sent into the world for the salvation of the world. The Spirit establishes the nature of righteousness: Jesus' death was not the result of a just verdict of the world; since he left the world and went to the Father, he has been vindicated as righteous. The Spirit demonstrates that Jesus, whom the disciples no longer see, is with the Father. And the Spirit establishes that the judgment has taken place when Jesus was exalted and went to the Father: the hour of his crucifixion is the hour of God's judgment of the world; Satan has been judged and has lost his power (Jn 12:31). Thus Jesus encourages the disciples to be witnesses of his message despite the resistance of the world: Jesus has been vindicated by God, the adversary has been judged, the judgment of unbelief is in process, and the Spirit convicts the unbelieving world of the sin of unbelief by confronting the world with the faith of the followers of Jesus.[240]

10. Finally, we need to examine the difficult passage Mt 10:23, a statement by Jesus that only Matthew records.

---

[237]Gnilka, *Mt*, 1:382.
[238]Besides the commentaries see D. A. Carson, "The Function of the Paraclete in John 16:7-11," *JBL* 98 (1979): 547-66; Billington 1995.
[239]Wilckens, *Joh*, 250-51; cf. Schnackenburg, *Joh*, 3:148-49 (ET, 3:130-31).
[240]See Schnackenburg, *Joh*, 3:150-51 (ET, 3:131-32).

Mt 10:23: "When they persecute you in one town, flee to the next; for truly I tell you, you will not have gone through all the towns of Israel before the Son of Man comes."

Some scholars think that those who accept the authenticity of this statement[241] must acknowledge "that Jesus was very much mistaken" unless they "reinterpret" the text.[242]

Volker Hampel concludes in a study of Mt 10:23 that Jesus instructs his closest co-workers in the context of a prophecy of their experience of the consummation that they should not leave Israel despite the suffering that they will have to endure collectively. The promise of salvation "includes the comforting assurance for those who are persecuted and who have to flee: Be steadfast, because the short period of the eschatological tribulation is not the last thing; the final reality is the full salvation of the consummation that comes after the tribulation. Jesus and his followers will experience this even before the disciples have reached the end of their flight through the cities of Israel, since redemption is imminent, the state of שָׁלוֹם (*šālōm*) of the consummation of God's reign." However, this prophecy was not fulfilled: "Neither the messianic enthronement of Jesus nor the beginning of the visible kingdom of God linked with Jesus' enthronement has taken place as the saying of Jesus had asserted and promised."[243]

The contradiction that scholars see is a consequence of interpreting the statements in terms of a "consistent eschatology": Jesus limited his and his disciples' missionary activity to Israel, and this mission cannot be completed because the Son of Man will appear soon. Scholars argue that Jesus' statement remained unfulfilled in a twofold sense: the missionary work of his followers went beyond the borders of Israel, and the Son of Man has not returned.[244] An eschatological interpretation in terms of a delay of the parousia arrives ultimately at the same conclusion, when scholars assume that the parousia of the Son of Man was expected to come within one or two generations.

Scholars who have looked for other interpretations, assuming that Jesus' prophecy in Mt 10:23 was indeed fulfilled, suggest various explanations.[245] (a) The coming of the Son of Man refers to a coming of the historical Jesus subse-

---

[241]The authenticity of this verse is supported by J. Schniewind, J. Jeremias, E. Sjöberg, C. Colpe, M. Künzi, H. Patsch, L. Goppelt, O. Betz; recently Hampel 1989, 23-24, 27; Davies and Allison, *Mt*, 2:189-90. The authenticity is questioned by R. Bultmann, E. Grässer, P. Vielhauer, H. E. Tödt, A. Vögtle, H. Merklein, R. H. Gundry; see Luz (*Mt*, 2:113), who is "very uncertain." Bammel (1961) disputes that the saying has any connection with a mission of the disciples.

[242]P. Vielhauer, "Gottesreich und Menschensohn in der Verkündigung Jesu," in Vielhauer 1965, 65; quoted in Hampel 1989, 27. Similarly, Luz, *Mt*, 2:114.

[243]Hampel 1989, 26, 27.

[244]See, for example, S. Wilson 1973, 17-18.

[245]For the discussion that follows above see Carson, *Mt*, 250; Davies and Allison, *Mt*, 2:19; see also Luz, *Mt*, 2:115-16 (Wirkungsgeschichte). For a redaction-critical explanation see Nepper-Christensen (1995), who argues that Matthew wanted to encourage his readers to reach as many towns in Israel as possible before the return of the Son of Man.

quent to the missionary activity of the Twelve and the Seventy-Two. This interpretation cannot explain the reference to a persecution of the disciples, however. Followers of Jesus were not persecuted before Jesus' death in either Judea
or Galilee. (b) The coming of the Son of Man refers to the public identification
of Jesus as the Messiah. Scholars who support this interpretation suggest different "dates" for this event. Some think of Jesus' resurrection;[246] this explanation,
however, hardly explains the urgency of the statement or the announcement of
persecution. Others suggest Pentecost;[247] however, the Holy Spirit is not a significant theme in the First Gospel, nor is the Spirit ever identified with the Son
of Man. Still other scholars think of the events after Pentecost that represent the
arrival of the kingdom of God. Again, the urgency of Jesus' statement fails to be
explained. (c) The coming of the Son of Man refers to Jesus' return (parousia).
Scholars who support this interpretation and do not allow for an error on Jesus'
part have to reinterpret "Israel" in terms of the world or the church. However,
an interpretation of "Israel" as a symbol for the church is highly unlikely for Matthew. Scholars who discount the motif of urgency interpret Jesus' statement in
the sense of an announcement of the church's missionary activity among Jews
as a permanent commission given to Jesus' followers.[248] (d) The dispensational
approach interprets Mt 10:23 in terms of Jesus' return, with the present era of
the church being a parenthesis that must be disregarded in the interpretation of
Jesus' statement. This view is hardly convincing, as the time of the Gentile mission and the era of the church consisting of Jewish Christians and Gentile Christians is hardly a "parenthesis" or a "time between" God's dealings with historical
Israel and the millennium. (e) The coming of the Son of Man refers to his coming
in judgment of Israel, with the destruction of Jerusalem and the temple as climax.[249] The coming of the Son of Man corresponds to the coming of the kingdom
of God: as the latter arrives in stages, so does the Son of Man. Important for this
interpretation is Jesus' repeated warning to his Jewish listeners about the consequences of their rejection of his message. The statement in Mt 10:23 marks that
stage in the coming of God's reign during which the judgment that Jesus had announced will take place. With the destruction of the temple "the age of the kingdom comes into its own, precisely because so many of the structured foreshad-
owings of the OT, bound up with the cultus and nation, now disappear. . . . The
Son of Man comes." This means in the context of Mt 10:23 that the envoys whom

---

[246]John Chrysostom, *Hom. Matt.* 34:1; Karl Barth, *Kirchliche Dogmatik III/2* (3rd ed.; Zürich:
Theologischer Verlag, 1974), 601 (ET, 499); Hampel 1989, 27-28.
[247]Calvin, Beza. The option that follows above has been suggested by N. B. Stonehouse and
P. Gaechter.
[248]Gnilka, *Mt,* 1:379; Davies and Allison, *Mt,* 2:190; Keener, *Mt,* 325.
[249]Feuillet 1961; France 1971, 140; Carson (*Mt,* 252-53), who also refers to J. Robinson 1957, 80,
91-92; Moule 1962, 90; see now prominently N.T. Wright 1996, 365, 470. For the explicaton
that follows above see Carson, *Mt,* 252-53; quotation, 252.

Jesus sends out to the towns and villages of Israel suffer in a time during which many of them are still connected with synagogues; they are encouraged not to give up in this time of persecution but to retreat strategically to the next town and there to continue their witness. They will not be able to reach every settlement of Israel before the Son of Man comes in judgment on the people of Israel. This explanation is perhaps more convincing than the others, although the connection between the coming of the Son of Man in judgment, the coming of the kingdom of God ("into its own"), and the destruction of the temple in A.D. 70 is not without difficulties.

The Geographical Outreach of the Twelve

The Gospel writers provide no account of the composition of the six teams of two disciples each, nor do they mention the areas or the Galilean towns and villages (fig. 5) that the disciples visited on their preaching tour.

The list of disciples in Mt 10:2-4 registers the disciples in pairs. This fact has been interpreted by some scholars as reflecting their sending out in pairs (Mk 6:7).[250] There is not enough evidence, however, to conclude that Matthew, who himself does not mention the sending in pairs of two, actually lists the pairs of disciples whom Jesus sent out to the Galilean villages. (The list of disciples in Acts 1:13, which also lists the disciples in pairs, does not agree with the "pairs" of Matthew.) Now, if historical reconstruction means that an attempt can be made to describe more fully events that the sources hint at with little detail, creatively bringing to bear the historical, social and geographical context, then Matthew's list of pairs of disciples is as good as any list suggested by any scholar for a possible record of the six teams of two disciples each embarking on a missionary tour through Galilee. If we assume that the disciples were to preach and heal in every Galilean town and village, with the exception of the large cities Tiberias and Sepphoris and towns that they had often visited, such as Capernaum and Nazareth, and if we include several Jewish settlements in the area that did not belong to Galilee politically, then the missionary tour of the disciples could have taken place in some fashion similar to that described below. For the 147 towns and villages that the following survey mentions one should consult the map *Iudaea-Palaestina* (TIR, 1993; scale 1:250,000), edited by Y. Tsafrir and L. di Segni.[251] Also helpful is the map by E. Höhne and H. Wahle (1979; scale 1:300,000); not as detailed is the map by D. Jericke and G. Schmitt (*TAVO*, 1990; scale 1:500,000). In the process of the efforts of the Archaeological Survey of Israel, 138 Galilean settlements of the Roman period have been discovered.[252] The information for the individual sites, most of which have not been excavated, has been taken from the gazetteer of the TIR volume *Iudaea-Palaestina*, edited by Y. Tsafrir, L. di Segni and J. Green. It has not been possible to ascertain for every settlement that it existed in the first century A.D. The names of the set-

---

[250]Jeremias 1959, 135; 1988, 226-27 (ET, 235-36).

[251]Map 69 in *BAGRW* (1994; scale 1:500,000), edited by J. P. Brown and E. M. Meyers, lists only a quarter of the settlements recorded by the TIR map. See also the maps in Freeman-Grenville 2003, 207-14, listing the sites mentioned in Eusebius's *Onomasticon.*

[252]M. Aviam, "Galilee: The Hellenistic to the Byzantine Period," *NEAEHL* 2:452-58, esp. 455. See the gazetteer of the TIR map for further bibliography on individual settlements; in the case of more important towns I refer to Hüttenmeister 1977 and to articles in *NEAEHL* (1993).

tlements are mostly Arab or modern Jewish place names, as the names of the ancient settlements usually are unknown.

1. Missionary outreach of two disciples—Simon Peter and his brother Andrew (?)—in the western part of Lower Galilee (24 towns and villages):

Geth Hefer: according to tradition the birthplace and tomb of the prophet Jonah.

Reina: Roman reservoir, aqueduct to Sepphoris, tombs.

'*Illut:* remains of settlement and a synagogue, tombs; perhaps identical with Aithelu (*t. Nid.* 1:9).

Mahalol: settlement in the western Jezreel Valley; mausoleum, tombs.

Simonias (Heb., Shimron): remains of settlement, rock-hewn caves, sarcophagi; rabbinic sources attest a synagogue for the second century and a small sanhedrin (court).[253]

Zebed: remains of buildings, oil presses, wine presses, tombs; perhaps identical with Zebod de Galila (*Gen. Rab.* 98:11).

Gabatha (Heb., Gĕvat): remains of a synagogue; olive and wine presses, cave-tombs, cisterns.

Tel Shem (Dabbešet): settlement in the Jezreel Valley.

Chorvat Zeror: settlement in the Jezreel Valley.

Chorvat Izhaqia: settlement in the Jezreel Valley; synagogue (third century) with Aramaic inscription.

Beth Shearim (Bēsara in Josephus, *Vita* 118-119):[254] settlement in the Jezreel Valley on the border of the territory of Ptolemais-Acco; administrative center for the estates of Queen Berenike ca. A.D. 45; remains of the settlement from Herodian times; seat of several rabbinic scholars in the second century; remains of a synagogue (third century).

Tel Risim: settlement in the Jezreel Valley.

Ramat Yishay: large settlement in the Jezreel Valley; remains of a (later) church.

Chivria: settlement in Lower Galilee; burial caves.

Chorvat Hazin: Hellenistic and Roman settlement in the Jezreel Valley.

'*Ardasqus:* near Beth Shearim; remains of settlement, tombs; seat of Rabbi Meir in the second century.

Tiv'on: settlement between the Jezreel Valley and Mount Carmel; remains of settlement; literary sources attest a synagogue from the second century.

Chorvat Buzin: large settlement in the Jezreel Valley in the Hellenistic and Roman period.

Chorvat Qoshet (Ch. Qasṭa): settlement in the Jezreel Valley, 14 km southwest of Tiberias; remains of a synagogue (?).

Kh. Umm Rashid: large settlement in the Jezreel Valley.

Kefar Sasai: settlement on the eastern border of the territory of Ptolemais-Acco; cisterns.

Usha: remains of settlement, mosaic floor; seat of the Sanhedrin after A.D. 135.[255]

Shephar'am: remains of a synagogue (?), tombs, mausoleum, cisterns; seat of the Sanhedrin in the second century after the Bar Kokhba Revolt.

Asochis (Shikhin, Kefar Sekanyah): city in the plain of Beth Netopha in Lower Galilee,

---

[253]L. Levine 2000, 359 n. 11.

[254]A. Negev, "Besara," *PECS* 152; Hüttenmeister 1977, 68-72, 523-24; N. Avigad and B. Mazar, *NEAEHL* 1:236-48; J. Pahlitzsch, *DNP* 2:593.

[255]Hüttenmeister 1977, 469-75.

ca. 6 km north-northwest of Sepphoris; production center for stone jars for Sepphoris.[256] There is evidence that Shikhin was a center of the early Christian mission in Galilee and in southern Syria during the first century (see §22.2).

2. Missionary outreach of two disciples—James son of Zebedee and his brother John (?)—in central Lower Galilee (25 towns and villages):

Chorvat Veradim: ca. 2 km west of Magdala; remains of a synagogue and a public building.

Arbela: remains of a synagogue; Josephus built a fortress nearby.

Kefar Chittaia: remains of buildings, tombs, synagogue (third century).

Kefar Nimra: remains of buildings; known for its weaver workshops (*Lam. Rab.* 2.22.4 [54a]).

Kafr Kena: remains of a synagogue, tombs; 6 km north of Nazareth; wrongly identified by pilgrims as the Cana of Jn 2:1;[257] ca. 3 km northeast lies *Chirbet Kenna,* with remains of buildings from the Roman period; perhaps to be identified with Garis (Josephus, *Vita* 395, 412).

Iaphia (mod. Yafa):[258] large town ca. 2 km southwest of Nazareth; according to Josh 19:12, one of the cities of Zebulun. The town was fortified by Josephus after A.D. 66; Titus killed most of the inhabitants in the summer of A.D. 67 (Josephus, *B.J.* 3.289-306). Remains of a synagogue (15 by 19 m). According to a later tradition, James son of Zebedee was born here.

Ginneigar: settlement in the Jezreel Valley; well, tombs.

Tel ʿAdashim: settlement in the Jezreel Valley.

el Mazraʿa: settlement in the Jezreel Valley; remains of buildings, mosaic, cisterns.

Tarbenet (Tarbanat):[259] settlement in Lower Galilee, bordering on the Jezreel Valley; according to *y. Meg.* 4:5 (75b), the town had a synagogue.

Arbela (mod. ʿAfula):[260] settlement in the Jezreel Valley, ca. 6 km northwest of Tiberias.

Sulem: the Shunem of the Old Testament; settlement in the Jezreel Valley.

Nain: settlement in the Jezreel Valley; remains of buildings, mosaic floor.

Chorvat Sahar: remains of buildings, rock-hewn tombs, sarcophagi, olive press, coins.

Chorvat Elef: remains of buildings, remains of a fortress or a synagogue, rock-hewn tombs.

Endor: large settlement in Lower Galilee; remains of buildings, olive press.

Tamra: remains of settlement; burial caves.

Kafr Misr: remains of a synagogue, spring, sarcophagi.

Exaloth: small village at the foot of Mount Tabor; border point in Lower Galilee; Roman mill and cemetery.

Dabaritta: administrative center in Lower Galilee; tombs, cisterns, mosaic pavement.

ʿEn Teʾena: settlement in Lower Galilee near Sepphoris.

Sejera (esh Shajara): synagogue, Jewish tombs.

el Khirbe: settlement near the road to Sepphoris.

Lavi: road station on the Tiberias-Sepphoris road in the Roman period; agricultural installations, synagogue (?), tombs.

---

[256]J. F. Strange, "Excavations at Sepphoris: The Location and Identification of Shikhin," *IEJ* 44 (1994): 216-27; 45 (1995): 171-87.

[257]L. I. Levine, *NEAEHL* 1:56; R. Riesner, *GBL* 2:752.

[258]Hüttenmeister 1977, 479-82; D. Barag, *NEAEHL* 2:659-60.

[259]See L. Levine 2000, 359 n. 8.

[260]Hüttenmeister 1977, 15-17; M. Dothan, *NEAEHL* 1:37-39.

Beth Maon:[261] seat of the priestly family Chuppah; a synagogue is attested.

3. Missionary outreach of two disciples—Philip and Bartholomew (?)—in the eastern part of Lower Galilee (26 towns and villages):

Damin: remains of buildings, synagogue, cisterns.
Kefar Shabtai: remains of buildings, synagogue (?), fortifications, wine presses.
Chorvat Sarona: remains of buildings, synagogue, tombs, church.
Chorvat Se'ara: remains of buildings, cisterns, synagogue (?).
Khirbet Ma'azer: settlement in Lower Galilee.
Khirbet Sara: remains of buildings, synagogue (?), cisterns, wine presses, rock-hewn tombs.
Chorvat Massal: remains of buildings, quarry, wine presses since the Persian period.
Tira (mod. Tirat el 'Amran): remains of a synagogue (?).
Khirbet Rib (Tirat el Khariba): remains of a synagogue (?), rock-hewn tombs.
Ne'oran: remains of buildings, cisterns.
Chorvat Qara: remains of buildings, cisterns, sarcophagi, synagogue (?).
Khirbet Buleiq: remains of settlement, mosaic, cisterns, wine presses.
et-Taiybeh: village in the northern Jezreel Valley; remains of buildings since the Hellenistic period.
Kefar Dan: remains of settlement, synagogue, olive press.
Kafrah: remains of buildings, cisterns, Jewish inscription.
Gebul: remains of synagogue, tombs.
Khirbet el Bira: remains of settlement, synagogue.
Sirin: mosaic pavement from the Hellenistic and Roman periods, olive press, vaulted spring.
Ulama: remains of buildings, synagogue (?), cisterns.
Kefar Iamma (Yabneel): remains of settlement, synagogue.
Khirbet Beit Jann (Beth Gan): remains of settlement, cisterns, rock-hewn tombs; synagogue (?).
Chorvat 'Atosh: remains of buildings, cistern, synagogue (?).
Ivzam (Khirbet Bassum): remains of buildings.
Chorvat Zedata: remains of buildings, mosaic floor, synagogue (?), cistern.
Sergunin:[262] village south of Tiberias; a synagogue (from which the Sea of Galilee is visible) is attested.

4. Missionary outreach of two disciples—Thomas and Matthew (?)—in central and western Galilee (23 towns and villages):

Chukkok (mod. Yaquq): village in Lower Galilee; synagogue, tombs.
Me'araia: seat of the priestly family Bilgah after A.D. 70.
Selamen: remains of buildings, aqueduct; fortified by Josephus in A.D. 66.
Mamliaḥ: seat of the priestly family Hezir after A.D. 70; remains of a synagogue.
Ailabon: seat of the priestly family Ha-Qoz; remains of a synagogue (?), tombs.
Beth Netopha: settlement in the plain of Beth Netopha (plain of Asochis); remains of a synagogue.

---

[261]Hüttenmeister 1977, 302-6.
[262]Hüttenmeister 1977, 390-92.

Gabara:[263] town in Lower Galilee; conquered by Vespasian as the first rebellious town; remains of buildings, tombs.

Kefar Iohannah: seat of the priestly family Yakhin; remains of buildings, cisterns, tombs.

Sogane (Sigoph): village in Lower Galilee; fortified by Josephus in A.D. 66.

Khirbet Miʿar (Yaʿad): remains of buildings, olive presses, cisterns, Roman tombs.

Saab: remains of buildings, cisterns, tombs.

Chabulon (Kabul): on the road from the Sea of Galilee to Ptolemais-Acco; headquarters of Josephus in A.D. 66; remains of buildings and cisterns. A bishop of Chabulon visited the Council of Nicea in A.D. 325.

Damun:[264] village in the plain of Acco; remains of settlement; church (at the latest A.D. 518).

Kefar Thamartha: remains of buildings, cisterns, tombs.

Abelim: remains of buildings, wall, synagogue (?), tombs.

Kochaba (mod. Kaukab): town in Lower Galilee; later a center of the missionary activity of Jesus' relatives (Julius Africanus; see Eusebius, *Hist. eccl.* 1.7.14);[265] remains of a Byzantine church beneath the mosque.[266]

Iotapata (Jotba):[267] most important Jewish fortress in Galilee; remains of the fortification walls, water installations, olive press, potter's kiln; settled since ca. 75 B.C.

Cana (*Chirbet Qana*):[268] administrative center in the plain of Asochis; remains of a synagogue; the Cana of Jn 2:1; situated ca. 14 km northeast of Nazareth.

Kefar Mandi: remains of settlement, sarcophagi.

Ruma: remains of synagogue.

Rimmon: village in Upper Galilee; rabbinic center after A.D. 135.

Turan: village on Mount Turan in Lower Galilee; remains of buildings, cisterns.

Mashkanah: settlement halfway between Tiberias and Sepphoris; remains of buildings, cisterns, tombs.

5. Missionary outreach of two disciples—James-Alphaeus and Thaddaeus (?)—in the western part of Upper Galilee (25 towns and villages):

Rama:[269] synagogue (third century), Aramaic inscription; remains of a church.

Shezor: remains of settlement, cisterns.

Nahf: remains of a public building (synagogue or church), tombs.

Beth Anath: wine-producing estate in Galilee.

Chorvat ʿAmud: remains of buildings, cisterns.

Chorvat Bata (mod. Karmiel):[270] remains of settlement from Hellenistic, Roman and Byzantine periods; the mosaic floor of the older church dates to A.D. 526/527.

Chorvat Kenes: remains of settlement.

Beth ha-Kerem: village and valley in Upper Galilee.

---

[263]E. A. Knauff, *DNP* 4:725-26.

[264]See L. di Segni, in Humphrey 1995-2002, 2:167.

[265]Bauckham 1990, 60-64; cf. Harnack 1924, 2:635-36 (ET, 2:102-3).

[266]Bagatti 1971, 122-25; cf. Bauckham 1990, 64.

[267]See "Yodefat," *IEJ* 45 (1995): 191-96 (excavation report); Aviam, *NEAEHL* 2:454.

[268]Hüttenmeister 1977, 246-49; L. I. Levine, *NEAEHL* 1:56; R. Riesner, *GBL* 2:752-53.

[269]Hüttenmeister 1977, 367-69; M. Aviam, *NEAEHL* 2:457.

[270]*SEG* XLII 1456. See Aviam, *NEAEHL* 2:456; L. di Segni, in Humphrey 1995-2002, 2:168.

Chorvat Tefen:[271] Hellenistic and Roman fortress; Jewish tombs.

Kisra: remains of buildings, wine presses, cisterns, tombs.

Baca: village in Upper Galilee on the border of the territory of Tyre.

Chorvat 'Eved: village in Upper Galilee; remains of buildings.

Caparasima: remains of buildings, mosaic, cisterns; situated in the territory of Ptolemais-Acco.

Tefen Area: remains of agricultural installations from Hellenistic and Roman times.

Ianoa: village in western Upper Galilee.

Beth Chobaia: village in western Galilee; seat of the priestly family Gamul.

Ga'aton: remains of settlement, Roman bridge.

Zenita: settlement on the border of the territory of Ptolemais-Acco.

Mi'ilya:[272] remains of buildings, remains (e.g., mosaic) of a Byzantine church.

edh Dhur: settlement in western Galilee; remains of a church.

Kabritha (mod. Tel Kabri):[273] town in western Galilee, already settled in prehistoric times; probably identical with the Rehob of Josh 19:24-26; springs feeding the aqueduct to Ptolemais-Acco are nearby; tombs, remains of a Byzantine church.

Kefar Amiko: remains of buildings.

Kafr Yasif: Hellenistic dedication for Hadad and Atargatis; remains of a synagogue (?).

Kafr el Makr: pagan and Jewish remains.

Khirbet Waziya:[274] cisterns, wine and olive presses, cave tombs; in the fourth/fifth century two churches were built, one of the largest churches in Galilee (37 by 32 m).

6. Missionary outreach of two disciples—Simon Cananaeus and Judas Iscariot (?)—in the mountainous eastern region of Upper Galilee (24 towns and villages):

Betsaida: see §9.3.

Chorazin: see §9.2.

Acchabaron: remains of walls, olive presses; fortifications built by Josephus; synagogue.

Sepph (mod. Safed): village in Upper Galilee; fortified by Josephus.

Biri: village in Upper Galilee.

Iannit (mod. Yavnith; Khirbet Banit): settlement; fortified by Josephus.

'Amuqa: synagogue (?), cave tombs.

Kefar Nevoraia (Nabratein):[275] village in Upper Galilee that evidently served as a market center for the surrounding settlements; remains of walls, buildings, vessels; remains of three synagogues (the largest, 16.9 by 11.6 m; the oldest, ca. A.D. 135).

Meroth (Khirbet Marus):[276] according to Josephus, situated on the northern border of Upper Galilee; settled in the Hasmonean period. The town had around one thousand inhabitants, who lived from the cultivation of olives, wine, wheat and vegetables. The town was oriented toward Tyre. Remains of a synagogue (11.4 by 17.9 m; ca. A.D. 400).

Qision: remains of a monumental building (synagogue?).

---

[271]M. Aviam, *NEAEHL* 2:453.

[272]M. Aviam, *NEAEHL* 2:457.

[273]A. Kempinski, *NEAEHL* 3:839-41.

[274]M. Aviam, *NEAEHL* 2:456-57.

[275]E. M. Meyers, *NEAEHL* 3:1077-79.

[276]Z. Ilan, *NEAEHL* 3:1028-31; M. Aviam, *NEAEHL* 2:454; Z. Ilan, "The Synagogue and Study House at Meroth," in Urman and Flesher 1995, 1:256-88; L. Levine 2000, 163, and passim.

ʿAlma: remains of buildings, synagogue, inscriptions.

Yarun ed Deir: remains of a synagogue or temple (later transformed into a church); burial caves; Greek inscription.

Barʿam (mod. **Kefar Birʿam**):[277] remains of settlement, tombs, two large synagogues (the largest, 15.2 by 20 m; third century.).

Gischala (mod. Gush Chalav; Arab., el-Jish):[278] mentioned in *m. ʿArak.* 9:6 as a town fortified since the time of Joshua; sources mention olive oil produced here (Josephus, *B.J.* 2.591-592) as well as silk. Further fortified by Josephus in A.D. 66; home of the Zealot leader John. According to Jerome, the hometown of the parents of the apostle Paul (*Vir. ill.* 5). The town was oriented toward Tyre. Remains of a synagogue (second century), tombs.

Sifsufa: remains of buildings, synagogue (?).

Chorvat Qiuma: remains of a synagogue (?).

Meron (mod. Mērōth):[279] village in Upper Galilee; remains of a synagogue (third century).

Thecoa (mod. **Khirbet Shemaʿ**):[280] situated opposite Meron; famous for olives; Rabbi Shammai is said to be buried here. Remains of a synagogue (9 by 18 m; third century).

Chorvat Rom: remains of settlement on the Meron ridge in Upper Galilee.

Chorvat Sartaba: remains of settlement.

Beth Dagon: remains of settlement.

Beersheba:[281] village on the boundary of Upper and Lower Galilee; fortified by Josephus.

Parod: village in Upper Galilee; tombs.

Kefar Hanania (mod. **Kafr ʿInān**):[282] village on the boundary of Upper and Lower Galilee; pottery industry with trade contacts with Ptolemais-Acco and towns east of the Jordan River; synagogue attested for the third century.

If the disciples planned to spend one day in each settlement, they could have finished their missionary tour within one month (not counting sabbath days). If they stayed two days in each settlement, their mission would have lasted two months.

The "Plentiful Harvest"

Matthew reports Jesus' saying about a "plentiful harvest" before the missionary discourse in the context of a summary statement (Mt 9:37), while Luke places the saying at the beginning of the sending out of the seventy-two disciples (Lk 10:2; cf. Jn 4:35).

Mt 9:35-38: "Then Jesus went about all the cities and villages, teaching in their syna-

---

[277]Hüttenmeister 1977, 31-38; N. Avigad, *NEAEHL* 1:147-49; L. Levine 2000, 178, and passim.
[278]E. M. Meyers and F. Vitto, *NEAEHL* 1:546-50; M. Aviam, *NEAEHL* 2:454.
[279]Hüttenmeister 1977, 311-14.
[280]Hüttenmeister 1977, 387-90; E. M. Meyers, *NEAEHL* 4:1359-61.
[281]M. Aviam, *NEAEHL* 2:454.
[282]Hüttenmeister 1977, 256-58, 526. On the pottery trade see D. Adan-Bayewitz, *Common Pottery in Roman Galilee: A Study of Local Trade* (Ramat-Gan: Bar-Ilan University, 1993).

gogues, and proclaiming the good news of the kingdom, and curing every disease and every sickness. [36]When he saw the crowds, he had compassion for them, because they were harassed and helpless, like sheep without a shepherd. [37]Then he said to his disciples, 'The harvest is plentiful, but the laborers are few; [38]therefore ask the Lord of the harvest to send out laborers into his harvest.'"

Lk 10:1-2: "After this the Lord appointed seventy[-two] others and sent them on ahead of him in pairs to every town and place where he himself intended to go. [2]He said to them, 'The harvest is plentiful, but the laborers are few; therefore ask the Lord of the harvest to send out laborers into his harvest.'"

The "plentiful harvest" (θερισμὸς πολύς, *therismos polys*) is related to the "harassed and helpless" people who came to Jesus and for whom Jesus had compassion (Mt 9:36a). Jesus likens them to "sheep without a shepherd" (Mt 9:36b)—that is, sheep who went astray, who are lost if nobody finds them and brings them back to the flock. This metaphor overlaps with the metaphor of bringing in the harvest, which refers to people who accept Jesus' message of the arrival of God's reign, thus acknowledging God's presence and authority in Jesus' person and ministry. The "workers" (ἐργάται, *ergatai*) whom God will "send out" (ἐκβάλλειν, *ekballein*) in Mt 9:38 are the Twelve, and in Luke's Gospel a further seventy-two disciples who are willing to be sent out. The urgency of the statement presumably is related to the small number of "harvest workers" who have to cope with a potentially huge harvest.

Axel von Dobbeler suggests that the "sheep without a shepherd" (Mt 10:6) should not be identified with the entire people of Israel but is, in the context of the prophetic critique of the rulers (Jer 50:6; Zech 11; Ezek 34), a reference "to the misery of *those* in Israel who have to suffer under a leadership that skins the people (this is the literal meaning of σκύλλω), brings them down and lets them languish."[283] This interpretation is implausible because of historical reasons: if we calculate the "leading circles" generously at 5 percent of the population, then Jesus' statement relates to 95 percent of the people, the vast majority of Jews in Galilee and in Judea. It is unlikely that the disciples had much contact with the "establishment" during their mission trip through the Galilean countryside.

The reference to the "Lord of the harvest" often is interpreted in terms of the final judgment. In Mt 3:12; 13:30, 39 this is indeed the reference of the metaphor of the harvest, following a broad tradition in which "harvest" was a metaphor for God's judgment, with God himself or the angels being those who do the "harvesting."[284] Seen in this context, Jesus' statement has the following meaning: the harvest that will be brought in on the day of judgment begins now, in the present, with the disciples who proclaim the message of the arrival of the kingdom of God, a message that divides the listeners into two "camps." The mes-

---

[283]Dobbeler 2000b, 30.
[284]Is 18:4; 27:12; Jer 51:53; Hos 6:11; Joel 3:13; *4 Ezra* 4:26-37; 9:17; *2 Bar.* 70:1-2; *b. B. Meṣīʿa* 83b; Mk 4:26-29; Rev 14:14-20. See Davies and Allison, *Mt,* 2:148-49.

sengers thus have the task of warning the people of the coming judgment and of offering to Israel a final opportunity for repentance.[285] We should note, however, that Matthew does not explicitly allude to the judgment in the context of Mt 9:37-38. Matthew uses metaphors with different meanings, one example being the "sheep" in Mt 10:6; 10:16. The term "harvest" does not necessarily allude to the final judgment.

The metaphor "harvest" is a metaphor for missionary work in this dominical saying.[286] Those who do the "harvesting" are Jesus' disciples, with their message of the dawn of God's reign. The tradition-historical background of the metaphor of harvesting as reference to the final judgment indicates that the missionary activity of the Twelve, and of the Seventy-Two, is an event of the last days, which have begun to set in with the arrival of the Messiah. The missionary work of the disciples is "not simply a prelude before the end but itself part of the complex of events that make up the end."[287] The problem that results from a plentiful harvest that is brought in now, in the present time, and the problem that there are but few harvest workers are solved not by an improved organization but by prayer. As Eduard Schweizer comments, "Man cannot create the new situation that is necessary; God alone will choose his messengers. Therefore prayer is needed."[288] And Oscar Cullmann observes insightfully, "Although it is God who performs his saving work with a view to his kingdom, we should pray for it, and this is confirmed by the fact that according to Jesus' preaching God does not need, but wants, our prayer."

Blaine Charette dismisses this interpretation in terms of a "missionary command" because the notion of "harvesting" people has no Old Testament precedent and because the connection of the two metaphors "sheep without a shepherd" and "harvesting people" is redactional: in Mk 6:34 there is no reference to a "harvest," while in Lk 10:2 the "sheep" are lacking. Charette wants to interpret the term "harvest" as a reference to the eschatological blessing that has been promised to Israel in passages such as Hos 6:11; Joel 3:18; Amos 9:13-15. The metaphor does not concern a harvest among people or of people, but a harvest *for* the people—that is, the blessings of the kingdom of God that are present in Jesus' ministry and that will be communicated to the people by the disciples very soon. According to Charette, Mt 9:37-38 does not call harvest workers to go to the lost crowds of people in order to save some of them; rather, the text challenges the workers to recognize the presence of the kingdom of God in their midst and to take the blessings of the messianic days in Jesus' authority to those who are helpless and who need God. It is only in *that* sense, Charette argues, that Mt 9:37-38 is a missionary

---

[285]Schweizer, *Mt,* 151 (ET, 234). For the remark that follows above see Charette 1990, 30.

[286]On the authenticity of the saying see Davies and Allison, *Mt,* 2:149 with n. 21; Luz, *Mt,* 2:80.

[287]Davies and Allison, *Mt,* 2:149; similarly Luz, *Mt,* 2:81.

[288]Schweizer, *Mt,* 151 (ET, 234). The quotation that follows above, commenting on Mt 9:38, is from Cullmann 1994, 35 (ET, 25 [J. Bowden erroneously translates "daß nach Jesu Verkündigung Gott unser Gebet *nicht braucht,* aber will" with "that according to Jesus' preaching God *not only needs,* but wants"]).

commission.[289] This interpretation assumes unnecessary alternatives: the missionary existence of the disciples depends on their recognition that the kingdom of God has become a present reality. The arguments that dispute that the harvest workers "go" to the people who need to be saved fail to convince: Jesus himself went, quite literally, to the people of Galilee, visiting their towns, villages and farmsteads, and clearly he introduces his disciples in Mt 9:37-38 into the very same ministry in which he had been engaged.

The "Salt of the Earth" and the "Light of the World"

Jesus describes his disciples in the Sermon on the Mount as "the salt of the earth" (τὸ ἅλας τῆς γῆς, *to halas tēs gēs* [Mt 5:13]) and "the light of the world" (τὸ φῶς τοῦ κόσμου, *to phōs tou kosmou* [Mt 5:14]). Just as salt is an indispensable ingredient, so also the disciples and their witness are essential and irreplaceable, despite the fact that they are ridiculed and persecuted for Jesus' sake (Mt 5:11-12). As salt exists for food, likewise the disciples live not for their own benefit or advantage but for the sake of the earth.[290]

The metaphor "light of the world" is even more explicit: the small group of Jesus' disciples is like a town on a hill whose lights can be seen at night from a distance (Mt 5:14); they are like an oil lamp on a stand, illuminating the entire house (Mt 5:15). In Mt 4:16 Matthew had explained Jesus' ministry in Galilee with a quotation from Is 9:1-2 (Heb. and LXX, 8:23—9:1) that spoke about light that is seen by the people sitting in darkness. Jesus' description of the disciples as "light of the world" thus explains their assignment as being analogous to his own mission.[291] The statement in Mt 5:16 shows that the metaphor "light of the world" not only describes a function of the nature of Jesus' followers but also formulates the disciples' task. As the "light of the world" they must let this light shine so that all can see it—all people in the world, everybody in the house.

T. W. Manson interprets the metaphor "light of the world" against the background of Is 42:6 as a reference to the Gentiles. Joachim Jeremias points to the expectation that God's eschatological light will shine from Mount Zion as a call to the nations to come to Jerusalem.[292] For Christian communities that read the Gospel of Matthew after Easter and after Pentecost, thus in a time when missionary work among Gentiles was successfully underway, such an "international" reading of Mt 5:13-14 would have been a distinct possibility. In the specific situation of Jesus describing to the disciples their task, however, the metaphors "salt of the earth" and "light of the world" do not necessarily speak of "world missions."

---

[289]Charette 1990, 31-33.

[290]Luz, *Mt,* 1:222-23; cf. Hagner, *Mt,* 1:99.

[291]Luz, *Mt,* 1:224; for the observation that follows above see ibid.

[292]T. W. Manson 1949, 92-93; Jeremias 1956, 75-78 (ET, 56).

Salvation-Historical Differences

The early Christian communities that were involved in missionary work did not take over the missionary instructions that Jesus had given to the Twelve. Three observations are important. (1) The verb "follow" (ἀκολουθεῖν, *akolouthein*) is used in the New Testament, with the sole exception of Rev 14:4, for the followers of Jesus during his earthly ministry. This shows that the early church was very much aware of the fact that the circle of disciples who followed Jesus before Easter represented a community that had a unique character and a unique, unrepeatable significance.[293] (2) Some instructions, such as those concerning the prohibited provisions, make sense in the specific situation of a short-term missionary tour to the towns and villages of Galilee, where Jesus and his disciples were already known and where the disciples could expect to receive room and board among the families and houses of the Galilean settlements. Here the hermeneutical difference between the descriptive and the prescriptive comes into play: the details of what the Gospel writers describe were not all equally normative for the early church. This does not exclude the possibility that Jesus' instructions have paradigmatic relevance in regard to, for example, missionary work among the economically poor and socially disenfranchised—a situation in which missionaries who travel with a lot of worldly ballast are more of a burden than a witness for the gospel. (3) Clearly, elements of Jesus' missionary instructions that pointed beyond this specific situation of the short-term missionary tour continued to be relevant for the early church: for example, the reference to suffering as the "social" context of missionary work, the description of fear as the denial of Jesus, the explanation of discipleship in terms of taking up one's cross, and the promise of reward as an encouragement for missionaries.

---

[293]Riesner 1988, 422; G. Kittel, *ThWNT* 1:214-15 (*TDNT* 1:215); Larsson 1962, 44-45; A. Schulz 1962, 64, 131.

11

THE MISSION OF THE SEVENTY-TWO

Luke reports a second sending out of disciples by Jesus "ahead of him in pairs to every town and place where he himself intended to go" (Lk 10:1). This mission of seventy-two disciples (Lk 10:1-16) is the subject of the following analysis.

The "central section" Lk 9:51—19:27[1] is the longest section in the Gospel of Luke, containing many passages unique to Luke. This "travel narrative," as this section is also called, is neither a purely metaphorical journey[2] nor a journey from Galilee to Jerusalem that can be dated with chronological precision.[3] The travel narrative is a summary of the last phase of Jesus' ministry, focusing on Jesus' movement toward Jerusalem under a theological perspective.[4]

Morton Enslin suggests that the travel narrative was composed by Luke to demonstrate that Jesus did not reject Gentiles but that he anticipated the Gentile mission in his "Samaritan ministry."[5] For evidence Enslin refers to (1) the comment about rejection in a Samaritan town at the beginning of the central section (Lk 9:52-53); (2) two alleged doublets: the healing of the Samaritan leper (Lk 17:11-19) and the sending out of the seventy[-two] disciples (Lk 10:1-12); (3) the striking references to Samaritans in the parable of the good Samaritan (Lk 10:25-37). However, the texts that suggest that Lk 9:51—18:14 is a unity are far too disparate to fit under the rubric "Samaritan mission." The notice about Jesus' rejection by Samaritans in Lk 9:53 hardly fits the supposed desire of Luke to portray Jesus as friendly to Samaritans.

Armin Baum compares Luke's travel narrative with other ancient travel reports and concludes that Luke's central section is more carefully structured and much more of one piece than are comparable texts. He argues, however, that "the vague geographical anchoring and the loose chronological links" show that

---

[1]Nolland, Lk, 2:529: 9:51—18:34; Bock, Lk, 2:957-58: Lk 9:51—19:44.
[2]Thus Schürmann (Lk, 2:1, 5), who therefore does not want to use the term "Reisebericht" ("travel narrative").
[3]Thus W. F. Arndt, The Gospel according to St. Luke (St. Louis: Concordia, 1956), 272.
[4]Bock, Lk, 2:961.
[5]Enslin 1980.

Luke "evidently had no interest in conveying topographical or ethnographical information," and that Luke wanted to focus on summarizing the numerous speeches that Jesus gave during the journey.[6] He concludes, after analyzing Luke's central section as a historical document, that Luke's information "provides a consistent, even if not complete picture of this journey. Jesus traveled along the Galilean-Samaritan border, avoiding Samaria, via Transjordan to Jerusalem." And he argues that there is therefore no cogent reason why Luke's travel narrative should be interpreted independently of the parameters set by Luke's prologue.[7] In regard to the practice of many scholars to play the theological organization of the material in the central section off against the historical authenticity of individual passages, Darrel Bock comments that Luke is very well able to present a general movement in the direction of Jerusalem in terms of a reliable description of Jesus' words and actions as he approached Israel's capital city, and that there is no reason why Luke should have invented the motif of a journey: "The journey is expressed in time, not direct geographic direction. Jesus is headed to Jerusalem and his fate there."[8]

Many scholars believe that the sending out of the disciples in Lk 10:1-24 has no valid claim to historical credibility.

The historicity of a second missionary tour of disciples is questioned for at least three reasons.[9] (1) Neither Mark nor Luke knows of a mission of disciples apart from the Twelve. (2) Instructions that Jesus gives to the Seventy-Two in Lk 10 appear also in Mt 9:37-38; 10:7-16, which indicates that Luke created in Lk 10 a literary doublet from Q material, with parallels to Mk 6:6b-13. Luke composed this doublet in order to emphasize that the task of missionary outreach is not restricted to the Twelve but that other disciples have been, and are, involved in their witness as well.[10] (3) Some scholars argue that the discourse in Lk 10:2-12, analyzed from a tradition-historical perspective, is not a unified composition: the "growth rings" that are noticeable demonstrate that the discourse developed during a lengthy process of transmission.[11] However, some scholars argue that the passage is a compositional unity.[12] Howard Marshall emphasizes that Luke follows his sources: it is improbable that he simply invented the second mission in order to solve the tension between Jesus' commission given to the Twelve and the existence of a larger group of evangelists in the post-Easter church.[13]

The following factors must not be overlooked in the discussion.[14] (1) The fact that neither Mark nor Matthew reports a second mission by the disciples may be taken precisely as an argument supporting the historicity of the mission in Lk 10. If every narrative that

---

[6]A. Baum 1993, 155-97; quotations from the summary, ibid., 198.

[7]A. Baum 1993, 203-337; quotation, 336.

[8]Bock, *Lk,* 2:961.

[9]Hoffmann 1972, 248-54; Braun 1991; Fitzmyer, *Lk,* 2:843-44.

[10]Fitzmyer, *Lk,* 2:844; cf. Bovon, *Lk,* 2:45-46.

[11]Hoffmann 1972, 287-311; Uro 1987, 97-116; Braun 1991, 287-91.

[12]S. Schulz 1972, 409.

[13]Marshall, *Lk,* 413.

[14]Marshall, *Lk,* 413; Bock, *Lk,* 2:987-91; J. Wenham 1991b, 3-44, esp. 7.

is extant in only a single Gospel must be regarded as a secondary literary creation, then doubts concerning historicity have to be cast over all the special material in the Gospel of Luke (or in the Gospel of Matthew). And one should not forget with regard to Luke's literary habits that he avoids doublets. (2) The numerous contacts between the mission of the Seventy-Two and the mission of the Twelve cannot automatically be used as an argument against the historicity of such a second mission: if Jesus indeed sent out followers on different occasions during his ministry with the assignment to proclaim his message of the kingdom and to heal the sick, it is to be expected that some instructions would be similar if not identical. (3) There were other occasions when Jesus sent disciples ahead (cf. Lk 9:51-56). There is no reason why he could not have sent a larger group of followers ahead as he traveled toward Jerusalem. (4) If Luke indeed thought it necessary to invent a second mission of disciples in order to demonstrate the necessity of a universal evangelistic ministry of the church or in order to justify the existence of a larger circle of Christian evangelists, then he relied on a rather weak and questionable foundation. Nothing in Lk 10 alludes to a universal mission of the disciples. And we must not forget the methodical criteria that Luke set out in Lk 1:1-4 for his account of Jesus' ministry. (5) If the account of the Seventy-Two is an invention—something that could hardly have remained unknown in early Christian circles—it is very difficult to imagine how this account could have achieved the intended effect. If the churches were ignorant of the invention and regarded the account as historical, the intended effects could have only been realized slowly. (6) Instead of creating a doublet to the sending out of the Twelve, Luke might have been better advised to "compose" a doublet of the calling of the Twelve (Lk 6:12-16) or to reformulate the missionary commission of the risen Christ (Lk 24:48-49; Acts 1:8), which probably would have been more directly effective. I conclude that there is no reason to doubt the historicity of a second sending out of disciples, a conclusion that also favors the historicity of the individual sections of the "travel narrative."

There is some dispute concerning the number of disciples whom Jesus sent out: The manuscript tradition mentions in Lk 10:1 both the number "seventy" and the number "seventy-two."

The external evidence for both numbers is equally strong. (1) The number "seventy" (ἑβδομήκοντα) is attested in ℵ A C L W Θ Ξ Ψ f[1,13] 𝔐 f q sy[p,h] bo. This reading is accepted by the translations RSV, NRSV, NASB, GN, as well as by A. Schlatter, W. Grundmann, E. Schweizer, E. E. Ellis, H. Schürmann.[15] (2) The number "seventy-two" (ἑβδομήκοντα δύο) is attested in P[75] B D 0181 pc lat sy[s,c] sa bo[ms] Adamantius. This reading is accepted by the Greek texts UBS[4] and NA[27] (with brackets), by the translations JB, NIV, TNIV, Lü, Eü, NEB, as well as by M.-J. Lagrange, T. Zahn, F. Godet, J. Ernst, I. H. Marshall, J. Fitzmyer, W. Wiefel, J. Nolland, D. Bock, F. Bovon, K. Aland.[16]

The discussion of the internal evidence considers what role a symbolic significance of the numbers "seventy" and "seventy-two" might have played. (1) The figure "seventy" may have a symbolic meaning, as it occurs repeatedly in the Old Testament and in Second Temple traditions. For example, there were 70 elders of Israel (Ex 24:1; Num 11:16-17, 24-25), 70 descendants of Jacob (Ex 1:5; Deut 10:22), 70 nations (Gen 10; *1 En.* 89:59; 90:22;

---

[15]See also M. Völkel, *EWNT* 1:891-92 (*EDNT* 1:368-69); recently Wilk 2002, 165 n. 81.

[16]K. Aland (in Metzger, *Textual Commentary,* 127) contends that the number "seventy-two" should be printed without brackets. On the discussion see B. Metzger 1958-1959; Jellicoe 1960.

Tanchuma, Toledot 32b), 70 sons of Jerubbaal (Judg 9:2), 70 years of exile (Jer 25:11), 70 members of the Sanhedrin (*m. Sanh.* 1:5-6), 70 languages in which Moses' commandments were heard (*b. Šabb.* 88b). (2) The number "seventy-two" also occurs in the Old Testament and in Jewish traditions: according to the Septuagint there are 72 nations (Gen 10-11), 72 translators of the Hebrew Bible (*Let. Arist.* 46-50), 72 members of local councils (*m. Zebaḥ.* 1:3; *m. Yad.* 3:5; 4:2), 72 princes and 72 languages of the world (*3 En.* 17:8; 18:2-3; 30:2). The number "seventy" plays a more important role in the tradition than does the number "seventy-two." A copyist who wanted to accommodate a symbolic meaning in the number would change a "seventy-two" into a "seventy" rather than vice-versa. This means that if there was a deliberate change in the transmission process, the number "seventy-two" is more likely to be original.

Did Luke see a symbolic meaning in the number of disciples? Many scholars assume that he did and interpret the number as implying a reference to the number of nations: Luke sees the later Gentile mission prefigured in the mission of these disciples, which favors the figure "seventy"[17] but does not exclude the number "seventy-two" if Luke follows the Septuagint. Howard Marshall surmises that Luke followed Gen 10 LXX and wrote the number "seventy-two," which was changed to "seventy" by later copyists who followed the Masoretic text of Gen 10 or were influenced by the more frequent occurrence and by the symbolic meaning of the number "seventy."[18] It is not certain at all, however, that the number "seventy-two" has a symbolic meaning in Lk 10:1: even though Luke does not restrict the mission of the seventy-two to Israel in Lk 10, there is no clear universal dimension that would make an allusion to the nations of Gen 10 plausible;[19] in addition, the selection of seventy elders by Moses is not alluded to in Lk 10 or anywhere in the book of Acts. A symbolic meaning of the number in Lk 10:1 seems rather unlikely. The criterion of the *lectio difficilior* favors the number "seventy-two," which is the number I accept for the disciples whom Jesus sent out on a missionary journey.

The mission of the seventy-two disciples took place probably in the initial phase of Jesus' orientation toward Jerusalem in the spring of A.D. 30.

The parallels to Lk 10:13-15 in Mt 11:20-24 often are judged to be problematic with regard to chronological considerations. In Lk 10 the woes against Chorazin, Bethsaida and Capernaum are pronounced in connection with the mission of the Seventy-Two, while in Mt 11 they are part of Jesus' answer to the question of John the Baptist, which Luke reports in Lk 7:18-35. Since Lk 7 and Mt 11 are thematically structured, the geographical location of this conversation is difficult to determine. A localization at the beginning of Jesus' orientation toward Jerusalem is a plausible possibility.[20]

The tradition that specifies names for some of the seventy[-two] disciples is problematic. Eusebius (*Hist. eccl.* 1.12.1) first points out that "there exists no catalogue of the seventy disciples" and that he therefore needs to rely entirely on oral tradition. He mentions Paul's co-workers Barnabas and Sosthenes, Matthias from Acts 1, Joseph Barsabbas of Acts 1, and Thaddaeus (1.12.1-5). The fact that Eusebius also mentions the

---

[17]K. H. Rengstorf, *ThWNT* 2:623-31 (*TDNT* 2:627-35); Völkel, *EWNT* 1:891-92 (*EDNT* 1:368-69).

[18]Marshall, *Lk,* 415.

[19]Fitzmyer, *Lk,* 2:846; Bock, *Lk,* 2:1015; for the objection that follows above see Bock, ibid. Differently J. M. Scott 2002, 51-55.

[20]Bock (*Lk,* 2:989), who relies for his reconstruction in part on Fitzmyer, *Lk,* 2:850-52.

Cephas of Gal 2:11 as a "man who bore the same name as the apostle Peter" (1.12.2) makes this tradition suspect.

11.1 The Strategy

The goal of the sending of the seventy-two disciples is twofold: (1) they are directed, as Jesus' heralds, to prepare his arrival in the towns and villages that they will visit (Lk 10:1); (2) they are to heal the sick and proclaim the good news of the arrival of God's reign (Lk 10:9).

Lk 10:1, 9: "After this the Lord appointed seventy[-two] others and sent them on ahead of him in pairs to every town and place where he himself intended to go. . . . [9]'Cure the sick who are there, and say to them, "The kingdom of God has come near to you.""'"

Luke does not harmonize the two elements here that stand in some tension with one another: the Seventy-Two are heralds, forerunners of Jesus, but at the same time they are missionaries who themselves preach and heal.

1. The Seventy-Two may be interpreted as heralds of Jesus who have been given the task of preparing his visit to various towns and villages, particularly if we interpret their mission in the framework of Jesus' final orientation from Galilee to Jerusalem. This view makes sense considering the wording of Lk 10:1.

Armin Baum reconstructs the historical situation as follows: "Jesus focused his preaching activity so far (Lk 4—9) mostly on Galilee; now he turns to areas that are mostly in a southerly direction, especially Transjordan. Since there is only a little time for preaching the gospel in this part of Palestine, compared with his Galilean ministry, he uses a special strategy during this journey. He sends ahead pairs of envoys who are to prepare his arrival in the individual villages. This allows Jesus to visit only those places that have demonstrated their openness to his message by welcoming his envoys. The preparatory activity of the heralds also allows shorter visits in the villages. He is thus able to evangelize the areas through which he will be traveling in a much shorter time compared with the preaching of the gospel in Galilee, which he had carried alone until the sending out of the Twelve."[21]

2. It is unlikely, however, that the Seventy-Two were directed simply to prepare for Jesus' arrival. The formulation of their assignment in Lk 10:9 implies a ministry of preaching and healing: the Seventy-Two are directed to engage in the same ministry of healing and preaching as the Twelve did before them (Lk 9:2), reproducing the ministry of Jesus. The search for accommodations is indeed referred to extensively: with regard to private homes in Lk 10:5-7, with regard to towns in Lk 10:8, 10-11. But the focus is on accommodations for the disciples themselves, not for Jesus. We should further note that if the seventy-two disciples were simply asked to prepare for Jesus' imminent arrival in thirty-six

---

[21]A. Baum 1993, 231-32; cf. ibid., 260-63.

towns and villages that he would visit during his journey to Jerusalem, they would not need to return to Jesus (cf. Lk 10:17): they could have waited in the villages that had welcomed them, and would welcome Jesus, which would have allowed them to prepare the population even more extensively for Jesus' arrival.

3. The location from which the Seventy-Two were sent out presumably was southern Galilee: Bethsaida is the last place that Luke had mentioned (Lk 9:11). Since Jesus was not welcomed in Samaria (Lk 9:51-56), he most probably moved to southern Galilee.[22]

4. The Seventy-Two are directed to preach the message of the arrival of the kingdom of God (Lk 10:9, 11) "in every town and place" (εἰς πᾶσαν πόλιν καὶ τόπον, *eis pasan polin kai topon* [Lk 10:1]) before Jesus would visit these places himself (Lk 10:1; cf. 13:22: "He went through one town and village [κατὰ πόλεις καὶ κώμας, *kata poleis kai kōmas*] after another, teaching as he made his way to Jerusalem"). If we interpret Lk 10 in the framework of Jesus' journey from southern Galilee to Jerusalem (avoiding Samaria [cf. Lk 9:51-56]), these towns and villages would have to be located in southern Galilee itself as well as in Perea east of the Jordan River.

The following towns are possible locations for a mission of the Seventy-Two: a route from Pella (Berenike) in the upper Jordan Valley south of the Sea of Galilee runs in a south-easterly direction across the plateau east of the Jordan through the Decapolis to Iabeis, Thesbe, Gerasa, Gadara, Philadelphia, Elealeh, Esbous, Livias, Betharba and Jericho. A more southerly route in the Jordan Valley runs from Pella (Berenike) via Salem, Aenon, Kh. el Givur, Kh. Basaliyye, Kh. Khiraf, Koreai, Phaselis and Archelais to Jericho.

The instruction to visit "every town and place" (Lk 10:1) means that the thirty-six pairs of missionaries could concentrate on at least thirty-six settlements during the necessary three days for a journey from Galilee to Jerusalem. If every missionary team, perhaps within a week, visited two towns, seventy-two places would be reached, and within two weeks they could have visited roughly 150 towns and villages. However, the assumption that Jesus would have visited thirty-six, or seventy-two, or 150 towns and villages during this journey with the intention of preaching, teaching and healing is not without problems: the focus on the search for accommodations in Lk 10:5-7 seems to indicate, assuming a literal-historical interpretation, that Jesus spent at least one night in each of the places that the Seventy-Two "prepared," which means that if he spent one day in each place, he would have needed six weeks for thirty-six towns (reckoning the sabbath as a day of rest), and for seventy-two towns twelve weeks (three months). Such a scenario is not impossible, but if Lk 10 is placed in the context of the last journey to Jerusalem, it is unlikely, especially since Luke does not mention any "follow-up" work by Jesus. Another difficulty is that it is not easy

---

[22]A. Baum 1993, 235.

to list even two dozen towns or villages for Perea (although we do not know the number of villages, which often have left little or no trace).

It is perhaps more plausible to interpret the reference in Lk 10:1 to towns and villages "where he himself intended to go" (ἤμελλεν αὐτὸς ἔρχεσθαι, *ēmellen autos erchesthai*) in terms of the coming of Jesus as the exalted Son of Man. The assertion in Lk 10:16 that the disciples will take the place of Jesus may support this interpretation.[23]

11.2 The Instructions

The instructions that Luke reports in Lk 10:1-12 for the ministry of the Seventy-Two generally correspond to the instructions for the Twelve.

1. The seventy-two disciples, who are distinguished from the Twelve—Lk 10:1 speaks of "other" (ἑτέρους, *heterous*) disciples—go in pairs of two (ἀνὰ δύο δύο, *ana dyo dyo*), thus thirty-six pairs, to the towns and villages between Galilee and Jerusalem. The reason for the pairing is, again, not only the increased security on the road and the mutual support during the preaching and healing activity but also the notion that the truth of assertions is confirmed by two witnesses (cf. Deut 19:15; Num 35:30).[24]

2. The activity of the disciples is described with reference to the "plentiful harvest" (θερισμὸς πολύς, *therismos polys* [Lk 10:2; cf. Mt 9:37-38]).

According to Jn 4:38 the disciples reap a harvest even though they have not toiled. There is no evidence in Lk 10:2 that this thought is present here[25]—that is, that missionaries always reap what they have not sown, that the work of the disciples is always "harvest work."[26]

The metaphor of harvesting, taken from everyday life in Palestine, may refer to the necessity of gathering the rich harvest as quickly as possible,[27] but this is not certain. Of course, the call to repentance is always urgent. The urgency of the missionary task that some scholars see in this passage, however, usually is determined by the assumed eschatological horizon—the imminence of the end that Jesus expects and proclaims.[28] If we interpret the kingdom of God that becomes a reality in the ministry of Jesus as an eschatological reality, then the statement in Lk 10:2a ("the harvest is plentiful, but the laborers are few") asserts that the eschatological gathering of the people of God takes place in the mission of the disciples.[29] In this interpretation the "harvest" is not the end or the final

---

[23]See Marshall, *Lk,* 416; Fitzmyer, *Lk,* 2:846.

[24]See Fitzmyer, *Lk,* 2:846.

[25]Contra Fitzmyer, *Lk,* 2:846; cf. Bovon, *Lk,* 2:50 n. 29.

[26]Thus Bultmann, *Joh,* 147 (ET, 199).

[27]Thus A. Sand, *EWNT* 2:360 (*EDNT* 2:146).

[28]Thus, for example, Hoffmann 1972, 289-93.

[29]See Marshall, *Lk,* 416.

judgment but the missionary successes of the disciples.[30] The description of the harvest as "plentiful" renders the interpretation in terms of an imminent judgment highly unlikely. The harvest is "plentiful," meaning that many people are ready to be "harvested" for Jesus' message of the dawn of God's reign.

3. The urgency of the mission of the Seventy-Two springs from the fact that "the laborers are few" (οἱ ἐργάται ὀλίγοι, *hoi ergatai oligoi* [Lk 10:2a]). The statement that follows formulates Jesus' exhortation to pray for more missionary workers but primarily underlines the urgency of the situation.[31] The term *ergatēs* ("worker, laborer") does not establish the "right to wages" for the missionaries, who, if that interpretation were correct, would have to be understood as wage laborers.[32] Even though Lk 10:7 refers to "wages," the focus clearly is on the directive to them to accept the hospitality that is offered, to accept room and board. The disciples are directed to participate in the table fellowship of the family and of the house that welcomed them, "not as beggars but as day laborers" (cf. Lk 10:2) who receive the meal they have earned, in the evening, after they have finished their work (Lk 10:7c).[33] Jesus' request makes sense when viewed with the evidence that the disciples visited numerous towns and villages and many accepted the message of God's kingdom.

4. The request to pray for more laborers implies at least a threefold message. (a) God is the Lord of missionary work; he alone is authorized to give directives, not the missionaries. He is the Lord of the harvest, which always remains his. The missionaries will always be dependent upon him. (b) God is the initiator of missionary work; he alone is authorized to send out missionaries. He sends laborers out to accomplish important tasks. (c) God is the provider for the missionaries; they can rely on him and expect that they will have enough to eat and to drink.

5. The prohibition against taking along provisions (Lk 10:4a) underlines God's faithfulness, on which the Seventy-Two can depend, and at the same time implies the short-term nature of their mission. The Seventy-Two are directed not to take along a purse (*ballantion*) or a bag (*pēran*) or an additional pair of shoes (*hypodēmata*). They should expect to receive their necessary provisions locally. Their missionary activity is only short-term, for this occasion.

6. The prohibition against greeting people (Lk 10:4b) underlines the "haste in the proclamation of the message."[34] The Seventy-Two are directed to avoid the long conversations and hospitable invitations that may easily arise during the journey. Human encounters are set in motion by initial greetings, without

---

[30]Fitzmyer, *Lk*, 2:846; for the comment that follows above see Carson, *Mt*, 235.

[31]See Marshall, *Lk*, 416.

[32]Contra Haraguchi 1993, 188, 190.

[33]Schürmann, *Lk*, 2:69; cf. Green, *Lk*, 414.

[34]P. Trummer, *EWNT* 1:416 (*EDNT* 1:173); cf. Marshall, *Lk*, 418; A. Baum 1993, 241-45; Bosold 1978.

which such encounters remain impersonal, perhaps even threatening. The prohibition of greeting people on the way is meant to underline not so much the urgency of the preaching ministry as the dedication of the missionaries to the task given them by Jesus. The proclamation of the kingdom of God creates relationships that transcend traditional courtesies.[35]

Joseph Fitzmyer comments, "*Impedimenta* cannot be tolerated in the preaching of the kingdom, and the curing of the sick must be handled with the speed expected of workers at harvest time. But the disciples must realize that they are not being sent to carry out ordinary social obligations and amenities, for what they are to preach and do will set them apart. There will be no time for ordinary greetings, scruples over what sort of food one eats, or searching for better quarters." Fitzmyer rightly rejects the interpretation of Bernhard Lang, who understands Jesus' directive as a prohibition against the missionaries having visitation with relatives during their missionary work.[36]

7. The search for accommodations should remain as uncomplicated as possible. The disciples are instructed to stay with the first family that welcomes them and not to hunt for better quarters. Armin Baum makes the suggestion that Jesus tells the disciples not to seek out the public institutions of the town (Lk 10:8-9) but to go first to private homes (Lk 10:5a).[37] The "public organs" would be the local synagogues and councils.

Several scholars suggest that Lk 10:5-7 refers to a "house mission," missionary efforts directed at the houses and families of the town.[38] This interpretation is not without problems, as Jesus instructs the missionaries, "Remain in the same house. . . . Do not move about from house to house" (Lk 10:7). Jesus hardly directs them to acquaint only one family with the message of the kingdom of God.[39] The text does not state that a "house mission" would be followed by a "city mission."[40] This conflict can be avoided if we interpret Lk 10:5-7 simply in terms of the accommodations of the missionaries who evangelize in the town, without assuming a particular charge to evangelize houses or families.[41]

The rather elaborate description of the greetings in Lk 10:5-6 can be explained against the background of the prohibition to greet people in Lk 10:4. Jesus emphasizes in Lk 10:5-6 God's loving care: if laborers earn their wages in everyday

---

[35]Fitzmyer, *Lk,* 2:847; the quotation that follows above, ibid., 2:844.
[36]Bernhard Lang, "Grußverbot oder Besuchsverbot? Eine sozialgeschichtliche Deutung von Lukas 10,4b," *BZ* 26 (1982): 75-79.
[37]A. Baum 1993, 246.
[38]Thus Marshall, *Lk,* 419; A. Baum 1993, 240 (the *Hausmission* that he describes seems to be in tension with his identification of the houses as "bases" for missionary work; cf. ibid., 248-49); Gehring 2000, 108-13.
[39]Marshall (*Lk,* 421) resolves this tension with the suggestion that Jesus gave more comprehensive sets of missionary instructions that perhaps were independent of each other, which Luke summarized without harmonizing tensions in his traditions.
[40]Thus Gehring 2000, 110-11.
[41]Thus correctly Carson, *Mt,* 246-47, with reference to Lk 10:5.

life by their work, so do the messengers of the kingdom of God, who totally depend upon God due to their lack of provisions. Jesus promises these missionaries that they will find a house, a family that will welcome them and provide them with room and board. The heads of the families who will welcome the Seventy-Two in their homes and whom they are to greet with the greeting of peace (Lk 10:5b) are described by Jesus as a "son of peace" (υἱὸς εἰρήνης, *huios eirēnēs* [Lk 10:6a; cf. NASB).[42] The TNIV translates "if the head of the house loves peace," the NIV has "if a man of peace is there," and the NRSV has "and if anyone is there who shares in peace." These people probably had already heard of Jesus and his message and might already have been sympathizers or received through the Seventy-Two the final impetus to accept Jesus' message. If the "greeting of peace" for the "sons of peace" demonstrates that the people welcomed Jesus' messengers as his representatives, their houses become strategic bases for the proclamation of the good news in that particular town or village.[43]

8. The reception in a town can be positive (Lk 10:8-9). The greeting of peace and eating and drinking are everyday actions that take place when hospitality is extended to guests; at the same time they point to the importance of relationships between people that are critical for successful missionary work.[44] The instruction to eat whatever is offered (Lk 10:8) may refer to invitations from influential people of the town or village who may desire to host banquets.[45] The comment in Lk 10:8b ("eat what is set before you") should not be interpreted as an allusion to the Gentile mission, in the course of which the Mosaic food laws can quickly become a problem for Jewish missionaries.[46]

9. The missionary activity of the Seventy-Two is described in Lk 10:9: "Heal the sick who are there and tell them, 'The kingdom of God is near you.'" This instruction corresponds with Jesus' own ministry and with the instructions for the Twelve (Lk 9:2; cf. Mt 10:7-8). The healings precede the proclamation, at least in Jesus' instructions. This may be an indication that the healing miracles should be seen as signs of the presence of the kingdom of God.[47]

10. Jesus speaks about opposition that the Seventy-Two may encounter. It is possible that they will be officially banished from some towns (Lk 10:10-12). Such an experience will not be exceptional (Lk 10:13-15). Jesus instructs his disciples that they should immediately leave the town when this happens and wipe the dust of the town publicly from their shoes, explaining the meaning of this

---

[42]Even Braun (1991, 306) accepts the greeting of peace and the "son of peace" as authentic saying of Jesus.

[43]A. Baum 1993, 248-49.

[44]See Casalegno 1994, 35-37.

[45]A. Baum 1993, 251.

[46]Contra, for example, Braun 1991, 284; Uro 1987, 68-69. See more recently Stenschke 1999a, 110-11.

[47]See Marshall, *Lk,* 421.

action to the townspeople (Lk 10:11). If they are rejected, so also the message of the kingdom of God is rejected. As a result, they should announce God's judgment and travel on to the next town.[48]

11.3 The Return of the Messengers

The Seventy-Two return to Jesus after an unspecified amount of time (Lk 10:17). They report "with joy" (μετὰ χαρᾶς, *meta charas*) of exorcisms that they performed: "Lord, even the demons submit to us in your name." Jesus answers by reporting a vision that he had: "I saw Satan fall like lightning from heaven" (Lk 10:18). The fall of Satan is described as a singular and sudden event that took place before the exorcisms that the Seventy-Two performed, presumably even before Lk 4:1-13.[49] Jesus' next remark reminds the missionaries that the authority that put the demons to flight is rooted in his establishment of their mission, and that the power with which Satan opposes the work of the missionaries has been placed under Jesus' authority. He assures the disciples that "nothing will harm" them (Lk 10:19),[50] neither snakes nor scorpions nor any other impediment that Satan's power may put before them. Heinz Schürmann interprets this promise of Lk 22:3, 53, as valid only until the beginning of Jesus' passion.[51]

Luke concludes his report of the return of the Seventy-Two with a comment by Jesus that curbs the disciples' enthusiasm that had been prompted by the exorcisms: "Do not rejoice that the spirits submit to you, but rejoice that your names are written in heaven" (Lk 10:20). To quote Schürmann again, "There is something even more important than exceptional charismatic power: the knowledge that they have been preordained by God for eternal salvation, that they have been recorded in heaven as having eternal life. . . . They must realize that it is more important that they themselves are listeners than that others listen to them (10:16)."[52]

---

[48]Schürmann, *Lk,* 2:76.
[49]Luke probably did not think of an event that took place before Jesus' coming into the world, and he presumably did not refer proleptically to Jesus' crucifixion and resurrection; see Schürmann, *Lk,* 2:90. Bovon (*Lk,* 2:58) seeks to reformulate Jesus' statement in "non-mythological" terms.
[50]Schürmann, *Lk,* 2:92.
[51]Schürmann, *Lk,* 2:93.
[52]Schürmann, *Lk,* 2:94, 95.

12

JESUS AND GENTILES

Jesus limited his ministry to his Jewish contemporaries. He preached and healed among the people who lived in Galilee, in synagogues and in the open. He preached and healed in Jerusalem, the Jewish capital. He spoke with peasants and artisans, with scribes and priests, with Sadducees and Pharisees. The Gospel writers also report contacts with non-Jews and relate that Jesus, on a few occasions, commanded his disciples to engage in missionary work among Gentiles. Did Jesus envision a Gentile mission? The majority of critical scholars suggest that he did not.

Bengt Sundkler argues that the Son of Man had only *one* mission as the Son of David: to transform the house of Israel into the house of the church; Jesus did not "go" as a missionary goes to pagans, but rather he remained in the "center"—the center of God's will. His "mission" was to go to the cross and thus to procure salvation for Israel. It was that event that made the Gentile mission possible.[1] Joachim Jeremias argues that Jesus squarely rejected the contemporary Jewish Gentile mission; Jesus did not engage in missionary outreach to Gentiles but limited his ministry to Israel and similarly prohibited his disciples from doing missionary work among non-Jews. Paul based his missionary work not on the words of Jesus but on Old Testament passages.[2] According to Jeremias, passages such as Mk 13:10 or Mk 14:9 that speak of an active Gentile mission of Jesus' followers are redactional reinterpretations of dominical sayings in a later period when the church was engaged in missionary work. He argues that Jesus expected, as did the Old Testament prophets, "the incorporation of the Gentiles in the kingdom of God promised by the prophets" and proclaimed this future event "as God's eschatological act of power, as the great final manifestation of God's free grace." The Gentile mission of the early church is "a part of the final fulfilment, a divine factual demonstration of the exaltation of the Son of Man, an eschatology in process of realization." The view that Jesus' eschatological outlook excluded the possibility of an active Gentile mission was quite influential.[3] T. W. Manson emphasizes that Jesus concentrated on the "lost sheep of the house of Is-

---

[1]Sundkler 1936, esp. 491-98; cf. earlier Soden 1924, 22.

[2]Jeremias 1952; 1956, 9-33 (ET, 11-39); the quotations that follow above, Jeremias 1956, 60, 63 (ET, 70, 75); similarly Kilpatrick 1955, independently of Jeremias; see also Gensichen 1971, 69; Ker 1988; Bosch 1969. See the history of research on this issue in Jáuregui 1981 (on Jeremias, 1476-87); Wilk 2002, 14-24.

[3]See Barrett 1988, 67-69; Hofrichter 1993, 14.

rael" because he hoped that the kingdom of God, which expands only through personal encounters, would transform the life of the Jewish people through the new community that he established with the disciples. The expected eschatological transformation of the world would be the work of a transformed Israel.[4] David Bosch concludes in his study on the Gentile mission in Jesus' eschatology that Jesus restricted his ministry to Israel, thus creating the precondition for a later worldwide missionary activity. The Gentile mission is not the result of a "delay of the parousia" but can be traced back to Jesus himself (Mk 13:10): "The risen and exalted Lord himself engages in missionary work in the form of the Holy Spirit through his messengers. For this reason a centrifugal mission is possible only after Pentecost. Jesus Christ himself, by the Spirit, goes to the nations and thus prepares the world for his return through his emissaries."[5] Missionary work is therefore "an eschatological process, an eschatological action." Geza Vermes believes that Jesus was xenophobic, as were his Jewish contemporaries.[6]

Stephen Wilson analyzes all relevant passages concerning the Gentiles in the Gospel of Luke and comes to the following conclusions:[7] (1) Jesus limited his ministry to Israel and directed his disciples to do the same. (2) In Jesus' teaching the Gentiles find a place in the kingdom of God, but only in the future when the kingdom becomes visibly manifest in the consummation. (3) The connection between the Gentiles and the kingdom of God seems to have been established by Jesus in contexts that hint at the imminence of the kingdom of God. (4) Jesus spoke with Gentiles who approached him, although in a cautious manner. These Gentiles found access to the kingdom of God as it was in the process of becoming a reality in a hidden manner. (5) There is no reliable evidence to suggest that Jesus anticipated or intended a Gentile mission.

David Sim argues in several recent studies that Matthew paints no positive picture of the Gentiles, especially in the passion narrative, where Pilate and the Roman soldiers are anything but heroes; the Matthean community was a Christian-Jewish sect that still moved within Judaism, and it was not actively involved in missionary work among Gentiles.[8] Ulrich Luz believes that Matthew propagates, at the end of this Gospel, the Gentile mission as substitute for the mission to Israel that Jesus had commanded according to Mt 10:5-6.[9] According to Luz, the command to a worldwide mission in Mt 28:19 is a correction of the earlier command of Jesus. The expression *panta ta ethnē* means, in deliberate opposition to the "lost sheep of the house of Israel," that "all Gentiles" (without Israel) should be reached. Luz argues that Matthew's theology is deeply anti-Jewish, and Matthew regards at least the leaders of the majority of Israel who do not believe in Jesus as apostate.[10] The attacks against the Pharisees and the scribes in Mt 23 violate not only Jesus' command to love one's enemies but also his command to be truthful: Matthew accuses Israel's leaders of sins that others committed. Forced to explain his position more clearly,[11] Luz acknowledges that Mt 28:16-20 does not exclude categorically a continuation of the mission to Israel; he argues, however, that for Matthew and his community there seems to have been

---

[4]T. W. Manson 1964 [1955], esp. 14-15, 18-21.

[5]Bosch 1959, 198-99; the quotation that follows above, ibid., 196; see now idem 1991, 25-31.

[6]Vermes 1983, 49.

[7]S. Wilson 1973, esp. 18.

[8]Sim 1995; 1998, with reference to Mt 5:46-47; 6:7-8, 31-32; 18:15-17.

[9]See Luz 1992; cf. idem 2000, with a protest against the alleged misunderstanding of his position. For a critique of Luz see Sim 1995; 1998; Kvalbein 2000.

[10]For Luz's understanding of "anti-Judaism" see *Mt,* 3:395-96. Apart from Mt 23 he refers to passages such as Mt 8:10-12; 11:16-24; 12:22-45; 13:10-17, 36; 16:1-12; 21:28-32, 46.

[11]See Luz 2000, 65.

no reason to be confident of any success, which is why they turned to the Gentile mission as the main task. Meinrad Limbeck formulates as the consensus of Roman Catholic exegesis that "the Gentiles" were not subject to Jesus' teaching and that the missionary commission in Mt 28:19-20 was not an authentic word of the historical Jesus.[12] Schuyler Brown suggests that Jesus may have been characterized by an "expectant universalism" but believes that the teaching and the behavior of the historical Jesus did not provide the post-Easter church any clear directives concerning a mission to Gentiles. By putting a commission to a universal mission into Jesus' mouth at the end of his Gospel, Matthew uses a *deus ex machina* in order to achieve a consensus in his community on the question of the Gentile mission.[13]

There is no doubt that soon after Easter the first Christians actively sought to convince Gentiles to accept their beliefs about Jesus Christ. How did this missionary activity begin among non-Jews? Scholars who believe that the "Great Commission" in Matthew 28:16-20 is unauthentic, to be interpreted as a later redactional composition rather than a directive of the historical Jesus, give two answers to this question. (1) The impetus to reach not only Jews but also Gentiles with the message of Jesus Christ came from Hellenistic Jewish Christians who had to leave Jerusalem and went to non-Jewish cities such as Antioch in Syria.[14] (2) The apostles realized in the 50s that only a minority of Jews accepted Jesus as the Messiah and so they decided to turn to non-Jews, especially Paul, who provides for this turn to the Gentiles a psychological (Rom 11:14) and a theological (Rom 11:28-29) explanation, defending it as a divine revelation (Rom 11:25).[15]

The consensus of historical-critical research deems the sayings in Mk 13:10; Mt 10:18; 28:16-20 to be redactional, thus inauthentic.[16] Some evangelical scholars have supported this view as well. Frederick Schmidt writes that these passages are (later) compositions of the evangelists and argues that there is no evidence that Jesus ever transcended the particularism of his Jewish contemporaries or overcame the barriers between Jews and Gentiles.[17] An often repeated argument against the authenticity of texts such as Mk 13:10 and Matthew 10:18 asserts that if Jesus had indeed left behind clear instructions for a Gentile mission, there would hardly have been so much discussion in the early church about whether Gentiles should be admitted to the churches. This argument overlooks the fact that the admission of Gentiles into the churches was never contested; rather, the debate concerned whether there were conditions that the Gentiles had to fulfill before they could be accepted into the church. Theodor Zahn had already underlined the fact that Jesus directed the disciples to engage in missionary work several times, declaring them to be

---

[12]Limbeck 1989, 44.

[13]S. Brown 1977, 21-32, esp. 32; cf. idem 1978; 1980.

[14]See, for example, Scobie 1984.

[15]See, for example, Barrett 1988, 69-71.

[16]See Hahn 1963, 32-33, 60-61, 101-103, 109-110; Kasting 1969, 108; Hengel 1971-1972, 20 (ET, 168 n.13, 170 n.23); Jeremias 1988, 134 (ET, 133-34); differently Bosch 1959, 149; Meinertz 1959, 770-71; Sautter 1985, 59-60; Wilckens 2002, 1.2:154-55. Brandenburger (1984, 31) argues that Mk 13:10 originates in pre-Markan tradition.

[17]F. Schmidt 1993, 103-4; for the observation that follows above see ibid., 104.

"fishers of people" when he called them, and gave them as apostles the task to make disciples of all nations.[18] In the following discussion the question of the historicity of Gospel sayings will repeatedly play an important role.

Again, no one questions that the early church engaged in missionary outreach, that Jewish Christians proclaimed the message of the Jewish Messiah to polytheists in the early years of the church, with the goal of establishing new communities of believers in Jesus. How did this revolutionary innovation come about if there was no Gentile mission in Israel or in Second Temple Judaism? How did this international and interracial mission come into existence if there were no Greek or Roman models for an active and deliberately organized program of expansion by a religious association? One possible answer is to refer to the significance of Jesus' death and resurrection for the faith of the early Christians, which provoked the opening up of the apostolic mission to include Gentiles.[19] However, the acceptance of the eschatological significance of Jesus' death and resurrection does not lead automatically to an active missionary work among polytheists, seen from a Jewish perspective, which expected the nations to take the initiative in coming to Zion. An expanded answer refers to the new presence of the Holy Spirit as characteristic of the arrival of the last days, for which a pilgrimage of the nations to Zion had been promised. This answer is not fully satisfactory either: the Qumran community had an understanding of itself as the covenant community of the last days that was in some ways similar to the self-understanding of the early church, but it never engaged in missionary work, especially not to pagans. Ernst Dassmann comments, "We must not forget that the problem with regard to the origin of the mission [of the early church] concerns really *only* the very first beginnings. Not much time passed before missionary work was generally accepted, including the Gentile mission without law and circumcision, which was much more difficult to defend theologically."[20] The word "only" is the operative word in this statement. The question remains: what is the connection between the early Christian missionary activity and Jesus of Nazareth?[21]

12.1 The Summaries

The fact that the Gospel writers hint at the effects of Jesus' ministry on non-Jews in their summaries is often ignored. Both Matthew and Luke include such comments in their very first summaries of Jesus' ministry after the calling of the disciples. It is important to remind ourselves at this point that summaries are "texts that do not describe individual events but a (durative) state of affairs that existed

[18]Zahn 1886, esp. 106-7.
[19]Thus Vanhoye 1990, esp. 550-51.
[20]Dassmann 1991, 39 (italics added).
[21]See N. T. Wright 1992, 11, 18, 22, 26.

over a longer period of time or (iterative) events that occur repeatedly within a longer time period. These states of affairs or events exist or happen simultaneously with the actual progress of the story."[22]

Mt 4:24-25: "News about him spread all over Syria, and people brought to him all who were ill with various diseases, those suffering severe pain, the demon-possessed, those having seizures, and the paralyzed, and he healed them. [25]Large crowds from Galilee, the Decapolis, Jerusalem, Judea and the region across the Jordan followed him" (NIV).

Mk 3:7-8: "Jesus withdrew with his disciples to the lake, and a large crowd from Galilee followed. [8]When they heard all he was doing, many people came to him from Judea, Jerusalem, Idumea, and the regions across the Jordan and around Tyre and Sidon" (NIV).

Lk 6:17-18: "He went down with them and stood on a level place. A large crowd of his disciples was there and a great number of people from all over Judea, from Jerusalem, and from the coast of Tyre and Sidon, [18]who had come to hear him and to be healed of their diseases" (NIV).

Besides the mostly Jewish areas of Judea, Jerusalem and Galilee, these summaries also mention Transjordan/Perea, Tyre, Sidon, Idumea, Syria and the Decapolis, areas having mostly pagan populations. Even though Jesus limited his teaching and healing ministry to the Jewish population and, from a geographical perspective, largely to Galilee, he quickly became known outside of the borders of Galilee and Judea. And it was not only Jesus' reputation that became known in the surrounding regions. According to Mark's account, Jesus traveled and ministered in all the areas that he mentions in Mk 3:7-8: he preaches in Galilee (Mk 1:14), he visits the region east of the Jordan River (Mk 5:1) and the territories of the cities Tyre and Sidon (Mk 7:24, 31), he spends time in Judea and Transjordan (Mk 10:1), and he goes to Jerusalem (Mk 11:11).[23] Matthew writes his Gospel from a geographical vantage point west of the Jordan River, and in Mt 4:24-25 he locates the influence of Jesus' ministry on all four points of the compass: Galilee in the northwest, the Decapolis in the northeast, Judea in the southwest, Transjordan in the southeast, with Jerusalem as the center of the world.[24]

Rudolf Pesch suggests that the regions that Mark mentions are not regions of Jesus' ministry but rather "the areas in which Christians lived at the time of the composition of the summary."[25] There is nothing in the text that could be regarded as evidence for this hypothesis. Equally hypothetical is the suggestion that Matthew does not describe the social and political reality of the influence of Jesus' ministry but provides instead a description

---

[22]Wendel 1998, 13; on redactional questions see ibid., 17-29.
[23]See Burkill 1966, 33.
[24]Davies and Allison, *Mt*, 1:420.
[25]Pesch, *Mk*, 1:200. The comment that follows above, pace Cousland 2002, 43-50, 63-68, and passim.

of an idealized Israel in the context of salvation-historical categories.

The regions mentioned by the Gospel writers that have a predominantly Gentile population include the northeast part of Palestine east of the Jordan River, the Decapolis, Syria, Tyre and Sidon in southern Syria, and Idumea. Northeast Palestine, "beyond the Jordan," included Gaulanitis, Trachonitis, Batanea and Panias (fig. 24). After the death of Herod I, his son Philip was the ruling tetrarch over this area from 4 B.C. until A.D. 34. The population in the areas that he controlled consisted of Jews, Syrians and Idumeans.[26] The coins that Philip had minted seem to indicate that the Jewish population of this region was not very conservative: he was the first Jewish ruler who depicted human beings on coins. The coins minted in Caesarea Philippi and in Bethsaida between 1 B.C. and A.D. 33 show images of Philip, Augustus, Tiberius and Julia. The reverse side of some coins depicted a temple—for example, the temple of Augustus in Caesarea Philippi.[27] Neither Josephus nor any other source reports resistance to these coins. It is a fair assumption that Jesus concentrated on the Jewish population of Batanea and Gaulanitis. But contacts with non-Jews could hardly be avoided in a densely populated region: in the Golan alone, between the Yarmuk River and Mount Hermon, the existence of 143 settlements of the early Roman period has been documented.[28] The Decapolis extended east of the Sea of Galilee from Damascus in the north to Philadelphia in the south.[29] The geographical scope of Syria is difficult to determine in the context of Mt 4:24. Jesus' perspective from Galilee had Syria to the north; politically, Syria was a Roman province that included Palestine (without Galilee, which Herod Antipas ruled at the time). However, it is neither necessary nor indeed plausible, considering these geographical factors, to exclude the possibility that Gentiles came to Jesus for healing.[30] In view of the sentence construction in Mk 3:7-8 and Lk 6:17, the reference to Tyre and Sidon seems to have Jews in mind who live in these cities or in the villages controlled by Tyre and Sidon. However, due to the symbolic force of these geographical names, perhaps Gentiles are also assumed.[31] These passages obviously are not evidence for an active missionary program to reach Gentiles, but they do show that the later Gentile mission of the early church was also motivated by the pull of Jesus' ministry, which had an effect on non-Jewish regions and people.

---

[26]Josephus, *B.J.* 3.58; *A.J.* 16.292; 17.25. See further §8.1 in the present work.
[27]Strickert 1995, esp. 166-69.
[28]See Z. U. Maoz, *NEAEHL* 2:536.
[29]For details see §§8.1; 9.3; 26.1. See Bietenhard (1977, 251), who interprets Mt 23:15 in terms of a Jewish proselytizing mission in the Diaspora "as was going on everywhere in the world of that time."
[30]See Smillie 2002, 87-88.
[31]Marshall, *Lk,* 242; Gundry, *Mt,* 64; Theissen 1992a, 59 (ET, 57); differently Bovon, *Lk,* 1:286; Cousland 2002, 54-57.

12.2 The Evidence in the Gospels

The Gospels indicate repeatedly that Jesus had contacts with Gentiles, and that these contacts were not simply, or not always, accidental in nature but indeed a part of his mission that his disciples were to continue at a later time.[32]

The Centurion in Capernaum

Mt 8:5-13/Lk 7:1-10; cf. Jn 4:46-54. The centurion (ἑκατόνταρχος) was a Gentile. Jewish-Christian readers of the Gospels would have understood this immediately. For them a *hekatontarchos* was an officer who served in the Roman army or in the army of a vassal king of the Roman Empire, and who generally was not a Jew.[33] This centurion came to Jesus with the request that he heal his slave (παῖς, *pais* [Mt 8:6]; δοῦλος, *doulos* [Lk 7:2])[34] by a word spoken from a distance, without Jesus visiting his house (Mt 8:8). Either the centurion wanted to spare Jesus from having to make a visit, as some scholars assume,[35] or Jesus asks a question that is friendly or disapproving or a test ("Should I come and heal him?"),[36] implying that Jesus does not want to come because he is not sent to Gentiles. The pagan centurion refuses to be turned away. He declares that he has full confidence in the unlimited power of healing of Jesus' word: as he can command his soldiers and his slaves and they obey him, so Jesus can issue a command and grant healing (Mt 8:9).

Robert Gagnon analyzes the twofold delegation that the centurion sends to Jesus in Lk 7:3-7 in terms of redactional activity of the author:[37] The first delegation, consisting of Jewish "elders," emphasizes that the Gentile mission can be reconciled with the Jewish traditions, with the argument that Gentile Christians (the centurion) have a pro-Jewish attitude. Luke includes the first delegation in order to remove Jewish concerns that the Christian churches disrupt the Jewish commonwealth. Gagnon argues further that Luke created the second delegation in order to give Jesus time to demonstrate his willingness to visit the house of a Gentile, while underlining at the same time the great humility of the centurion. Luke uses this second delegation to admonish influential patrons of the Christian church

---

[32]See Bosch 1959; Wilk 2002 (who disregards historical questions entirely); on the Gospel of Matthew see Cerfaux 1957; Uro 1987; Weaver 1990; Grilli 1992; Tisera 1993; LaGrand 1995; on the Gospel of Mark see Böttger 1981; Kato 1986 (with tradition- and redaction-critical analyses and eliminations); on Luke-Acts see Wilckens 1974; Burchard 1970; S. Wilson 1973; Kee 1990a; Lane 1996; on the Gospel of John see W. Oehler 1936; 1941; Ruiz 1987; Okure 1988; Köstenberger 1998a.

[33]See Burchard 1993, 278-79; Wegner 1985, 60-69. An exception is mentioned by Josephus, *B.J.* 2.578.

[34]Gnilka, *Mt,* 1:301; Davies and Allison, *Mt,* 2:21; Luz (*Mt,* 2:14) and others interpret in terms of a son. The issue is debated; see Wegner 1985, 41-46; Burchard 1993, 281.

[35]For Mt 8:7 interpreted as consent or as a friendly question see Catchpole 1992, 525-27; interpreted as showing respect for Jewish sensibilities, Stenschke 1999a, 105.

[36]Wegner 1985, 375-80; Gnilka, *Mt,* 1:301; Davies and Allison, *Mt,* 2:21-22; Luz, *Mt,* 2:14.

[37]Gagnon (1994, esp. 138-45), who argues against Wegner (1985, 238-55) and Dauer (1984, 39-125), who see traditional material in this motif.

to behave with the same humility concerning other Christians. Apart from Gagnon's liter-ary-critical decisions, which are not unproblematic, this reconstruction is implausible: (1) The report of the first delegation is linked less with general Jewish traditions than specif-ically with the argument that Jesus has to help this Gentile because he financed the local synagogue. The Jewish elders argue over the categories of honor and obligation.[38] (2) The view that there is an allusion to the Gentile mission of the church has no basis in Lk 7:1-10: it is not the centurion who is healed but his slave, and Jesus never comes into direct contact with the Gentile centurion. (3) The second delegation is not necessary in order to demonstrate the humility of the centurion: the first delegation could serve this purpose just as well. We should further note that the members of the second delegation do not ask Jesus to help a humble person; rather, they declare that there is no need for Jesus to visit the centurion's house.[39] Perhaps the centurion thought that the Jewish elders might misrepresent his request before Jesus, perhaps in terms of an existing obligation: the cen-turion asks friends (who know him) to tell Jesus that he has no claims on Jesus' help. The fact that neither Matthew nor Luke emphasizes the conversion of Gentiles confirms the historical authenticity of this passage.[40]

Jesus responds to the centurion's request with the statement "Go; let it be done for you according to your faith" (Mt 8:13). This response indicates that the mir-acle happens for the benefit of the centurion. It is the sick slave who is healed, but the miracle happens "for" the centurion (γενηθήτω σοι, *genēthētō soi*), who is concerned for his slave who is ill and whom he could not help himself.[41] Jesus comments on the surprising confidence of the Gentile centurion by asserting, "Truly I tell you, in no one in Israel have I found such faith" (Mt 8:10). This re-sponse does not compare the great faith of the centurion with the unbelief of Israel but rather contrasts his faith with the "little" faith of the Jews (cf. Mt 8:26) among whom he preaches and heals. The great faith of the Gentile centurion consists not only in his confidence in Jesus' unlimited power but also, as Chris-toph Burchard asserts, in his confidence "that Jesus brings salvation even to those who do not belong to Israel and who have no natural claims for this. And this is exactly what the crowds are lacking. They believe in Jesus' miracle-work-ing power as well, they later accept miracles performed λόγῳ (*logō*, 'with a word,' 8:16), Jesus attests for some of them that they have faith (9:2, 22, 29). But they do not believe in Jesus' universal mission."

In Mt 8:11 Jesus takes up the tradition of the nations' pilgrimage to Zion and adds the promises of the coming messianic time of salvation and of the kingdom of God:

Mt 8:11: "I tell you, many [πολλοί] will come from east and west and will eat with Abraham and Isaac and Jacob in the kingdom of heaven."

---

[38]Green, *Lk*, 287.

[39]Bock, *Lk*, 1:639. For the observation that follows above see Green, *Lk*, 287.

[40]Wegner 1985, 403-28; Gnilka, *Mt*, 1:305; Davies and Allison, *Mt*, 2:18; cf. Schürmann, *Lk*, 1:394, on Lk 7:9.

[41]Burchard 1993, 285; the quotation that follows above, ibid., 285-86.

The "many" describes the Gentiles, who are contrasted in Mt 8:12 with the "heirs of the kingdom," meaning the Jews.[42] The temporal reference is not to the present reality of Jesus' ministry but to a future event in the eschaton.[43] Jesus does not teach the future salvation of many Gentiles in contrast to a future condemnation of Israel, nor does he teach the return of the Jews from the Diaspora.[44] Rather, Jesus emphasizes the fundamental nature of the Gentile centurion's faith:[45] he comments on the faith of the Roman centurion by reminding the listeners that the nations[46] will be called by God in the eschatological time of salvation, when they will receive salvation at the "table" of the patriarchs— that is, become members of God's kingdom. Jesus separates the kingdom of God from the conditions stipulated in the Old Testament and in Second Temple Judaism: he challenges the privileged position of Israel, he revokes membership in Israel as *conditio sine qua non* for salvation, he teaches the future integration of Gentiles (as Gentiles) in the kingdom of God.[47]

The Demon-Possessed Man in Gadara

Mt 8:28-34/Mk 5:1-20/Lk 8:26-39. The Gospels report that Jesus freed from demons a man who lived in Gergesa,[48] on the eastern shore of the Sea of Galilee. This man evidently was a non-Jew, a polytheist. The repeated reference to pigs[49] "underlines that this is not a negligible detail of the narrative" but conveys to the readers that the man was a pagan and that the miracle took place in a pagan context.[50]

The discussion concerning the historicity of the passages focuses usually on the geographical location of the episode. Franz Annen correctly points out that it cannot be established during which stage of the tradition the name "Gerasene" (or "Gergesene") would have been introduced into the narrative.[51] The following observations are relevant.

---

[42]Some scholars relate those who come from east and west to the Jewish Diaspora; see E. P. Sanders 1985, 119-20; Allison 1989. On the authenticity of the saying see Jeremias 1956, 48.

[43]S. Wilson 1973, 3-4, contra Hahn (1963, 26), who includes a present reference of Jesus' statement.

[44]See Davies and Allison, *Mt,* 2:27-28; Allison 1989; Theissen 1992a, 47-48 (ET, 45-46). Burchard (1993, 286) interprets in terms of those Christians who have been reached by the Christian mission.

[45]See Gnilka, *Mt,* 1:303.

[46]Davies and Allison (*Mt,* 2:27-28) interpret not in terms of Gentiles but in terms of unprivileged Jews.

[47]See Bürkle 1979, 35 (who overemphasizes the obedience to the law); S. Wilson 1973, 4.

[48]On the text-critical discussion with regard to the location see §9.3.

[49]Mk 5:11, 12, 13, 16; Mt 8:30, 31, 32; Lk 8:32, 33. On pigs in the first century and in the context of Second Temple Judaism see Annen 1976, 162-73.

[50]Annen 1976, 182; Marcus, *Mk,* 342; Witherington, *Mk,* 178-79; Ådna 1999b, 293-94. J. Williams (1995, 108-12) does not comment on the ethnic identity of the man. For the interpretation that follows above see also Schnabel 1994, 51-52.

[51]Annen 1976, 196.

(1) Mark, Matthew and Luke show no particular interest in the city. (2) The text-critical uncertainty—the manuscripts variously have Gadara, Gerasa or Gergesa—makes it unlikely that the geographical location of this spectacular exorcism was pure invention (which would support the reading "Gerasa"). (3) The fact that Jesus repeatedly visited regions outside of the Jewish territory (see §9.3) and that he had followers from the regions of Tyre and Sidon (Mk 3:7-8; Lk 6:17) and the Decapolis (Mt 4:25) indicates that the assumption is historically plausible that Jesus performed miracles in the region east of the Sea of Galilee.

The suggestion by Rudolf Pesch that the pericope shows, in the context of Mk 4, the attempt of the author to emphasize the Gentile mission of the church as a result of Jesus' rejection by the Jews[52] is unconvincing. (1) The parable of the sower, the parable of the growing seed and the parable of the mustard seed (Mk 4:1-34) speak of the success of the kingdom of God, not its failure. This is confirmed specifically by the reference to the "other boats" in Mk 4:36 that accompanied Jesus to the other side of the lake. (2) The narrative of the healing of the demon-possessed man in Mk 5:1-20 can easily be integrated into the topographical context of Mk 4—5. And there is nothing in the narrative that would make it impossible to link Mk 5:1-20 in the context of Mk 4—5 with the chronology of the other events of these chapters. (3) The numerous vivid details that describe this miracle may well come from an eyewitness account of one of the followers of Jesus, or from accounts of people living in the area who later recalled the healing of this notorious demoniac.

R. H. Lightfoot suggests that Christian communities in the Decapolis used and developed this story in order to show how the Christian mission started in this area.[53] This suggestion is implausible for at least four reasons. (1) This hypothesis cannot explain why this particular story was used and "developed" in terms of contacts with Gentiles. (20 The narrative of Mk 5:1-20 contains clear references to a Gentile context, but the evangelist does not describe the demoniac explicitly as a Gentile. (3) The passage does not belong to a section of the Gospel narrative that describes Jesus' ministry in Gentile territory. (4) The "amazement" of people in the Decapolis (Mk 5:20) cannot easily be linked with conversions.

Rudolf Pesch regards Mk 5:1-20 as a "missionary story" (*Missionserzählung*), on the assumed third level of development.[54] This has rightly been criticized by Franz Annen, who argues that a missionary story or sermon that intends to win over Gentiles for faith in Jesus Christ and for the church would hardly describe the "human condition" of Gentiles as demon-possessed, and it would hardly emphasize their uncleanness or their affinity with pigs.[55] Annen, who interprets the pigs and the nakedness of the demoniac as references to paganism that were developed by the evangelist, locates the *Sitz im Leben* of the narrative in the Jewish Christians' discussions about the Gentile mission: the story is intended to show that Jesus liberated even Gentiles from their "possession" by the pagan deities. He claims that the Hellenistic Jewish Christians argued with the story of Mk 5:1-20 against Judaizers in the church, emphasizing that Jesus himself freed a Gentile from his uncleanness. Robert Gundry correctly argues that this reconstruction is unconvincing: the episode

[52]Pesch, *Mk*, 1:279-82, 292-93. For the critique that follows above see Gundry, *Mk*, 255.
[53]R. Lightfoot 1935, 89-90; cf. Hofrichter 1993, 14. For the critique that follows above see Gundry, *Mk*, 265.
[54]Pesch, *Mk*, 1:293.
[55]Annen 1976, 187; on the alleged secondary character of the narrative see ibid., 159-62, 182-84, followed recently by Ådna 1999b, 296-300.

of the pigs is an integral part of the miracle story and cannot be eliminated without destroying the narrative as a whole.[56]

Jesus heals a man who was possessed by a "legion" of demons (Mk 5:9), who lived in a necropolis ("he lived among the tombs" [Mk 5:3]), who howled "on the mountains" and bruised himself with stones (Mk 5:5). The healed man wanted to join Jesus' disciples, a request that was denied (Mk 5:18). Rather, Jesus asked him to "go home" (*oikos*, "house, family") and tell his family and friends "how much the Lord has done" and "what mercy" he had been shown (Mk 5:19).[57] The evangelist records a tradition according to which Jesus directs a Gentile to proclaim among his (Gentile) family and friends the good news of the mercy that the God of Israel extends to the Gentiles.[58] The Gerasenes cannot interpret the events that transpired by themselves; they need the testimony of the healed man to understand them.

Rudolf Pesch correctly observes that the fact that the healed demoniac receives a proclamation assignment is singular in the Synoptic miracle tradition.[59] However, he does not see this as indicative of the authenticity of this feature but as a comment of the redactor, who uses the concluding "notice of admiration" to indicate the effect of the missionary work that he hopes for. This is implausible: a redactor who is familiar with the reality of the active Jewish-Christian Gentile mission after Easter and who wants to describe the results of missionary work that the church hopes for would hardly be content to note the admiration of Gentiles: he surely would "note" their faith in Jesus. The fact that Mk 5:20 does not mention the "faith" of the people who hear of the miracle argues against the assumption of a redactional creation in the context of the Gentile mission of the church.

According to Mk 5:20/Lk 8:39, the healed Gadarene man complied with Jesus' directive: "And he went away and began to proclaim in the Decapolis how much Jesus had done for him; and everyone was amazed."[60] The result of this "proclamation" is not recorded, but Jesus' instruction for the healed Gentile implies that a positive outcome of his witness was not considered futile.[61]

The Woman in Syro-Phoenicia

Mt 15:21-28/Mk 7:24-31. Mark records Jesus' visit in Gentile territory beginning in Mk 7:24.[62] He travels to the territory of Tyre (Mk 7:24) and, via Sidon, into the

---

[56]Gundry, *Mk*, 257-58; cf. Twelftree 1993, 74-76. The argument in Ådna 1999b, 298 n. 72, is unconvincing.

[57]Mk 5:19: Ὕπαγε εἰς τὸν οἶκόν σου πρὸς τοὺς σούς καὶ ἀπάγγειλον αὐτοῖς ὅσα ὁ κύριός σοι πεποίηκεν καὶ ἠλέησέν σε. The ὅσα-clause interprets the events of 5:1-17 (cf. Lk 8:39).

[58]Kato 1986, 59; for the following observation see Stenschke 1999a, 108.

[59]Pesch, *Mk*, 1:293; for the discussion that follows above see ibid., 1:294.

[60]Mk 5:20 καὶ ἤρξατο κηρύσσειν ἐν τῇ Δεκαπόλει ὅσα ἐποίησεν αὐτῷ ὁ Ἰησοῦς.

[61]Stenschke 1999a, 108.

[62]Matthew omits the corresponding geographical notices. A.-J. Levine (1988, 131-64) suggests that Mark emphasizes the motif of Gentile mission more clearly than Matthew does.

region of the Decapolis (Mk 7:31) before he sails across the Sea of Galilee and arrives in the area of Dalmanutha (Mk 8:10). In the territory controlled by Tyre he meets a Syro-Phoenician woman who asks him to heal her daughter who was possessed by an evil spirit (Mk 7:25-26). Initially Jesus, following a traditional Jewish position, emphasized the salvation-historical difference between Jews and Gentiles: "Let the children be fed first, for it is not fair to take the children's food and throw it to the dogs" (Mk 7:27).

Gerd Theissen explores the local background of the miracle story in detail.[63] Tyre was a wealthy city that bought agricultural products in the hinterland, including northern Galilee. Since Tyre was strong enough to buy up wheat in times of crisis, it had more leverage than the Galilean population, which often was the loser in the struggle for the distribution of food. Theissen speculates that there may have been a local proverb that Jesus alluded to in his answer. Even though the woman was a Syro-Phoenician by birth, she is described as a "Hellene" (Ἑλληνίς, *Hellēnis* [Mk 7:26]), which seems to indicate that she belonged to the privileged group of the Greek citizens of Tyre.

As the Greek woman meets Jesus, the situation differed from the usual "balance of power" in the region: the privileged woman pleads for help from an itinerant Galilean preacher who belongs to the population that often got the short end of things.[64] When Jesus reminds the woman of the fact that Jews do not help Gentiles, the woman responds by pointing out that the "children" do not have to be robbed of their privileges if the "dogs" also receive from the bread. The point of the metaphor "is no longer the contrast between children and dogs but the solidarity of child and domestic animal where subordination does not exclude togetherness."[65] In other words, Jesus can fulfill her request without jeopardizing the salvation-historical principle that distinguishes between Jews and Gentiles. The singular case is transformed into Jesus' behavior toward Gentiles more generally: "he could not escape notice" (Mk 7:24b). The people who lived in the hinterland of Tyre discovered that Jesus was in the area, with the result that they came to him. Jesus' significance as one who heals is recognized and acknowledged beyond the borders of Israel.[66] The Christian readers of Matthew and Mark possibly detected a recognition of Jesus' messianic dignity in *kyrie,* which the woman uses to address him (Mk 7:28/Mt 15:27). The pagan woman recognizes Jesus as the Lord "in a moment of inspiration."[67] Matthew notes, as in the case of Jesus' encounter with the centurion, that Jesus praises the woman's faith as "great

---

[63]Theissen 1992a, 63-85 (ET, 61-80); see also Feldmeier 1994a, 211-12.
[64]Theissen 1992a, 83 (ET, 79). The narrative analysis by J. Williams (1995, 117-21) is one-sided.
[65]Feldmeier 1994a, 213; for the observation that follows above see Kato 1986, 86.
[66]See Kato 1986, 88. Feldmeier (1994a, 226) suggests that the *Sitz im Leben* of this pericope was the justification of the Gentile mission.
[67]Burkill 1966, 35. The suggestion by Feldmeier (1994a, 223-24) that Jesus reflected on and then changed his view about Gentiles has no foundation in the text.

faith" (Mt 15:28). Jesus grants her request and heals her daughter. The "great faith" of the woman, consisting in the acknowledgment of the favored position of the Jews while expecting at the same time that Jesus would heal her (Gentile) daughter, presumably was the result of her desperation concerning her daughter's condition. The Gospel writers do not even hint at the possibility that the woman became a follower of Jesus. However, the account clearly demonstrates that Jesus does not limit the mercy of the dawning reign of God to Jewish people who are plagued by demons: he makes this divine mercy available to Greeks as well when they approach him with believing expectation.[68]

The Deaf-Mute Man in the Decapolis

Mk 7:32-37. Mark reports the continuation of Jesus' journey after leaving Tyre. Jesus travels in a northern curve to the territory of Sidon and to the region of the Decapolis before returning to the Sea of Galilee. He heals a deaf-mute man, whose name is not mentioned, in a city belonging to the Decapolis. The astonishing acclamation in Mk 7:37b ("He has done everything well; he even makes the deaf to hear and the mute to speak"), not found anywhere else in the Gospel of Mark,[69] is spoken by Gentiles. Zenji Kato observes that "the Gentiles in the Decapolis recognize that the time of salvation that the prophet Isaiah had announced for Israel has become present in Jesus' mighty acts."[70] Jesus requests that the people not tell others about the miracle "because the salvation-historical distinction between Jews and Gentiles continues to exist, despite Israel's obstinacy." Again, however, the news of Jesus' mighty acts cannot be suppressed (Mk 7:36).

The Four Thousand People East of the Sea of Galilee

Mk 8:1-10/Mt 15:32-39. There is no doubt that the account of Mk 8:1-10 is located in pagan territory, as Jesus is still in the region east of the Sea of Galilee.[71] Joachim Gnilka notes that compared with Mk 6:41 (the miracle of the feeding of the five thousand), a reference to Jesus' looking up to heaven is omitted and the blessing is replaced by thanksgiving.[72] These details may be less linked with the "Hellenistic narrator": they can readily be explained from the Gentile context. Zenji Kato describes the story of the feeding of the four thousand as the crowning conclusion of Jesus' journey to the Gentile regions bordering on Galilee: the "great crowd" (πολλὺς ὄχλος, *pollys ochlos*) consists of "Gentiles who have heard the proclamation of the healing performed by

---

[68]See Schnabel 1994, 52-53.
[69]Pesch, *Mk*, 1:399; Kertelge 1970, 160; Kato 1986, 93.
[70]Kato 1986, 93; the quotation that follows above, ibid., 94.
[71]See Pesch, *Mk*, 1:400; Gnilka, *Mk*, 1:304, is not particularly helpful.
[72]Gnilka, *Mk*, 1:303; for the comment that follows above see ibid., 1:301.

Jesus in 7:31ff. and who have recognized that Jesus is the bringer of salvation."[73] Even though Jesus is not reported to have preached or taught before Gentiles, his sojourn in pagan territory has a dramatic conclusion, analogous to Mk 6:30-44: "Gentiles are granted as much a share in the eschatological table fellowship as the Jews."[74] The account of the first feeding miracle (Jews) does not mention hunger. Jesus did not want to leave the people like sheep without a shepherd; he ministered to the people of Israel as the true shepherd. In the account of the second feeding miracle (Gentiles) Jesus helps the people because they are hungry.

Some scholars interpret the second feeding miracle against the background of the Gentile mission of the early church: while it is the disciples who (want to) take the initiative during the first multiplication of bread (Mk 6:35-36) in order to feed "the sheep without a shepherd" (Mk 6:34), in the second feeding miracle it is Jesus who takes the initiative when he explains to his disciples why he has mercy on these people, some of whom have come "from a great distance" (Mk 8:3). Peter Hofrichter argues that Mark wants to emphasize the Gentile mission "that still needs to be explained" as a valid program beside the Jewish mission of the Twelve. He argues that the mission among Jews is indicated by the five pieces of bread and the five thousand people (5 times 1,000 symbolically representing the five books of Moses, the Pentateuch) and by the twelve baskets (for the twelve tribes of Israel) in Mk 6:38, 43, 44, while the reference to Gentiles can be seen in the seven pieces of bread and the seven baskets (for the seven days of creation and the seven Noahic commandments) and in the four thousand people (4 times 1,000 for the four corners of the compass) in Mk 8:5, 8, 9.[75] Such interpretations are unconvincing. Apart from questionable tradition- and redaction-critical presuppositions, they break down in view of the fact that Mk 8:9 specifically speaks of "about [ὡς, hōs] four thousand people," which means that Mark clearly thinks of a concrete number of people, not of a symbol. And it is unclear how readers should detect in the reference to seven pieces of bread that could be eaten or that were left over a reference to the Gentile mission, in which missionaries aimed at winning people for faith in Jesus Christ.[76]

The Action in the Temple

Mt 21:12-13/Mk 11:15-17/Lk 19:45-46. Jesus' action in the Jerusalem temple was not intended as a religious or political act with the goal of "cleansing" or reforming the temple or the temple cult, but rather as a prophetic symbolic action. Crucial for the correct understanding of Jesus' action is the direct speech that the Gospel writers use to summarize Jesus' teaching on this occasion. Jesus quotes Is 56:7 and Jer 7:11: "He was teaching and saying, 'Is it not written, "My house shall be called a house of prayer for all the nations"'?[77] But you have made it a

---

[73]Kato 1986, 98, following Pesch, *Mk*, 1:399.
[74]Kato 1986, 98.
[75]Hofrichter 1992, 145-48; cf. Senior 1982.
[76]See Gundry (*Mk*, 396-400), who argues against a symbolic interpretation.
[77]Mk 11:17, quoting Is 56:7 LXX: ὁ γὰρ οἶκός μου οἶκος προσευχῆς κληθήσεται πᾶσιν τοῖς ἔθνεσιν.

den of robbers."[78] The reference to the "nations" (ἔθνη, *ethnē*)[79] and the designation of the temple as a "den of robbers" provide the interpretation of the temple action.

The quotation from Jer 7:11 is taken from a prophecy in which Jeremiah announces the destruction of the (Solomonic) temple:

> Jer 7:13-15: "And now, because you have done all these things, says the LORD, and when I spoke to you persistently, you did not listen, and when I called you, you did not answer, [14]therefore I will do to the house that is called by my name, in which you trust, and to the place that I gave to you and to your ancestors, just what I did to Shiloh. [15]And I will cast you out of my sight, just as I cast out all your kinsfolk, all the offspring of Ephraim."

Doubts concerning the authenticity of the allusion to Jer 7:11 with the term "den of robbers" in Mk 11:17[80] are unwarranted: Jer 7:11 was never used in the early church (apart from Mk 11:17) in the context of a critique of the Jerusalem temple. And Jewish sources confirm for the Second Temple period that some Jews accused the temple establishment of corruption and that they spoke of "robbers" in this connection.[81]

The quotation from Is 56:7 emphasizes the universal significance of the presence of Yahweh in Israel. Jesus does not simply indict Israel for its behavior and failure; he proclaims (with Jer 7:11) the end of the temple cult and thus the end of the significance of the temple for procuring holiness for Israel.[82] Rudolf Pesch comments, "Jesus advocates in the court of the Gentiles the holiness of the entire temple precinct. He teaches that the worship of Yahweh by the Gentiles, who are allowed in this court, should be made possible. Jesus does not demonstrate for a cult without sacrifices, he does not disturb the sacrifices in the inner temple court. The sacrifices were not dependent upon the sale of offerings and sacrificial animals in the court of the Gentiles. The visitors to the temple could bring their own sacrifices, and the pilgrims could buy sacrifices on the Mount of Olives, where the Bene Hannan maintained four markets for temple offerings."[83]

Jostein Ådna interprets Jesus' action in the temple as an "hour of decision" for Israel: "If Israel, guided by its leaders in the Jerusalem temple, in view of the dawning kingdom of God in the person and in the ministry of Jesus, would repent in this last and final hour, the imminent catastrophe of destruction could still be prevented. If Israel repents and ends the den-of-robbers status of the temple, the threat of destruction will be replaced by the promise of Is 56:7. . . . The 'taking down' of the old temple and its replacement by the new

---

[78]Jer 7:11a: μὴ σπήλαιον λῃστῶν ὁ οἶκός μου; Mk 11:17/Mt 21:13/Lk 19:46 agree in writing σπήλαιον λῃστῶν.

[79]On questions of historicity see Kato 1986, 109-10.

[80]See R. Bultmann 1995, 36, 59 (ET, 36, 57); E. P. Sanders 1985, 66, 363-64, 367.

[81]Evans 1995, 319-44, 362-63, with reference to Josephus, *A.J.* 20.181, 206-207; 1QpHab VIII, 12; IX, 5; XII, 10; *T. Mos.* 7:6; *Tg. 1 Sam.* 2:17, 29; *Tg. Jer.* 8:10; 23:11; *t. Menaḥ.* 13:18-19.

[82]Contra Böttger 1981, 77-78.

[83]Pesch, *Mk,* 2:199.

sanctuary established by God's hands (cf. Ex 15:17) *can possibly* assume the form of a transformation instead of a destruction. The prerequisite that is necessary for this to happen is the repentance of the people."[84] Ådna asserts that "the rights or the interests of the Gentiles in the temple" were not the main focus of Jesus' action in the temple. Rather, the focus is on the "positive future of the temple," which will happen if and when Israel repents and follows Jesus' call to believe in the good news of his message. "If the priests and the people repent and if the imminent destruction of the temple is thus avoided, then the eschatological era of salvation that has been promised will become reality, and it will emanate from Zion and attract the Gentile nations as well." This interpretation is not fully convincing: after encountering rather consistent opposition from the Jerusalem authorities and from leading scribes, Sadducees and Pharisees, Jesus would hardly have had much hope that his call to repentance and faith in the good news of the present arrival of the kingdom of God would be heard and accepted. Jesus' prophecies concerning his death, which became more numerous, as well as his statements during the last week in Jerusalem—Jesus announces the destruction of the temple (Mt 24:1-2/ Mk 13:1-2/Lk 21:5-6) without prophesying its rebuilding—confirm this impression. This means that Jesus' action in the temple is not an "hour of decision" but rather the announcement of the "hour of judgment" of the temple and its leaders, and the announcement of the "hour of salvation for the nations" who henceforth, independently of the temple, will worship the God of Israel.[85]

Jesus used his dramatic action in the temple to proclaim the end of Israel's sacrificial cult and at the same time the inauguration of the temple as the eschatological house of prayer for the nations. It is important to note in this connection that Jesus saw his impending death and resurrection as "the beginning of a new spiritual temple in the form of the community of his disciples."[86] Peter, who confesses Jesus as the Messiah, is the foundation of a new "house" that is now being established in Israel. Jesus' action in the temple marks "a decisive hour of salvation-history."[87] This is reflected in the violent reaction of the chief priests and the scribes: they began looking for a way to kill Jesus (Mk 11:18).

The Other Tenants of the Vineyard

Mt 21:33-46/Mk 12:1-12/Lk 20:9-19. In the parable of the tenants of the vineyard Jesus indicts the religious establishment of Jerusalem, the "tenants" of the "vineyard," which is Israel,[88] for their failure in leading the people of God. Jesus announces that their responsibility for Israel is about to come to an end.[89]

---

[84] Ådna 2000a, 284; the quotations that follow above, ibid., 362.

[85] Ådna (2000a, 363) criticizes the interpretation by Rudolf Pesch as "nachträgliche Schriftgelehrsamkeit" ("subsequent scribal erudition") that seeks to combine aspects that are too numerous and too diverse. This critique is unfair and unwarranted.

[86] Riesner 1995a, 1869. Cf. Köstenberger and O'Brien 2001, 78-79

[87] Kato 1986, 111.

[88] See particularly Is 5:1-7; also Is 27:2-6; Jer 2:21; 12:10; Hos 10:1; Ezek 15:6; 19:10; Ps 80:1-18; 4Q500; for the evidence in rabbinical writings see Str-B 2:563-64.

[89] On the historical realism of the parable see Martin Hengel, "Das Gleichnis von den Weingärtnern Mc 12:1-12 im Lichte der Zenonpapyri und der rabbinischen Gleichnisse," *ZNW* 59 (1968): 1-39; on the authenticity of the parable see Snodgrass 1983, 31-40; Evans 1995, 381-406.

Ulrich Mell interprets the parable of the renting of the vineyard to tenant farmers as a "Palestinian Jewish-Christian judgment speech (*Gerichtsüberführungsrede*) about the definitive end of Israel's salvation of election" that declares to the Jewish dialogue partner "that the soteriology on which he relied absolutely, guaranteeing him as a Jew (with circumcision on the eighth day) the status of election, has been abrogated once and for all."[90] The Jewish listeners can become new covenant partners of God only if and when they free themselves from the notion that the Jewish nation is the only people that God has chosen. At the same time, Mell argues, the parable teaches that Gentiles can become direct new covenant partners God also (e.g., a God-fearer) without taking the detour via integration into the synagogue.[91]

The parable does not indicate who the new covenant partner will be—repentant Jews or repentant Gentiles—and does not demonstrate any "strategy of missionary theology." This does not mean, however, that the allegory has lost its communicative power; rather, it is evidence for the authenticity of the parable in the situation before Easter. Jesus announced to Israel's leaders before his death that their function, which was closely tied to the temple and to the Torah, will come to an end and that God will choose other leaders through whom he will achieve his goals for Israel.

The Parable of the Wedding

Mt 22:1-10; cf. Lk 14:16-24. The parable of the wedding speaks of guests who are invited to a wedding banquet (a symbol for Israel) but turn down the invitation with all kinds of explanations and excuses. This prompts the invitation of other guests who accept and come, an invitation to substitute guests often interpreted in terms of the universal mission of the church.[92] The traditional barriers for friendly relations with the king are taken away, the "natural" invitees refuse to come, and the servants of the king go out to the places "where a main street cuts (through) the city boundary and go (out) into the open country"[93] to invite anyone they can find as new wedding guests.

The readers of Matthew's Gospel are familiar with the Gentile mission as a historical and contemporary reality; they surely would have interpreted the substitute guests as a reference to the Gentile mission. In Mt 8:11-12 Jesus stated that many people will come "from east and west" and eat "with Abraham and Isaac and Jacob in the kingdom of heaven" while the "heirs of the kingdom" remain outside. The banquet feast of the substitute guests in Mt 22:8-10 and the reference to the servants who "went out" (ἐξελθόντες, *exelthon-*

---

[90]Mell 1994, 152, 151.

[91]Mell 1994, 152; for the observation that follows above see ibid.

[92]Hahn 1963, 28-29; Bosch 1959, 124-25; Vögtle 1996, 26-27; Davies and Allison, *Mt*, 3:202; Luz, *Mt*, 3:237-38, 243-44. S. Wilson (1973, 6-7) is uncertain.

[93]BDAG, s.v. "διέξοδος," 244; cf. W. Michaelis, *ThWNT* 5:112 (*TDNT* 5:108-9); G. Schneider, *EWNT* 1:776 (*EDNT* 1:322); Davies and Allison (*Mt*, 3:203) and Luz (*Mt*, 3:243) think of the borders of the royal territory.

tes) suggest such an interpretation in terms of Gentiles. It should not be doubted that the invitation of new guests is an authentic element of a parable told by Jesus. Anton Vögtle remarks that "since the kingdom of God must achieve its goals, the feast must be celebrated by all means, even with a 'full house.'"[94]

Most scholars think that the doubling of the command to invite others in Lk 14:21c-23 is redactional.[95] In the Lukan version the initial guests who decline the invitation usually are interpreted in terms of the Jewish leadership, particularly the Pharisees. The first group of substitute guests is interpreted in terms of the population in general, particularly the "tax collectors and sinners," and the second group of substitute guests in terms of Gentiles.[96] Rather unconvincing is Vögtle's interpretation of what he calls "the allegorizing Lukan version": the guests who decline the invitation are those Jews who reject the church's preaching about Jesus; the first group of substitute guests stands for the ongoing Gentile mission, while the command to invite further guests is "the commission to continue the Gentile mission."[97]

The Nations and the Return of the Son of Man

Mk 13:10; cf. Mt 10:18. Jesus, in his discourse about the time that will pass until God's judgment comes upon Jerusalem and the world, announces that his message will be proclaimed to Gentiles: "And the good news must first be proclaimed to all nations."[98]

Zenji Kato suggests that Mark formulated the sentence himself, analogous to Mk 14:9, arguing that Jesus announces the proclamation of the gospel among all nations despite the fact that he maintained until this point the salvation-historical dissimilarity of Jews and Gentiles. He believes that "the killing of Jesus by the leaders of the Jewish people entails the new epoch in salvation-history."[99] The members of Mark's community were convinced that the gospel could be preached to all nations now that the traditional distinction between Jews and Gentiles has been abolished as a result of Jesus' death. When scholars interpret Mk 13:10 as a redactional composition of Mark[100] or as a traditional early Christian gloss,[101] they often presuppose the view that Jesus expected his imminent parousia (second coming). And critical scholars usually reject the possibility of genuine prophecy. R. T. France offers a different explanation: Mk 13:10 does not refer to Jesus' return but to

---

[94]Vögtle 1996, 25. Most interpreters who see a reference to the Gentile mission interpret on the level of redaction.

[95]See Fitzmyer, *Lk,* 2:1052; Bovon, *Lk,* 2:507; Nolland, *Lk,* 2:754; Weder 1978, 184 n. 78; Vögtle 1996, 20, 23.

[96]Fitzmyer, *Lk,* 2:1053.

[97]Vögtle 1996, 37.

[98]Mk 13:10: εἰς πάντα τὰ ἔθνη πρῶτον δεῖ κηρυχθῆναι τὸ εὐαγγέλιον.

[99]Kato 1986, 148

[100]See Taylor, *Mk,* 507; Pesch, *Mk,* 2:285; Marxsen 1959, 119-20; Stuhlmacher 1968, 284 n. 2; Strecker 1972, 98-101. For arguments against the evaluation of Mk 13:10 as redactional see Hahn 1963, 57-63.

[101]See Cranfield, *Mk,* 399-400; Hahn 1963, 62-63; Brandenburger 1984, 30-32; G. Beasley-Murray 1993, 402-3. For arguments against this view see Gundry, *Mk,* 768.

the destruction of Jerusalem.[102] If we assume that Jesus expected an interval of time between the events of his imminent death and resurrection and his parousia, then the statement in Mk 13:10 can be understood as a prophetic assignment to engage in missionary work among Gentiles. The following arguments support the authenticity of Mk 13:10 as a genuine saying of Jesus. (1) Jesus demonstrated an interest in Gentiles and their faith in Yahweh in his symbolic action in the temple (Mk 11:17).[103] (2) The interest for winning Gentiles to messianic salvation has Old Testament roots (Is 42:6; 49:6, 12; 52:10; 57:1-8; 60:6; Ps 96) and is present in early Jewish texts (*Pss. Sol.* 8:17, 43; 11:1). (3) When Jesus prophesied his coming suffering and death, he spoke about the rejection by the Jewish authorities. Since the Jerusalem temple was the center of their authority, it is not at all surprising if the temple is no longer an "attraction" for the nations in Jesus' vision of the future. It is plausible, therefore, that Jesus announced that the Old Testament expectation of the gathering of the nations on Mount Zion would be replaced by a missionary activity of his disciples, who would carry the messianic salvation to the nations.[104] (4) If Jesus indeed reckoned with a period of international evangelization after his death and resurrection, then he provided his disciples with a resolution to the tension between his message of the kingdom of God as an eschatological event and his ethical instruction. This implies or assumes the continuation of the present conditions of life on earth after the Fall, which is not fundamentally motivated by the expectation of an imminent end of the world. Jesus undeniably taught both of these perspectives. (5) The early church accepted and engaged in missionary work among Gentiles without disagreements about the necessity of a Gentile mission. The debates that we encounter in the book of Acts and in the letters of Paul concerned the status of converted Gentiles in the church and the specific relations between Jewish Christians and Gentile Christians. The question is never raised whether the followers of Jesus the Messiah should wait for the gathering of the nations in Jerusalem, prompted by God himself, or whether they should take the initiative for international missionary outreach—a fact that confirms the origin of the Gentile mission in the proclamation of Jesus.

The expression "all nations" (πάντα τὰ ἔθνη, *panta ta ethnē*) must be related to the geographical perspective of the disciples, which is not, as we will see (§16.2), limited to the Roman Empire but extends from Scythia to Ethiopia, from Spain to possibly India. Jesus identifies the assignment that he gives to the disciples in the context of warnings concerning the future, the proclamation of the good news among all nations—that is, before Jews and non-Jews, in Judea and Galilee but also the regions beyond.[105] Since the verb *kēryssein* ("to announce, make known, proclaim") usually is employed with the dative as indirect object, the formulation *eis panta ta ethnē* should be interpreted in a locative sense: "among all nations."[106] The expression "first" (πρῶτον, *prōton*) refers to the state-

---

[102]France, *Mk,* 498-505, 516-17; cf. N. T. Wright 1996, 339-66. For cogent arguments against this interpretation see Carson, *Mt,* 492-94.

[103]See Evans, *Mk,* 310; for the argument that follows above see ibid.; see also Bosch 1959, 157.

[104]See Gundry, *Mk,* 766; for the argument that follows above see ibid., 767.

[105]See S. Wilson 1973, 23-24; J. Williams 1998, 142-43. Kilpatrick (1955) sees only a mission to Diaspora Jews; for arguments against this interpretation see Gundry, *Mk,* 768.

[106]And not in the sense "to all nations"; see Gundry, *Mk,* 769.

ment in Mk 13:7 that "the end is still to come" when false messianic pretenders appear and when Jesus' followers hear of new wars. Before the end of the world, which is the next "date" in God's calendar, the good news must "first" be announced to all nations. The text does not say that the end of world comes as soon as "all nations" have heard the good news announced: Jesus does not make his return and the end of history dependent upon the missionary activity of his disciples. The "beginning of the birth pangs" (Mk 13:8) refers to the entire period between Jesus' first coming (or Pentecost) and his return (parousia). During this time the disciples are witnesses of the gospel in the world; they will endure persecution (Mk 13:9, 11) and they face the danger of seduction (Mk 13:7). The time of the messianic birth pangs of the "last days" receives a positive significance through the *prōton,* however: the time before the end, with its tribulations, is the time of missionary activity among Gentiles and thus the time of the fulfillment of the old prophecies that anticipated the conversion of the nations.[107] The term δεῖ (*dei,* "must") refers to God's plan for salvation-history, to God's purposes for the time of the "last days": the assignment of the disciples is and remains, as an assignment given by Jesus, the universal proclamation of the gospel, even in precarious times and in dangerous situations.

The parable of the sheep and the goats (Mt 25:31-46), placed by Matthew in the context of Jesus' eschatological discourse, speaks about "all nations" (πάντα τὰ ἔθνη, *panta ta ethnē* [Mt 25:32]) standing before the throne of God to be judged. Stephen Wilson interprets this expression in terms of Gentile nations and argues that the Gentiles will be judged on the basis of the assumption that they have not heard the gospel, which suggests that Jesus did not envision a Gentile mission.[108] It is more plausible, however, to interpret "all nations" in Mt 25:32 in the sense of "all people," including the followers of Jesus, who will be declared righteous in the last judgment.[109] People's fate in the last judgment will be decided on the basis of their reaction to "one of the least of these brothers" (Mt 25:40)— that is, the followers of Jesus who carry out their assignment to proclaim the good news despite hunger, thirst, illness or imprisonment.

The Proclamation of the Gospel in the Entire World
Mk 14:9/Mt 26:13. When Jesus is anointed by a woman in Bethany shortly before his arrest, he states, "Truly I tell you, wherever the good news is proclaimed in the whole world [εἰς ὅλον τὸν κόσμον], what she has done will be told in remembrance of her."

---

[107]See J. Thompson 1971, 25.
[108]S. Wilson 1973, 5.
[109]Davies and Allison, *Mt,* 2:422-23; Gnilka, *Mt,* 2:370-71; Hagner, *Mt,* 2:742; Carson, *Mt,* 520-52; for the observation that follows above see ibid. See also Gray (1989), who provides a history of interpretation (with the statistical information, which exegetically is hardly relevant, that 537 of 914 interpreters understand the phrase *panta ta ethnē* in terms of the judgment of humanity; see ibid., 348).

Some scholars regard this sentence as a secondary gloss,[110] while others contend for its authenticity,[111] pointing out, for example, that the woman remains anonymous. Joachim Jeremias accepts the statement as a saying of Jesus but relates it to Jesus' return, not to missionary activity in the world;[112] in view of the iterative sense of the phrase ὅπου ἐάν (*hopou ean*, "wherever"), this interpretation is implausible. Equally unlikely is an interpretation in terms of the angels remembering the woman before God:[113] even though there are a good number of texts that speak of a remembrance in heaven or before God, the remembering that Jesus speaks of in Mk 14:9/Mt 26:1 in the context of the passion narrative is more plausibly linked with human activity (cf. 1 Cor 11:25).[114]

Jesus speaks again of an international, worldwide proclamation of the good news at the beginning of the passion story.

The Confession of the Centurion at the Cross

Mk 15:39/Mt 27:54; cf. Lk 23:47. The first person who may have had an inkling of the significance of Jesus' death was a pagan. The centurion who observed Jesus' death commented, "Truly this man was God's Son!"[115]

Critics argue that this statement is redactional, but there are good arguments that support the authenticity of the verse.[116] Zenji Kato observes that Mark unites the entire passion narrative with the *amēn* saying of Jesus in Bethany at the beginning of the passion narrative (Mk 14:9) and the *amēn* saying of Jesus in the confession of the centurion immediately after Jesus' death (Mk 15:39): "By pointing to the possibility of salvation for all people at the beginning and at the end of the passion, the Gospel emphasizes that the Markan passion story signifies a definitive turn in God's history of salvation. The killing of Jesus by the authorities marks the decisive turn in salvation-history."[117]

The centurion's comment does not need to be understood as a full "Christian confession." It makes good sense in the context of the veneration particularly of Caesar Augustus as "son of god." The centurion ascribes a dignity to Jesus that he used to link with Augustus: he asserts that (not Caesar but) Jesus is *divi filius*, "god's son."[118]

---

[110]R. Bultmann 1995, 37 (ET, 36-37); Kato 1986, 155-59; Gnilka, *Mk*, 2:225.

[111]Taylor, *Mk*, 534; Cranfield, *Mk*, 417-18; Evans, *Mk*, 362.

[112]J. Jeremias, "Markus 14,9," *ZNW* 44 (1952-53): 103-7; idem 1956, 19 (ET, 22-23).

[113]Pesch, *Mk*, 2:335-36, following Stuhlmacher 1968, 207; see also Gundry, *Mk*, 818, with reference to numerous texts in support of this interpretation.

[114]See Evans, *Mk*, 362.

[115]Mk 15:39: ἀληθῶς οὗτος ὁ ἄνθρωπος υἱὸς θεοῦ ἦν; Mt 27:54 is shorter: ἀληθῶς θεοῦ υἱὸς οὗτος. Lk 23:47 reads: ὄντως ὁ ἄνθρωπος οὗτος δίκαιος ἦν ("Certainly this man was innocent.")

[116]Kato (1986, 162-75) argues against authenticity. For a cogent critique of this position see Carson, *Mt*, 582; T. Kim 1998, 240. See also Earl S. Johnson, "Is Mark 15.39 the Key to Mark's Christology?" *JSNT* 31 (1987): 3-22; idem, "Mark 15.39 and the So-Called Confession of the Roman Centurion," *Bib* 81 (2000): 406-13.

[117]Kato 1986, 160. J. Williams (1995, 183-87) does not discuss the ethnic identity of the centurion (but see idem 1998, 144).

[118]See Evans, *Mk*, 510; T. Kim 1998, 240. Others suggest a "minimalist" interpretation for an authentic declaration of the centurion; see Stenschke 1999a, 137-38.

In regard to Jesus' prophetic announcement of a Gentile mission, Ernest Best has insightfully pointed out that major parts of Jesus' teaching have no connection with the Torah and thus can be lifted without difficulty from their Jewish context and applied to Gentiles who become followers of Jesus.[119] Examples are Mk 8:35 and Mk 2:17: "For those who want to save their life will lose it, and those who lose their life for my sake, and for the sake of the gospel, will save it"; "Those who are well have no need of a physician, but those who are sick; I have come to call not the righteous but sinners."

A final comment concerns Mary's canticle of praise in which Gentiles, specifically "God-fearers," possibly are referred to: "Surely, from now on all generations will call me blessed. . . . His mercy is for those who fear him from generation to generation" (Lk 1:48b, 50). At least for Luke, this statement transcends the boundaries of the Jewish people and refers to the Gentiles who will hear and accept the good news of Jesus.[120] The plural nouns in the construction *eis geneas kai geneas* in 1:50a (English versions translate with singular nouns: "from generation to generation") differ from the standard Old Testament phrase, which is formulated in the singular;[121] they could very well refer to later generations outside of Israel, as the reference to God's promises for "Abraham and his descendants" (Lk 1:55) at the end of the Magnificat points to the promises for the nations given to Abraham.[122] Simon's prophecy on the occasion of Jesus' presentation in the temple includes the statement "For my eyes have seen your salvation, which you have prepared in the presence of all peoples, a light for revelation to the Gentiles and for glory to your people Israel" (Lk 2:30-32). The allusion to Is 42:6 and Is 49:9 makes it clear that Simon speaks of the universal scope of the life of Jesus and its effects.

12.3 The Missionary Commission after Easter

After his resurrection Jesus gave his disciples the assignment to go to "all nations" (πάντα τὰ ἔθνη, *panta ta ethnē* [Mt 28:19]), "to the ends of the earth" (ἕως ἐσχάτου τῆς γῆς, *heōs eschatou tēs gēs* [Acts 1:8]), and announce to them the good news of God's salvation made possible through the life and death and resurrection of Jesus Christ, to invite all people to become followers of Jesus, and to teach them the word of God as Jesus had taught them.

Mt 28:18-20

The "Great Commission" of the risen Jesus Christ in Mt 28:18-20 is the final section in the First Gospel. Matthew clearly regards Jesus' command to engage in international missionary activity as "the last word of the exalted Jesus to the disciples."[123]

Mt 28:18-20: "All authority in heaven and on earth has been given to me. [19]Go therefore and make disciples of all nations, baptizing them in the name of the Father and of the

---

[119]See Best 1984, 1-30.

[120]Klauck 1997; Bovon, *Lk,* 1:89.

[121]Ps 32:11; 48:12; 78:13; 88:2, 5; 101:13; 118:90; 134:13; 145:10 LXX: *eis genean kai genean* (Heb., לְדֹר וָדֹר).

[122]Klauck 1997, 136-37; Fitzmyer, *Lk,* 1:361; differently Marshall, *Lk,* 85.

[123]Thus the heading in Gnilka, *Mt,* 2:501, commenting on Mt 28:18-20.

Son and of the Holy Spirit, [20]and teaching them to obey everything that I have commanded you. And remember, I am with you always, to the end of the age."

The interpretation of this passage is disputed in more ways than one, and the literature is immense.[124] Among the questions discussed are the following: What is the genre of the text? Is Mt 28:16-17 part of the pericope? Is the passage a composition of the evangelist or an authentic statement of Jesus? What does the expression *panta ta ethnē* ("all nations") mean? How should we understand the trinitarian formulation of the command to baptize?

The critical consensus of contemporary scholarship assumes that Mt 28:18-20 cannot be traced back to Jesus, as it reflects later missionary theology and early Christian baptismal practices.[125] The question of the authenticity of the missionary commission is important: if there was indeed no Jewish Gentile mission, if the early Christian missionary activity among Gentiles was a complete innovation, then the question of the historical causes of the Gentile mission of the first Christians is highly significant.

Opponents of the authenticity of the passage offer the following arguments. (1) Jesus did not envision a Gentile mission; the early church accepted the notion of a Gentile mission only after long and difficult struggles.[126] (2) The trinitarian baptismal formula reflects an advanced level of theological and christological reflection. The book of Acts reports only baptisms "in the name of Jesus." Scholars argue, therefore, that the trinitarian baptismal formula was composed by Matthew or is derived from the pre-Matthean liturgical tradition of the church.[127] (3) The debates and "birth pangs on the path to the Gentiles"[128] that the book of Acts relates become unintelligible if there was an unequivocal word of Jesus about an international, worldwide mission to Gentiles, a word known to the first followers of Jesus.[129]

These arguments are unconvincing. (1) The struggles and debates that Luke and Paul report did not concern the Gentile mission as such; only the mode of the Gentile mission was contested. The main issue that was fiercely debated was whether converted Gentiles must be circumcised and taught to obey certain stipulations of the Torah, an issue that was not addressed in Jesus' missionary commission. (2) Since there is no agreement among scholars concerning the tradition-historical origins or concerning the genre of Mt

---

[124]See, besides the commentaries, particularly O. Michel 1941; Trilling 1964, 21-51; Lange 1973; Hubbard 1974; D. Palmer 1974; Hahn 1980; Donaldson 1985, 170-90; Legrand 1987; Grilli 1992, 185-89; Lagrand 1995, 235-47; Köstenberger and O'Brien 2001, 101-6. See the bibliography in Hagner, *Mt,* 2:878-80.

[125]See, for example, J. Lange 1973, 170, 306, 308, 316-18, 349, 482, with an attempt to prove the redactional composition of Mt 28:16-20 in individual stages (Mt 28:18b, 19a, 20a, 20b, 16-18a).

[126]See Schweizer, *Mt,* 347 (ET, 529)

[127]See, for example, Gnilka, *Mt,* 2:505; Hahn 1980, 18, 23-24; Schneider 1982, 192; Wilckens 2002, 1.2:185.

[128]Feldtkeller 1993, 23.

[129]See Bornkamm 1959; Strecker 1971, 208-14; cf. Luz (*Mt,* 4:430-36), who comments that "Mt 28:18b-20 is not a 'logion of the Lord' but a . . . 'logion in the Lord'" (436).

28:16-20, even scholars who reject the authenticity of the passage argue that it is anchored in the "Easter events." Ferdinand Hahn writes, "Thus Mt 28:16-20 rests largely on an insight that the disciples were given successively, but it is an insight that became possible and necessary as a result of the Easter event."[130] If Jesus indeed rose from the dead, I see no reason to deny the possibility that the missionary commission was spoken by Jesus himself. (3) In regard to the trinitarian formula, it is of course impossible to hypothesize what the risen Jesus could or could not have said. As far as the disciples are concerned, it is possible that they would have hardly been able, initially, to grasp the implication of the triadic formulation, which is that Jesus shares the divine dignity of the one and only God. We should note at the same time that the book of Acts does not provide us with an elaborate description of baptisms in the early church: passages such as Acts 2:38 (Peter: Jerusalem), Acts 8:16 (Samaria) and Acts 19:5 (Paul: the disciples of John in Ephesus) do not necessarily report the "baptismal formula" that the early Christian missionaries used when they baptized new converts. Further, it must be noted that it is unclear in Mt 28:19 "whether the triadic formula was even understood in a dogmatic sense."[131] It is unlikely that Matthew "invented" the triadic formula and forced it upon the Christian communities for which he writes his Gospel. He evidently encountered it in the traditions that he used.[132] Martin Hengel and Anna Maria Schwemer point out that as a matter of principle, references to a trinity of Father, Son and Spirit were intelligible in Syria, as there are numerous examples of a triad of deities with a supreme god, a mother goddess and a son.[133] Inscriptions of a Ḥaṭrā that come in part from the Hellenistic temple of the city often contain appeals to a divine family: Māran the Lord (father), Mārtan the Lady (mother) and Barmārēn the "Son of our Lord." Māran is identical with the sun-god Shamash (Helios), Mārtan probably is identical with the moon god (Selene), and Barmārēn is identified with the moon god Sin and, in the *interpretatio graeca,* with Dionysos and Apollo.[134] Ernst Lohmeyer attempts to trace a tradition-historical development from the "formula" God, Son of Man, Angel (*1 En.* 39:5-7; 51:3-4; 61:8-10) via John the Baptist with the triad God, the Coming One, the Spirit, all the way to Jesus.[135] This hypothesis cannot be proven from the texts, however, nor is it plausible.

Suggestions regarding the history of tradition and redaction cannot be discussed in detail here. Some pertinent remarks on a few important issues must suffice. Otto Michel argues that the element of teaching needs to come before baptism; the reversal of this sequence indicates, in his view, "the literary integration of the baptismal formula into the original text."[136] This argument neglects the fact that the conversion accounts in the book of Acts do not report extensive "ecclesial instruction" before converts were baptized: it appears that the first missionaries baptized immediately upon confession of faith in Jesus Christ. Hans-Werner Bartsch suggests with regard to the redactional history of the passion and Easter accounts that Jesus' crucifixion, resurrection and appearance were initially seen as events of the parousia, which, eventually, did not come to pass. He argues that

---

[130]Hahn 1980, 24.

[131]Sand (*Mt,* 595), who assumes pre-Matthean tradition for the baptismal formula.

[132]See Best 1984, 2.

[133]Hengel and Schwemer 1998, 204-6 (ET 1997, 123, 398 n. 662), with reference to Jacob Hoftijzer et al., *Dictionary of the North-west Semitic Inscriptions* (Handbuch der Orientalistik 1.21; Leiden: Brill, 1995), 51-61, 683, 684, s.v. "*mrn*"; Tubach 1986.

[134]Tubach 1986, 255-487; on the inscriptions, 255-70; on Māran, 295-300; on Mārtan, 448-58; on Barmārēn, 270-76, 300-448.

[135]E. Lohmeyer 1951, 30-31.

[136]O. Michel 1941, 264.

Mt 28:16-20 reflects the attempt of the evangelist to harmonize the various expectations of Christians: Matthew no longer reports a fulfilled parousia, but he does not want to give up the connection between passion story, resurrection and parousia, thus distinguishing himself from Luke. By incorporating the Great Commission, he manages to integrate the disciples into the events of the parousia: "The mission belongs to the epiphany, the Kyrios reveals himself in its effectiveness [i.e., of the mission] as Lord over the whole world. . . . The parousia is already a reality and yet is expected with every manifestation of his reign."[137] Other scholars argue that Mt 28:16-20 was a redactional programmatic text that Matthew developed from Jesus' command in Mt 10:5-6, introducing corrections.[138] Donald Carson points out that scholars need to resist the temptation to regard the "tradition" as authentic but not the "redaction."[139] Scholars such as Otto Betz, Robert Gundry, Donald Carson, Donald Hagner and more recently Peter Stuhlmacher defend the authenticity of Mt 28:16-20 against critics who see no possibility for placing this text at the beginning of the early Christian missionary history.[140] Stuhlmacher, for example, interprets Mt 28:16-20 as an "ancient authentic tradition" upheld by the pillar apostles in Jerusalem. This tradition "was known in Jerusalem both among the Aramaic-speaking and the Greek-speaking members of the early church, and it contained right from the beginning the universal command to baptize and to do missionary work. James (Jesus' brother), John and Peter stood in this tradition when they acknowledged for Paul (and Barnabas) at the Apostles' Council the right to engage in missionary work among Gentiles." Stuhlmacher points out that this interpretation allows the interpreter "to dispense with a good number of hypotheses that unnecessarily complicated our understanding of the development of the early Christian mission."[141] (1) The complicated tradition- and redaction-history of the text, as suggested by, for example, Günther Bornkamm and Ferdinand Hahn,[142] is unnecessary. It is entirely sufficient to assume the existence of a traditional text in Jerusalem that was redacted by the evangelist in light of the emphases of his Gospel. (2) The theory that the early church initially engaged in missionary work only among Jews, waiting for the universal kingdom of God, including the pilgrimage of the nations to Zion to happen at the "end of days,"[143] is both unnecessary and misguided. The same holds true for the claim that there were bitter controversies between Jewish Christians in Jerusalem who held a particularistic position and Stephen and his friends who wanted to initiate personally the eschatological pilgrimage of the nations to Zion through his missionary work.[144] (3) Equally erroneous is the postulation that there was a diversity of arguments and practices with regard to the mission of the church—for example, the different approaches and emphases of the missionary activity of the itinerant prophets of the Q community, of the mission of Peter and the Twelve,

---

[137]Bartsch 1959, 27-41, esp. 40-41.

[138]Luz 1993, 27; for a critique of Luz's position see Stuhlmacher 1999, 112-13; 1992-1999, 2:171-72; Kvalbein 2000.

[139]Carson, *Mt,* 592.

[140]O. Betz 1994, 25; Gundry, *Mt,* 596; Carson, *Mt,* 591-98; Hagner, *Mt,* 2:883; Stuhlmacher 1999; 1992-1999, 2:170-71 (correcting his earlier view; cf. 1992-1999, 1:215-16 and 1981, 112-13); for the quotations that follow above see 1992-1999, 2:170; 1999, 122. For a rigorous defense of the historicity Jesus' resurrection see now N. T. Wright 2003.

[141]Stuhlmacher 1999, 122; for the arguments that follow above see ibid.

[142]Bornkamm 1959; Hahn 1963, 52-63; 1980.

[143]See Jeremias 1956, 61. This view was very influential.

[144]Hahn 1963, 43-48; on the Hellenistic Jewish Christians see ibid., 48-65; cf. Stuhlmacher 1968, 210-15. (Hahn is critiqued in Stuhlmacher 1999, 122 with n. 67).

and of the mission of Paul the apostle.[145] Dispensing with such theories and placing Mt 28:16-20 at the beginning of the early Christian mission results in a twofold benefit: first, the astonishing fact that the legitimacy of the Gentile mission is never questioned in the New Testament becomes intelligible; second, the missionary work of Peter, of Stephen, of Philip, and of Paul, as well as the missionary theology that James presented at the apostolic council (Acts 15) makes sense.[146]

There is no agreement concerning the genre of Mt 28:16-20. Joachim Gnilka remarks that "the diversity of suggestions is more depressing than convincing."[147]

The following suggestions have been made: cult legend, enthronement hymn, farewell speech, theophany, covenant renewal, missionary document, commissioning narrative, official ecclesiastical decree.[148] Benjamin Hubbard classifies the text as a "primitive apostolic commissioning," which is more plausible than most of the other suggestions. He lists seven elements of such a commissioning:[149] introduction, confrontation, reaction, commission, protest, reassurance, conclusion. Two of these elements are missing in Mt 28:16-20: protest and conclusion, unless the reference to the doubts of the disciples in Mt 28:17 should be understood as "protest." Discussions of the various suggestions[150] show that this explanation is generally more plausible. Peter Stuhlmacher observes, "In vv. 16-17a we find statements of place, view and worship of the risen Christ. The risen Christ presents himself to the hesitating disciples as the Son of Man, who has been given the authority of universal rule (vv. 17b-18) and who gives to the disciples in vv. 19-20a the global commission, which he confirms in v. 20b by the formula of assurance."[151] However, the classification of the text as a commissioning narrative is not without problems. The Old Testament texts cited in support of this classification do not follow a fixed scheme. Some scholars therefore argue that the text is unique and cannot be derived from any known genres.[152]

The missionary commission of the disciples in Mt 28:16-20 contains allusions to Old Testament language. This text, however, is unique and must be interpreted as such.[153]

The missionary commission in Mt 28:18-20 consists of the following elements:[154]

---

[145]Burchard 1980, 20-23.
[146]Stuhlmacher 1999, 123-27.
[147]Gnilka, *Mt*, 2:502.
[148]R. Bultmann 1995, 310 (ET, 306): cult legend; Bornkamm 1959, 292: enthronement hymn; Frankemölle 1984b, 51-67: covenant renewal; E. Lohmeyer 1951, esp. 23-28: missionary document; Hubbard 1974: commissioning narrative; Malina 1970; Lange 1973, 351-54: official decree.
[149]With reference to Gen 12:1-4; Ex 3:1-10; Josh 1:1-11; Is 6; 49:1-6.
[150]Carson, *Mt*, 591-92; Gnilka, *Mt*, 2:502-4; Stuhlmacher 1999, 110-11, 114-15; 1992-1999, 2:169.
[151]Stuhlmacher 1999, 115.
[152]Carson, *Mt*, 592; Gnilka, *Mt*, 2:504; cf. Hahn 1980, 30-31; H. J. Michel 1973, 58-59.
[153]Gnilka, *Mt*, 2:504; see similarly Hagner, *Mt*, 2:883; T. Heckel 1999, 68; Luz, *Mt*, 4:432-33.
[154]Cf. the structure suggested by Gnilka, *Mt*, 2:502.

v. 18b	word of authority	Ἐδόθη μοι πᾶσα ἐξουσία ἐν οὐρανῷ καὶ ἐπὶ τῆς γῆς
v. 19a	word of commission	πορευθέντες οὖν
v. 19b		μαθητεύσατε πάντα τὰ ἔθνη
v. 19c		βαπτίζοντες αὐτοὺς
v. 19d		εἰς τὸ ὄνομα τοῦ πατρὸς καὶ τοῦ υἱοῦ καὶ τοῦ ἁγίου πνεύματος
v. 20a		διδάσκοντες αὐτοὺς τηρεῖν πάντα ὅσα ἐνετειλάμην ὑμῖν
v. 20b	word of promise	καὶ ἰδοὺ ἐγὼ μεθ᾽ ὑμῶν εἰμι πάσας τὰς ἡμέρας ἕως τῆς συντελείας τοῦ αἰῶνος

The word of authority, formulated in the aorist, is followed by a word of commission, formulated with an imperative and three participles. The present tense of the word of promise that concludes the text underlines the duration of the promise. The frequent use of πᾶς (*pas*) "all" is striking: "all power" (πᾶσα ἐξουσία, *pasa exousia*), "all nations" (πάντα τὰ ἔθνη, *panta ta ethnē*), "to obey everything" (τηρεῖν πάντα, *tērein panta*), "always" (πάσας τὰς ἡμέρας, *pasas tas hēmeras* [lit., "all days"]).

1. The word of authority: Jesus places the following assertion at the beginning of his commission for the disciples: "All authority in heaven and on earth has been given to me" (Mt 28:18). The presupposition of missionary work is "the risen Lord with his authoritative word. . . . The only 'power which decides' is now Jesus Christ; his word has universal significance."[155] The authority over heaven and earth that has been given to Jesus is the authority given by God the Creator. Adolf Schlatter comments that with this assertion, "monotheism is protected against any upset."[156] Jesus possesses authority not only as a result of the resurrection[157] but also as a result of his messianic dignity.[158] What has changed with respect to the time before the crucifixion and the resurrection is the realm in which Jesus possesses absolute authority: he now has authority over the entire heaven and over the entire earth, thus over the entire universe, the entire creation.[159] This comprehensive authority was given to Jesus by God. The authority of the Father is conveyed *entirely* through the Son.

The formulation of the word of authority very probably alludes to Dan 7:13-14,[160] where the Son of Man, who had been humiliated and had suffered, receives universal authority:

---

[155]Baumbach 1967, 890, with reference to W. Foerster, *ThWNT* 2:563 (*TDNT* 2:566); cf. Hahn 1980, 24.

[156]Schlatter, *Mt*, 798; cf. Hahn 1980, 34.

[157]Contra Gnilka, *Mt*, 2:507.

[158]Cf. the emphasis in Mt 7:29; 9:6 (he forgives sins as God does); 10:1, 7-8; 11:27; 22:43-44; 24:35 (his words, like those of God, will not pass away). See Carson, *Mt*, 594; note Gnilka, *Mt*, 2:508: "Die neue Dimension ist die Teilhabe an der göttlichen Schöpfermacht."

[159]See Carson, *Mt*, 594.

[160]Differently Hahn 1980, 27-28. See also the discussion in Luz, *Mt*, 4:434.

Mt 28:18b   ἐδόθη μοι πᾶσα ἐξουσία   ἐν οὐρανῷ καὶ ἐπὶ τῆς γῆς

Dan 7:14 LXX   ἐδόθη αὐτῷ ἐξουσία   καὶ πάντα τὰ ἔθνη τῆς γῆς κατὰ γένη
                                                  καὶ πᾶσα δόξα αὐτῷ λατρεύουσα
                                                  καὶ ἡ ἐξουσία αὐτοῦ ἐξουσία αἰώνιος

Jesus, the crucified Son of Man, is granted divine authority as the climax of his vindication (cf. Phil 2:5-11). With this turning point of salvation history, the kingdom of God, which Jesus had proclaimed and was most closely connected with his messianic identity and ministry, received a new dimension of power.[161]

Some scholars want to distinguish a theocratic concept of power in Dan 7:14 from a creation-theological understanding of power in Mt 28:18, but this analysis is misleading. It is correct that Matthew emphasizes participation in the divine power of the Creator as a new dimension of Jesus' ministry with the phrase ἐν οὐρανῷ καὶ ἐπὶ τῆς γῆς (en ouranō kai epi tēs gēs).[162] One must not forget, however, that the passive construction ἐδόθη μοι (edothē moi, "has been given to me") implies the theocratic origin and foundation of Jesus' authority. Also erroneous is the suggestion that Jesus spoke of the subjugation of the nations under his power through the mission of his disciples. Joachim Gnilka correctly asserts that Jesus wants to grant his salvation to all nations, not conquer them.[163]

The exalted Son of Man is Lord over all people and over all things, over heaven and earth and therefore over all nations. The universal perspective of this introductory sentence is maintained prominently in the word of commission that follows, emphasized in three ways by two comments each:[164] (a) Jesus has been given "all authority" (πᾶσα ἐξουσία, pasa exousia [Mt 28:18]), which is true "in heaven and on earth" (ἐν οὐρανῷ καὶ ἐπὶ τῆς γῆς, en ouranō kai epi tēs gēs), thus in all realms of creation. (b) The disciples are directed to make disciples of "all nations" (πάντα τὰ ἔθνη, panta ta ethnē [Mt 28:19]), which is linked with baptism "in the name of the Father and of the Son and of the Holy Spirit," thus with God in all dimensions of his engagement with his creation. (c) The disciples are to teach the nations "everything that I have commanded you" (πάντα ὅσα ἐνετειλάμην ὑμῖν, panta hosa eneteilamēn hymin [Mt 28:20]), which happens in the presence of and with the help of Jesus "all days to the end of the age" (πάσας τὰς ἡμέρας ἕως τῆς συντελείας τοῦ αἰῶνος, pasas tas hēmeras heōs tēs synteleias tou aiōnos).

The universal perspective implies an exclusive dimension. Theo Heckel comments, "All authority means: there can be no authority that is not maintained by Jesus. Jesus' authority is an exclusive authority. All nations: there can be no nation that would not need the Christian message brought to it. The phrase 'all days,' a

---

[161]Carson, Mt, 595.
[162]Emphasized by Vögtle 1964, 268-69; Gnilka, Mt, 2:508. For the critique that follows above see Stuhlmacher 1999, 110.
[163]Gnilka, Mt, 2:508.
[164]Landmesser 2001, 15-16; cf. ibid. for the following remarks.

reference to completeness, has an exclusive connotation as well. . . . There can be no time that would not be qualified by Christ's presence."[165]

2. The commission: The assignment that Jesus gives to his disciples is connected with his universal authority in two ways. First, the disciples are directed to go out and to win new disciples because Jesus possesses this authority *now*. The new era of messianic authority changes the conditions of the activity of the disciples. The universality of his claims that were present in his ministry before his death and resurrection only in latent and tentative ways can now be proclaimed publicly as the disciples embark on an international mission.[166] Second, the disciples go out depending on Jesus' universal authority, which guarantees that the Lord has "everything in heaven and on earth" under control.

The commission lists four activities: going, winning disciples, baptizing and teaching. In the Greek text only the winning of disciples is formulated with a finite verb, construed as an imperative (μαθητεύσατε, *mathēteusate*). The "going" is either implicitly imperatival or it is the preceding condition for the implementation of the subordinate regulations "baptizing" and "teaching," which are "essential consequences when people have been won as disciples."[167]

Some scholars interpret the imperative aorist μαθητεύσατε (*mathēteusate*, "make disciples") with the three participles πορευθέντες (*poreuthentes*, "going"), βαπτίζοντες (*baptizontes*, "baptizing") and διδάσκοντες (*didaskontes*) "teaching," arguing that the winning of disciples (imperative) is realized in going as a precondition, and in baptizing and teaching as an implementation of the imperative.[168] Other scholars link the going with the winning of disciples: the going and the winning of disciples (*poreuthentes, mathēteusate*) are imperatives, while the two participles in the present tense (*baptizontes, didaskontes*) are descriptions of the process of winning disciples: new disciples are baptized and taught.[169]

a. The disciples are directed to "make disciples" (μαθητεύσατε, *mathēteusate* [Mt 28:19]) among all nations of the world. Disciples are people who hear, understand and practice Jesus' teaching (Mt 12:46-50). Disciples are people who live in community, in fellowship with teachers and with other followers of Jesus. It is impor-

---

[165]T. Heckel 1999, 71. Heckel (ibid., 73) interprets the phrase *"everything* that I have taught you" in terms of the Gospel of Matthew: the evangelist has Jesus directing his disciples to teach the nations all the commandments that are reported in the text of his Gospel and none other. This interpretation is untenable: it assumes the inauthenticity of the commission, it implies that Matthew was willing to claim Jesus' authority for the Gospel that he has just written, and it neglects the fact that the Gospel of Matthew, as all the other Gospels, would have been widely known among the early Christian churches because of the constant travels of missionaries and teachers and the communication by letters among the Christian communities. See Bauckham 1998.

[166]See Carson (*Mt*, 595), who comments, "His promotion to universal authority serves as an eschatological marker inaugurating the beginning of his universal mission."

[167]Hahn 1980, 35. On the imperatival sense of *poreuthentes* see below.

[168]See Schweizer, *Mt*, 348 (ET, 532); Gnilka, *Mt*, 2:508; Hagner, *Mt*, 2:886-87.

[169]See Grundmann, *Mt*, 578-79.

tant to note with regard to the context of Jesus' commission to international missionary work that there is no command to proclaim the gospel, no emphasis on preaching the good news. Joachim Gnilka concludes from this fact, correctly I believe, that Jesus' commission is directed "toward the building of the church, the establishment of congregations, beyond the missionary work and mediated by it, as it were."[170] The directive to train people as disciples is given to the Twelve (here, the Eleven), whom Jesus had called to be trained as fishers of people: they are the paradigm for all followers of Jesus, for all future disciples. All people are to be won over to become disciples, people who follow and obey Jesus.

David Hill argues that such a directive cannot be authentic in view of the later opposition to Paul's Gentile mission.[171] This argument is not cogent for at least two reasons. (*i*) There were other aspects of Jesus' teaching that took the disciples some time to understand and come to terms with. (*ii*) The later debates did not represent opposition to the Gentile mission as such; rather, they involved the issue of entrance requirements for Gentiles who wanted to join the (new) people of God.

The directive to "make disciples" demonstrates the ecclesiological dimension of the mission of the Twelve: missionary work and church must not be separated, since the very goal and purpose of missionary work is the creation of a community of disciples.[172]

   b. The disciples are directed to "go" (πορευθέντες, *poreuthentes* [Mt 28:19]). In the context of the command to win followers of Jesus and in the context of the geographical address "all nations," the "going" of the disciples is a directive as well.

Some scholars deduce from the participial form *poreuthentes,* which is given before the imperative "make disciples," that there is a command to win disciples but no command to go. Matthew challenges Christians, it is argued, to be missionaries "by going"—that is, wherever they may live. In view of a worldwide church today, this interpretation is not entirely wrong. In most countries and regions there are so many churches that Christians do not have to "go" far in order to introduce people to the message of Jesus Christ. However, at least three considerations show that the participle *poreuthentes* cannot be denied an imperatival sense. (*i*) If a participle modifies an imperative as an adverbial qualification and precedes the imperative, it usually has an imperatival meaning.[173] (*ii*) Since the context affirms that the activity of the disciples is to reach "all nations," it is implausible to assume that the "going" has no imperatival significance whatsoever, unless we assume that Jesus (or Matthew) wanted the disciples to stay in Jerusalem and wait for the nations gathering on Mount Zion. (*iii*) The missionary commission of Jesus is extant in other formulations as well,[174] with Acts 1:8 clearly describing a geographical movement from the center (Jerusalem, Judea) to the periphery (ends of the earth). It is quite a stretch, therefore, to mini-

---

[170]Gnilka, *Mt,* 2:509.
[171]Hill, *Mt,* 362.
[172]See Baumbach 1967, 89l; Legrand 1987, 21-22, 27.
[173]See Carson, *Mt,* 597.
[174]Lk 24:45-49; Jn 20:21; Acts 1:8; cf. Mt 4:19; 10:16-20; 13:38; 24:14.

mize the significance of "going" in Jesus' directive. The participle *poreuthentes* serves not simply to emphasize the ensuing finite verb *mathēteusate* ("make disciples"): it is the prerequisite of winning disciples. Johannes Nissen argues that Christian missionary activity that refrains from emphasizing the "going" loses its problematic focus on the geographical component and becomes a "mission in six continents." Among other things, this interpretation is anachronistic: after Easter we find communities of believers in Jesus as the Messiah in Jerusalem and probably in several towns in Judea and in Galilee; without a "geographical component" there would have been no "mission" in this specific historical context. It goes without saying that the emphasis on geographical expansion must not be linked with a "crusading mind" or with the coercive violation of other cultures: Paul clearly emphasized the "geographical component" of missionary work, and surely he was not a violent "crusader" (and the crusaders of the Middle Ages were anything but missionaries).[175] Similarly, J. S. Hong suggests that the term "going" has not only a geographical meaning but also a moral one, referring to the totality of behavior in everyday life, which should be a testimony for Jesus Christ. Hong's concern to emphasize consistent discipleship is understandable, but the formulations of Mt 28:19 are hardly adequate evidence for his view.

The disciples are directed to go to people who have not heard of Jesus or of the message that he proclaimed, and announce to them the good news of salvation that Jesus had preached and procured.

c. The disciples are directed to "baptize" (βαπτίζοντες, *baptizontes* [Mt 28:19]). The reference to winning disciples is followed by a reference to baptism. The fact that the text does not mention the instruction of new converts before baptism should not be regarded as a problem, since not even the central process of the preaching of the gospel is mentioned.[176] At the same time it surely is significant that baptism is mentioned after the winning of disciples: it is people who have been converted to faith in Jesus Christ who are baptized (not vice versa, baptized people being made into disciples by the teaching of the church). Baptism is not the means by which people become disciples. Rather, baptism characterizes and explains the winning of disciples:[177] disciples are people who follow Jesus, who have received purification from their sins and put Jesus' teaching into practice.

Otfried Hofius, speaking as a representative of mainline churches, emphasizes in an exegetical and theological study on faith and baptism in the New Testament the following points.[178] (*i*) The baptismal practice that we find in the New Testament presupposes that

[175]Contra J. Nissen 1999, 22, 32. Regarding the comment that follows above see Hong 1994.
[176]Gnilka, *Mt,* 2:508.
[177]See Carson, *Mt,* 597; Gnilka, *Mt,* 2:509; cf. Hofius 1994, 135-36.
[178]Hofius 1994; the quotations that follow above, 137, 141, 143, 151, 147, 151, 156 n. 68. For the statistics below of baptized Christians in Europe and Northern America see David B. Barrett et al., *World Christian Encyclopedia* (2nd. ed.; 2 vols.; Oxford: Oxford University Press, 2001), 1:14-15. The statistics are the numbers for "affiliated Christians," defined by Barrett as "church members; all persons belonging to or connected with organized churches, whose names are inscribed, written or entered on the churches' books, records, or rolls" (1:27). It seems a fair assumption that this number corresponds more or less to the number of people who have received Christian water baptism.

conversion comes before faith in Jesus Christ and baptism. (*ii*) The baptism texts of the New Testament do not stipulate that the person who is to be baptized *must* believe first: they only describe the reality of "the missionary situation of the earliest church," which, however, is irrelevant for the material relationship between faith and baptism because the determination of this relationship must be a *theological* determination. (*iii*) Faith surely has to do with knowledge of faith, confession of faith and life in the faith, but it is not a human work; rather, it is "a reality objectively stipulated and initiated by God," meaning that it is God's work and God's gift, given through Jesus' death on the cross and his resurrection "as the definitive realization of salvation." (*iv*) Baptism validly announces and effectively conveys what Jesus as the crucified and risen one represents and what he has done for the individual. The person who receives baptism is always and only the recipient of a gift; his or her will does not matter. Because baptism has its basis solely in God's act of salvation in the death and resurrection of Jesus, "it is by itself valid and effective. . . . Because it is not faith that makes baptism valid and effective, unbelief does not render it invalid or ineffective." (*v*) Because neither faith nor baptism is a human work, because it is solely God's act of salvation in Jesus Christ that constitutes both faith and baptism, faith demands baptism but is not dependent upon it, and baptism aims at faith but does not depend upon it. This means that faith that has been prompted by the preaching of the gospel may chronologically precede baptism, as baptism may chronologically precede coming to faith. Both forms of baptism therefore are legitimate: adult baptism (in missionary situations), and infant baptism (in Christian churches), where parents who believe in Jesus Christ bring their babies to Jesus "that he might touch them" (Mk 10:13).

This understanding of faith and baptism, though traditional, is highly problematic for at least six reasons. (*i*) Since the New Testament reports only one baptismal practice, with faith preceding baptism, and since no New Testament author develops a full doctrine of baptism, we may conclude confidently that the early Christian doctrine of baptism corresponds with the early Christian praxis of the rite of baptism. (*ii*) One tragic result of the Constantinian legalization of Christianity in the fourth century was that the church that baptized exclusively was convinced before long that the time of the "missionary situation" had come to an end. In reality, however, there is a new "missionary situation" in every family in which a baby is born. The "missionary situation" will never end until the second coming of Jesus Christ. (*iii*) The assertion that faith is God's "work" and gift is correct, as is the assertion that the central focus of baptism in the name of Jesus Christ is the death and resurrection of Jesus, not the will or the decision of a person. It is somewhat simplistic, however, when Hofius maintains that phrases such as "he was baptized" or "they were baptized" (Acts 2:41; 8:12, 13; 9:18; 16:15, 33; 18:8; 19:5; German versions have "er ließ sich taufen" or "sie ließen sich taufen," implying a conscious decision of the new believers to accept baptism) refer "only to the process itself as it is practiced in the missionary situation." It is special pleading if we eliminate implied theological convictions in these phrases: when Saul "got up and was baptized" (ἐβαπτίσθη, *ebaptisthē* [Acts 9:18]), the term *ebaptisthē* is as much a "genuine" passive voice as in Rom 6:3 and in other passages where Saul was baptized because he was willing to be baptized; he wanted to be baptized because he had come to faith in Jesus Christ. Baptism is not a completely passive experience ("reines Widerfahrnis"), but rather is the answer of faith to God's grace. (*iv*) The effort to validate infant baptism with reference to Jesus blessing the children (Mk 10:13) fails, still, because it has not been possible to locate water in the context of Mk 10 (the Jordan River in Mk 10:1 is too distant). We must be careful not to create a dichotomy between theological arguments and historical reality, as proponents of infant baptism appealing to Mk 10:13 do, taking into consideration the significance of the death and resurrection of Jesus Christ as historical events with theological *and* historical significance. (*v*) If salvation was "definitively realized" with Jesus' death on the cross and his resurrection, and if every baptized person has received salvation as the effect of the death and resurrection of Jesus as a gift, then the question becomes acute whether all baptized people have salvation. Does Hofius really want to claim that basically every person living in the "baptized Western world" has received salvation? This would mean that in 1900 a total of 96.6 percent of all North Americans and 94.5 percent of all Europeans had "salvation," and in 1990 a total of 85.3 percent of North Americans and 76.2 percent of Europeans—this would be practically tantamount to arguing for the universal salvation of all people born in the "Christian countries" of the West. In regard to the unbelief of a baptized person, Hofius comments that this is "a phenomenon that is virtually impossible to explain and categorize." The unbelief of a baptized European or American is a mystery only if we are so convinced of the "theological correctness" of infant baptism that we are under no circumstances willing to reconsider our exegesis of the relevant New Testament texts or to reconsider our baptismal practices. The leading Nazis and the managers of the concentration and extermination camps were all baptized; was their baptism really "valid and effective," independent of the horrible nature of their "unbelief in practice"? Hundreds of thousands of baptized church members left the mainline churches in Europe over the past couple of decades, leaving their newborn children unbaptized; was the baptism of these unbelievers who broke ranks still "effective." When the number of "confessing" agnostics or atheists among those who had been baptized was relatively small, it was easier to speak of an unexplainable phenomenon. When their number increases as dramatically as is happening in Europe, the quantitative reality becomes a qualitative issue—not in terms of a modification of the theology of the grace of God, who elects and graciously saves the sinner, but in terms of an honest rethinking of the baptism texts of the New Testament. If God's grace becomes effective in baptism, independent of the faith or lack of faith of the person who is baptized, then the quality and the effectiveness of the grace of God becomes a problem when baptized persons never confess faith in Jesus Christ or when such persons disregard the will of God, as, for example, racists or criminals who mistreat God's creatures. (*vi*) Hofius, who presented his study before the theological commission of the synod of the Lutheran Church in Württemberg in southern Germany, asserts that all church officials should be removed from office who propagate or practice "rebaptism" (anabaptism) or see it as a possibility. Hofius's plea would be more credible if he had argued in his discussion of faith and the death and resurrection of Jesus that all church officials should be removed who do not believe in the atonement that results from Jesus' death or in the bodily resurrection of Jesus on the third day. The teaching of the New Testament about baptism and the praxis of baptism in the early church not only demand a baptism in the name of the Father, the Son and the Holy Spirit but also connect baptism with the proclamation and believing acceptance of the gospel. And this means that the baptism of people who have come to faith is always legitimate, whether the new converts are polytheistic pagans of the Greco-Roman world or postmodern neo-pagans who were "baptized" as infants and came to faith in Jesus Christ later in life.

Günther Baumbach suggests that the church "has a missionary effect less by what it says than by what it does: by baptizing and by exemplified teaching."[179] This view is as erroneous as it is anachronistic. How could the Jerusalem church in the first century hope to have a missionary effect by baptizing? It could not. The lack of a command to preach the gospel is surely not a valid argument in favor of this view: as Jesus preached the good news in Galilee and as the Twelve were instructed to preach the good news on their mis-

---

[179]Baumbach 1967, 891.

sionary tour in Galilee, so the preaching of the gospel is an implicit necessity between the references to "going" and the reference to "making disciples."

The phrase "in the name of" (εἰς τὸ ὄνομα, *eis to onoma*) is a formula of transfer: the person who has come to faith in Jesus, the new disciple, enters into a new relationship to God, who now is Lord—depicted in baptism.[180] Since baptism is a feature common to all believers in Jesus, the command to baptize implies, for Matthew, a confessional commitment to the church worldwide.[181]

d. The disciples are directed to "teach" (διδάσκοντες, *didaskontes* [Mt 28:20]). Discipleship arises from teaching and becomes permanent through teaching. Joachim Gnilka comments that again "the establishment of congregations is the focus, their consolidation and the shaping of their life which is achieved as the baptized become more and more familiar with the teaching, not only intellectually but also in the praxis of everyday life."[182] Throughout his Gospel, Matthew connects teaching with doing, with the will of God as proclaimed by Jesus, with righteousness—hence the phrase in the missionary commission "to obey everything that I have commanded you" (τηρεῖν πάντα ὅσα ἐνετειλάμην ὑμῖν). Matthew characteristically ties the teaching of the disciples to the teaching of Jesus, and likewise characteristic is his emphasis that they have been directed to teach the new followers of Jesus to keep what Jesus taught—that is, to obey his words.[183] The true church of Jesus Christ exists "only where disciples of Jesus live in fellowship and seek to fulfill the will of their Lord and continue to receive new strength from God's mercy."[184] Jesus emphasizes with this directive at least the following points.[185] (*i*) The teaching of the missionaries focuses on the instructions of Jesus, not on the Mosaic law: his words are, like the words of the sacred Scriptures, more permanent than heaven and earth (Mt 24:35), and their authority is like Yahweh's authority.[186] The climax of salvation history does not abrogate God's earlier revelation (Mt 5:17-20), but its focus has shifted to Jesus the Messiah. (*ii*) The disciples are to teach "everything" (πάντα ὅσα, *panta hosa*) that Jesus taught, thus without making distinctions, "to the end of the age" (ἕως τῆς συντελείας τοῦ αἰῶνος, *heōs tēs synteleias tou aiōnos*), thus without later repeal. (*iii*) The teaching of the disciples in their missionary work and in their involvement in the local congregations is not mere dogma presented in theoretical propositions and memorized by the new converts; rather, it is, teaching with a

[180]On the trinitarian "formula" see Carson, *Mt,* 598. Note Davies and Allison (*Mt,* 3:684), who point out that the phrase "need not imply the recitation of a fixed formula."
[181]See Luz, *Mt,* 4:452.
[182]Gnilka, *Mt,* 2:509; for the remarks that follow above see ibid., 2:510.
[183]Alfred Zimmermann (1984, 154) argues that *didaskein* should be connected with the Torah. There is no evidence in the text for this view.
[184]Hahn 1980, 35.
[185]See Carson, *Mt,* 598-99.
[186]Cf. Ex 29:35; Deut 1:3, 41; 7:11; 12:11, 14.

content that can and must be put into practice in everyday life (τηρεῖν, *tērein*). (*iv*) The disciples convey what they as eyewitnesses have received from Jesus to new converts, who then as "earwitnesses" will pass on the truth of Jesus Christ to the next generation. As the truth and the salvation of God's revelation in Jesus Christ are preserved faithfully in each generation (τηρεῖν, *tērein*), the future generations will stay in contact with the risen Lord. (*v*) The disciples follow Jesus by going to other towns, by making disciples among the people in the places they visit, by baptizing and by teaching. The community of Jesus' followers expands with an inner necessity, a necessity that is bound up with Jesus' missionary commission and with his divine power.[187]

e. The disciples are directed to reach "all nations" (πάντα τὰ ἔθνη, *panta ta ethnē* [Mt 28:19]). The expression *panta ta ethnē* can be interpreted either in terms of all "nations" without distinguishing Jews from non-Jews,[188] or in terms of excluding Israel and the Jews to refer to all the non-Jewish people(s), meaning all "Gentiles."[189] The following observations show that the first option is more plausible. (*i*) The term *ethnē* signifies in Mt 24:7; 24:14; 25:32 "all nations," without any restrictions.[190] These passages are linked with the last judgment, but this does not prohibit an interpretation of Mt 28:19 in terms of "all nations":[191] the missionary work of the disciples procures salvation for people in the last judgment, and their mission is the only "date" between the present and the second coming of Jesus, which is connected with the last judgment. (*ii*) Jesus asserts in the immediate context of Mt 28:19 that he has been given "all authority in heaven and on earth." This claim, formulated against the background of Dan 7:13-14, permits no restriction of the missionary commission. It is impossible to relate the authority of the risen Lord to the entire earth while excluding Israel from the mission of his disciples.[192] (*iii*) Jesus gave his disciples unambiguous instructions in Mt 10:5 when he restricted their missionary work to the Jewish population of Galilee. After his resurrection, Jesus repealed this restriction. If he

---

[187]Legrand (1987, 27) speaks of the ethical dimension of the Christian mission: "the concern for justice and righteousness, for effective love, for a life worthy of the children of God."
[188]Thus the usual meaning of *ethnē* in the Septuagint. See K. L. Schmidt, *ThWNT,* 2:366-67 (*TDNT* 2:369-70); Hahn 1963, 109-11 (ET, 126-27); Trilling 1964, 26-28; Hubbard 1974, 84-87; S. Brown 1977, 29; J. P. Meier 1977; Hahn 1980, 35; Frankemölle 1982, 114; 1984, 119-23; A.-J. Levine 1988, 46; Kruijf 1993; Wasserberg 1998, 203-6; Stuhlmacher 1999, 117; Kvalbein 2000, 54-55; Köstenberger and O'Brien 2001, 99-100; Landmesser 2001, 15-17; see also in the commentaries Carson, *Mt,* 596; Davies and Allison, *Mt,* 3:684; Gnilka, *Mt,* 2:361-62, 371; Hagner, *Mt,* 2:887; Luz, *Mt,* 4:447-51.
[189]Cf. *Pss. Sol.* 9:9. Thus E. Lohmeyer 1951, 36; Walker 1967, 111-12; Lange 1973, 270, 302-3; Hare and Harrington 1975; Legrand 1987, 23; A.-J. Levine 1988, 186-92; Hre Kio 1990; Luz 1992, 408-9; Dobbeler 2000b, 31-32; Wilk 2002, 129.
[190]In Mt 4:15; 6:32; 10:5, 18; 12:18-21; 20:19 the term *ethnē* refers to non-Jews (i.e., Gentiles); the references in Mt 20:25-26 and 24:9 are unclear, but the probable meaning is "all nations."
[191]Contra Hre Kio 1990, 234-35.
[192]See Kvalbein 2000, 54-55.

introduced at the same time a new restriction, then we would expect clear information concerning the exclusion of Israel from the disciples' sphere of missionary ministry. If in Mt 28:19 Matthew replaces Israel with Gentiles, "the narrative expectation suggests that Matthew would prepare the Gentile mission among non-Jews with the help of unmistakable text signals . . . in order not to ask too much of the reader at the end."[193] (*iv*) The commission in Mt 28:19 does not contradict the commission of Mt 10:5-6 but rather expands it.[194] (*v*) The evangelist did not report in Mt 10 the return of the Twelve from their missionary work in Israel. This means that the mission to Israel (i.e., to the Jews), in terms of the narrative structure of the Gospel of Matthew, has not ended.[195] (*vi*) The reference in Mt 10:18 to governors and kings as authorities who investigate and abuse the missionary disciples presupposes a mission in areas outside of Judea and Galilee, and this in the context of the mission to Israel that evidently is not replaced by a mission to Gentiles.[196] (*vii*) The rejection of Jesus by the leading political and religious authorities reached its climax in the crucifixion. Does this mean that Jesus blamed all Jews for their failure by excluding them from the missionary proclamation of the disciples that offered nothing less than God's forgiving grace? That is improbable. There was no prophecy in the Old Testament that would have suggested such a scenario. (*viii*) Jesus experienced not only opposition and rejection but also acceptance and faith in his message and mission: there were thousands of sympathizers and followers in Galilee. This clearly means that there was a realistic hope for future missionary successes among the Jewish population. (*ix*) Jesus told the disciples that the time of their international world mission comes to an end only when he returns to establish the kingdom of God as a visible reality on a new earth with a new heaven. The disciples did not know when this would happen. Jesus had indicated, however, that the time until these events of the end might be longer than many expect (cf. the parables in Mt 25). The disciples thus had to reckon with years or decades in which they would be responsible for the implementation of Jesus' missionary commission. Given this context, it is implausible that they would have excluded their Jewish compatriots and the Jews who would be born in the coming years from their preaching of salvation through Jesus the Messiah. Jesus had not announced a mass conversion of Jews for the future (whether Paul provides such a prophecy in Rom 11:26 is debated [see below]). This means that Jews need to hear the message about Jesus now, and again and again. (*x*) The Twelve did in fact preach the good news of Jesus Christ after Easter among Jews, first in Jerusalem and then in the Jewish Diaspora. Paul understood his own mission-

---

[193]Wasserberg 1998, 204.
[194]See Gnilka, *Mt,* 2:508-9; Sand, *Mt,* 596; Landmesser 2001, 15 n. 40.
[195]Stuhlmacher 1999, ET, 30; Kvalbein 2000, 55.
[196]See Kvalbein 2000, 55.

ary commission in terms of a mission to Gentiles, but he also primarily preached in synagogues before Jews. His statements in Rom 11:11-14 demonstrate that his grief on account of the unbelief of Israel (Rom 9:1-5) did not exclude the hope that Jews would be converted: he hopes that the eschatological reality of life in the Gentile-Christian churches will make Jews "jealous," prompting them to come to faith in Jesus Christ. (*xi*) The Christians of the second century still evangelized Jews.[197] Justin Martyr reports that Jews are converted "daily" and join the churches (*Dial.* 39.1-2).

To summarize: Jesus' commission to go to "all nations" rescinds the restriction of missionary work to Israel (Mt 10:5) without excluding Israel (i.e., the Jewish people) from the mission of the disciples. This means that Israel is absorbed into the world of the nations—a relativizing of the preeminent status that Israel had enjoyed as the one and only people of God. This quite likely was shocking.[198] Israel has fulfilled its salvation-historical role with the conclusion of the salvific work of Jesus the Messiah in his death on the cross, his resurrection and his exaltation to the right hand of God. Israel will enjoy the fruit of this work as *primus inter pares* (cf. Rom 1:16).

Axel von Dobbeler summarizes the salvation-historical explanations with regard to the relationship between the mission to Israel (Mt 10:5-6) and the mission to the nations (Mt 28:19) with two models and suggests a third model of his own. (*i*) According to the "substitution model" (*Substitutonsmodell*), Matthew believed that the people of Israel have lost their salvation-historical status to the Gentile church: the sending of the disciples to Israel is replaced by the commission to go to the nations. The reason for the substitution is Jesus' rejection by the Jews.[199] This explanation is implausible for various reasons. Note, for example, that Matthew never speaks in general terms of the guilt of Israel or of the Jews for the death of Jesus, and he never asserts that Israel as a whole has been rejected (Mt 21:43 and Mt 27:25 are not to be interpreted in this sense). (*ii*) The "delimitation model" (*Entschränkungsmodell*) interprets the universal commission of Mt 28:19-20 as a repeal of the particularistic limitation of the missionary activity of the disciples who had been directed to minister only among Jews in Mt 10:6. The disciples understood their commission after Easter to be an expansion of their earlier commission.[200] Dobbeler praises this model for its emphasis on the continuity between Israel and the church but criticizes that "Israel loses its salvation-historical position over against the nations"—that is, that Israel becomes an addressee of the mission of the disciples just as the nations.[201] (*iii*) The "complementary model" (*Komplementaritätsmodell*) assumes that "early Christian ears" would not have heard tensions between Mt 10:5-6 and Mt 28:19-20. The sending to Israel and

---

[197]See Skarsaune 2000.

[198]Thus Hagner, *Mt*, 2:887, with regard to the Jewish-Christian readers of the Gospel of Matthew; for the comment that follows above see ibid.; see also Stuhlmacher 1999, 117 n. 52.

[199]See Walker 1967, 145; Lange 1973, 302.

[200]Bosch 1959, 190-91; Hahn 1963, 111 (ET, 127-28); Vögtle 1964, 284-85; Strecker 1971, 117-18; Frankemölle 1984b, 121; Gnilka, *Mt*, 1:362-63; 2:508-9; Sand, *Mt*, 596.

[201]Dobbeler 2000b, 26, 27; for the following comments cf. ibid. 27-41, who follows Luz, *Mt*, 2:91.

the sending to the Gentiles have different goals and different assignments. For Israel, the proclamation of the kingdom of God signifies the restoration of the people of God; for the Gentiles, the focus is on the conversion from dead idols to the living God.

According to the summary in Mt 4:17, Jesus called all Israel to repent; in Mt 11:20 he pronounced judgment on towns that have not repented; in Mt 12:41 he contrasted the unrepentant people whom he encounters with the inhabitants of Nineveh who repented after Jonah's preaching. These passages indicate that the disciples' mission to Israel demanded repentance, turning back to God, as does the mission to the Gentiles: God's judgment can fall upon Israel just as it will fall upon the Gentiles. And God's "Emmanuel" does not force Israel to be obedient to the dawn of God's kingdom as he does not force the Gentiles to believe. Günter Wasserberg suggests that for Matthew, the *ethnē* should be made into proselytes because the "Matthean mission" in Mt 5:17-20 and Mt 23:3 is valid, which means that the Gentile mission is a "mission with circumcision."[202] This interpretation clearly is wrong. Not only does it make the Gospel of Matthew responsible for the theological position of the "Judaizers" who demanded the circumcision of the converted Gentile Christians in Antioch and in the churches that Paul had established, for which there is no evidence whatsoever, but also it fails to see that while Matthew indeed portrays Jesus as speaking of the continued validity of the law, he radicalizes the latter (particularly in the Sermon on the Mount) and thus modifies it.

Florian Wilk relates the phrase *panta ta ethnē* in Mt 28:19 to Gentiles, while asserting that this does not mean that he has to decide whether the missionary commission limited to Israel in Mt 10:5-8 is expanded or repealed in Mt 28:18-20:[203] the overall concerns of Matthew show that the commission of Mt 10:5-8 is complemented in Mt 28:19.[204] The disciples have "two different assignments: on the one hand, they are to gather Israel around Jesus as the messianic shepherd; on the other hand, they are called to integrate the nations into their own community as disciples of the Son of Man." Wilk emphasizes that these two commissions are not unrelated: they are connected in Jesus, the one who commands both missions, and in Abraham, whose children they are both as restored Israel and as converted Gentiles. It is preferable, however, not to think of two commissions with two different assignments, as this could mean that the disciples were expected to gather the Jewish believers in Jesus the Messiah and the Gentile Christians into separate communities, which would contradict their common status as descendants of Abraham. Wilk's analysis demonstrates that scholars should consider whether Mt 28:18-20 should not indeed be interpreted in terms of a single assignment that Jesus gave to his disciples: a commission to preach the good news to "all nations" that expands the commission of Mt 10:5-8, as the scope of the disciples' missionary ministry now includes the Gentiles as well.

The messianic commission to go to "all nations" would have reminded the disciples with regard to geographical and ethnographical implications of the table of nations in Gen 10, which had retained a continuous significance for both the Israelite and the Jewish tradition as a valid "description" of the world.[205] How much did an average Galilean know about regions and nations within and beyond the

[202]Wasserberg 1998, 205.
[203]Thus the alternative as formulated by Luz, *Mt,* 2:92.
[204]Wilk 2002, 126-31, the quotation that follows above, 129.
[205]J. M. Scott 1994, 492-522; 1995, 5-56.

borders of the Roman Empire? The question of the disciples' geographical conceptions will be discussed later (§16.2). It will become clear that the geographical horizon of the disciples was not limited to the confines of the Roman Empire.

Karl Holl maintained in his 1912 lecture on "the missionary method of the early and the medieval church" that the mission of the church in the first centuries was limited to the regions controlled by the Roman Empire. "Where it went beyond these borders, especially in the East, this was like a collateral success. The primitive church believed that its obligations were fulfilled if it managed to reach the borders of the Roman Empire. This is how world mission was understood."[206] In §16.2 we will see that this view is seriously flawed.

Luke, in the second volume of his account, mentions Parthia (Acts 2:9) and Ethiopia (Acts 8:27), regions outside of the eastern and southern borders of the Roman Empire.[207]

Matthew returns to the beginnings at the end of his Gospel: "This is an account of the origin of Jesus the Messiah the son of David, the son of Abraham" (Mt 1:1 [TNIV margin]). The divine blessings promised to Abraham and, through Abraham, to all nations (Gen 12:3) are now fulfilled in Jesus the Messiah. The repetition of the blessing given to Abraham in Gen 18:18 LXX and Gen 22:18 LXX also speaks of "all nations" (πάντα τὰ ἔθνη, *panta ta ethnē*).

Proponents of the North American "church growth movement" argue on anthropological and sociological grounds that missionaries should plan to reach "people groups" with the gospel message—that is, groups with their own identity with respect to language, religion, geographical location, worldview and values. In an effort to provide this program with a theological-exegetical basis, they refer to the *panta ta ethnē* to whom Jesus sent his disciples.[208] These missiologists argue that *ethnos* means "tribe, people group." Edward Dayton remarks that "it is probably preferable to render Matthew 28:19 as 'Go, then, to all *peoples* everywhere and make them my disciples . . . ' rather than 'all *nations*.' . . . The latter term indicates the notion of a political unit such as a state which may in fact have numerous 'peoples' as component parts of the nation. . . . The commission to make disciples of all peoples does not refer simply to constituting fellowships of disciples in all the political units which are today recognized as nations. Rather it is aimed at all peoples who exist in states of natural cohesion because of shared language and life. . . . In some cases these will be ethnic units. In other cases, they may be subcultural groupings or social caste units within a single ethnic unit. . . . The Greek word comes closest to modern anthropological terms for labeling people groups."[209] Peter Wagner and Edward Dayton write, "The people approach is biblical.

---

[206]Holl 1912, 3.

[207]P. S. Alexander (*ABD* 2:983-84) omits Ethiopia.

[208]See Donald McGavran, *The Bridges of God: A Study in the Strategy of Missions* (London: World Dominion Press, 1955); idem, *Understanding Church Growth* (Grand Rapids: Eerdmans, 1970); H. C. Goerner, *All Nations in God's Purpose* (Nashville: Broadman, 1979).

[209]E. Dayton and D. A. Fraser, *Planning Stategies for World Evangelization* (Grand Rapids: Eerdmans, 1980), 119.

Our Lord's Great Commission, as translated in the Good News Bible reads: 'Go, then, to all peoples (*panta ta ethne*) everywhere and make them my disciples . . .' (Matt. 28:19). . . . A people is a significantly large sociological grouping of individuals who perceive themselves to have a common affinity for one another."[210] They argue that missionary work should adopt the "homogeneous unit principle" and seek to plant churches in homogeneous people groups.

I agree that the quantitative growth of the church is a legitimate concern of missionary work, that the church indeed often has success in specific social or cultural contexts where people do not have to cross cultural barriers, that God can cause the conversion of entire people groups, as the "church growth movement" has emphasized, and that sociological and anthropological categories may be very helpful in formulating strategies of evangelism and missionary outreach. This does not change the fact, however, that in regard to the linguistic meaning of the Greek term *ethnē* a collective plural has an all-embracing force,[211] and that it is illegitimate to read a contemporary socioanthropologic definition back into the phrase *panta ta ethnē*. Further, it is doubtful on biblical and theological grounds whether the "homogeneous unit principle" is valid as a guideline for missionary strategy and church growth.[212] The following five arguments need to be considered. (*i*) The early church proclaimed the gospel to all people, to Jews and pagans, slaves and free, rich and poor. There is no evidence for a strategy that took into account social or cultural identities and peculiarities for the "effectiveness" of church-planting efforts. (*ii*) The removal of barriers that separate people from each other is not simply a result of the gospel but an essential part of its nature. Conversion means integration into a community, a new "humanity," the people of God whose identity is defined no longer by race, social status or gender but by Jesus Christ. (*iii*) The early church did not just grow; it grew across cultural barriers: despite difficulties, Jewish Christians and Gentile Christians lived together in local congregations. (*iv*) Each congregation was expected to demonstrate the unity of its members. Unity is not the unity of different congregations but rather the unity of the different believers within the local congregation. Unity of the church is not to be confused with uniformity of church members, suppressing or eliminating their diversity. (*v*) The apostles never attempted to disprove the accusation that believers in Jesus Christ abandon or betray their culture. The apostle Paul especially was concerned that the unity of the church not be compromised as a result of social or ethnic reasons. René Padilla argues that if the conclusions of the "church growth movement" are correct, "it is quite evident that the use of the homogeneous unit principle for church growth has no biblical foundation. Its advocates have taken as their starting point a sociological observation and developed a missionary strategy; only then, a posteriori, have they made the attempt to find biblical support. As a result the Bible has not been allowed to speak. . . . The analysis above leads us to conclude that the 'Church Growth' emphasis on homogeneous unit churches is in fact directly opposed to the apostolic teaching and practice in relation to the expansion of the

---

[210]C. Peter Wagner and Edward R. Dayton, "The People-Group Approach to World Evangelization," in *Unreached Peoples '81* (Elgin, Ill.: Cook, 1981), 19-35, esp. 21, 23.

[211]Carson (*Mt*, 596), who comments that nobody demands a "city movement" on the basis of Acts 8:40.

[212]For the critique that follows above see René Padilla, "The Unity of the Church and the Homogeneous Unit Principle," *International Bulletin of Missionary Research* 6 (1982): 23-30; J. Robertson McQuilkin, *How Biblical Is the Church Growth Movement?* (Chicago: Moody, 1973); recently also Turner 1995, 163-64.

church. No missionary methodology can be built without a solid biblical theology of mission as a basis. What can be expected of a missiology that exhibits dozens of books and dissertations dealing with the 'Church Growth' approach, but not one major work on the theology of mission?"[213]

Another question often has been raised by mission leaders: Does Jesus' missionary commission demand, for example, in the context of Mt 24:14, that *all unreached* peoples must be reached with the gospel message? Or does it demand that missionaries must reach *all* people of *each* generation in the *entire* world before Jesus Christ returns? It is safe to conclude that the timing of Jesus' second coming does not depend upon the missionary activity of the church or upon the obedience of Christians to the missionary commission.

3. The word of promise: Jesus concludes the missionary commission with the promise of his abiding presence: "And remember, I am with you (ἐγὼ μεθ' ὑμῶν, *egō meth' hymōn*) always, to the end of the age" (Mt 28:20). With this promise Jesus takes the place of Yahweh "and assumes his function with regard to the new people of God."[214] The formulation in the present tense (εἰμι, *eimi*) and the reference to, literally, "all days" (English versions usually have the translation "always") promise permanence. The time until the return of Jesus Christ is the time of the missionary work of the church, a time in which Jesus' disciples experience the presence of the risen Lord precisely as they are sent and as they go.[215] This is the christological dimension of missions, the grounds and the final reality of missionary work.[216] The missionary commission of Mt 28:18-20 formulates indeed "for the first time in the history of religions" a claim "which leaves no room for other religions."[217] This claim means with regard to the biography of the addressees of missionary proclamation "discontinuity over against the pagan past" and with regard to cultural identity "the disposal of pagan legacy." As the messianic era has been fully inaugurated with the death and resurrection of Jesus, as Jesus the Messiah has initiated the reign of God, which is to reach the ends of the earth, the disciples can now leave Israel "without being afraid that they move away from the sanctifying presence of God, because this presence goes with them in Jesus, who is with them always, and thus the boundaries of the [holy] land are expanded to incorporate all nations."[218]

---

[213]Padilla, "Unity of the Church," 29-30.
[214]Gnilka, *Mt*, 2:510, with reference to Gen 26:24; Ex 3:12; Deut 20:1, 4; 31:6; Josh 1:9; Judg 6:12, 16; Is 41:10; 43:5.
[215]See Carson, *Mt*, 599; cf. Robert E. Coleman, "The Promise of the Great Commission," *EvJ* 9 (1991): 75-85.
[216]Legrand 1988, 26-27.
[217]Feldtkeller 1993, 22; the quotation that follows above, ibid.
[218]K. E. Wolff 1989, 274.

Lk 24:46-49

Luke reports a missionary commission of the risen Christ in his account of the Easter events for the evening of the day of resurrection, when Jesus appeared to the disciples in Jerusalem.

Lk 24:46-49: "And he said to them, 'Thus it is written, that the Messiah is to suffer and to rise from the dead on the third day, [47]and that repentance and forgiveness of sins is to be proclaimed in his name to all nations, beginning from Jerusalem. [48]You are witnesses of these things. [49]And see, I am sending upon you what my Father promised; so stay here in the city until you have been clothed with power from on high.'"

The formulation of these sentences reminds the biblically informed reader of Isaiah's description of the Servant of the Lord.[219] Luke omits a geographical list of regions to be reached by the missionary work of the disciples; he will supply such a list later in Acts 1:8. And unlike Matthew, Luke does not formulate in the imperative but rather in the indicative. Luke emphasizes the following points.

1. The mission of the disciples is founded upon a word of the risen Christ and in a word of Scripture.[220] Luke focuses his formulation of the missionary commission on the content of the gospel, establishing the witness of the disciples to the nations on the Scriptures of Israel.

2. The phrase "you are witnesses of these things" (ὑμεῖς μάρτυρες τούτων [Lk 24:48]) corresponds to the formulation in Acts 1:8 "you will be my witnesses" (ἔσεσθέ μου μάρτυρες). On the assumption that these are authentic words of Jesus, we have here the earliest New Testament evidence for the meaning of "a witness" or "to give witness" (μαρτύς/μαρτυρεῖν, martys/martyrein) in the sense of "proclaimer of Jesus Christ/to proclaim Jesus Christ."[221] The term "witness," originally a legal term ("one who testifies in legal matters"), connects the elements of personal presence, interpretation of what has been seen and experienced, and standing up for what one is witnessing to.[222] Birger Gerhardsson convincingly argued that the terms "witness" (μάρτυς, martys; Heb., עֵד, 'ed) and "testimony, witness" (μαρτύριον, martyrion; Heb., עֵדוּת, 'edût), interpreted against a Jewish-rabbinic background, connote in a legal sense the credibility of eyewitness accounts.[223]

---

[219]T. Moore 1997, with reference to Is 58:6; 61:1 (forgiveness); 2:2; 25:6-7; 52:10; 56:7; 61:11; 66:18, 20 (all nations); 43:10, 12; 44:8 (witnesses); 44:33; 61:1 (God's Spirit). Pao (2000, 84-91) sees Is 49:6 as background of Lk 24:46-47.
[220]Best 1984, 4; Talbert 1992, 28-29; the second point was particularly emphasized by Freitag (1917, 126-28).
[221]On μάρτυς/μαρτυρία/μαρτυρεῖν in the New Testament see Strathman, ThWNT 4:477-520 (TDNT 4:474-514); A. A. Trites, NIDNTT 3:1038-50; J. Beutler, EWNT 2:969-73 (EDNT 2:393-95); L. Coenen, ThBLNT 2:1767; I. H. Marshall 1970, 41-44, 159-61; Nellessen 1976; Trites 1977; Frizzi 1984; Gebauer 1998; Zmijewski, Apg, 92-95.
[222]BDAG 619; J. Beutler, EWNT 2:970 (EDNT 2:393).
[223]Gerhardsson 1961, 182-85, 222. Cf. P.Oxy. 105, 13, where μαρτυρῶ (martyrō) is used, parenthetically, to emphasize the correctness of a statement (BDAG 617, s.v. "μαρτυρέω").

Lucien Cerfaux interprets only the preaching of the Twelve in Jerusalem as "witness" (*martyrion*) in a Lukan sense: only the Twelve could stand before the Jews as eyewitnesses of the ministry of Jesus and especially of the resurrection of Jesus. Since Paul was not an eyewitness in the sense that the Twelve were direct witnesses, Paul's missionary preaching was not "witness."[224] Christoph Burchard argues that for Luke, the term "witness" refers only to the guarantee ("Bürgschaft") of the apostles for the truth of the gospel as eyewitnesses and thus does not describe their preaching; witnesses do not "propagate the truth, they only establish truth."[225] Since Luke can indeed describe the saving message of Jesus Christ in general as "witness,"[226] Jacob Kremer characterizes "mission" and "witness" as practically synonymous terms: the "witness" of the apostles is their international missionary work.[227]

According to Lk 24:48, a larger group of disciples receives the commission to be "witnesses" of Jesus. According to Acts 1:8; 2:40; 3:15; 4:33; 5:32, it is the Twelve who are "witnesses," particularly in their function as eyewitnesses of the resurrection (Acts 10:39; 13:31). However, Stephen is also called "witness" (Acts 22:20), and Paul was called by the risen Lord to "witness" just as the Twelve had done (Acts 22:15; 26:16; cf. 18:5; 20:24; 23:11; 28:23). For Luke, "witnesses" are the early Christian preachers who proclaim the message of Jesus Christ authentically and without distorting it—both the "external events" linked with the life, death and resurrection of Jesus of Nazareth, and the "internal significance" of Jesus the Messiah and his procurement of salvation for people. The term "witness" also implies the personal involvement and engagement of the apostles.[228] The term διαμαρτύρομαι (*diamartyromai*) "to make a solemn declaration about the truth of something, testify, bear witness to" is thus a technical term in the book of Acts, describing the missionary work both of the Twelve and of Paul. The content of the witness is primarily "the exalted Lord Jesus, his word and his ministry":[229] Jesus' life and ministry (Acts 1:21-22), his death and resurrection, his vindication and his exaltation (Acts 1:22), the salvation "from this corrupt generation" (Acts 2:40), the word of the Lord (Acts 8:25), the necessity of conversion and faith in the Lord Jesus Christ (Acts 20:21), the gospel of the grace of God (Acts 20:24), the message of Jesus (Acts 23:11), the kingdom of God (Acts 28:23).[230]

Critical scholars have suggested that Luke's concept of "witness" should be interpreted in the context of the question of identity and continuity. Luke was (allegedly) a Christian of the third generation, and as the delay of the parousia resulted in an identity crisis of the Christian movement at the end of the first century, he faced the dual challenge of protecting the Jesus tradition against falsification and legitimizing it for a mostly Gentile-Christian church by providing a salvation-historical context.[231] This reconstruction is quite implausible for at least the following reasons. (a) If Luke, the companion of Paul, was indeed the author of the book of Acts, this reconstruction becomes immaterial. (b) Luke uses the concept of "witness" to describe the work of missionaries, not events within the church.

[224]Lucien Cerfaux, "Témoins du Christ," *Angelicum* 20 (1943): 166-83; on the discussion of Luke's concept of "witness" see Trites 1977, 128-53; Gebauer 1998.
[225]Burchard 1970, 130-35; quotation, 132.
[226]Brox 1961, 49, 68.
[227]Kremer 1982.
[228]Beutler, *EWNT* 2:970 (*EDNT* 2:394); cf. H. Strathman, *ThWNT* 4:496 (*TDNT* 4:492-93).
[229]Nellessen 1976, 278.
[230]J. Beutler, "μαρτυρέω," *EWNT* 2:958-64 (*EDNT* 2:389-91); cf. Strathmann, *ThWNT* 4:518-19 (*TDNT* 4:511-12); Brox 1961, 67; Schneider 1970, 64-65; Gebauer 1998, 57.
[231]Brox 1961, 54; Plümacher 1978a, 516-19; Schneider 1970, 74; Roloff 1993, 204-6, 210-12; Gebauer 1998, 58-59; Pokorný 1998, 75-78.

(c) The "external factual level" on which the witness of the apostles becomes significant, guaranteeing the reliability of the preaching of Jesus' death and resurrection, not only was important for later churches, which had no longer direct knowledge of Jesus,[232] but also was indispensable already in the first decades after A.D. 30 for people who had not seen the risen Christ personally—Jews and Gentiles in Damascus and Antioch, in Athens and Corinth, in Ephesus and Rome.

In Lk 24:48 the witness of the apostles concerns the suffering of Jesus as the Messiah, his resurrection on the third day, the proclamation of the necessity of conversion in the name of Jesus Christ, a proclamation that begins in Jerusalem and is addressed to all nations.[233]

3. The disciples are sent "to all nations" (εἰς πάντα τὰ ἔθνη, *eis panta ta ethnē* [Lk 24:47]). This expression may again refer either to the nations without Israel, thus the "Gentiles,"[234] or to all nations, including Israel.[235] The context shows that "all nations" includes Israel (i.e., the Jews): first, the term is followed by the phrase "beginning from Jerusalem," and second, Luke takes up Lk 24:47 in Acts 1:8, where he mentions, apart from Jerusalem and Judea ("Israel"), also Samaria and the "ends of the earth" as the goal of the missionary work of the disciples.[236] Günter Wasserberg observes that "the phrase εἰς πάντα τὰ ἔθνη in Lk 24:47 is a conclusion as well as the preparation for the second volume of Luke's work, and it refers to the fact that the salvation of the world comes from within Israel. It thus *has* to begin among the Jews in Jerusalem, before successively reaching the world of the nations." From a formal point of view it is true that "the motif of an explicit commission" is missing in Lk 24:47-48 (as well as in Acts 1:8).[237] This fact is not vital, however: Jesus announces that the disciples will be witnesses among "all nations" and "to the ends of the earth," an announcement that amounts to a directive that cannot be fulfilled without going from Jerusalem to other towns, from Judea to other regions. The presence of the prepositions εἰς (*eis,* "to") and ἕως (*heōs,* "to") also indicates that this announcement implies a sending and is therefore a missionary commission.

4. The directive to begin their witnessing in Jerusalem (ἀρξάμενοι ἀπὸ Ἰερουσαλήμ [Lk 24:47]) indicates a reversal of the direction that the Old Testament promises assumed. Whereas the Jews expected the nations to come from "outside" to Jerusalem as the center of the world, Jesus tells his disciples that they will begin in Jerusalem and then move out to the nations.[238]

---

[232]Gebauer (1998, 59, 62), who notes correctly, however, that Luke speaks of the witness of the apostles "exclusively in the context of their missionary preaching" (61).
[233]Hahn 1963, 113 (ET, 130); Senior 1983, 257-60; Barbi 1990, 129-30; Gebauer 1998, 59.
[234]Kremer 1982, 149.
[235]Bock, *Lk,* 2:1940-41; Marshall, *Lk,* 906; Hahn 1980, 17-18; Wasserberg 1998, 200-206.
[236]See Wasserberg 1998, 201; the quotation that follows above, ibid., 203.
[237]Kremer 1982, 147.
[238]Green, *Lk,* 857.

Acts 1:8

Luke notes in the first paragraph of the second volume of his account of Jesus and the movement that he initiated a second post-Easter missionary commission, which includes an assignment to worldwide ministry.

Acts 1:8: "But you will receive power when the Holy Spirit has come upon you; and you will be my witnesses in Jerusalem, in all Judea and Samaria, and to the ends of the earth."

Jesus Christ emphasizes at least five matters in connection with the commission to international missionary work.

1. Jesus is the disciples' principal, who, as the crucified and risen Christ, mandates their ministry, as the one who "presented himself alive to them" after the crucifixion.[239] He sends the disciples out as his witnesses (μου μάρτυρες, *mou martyres* [Acts 1:8]). The personal pronoun μου (*mou*) is emphasized by virtue of being placed first: the disciples will not testify to their own experiences; they testify to the resurrection of Jesus, who died as Israel's Messiah for the atonement of sins.

2. The apostles are given the assignment to be witnesses (μάρτυρες, *martyres*).[240] The significance of what it means to be a witness can be gleaned from the continuation of Luke's account of the disciples' ministry in the book of Acts.

Rudolf Pesch describes the content of the disciples' witness as follows: "For the Christ who had to suffer and be raised from the dead according to the Scriptures (Lk 24:48-49), for his resurrection (Acts 1:21; 2:32; 3:15; 4:33; 10:41; 13:31), for his resurrection and exaltation (5:31-32), for the repentance and forgiveness of sins granted by God in Jesus' name (Lk 24:47-48; Acts 5:31-32; 10:42), finally, for everything that he did in the land of the Jews and in Jerusalem (10:39); as witnesses of the ascension (1:9-11), the apostles are also witnesses, guarantors, for his parousia."[241]

3. The Holy Spirit is the power (δύναμις, *dynamis*) that the disciples need in order to fulfill the assignment of international missionary work. The Holy Spirit is "the promise of the Father" (Lk 24:49; Acts 1:4; 2:38), and he is sent by the risen Lord (Lk 24:49). Jesus leads the mission of the disciples by his Spirit, who is identical with the Spirit of God promised for the last days by the prophets. In other words, Jesus continues his divine mission by the Spirit through the mission of the apostles, who do God's work until he, Jesus, returns.[242]

4. The apostles are given a description of the route that their witness will take: "You will be my witnesses in Jerusalem, in all Judea and Samaria, and to the ends of the earth" (Acts 1:8). Jesus traveled from Galilee to Jerusalem (Lk

---

[239]Acts 1:3: ζῶντα μετὰ τὸ παθεῖν αὐτόν.
[240]Acts 1:8: ἔσεσθέ μου μάρτυρες (future with imperatival meaning).
[241]Pesch, *Apg*, 1:69.
[242]Kremer 1982, 154; Barbi 1990, 131-34.

23:5; Acts 10:37); the disciples will travel from Jerusalem to the ends of the earth, with Judea and Samaria being stations on this route. The phrase "to the ends of the earth" (ἕως ἐσχάτου τῆς γῆς, *heōs eschatou tēs gēs*) alludes to Is 49:6, where Yahweh says of his Servant, "I will give you as a light to the nations, that my salvation may reach to the end of the earth" (ἕως ἐσχάτου τῆς γῆς, *heōs eschatou tēs gēs*).[243] This prophecy of Isaiah does not only state that the mission of the Servant will reach Gentiles: it asserts that this mission will extend "to the end of the earth." This prophecy is taken up also in Acts 13:47 where a twofold motif is emphasized: God's salvation is now open to the Gentiles as well, and God's salvation is universal in reach. In Acts 1:8, the abbreviated allusion to the phrase "to the end of the earth" has first of all a geographical meaning:[244] "Jerusalem," "Judea" and "Samaria" are geographical terms, which indicates that the phrase "end of the earth" should be taken as such as well. This also means that Acts 1:8 is not simply the "Lukan version" of the Matthean missionary commission but rather an independent, specific commission of the risen Christ.

5. We turn to the geographical terms. Jerusalem is the center of the mission of Jesus' followers, the point of departure of their missionary work. The term "Judea" (Ἰουδαία, *Ioudaia*) evidently includes Galilee: in Lk 9:31 Luke refers to "the church" of Judea, Galilee and Samaria, while in Acts 1:8 only Judea and Samaria are mentioned as areas in which the disciples are directed to preach the gospel. Apart from Acts 9:31, Galilee is never mentioned in the book of Acts. Samaria (Σαμάρεια, *Samareia*) is the region between Judea and Galilee. The phrase "to the end of the earth" (ἕως ἐσχάτου τῆς γῆς, *heōs eschatou tēs gēs*) does not refer to Rome,[245] nor to the Jewish Diaspora or to the "land Israel,"[246] nor to Spain or Ethiopia,[247] nor to the Gentiles,[248] but literally to the farthest reaches of the inhabited world (known at the time).[249]

Scholars who interpret the phrase in terms of Rome, the capital of the Roman Empire, advance two arguments. (a) The structure of the book of Acts: Luke traces the history of the early Christian mission from Jerusalem (Acts 1—7) to Rome (Acts 28). (b) The verse *Pss. Sol.* 8:15, which says of God, "He brought someone from the end of the earth, one

[243]There are further allusions to Is 49:6 in Lk 2:32; 24:46-47 and in Acts 13:47. See Pao 2000, 84-100. In the Greek phrase, *eschatos* is singular ("the end of the earth"), which is translated by most versions as a plural; see the discussion below.
[244]See Ellis 1991, 278, with reference to Bruce, *Acts,* 37-38; Conzelmann, *Apg,* 27 (ET, 7).
[245]Conzelmann, *Apg,* 27 (ET, 7); Haenchen, *Apg,* 112 (ET, 143-44 with n. 9); Schille, *Apg,* 72; Fitzmyer, *Acts,* 206; Bruce 1977, 447-48. Against this interpretation, with cogent arguments, see T. Thornton 1977-1978. Barrett (*Acts,* 1:80) interprets the phrase in terms of Rome as representative of the entire world.
[246]Jewish Diaspora: Rengstorf 1962, 186-87; Israel: D. Schwartz 1986; as (rejected) possibility in W. Davies 1974, 279.
[247]Spain: Ellis 1991; Ethiopia: T. Thornton 1977-1978; cf. Aus 1979, 244-46.
[248]Unnik 1966; Pao 2000, 93-94 (with reference to the background in Is 32:15).
[249]See Rosner 1998, 218-19; J. M. Scott 2002, 58-60.

who attacks in strength; he declared war against Jerusalem, and her land." This text is interpreted as a reference to the invasion of the East by the Roman general Pompey, which began in Rome and ended in Jerusalem. This interpretation is unconvincing for the following reasons.[250] (a) The phrase "end of the earth" in *Pss. Sol.* 8:15 probably is an allusion to Jer 6:22, a reference to the invasion of the Babylonians. (b) Pompey was indeed a "Roman," but he came into the East in 67 B.C. as a Roman general who had commanded troops between 77-71 B.C. in Spain, which means that "end of the earth" in *Pss. Sol.* 8:15 could also be a reference to Spain. (c) The phrase "end of the earth" had a fixed meaning in the sense of the far reaches of the inhabited world, a meaning that never was restricted to the city of Rome. (d) In Acts 28 Rome is not portrayed as the goal or the fulfillment of the early Christian mission but rather as a new starting point from which the gospel was proclaimed "with all boldness and without hindrance" (Acts 28:31). (e) Rome was the capital of the Roman Empire and possibly the location where Luke wrote the book of Acts: it would have been absurd in any situation to label the center of the *Imperium Romanum* as "end of the earth."

The phrase "end of the earth" is identified with Ethiopia, based on the story in Acts 8:26-40, which speaks of an Ethiopian who was "returning home" (Acts 8:28) from Jerusalem, was evangelized and baptized by Philip, and "went on his way rejoicing" (Acts 8:39). This interpretation is implausible:[251] (a) Luke does not actually state that there was missionary work going on in Ethiopia; at best he leaves his readers guessing whether such was the case, and he leaves this "missionary" anonymous. (b) Luke does not report the conversion of the Ethiopian as the end or climax of the apostles' mission but rather places it between the missionary work in Judea and missionary work in Samaria.

The interpretation of the phrase "end of the earth" in terms of the Jewish Diaspora of Israel as the Holy Land also is implausible. (a) The prophecy of Is 49:6 and the eschatological hopes in Second Temple Judaism expected the conversion not only of (apostate) Jews but also of Gentiles. (b) The Lukan narrative in the book of Acts reports the progress of the early Christian mission not just to regions politically controlled by Gentiles but to Gentiles personally: non-Jews are converted to faith in Jesus Christ. Clearly, Acts 1:8 does not restrict the preaching of the gospel to Jews.

The interpretation of the phrase "end of the earth" in ethnic rather than geographical terms—the "end of the earth" would then be identical with "all nations" or "the Gentiles"[252]—is equally implausible.

The phrase "the ends of the earth" (τὰ ἔσχατα τῆς γῆς, *ta eschata tēs gēs*), formulated with the plural *eschata* ("ends"), designates the farthest regions of the earth—"for example, the Arctic on the North, India on the East, Ethiopia on the South and Spain on the West."[253] The following details are relevant.[254]

a. The western border of the known world in the Roman period was Gaul or Germania on the Atlantic Ocean as well as Britannia, which Emperor Claudius had annexed in A.D. 43, or, further south, Spain and particularly the city of

[250]For the arguments that follow above see Ellis 1991, 279, 281 (ET, 125-26, 128).
[251]Ellis 1991, 281 (ET, 128).
[252]Huffard 1991, 6.
[253]Ellis 1991, 279-80 (ET, 126), with reference to Strabo 1.1.6; 1.2.31; 2.3.5; 2.4.2; Philostratus, *Vit. Apoll.* 6.1.1; Philo, *Cher.* 99; *Somn.* 1.134; *Migr.* 181. See Romm 1992, 11-41.
[254]See Unnik 1966; Best 1984, 3; Ellis 1991, 280-81 (ET, 126-28); Romm 1992, 11-41.

Gades/Gadeira west of the Strait of Gibraltar. Strabo describes Gades as a city "at the end of the earth."[255] This region with the "promontory of Iberia which they call the Sacred Cape is the most westerly point of the inhabited world." Diodorus Siculus located Gades also "at the end of the inhabited world."[256] Strabo further describes the "Islands of the Blest" (the Canary Islands) as lying "to the westward of the most western Maurusia [Morocco]."[257]

b. The northern border was the Arctic (known to geographers of the first century) or, in terms of inhabited regions, Scythia. The Scythians were a people "at the end of the earth," according to the Roman poet Propertius (ca. 50-5 B.C.), in a comment on the city of Borysthenes, which Greek colonists had founded on the northwestern coast of the Black Sea.[258] Both the Greeks and the Romans used the term "Scythia" as a designation for the regions to the north and the east of their sphere of control: the region from the river Danube to the river Don, as far as the Caucasus Mountains to the Volga River. Scythia was regarded as a desolate steppe inhabited by nomadic cattle breeders and archers, savage and uncivilized people who practiced blinding, scalping, flaying, tattooing and the drinking of wine unmixed with water.[259]

c. The southern "end of the world" was Ethiopia. Homer (Od. 1.23) described the Ethiopians as "the farthermost of men" (ἔσχατοι ἀνδρῶν, eschatoi andrōn), living "at the ends of the earth on the banks of Oceanus" (ἐπὶ τῷ ὠκεανῷ ἔσχατοι, epi tō ōkeanō eschatoi [in Strabo 1.1.6]). Herodotus (3.25) mentions an army that marched to Ethiopia "to the ends of the earth" (τὰ ἔσχατα γῆς, ta eschata gēs).

d. The eastern "border" of the earth was thought to be beyond India and the Seres, the silk people (China). Procopius, writing in the sixth century, refers to Roman soldiers posted on the eastern border of Persia and India as living "at the ends of the inhabited world."[260]

In Acts 1:8 Luke formulates not with the plural ("ends of the earth," as most English versions translate) but with the singular, "the end of the earth." Does this mean that he thinks specifically of Spain, after all?[261]

---

[255]Strabo 3.1.8: ἐσχάτη τῆς γῆς; cf. 1.2.31; the quotation that follows above, 2.5.14: δυσμικώτατον τῆς οἰκουμένης; cf. 3.1.4. Further evidence is Lucanus, Pharsalia 3.454. See Ellis 1991; Riesner 1994, 272.

[256]Diodoros Siculus 25.10.1: τὰ ἔσχατα τῆς οἰκουμένης. For further evidence see Juvenal, Sat. 10.1-2; Silius, Punica 17.637.

[257]Strabo 1.1.5: πρὸ τῆς Μαυρουσίας εἰσιτῆς ἐσχάτης πρὸς δύσιν.

[258]Propertius 2.7.18: gloria ad hibernos lata Borysthenidas.

[259]See P. Kretschmer, PW 2.A (1921): 923-42; C. Danoff, KP 5:241-42; D. C. Braund, OCD 1374-75; Renate Rolle, Die Welt der Skythen (Lucerne: Bucher, 1980; ET, The World of the Scythians [Berkeley: University of California Press, 1989]); Heinen 2001.

[260]Procopius, De bellis 2.3.52: ταῖς τῆς οἰκουμένης ἐσχάταις; cf. 6.30.9. On contacts with India see §16.2 in the present work.

[261]Thus Unnik 1966; Ellis 1991, 282-86.

Earle Ellis suggests that the reference to the "end [sg.] of the earth" in Acts 1:8b refers to Spain, where Paul plans to engage in missionary work. He advances the following arguments. (*i*) Terms such as "end of the earth" and "limits of the West" are frequently used for Spain.[262] (*ii*) If Luke wanted to refer to a worldwide mission extending as far as the border regions of the earth, he could have done so with the plural ἐσχάτων (*eschatōn*) or ἐσχάτους (*eschatous*) without losing the allusion to Is 49:6 (especially at Acts 13:47). (*iii*) The total plan of the book of Acts supports a reference to Spain, particularly to Gades, in view of the phrase "the limits of the West" (τὸ τέρμα τῆς δύσεως) in *1 Clem.* 5:7, referring to the apostle Paul's mission to Spain, presupposing his release from his imprisonment in Rome (see §27.4 in the present work). These arguments are not fully convincing. (*i*) The directive of Acts 1:8 is not given to Paul but to the Twelve. And the allusion to Is 49:6 in Acts 13:47 applies the Isaiah passage not just to the mission of Paul but to the mission of Paul and Barnabas, who are both mentioned explicitly in Acts 13:46. (*ii*) The singular ἐσχάτου (*eschatou*), which corresponds to the wording of Is 49:6, refers already in the Isaiah passage to a worldwide mission that reaches the Gentiles. The argument that Luke would have used the plural if he truly wanted to emphasize a mission to the bounds of the earth universally is unpersuasive. In the context of the allusion to Is 46:6 we are not forced to interpret the singular *eschatou* in terms of a singular goal of the mission of the disciples: Luke defines the mission of the disciples as a mission to the nations.[263] (*iii*) The "total plan" of the book of Acts does not mention Spain at all. If it is wrong, on account of the structure of Acts, to identify the "end of the earth" with the city of Rome, it is equally wrong to import Paul's plans to visit Spain from Rom 15:23-25, 28 to the commission in Acts 1:8. I agree that Luke, as Paul's companion, knew of the apostle's plans to go to Spain. To argue, however, that Luke omits a reference to a "mission in Gades" because this mission had not been completed by the time Luke wrote Acts[264] implies a hypothesis concerning the time of composition of the book of Acts that must remain speculative. And it is an argument that fails to convince: if Paul's mission to Spain was ongoing when Luke completed the book of Acts, then a reference to this mission would have been indeed an ideal climax and a fitting conclusion for his account of the missionary work of the early church. And if Luke wrote the book of Acts after the completion of Paul's mission to Spain, we would expect a reference to this mission even more. It is possible, as Ellis argues, that Luke did not mention the mission to Spain because he did not want to draw attention to the fact of Paul's release from prison so as to protect Paul or the Roman officials who released him. But this explanation still does not explain why Luke is completely silent concerning missionary work in Spain: he is not afraid to state, in the last line of his book, that Paul proclaimed the kingdom of God and taught about the Lord Jesus Christ "with all boldness and without hindrance" (Acts 28:31).

The phrase "to the end(s) of the earth" in Acts 1:8 describes the geographical scope of the missionary assignment of the disciples: they will have fulfilled their commission only when they have penetrated to the borders of the earth. The mission of the disciples is world mission. Jesus directs his disciples to initiate an

---

[262]Josephus, *C. Ap.* 1.67; Tacitus, *Hist.* 4.3; Strabo 1.2.31; 1.4.6; 2.1.1; 2.4.3-4; 3.1.2; 3.5.5; Philostratus, *Vit. Apoll.* 5.4; 4.47; Pliny, *Nat.* 3.1.3-7; Livy 21.43.13; 23.5.11.

[263]See Schneider, *Apg,* 1:203 with n. 41; Pesch, *Apg,* 1:70; Zmijewski, *Apg,* 59; Best 1984; E. Schnabel, *ThBLNT* 1:32.

[264]Ellis 1991, 284 (ET, 130-31); for the comments that follow above see ibid.

international and universal mission that begins in Jerusalem, reaches the surrounding regions of Judea (including Galilee) and Samaria, and then extends as
far as the border regions of the earth. In §16.2 I will discuss more fully these
geographical conceptions, which most probably were linked with this directive
of Jesus in the minds and the planning of the disciples.

Mk 13:10; 14:9

The Gospel of Mark does not record an explicit missionary commission. Mark
left several signals in the text, however, that challenge Christians who read his
book to see that Jesus wanted the Gentile mission. In his account of Jesus' prophetic action in the temple, Mark alone recounts that Jesus explained his action
with reference to Is 56:7, reclaiming the temple as a "house of prayer for all nations" (Mk 11:17). It is unclear whether Mark intended the tearing of the curtain
in the temple at the time of Jesus' death (Mk 15:38) to symbolize the opening
of the worship of Yahweh to Gentiles.[265] On the cross Jesus laments his abandonment by God with words from Ps 22:2: "My God, my God, why have you
forsaken me?" (Mk 15:34). Mark (and his readers) may have had in mind the
entirety of Ps 22, in which the sufferer passes through death to life (Ps 22:15-
26), and in which the psalmist speaks of the worship of God by the "ends of
the earth" and of the proclamation of the rescue that God provided (Ps 22:27-
31). If the quotation of Ps 22:2 indeed was meant to remind the readers of the
entire contents of that psalm, then Mark might have wanted to emphasize that
the suffering of Jesus did not signify the end of all hope but the beginning of
the hope for salvation among the nations.[266] The first person who makes a positive statement about Jesus after the crucifixion is a Gentile (Mk 15:39).

Two passages in the Gospel of Mark refer explicitly to a Gentile mission (Mk
13:10; 14:9).

Mk 13:10: "And the good news must first be proclaimed to all nations."

Mk 14:9: "Truly I tell you, wherever the good news is proclaimed in the whole world,
what she has done will be told in remembrance of her."

In Mk 13:10 the term "must" (δεῖ, dei) implies a necessity that God placed upon
the community of Jesus' followers:[267] in the time before the end, the good news
that Jesus had preached will be preached to all nations (i.e., to Gentiles). The
statement in Mk 14:9 announces a universal ministry of Jesus' followers, whose
message of the good news will include a reference to Jesus' anointing by a
woman before the crucifixion. Joachim Jeremias argues that both passages do

---

[265]Thus Best 1984, 8.
[266]See T. Schmidt 1994.
[267]Best 1984, 8.

not refer to human proclamation but "to an apocalyptic event, namely, the angelic proclamation of God's final act."[268] This interpretation is unconvincing. The disciples who had been called to be trained as fishers of people (Mk 1:17) are portrayed here as engaged in a worldwide ministry of preaching the good news.

Some scholars suggest that the ending of Mark's Gospel can be read as a "missionary commission." According to the most reliable Greek manuscripts, the Gospel ends with Mk 16:8.

Mk 16:6-8: "But he said to them, 'Do not be alarmed; you are looking for Jesus of Nazareth, who was crucified. He has been raised; he is not here. Look, there is the place they laid him. [7]But go, tell his disciples and Peter that he is going ahead of you to Galilee; there you will see him, just as he told you.' [8]So they went out and fled from the tomb, for terror and amazement had seized them; and they said nothing to anyone, for they were afraid."

An investigation of the motifs that are related in Mk 16:8 as the reaction of the women[269] shows that "terror" or "fear" and "amazement" often are portrayed in Mark's Gospel in a positive sense, as awe after a miracle (Mk 4:41; 9:6; cf. 5:15, 33; 6:19-20; 10:32) and as amazement after exorcisms (Mk 2:12; 5:42). The readers can identify with the likable women: terror and fear are legitimate reactions to the manifestation of divine power. At the same time Mark challenges his Christian readers to reflect on their own reaction to the news of Jesus' resurrection: are they silent, like the women, or do they leave the fear behind and participate in the proclamation of the resurrection of the Messiah? If this is indeed a plausible interpretation of the ending of Mark's Gospel, then it could be described as a rhetorical missionary commission.

The shorter ending of Mark's Gospel, inserted after Mk 16:8,[270] provides a brief account of the activities of the woman and concludes with an implied missionary commission of the disciples by Jesus.

"But all that they had been told they reported briefly to those with Peter. But after these things, even Jesus himself sent out by means of them, from east to west, the sacred and imperishable proclamation of eternal salvation. Amen."

This supplement, dated probably between A.D. 100 and 150,[271] emphasizes the importance of Peter and the people around him for the universal proclamation of Jesus Christ.[272] This text is authentic, but it is a later compilation meant to pro-

---

[268]Jeremias 1956, 20 (ET, 23); see also Kilpatrick 1955.
[269]For the observations that follow above see Boomershine 1981, esp. 228-30, 237-38.
[270]Mk 16:8 with the shorter ending is attested by MSS L Ψ 083 099 274^mg 579 *l* 1602 k sy^hmg sa^mss bo^ms aeth^mss. The translation that follows above is from Evans, *Mk*, 544.
[271]Aland 1979, 264-66, contra Theodor Zahn, who dated the shorter ending to the beginning of the fourth century. The literature on the endings of the Gospel of Mark is immense; see recently Evans, *Mk*, 540-43.
[272]T. Heckel 1999, 280.

vide Mark's Gospel with an ending akin to the endings of Matthew's and Luke's Gospels, although it does reflect missionary concerns in the first half of the second century.

The longer ending, Mk 16:9-20, is a text that, according to Irenaeus, formed the ending of Mark's Gospel since around at least A.D. 180. It contains an explicit missionary commission:

Mk 16:15: "Go into all the world and proclaim the good news to the whole creation" (πορευθέντες εἰς τὸν κόσμον ἅπαντα κηρύξατε τὸ εὐαγγέλιον πάσῃ τῇ κτίσει).

This text, although not part of the original Gospel of Mark, is based on elements from Mt 28:16-20 and possibly from the theme of the book of Acts, presented in an abbreviated and summarized version.[273]

John 20:21

The missionary commission in the Gospel of John is the least detailed of the commissions but is perhaps the most striking directive from a theological point of view:

Jn 20:21: "Peace be with you. As the Father has sent me, so I send you."

In regard to the authenticity of this commission, the following similarities between Jn 20:21 and Lk 24:36-37 should be noted.[274] (1) Jesus shows his wounds (Jn 20:22; Lk 24:39). (2) Both passages mention the Holy Spirit (Jn 20:22; Lk 24:49). (3) Jesus refers to sin (Jn 20:24; Lk 24:47). Rudolf Schnackenburg concludes that "the connection with the Synoptic tradition, particularly with the missionary commission in Mt 28:18-20 and with the word of authority in Mt 18:18 (cf. 16:19)" is unmistakable.[275] The argument is correct, at least on a linguistic level, that the sending "into the world" in Jn 17:18 cannot simply be identified with the sending to the "nations" in Mt 28:19, but must be understood in a "qualitative" sense as a sending into the realm that is distant from God. One should not overlook the fact, however, that the pagan nations constitute "the realm distant from God" par excellence.

Jn 20:21 lacks a reference to the geographical scope of the disciples' mission. The universalistic perspective of the Fourth Gospel suggests that the author and his readers thought in terms of Jews and Gentiles as the target of the sending of the disciples.[276] Jesus' statement asserts the following.

1. The sending of the disciples and of the community of Jesus' followers takes place in the context of peace, and it proclaims and offers peace. Jesus had

---

[273]Evans, *Mk*, 550; T. Heckel 1999, 283; Kelhoffer 2000, 97-101, 123-50.
[274]Best (1984, 5-6), who concludes that these two commissions shared a common tradition.
[275]Schnackenburg 1984, 61; for the remark that follows above see ibid., 62.
[276]Best 1984, 6. Olsson (1986-87, 185-88) thinks that the Johannine mission model is directed inwardly. Reinbold (2000, 274, 297) sees no missionary motif at all. Both positions are unconvincing.

already greeted the disciples with the greeting of peace (Jn 20:19); the repetition of the *shalom* blessing in Jn 20:21a emphasizes the meaning of the term "peace." Jesus had passed "his peace" to the disciples before his death (Jn 14:27): on the day of his resurrection he confirmed that he possesses peace and passes it on to his disciples, who had been hiding in fear during the last days. The peace that Jesus gives is an important foundation for the mission of the disciples, a mission that demonstrates and confirms the reliability of life with Jesus Christ in the midst of political uncertainty, social insecurity and personal vulnerabilities. The message of the disciples is about peace: about the restoration of peace with God through Jesus' death on the cross, about the atonement and forgiveness of sins, about the reconciliation of rebellious humankind with God.

2. The disciples are the envoys of Jesus, in whom God reveals himself to the world. Statements such as "Whoever sees me sees him who sent me" (Jn 12:45), and "No one comes to the Father except through me" (Jn 14:6), which were valid for Jesus, are not valid for the disciples: they are given the task of making God and his Messiah visible and of showing people the way to God the Father and his Son. The content of the disciples' mission is determined by the content of Jesus' mission. Jesus revealed the Father when he, like a good shepherd, risked his life for the world and eventually laid down his life (Jn 10:11, 15) so that the world might be "sanctified in the truth" that is Jesus himself (Jn 17:17); thus the disciples are directed, as envoys whom Jesus sends into the world (Jn 17:18), to help people find forgiveness for their sins and obtain salvation and eternal life (Jn 3:16).[277] The sending of the disciples is not an end in itself, and it does not serve the promotion of their own image: they are signposts to the Son and to the Father, and thus signposts to salvation and eternal life. Mission thus defined obligates the disciples to humility in their self-image, to holiness in their behavior, and to sacrificial love in their missionary work. By virtue of being sent by Jesus, the disciples are co-workers of God the Father: they do the work of the Son (Jn 13:12-14), by whose ministry all of God's creatures are to believe in God and receive salvation (Jn 6:29). Jesus was sent by God in order to do the "work" that the Father had entrusted to him, and Jesus faithfully carried out this work, with unreserved engagement and unselfish willingness to suffer, until it was "finished" in his death. And it is this work that the disciples are commissioned to continue.

3. The sending of the disciples as envoys and representatives of Jesus, God's own representative and envoy, confers on the disciples and their message the authority of the Son, who spoke and acted with the authority of the Father.[278]

---

[277]See Wilckens, *Joh,* 313. On Jesus as the eschatological Davidic messianic shepherd in the Gospel of John see Köstenberger 2002.

[278]Schnackenburg, *Joh,* 3:384-85 (ET, 3:324); for remark that follows above see ibid., 324; see also Köstenberger and O'Brien 2001, 222.

Since the sending by the Father continues (perfect tense, ἀπέσταλκεν), the disciples are given a share in the mission of Jesus.

4. The disciples sent by Jesus are missionaries who are enabled by God: they receive the Spirit of God (Jn 20:22). The Spirit empowers them to serve in a hostile world (Jn 15:25-26), and the Spirit guarantees the effectiveness of their mission (Jn 16:8-11).[279]

5. John does not specify the sending in Jn 20:21 in terms of the addressees. The target of the mission of the disciples can be supplied, however, from Jn 17:18: "As you have sent me into the world, so I have sent them into the world." The disciples are sent to the "world" (κόσμος, kosmos), meaning all human beings who are distant from and antagonistic toward God, despite the fact that the disciples will encounter hatred (Jn 17:14).[280] This "world" includes "Greeks," some of whom wanted to see Jesus during a Feast of Passover in Jerusalem (Jn 12:20-21).

6. John does not limit Jesus' commission to the disciples who are present. He never calls them "apostles" in the narrow sense of the word. According to Rudolf Schnackenburg, "they represent for him the entire community of believers."[281]

Conclusion

The four missionary commissions are very different. Rather than being a problem, this indicates that Matthew, Mark, Luke and John did not "create" a "Great Commission" as a result of their personal ecclesiastical concerns: they recount, with specific emphases and concerns, the directive that Jesus gave to the disciples in terms of international missionary work in a universal scope.

Ernest Best argues that the early Christian tradition of a "revelation" of the Gentile mission cannot be authentic for four reasons. (1) This tradition is not mentioned in the encounter between Peter and Cornelius (Acts 10) or in Peter's explanation of his activities in Caesarea (Acts 11:1-18). (2) This tradition is not mentioned in connection with the apostolic council (Acts 15). (3) This tradition is not mentioned in connection with the discussions in Jerusalem reported in Gal 2:1-10; had there been a commission for international missionary work, it would not have been Paul and Peter who divided missionary spheres of work but rather Paul and the Twelve. (4) The Gospel of Mark does not seem to be aware of a missionary commission. This indicates that the tradition of such a commission must have arisen after these events. Since Eph 3:5 links the revelation of the mystery of the acceptance of converted Gentiles into the community of God's people with apostles and with prophets, this might indicate that a Christian prophet was responsible for the creation of a dominical missionary commission directing the Twelve to engage in missionary work among Gentiles.[282] These arguments, as persuasive as they might seem at first sight, do not convince. (1) It is always problematic if one has to rely on arguments from silence.

---

[279]See also Jn 14:16-17, 26; cf. Burge 1987, 199-204.
[280]See Schnackenburg, *Joh,* 3:385 (ET, 3:324).
[281]Schnackenburg, *Joh,* 3:385 (ET, 3:324).
[282]Best 1984, 28-29.

(2) The first two arguments are not cogent: the Gentile mission as such was not contested in either Acts 11:1-18 or in Acts 15. Luke's account in Acts 10:1—11:18 focuses, in a general sense, on the behavior of Jewish-Christian missionaries who stay in the homes and families of pagans, where they cannot follow the purity and food laws of the Torah. A second focus of Luke is the acceptance of Gentiles who have come to faith in Jesus, the crucified and risen Christ, into the community of God's people without their first having become Jews (the implication of circumcision). The account in Acts 15 focuses specifically and explicitly on the admission of Gentile Christians to the church without circumcision. In Jesus' missionary commission to the disciples neither the obedience of the missionary to the Torah nor the issue of the necessity or nonnecessity of circumcision for Gentile converts had been addressed. Jesus' missionary commission did not describe the modus operandi of the Gentile mission. This means that a reference to Jesus' missionary commission would not have advanced or solved the problems addressed in the discussion of Acts 11:1-18 and Acts 15. (3) The agreement between Paul and Peter according to Gal 2:1-10 will be discussed more fully later (§25.1). Suffice it to say at this point that Gal 2:1-10 must be interpreted in the context of a very early phase in the missionary work of the apostles, perhaps three or four years after Easter, at a time when the Twelve are based in Jerusalem and engage in missionary work from there and when they were confronted with the necessity of accepting a new and leading missionary to the Gentiles, the rabbi Saul/Paul from Tarsus, who had persecuted Christians, who did not belong to the followers of Jesus before Easter, who did not belong to the Jerusalem church, and who was involved in missionary work among Jews and particularly Gentiles since his dramatic conversion near Damascus. The leading apostles in Jerusalem agreed that they would impose no conditions on the missionary work of Paul and Barnabas, under which many Gentiles were converted. A reference to Jesus' missionary commission, again, would not have advanced the discussion during this missionary conference in Jerusalem.

There have been several attempts to reconstruct from the Gospels on the basis of literary-critical operations an "original" text of the missionary commission.[283] These efforts have not produced unified results and probably are unnecessary. It is quite possible that Jesus spoke repeatedly about the future missionary task of the disciples after the resurrection. It may be quite significant that the context of the missionary commissions in Matthew, Luke and John are different: (1) The geographical location and the time of the commissions are different: Mt 28:16 has the disciples in Galilee on "the mountain" at an unspecified time after the resurrection; Lk 24:36 and Jn 20:19 locate the disciples in Jerusalem and date the commission to the evening of the day of the resurrection. (2) The group that receives the commissions varies: Mt 28:16 speaks of the eleven disciples of Jesus; Lk 24:33, 36 speaks of the eleven disciples and of "their companions"; in Jn 20:19 there are ten disciples (without Thomas) and, in view of John's use of the term "disciple," a reference probably to all believers in Jesus.

Even though the four passages are very different, they display several fundamental similarities.[284] (1) The encounter with the risen Jesus Christ is an integral part of the missionary commission given to the disciples. The missionary message of the disciples focuses, not by accident, on the Risen One, who had been crucified but whom God had raised from the dead. (2) Jesus conveys to

---

[283]See Hubbard 1974, 101-22.
[284]See Best 1984, 6-7; Wilckens, *Joh,* 313.

his disciples after his resurrection a commission; he gives them an assignment. The disciples are envoys sent by Jesus the Messiah. They do not preach themselves or their interpretation of Torah but rather God's revelatory acts in and through Jesus. (3) Jesus sends the disciples to the nations, into the world, to the ends of the earth. The missionary work of the disciples includes pagans but does not exclude Jews. They are to begin to reach people with the message of salvation in Jesus Christ in Jerusalem and Judea, but they are directed to reach regions beyond Israel as well. (4) Jesus promises the disciples his continued presence, the presence of the Holy Spirit of God, empowering their mission with divine authority.

13

SUMMARY

The early Christian missionary work began in Galilee with Jesus' preaching and healing ministry. During his three years of public ministry Jesus could easily have visited the 175 towns and villages on his travels through Lower and Upper Galilee. It would have been difficult to find anyone among the approximately two hundred thousand people living in Galilee who had not heard about Jesus, and presumably there would not have been many people who had not personally encountered him during these three years. Most of the half a million Judeans would only have heard about Jesus, including many of the one hundred thousand inhabitants of Jerusalem. Jesus proclaimed the dawn of God's kingdom in synagogues, in private homes and in the open air, before pious audiences, and before "sinners" such as the tax collectors and their politically problematic and ethically unreliable friends. He had learned disputes with scribes, experts of the law, but he also had conversations with uneducated rural folk. He had contacts with members of the small upper class, even though he avoided the Galilean capitals of Sepphoris and Tiberias. But he concentrated his efforts on the unprivileged, the peasants and the fishermen, rural wage laborers and tenant farmers, day laborers and serfs, artisans and traders, beggars and prostitutes. Jesus sought encounters with men and with women, and he did not refuse to deal with children. He spoke before large crowds of people numbering in the thousands, and he had private conversations with individuals who came with questions or with whom he initiated contact. Jesus understood himself to have been sent by God to gather the "lost sheep of the house of Israel," thus establishing the reign of God, who had promised through the prophets to return to his people and grant salvation to those who would repent.

Jesus gathered disciples, notably the Twelve, to train them as "fishers of people." In symbolic representation of the twelve tribes of Israel, the people of God, Jesus initiates with the calling and commissioning of the Twelve the restoration of Israel that was expected for the last days. Jesus emphasized that this eschatological restoration is connected with himself laying down his life as a ransom for many (Mk 10:45) and with his resurrection. As he had come to call sinners

(Mt 9:13), to serve and sacrificially to devote his life for the benefit of others (Mk 10:45), to seek and to save the lost (Lk 19:10), to open the eyes of the blind (Jn 9:39), so the Twelve are called to emulate and to continue this mission now and in the future. Jesus introduced his disciples to this task in the course of his ministry in Galilee: he gave them a role in his ministry of preaching and healing, and he sent them out on a short tour through the towns and villages of Galilee with the assignment to preach the message of the dawn of God's reign, to heal the sick and to liberate people from evil spirits. The Twelve learned from Jesus and from their own experiences that many people accept the message of the arrival of the kingdom of God and his presence in Jesus and in his ministry. But they also learned that many people reject their message and oppose their ministry. They learned from Jesus and from their own experiences that many do not recognize the dawn of the new time of salvation, and therefore it is necessary for them to go, literally, to people, overcoming geographical distances and personal barriers as well as ethical and theological obstacles so that all people in the towns and villages of Galilee may hear of God's forgiving and healing love and be drawn into the presence of God's kingdom.

Jesus did not initiate contact with non-Jews, Gentiles, polytheists, but neither did he avoid such contacts at all costs. He healed pagans; he heard the request of polytheists to heal their relatives or their friends. The Gospel writers repeatedly mention the impact of Jesus' ministry on the non-Jewish regions surrounding Galilee. It is plausible to assume that among the sick who came or who were brought to Jesus were many polytheists: it was not far from Tyre or Sidon, from Gaulanitis or the cities of the Decapolis to reach Jesus, who was based in Capernaum and traveled throughout Galilee and sometimes into regions beyond. Still, contact with Gentiles was not a major focus of Jesus' ministry; the relevant comments of the Gospel writers are made in passing. However, Jesus taught on several occasions that the time has arrived in which the promises of the prophets who spoke of the nations finding salvation would be fulfilled. Jesus' action in the temple, announcing God's judgment on the temple and the dawn of the era of Gentiles worshiping Yahweh in Zion, and his announcement of the destruction of the temple point out that God's saving presence is no longer tied to the institutions and practices of Israel. Jesus taught that the message of the arrival of the kingdom of God, which seeks the lost and saves the sinner, would be preached among all nations before the end of the present age (Mk 13:10). And after his death and resurrection Jesus gave his disciples the commission to international and universal missionary work (Mt 28:18-20; Lk 24:47; Jn 20:21; Acts 1:8): they are directed to go to "all nations" (*panta ta ethnē* [Mt 28:19]), to "the ends of the earth" (*heōs eschatou tēs gēs* [Acts 1:8]).

The early Christian mission to Gentiles has its germinal roots in an assignment from Jesus. This truth, contested by much of critical scholarship, is supported by at least four facts. (1) Jesus anticipated that he would be rejected by the Jewish authorities, who essentially determined, by virtue of controlling the temple, what was theologically acceptable in Israel and what was not. It is more than plausible in this context that Jesus interpreted the Old Testament hopes and expectations concerning the gathering of the nations in Zion in terms of a mission of his disciples that would move from Jerusalem to the nations, offering them God's grace and mercy at the very places where they live. (2) Jesus expected that he would be killed and that he would be raised from the dead on the third day. It is only natural that he would have passed on his messianic mission to his disciples and co-workers, who would continue to preach his message. The view that Jesus expected the immediate, apocalyptic end of the world during his lifetime has no basis in the text of the Gospels. (3) Jesus' proclamation included the conviction that God's reign becomes a reality among his followers but does not yet encompass the entire world: besides the good seed leading to a full harvest, weeds are growing also. This duality of the kingdom of God and the kingdom of this world implies the necessity of a universal mission. (4) The Gentile mission as such was never a controversial issue in the early church. The debates that some New Testament documents record concerned only the status of converted Gentiles and the practical, everyday relationships between Jewish Christians and Gentile Christians. There is no evidence that the apostles in Jerusalem or the Jerusalem church at large ever discussed whether Gentiles should be actively approached with the message that was preached to Jewish audiences or whether it was advisable to wait for the nations coming to Jerusalem as a result of their own initiative, as promised by the prophets. The early Christian conviction that followers of Jesus should evangelize the problematic Samaritans, Ethiopians passing through the area, polytheists in Antioch, Rome and many other cities of the Roman Empire goes back to Jesus himself.

The hypothesis of Joachim Jeremias that was so influential in New Testament scholarship has proven untenable: (1) With his comment in Mt 23:15 Jesus did not reject contemporary Jewish missionary work among Gentiles but rather the Pharisees' blocking people from welcoming and accepting the dawn of God's reign, whose arrival he proclaimed and whose presence he demonstrated in his miracles of healing and liberation. (2) Jesus did not seek to initiate or establish intensive contacts with Gentiles, but neither did he restrict his ministry and its effects exclusively to Jews: he spoke with Gentiles directly, and he influenced many Gentiles indirectly who heard of him, both within and outside of Galilee. (3) Jesus gave his disciples the assignment to go to all nations and proclaim the good news of the arrival of God's reign among Gentiles, beginning in Jerusalem and stopping only at the ends of the earth.

Jesus' missionary commission to the disciples initiated a new phase in the history of God's people: the universal and international dimension of God's history with the world that Israel had expected for the last days. The promise of blessing that YHWH had given to Abraham for his descendants and for the "families of the earth" (Gen 12:1-3) is now fulfilled in the one "seed" through whom God's blessing is granted to the nations of the earth: through Jesus the Messiah, and through the disciples whom he called and commissioned. The universal and international mission of the followers of Jesus, a *novum* in the history of religions and in the history of thought, was initiated, inaugurated and established by Jesus of Nazareth.

PART III

BEGINNINGS

*The Mission of
the Apostles in Jerusalem*

14

THE APOSTLES AS ENVOYS OF
JESUS THE MESSIAH

The effective origins of the early Christian missionary activity lie in the Easter events, in the encounter of the disciples with the risen Christ, and in the events at Pentecost in A.D. 30. I speak of *effective* origins because I link the *historical origins* of the missionary work of the early church with the calling of the twelve disciples as "fishers of people" (Mk 1:17) and the sending of the disciples on a short-term tour through the towns and villages of Galilee (Mt 10:1-15). It is indeed appropriate to view the Easter events as a "decisive new start"[1] because the encounter with the risen Jesus Christ granted the disciples "in a very direct sense justification and reconciliation," as the repeated "Peace be with you" shows, and as it convinced them "that the crucified and risen Christ is the one mediator and reconciler whom God has vindicated over against his oppressors, making him 'Lord and Messiah' (Acts 2:36)." In the encounter with the risen Lord, who forgave their failure and opened their eyes regarding the true nature of his messianic dignity, the earlier commission for the disciples[2] was renewed: they are envoys of the crucified and risen Messiah, who will return for the last judgment.

14.1 The Commission by the Risen Christ
Luke reports the confirmation of the disciples' missionary commission in Acts 1:4-8 in the context of his account of the events at Pentecost (Acts 2), specifying Jesus' assignment in terms of nature and content and of time and space. I analyzed the missionary commission of Acts 1:8 in §12.3. What remains to be discussed is the context of the missionary commission in the setting of the historical beginnings of the community of Jesus' followers in Jerusalem. Luke makes several important observations.

---

[1]Stuhlmacher 1981, 112; the quotation that follows above, ibid., 113. For a rigorous exposition of Jesus' resurrection as an historical event see now N. T. Wright 2003.
[2]Paul speaks of ἀπόστολοι πάντες in 1 Cor 15:7.

1. Jerusalem is the capital of Israel, the center of the people of God, the goal and finish of Jesus' ministry, the place where God poured out the promised Holy Spirit, the location of the first community of followers of Jesus after Easter.[3] It would have been plausible to choose Galilee, perhaps Capernaum, as the site of the first community of Jesus' followers: all the leading disciples were Galileans, the last encounters with the risen Christ had taken place in Galilee (Jn 21:1-14; Mt 28:16-17), and Jerusalem was the place of Jesus' execution and a city controlled by the powerful enemies of the movement initiated by Jesus. However, Peter and the other men and women who had traveled and worked with Jesus over the preceding three years stayed in Jerusalem.[4] And Jerusalem was not only the scene of the future salvation of the eschaton but also the place of the moment of truth, the place of trials and persecution.[5] The disciples therefore were directed not to leave Jerusalem but to begin with their testimony of the good news of Jesus Christ right there in the center of Israel's faith and practice. Adolf Schlatter observes that "without the Jerusalem church there would never have been a church anywhere. . . . Jesus did not tell them to leave Jerusalem, which remained unrepentant and was heading toward judgment; rather, when he called them to be his witnesses and when he placed on them the obligation to speak and act in his name, he bound them first with solemn obligation to Jerusalem in order that his message might proceed from here to the nations."[6] The church (*ekklēsia*) of the followers of Jesus in Jerusalem, initially under the leadership of the Twelve, understood itself as the people of God of the last days.

Luke and Paul use the term ἐκκλησία (*ekklēsia*) as a designation both for the self-understanding of the first followers of Jesus and for the assemblies of the early Christians.[7] The expression *ekklēsia tou theou,* "assembly or congregation or church of God" (Gal 1:13; 1 Cor 15:9; Phil 3:6), is of fundamental importance.[8] For the Greco-Roman world the term *ekklēsia* designated the regularly summoned legislative body, the "assembly" of the free men of the city (*polis*) who were eligible to vote. The "relevant component" of the term *ekklēsia* for the young movement of believers in Jesus Christ tied in with this usage: *ekklēsia* is "where people assemble in order to be 'Ekklesia.'" The term thus describes the

---

[3]Pesch, *Apg,* 1:66.

[4]See Stuhlmacher 1989, 146-45.

[5]Stuhlmacher 1981, 113.

[6]Schlatter, *Lk,* 452.

[7]Acts 5:11; 7:38; 8:1, 3; 9:31; 11:22, 26; 12:1, 5; 13:1; 14:23, 27; 15:3, 4, 22, 41; 16:5; 18:22; 19:32, 39, 40; 20:17, 28; Rom 16:1, 4, 5, 16, 23; 1 Cor 1:2; 4:17; 6:4; 7:17; 10:32; 11:16, 18, 22; 12:28; 14:4, 5, 12, 19, 23, 28, 33, 34, 35; 15:9; 16:1, 19, 19; and 9 times in 2 Corinthians, 3 in Galatians, 9 in Ephesians, 2 in Philippians, 4 in Colossians, 4 in 1-2 Thessalonians, 3 in 1 Timothy, 1 in Philemon.

[8]See also 1 Cor 1:2; 10:32; 11:16, 22; 2 Cor 1:1; 1 Thess 2:14; 2 Thess 1:4; 1 Tim 3:5, 15; Acts 20:28. For the analysis that follows above see Kraus 1999, 33-38. See also BDAG 303-4; J. Roloff, *EWNT* 1:998-1011 (*EDNT* 1:410-15); Merklein 1987, 296-318; Roloff 1993, 83-85; Kraus 1996, 122-30; Seccombe 1998. The quotations that follow above are from Kraus 1999, 33; BDAG 303.

assembly of Christians for purposes of "worship and discussion of matters of concern to the community." The connection of the term, as understood in the early church, with the Old Testament and thus with salvation-history is disputed. Emil Schürer suggests that the term *ekklēsia* represents the "ideal" self-understanding of Jews, while the term *synagōgē* expresses the empirical reality of the Jewish communities. This explanation was influential for a long time but finds little support today, as it perhaps is too reminiscent of Luther's distinction between the visible and the invisible church (*ecclesia visibilis* and *ecclesia invisibilis*). Leonhard Rost suggests that the term *ekklēsia* was taken over from the Septuagint, where it translates the Hebrew *qāhal,* a term that designates the assembly of Israel. This explanation is widely accepted but faces at least three problems. First, the Septuagint uses the term *synagōgē* as designation for the "congregation" or "assembly" of Israel more frequently than the term *ekklēsia*. Second, the expression *qĕhal 'ēl* is translated in the Septuagint not as *ekklēsia theou* ("assembly of God") but as *ekklēsia kyriou* ("assembly of the Lord"). Third, the New Testament never links the term *ekklēsia* with a quotation from or an allusion to the Old Testament. Considering these facts, several scholars suggest that the expression *ekklēsia tou theou,* as used in the earliest Christian formulations, should be understood in connection with apocalyptic texts in which *qĕhal 'ēl* describes the "eschatological company of God" (cf. 1QM IV, 10; 1QSa I, 25).[9] Against this background, the term *ekklēsia* designates "the people among whom God's reign has already made powerful inroads. The conditions of admission to the kingdom of God (1 Cor 6:9-10) and to the 'Ekklesia' (1 Cor 5:11) are thus identical."[10] The early church in Jerusalem understood itself as the "initial place of the eschatological gathering of Israel that was beginning to take place, and thus as 'the eschatological company of God.'"

2. The connection of Acts 1:8 with the missionary program of Isaiah, indicated by the phrase "to the end(s) of the earth" (ἕως ἐσχάτου τῆς γῆς, *heōs eschatou tēs gēs* [cf. Is 49:6]), emphasizes a three-phase plan besides the geographical references: the beginning of the time of salvation for Jerusalem, the restoration of Israel, and the inclusion of the Gentile nations in the people of God.[11] The missionary commission in Acts 1:8 is the second part of Jesus' answer to the question of the disciples who wanted to know when the kingdom would be restored to Israel (Acts 1:6). Jesus first rejects speculations about times and periods as futile because only God the Father knows the chronological progress of salvation history (Acts 1:7). He points out, secondly, that the restoration of Israel expected for the last days is now beginning in and through their missionary activity starting in Jerusalem and extending unto the ends of the earth (Acts 1:8) and thus fulfilling the expectation of the conversion of the nations.

3. The life of the disciples stands not under the authority of their own personal ideas and hopes: the determination of time with its periods and epochs, and thus the determination of the duration of the last days that have begun and the duration of their missionary work, is the prerogative of the Father, who guides history as Lord of history according to his plan. Rudolf Pesch comments

---

[9]See K. Stendahl, *RGG* 3:1298-99; Stuhlmacher 1965, 210-12; Roloff, *EWNT* 1:1000 (*EDNT* 1:411).

[10]Kraus 1999, 34; the quotation that follows above, ibid., 36; cf. Seccombe 1998, 357-58.

[11]See recently Pao 2000, 91-95.

that "no phase of the history of the church and of its missionary work is work planned by the apostles, but is God's assignment on the basis of God's power."[12] Speculations about the periods of salvation history must not occupy their reflection, life and work. Their central concern must be empowerment for their missionary task: they are to make sure that salvation is taken to all nations.

Rudolf Pesch observes that this text "does not confirm the view that Luke regarded the promised Spirit who was poured out at Pentecost as the 'substitute' for the expectation of an imminent parousia, nor does it confirm the view that he 'decisively renounced all expectation of an imminent end.' Part of Luke's theological achievement is precisely the fact that he linked the expectation of the parousia as a 'constant expectation' with the review (and prospect) of the history of missionary work and that he emphasizes the imminent expectation as constitutive reality of Christian existence."[13] Philipp Vielhauer argues that Luke's thinking was noneschatological, as not only the content but also the very existence of the book of Acts supposedly demonstrates.[14] This view does not agree with the facts: note, for example, that Mark wrote a Gospel despite an intensive expectation of an imminent parousia,[15] and that Paul, while speaking about the possibility of the return of Jesus in the near future (1 Thess 4:13—5:3), pursued at the same time a missionary program that included short-, medium- and long-term strategies.

4. The apostles are assured that their missionary commission corresponds both to sacred Scripture and to divine promise: the work that they will do by order of Jesus the Messiah and in the power of the Spirit is the work of God himself.[16] The promise of the Spirit in Lk 24:47-49 and in Acts 1:4-5, 8 assures the readers of the book of Acts "that the disciples fully understand the significance of the events which are about to take place, and so will be effective guarantors of the 'witness' which they are about to give."[17] These two texts describe the Spirit primarily as prophetic empowering for witness of God's acts in and through Jesus Christ: "You will receive power when the Holy Spirit has come upon you; and you will be my witnesses" (Acts 1:8a).[18] The continuation of the book of Acts shows that the function of the "Spirit of prophecy," who was promised by the prophet Joel and whom the disciples received, is not limited to empowerment for witness. Rather, the Spirit gives them insight into and orientation for questions that arise in the context of their leadership in the ekklēsia (Acts 5:3, 9; 15:28). The work of the Holy Spirit is a tangible reality not just in the ministry of the Twelve: it is a reality that also determines the

---

[12]Pesch, Apg, 1:68-69.
[13]Pesch, Apg, 1:70, with quotation of Conzelmann, Apg, 26-27 (ET, 6-7), and Haenchen, Apg, 150 (ET, 143).
[14]Vielhauer 1950, 26; cf. Conzelmann 1962, 6 (ET, 14); Haenchen, Apg, 105-6 (ET, 94-96); S. Wilson 1973, 77.
[15]Franklin 1975, 26; Maddox 1982, 131-32.
[16]Pesch, Apg, 1:69.
[17]Turner 1996a, 342.
[18]Menzies 1991, 198-204; Mainville 1991, 141-54; Turner 1996a, 343-44.

ministry and the life of other Christians and missionaries.[19]

5. The disciples are envoys, *apostoloi,* sent by Jesus (Acts 1:2, 25-26). The meaning of this term and its significance for the early Christian *apostolos* is elucidated in Acts 1:4-8: Jesus the crucified and risen Messiah is the one who sends and commissions; the disciples proclaim his message as his representatives; the authority of the disciples is delegated authority, with the decisive and final authority belonging to Jesus the Son and God the Father; the disciples will act on their own but always as Jesus' representatives. As envoys, they are "witnesses" of Jesus (Acts 1:8), specifically of his life, death and resurrection (Acts 1:21-22).

14.2 The Reconstitution of the Twelve

Luke reports the election of a disciple replacing Judas Iscariot in the weeks between Easter and Pentecost (Acts 1:15-26). The reason that is given for this election demonstrates the fundamental significance of the Twelve for the identity, development and missionary work of the church that confesses faith in Jesus the crucified and risen Messiah. Peter, as spokesman of the Twelve and the other followers of Jesus who are present, lays out specific conditions for the man who would replace Judas (Acts 1:21-22).

Acts 1:21-22: "So one of the men who have accompanied us during all the time that the Lord Jesus went in and out among us, [22]beginning from the baptism of John until the day when he was taken up from us—one of these must [δεῖ] become a witness with us to his resurrection [μάρτυρα τῆς ἀναστάσεως αὐτοῦ σὺν ἡμῖν]."

Two men who fulfilled these conditions stepped forward, willing to be included in the circle of the Twelve. They both knew Jesus from the beginning of his ministry, they had come to faith in the reality and the effectiveness of God's reign in Jesus and in his ministry of healing and liberation, and they had seen seen him after his crucifixion and resurrection. The two candidates were Joseph-Barsabbas, who was also called Justus, and Matthias, who eventually was chosen by the casting of lots. Both men were willing to be witnesses of Jesus and to "catch people" together with the Twelve. At least the following elements of this event are important for the early Christian missionary work.

1. The continuation of history and the message of Jesus is determined by divine "necessity" and is thus the result of the work and the will of God.[20] Insight into this divine necessity is not the private viewpoint of Peter but evidently the result of intensive reflection on relevant passages of sacred Scripture in which the Holy Spirit speaks (Acts 1:16): Peter quotes Ps 69:26; 109:8 to explain the fate of Judas (Acts 1:20). Peter does not act unilaterally but fulfills a directive

---

[19]Acts 6:3, 5; 9:31; 11:24, 28; 13:52; 15:28; 20:23, 28; 21:4, 11; cf. Turner 1996a, 344, 349, 401-18, arguing against Menzies 1991, passim, esp. 210.

[20]See Reasoner (1999), who regards "divine necessity" as the theme of the Book of Acts.

given by the Holy Spirit to David. The casting of lots ascertains that it is God himself who chooses the twelfth apostle.

2. The reconstitution of the circle of the Twelve after Judas's exit is not motivated by organizational requirements: such issues become relevant only later in connection with the problem of caring for the widows in the church (Acts 6:1-7). The motivation for the election of a twelfth disciple is linked with the authority of the apostles appointed by Jesus and in the symbolic significance of the number "twelve." The early church claims to represent the eschatological gathering of all Israel by reconstituting the circle of the Twelve as the beginning of the restoration of Israel.[21] Many scholars interpret the circle of the Twelve as "the eschatological, true Israel, witnesses before the entire people of Israel gathered together in Jerusalem for Pentecost, and indirectly before all nations."[22] This is correct, but it is only hinted at in the opening chapter of the book of Acts. Luke establishes a more direct and explicit link with Jesus and his resurrection, mentioned twice (Acts 1:17, 21-22): there must be twelve witnesses because Jesus had called and commissioned twelve disciples (Acts 1:13; cf. Lk 6:12-16). Luke describes the Twelve as witnesses of Jesus' life and ministry, called and commissioned by Jesus himself. They are witnesses of his death and resurrection and are sent by Jesus to the ends of the world. The symbolic significance of the Twelve, pointing to the inaugurated restoration of Israel, becomes evident in the qualifications required of candidates to replace Judas Iscariot: these are not national criteria connected with the twelve tribes of Israel, but criteria exclusively linked with Jesus.[23]

3. A central task of the Twelve is to witness to Jesus' resurrection. Jesus sends them from Jerusalem to the ends of the earth as his "witnesses" (Acts 1:8), and Matthias is chosen as the twelfth "witness of the resurrection" (Acts 1:22). The modern meaning of "witness" is more comprehensive than that of the Greek terms μάρτυς (martys) and μαρτυρία (martyria) in the book of Acts:[24] Luke uses the term "witness" nearly always for the Twelve,[25] sometimes for Paul.[26] The Twelve, and Paul on the road to Damascus, have seen the risen Jesus and thus are able to testify, as (eye)witnesses, to the truth of the message of Jesus as the crucified and risen Messiah.

4. The leaders of the early church were highly conscious of the missionary

[21]See Pesch, *Apg,* 1:91; Clark 1998, 170-71; see also Ravens 1996; Seccombe 1998.
[22]Pesch, *Apg,* 1:91.
[23]See Pao 2000, 126-27.
[24]See R. P. Casey, "μάρτυς," in *Begs.* 1.5:30-37; H. Strathmann, *ThWNT* 4:477-520 (*TDNT* 4:474-512); J. Beutler, *EWNT* 2:958-73 (*EDNT* 2:389-95); Brox 1961; Nellessen 1967; Trites 1977; Barrett 1994b; see particularly Bolt 1998, which I follow for the remarks that follow above.
[25]Lk 24:48; Acts 1:8, 22; 2:32; 3:15; 5:32; 10:39, 41; 13:31.
[26]Acts 22:15; 26:16; cf. 22:18; 23:11.

commission to be witnesses right from the beginning. The popular view is unfounded that claims that Jesus' disciples and the Jerusalem church needed to be forced to engage in missionary outreach, which took place only after and as the result of the persecution that followed the death of Stephen (on this question more fully see §16.4).

Carleton Paget suggests that Jewish Christianity initially consisted of practicing Jews who operated within a Jewish context and differed from non-Christian Jews only in their conviction that Jesus of Nazareth was the Messiah; these Jewish Christians did not envision any negative consequences that their allegiance to Jesus might have for their continuing obligations to their inherited faith.[27] This view clearly is wrong. First, there never was a Jewish-Christian "consensus" of this nature. Second, changes and controversies did not result from the "decision" of some Christians to engage in missionary work among Gentiles. The cause for the alienation of Jews and Jewish Christians was not the Gentile mission but the conviction that Jesus was the messianic Son of Man and Son of God, the conviction that the apostles were the representatives of the messianic people of God, the conviction that the present time was the messianic end time, the conviction that the present messianic days brought the fulfillment of the old expectations for the conversion of the nations, and the conviction that Jesus had appointed them to "catch people" and thus to play a crucial role in the conversion of Gentiles.

Peter Bolt emphasizes that the concept of the witness is connected with the Twelve and with Paul as the "thirteenth witness."[28] He seems to downplay the significance of Stephen, however, when he describes his role as merely a "supporting role." Luke describes Stephen as a man "full of faith and the Holy Spirit" (Acts 6:5); he is "full of grace and power" and performs "great wonders and signs among the people" (Acts 6:8). He proclaims and defends in the synagogues of Jerusalem the message of Jesus with wisdom and in the power of the Holy Spirit (Acts 6:9-10). According to Luke, Stephen was the first early Christian preacher to argue that the temple with its sacrifices is no longer the place of God's atoning presence, a position that he defended with courage in a speech before the Sanhedrin (Acts 7:2-53). Since Paul calls Stephen a "witness" of Jesus (Acts 22:20), there is no reason to assume that here the term has a meaning different from those passages in which Luke describes the Twelve or Paul as "witnesses." It is true that Luke describes nearly exclusively the Twelve as "apostles" (*apostoloi*) and that he uses this term for Paul hardly at all. However, as Luke describes the missionary work of Paul, whom the risen Lord has sent to Jews and to Gentiles as his messenger and witness, in great detail, more extensively in fact than the missionary work of Peter or of any other apostle, it is permissible to assume that Luke provides his account of Paul, missionary among Gentiles, in order to give to his Christian readers a pattern to follow in their own missionary work.[29]

14.3 The Leadership of Peter

According to the unanimous testimony of the New Testament writers, Peter was a spontaneous, enthusiastic, eloquent disciple of Jesus with unquestioned lead-

---

[27]Paget 1999, 742; for the remark that follows above see ibid., 743.

[28]Bolt 1998, esp. 192-94, 210-12, with reference to Burchard 1970; on Stephen see Bolt 1998, 192-93, and esp. 202-3.

[29]See I. H. Marshall 2000b, 112.

ership qualities. The disciple lists consistently mention Peter in first place.[30] The missionary work of Peter will be treated in detail in §21. Here I will focus on his function as leader of the disciples and of the church in connection with the dominical saying in Mt 16:18-19.

Mt 16:18-19: "And I tell you, you are Peter, and on this rock I will build my church, and the gates of Hades will not prevail against it. [19]I will give you the keys of the kingdom of heaven, and whatever you bind on earth will be bound in heaven, and whatever you loose on earth will be loosed in heaven."

The interpretation of this passage historically focuses on two explanations. (1) Matthew emphasizes Peter's unique role: he is not only the leader of the Twelve but also possesses a specific and unrepeatable position as the foundation stone of the church. (2) Peter is *primus inter pares;* he has a "typical" role: he shares the "power of the keys," according to Mt 18:18, with the church. If one takes into account the complex description of Peter in the Gospels of Matthew and of Mark as well as in the book of Acts, it is difficult to avoid the conclusion that neither of these two interpretations is correct to the exclusion of the other. As Peter was the first disciple to confess faith in Jesus as the Messiah, and as Peter clearly was the leading apostle in the Jerusalem church during the first years, he had a unique salvation-historical role. In this sense he is indeed the "foundation stone" of the church. At the same time he is the "typical" disciple, with regard both to his responsibility and to his failures.[31]

The authority to "bind" and to "loose" has been interpreted as (1) an announcement of forgiveness for the repentant sinner and a condemnation of church members who continue to sin; (2) an authority to permit and to prohibit various ways of behaving in the church. If we interpret the "theoretical" saying in Mt 16:18 against the background of Luke's account of the ministry of Peter in Jerusalem and in Samaria (Acts 1—11), the second option seems more likely: the authority of Peter appears to have been a teaching authority rather than a disciplinary power.[32]

Peter Dschulnigg asserts that according to Mt 16:16-19, Peter is portrayed as having a teaching authority, a disciplinary authority and the authority to excommunicate, and he concludes that Peter "presumably helped to legitimize the separation of the Jewish Christians from the synagogue controlled by the Pharisees and the establishment of a new people of God oriented entirely toward the message of Jesus and the confession of Jesus as

---

[30]Mk 3:16-19; Mt 10:2-4; Lk 6:14-16; Acts 1:13. Cf. Böcher 1996, 269-70; for a summary of the research on Peter see Gnilka 2002, 9-18, and on Peter's position among the disciples, ibid., 44-58.

[31]Bock 1987, 264; Buckwalter 1998; on Acts 2:33 see Mainville 1991, 49-140, 155-245; on the quotation of Ps 16 see also Schaper 1995, 165-68.

[32]Some interpreters combine both elements; see Dschulnigg 1989, 169-70 with n. 30.

Messiah and Son of God."[33] I do not dispute that Peter had a decisive role and voice in questions of the teaching of the new community of followers of Jesus. But Dschulnigg's hypothesis remains implausible: the separation from "the synagogue" was not a decision made by Jewish Christians but a consequence of the fact that Jewish Christians soon ceased to be tolerated by the local synagogues. The experience of the apostle Paul, whose missionary preaching in synagogues provides the only concrete data that we have, indicates that this often happened within a few weeks. In *this* question Peter's teaching authority was not needed. The "legitimacy" of the new group of people who were independent of the synagogue had been established by Jesus and by his calling and commissioning of the Twelve, by the table fellowship that Jesus enjoyed with tax collectors and sinners, and by the new community of his followers. And we should not forget that the Qumran Essenes, equally independent of "the synagogue," do not seem to have been concerned at all about the latter's acknowledgment of their "legitimacy."

Luke mentions Peter in the first chapters of the book of Acts in the following literary and historical contexts. (1) Peter is mentioned as the first disciple in the apostle list in Acts 1:13, a fact that evidently indicates his leadership position. (2) Peter took the initiative on the occasion of the election of a twelfth disciple in the upper room (Acts 1:15). (3) A few weeks later, at Pentecost, Peter was the spokesman of the 120 followers of Jesus, explaining the events connected with the outpouring of the Holy Spirit. This explanation presented an opportunity to give an account of the significance of Jesus, and Peter spontaneously exhorted the listeners to repent and be baptized in the name of Jesus the Messiah (Acts 2:14, 37-38). (4) On one occasion Peter was instrumental in the healing of a lame man who was begging at the Beautiful Gate of the temple. When people excitedly congregated in Solomon's Portico, Peter gave a speech and explained the good news of Jesus (Acts 3:11-26). (5) Peter was arrested in the temple together with John; when he was brought before the Sanhedrin on the morning of the next day, he explained before the "rulers of the people and elders" the message that he had proclaimed in the temple (Acts 4:3, 8-12). (6) When a couple who belonged to the community of the followers of Jesus wanted to manipulate the church through false information concerning their charitable giving, Peter was the leading apostle who dealt with this serious incident (Acts 5:2, 3, 8). (7) Peter performed extraordinary miracles in Jerusalem (Acts 5:15) with the result that news about the community of believers in Jesus spread to the surrounding region and towns (Acts 5:16). (8) When the apostles were arrested (Acts 5:18), Peter was again the spokesman (Acts 5:29). (9) When the apostles received news of the conversion of large numbers of Samaritans resulting from the missionary work of Philip, the Jerusalem church sent Peter and John north to consolidate the new believers and churches (Acts 8:14). (10) Peter engaged in missionary work in the cities of the coastal plain (Acts 9:32), and in the plain of Sharon many people were converted (Acts 9:35). (11) During a visit to be-

---

[33]Dschulnigg 1989, 170; quotation, ibid., 181.

lievers in Lydda, Peter was called by believers in Joppa after a Christian woman had passed away (Acts 9:38). (12) Peter received a divine revelation that taught him that Gentiles who had been converted to believe in Jesus the Messiah should be admitted to the community of the people of God with no stipulation of halakic rules of purity and behavior for the Gentile believers (Acts 10:9-18). (13) Peter played a major role in the conversion of Cornelius, a Roman centurion in Caesarea (Acts 10:24-48). (14) When the Jerusalem church asked Peter to explain his initiative in Caesarea, he defended his behavior and the admission of Gentiles into the church by referring to the revelation that he had received from God and to the reception of the Holy Spirit that the converted Gentiles had experienced (Acts 11:1-18). (15) Peter was arrested by Herod Antipas and was about to be executed, as this would have pleased the Jews in Jerusalem (Acts 12:3). After his miraculous liberation from prison, he made his escape, left Jerusalem, and went to "another place" (Acts 12:17) that Luke does not specify. (16) On the occasion of the apostolic council, when the debate was heating up, Peter took the floor and reminded "the brothers" that "in the early days God made a choice among you, that I should be the one through whom the Gentiles would hear the message of the good news and become believers" (Acts 15:7).

14.4 The Events of Pentecost

The first evangelistic sermon in the book of Acts is directly linked with the outpouring of the Holy Spirit at the Feast of Pentecost, fifty days (seven weeks and one day) after Passover, thus on May 27 in A.D. 30. According to the Jewish calendar, this was the Feast of Weeks (Heb., *ḥag šabûʿôt*) or the Feast of Harvest (Heb., *ḥag haqaṣîr*), the celebration at the conclusion of the wheat harvest, the second of the three great pilgrimage festivals of Israel, (later) connected with the Sinaitic covenant and the giving of the law. During this feast Jesus' promise that he would send the Spirit upon the disciples was fulfilled. It was as a result of these events that the Twelve and the other followers of Jesus who were in Jerusalem at the time (Acts 2:1: "they were all [πάντες] together in one place") made a public appearance for the first time. The "publication" of the message of Jesus the Messiah and Kyrios took place both in the language miracle and in a sermon that Peter preached. The outpouring of the Holy Spirit at Pentecost "was the *kairos* at which Jesus' disciples who had gathered again in Jerusalem began their missionary activity."[34]

The authenticity of the speeches that Luke records in the book of Acts is disputed. Since Martin Dibelius's influential essay "The Speeches in Acts and Ancient Historiography" (1949), many scholars argue that the speeches of Acts are free compositions of the author, with the kerygmatic speeches reflecting the preaching of the gospel familiar to the

---

[34]Stuhlmacher 1981, 113.

author around A.D. 90.[35] Ulrich Wilckens, in his study *The Missionary Speeches in the Acts of the Apostles,* concludes that the missionary speeches of Peter and of Paul, delivered before Jews and God-fearers (Acts 2:14-36; 3:12-26; 4:8-12; 5:29-32; 10:34-43), have a common structure, that they are the composition of the author of Acts, and that they do not contain early kerygmatic traditions, in contrast to the missionary speeches before Gentiles (Acts 14:15-17; 17:22-31), which can be traced to a pattern found in Paul's letters (e.g., 1 Thess 1:9-10).[36] Wolfgang Reinbold argues that Peter's first speech at Pentecost (Acts 2:14-41) was "more or less freely composed," and that the speech in the temple (Acts 3:12-26) is a product of the author and certainly not a helpful source "to reconstruct the propaganda of the historical Peter." He argues similarly that the hearing before the Sanhedrin (Acts 4:1-22) is an "ideal scene" with little information that is historically reliable, and the speech before Gamaliel (Acts 5:34-39) is "freely composed," a complete invention of the author.[37]

However, if the speeches in the book of Acts are compared with the speeches that Thucydides and Polybius incorporated in their historical works, it can be shown that Luke evidently followed the same practices that these Greek historians used.[38] Thucydides writes with regard to speeches that are incorporated in historical account, "With reference to the speeches in this history, some were delivered before the war began, others while it was going on; some I heard myself, others I got from various quarters; it was in all cases difficult to carry them word for word [τὴν ἀκρίβειαν] in one's memory, so my habit has been to make the speakers say what was in my opinion demanded of them by the various occasions, of course adhering as closely as possible to the general sense of what they really said [τῆς ξυμπάσης γνώμης]" (1.22.1). Polybius, who lived in the second century B.C., writes that a historian must not include freely invented speeches; rather, he must, in contrast to the poet who writes tragedies, "record what really happened and what really was said" (2.56.10-12). In a critique of the work of Timaios he writes, "But to convince those also who are disposed to champion him I must speak of the principle on which he composes public speeches, harangues to soldiers, the discourses of ambassadors, and, in a word, all utterances of the kind, which, as it were, sum up events and hold the whole history together. Can anyone who reads these help noticing that Timaios had untruthfully reported them in his work, and has done so of set purpose? For he has not set down the words spoken nor the sense of what was really said, but having made up his mind as to what ought to have been said, he recounts all these speeches and all else that follows upon events like a man in a school of rhetoric attempting to speak on a given subject, and shows off his oratorical power, but gives no report of which was actually spoken. The peculiar function of history is to discover, in the first place, the words actually spoken, whatever they were, and next to ascertain the reason why what was done or spoken led to failure or success. For the mere statement of a fact may interest us but is of no benefit to us: but when we add the cause of it, study of history becomes fruitful. For it is the mental transference of similar circumstances to our own times that gives us the means of forming presentiments of what is about to happen, and enables us at certain times to take precautions and at others by reproducing former conditions to face with more confidence the difficulties that menace us. But a writer who passes over in silence the speeches made and the

---

[35]Dibelius 1949; see earlier Jülicher 1906, 404.
[36]Wilckens 1974.
[37]Reinbold 2000, 45, 46, 48, 51.
[38]See Bruce 1985a, 2582-88; 1990; Hemer 1989, 415-26; Porter 1990; Gempf 1993b; A. Baum 1996a.

causes of events and in their place introduces false rhetorical exercises and discursive speeches, destroys the peculiar virtue of history. And of this Timaios especially is guilty, and we all know that his work is full of blemishes of the kind" (12.25a.3-25b.4).

Also, the fact that the speeches in the book of Acts reflect different historical and theological perspectives hinders the argument that Luke has freely invented the speeches in Acts.[39] Narrative studies of the book of Acts show that the speeches clearly do not repeat some basic pattern or scheme in stereotypical fashion: they have distinct characteristics with regard to both content and effect. Robert Tannehill has further shown that although Luke indeed addresses his readers with his book, the speeches of Acts are not formulated for the readers and thus need to be interpreted in terms of their connectedness with their particular context.[40]

These arguments do not prove, of course, that Peter preached the sermon recorded in Acts 2:14-36 on this particular Feast of Pentecost in A.D. 30. However, the confidence of Gerd Lüdemann clearly is misplaced when he claims that "the Acts account of the events of Pentecost is certainly unhistorical in its present form. Peter did not make a speech on the first day of Pentecost in Jerusalem, certainly not with the sort of content that is reproduced in Acts."[41] It seems that the question of whether Jesus indeed rose from the dead is decisive: if Peter indeed encountered the risen Lord, there is no reason why he could not have said what Luke reports in Acts 2.[42]

Peter explains to his listeners the speech miracle with a quotation from Joel 3:1-2 LXX: the glossolalia they are hearing is the Spirit of prophecy praising God (Acts 2:11).[43] Glossolalia was a phenomenon unknown in early Judaism, hence the need for Peter's explanation. The further citation of Joel 3:3-5 LXX, which no longer directly elucidates the speech miracle, aims at the statement "Everyone who calls on the name of the Lord shall be saved" (Joel 3:5a = Acts 2:21). Peter interprets this Old Testament statement in a consistently christological manner, as Max Turner explains: "Peter is to argue that Jesus has been made 'Lord' (2:36), and closely identified with 'the Lord God' of Acts 2:39 = Joel 3:5b (and Acts 2:21 = Joel 3:5a); so closely that those who call on God in baptismal repentance undertake that rite 'in (ἐπί) the name of Jesus Christ' (2:38)." Peter explains the theological foundation of his application of Joel 3 to Jesus the Lord and to the people who are listening to his sermon. Peter argues in three stages.[44] (1) The prophecy of Joel has been fulfilled in the ministry and in the death of Jesus (Acts 2:22-24). (2) Jesus has been raised from the dead, and therefore he is the eschatological Son of David, of whom David spoke in Ps 16 (Acts 2:25-32). (3) Since Jesus has been exalted by God, the person whom David calls "my Lord" and who is addressed by the Lord (i.e., by God) and who received dominion (Ps

---

[39]For details see Bruce 1985a, 2582-88.

[40]Tannehill 1991, 400-401 with n. 4; on Peter's sermon at Pentecost see ibid., 402-4.

[41]Lüdemann 1987, 54 (ET, 48); cf. recently Reinbold 2000, 44-45.

[42]On the historicity of Acts 2 see further Bock 1987, 156-87; Turner 1996a, 268-69 with n. 3-4.

[43]See also Acts 10:46; 19:6. For the interpretation that follows above see Turner 1996a, 267-315; quotation, 272. See also Sloan 1991.

[44]Turner 1996a, 273. I will discuss the fourth stage in the next section.

110:1) is none other than Jesus himself: Jesus the Messiah has become Lord (Acts 2:33-36), the coregent of God (cf. Acts 10:46; 19:6).[45]

The explanation that the Spirit of God is the Spirit of Jesus, that Jesus is "Lord" of the Spirit, that Jesus "poured out" the Spirit must have been surprising and provocative for Peter's Jewish listeners: according to Jewish conviction, only God can pour out the Spirit, since the Spirit of God is the active presence of the one true God revealing himself personally to his creation. In the biblical and Jewish tradition such a claim was made with respect neither to the coming redeemer nor to any other person. What was the justification for this claim that Peter made? Luke answered this question in Lk 24:49: Jesus had promised that he would send the Spirit.[46]

　　The theological significance of the events at the Feast of Pentecost of A.D. 30 possibly is linked not only with the significance of Jesus the Messiah and the early Christian view of salvation history but also with the theology of the Jewish Feast of Weeks. In regard to the latter, there is no consensus, however. Some scholars argue that the events of Pentecost should not be interpreted against the background of the Sinaitic covenant and the Mosaic law,[47] while others see such connections to Moses and to Sinai in Acts 2.[48] If the description of the outpouring of the Spirit was formulated against the background of Jewish traditions about the giving of the law at Sinai,[49] Peter makes in Acts 2 the following three points in addition to his main emphasis that the risen and exalted Jesus is the Lord who has poured out the Spirit. (1) God has made the promised second climax of his revelation a reality, after the revelation at Sinai, after the giving of the covenant and after the giving of the law: the outpouring of his Spirit on all flesh, the gracious gift of Jesus the Messiah, who has been exalted at the right hand of God and is thus Lord himself and who has poured out the Spirit. (2) The Feast of Weeks, celebrating the first fruits of the wheat harvest (Ex 34:22), had become the feast in which Israel remembered that God gave the Torah on Mount Sinai. Jewish exegesis concludes from Ex 19:1-4 that the day of the giving of the Torah was the same day as the day of the exodus from Egypt; the Feast of Weeks therefore was the feast of covenant renewal. This background receives new, eschatological significance in the context of the inauguration of the "new covenant" on account of the death of Jesus (cf. Jesus' words during the Last Supper). Rudolf Pesch comments, "The Torah is replaced by the gift of the Spirit that had been promised with the new covenant (Jer 31:31-34), a gift that helps the new community fulfill the Torah (cf. Rom 8:4). . . . The fire of the Spirit, given at Pentecost, constitutes the grounds for the ability to fulfill the Torah, God's social order for his people now interpreted in a definitive way by Jesus, who rectifies all distortions, for its translation in the respective social reality of the new society of the church."[50] (3) Just as Moses climbed Mount Sinai and received the Torah from God, which he passed on to Israel, accompanied by visible signs of God's presence, so also Jesus ascended to God's right hand and poured out the gift of God's Spirit upon the people of the (new) covenant. Thus the events of Pentecost belong to the fulfillment and to the renewal of God's covenant with Israel, in which the Spirit will have a major role.[51]

---

[45]See Turner 1996a, 275-76.
[46]Turner 1996a, 277-79.
[47]See Bock 1987, 182-83.
[48]See Turner 1996a, 280-89; Pao 2000, 131.
[49]See especially Philo, *Decal.* 33-37, 46-47. See Wedderburn 1994, 29-39.
[50]Pesch, *Apg,* 1:108, 113.
[51]Turner 1996a, 280-89; cf. idem 1998.

The effective significance of the Holy Spirit for the missionary work of the apostles is explained by Luke in the subsequent narrative in the book of Acts.[52] (1) When Peter and John were required to justify their preaching before the Sanhedrin, Peter, "filled with the Holy Spirit," explained the message and the ministry of the apostles (Acts 4:7-8). (2) When the Jerusalem church prayed after the release of Peter and John from prison, the believers were "all filled with the Holy Spirit" so that they "spoke the word of God with boldness" (Acts 4:31-32). (3) When the apostles stood before the Sanhedrin for the second time, they again referred to the Holy Spirit, "whom God has given to those who obey him" (Acts 5:32). This means that the witness of God's Spirit becomes visible and audible in the proclamation of the apostles, to which the members of the Jewish council should become obedient as well![53] (4) When the ministry of the Jerusalem church needed to be consolidated by the election of further co-workers, the leadership looked for members who had a good reputation and were "full of the Spirit and of wisdom" (Acts 6:3). (5) When Stephen stood before the Sanhedrin and defended and explained the message that he proclaimed in the synagogues of Jerusalem, the members of the council "could not withstand the wisdom and the Spirit with which he spoke" (Acts 6:10). Stephen rebuked them for resisting the Holy Spirit (Acts 7:51). The events that happen in connection with and through the apostles are the work of the Holy Spirit. Resistance against the community of the followers of Jesus the Messiah is resistance against God's Spirit. When Stephen was killed, he died "filled with the Holy Spirit" (Acts 7:55). (6) In Samaria God poured out the Spirit on the new converts through the mediation of Peter and John (Acts 8:14-17). (7) The conversion of the first foreigner, an official of the Ethiopian court, was the result of the work of the Spirit, who said to Philip, "Go over to this chariot and join it" (Acts 8:29). (8) When Saul of Tarsus was converted, Ananias, a Christian from Damascus, assured him that he would regain his sight and that he would be "filled with the Holy Spirit" (Acts 9:17). (9) Luke summarizes the success of the missionary work in Judea, Galilee and Samaria by pointing to the Holy Spirit: "Meanwhile the church throughout Judea, Galilee, and Samaria had peace and was built up. Living in the fear of the Lord and in the comfort of the Holy Spirit, it increased in numbers" (Acts 9:31). (10) The conversion of the first Gentile was connected with the work of the Spirit, who said to Peter, "Look, three men are searching for you" (Acts 10:19). When Cornelius and the other listeners heard and accepted Peter's message, they received the Holy Spirit, which prompted Peter to baptize them without delay—that is, to accept them into the people of God without circumcising them or stipulating that they keep all the commandments of the Torah (Acts 10:44-48). Back in Jerusalem, Peter explained his actions in Caesarea with the

---

[52]See Barbi 1990, 138-45; Shelton 1991; Turner 1996a, 349-52.
[53]See Pesch, *Apg*, 1:217.

argument that the Gentiles had received "the same gift that he gave us when we believed in the Lord Jesus Christ," which is sufficient reason why they must be admitted as full members into God's people (Acts 11:12, 15-17; 15:8). (11) Barnabas, a well-respected member and coworker in the Jerusalem church who was sent to Antioch, the capital of Syria, to engage in missionary work was "a good man, full of the Holy Spirit and of faith" (Acts 11:24). (12) The missionary work on Cyprus and in Galatia by Paul and Barnabas was a result of the initiative of the Holy Spirit (Acts 13:2, 4). (13) Paul, "filled with the Holy Spirit," confronted the magician Elymas (Acts 13:9). (14) The new followers of Jesus in Pisidian Antiocheia were "filled with joy and with the Holy Spirit" despite the persecution that they had to endure (Acts 13:52). (15) The results of the apostolic council are traced back to the Holy Spirit (Acts 15:28). (16) It was God's Spirit who prevented Paul from preaching the gospel in the provinces of Asia and Bithynia (Acts 16:6-7). (17). The men in Ephesus who had only heard of John's baptism of repentance received the Holy Spirit (Acts 19:6). (18) The Spirit told Paul through Christian prophets that he would be arrested in Jerusalem, an announcement that did not, however, prevent Paul from traveling to Jerusalem (Acts 20:23; 21:4, 11). (19) The elders of the church in Ephesus were appointed as *episkopoi* ("overseers") by the Holy Spirit (Acts 20:28).

The function of the Holy Spirit can be summarized in five areas, following Max Turner, who emphasizes that the Spirit received by those who come to faith in Jesus the Messiah is, according to the description in the book of Acts, the Spirit of prophecy promised by Joel and poured out by the risen Lord at Pentecost.[54] (1) The Spirit grants visions and dreams that convey divine revelation.[55] (2) The Spirit grants revelatory words, instructions and guidance.[56] (3) The Spirit grants wisdom and revelatory discernment.[57] (4) The Spirit inspires "invasive charismatic praise" (glossolalia).[58] (5) The Spirit inspires preaching, witness and teaching.[59] Turner concludes, "Luke evidently regards the promise made to believers to be a Christianized version of Joel's promise: the gift of prophecy. In that sense Acts 2:14-39 is genuinely programmatic for the pneumatology of Acts. . . . Luke does not spell out his pneumatology, like Paul, in terms of the fulfillment of Ezekiel 36, and new creation, but in terms of Joel 3:1-5 (EVV 2:28-32)."[60]

---

[54]Turner 1996a, 349-50.

[55]Acts 2:17; 7:55-56; cf. 9:10-18; 10:10-20; 16:9-10; 18:9-10; 22:17-18, 21; 23:11, with the Spirit mentioned explicitly in 10:19; 16:6-7.

[56]Acts 1:2; 8:29; 10:19; 11:12, 28; 13:2, 4; 15:28; 16:6-7; 19:21; 20:22, 23; 21:4, 11; see further 1:16; 4:25; 7:51; 28:25, where the revelation occurs through the Old Testament.

[57]Lk 21:15; Acts 5:3; 6:3, 5, 10; 9:31; 13:9; 16:18.

[58]Acts 2:4 (Jerusalem); 10:46 (Caesarea); 19:6 (Ephesus).

[59]Acts 1:4, 8; 4:8, 31; 5:32; 6:10; 9:17; teaching: 9:31; 18:25 (?).

[60]Turner 1996a, 351-52, formulated in part as a critique of Dunn 1970, 46, and passim; see also Turner 1998.

14.5 The First Missionary Sermon

The Pentecost pilgrims are shaken when they hear Peter explain that Jesus, who had been crucified, was the Messiah, the promised Son of David, that he rose from the dead and that he is the Lord who poured out the Spirit of the last days. They were "cut to the heart" and asked Peter and the other apostles, "Brothers, what should we do?" (Acts 2:37). Peter had begun his explanation with the declaration, directed to the "entire house of Israel," that "this man, handed over to you according to the definite plan and foreknowledge of God," whom "you crucified and killed by the hands of those outside the law" (Acts 2:23), is the Messiah and the exalted Lord. When the listeners inquire about the consequences of these events for themselves, Peter's sermon takes a missionary turn: he challenges them to repent, to receive forgiveness of their sins through faith in Jesus Christ, and to be baptized.

Acts 2:38-40: "Peter said to them, 'Repent, and be baptized every one of you in the name of Jesus Christ so that your sins may be forgiven; and you will receive the gift of the Holy Spirit. [39]For the promise is for you, for your children, and for all who are far away, everyone whom the Lord our God calls to him.' [40]And he testified with many other arguments and exhorted them, saying, 'Save yourselves from this corrupt generation.'"

This is the last step in Peter's sermon. Max Turner describes the connection between Peter's explanation of the outpouring of the Spirit and the call to repentance: "The nature of the exaltation in question, and of the gift which flows from it, involves such a close identification with 'the Lord' of Joel's citation that Jesus may be presented as the Redeemer upon whose name men should call for salvation (Acts 2:38-39)."[61] Peter, and with him the other apostles, emphasizes as least six points.[62]

1. Since the Spirit of God has been poured out, as promised by Joel, the last days have begun and the new covenant has been inaugurated. This is the reason why even Jews need to be "saved" and thus are called to repentance. In view of the messianic period, being born in Israel is no longer sufficient. There is time before the coming of the Day of the Lord to repent and receive salvation (Acts 2:38).

2. Salvation is linked with calling upon the name of the "Lord Jesus the Messiah"—that is, with the recognition and acknowledgment of Jesus' messianic dignity, with the understanding that his death on the cross achieved the atonement for sins, with the "theo-logic" of his resurrection from the dead and his exaltation to the right hand of God, with his position as Lord who pours out the Spirit of God, a position that he has as the crucified, risen and exalted Messiah.

3. Salvation is linked with water baptism, a personal demonstration of repen-

---

[61]Turner 1996a, 273.
[62]See Pesch, *Apg*, 1:126.

tance and acknowledgment of Jesus as the crucified Messiah and risen Lord who sends the Spirit. This confession of Jesus as Messiah and Lord is the reason why baptism is linked with "the name of Jesus Christ."

4. Salvation through repentance and baptism entails reception of the Holy Spirit and integration into the people of God's new covenant. Acceptance of the missionary message is the "prerequisite of baptism"[63] and of integration into the community of the people of God.

5. The salvation of Jews signifies that the restoration of Israel has begun in the gathering of the community of the followers of Jesus the Messiah and Lord from among the "house of Israel," which has proven to be a "corrupt genera-tion" in the crucifixion of the Messiah. Peter's designation of his Jewish contem-poraries as a "corrupt generation" (ἡ γενεὰ τῆς σκολιᾶς ταύτης, *hē genea tēs sko-lias tautēs* [Acts 2:40]) refers back to the generation of Israel in the desert.[64] Peter "actualizes God's great act of liberation in the history of his people and the tragic reaction of unbelief with its consequences." The typology of the "corrupt" gen-eration of the desert implies "an ominous announcement of impending judg-ment." Peter calls on his Jewish listeners to be rescued from their rejection of God's second great act of liberation and to accept God's act of salvation that took place in the death and resurrection of Jesus the Messiah.

6. The gathering of the new people of God in Israel is accompanied by the promised ingathering of "all who are far away" (Acts 2:39), the Gentiles, to whom God's promise applies as well.

---

[63]Pesch (*Apg*, 1:126), who refers to Lk 8:13; Acts 11:1; 17:11.

[64]Deut 32:5: "Yet his degenerate children have dealt falsely with him, a perverse and crooked gen-eration" (LXX: γενεὰ σκολιὰ καὶ διεστραμμένη); cf. Ps 78:8; *Tanhuma,* B Shelach 9 (33a); *Num. Rab.* 16.9 (69a); *b. Soṭah* 34b. See Lövestam 1983, 84-85; the quotations that follow above, ibid., 90. Arguing against Haenchen, Lövestam points out that this phrase is not simply a formulation of the missionary language of the early Christians: apart from the Gospels and Acts 2:30; Phil 2:15; Heb 3:10, the phrase is not used in the New Testament (ibid., 91-92 with n. 32).

15

PRIORITIES AND CONVICTIONS OF
THE JERUSALEM APOSTLES

Luke and James mention three places where the followers of Jesus in Jerusalem were meeting: (1) The so-called upper room (τὸ ὑπερῷον, *to hyperōon* [Acts 1:13]), where 120 believers "were staying."[1] This was the place where the speech miracle at the Feast of Pentecost took place (Acts 2:1-2). The use of the definite article indicates that Luke was familiar with the local tradition concerning the localization of this room.[2] Luke visited Jerusalem at least in connection with Paul's last visit in the Jewish capital. This "upstairs room" may have been the meeting place of the Jerusalem church when James the brother of Jesus was the leader of the Christian community (Acts 12:12).[3] This first meeting place of the Jerusalem church was located on the southwest hill in close proximity to the Essene quarter, as very probably was true also for the room where Jesus had celebrated the Last Supper before his trial.[4] (2) The house of Mary the mother of John Mark had an entrance with a gate (πυλών, *pylōn* [Acts 12:12-14]), and thus evidently was an elegant house. (3) The reference to a Christian συναγωγή (*synagōgē* [Jas 2:2-3]) in the letter of James, written probably before A.D. 62, may indicate a building;[5] since the context discusses the behavior of Christians, it is more plausible, however, to interpret the term as "congregation."[6]

During excavations on the grounds of the Dormition Abbey, situated on Mount Zion near the so-called Tomb of David, conducted by E. Eisenberg in 1983/1984, remains of poorly

---

[1] Acts 1:13: οὗ ἦσαν καταμένοντες is a periphrastic construction with the imperfect; see Schneider, *Apg*, 1:205 n. 62; Riesner 1995a, 1839.

[2] Riesner 1995a, 1841, with reference to Mussner, *Apg*, 18; see also Riesner 1995b, 206.

[3] Thus Riesner 1995a, 1840, with reference to W. Schrage, *ThWNT* 7:836 (*TDNT* 7:837); Maser 1993, 277-81; see also Bargil Pixner, "Jerusalem's Essene Gateway—Where the Community Lived in Jesus' Time," *BAR* 23 (1997): 22-31, 64-66.

[4] See Riesner 1995a; Pixner 1994, 219-28.

[5] Riesner 1995a, 1841; cf. idem 1995b, 207, where Riesner speaks of Jewish-Christian synagogues in Jerusalem.

[6] Thus Mussner, *Jak*, 117; Davids, *Jas*, 108.

built houses were discovered that date to the Herodian or early Roman period. The coins from the time of the First Jewish Revolt (A.D. 66-70) that were found at the site stop in A.D. 67/68, leading Bargil Pixner to suggest that these houses perhaps belonged to Christians[7] who fled in A.D. 67/68 to Pella, following the directive of a prophetic oracle.[8]

15.1 The Life of the Jerusalem Church

Luke describes the life of the messianic community of the followers of Jesus in Jerusalem in the first chapters of the book of Acts in five summary statements (Acts 1:14; 2:42-47; 4:31-35; 5:12-16; 5:42).

Acts 1:14: "All these were constantly devoting themselves to prayer, together with certain women, including Mary the mother of Jesus, as well as his brothers."

Acts 2:42-47: "They devoted themselves to the apostles' teaching and fellowship, to the breaking of bread and the prayers. [43]Awe came upon everyone, because many wonders and signs were being done by the apostles. [44]All who believed were together and had all things in common; [45]they would sell their possessions and goods and distribute the proceeds to all, as any had need. [46]Day by day, as they spent much time together in the temple, they broke bread at home and ate their food with glad and generous hearts, [47]praising God and having the goodwill of all the people. And day by day the Lord added to their number those who were being saved."

Acts 4:31-35: "When they had prayed, the place in which they were gathered together was shaken; and they were all filled with the Holy Spirit and spoke the word of God with boldness. [32]Now the whole group of those who believed were of one heart and soul, and no one claimed private ownership of any possessions, but everything they owned was held in common. [33]With great power the apostles gave their testimony to the resurrection of the Lord Jesus, and great grace was upon them all. [34]There was not a needy person among them, for as many as owned lands or houses sold them and brought the proceeds of what was sold. [35]They laid it at the apostles' feet, and it was distributed to each as any had need."

Acts 5:12-16: "Now many signs and wonders were done among the people through the apostles. And they were all together in Solomon's Portico. [13]None of the rest dared to join them, but the people held them in high esteem. [14]Yet more than ever believers were added to the Lord, great numbers of both men and women, [15]so that they even carried out the sick into the streets, and laid them on cots and mats, in order that Peter's shadow might fall on some of them as he came by. [16]A great number of people would also gather from the towns around Jerusalem, bringing the sick and those tormented by unclean spirits, and they were all cured."

Acts 5:42: "And every day in the temple and at home they did not cease to teach and proclaim Jesus as the Messiah."

Other summaries describe the progress of the gospel in Jerusalem and other re-

---

[7]Pixner 1994, 403-7.
[8]See Eusebius, *Hist. eccl.* 3.5.3; Epiphanius, *Pan.* 29.7.7 (GCS 25.330).

gions (Acts 6:7; 9:31; 12:24; 16:5; 19:20; 28:30-31).

Acts 6:7: "The word of God continued to spread; the number of the disciples increased greatly in Jerusalem, and a great many of the priests became obedient to the faith."

Acts 9:31: "Meanwhile the church throughout Judea, Galilee, and Samaria had peace and was built up. Living in the fear of the Lord and in the comfort of the Holy Spirit, it increased in numbers."

Acts 12:24: "But the word of God continued to advance and gain adherents."

Acts 16:5: "So the churches [in Syria, Cilicia, southern Galatia] were strengthened in the faith and increased in numbers daily."

Acts 19:20: "So the word of the Lord grew mightily and prevailed."

Acts 28:30-31: "He lived there two whole years at his own expense and welcomed all who came to him, [31]proclaiming the kingdom of God and teaching about the Lord Jesus Christ with all boldness and without hindrance."

These summary statements mark the transition from one event or from one phase of growth to the next. They confirm that the preaching of the gospel of Jesus Christ made progress, and they confirm that the expansion of faith in Jesus the Messiah was remarkable and reached more and more people and regions as a result of what God was doing.[9]

Ulrich Wendel compares the summary statements in the book of Acts with the summary statements in the Gospel of Luke and demonstrates that "each summary account had an independent summary *Vorlage*," meaning that the view of Ernst Haenchen and many other scholars that the summary statements are entirely Luke's composition is erroneous.[10] The summary statements of Acts intend to express Luke's conviction that the community of Jesus' followers that God himself established in Jerusalem "can happen again in the reality of the readers. The church is 'put into force' by God. The summaries of Acts present a model rather than parenesis, 'gospel' rather than 'law.'" Wendel notes the following elements in the summaries in Acts: apostolic teaching; prayers; fear (awe) in the congregation; signs and wonders performed by the apostles; fellowship: the personal attitude; fellowship: the resulting behavior (sale of possessions, sharing of resources); frequency of meetings: daily, public assemblies; meetings in private houses; breaking of bread (and/or common meals); rejoicing in the congregation; unequivocal hearts; reputation of the church spreading in the larger community; church growth; men and women in the church.

The Teaching of the Apostles
Luke's first description of the church mentions that the believers "devoted them-

---

[9]Rosner 1998, 221-23.
[10]Wendel 1998, 71; see generally 51-72; contra Haenchen, *Apg,* 157 (ET, 151); contra Horn 1983, 36-39, and passim. For the observation that follows above see Wendel 1998, 84-109; on the individual themes, 81.

selves to the apostles' teaching" (διδαχῇ τῶν ἀποστόλων, *didachē tōn apostolōn* [Acts 2:42]) as a basic characteristic of the Jerusalem church. The "teaching of the apostles" is "the tradition of Jesus that has been responsibly transmitted and interpreted and that includes the proof from the Old Testament (reading the Old Testament with newly opened eyes)."[11] One should refrain from assuming a contradiction between the "proclamation of the apostles" as preaching of Jesus Christ and "teaching and tradition:"[12] The proclamation of Jesus is grounded in the "tradition" of what the disciples and other followers of Jesus of Nazareth had seen and heard, and the proclamation of Jesus as Messiah and exalted Lord contains "teaching."

Luke does not specify the "apostles' teaching" in Acts 2:42, but he does provide a lengthy account of Peter's preaching. This warrants the conclusion that the sermons and speeches of Peter, who acts as representative and spokesman of the apostles,[13] provide the substance and content of the "teaching of the apostles." If this assumption is correct, we are justified in summarizing the apostles' teaching in three basic points. (1) Peter preaches in Jerusalem the necessity of repentance, of turning back to God, in view of God's eschatological acts in the death and resurrection of Jesus and in the outpouring of the Spirit of prophecy.[14] (2) Peter proclaims God's offer of messianic salvation through Jesus, who is the Messiah: after Jesus' ministry, death, resurrection and exaltation, salvation can be found only in connection with, in personal allegiance to, faith in Jesus. God offers his messianic salvation not only to Jews, for whom there is now no other way open to salvation, but also to Gentiles.[15] Salvation means forgiveness of sins,[16] reception of the Holy Spirit,[17] rescue from enemies who rebel against God,[18] integration into the community of the messianic people of God who worship Jesus the Messiah, who experience healing liberation from illness, demonic oppression and material selfishness.[19] (3) Peter proclaims Jesus as *kyrios* and *christos,*[20] as Son of David and as God's Servant,[21] as holy and righteous and as

---

[11]Pesch, *Apg,* 1:133; see the older study Rétif 1953. H.-F. Weiss (*EWNT* 1:770 [*EDNT* 1:320]) speaks in this context of "the firmly established tradition of instruction in the Church"; this definition is dependent upon the assumption of a late date for the book of Acts.

[12]Contra Jervell (*Apg,* 155), who refers to Conzelmann, *Apg,* 37 (ET, 23); Weiser, *Apg,* 1:104.

[13]Bayer 1998, 261-62, with reference to Acts 2:14, 37, 42; 3:4, 12; 4:7-8, 13, 19, 24, 32; 5:2-3, 29; 6:2; 8:14; for the observation that follows above see ibid., 262-74.

[14]Acts 2:38, 40; 3:19; 5:31; cf. 8:22; 10:42-43; 15:8.

[15]Acts 2:21, 39; 3:26; 10:34-35, 36, 43, 45; 11:18. For the point that follows above see J. Green 1998, 90-95.

[16]Acts 2:38; 3:19; 5:31; 10:43; cf. 13:38; 15:9; 22:16; 26:18.

[17]Acts 2:38; 9:17; 10:43-44; 11:15-17; 15:8.

[18]Acts 2:40; cf. the exodus typology in 3:17-26; 7:25.

[19]Acts 2:1, 44-45; 3:1—4:12; 4:32—5:11; 5:12-16; 8:7.

[20]*Kyrios:* 2:21, 34, 36; 10:36; *christos:* 2:31, 36, 38; 3:18, 20; 4:10; 10:36.

[21]Son of David: 2:29-31; Servant of God: 3:13, 26; 4:27, 30.

"Leader and Savior that he might give repentance to Israel and forgiveness of sins,"[22] as prophet like Moses and as judge.[23] Peter emphasizes that Jesus has been confirmed by God through mighty signs and wonders and that God vindicated him as Kyrios and Messiah.[24] And he argues that it was according to God's deliberate plan that Jesus was handed over to the wicked so that people would have salvation through Jesus' death.[25]

If the phrase "teaching of the apostles" describes the entire preaching of the apostles, both the word that seeks to win outsiders and the instruction of believers,[26] the missionary proclamation of the apostles is included as well. Luke repeatedly uses "the word" to describe the apostolic preaching of the message of Jesus Christ. The absolute ὁ λόγος (ho logos, "the word") and the fuller ὁ λόγος τοῦ θεοῦ (ho logos tou theou, "the word of God") or ὁ λόγος τοῦ κυρίου (ho logos tou kyriou, "the word of the Lord") belong to the missionary language of the early Christians.[27] Several statements in Acts 4 are characteristic.

Acts 4:4, 29, 31: "But many of those who heard the word [τὸν λόγον] believed; and they numbered about five thousand. . . . [29]'And now, Lord, look at their threats, and grant to your servants to speak your word with all boldness [μετὰ παρρησίας πάσης λαλεῖν τὸν λόγον σου]. . . .' [31]When they had prayed, the place in which they were gathered together was shaken; and they were all filled with the Holy Spirit and spoke the word of God [τὸν λόγον τοῦ θεοῦ] with boldness."

The significance of missionary preaching for the Jerusalem church is demonstrated in the petition of the prayer in Acts 4:29: while the Jewish leaders engage in tactical deliberations on how to oppress the church, the believers ask God in this prayer—the longest prayer recorded by any New Testament writer—for courage to proclaim "the word of God." The church prays for strength to continue to engage in frank, unreserved missionary work.[28] The "growth of the word" (Acts 6:7; 12:24; 19:20) describes "the addition of individual newly converted Christians," thus the numerical growth of the churches as new converts join the congregation.[29] The fact that Luke explicitly emphasizes the growth of "the word" highlights the inherent power of the apostles' message of Jesus Christ as the Word of God. Luke's formulations emphasize the dynamic of the growth of the church, which is quite independent of the apostles; they empha-

---

[22]Acts 5:31; holy and righteous: 3:14; 4:27, 30.
[23]Prophet like Moses: 3:22; judge: 10:42.
[24]Acts 2:22, 36; 3:26; 10:38.
[25]Acts 2:23. On the Christology of Judean Jewish Christianity see now Hurtado 2003, 155-216.
[26]Schneider, *Apg,* 1:286 with n. 15.
[27]H. Ritt, *EWNT* 2:887 (*EDNT* 2:359), with reference to Acts 4:31; 6:2, 7; 8:14; 11:1; 13:5, 7, 44, 46; 16:32; 17:13; 18:11; "word of the Lord": 8:25; 13:44, 48, 49; 15:35, 36; 16:32; 19:10, 20.
[28]See Pesch, *Apg,* 1:178.
[29]Wendel 1998, 261, 262.

size the *extra nos* character of the preaching of the gospel, whose success is grounded not in the messenger but in God; they emphasize that the growth of the church is not commanded by the apostles but is the result of the work of God. When the growth of the church caused difficulties in the congregation, the Twelve emphasized the priority of preaching and of prayer (Acts 6:2-4).

Acts 6:2-4: "And the twelve called together the whole community of the disciples and said, 'It is not right that we should neglect the word of God [τὸν λόγον τοῦ θεοῦ] in order to wait on tables. ³Therefore, friends, select from among yourselves seven men of good standing, full of the Spirit and of wisdom, whom we may appoint to this task, ⁴while we, for our part, will devote ourselves to prayer and to serving the word [τῇ διακονίᾳ τοῦ λόγου].'"

The apostles solved the problem caused by the growth of the congregation and by the limited time they had as leaders to deal with practical matters, such as providing food for widows, on the basis of the primacy of the preaching and teaching responsibility of the church leaders.[30] The apostles felt obligated to emphasize and act according to this responsibility: they stuck to their priorities, and they resolved the tensions by appointing co-workers to take care of the widows. As a result of these decisions "the word of God" and thus the church continued to grow (Acts 6:7).

Acts 6:7: "The word of God continued to spread [ὁ λόγος τοῦ θεοῦ ηὔξανεν]; the number of the disciples increased greatly in Jerusalem, and a great many of the priests became obedient to the faith."

David Pao recently described the "itinerary of the word of God" in the book of Acts:[31] the "word" travels from Jerusalem (Acts 4:4, 29; 6:4, 7; 10:36) and Judea (Acts 12:24) to regions outside of Judea (Acts 8:4): to Samaria (Acts 8:14, 25) and Caesarea (Acts 11:1), to Phoenicia, Cyprus and Antioch in Syria (Acts 11:19; 15:35), to Cyprus and Galatia (Acts 15:36), specifically to Salamis and Paphos (Acts 13:5, 7), to Antiocheia (Acts 13:26, 44, 46, 48), to Lystra (Acts 14:3) and Perge (Acts 14:25); then to Macedonia and Achaia: to Philippi (Acts 16:32), Beroea (Acts 17:11, 13) and Corinth (Acts 18:5, 11); and finally to the province of Asia: to Ephesus (Acts 16:6; 19:10, 20) and Miletus (Acts 20:32).

The suggestion that according to Luke "the word does not appear in a city twice"[32] is unconvincing, however: the "word" is mentioned repeatedly for Jerusalem and for Judea (Acts 4:4, 29; 6:4, 7; 10:36), as well as for Antioch in Syria (Acts 11:19; 15:35). The view that Luke deliberately uses distinctive references to "the word of God" and to "the word

---

[30]Cf. Pesch, *Apg,* 1:232.

[31]Pao 2000, 150-56, in the context of a literary interpretation of the passages in which the phrase "the word of God" or "the word of the Lord" occurs.

[32]Pao 2000, 154-55; quotation, 154.

of the Lord" is a literary rather than a historical assessment. We should not forget that authors rarely are concerned about word statistics.

Fellowship

The second characteristic of the early church in Jerusalem is "fellowship" (κοινωνία, *koinōnia*), the personal, fraternal coherence of the individual members of the congregation. In Acts 2—4 the term *koinōnia* describes "the unanimous frame of mind and the resulting communal (social!) behavior which extends to the material resources."[33] According to a different definition, *koinōnia* describes "the participation in the salvation that has been opened up by Jesus; it is the specific social place of this salvation where all are linked with each other, as sinners who have been saved, by the holy Spirit in *agape*."[34] In regard to the fellowship of the Jerusalem church, we may distinguish attitude and action: the attitude within the church toward other believers and the actions that result from this attitude. In the first months and years of the existence of the Jerusalem church the attitude and the actions of *koinōnia* prompted believers to sell their possessions and share their resources.[35]

Luke uses the term *koinōnia* only in Acts 2:42, explaining it in Acts 2:44 with the statement that all believers "were together" (ἦσαν ἐπὶ τὸ αὐτό, *ēsan epi to auto*). This latter expression probably has no local meaning ("all believers were gathered at one place")[36] but rather emphasizes the unity of the congregation, which is described in Acts 2:46 with the term ὁμοθυμαδόν (*homothymadon*), rendered as "with one mind" in the NASB.[37] The translation in the TEV of Acts 2:44 is correct: "All the believers continued together in close fellowship." The comment in the summary statement in Acts 4:32 that "the whole group of those who believed" in Jerusalem "were of one heart and soul" (ἦν καρδία καὶ ψυχὴ μία, *ēn kardia kai psychē mia*) relates at least to the unity of the church in prayer, as "fellowship in the church" is always "fellowship in prayer" in the summary statements.[38] However, since the early Jewish parallels to the phrase "one heart (and soul)"[39] speak of unity in verbal utterances, the comment may also describe the theological unity of the congregation. Ulrich Wendel's caveat is appropriate, however, that Luke does not describe the church "as a realm free of conflict."

---

[33]Zmijewski, *Apg,* 158.

[34]Pesch, *Apg,* 1:133.

[35]See Wendell 1998, 120-61.

[36]BAA, s.v. "ἐπί," 584 (III.1.a.ξ); BDAG, s.v. "ἐπί," 363 (1.c.β); W. Radl, *EWNT* 1:433 (*EDNT* 1:179-80); W. Köhler, *EWNT* 2:57 (*EDNT* 2:22); Schneider, *Apg,* 1:287.

[37]See Wendell 1998, 121-24; Roloff, *Apg,* 64; Pesch, *Apg,* 1:132. Cf. BDAG 706, s.v. "ὁμοθυμαδόν": "with one mind/purpose/impulse"; F. W. Danker cites Acts 2:46 for this meaning and comments that the NRSV and other versions are correct in assuming the weakened meaning "together" in texts such as Acts 5:12.

[38]Wendel 1998, 128; the quotation that follows above, ibid., 129.

[39]Philo, *Mos.* 1.86; 4 Macc 8:29; cf. 1 Chron 12:39; see Wendel 1998, 124, 128.

The fellowship of the Jerusalem believers became visible in specific actions: they had "all things in common" (Acts 2:44) and they "would sell their posses-sions and goods and distribute the proceeds to all, as any had need" (Acts 2:45).[40] In Acts 4:32, 34-35 Luke repeats this description. In Acts 4:37 Joseph-Barnabas, a Jewish Christian from Cyprus, is presented as an examplar of this behavior, while in Acts 5:1-11 Ananias and Sapphira are shown to violate it. Ul-rich Wendel analyzes the relevant passages in Luke's Gospel—the exhortation to lend money (Lk 6:30, 34-35); the exhortation to renounce possessions (Lk 12:33-34), the parable of the clever manager (Lk 16:1-13), and the repentance of Zacchaeus the tax collector (Lk 19:1-10). He demonstrates that in these pas-sages, as well as in Acts 2:45; 4:34, 37; 5:1, 4, 8, the focus is on the sale of pos-sessions. In other words, Luke describes not an early Christian "community of goods" but the renunciation of monetary assets for the sake of the poor.[41] In Acts 5:1-11 Luke underlines that the giving away of resources was voluntary. Luke does not present his readers with maximalist demands; he does not describe a community that denies the appropriateness of private property (as in a monastic order); he does not propagate a world-denying "love-communism" (Max We-ber). Rather, Luke presents a pragmatic ethic of possessions that places the needs of the poor in the center. He does not idealize a past mode of behavior in the Jerusalem church but describes a way of behavior that is focused on the community and can be practiced in all Christian communities. The view that Luke has a "bourgeois" concept of the church is wrong.[42] Luke repeatedly re-minds his readers that the Jerusalem church (as a model for other churches) ex-pected its wealthy members to sacrifice their private property or encouraged them to sell property voluntarily and with joy.

Brian Capper suggests that Luke wanted to remind his readers of the Greco-Roman de-scriptions of the "golden age," making the point that the idyllic conditions that prevailed at the beginning of the history of humankind were realized, for a moment, at the begin-ning of the history of the church. If this had been Luke's intention, he would have made the theological point that the events in Jerusalem that were initiated by the death and the resurrection of Jesus have fundamental significance for the history of the world.[43]

Luke reports that the Jerusalem church numbered several thousand believers,

---

[40]Acts 2:44b-45: εἶχον ἅπαντα κοινὰ καὶ τὰ κτήματα καὶ τὰς ὑπάρξεις ἐπίπρασκον καὶ διεμέ-ριζον αὐτὰ πᾶσιν καθότι ἄν τις χρείαν εἶχεν.

[41]Wendel 1998, 134-61. When Wendel speaks of the "concept of the skimming of capital for the sake of the needy" (160), it sounds too technical. For the traditional view see Capper 1995, with the description of a possible Essene background.

[42]Contra Plümacher 1978a, 516-17. I adopt the critique in Wendel 1998, 161, and others. On Max Weber's notion of world-denying love-communism (*Liebeskommunismus*) see Robert N. Bellah, "Max Weber and World-Denying Love: A Look at the Historical Sociology of Religion," *Journal of the American Academy of Religion* 67 (1999): 277-304.

[43]Capper 1998, 504-12; see particularly Hesiod, *Op.* 106-201; Virgil, *Georg.* 1.125-129.

and so *koinōnia* was possible only in meetings that took place in private houses. As Werner Vogler correctly points out, it was only here that "everyone could know everybody. Only here everybody could have contact with everyone. Only here . . . could they take care of each others' material needs."[44] The fellowship that was practiced in the homes of the believers had missionary consequences: these meetings were so attractive that unbelievers started to attend. Luke notes that "day by day the Lord added to their number those who were being saved" (Acts 2:47).

The Breaking of Bread

The expression "breaking of bread" (κλάσις τοῦ ἄρτου, *klasis tou artou* [Acts 2:42]) refers primarily to the communal meals of the Jerusalem believers. According to Acts 2:46-47, these seem to have taken place not only in private homes but also in the temple, thus in public.

This interpretation of Acts 2:42 is based on the construction of the Greek sentence. In the hypotactical sentence in Acts 2:46-47 the main clause (μετελάμβανον τροφῆς ἐν ἀγαλλιάσει καὶ ἀφελότητι καρδίας) is preceded by two participial clauses that are coordinated by the conjunctions τε . . . τε (καθ᾽ ἡμέραν τε προσκαρτεροῦντες ὁμοθυμαδὸν ἐν τῷ ἱερῷ // κλῶντές τε κατ᾽ οἶκον ἄρτον).[45] Ulrich Wendel observes that "the eating of food is primary as the statement of the main clause. Both the 'sojourn in the temple' and the 'breaking of bread in houses' are dependent on this statement."

The believers in Jerusalem shared meals in private houses and on the occasion of their daily visits to the temple. The breaking of bread remembers Jesus' death and is neither identified with nor explicitly distinguished from everyday meals. It probably is misguided to ask whether Luke has in mind ordinary meals or the eucharistic celebration: evidently the two were closely connected in the early period of the church.[46] The public assemblies, accompanied by shared meals, took place on a daily basis, which was not necessarily the case as far as the breaking of bread in the eucharistic sense is concerned.

Ulrich Wendel combines Lk 14:1-24; 22:7-38; 24:28-35; Acts 27:33-38 for the formulation of a "Lukan theology of meals"[47] which demanded "that the church should invite outsiders to their meals, that Christ can be acknowledged during these meals and that there is an invitation to salvation and repentance." If indeed such meals "have their place at the point of contact with the gospel, if they aim at hoped-for conversions or if they seal and joyfully celebrate a conversion that took place, it is no longer difficult to classify the meal in Acts 2:46 . . . Luke thinks of a public meal as a missionary offer of salvation." Luke emphasizes that "the congregation comes together at a public place and shares a meal. Their fellow-

---

[44]Vogler 1982, 788, for the remark that follows above see ibid., 788-89.
[45]Wendel 1998, 183; the quotation that follows above, ibid.
[46]See Zmijewski, *Apg,* 159.
[47]Wendel 1998, 181-231; the quotations that follow above, 219, 220.

ship is deliberately opened up for people who have not yet accepted the gospel. Fellowship on this social level is formative. The offer of salvation for non-Christians is made in the context of this fellowship. Luke accords this meal the theological quality of making Christ recognizable." Wendel clearly interprets the passages that he selected for his "theology of meals" theologically, while providing simultaneously a historical evaluation. The latter appears plausible, though I find no clear evidence for a "theological quality" of the meals of the Jerusalem church in the book of Acts.

The expression "breaking of bread" is still used in some ecclesiastical traditions as a term for the Lord's Supper (e.g., the Brethren Assemblies); a term that has become more widely used is "the Eucharist," derived from the Greek εὐχαριστία (*eucharistia*), "thankfulness, thanksgiving."[48]

Prayer

The fourth characteristic of the Jerusalem church that Luke mentions is the "prayers" (προσευχαί, *proseuchai*) of the believers. The plural implies a regular prayer praxis, perhaps also a reference to the Jewish prayers and times for prayer in which the Jewish Christians of Jerusalem continued to participate, and of course a reference to the congregational prayers of the Christian believers.[49] Luke points out repeatedly that the prayer of the church was a significant factor for missionary work. Prayer did not initiate the mission of the disciples, it is not the primary presupposition of their mission, but it is mentioned at key points in the progress of the history and missionary work of the early church. (1) Before the Feast of Pentecost the followers of Jesus wait for the fulfillment of Jesus' promise of the Spirit while praying (Acts 1:14). (2) The disciples pray during the election of a twelfth apostle (Acts 1:24-25). (3) The sensational healing of a lame man at one of the temple gates happened in connection with the prayer routine of the church leaders: "one day Peter and John were going up to the temple at the hour of prayer, at three o'clock in the afternoon" (Acts 3:1). (4) Prayer is part of the fundamental priorities of the leadership of the church (Acts 6:4). (5) The Samaria mission was accompanied by prayer for the reception of the Holy Spirit (Acts 8:15). (6) The conversion of Saul of Tarsus is linked with prayer (Acts 9:11). (7) The reaction of the Jerusalem church to external pressure and to God's intervention is prayer (Acts 4:23-31).

Acts 4:23-24, 31: "After they were released, they went to their friends and reported what the chief priests and the elders had said to them. [24]When they heard it, they raised their voices together to God and said, 'Sovereign Lord, who made the heaven and the earth, the sea, and everything in them. . . .' [31]When they had prayed, the place in which they were gathered together was shaken; and they were all filled with the Holy Spirit and spoke the word of God with boldness."

---

[48]See J. Wanke, *EWNT* 2:731-32 (*EDNT* 2:296).
[49]Zmijewski, *Apg,* 159, with reference to Acts 2:46; 3:1; as well as 1:14-15; 4:24-30; 12:12.

The prayer of the Jerusalem church in Acts 4:24-30, with its specific reference to historical events and its petition for strength to continue missionary work, has a paradigmatic character. (1) The community of believers who are united in prayer form the place where salvation history is interpreted. The church that prays is the location where the sacred Scriptures are interpreted, where Christians "recognize the structural congruence of the history of the church with Israel's prophecy and with Jesus' history, as thus being under the guidance of God, the Creator, the Lord of history."[50] (2) The church united in prayer is the place where God answers the prayer for strength to engage in courageous missionary work, to confess Jesus the Messiah without fear even under external pressure. The connection between courageous witness and the Holy Spirit characterizes many passages in the book of Acts. Luke emphasizes that God's Spirit guides the mission of the church.[51]

Clearly the Jerusalem church was "not a free association of like-minded people for the purpose of heightened religious self-realization of the individual, but the concrete expression of the given reality of the power of salvation."[52] This reality is an effective reality in a missionary sense: the history of Jesus the Messiah and the significance of his life, death and resurrection, which continues to be proclaimed, are the powerful word of God, the Lord of history and of creation.

Growth

Luke repeatedly refers to the growth of the church in his account of the history and of the mission of the early church, both in summary statements and with regard to specific situations.[53] By repeating in his summary statements references to the growth of the church, Luke highlights in a remarkable manner this facet in comparison to other ecclesiological aspects. This may explain why he refers to the growth of the church last, thus in an emphasized position, in the comprehensive summary statement in Acts 2:42-47.[54] As individual people come to faith in Jesus Christ, the church grows numerically. Ulrich Wendel correctly notes that "the effect of the gospel is related not only to the salvation of many individuals but also to the local congregations as a whole, as they become larger."

15.2 Active Outreach in Jerusalem

According to Acts 1:8, Jesus commissioned the disciples to preach the good

---

[50]Pesch, *Apg,* 1:178.
[51]Cf. Acts 1:8; 4:29-31; 8:26, 29, 39; 10:19, 47; 11:15; 13:2; 16:6-7; 19:21; 20:22, 23; 21:4, 11. See Bieder 1960; Shelton 1991, 125-26; Kurichianil 1994.
[52]Roloff, *Apg,* 66; quoted also in Pesch, *Apg,* 1:133.
[53]Acts 2:47; 5:14; 6:7; 9:31; 12:24; 16:5; 19:20.
[54]See Wendell 1998, 260; the quotation that follows above, ibid., 261.

news starting in Jerusalem and in Judea. As we will see in §§16.2-3, the Twelve seem to have stayed in Jerusalem initially and proclaimed the gospel in the Jewish capital.

Missionary Work in Jerusalem

The visible success of the missionary work of the disciples in Jerusalem became evident in the fact that men and women came to faith in Jesus the Messiah on a daily basis (Acts 2:47; 5:14; 6:7). These conversions evidently happened in connection with the active assemblies of believers in private homes, prompting even priests to come to faith in Jesus the Messiah (Acts 6:7b), as well as in visits by the inhabitants of neighboring towns and villages of Judea who brought their sick to the apostles in Jerusalem (Acts 5:16).

Jerusalem (Ἰερουσαλήμ, *Hierousalēm;* Ἱεροσόλυμα, *Hierosolyma* [fig. 6])[55] was the capital of Israel from 1010 to 930 B.C. after the conquest by King David, and the capital of Judea from 930 to 587 B.C. After the fall of Samaria in 722 B.C., Jerusalem was again the religious and economic center of the entire nation. After the destruction of the city by the Babylonians, the Persian king Kyros in 538 B.C. permitted the return of the exiled Jews, who resettled Jerusalem in several waves under the leadership of Sheshbazzar, Zerubbabel and Jeshua and rebuilt the city and the temple. Nehemiah, the governor of Judea, was able to rebuild the city walls after 445 B.C. The political stability under Ptolemaic rule was responsible for a considerable growth of the population: according to Hecataeus, Jerusalem had 120,000 inhabitants around 250 B.C. (Josephus, *C. Ap.* 1.197). This figure probably is inflated, but it does clearly indicate that Jerusalem was a major urban center at the time. Around 200 B.C. Judea came under Seleucid rule; after 132 B.C. Jerusalem was again the capital of a large kingdom under John Hyrcanus and Alexander Jannaeus. New living quarters were built in the northern part of the city and enclosed with a second wall. After Pompey conquered Jerusalem in 64 B.C., Judea was ruled by the Roman governor Gabinius of Syria. In 37 B.C. the Idumean nobleman Herod, whose father had ruled over Judea as Roman regent, besieged Jerusalem for five months. With Roman help he managed to drive out the Hasmonean Mattathias Antigonus (Josephus, *A.J.* 14.468-486; *B.J.* 1.345-357).

Herod I (the Great), installed as king by the Romans, ruled over Judea, Galilee and several adjacent territories. He was the most energetic of the Roman client kings.[56] He rebuilt Jerusalem as a Greco-Roman capital and the seat of his court.[57] Herod's ambitious building program changed the city significantly: within one generation Jerusalem became one of the most beautiful capital cities of the Eastern Mediterranean. He rebuilt

---

[55]G. Beer, PW 9 (1916): 928-58, esp. 940-58; C. Colpe, *KP* 2:1142-44; Hüttenmeister 1977, 192-243, 525-26; P. Welten, *TRE* 16 (1987): 597-99; R. Riesner, *GBL* 2:661-77; Philip J. King, *ABD* 2:747-66; B. Mazar et al., *NEAEHL* 2:698-804, especially N. Avigad and H. Geva, "Second Temple Period," ibid., 2:717-57; Klaus Bieberstein, *DNP* 5:901-9; Jeremias 1963; Avigad 1983; Burgoyne 1988; Bieberstein and Bloedhorn 1994.

[56]D. M. Jacobson, "Three Roman Client Kings: Herod of Judaea, Archelaos of Cappadocia and Juba of Mauretania," *PEQ* 133 (2001): 22-38.

[57]On the Roman context see MacMullen 2000, 22-24; cf. Hesberg 1996.

several living quarters and erected impressive public buildings (theater/amphitheater,[58] hippodrome,[59] agora, senate building). Jerusalem could boast a Greek library: Nicolaus of Damascus wrote most of the 144 volumes of his universal history in Jerusalem (but Jerusalem had no academy, no rhetorical school, no center for philosophical studies). On the occasions of celebrations honoring Caesar, Herod organized plays in the theater, athletic games with races and wrestling matches, chariot races and fights between convicted criminals and animals (Josephus, *A.J.* 15.268-274). He built palaces and luxurious villas in the upper city; in the western section he built his royal palaces on a huge podium (330 by 130 m) with three large towers (named Phasael, Hippicus and Mariamme).

Herod's largest building project was the enlargement of the temple complex (250 by 250 m), which included a rebuilding of the temple, begun in 22 B.C. (Josephus, *A.J.* 15.268-296; *B.J.* 5.184-237).[60] The retaining walls, which reached a height of about 50 m, towered 30 m above the streets of the city (the stones weighed 2 to 5 tons; the huge stones of the *nidbakh rabba,* which stabilized the wall as a "girdle," weighed 100 tons; the largest stone of the wall that has been discovered measures 12 by 4 by 3 m and weighs about 400 tons). Most of these stones were quarried from the area south of the Antonia Hill. James the brother of Jesus was pushed to his death from the southeast corner of the wall in A.D. 62, to be buried in the Kidron Valley (Eusebius, *Hist. eccl.* 2.23.12-18). From the west, visitors entered the temple complex through four gates (the gate at Wilson's Arch, Warren's Gate, Barclay's Gate, the gate at Robinson's Arch). From the south, visitors entered through the Huldah Gates (6.5 m wide); the eastern gate was the Susa Gate.[61] The outer court was surrounded on three sides by colonnaded halls (porticoes) 13 m high by 16 m wide; the eastern portico was called Solomon's Portico (Josephus, *A.J.* 20.221; Jn 10:23; Acts 3:11; 5:12); the southern portico had four rows of imposing columns and was called the Royal Portico (300 m long). This outer court, the spacious court of the Gentiles, was separated from the inner temple courts by a stone balustrade that displayed Greek and Latin inscriptions warning non-Jews, on penalty of death, against walking into the inner court, where the laws of purification were rigorously obeyed. Jews who entered the temple area proper crossed the outer court, passed through this wall, and ascended a flight of steps onto the huge platform (485/470 by 315/280 m) on which stood the temple itself. The visitor first had to cross the rampart (*hel*), which was about 5 m wide. From the rampart (probably) nine gates gave access to the temple's own wall, which was quite thick and about 20 m high (lower on the eastern side). Within this wall the temple was divided into the court of the women, the court of the Israelites and the sanctuary. The court of the women (67.5 by 67.5 m), on the eastern side, allowed the presence of women; here all communal functions of the temple cult took place. On the western side fifteen semicircular stairs led to the Nicanor Gate, which led to the inner (Israelites') court (67.5 by 5.5 m) and, separated by a partition 50 cm high (Josephus, *B.J.* 5.226), the court of the priests (93.5 by 67.5 m) with the altar (15 by 15 m) and the slaughterhouse; it was here that most of the ritual functions of the temple

---

[58]Recently eleven blocks were found that have been interpreted as theater seats; see R. Reich and Y. Billig, "A Group of Theatre Seats Discovered Near the South-Western Corner of the Temple Mount," *IEJ* 50 (2000): 175-184.
[59]See Z. Weiss, in Humphrey 1995-2002, 2:23, 26.
[60]On the excavations in the area of the temple see H. Geva, *NEAEHL* 2:736-44. On the temple see Schwier 1989; Ådna 1999a; Dan Bahat, "The Herodian Temple," in *CHJ* 3:38-58; B. Chilton et al., *DNTB* 1167-83.
[61]On "traffic" in the temple complex see Sawicki 2000, 48-54.

were carried out. Twelve stairs led up to the temple building proper, which measured 50 by 50 m and stood 60 m high. The porch (5.5 m wide) had a gold candlestick above the door to the sanctuary, which was decorated in gold and had a vine trailing over cedar posts. The sanctuary (20 by 10 m) housed the gold vessels, the menorah, the table for the shewbread and the altar for burning incense. The holy of holies measured 10 by 10 m and was accessed from the sanctuary to the east through two curtains; its walls probably were covered with gold foil, and part of the bedrock (*shetiyah*) protruded above the floor. The sanctuary and the holy of holies were surrounded by thirty-eight cells used by the priests, while various chambers in the three inner courts housed ritual baths, wood, oil, priestly vestments and the temple treasures, including money deposited by private citizens. This enormous complex could accommodate 75,000 people,[62] and it emphasized the division of city and temple—a fact that Josephus comments on (*A.J.* 15.400).[63] Below the surface of the temple were huge cisterns that could hold 1,765,750 cu. ft. of water.

The main street of Jerusalem was 10 m wide, paved with stone slabs measuring 2 by 4 m (with a sewer beneath the street up to 4 m deep). It ran from northwest to south, leading from the new city via the Tyropoeon Valley to Robinson's Arch at the southwest corner of the temple mount. A bridge 3.6 m wide, 13 m long and 17.5 m high linked the temple mount with the city. From Robinson's Arch the street continued south to the Siloam Pool and one of the city gates; another street led north to the Antonia fortress.

After the death of Herod I in 4 B.C., his son Archelaos ruled in Jerusalem, Judea and Samaria as ethnarch. Unrest among the population prompted the Romans to intervene: Varus, the Roman procurator in Syria, occupied the city and had many citizens executed (Josephus, *A.J.* 17.250-264, 286-297). Archelaos was sent into exile to Vienne in Gaul in A.D. 6; Judea became a Roman province with Caesarea, the harbor city that Herod had built, as the seat of the governor. A Roman garrison was stationed in the Antonia fortress on the northwestern corner of the temple mount, built around a central courtyard (the so-called Lithostrotos), with four towers. The praetorium probably was located in the old Hasmonean palace on the western slopes of the Tyropoeon Valley opposite the temple mount.[64] In the period A.D. 6-66 fourteen Roman procurators ruled in Judea and thus in Jerusalem, increasingly disregarding the sensibilities of the Jewish population and provoking tensions that repeatedly triggered violent incidents—for example, at the time of Pontius Pilatus (A.D. 26-36), who used temple funds to build an aqueduct for Jerusalem (Josephus, *A.J.* 18.60-62; *B.J.* 2.175-177). The new living quarters in the northern part of the city occupied the hill Bezetha. The remains of the luxurious villas of the new city that have been discovered confirm the wealth of the citizens who lived here, but also the fact that they scrupulously followed the purity laws: the villas have at least one ritual bath (*miqveh*), and some have two or three. The floors were laid out with mosaics with flower or geometric motifs, and walls were decorated with frescoes. The most luxurious villa (in area P), with its numerous ritual baths, has been interpretred as the living quarters of a high priestly family. Agrippa I began to build a third wall for the defense of the new city between A.D. 41 and 44; it was finished not before A.D. 66. During Agrippa's reign the work on the temple was completed; many of the people who had worked on the temple also were employed in paving the streets of the city.

The most important institution in Jerusalem, apart from the temple, was the Sanhedrin, which decided religious and civil questions. The meeting place of the Sanhedrin was

---

[62]Blue 1998, 483 n. 33.
[63]Hesberg 1996, 12.
[64]B. Pixner, *ZDPV* 95 (1973): 65-86; R. Riesner, *GBL* 3:1222.

moved around A.D. 30 from the chamber of the hewn stone in the court of the priests to the "shops" (*m. Sanh.* 41:2; *b. Sanh.* 88b)—that is, presumably to the Royal Portico on the southern end of the temple mount. The Essene quarter was in the southwestern part of the city, as was the Essene gate mentioned by Josephus (*B.J.* 5.145).[65]

Jerusalem had at least 60,000 inhabitants around A.D. 45, probably even between 100,000 and 120,000 inhabitants.[66] Every year the temple was visited by hundreds of thousands of pilgrims who secured the livelihood of the city's inhabitants. Many older Jews living in the Diaspora returned to Jerusalem; many of them were impoverished. Numerous graves have been discovered in the vicinity of the city: apart from relatively simple chambers hewn in the rocks, there are ornate and monumental graves, as, for example, the mausoleum of Herod I and of Queen Helena of Adiabene, who had converted to Judaism and helped the Jews with food subsidies during the reign of Claudius (Josephus, *A.J.* 20.51-52, 95-96). There were numerous synagogues in Jerusalem, some of them for the Diaspora Jews living in the city. The "synagogue of the freedmen" mentioned in Acts 6:9 is possibly the building mentioned in a dedicatory inscription (*CIJ* II 332-35). At the conclusion of Rome's suppression of the First Jewish Revolt, Titus destroyed the temple in September of A.D. 70, after having destroyed large parts of the city since June.

According to the book of Acts, the missionary work of the early church in Jerusalem had a threefold thrust: (1) public proclamation of the gospel in the temple (i.e., on the temple mount) by the apostles (Acts 3:1; 4:1-2; 5:12, 20-21, 42); (2) proclamation of the gospel in the synagogues (Acts 6:8-10) by Stephen and presumably by other followers of Jesus; (3) the attraction of the communities of the believers who had fellowship in private homes, who celebrated common meals, who cared for each other financially, who worshiped God, and who taught and explained the good news of Jesus the Messiah (Acts 2:46-47; 5:42). The comment in Acts 8:3 that Saul entered "house after house" in order to drag off both men and women whom he arrested and committed to prison may plausibly be taken as an indication of house churches that actively proclaimed the gospel and attracted new converts.[67]

The missionary work of the apostles is grounded in the conviction that salvation can be found only in Jesus. When Peter and John are forced by a general assembly of the Sanhedrin to give an account of their preaching, Peter states,

Acts 4:12: "There is salvation in no one else, for there is no other name under heaven given among mortals by which we must be saved."

Many critical scholars attribute this statement to Lukan redaction, as they do most of Pe-

---

[65]B. Pixner, "The History of the 'Essene Gate' Area," *ZDPV* 105 (1989): 96-104, plates 8-16a; Riesner 1995a.

[66]M. Avi-Yona (*IEJ* 11 [1961]: 93) reckons 120,000 inhabitants before A.D. 70; Ben-David (1974, 57) estimates between 90,000 and 110,000; J. Scheckenhofer (*Die Bevölkerung Palästinas um die Wende der Zeiten: Versuch einer Statistik* [Munich: Vögel, 1978], 26-31) assumes 120,000; H. Geva (*NEAEHL* 2:721) reckons 80,000; Reinhardt (1995b, 263) estimates between 100,000 and 120,000 around A.D. 45.

[67]Vogler 1982, 789, with reference to Acts 12:12.

ter's speech in Acts 4:8-12. Jacob Jervell, for example, writes, "Preformed tradition is extant only in v. 11. . . . It is very difficult to know what happened historically. This is not a faithful historical account."[68] However, at least two considerations support the view that Peter indeed said what Luke reports. (1) The first few years after Jesus' death and resurrection saw an unprecedented development of theological reflection, and there is nothing in Acts 4:12 that does not fit into the framework of the earliest convictions of the early Christians in Jerusalem.[69] (2) The apostles were convinced that Jesus was the Messiah, the promised Redeemer of Israel: if the salvation of Israel is connected with the Messiah,[70] and if Jesus is the Messiah, and if his death, resurrection and exaltation possess redemptive significance, then Peter's assertion that salvation can now be obtained exclusively through Jesus has a solid and convincing basis.

The salvation that Peter refers to is salvation "from this corrupt generation" (Acts 2:40). Salvation therefore implies separation from the unbelieving and disobedient people and affiliation with the true people of God of the last days, with the community of people who believe in Jesus as God's Messiah and who have received the Spirit of prophecy promised by God through Joel, the Spirit who conveys new life corresponding with this new loyalty.[71]

Peter's confessional statement is interpreted in terms of an "exclusivist position" not by evangelical scholars only. Jürgen Roloff, for example, describes the conviction of Luke expressed in Acts 4:12 as follows: "As a result of his resurrection, God made Jesus the sole foundation of salvation."[72] And Rudolf Pesch speaks of the "exclusivity (and universality) of the mediation of salvation by Jesus Christ, the Messiah from Nazareth."[73] When some modern interpreters deny that the statement in Acts 4:12 describes Jesus' significance in terms of consistent exclusivity, such a denial seems to be a consequence of the contemporary religious pluralism promulgated by, for example, Paul Knitter and John Hick.

Clark Pinnock, for example, thinks that the commentaries (of F. F. Bruce, E. Haenchen, R. N. Longenecker, H. Conzelmann) are disappointing because they treat the book of Acts as a historical rather than a theological text, and because they regard Acts 4:12 as proof for the exclusivist paradigm.[74] Pinnock seems to have chosen to interpret Acts 4:12 in nonexclusivist terms no matter what the text actually says. The authorities to whom he appeals for a more "inclusive" interpretation do not include a single commentator on the book of Acts. Pinnock rightly asserts that the text does not answer the question of the eschatological fate of people who have never heard the gospel. He is wrong, however,

---

[68]Jervell, *Apg,* 183; cf. Lüdemann 1987, 61-65 (ET, 55-60); Conzelmann, *Apg,* 41 (ET, 32); Schneider, *Apg,* 1:342; Weiser, *Apg,* 1:121-24; Roloff, *Apg,* 80; similarly Fitzmyer, *Acts,* 297; Zmijewski, *Apg,* 208-9. Pesch (*Apg,* 1:163), however, has more confidence in the tradition.
[69]Marshall, *Acts,* 90; cf. Witherington, *Acts,* 194.
[70]Jervell, *Apg,* 179.
[71]Barrett, *Acts,* 1:231.
[72]Roloff, *Apg,* 82.
[73]Pesch, *Apg,* 2:167; cf. Munck, *Acts,* 34; Weiser, *Apg,* 1:121, 127; Schille, *Apg,* 132. See also Marshall, *Acts,* 101.
[74]Pinnock 1993, 107-15, esp. 108 n. 3.

when he states that the text expresses the incomparable power of the name of Jesus that saves people who hear and who respond, without commenting on the fate of the Gentiles. Peter ties salvation, including salvation in God's final judgment, to confessing faith in Jesus Christ, with regard not only to Gentiles but also to Jews.

The interpretation of Acts 4:12 in the sense of the exclusive redemptive significance of faith in Jesus Christ is supported at least by the following arguments. (1) The context of Acts 4:12 focuses on Jews, not on Gentiles, particularly on the members of the Sanhedrin who were responsible for Jesus' execution and who are now listening to Peter's explanations. (2) Peter asserts that the salvation granted by God is not attainable through any other means (οὐκ ἔστιν ἐν ἄλλῳ οὐδενί, *ouk estin en allō oudeni*) or through any other name (οὐδὲ ὄνομά ἐστιν ἕτερον, *oude onoma estin heteron*) than that of the crucified and risen Jesus, the Messiah from Nazareth (Acts 4:10, 12). Implied in this statement is the conviction that all other paths to salvation have become invalid, including the cult in the Jerusalem temple for which the chief priests who are present are responsible. (3) Peter refers to persons (*onoma,* "name") "under heaven" (ὑπὸ τὸν οὐρανόν, *hypo ton ouranon*), meaning "on earth, throughout the earth,"[75] in the entire world. Acts 2:5 similarly speaks of Diaspora Jews "from every nation under heaven" (ἀπὸ παντὸς ἔθνους τῶν ὑπὸ τὸν οὐρανόν), meaning from the entire world. Peter's reference to "mortals" (NRSV) or "human beings" (RSV, NIV, NASB translate ἐν ἀνθρώποις, *en anthrōpois,* with "among men") in Acts 4:12 relates generally to "all people in the world." (4) Peter's assertion that salvation is possible only through the crucified and risen Christ implies the universal perspective of the earth "under heaven" that necessitates the universal significance of Jesus, and thus implies the exclusive significance of Jesus for the salvation of humankind, Gentiles included. This conclusion corresponds to the fact that Jews claimed particularistic exclusivity of salvation for God's revelation in the temple and the sacrificial cult: if there is no other possibility to obtain salvation (now) for Jews except faith in Jesus the crucified and risen Messiah, then there can be no hope whatsoever that non-Jews might find salvation through any other means, since the God who reveals himself in Israel, mercifully granting forgiveness and salvation, is the one and only God. The conclusion that for the early Christians the life, death and resurrection of Jesus the Messiah have exclusive redemptive significance can be avoided only if one postulates that Peter's conclusion is impossible.

Clark Pinnock correctly points out that scholars who read meanings into Acts 4:12 that are not in the text are influenced by some particular interest. Pinnock's formulations clearly indicate that he falls under his own verdict of prejudiced exegesis: he labels those who interpret Peter's statement in an "exclusive" sense as restrictive hard-liners who ma-

---

[75] BDAG 737, s.v. "οὐρανός 1b"; BAA 1202, s.v. "οὐρανός 1b."

nipulate the text on opportunistic grounds, whereas those who interpret the text as he does are "more generous"—and who does not want to be generous! Pinnock at least is honest when he clarifies that he wants to avoid the "utterly repugnant" notion that Acts 4:12 excludes the majority of the world's population from eschatological salvation. Since he identifies himself as an evangelical, Pinnock is unwilling to criticize Peter, and so he refuses to interpret Acts 4:12 as the vast majority of exegetes do and then conclude that this theological position is misguided. He prefers to speculate concerning the possibility of salvation for those who have never heard the gospel in *limbus,* the intermediate state between death and resurrection. He may believe that this notion agrees with God's love and fairness,[76] but he can find no exegetical justification for this position.

The conviction that faith in Jesus Christ constitutes the only chance for salvation, for every human being no matter where he or she lives, is "the basis and the driving force of the Christian mission."[77] The disciples were convinced that the death and resurrection of Jesus, the promised Messiah, inaugurated the messianic era of salvation, the time in which God would gather the nations on Mount Zion, as he had promised through the prophets. James argues at the apostolic council that the gathering of the nations could become a reality only after Jesus had completed the ministry for the house of Israel, an integral part of which was his death and his resurrection.

Acts 15:15-18: "The words of the prophets are in agreement with this, as it is written: [16]'After this I will return and rebuild David's fallen tent. Its ruins I will rebuild, and I will restore it, [17]that the remnant of men may seek the Lord, and all the Gentiles who bear my name, says the Lord, who does these things' [18]that have been known for ages" (NIV) (cf. Amos 9:11-12).

The Twelve understood, they comprehended the task assigned to them by Jesus for the time until he would return and usher in the consummation of the kingdom of God in a visible and final way: Jesus had called them from the beginning to follow him and be trained as "fishers of people," winning people for faith in Jesus' message of the arrival of God's reign (Mk 1:17); Jesus had given them practical experience in the implementation of this assignment (Mk 6:7-13/Mt 10:1-15/Lk 9:1-6); Jesus confirmed their commission before his ascension and described it as an assignment that was universal in scope and international in extent and was the answer to the question of when God would restore the kingdom to "Israel" (Acts 1:8). The disciples had grasped the significance of their commission: they restored the full number of twelve apostles as "witnesses of the resurrection" of Jesus (Acts 1:21-22), and they began to proclaim with confidence and with courage the message of salvation through Jesus the Messiah. The disciples were convinced—the results of the apostolic council make this very clear—that the proclamation of the significance of Jesus Christ would bring

---

[76]Pinnock 1993, 114 n. 18.
[77]Brox 1983, 27.

about the gathering of the nations and the affiliation of Jewish and Gentile believers with the kingdom of God, promised by the prophets as the final event
before the consummation. As witnesses among the nations, the Twelve have a
part in the fulfillment of God's plan of salvation.

Did all Jewish Christians in Jerusalem engage in active missionary work? John Penney argues that Luke was convinced that all believers in Jesus received the Holy Spirit because
the new people of God had been called in its entirety and as a community to fulfill the
role of the anointed Servant of Yahweh in Is 42; 47; 49; in other words, each and every
follower of Jesus is obligated, from the first day of his or her conversion, to give verbal
witness of the gospel.[78] This view is unconvincing. We note, first, that according to Is 40—
66, the witness to the nations consists not only of the proclamation inspired by the Spirit
but also of the life that God's Spirit has restored. Second, the evidence of the book of Acts
does not allow the conclusion that new converts are expected to engage in missionary
work.[79] According to the summary statements about the life of the early church, the first
Christians and the new converts devoted themselves to the teaching of the apostles, to
the breaking of bread, to prayers, to the worship of God with joy and thanksgiving, and
to committed service for the poor in the congregation (Acts 2:42-47). Luke does not report
that the new converts gave witness of Jesus. His account leaves the impression that the
proclamation of the gospel before outsiders was the task particularly of the Twelve (Acts
4:32-37; 5:12-16) and of other Spirit-filled Christians such as Barnabas, Philip, Stephen,
Paul, John Mark, Silas, Timothy and Apollos, and he knows other Christians who engaged
in missionary work (Acts 8:4; 11:19-20). The prayer of the Jerusalem church for courage
to speak the word of the Lord with boldness (Acts 4:29) constitutes no proof that all members of the Jerusalem church were active in evangelism: the expression οἱ ἴδιοι (hoi idioi),
"their own," in Acts 4:23 should be linked, in the context of Acts 4:29, 30 and Acts 4:33;
5:12, with the apostles as "leaders in speech and action."[80] The conversion stories of the
Samaritans, of Cornelius and his family and of the twelve men in Ephesus explicitly mention the reception of the Holy Spirit by the new converts but never mention an evangelistic or missionary activity on their part. It surely is a plausible assumption that the new
converts told their relatives, friends and acquaintances of the new-found faith, and in
terms of "missionary tactics" the witness and testimony of new converts surely is effective.
However, there is no exegetical warrant for the position that this must be the case, that
new converts must be witnesses, or that their testimony will always be effective.

The Conversion of Pharisees and Essenes
Luke reports the conversion of Pharisees for the time after A.D. 40 (Acts 15:5).
Paul the apostle, who came to faith in Jesus the Messiah presumably in A.D. 31/
32, was himself a Pharisee (Phil 3:5). His aggressive activities against Christians
in A.D. 30/31 might have been motivated in part by the fact that some of his
Pharisee friends had accepted Jesus as the Messiah.

It is possible that Essenes came to faith in Jesus as the Messiah at a very early

---

[78]Penney 1997. He suggests that new converts have the most effective evangelistic witness.
[79]Turner 1997, 94-95.
[80]See Barrett, Acts 1:242-43. The NRSV renders οἱ ἴδιοι as "friends," while the NIV and TNIV translate it as "their own people."

time, possibly even before the persecution that followed the death of Stephen in A.D. 31/32. Luke's comment in Acts 6:7 is interpreted by some scholars in this sense.

Acts 6:7: "The word of God continued to spread; the number of the disciples increased greatly in Jerusalem, and a great many of the priests became obedient to the faith."

It appears that there were but few priests in the Pharisaic movement, whereas the Essenes and the Sadducees included a majority of priests as members. A mass conversion of Sadducees to the Christian faith is hardly likely, as their leading representatives in the Sanhedrin had been involved in the trial that condemned Jesus to death. The Essenes represented an apocalyptic movement characterized by intense messianic expectations, and they understood themselves as the eschatological sanctuary, similar to the self-understanding of the early church; they were more likely to come to faith in Jesus as the Messiah.[81] The first new converts were "devout Jews living in Jerusalem" (Acts 2:5). They heard the sound on the occasion of the miraculous events at the Feast of Pentecost in A.D. 30. Since the upper room in which the Twelve and other followers of Jesus met probably was located in the immediate vicinity of the Essene quarter, the assumption is plausible that Essenes were present when Peter explained the speech miracle in terms of the coming of the Holy Spirit, and it is possible that perhaps a larger number of Essenes were converted.[82] It may be significant in this respect that the casting of lots, used in the election of Matthias as the twelfth disciple, is not attested among Pharisees but has parallels among the Qumran Essenes.[83] The sharing of possessions also has parallels in the Essene movement.[84] Stephen calls Jesus "the righteous one" (Acts 7:52), a term used in the Enoch literature, which was close to the milieu of the Essenes, as a messianic title (*1 En.* 38:2; 53:6). Stephen is buried by "devout men" (Acts 8:2), a term that may refer to Essene friends. It has been suggested that the Christian Ananias in Damascus was a former Essene as well (see §20.5).

Possibly the chronology of Jesus' Last Supper is linked with the Essenes as well. According to the Synoptic Gospels, Jesus celebrated a Passover seder (Mk 14:12-16; Lk 22:7-13), while the Gospel of John identifies the day of Jesus' crucifixion with the day of preparation for

---

[81]Riesner 1995a, 1862, 1869, with reference to C. Spicq, *RevQ* 1 (1958-1959): 365-390; K. Schubert, in Maier and Schubert 1973, 130; Grappe 1992, 52-73.

[82]Riesner 1995a, 1862-63; for the observations that follow above see ibid.; see also Capper 1995, 341-50.

[83]1QS VI, 16-22; IX, 7; see W. A. Beardslee, "The Casting of Lots at Qumran and in the Book of Acts," *NovT* 4 (1960): 245-52; Annie Jaubert, *L'élection de Matthias et le tirage au sort* (TU 112; Berlin: Akademie-Verlag, 1973), 274-80; Riesner 1995a, 1875.

[84]Cf. Acts 2:42, 44-45; 4:32, 34-35. See D. L. Mealand, "Community of Goods at Qumran," *ThZ* 31 (1975): 129-39; Klauck 1989, 69-100; B. J. Capper, "Community of Goods in the Early Jerusalem Church," *ANRW* II.26.2 (1995): 1730-74; Riesner 1995a, 1877.

the Passover (Jn 18:28; 19:14). Some scholars suggest that this problem can be solved with reference to the solar calendar that was in use among the Essenes. According to the solar calendar, each new quarter of the year began on a Wednesday, and the Jewish feasts were always celebrated on the same day of the week, the Feast of Passover always on a Tuesday evening. This means that Jesus could have celebrated a Passover meal with his disciples on the night from Tuesday to Wednesday according to the solar calendar, while the priests who followed the traditional lunar calendar celebrated the Passover on Thursday night. This chronology is already found in the *Didascalia Apostolorum* (5.12-18).[85]

15.3 Forms of Organization

The evidence in the book of Acts provides few details concerning the organization of the earliest community of believers in Jesus in Jerusalem. Luke mentions three groups of people who had leadership functions: the Twelve, the Seven and the Elders.

The Twelve

The apostles are mentioned repeatedly in the book of Acts.[86] The term "the twelve apostles" occurs in Acts 1:26, and the term "the Twelve" in Acts 6:2. According to Luke's account, the Twelve were responsible for the following areas and activities in the first years of the existence of the Jerusalem church:[87] (1) teaching and prayer (Acts 6:4); (2) evangelism in Jerusalem, Judea, Samaria and in the regions to the ends of the earth (Acts 1:8); (3) consolidation of churches in other regions, such as Samaria and Antioch in Syria (Acts 1:8; 8:14-25; 9:32-35; 11:22); (4) decisions regarding developments in the Gentile mission (Acts 11:1-18; 11:22-24; 15:1-29); (5) decisions regarding disciplinary issues in the Jerusalem congregation (Acts 5:1-11); (6) appointment of co-workers in the Jerusalem congregation (Acts 6:1-6).

Luke describes the Twelve as leaders of the Jerusalem church, with Peter as *primus inter pares*, until Acts 11:1.[88] The persecution in the year A.D. 31/32 brought no changes in the leadership position of the Twelve, when many Christians were forced to leave the city after the martyrdom of Stephen, including a number of prominent, leading Christians who left Jerusalem permanently (Acts 8:1). This phase of the earliest history of the Jerusalem church came to a close in A.D. 41/42 when Herod Agrippa I (A.D. 41-44) started a new persecution of

---

[85] Annie Jaubert, *La date de la Cène* (Paris: Gabalda, 1957); idem, *NTS* 7 (1960-1961): 1-30; idem, *NTS* 14 (1967-1968): 145-64; E. Ruckstuhl, *Die Chronologie des Letzten Mahles und des Leidens Jesu* (Einsiedeln: Johannes-Verlag, 1963); idem, *Jesus im Horizont der Evangelien* (Stuttgart: Katholisches Bibelwerk, 1988), 101-84; J. Carmignac, *RevQ* 5 (1964): 59-79; Pixner 1994, 219-28; for a list of further authors who support this solution see Riesner 1995a, 1887 n. 583.

[86] Acts 1:2; 2:37, 42-43; 4:33, 35-37; 5:2, 12, 18, 29, 40; 6:6; 8:1, 14; 9:27; 11:1; 15:2, 4, 6, 22-23; 16:4; cf. the list of Jesus' disciples in 1:13.

[87] See Dumais 1990, 50-54; Vidal Manzanares 1995, 233. Bartchy (2002, 98-101) is overly skeptical.

[88] For the subsequent analysis I follow Bauckham 1995b, 427-44, which Bartchy (2002) ignores.

the Christians. In the course of this persecution several church members were tortured, and one of the Twelve, James (the son of Zebedee and the brother of John) was killed (Acts 12:1-2). Peter was arrested during the Feast of Passover and was to be executed publicly after the feast (Acts 12:3-4).[89] He escaped miraculously after the church had prayed fervently (Acts 12:5, 6-12). It seems that this persecution in the twelfth year after Jesus' death and resurrection ended the leadership of the Twelve in the Jerusalem church: when Barnabas and Paul visit Jerusalem in connection with the famine relief that the church in Antioch had organized in A.D. 44, they meet "elders" (πρεσβύτεροι, *presbyteroi*) of the church in Jerusalem (Acts 11:30). These elders evidently replaced the Twelve as the leadership team of the Jerusalem church, with James the brother of Jesus being the senior pastor (Acts 12:17; 15:13; 21:18 [see below]). Peter had been the chief spokesman and leader of the church in Jerusalem and its missionary outreach in Samaria and in the coastal plain, proclaiming the gospel to Jews and to Gentiles, a task that was taken over by James (Acts 12:17; 15:13; 21:18).

Acts 12:17: "He motioned to them with his hand to be silent, and described for them how the Lord had brought him out of the prison. And he added, 'Tell this to James and to the believers.' Then he left and went to another place."

Acts 15:13: "After they finished speaking, James replied, 'My brothers, listen to me.'" (Note the context, Acts 15:6-7, 12: "The apostles and the elders met together to consider this matter. [7]After there had been much debate, Peter stood up and said to them, 'My brothers, . . .' [12]The whole assembly kept silence, and listened to Barnabas and Paul as they told of all the signs and wonders that God had done through them among the Gentiles.")

Acts 21:18: "The next day Paul went with us to visit James; and all the elders were present."

It is not certain whether the Twelve were replaced after A.D. 41/42 by a group of three leaders consisting of "the prominent ones," the "influential men" (οἱ δοκοῦντες, *hoi dokountes*), also called "the pillars" (οἱ στῦλοι, *hoi styloi*): James the brother of Jesus, Peter and John (Gal 2:9; cf. 1:9), with James as *primus inter pares*.[90] The designation "the pillars" surely expresses the conviction that they were "the center and the decisive authorities of the redemptive community, as well as the conviction that this center can be located naturally and rightfully at no other place than Jerusalem." Paul does not speak of a leadership committee or of an "office," however, and presumably does not imply such either. During the events described in Gal 2:1-10 Peter evidently merely visited Jerusalem; that is, his authority was no longer tied to the Jerusalem church. Also, we must remember that the apostles did not act independently of the church: important

---

[89]On the meaning of ἀναγαγεῖν τῷ λαῷ in 12:4 see Barrett, *Acts,* 1:576.
[90]Thus Roloff 1993, 80; the quotation that follows above, ibid.

decisions were made by the entire congregation (Acts 1:23; 6:5; cf. 11:22; 15:22). The suggestion by F. Scott Spencer that "throughout the Book of Acts a non-hierarchical, democratic process characterizes church government in general and the appointment of ministers in particular"[91] perhaps employs somewhat overstated terminology, but it does describe the heart of the matter.

Finally, we need to note the astonishing and spontaneous flexibility that the Twelve demonstrated. The appointment of seven men to be responsible for the care of the widows in the church (Acts 6:1-6) is preceded by the willingness of the Twelve to admit personal failure and personal limitations. The Twelve were quickly willing to delegate administrative tasks in view of the need to concentrate on the primary tasks that the risen Christ had given to them. The role of Peter was discussed in §14.3; his missionary activity will be discussed in §21.

The Seven

The appointment of the Seven is reported in Acts 6:1-7 (see also §19.1). Stephen probably was the leader of this group: he is mentioned first in the list in Acts 6:5, and in Acts 6:10 he is singled out as powerful and influential preacher. The Seven took care of administrative tasks and charitable ministries in the church,[92] at least initially. The suggestion that they had two additional tasks, as leaders of the Hellenistic Jewish Christians in the congregation and as "outposts" of the missionary outreach of the Jewish and Gentile Hellenists,[93] cannot be substantiated exegetically from Acts 6—7. The fact that Stephen and Philip were engaged in evangelism does not warrant the suggestion that the Seven were "evangelists" and should therefore be distinguished from the later office of "deacons" (cf. Rom 12:7; 1 Tim 3:8). As the Twelve did not mind being involved in administrative and charitable tasks if circumstances demanded it, so also the Seven did not shrink from proclaiming the gospel of Jesus Christ when they were presented with opportunities to do so.

The view of some scholars concerning the early church seems to owe more to later ecclesiastical demarcations and sensibilities concerning areas of responsibility that are read back into the first century than to straightforward exegesis of the text. German scholars who use the word *Amt* ("office, agency, bureau") should consider whether the realities of modern state and ecclesiastical bureaucracies influence their exegesis or their reconstruction of early Christian developments. Paul was at different times in differing roles, sometimes simultaneously: cross-cultural missionary traveling from region to region, evangelist in a city, pastor of a local congregation, counselor, coordinator of the affairs of churches in an interregional framework (the bishop or superintendent of today), leader of a missionary team, teacher of co-workers, teacher of new converts, theologian, author of theological writings, author of hymns (perhaps), and leather worker who needed to

[91]F. Spencer 1992, 196-98; cf. Bauckham 1995b, 428 with n. 38.
[92]H. W. Beyer, *ThWNT* 2:909 (*TDNT* 2:907).
[93]Löning 1987, 83; cf. Burchard 1984, 25-26; Zmijewski, *Apg,* 287.

earn money. A missionary who explores new territory without any existing models, who is ready to value co-workers more than self, who is prepared to carry the cross daily, is not the "head of a department" or an "office boss." A missionary tackles the tasks at hand, using every opportunity for preaching the good news of Jesus Christ, and striving to nurture new believers in any way necessary. Luke's account in Acts 6 shows that conflicts may arise despite selfless service and dedicated ministry. But Acts 6 also demonstrates that such conflict can be solved ad hoc if those involved have the will to find solutions, if they are prepared to admit mistakes, be flexible and delegate tasks, and if they focus on what is of central importance.

Jürgen Roloff criticizes Luke's account in Acts 6:1-6 for addressing the conflict "only very briefly," for omitting a "self-critical admission of the inadequate provision for the tables" and for focusing entirely on the solution of the conflict.[94] I find this critique incomprehensible. A "self-critique" of the Twelve is not missing at all: the appointment of seven co-workers implies the admission of the Twelve that they had failed the widows and that the solution of the problem is not an intensified involvement on their part; their emphasis of the danger that the proclamation of the gospel might be neglected implies the admission that they had misjudged the time required to adequately care for the needy in the congregation. Why should the "certainty" with which the Twelve solve the problem be "astonishing"? Roloff is right when he asserts that "the apostles recognize as a result of the conflict what must be done, and they act accordingly. The conflict is thus evacuated of all elements of crisis." Why should the apostles not have been able to achieve just that? Christianity never would have taken hold or survived without the ministry of the Twelve; we should not doubt their abilities to solve conflicts.

Gerd Theissen interprets the group of the Seven as "a first attempt to create local authorities for Jerusalem besides the supraregional authorities of the Twelve. The new group is not (at least in theory) in competition with the superior group, but is subordinate to it. In practice, however, tensions could arise." The cause of the problem was the rapidly growing size of the church, which confronted members with the difficulty of having to care for more and more needy people, especially widows. Theissen surmises that the constitution of the group of the Seven may have been motivated by the attempt to provide a balance to the predominance of the "Hebrew" Jewish Christians represented by the Twelve, creating a smaller group of leaders whose authority was restricted in geographical terms, limited to ministry in Jerusalem. When Stephen died and persecution ensued, the Twelve evidently were not in Jerusalem but were engaged in missionary work elsewhere.[95] Theissen's suggestion that the Seven represented a "local board" that was responsible for the church in Jerusalem, whereas the authority and the ministry of the Twelve were related to all of Israel, is not supported by the text. In view of Jewish parallels,[96] the term "the Seven" (Acts 6:3; 21:8) sim-

---

[94]Roloff 1991, 117-18; the quotations that follow above, 118.
[95]Theissen 1996, esp. 326-31, quotation 328.
[96]See Josephus, *A.J.* 4.214; *B.J.* 2.571; *b. Meg.* 26a; *y. Meg.* 3:74a [16]; see also the group of seven men who organized communal meals in Palmyra, and the Septemviri in Rome (Tacitus, *Ann.* 3.64).

ply means that seven men were chosen for the assignment of taking care of specific tasks,[97] or that a new church office was established consisting of seven men.[98] The view that the Seven represented the leadership of the Jerusalem church is implausible in view of the context of Acts 6. The Twelve are present in Jerusalem exercising authority in the congregation, which does not preclude the possibility that they were engaged in missionary travels in Judea and the surrounding regions. It is only after Acts 11:30 (cf. Acts 15:2, 4, 22; 16:4) that the "Elders" appear as a group besides the apostles, with the latter evidently having left Jerusalem. And there is no hint in the text that these "Elders" were synonymous with the Twelve. There is also no hint that the "first attempt" to create a group of leaders with local authority in Jerusalem failed.[99] Luke does not link the Seven with tasks that are connected with the leadership of the congregation at large, nor does he report any activities on their part that would imply such an authority. Apart from these caveats, Theissen's endeavor to write the history of the early church "with the sources" and not against the sources is to be welcomed, and his suggestions are largely persuasive: the congregation of the followers of Jesus in Jerusalem grew rapidly; difficulties arose regarding the provision of food for the widows who belonged to the Jews from the Diaspora who had returned to Jerusalem; the church or the apostles appointed a group of seven men who were given the task of solving this problem; when the Christians were persecuted after the death of Stephen, the Twelve were unaffected because they were engaged in missionary work elsewhere; the supraregional ministry of the Twelve made it necessary to institute leaders of the Jerusalem congregation.[100]

The Seven worked alongside the Twelve,[101] responsible for the financial affairs of the congregation and for the daily care of the needy believers. The Seven clearly were not an independent authority in the Jerusalem church, as the appointment by the congregation and by the Twelve in Acts 6:6 shows.

When the Twelve left Jerusalem, the latter reality might have changed. On the other hand, some members of the group of the Seven left Jerusalem and Judea after Stephen's martyrdom: at least Philip, possibly others or even all of the Seven who were Stephen's colleagues. If the group of the Seven ceased to exist, possibly, in A.D. 31/32, and the Twelve left Jerusalem in A.D. 41/42, then the Seven can hardly be identical with the "Elders" of (Acts 11:30).[102]

---

[97]Barrett, *Acts*, 1:312.

[98]Zmijewski, *Apg*, 285.

[99]Contra Theissen 1996, 328 n. 14.

[100]Theissen (1996, 328 n. 14) speaks of a "need resulting from structural necessities," following Zahn, *Apg*, 223-37.

[101]See Conzelmann 1969, 44 (ET, 58); Zmijewski, *Apg*, 287.

[102]See T. M. Lindsay, *The Church and the Ministry in the Early Centuries* (London: Hodder & Stoughton, 1902), 115-17; A. M. Farrar, "The Ministry in the New Testament," in *The Apostolic Ministry* (ed. K. E. Kirk; London: Hodder & Stoughton, 1946), 133-42.

The Elders

A group called the "Elders" (πρεσβύτεροι, *presbyteroi*), exercising the leadership function in the Jerusalem church, is mentioned in Acts 11:30; 21:18; they are mentioned alongside the apostles in Acts 15:2, 4, 6, 22, 23; 16:4. This "church council" could be understood as analogous to a Jewish sanhedrin (*synedrion*); Greek-speaking readers of the book of Acts would have been reminded of the γερουσία (*gerousia*), the "council of elders" of Hellenistic cities.[103]

Some scholars suggest that the Elders were the successors of the Seven.[104] In terms of direct successors in a chronological sense this view is implausible, as has just been demonstrated. Equally implausible is the view that the first attempt to create a group with local authority leading the Jerusalem church failed, later to be realized with the formation of the council of Elders.[105] According to Acts 6:2-4, the Seven had purely administrative and charitable functions and responsibilities. If Stephen and Philip engaged in missionary work simultaneously (or later), this does not prove that the Seven were the spiritual leaders of the Jerusalem church and the local "substitute" for the apostles who traveled. The wider ministry of Stephen and Philip simply shows that the Seven, at least some of them, did not understand their responsibilities in an institutionalized sense as an "office" that limited their competence. We do not know whether the establishment of the group of the Seven failed; we only know that the leading representative of this group, Stephen, died as a martyr and that another member of the group, Philip, did missionary work in neighboring regions. We suspect that the five remaining members of the Seven had to leave Jerusalem after Stephen's death. We do not know whether they returned to Jerusalem after a few months or whether other believers assumed their responsibilities. We do not know whether the group of the Seven was reconstituted by the appointment of other co-workers. The Seven, or a smaller or a larger group of administrative assistants who cared for the needy, may have existed alongside the Elders. It is impossible to draw any conclusions from Luke's silence about the Seven after Acts 7.

Luke does not provide names of the Elders. If Richard Bauckham's interpretation of the bishops' list of Eusebius (*Hist. eccl.* 4.5.1-4) is correct, we know the names of these Elders.[106]

Eusebius's list first mentions the names of the leaders of the Jerusalem church from James the brother of Jesus until the time of Hadrian:

    1. James (A.D. 42-62)
    2. Symeon (A.D. 62 until 117 at the latest)
    3. Justus (until A.D. 138 at the latest)

The next twelve names represent men who can be dated, in connection with the apocryphal letter of James to Quadratus, to the time of James the brother of Jesus. The six persons mentioned in this letter—Philip, Senikus, Justus, Levi,

---

[103]J. Rohde, *EWNT* 3:358 (*EDNT* 3:149).
[104]For example, Bruce, *Acts*, 277.
[105]Thus Theissen 1996, 328 n. 14.
[106]Bauckham (1990, 73-76), who relies on Broek 1988. See further my discussion in §22.1.

Aphre, Judas—correspond to the last names in Eusebius's list. In other words, the twelve men in the second part of Eusebius's list are Jewish Christians who worked with James in Jerusalem:

4. Zacchaeus	10. Senekas (Senikus)
5. Tobias	11. Justus
6. Benjamin	12. Levi
7. John	13. Ephres (Aphre)
8. Matthias	14. Joseph
9. Philip	15. Judas

If this reconstruction is correct, then these twelve (!) men represented, together with James, the leadership council of the Jerusalem church. John (7), Matthias (8) and Philip (9) could have belonged to the Twelve; that is, they may have been disciples of Jesus who stayed in Jerusalem. Levi (12) and Zacchaeus (4) could be identical with the followers of Jesus with those names mentioned in the Gospels. Justus (11) perhaps is identical with the Justus Barnabas mentioned in Acts 1:23, a prominent member of the Jerusalem church. Joseph (14) and Judas (15), the last two persons, could be identical with the brothers of Jesus with those names (Mk 6:3), or with other leading members of the Jerusalem church who had these common names (for Joseph see Mk 15:40, 47; for Judas Barsabbas see Acts 15:22, 27, 32).

Scholars used to argue that a "council of elders" or a presbyterial constitution is testimony to a conservative structure that implies a consolidation of the church in legal terms and a self-understanding in institutional terms. This development implied, it is argued, that the church began to understand itself as guarantor and tradent of tradition. This new self-understanding, it is further argued, contradicted the charismatic nature of the Pauline churches, which were guided by prophecy and teaching, and arose not before the end of the first century.[107] (1) This view presupposes a contradiction between institutional leadership and charismatic guidance by the Holy Spirit, an assumption that is both problematic and entirely unnecessary. (2) The assumption that a group of people could exist and have a clear identity over a longer period without "tradition" is highly questionable. (3) The view that the council of elders reflects an institutionalization of the church has no basis in the text. According to Luke's account, the driving force in the Jerusalem church was not an office or an "institution" but rather the good news that the risen Christ commissioned his followers to proclaim, and the Spirit of God who moves people to receive and believe this message.[108] And the late date that scholars assume for the book of Acts and the Pastoral Epistles,

---

[107]See Lothar Coenen *ThBLNT* 2:1160-61, following Heinrich Greeven, "Propheten, Lehrer und Vorsteher bei Paulus: Zur Frage der 'Ämter' im Urchristentum," *ZNW* 44 (1952-1953): 1-43; Campenhausen 1963, 69-75, 82 (ET, 60-66, 78).
[108]See Barrett, *Acts,* 2:xcvi; cf. idem 1993, 78-80.

which is the presupposition for their reconstruction of the history of the early church, is by no means as certain as they assume. To view the history of the early church in terms of a development toward "early catholicism" has no exegetical basis in Luke's account of the Twelve and of the Elders and their responsibilities, apart from the fact that the term "early catholicism" is rather problematic for the first and second centuries anyway.[109]

James the Brother of Jesus

James the brother of Jesus became leader of the Jerusalem church not simply on account of being a relative of Jesus; even his commission by the risen Christ (1 Cor 15:7) and his status as apostle and "pillar" (Gal 1:19; 2:9) do not fully explain his role as the senior leader responsible for the congregation in Jerusalem (cf. Acts 12:17). Jürgen Roloff correctly observes that "his charismatic authority was decisive, which allowed him not only to keep together the diverse forces and trends in the Jerusalem church but also to exert influence that reached far beyond Jerusalem."[110]

There is no evidence for the view that James took decisions with "charismatic" and "solitary" authority as "authoritative leader of the early church."[111] Acts 21:18 can hardly serve as proof for this view: Luke reports that Paul and his co-workers who were traveling with him "went in to James; and all the elders were present," and continues to formulate in the plural: "After greeting them, he related one by one the things that God had done among the Gentiles through his ministry. And when they heard it, they glorified God. And they said to him, 'You see, brother, how many thousands there are among the Jews of those who have believed; they are all zealous for the law, and they have been told about you that you teach all the Jews who are among the Gentiles to forsake Moses, telling them not to circumcise their children or observe the customs. What then is to be done? They will certainly hear that you have come. Do therefore what we tell you'" (Acts 21:19-23 [RSV]). It is rather improbable that the Jerusalem church had a single "spiritual leader," James, with the elders who "surrounded him" being responsible for "the administrative-technical affairs."[112] Note the following observations. (1) If the Jerusalem church had a leadership team of twelve men in its first years, and if they appointed a group of seven men to take care of practical matters such as serving at tables, then the assumption that the church, which continued to grow numerically, would be able or willing to function with only a single "spiritual" leader and a group of assistants is highly unlikely. (2) Since Luke does not inform his readers about the names or the functions of these elders, the suggestion

---

[109]See Zettner 1991, 86-90; Pokorný 1998, 76-77.

[110]Roloff 1993, 81; cf. Hengel 1985, 75-79. In addition to the New Testament references to James, see the later testimony of Hegesippus (Eusebius, *Hist. eccl.* 2.23.4-24); Epiphanius, *Pan.* 29.4; 78.13-14; *Ps.-Clem. Recogn.* 1.33-71; on the latter see Lüdemann 1983, 230-48 (ET, 171-85). On James see Schmithals 1963; Hengel 1985; E. Ruckstuhl, "Jakobus," *TRE* 16 (1987): 485-488; Pratscher 1987; Ward 1992; Bauckham 1995b; 1996a; Painter 1997; Chilton and Evans 1999c; Ådna 2000b; Reinbold 2000, 36-37, 80-83; Chilton and Neusner 2001; McLaren 2001.

[111]Roloff 1993, 81.

[112]Ibid.

that they were administrative executives remains an argument from silence. (3) The plural forms of the verbs in Acts 21:19-23 clearly show that James did not exercise or claim to have "solitary authority": he evidently was integrated, as *primus inter pares,* into the council of elders that reached theological and practical decisions together (the request made of Paul involved theological concerns: they want to demonstrate that the church has not abandoned the Torah in toto; and also practical concerns: they want to protect the person and the missionary work of Paul). I also fail to detect a "noticeable aversion" to James on the part of Luke, as some have claimed:[113] Luke does not suppress the eminent significance of James; rather, he describes him as a decisive authority at one of the most important bifurcations of the early church (Acts 15:13-21).

James was the leader of the Jerusalem church until his death as a martyr in A.D. 62, an event that is reported by Josephus (*A.J.* 20.199-203).[114] His status as an apostle does not automatically imply that he saw himself as responsible for the proclamation of the gospel in unreached areas. It is unclear whether 1 Cor 9:5 ("Do we not have the right to be accompanied by a wife, as the other apostles and the brothers of the Lord and Cephas?") proves that James, one of Jesus' brothers, was personally involved in missionary travels or that he was married.[115] Since James was recognized by Paul as an influential "pillar" of the Jerusalem church (Gal 2:6-10), responsible for important missionary advances, he must at least have had competence and capabilities for missionary outreach among Jews. This is demonstrated by his decisive contribution during the apostolic council in Jerusalem that discussed and decided the modalities of missionary work among Gentiles (Acts 15:13-21). This view also agrees with the information provided by Hegesippus that James won some members of the "seven parties" of the Jews for faith in Jesus as Messiah, linked with the comment that many leaders of the Jewish people were converted.[116]

    After the Roman procurator Festus died and before the new governor Albinus arrived in Jerusalem, the Sadducean high priest Ananus arraigned several people accused of having broken the law, among them "James, the brother of Jesus who was called the Christ," and had them stoned (Josephus, *A.J.* 20.200).

James McLaren suggests that James was executed not because of his function as leader of the Christians in Jerusalem but because he was involved in the political intrigues of those who opposed Ananus the high priest.[117] This suggestion does not seem plausible. The implied scenario requires that James, who grew up in Galilee, had become a follower of Jesus and accepted and taught the message that Jesus taught, had joined the political op-

---

[113]Hengel 1985, 91; followed by Roloff 1993, 80 n. 56.
[114]On James's death see P. Winter, in Schürer 1:428-41; Ward 1992, 784-86; McLaren 2001.
[115]See Schrage, *1 Kor,* 2:293; differently Reinbold 2000, 82.
[116]Hegesippus, in Eusebius, *Hist. eccl.* 2.23.8-10 (πολλῶν οὖν καὶ ἀρχόντων πιστευόντων); see also *Ps.-Clem. Recogn.* 1.33-71. Pratscher (1987, 110-11, 121), Reinbold (2000, 82-83) and other scholars have claimed that the description of James by Hegesippus is legendary. There is no solid historical reason to doubt Hegesippus, however.
[117]See McLaren 2001, 1-25.

position against the current high priest, and had become so influential in Jerusalem that the high priest felt threatened by him and became convinced of the need to kill him. Such a scenario is not inherently impossible, but it presupposes a political program and political machinations by a Christian leader of the first generation, which seems unlikely. It is difficult if not impossible to specify what the specific goals of political agitation against the high priest might have been.

16

VISION, STRATEGY AND METHODS

This chapter discusses questions related to the geographical vision, the missionary strategy and the missionary methods that are referred to or implied in the New Testament sources in connection with the missionary outreach of the Twelve and of other Jewish-Christian missionaries from Jerusalem.

16.1 The Missionary Vision of the Disciples
Missionary Work Among Jews

Jesus had preached and healed among his Jewish contemporaries. He had sent his disciples on a preaching tour through Galilee with the assignment to minister to the "lost sheep of the house of Israel" (Mt 10:6). After Easter he commissioned the Twelve to engage in missionary work that was universal in scope (Mt 28:19; Acts 1:8), beginning in Jerusalem and in Judea. Luke reports in the first chapters of his account in the book of Acts the preaching of the Twelve in Jerusalem (Acts 2—7) and in Judea and Samaria (Acts 8—9) as missionary outreach among Jews. Paul understood himself as "apostle to the Gentiles" (Rom 11:13), but invariably he went first to the Jews (Rom 1:16; Acts 9:15). The first missionaries, without exception, were Jews. The first congregations were Jewish-Christian churches; that is, their members were Jews who had come to faith in Jesus as the Messiah: this was true in Jerusalem and in Damascus, initially in Antioch in Syria, and most churches outside of Palestine probably started with converted Jews, proselytes and God-fearers who had come to faith in Jesus Christ through the evangelistic activity of the early Christian missionaries in synagogues. The book of Acts does not describe the transition from missionary outreach among Jews to missionary outreach among Gentiles as a process that eventually abandoned missionary work among Jews. Luke's account of Paul's first preaching activity in Rome describes his proclamation as exhortation to the Jews, some of whom "were convinced by what he said" (Acts 28:24).[1] The Jews remain addressees of the Christian message throughout the book of Acts: Luke repeatedly

---

[1]Ellis 1991, 277; for the observation that follows above see ibid., 277-78.

reports the positive reaction of many individual Jews to the preaching of the missionaries[2] as well as mass conversions of Jews.[3] Jacob Jervell observes, "God's original intentions remain unchanged. Salvation comes to God's people."[4] It is impossible for the Twelve and other missionaries who have been commissioned by Jesus to preach the gospel to exclude their Jewish compatriots from the offer of salvation that their message entails.

Jacob Jervell is correct when he points out that Luke does not intend to assert in Acts 15:14 that "Israel is now no longer the people of God or is replaced by a new people consisting of Gentiles . . . for Luke, the salvation of the Gentiles is a part of the promises for Israel."[5] By his account of Paul's "path" from Jerusalem to Rome, Luke does not want to promote the notion that there was a "break between the church and Judaism."[6] However, it is not only Gentiles who are saved "as individual persons"; the same is true for Jews as well. The early Jewish-Christian missionaries offer salvation to Israel as a nation, but also individual Jews need to come to a decision of whether to accept or reject the message of Jesus the crucified and risen Messiah. The converted Gentiles are indeed linked in Acts 15:14 with Israel. However, this connection with the *one* people of God transforms not only the converted Gentiles but also the converted Jews as the entity "Israel": a new people of God is established, consisting of everyone who believes in Jesus the Messiah. On the interpretation of Acts 15:14 see further §25.4.

Missionary Work Among Gentiles

The early Christian missionary activity among polytheists was not an innovation introduced by Paul, the Diaspora Jew from Tarsus; it has its roots in Jesus' ministry (see §12).[7] The proclamation of Jesus that the time is fulfilled and the reign of God is arriving (Mk 1:14-15; Mt 4:17)—a message that Jesus commissioned his disciples to preach as well (Mt 10:7/Lk 10:9)—had universal consequences for the nation. Understood against the background of prophecies such as Is 2:2-5 (= Mic 4:1-5); 49:1-6; Zech 8:20-23, these consequences of Jesus' ministry were inevitable.

Is 2:2-5: "It shall come to pass in the latter days that the mountain of the house of the LORD shall be established as the highest of the mountains, and shall be raised above the hills; and all the nations shall flow to it, [3]and many peoples shall come, and say: 'Come, let us go up to the mountain of the LORD, to the house of the God of Jacob; that he may teach us his ways and that we may walk in his paths.' For out of Zion shall go forth the law, and the word of the LORD from Jerusalem. [4]He shall judge between the nations, and shall decide for many peoples; and they shall beat their swords into plowshares, and their

---

[2]Acts 11:19; 13:43; 14:1-2; 16:1; 17:1-4, 10-11; 18:4; 19:10; 20:21; 28:24.
[3]Acts 2:41, 47; 4:4; 5:14; 6:1, 7; 9:42; 12:24; 13:43; 14:1; 17:11-12; 21:20. See Jervell 1984, 15-16.
[4]Jervell 1991, 24.
[5]Jervell 1991, 18-19; the quotations that follow above, 19.
[6]Contra Roloff, *Apg,* 12; similarly Mussner (1991, 36-38), who, however, interprets this "anti-Judaism" in a theological sense and not in a political or racist sense (39-40).
[7]See McKnight 1992, 260; Schnabel 1994.

spears into pruning hooks; nation shall not lift up sword against nation, neither shall they learn war any more. ⁵O house of Jacob, come, let us walk in the light of the LORD." (RSV)

Is 49:1-6: "Listen to me, O coastlands, and hearken, you peoples from afar. The LORD called me from the womb, from the body of my mother he named my name. ²He made my mouth like a sharp sword, in the shadow of his hand he hid me; he made me a polished arrow, in his quiver he hid me away. ³And he said to me, 'You are my servant, Israel, in whom I will be glorified.' ⁴But I said, 'I have labored in vain, I have spent my strength for nothing and vanity; yet surely my right is with the LORD, and my recompense with my God.' ⁵And now the LORD says, who formed me from the womb to be his servant, to bring Jacob back to him, and that Israel might be gathered to him, for I am honored in the eyes of the LORD, and my God has become my strength—⁶he says: 'It is too light a thing that you should be my servant to raise up the tribes of Jacob and to restore the preserved of Israel; I will give you as a light to the nations, that my salvation may reach to the end of the earth'" (RSV).

Zech 8:20-23: "Thus says the LORD of hosts: Peoples shall yet come, even the inhabitants of many cities; ²¹the inhabitants of one city shall go to another, saying, 'Let us go at once to entreat the favor of the LORD, and to seek the LORD of hosts; I am going.' ²²Many peoples and strong nations shall come to seek the LORD of hosts in Jerusalem, and to entreat the favor of the LORD. ²³Thus says the LORD of hosts: In those days ten men from the nations of every tongue shall take hold of the robe of a Jew, saying, 'Let us go with you, for we have heard that God is with you'" (RSV).

Jesus challenged Israel, in the Sermon on the Mount, to be the light of the world and the salt of the earth (Mt 5:13-16). He did not reject Gentiles who came to him and asked him for help (Mk 5:1-20; 7:24-30; Mt 8:5-13; Jn 12:20-22). Jesus announced the dawn of the age in which Gentiles would have a share in the blessing of God's kingdom (Mt 8:11-12/Lk 13:28-29). He pointed out to his disciples that the end of the present age would not arrive before the gospel of the kingdom of God had been preached in the entire *oikoumenē*, among "all nations" (Mt 24:14; Mk 13:10). Jesus commissioned his disciples after his victory at the cross and in the resurrection to go to the "end(s) of the earth" (Acts 1:8) and make disciples of all nations, to preach the good news of salvation procured by Jesus Christ to all people and to teach them what Jesus had taught (Mt 28:19).

The "Mystery"

The early church was familiar with Jesus' missionary commission to the Twelve to travel as "fishers of people" from Jerusalem and Judea to the ends of the earth. The early church knew that in view of the messianic days that had begun, Gentiles who came to faith in Jesus the Messiah joined the community of believers who had been granted forgiveness of sins. Paul described this early Christian conviction as a "mystery" (Eph 3:5-6; Col 1:26-27).

Eph 3:4-6: "When you read this you can perceive my insight into the mystery of Christ, ⁵which was not made known to the sons of men in other generations as it has now been revealed to his holy apostles and prophets by the Spirit; [6]that is, how the Gentiles are fellow heirs, members of the same body, and partakers of the promise in Christ Jesus through the gospel." (RSV)

Col 1:24-27: "Now I rejoice in my sufferings for your sake, and in my flesh I complete what is lacking in Christ's afflictions for the sake of his body, that is, the church, [25]of which I became a minister according to the divine office which was given to me for you, to make the word of God fully known, [26]the mystery hidden for ages and generations but now made manifest to his saints. [27]To them God chose to make known how great among the Gentiles are the riches of the glory of this mystery, which is Christ in you, the hope of glory." (RSV)

The term "mystery" (μυστήριον, *mystērion*) is to be understood against the background of passages such as Dan 2:18, 19, 27, in the Old Testament, or *1 En.* 52:1-4; *4 Ezra* 14:5, and other texts in the apocalyptic tradition of Second Temple Judaism. In these texts the term "mystery" stands for the future action or intervention of God by which he implements his plan. It designates God's eschatological acts that are cosmic in scope. It describes the "mystery" that has been revealed to elect people.[8] In the New Testament the "mystery" usually is linked with membership in the people of God (Rom 11:25; 16:25-27; Eph 3:3, 4, 9; Col 1:26-27; 1 Tim 3:16). The following details are important.

1. The conversion of the Gentiles that was expected for the time of the last days, for the days of the Messiah, and their admission into the people of God is a "mystery" that was revealed to the apostles. It is not necessary to assume a later stage in the development of the tradition if Col 1:26 asserts that God has revealed the "mystery" to all believers, while Eph 3:5 speaks of a revelation of the "mystery" to the leaders of the church. The latter reference is not evidence for the view that in the early church revelation eventually was restricted to "officials." Revelation to a limited group belonged to the tradition of the term "mystery" right from the beginning (cf. Mt 28:16-20).[9] The early church was convinced that the ongoing missionary work among Gentiles, who, if they come to faith in Jesus Christ, are integrated the people of God as the locus of salvation, was not the result of groundbreaking new exegetical work on some particular Old Testament passages, nor the result of meditation on the significance of the life of Jesus, but the result of a direct revelation from God.

2. The "mystery" that God has revealed to the apostles consists of five fundamental facts (Eph 3:6). (a) The Gentiles who have been converted to faith in Jesus are "fellow heirs" (συγκληρονόμα, *synklēronoma*). This means that the Gen-

---

[8]See H. Krämer, *EWNT* 2:1099-11 (*EDNT* 2:446-49); G. Finkenrath, *NIDNTT* 3:501-506; M. Vahrenhorst, *ThBLNT* 2:1431-35; BDAG, s.v. "μυστήριον 1b," 662; Caragounis 1966; Bockmuehl 1990. Günther Bornkamm (*ThWNT* 4:809-34 [*TDNT* 4:802-28]) wanted to derive the term from the mystery religions, representing the view of an older generation of scholarship that has largely been abandoned.
[9]See Best, *Eph,* 307.

tiles not only receive the blessing of Abraham (Gen 12:2-3), but also that they are counted among his children. The Gentile Christians belong to the heirs of the blessing of Abraham, together (σύν, *syn*) with the Jewish Christians. (b) The Gentiles who believe in Jesus are "members of the same body" (σύσωμα, *sysōma*): they are, together (σύν, *syn*) with the Jewish Christians, a part of the body of Christ and thus have equal status with the Jewish believers. (c) The Gentiles are "partakers of the promise" (συμμέτοχα, *symmetocha*). They have received, together (σύν, *syn*) with the Jewish Christians, the Holy Spirit.[10] (d) The Gentile believers receive this manifold blessing "in Christ Jesus"—that is, in the "realm" of Israel and its Messiah. Only here do they become heirs of the blessing of Abraham. (e) The foundation and the implementation of God's plan of salvation that reaches the Gentiles in the missionary work of the early church is the "gospel," the good news of the death, resurrection and exaltation of Jesus Christ, who has broken down the dividing wall of hostility between Jews and pagans (Eph 2:14-17).[11]

3. God has revealed this mystery "to his holy apostles and prophets by the Spirit" (Eph 3:5). According to Eph 2:20, the apostles and prophets constitute the foundation of the church; in other words, Paul refers to the Jerusalem apostles and to Christian prophets as well as to himself (Eph 3:3). This means that the revelation of the "mystery" is evidently connected with Jesus' missionary commission,[12] with Peter's vision before his visit to Cornelius in Caesarea,[13] and with the vision of Ananias and of Saul/Paul[14] in Damascus.[15]

Critical scholars often assume that the connection of the "mystery" with the Gentile mission was a post-Pauline development, linked with the supposition that the letters to the Ephesians and to the Colossians were not written by the apostle Paul. The different meaning of "mystery" in the two letters often is used as an argument against Pauline authorship: it is alleged that the meaning of *mystērion* in Eph 3:5-6 is different from its meaning in the letters that are generally accepted as authentic: 1 Cor 2:7; 4:1; 13:2; 14:2; 15:21; Rom 16:25-26; Col 1:26-27. This view is unconvincing. There is no valid reason why Paul could not have written all of these passages. (a) In the first letter to the Corinthians the *mystērion* is focused on the salvation that became a reality as a result of Jesus' death on the cross, and that cannot be understood on the basis of human wisdom but is revealed by God to those who love him (1 Cor 2:10). When Paul uses the plural "mysteries" in 1 Cor 4:1, he evidently refers to diverse aspects that the *mystērion* incorporates. This means that the content of the *mystērion* can be described in varying terms. (b) In Rom 16:25-26 Paul connects the announcement or proclamation of the *mystērion* with his (Gentile) mission. (c) In Col

---

[10]See Barth, *Eph*, 1:338; O'Brien, *Eph*, 235.
[11]See O'Brien, *Eph*, 236.
[12]Mt 28:16-20; Lk 24:47; Jn 20:21; Acts 1:8.
[13]Acts 10:1—11:18.
[14]Acts 9:15; 22:15, 21; 26:14-18; Gal 1:12, 15-16.
[15]See Best 1984, esp. 23-25; idem, *Eph*, 135-36, 300-301, 309; on Paul before Damascus see O'Brien, *Eph*, 228-29.

1:26-27 the term *mystērion* describes the fundamental content of the message that the apostle preaches: "Christ in you, the hope of glory." Paul calls this mystery an "open" or "revealed" mystery that is known among the Gentiles. One of the hopes of the prophets was that the nations would find God in the last days and receive salvation, a hope that corresponds with the apocalyptic usage of "mystery." (d) This understanding of *mystērion* as eschatological fulfillment of God's plan of salvation in the crucified and risen Jesus Christ corresponds with the meaning of *mystērion* in the letter to the Ephesians: the "mystery" of the will of God consists of ushering in the "fullness of time" and "to gather up all things in him, things in heaven and things on earth" (Eph 1:10), with particular reference to the Gentiles (Eph 3:6), who have now gained access to the people of God as people of salvation. It is this mystery that Paul proclaims (Eph 3:3, 4, 9).[16] (e) Paul uses the term *mystērion* with different nuances of meaning. If scholars claim that this is impossible, then either they see Paul as inflexible and uncreative or they fail to understand the linguistic difference between meaning and reference.[17] In Rom 11:25 Paul describes with salvation-historical emphasis the restoration of Israel after the ingathering of the full number of the Gentiles as "mystery"; in 1 Cor 15:51 he describes with eschatological nuance the transformation of believers into spiritual bodies on the day of the resurrection; in Col 1:26 he describes with christological concentration the fulfillment of God's eternal plan of salvation among the Gentiles; and in Eph 3:6-7 he describes with ecclesiological emphasis the incorporation of the believing Gentiles into the community of the people of God—all are facets of the one new reality that resulted from the death, resurrection and exaltation of Jesus Christ.[18]

4. The knowledge of this "mystery" is something new that God has "now" (νῦν, *nyn*) revealed (Eph 3:5; Col 1:26); "in former generations this mystery was not made known to humankind" (Eph 3:5; cf. Rom 16:25-27; Col 1:25-27). This does not mean that the gospel was an innovation.[19] There is of course a continuity between the Old and the New Testaments, especially with regard to the gospel, "which he promised beforehand through his prophets in the holy scriptures" (Rom 1:2; cf. Rom 3:21; Gal 3:8), also with respect to the Gentiles, whom some of the prophets had promised God's blessing in the last days. What was new was the manner in which salvation reached the nations: it had not been known that both Jews and Gentiles were to receive salvation through faith in the Messiah crucified and raised from the dead, and that both Jews and Gentiles who believe in Jesus the Messiah would be incorporated into one community of salvation, the "body of Christ."[20] When Jesus called the disciples to become "fishers of people," surely they thought in terms of winning Jews, not Gentiles; when they traveled with Jesus through Galilee and when they were sent on a short-term missionary tour through Galilee, they preached only to Jews. To be a dis-

---

[16]O'Brien, *Eph,* 109-10, 237; cf. Roels 1962, 165-69; R. Meyer 1977, 30-34, 55-60; Turner 1995, 42, 145-46.
[17]See Cotterell and Turner 1989, 82-90, esp. 89 on *mystērion*.
[18]See S. Kim 1981, 22-23.
[19]Dunn 1994, with respect to Paul.
[20]See O'Brien, *Eph,* 232.

ciple of Jesus meant, in the case of the Twelve, to be called to proclaim the good
news of the dawn of God's reign, but it did not include international missionary
work that was universal in scope.[21] The commission to go to the nations "to the
end(s) of the earth" and to make disciples of all nations was something entirely
new that God needed to reveal. The difficulties and tensions that the first Christians faced with regard to the acceptance of converted Gentiles into the people
of God illustrates and confirms this necessity: it was only after receiving a vision
from God, repeated three times, that Peter was willing to visit a Gentile and proclaim to him the good news (Acts 10:1—11:18); and yet a few years later in Antioch he acted contrary to the convictions, legitimized by God, that he gained
in that visionary experience when Jewish Christians pressured him because of
his table fellowship with Gentile Christians (Gal 2:11-14). Paul constantly was
forced to defend his theology and behavior against Jewish Christians who demanded that Gentile Christians be circumcised and keep further commandments
of the Torah. If Matthew and the other evangelists had been able to "develop"
the conception of a Gentile mission on the basis of the Jesus tradition, then they
would not have composed missionary commissions that instructed the disciples
to engage in missionary outreach among Gentiles.[22] And it is improbable to assume that the Gentile mission would have developed spontaneously anyway,
without divine revelation:[23] we must not forget that there was no Jewish mission
among Gentiles, and there were no models in the Greco-Roman world for a deliberately planned and organized international initiative that was universal in
scope.

Missionary Work in Villages and Cities

The Twelve and other early missionaries must have reflected on the task that
Jesus had assigned: to proclaim the good news of the dawn of the reign of God
among Jews and Gentiles, in Jerusalem and Judea and in regions as yet unknown to them. As they reflected on Jesus' missionary commission, they could
hardly have overlooked the fact that Jesus was a preacher and teacher who did
not wait for people to come to him: he had taken the initiative and traveled to
the hamlets, villages and towns of Galilee (Mk 6:56), but also he preached in
Jerusalem, the major urban center of Judea.

Comments on the geographical movement of Jesus in Mk 6:6 (*periēgen* . . .
kyklō), Mk 9:35 and Lk 4:43 seem to indicate that Jesus planned his preaching
tours through the Galilean towns and villages. We have seen that Jesus and his
disciples presumably visited many if not most Galilean settlements more than
once. It seems plausible to assume that the disciples were guided by Jesus' ex-

---

[21]See Best 1984, 1.
[22]See Best 1984, 10.
[23]Thus Best 1984, 28.

ample when they reflected upon the specific realization of the missionary commission that they had received from him. They must have decided that their assignment included reaching as many people as possible in all the towns and villages in the regions that they would visit.

Missionary Work Among All Types of People

Jesus had addressed his message of the arrival of the reign of God to all people: to the simple and to the educated, to powerless Galilean peasants and to influential members of the Jewish establishment, to people with bad reputations and to people who were consistently pious. Jesus compares the arrival of the kingdom of God to a dragnet in which "all kinds of fish" are caught (Mt 13:47). He had emphasized that the sorting of the catch takes place only on the future day of judgment (Mt 13:48-50). The disciples had followed, lived with and observed Jesus for three years and faced the same challenge: their missionary commission directed them to continue the ministry of Jesus, which means that they were sent as "fishers of people" to catch all kinds of people, anyone who was prepared to listen to their message and to accept faith in Jesus the Messiah—without consideration for the traditional social and religious barriers.

Because Jesus had commissioned the Twelve to "fish" not only among Jews but also among all nations to the ends of the earth, they faced an entirely novel situation. The prophets had spoken of a time when the nations would come to Mount Zion to worship the true God (Is 2:2-5/Mic 4:1-5; Zech 8:20-23). Jesus' message of the arrival of the kingdom of God implied a redefinition of the kingdom of God: the traditional symbols of Israel's identity—Torah, temple, sabbath, food laws, nation, land—were missing; they had no function in Jesus' teaching.[24] Jesus' commission to engage in international missionary outreach redefines the vision of the prophets of the pilgrimage of the nations to Mount Zion: the nations do not travel to Jerusalem; rather, the Twelve are directed to travel to the nations. The expected movement from the periphery to the center is replaced by a movement from the center, Jerusalem as the location of the death and resurrection of Jesus the Messiah, to the periphery, the ends of the earth. A basically stationary model of communication—Yahweh reveals himself on Mount Zion, the nations are attracted by the temple on Mount Zion, the Gentiles travel to Jerusalem and convert to worshiping Yahweh—is transformed into an essentially mobile model of communication: the followers of Jesus carry their conviction about Jesus the Savior from Jerusalem to the outside world, to Damascus and to Antioch, to Athens and to Corinth, to Rome and to Ephesus, to Spain and perhaps to India.

Missionary Work in Word and Deed

The basic missionary strategy was simple: the early Christian missionary

---

[24]See N. T. Wright 1996, 369-442, 467-72.

wanted to reach as many people as possible with the message of Jesus and convince them of the truth of his teaching and of the significance of his life, death and resurrection—"in the whole world" (ἐν παντὶ τῷ κόσμῳ, *en panti tō kosmō* [Col 1:6]), whether Jews or Gentiles. The early Christian missionaries are described in the New Testament as messengers who follow the example of Jesus and who are faithful to his directive to preach and to heal (Mt 10:7-8) and to make disciples, whom they instruct to obey the teachings of Jesus (Mt 28:19-20). They proclaim the gospel as the word of God, they heal sick people, they establish communities of followers of Jesus that are characterized by selfless love and mutual care.

The preaching of the apostles focused on the atoning death of Jesus, who had been raised from the dead and who commands as risen Lord both Jews and Gentiles to return to the true and living God. The Jews were to turn to Yahweh, who had revealed himself in Jesus the Messiah. The Gentiles were to turn to the only true God, whose revelation in Jesus Christ the Savior provided the only possibility to receive forgiveness for sins.[25]

Michael Goulder has argued in several publications that there were two competing missions in early Christianity: the mission of the "pillar apostles" in Jerusalem (the "Petrines") and the mission of Paul and Barnabas in Antioch (the "Paulines").[26] He contends that the two missions were divided with regard to the Old Testament and Jewish food laws, with regard to the role of visions, with regard to healing miracles, with regard to the financial support of the missionaries, with regard to the roles of apostles and elders in the local congregations, and with regard to the person and significance of Jesus. The Petrines confessed Jesus as the Messiah and regarded the incarnation Christology of the Paulines as blasphemy. Matthew was a liberal Petrine, Mark a Pauline, John an ultra-Pauline, Luke an irenic Christian who wanted to be friendly to both sides of the divide.[27] Goulder's reconstruction, which takes up in modified form the theories of F. C. Baur, fails because (1) the Jerusalem apostles did not authorize the activities of the opponents of Paul's mission who were responsible for the controversies in the churches in Galatia and in Achaia, particularly in Corinth; (2) there was fundamental agreement between Paul, Peter, John and James in theological, christological and missiological questions (cf. Acts 15; Gal 1-2; 1 Cor 15:3-11).

16.2 Geographical Considerations

The disciples had been directed by Jesus to preach the gospel among Jews and Gentiles: in villages and in towns, among every kind of people, among all nations to the end of the earth. Before examining the question of which theoretical and practical options existed for the disciples in regard to the strategic planning and tactical implementation of this assignment, we need to survey the geo-

---

[25]See 1 Cor 15:3-5; 2 Cor 5:21; Rom 4:25; Acts 2:36; 5:30-31; 10:34-43; 13:25-41; 17:30.
[26]Goulder 1994; 1996a; 1996b; 2001.
[27]See Goulder 1994, 8-23, using a "loyalty test" for establishing these classifications. For the position of the Petrines see idem 2001, 16-46, 197-210.

graphical knowledge available in the Greco-Roman world. People in the first century were rather well informed about numerous regions between the borders of the Roman Empire and the "ends of the earth."

Greek and Roman Geography

The following survey of the geographical knowledge of the ancient world is based on the following primary sources:[28] *periploi* (lit., "voyages around," descriptions of sea voyages), *itineraria* (descriptions of routes on land), administrative handbooks, maps, geographical writings, historical writings, reports by traveling philosophers, light fiction. The following survey focuses on the time between 400 B.C. and A.D. 100.

1. The term *periplus* designates both a voyage along the coast and the register in which sailors noted details of the various sea routes. A periplus is a kind of log book in which names of places, rivers, mountains and distances were listed, augmented by information about shallows, currents, surf, winds, availability of fresh water, bays, anchorages and harbors. Despite the fact that such log books were in use throughout antiquity, no originals or copies have been preserved. What has survived are literary descriptions of coasts (periploi) derived from these log books and based on the personal experiences of the author. Some classical scholars assume that Homer used such periploi when he wrote the work *Odyssey.*[29]

The earliest preserved periplus is that of Hanno of Carthage (fifth century B.C.), which describes an expedition along the west coast of Africa from the pillars of Heracles as far as (modern) Sierra Leone.[30] The periplus of Himilco of Carthage (fifth century B.C.) that described the voyage along the west coast of Europe as far as Britain was not preserved. Scylax from Caria (fifth/fourth century B.C.), following orders from the Persian king Darius, circumnavigated the Arabian peninsula from the mouth of the Indus River to Suez (Herodotus 4.44) and wrote a periplus.[31] Nearchos from Crete, the "admiral" of Alexander the Great, sailed down the Indus River in the fall of 325 B.C. and circumnavigated the coast from southern India to the Tigris in six months. His periplus about this voyage is the basis for the description of India by Flavius Arrianus (see below). Patrocles, the commander of the Seleucid fleet, wrote a periplus about his expedition of 286-

---

[28]For the discussion that follows above see Dilke 1998; Harley and Woodward 1987, 130-256; Olshausen 1991.

[29]Dilke 1998, 130-40l; Olshausen 1991, 81-82. Dueck (2000, 40-45) proves that some descriptions and basic conceptions of Strabo derive from periploi.

[30]See K. Bayer, ed., "Der Fahrtenbericht des Hanno: Text und Übersetzung," in *C. Plinius Secundus d.Ä: Naturkunde; Lateinisch-deutsch* (vol. 5; ed. G. Winkler; 5th ed.; Tusculum; Zürich: Artemis, 1993), 337-53; cf. W. Huss, "Das afrikanische Unternehmen des Hanno," in ibid., 354-63.

[31]Skylax, *FGrH* 709 F 1-7; *Periplus Scylacis, GGM* I 15-96. On Scylax see F. Gisinger, "Skylax Nr. 2," PW 3.1A (1927): 619-46; Romm 1992, 84-85.

281 B.C. to the Caspian Sea.[32] Pytheas of Massalia (mod. Marseille) wrote a periplus about his voyage of around 320 B.C. from southern France to Britain, Thule (Iceland, or the Feroer islands)[33] and into the Baltic Sea. The periplus has not been preserved.[34] Pytheas was the first to describe the tides. The critique of Pytheas that has occasionally been derisive since Dikaiarchos, particularly in Strabo, was linked with the conviction that the northern regions were too cold to be inhabited; the critics did not know of the Gulf Stream and were victims of the prejudice that a mathematician on a ship west and north of Hispania could only be a swindler. Agatharchides from Cnidus (ca. 215-145 B.C.), a historian and geographer at the Ptolemaic court in Alexandria, wrote a periplus titled "On the Erythraean Sea" (περὶ τῆς Ἐρυθρᾶς θαλάσσης), in five books, in which he describes the regions from the Indian Ocean to the Red Sea.[35] Menippus, a geographer from Pergamon, wrote a periplus about the Black Sea (*Periplus Ponti Euxini*) between 36 and 25 B.C. His "Periplus of the Inner Sea" (i.e., of the Mediterranean) describes in three books Europe, Asia and Africa, noting the coastline and harbors, and provides historical information.[36] The *Periplus Maris Erythraei* was written between A.D. 40 and 70, describing routes and harbors for the voyage from Alexandria to Arabia and to India (see below). Flavius Arrianus (A.D. 86-160), the imperial legate in Cappadocia, wrote a periplus of the Black Sea.[37]

2. *Itineraria* are the terrestrial equivalent of the periploi; they are records

---

[32]*FGrH* 712 F 1-8. Cf. F. Gisinger, "Patrokles Nr. 5," PW 18.4 (1949): 2263-73.

[33]Iceland is (at the coast marked by the volcano Hekla) about 830 km from the island of Lewis on the west coast of Britain, a passage that Pytheas was able to sail in six days (Strabo 1.4.2; cf. Pliny 2.186-187; 3.104). Pytheas saw the polar sea, according to Pliny one day's distance from Iceland: "One day's sail from Thule is the frozen Ocean [*mare concretum*], called by some the Cronian Sea" (Pliny 4.16.104; see also Strabo 1.4.2).

[34]Hans J. Mette, ed., *Pytheas von Massalia* (Berlin: de Gruyter, 1952), frg. 1-9b.14-15. Cf. C. F. C. Hawkes, *Pytheas: Europe and the Greek Explorers* (Oxford: Blackwell, 1977); Aujac 1987b, 150-51. Hawkes (*Pytheas,* 41-44), dates Pytheas's voyage to Britain and Thule to 325 B.C. and argues for Iceland as the northwestern end of the journey (33-37); for the observation that follows above see ibid., 45.

[35]Agatharchides, *De mari Erythraeo, GGM* I 111-95 (excerpta); *FGrH* 86; Stanley M. Burstein, *Agatharchides of Cnidus: On the Erythraean Sea* (London: Hakluyt Society, 1989); D. Woelk, *Agathar chides von Knidos 'Über das Rote Meer': Übersetzung und Kommentar* (Freiburg im Breisgau: Bamberg, 1966). Cf. E. Schwartz, PW 1 (1893): 739ff.; K. Reinhardt, PW 22 (1953): 763ff.; H. Gams, *KP* 1:115-16; K. S. Sacks, *OCD* 36; Fraser 1972, 1:539-50; Dihle 1994, 86-90.

[36]*Menippi Periplus Maris Interni, GGM* I 563-72; *Fragmenta, GGM* I 572-73; Diller 1986, 151-56 (commentary, 156-64). Cf. F. Gisinger, "Menippos Nr. 9," PW 15.1 (1931): 862-88; F. Lasserre, "Menippos Nr. 6," *KP* 3:1217-19.

[37]*GGM* I 370-401; A. G. Roos and G. Wirth, eds., *Flavii Arriani quae extant omnia* (3rd ed.; 2 vols.; Leipzig: Teubner, 1967-1968), 1:103-28. See Everett L. Wheeler, "Flavius Arrianus: A Political and Military Biography" (Ph.D. diss.; Duke University, 1977), 195-201. The anonymous "Periplus of the Black Sea" probably was written after A.D. 550; see Diller 1986, 102-13 (newly reconstructed text, 118-38; commentary, 138-46).

about the logistics for travels on land, with information on stations, distances, road conditions, tolls, accommodations.[38] Itineraries existed already around 1900 B.C. in Babylonia. Whereas the Greeks comprehended the world from the sea and described sea routes, the Romans focused on the overland connections between towns. The emperor and the provincial governors needed a travel plan narrative that made it possible to plan daily travel, and subordinate officials of the various administrations, merchants and tourists (e.g., traveling geographers of pilgrims) were dependent upon descriptions of land routes as well. Flavius Vegetius advises officers to use *itineraria*, providing the following reason:

Vegetius, *Epitoma rei militaris* 3.6.4: "First, he should have itineraries of all regions (*itin-eraria omnium regionum . . . plenissime debet habere*) in which the war is being waged written out in the fullest detail, so that he may learn the distances between places (*lo-corum intervalla*) in terms of the number of miles (*passum numero*) and the quality of roads (*viarum qualitate*), and examine short-cuts, by-ways, mountains and rivers, accu-rately described (*ad fidem descripta*). Indeed, the more conscientious generals reportedly had itineraries of the provinces in which the emergency occurred not just annotated but illustrated [i.e. coloured maps] as well (*itineraria provinciarum . . . non tantum adnotata, sed etiam picta*), so that they could choose their route when setting out by the visual as-pect (*verum aspectu oculorum*) as well as by mental calculation (*consilio mentis*)."[39] In the comments that follow, Vegetius gives advice on how to use guides who are familiar with the localities.

The *Itinerarium Burdigalense* (or *Hierosolymitanum*) purports to document a pilgrimage from Bordeaux in France to Jerusalem in A.D. 333, including a description of places of interest. The *Peutinger Table,* named after its owner, Konrad Peutinger (1465-1547), is the medieval exemplar (1200) of a Roman world map of the fourth century, representing the inhabited world from Spain and the east coast of Britain to China on a parchment scroll measuring 6.8 m by 34 cm (approx. 22 by 1 ft.). Scholars assume that the sources used for the production of this map reach back to the first century.[40] The map is not ac-cording to scale, but "the dense and topologically correct network of roads (with posting-stations and distances) has a practical value like the Itineraries." Excavations on the northern shore of Lago di Bracciano in Italy unearthed sil-

---

[38]W. Kubitschek, "Itinerarien," PW 9 (1916): 2308-63; G. Radke, *KP* 2:1488-90; N. Purcell, *OCD* 775; Dilke 1998, 112-29; Olshausen 1991, 87-90; Isaac 1996, esp. 154-55.

[39]The English translation follows N. Milner, ed., *Vegetius: Epitome of Military Science* (Trans-lated Texts for Historians 16; Liverpool: Liverpool University Press, 1993), 73-74. On Vegetius see below.

[40]Konrad Miller, *Die Peutingersche Tafel* (Stuttgart: Brockhaus, 1962 [1916]); Ekkehard Weber, *Tabula Peutingeriana: Codex Vindobonensis 324* (Graz: Akademische Druck- und Verlagsan-stalt, 1976); Luciano Bosio, *La Tabula Peutingeriana: Una descrizione pittorica del mondo antico* (I monumenti dell'arte classica 2; Rimini: Maggioli, 1983). Cf. N. Purcell, *OCD* 1151; the quotation that follows above, ibid.; Dilke 1998, 113-20; 1987, 238-42; Austin and Rankov 1995, 115; D. F. Graf, in Humphrey 1995-2002, 1:242.

ver cups dating between A.D. 10 and 50 on which was engraved an itinerary depicting the route from Gades (mod. Cadiz, western Spain) via Cordoba, Tarragona, Narbonne, Nîmes, Sisteron, Turin, Piacenza, Rimini, Fano and Bevagna to Rome (*CIL* XI 3281-84). The most extensive itinerary that has been preserved is the *Itinerarium provinciarum Antonini Augusti* from the time of the emperor Caracalla (211-217), representing a private route book for the entire Roman Empire.[41]

3. The only extant *administrative handbook* (*notitia dignitarum*, a "list of offices") dates to the fifth century[42] and is therefore not relevant for a description of geographical knowledge in the first century. Material from archives (e.g., from the provincial capitals of the Roman Empire), which contained relevant information for geographical knowledge, has been preserved only rarely and always in fragmentary form (see below).

Some Greek cities had a register of streets. In Erythrai (Erythrae), one of the twelve cities of the Ionian League, an inscription was found dating to 340 B.C. that records the public streets of the city. The register lists both for the "public roads" (ὁδοὶ δημοσίαι) and for the "foot paths" (ὁδοὶ ἀνδρόβασμοι) the starting point and the end point and often includes prominent landmarks.[43] The streets mentioned in lines 1-15 proceed from the agora, which leads to the assumption that this register lists those streets that had to be maintained by the *agoranomos,* the official who was responsible for overseeing the market. It can be assumed that many cities had registers of streets and roads listed on public inscriptions.

4. *Maps* of regions and cities existed from the earliest times in the ancient Near East.[44] In Babylonia maps of houses and temples were recorded on clay tablets as early as 2300 B.C. The earliest city map drawn to scale was found in Nippur and dates to 1500 B.C., depicting the temple of Enlil, city walls, canals, storage houses and a park. The earliest world map, recorded on a Babylonian clay tablet, dates to 600 B.C.[45] Rudimentary topographical sketches can be found on

[41]Cuntz 1929, 1-85; see also Konrad Miller, *Itineraria Romana: Römische Reisewege an der Hand der Tabula Peutingeriana dargestellt* (Bregenz: Husslein, 1988 [1916]). For example, §482 in the section on Britain states (following Olshausen 1991, 89), "Thus also from Caernarvon to Chester 109.631 kilometers, from there to Caerhin 35.556 kilometers, from there to St. Asaph (?) 26.667 kilometers, from there to Chester 47.408 km."

[42]See Otto Seeck, ed., *Notitia dignitatum, accedunt Notitia Urbis Constantinopolitanae et latercula provinciarum* (Berlin: Weidmann, 1876; repr., Frankfurt: Minerva, 1962); Eduard Böcking, ed., *Notitia dignitatum et administrationum omnium tam civilium quam militarium in partibus orientis et occidentis* (2 vols.; Bonn: Marcus, 1839-1853); cf. E. Polaschek, "Notitia Dignitatum," PW 17.1 (1936): 1077-1116; A. Lippold, *KP* 4:166-68; R. S. O. Tomlin, *OCD* 1049.

[43]First edition: A. Fontrier, *Mouseion* 5 (1884-1885) 19: no. 235; republished in *I. Erythrai* I 151. The fifty-two lines are preserved only in fragments.

[44]W. Kubitschek, PW 10 (1919): 2022-2149; F. Lasserre, *KP* 3:130-35; N. Purcell, *OCD* 920; R. K. Sherk, "Roman Geographical Exploration and Military Maps," *ANRW* 2.1 (1974): 534-62; North 1979; Harley and Woodward 1987, 1:105-257; Dilke 1998, 11-20; Olshausen 1991, 91-95.

[45]Millard 1987, 109-10.

Egyptian vases dating to 3500 B.C. Information with more advanced cartographic value can be found on a depiction of the conquest of Canaan by Sethos I (1318-1304 B.C.). The earliest topographical map, the so-called Turin Papyrus, dating to the Ramses period (1292-1070 B.C.), records the location of gold mines, barracks of the workers and the roads between the Nile and the Red Sea in the area of Wadi al-Ḥammamat.[46] Greek cartography made enormous progress between 600 B.C. and A.D. 200, particularly in theoretical and hypothetical areas. The Romans were more interested in practical applications.[47] Greeks and Romans had different terms for what we call a "map" or "world map" today,[48] which indicates that maps were not esoteric objects that interested only a handful of specialists; rather, the wider public knew them well.

γῆς περίοδος	"way around the earth": map;[49] book on geography[50]
πίναξ	"board, plank, plate": map[51]
σφαῖρα	globe, sphere
σχηματογραφία	plan or map of a country[52]
ἰχνογραφία	"tracing out": ground plan[53]
διάγραμμα	sketch, diagram[54]
forma	"form": map, plan[55]
tabula	"tablet": map[56]
descriptio	"sketch": world map[57]
sphaera	cf. σφαῖρα
itinerarium pictum	map with pictorial drawings[58]
mappa	"table cloth, napkin" (medieval Lat.): map (*mappa mundi,* "world map")[59]
charta	"papyrus" (Renaissance Lat.): map, table

The earliest Greek world map is traced back to Anaximander (610-546 B.C.), a student of Thales from Miletus.[60] Around 500 B.C. Hekataios of Miletus wrote a

---

[46]See A. F. Shore, "Egyptian Cartography," in Harley and Woodward 1987, 1:117-29. See also <http://members.tripod.com/oceanoz/gold.html>.

[47]Aujac 1987a, 130; Dilke 1987b, 201.

[48]For the list that follows above see Dilke 1998, 169-70.

[49]Herodotus 4.36; 5.49; Arrian, *Nub.* 206.

[50]Aristotle, *Pol.* 1262a19; *Rhet.* 1360a34; *Mete.* 350a16.

[51]Herodotus 5.49; Plutarch, *Thes.* 1; Strabo 1.1.11 (πίναξ γεωγραφικός).

[52]P. Meyer 1.20 (second century B.C.); PSI 10.1118.10 (first century A.D.).

[53]Vitruvius 1.2.2.

[54]Julian, *Epist.* 7 (403 CD).

[55]Lex Thoria (111 B.C.); Cicero, *Fam.* 2.8.1; Vespasian inscription from Arausio (mod. Orange, in southern France); Suetonius, *Aug.* 31.

[56]Cicero, *Att.* 6.2.3; Propertius 4.3.37.

[57]Vitruvius 8.2.

[58]Vegetius 3.6.

[59]Gromatici 358.12 (sixth century). Cf. *OCD.*

[60]See the information provided in Agathemeros 1.1 (*GGM* II 471); Diogenes Laertius 2.1.1-2; Strabo 1.1.11 (τὸν μὲν οὖν ἐκδοῦναι πρῶτον γεωγραφικὸν πίνακα). See Aujac 1987a, 134.

two-part work titled "Journey Around the World" (Περίοδος γῆς, *Periodos gēs*), which includes a world map (see fig. 7).[61] His commentary on the world map begins in Spain and moves via Europa (Εὐρώπη), Asia (Ἀσίη), Egypt (Αἴγυπτος) and Libya (Λιβύη) to the Pillars of Heracles (Strait of Gibraltar). In his map he divides the world into halves (Europe and Asia), separated by the Mediterranean and the Phasis River (mod. Rioni). The southern half was divided in two parts by the Nile, and the northern half likewise by the Ister River (mod. Danube). It is unclear whether Libya (Africa) was a third continent; it seems to have belonged to Asia. At edges of the continents lived fabled peoples. W. Spoerri comments that this work was written "as a full 'scientific' presentation of the geographical knowledge of the entire world and its inhabitants, without intending practical application. He lists the ἔθνη [*ethnē*]: their borders (rivers), cities, rivers, mountains, gulfs, harbors; the nature of the land (ground, flora, fauna); primeval history. . . . He has strong ethnic interests (way of life, customs, θαυμάσια), a tradition that goes back to Homer and that was stimulated by Ionian navigation and Greek physics."[62] Herodotus (485-425 B.C.) mentions a bronze board (πίναξ, *pinax*) with the engraving of the outlines (περίοδος, *periodos*) of the world with rivers and seas (5.49). When Aristagoras of Miletus went to Greece around 500 B.C. to recruit allies for the war against the Persians, he carried this board with him. This comment demonstrates that maps of the inhabited world that provided useful information were manufactured in Ionia, evidently particularly in Miletus. Aristagoras was able to show on his map the regions that one had to cross during a journey from Ionia to Persia: Lydia, Phrygia, Cappadocia, Cilicia, Armenia, Matiene (Matiane) and Kissia (Elam) with the city of Susa.[63]

Theophrastus (ca. 372-288 B.C.), the associate and successor of Aristotle, confirms the familiarity with maps in Athens for the third century B.C. He states in his testament that the panels (πίνακας, *pinakas*) with the maps (γῆς περίοδοι, *gēs periodoi*) should be set up in the colonnade with the lower roof in the small hall beside the temple of the Muses.[64]

Eratosthenes from Cyrene (275-194 B.C.), a student of Zeno the Stoic and Callimachus the poet, was the head of the royal library in Alexandria. He wrote the first work with the title "Geography" (Γεωγραφικά, *Geōgraphika*), which is

---

[61]Only fragments are preserved: *FGrH* 1 F 1A 7-47. On Hekataios (Hecataeus) see F. Jacoby, PW 7.2 (1912): 2667-69; PWSup 2 (1913): 341-473; W. Spoerri, "Hekataios Nr. 3," *KP* 976-80; S. R. West, *OCD* 670-71; Dilke 1998, 56-57; Aujac 1987a, 134. The map of Hekataios can be reconstructed on the basis of the critique by later Greek geographers.

[62]Spoerri, *KP* 977-78.

[63]Aujac 1987a, 135; on the contributions of Pythagoras, Herodotus and Democritus see ibid., 135-40.

[64]Diogenes Laertius 5.51.

known mostly through Strabo.[65] In the third book of this work he develops a world map (see fig. 8) whose axis of coordinates stood on Rhodes: the parallel of latitude is determined by the Pillars of Heracles (Strait of Gibraltar), the meridian by Lysimacheia in Thrace and Syene (mod. Assuan, on the western shore of the Nile River). He adds to this division, which already had been suggested by the Sicilian Dikaiarchos, seven additional parallels of latitude and eight additional meridians: his map describes the world from the island of Thule (Iceland) in the north to Taprobane (Ceylon) in the south, from the west coast of Iberia (Spain) in the west to India in the east. "He strives to include in his map only points that have been astronomically confirmed; where these are not available, he uses information from log books." In his book *On the Measurement of the Earth* (Περὶ ἀναμετρήσεως τῆς γῆς), also lost, Eratosthenes calculated the earth's circumference on the basis of the known north-south meridian of Alexandria and Syene, and the difference of the angle of incidence of the sun rays at both places. His figure of 252,000 stadia corresponds to 39,690 km (on the basis of Egyptian stadia of 157.50 m), or 45,007 km (on the basis of Olympic stadia of 60 m), which is astonishingly precise: modern measurements record the circumference of the earth at the equator at 40,075 km!

Archimedes of Syracuse (287-212 B.C.), who met Eratosthenes in Alexandria, constructed several globes. Two of his globes were taken to Rome in 212 B.C. after the destruction of Syracuse, where they were described by Cicero.[66] Poseidonios of Apameia on the Orontes (135-51 B.C.), a Stoic philosopher, historian and geographer who was educated in Athens, lived on Rhodes, and visited Spain, Gaul and Italy, is said to have constructed a globe as well. A world map is also linked with him (see below on his geographical work).

Marcus Vipsanius Agrippa (64-12 B.C.), a friend of Augustus, served in numerous political and military offices and posts in (in alphabetical order) Aquitania, Asia, Illyricum, Italy, Gallia, Germania, Macedonia, Pannonia, Sicily, Spain, Syria. He wrote a commentary in which he gives directions for setting up a world map in Rome.[67] His sister Vipsania Polla and Augustus completed Agrippa's project: the world map was set up on a wall of the Porticus Vipsania east of the Via Lata (mod. Via del Corso).

---

[65]Hugo Berger, ed., *Die geographischen Fragmente des Eratosthenes* (Leipzig: Teubner, 1880; repr., Amsterdam: Meridian, 1964), 1-382. Cf. J. Mau, *KP* 2:344-45; P. M. Fraser, *OCD* 553-54; Fraser 1972, 1:309-10, 330-33, 525-39; Aujac 1987b, 154-57; Jerker Blomqvist, "Alexandrian Science: The Case of Eratosthenes," in Bilde et al. 1992, 53-69; Dilke 1998, 32-39, 60-63; Dueck 2000, 56-59. The quotation that follows above is from Olshausen 1991, 94.

[66]Cicero, *Rep.* 1.14; cf. Aujac 1987b, 159-60.

[67]See Paul Schnabel, "Die Weltkarte des Agrippa als wissenschaftliches Mittelglied zwischen Hipparchos und Ptolemaios," *Philologus* 90 (1935): 405-40 (with a copy of Agrippa's *Demensuratio Provinciarum* [425-40]); Dilke 1998, 41-53; idem, "Maps in the Service of the State: Roman Cartography to the End of the Augustan Era," in Harley and Woodward 1987, 1:201-211, esp. 207-9; Brodersen 1995, 268-87; Dueck 2000, 127-29.

Kai Brodersen argues that this world map never existed: Agrippa's project produced only the *Commentarii,* which listed, in a monumental inscription, regions, cities, distances, mountains, rivers, islands, as well as the names of tribes and peoples, describing for the public in Rome the entire *oikoumenē.*[68]

Pliny the Elder voiced amazement at Agrippa's measurements (*conputatio mensurae*) for Spain, which did not correspond to reality: "Agrippa was a very painstaking man, and also a very careful geographer; who, therefore, could believe that when intending to set before the eyes of Rome a survey of the world [*orbem terrarum urbi spectandum propositurus esset*], he made a mistake, and with him the late lamented Augustus?" (*Nat.* 3.3.17). The commentary and the map evidently were used by Orosius and Eratosthenes, and probably by Strabo and later geographers as well. It is reasonable to assume that the increasing availability of maps in the Augustan period is connected with preliminary studies for this map.[69] For example, the map of M. Vipsanius Agrippa may have been the source for the world map depicted on the tapestry that Queen Kypros, granddaughter of Herod I and wife of Agrippa I, gave to Gaius Caligula as a gift (perhaps) in A.D. 39; this occasion was celebrated in an epigram by Philip of Thessalonike, written probably in A.D. 40 (*Anthologia palatina* 9.778). In regard to the scale of ancient maps, recent studies seem to confirm the conclusion that the Romans were not interested in producing maps that were true to scale, except for urban land registers. The ancient perception of geographical space was linear.[70]

5. The *geographical works* of Greek and Roman authors are in many cases lost. What often has survived are quotations in the writings of other authors—for example, in historical texts. For the period of interest to us, the following authors must be mentioned. Around 200 B.C. Demetrios of Kallatis, a Greek city on the western shores of the Black Sea, wrote around a description of Europa and Asia in twenty books (Περὶ Εὐρώπης καὶ Ἀσίας, *Peri Eurōpēs kai Asias*), which were used by Agatharchides.[71] Eratosthenes, who around 200 B.C. wrote the first work with the title *Geōgraphika,* has already been mentioned. Agatharchides of Cnidus (ca. 150 B.C.), whose periplus on the Red Sea has been mentioned, wrote a geography of Asia in ten books (Ἀσιατικά, *Asiatika*), which

---

[68]Brodersen 1995, 280-84; cf. Dueck 2000, 128; see also J. M. Scott 2002, 14-15.

[69]Austin and Rankov 1995, 113-14, referring to Vitruvius, *De architectura* 8.2.6; Propertius, *Elegies* 1.6.19-20; 10.29ff.; Ovid, *Heroides* 1.31ff. For the observation that follows above see J. M. Scott 2002, 5-22.

[70]Isaac 1996, with reference to Pietro Janni, *La mappa e il periplo: Cartografia antica e spazio odologico* (Rome: Bretschneider, 1984); Nicholas Purcell, "Maps, Lists, Money, Order and Power," *JRS* 80 (1990): 178-82.

[71]*FGrH* 85 2A 202-204; cf. Diogenes Laertius 5.83. See H. Gärtner, "Demetrios Nr. 20," *KP* 1:1467. On Kallatis see John Hind, "Megarian Colonisation in the Western Half of the Black Sea (Sister- and Daughter-Cities of Herakleia)," in Tsetskhladze 1998, 131-52, esp. 140-41; Alexandru Avram, "P. Vinicius und Kallatis," in ibid., 115-29.

included a description of Egypt, Ethiopia and Arabia. He also wrote a geography of Europe in forty-nine books (Εὐρωπιακά, *Eurōpiaka*). Both survive only in fragments.[72] His books were used by Artemidoros, Diodorus and Strabo. Apollodoros of Athens (ca. 180-120 B.C.), who lived also in Alexandria and Pergamon, wrote, besides philological texts, a comprehensive commentary in twelve books on the Homeric *Catalogue of Ships* (Περὶ τοῦ νεῶν καταλόγου, *Peri tou neōn katalogou*), explaining the Homeric geography and subsequent changes. Extensive quotations survive in Strabo's *Geography*.[73] The intellectual authority of Apollodoros gave rise to forgeries that appeared under his name in the first century B.C., among them a geographical guide (Γῆς περίοδος, *Gēs periodos*). Between 104 and 101 B.C. Artemidoros of Ephesus, well traveled in the regions of the Mediterranean (e.g., Spain, Gaul, Egypt and Rome), wrote eleven geographical books (e.g., Περίπλους, *Periplous;* Τὰ γεωγραφούμενα, *Ta geōgraphoumena;* Γεωγραφίας βιβλία, *Geōgraphias biblia;* ᾽Ιωνικὰ ὑπομνήματα, *Iōnika hypomnēmata*), which are frequently quoted by Strabo and other geographers. Among his sources are Agatharchides (for the eastern regions and Ethiopia) as well as the geographers of Alexander the Great and Megasthenes (for India).[74]

Around 90 B.C. Skymnos of Chios wrote a description of Asia (with Libya and Africa) and Europe; only fragments survive. The title Περιήγησις (*Periēgēsis*), literally "leading around and explaining," represents a travel guide. It includes extensive descriptions of historical questions (e.g., the establishment of colonies), references to mythology and paradoxical descriptions (e.g., the poor vegetation of Britain).[75] Poseidonios of Apameia on the Orontes (135-51 B.C.), a Stoic philosopher who was educated in Athens and lived on Rhodes, was also a historian and geographer who visited Spain, southern Gaul and Italy. About thirty titles of his substantial body of works have been preserved, although only in fragmentary form.[76] In his book "On the Ocean" (Περὶ ᾽Ωκεανοῦ, *Peri Ōkeanou*) he wanted to move beyond a description of earth to a history of the earth. He de-

---

[72] *FGrH* 86 2A 205-206, 206-22; 3B 741. Cf. E. Schwartz, PW 1 (1893): 739-41; K. Reinhardt, PW 22 (1953): 558-26; H. Gams, *KP* 1:115-16.

[73] *FGrH* 244. Cf. Gärtner, "Apollodoros Nr. 5," *KP* 1:438-39; K. S. Sacks, "Apollodoros 6," *OCD* 124.

[74] *GGM* I 574, 576; *FGrH* 438. Cf. H. Gärtner, "Artemidoros Nr. 1," *KP* 1:617; E. H. Warmington and S. Hornblower, "Artemidoros (2)," *OCD* 182.

[75] *GGM* I 196-237; Diller 1986, 165-76: "Fragmenta periegeseos ad Nicomedem regem" (Pseudo-Scymni). Cf. F. Gisinger, PW 3.A (1897): 664-72; F. Lasserre, *KP* 5:240.

[76] L. Edelstein and I. G. Kidd, eds., *Posidonius I: The Fragments* (2nd ed.; Cambridge: University Press, 1989 [1972]); W. Theiler, ed., *Posidonios: Die Fragmente* (Berlin: de Gruyter, 1982); I. G. Kidd, ed., *Posidonius II-III: The Commentary; The Translation of the Fragments* (Cambridge: Cambridge University Press, 1988). Cf. M. Pohlenz, PW 22 (1954): 560-826; H. Dörrie, "Poseidonios 2," *KP* 4:1080-84; I. G. Kidd, *OCD* 1231-33; Aujac 1987c, 168-69; Dihle 1994, 90-93.

scribed foreign peoples on the basis of his theory of culture: the inhabitants of
the Iberian peninsula, which he had visited, but also the Germans and the Celts.
It is very possible that much of Caesar's and Tacitus's information about Germania came from Poseidonios.

Strabo (64 B.C.-A.D. 21) of Amaseia in Pontus[77] visited, on several journeys,
"the entire world"[78]—that is, Asia Minor, Greece, Italy, Sardinia, Egypt, Syria
and Armenia. His book Γεωγραφικα Ὑπομνήματα (Geōgraphika Hypomnēmata),
compiled after 20 B.C. and written probably in Alexandria between A.D. 18 and
24, describes in seventeen books the entire world known at the time.[79] Strabo's
work is not a synthesis of his research and reading: he used a limited number
of sources—particularly Eratosthenes, Hipparchos, Polybius, Poseidonios, Artemidoros, Apollodoros, Demetrios, Ephoros—as something like testimonies
of eyewitnesses, although he did not utilize their information uncritically.[80]
Still, Strabo's work must be regarded as "the richest source of ancient geography."[81] In contrast to Eratosthenes, Strabo is not interested in cartography as
the proper subject of geography. Rather, he focuses on practical geography.[82]
He describes with encyclopedic erudition (πολυμαθεία, polymatheia [1.1.12]),
on the basis of Greek ethnographical traditions, the entire oikoumenē from the
perspective of the Roman Empire.[83] After the prolegomena in books 1—2,
where he discusses the importance of geography and provides a critique of
his predecessors, he describes Spain (book 3); Gaul, Britannia and the Alps
(book 4); Italia and Macedonia (books 5—6); northern Europe from the Rhine

---

[77]G. Kramer, ed., *Strabonis geographica* (3 vols.; Berlin: Teubner, 1844-1852); A. Meineke, ed.,
Strabonis geographica (3 vols.; Leipzig: Teubner, 1852; repr., Graz: Akademische Druck- und
Verlagsanstalt, 1969); Horace L. Jones, ed., *The Geography of Strabo* (8 vols.; LCL; Cambridge,
Mass.: Harvard University Press, 1917-1930); Christoph G. Groskurd, ed., *Strabons Erdbe-
schreibung in siebzehn Büchern* (4 vols.; Berlin: Nicolai, 1831-1834). Cf. E. Honigmann, PW
4.A (1900): 76-155; François Lasserre, *KP* 5:381-85; N. Purcell, *OCD* 1447; F. Lasserre, ed., *Strabon: Géographie* (9 vols.; Paris: Les Belles Lettres, 1969-1981); Dilke 1998, 62-65; Aujac 1987c,
173-75; Dihle 1994, 96-100; Syme 1995; Dueck 2000; idem, "The Date and Method of Composition of Strabo's 'Geography,'" *Hermes* 127 (1999): 467-78.
[78]Olshausen 1991, 79.
[79]Dueck 2000, 146-51. Some scholars suggest that Strabo wrote *Geography* in the first century
B.C. and that he edited a revised version, perhaps after A.D. 19; some scholars suggest that the
work appeared posthumously.
[80]For example, he accuses Eratosthenes of denying Homeric geographical knowledge that
needs to be taken seriously and of not recognizing errors in cartography (1.2-2.1). On Strabo's
use of his sources see Aujac 1966, 19-82; Dueck 2000, 180-86.
[81]Lasserre, *KP* 5:385.
[82]Olshausen 1991, 79. In regard to physical geography (volcanism, atmospheric conditions,
winds, climate, rivers), his information does not reach the level of expertise of his predecessors—for example, Eratosthenes: according to Aujac (1966, 306, 309), Strabo "wanted to reign
rather than discover" ("préoccupé de gouverner plus que de découvrir"), the result of which
was that his predecessors left only an "écho affaibli" in his work.
[83]Dueck 2000, 107-15, 165, 186-87.

River to Illyricum, Epirus, Thessalia and Macedonia (book 7); Greece and the
islands of the Ionian and the Aegean Seas (books 8—10); the northern regions
of Asia from the Tanais River (mod. Don) to India with Iberia, Albania, the
Caucasus, Parthia, Bactria, Media and Armenia (book 11); Cappadocia, Pontus,
Paphlagonia, Bithynia, Galatia, Lycaonia, Pisidia, Mysia and Phrygia (book
12); the Troas and the Aeolis, Ionia, Caria, Lycia, Pamphylia, Cilicia and Cyprus
(books 13—14); India and the Persian Gulf (book 15); Assyria, Syria and Arabia (book 16); Egypt, Libya and Mauretania (book 17). For Strabo, the
oikoumenē is "the world which we inhabit and know" (1.4.6)—that is, the
world of the Roman Empire (17.3.24-25). The kingdoms and regions on the
borders of the Roman Empire, which are not Roman provinces or which are
not under direct Roman control—particularly the Parthians, the Indians and
the Ethiopians—acknowledge the power of Rome and the glory of the emperor Augustus (for the Parthians see 6.4.2 15.1.4; for the Indians, 15.1.73; for
the Ethiopians, 17.1.54).[84]

In book 14 Strabo describes Tarsus, the city in which the apostle Paul was born, as follows: "As for Tarsus, it lies in a plain; and it was founded by the Argives who wandered
with Triptolemus in quest of Io; and it is intersected in the middle by the Cydnus River,
which flows past the very gymnasium of the young men. Now inasmuch as the source of
the river is not very far away and its stream passes through a deep ravine and then emp-
ties immediately into the city, its discharge is both cold and swift; and hence it is helpful
both to men and to cattle that are suffering from swollen sinews, if they immerse themselves in its waters. The people at Tarsus have devoted themselves so eagerly, not only
to philosophy, but also to the whole round of education in general, that they have surpassed Athens, Alexandria, or any other place that can be named where there have been
schools and lectures of philosophers [σχολαὶ καὶ διατριβαὶ φιλοσόφων]. But it is so different from other cities that there the men who are fond of learning are all natives
[ἐπιχώριοι], and foreigners [ξένοι] are not inclined to sojourn there; neither do these natives stay there, but they complete their education abroad; and when they have completed
it they are please to live abroad, and but few go back home. But the opposite is the case
with the other cities which I have just mentioned except Alexandria; for many resort to
them and pass time there with pleasure, but you would not see many of the natives either
resorting to places outside their country through love of learning or eager about pursuing
learning at home. With the Alexandrians, however, both things take place, for they admit
many foreigners and also sent not a few of their own citizens abroad. Further, the city of
Tarsus has all kinds of schools of rhetoric [σχολαὶ . . . τῶν περὶ λόγους τεχνῶν]; and in
general it not only has a flourishing population but also is most powerful, thus keeping
up the reputation of the mother-city [μητρόπολις].[85] The following men were natives of
Tarsus: among the Stoics, Antipater and Archedemus and Nestor; and also the two Athen-
odoruses, one of whom, called Cordylion, lives with Marcus Cato and died at his house;
and the other, the son of Sandon, called Cananites after some village, was Caesar's

---

[84]Dueck 2000, 107-15. On Strabo's description of India see Romm 1992, 97-116.
[85]This means despite the fact that so many capable men have left the city and never returned;
see the comment on this sentence in Jones, ed., *The Geography of Strabo.*

teacher and was greatly honoured by him; and when he returned to his native land [εἰς τὴν πατρίδα], now an old man, he broke up the government there established, which was being badly conducted by Boethus, among others, who was a bad poet and a bad citizen, having prevailed there by currying the favour of the people. . . . Finding the city in this plight, Athenodorus for a time tried to induce both Boethus and his partisans to change their course; but since they would abstain from no act of insolence, he used the authority given him by Caesar, condemned them to exile, and expelled them. These at first indicted him with the following inscription on the walls: 'Work for young men, counsels for the middle-aged, and flatulence for old men'; and when he, taking the inscription as a joke, ordered the following words to be inscribed beside it, 'thunder for old men,' someone, contemptuous of all decency and afflicted with looseness of the bowels, profusely bespattered the door and wall of Athenodorus' house as he was passing by it at night. Athenodorus, while bringing accusations in the assembly [ἐν ἐκκλησίᾳ] against the faction, said: 'One may see the sickly plight and the disaffection of the city in many ways, and in particular from its excrements.' These men were Stoics; but the Nestor of my time, the teacher of Marcellus, son of Octavia the sister of Caesar, was an Academician. He too was at the head of the government of Tarsus, having succeeded Athenodorus; and he continued to be held in honour both by the prefects and in the city. Among the other philosophers from Tarsus, 'whom I could well note and tell their names' [Homer, *Il.* 3.235], are Plutiades and Diogenes, who were among those philosophers that went round from city to city [περιπολιζόντων] and conducted schools in an able manner. Diogenes also composed poems, as if by inspiration, when a subject was given him—for the most part tragic poems; and as for grammarians [γραμματικοί] whose writings are extant, there are Artemidorus and Diodorus; and the best tragic poet among those enumerated in the 'pleias' was Dionysides. But it is Rome that is best able to tell us the number of learned men [φιλόλογοι] from this city; for it is full of Tarsians and Alexandrians. Such is Tarsus" (Strabo 14.4.12-15).[86]

In the early first century A.D. Isidoros from Charax in southern Babylonia wrote a book titled "Parthian Stations" (Σταθμοὶ Παρθικοί), a description of the Parthian royal road from Antioch in Syria via Zeugma on the Euphrates, Seleukeia on the Tigris and Ecbatana on the Caspian Sea to Alexandropolis in Arachosia. His book on surveying the earth, which included information on the distances between towns and on the size of islands, has survived in only one fragment.[87]

In the winter of A.D. 43/44 Pomponius Mela of southern Spain wrote a three-volume work titled *De Chorographia,* which is regarded as the oldest complete Latin geography. The book is written in the form of a periplus, describing the regions located beyond the coast. The descriptions therefore are superficial. Pomponius Mela presents the coasts from Mauretania to Egypt (1.25-60); Arabia and the Asian coast of the Mediterranean, Syria and the Bosporus (1.62-101); the Black Sea (1.102-2.24); the Aegean, the Adriatic and the Tyrrhenian Seas to

---

[86]On the description of Tarsus see Welles 1962, 54-56.
[87]Isidoros, *GGM* I 244-54; *FGrH* 781. Cf. Weissbach, PW 9 (1916): 2064; W. Spoerri, "Isidoros Nr. 5," *KP* 2:1461; N. Purcell, *OCD* 768.

Gades in Spain (2.25-112); the Ocean as far as the Baltic, and the northern peoples as far as the border to Asia (*confinia Asiae*) (3.1-36); the Caspian and the peoples living in this region (3.37-45); the islands of the north and the east (3.46-66); the coasts of the *Mare Rubrum* from the Indus to the Ganges (3.67-71); and the coasts of the Persian Gulf as far as Libya and Mauretania (3.72-107).[88]

Gaius Plinius Secundus (A.D. 23/24-79), also called Pliny the Elder, came from Novum Comum (mod. Como) and occupied highest military posts. Besides other works, he wrote *Naturalis historiae,* a "natural history" in thirty-seven books. He states in the preface that his work rests on twenty thousand facts culled from two thousand books.[89]

Pliny, *Nat.* praefatio 17: "As Domitus Piso says, it is not books but store-houses that are needed; consequently by perusing about 2,000 volumes, very few of which, owing to the abstruseness of their contents, are ever handled by students, we have collected in 36 volumes 20,000 noteworthy facts obtained from one hundred authors that we have explored, with a great number of other facts in addition that were either ignored by our predecessors or have been discovered by subsequent experience. Nor do we doubt that there are many things that have escaped us also; for we are but human, and beset with duties, and we pursue this sort of interest in our spare moments, that is at night."

After an index and a table of contents, Pliny lists the authors of his sources in book 1 and of the cosmology in book 2.

In book 6 (Asia) he mentions the following sources: "Roman authorities [*ex auctoribus*]: Marcus Agrippa, Marcus Varro, Varro of Atax, Cornelius Nepos, Hyginus, Lucius Vetus, Pomponius Mela, Domitius Corbulo, Licinius Mucianus, Claudius Caesar, Arruntius, Sebosus, Fabricius Tuscus, Titus Livy the son, Seneca, Nigidius. Foreign authorities [*externis*]: King Juba, Hecataeus, Hellanicus, Damastes, Eudoxus, Dicaearchus, Baeto, Timosthenes, Patrocles, Demodamas, Clitarchus, Eratosthenes, Alexander the Great, Ephorus, Hipparchus, Panaetius, Callimachus, Artemidorus, Apollodorus, Agathocles, Polybius, Timaeus of Sicily, Alexander the Learned, Isidore, Amometus, Metrodorus, Posidonius, Onesicritus, Nearchus, Megasthenes, Diognetus, Aristocreon, Bion, Dalion, the younger Simonides, Basilis, Xenophon of Lampsacus."

Pliny begins with a description of countries and regions. He describes in the manner of a periplus Europe (3—4), Africa (5.1-46) and Asia (5.47—6.207); in

---

[88]K. Frick, ed., *Pomponii Melae De choreographia libri tres* (Stuttgart: Teubner, 1968); Brodersen 1994; Romer 1998. Cf. F. Gisinger, "Pomponius 104," PW 21 (1952): 2360-2411; F. Lasserre, "Pomponius 5," *KP* 4:1039; Olshausen 1991, 75; Dilke 1998, 65-66.

[89]*C. Plinius Secundus d. Ä: Naturkunde; Lateinisch-deutsch* (ed. R. König, G. Winkler and K. Brodersen; 37 vols.; Tusculum; Zürich: Artemis & Winkler, 1973-1999); H. Rackham, ed., *Pliny: Natural History* (10 vols.; LCL; Cambridge, Mass: Harvard University Press, 1938-1963). Cf. K. Ziegler et al., "Plinius 5," PW 21.1 (1951): 271-439; R. Hanslik, "Plinius Nr. 2," *KP* 4:928-37; N. Purcell, *OCD* 1197-98; Dihle 1980, 174-90; Dilke 1998, 66-71. The translation by Rackham is based on an unreliable text (cf. Purcell, *OCD* 1197-98); occasionally it is corrected on the basis of a comparison with König, Winkler and Brodersen's text and German translation.

an appendix he describes the size of the continents and climate tables. He continues with a discussion of anthropology, zoology, botany, medicine, pharmacology, metallurgy, mineralogy and art history (7-37). The geographical volumes describe, in more detail, Spain, southern Gaul, Italy, islands (Balearic, Corsica, Sardinia, Sicily, Malta, etc.), Gallia Transalpina, Gallia Cisalpina, the Alps, Dalmatia, Macedonia, Epirus, upper Danube region, Pannonia, lower Danube region, Illyricum, Adriatic islands, Greece (Epirus, Achaia, Attica, Thessalia), Macedonia, Thrace, the Aegean, the Aegean islands (with Crete), the regions around the Black and the Azov Seas, the islands of the northern ocean (with Helgoland or Bornholm, and Scandinavia), Germania, Britannia, Ireland, Thule, Gaul (with Belgica), Spain, Mauretania, the northern coast of Africa, Numidia, Tunesia, Cyrenaica, Libya, Egypt, Arabia, Syria, Idumea, Palestine, Samaria, Decapolis, Phoenicia, inner Syria, Mesopotamia, Isauria, Pisidia, Lycaonia, Pamphylia, Lycia, Caria, Lydia, Ionia, Aeolis (Mysia), Troas, Cyprus, Rhodes, the islands before the Ionian coast, Mysia, Phrygia, Galatia, Bithynia, the Black Sea, Paphlagonia, Cappadocia, Armenia, Media, Scythia, China, India, Ceylon, the Persian Gulf, Parthia, Mesopotamia, Arabia, the Red Sea, Ethiopia.

The following quotations are meant to give an impression of the rich detail that could be researched in the first century. In his description of the province of Baetica in eastern Spain, Pliny writes, "Its towns [*oppida*] number in all 175, of which 9 are colonies, 10 municipalities of Roman citizens, 27 towns granted early Latin rights, 6 free towns, 3 bound by treaty to Rome and 120 paying tribute. Worthy of mention in this district, or easily expressed in Latin, are: on the ocean coast beginning at the river Guadiana, the town Ossonoba, surnamed Aestuaria, at the confluence of the Luxia and the Urium; the Hareni Mountains; the river Guadalquivir; the winding bay of the coast of Curum, opposite to which is Cadiz, to be described among the islands; the Promontory of Juno; Port Vaesippo; the town of Baelo; Mellaria, the strait entering from the Atlantic; Carteia, called by the Greeks Tartesos; Gibraltar. Next, on the coast inside the straits, are: the town of Barbesula with its river; ditto Salduba; the town of Suel; Malaga with its river, one of the treaty towns. Then comes Maenuba with its river; Firmum Julium surnamed Sexum; Sel; Abdara; Murgi, which is the boundary of Baetica" (3.1.7). The city of Caesaraugusta (mod. Saragossa) in western Spain is described as follows: "Caesaraugusta, a colony that pays no taxes, is by the river Ebro; its site was once occupied by a town called Salduba, belonging to the district of Edetania. It is the centre for 55 peoples; of these with the rights of Roman citizens are the Bilbilitani, the Celsenses (once a colony), the Calagurritani (surnamed Nasici), the Ilerdenses belonging to the race of the Surdaones next to the river Sicoris, the Oscenses of the district of Suessetania, and the Turiassonenses; with the old Latin rights are the Cascantenses, Ergavicenses, Graccurritani, Leonicenses and Osicerdenses; bound by treaty are the Tarracenses; tributary are the Arcobrigenses, Andelonenses, Aracelitani, Bursaonenses, Calagurritani surnamed Fibularenses, Conplutenses, Carenses, Cincienses, Cortonenses, Camanitani, Ispallenses, Ilursenses, Iluberitani, Jacetani, Libienses, Pompelonenses and Segienses" (3.4.24). At the end of his description of Europe, Pliny summarizes: "Having completed the circuit of Europe we must now give its complete dimensions, in order that those who desire this information may not be left at a loss. Its length from the Don to Cadiz is given by Artemidorus and Isidorus as 7,714 miles. Polybius stated the breadth of Europe from Italy to the ocean as 1,150 miles, but its exact magnitude had not been ascertained even in his day. The length of Italy itself up to the Alps is 1,020 miles, as we stated [4.3.43]; and from the Alps through Lyons to the harbor of the Morini, the port on the British channel, the line of measurement that Polybius appears to take, is 1,169 miles, but a better ascertained measurement and a longer one is that starting also from the Alps but going northwest through the Camp of the Legions in Germany to the mouth of the Rhine—1,243 miles" (4.37.121-122).

Pliny's description of Egypt begins with this sentence: "In addition to boasting its other glories of the past Egypt can claim the distinction of having had in the reign of King Amasis 20,000 cities; and even now it contains a very large number, although of no importance. However, the City of Apollo is notable, as is also the City of Leucothea and the Great City of Zeus, also called Thebes, renowned for the fame of its hundred gates, Coptos the market near the Nile for Indian and Arabian merchandise, and also the Town of Venus and the Town of Jove and Tentyris, below which is Abydos, famous for the place of Memnon and the Temple of Osiris, in the interior of Libya seven and a half miles from the river" (5.11.60).

On the Scythians: "Beyond are some tribes of Scythians. To these the Persians have given the general name of Sacae, from the tribe nearest to Persia, but old writers call them the Aramii, and the Scythians themselves give the name of Chorsari to the Persians and call Mount Caucasus Croucasis, which means 'white with snow.' There is an uncountable number of tribes, numerous enough to live on equal terms with the Parthians; most notable among them are the Sacae, Massagetae, Dahae, Essedones, Astacae, Rumnici, Pestici, Homodoti, Histi, Edones, Camae, Camacae, Euchatae, Cotieri, Authusiani, Psacae, Arimaspi, Antacati, Chroasai and Oetaei; among them the Napaei are said to have been destroyed by the Palaei. Notable rivers in their country are the Mandragaeus and the Caspasus. And in regard to no other region is there more discrepancy among the authorities, this being due as I believe to the countless numbers and the nomadic habits of the tribes. The water of the Caspian Sea itself was said by Alexander the Great to be sweet to drink, and also Marcus Varro states that good drinking water was conveyed from it for Pompey when he was operating in the neighborhood of the river during the Mithridatic War" (6.19.50-51).

On the Seres (China): "After leaving the Caspian Sea and the Scythian Ocean our course takes a bend towards the Eastern Sea as the coast turns to face eastward. The first part of the coast after the Scythian promontory is uninhabitable on account of snow, and the neighboring region is uncultivated because of the savagery of the tribes that inhabit it. This is the country of the Cannibal Scythians who eat human bodies; consequently the adjacent districts are waste deserts thronging with wild beasts lying in wait for human beings as savage as themselves. Then we come to more Scythians and to more deserts inhabited by wild beasts, until we reach a mountain range called Tabis which forms a cliff over the sea; and not until we have covered nearly half of the length of the coast that faces northeast is that region inhabited. The first human occupants are the people called the Chinese, who are famous for the woolen substance obtained from their forests; after soaking it in water they comb off the white down of the leaves, and so supply our women with the double task of unraveling the threads and weaving them together again; so manifold is the labor employed, and so distant is the region of the globe drawn upon, to enable the Roman matron to flaunt transparent raiment in public. The Chinese, though mild in character, yet resemble wild animals, in that they also shun the company of the remainder of mankind, and wait for trade to come to them. The first river found in their territory is the Psitharas, next the Cambari, and third the Lanos, after which come the Malay Peninsula, the Bay of Cirnaba, the river Atianos and the tribe of the Attacorae on the bay of the same name, sheltered by sunbathed hills from every harmful blast, with the same temperate climate as that in which dwell the Hyperborei" (6.20.53-55). The rivers and mountains that Pliny mentions in this description, some of them mentioned in other contemporary sources, cannot be identified. The mountains of Chryse are, according to the *Periplus Mari Erythraei* (63), the easternmost point of the known world. Identifications with Malaysia, Birma or Sumatra, for example, are not helpful.[90]

On India: "We now come to the point after which there is complete agreement as to the races—the range of mountains called the Hemodian Mountains [the Himalayas]. Here begins the Indian race, bordering not only on the Eastern Sea but on the southern also, which we have designated the Indian Ocean. The part facing east stretches in a straight line until it comes to a bend, and at the point where the Indian Ocean begins its total length is 1,875 miles [2,775 km]; while from that point onward the southerly bend of the coast according to Eratosthenes covers 2,475 miles [3,663 km], finally reaching the river Indus, which is the western boundary of India. A great many authors however give the entire length of the coast as being forty days' and nights' sail and the measurement of the country from north to south as 2,850 miles [4,218 km]. Agrippa says that it is 3,300 miles long and 1,300 miles broad [4,884 and 1,924 km]. . . . In that country the aspect of the heavens and the rising of the stars are different, and there are two summers and two harvests yearly, separated by a winter accompanied by etesian winds, while at our midwinter it enjoys soft breezes and the sea is navigable. Its races and cities are beyond counting, if one wished to enumerate all of them. . . . Those who accompanied Alexander the Great have written that the region of India subdued by him contained 5,000 towns, none smaller than Coos,[91] and 9,000 nations, and that India forms a third of the entire surface of the earth, and that its populations are innumerable, which is certainly a very probable theory, inasmuch as the Indians are almost the only race that has never migrated from its own territory. . . . Diognetus and Baeton, the surveyors of his expeditions [i.e., of Alexander the Great], write that the distance from the Caspian Gates to the Parthian City of Hecatompylos is the number of miles that we stated above [6.17.44: 133 miles, or 197 km];[92] from thence to the city of Alexandria of the Arii, which Alexander founded, 575 miles [851 km], to the city of Crangae, Prophthasia, 199 miles, [294 km] to the town of Arachosii 565 miles [836 km], to Kabul 175 miles [259 km], and thence to Alexander's Town 50 miles [74 km] (in some copies of this record we find different numbers): this city is stated to be situated immediately below the Caucasus; from it to the river Kabul and the Indian town of Peucolatis 237 miles [351 km], and thence to the river Indus and the town of Taxila 60 miles [89 km], to the famous river Jhelum 120 miles [177 km], to the not less notable Beas 390 miles [577 km]—this was the terminus of Alexander's journeys, although he crossed the river and dedicated altars upon the opposite bank. The king's actual dispatches also agree with these figures" (6.21.56-62). Pliny continues with an elaborate description of the tribes in northern India and of the Ganges and Indus regions. Finally he provides information about sea routes from Arabia and Egypt to India (6.26.101-106).

Pliny's description of travel opportunities to India seems to suggest that a voyage to India was hardly remarkable: "The following period considered it a shorter and safer route to start from the same cape and steer for the Indian harbor of Sigerus, and for a long time

---

[90]See G. Winkler, ed., *C. Plinius Secundus d. Ä: Naturkunde,* book 6, 189; on Okelis, see ibid., 211.

[91]The comparison with Coos probably goes back to Onesikritos, who accompanied Alexander the Great, who came from this not very large polis.

[92]See Seibert 1985, 25.

this was the course followed, until a merchant discovered a shorter route, and the desire for gain brought India nearer; indeed, the voyage is made every year, with companies of archers on board, because these seas used to be very greatly infested by pirates. And it will not be amiss to set out the whole of the voyage from Egypt, now that reliable knowledge of it is for the first time accessible. It is an important subject, in view of the fact that in no year does India absorb less than fifty million sesterces of our empire's wealth, sending back merchandise to be sold with us at a hundred times its prime cost. Two miles from Alexandria is the town of Juliopolis. The voyage up the Nile from there to Keft is 309 miles [357 km], and takes twelve days when the midsummer tradewinds are blowing. From Keft the journey is made with camels, stations being placed at intervals for the purpose of watering; the first, a stage of 22 miles, is called Hydreuma; the second is in the mountains, a day's journey on; the third at a second place named Hydreuma, 85 miles from Keft; the next is in the mountains; next we come to Apollo's Hydreuma, 184 miles from Keft; again a station in the mountains; then we get to New Hydreuma, 230 miles from Keft. There is also another Old Hydreuma known by the name of Trogodyticum, where a guard is stationed on outpost duty at a caravanserai accommodating two thousand travelers; it is 7 miles from New Hydreuma. Then comes the town of Berenice, where there is a harbor on the Red Sea, 257 miles [380 km] from Keft. But as the greater part of the journey is done by night because of the heat and the days are spent at stations, the whole journey from Keft to Bernice takes twelve days. Traveling by sea begins at midsummer before the dogstar rises [July 18] or immediately after its rising, and it takes about thirty days to reach the Arabian port of Cella or Cane [Okelis] in the frankincense-producing district. . . . The most advantageous way of sailing to India is to set out from Cella [Okelis]; from that port it is forty days' voyage, if the Hippalus is blowing, to the first trading-station in India, Muziris" (6.26.101-104). Okelis is a harbor on the Arabian coast of the Bab el-Mandeb (cf. *Periplus Maris Erythraei* 25) and is identified with the lagoon Shykh Sai'id or with Khawr Ghurayrah.

The geographical work of Pliny, written not as a contribution to research and scholarship, has to be understood in the context of literary-scientific general education. Albrecht Dihle observes that Pliny "combines many geographical details with moralizing observations for the benefit of his readers, and in many passages he strives to provide a pleasing presentation of the dry material that would meet stylistic criteria."[93]

In A.D. 124 Dionysios of Alexandria wrote a "Description of the Inhabited Earth" (Περιήγησις τῆς οἰκουμένης, *Periēgēsis tēs oikoumenēs*) in hexameters, possibly for use in schools. He describes the shape of the earth and of the oceans, Libya (Africa), Europe, the islands of the Mediterranean and of the "outer ocean," and Asia.[94] Around A.D. 150 Pausanias from Magnesia ad Sipylum in Lydia (?) wrote a "Description of Greece" (Περιήγησις τῆς Ἑλλάδος, *Periēgēsis tēs Hellados*), which was based on observations that he had made on his travels. Even though he is particularly interested in the description of ancient

---

[93]Dihle 1980, 175.
[94]Dionysios, *Orbis descriptio, GGM* II 104-75. Cf. R. Böker, "Dionysios Nr. 30," *KP* 2:73-74; E. H. Warmington and J. S. Rusten, "Dionysius (9)," *OCD* 478.

works of art, it is obvious that he has traveled widely, visiting not only Greece but also Asia Minor, Syria, Palestine, Egypt and Rome.[95]

Claudius Ptolemaios of Alexandria (A.D. 90-168), mathematician, astronomer and geographer, provides in his main geographical work Γεωγραφίας Ὑφήγησις (*Geographias Hyphēgēsis*) a "Guide to Map the World," which consists of a theoretical part (book 1), a description of the countries of the three continents Europe, Libya (Africa) and Asia (books 2—7), and a breakdown of the world map into twenty-six individual maps of smaller areas (book 8).[96] Ptolemaios describes the world from Ferro, the westernmost of the Canary islands, to Sera (China) in the east (180 degrees of longitude), and from Thule to Agisymba (Chad?) in the interior of Africa (80 degrees of latitude). The description of countries and regions contains 8,100 fixed geographical points including towns, mountains, mouths of rivers and sixty-eight names of peoples. Longitude is measured from zero meridian, which was located at the "Isles of the Blessed" in the far west; latitude was measured from the equator. Books 2—3 describe western and eastern Europe (with the first reference to the Frisians, Langobards, Saxons and Sudetes); book 4: Libya; book 5: western Asia as far as the Euphrates; book 6: near east, central and northern Asia (Scythia) and China (Serike); book 7.1-4: India, southeast Asia (Sinai; the most eastern place is "Cattigara," perhaps Kiau-chi [mod. Hanoi in Vietnam]), Ceylon (Taprobane).

The description of Bactria may serve as an example: Ptolemaios first describes the borders (6.11.1) and rivers (6.11.2-6) before he lists the towns, including longitude and latitude (11.7-9): "Towns of Baktrianē lying on the River Ōxos are these: Chatracharta 110° 44°10', Charispa 113° 43°, Choana 113° 42°, Surogana 117°30' 40°30', Phratu 118° 39°20'. On the other rivers (are situated): Alichodra 118° 39°20', Chomara 116°30' 43°30', Kuriandra 109°30' 42°10', Kauaris 111°20' 43°, Astakana 112° 43°20', Tosmuanassa 108°30' 41°20', Menapia 113° 41°20', Eukratidia 115° 42°, Bactra Royal Residence 116° 40°, Ostobara

---

[95]Nikolaos D. Papachatze, ed., *Pausaniou Hellados Periegesis* (5 vols.; Athens: Ekdotike Athenon, 1974-1981); Maria H. Rocha-Pereira, ed., *Pausaniae Graeciae descriptio* (2nd ed.; Leipzig: Teubner, 1989). Cf. O. Regenbogen, "Pausanias Nr. 17," PWSup 8 (1956): 1008-97; F. Lasserre, "Pausanias Nr. 7," *KP* 4:570-72; A. J. S. Spawforth, "Pausanias (3)," *OCD* 1129; Christian Habicht, *Pausanias und seine "Beschreibung Griechenlands"* (Munich: Beck, 1985); English: *Pausanias' Guide to Ancient Greece* (Sather Classical Lectures; Berkeley: University of California Press, 1985); Swain 1998, 330-56.

[96]Carl F. A. Nobbe, ed., *Claudii Ptolemaei Geographia* (2 vols.; Leipzig: Teubner, 1843-1845 [1898]; repr., Hildesheim: Olms, 1966]. A new edition of the Greek text and a translation of book 6 has been published: Helmut Humbach and Susanne Ziegler, eds., *Ptolemy: Geography, Book 6: Middle East, Central and North Asia; Part I: Text and English/German Translations* (Wiesbaden: Reichert, 1998). For an older study on the manuscripts of Ptolemaios's *Geography* and their history see Paul Schnabel, *Text und Karten des Ptolemäus* (Leipzig: Koehler, 1939). See also E. Polaschek, "Ptolemaios als Geograph," PWSup 10 (1965): 680-833; F. Lasserre, *KP* 4:1224-32, esp. 1229-32; G. J. Toomer, "Ptolemy (4)," *OCD* 1273-75; O. A. E. Dilke, "The Culmination of Greek Cartography in Ptolemy," in Harley and Woodward 1987, 1:177-20; idem 1998, 72-86; Olshausen 1991, 75-76, 95.

109°30′ 45°20′, Marakanda 112°30′, 39°45′, Marakodra 115°20′ 39°20′."[97]

Greek text: Πόλεις δέ εἰσι τῆς Βακτριανῆς πρὸς μετῷ ῎Ωξῳ ποταμῷ αἵδε· Χαράχαρτα ρια μδ Ζαρίασπα ἢ Χαρίσπα ριε μδ Χόανα ριζ μβ Σουρογάνα ριζ μ Φράτου ριθ λθ γ· πρὸς δὲ ταῖς ἄλλαις ποταμίαις αἵδε· ᾿Αλιχόρδα ρζ μγ Χόμαρα ρ μγ Κουριάνδρα ρθ μβ Καυαρίς ρια γ μγ ᾿Αστακάνα ριβ μβ γ ᾿Εβουσμουάνασσα ἢ Τοσμου ἄνασσα ρη μα γ Μεναπία ριγ μα γ Εὐκρατιδία ριε μβ· Βάκτρα βασίλειον ρι μα ᾿Εστόβαρα ρθ με γ Μαρακάνδα ριβ λθ δ Μαρα-κόδρα ριε γ λθ γ.

In book 7.5 Ptolemaios provides a summary description of the world map, with a discussion of the borders that separate the *oikoumenē* from the "unknown earth" (ἄγνωστος γῆ, *agnōstos gē*) and reference to the oceans that surround the continents. Book 8 discusses the drawing of maps that depict one or more countries of the inhabited world, ending with a list of the most important towns and islands, with latitudes and longitudes. The work of Ptolemaios represents "the climax of ancient cartography, at the same time its end."[98] For the thousands of facts that he included in his geography, Ptolemaios was able to rely on the work of Roman land surveyors (*agrimensores, mensores, gromatici*), among them freedmen and slaves who had compiled countless geographical facts during expeditions of Roman armies. The legions of Rome had surveyed one sixth of the globe.[99]

6. The *historical writings* of ancient authors often included geographical information. The work of the Greek historian Xenophon (ca. 425-355 B.C.), still valued by Caesar and Cicero three hundred years later, demonstrates an intensive interest in geographical information. The *Anabasis* and the *Hellenika* confirm Xenophon's interest in observations on countries and people, on manners and customs, on geographical and topographical information.[100] Ephoros of Kyme in Asia Minor (ca. 405-330 B.C.) wrote a universal history in thirty volumes (Ἱστορίαι, *Historiai*), which unfortunately is lost. We know, however, that he provided a survey of the world in book 5. It appears that each book was devoted to a particular re-

---

[97] Translation according to Humbach and Ziegler, *Ptolemy: Geography*, 159-63.

[98] Olshausen 1991, 76.

[99] Bernecker 1989, 331. On the Roman land surveyors see Friedrich Blume, Ed., *Die Schriften der römischen Feldmesser* (2 vols.; Berlin: Reimer, 1848-1852; repr., Hildesheim: Olms, 1967); O. A. W. Dilke, *The Roman Land Surveyors: An Introduction to the Agrimensores* (Newton Abbot: David & Charles, 1971); idem, "Roman Large-Scale Mapping in the Early Empire," in Harley and Woodward 1987, 1:212-33; Sherk 1974.

[100] C. L. Brownson, ed., *Xenophon: Anabasis* (LCL; Cambridge, Mass.: Harvard University Press, 1998); P. Krentz, ed., *Xenophon: Hellenika* (Classical Texts; Warminster: Aris & Phillips, 1989-1995); W. Müri and B. Zimmermann, eds., *Xenophon: Anabasis; Griechisch-deutsch* (2nd ed.; Tusculum; Düsseldorf and Zürich: Artemis & Winkler, 1997); G. Strasburger, ed., *Xenophon: Hellenika; Griechisch-deutsch* (2nd ed.; Tusculum; Düsseldorf and Zürich: Artemis & Winkler, 1988). Cf. M. Treu and H. R. Breitenbach, "Xenophon Nr. 6," PW 9.A (1967): 1569-2052, esp. 1579-1638, with a complete list of all geographical facts in *Anabasis;* F. Lasserre, "Xenophon Nr. 5," *KP* 5:1422-30, esp. 1423; C. J. Tuplin, *OCD* 1628-31; Olshausen 1991, 63.

gion—for example, southern Greece, central Greece, Macedonia, Sicily, Persia. Polybius describes Ephoros as the first universal historian; Diodorus Siculus and Nicolaus of Damascus excerpted long passages. Strabo, Polyaenus and Plutarch are in part dependent upon him.[101]

Polybius of Megalopolis in Arcadia (ca. 200-118 B.C.) had gained political and military experience in Greece, Spain, Africa and Asia Minor. He is the only Hellenistic historian of whose writings larger parts have survived: about one third of the forty volumes of his universal history ('Ιστορίαι, *Historiai*).[102] Polybius summarized the principles that a historian needs to observe: personal political or military experience, study of the sources, study of the scenes of historical events in terms of personal presence and practical experience (αὐτοπαθεία, *au topatheia*), also with reference to geographical factors (12.25e.1; 12.25h.4; 12.25i.2). He emphasizes that it is important that the historian becomes acquainted with "cities, places, rivers, lakes, and in general all the peculiar features of land and sea and the distances of one place from another"(12.25e.1).[103] Polybius repeatedly includes excursuses to explain the geographical place of the historical events that he describes. As a result we have extensive descriptions of Sicily (1.41.7-42.6), northern Italy (2.14.3-17.12), Byzantion (4.38-46), the Black and the Azov Seas (4.39-42), Media (5.44.4-11), Seleukeia in Syria (5.59.3-11) and Carthage (10.9-11). Book 34, with a survey of the geography of the entire world, unfortunately has not survived (cf. Strabo 8.1.1). Book 40 provided a general index, making the geographical information easily accessible. Even though Polybius was no expert in the area of general and astronomical geography, he wrote a treatise "On the Habitability of the Equatorial Region" (Περὶ τῆς περὶ τὸν ἰσημερινὸν οὐκήσεως, *Peri tēs peri ton isēmerinon oukēseōs*), of which only the title survives.

Diodorus Siculus of Agyrion in Sicily finished his "Library" (Βιβλιοθήκη, *Bibliothēkē*), a universal history in forty volumes, probably in 30 B.C., of which

---

[101] *FGrH* 70. Cf. H. Gärtner, *KP* 2:299-301; K. S. Sacks, *OCD* 529-30.
[102] Theodor Büttner-Wobst, ed., *Polybii historiae* (5 vols.; Leipzig: Teubner, 1893-1922; repr., Stuttgart: Teubner, 1993); W. R. Paton, ed., *Polybius: The Histories* (6 vols.; LCL; Cambridge, Mass.: Harvard University Press, 1922-1927). See K. Ziegler, "Polybios Nr. 1," PW 21.1 (1952): 1440-1578; idem, "Polybios Nr. 3," *KP* 4:983-91; P. S. Derow, *OCD* 1209-11; F. W. Walbank, *Polybius* (Sather Classical Lectures 42; Berkeley: University of California Press, 1972); idem, *A Historical Commentary on Polybius* (Oxford: Clarendon, 1977); K. Stiewe and N. Holzberg, eds., *Polybios* (WF 347; Darmstadt: Wissenschaftliche Buchgesellschaft, 1982); Aujac 1987c, 161-62; Olshausen 1991, 50-54; F. W. Walbank, *Polybius, Rome, and the Hellenistic World: Essays and Reflections* (Cambridge: Cambridge University Press, 2002).
[103] Polybius 12.25e.1: περὶ τὴν θέαν τῶν πόλεων καὶ τῶν τόπων περί τε ποταμῶν καὶ λιμένων καὶ καθόλου τῶν κατὰ γῆν καὶ κατὰ θάλατταν ἰδιωμάτων καὶ διαστημάτων. In regard to θέα, Arno Mauersberger (*Polybios-Lexikon* [4 vols.; Berlin: Akademie-Verlag, 1956-1998], 1:1140) gives as the first meaning "d. Ansehen: Augenschein = eigene Besichtigung v. Örtlichkeiten"—personal inspection of places.

only fifteen volumes have survived intact.[104] Diodorus uses specialized geographical literature in places where he wants to describe the geographical location of historical events. For his description of events in Asia, Egypt, Ethiopia, Arabia and the area of the Red Sea he uses the *Asiatika* and the periplus of Agatharchides (1.30-41; 3.2-37; 2.48-54; 3.12-48). For India and Taprobane (Ceylon) he uses Megasthenes (2.35-42:55-60; 18.5-6) and Kleitarchos, the historian of the history of Alexander the Great. For the western regions of the world he uses the histories of Timaios (5.2-23) and of Poseidonios (5.24-40). Further sources that Diodorus uses are Hekataios, Ktesias, Dionysios Skytobrachion, Ephoros, Duris, Philinos and Polybius.[105] Gaius Sallustius Crispus (86-34 B.C.) wrote a contemporary history for the period 78-67 B.C. in five volumes (*Historiae*), only fragments of which have survived. His work contains descriptions of Pamphylia, Sardinia, Corsica, Carthage, the Taurus Mountains, Crete, the Black Sea, southern Italy and Sicily.[106] Gaius Iulius Caesar (100-44 B.C.) included several geographical and ethnographical excurses in his *commentarii* on the war in Gaul, the seven books on the *Bellum Gallicum:* on Gaul and its inhabitants, on the Belgians, the Nervians, the Suebes, on the rivers Maas and Rhine, on Britain and its inhabitants, on the Germans and on the Ardenne Mountains.[107]

Titus Livius (Livy [59 B.C.-A.D. 17]), Roman historian and friend of Augustus, did not travel much and had little political or military experience, which is reflected in the small role that geography plays in his historical work *Ab urbe condita libri.* However, most of the 142 volumes of this work have not survived, and in the extant passages we do find geographical descriptions of Gaul, Germania and Britannia.[108] Pompeius Trogus from Gallia Narbonensis wrote his main work, *Historiae Philippicae,* between 30 and 1 B.C. He described in forty-four volumes the

---

[104]F. Vogel and K. T. Fischer, eds., *Diodori Bibliotheca historica* (6 vols.; Bibliotheca scriptorum Graecorum et Romanorum Teubneriana.Teubner: Leipzig, 1964-1969 [1888-1906]); C. H. Oldfather, ed., *Diodorus Siculus: Library of History* (12 vols.; LCL; Cambridge, Mass.: Harvard University Press, 1976-1993 [1933-1967]); G. Wirth and O. Veh, eds., *Diodoros: Griechische Weltgeschichte* (3 vols.; Bibliothek der griechischen Literatur; Stuttgart: Hiersemann, 1992-1998). See K. S. Sacks, *OCD* 472-73; Olshausen 1991, 31; Dihle 1994, 105-6.

[105]See M. von Albrecht, "Diodoros Nr. 12," *KP* 2:41-42; Olshausen 1991, 31-32; K. S. Sacks, *OCD* 472-73. On Ktesias see Romm 1992, 86-88.

[106]J. C. Rolfe, ed., *Sallust* (rev. ed.; LCL; London: Heinemann; Cambridge, Mass.: Harvard University Press, 1931); P. McGushin, ed., *Sallust: the Histories* (2 vols.; Clarendon Ancient History Series; Oxford: Oxford University Press, 1992-1994); W. Eisenhut and J. Lindauer, eds., *Sallust: Werke; Lateinisch und Deutsch* (2nd ed.; Tusculum; Zürich: Artemis & Winkler, 1994). Cf. C. B. R. Pelling, *OCD* 1348-49; Olshausen 1991, 58.

[107]Caesar, *Bell. gall.* 1.1.5-7; 2.3-5; 2.15.3-6; 4.1-3; 4.10; 5.12-14; 6.11-28; 6.29.4. For the discussion on the authorship of the excurses see Helga Gesche, *Caesar* (EdF 51; Darmstadt: Wissenschaftliche Buchgesellschaft, 1976), 83-87. Since the studies of F. Beckmann (1930) and D. Rasmussen (1967), the arguments used to support non-Caesarean authorship generally are no longer regarded as valid.

[108]Livy, 103.104; Tacitus, *Agr.* 10.3. A. C. Schlesinger, ed., *Livy* (14 vols.; LCL; London: Heinemann, 1951); H. J. Hillen and J. Feix, eds., *Livius: Römische Geschichte* (11 vols., Lateinisch-

history of the Mediterranean world until his own time.[109] Only excerpts by M. Iunianus Iustinus (ca. A.D. 300) are extant. In the first forty volumes he described in excursuses the geographical aspects of the events narrated in chronological sequence. For example, he discusses the location of the Aeolian and Ionian cities, Egypt, Sicily, Africa, Carthage, Palestine and Asia Minor. The last four volumes follow a geographical order; Pompeius describes the eastern and the western regions: Parthia, Arabia, Armenia, Rome and Spain.

Cornelius Tacitus (A.D. 56-120) wrote a biography of Agricola, his father-in-law, who had been governor in Britain, in which he included geographical descriptions of Britain, Hibernia and Caledonia (*Agr.* 10-12.24.25). In the book about Germania and its inhabitants (*De origine et situ Germanorum*), unique in Roman literature as a book about a foreign people, he describes the borders and the nature of the country (1-5), the public and private life of the inhabitants (6-15.16-27) and individual tribes (28-46). This geographical and ethnographical interest of Tacitus is less evident in his major historical works, the *Historiae* and the *Annales,* which, however, have not survived intact or remained unfinished. We do find geographical descriptions in connection with the uprising of the Batavians in Germania and the Jewish revolt in Judea (*Hist.* 4.12; 5.23; 5.6-8; 5.11-12). In the *Annales* Tacitus generally dispenses with detailed geographical information, but we still find numerous comments about Germania, Britannia, Thrace, the northeastern coast of the Black Sea, Asia Minor, Armenia, Mesopotamia and Egypt.[110]

Appian from Alexandria finished in A.D. 165 a "Roman History" ('Ρωμαϊκὴ ἱστορία, *Rōmaikē historia*) in twenty-four volumes. The work begins with a survey

---

deutsche Gesamtausgabe; Tusculum; Zürich: Artemis & Winkler, 1991-1998 [1972-1987]). The accusation of geographical ignorance (M. Fuhrmann, *KP* 3:696) probably is unjustified, considering the size of Livy's work; cf. Olshausen 1991, 47-49; J. Briscoe, *OCD* 877-79.

[109]Otto Seel, ed., *Pompei Trogi fragmenta* (Bibliotheca scriptorum Graecorum et Romanorum Teubneriana; Leipzig: Teubner, 1956); idem, ed., *Historiae Philippicae: Weltgeschichte von den Anfängen bis Augustus; Pompeius Trogus, im Auszug des Justin* (Bibliothek der alten Welt, römische Reihe; Zürich: Artemis, 1972). Cf. P. L. Schmidt, *KP* 4:1031-33; A. Spawforth, *OCD* 1217; Olshausen 1991, 54-55.

[110]M. Winterbottom and R. M. Ogilvie, eds., *Cornelii Taciti Opera Minora* (Oxford: Clarendon, 1975); C. H. Moore and J. Jackson, eds., *Tacitus: The Histories, The Annals* (4 vols.; LCL; Cambridge, Mass.: Harvard University Press, 1969 [1925-1937]); A. Städele, ed., *Tacitus: Agricola, Germania; Lateinisch und Deutsch* (Tusculum; Zürich: Artemis & Winkler, 1991); E. Heller, ed., *Tacitus: Annalen; Lateinisch und Deutsch* (3rd ed.; Tusculum; Zürich: Artemis & Winkler, 1997); J. Borst, ed., *Tacitus: Historien; Lateinisch und Deutsch* (5th ed.; Tusculum; Zürich: Artemis & Winkler, 1984). Cf. S. Borzsák, "Cornelius Nr. 395," PWSup 11 (1968): 373-512; M. Fuhrmann, *KP* 5:486-93; R. H. Martin, *OCD* 1469-71; Olshausen 1991, 29-30; Dieter Flach, *Tacitus in der Tradition der antiken Geschichtsschreibung* (Göttingen: Vandenhoeck & Ruprecht, 1973); Günther Wille, *Der Aufbau der Werke des Tacitus* (Heuremata 9; Amsterdam: Grüner, 1983); H. Y. McCulloch, "The Historical Process and Theories of History in the 'Annals' and 'Histories' of Tacitus," *ANRW* II.33.4 (1991): 2928-48; Anthony R. Anthony, "The Life and Death of Cornelius Tacitus," *Historia* 49 (2000): 230-47.

of the geography of the Roman Empire (1 *praef.* 1-5) and then follows an ethno-graphical outline, describing the various people that have been conquered by Rome: the Italians, Samnites, Celts, Sicilians, Iberians, Hannibal, Carthaginians, Ionians, Syrians, Parthians, Mithradates, the civil wars, the wars in Egypt, the wars against the Dacians, against the Jews and against the Pontic peoples, as well as the Arabs.[111] Flavius Arrianus (A.D. 86-160) wrote a "Periplus of the Black Sea," previously mentioned, and also a description of the history of Bithynia (eight books), Parthia (seventeen books) and India (forty-three chapters). His history of Alexander the Great (seven books) also contains geographical descriptions.[112]

7. Some *philosophers* included geographical descriptions in their texts, usu-ally the result of personal travels. Publius Aelius Aristides (A.D. 117-181) of Hadrianutherai (Hadriani) in Mysia, a representative of the Second Sophistic who taught in Smyrna, is a good example.[113] While living in Alexandria, he vis-ited the pyramids, Memphis, the labyrinth at Lake Moeris, the Kanopus Valley and the Nile Delta. He used local translators who introduced him to the history, religion and language of Egypt. During his investigation of the sources of the Nile he traveled beyond the first cataract to Elephantine, Syene and Phylae, the last Roman station, where he met an Ethiopian delegation. A slave helped him to write journals (ὑπομνήματα, *hypomnēmata*) that he later used as basis for his "Egyptian Discourse" (Αἰγύπτιος [*Or.* 36]).

8. In works of *light fiction* foreign countries and peoples occur from time to time as well. Adventure stories often were placed in exotic milieus. A compre-hensive fragment of a play by Chariton was found on a papyrus of the second century A.D. that describes the adventures of a couple of Greek lovers at the court of an Indian king.[114] Specialists in Indian studies point out that the gibber-

---

[111]H. White, ed., *Appian: Roman History* (4 vols.; LCL; London: Heinemann, 1912-1913); P. Vi-ereck and A. G. Roos, eds., *Appiani Historia Romana* (3 vols.; Leipzig: Teubner, 1897-1881; repr., 1962); Otto Veh and Kai Brodersen, eds., *Appian von Alexandreia: Römische Ge-schichte* (2 vols.; Stuttgart: Hiersemann, 1987-1989). Cf. E. Schwartz, "Appianus Nr. 2," PW 2.1 (1895): 216-37; J. Werner, *KP* 1:463-65; K. Brodersen, *OCD* 130; Olshausen 1991, 25-26; Swain 1998, 248-53.

[112]Roos and Wirth, *Flavii Arriani*, 1:1-390 (Ἀλεξάνδρου Ἀνάβασις); 2:1-73 (Ἰνδική), 197-223 (Βιθυνικά, frg.), 224-52 (Παρθικά, frg.); P. A. Brunt, *Arrian* (LCL; 2 vols.; Cambridge, Mass.: Harvard University Press, 1976-1983). See E. Schwartz, "Arrianus Nr. 9," PW 2 (1895): 1230-47; G. Wirth, *KP* 1:605-6; A. B. Bosworth, *OCD* 175-76; Wheeler, "Flavius Arrianus," 260-328, 399-419; Philip A. Stadter, *Arrian of Nicomedia* (Chapel Hill: University of North Carolina Press, 1980); on Arrianus's *Indike* see ibid., 7-9; A. Brian Bosworth, *A Historical Commentary on Arrian's History of Alexander* (2 vols.; Oxford: Clarendon, 1980-1995); Olshausen 1991, 35-37; Swain 1998, 242-48.

[113]See R. Klein 1981, 71-108, esp. 75-76; Swain 1998, 254-97; C. A. Behr, ed., *P. Aelius Aristides: The Complete Works* (2 vols.; Leiden: Brill, 1981-1986), 1:1-4.

[114]P.Oxy. 413; for the translated text see D. L. Page, ed., *Select Papyri* (5 vols.; LCL; Cambridge, Mass.: Harvard University Press, 1950), 3:336-44; cf. Mario Andreassi, *Mimi greci in Egitto: Chariton e Moicheutria* (Bari: Palomar, 2001); Dihle 1994, 113.

ish spoken by the Indian persons in the play is reminiscent of a Dravidic language.

Jewish Geography

The Jewish people do not seem to have had their own geographers. However, we do find geographical knowledge and information in the Old Testament, particularly in connection with the exodus story. The list of resting places in the desert (Num 33) is an itinerary.[115] We find geographical descriptions of borders (e.g., Num 34:2-12) and topographical information on the settlement areas of the individual tribes (Josh 15—19). The table of nations in Gen 10 lists the peoples of the world primarily on the background of relationships, but geographical details are included there as well.[116] The geographical conception of Gen 10 evidently has dominated Jewish geography for hundreds of years.[117] The map that we can reconstruct on the basis of the geographical information provided in *Jubilees* (second century B.C.; see fig. 9) confirms this suggestion. The author of *Jubilees* might well have consulted a world map while writing *Jub.* 8—10. The geography of Josephus also confirms the lasting influence of Gen 10.

Flavius Josephus, a member of the priestly aristocracy in Jerusalem, included in his *Bellum Judaicum* geographical descriptions of Galilee, Samaria, Judea (*B.J.* 3.3), Jericho and the Dead Sea (4.8) and Jerusalem (5.4-5), but they are not extensive. In *Antiquitates Judaicae,* a history of Israel and the Jewish people in twenty books, there are no extensive geographical excursuses, a fact that scholars explain with reference to the tradition of the Jewish sources that Josephus used.[118] This does not mean, of course, that Josephus possessed no geographical knowledge. The speech of Agrippa II (A.D. 50-93) that Josephus recounts in connection with the beginning of the Jewish revolt against the Romans in A.D. 66 in the Hasmonean royal palace includes a list of towns and peoples that could not resist the might of Roman legions (*B.J.* 2.345-401). There are good reasons to believe that the basic content of the speech is authentic.[119]

Agrippa II mentions Athens, Sparta and Macedonia (*B.J.* 2.358-361), Egypt and Arabia (2.362), the regions east of the Euphrates, north of the Danube, south of Libya, and in the west Gadeira (mod. Cadiz) and Britannia as the "new world beyond the ocean" (2.363), the wealthy Gauls, the strong Germans, the intelligent Greeks (2.364), the five hundred cities of Asia, the Heniochoi and the Kolchoi on the Black Sea coast, the Tauroi on the

---

[115]See G. Davies 1979.

[116]See Millard (1987, 115), who points out that the writing material in Palestine and Syria (papyrus) is a major reason why more texts have not been discovered in these regions.

[117]On Jewish geography see P. S. Alexander, *ABD* 2:977-87; J. M. Scott 1995, 14-56; Bechard 2000, 171-209; on *Jub.* 8—9 see Alexander, *ABD* 2:980-82; Bechard 2000, 188-95; J. M. Scott 2002, 23-43.

[118]Olshausen 1991, 38. On the influence of Gen 10 on *A.J.* 1.120-147 see Bechard 2000, 195-209.

[119]See M. Smith, "The Troublemakers," *CHJ* 3:502-3.

Crimean, the peoples of the Bosporus, the peoples living at the Black Sea and the Azov
Seas (2.366), Bithynia and Cappadocia, the people living in Pamphylia, the Lycians, Cilicians, Thracians (2.368), the Illyrians, the invading Dacians, the Dalmatians (2.369-370),
the Gauls (2.371-373), the Iberians, Lusitanians, Cantabrians (2.374-375), the Germans
(2.377), the Britons (2.378), the Parthians (2.379), Carthage, Cyrene and the African tribes
of the Marmaritai, Syrtes, Nasamones, Maurians and Numidians (2.380-381), the Ethiopians (2.382), Egypt and Arabia (2.385-386). Because Rome rules over "myriads of other nations" (ἔθνη μυρία [2.361]), "all the peoples of the world" (τῶν κατὰ τὴν οἰκουμένην [ ]
πάντων [2.364]), "almost every nation under the sun" (πάντων δὴ σχεδὸν τῶν ὑφ᾽ ἡλίῳ
[2.380]), because indeed "in the habitable world all are [under the] Romans" (οἱ μὲν γὰρ
ἐπὶ τῆς οἰκουμένης πάντες εἰσι ῾Ρωμαῖοι [2.388]), the Jewish people should not have any
illusions about finding allies if they rebel against Rome; such allies would have to be recruited "from the uninhabited wilds" (ἐκ τῆς ἀοικήτου [2.388]), as even the royal house of
Adiabene, which had converted to Judaism, would not come to their aid, since they lived
beyond the Euphrates and since the Parthians would not permit it anyway (389).

Josephus reports that soldiers from Thrace, Germania and Gaul fought in the army of
Herod I (*B.J.* 1.672). He repeatedly mentions Germans and Germania (*B.J.* 1.672; *A.J.*
19.119, 125), Gaul and Gauls (*B.J.* 1.5, 397, 673; 2.371; *A.J.* 1.123), Spain and Spaniards
(*B.J.* 2.374; *A.J.* 1.125), Libya and Libyans (*B.J.* 2.115-116; *A.J.* 1.132-133, 137); Egypt and
Egyptians (546 times), Arabia and Arabs (*B.J.* 1.99, 101; *A.J.* 2.32), Persia and Persians (*A.J.*
1.143; *C. Ap.* 1.13), Scythians (*B.J.* 7.90, 244; *A.J.* 1.124; *C. Ap.* 2.269). Josephus is informed
about the "ends of the earth": in the north the Scythians and Germans (see above), in the
west Gades (*B.J.* 2.363), in the south Ethiopia (*B.J.* 2.382; *A.J.* 1.131; *C. Ap.* 1.169), in the
east India (*B.J.* 2.385; *A.J.* 1.38; *C. Ap.* 1.144) and even China (*A.J.* 1.147). As far as India
is concerned, Josephus knows the pertinent works of Megasthenes and Philostratus.[120] He
believes that the Indians are descendants of Shem (*A.J.* 1.147).

The geography of the Jewish *Apocalypse of Enoch* (*1 Enoch*), written and compiled in
the first century B.C., is less directly connected with the tradition of the table of nations in
Gen 10. This writing often is described as "mythological" or "mystical," but this description
should not be allowed to obscure the fact that the author condenses cosmological and
geographical phenomena into a model of the world, parts of which were evidently visu-
alized, perhaps with the help of an actual map, certainly with a mental world map. The
schematic description of the *oikoumenē* in *1 En.* 77 mentions the Mediterranean Sea, the
Indian Ocean and the Persian Gulf, the seven highest mountains, the seven largest rivers
and the seven largest islands. The description of the mountains, rivers and islands is not
sufficiently detailed to allow geographical identifications in each case. In regard to the
seven highest mountains, the author at least mentions that they are covered with snow (*1
En.* 77:4). In regard to the rivers, the Tigris, the Euphrates and the Nile can be identified
with relative certainty; perhaps the author thinks further of the Don and the Danube. Five
of the seven largest islands are located in the Mediterranean and thus are easily identified;
another island might be Bahrain.[121]

The Geographical Perspective of the Apostles

Jesus commissioned his disciples to go to "all nations" and to travel to "the ends
of the earth" (Mt 28:19; Acts 1:8). This raises the important question of how the

---

[120]See Josephus, *A.J.* 10.227-228; 11.33, 186, 216, 272; *C. Ap.* 1.144.
[121]P. S. Alexander, *ABD* 2:983-84.

disciples specifically understood and interpreted this assignment. Another question is whether they took this assignment seriously, and if they did, how they conceived the actual and practical implementation of the assignment.

In regard to the term "nations" (ἔθνη, *ethnē*), the disciples thought of all peoples of the world, including Israel, and the phrase "to the ends of the earth" must have been interpreted in terms of Ethiopia in the south, India in the east, Scythia in the north and Spain in the west (see §12.3).

How much did the average Galilean know about regions and peoples beyond the borders of the Roman Empire? This question cannot be answered with complete certainty, as both the quality and the quantity of the geographical information that the early church had is unknown: neither the New Testament nor the Christian literature of the second century provides much information in this regard. However, a discussion of this question needs to consider the following factors.

1. All the first missionaries were Jews. Traveling Jews could expect to be accommodated in the synagogues of the Jewish communities in the Diaspora cities. And they could expect to obtain further information concerning more distant regions and towns in which Jews lived or where Jews traveled as merchants.

2. The apostles would have had no difficulties procuring information about regions they were interested in and about the towns and the populations they hoped to reach with the gospel, even about regions beyond the borders of the Roman Empire. Merchants in the markets of the large cities and towns often had such information. Also, we should not forget that the influence of the Roman Empire did not end at fixed borders: archaeological discoveries show that Roman rule affected areas about 200 km (125 mi.) beyond the borders of the provinces that were under direct Roman administrative control, and that the economic influence of Rome extended 200 km further.[122] Strabo complains at the beginning of his chapter on India about the merchants who sometimes had reached the Ganges River in east India, but who are *idiōtai,* that is, people who have no professional knowledge;[123] they are useless for providing information for a report on the history of the places that they have seen (15.1.4). This is not a complaint concerning a basic lack of information that forces him to rely on early Hellenistic sources (mostly Megasthenes and Eratosthenes);[124] it is a complaint concerning a lack of *scientific* information that makes it impossible for him to write a detailed history of individual cities and regions.

---

[122]Austin and Rankov 1995, 26.

[123]LSJ, s.v. "ἰδιώτης III." The translation of the term in Strabo 15.1.4 as "private citizen" (thus H. L. Jones) is useless: all India merchants were "private citizens." The text reads: καὶ οὐδὲ πρὸς ἱστορίαν τῶν τόπων χρήσιμοι.

[124]See Dihle 1964, 93.

3. Several of the leading disciples had been fishermen. They could easily obtain information from sailors in the harbor cities of the Mediterranean concerning other regions of the world. The information that one could glean from a periplus was not necessarily up to date, but captains who sailed these routes would have been ready sources of information for the latest news about many places.

4. The early Christian missionaries did not need information about other peoples or cities that was highly specialized or detailed, as they did not plan complex military actions or risky business ventures that depended on many diverse factors. The information essential for the missionaries was about population centers and roads. Such information could easily be obtained at the markets of the cities and towns in which the missionaries were presently active. And since the missionaries traveled the major roads of the Roman Empire on foot, they could not fail to make the acquaintance of dozens or hundreds of "international" merchants who would have relevant information.

Mithradates is said to have massacred on a single day in 88 B.C. about eighty thousand Roman or Italian merchants (Valerius Maximus 9.2.4 ext. 3). In 69 B.C. Cicero referred to the fact that Gaul was full of Roman merchants ("refertia Gallai negotiatorum est, plena civium Romanorum" [*Font.* 5.11]). In a speech delivered in 67 B.C. he refers to daily reports received by Roman *equites* (knights), who were leading merchants and businesspeople, about the situation in Asia Minor ("equitibus Romanis, honestissimis viri, adferuntur ex Asia cotidiae litterae" [*Leg. man.* 2.4]). And Cicero reports that these businesspeople (*publicani*) have their own courier service (*tabellarii* [*Att.* 5.15.3; *Fam.* 8.7.1]).[125]

5. In some cities it was possible to receive "information" about other regions and peoples through inscriptions and reliefs at public buildings. Statues representing fourteen nations, made by Coponius, could be seen in the temple of Venus Victrix that Pompey had built after his victories in Libya (79 B.C.), Europe (71 B.C.) and Asia (69 B.C.).[126] Another place in Rome where people could see the nations and peoples of the empire was the *Porticus ad nationes,* reportedly built by Augustus.[127] The pictorial program of this hall perhaps is found in Virgil's description of the threefold triumph of Augustus in 29 B.C.: Augustus surveyed the gifts of the nations and affixed them at the pillars of the temple of Apollo on whose threshold he sat. A catalogue of nations mentions the Africans, Thessalians, Carians, Scythians, the Euphrates, the Morians (Britannia), the Rhine River (for Gaul and Germania), the Dahae (Scythia) and Araxes (Armenia).

[125]Austin and Rankov 1995, 94, 105.
[126]Represented are Pontus, Armenia, Paphlagonia, Cappadocia, Media, Kolchis, Iberia, Albania, Syria, Cilicia, Mesopotamia, Phoenicia/Palestine, Judea, Arabia. See Cancik 1997, 130-32.
[127]Pliny, *Nat.* 36.39; Servius, *Commentarius in Vergilii Aeneida* 8.721; Virgil, *Aen.* 8.725. Cf. Cancik 1997, 132-33; for the description that follows above see 133.

Another example of public buildings displaying information about foreign nations can be found in the city of Aphrodisias in Asia Minor. The street (90 m long) that led to the Sebasteion, the temple of Aphrodite, Divi Augusti and the Demos, was lined with porticoes that were three stories high (12 m), with the two upper stories decorated with forty-five reliefs each. The 190 reliefs portrayed emperors, gods, mythological figures, allegories (e.g., Day and Ocean) and the nations of the Roman Empire.[128] The allegorical figures were the "universal context" for the "universal" empire in which the nations live. The latter are represented as female figures; inscriptions above the individual reliefs identify the *ethnos,* which sometimes is characterized by a specific attribute.

The following reliefs of nations, of which originally probably fifty existed, with thirteen depicting barbarian peoples, can be identified on the basis of the present state of research: the islands Sicily, Crete and Cyprus, the Callaeci (northwestern Spain), Rhaeti (Danube and Rhine rivers), Trumpilini (Italian Alps), Pirouostae and Andizetae (Pannonia), Iapodes (Illyricum), Daci (north of the Danube River), Dardani and Bessi (Thrace), Bospori (north of the Black Sea), Iudaei (Jews), Arabi (Arabs) and Aegyptii (Egyptians).

Several factors and considerations are illuminating. (a) The nations represent the *Imperium Romanum* of the emperor Augustus, with particular emphasis on his victories and on the expansion of the borders of the empire that he achieved (see Augustus, *Res gestae* 26). (b) The fact that some of the nations are unknown, exotic peoples suggests that they have been selected from a list that contained many more than fifty names. With one exception (the Trumpilini), all nations are mentioned by Strabo. (c) The subtle characterization of the nations evidently was based on existing models, probably a "province series" in Rome, possibly as an imitation of the *simulacra gentium,* the "portrait of the nations," which Augustus had displayed in his *Porticus ad nationes.*[129] (d) The nations possibly were depicted in the sequence of their geographical location from west to east. (e) The large number of nations depicted and their exotic names evidently symbolize the conviction that the borders of the Roman Empire are identical with the ends of the earth (see below, "Maximum Perspectives"). (f) These iconographical representations did not intend to describe the geographical composition of the Roman Empire; rather, they use ethnic stereotypes to formulate a spatial conception of dominion that included regions beyond the confines of the empire.[130]

An inscription on the triumphal arch in Laodikeia, written around A.D. 250, informed the citizens that the man who was honored by this dedication had held

[128]See R. R. R. Smith, "*Simulacra gentium:* The *Ethne* from the Sebasteion at Aphrodisias," *JRS* 78 (1988): 50-77; idem 1990 (interpretation, ibid., 92-95); cf. also Cancik 1997, 133-35.

[129]Servius, *Commentarius in Vergilii Aeneida* 7.721; see R. R. Smith 1990, 92, with reference to Platner and Ashby 1965, s.v. "Porticus ad Nationes."

[130]Bendlin 1997, 37.

(priestly) offices in Europe, Libya, Asia and Egypt.[131]

6. Paul, a citizen of Tarsus and of Rome, presumably Matthew-Levi the tax collector, and also Hellenistic Jewish Christians all were familiar with Greek education. This means that they would have been able to obtain needed information from libraries and archives in the capital cities of the provinces and in other towns. Paul might have been able to consult some of the geographical works described above in the libraries of, for example, Tarsus, Jerusalem or Antioch. He would have been able to visit archives that stored *commentarii* on expeditions and military campaigns, which included geographical and ethnographical information. The writings of Strabo and Diodorus confirm that written and oral accounts on military campaigns were important sources for geographical information; the campaigns of Pompey, Julius Caesar and Marcus Antonius (Mark Antony) are good examples.[132] Paul's contact with Sergius Paulus, proconsul on Cyprus, might have been important in this context.

Libraries (βιβλιοθήκη, *bibliothēkē*) were part of the basic infrastructure of Hellenistic cities, an integral part of their identity, as were gymnasiums, theaters, odeions or temples.[133] Libraries existed in the East for a long time. The first known founder of a library was the Assyrian king Tiglath-Pileser I (1115-1077 B.C.). In Greece collectors of books are known since the sixth century B.C. Rulers such as Polykrates or the Attalid kings in Pergamon had libraries, but philosophers and scientists such as Euripides and Aristotle owned collections of books, or rather scrolls, as well. The first and most famous library in the Greek world was the library of Alexandria, established in 300 B.C.[134] The library was housed in a room of the museion and was organized in six groups of subjects for poetry and six groups of subjects for prose. The approximately 490,000 volumes (which corresponds to 100,000 modern books) were displayed in alphabetical order by the first librarian, Zenodotos. The smaller library in the Serapeion had about 42,800 volumes. In 12 B.C. Augustus donated an additional small library, which was housed in the temple of Divus Iulius. Famous librarians in Alexandria included Kallimachos of Cyrene, who provided a complete bibliographical overview of all Greek writings in 120 volumes (*pinakes*), Eratosthenes the geographer, Aristophanes of Byzantion and Aristarchus. Antioch on the Orontes had a library since the time of Antiochos III (223-187 B.C.) at the latest, with Euphorion of Chalkis as librarian. Eumenes II (197-160 B.C.) founded the library of Pergamon, which had at least 200,000 books, which Marcus Antonius is said to have given to Cleopatra as

---

[131] *I. Laodikeia* 46.

[132] See Strabo 11.4.1-8; 14.10-11 (Theophanes); 4.2.3-5.5; 7.1.2-5 (Caesar), 11.6.3 (Dellius). Cf. Austin and Rankov 1995, 89.

[133] K. Preisendanz, *KP* 1:892-96, 896-97; P. J. Parsons, *OCD* 854-55; H. Gamble, *DNTB* 646-47; Gerald J. Argabright, "The Development and Use of Books in Ancient Greece" (M.A. thesis; University of Ohio, 1979); Rudolf Fehrle, *Das Bibliothekswesen im alten Rom: Voraussetzungen, Bedingungen, Anfänge* (Wiesbaden: Reichert, 1986); Horst Blank, *Das Buch in der Antike* (Munich: Beck, 1992); Sylvia Usener, *Isokrates, Platon und ihr Publikum: Hörer und Leser von Literatur im 4. Jahrhundert v. Chr.* (Tübingen: Narr, 1994); Wolfram Hoepfner, "Zu griechischen Bibliotheken und Bücherschränken," *AA* (1996): 25-36; Casson 2001; Hoepfner 2002.

[134] See Fraser 1972, 1:305-35; Casson 2001, 31-47.

a gift (Plutarch, *Ant.* 58.9). The library of Pergamon was housed in three rooms on the upper level of the west portico (10 by 7 m) of the temple of Athene Polias. The scrolls of papyrus and parchment were kept on wooden shelves in cupboards.[135] A fourth room, with statues of Athene and of poets, was used for meetings of scholars. The portico, which was open on one side, was used as a study and reading room. The monumental building of the Celsus library in Ephesus, which could house about 30,000 book scrolls, was erected in the time of Hadrian, but it is fair to assume that the holdings of the library largely existed already in the first century. The Trajan library in Rome owned probably about 20,000 books. The Roman architect Marcus Vitruvius (end of the first century B.C.) gave the advice to orient the rooms of libraries toward the east in order to guarantee good light and to control humidity (*De architectura* 6.4.1). The holdings of the large libraries were made accessible through catalogues (*indices*). In the library of Pantaenus in Athens (second century) the conditions for visiting and using the library were inscribed on stone: "No book is to be taken out since we have sworn an oath. The library is to be open from the first hour until the sixth."[136] Scholars assume that in many cities the gymnasia had libraries, which probably were superior to modern school libraries with regard both to needs and to means.[137] We know, for example, that the ephebes of the Ptolemaion in Athens had to buy one hundred books every year for the library. In some cases the scope of private collections of books was substantial. Cicero and his friend Atticus employed slaves who organized and maintained their considerable collections. Cicero comments that Atticus has *plurimi librarii,* and he complains that one of his library slaves was a thief.[138] Seneca the Younger (A.D. 4-65) cracks jokes about the fashion of wealthy people to have a private library in order to be considered cultured (Seneca, *Dial.* 9.9.4-7). People who were interested in buying books could contact book dealers, whom Euripides attests for Athens as early as the fifth century (*Fragmenta* 327). Xenophon reports the export of books from Athens to the Black Sea (*Anab.* 7.5.14). In large Jewish communities in Antioch, Alexandria, Rome and perhaps Tarsus there were presumably some wealthy Jews who had private libraries. It is fair to assume, for example, that the Alexandrian synagogue had a large library.[139]

Archives (ἀρχεῖον, *archeion*) were housed in public buildings, at royal courts and often in temples. The law of the gymnasiarchs of Beroea in Macedonia stipulates, among other matters, "Since the rest of the officials all hold office according to a law, and since the laws concerning the gymnasiarchs are deposited in the public archives in the cities which have gymnasia and set up training, it is proper that the same is carried out here and that (the law) which we have given to the Exetastai is displayed in the gymnasium, after it has been inscribed on a stele, and (that it) will also be kept in the public archive. . . . The city decided that the law concerning the gymnasiarchs that has been introduced by Zopyros son of Amyntas, the gymnasiarch, and from Asklepiades son of Heras and Kallippos son of Hippostratos shall be valid and shall be kept in the public archive and that it shall be applied by the gymnasiarch and that it shall be displayed in the gymnasium, after it has

---

[135]Hoepfner ("Bibliotheken und Bücherschränken," 25-36) suggests that the wooden shelves stood under large windows, at a distance of 50 cm from the walls for the protection of the scrolls. This theory is not accepted by all scholars; see W. Röllig, *DNP* 9:552; Casson 2001, 49-53.

[136]R. E. Wycherley, *The Athenian Agora, Vol. 3* (Princeton: American School of Classical Studies, 1957), I 2729. See J. Camp 2001, 198.

[137]See Preisendanz, *KP* 1:893.

[138]Cicero, *Att.* 4.4a.1; *Fam.* 13.77.3; Nepos, *Atticus* 13.3. On Cicero see Casson 2001, 70-74.

[139]See Noack 2000, 27 with n. 112.

been inscribed on a stele."[140] An inscription found in Priene, with a decree of Laodikeia honoring judges whom Priene had sent, stipulates that a copy of the document on a white wooden board is to be deposited in the treasure house of Artemis in Laodikeia.[141] Even villages had archives: Orkistos in Phrygia and Takina in the border area of Phrygia and Pisidia employed an official who was responsible for the archive (γραμματοφύλαξ, *grammatophylax*). Archives are attested also for villages near Philadelphia, Magnesia and in the Kaystros Valley. Christoph Schuler comments, "Even though these testimonies are sparse, they prove the existence of archives in rural communities. The other material from rural communities presupposes archives, because where village assemblies gather and make decisions, where communities determine matters related to communal property and public revenue and benefactions, a local archive is indispensable."[142] The Christian scholar Julius Africanus, who lived in Emmaus-Nikopolis in Judea in the third century, used the archives of Edessa for his history of the kings of Edessa, and he also used books from the temple library of Sinope in Pontus.[143]

7. Hellenistic education enabled those who were interested in other peoples to make independent observations. Agatharchides of Cnidus was "certainly not one of the leading lights of Hellenistic philosophy or science,"[144] as Albrecht Dihle remarked; however, he not only unprejudicially registered unusual phenomena but also sought to understand them. "We never find a precipitate value judgment, as we might well expect from the representative of a superior civilization, analogous to the judgments of Chinese annalists or European travelers of the nineteenth century." He does not trace differences in civilization immediately back to the "nature" of primitive peoples but rather repeatedly cites conditions of climate or suggests anthropological, philosophical or moral explanations. Hellenistic scholars were capable of an "ethnography that went far beyond pure description" if they had "the gift of unprejudiced observation," as they worked with a full complement of "physical, psychological, medical and social-political concepts."

8. Followers of Jesus and sympathizers of the new movement who had influential positions may well have had geographical, ethnographical and political knowledge that was important for the planning of further missionary advances. Luke mentions Chuzas, an administrator of Herod Antipas (Lk 8:3); Manaen, a friend of the young Herod Antipas (Acts 13:1); Sergius Paulus, the Roman procurator on Cyprus, who was converted to the Christian faith during the missionary work of Barnabas and Paul on Cyprus (Acts 13:7-12); the Asiarchs in Ephesus

---

[140]*SEG* XXVII 261; *SEG* XLIII 381; the translation follows *HGIÜ* III 486; cf. P. Gauthier and M. B. Hatzopulos, *La loi gymnasiarchique de Beroia* (Meletemata 16; Paris: Boccard, 1993). "Exetastai" are auditors of public accounts.

[141]*I. Laodikeia* 5, lines 35-36: τοὺς δὲ ἐξεταστὰς [ἀν]αγράψαντας αὐτὸ εἰς λεύκωμα θεῖναι ἐν τῶι Ἀρ[τέμιδ]ος θησαυρῶ[ι]. This archive is attested also in the inscriptions nos. 85, 123.

[142]Schuler 1998, 242-43; quotation, 243.

[143]Moses of Chorene, *History of Armenia* 2.10; see Markschies 1997, 281 with n. 83.

[144]Dihle 1962, 40; for the observations that follow above see ibid., 27-40; quotations, 29, 40.

whom Paul knew (Acts 19:13); the royal official in Capernaum mentioned by John (Jn 4:46).

9. Albrecht Dihle, one of the foremost specialists on the contacts between the Greco-Roman world and the regions in the eastern part of the Roman Empire, points out that Christians were much better prepared than their pagan contemporaries to obtain information from sailors and merchants about other nations.[145] Guy Stroumsa identifies two factors that explain why it is plausible to assume that Christians, at least in the second and third centuries, were in an excellent position to obtain information about foreign nations from sailors and merchants: their missionary activity and their lack of solidarity with the Hellenistic literary tradition.[146] Thus we find Clement of Alexandria, in the second century, providing an astonishing description of India in general and of the Brahmans in particular (*Strom.* 1.15.71). Clement's description of India is independent of the presentations of his Greek and Roman contemporaries, and it includes details—for example, the first explicit reference to Buddhism,[147] which he may have received from his teacher Pantaenus, who had spent time in India as a missionary. Jerome (347-420) is the first Western author to mention the legend of the birth of Buddha, referring specifically to Buddhist sources.[148] Stroumsa offers a twofold explanation for this curiosity and openness concerning ethnographical information: (a) the religious "universalism" of the early Christians; that is, their conviction that all nations have been created by the God of Israel, the Father of Jesus Christ, and that all human beings therefore may be regarded as a unity, one single group of people who all need salvation; (b) the cultural "relativism" of the early Christians; that is, their distance from the literary and the philosophical traditions of their time.[149] Stroumsa refers to the apostle Paul and to an important passage in the *Epistle to Diognetus,* which was written by a Christian in the second century. Some statements from Paul and 1 Peter also need to be presented here.

Diogn. 5:1-5: "For Christians are no different from other people in terms of their country, language, or customs [Χριστιανοὶ γὰρ οὔτε γῆ οὔτε φωνῇ οὔτε ἔθεσι διακεκριμένοι τῶν λοιπῶν εἰσὶν ἀνθρώπων]. ²Nowhere do they inhabit cities of their own [πόλεις ἰδίας], use a strange dialect [διαλέκτῳ τινὶ παρηλλαγμένῃ], or live life out of the ordinary [βίον παράσημον]. ³They have not discovered this teaching of theirs through reflection or through the thought of meddlesome people, nor do they set forth any human doctrine,

---

[145]See Dihle 1964, 91.

[146]Stroumsa 1996, 357; on Clement of Alexandria see ibid., 356-58.

[147]A. Dihle, "Indische Philosophen bei Clemens Alexandrinus," in Dihle 1984, 78-88; cf. idem 1983, 95-96.

[148]Jerome, *Jov.* 1.42 (see B. Breloer and F. Bömer, *Fontes historiae religionum indicarum collegerunt* [Bonn: Röhrscheid, 1939], 173); cf. A. Dihle, "Buddha und Hieronymus," in Dihle 1984, 98-101.

[149]Stroumsa 1996, esp. 340-41, 346-47, 354-58.

as do some. [4]They inhabit both Greek and barbarian cities, according the lot assigned to each [κατοικοῦντες δὲ πόλεις ἑλληνίδας τε καὶ βαρβάρους ὡς ἕκαστος ἐκληρώθη]. And they show forth the character of their own citizenship in a marvelous and admittedly paradoxical way by following local customs in what they wear and what they eat and in the rest of their lives [καὶ τοῖς ἐγχωρίοις ἔθεσιν ἀκολουθοῦντες ἔν τε ἐσθῆτι καὶ διαίτῃ καὶ τῷ λοιπῷ βίῳ]. [5]They live in their respective countries, but only as resident aliens [πατρίδας οἰκοῦσιν ἰδίας, ἀλλ' ὡς πάροικοι]; they participate in all things as citizens, and they endure all things as foreigners. Every foreign territory is a homeland for them, every homeland foreign territory [πᾶσα ξένη πατρίς ἐστιν αὐτῶν, καὶ πᾶσα πατρὶς ξένη]."

Rom 1:14-16: "I am a debtor both to Greeks and to barbarians ["Ελλησίν τε καὶ βαρβάροις], both to the wise and to the foolish[15]—hence my eagerness to proclaim the gospel to you also who are in Rome. [16] For I am not ashamed of the gospel; it is the power of God for salvation to everyone who has faith, to the Jew first and also to the Greek ['Ιουδαίῳ τε πρῶτον καὶ "Ελληνι]."

Col 3:11: "In that renewal there is no longer Greek and Jew [οὐκ ἔνι "Ελλην καὶ 'Ιουδαῖος], circumcised and uncircumcised, barbarian [βάρβαρος], Scythian [Σκύθης], slave and free; but Christ is all and in all!"

Gal 3:28: "There is no longer Jew or Greek [οὐκ ἔνι 'Ιουδαῖος οὐδὲ "Ελλην], there is no longer slave or free, there is no longer male and female; for all of you are one in Christ Jesus."

1 Pet 1:1-2, 17: "Peter, an apostle of Jesus Christ, To the exiles [παρεπιδήμοις] of the Dispersion [διασπορᾶς] in Pontus, Galatia, Cappadocia, Asia, and Bithynia, [2]who have been chosen and destined by God the Father and sanctified by the Spirit to be obedient to Jesus Christ and to be sprinkled with his blood: May grace and peace be yours in abundance. . . . [17] If you invoke as Father the one who judges all people impartially according to their deeds, live in reverent fear during the time of your exile [τὸν τῆς παροικίας ὑμῶν χρόνον]."

1 Pet 2:11: "Beloved, I urge you as aliens and exiles [ὡς παροίκους καὶ παρεπιδήμους], to abstain from the desires of the flesh that wage war against the soul."

Christians of the first century believed, as did Jews, that there was one God, who created all human beings. Christians further believed that this one God had sent his Son into the world to procure forgiveness for all who believe in Jesus Christ. They understood the oneness of humankind not only in terms of creation but also in terms of salvation—that is, not only as a past reality but also as a present reality. As a result, the ethnological, cultural and religious boundaries between the nations had become ultimately irrelevant: the Jewish taxonomy of Jews and Greeks, Israel and the *gōyîm* (the nations), is as immaterial as the Greek taxonomy of Greeks and barbarians. The identity of Christians cannot be described with ethnological concepts: Christians, no matter where they live, are always "strangers," "exiles," "resident aliens." They find their identity not in their affiliation with a people or a city but rather in the new family to which they belong, as sons and daughters of God, as a result of their faith in Jesus Christ. In the

Greco-Roman world the main criteria of personal identity were ethnic affiliation, cultural reality and religious praxis.[150] The passages quoted above show that the Christians of the first and second centuries were aware of their peculiarities. At least by the second century their theological position implied a relativizing of the Greek cultural tradition, which prompted an "ethnological curiosity" concerning other cultures. We have already noted Clement of Alexandria, *Strom.* 1.15. The theological convictions of the early Christians did not automatically lead to anthropological interests: as cultural realities became irrelevant for one's own identity, they become secondary for the preaching of the gospel as well, which focused primarily on the sins of people and on God's intervention to procure salvation through Jesus Christ.

Minimal Perspectives

As the disciples reflected on their assignment to reach the ends of the earth with the good news of Jesus Christ, they could have thought in terms of the geographical scope of the Jewish Diaspora. When Luke lists in Acts 2:9-11 the regions from which the Jewish pilgrims came to Jerusalem for the Feast of Pentecost, he may be describing regions that the disciples later would reach as missionaries: Parthia, Media, Elam, Mesopotamia, Judea, Cappadocia, Pontus, Asia, Phrygia, Pamphylia, Egypt, Libya, Rome, as well as the Cretans and Arabs. Interestingly, the Greeks (Achaia) are missing from the list.[151]

Judea (*Ioudaia*), listed between Mesopotamia and Cappadocia, probably is "larger Judea," which included Syria according to biblical traditions and in the context of messianic expectations.[152] If we interpret the list against the background of Gen 10,[153] then the regions that Luke mentions are divided between the sons of Noah as follows: to Shem belong Parthia, Media, Elam, Mesopotamia; to Ham belong Judea, Egypt, Libya, Cretans and Arabs; to Japheth belong Cappadocia, Pontus, Asia, Phrygia, Pamphylia, Rome.

It is quite possible that there were Jewish citizens and Jewish communities in many cities of these regions that could not (yet) be documented because they are not mentioned in Greek or Roman sources or because archaeologists have not unearthed relevant evidence such as Jewish epitaphs or synagogues.[154] Aphrodisias in Caria is a good example: until recently, scholars were not

---

[150]Stroumsa 1996, 342; for the remark that follows above see ibid., 355. On cultural identity in the Roman Empire see Laurence and Berry 1998; Stephan 2002; on Christians in Asia Minor as "strangers" see Stephan 2002, 294-328.

[151]See Bechard 2000, 211-24, with a critical discussion of Ernst Haenchen's view, 219-21.

[152]See Martin Hengel, " Ἰουδαία in der geographischen Liste Apg 2,9-11 und Syrien als 'Grossjudäa,'" *RHPR* 80 (2000): 51-68. On the text-critical discussion see Wedderburn 1994, 29-47; Bechard 2000, 212 n. 112.

[153]J. M. Scott 1994, 528-30; Bechard 2000, 222-24, esp. 223 n. 142; J. M. Scott 2002, 68-84.

[154]Kraabel 1983, 181.

aware that a Jewish community existed in this city, but two long inscriptions from the second century have been discovered that list names and professions of many Jews of Aphrodisias (see §6.2; 27.3). We must not assume that all Jewish communities were as influential as the Jews in Sardis (see §30.2) or Aphrodisias: the small synagogue of Priene consisted of a simple room measuring 12.6 by 13.7 m.[155]

Maximum Perspectives

Reflecting on their assignment to reach the ends of the earth with the good news of Jesus Christ, the disciples could have thought in terms of the known world from a Greco-Roman perspective. This possibility is particularly plausible if they interpreted the phrase "to the end(s) of the earth" in a geographical sense. We have seen that at least educated people had a lot of information about many regions beyond the Mediterranean world "at the ends of the earth" by the first century. In border regions such as Judea and Syria many people, particularly merchants, possibly had more information than did many people in Rome itself. In what follows I devote particular attention to the contacts with India, since there are traditions about early Christian missionary work in this region at the eastern "end of the earth" (see §22.12).

Contacts with India

Contacts between the Mediterranean world and India had existed for a long time.[156] Mesopotamian ships sailed from the Persian Gulf to India already in 2800 B.C. Phoenician, Arab and Indian ships sailed this route for hundreds of years. Herodotus (485-425 B.C.) described in an ethnographical excursus not only Egypt, Phoenicia, Mesopotamia and Scythia but also India (3.98-106). The material for passages is based in part on extensive travels to these regions. The

---

[155]L. Levine 2000, 249.

[156]See Tarn 1984 [1938], new preface by Frank L. Holt (iii-xvii); Narain 1957; Fraser 1972, 2:173-84; L. Mooren, "The Date of SB V 8036 and the Development of the Ptolemaic Maritime Trade with India," *Ancient Society* 3 (1972): 127-33; Bivar 1983, 181-231; Frank L. Holt, *Alexander the Great and Bactria: The Formation of a Greek Frontier in Central Asia* (Mnemosyne Supplements 104; Leiden: Brill, 1988); Posch 1995; Jeffrey D. Lerner, *The Impact of Seleucid Decline on the Eastern Iranian Plateau: The Foundations of Arsacid Parthia and Graeco-Baktria* (Historia: Einzelschriften Heft 123; Stuttgart: Steiner, 1999); Boussac and Salles 1995; Frank L. Holt, *Thundering Zeus: The Making of Hellenistic Bactria* (Berkeley: University of California Press, 1999); H. Sidky, *The Greek Kingdom of Bactria: From Alexander to Eucratides the Great* (Lanham, Md.: University Press of America, 2000); Hölbl 2001, 57-58, 204. For contacts between Rome and India see Dihle 1964; 1974; 1978; Sidebotham 1986; Drexhage 1988; Singh 1988; Begley and Puma 1991; see also the anthology by Jacques André and Jean Filliozat, *L'Inde vue de Rome: Textes latins de l'Antiquité relatifs à l'Inde* (Paris: Les Belles Lettres, 1986); Sherwin-White and Kuhrt 1993; Cimino 1994; Ball 2000, 123-33; K. Karttunen, *DNP* 5:966-69. The interest in this topic continues to grow as a result of new and numerous archaeological discoveries in western, central and southern India.

Persian king Darius I conquered northwestern India. The Indian princes still paid tribute to the Persians at the time of Darius III. The tablets of Persepolis document for the early fifth century B.C. the organization and maintenance of the royal route from the periphery of India to Sardis in Asia Minor. India (Heb., וֹדוּ, *Hôddû;*[157] Gk., Ἰνδίκη, *Indikē*) was known to the Jews living in exile in the Persian Empire by the fourth or third century B.C. at the latest: Esther 1:1; 8:9 LXX mention India (or the Indus River) as the eastern border of the empire of King Ahasuerus; in 1 Esd 3:2 and in Additions to Esther 13:1; 16:1 India is mentioned in the context of the description of the geographical scope of the Persian Empire.

The march of Alexander the Great through the eastern Persian regions of Sogdiana and Bactria and through the Cophen Valley (mod. Kabul) to India in 327-324 B.C.[158] triggered an enormous expansion of geographical knowledge of India and Arabia among the Greeks.[159] Numerous accounts of Alexander's march described India; two well-known examples are Kleitarchos's history of Alexander and Flavius Arrianus's *Anabasis,* written on the basis of contemporary sources.

The royal court of Alexander played a major role in this expansion of knowledge. The official accounts "could provide a solid basis for any scientific interests. The observations that were made by various participants in the military campaigns by order of the king were collected and recorded in journals that were kept for just this purpose. The bematists, for example, measured and calculated distances and travel times in connection with the movements of the army."[160] Some bematists published their observations in monographs called *stathmoi* ("stages"), which provided the framework for Eratosthenes' geography of Asia. Alexander not only retained surveyors in his entourage but also founded new cities, whose Greek-Macedonian citizens—veterans of his army and volunteers from among the mercenaries—were intended as occupying forces to control the surrounding regions and the lines of communication.[161] Cities that were important for travel to India included Alexandria in Artakoana/Ariana (mod. Herat, on the Hari River),[162] Alexandria in Arachosia (mod. Kandahar),[163] Alexandria Oxiana (Termez [?], on the Oxus River),[164] Alexandria in Paropamisos (or *sub Caucaso,* perhaps Begram, mod. Jebal Seraj, in the central Hindukush on the Kabul

---

[157]The Hebrew terms is probably derived from Old Persian *hidav,* which can be traced back to the Sanskrit term *sindhu,* which means "river" and also designates the Indus River.

[158]See Seibert 1985, 125; Bosworth 1988, 119-56; 1996, 69-97, 133-56, 186-200.

[159]Dihle 1962; 1964, 91; 1994, 54-66. On Arabia see Peter Högemann, *Alexander der Grosse und Arabien* (Munich: Beck, 1985); Seibert 1985; on the march to India see Seibert 1985, 143-84.

[160]Olshausen 1991, 84. For the observation that follows above see A. B. Bosworth, *OCD* 238.

[161]See Fraser 1996, 240-43, with a list of fifty-seven cities; the foundation by Alexander is not secure in each case; see also N. G. L. Hammond, "Alexander's Newly-founded Cities," *GRBS* 39 (1998): 243-69.

[162]See Fraser 1996, 109-31.

[163]Fraser 1996, 132-40.

[164]See Fraser 1996, 153-56, with arguments against the identification with Ai-Khanum.

River),[165] Alexandria Eschate in Sogdiana (mod. Leninabad/Khojand, on the Jaxartes River),[166] Nikaia (on the west bank of the Hydaspes River, mod. Jhelum) and Bucephala (on the east bank of the Jhelum River, near mod. Jelalapur),[167] Alexandria Rambakia west of the Indus Delta (mod. Las Bela, on the Porali River),[168] Alexandria (Multan [?], on the confluence of the rivers Akesines [Chenab] and Indus), Alexandria Patala (on the mouth of the Indus)[169] and several garrisons in the northern Punjab.[170] Some of these cities were overrun by nomads, and some were reestablished by the first Seleucid rulers in the third century B.C. One of these new foundations evidently was Ai Khanum in northern Afghanistan on the confluence of the rivers Oxus (mod. Amu Darya) and Kokcha, a city whose ancient name is unknown, excavated between 1965 and 1978.[171]

Since the time of Alexander the leaders of expeditions to India recorded their voyages in published reports (see above). Androsthenes of Thasos wrote a "Paraplous of India" in 325 B.C. Nearchos of Crete, who sailed down the Indus River in 325 B.C. with Alexander's fleet, continuing to Babylonia, described his voyage in a paraplus, which, however, has not survived. Patrokles also wrote about India.[172]

Seleukos I Nikator (311-281 B.C.) controlled the eastern part of the empire after Alexander's death. He ceded the claims of his dynasty located on Persia's eastern satrapies in India to the Indian ruler Chandragupta (ca. 324-300 B.C.) because he wanted to have peace on the eastern border. Chandragupta had defeated the Nanda dynasty that ruled in Maghada in the central basin of the Ganges River, conquered northern India and established the Mauryan dynasty. The ambassador of Seleukos I at the court of Chandragupta between 304 and 292 B.C. was Megasthenes, an Ionian from Asia Minor. Megasthenes reports in his work *Indika,* written around 290 B.C. but surviving only in fragments,[173] that 118 "tribes" live in India. He describes the successful, absolutist rule of Chandragupta and he mentions the Persian royal road to northwestern India. In one passage he mentions Indians and Jews together:

---

[165]See Fraser 1996, 140-50; on the French excavations between 1936 and 1946 see 147 with n. 80.

[166]See Fraser 1996, 151-61; for Russian excavation reports see 151 n. 92.

[167]See Fraser 1996, 161-62. The founding of Bucephala-Alexandria commemorated Alexander's favorite horse.

[168]See Fraser 1996, 164-66.

[169]Seibert 1985, 168-69; Fraser 1996, 71.

[170]Bosworth 1988, 247-49; D. N. Wilber, "Alexandrian Foundations," *PECS* 39-40.

[171]Posch 1995, 15. On Ai Khanum see ibid., 15-23; P. Bernard et al., *BEFEO* 68 (1980): 1-87, with a report on the first campaign of excavations in 1978; idem, "Problèmes d'histoire coloniale grecque à travers l'urbanisme d'une cité hellénistique d'Asie centrale," in *150 Jahre Deutsches Archäologisches Institut* (Mainz: Zabern, 1981), 108-20; S. Sherwin-White, *OCD* 47; Fraser 1996, 154-56. Excavations: Paul Bernard, *Fouilles d'Aï Khanoum I-IV* (Mémoires de la Délégation archéologique française en Afghanistan; Paris: Klincksieck, 1973-1985).

[172]*FGrH* 711 F 1-5 (Androsthenes); 133 (Nearchos; 3:592); 712 T 1-6, F 1-8 (Patrokles).

[173]*FGrH* 715 T 1-7, F 1-34. All later Hellenistic authors who describe India depend on Megasthenes; see Dihle 1964, 89-97; Sedlar 1980, 262.

"All the opinions expressed by the ancients about nature are found also among the philosophers outside Greece, some among the Indian Brahmans [τὰ μὲν παρ' Ἰνδοῖς ὑπὸ τῶν Βραχμανων] and others in Syria among those called Jews [τὰ δὲ ἐν τῇ Συρίᾳ ὑπὸ τῶν καλουμένων Ἰουδαίων]."[174]

Emperor Asoka (ca. 273-236 B.C.),[175] the grandson of Chandragupta and third Mauryan emperor, finished the military conquest of the Indian subcontinent.

Asoka's Rock Edict 13 mentions *Yonas* ("Greeks") and *Cambojas* ("Iranians"); a bilingual, Greek-Aramaic inscription discovered in 1957 near Kandahar and a Greek inscription discovered in 1964 in Old Kandahar (*SEG* XX 326) made it possible to identify them in Shahr-i Kohna (Old Kandahar).[176] The manifest of Asoka reads, "Ten years having passed since his coronation, King Priyadarśî (Piodasses) has been showing piety to the people. And since then, he has rendered the people more pious, and all people prosper on the whole earth. And the king abstains from the slaughter of living beings, and other people including the king's hunters and fishermen have given up hunting. And those who could not control themselves have now ceased not to control themselves as far as they could. And they have become obedient to their father and mother and to the old people contrary to what was the case previously. And henceforth, by so acting, they will live in an altogether better and more profitable way."

---

[174]*FGrH* 715 F 3 (= Clement of Alexandrien, *Strom.* 1.72.5; in *GLAJJ* I 45-46). Diogenes Laertius (1.9) states that Jews and Brahmans both descend from the "magoi." See Hengel 1969, 467 (ET, 257). On Megasthenes see Sherwin-White and Kuhrt 1993, 93-100; on the empire of Chandragupta see ibid., 97-101.

[175]On Asoka (Ashoka) see Seneviratna 1994; on the state of research see Ananda W. P. Guruge, in Seneviratna 1994, 127-61; see also Thapar 1961, 41-49; idem, *OCD* 189; Sherwin-White and Kuhrt 1993, 101-3; K. Karttunen, *DNP* 2:101.

[176]See Eugen Hultzsch, ed., *Inscriptions of Asoka* (Corpus inscriptionum Indicarum 1; Oxford: Clarendon, 1925; repr., Delhi: Indological Book House, 1969]); Daniel Schlumberger et al., "Une bilingue Gréco-Araméenne d'Asoka," *JA* 146 (1958): 1-48; Louis Robert, "Observation sur l'inscription Grecque," *JA* 146 (1958): 7-18; Pierre H. L. Eggermont and Jacob Hoftijzer, *The Moral Edicts of King Asoka; Included: the Greco-Aramaic Inscription of Kandahar and Further Inscriptions of the Mauryan Period* (ed. P. H. L. Eggermont and J. Hoftijzer; Textus Minores 29; Leiden: Brill, 1962, 42-46); D. Schlumberger, "Une nouvelle inscription grecque d'Asoka," *CRAI* (1964): 126-40; L. Robert, "Communication," in ibid., 134-40; E. Benveniste, *Journal Asiatique* 252 (1964): 137-57; Ulrich Schneider, *Die großen Felsen-Edikte Aœokas: Kritische Ausgabe, Übersetzung und Analyse der Texte* (Wiesbaden: Harrassowitz, 1978), 119; Lars Rydbeck, "Εὐσέβειαν ἔδειξεν τοῖς ἀνθρώποις: The Significance of the Bilingual Asoka Inscription for New Testament Philology and for Research into the Notion of Hellenism," in Fornberg and Hellholm 1995, 591-96. The translation follows Dines Chandra Sircar, *Inscriptions of Aœoka* (3rd ed.; New Delhi: Ministry of Information and Broadcasting, 1975), 44-45. Greek text and English translation are found also in Rydbeck, "Εὐσέβειαν ἔδειξεν τοῖς ἀνθρώποις," 593; see also <http://depts.washington.edu/ebmp/Asoka.txt>. German translation, *HGIÜ* II 321. On the inscriptions of Asoka see also Beni Madhab Barua, *Aœoka and His Inscriptions* (2nd ed.; 2 vols.; Calcutta: New Age, 1955); P. H. L. Eggermont, "Indien und die hellenistischen Königreiche," in *Aus dem Osten des Alexanderreiches: Völker und Kulturen zwischen Orient und Okzident; Iran, Afghanistan, Pakistan, Indien* (FS K. Fischer; ed. J. Ozols and V. Thewalt; Cologne: DuMont, 1984), 74-83; Ananda Guruge, "Emperor Aœoka and Buddhism," in Seneviratna 1994, 27-65.

When the Parthians, coming from central Asia, invaded Persia and established the Parthian Empire in 247 B.C. under Arsaces, the communication between the heartland of the Seleucid Empire in the west and the eastern territories was temporarily interrupted. Diodotus managed around this time to detach Bactria, to the east of Parthia, from the Seleucid Empire and to establish a kingdom ruled by Greeks with Baktra (mod. Balkh, Afghanistan) as capital, situated on the road from Ecbatana to the (north)eastern regions of the former Persian empire.[177] This region had been conquered by Alexander the Great; Baktra was the place where he had left his baggage train and where he stayed during the winter of 329 B.C.

Several Greek and Roman historians wrote an account of the history of the Bactrian kingdom (i.e., "India"): Demodamas of Halikarnassos and Dionysios in the third century B.C.; Basilis in the third/second century B.C.; Daimachos of Plataiai in the second century B.C.; Alexander Polyhistor of Miletus in the second/first century B.C.; Apollodoros of Artemita, Pompeius Trogus of southern Gaul, Orthagoras, Annaeus Seneca in the first century B.C. (as well as Chrysermos of Corinth, who cannot be dated). Unfortunately, only fragments are preserved.[178] The exploration of this region made progress only in 1964 when French archaeologists discovered the first Greek-Bactrian city at the confluence of the rivers Kokcha and Oxus near Ai Khanum.

The Bactrian king Demetrius (190-167 B.C.) occupied the Punjab and controlled northwestern India. This invasion of India by Bactrian Greeks is mentioned by Apollodoros.[179] The most famous Indo-Greek king was Menander (Menander Soter, ca. 158-148 B.C.), who resided in Pushkalavati and became a revered figure of Buddhism under the name Milinda.[180] The Bactrian kings controlled India from the northwest to the mouth of the Indus; in the east their empire probably included the region north of Bombay. In 128 B.C. the Indo-Greek empire of Bactria was invaded and conquered by the Tochari and Sacae, tribes from central Asia.[181] Maues was the first ruler of the Sacae; he resided in Taxila (mod. Sirkap; see §22.12) and issued coins. He was followed by Azes I, Azilises and, at the end of the first century B.C., Azes II. In the first century A.D. the Sacae were pushed to the south by the Indo-Parthians under the ruler Gondophares and by the central Asian tribes related

---

[177]Seibert 1985, 25; for the observations that follow above see ibid., 127, 134.

[178]*FGrH* 287 F 3 (Chrysermos; cf. 293 F 2); 428 F 2-3 (Demodamas); 644 F 2-3 (Annaeus Seneca); 713 F 1-5 (Orthagoras); 716 T 1-3, F 1-6 (Daimachos); 717 T 1, F 1 (Dionysios); 718 T 1-2, F 1 (Basilis), 237 F 18 (Alexander Polyhistor); 779 F 3C 773-776 (Apollodorus). In the second/third century A.D. the gnostic Bardesanes of Edessa wrote about India (*FGrH* F 1-3).

[179]Apollodoros, *FGrH* 779; cf. Strabo 11.11.1; 15.1.3. See Dihle 1978, 124.

[180]On Menander see F. L. Holt, "Menander (2)," *OCD* 957; Narain 1957, 74-100; idem, "The Greeks of Bactria and India," *CAH* 8:388-421, esp. 406-12 (2nd ed., 1989); Tarn 1984, 225-69.

[181]On the arrival of the Yuezhi (of Chinese primary sources) in Bactria see Posch 1995, 84-88. The territory controlled by Indo-Greek kings was limited henceforth to southern Afghanistan and northwestern India (Strabo 11.8.2-3).

to the Sacae, the Tochari and the Kushan (the "Assi" of Strabo [see 11.8.2]).

Gondophares, satrap of the eastern regions of Parthia, revolted in A.D. 19 to establish his own empire in the region of Kabul, Arachosia and Gandhara (mod. Afghanistan and Pakistan). The inscription of Takht-i-Bahî (near Peshawar) dating to the year 103 of the Vikrama era allows us to date Gondophares' reign to A.D. 20-46 (or longer).[182]

Gondophares, whom according to early Christian tradition the apostle Thomas is said to have met (see §21.9), is mentioned in the following sources: (1) In literary sources: the apocryphal *Acts of Thomas,* dating to the third century A.D., discovered 1822 in Paris, and the *Vita Apollonii* of Philostratus (ca. A.D. 200). (2) In the Takht-i-Bahî inscription of A.D. 103, discovered in 1871 near Peshawar. Whether other inscriptions refer to Gondophares is contested. (3) On numerous coins that were found in an area extending from Seistan to Taxila and Jammu (about 1,600 km).[183] The coins that Gondophares issued indicate that he called himself "King," "King of Kings," "Sole Ruler, called Shah," the "Great," the "Savior." He unified areas that recently had been controlled by various Indo-Greek, Indo-Scythian and Kushan kings. The western areas of his kingdom, Arachosia and Seistan, were under the administrative control of his brother Orthagnes (A.D. 25-55);[184] the eastern areas, with Taxila as the main center, were governed by Aspavarma (A.D. 1-35) and Sasan (A.D. 35-55). Taxila probably was conquered in A.D. 25 when Gondophares defeated Azes II, the ruler of the Sacae.[185] After Gondophares' death his empire disintegrated.

Taxila probably was Gondophares' capital. Philostratus reports that the name of the king of India who resided in Taxila was Phraotes and that he was independent of the Parthian king Vardanes, with the result that he also controlled the satrapy of Gandhara, with the exception of the wild tribes at the borders of his territory, whom he managed to keep quiet through payments of money. Vardanes was indeed the Parthian king, residing in Babylon, between A.D. 41 and 45, and the Kushan were active during this time in the region in which Gondophares established his empire. Epigraphical and numismatic sources confirm that the Indo-Parthian king Gondophares ruled the city of Taxila through his governor Aspaverma. As a result there is sufficient evidence that allows us to identity the Phraotes mentioned by Philostratus with Gondophares. "Phraotes" presumably is a title, perhaps the Grecized form of the Pali word *apratihata,* which means "the Invincible."[186] This title did not only correspond to historical reality; it also appears on one of his copper coins.[187] In Taxila 744 coins of Gondophares were found, which is hardly accidental.

---

[182]R. M. Smith (1997, 103, 107, 109-18) dates his reign to A.D. 19-48.

[183]On Gondophares see Dar 1988, 16-30; cf. ibid. 22, for a reproduction, transcription and translation of the Takht-i-Bahî.

[184]"Orthagnes" is the name given in Greek sources; in Kharoshthi he is called "Gadana." See Dar 1988, 27.

[185]See John H. Marshall, *Taxila: An Illustrated Account of Archaeological Excavations Carried Out at Taxila under the Orders of the Government of India between the Years 1913 and 1934* (3 vols.; Cambridge: Cambridge University Press, 1951), 1:64.

[186]Ernst Herzfeld, *Archäologische Mitteilungen aus Iran* (Berlin: Reimer, 1929), 133; cf. Marshall, *Taxila,* 64.

[187]Dar 1988, 19: "Maharajasa . . . sa dhramikasa. Apratihatasa devavratasa Guduphrasa." Waldmann (1996, 10) thinks that Patala/Minnagara, located on the southern course of the Indus River, was the capital. However, his reference to *Periplus Maris Erythraei* is not sufficient to invalidate the archaeological evidence (which Waldmann does not consider).

In the second half of the first century A.D. Kujala Kadphises, the ruler of the Kushan, managed to unify the central Asian tribes that Chinese sources call the "Yuezhi." The most important centers of the empire of the Kushan were Push-kalavati and Mathura. Around A.D. 59 they managed to occupy the northern areas of the Punjab, including the city of Taxila. Under Kaniska I (after A.D. 78) the Kushan controlled most of northern India, Afghanistan and parts of central Asia.[188] The Kushan were regarded at the time as one of the four great Eurasian powers, besides China, Rome and Parthia. As heirs of Hellenistic Bactria, they had contacts with the Mediterranean world in the west, and as nomadic people from central Asia they mediated contacts between China in the east and India in the south.

In regard to the Jews, the earliest evidence for familiarity with India or at least Indian products dates to the third century B.C. In *1 En.* 30—32, a text dating to around 200-150 B.C., Aramaic fragments of which were found in Qumran (4Q201-202), we read of a utopian journey of Enoch to the regions beyond the Erytraean Sea (Indian Ocean), thus evidently to India.[189] This "account" implies familiarity with the trade in aromatic spices and with the places of origin of the various ingredients. On the markets of Syria and Judea one could buy Indian items such as ivory, ebony, sandalwood and exotic animals. It seems that generals could acquire Indian elephants along with Indian riders: when the Syrian king Antiochos V (164-162 B.C.) fought the rebellious Jews at Beth-Zur and Beth-Zechariah, "thirty-two elephants accustomed to war" and their "Indian drivers" were present (1 Macc 6:30, 37); 1 Macc 6:34-37 presents an elaborate description of the handling of these war elephants from India. Coins of Antiochos III (223-187 B.C.), found in Caesarea Philippi north of the Sea of Galilee, depict on the reverse an elephant walking to the right. Nicolaus of Damascus, the adviser of Herod I, met the members of an Indian embassy in Antioch (Syria) who were on their way to Rome. The letter to Augustus that the three ambassadors carried with them was written in Greek by the Indian king Porus (Strabo 15.1.72-73). It is not known whether Nicolaus described India in his 144 volume universal history, which he wrote largely in Jerusalem.[190]

The Greeks encountered religious traditions with distinct doctrinal content

---

[188]On the Kushan see Bivar 1983, 192-203.

[189]Denis 1970, 26-27; Hengel 1969, 377 n. 589 (ET, 2:138 n. 635). J. T. Milik (*The Book of Enoch: Aramaic Fragments of Qumrân Cave 4* [Oxford: Clarendon, 1976], 27) dates *1 En.* 6—36 to around 250 B.C.

[190]The surviving fragments (*FGrH* 90) demonstrate that he wrote on the history of Assyria, Babylonia, Media (F 1-6), Greece (F 7-14), Syria, Judea (F 17-20) and Rome (F 69-70). See Dueck 2000, 133. For the coin of Antiochos III (minted in Ecbatana) see Newell, *Coinage of the Eastern Seleucid Mints,* no. 631; Houghton, *Coins of the Seleucid Empire,* no. 483; an image can be seen at <http://www.pepperdine.edu/seaver/religion/isar/CoinPages/w422Ecb.htm>.

for the first time in Bactria and India. Whereas the Greeks of the West quickly
lost interest in the cultures of the east after Alexander's conquest of Persia, many
of the Greeks who lived in these regions adopted local religions, especially Buddhism. The Buddhist Pali text *Milinda's Questions* (Milindapañha)[191] describes
the conversion of the Bactrian king Menander (ca. 115-90 B.C.) to Buddhism, the
direct result of a public disputation between Menander and the monk Nagasena
living in Patna about nirvana, about the existence or nonexistence of the soul,
about reincarnation, karma and other Buddhist teachings. The disputation is
said to have taken place in a monastery in Sagala in which eighty thousand
monks lived. King Milinda arrived at the monastery with an entourage of five
hundred Greeks and became convinced of the truth of (Hînayâna) Buddhism as
a result of Nagasena's answers.[192]

Buddhism reached these areas around 200 B.C., when the emperor Asoka adopted Buddhism, one of many versions of Indian ascetic spirituality, and actively supported its
expansion. After his conversion Asoka decided to disavow military conquests, which
only bring suffering on innocent people. He wanted instead to prevail by *dhamma*
("righteousness," Gk., εὐσέβεια, *eusebeia*). Rock Edict 13 asserts, "So, what is conquest
through Dharma is now considered to be the best conquest by the Beloved of the Gods
[i.e., Asoka]. And such a conquest has been achieved by the Beloved of the Gods not
only here in his own dominions but also in the territories bordering on his dominions,
as far away as at the distance of six hundred yojanas, where the Yavana king named
Antiyoka is ruling and where, beyond the kingdom of the said Antiyoka, four other
kings named Turamaya, Antikini, Maka and Alikasundara are also ruling."[193] Antiyoka is
Antiochos II Theos of Syria (262-247 B.C.), Turamaya (or Tulamaya) is Ptolemy II Philadelphos of Egypt (285-246 B.C.), Antikini (or Antekina) is Antigonos Gonnatas (283-239
B.C.), Maka (or Makas) is Bagas of Cyrene in northern Africa (308-248 B.C.), Alikasundara (or Alikasudala) is Alexandros, deputy of Antiochos I Soter in Sardis (ca. 246
B.C.). There is debate whether Asoka's *dhamma* should be understood in terms of an
active propagation of Buddhist religion—that is, whether the sending of envoys to all
regions of the Indian subcontinent, to the northwest (the Hellenized states beyond the
Indus River) and to Ceylon (Sri Lanka) represents a Buddhist "missionary" program. Reinhold Merkelbach interprets the text in terms of Asoka sending out "missionaries" commissioned "to convert the people to the right way of life".[194] Several scholars of the history of India agree with this interpretation and accept the Buddhist Pali sources from

---

[191]Isaline B. Horner, *Milindapañha, Milinda's Questions: Translated from the Pali* (2 vols.; London: Luzac, 1963-1964); Édith Nolot, *Entretiens de Milinda et Nagasena* (Paris: Gallimard,
1995).

[192]Carsten Colpe ("Development of Religious Thought," *CHI* 3:819-65, esp. 848) accepts this account as deriving from historical facts. Tarn (1984, 268-69) assumes a political motivation for
Menander's conversion and thus is skeptical with regard to the religious impetus of his adoption of Buddhism. George Woodcock (*The Greeks in India* [London: Faber, 1966], 112-13) defends a more positive evaluation.

[193]See recently R. Merkelbach, "Wer war der Alexandros, zu dem Aœoka eine Gesandtschaft
geschickt hat?" *EA* 32 (2000): 126-28.

[194]Merkelbach, "Wer war der Alexandros?" 126.

Sri Lanka that speak in this connection of a decision of the third council of Pataliputra as historical.[195] Other India specialists interpret the envoys who are described in some inscriptions as *dhamma-mahāmattas* ("office bearers of *dhamma*") as ambassadors whose task was to take care of the social needs of the Indian population and to attend to diplomatic relations with the neighboring Hellenistic kingdoms of western Asia.[196] It is important to note in this discussion that several relevant inscriptions stipulate that all religious groups should be supported financially in a nonpartisan way.[197] This seems to make an expansionist missionary program of Asoka unlikely. Finally, some scholars doubt whether *dhamma,* as understood by Asoka, was specifically Buddhist in the first place: the ethical ways of life that Asoka propagated are present in Jaina and other Sramanic groups of the time as well.[198]

Since Eudoxus of Kyzikos on the Marmara Sea sailed in 116 B.C. to India,[199] the Greeks knew that the monsoon winds could be exploited for the voyage to India (thus Strabo; according to *Periplus Maris Erythraei* 57.19, it was a captain named Hippalos who made this discovery). In the decades following this discovery the trade contacts between Egypt and India became closer.[200] Ptolemy XII (80-58 B.C.) created the office of "strategos of the Red and Indian Sea."[201] Cleopatra's plan to flee to India after the defeat of Actium in 31 B.C. certainly was not utopian.[202] When Egypt became a Roman province under Augustus, maritime trade with India received an enormous impetus.[203] In earlier years only about twenty ships sailed to India every year. At the beginning of the first century A.D. about 120 ships sailed every year, leaving Myos Hormos on the Red Sea in June/July and returning from India in December/January (Strabo, 2.5.12; 17.1.13). Archaeologists found 5,400 Roman *denarii* and 800 *aurei* (gold coins) in southern India, dating largely to the time of Augustus and Tiberius (but which could have been used as means of payment in later times), as well as Roman pottery.

Merchandise destined for India was shipped to Alexandria and then transported on the river Nile as far as Koptos (mod. Qift). At Koptos the goods were loaded onto camels and transported across to port cities in the Red Sea, particularly ʾAbu Shaʾar, Myos Hormos (mod. Quseir el-Qadim) and Berenike

---

[195]S. Richard Gombrich, "Aśoka—The Great Upāsaka," in Seneviratna 1994, 1-10, esp. 7-8; Ananda Guruge, "Emperor Aśoka and Buddhism," in ibid., 27-65, esp. 46-57, with reference to Rock Edicts 2, 5, 13; Anuradha Seneviratna, "Aśoka and the Emergence of a Sinhala Buddhist State in Sri Lanka," in ibid., 79-98; see also Ström 1994, 18; Clemen 1929, 233-34.

[196]Thapar 1994, 21-22. T. W. Rhys Davids (*Buddhist India* [London: Fisher-Unwin, 1902], 298-302) was also skeptical as far as a "missionary program" was concerned.

[197]Rock Edicts 8, 12; Pillar Edicts 7. See Thapar 1994, 22.

[198]Thapar, 1994, 22.

[199]See Dihle 1974, 111-15; 1978, 119-23.

[200]See Warmington (1928), who dates Hippalus to the time of emperor Tiberius (ibid. 46).

[201]Hölbl 2001, 204.

[202]Plutarch, *Ant.* 81. See Dihle 1978, 121.

[203]For the observations that follow above see Casson 1989, 11-12, 283-85, 289-91.

(mod. Bender el-Kebir). The route from Koptos to Myos Hormos was only 174 km (108 mi.) long, the shortest route across the desert east of the Nile. The northeasterly route from Kaina (mod. Qena), north of Koptos, to ʾAbu Shaʾar was 184 km long and passed via Mons Porphyrites or Mons Claudianus, two mines worked by the Romans. The route from Koptos to Berenike, which Hadrian fortified, is 392 km long, nearly twice the length of the route from Koptos to Myos Hormos.[204]

Pack camels can cover about 4 km (2.5 mi.) per hour, thus 24-32 km (15-20 mi.) per day. This means that they would need between twelve and sixteen days for the route from Koptos to Berenike (Pliny, *Nat.* 6.26.102, mentions twelve days). Along this route fifteen fortified stations are known (or are presumed), with further cisterns between these stations. For the route from Koptos to Myos Hormos nine fortified stations and two unfortified rest stops are known; a caravan would have needed between five and seven days for this route. The first stations were fortified already in the second century B.C. Under Augustus many stations were fortified as garrisons (square layout with a lateral length of 50 to 60 m, and a well in the center).[205]

The import of goods from India and Arabia by the shipping trade used the same routes, with an import tax of 25 percent. The large freight ships that could carry well over one thousand tons left the Egyptian ports in June/July, sailing with the north wind through the Red Sea, catching the southwest monsoon south of the Gulf of Aden.[206] The captains wanted to reach the west coast of India before the month of August, when navigation became dangerous due to the wind conditions. The approximately two thousand nautical miles from the straits of Aden to Muziris on the southwest coast of India could be covered in about twenty days (with favorable winds the sailboats could reach speeds of four to seven knots). The return journey began in December/January, during the northeast monsoon. One result of the India trade of Roman and Egyptian merchants was the decline of Eudaimōn Arabia, the old trading post on the entrance to the Red Sea (*Periplus Maris Erythraei* 26.8), a fact that demonstrates that even the Indian ships sailed as far as Egypt.[207]

A papyrus, dating between 200 and 150 B.C. and written probably in Alexandria, records a loan agreement with the purpose of financing a trading venture to India. The merchants who borrowed money formed an international consortium, perhaps a feature of the trade with India that was rather com-

---

[204]See S. E. Sidebotham and R. E. Zitterkopf, "Routes Through the Eastern Desert of Egypt," *Expedition* 37.2 (1995): 39-52; idem, "Survey of the Via Hadriana: The 1997 Season," *Bulletin de l'Institut Français d'Archéologie Orientale* 98 (1998): 353-65.

[205]See Valerie A. Maxfield, "The Eastern Desert Forts and the Army in Egypt during the Principate," in D. Bailey 1996, 9-19, esp. 11-12.

[206]*Periplus Maris Erythraei* 49.16.31-32: "For those sailing to this port from Egypt, the right time to set out is around the month of July, that is Epeiph."

[207]See Casson 1989, 20.

mon. In this particular case the five partners have Greek names; one came from Sparta, another from Massalia (mod. Marseilles) in southern Gaul. The lender has a Greek name, and the banker who handled the funds probably was a Roman. Of the five sureties, one was a merchant from Carthage in northern Africa, and four were soldiers, one of whom came from Massalia, one from Elia in southern Italy, one from Thessalonike in Macedonia.[208] Another papyrus contains the register for the poll tax of the town of Arsinoe for the year A.D. 72/73, mentioning a certain "Gaion, also called Diodoros," who is reported to be in India (and perhaps lives there).[209] It seems that wealthy Egyptian families had agents in the ports of the Red Sea who supervised trade with Africa, Arabia and India. A certain Marcus Julius Alexander belonged to these families that were involved in the trade with India; he evidently was a member of the wealthy Jewish family in Alexandria to which Philo belonged. Marcus probably was Philo's nephew. He had agents in Myos Hormos and Berenike.[210] Xenophon of Ephesus writes, in his second-century novel *The Ephesian Story of Anthia and Habrocomes,* in a rather matter-of-fact manner about a "maharajah from India" who came to Alexandria to see the city and to engage in trade.[211] Strabo had not visited India (although he visited Armenia). For his description of India in books 11 and 15 he relies on Megasthenes, Onesikritos and Nearchos, who had accompanied Alexander to India. He devotes a long passage to a description of the customs and religions of India (15.1.59-70).

Using Megasthenes as his source, Strabo describes the way of life of the Brahmans. We learn that they speak more about death than about other subjects: "For they believe that the life here is, as it were, that of a babe still in the womb, and that death, to those who have devoted themselves to philosophy, is birth into the true life, that is, the happy life [εἰς τὸν ὄντως βίον καιτὸν εὐδαίμονα]; and that they therefore discipline themselves most of all to be ready for death; and that they believe that nothing that happens to mankind is good or bad, for otherwise some would not be grieved and others delighted by the same things, both having dreamlike notions, and that the same persons cannot at one time be grieved and then in turn change and be delighted by the same things. As for the opinions of the Brahmans about the natural world, Megasthenes says that some of their opinions indicate mental simplicity, for the Brahmans are better in deeds than in words [ἐν ἔργοις γὰρ αὐτοὺς κρείττους ἢ λόγοις εἶναι], since they confirm most of their beliefs through the use of myths; and that they are of the same opinion as the Greeks about many things; for example, their opinion that the universe was created

---

[208]U. Wilcken, "Punt-Fahrten in der Ptolemäerzeit," *Zeitschrift für ägyptische Sprache und Altertumskunde* 60 (1925): 86-102; Casson 1989, 31-32.

[209]P. Lond. 260. See Carl Wessely, ed., *Studien zur Palaeographie und Papyruskunde* (18 vols.; Amsterdam: Hakkert, 1901-1924), 4:72-79, esp. 74, line 549. Cf. Casson 1989, 32.

[210]Alexander Fuks, "Notes on the Archive of Nicanor," *Journal of Juristic Papyrology* 5 (1951): 207-16, esp. 214-16. Cf. Casson 1989, 32.

[211]Xenophon, *Ephesiaca* 3.

and is destructible, as also the Greeks assert, and that it is spherical in shape, and that the god who made it and regulates it pervades the whole of it; and that the primal elements of all things else are different, but that water was the primal element of all creation; and that, in addition to the four elements, there is a fifth element of which the heavens and the heavenly bodies are composed; and that the earth is situated in the center of the universe. And writers mention similar opinions of the Brachmanes about the seed and the soul, as also several other opinions of theirs. And they also weave in myths, like Plato, about the immortality of the souls and the judgments in Hades and other things of this kind" (15.1.59).

Archaeological discoveries as well as epigraphical and literary Indian texts confirm that Greeks and Romans lived in colonies in India.[212] References to *Yavanas* in early Pali and Sanskrit texts designate, in a generalizing sense, Greeks, Indo-Greeks and Egyptian-Roman merchants. The presence of *Yavanas* in western Deccan is documented for a time during which trade with the outside world increased considerably: gifts for centers of Buddhist monks indicate that the *Yavanas* actively strove to be accepted by the local trade networks. In eastern Deccan and in southern India, the *Yavanas* evidently were direct players in the local trade. In Arikamedu (Ποδούκη, Poduke; mod. Virapatnam),[213] situated on the Tamil coast about 4 km south of (modern) Pondicherry, Roman glassware, lamps and Arretine pottery have been found. Arikamedu-Poduke is mentioned in *Periplus Maris Erythraei* (60.20) and by Greek geographers (Ptolemaios 7.1.14.). Evidently this Indian port city had contacts with the West as early as the second century B.C. The "Roman period" of Arikamedu dates to the early first century B.C.

Ongoing excavations in Arikamedu have uncovered an "industrial complex" or market with a warehouse (50 m long), "tanks" for storing goods or agricultural products and evidence for port facilities and for living quarters. Amphora that were found indicate that the Greek islands—Cos, Cnidus, Rhodes—dominated the maritime trade with India since the second century B.C., whereas several ports of Campania (Pompeii), Istria and southern Spain were the main export harbors at the end of the first century B.C. and in the first century A.D.[214] Imported goods included wine, olive oil, fish sauce (*garum,* from southern Spain) and pottery (*terra sigillata*). Since no *terra sigillata* have been found at any other place in southern India, scholars presently assume that these imports confirm the constant presence of people from the Mediterranean world: Greeks, Romans, Phoenicians, Syrians

---

[212]See Himanshu Prabha Ray, "The Yavanas in India," in Boussac and Salles 1995, 75-95. On archaeological research in India see Chakrabarti 1998.
[213]Vimala Begley, "Arikamedu Reconsidered," *AJA* 87 (1983): 461-81; idem, "Changing Perceptions of Arikamedu," in Begley 1996, 1-39; Casson 1989, 228-29; Chakrabarti 1998, 233-34; Allchin 1995, 147-49; K. Karttunen, *DNP* 1:1081; Ball 2000, 128-29. French archaeologists were the first to investigate Arikamedu (1941-1944); other important archaeologists are Mortimer Wheeler (1945) and J.-M. Casal (1947-1950), and more recently V. Begley and others (1989-). The identification of Arikamedu with the town of Poduke mentioned in Greek sources can be regarded as certain.
[214]See Elizabeth L. Will, "Mediterranean Shipping Amphoras from the 1941-1950 Excavations," in Begley 1996, 317-49.

(and Jews?).[215] It is unknown how many Westerners lived in Arikamedu or to what extent they controlled or dominated local trade. *Periplus Maris Erythraei* mentions that the wine transported to India was sold on Indian markets (49.56). The ships leaving Arikamedu carried textiles, pearls of semiprecious stones, glass, armbands made of shells. Fragments of two perfume bottles (*unguentarium*) confirm trade with Gaza or Nabatea, and fragments of Fayence containers confirm trade with Egypt.[216] A bowl found in Arikamedu, dating to the second part of the first century A.D., carries the stamp of the producer, Sertorius. This bowl presumably originated in the workshops of C. Sertorius Ocella and Q. Sertorius, whose products were found also in Corinth and Alexandria.[217] A denarius with a depiction of Tiberius from the mint of Lugdunum (mod. Lyon) was probably also found in Arikamedu.[218] A jar found in Myos Hormos (mod. Quseir el-Qadim) on the Egyptian coast of the Red Sea is inscribed in Tamil-Brahmi script with the name of an Indian man, Kanan, dating to the first century A.D. (on paleographical grounds). This Kanan might be identical with the man whose name is inscribed, with a similar script, on a shard of a large earthen jar found in Arikamedu.[219] Vimala Begley dates the "golden age" of Arikamedu-Poduke from 50 B.C. until A.D. 50. Poduke had regular contacts with the West until about A.D. 200.

The portrait of a young girl found in Didarganj, northeast of Benares, indicates that at least some of the Western merchants who lived in the eastern regions of India were accompanied by their wives.[220] Tamil texts inform us that the town of Kamara-Chaberis, situated on the mouth of the Kaveri River (Cauvery) near Tranquebar, presumably identical with Kavirippattinam, had a thriving port in which one could see *Yavanas* (Westerners).[221] Dio Chrysostom, a Stoic popular philosopher from Bithynia who visited the countries in the East after being exiled from Rome in A.D. 82, reports that Indian spectators attended games in Alexandria (*Or.* 32.40). Xenophon of Ephesus mentions in the second/third century an Indian rajah who visited Alexandria as a tourist and merchant (*Ephesiaca* 3.11.2).[222]

---

[215]See Begley, "Changing Perceptions," 22.

[216]See Kathleen W. Slane, "Other Ancient Ceramics Imported from the Mediterranean," in Begley 1996, 351-68, esp. 352, 367, with nos. 54-55 (figs. 7, 29-32) and nos. 49-52.

[217]Slane, "Other Ancient Ceramics," no. 27.

[218]Begley, "Changing Perceptions," 6; for the observation that follows above see ibid., 8.

[219]See D. Whitcomb and J. H. Johnson, *Quseir al-Qadim 1978 Preliminary Report* (Princeton, N.J.: American Research Center in Egypt, 1979), fig. 27.2; I. Mahadevan, "Pottery Inscriptions in Brahmi and Tamil-Brahmi," in Begley 1996, 287-315, fig. 5.22; Begley, "Changing Perceptions," 23-24. The name "Kanan" probably is derived from "Kanha" or "Kana" and is identical with "Krishna."

[220]See Casson 1989, 25 n. 26, with reference to D. Schlumberger, "Coiffures féminines similaires à Rome et dans l'Inde," in *Mélanges d'archéologie et d'histoire* (FS A. Piganiol; ed. R. Chevallier; 3 vols.; Paris: l'École des Hautes Études en Sciences Sociales, 1966), 1:587-95.

[221]P. Meile, "Les Yavanas dans l'Inde tamoule," *JA* 232 (1940): 85-123; Warmington 1928; Casson 1989, 228. On Kamara (or Chaberis Emporion) see *Periplus Maris Erythraei* 60.20; Ptolemaios 7.1.13. Excavations brought a Buddhist temple to light; see Chakrabarti 1998, 234.

[222]On Indian inscriptions in Egypt see R. Salomon, "Epigraphic Remains of Indian Traders in Egypt," *JAOS* 111 (1991): 731-36.

A significant text documenting both the geographical knowledge in the first century regarding the regions of the Indian Ocean and the economic relations between Rome and the Orient is the *Periplus Maris Erythraei*, written between A.D. 40-70, thus during the time of the first major missionary expansion of the Christian faith.[223] The title "Periplus" is somewhat misleading: in contrast to the traditional periploi, this text is not a guide for sailors but a handbook for merchants. The author evidently was an Egyptian Greek who knew the voyage to India from personal experience as a merchant. The accuracy with which the author transcribes Indian names and terms into Greek confirms that his information rests on personal knowledge. The text informs about goods that could be bought or sold in the various ports that are mentioned. The text also provides information about the rulers of the port cities or regions that are mentioned, and also records anthropological and historical information as well as natural phenomena.

Information that the author provides, often merely in passing, can be combined into a political map of northeastern Africa, Arabia and (western) India. On the region east of the Persian Gulf we learn, among other things, the following facts. The kingdom of Persis extended from the southern end of the Persian Gulf to Omana (33.11.12; 36.12.3-4), where the territory of the Indo-Persian kings began. First comes a district inhabited by the Parsidai (37.12.13-14); next is "Scythia" ("Indoscythia" in Ptolemaios 7.1.55; mod. Sind), with the most important port of the region, Barbarikon at the mouth of the Indus (38.12). The capital of "Scythia" is identified as Minnagar, a town up the river Indus. The Parthian invasion of the Sind brought the rule of the Sacae in this region to a close.

India proper began in the Gulf of Kutch (41.14.2-3), where the Sacae ruled at the time,[224] pushed to the south by the Parthians (38.12-13). This region, called Ariake, ex-

---

[223] *GGM* I 257-305 (commentary, ibid., 1:xcv-cxi; with maps, no. 11); B. Fabricius, *Der Periplus des Erythräischen Meeres von einem Unbekannten; Griechisch und Deutsch* (Leipzig: Veit, 1883); Wilfred H. Schoff, *The Periplus of the Erythraean Sea: Travel and Trade in the Indian Ocean by a Merchant of the First Century* (2nd ed.; New Delhi: Oriental Books, 1974 [1912]); Hjalmar Frisk, *Le Périple de la mer Érythrée* (Göteborgs Högskolas Årsskrift 33; Göteborg: Elanders, 1927); Casson 1989. See Sudhakar Chattopadhyaya, *The Periplus of the Erythraean Sea and Ptolemy on Ancient Geography of India* (Calcutta: Prajñā, 1980). The quotations that follow above are from Casson 1989. Recent studies on the Nabatean kings have shown that "Malichus, king of the Nabataeans" in Petra, mentioned in *Periplus Maris Erythraei* 19.6.28-29, can only be Malichus II, who ruled between A.D. 40 and 70; see G. Bowersock, *JRS* 61 (1972): 233; Casson 1989, 6-7; Jean-Francois Salles, "The Periplus of the Erythraean Sea and the Arab-Persian Gulf," in Boussac and Salles 1995, 115 n. 1. Attempts to save the older date of the third century (see H. von Wissmann, *ANRW* II.9.1 [1976]: 434-35) are unconvincing. The periplus is written in Greek, and the diction is that of a merchant, similar to the Greek of Egyptian papyri documenting business transactions. For the discussion that follows above see Casson 1989, 7-47.

[224] Indian and Greek sources describe the Iranian-speaking nomads who came from central Asia and settled in the Sind between 140 and 100 B.C. as "Saka," while Greek sources sometimes call them "Scythians." The first king of this empire was Maues (ca. 100 B.C.), with Taxila as the capital. The last king was Azes II, who was deposed around A.D. 20 by the Parthian Gondophares. See Bivar 1983, 192-97.

tended as far as (modern) Bombay. The main port of the kingdom of the Sacae was Barygaza, which boasted to be the largest harbor of India. In the time in which *Periplus Maris Erythraei* was written, Manbanos was king, one of the greatest rulers of the Sacae, with the capital in Minnagara (41.14), situated north of Barygaza. The Kushan ("Bactrians" in the terminology of the author [47.16.6]) lived north of the Sacae. South of the Sacae we find the mighty Andhra. It seems that the Sacae had occupied several important port cities of Andhra just before the arrival of the author of the periplus. South of Andhra we find the three large kingdoms of southern India: the Chera (54.17), the Panya or Pandya (54.18) and the Chola. The political information ends with comments on the "kingdom of Pandion," meaning Panya (Pandya), which extended on the east coast of India as far as Kolchoi in the Gulf of Mannar (59.12.22-24).[225] The next port cities that the author mentions—Argaru, Kamara, Poduke, Sopatma (59.20.1; 60.20.6)—must belong to the kingdom of the Chola. For the ports up to the Ganges Delta no political information is provided either.

The most important harbors on the northwestern coast of India were Barbarikon (in the Indus Delta) and Barygaza (Βαρύγαζα; mod. Broach);[226] on the southwest coast (Malabar): Muziris (Μουζιρίς; mod. Cranganore)[227] and Nelkyanda (Νέλκυνδα; mod. Niranom-Pirakkād);[228] on the east coast: Masalia, Desarene and Ganges. The author of *Periplus Maris Erythraei* mentions seventeen or eighteen emporia and harbor cities on the west coast between Bombay and the southern tip of India on Cape Comorin: Semylla (mod. Chaul), Mandagora (mod. Bankot), Palaipatmai (mod. Dabhol), Melizeigara (mod. Jaigarh), Byzantion (mod. Vijayadurg), Toparon (?), Tyrannosboas, the Sesekreienai Islands (mod. Vengurla Rocks), the island of the Aigidioi (mod. Goa), the island of the Kaineitoi (mod. Oyster Rocks), the White Island (mod. Pigeon Island), Naura (mod. Mangalore), Tyndis (mod. Ponnani), Muziris, Nelkynda/Bakare, the Red Mountain (mod. Varkkallai), Balita (mod. Vilinjam), Komar (mod. Cape Comorin) (53.17; 58.19).[229] In some regions the trade between Rome and India increased the significance of urban centers.[230] The development of trade was accompanied in some areas by a noticeable increase of religious centers, mostly Buddhist.[231]

Direct trade with the harbors on the Indian east coast was less important, since the large ships of the Roman-Egyptian merchants could not navigate between the southern tip of India and the northern tip of Ceylon (the so-called Adam's Bridge): to reach the east coast they had to sail around the island. Trade with the east coast of India usually was carried

---

[225]King Pandion sent an embassy to Augustus in 20 B.C.; see Strabo 15.1.4.

[226]B. G. Gokhale, "Bharukaccha/Barygaza," in Pollet 1987, 67-79; Karttunen, *DNP* 2:458; E. H. Warmington and R. Thapar, *OCD* 234.

[227]K. Karttunen, *DNP* 8:567.

[228]O. Stein, PW 16.2 (1935): 2281-85; K. Karttunen, *DNP* 8:810.

[229]Schoff, *Periplus of the Erythraean Sea;* Casson 1989, 296-99.

[230]Chakrabarti 1998, 183-84 (Sind), 217 (Wari-Bateshwar in the lower Ganges Valley), 226-27 (the coast of Gujarat, with the harbor city of Barygaza), 228 (Maharashtra, with the coastal cities Surpara-ka and Kalyana, and the emporia Pratisthana and Tagara in the interior); 232-33 (Tamilnadu, with the empires of the Chola and Panya); 234 (Andhra, with the Godavari Delta); on the coast of Kerala (with the harbor city of Muziris), which was important for trade, no ancient cities have been found as of yet, a fact that may be due to a variety of reasons (231-32).

[231]For the Godavari Delta on the east coast see Chakrabarti 1998, 234-35. Vijayapuri, the capital of the Ikshakus, had a dozen rest houses with colonnaded halls and public baths, as well as eighteen Brahman temples and over thirty Buddhist institutions.

out by middlemen who had smaller ships or who brought export goods from the harbors of the east coast via overland routes to the west coast.[232] According to Pliny, there were trade contacts with Ceylon at the time of the emperor Claudius (*Nat.* 6.84-85); these contacts become more intensive only in the fourth century, however.[233]

The Greek and Roman merchants bought a great number of luxuries in India: in Barbarikon and Barygaza (39.13; 48.16; 49.16) costus, bdellium, *lykion,* nard, myrrh, indigo, turquoise, lapis lazuli, onyx, agate, ivory, cotton cloth, fine cotton garments, silk cloth and yarn, Chinese pelts, pepper; in Muziris and Nelkyanda (56.18; 59.20) nard, malabathron (leaf of the *Cinnamomum tamala*), pepper, pearls, ivory, tortoise shell, transparent gems, diamonds, sapphires, silk cloth, fine cotton garments; in Masalia, Desarene and Ganges (62.20; 63.21) nard, malabathron, pearls, ivory, fine cotton garments. The merchandise that the Roman-Egyptian ships brought to India included Italian and Laodicean wine (6.2; 49.16), metals (lead, tin, copper), and especially expensive items such as drugs and cosmetics (antimony, realgar, orpiment, storax), silverware, glassware, coral, multicolored textiles (39.13; 49.16; 56.18; 60.20). The merchants from Roman Egypt sold to the local kings fine ointments, vintage wines, luxury clothing, slave girls for the harem and slave boys who could play musical instruments (49.16). On the northwestern coast of India the Roman merchants exchanged their goods for import merchandise, which seems to be the main reason why archaeologists have found few Roman coins in northern India.[234] In the harbors of the southwest coast they had to pay "a great amount of money" (i.e., cash) for the Indian (and Chinese) luxury items (56.18; cf. 24.8; 39.13).[235] The trade relations between the Greco-Roman and the Indian worlds was "without doubt" very intensive in the early imperial period.[236]

Apart from a single exception, the author of *Periplus Maris Erythraei* seemed uninterested in religious questions. Referring in 58.19 to the shrine of the goddess Durga near Cape Comorin, the author comments, "Men who wish to lead a holy life for the rest of their days remain there celibate; they come there and they perform ablutions. Women do the same. For it is said that at one time the goddess remained there and performed ablutions."

Pomponius Mela describes the coast of India as far as the Ganges River in the third book of his work *Chorographia* (3.67-71).

He writes in 3.67, "The Palibothri hold the coastline from Point Tamus [Cape Negrais?] to the Ganges. From the Ganges to Point Colis, except where it is too hot to be inhabited, are found black peoples [*atrae gentes*], Aethiopians so to speak. From Point Colis to the Indus the shores are straight, and peoples live there who are timorous and quite prosperous because of the sea's riches [*timidique populi et marinis opibus affatim dites*]."

Pliny describes India extensively (*Nat.* 5.9.47; 6.21.56-26.106). Flavius Arrianus's

---

[232]For a discussion of relevant archaeological, epigraphical and literary sources see Himanshu Prabha Ray, "The Yavanas in India," in Boussac and Salles 1995, 75-95, esp. 83-85; idem, "A Resurvey of 'Roman' Contacts with the East," in ibid., 97-114.

[233]See Dihle 1974, 110-15; 1978, 139-45.

[234]Raschke 1978, 665.

[235]See Casson 1989, 31.

[236]Hans-Joachim Drexhage, "Indienhandel," *DNP* 5:971.

Indikē,[237] based on the paraplus of Nearchos, was a byproduct of this work on the history of Alexander the Great. Ptolemaios also includes a wealth of information about India in his *Geographica* (7.1).[238]

Ptolemaios mentions the following important cities on the west coast of India, many of which cannot be identified with certainty: Syrastrene, Monoglosson, Larike, Barygaza, Nousaripa, Poulipoula, Ariake Sadenoi, Souppara, Dounga, Semyla, Mandagara, Battepatna, Byzantion, Khersoneses, Armagara, Nitraiai, Limyrike, Tyndis, Bramagara, Kalaikaris, Mouzeris, Podoperoura, Semne, Koreoura, Bakare, Melkyda, Elankoros, Kottiara, Bambala, Komaria. In places where this list diverges from *Periplus Maris Erythraei,* the two texts perhaps reflect different historical periods.

As far as contacts with China are concerned, Chinese silk had long been known in the Greco-Roman world before there was a marked increase of imports in the first century B.C.[239] Since this time, references to the "Seres" (Σῆρες), the "silk people," become more frequent: Caesar mounts *vela* of the Seres in the theater, Cleopatra wears silk clothes, and Tiberius makes critical remarks on clothes made of silk as luxury items.[240] The image of the Seres as typical people at the eastern or northeastern end of the inhabited world probably goes back to Poseidonios, whom Strabo uses as a source. The first reference in Western texts to the Seres is connected with an expedition organized by Greeks from Bactria that visited the tribes of central Asia in the second century B.C.[241] The first explicit and reliable reference in Greco-Roman literature to China as the land from which silk originates is found in *Periplus Maris Erythraei,* dating to the first century A.D. In regard to direct contacts with China, official Chinese chronicles mention a voyage of a certain Zhang Qiang (Chang Chi'en), an envoy of Emperor Wu Ti (140-87 B.C.) of the Han dynasty, who traveled in the context of a political mission to the West and reached Bactria.[242] Several years after Zhang Qiang's voyage, Parthia and China maintained diplomatic relations. During the years A.D. 73-79 a Chinese army under Pan Ch'ao occupied the region around Khotan and Turfan. The *pax sinica* was intended to secure the trade with the West. The Chinese merchants transported their goods as far as Dunhuang or beyond the Great Wall to Louisville, Lou-Lan, where they were sold to central Asian middlemen from Parthia, Sogdiana, Kushan or India who transported them to the West.

---

[237]Roos and Wirth, *Flavii Arriani,* 2:1-73.

[238]See Chattopadhyaya, *Periplus of the Erythraean Sea;* for the observation that follows above see ibid., 95.

[239]For the discussion that follows above see Casson 1994, 123-26; see also Ball 2000, 133-39.

[240]Cassius Dio 43.24.2; Tacitus, *Ann.* 2.33.

[241]Apollodoros, *FGrH* 779 F 7 (Apollodoros lived in Artemita in the early first century B.C.). See Dihle 1964, 92; 1983, 201.

[242]See William Watson, "Iran and China," *CHI* 3:537-58, esp. 540-42. On the trade relations with China see V. G. Lukonin, "Political, Social and Administrative Institutions: Taxes and Trade," *CHI* 3:681-746, esp. 738-44.

Around A.D. 100 a certain Alexandros explored for the first time the sea route to China; he reached Kattigara, the easternmost fixed point of the world since Ptolemaios.[243] Before A.D. 100 there were two routes to India (see fig. 22).[244]

1. The first route was the royal road through Parthia and via the so-called Silk Road[245] to China. This route proceeded from Antioch in Syria in a northeasterly direction via Zeugma to Edessa, from there in a southeasterly direction via Dura Europos to Seleucia (Kutal-Imara), again in a northeasterly direction via Artemita and Ecbatana (Hamadan) through the Caspian Gates south of the Caspian Sea to Hekatompylos (Damghan, the capital of Parthia), and in an easterly direction to Marv (Antiochia Margiana, Mary in Turkmenia). From Marv one could travel in a northeasterly direction to Samarkand (Maracanda) and via Farghana through the Terek Pass in the Pamir Mountains to Kashgar, or in a southeasterly direction via Balkh (the capital of Bactria) via the Tuan-Murun Pass to Kashgar. From Kashgar one would travel in a southeasterly direction (via Yarkand, Khotan and Loutan) or in a northeasterly direction (via Aksu and Turfan), passing the Taklimakan Desert of the Tibetan Plateau to An-hsi, and inside the Great Wall to Lo-yang and Xian (Chang'an).

In the first century A.D. both Indians and Chinese lived in Khotan (Yotqan). Coins dating to this time have Chinese script on the obverse and Indian Prakrit letters on the reverse. The available information about the political history of Khotan comes nearly entirely from Chinese sources. Between A.D. 58 and 75 the general of Khotan named Hsiu-mo-pa rebelled against the king of So-chü (Yarkand) and made himself king of Khotan. His successor Kuang-te, the son of his older brother, destroyed Yarkand and expanded the power of Khotan as far as Shu-lo (Kashgar). Since the second century A.D. Khotan was an important cultural and religious center.[246]

---

[243]Ptolemaios 1.14. See Dihle 1962, 90; 1978, 147. For the sea route via Indonesia, mentioned since the fifth century, see O. W. Wolters, *Early Indonesian Commerce: A Study of the Origins of Srivijaya* (Ithaca, N.Y.: Cornell University Press, 1967), 35, quoted in Casson 1989, 27. Kattigara has been identified with almost every harbor city between Singapore, Manila and Canton; see A. Hermann, PW 11.1 (1921): 46-50, s.v. "Kattigara"; E. Polaschek, PWSup 10 (1965): 703; Casson 1978, 148.

[244]Cf. *Periplus Maris Erythraei* 64.21; Ptolemaios 1.17.4. See James O. Thomson, *History of Ancient Geography* (Cambridge: Cambridge University Press, 1948), 177-81, 306-12; William Watson, "Iran and China," *CHI* 3:537-58, esp. 544-48; Joseph Needham, *Science and Civilisation in China* (7 vols.; Cambridge: Cambridge University Press, 1954-1971), 1:181-82 ("Introductory Orientations"), 4.3:17-18 ("Physics and Physical Technology: Civil Engineering and Nautics"); J. Ferguson, "China and Rome," *ANRW* II.9.2 (1980): 581-605; Dihle 1983; Casson 1989, 26-27.

[245]The name "Silk Road" goes back to the German geographer Ferdinand von Richthofen, who coined it in 1875. On the myth of the Silk Road, which never existed as an "organized" route to China, see Ball 2000, 137-39.

[246]See R. E. Emmerick, *Tibetan Texts Concerning Khotan* (London: Oxford University Press, 1967); idem, "Iranian Settlement East of the Pamirs," *CHI* 3:263-75, esp. 265-66; Harold W. Bailey, *Khotanese Texts* (London: Cambridge University Press, 1969); idem, *The Culture of the Sakas in Acient Iranian Khotan* (Delmar, N.Y.: Caravan, 1982).

2. The second route, via India, allowed the traveler to avoid the politically unstable regions east of the Roman Empire. One could travel from western India north through Bactria, continuing on the Silk Road through the Pamir Mountains to Kashgar and via An-hsi to Xian, or from eastern India via the Ganges Delta to Tamralipti (Tamluk) and Pataliputra (Patna), and from there via Mathura to Bactria and join there the Silk Road.

Periplus Maris Erythraei provides the following information about China: "Beyond this region [i.e., the Ganges Delta], by now at the northernmost point, where the sea ends somewhere on the outer fringe, there is a very great inland city called Thina from which silk floss, yarn, and cloth are shipped by land via Bactria to Barygaza and via the Ganges River back to Limyrike. It is not easy to get to this Thina; for rarely do people come from it, and only a few" (64.11-17). This is the oldest known reference to Thina. Ptolemaios speaks of "Sinai or Thinai, the capital" (7.3.6) but usually relates "Sinai" only to the country (7.3.1). Both terms derive via Sanskrit from Ch'in, the name of the great dynasty (221-206 B.C.) that unified China and whose first ruler began to build the Great Wall. The capital was Hien-yang, later known as Si-gnan-fu, on the Wei River, near the confluence with the Ho-ang-ho River (in the modern province of Shen-si).[247]

Ptolemaios records a remarkable number of facts about China.[248] He knows the borders (6.16.1); mountains: Anniba, Auxakia, Asmiraia, Kasia, Thaguron, Emoda, Ottorokorras (6.16.2); the most important rivers with their sources: Oichordas, Bautes (6.16.3); the peoples living in Serike (Anthropogagoi [i.e., "cannibals"], Anniboi, Sizyges, Damnai, Piaddai, Oichardai, Garenaioi, Nabannai, Issedones, Throanoi, Ethaguroi, Aspakarai, Batai, Ottorokorrai); and cities for which he provides (as he does for the mountains and rivers) longitude and latitude: Damna, Piada, Asmiraia, Tharrana, Issedon Serike, Aspakara, Drosache, Paliana, Abragana, Thogara, Daxata, Orosana, Ottotokorra, Solana, Sera Metropolis (6.16.6-8).

The earliest reliable evidence for the presence of Jews in China comes from Khotan (Sinkiang province) in western China, dating to the eighth century A.D. Jews lived on the eastern coast and in the interior of China by the ninth century at the latest. During unrest in Canton in A.D. 878/879, about 120,000 Moslems, Jews and other foreigners were killed. In the ninth century the emperor extended an invitation to a thousand Jews, probably from India or Persia, to settle with their wives and children in Kaifeng (Hunan province).[249] David Selbourne recently translated a travel narrative of the Jewish merchant Jacob d'Ancona, from 1270 (four years before Marco Polo), who is said to have traveled to China, where he encountered a Jewish community in the city of Zaitun (mod. Quanzhou);[250] the authenticity of this narrative can be clarified only when the manuscript can be examined, which the owners thus far have not allowed.

---

[247]See Schoff, *Periplus*, 261; Casson 1989, 238.

[248]The orthography of Chinese names follows the translation by Humbach and Ziegler, *Ptolemy: Geography*, 201-11.

[249]See Rudolf Loewenthal, "China," *EncJud* 5:468-71.

[250]Jacob d'Ancona, *The City of Light* (ed. D. Selbourne; Secaucus, N.J.: Citadel, 2000 [1997]). In 1972 official figures listed twenty-one Jews living in China: fifteen in Shanghai and six in Harbin; see I. Eber, "China," *Encyclopaedia Judaica Decennial Book 1973-1982* (Jerusalem: Keter, 1982), 208-9.

Conclusions

There is sufficient evidence to conclude that Jesus' disciples and the first apostles thought in terms of the Greco-Roman "maximum perspective." (1) Soon after Pentecost, Jerusalem Christians had contacts with an Ethiopian who converted to faith in Jesus (Acts 8:27-39). (2) Paul mentions Scythians in Col 3:11, suggesting the possibility that a converted Scythian slave was a member of the church in Colossae. Apparently Johann Bengel was the first to make this suggestion: "Fortasse Colossis erat unus alterque Scytha Christianus."[251] (3) Paul plans further missionary work in Spain (Rom 15:24, 28) and writes a long letter to the Christians in Rome in the context of these plans, in which the church in Rome is to play a major role. (4) India is not mentioned in the New Testament, but it was known to the Jews. However, Gaza is mentioned in Acts 8:26—Gaza, the ancient harbor city that was under direct Jewish influence since 99 B.C., was ruled by Herod I since 37 B.C., and was famous as a center of trade with Arabia that reached as far as India.

If Jesus' disciples indeed thought in terms of the geographical maximum perspective, the question arises whether they would have felt responsible for reaching all regions and peoples known at the time with the gospel of Jesus Christ. Many scholars do not even raise this question; others label the question as anachronistic. This possibility should not be dismissed hurriedly, however. Many Christians in the first century were willing to die for their faith in Jesus Christ. They risked much more for their convictions than ever would many critics of early Christian traditions. Sacrifice and courage were all that the apostles needed in order to travel to Germania or Spain, to Ethiopia or to Scythia or to India. The later traditions of early Christian missionaries in India, Scythia and Ethiopia may be not mere legends after all.

James Scott suggests that the missionary program of the early Christians was based, in geographical terms, on the table of nations in Gen 10, which, he argues, is important both for the structure of the book of Acts and for Pauline texts. According to Scott, the apostles divided the missionary task in geographical spheres of responsibility along the lines of the regions in which the sons of Noah lived: Peter was responsible for the mission to "Shem" (Acts 2:1—8:25), Philip for the mission to "Ham" (Acts 8:26-40), and Paul for the mission to "Japheth" (Acts 9:1—28:31).[252] This suggestion is attractive from a tradition-historical point of view and can illuminate some details of the geographical route of the apostle Paul, but it is unconvincing on historical grounds. The following five factors need to be considered. (1) It has not been demonstrated that Paul "consulted" the table of nations in Gen 10 when he made tactical decisions concerning the cities in which he would do missionary work. (2) The fact that Paul was open to divine guidance suggests a basic flexibility that appears to make geographical aspects a secondary concern. (3) The suggestion that Paul's

---

[251]Bengel, *Gnomon Novi Testamenti,* 806; cf. Michel, *ThWNT* 7:450-51 (*TDNT* 7:449-50); D. Campbell 1996. See §27.3 in the present work.

[252]J. M. Scott 1994, 522-44; 1995, 135-80; 2000 (on the list of nations in Acts 2:9-11); 2002, 56-96.

vehement reaction in Antioch concerning Peter was motived by the fact, criticized by Paul, that Peter and the "men from James" did missionary work in the "Japheth region," thus violating the earlier territorial agreement,[253] is hardly convincing: the dispute in Antioch did not concern geographical or territorial jurisdictions but rather the relations between converted polytheists and messianic Jews. (4) If 1 Pet 1:1 lists regions in which Peter not only knows Christians but also was involved in missionary work, then Scott's thesis founders on the overlap of missionary areas in Asia Minor in which both Paul and Peter were active. The assumption that Peter was involved in missionary work in these areas *before* the apostolic council (i.e., between A.D. 42-48)[254] is hypothetical. The assertion that Peter and his emissaries "intruded" into areas that Paul regarded as "his territory" is not only hypothetical but also groundless: it founders on the entirely unpolemical reference to the missionary activity of Peter in 1 Cor 9:5. The assumption that Peter followed the geographical identifications of *Jub.* 8—9 according to which all of Asia Minor was included in his "jurisdiction" for Shem, which caused the conflict and misunderstandings among the apostles, likewise is hypothetical. (5) We must recall that the identification of the descendants of Noah and his sons in the various Jewish (and early patristic) traditions is not uniform. For example, in regard to the descendants of Japheth, we find the following variations:[255]

Gomer		Galatians (Josephus), Phrygia (Targum), Cappadocians (Hippolytus)
	Ashkenaz	Reginians (Josephus), Asia (Targum), Thelez (Pseudo-Philo), Sarmatai (Hippolytus)
	Riphath	Paphlagonians (Josephus), Parthians (Targum), Lud (Pseudo-Philo), Adiabene (*Genesis Rabbah*)
	Togarmah	Phrygians (Josephus), barbarians in northern Europe (Targum), Armenians (Hippolytus)
Magog		Scythians (Josephus), Germans (Targum), Celts/Galatians (Hippolytus)
Madai		Medes
Javan		Ionians/Greeks
	Elishah	Aeolians (Josephus), Hellas (Targum), Sikeloi (Hippolytus)
	Tarshish	Tarsus/Cilicia (Josephus), Iberians/Spain (Hippolytus)
	Kittim	Cyprus (Josephus), Achaia (Targum), Italy (Targum), Romans (Hippolytus)
	Dodanim	Rhodes (1 Chronicles), Dardania (Targum)
Tubal		Iberians/Spain (Josephus), Europe from Bulgaria to France (*Jubilees*), Bithynia (*Genesis Rabbah*)
Meshech		Cappadocians (Josephus), Mysia (Targum), Spain/France (*Jubilees*), Illyricum (Hippolytus)
Tiras		Thracians (Josephus; Targum), the islands in the Mediterranean except Crete (*Jubilees*)

16.3 Strategy and Tactics

Today questions of strategy and tactics are discussed in terms of the military,

---

[253]J. M. Scott 1995, 149-62, esp. 150, 158-59.

[254]See J. M. Scott 1995, 161 n. 122; Scott does not, however, commit to this view; for the comments that follow above see ibid., 161-62.

[255]For the data that follows above see J. M. Scott 1995, 48-49 (table 3).

politics and the business world. In the ancient world strategic and tactical considerations are found primarily in the first two areas: the military and rhetoric. Strategy is concerned with the planning of an engagement and with the question of how plans can and should be realized in specific operations, while tactics deal with the phase immediately before the operation as well as with the actions and reactions on the battlefield. These two areas are not always distinguished, neither today nor in antiquity. The literary sources are less concerned with strategic deliberations; they focus more strongly on tactical interests.[256]

Carl von Clausewitz defined the conduct of war as "the arrangement and conduct of combat. If this combat were a single act, there would be no necessity for any further subdivision. But combat is composed of a more or less large number of single acts, each complete in itself, which we call engagements . . . and which form new units. From this two different activities spring: individually arranging and conducting these single engagements and combining them with one another to attain the object of the war. The former is called tactics, the latter, strategy. . . . According to our classification, therefore, tactics teaches the use of the armed forces in engagements, and strategy the use of engagements to attain the object of the war."[257] Strategy "must therefore give an aim to the whole military action, which aim must be in accordance with the object of the war. In other words, strategy maps out the plan of the war, and to the aforesaid aim it affixes the series of acts which are to lead to it; that is, it makes the plans for the separate campaigns and arranges the engagements to be fought in each of them."[258] Clausewitz discusses under the heading "strategy" moral quantities (the spirit and the moral qualities of the military and political leadership, public opinion, the moral effect of victory or of defeat), the talents of the commander and of the army, boldness, perseverance, superiority in numbers, surprise, stratagem, assembly of forces in space, assembly of forces in time, the strategic reserve, the economy of forces, the geometrical element in the disposition of the forces, the suspension of action in warfare, the character of modern war, tension and rest as the dynamic law of war. Tactics is "the construction of the engagement," which Clausewitz defines as combat in which "the object is the destruction or the overcoming of the opponent," in accordance with his definition of war as "an act of force to compel our adversary to do our will." He states that "conflict between men really consists of two different elements: hostile feeling and hostile intention," and he asserts that "all war presupposes human weakness, and against that it is directed," with the goal to win the victory, which consists "not merely in the conquest of the battlefield, but in the destruction of physical and moral forces."

Modern dictionaries define strategy generally as "a plan for successful action

---

[256]See Fergus Millar, "Emperors, Frontiers and Foreign Relations, 31 BC to AD 378," *Britannia* 13 (1982): 1-23, esp. 21; Austin and Rankov 1995, 12.

[257]Karl von Clausewitz, *On War,* in *The Book of War* (trans. O. J. M. Jolles; New York: Modern Library, 2000), 329-30. Cf. the most recent German edition: Carl von Clausewitz, *Vom Kriege* (19th ed.; 3 parts in 1 vol.; Bonn: Dümmlers, 1980), 270-71.

[258]Clausewitz, *On War,* 390 (*Vom Kriege,* 345). For the remarks that follow above see *On War,* on "strategy," 390-449 (*Vom Kriege,* 345-416), on "tactics," 452, 455 (*Vom Kriege,* 419, 422), the definition of "war," 264 (*Vom Kriege,* 191-92), on "conflict," 265 (*Vom Kriege,* 193), on "weakness," 491 (*Vom Kriege,* 465), on "conquest," 260 (*Vom Kriege,* 182-83).

based on the rationality and interdependence of the moves of the opposing participants," as "the science and art of employing the political, economic, psychological, and military forces of a nation or group of nations to afford the maximum support to adopted policies in peace or war . . . a careful plan or method: a clever stratagem, the art of devising or employing plans or stratagems toward a goal."[259] In the following chapters, for the terms "strategy" and "tactics" this general meaning is presupposed, leaving out of consideration the military dimension of their usage. Such a caveat is necessary not only on church-historical grounds—there are the bad memories of the crusades, which were the antithesis of missionary work as understood by the apostles in the first century—but also on hermeneutical grounds, as is demonstrated by Clausewitz's comment on the use of force made in the paragraph that immediately follows his definition of war:

"Now philanthropic souls might easily imagine that there was an artistic way of disarming or overthrowing our adversary without too much bloodshed and that this was what the art of war should seek to achieve. However agreeable this may sound, it is a false idea which must be demolished. In affairs so dangerous as war, false ideas proceeding from kindness of heart are precisely the worst. As the most extensive use of physical force by no means excludes the co-operation of intelligence, he who uses this force ruthlessly, shrinking from no amount of bloodshed, must gain an advantage if this adversary does not do the same. Thereby he forces his adversary's hand, and thus each pushes the other to extremities to which the only limitation is the strength of resistance on the other side. This is how the matter must be regarded, and it is a waste—and worse than a waste—of effort to ignore the element of brutality because of the repugnance it excites."[260]

The early Christian missionaries endured persecution; in some cases they willingly risked death, more often they had to flee, ceding the "battlefield" to the enemy, accepting "personal defeat" for the following reasons. (1) The first Christians were a minority, even in Jerusalem, where there were thousands of believers in Jesus Christ, according to Luke. They were a minority with no political access and with no chance of initiating any countermeasures. This, however, is only a superficial reason, not the real grounds for their renunciation of force. (2) The first Christians practiced Jesus' command to love one's enemies and relinquish force.[261] Exhortations to endure injustice can be found also in Greek and Roman writings as well as in the Old Testament and in other Jewish texts.[262]

---

[259]These are the definitions of the *OED* and of Merriam-Webster. For German definitions see G. Wahrig, *Deutsches Wörterbuch* (9th ed.; Munich: Mosaik, 1988), 1239.

[260]Clausewitz, *On War*, 265 (*Vom Kriege*, 192).

[261]Mt 5:38-48; Lk 6:27-36; cf. Peter and Jesus in the passion narrative: Mt 26:51-52; Mk 14:47; Lk 22:49; Jn 18:11.

[262]Ex 23:4-5; Prov 24:17; 25:21; Philo, *Virt.* 23.117; 1QS X, 17-18; *T. Benj.* 4.3; *T. Jos.* 18:2; Plato, *Gorg.* 469c; Thucydides 4.19.1-4; Diogenes Laertius 8.23; Seneca, *Ben.* 4.26.1; *Ira* 2.33.2; Epictetus, *Diatr.* 3.22.54. See Bovon, *Lk,* 1:313; Luz, *Mt,* 1:293.

However, in Mt 5:38-42 no motivation is given for the renunciation of force, which is significant. Ulrich Luz observes that "a resigned element is missing: 'Give in, for there is no other course of action.' An optimistic calculating is missing: 'By giving in, you make friends of your enemies.' Any hint which could explain these demands as prudent and reasonable is missing."[263] The exhortation to love one's enemy and to relinquish violence is not just a provocative protest against the vicious cycle of violence as a "sigh of the oppressed" but the expression and consequence of the arrival of the kingdom of God, which comes to people in Jesus' ministry as "limitless love of God for the people which on its part makes possible the love of humans among themselves and even for their enemies." The first Christians wanted to bring God's forgiveness and love to people, following the example of Jesus, who forgave his enemies and who let himself be condemned and remained hanging on the cross despite his messianic authority. This "strategic" goal discounts any tactical measure that would force other people, whether sympathetic, indifferent or hostile, to do their (or God's) will. (3) The leaders of the Jerusalem church wanted to "catch" people as *apostoloi* sent by Jesus; that is, they wanted to win them for faith in Jesus as Messiah, which is the opposite of destroying them. Opponents of the early Christian missionaries were not only Sadducees and the scribes of the Sanhedrin who arranged for their arrest and forced their expulsion: their mission addressed all people who had not (yet) accepted Jesus as Messiah, who thus rejected God's new redemptive revelation and who were in *that* sense the enemies of God (Rom 5:10). When God seeks reconciliation with his enemies by sending his Son to die on the cross, his messengers can hardly afford to encounter people with "hostile feeling" (Clausewitz): they do not pursue hostile intentions but rather seek to help people accept God's offer of forgiveness and salvation. Missionaries do not fight against people but against arguments and the pride that sets itself up against the true knowledge of God (2 Cor 10:4-5), not against flesh and blood but "against the cosmic powers of this present darkness, against the spiritual forces of evil in the heavenly places" (Eph 6:12). This is why they do *not* fight "according to human standards" (2 Cor 10:3). Missionaries do not seek to take advantage of human weakness, but they fight with "the weapons of righteousness for the right hand and for the left" (2 Cor 6:7); that is, their weapons consist of the righteousness that they have received from God because of their faith in Jesus Christ and that thus characterizes their moral behavior.[264] They are weapons of "light" (Rom 13:12), the "sword of the Spirit, which is the word of God" (Eph 6:17)—that is, the message of the gospel with which God has entrusted them, which God has made possible and makes effective. They do not want to "destroy" combatants or "conquer" battlefields. They want to win peo-

---

[263]Luz, *Mt*, 1:294 (ET, 1:326-27); for the remarks that follow above see ibid., 1:295-96 (ET, 1:328).
[264]See Martin, *2 Cor*, 178-79; Thrall, *2 Cor*, 1:461-62.

ple and integrate them into the community of the followers of Jesus, to whom they themselves belong.

It is not certain whether the reference to the right hand and the left hand in 2 Cor 6:7 is intended to refer to weapons of attack and weapons of defense, to the sword and the shield.[265] Paul probably simply emphasizes the completeness of the equipment.

I define "missionary strategy" as the reflection on the assignment given to the disciples by Jesus to reach "all nations" as far as "the ends of the earth," including planning for the fulfillment of this assignment in specific actions in Jerusalem, in Judea, in Samaria and in the provinces and regions outside of Palestine. And I define "missionary tactics" as the preparation of the specific evangelistic outreach of a missionary or a team of missionaries in a particular region or city, and the concrete implementation of the missionary work, adapted to local conditions and peculiarities, from the first contact and the proclamation of the gospel before Jews and Gentiles to the establishment of a community of believers in Jesus Christ.

First the question needs to be raised whether the Roman emperors pursued a global strategy with which we might compare the early Christian mission, whose missionaries aspired to carry the message of Jesus Christ to the "ends of the earth." After surveying several examples of strategic planning in the Greco-Roman world, I will attempt to answer the question of what kind of strategic thinking and planning may be presupposed for the early Christian missionaries.

Rome and Global Strategies

Did the Roman emperors pursue a comprehensive geopolitical strategy? Edward Luttwak, in a larger study, answers this question positively. He distinguishes three phases: (1) The strategy of the Julian-Claudian emperors relied on the instrument of "forceful suasion." (2) During the time of the Flavian and Antoninian emperors "scientific borders" were established that served the sole purpose of defending the empire (preclusive forward defense). (3) In the third century the emperors developed in depth a system of elastic defense. In more recent studies, Arthur Ferrill and Everett Wheeler also argue that the Roman emperors pursued a global strategy.[266] Others question the position of these scholars. John Mann analyzes empirical and archaeological facts and argues that every border of the Roman Empire had its own explanation, that a unified strategic principle is neither necessary nor recognizable. Benjamin Isaac ar-

---

[265]Thus Lietzmann, *1-2 Kor,* 128; Bultmann, *2 Kor,* 174 (ET, 172); A. Oepke, *ThWNT* 5:293 (*TDNT* 5:294); G. Schneider, *EWNT* 1:365 (*EDNT* 1:152).

[266]Luttwak 1976; Ferrill 1991; Everett L. Wheeler, "Methodological Limits and the Mirage of Roman Strategy," *Journal of Military History* 57 (1993): 7-41, 215-40. The standard work by Delbrück (1964-1966) is not very helpful for this issue.

gues that there was no comprehensive strategy that Roman military commanders followed, as decisions were made by ad hoc groups. Fergus Millar describes the emperors as rulers who only rarely took the initiative, usually
reacting merely ad hoc to events.[267] For the people who lived in the provinces
experienced the presence of the emperor not in a stream of decisions and laws
but rather in statues and inscriptions. Theoretically the governors in the provinces were responsible for everything that happened in their province, but the
small Roman administrative staff—a higher official in Roman provincial administration was "responsible" for 350,000 people—probably did not prompt any
expectations that its actions would be the expression of a consistent provincial
policy.[268] Charles Whittaker argues that while one should not deny that the Roman emperors and senate did some strategic thinking, there is no evidence for
a global strategy in terms of an integrated pursuit of specific mid-range and
longer-range political goals.[269]

Evidence for strategic thinking can be found in, for example, the *Historia Romana* of Velleius Paterculus (2.106), written in A.D. 29/30, in which he praises the "precaution" of
Tiberius, who sent the fleet to the Elbe River in order to supply the army with provisions.[270] Strabo (2.5.8) and Appian (*Prooemium* 5) comment that the border regions of
the barbarians are not profitable, comments that probably reflect an evaluation of the economic consequences of an annexation.[271]

The ideological goal, deeply anchored in the Roman psyche, to expand the
power of Rome *sine fine*[272] must be distinguished from a strategy that discusses
various options of operative procedure and carefully weighs possible consequences. Ideology and strategy are not the same thing.[273]

The Roman border ideology distinguished between direct rule over an area (ἀρχή, *archē*)
and indirect rule (ἡγεμονία, *hēgemonia*). The cosmological worldview that existed already
in the time of the Roman Republic was propagated by Augustus: the city of Rome, situated
in the center of the world, has the right to control the nations (*gentes*) outside the boundaries of Roman rule (*termini imperii*) through kings and through alliances, and to expand
the borders (*termini*) through justified wars (*belli iusti*). In this worldview the world con-

---

[267]J. Mann 1974; 1979; Isaac 1993, 19-53, 372-418; Millar 1992 (cf. Bleicken 1982); 1993; 1996.
[268]Bendlin 1997, 41 with n. 21.
[269]C. Whittaker 1994; idem, "Where Are the Frontiers Now?" in D. Kennedy 1996, 25-42.
[270]Strabo's comment (7.1.5) that Tiberius "saw the sources of the Ister" (i.e., the Danube River)
     after his successful campaign against the northern tribes beyond the Alps in the year 15 B.C.
     probably reflects both scientific and military interests. See Bernecker 1989, 59.
[271]See F. Lassère, "Strabon devant l'empire romain," *ANRW* II.30 (1983): 867-96.
[272]David Potter ("Emperors, Their Borders and Their Neighbours: The Scope of Imperial *man-
     data*," in D. Kennedy 1996, 49-66, esp. 60) shows that the annexations made by Tiberius,
     Claudius, Nero, Hadrian, Antoninus and Marcus Aurelius can be explained with the character
     of these emperors rather than with an ideology of world conquest.
[273]Whittaker, "Where Are the Frontiers Now?"

sisted of three areas: in the center, the civilized world (i.e., the territories under Roman administration); next, the territories not governed by Rome but under Roman rule; finally, at the periphery the *gentes externae*, who extend as far as the *oceani*. When Virgil spoke of a "empire without end" (*imperium sine fine* [*Aen.* 1.279, 287]), he did not describe a Roman strategy of world conquest but rather expressed the claim to the unrestricted *right* to rule as far as the Oceanus, to the end of the world.

The Roman emperors of the first century did not maintain a central intelligence service that would have been useful for strategic planning. This also makes it unlikely that Rome pursued a comprehensive geopolitical strategy.

The *frumentarii*, couriers between Rome and the provincial capitals who were stationed in the Castra Peregrina on Mons Caelius, were something like a security agency, which, however, was not organized as a military intelligence service. Similarly the bureau of the procurator *ab epistulis*, who was responsible for the imperial correspondence, who sometimes also dealt with foreign embassies (Statius, *Silvae* 5.1.85-100), and who employed an archivist (*scriniarius* [*CIL* X:527]), evidently was not responsible for evaluating the existing news for strategic purposes. Information that was relevant for the military was collected by the procurators in the border provinces.[274]

Examples of Strategic Planning in Antiquity

Using the criterion of Polybius, the great Greek historian, according to which the historian who has personal and pertinent experience can write about battles with greater knowledge and authority (12.28a.7-10; 3.48.12), several authors are relevant for a description of military strategy and tactics: Cato,[275] Caesar, Cicero, and Sallust in the second and first centuries B.C.; Flavius Josephus, Frontinus, Tacitus and Velleius Paterculus in the first century A.D.; Flavius Arrianus[276] and Cassius Dio in the second and third centuries; Ammianus Marcellinus in the fourth century. Authors of military handbooks include Polybius[277] and Asklepiodotos[278] in the second and first centuries B.C.; Aelianus,[279] Onasander[280] and

---

[274]Austin and Rankov 1995, 135-41.

[275]M. Porcius Cato, the most famous figure in Rome in the second century B.C., composed a military treatise titled *De re militari,* which has not survived. It probably was used by Flavius Vegetius; see Delbrück 1964-1966, 2:211-12.

[276]Roos and Wirth, *Flavii Arriani,* 2:129-176; cf. Wheeler, "Flavius Arrianus," 329-78.

[277]Polybius's work on military tactics (cf. 9.20.4) is lost.

[278]Asklepiodotos's work on tactics (τακτικὰ κεφάλαια) discussed in twelve chapters the military battle formations on the battlefield; apparently he had no interest in questions of military strategy. See C. H. Oldfather and W. A. Oldfather, *Aeneas Tacticus, Asclepiodotus, Onasander* (LCL; Cambridge, Mass.: Harvard University Press, 1962 [1923]), 244-332; Lucien Poznanski, *Asclépiodote: Traité de Tactique; Texte établi et traduit* (Paris: Les Belles Letters, 1992).

[279]H. Köchly and W. Rüstow, *Asclepiodotos' Taktik, Aelianos' Theorie der Taktik,* in *Griechische Kriegsschriftsteller: Griechisch und Deutsch, mit kritischen und erklärenden Anmerkungen* (2 vols. in 3; Osnabrück: Biblio Verlag, 1969 [1855]), 2.1:218-470.

[280]Oldfather and Oldfather, *Aeneas Tacticus, Asclepiodotus, Onasander,* 368-526.

Polyaenus[281] in the first and second centuries A.D.; Flavius Vegetius[282] in the fourth century; the author of Περὶ Στρατηγίας (*Peri Stratēgias;* Pseudo-Mauricius)[283] in the sixth century.

The military campaign of Alexander the Great, without parallel in the ancient world, taking him from Macedonia to Egypt, Persia and India, had profound and lasting effects in areas thousands of kilometers away from his home base. No people and hardly any of the larger cities between Corinth in the west and Barbarikon on the mouth of the Indus River were untouched by the influence of Greek culture and its institutions, not even Judea. The strategic methods and tactical maneuvers of the Macedonian general were well known, at least for interested observers. More than 450 years after Alexander's death Greco-Roman authors still discussed him: one of the most important descriptions of Alexander is the *Anabasis* of Flavius Arrianus, a work that describes in seven books Alexander's campaigns. Alexander's military strategy relied on four elements:[284]

(1) Securing the base. Alexander made sure, with force if necessary but also through tax reductions, that he had the support of the cities of Macedonia, Thessaly, Boeotia, Attica, Achaia and Asia Minor. (2) Neutralization of enemy cities. Alexander conquered the harbor cities of the Persian allies and thus denied the Persian fleet, which he could never hope to defeat directly, its operational base. (3) Destruction of the enemy. Alexander engaged the Persian army and defeated it numerous times, at the end decisively. (4) Consolidation. Alexander conquered the Persian capital as well as the Persian territories as far as India and appointed governors in the provinces.

With regard to the specific tactical procedures of Alexander, the following factors are important.

(1) Alexander was superb at solving logistical problems. During his campaign against the Persians he had to supply an army of thirty thousand to fifty thousand soldiers. Among the reasons why he managed this feat is that he considered climate, geography, transport resources and harvest times in the course of his planning; other factors were the limitation of the baggage train, the active acquisition of intelligence concerning the area controlled by the enemy, and the capitulation of enemy garrisons that resulted from negotiations of advance troops. Similarly, Hannibal's long voyage of 1,500 km through Gaul and across the Alps to Italy in 218 B.C. was the result of careful advance planning: the agents that he

[281]E. Woelfflin and J. Melber, *Polyaeni strategematon libri viii* (Stuttgart: Teubner, 1970 [1887]); cf. Friedel Schindler, *Die Überlieferung der Stratagamata des Polyainos* (Vienna: Österreichische Akademie der Wissenschaften, 1973).

[282]For the Latin text and a German translation see Friedhelm Müller (1997); also the English translation by Nicholas Milner (1993) and the Teubner edition by Alf Önnerfors (1995). In regard to the English translation by Leo Stelten (1990) see the scathing critique in *Gnomon* 65 (1993): 494-98.

[283]George T. Dennis, *Maurice's Strategikon: Handbook of Byzantine Military Strategy* (Philadelphia: University of Pennsylvania Press, 1984).

[284]See Delbrück 1964-1966, 1:178-235; John F. C. Fuller, *The Generalship of Alexander the Great* (New Brunswick, N.J.: Rutgers University Press, 1960); Engels 1978; May et al. 1984, 19-41.

sent ahead of his army arranged alliances with the tribes in Gaul, organized supplies and investigated the best routes.[285] (2) Alexander was extremely flexible both in the planning and in the execution of battles, which often demanded courage bordering on audacity. He was, for example, able to turn the disadvantage of a defensive drawback into the advantage of offensive action. Similarly, the successes of the Seleucid army in the third and second centuries B.C. can be explained partly in terms of the flexibility with which its generals planned the reaction to enemy ambushes and blockages of roads.[286] (3) Alexander was able to make tactical use of the technical diversification of weapons and other war matériel.

Julius Caesar knew the significance of strategic information about the enemy, which was necessary in order to plan the course of a military campaign and to plan the procurement of the required resources. In *Bellum Gallicum* he describes extensively the preparations for the invasion of Britannia in 55 B.C. Since he was able to obtain only scant information about the size of the island, about the tribes living there, about their strength, their manner of doing battle, their constitution and the quality of the harbors from traders, he sent the tribune C. Volusenus to collect this information. Since this proved to be unsuccessful, he decided to cross the channel to Britannia, even though the time of the year was unfavorable for a military campaign, "in order to see into the character of the people and to know their localities, harbors, and landing-places" (*genus hominum perspexisset, loca portus aditus cognovisset* [*Bell. gall.* 4.20.2-4]). Caesar knew that geographical, ethnic, social, political, military and psychological information about the enemy is of crucial importance for the planning of a campaign. The fact that he landed in Britannia without having such vital information made the venture risky—Polybius would not have been pleased.[287] In his description of the Gauls, Caesar repeatedly refers to their weaknesses (from a Roman point of view), which he took into account in his military planning: their instability, unreliability, arrogance, lack of stamina after setbacks, and divisions among their tribes and even in their families (*Bell. gall.* 3.19.6; 4.5; 6.11; 7.42.2). His descriptions of the Germans demonstrates detailed knowledge about their religion, way of life, military training, agriculture, land ownership (inhibited by the aristocracy), courage, behavior in defensive or offensive battles, civil constitution, hospitality, relationship with the Gauls, game population (*Bell. gall.* 6.21-28).

Ammianus Marcellinus, a Greek from Antioch in Syria and a Roman historian, had ten years of military experience as *protector domesticus* (15.5.22) and had

---

[285]See May et al. 1994, 53; Max Zlattner, *Hannibals Geheimdienst im Zweiten Punischen Krieg* (Xenia 39; Konstanz: Universitätsverlag, 1997).

[286]See Bar-Kochva 1976, 204-5.

[287]Note the comment by Polybius (3.48) that an experienced and responsible general, in this case Hannibal, does not move into an area for which he lacks detailed geographical, political and social information; similarly Vegetius, *Epitoma* 3.6. See Austin and Rankov 1995, 13, 99-101.

served in intelligence and as general officer. In the writing of his *Roman History*
he could build not only on the *Historiae* of Tacitus but also on his own military
experience, and thus was totally dependent upon the report of eyewitnesses
and official documents (15.1.1; 16.12.70), the other sources of his description.[288]

An analysis of Ammianus's historical narrative shows that he reflected on the following
elements of military strategy. (1) Collection and evaluation of strategic information about
topographical and chronological facts as well as about the strength, movements and plans
of the enemy. The collection of information relied on the relatively simple "methods" of
personal observation and inquiry from people with pertinent knowledge, in the context
of diplomatic missions, through espionage activities, through merchants who visited markets in border areas, less frequently through active reconnaissance. Ammianus knew, for
example, that knowledge of the language of the enemy was important: Hariobaudes was
sent by Emperor Julian in the spring of 359 to investigate the Alemans' war preparations
"for he was thoroughly acquainted with the language of the savages" (*sermonis barbarici
perquam gnarus* [18.2.2]); that is, he fluently spoke the local Aleman dialect.[289] (2) Strategic planning: continued supply of food and weapons at the right time and at the right
place are decisive, as is the availability of sufficient troop strength for the efficient realization of the military goals. Ammianus is convinced that "careful planning is victorious
over nearly all difficiulties" (*sed ut est difficultatum paene omnium diligens ratio uictrix*
[17.8.2]). (3) Execution of the operation: defensive or offensive actions, concentration of
superior battle strength, focus on the main goal with a simultaneous limitation of secondary goals. The decisive elements of military tactics are twofold: (1) the procurement of
tactical information through reconnaissance units of the army (*procursatores*), scouts (*ex-
ploratores*, κατασκόποι) and spies (*speculatores*), through personal observations (autopsy)
of the commanding general or an officer and through enemy sources such as prisoners,
deserters (*perfugae*), refugees or the local population, sometimes also through hearsay
(*rumor, fama*); (2) implementation of operations that have different tactical needs, as in,
for example, siege operations in which technical details of the machines are important,
or battles in the open field.

Flavius Vegetius collected the available material on military matters from older
sources in his work *Epitoma rei militaris,* which served as a military handbook
and textbook until the nineteenth century.[290] Vegetius probably dedicated this
work to Emperor Theodosius I (379-395), describes himself as a Christian (*Epitoma* 1 prol. 1; 2.5.3), and was similar to a finance minister and seems to have

---

[288]Besides the editions and translations by John C. Rolfe and Wolfgang Seyfarth see Norman J.
E. Austin, *Ammianus on Warfare: An Investigation into Ammianus' Military Knowledge* (Collection Latomus 165; Brussels: Latomus, 1979), 12-21; for the comments that follow above
see ibid, 22-163. See also Jan Willem Drijvers and David Hunt, eds., *The Late Roman World
and Its Historian: Interpreting Ammianus Marcellinus* (London: Routledge, 1999).
[289]On the tactical collection of information see Austin and Rankov 1995, 40-86. Translators are
documented on inscriptions: *CIL* III 10505, 10988, 14349, 14507; cf. Austin and Rankov 1995,
28-29.
[290]On Flavius Vegetius see Delbrück 1964-1966, 2:211-13; A. R. Neumann, "Vegetius," PWSup
10 (1965): 992-1020; idem, *KP* 5:1151-52; J. B. Campbell, *OCD* 1584; see also Milner, ed., *Vegetius,* xxxi-xxxvii; F. L. Müller, ed., *Publius Flavius Vegetius Renatus,* 12-25.

occupied the most influential position at the imperial court. He is the only military historian of antiquity who advises officers to use maps (3.6.4). Since Julius Caesar, a general, and Agrippa, an admiral, both supported the production of maps, we may safely assume that the military use of maps, itineraries and periploi was customary by the first century B.C.[291] Pliny provides relevant evidence for the first century A.D.

Pliny reproaches the expeditions of Domitius Corbulo (between 58 and 63 B.C.) to be responsible for making an erroneous designation of the Caspian Gates, as even "maps of the region sent home from the front have this name written on them" (*Nat.* 6.15.40). The expedition mentioned in *Nat.* 6.35.181 that was given the task to explore (*ad explorandum*) Ethiopia is linked in 12.8.19 with a map (*forma*) of Ethiopia that showed that there are few trees between Syene and Meroë.

A passage by Suetonius demonstrates that a distrustful emperor and an active general could notice dangers linked with geographical maps: Domitian commanded the execution of the consul Mettius Pompusianus not only because it was commonly reported that his horoscope predicted that he would rule the empire, and because he gave two of his slaves the names of Carthaginian generals, but also because he "carried about a map of the world on parchment (*quod depictum orbem terrae in membrana[s]*) and speeches of kings and generals from Titius Livius" (*Dom.* 10.3). The increasing use of parchment made it easier for travelers to carry maps.[292]

Several geographers recognized the fact that geographical information is of utmost importance for strategic military planning. Strabo refers to several military debacles that resulted from a lack of geographical information, and he points out that many courageous operations were successful "due to acquaintance with the regions involved" (1.1.17). Strabo believes that geographical knowledge is a necessary part of the instruments of the government of a ruler. At the same time he seeks to prove that his *Geography* is useful for the public as well (1.1.22). For Pliny, the description of geography is more useful than delightful on account of the difficulties that need to be overcome (*qui difficultatibus victis utilitatem iuvandi praetulerint gratiae placendi* [*Nat.* praef. 16]).[293]

Any discussion of the existence of a comprehensive, global strategy must recall that over 95 percent of the roughly three hundred institutes for strategic studies working in over fifty countries have existed only since the 1960s.[294] Observers of general staffs in the two world wars repeatedly pointed out that a "global strategy" existed only in very rare situations. Most decisions were made in the context of the interplay of thousands of often accidental facts, suggestions and events.

---

[291]See Dilke 1987a, 253.
[292]See Dilke 1987a, 254.
[293]Isaac 1996, 153-54.
[294]Isaac 1993, 378; for the comment that follows above see ibid.

Several sources for strategic information were available for a Roman governor. (1) Personal acquaintance with the province through a tour of inspection after taking office. The periplus of Flavius Arrianus is a pertinent example. (2) The client rulers in the provinces and in the border regions. The numerous diplomatic contacts that Josephus reports between the various kings and tetrarchs of Judea/Galilee and the Roman legates in Syria are a good example.[295] (3) The archives that were available to the staff (*officium*) of the governor, potentially containing information on a vast variety of issues. Between 100 and 150 persons worked in the "headquarters" of a province: officers of the general staff (*cornicularii, beneficiarii*), couriers (*frumentarii, speculatores*), people responsible for interrogations (*quaestionarii*), translators (*interpretes*), interpreters of portents and miraculous signs (*haruspices*), archivists (*librarii*), secretaries (*notarii*), tax collectors (*exacti*), stenographers (*exceptores*). In provinces in which three legions were stationed, the number of officials could increase to between 300 and 450 persons. For example, officials in the archives of the governor kept records in which each solder was listed with name and individual characteristics,[296] sometimes with the name of the horse assigned to him. Since the Roman army in Syria had about 30,000 soldiers in A.D. 150, including 7,000 cavalry, with 1,200 recruits every year, the archives in Antioch, the provincial capital, were constantly busy. The archivists also catalogued copies of documents and of letters that were sent to, for example, the individual commanders or to Rome. The archives presumably also stored the *commentarii* (lit., "memory aids"), the reports that the governors or the superior officers wrote about their expeditions and campaigns.[297] (4) The army officers who in many cases had served for several years in the province. A new procurator could be better informed about his province and about the border regions in a short time than could some official in Rome.[298]

In Egypt, and surely in other provinces, civilians were able to ask for copies of documents stored in the official archives. A papyrus that was discovered in Oxyrhynchus, dating to about A.D. 150, records a payment made to a "searcher of the archives of the prefect" (αἱρέτῃ ἡγεμονικῆς βιβλιοθήκ[ης] [P.Oxy. 1654]).[299]

At this point we need to take note of the *Onomastikon of the Biblical Place-Names,* written by the first Christian church historian, Eusebius, around A.D. 293.[300] This work is

---

[295]Josephus, *A.J.* 16.270; 18.150-154; 19.300-311, 326-327, 340-342; 20.1.

[296]Note P.Oxy. 1022: "Marcus Antonius Valens, 22 years old, mark on the right side of the forehead."

[297]The only autobiographical *commentarii* of a military general preserved in their entirety are Caesar's books on the Gallic War and on the Civil War. See A. von Premerstein, PW 4 (1901): 757-59; A. Lippold, *KP* 1:1257-59.

[298]Austin and Rankov 1995, 142-69.

[299]Austin and Rankov 1995, 160.

[300]For the observations that follow above see Isaac 1996.

unique in ancient geographical literature: it focuses deliberately on regional areas, specifically on Judea/Palestine, Arabia and Syria. The *Onomastikon* contains over nine hundred *lemmata* (dictionary entries) that mention twenty-nine cities and hundreds of villages, with references to mountains, plains, deserts, rivers and roads. Eusebius did not include a map; he presents his information in the format of the *itineraria*—that is, verbally with reference to distances that generally are correct.

The Strategy and Tactics of the Early Christian Missionaries

In the military, as well as in everyday life, strategic thinking generally means that what is unknown becomes known through proactive engagement in order to find out "what is on the other side of the hill" (Duke of Wellington).[301] If strategy is understood in this way, the most important factor in the strategic reflections of the apostles may have been the notion that their experiences in Jerusalem, the Jewish capital, or in Antioch, the Syrian metropolis, could be transferred to other large cities in the Roman Empire, and that their experiences in smaller towns and in villages could be applied in the towns and villages of other regions, both in the provinces of Roman Empire and beyond its borders. The following strategic goals and tactical measures of the early Christian missionaries can be described (for Paul see §24.3).

The strategic conception of the missionary outreach of the apostles can be described as follows.

1. Obedience to the missionary commission by Jesus Christ. The New Testament sources provide no evidence that the question of the suitability of followers of Jesus for missionary work was ever an issue.[302] The disciples came from very different backgrounds, as Rainer Riesner observes: "Beside the Galilean fishermen we find the man from the Jewish town of Karioth, beside the tax collector in the service of the political rulers we find a former partisan of the Zealots."[303] What Riesner says concerning the education of Jesus[304] applies *mutatis mutandis* to the disciples as well, at least some of them: "His devout parental home, . . . the visits to the synagogues in Nazareth and the surrounding region and the regular pilgrimages to Jerusalem could have provided him with a great deal of information, particularly about the Scriptures. As an attentive listener he would have learned much about exegesis and techniques of passing on tradition, even though he did not attach himself to a teacher." Jesus certainly was capable of matching wits with learned scribes. Luke informs us in the book of

---

[301]Austin and Rankov 1995, 7.

[302]See Padberg (1995, 50-51), with regard to the missionaries of the seventh century, who comments that at least initially the entire strategy was the obligation to be obedient to the sending principle.

[303]Riesner 1988, 411, with reference to Jn 6:71; Mt 9:9/Mk 2:14/Lk 5:27-28; Mt 10:3; Mk 3:17; Lk 6:15/Mt 10:4/Acts 1:13.

[304]See Riesner 1988, 206-45; the quotation that follows above, 244; on Jewish education see ibid., 97-206.

Acts that the same was true for some of his disciples. Matthew-Levi, formerly a
tax collector, must have been able to read and to write, and he must have been
fluent in Greek. Peter, Andrew and Philip came from Bethsaida (Jn 12:21), a village in the immediate vicinity of the city of Julias, which Herod Philip built; they
must have spoken Greek as well. The comment in Jn 12:21 confirms this for
Philip. The Galilean fishermen did not belong to the rural lower classes, but to
the commercial middle class. As Riesner suggests, it can be assumed that some
if not most of the Twelve came from devout families and would have had, like
Jesus, a solid basic education in the parental home, the synagogue and elementary school.[305] Jesus intended to train the disciples as "fishers of people," and he
commissioned them to engage in international missionary outreach after Easter.
If the disciples took Jesus seriously—and they were at least convinced that Jesus
was the Messiah!—and if they were prepared to be obedient and fulfill Jesus'
commission, then the assumption that they reflected specifically and in detail
about the implementation of their assignment is entirely plausible.

2. Proclamation of the good news of God's redemptive action in Jesus Christ
to as many people as possible, to Jews and to Gentiles, in all regions and among
all peoples, at every opportunity. Peter preaches to Jews in Jerusalem, the Jewish capital (Acts 2—4), and to Gentiles in Caesarea, the seat of the Roman governor (Acts 10). He is engaged in missionary work in Judea (Acts 2—4), Samaria
(Acts 8:25) and towns in the coastal plain (Acts 9:32—10:48). When he is arrested and dragged before the Sanhedrin together with John, where the leaders
of the Jewish people confront him, he uses the opportunity to explain their message of Jesus the Savior (Acts 4:8-12). This happened repeatedly (Acts 5:27-32).
The preaching takes place in houses (Acts 2:46-47), the Jerusalem temple (Acts
2:46; 5:12-13) and synagogues (Acts 6:8-9; 9:20). Some scholars argue that since
the book of Acts never specifically mentions missionary activity taking place in
private homes, one should not assume that the gatherings in houses had an
evangelistic dimension.[306] Even though this assessment is correct as far as explicit comments in Acts are concerned, it does not do justice to the historical
context in the first century: there was no reason whatsoever to exclude family
members and friends who did not (yet) accept faith in Jesus as the Messiah from
the gatherings in private homes. Since Luke links a comment in Acts 2:47 about
daily conversions with a comment in Acts 2:46 about daily gatherings in the
temple and in houses, the conclusion is at least plausible that inhabitants of Jerusalem were converted in house meetings organized by the followers of Jesus.

3. Establishment of communities of followers of Jesus, in which the God of
Abraham was worshiped as the only true God and in which Jesus was accepted
and believed as Messiah and Savior. It seems fair to assume that the apostles

[305]Riesner 1988, 413.
[306]See Blue (1998, 486), who emphasizes the gatherings in the temple; cf. ibid., 483, 485-86.

presupposed in their strategic deliberations that Jesus' commission to go to all nations to the ends of the earth and to establish communities of followers of Jesus was a feasible assignment that could be carried out (see §16.4).

The tactical actions of the early Christian missionaries can be observed in different situations and contexts.

1. Travels to towns and villages in which there were no followers of Jesus as of yet. Cities and towns were particularly important as goals of the missionary outreach of the early Christians. Philip traveled through "all the towns" of Samaria (Acts 8:40), and Paul, himself "a citizen of an important city" (Acts 21:39), engaged in missionary work "in the cities of the Mediterranean world."[307]

The "homelessness" connected with the travels of missionaries often has been compared to the lifestyle of Cynic itinerant philosophers. However, this religion-historical background is neither historically plausible nor useful in terms of missionary tactics (see §§10.2; 18.5). Whether the homelessness of the early missionaries was "ascetic" is an open question: the prohibition of provisions in Mt 10:9-10 more likely reflects a unique, short-time missionary tour of the disciples in Galilee, where they were known to many people and could anticipate receiving hospitality and meals. When Paul says that he often went hungry (1 Cor 4:11; 2 Cor 11:27), he describes not a program of asceticism but the consequences of a lack of financial resources, which sometimes resulted from his refusal, in missionary pioneer situations, to be supported by a *patronus.*

In ancient monasticism, including the way of life of the early medieval missionaries, ascetic homelessness was interpreted in terms of the conception of the *peregrinatio,* whose central idea was the renunciation of worldly things.[308] The relevant sources appeal to biblical texts such as Gen 12:1; Mt 16:24; 19:29; Lk 14:26. However, the early Christian missionaries hardly resemble the early medieval missionaries or monks with their program of the "renunciation of the world" and the "exchange of earthly for spiritual kinship."

2. The early Christian missionaries did not travel alone but rather at least in pairs. Possibly they traveled in larger teams on occasion. Jesus had sent them out in pairs, but this missionary tour through the Galilean villages was limited in terms of its duration. Jesus' surrounding of himself with a larger group of "fishers of people" presumably was a model for early Christian missionaries. The apostle Paul led such a team of missionary co-workers (see §28.4). In regard to Peter, we know that he traveled at least with his wife (1 Cor 9:5), and according to early Christian tradition he was accompanied by John Mark on occasion.

3. Women had responsible functions and duties. This clearly was the case with Priscilla in Corinth, Rome and Ephesus;[309] the four daughters of Philip in Caesarea (Acts 21:9); Lydia, Euodia and Syntyche in Philippi;[310] Phoebe in Cenchreae (Rom 16:1-2); Maria, Tryphaena, Tryphosa and Persis in Rome (Rom

---

[307]Sievernich 1990, 105.
[308]See Padberg 1995, 61-62; for the observation that follows above see ibid., 61 n. 2.
[309]Acts 18:26; 1 Cor 16:19; Rom 16:3-5; 2 Tim 4:19 (Prisca).
[310]Acts 16:12-15, 40; Phil 4:2-3.

16:2, 12); perhaps also in Rome the mother of Rufus (Rom 16:13), Julia the wife of Philologus, and the sister of Nereus (Rom 16:15).

The role of women in the early Christian mission can hardly be explained without Jesus' behavior toward women, which was strikingly novel for its time.[311] Jesus addressed his message of the arrival of the kingdom of God as well as his healing ministry to both men and women.[312] His teaching about marriage and divorce placed the dignity of women on the same level as that of men.[313] He had personal conversations with women.[314] He allowed women to accompany him on his travels and to support him with their financial resources.[315] It is therefore not surprising that Luke's account in the book of Acts describes women as full members of the churches, a fact that is not simply presupposed but is stated specifically. In Jerusalem women are present when the disciples come together in the upper room (Acts 1:14). They receive the Holy Spirit together with the men (Acts 2:17-18). More and more women are converted (Acts 5:14), including widows (Acts 6:1). In Samaria both men and women are baptized (Acts 8:12). When Saul/Paul travels to Damascus, he intends to arrest women as well (Acts 9:2). Later Paul is accompanied by the women and children of the church in Tyre when he goes down to the harbor (Acts 21:5). In Corinth and in other churches women participate in public prayers and prophecy (1 Cor 11:2-16; 14:33). Paul and Peter specifically address women in their exhortations for the congregations.[316] The following Christian women, most of them leading disciples and missionary workers, are mentioned by name: in Jerusalem, Mary the mother of Jesus (Acts 1:14), Mary the mother of John Mark (Acts 12:12-13), Sapphira (Acts 5:1-11); in Joppa, Tabitha (Acts 9:36); in Lystra, Eunice (Acts 16:1; 2 Tim 1:5); in Corinth, Chloe (1 Cor 1:11); in Colossae, Apphia (Philem 2); in Laodikeia, Nympha (Col 4:15); in Thyatira, Jezebel (Rev 2:20-25); in Athens, Damaris (Acts 17:34).

These women did not only pray (1 Tim 5:5) and serve in charitable roles or as deaconesses, such as Tabitha in Joppa, Lydia in Philippi, or Phoebe in Cenchreae or Corinth:[317] they were active in the house churches[318] and in missionary contexts. Priscilla and Aquila are "co-workers" (συνεργοί, *synergoi*), Priscilla the wife is mentioned before her husband, and the gratitude of the churches is extended to her also (Rom 16:3-4). Mary, Tryphaena and Tryphosa "worked hard" in Rome (Rom 16:6, 12), comparable to the hard work of Paul's own missionary ministry. In Philippi, Euodia and Syntyche "struggled" beside Paul "in the work of the gospel, together with Clement and the rest of my co-workers" (συνεργοί, *synergoi* [Phil 4:3]); that is, they were actively involved in spreading the gospel

[311]See Weiser 1983, 164; for the observations that follow above see ibid., 159-62, 164-65.
[312]Mk 5:25-34; 7:24-30; Lk 7:36-50; 13:10-17.
[313]Mk 10:2-12/Mt 5:31-32/Lk 16:18.
[314]Mk 7:26-29; Lk 10:38-42; Jn 4:7-27.
[315]Mk 15:40-41/Mt 27:55-56/Lk 23:49; Lk 8:1-3; 23:27.
[316]Eph 5:22—6:9; Col 3:18—4:1; 1 Tim 2:8-15; Tit 2:1-10; 1 Pet 2:18—3:7.
[317]Acts 9:36-42; 16:15; Rom 16:2.
[318]Acts 12:12-13 (Mary in Jerusalem); 16:15, 40 (Lydia in Philippi); 1 Cor 16:19 (Priscilla in Ephesus); Rom 16:5 (Priscilla in Rome); Rom 16:5 (Julia and other women in Rome); Col 4:15 (Nympha in Laodikeia); Philem 1-2 (Apphia in Colossae); 1 Cor 1:11 (Chloe in Corinth).

and winning people for faith in Jesus Christ, and evidently they were involved in the intellectual, theological and spiritual battle with the opponents with whom Paul had to contend (Phil 1:27-28).[319]

4. Intelligent, sober evaluation of missionary opportunities. The disciples had learned as they accompanied Jesus that there would be not only success but also indifferent rejection of the good news that they preach, and even intense opposition and persecution. Jesus had instructed them that if people in one house or town do not want to hear their message, they should leave and move on to the next (Mt 10:14; Mk 6:11; Lk 9:5; 10:10-11; cf. Acts 13:51). And if they started to preach the good news in a town and encountered organized opposition, they were instructed to move on as well, in a hurry if necessary (Mt 10:23; cf. Acts 12:17; 14:6, 19-20). Plans were not executed without regard for changed circumstances. When Paul and his co-workers wanted to travel through the province of Asia in the spring of A.D. 49 but were hindered from engaging in missionary work (presumably in Ephesus), they reacted in a consistently flexible manner: they started to plan missionary outreach in Bithynia. In route to the northern regions of Asia Minor, they recognized that this new plan could not be carried out either. When they came to Troas, they realized with the help of divine revelation and in the context of discussion that God wanted them to engage in missionary work in Europe. Thus they embarked on a ship, sailed to Macedonia and came to the realization during their visit to Philippi that God had given them an open door in this city (Acts 16:6-12).

5. Establishing contact with Jews in synagogues, proclaiming Jesus as the promised Messiah. The missionary outreach to Jews was not limited to Jerusalem and Judea; it continued in the Diaspora synagogues, as Luke regularly reports with regard to the missionary work of Paul.[320]

6. Establishing contact with non-Jews, proselytes and God-fearers, both in synagogues and in the market (*agora*) and also in private homes. Familiarity with indigenous languages was not an issue for the Jerusalem missionaries, if we assume that they could speak Greek. At least in the cities in the eastern part of the Roman Empire, the Jewish Christian missionaries would have had no problems being understood. Christine Mohrmann comments that "the possibility of this initial unity of language was due to the political and cultural conditions in the Roman Empire."[321] At the same time there is enough evidence to suggest that the first missionaries, who without exception were followers of Jesus, whose mother language was Aramaic, were aware of the importance of the translation of the good news into other languages, as references to the Hebrew,

---

[319]See Weiser 1983, 179.
[320]Reinbold (2000, 117-225) argues that Luke's account is "stylized"; that is, Paul did not preach in synagogues. For a critique see §24.2 in the present work.
[321]Mohrmann 1954, 104. On this question see also Riesenfeld 1969.

Greek, Latin and Lycaonian language in the New Testament demonstrate.[322]

7. Gathering the converts in congregations whose assemblies were open to visits of curious and interested unbelievers. The establishment of communities of believers in Jesus Christ was not the result of a separation from the synagogue (or from "Judaism") sometime in the last decades of the first century but rather a direct result of Jesus' missionary commission. If people accept and confess faith in Jesus the Messiah and Savior and become followers of Jesus, and if this happens through the Christian missionaries teaching "everything" that Jesus taught, then independent meetings are the inevitable result, if and when the leaders of the local synagogue decide that the message about Jesus should no longer be given a forum in the synagogue services, and if and when the local synagogue decides not to tolerate Gentiles who were converted to faith in Israel as a result of their faith in Jesus but who were not circumcised. Jesus himself, with his group of followers, of which the Twelve were a nucleus, was an example for gathering into communities people who had repented and accepted the good news of the arrival of God's reign and forgiveness. The Christians in Jerusalem quickly realized that they had to organize in order to take care of matters that the local Jewish authorities or synagogues denied them—for example, the support of widows. The fact that the first Christians met in private homes was not a tactical measure but a necessity, and it was not all that remarkable in light of the existence of Jewish synagogues in private houses. The phenomenon of hospitality, which for many societies in the first-century world was a matter of course, should not be accorded too much symbolic value.[323] It is doubtful, for example, that "human beings in antiquity" had a "feeling of the numinous" when they encountered a stranger.

8. Expectation of surprising success. The Twelve witnessed in Jerusalem that several thousand people could find faith in Jesus Christ within a very short time. Peter's experience in Caesarea taught them that even officers of the Roman army could be converted very unexpectedly. They had learned in Damascus that even actively violent enemies of the Christians could be converted. Both poor people and influential people were converted. The people converted through the preaching ministry of the Jerusalem apostles and other missionaries, as described by Luke in Acts 1—12, had a low social position and were relatively poor. At the same time he mentions six Christians who had a higher social position because they were wealthy: Barnabas, Ananias and Sapphira, and Mary the mother of John Mark owned houses or real estate that they could sell. Cornelius and the Ethiopian official were Gentiles with a higher social standing.[324]

---

[322]Jn 5:2; 19:13, 17, 20; 20:16; Acts 9:36; 14:11; 21:40; 22:2; 26:14; Rev 9:11; 16:16.
[323]Contra Rusche 1958. For a critical discussion of hospitality from an anthropological perspective see Gittins 1994. The quotation that follows above is from Rusche 1958, 45.
[324]See Beydon 1986; for the remark that follows above see ibid., 338-39.

References to the higher social position of new converts to the Christian faith underline the effectiveness of the early Christian mission: the houses of the wealthier church members served as places of assembly, and their real estate served to help poorer Christians. The newly converted Roman military officer who is stationed in Caesarea and who hails from another region of the Roman Empire (which Luke does not identify) and the converted Ethiopian official who returns home are presented by Luke, who describes the geographical expansion of the Christian faith, probably as examples of the mobility that drives the early Christian mission.

9. Trust in God regarding the success of their missionary work. The early Christian missionaries knew that conversions of people, whether Jew or Gentile, could neither be planned nor manufactured through some specific measure. The apostles were not under "pressure to succeed." They knew themselves to be entirely and directly dependent upon the will and the work of God through the Holy Spirit, who alone could convince people of the truth of the message about God's revelation and offer of salvation in Jesus, the crucified and risen Messiah.

10. Gentiles need salvation. What did the early Christian missionaries think about pagans? This question often is answered with reference to Jewish attitudes as expressed in, for example, Wis 14:23-31.[325] Luke, the one New Testament author who writes specifically about the progress of the early Christian mission, provides the following "portrait" of Gentiles:[326] Gentiles are ignorant, lacking the light of the knowledge of the true God; they reject God's revelation and God's intentions in history; they worship many deities in their ignorance and hardly distinguish between humans and gods; they are enslaved to magic and witchcraft; they are more interested in their own material advantage than in the well-being of others; they are involved in moral aberrations; they are under the power of Satan, some of them in a visible manner. Unless they repent, they stand helpless before the judgment of God.

Since we have more detailed material with regard to the missionary work of Paul that illuminates the issues of missionary strategy and tactics, these matters will be discussed more extensively at a later point (§28).

16.4 Motivation and Reality

The Feasibility of Going to "All the Nations"

The apostles were convinced that the coming of Jesus signified the arrival of the "last days" and that God would establish his universal reign very soon. The "imminent expectation" was a dominant element already in Jesus' proclamation: he called people to repentance because the kingdom of God is presently arriving,

---

[325]See Hanson 1985, 144-45; Grant 1986, 46.
[326]For the observations that follow above see Stenschke 1999a; summary, 378-88.

he spoke of the return of the Son of Man, and he announced the destruction of the temple (see §9.1). At the same time Jesus rejected attempts to calculate a date for the parousia,[327] as only God knows the time and the hour of the last judgment. Jesus called his disciples to be watchful because "the end" is near, when "these things" will take place; at the same time he called them to engage in the work that he commissioned them to do, illustrated in the parable of the faithful and the unfaithful servants and in the parable of the talents, pointing out that the return of the Lord may be delayed, just as the bridegroom in the parable of the wise and the foolish virgins tarries until midnight (Mt 24:45—25:29).

Peter Stuhlmacher correctly points out that in the context of this teaching about a delayed parousia, the apostles' expectation of the imminent "end" did *not* become the basic theological problem that Albert Schweitzer and others saw in the early church.[328] On the one hand, the apostles spoke and wrote about the fact that they lived "in the last days"[329] and they prayed earnestly and regularly for the return of Jesus with the prayer call *marana tha* ("Our Lord, come!" [1 Cor 16:22; Rev 22:20]). On the other hand, this "imminent expectation" did not make them count the hours until the arrival of the end: they actively engaged in the proclamation of the good news of Jesus Christ in Jerusalem, Judea, Samaria and beyond the borders of Palestine.[330] The "eschatological factor" was not the most important factor for the intensive missionary work of the early church. Paul engaged in missionary outreach in Corinth and Ephesus for several years, he repeatedly visited existing churches in southern Galatia, in Macedonia and in Achaia, and he sent co-workers and letters to churches, all of which demonstrates that the early Christian missionaries did not try to preach the gospel in as many towns and regions as possible. Rather, they recognized right from the beginning the necessity of consolidating the new churches, and they were willing and prepared to involve co-workers and utilize resources such as time, energy and literary activity for this task without abandoning their eschatological convictions.

At the same time their conviction that Jesus Christ might return soon must have influenced the planning of their missionary work. The question of how the apostles intended to fulfill Jesus' assignment to preach the good news to *panta ta ethnē* ("all nations") must be answered in the context of their conviction to live in the "last days." This means for the "tactical" implementation of their missionary commission—we must not forget that the apostles were not naive—that they would not have understood Jesus' assignment in the sense that they must

---

[327]Mt 24:23-28/Mk 13:21-22; Lk 17:23-24.
[328]Stuhlmacher 1992-1999, 1:94, with reference to A. Schweitzer, *Das Messianitäts- und Leidensgeheimnis: Eine Skizze des Lebens Jesu* (3rd ed.; Tübingen: Mohr, 1956).
[329]Gal 4:4; 1 Thess 2:19; 3:13; 5:23; 1 Cor 10:11; Rom 13:11; Eph 1:7-10, 20-23; Heb 1:1-2; 9:26; Jas 5:1-9; 1 Pet 1:19-21; 2 Pet 3:3; Jude 18; 1 Jn 2:18.
[330]See Unnik 1960, 360; followed by Reinhardt 1995a, 252.

present the gospel to every single human being in all provinces and regions, in every city, town and village of the *oikoumenē*. When Paul states in Rom 15:19 that he has "fully proclaimed the good news of Christ" by the power of God's Spirit "from Jerusalem and as far around as Illyricum," and that he therefore intends to travel to Spain and begin missionary work there, he does not claim that he has personally presented the gospel to every human being in the eastern provinces of the Roman Empire. At the same time he clearly is convinced that he has fulfilled the task of a pioneer missionary, making sure that people hear the gospel before Jesus' return (cf. Mk 13:10), or that this task will be fully carried out by his co-workers and other missionaries. The question arises, therefore, whether the apostles had, or could have had, a plan for the implementation of Jesus' missionary commission.

The Planning of International Missionary Work

Did the Twelve leave the specific and practical implementation of the missionary commission to preach the gospel of Jesus Christ to all nations from Jerusalem to the ends of the earth to the circumstances of more or less random historical events and developments?[331] This is the impression one might get from an initial reading of Luke's account of the earliest missionary activities of the Jerusalem apostles in the book of Acts.

1. The first missionary sermon, preached by Peter on the Feast of Pentecost in A.D. 30 in Jerusalem, according to Luke, seems to have been a spontaneous speech: he explains to the surprised crowd the significance of the miraculous events linked with the arrival of the Holy Spirit, promised by the prophets for the last days and now realized as a consequence of the exaltation of Jesus, the crucified and risen Messiah (Acts 2:12-14, 37-38).

2. The Twelve seem to have stayed in Jerusalem in the months following Pentecost (Acts 8:1). Luke does not hint at any missionary travels of the Jerusalem apostles to the surrounding Jewish areas, let alone at outreach to pagans.

3. The first "travels" that Luke mentions in the book of Acts concern the flight of Jewish Christians from the Jerusalem church who had to leave the city after Stephen had been killed; they traveled to Judea, Samaria, Phoenicia, Cyprus and Syria and proclaimed the gospel (Acts 8:1, 4-5; 11:19). Luke explicitly comments that "the apostles" (i.e., the Twelve) were spared in this persecution (Acts 8:1), which evidently means that they stayed in Jerusalem. The first larger-scale geographical expansion of the church took place in Samaria, a missionary outreach for which Philip was responsible, who was one of the Seven (Acts 8:5), not the Twelve. The beginning of the Samaria mission does not seem to have been the

---

[331]Note Bruce 1985b, 652: "The first presentation of the gospel to Gentiles . . . took place informally and almost accidentally." Similarly Soden 1924, 28; also Frend 1974, 32-33, with regard to the mission of the early church in general.

result of strategic planning but rather a spontaneous development in the course of a persecution that Jerusalem Jews organized against Jewish Christians. Some scholars argue that even Paul turned from the Jews to the Gentiles only after his preaching was rejected in the synagogues.[332]

4. Luke emphasizes repeatedly that new missionary ventures of the missionaries were initiated by supernatural directives: Philip is directed by an "angel of the Lord" to go to the road that goes down from Jerusalem to Gaza (Acts 8:26), where he meets the Ethiopian official. Cornelius is being prepared for his conversion by a "vision" (horama) of an "angel of the Lord" (Acts 10:3-8), while Peter falls into a "trance" (ekstasis) in which he sees the open heaven and hears the voice of the Lord (Acts 10:10-16). Paul is prevented by the Holy Spirit from traveling to the provinces of Asia and Bithynia (Acts 16:6.7). In a "vision" (horama) that he receives at night he is called to Europa by a Macedonian man (Acts 16:9-10).

5. New missionary actions sometimes are influenced by external circumstances. For example, Paul goes to southern Galatia, where he engages in missionary work "because of a physical infirmity" (Gal 4:13). Plans for his desired visit to Rome had to be postponed repeatedly (Rom 1:10-11, 13).

Many scholars conclude on the basis of this evidence that the first Christians had to be "forced" (by God) to do missionary work: if they had not been dispersed in the persecution following the death of Stephen, they would have felt no urgent need to leave Jerusalem. This position has been argued again recently by Andreas Feldtkeller: "The actual booster charge for the breathtaking development was, according to the material in the Acts of the Apostles, an event in which the church was entirely passive: the expulsion of Torah-critical Christians belonging to Stephen's circle from Jerusalem (Acts 8:1)."[333] Feldtkeller asserts that according to Acts 11:20, the first deliberate missionary activity among Gentiles took place in Antioch under the leadership of Paul and Barnabas. The leading apostles of the Jerusalem church, it is argued, were a conservative group that never was responsible for new ventures.[334]

Wolfgang Reinbold argues that the Twelve (or the Eleven) did not engage in missionary work, as we have no reliable information about them; the early patristic traditions do not record historical memories but merely present hypotheses with widely differing quality. The Twelve stayed in Jerusalem to announce there symbolically the coming kingdom of God; they soon lost their function because the expected end did not come.[335] This is an extreme position that very few scholars embrace. The following facts show that this view

---

[332]See Dumais 1993, 120-21.
[333]Feldtkeller 1993, 31; for the remark that follows see ibid., 32-33. Similarly Zahn 1886, 113-16; Würz 1922, 8-12; Pieper 1929, 10-11; Burchard 1978, 336-40; Brox 1983, 27; Gaventa 1982, 416; McKnight 1997, 390; Hengel and Schwemer 1998, 394; Witherington 2001, 188.
[334]See Marshall, Acts, 156; similarly Köstenberger and O'Brien 2001, 139.
[335]Reinbold 2000, 263-64, following Campenhausen 1963, 16-17 (ET, 14-15).

is untenable (see also §22). Reinbold's study shows how literary-critical hypotheses dismantle primary sources and hover in a historical vacuum despite the historical-critical pathos of the author. If the Twelve did not learn from Jesus to do missionary work, if they did not receive a missionary commission from Jesus, if most local churches came into existence without the work of missionaries, if Paul the missionary was an atypical figure—a lone wolf whose project of missionary work in the urban centers of the Greco-Roman world was not taken up by any other Christian in the early church before or after him—if "the church" expanded mostly through everyday private and occupational contacts of anonymous sisters and brothers like a "constant fermentation," if sermons played a role only in rare cases, not even in the mission of Paul,[336] then one may ask the question, somewhat tongue-in-cheek, whether the author wishes to abolish in his church or denomination pastors, superintendents and bishops alongside missionaries and evangelists and sermons outside the Sunday worship services in order to reverse the dramatic decline of the mainline churches (in Germany and in Europe), expecting renewed church growth only through "individual propaganda." Reinbold's explanation of the growth of the church in the first centuries is completely unconvincing. He would make two factors responsible for the dramatic growth of the early church: (a) Christians brought up their children as Christians; (b) if every Christian believer won a single pagan neighbor to faith in Jesus Christ within one generation, the growth of the church can be explained statistically. But regardless of how high (or low) the growth rates of the Christian churches may have been in the first centuries, the dynamic missionary force of the apostle Paul certainly was not unique, and the lack of authentic evidence for the missionary outreach of the Twelve that Reinbold would find acceptable must not be taken as proof of their missionary inactivity. It is difficult to avoid the impression that Reinbold has decided not to find any missionaries in the New Testament apart from Paul. He argues that the missionary commission in Mt 28:19-20 does not go back to Jesus and thus did not make the Twelve (or Eleven) into missionaries; Mt 28:19-20 is not even evidence for the existence of missionaries at the time of first readers of the Gospel of Matthew: even though we cannot exclude the possibility that the first readers of the Gospel reached Gentiles with the good news of Jesus Christ and taught them to become disciples, this is not certain, since "we simply know nothing about the reaction of the addressees to the final word of the First Gospel."[337] Perhaps Reinbold's radical position is not radical enough. If Jesus did not rise from the dead, if he failed with his proclamation of the imminent arrival of the kingdom of God, if his death on the cross was accorded atoning efficacy only by later followers who engaged in theological reflection, then not only can we do without missionaries who proclaim the good news of salvation in Jesus Christ with personal involvement and a sense of urgency, accepting joyfully missionary work as their life calling, but also the "propaganda" of individual Christians becomes superfluous as well because they have nothing to offer to devout Jews and happy polytheists.

The following observations demonstrate that the apostles were indeed aware of their responsibility for the implementation of Jesus' missionary commission, including the assignment to preach the good news among the Gentiles. Since there were no Jewish or non-Jewish examples and models for international outreach, the missionary responsibility that the actions of the Twelve imply and

---

[336]Reinbold 2000, 280-83, 342-47; on "fermentation," 345; on the children of Christians, 351.
[337]Reinbold 2000, 274-75, 296-98; quotation, 297.

demonstrate can be explained only on the basis of an existing "Great Commission" given by Jesus.

1. Luke reports very selectively, a fact that we must not forget. Even though he records in Acts 1:13 for the second time a list of the Twelve/Eleven (cf. Lk 6:14-16), he describes only the activities of Peter, and these are limited to the first twelve years from A.D. 30 to 41 (Acts 1—12). He keeps silent about the approximately twenty-five years between his departure from Jerusalem in A.D. 40/41 and his death in Rome around A.D. 67 (date uncertain). The only exception is his participation in the apostolic council in Jerusalem that Luke reports (Acts 15). John and his brother James are the only other members of the Twelve mentioned by Luke, and always in connection with Peter: John prays (Acts 3:1), he is present when a lame man is healed (Acts 3:4), he is arrested (Acts 4:3), he defends himself before the Sanhedrin (Acts 4:19), he travels with Peter to Samaria (Acts 8:14-15, 25); in regard to James, Luke only notes his execution (Acts 12:2). The missionary work of Paul also is reported selectively by Luke. He does not describe Paul's activities between his conversion and missionary call in A.D. 31/32 and his involvement in the activities of the church in Antioch after A.D. 42. He does not mention the establishment of the churches in Colossae, Laodikeia and Hierapolis, which probably date to the time of Paul's extended stay in Ephesus. He does not mention Paul's plans to travel to Spain, nor does he mention the collection that Paul had organized in the churches in Macedonia and Achaia, which was the reason why he traveled to Jerusalem before embarking on his missionary journey to Spain. If Luke provided us with a reliable description of Paul's missionary work without giving us a complete picture[338]—over half of the material in the book of Acts concerns Paul—it is methodologically unwarranted to draw any conclusions from Luke's silence concerning the activities of the Twelve. The lists of the names of the Twelve (Acts 1:13-14), the Seven (Acts 6:5) and the Five (Acts 13:1), not to mention the numerous names mentioned in the greeting lists of the New Testament letters (e.g., in Rom 16), prove the following. (a) We know relatively little about the leading missionaries, preachers and teachers of the early churches. (b) Luke lets persons whom he no longer "needs" for his historical purposes simply disappear. (c) Luke clearly knew much more than he includes in his account. (d) It is thus obvious that earliest Christianity was "not an anonymous movement in which 'collective creativity' predominated, but that everything depended on the authority of the individual teachers and prophets."[339]

2. Luke's silence concerning the congregational and the missionary activities of the Twelve is all the more remarkable because he begins his account of the missionary outreach of the early Christians in Jerusalem and of the expansion

---

[338]I. H. Marshall 1992a, 91-98.
[339]Hengel and Schwemer 1998, 333-36 (ET, 219-21); quotation, 335-36 (ET, 220).

of the Christian faith to Syria, Galatia, Macedonia and Achaia and to Rome with another missionary commission of Jesus to the Twelve (Acts 1:8: cf. Lk 24:46-49), with another list of the names of the Twelve (Acts 1:13; cf. Lk 6:13-16) and with a relatively long report about the election of Matthias as the new twelfth disciple (Acts 1:15-26).

3. Luke reports that the Jerusalem apostles had enormous courage. They were willing to oppose the directives of the Sanhedrin, the institution that had indicted Jesus and condemned him to death and that explicitly prohibited the apostles from preaching about Jesus. The Twelve refused to discontinue their public proclamation, and they refused to limit their activities to private homes (Acts 4:18-20; 5:28-29). This unflagging courage, which was coupled with their willingness to suffer, stands in contrast to the view that the Twelve were conservative, somewhat timid teachers and leaders of the Jerusalem church who were more concerned with the preservation of what had been achieved and who were neither willing nor able to think about new ventures, or strategize new missionary initiatives, or personally engage in evangelistic activity in more distant towns or provinces.

4. The extended prayer of the Jerusalem church in Acts 4:24-29 confirms the supposition that Luke knows more about the missionary involvement of the Jerusalem church and its leaders than he reports. After Peter and John were released by the chief priests who had arrested them, the believers pray, in view of the "rage" of the Gentiles (Acts 4:25, quotation from Ps 2:1) and in the context of threats by the political establishment in Jerusalem (Acts 4:29a), that God may grant them "boldness" (*parrēsia*) to proclaim the word of God (Acts 4:29b). To assume that church members could pray in this manner while their leaders were incapable of new missionary initiatives is unconvincing.

Scholars argue that the prayer in Acts 4:24-30 is a Lukan composition and therefore does not reflect actual historical events.[340] This view is contradicted by a detailed analysis of the narrative framework and of the prayer itself, which leads Rudolf Pesch to the conclusion that "4:23-31 belongs in its basic content to the narrative complex provided by Luke beginning in 3:1."[341] It is unclear how we should envision the congregation saying this prayer. It is possible that a church member spoke the prayer on behalf of the entire congregation, or the congregation may have repeated each individual statement after the person leading in prayer.[342]

5. Paul evidently started to engage in missionary work immediately after his conversion and call to preach the gospel among the Gentiles, specifically in

---

[340]See Barrett, *Acts,* 1:241-42; Fitzmyer, *Acts,* 307; Zmijewski, *Apg,* 225-26.

[341]Pesch, *Apg,* 1:173-75; quotation, 175; cf. Marshall, *Acts,* 104. Jervell (*Apg,* 190) reckons with traditions "from the old, first generation of Jewish Christians."

[342]Marshall, *Acts,* 103 with n. 1.

Arabia-Nabatea, a region that had Jewish communities. However, since the (pagan) ethnarch under King Aretas IV wanted to arrest him, it is a plausible assumption that Paul reached Nabatean Arabs with the gospel (see §26.1).[343] If Paul indeed implemented the assignment that the risen Christ had given to him to reach Gentiles with the gospel, then it is equally plausible that the Twelve not only "heard" their commission to become "fishers of people" but also obediently followed the directives that Jesus had given to them.

6. The Sanhedrin was concerned that the movement that Jesus had initiated and that was now promoted by his disciples as a messianic movement might be "spreading further among the people" (Acts 4:17).[344] This text does not speak of missionary preaching among Gentiles; the term *laos* refers here to the Jewish people. But this comment confirms the dynamic vitality of the Jerusalem church and its leadership, whose activities evidently aimed at and resulted in the growth of the number of believers. Luke notes later that the high priest accuses the apostles during a general assembly of the Sanhedrin that they "filled Jerusalem" with their teaching (Acts 5:28).[345] This statement is not explicit evidence for a missionary strategy of the Twelve, but it does not exclude the possibility that their intention indeed was to "fill" Jerusalem with the message of Jesus the Messiah, to make sure that every citizen heard of the resurrection of Jesus and of his vindication as the exalted Messiah at the right hand of God.

7. The fact that the Twelve were initially active in Jerusalem is not simply a reflection of Luke's perspective, which focuses on Jerusalem. It corresponds to the Jewish geographical conception of Jerusalem being the center of the world,[346] and it corresponds to the Old Testament prophecies and the early Jewish expectations of the return of the Jews from exile, who would come to Jerusalem from all corners of the earth, together with the nations that gather on Mount Zion to worship Yahweh.[347] It would have been natural in the context of such expectations that the leaders of the Jerusalem church stay in Jerusalem, on Mount Zion, rather than go to Galilee or travel to other regions. It is important to note in this context also that the early church understood itself to be God's eschatological people and the "temple" of the messianic days. The Twelve could easily have understood Jesus' assignment to mean that they were called to proclaim the arrival of God's reign and God's offer of forgiveness through Jesus the Messiah to Jews, Diaspora Jews and Gentiles who came to Jerusalem. Also, we should not stipulate that the bond between the Twelve and Jerusalem was very rigid.[348]

8. When the apostles looked for a replacement for Judas Iscariot—for a dis-

---

[343]Cf. Gal 1:17; 2 Cor 11:32-33.
[344]Acts 4:17: ἵνα μὴ ἐπὶ πλεῖον διανεμηθῇ εἰς τὸν λαόν.
[345]Acts 5:28: πεπληρώκατε τὴν Ἰερουσαλὴμ τῆς διδαχῆς ὑμῶν.
[346]See J. M. Scott 1994, 492-522.
[347]Cf. Is 2:2-3; 11:12; 43:5-6; 49:12; 60:3-16; Zech 8:20-23; Tob 13:11-13.
[348]O. Betz 1994, 26, with reference to Acts 8:25; Gal 1:18-19; 1 Thess 2:14.

ciple willing to leave his "nets," to give up his livelihood, to spend his time and
energy winning people to faith in Jesus Christ—there were quickly not one, but
two candidates who were willing to be involved in missionary work: Joseph
Barsabbas, who also was called Justus, and Matthias (Acts 1:23). We must not
forget the circumstances in which Joseph and Matthias volunteered to join the
Twelve: Jesus had been executed a few weeks earlier, and the hostility of the
Jewish establishment against the followers of Jesus had not diminished. As the
events of the following months and years demonstrated, it was potentially dangerous to belong to the leadership council of the Jesus movement. Since Joseph
and Matthias had accompanied Jesus during his travels in Galilee, they would
have been able to picture their future ministry: they would leave their professions and their homes and families, they would walk long distances, they would
have to cope with opposition. There was no organization or structures. And the
question of how Gentiles who came to faith in Jesus would be included in the
community of the followers of Jesus had not been thought through. The fact that
there were several candidates for Judas's position among the Twelve confirms
the willingness and the preparedness of the earliest followers of Jesus to engage
courageously in missionary work.

9. The missionary initiative of the Twelve can be discussed not just in terms
of circumstantial evidence. Specific, albeit scattered, pieces of evidence support
this conclusion. (a) The Jerusalem church sent Peter and John to Samaria as a
reaction to reports that Samaritans had come to faith in Jesus (Acts 8:14). There
is no hint that the news from Samaria surprised the apostles.[349] On the contrary:
after their arrival and their consolidation of the missionary work that Philip had
started, Peter and John themselves visit Samaritan villages, preaching the gospel.

Acts 8:14, 25: "Now when the apostles at Jerusalem heard that Samaria had accepted the
word of God [τὸν λόγον τοῦ θεοῦ], they sent Peter and John to them. . . . [25]Now after Peter
and John had testified and spoken the word of the Lord [τὸν λόγον τοῦ κυρίου], they returned to Jerusalem, proclaiming the good news to many villages of the Samaritans."

The reaction of the Jerusalem apostles to the missionary report from Samaria indicates that the central process of the missionary work of the early church was
the proclamation and acceptance of the message of Jesus Christ as word of God,
and that the apostles were personally and directly involved in this process. (b)
The Twelve had contact with Saul/Paul when he returned to Jerusalem for the
first time after his conversion. They listen to a report about his conversion, and
they are informed "how in Damascus he had spoken boldly in the name of
Jesus" (πῶς ἐν Δαμασκῷ ἐπαρρησιάσατο [Acts 9:27]). Clearly the apostles were
interested in hearing not only about the conversion of Saul, the prominent rabbi
who was a Pharisee; they also wanted to hear about details of his missionary

[349]Dunn, *Acts,* 110.

work in Damascus. (c) Peter traveled through all the areas of Judea, Galilee and Samaria (διερχόμενον διὰ πάντων, *dierchomenon dia pantōn* [Acts 9:32a]) as well as to cities in the coastal plain (Acts 9:31-32).[350] Evidently Peter was not on an "inspection tour" as "bishop" of Jerusalem but rather on a missionary journey: Luke notes in Acts 9:35 the conversion of citizens of Lydda and inhabitants in the plain of Sharon. He had already mentioned a missionary activity of Peter in "many villages of the Samaritans" (Acts 8:25). (d) When the first Gentiles were converted to faith in Jesus Christ in Caesarea, the seat of the provincial governor, Peter not only was present but also played a decisive role (Acts 10:1—11:18). (e) When the first reports arrive in Jerusalem that the message of Jesus had reached Antioch, the leadership of the church immediately recognized their responsibility for the consolidation of the missionary work in the provincial capital of Syria (Acts 11:19-24). (f) All the first co-workers of Paul whose missionary work reaches both Jews and pagans are Jewish Christians from Jerusalem: Barnabas, John Mark and Silas. (g) The missionary outreach of the Jerusalem apostles is not explained by Luke with reference to the sacred Scriptures but is narrated as matter-of-fact actions of the apostles. This means that the apostles' conviction of the universal significance of God's redemptive revelation in the death and resurrection of Jesus the Messiah, linked with the conviction that they were responsible for the proclamation of this message among Gentiles, did not develop gradually as a result of negative experiences among their Jewish contemporaries or as a result of a study of the prophecies concerning the salvation of the nations in the sacred Scriptures.[351] Both convictions were alive and courageously held from earliest times in the Jerusalem church.

10. The Twelve were the responsible authorities of the Jerusalem church, in Luke's account, until Acts 11:1, thus until A.D. 41/42, with Peter as principal leader. This changed when Herod Agrippa I (A.D. 41-44) organized another persecution of the Jerusalem church, during the course of which James, John's brother, was killed (Acts 12:1-2) and Peter was about to be executed publicly during the Feast of Passover (Acts 12:3-4). It appears that the Twelve left Jerusalem during this time and that the leadership of the church was passed on to a group of "Elders" whose principal leader was James the brother of Jesus (Acts 11:30; 12:17; 15:13; 21:18). Chapter 12 of the book of Acts represents an important turning point in the history of the Jerusalem church and of the early Christian mission. At the end of Acts 12 Peter leaves the Jewish capital and travels "to another place" (Acts 12:17). In Acts 13 Luke gives an account of the missionary

---

[350]Correctly NASB, NIV, TNIV, LÜ, GN; Haenchen, *Apg*, 326 n. 1 (ET, 338 n. 1); Barrett, *Acts*, 1:479; Fitzmyer, *Acts*, 442, 444; Jervell, *Apg*, 295; as a possibility, Pesch, *Apg*, 1:318 n. 7. Less plausible is a reference to the "saints" mentioned in Acts 9:32b—that is, Peter "went here and there among all the believers" (NRSV)—as assumed by Conzelmann, *Apg*, 68 (ET, 76); Pesch, *Apg*, 1:318.

[351]Contra Dumais 1993, 120-22, and others.

initiative of Paul and Barnabas on Cyprus and in the province of Galatia to cities in Pamphylia, Phrygia and Lycaonia. It appears from Luke's account in Acts 11—12 that the leadership demands in the oldest and probably largest church at the time, the congregation in Jerusalem, were no longer compatible with the leadership demands of the missionary work of the church.[352] It is impossible to say whether the persecution provoked by Agrippa I was the cause for this change or only the spark that triggered the implementation of plans that already had been discussed. It should not be doubted, however, that Peter did not leave Jerusalem in order to retire: his ministry as traveling missionary (cf. 1 Cor 9:5) may well have multiplied his influence.

This scenario agrees with later traditions according to which the twelve disciples stayed in Jerusalem for twelve years, after which they embarked on the universal and international mission that Jesus had directed them to engage in. The following primary sources mention a departure of the Twelve from Jerusalem twelve years after Jesus' death and resurrection (i.e., A.D. 40/41) to reach the regions that had been assigned to them for missionary proclamation.[353]

Acts Pet. 5 (ca. A.D. 180-190?): "While they were grieving and fasting, God was already preparing Peter at Jerusalem for the future. After the twelve years had passed, according to the direction of the Lord to Peter, Christ showed to him the following vision, saying, 'Peter, Simon, whom you expelled from Judaea after having exposed him as a magician, has forestalled you at Rome. . . . But do not delay. Go tomorrow to Caesarea, and there you will find a ship ready to sail to Italy.'"

Apollonius (ca. A.D. 200; in Eusebius, *Hist. eccl.* 5.18.14): "Moreover, he says, as though from tradition, that the Saviour ordered his apostles not to leave Jerusalem for twelve years [προστεταχέναι τοῖς αὐτοῦ ἀποστόλοις ἐπὶ δώδεκα ἔτεσιν μὴ χωρισθῆναι τῆς Ἰερουσαλήμ]."

Acts Thom. 1:1 (ca. A.D. 200-240): "At that time we apostles were all in Jerusalem—Simon called Peter, and Andrew his brother, James the son of Zebedee, and John his brother, Philip and Bartholomew, Thomas and Matthew the taxgatherer, James the son of Alphaeus and Simon the Cananaean, and Judas the son [brother?] of James—and we portioned out the regions of the world [καὶ διείλαμεν τὰ κλίματα τῆς οἰκουμένης], in order that each one of us might go into the region that fell to him by lot [ὅπως εἰς ἕκαστος ἡμῶν ἐν τῷ κλίματι τῷ λαχόντι αὐτῷ], and to the nation to which the Lord sent him [καὶ εἰς τὸ ἔθνος ἐν ᾧ ὁ κύριος αὐτὸν ἀπέστειλεν πορευθῇ]."

Origen (A.D. 185-254; in Eusebius, *Hist. eccl.* 3.1.1): "Such was the condition of things among the Jews, but the holy Apostles and disciples of our Saviour were scattered throughout the whole world [τῶν δὲ ἱερῶν τοῦ σωτῆρος ἡμῶν ἀποστόλων τε καὶ μαθητῶν ἐφ' ἅπασαν κατασπαρέντων τὴν οἰκουμένην]. Thomas, as tradition relates, obtained by lot

---

[352]Bauckham 1995b, 436. On this subject see more extensively §15.3 in the present work.
[353]See Harnack 1893-1904, 2.1:243-44; Kaestli 1981; Junod 1981; Weidmann 1999, 18-19. For an introduction to the apocryphal Acts of various apostles see §22.2 in the present work.

Parthia, Andrew Scythia, John Asia (and he stayed there and died in Ephesus), but Peter seems to have preached to the Jews of the Dispersion in Pontus and Galatia and Bithynia, Cappadocia, and Asia, and at the end he came to Rome. . . . This is stated exactly by Origen in the third volume of his commentary on Genesis."

The following texts speak more generally about a universal and international mission of the Twelve:[354]

1 Clem. 42:1-4 (ca. A.D. 90-100): "The apostles were given the gospel for us by the Lord Jesus Christ, and Jesus Christ was sent forth from God [ἐξεπέμφθη]. ²Thus Christ came from God and the apostles from Christ. Both things happened, then, in an orderly way according to the will of God. ³When, therefore, the apostles received his commands [παραγγελίας οὖν λαβόντες] and were fully convinced through the resurrection of our Lord Jesus Christ and persuaded by the word of God, they went forth proclaiming the good news [ἐξῆλθον εὐαγγελιζόμενοι] that the Kingdom of God was about to come, brimming with confidence through the Holy Spirit. ⁴And as they preached throughout the countryside and in the cities, they appointed the first fruits of their ministries [κατὰ χώρας οὖν καὶ πόλεις κηρύσσοντες καθίστανον τὰς ἀπαρχὰς αὐτῶν] as bishops and deacons of those who were about to believe, testing them by the Spirit."

Pre. Pet. 3a (A.D. 100-120; Agraphon 10; in Clement of Alexandria, *Strom.* 6.5.43): "Therefore Peter says that the Lord said to the apostles [διὰ τοῦτό φησιν ὁ Πέτρος εἰρηκέναι τὸν κύριον τοῖς ἀποστόλοις], 'If then any of Israel will repent and believe in God through my name, his sins shall be forgiven him: and after twelve years go out into the world [μετὰ δὲ δώδεκα ἔτη ἐξέλθετε εἰς τὸν κόσμον], lest any say, "We did not hear." ' "

Pre. Pet. 3b (Agraphon 9; in Clement of Alexandria, *Strom.* 6.6.48): "For example, in the Preaching of Peter the Lord says, 'I chose you twelve, judging you to be disciples worthy of me, whom the Lord willed, and thinking you faithful apostles I sent you into the world to preach the gospel to men throughout the world [καὶ ἀποστόλους πιστοὺς ἡγησάμενος εἶναι πέμπω ἐπὶ τὸν κόσμον εὐαγγελίσασθαι τοὺς κατὰ τὴν οἰκουμένην ἀνθρώπους], that they should know that there is one God; to declare by faith in me [Christ] what shall be, so that those who have heard and believed may be saved, and that those who have not believed may hear and bear witness, not having any defense so as to say, "We did not hear." ' "

Ep. Apos. 30 (A.D. 100-150?): "But he said unto us, 'Go you and preach to the twelve tribes and preach also to the gentiles and to the whole land of Israel from sunrise to sunset and from South to North, and many will believe in the Son of God.' "[355]

Acts Pet. 12 Apos. 1:9-20; 5:11-14 (second/third century; NHC VI,1): "And in our hearts, we were ¹⁰united. We agreed to fulfill the ministry to which the Lord appointed us. And

---

[354]Note also Eusebius, *Comm. Ps.* (PG 23 697c [fourth century]): οἱ τοῦ σωτῆρος ἡμῶν μαθηταὶ καὶ ἀπόστολοι, καὶ εὐαγγελισταί, ἥ τε λοιπὴ αὐτοῦ στρατεία . . . κτῆμα ἴδιον ποιησάμενοι, διενείμαντο εἰς ἀλλήλους . . . [τῶν . . . ἀποστόλων ἕκαστος] τὰ ἐξ ἐθνῶν ἐκληροῦτο σκύλα.
[355]Hornschuh (1965, 90-91) argues that this formulation shows that the concept of the Gentile mission was no longer understood as a matter of course by the readers of this text. I find no evidence for this view, neither here nor in *Ep. Apos.* 36.

we made a covenant with each other. We went down to the sea at an [15]opportune moment, which came to us from the Lord. We found a ship moored at the shore ready to embark, and we spoke with the sailors of the [20]ship about our coming aboard with them. . . . [5:11]'We are strangers and servants of God. It is necessary for us to spread the word of God in every city harmoniously.' "[356]

Ep. Pet. Phil. 134:18-26; 140:7-15, 23-27 (second/third century; NHC VIII,2): "Then the apostles answered [20]and said, 'Lord, we would like to know the deficiency of the aeons and their pleroma.' And: 'How are we detained in this dwelling place?' [25]Further: 'How did we come to this place?' And: 'In what manner shall we depart?' . . . [140:7]Then Peter and the other apostles saw [him] and they were filled with a holy spirit. [10]And each one performed healings. And they parted in order to preach the Lord Jesus. And they came together and greeted each other [15]saying, 'Amen.' . . . [23]Then the apostles parted from each other [25]into four words in order to preach. And they went by a power of Jesus, in peace."[357]

Fragments of Polycarp a, 5-12 (third century): ". . . went out in the whole inhabited world so that each one of them might complete his course within the regions which were assigned to them, while they completed the preaching about the kingdom of heaven throughout the whole of his creation, according to the testimony of the apostle."[358]

Didascalia Apostolorum 23 (ca. A.D. 250): "But when we had divided the whole world into twelve parts, and were gone out to the gentiles into all the world to preach the word, at that time Satan made ready and stirred up the people to send after us false apostle for the destruction of the word."[359]

Acts Phil. 8:1 (fourth century): "It came to pass when the Savior divided the apostles according to city and country, so that each one of them would depart to the place that had been allotted to him [ἐγένετο ὅτε ὁ σωτὴρ ἐμέριζεν τοὺς ἀποστόλους κατὰ πόλιν καὶ χώραν πορευθῆναι ἕνα ἕκαστον αὐτῶν ἐπὶ τὸν κεκληρωμένον αὐτοῖς τόπον, καθὼς ἐκληρώθησαν]. It fell on Peter to go to Rome, Thomas to go to all the regions of Parthia and India, Matthew to go to the innermost regions of Pontus,[360] Bartholomew to go to Lycaonia, Simon Cananaeus to go to Spain, Andrew to go to Achaia, John to go to Asia, and Philip to go to the country of the Greeks. This was the decree that the Saviour had ordained [αὕτη γάρ ἐστιν

---

[356]Translation from J. M. Robinson, ed., *Nag Hammadi Library,* 289-91. Molinari (2000, 249-51) suggests that the final redaction of the text was completed in Alexandria immediately after the persecution under Decius.

[357]Translation from J. M. Robinson, ed., *Nag Hammadi Library,* 434-37.

[358]Weidmann 1999, 42; Coptic text, ibid., 17; commentary, ibid., 60-73; on the dating of the fragments of Polycarp extant in Coptic (Sahidic), kept in the Harris Collection in the British Museum in London, see ibid., 146-47; the fragments have been known since 1926 but were published only recently. Weidmann dates the tradition of the apostolic "missionary report" to the second/third century (ibid., 61).

[359]Translation from A. Vööbus, ed., *The Didascalia Apostolorum,* 2:212, lines 7-11. For a German translation see H. Achelis and J. Fleming, eds., *Die syrische Didaskalia,* 77, 120-21. The Latin text reads: Cum autem diuidissemus inter nos duodecim uncias saeculi et exiuimus ad gentes ut in omni mundo praedicaremus verbum.

[360]MS Xenophontos 32 (A) makes Matthew responsible for the missionary work in Judea; cf. the text in Bovon, Bouvier and Amsler 1999, 237.

ἡ ὑπὸ τοῦ σωτῆρος διατεταγμένη διάταξις]" (Athen 345).[361]

Syriac Acts of John (ca. A.D. 500): After Jesus' ascension and the arrival of the Holy Spirit at Pentecost, the apostles are filled with the desire to depart. The apostles give speeches in which they address the necessity of worldwide missionary work. After they are finished, they separate: "Each traveled to the country and the region for which he had received responsibility through the grace."[362]

What is the historical value of these texts? The tradition about a division of the world into areas of missionary responsibility often is regarded as legendary, having no historical value. At least four reasons are given.[363] (a) The oldest sources do not contain a complete list of the twelve apostles and their missionary areas.[364] (b) The sources present no coherent tradition about the division of the world among the apostles.[365] (c) The earliest texts list five apostles—Thomas, Andrew, John, Peter and Paul—on whose life and ministry other authors wrote *acta,* which means that these apostles already played an important role in the tradition.[366] (d) The twelve years that are mentioned in some sources fit the twelve apostles too neatly.[367]

These arguments may be evaluated as follows. In regard to the first objection, we cannot avoid the suspicion that this is a *petitio principii:* the possibility that Jesus' disciples planned a worldwide missionary ministry and divided the world into separate areas of missionary work is possibly rejected from the outset and does not depend on the content of the texts from the second and third centuries. Adolf von Harnack, after reading the apocryphal Acts as "apostolic legends," comments that "according to their literary genre they belong to the descriptions of undiscovered countries and peoples."[368] The "legends" that Origen quotes may, however, have "in one or another case" a historical core because Origen "surely did not 'invent' anything." Critical scholars who are skeptical of the historical value of the Jesus tradition in the Gospels or of the traditions about Peter and Paul in the book of Acts, who reject the authenticity of Jesus' miracles, who

---

[361]See also *Acts Phil.* 3.2: Andrew is sent to Achaia and Thrace, Thomas to India, Matthew to the cave dwellers (*tryglodytai,* a term frequently used for the Nubians and Ethiopians, as well as for the African coast of the Red Sea; see F. Lasserre, "Tryg[l]odytai," *KP* 5:977).

[362]According to Kaestli 1981, 256; cf. Junod and Kaestli 1983, 2:706. For the Syriac text see William Wright, *Apocryphal Acts of the Apostles, Edited from Syriac Manuscripts* (2 vols.; Hildesheim: Olms, 1990 [1871]), 1:4-65; 2:3-60.

[363]W. Bauer, in Hennecke and Schneemelcher 1959-1964, 2:17-19; Lipsius 1883-1890, 1:11 ("Die Legende von der Aposteltheilung"); Kaestli 1981; Brox 1982, 195-96; Lampe and Luz 1987, 212; Weidmann 1999, 60; Amsler 1999, 298, following Kaestli.

[364]Junod 1981, 243; Weidmann 1999, 60.

[365]Kaestli 1981, 264; Weidmann 1999, 61.

[366]Junod 1981, 248; McDonald 1992, 178; Weidmann 1999, 60.

[367]W. Bauer, in Hennecke and Schneemelcher 1959-1964, 2:19.

[368]Harnack 1924, 1:108-9 with n. 1; the quotation that follows above, ibid.

reject the historicity of Jesus' resurrection and of missionary commissions given by Jesus to the Twelve, will read the apocryphal Acts with uttermost skepticism. This is consistent, but hardly convincing.[369] In regard to the specific argument of the first objection, it surely is a fair assumption that if the apocryphal Acts contained complete lists of the twelve apostles, this fact would be regarded as evidence for aetological legends (analogous to the lists of disciples in the canonical Gospels whose authenticity is rejected by scholars). Luke had much more information about the history of the church and of the missionary expansion of the church in the first century than he includes in the book of Acts. Yet he fails to report the origins of the churches in Damascus, Rome, Tyre, Sidon, Smyrna (the rival of Ephesus) and Pergamon. He makes no reference to Paul's missionary work in the first ten years or so after his conversion, and he makes no reference to Peter's missionary work during the twenty-five years after his departure from Jerusalem. It was only Eusebius, in the fourth century, who attempted to provide a complete survey of the history of the church. To demand complete lists of apostles is therefore highly problematic.

The second objection has similar problems. If the sources from the second and third centuries presented a coherent and consistent tradition, then this would be used as an argument against the authenticity of such a conference in Jerusalem twelve years after Easter. It is a fact that no early Christian text that reports or claims to report historical events attempts to provide a comprehensive historical account. It is precisely the missing "coherence" that may indicate that Christian authors of the second and third centuries had information about the ministry of the apostles. Since they did not write a comprehensive history of the early church, they passed on the information that they had in a selective and uncoordinated manner.

Third, it must be noted that the apocryphal Acts of Thomas, of Andrew, of John, of Peter and of Paul do not explain the tradition of the worldwide missionary work of the twelve apostles in a compelling manner. The latter is mentioned only in the Acts of Thomas and of Peter; it has not been possible to confirm an influence of the Acts of Andrew and of John on this tradition. Adolf von Harnack and others argue that the rise of "missionary legends" around A.D. 200 can be explained with the growing ambition of "the countries" to be able to claim that they received the Christian faith as early as possible and from an apostle.[370] This argument is discredited by Harnack himself: the churches in northern Africa and in Gaul do not "need" (at this time) an apostolic founder. We also should recall that the apostles function as a group in the early noncanonical Acts, without reference

---

[369]W. Bienert (in Hennecke and Schneemelcher 1987-1989, 2:18-20) arrives at a more cautious evaluation: "Whether and to what degree these Acts report historically reliable events besides miraculous legends is often difficult to say."

[370]Harnack 1924, 1:108; for the remark that follows above see ibid., 108-9.

to a command, commission or initiative of Jesus Christ or of Peter, and that they do not include a complete list of the apostles and their missionary areas.[371]

Fourth, while it is correct that the number of twelve years fits the twelve apostles, it may safely be assumed that if the tradition mentioned another figure, the critics still would not take it seriously as a chronological reference to the beginning of the worldwide mission of the Twelve. Ernst Haenchen rejects the number 120 in Acts 1:15 as historically worthless, as it (allegedly) has a symbolic significance, but he also rejects the figures that Luke mentions for the people who are converted in Jerusalem, even though he is unable to provide symbolic explanations for the three thousand converts or for the five thousand Christians in Jerusalem.

A refutation of the objections listed above does not prove, of course, the authenticity of the tradition of a "planning conference" of the Twelve during which they discussed and strategized the implementation of Jesus' missionary commission in a universal and international scope. The following twofold consideration shows, however, that the tradition that the Twelve were active in Jerusalem for twelve years before they decided to embark on a universal missionary activity may well be historical.[372] (a) The early church fathers, such as Tertullian and Hippolytus, treated the apocryphal Acts favorably. The distrust that we find in Eusebius (*Hist. eccl.* 3.3.5) eventually turns into outright rejection, but only after the closure of the New Testament canon; another reason might have been the fact that the heretical Manicheans valued these texts highly.[373] (b) The Indian local color of *Acts of Thomas* and historical and archaeological advances in our knowledge of the history of India in the first century indicate that a mission of Thomas to India is plausible (see §22.12). It therefore is not impossible that other chips of information in the apocryphal Acts may potentially claim plausibility in regard to activities of the Twelve.

11. The last piece of evidence for an active Gentile mission of the Twelve is found in Paul's letter to the Roman Christians. According to Rom 15:20, it is an important principle of his missionary strategy that he "not build on someone else's foundation"; that is, he will not engage in missionary work in areas where other missionaries are active. This principle causes Paul to leave the eastern areas of the Mediterranean world and plan to begin missionary work in Spain, and it confirms the existence of other early Christian missionaries who preached the gospel among Gentiles.[374] Paul states in 1 Cor 9:5 that other apostles, the brothers of the Lord and Cephas-Peter take their wives along (περιάγειν, *periagein*) on their missionary journeys. This comment proves that among the pio-

---

[371]Weidmann 1999, 61.
[372]Thus Harnack 1893-1904, 2.1:244. Most scholars are skeptical; see Schäferdiek 1991, 69.
[373]W. Bienert, in Hennecke and Schneemelcher 1987-1989, 2:20.
[374]Thus Pieper 1929, 9.

neer missionaries who evidently engaged in missionary work among Gentiles there were Jerusalem apostles. In 1 Cor 15:10 Paul notes that even though he is the least of the apostles, by God's grace he "worked harder than any of them" (περισσότερον αὐτῶν πάντων ἐκοπίασα): since he writes to the Corinthian Christians primarily not as a church leader but as a missionary—Paul is engaged in missionary work at the time when he writes to the Corinthians—this comment also implies that "the Twelve" and "all the apostles" (1 Cor 15:5, 7) were active as missionaries.[375] Finally, we should not forget that even the conservative Jewish Christians who demanded that Gentile Christians be circumcised and keep the traditional Jewish purity and food laws were engaged in "missionary" activity (cf. Gal 6:13)!

I conclude, therefore, that other apostles also planned and organized missionary outreach, consolidated new congregations, appointed co-workers, and presumably also reflected on the missionary commission that Jesus gave them as well as on the good news of Jesus Christ that they proclaimed, perhaps even in written form. It may be true that nobody worked as intensively, effectively and internationally as Paul did.[376]

Motivating Factors

What was the inner motivation that helped the early Christian missionaries to be and to remain involved in evangelistic activity? Which motivating factors were important?

1. Both the Gospel writers and Luke in the book of Acts[377] impress upon the Christian communities the missionary commission of the risen Christ as the foundation of the missionary work of the church. The calling to be "fishers of people"[378] linked the missionary task with Jesus as well, as a central, fundamental assignment that Jesus gave to his followers.

2. The Gentile mission is a prerequisite for the parousia, for Jesus' second coming. According to Mk 13:10, Jesus described missionary outreach among the nations as a necessary development before the end can come. When the disciples expressed the conviction that the end of the present aeon is near (Acts 1:6), Jesus did not correct them, but he connected his answer concerning the timing of the end with a renewed commission to engage in international missionary work among the nations to the ends of the earth (Acts 1:8). The apostles were convinced that Jesus was the promised Messiah (Acts 2:36), that the time had come when the nations are gathered, and that Jesus has given them an important task in the context of these events of the last days. This eschatological un-

---

[375]Bruce 1993, 688.
[376]See Becker 1987, 104; Schrage, *1 Kor,* 3:69-70.
[377]Mt 28:19-20; Mk 13:10; Lk 24:47; Jn 20:21 (cf. Mk 16:15); Acts 1:8.
[378]Mt 4:19; Mk 1:17; Lk 5:10; cf. Mt 13:47.

derstanding of history was central for Paul. He argues that Israel has rejected the gospel "until the full number of the Gentiles has come in" (Rom 11:25).[379] The time until the return of Jesus Christ is the time of missionary work among the nations. Whether the phrase "full number of the Gentiles" refers to the conclusion of the Gentile mission[380] or to a fixed number of Gentiles whom God has preordained to be converted[381] does not change the thrust of Paul's basic argument at this point.[382] It should be noted that Paul does not use these eschatological convictions when he exhorts the churches to be active for the gospel (see §28.6). The second coming of Jesus is never used as an argument to speed up the missionary work or to reach out to new regions.

This eschatological view of history played a major role as a motivating force in the early medieval missionary activity, as is shown by the pastoral letter of Pope Gregory the Great of June 22, 601. Pope Gregory argues the necessity of intensive missionary work on the basis of the coming end of the world.[383] Lutz von Padberg comments that in the pope's argumentation "the Gentiles are prepared for their conversion by the work of God, while the missionaries react to the divine plan of salvation with their obedience to the missionary commission. This connection shows again why the messengers of faith believed it to be unnecessary to interact more intensively with the pagan's belief in idols, as the latter could hardly play a decisive role in the last days of the world."

3. The apostles were convinced that Jesus was the only answer to the lostness of humankind, that there was nobody else through whom people could be saved (Acts 4:12). They held this conviction with regard to the Jewish faith, aware of the consequences this had for the Jerusalem temple, for the sacrifices and for the purity laws of the Torah. And they held this conviction even more firmly with regard to the beliefs of the Gentiles, whose gods were false gods and whose sacrifices achieved nothing.

Greg Beale argues that the realization of the "new creation" that has begun with the death and the resurrection of Jesus Christ as the "last Adam"[384] takes place in the universal mission of the disciples who fulfill the task that God had given to Adam and to Israel, as they go to the ends of the earth.[385]

We have seen in §§4; 5 that neither Adam nor Israel (nor Noah) received a divine commission to go "to the end of the earth." The command to Adam in Gen 1:28, "Be fruitful and multiply, and fill the earth and subdue it; and have dominion over the fish of the sea

[379]Rom 11:25: ἄχρις οὗ τὸ πλήρωμα τῶν ἐθνῶν εἰσέλθῃ.
[380]Wilckens, Röm, 2:254; Munck 1954, 39-41; Aus 1979 , 232-42; Hübner 1984, 112-13; N. T. Wright 1992, 249-51.
[381]Michel, Röm, 355; Schlier, Röm, 339; Käsemann, Röm, 303; Cranfield, Rom, 2:575; Dunn, Rom, 2:680; Moo, Rom, 719; Refoulé 1984, 83-85.
[382]Fitzmyer, Rom, 622.
[383]Padberg 1995, 41-48, esp. 42-46; the quotation that follows above, ibid., 48.
[384]Gal 6:14-15; 2 Cor 5:14-17; Col 1:15-18; Rev 1:5; 3:14.
[385]Beale 1997, 28-29.

and over the birds of the air and over every living thing that moves upon the earth," speaks of fertility and procreation that result from the successions of the generations,[386] from rule over the animal world and the material world. The divine command formulates a cultural and civilizational mission. The blessing of the creation, which is the basis of this commission, is repeated after the flood as a directive given to Noah (Gen 9:1-7). Again the text does not refer to going to "the ends of the earth," nor is this the case in the blessing of Abraham in Gen 12:3. The New Testament texts that speak of the "new creation," understood in the context of the early Christian conviction that Jesus is present in the "house" of his church as the new people of God, focus on the new reality of the community of the followers of Jesus, not on world missions. Note the following texts:

Gal 6:15: "For neither circumcision nor uncircumcision is anything; but a new creation is everything [ἀλλὰ καινὴ κτίσις]!"

2 Cor 5:14-17: "For the love of Christ urges us on, because we are convinced that one has died for all; therefore all have died. [15]And he died for all, so that those who live might live no longer for themselves, but for him who died and was raised for them. [16]From now on, therefore, we regard no one from a human point of view; even though we once knew Christ from a human point of view, we know him no longer in that way. [17]So if anyone is in Christ, there is a new creation [εἴ τις ἐν Χριστῷ, καινὴ κτίσις]: everything old has passed away; see, everything has become new [ἰδοὺ γέγονεν καινά]!"

If Jesus as "the firstborn from the dead" (Col 1:18; Rev 1:5) is "the beginning of God's creation" (ἡ ἀρχὴ τῆς κτίσεως τοῦ θεοῦ [Rev 3:14]), then the people of God who belong to Jesus as his "body" belong to the new creation. This assurance implies the obligation to live as "new creation." The life of the church as the community of the new creation is directed, initially, to Jesus Christ himself (2 Cor 5:15). Since Jesus as the "head of the body" is the beginning of the new creation, since Jesus fulfilled the mission that God had given to him, to reconcile the world through his death on the cross (Col 1:18-20), and since Jesus involves his disciples as "fishers of people" who go "to the ends of the earth" in this mission, the missionary work of the apostles can indeed be understood as a central aspect of the realization of the new creation.

Col 1:18-20: "He is the head of the body, the church; he is the beginning, the firstborn from the dead [ὅς ἐστιν ἀρχή, πρωτότοκος ἐκ τῶν νεκρῶν], so that he might come to have first place in everything. [19]For in him all the fullness of God was pleased to dwell, [20]and through him God was pleased to reconcile to himself all things [δι᾽ αὐτοῦ ἀποκαταλλάξαι τὰ πάντα εἰς αὐτόν], whether on earth or in heaven, by making peace through the blood of his cross."

We note, however, that in this text the "action" by which the new creation becomes a reality as a world that has been reconciled with God as the acting subject is not linked with the missionary activity of the disciples. It therefore is not

---

[386]Westermann, *Gen,* 222.

helpful, in my view, to describe the missionary work of the church as fulfillment of the divine commission given to Adam and to Israel to subjugate the earth as God's viceroy.[387] The church subdues neither people nor the world but rather serves people and the world unselfishly and sacrificially. The missionaries of the church do not make the kingdom of God a reality: they proclaim the kingdom of God and teach the followers of Jesus everything that Jesus commanded, so that the reality of the kingdom of God, as the reality of the new creation, increasingly and visibly takes shape in the communities of believers and in the individual Christians.

16.5 Difficulties and Challenges
The Lack of Suitable Models

The first challenge for the early Christian missionaries was the lack of models for an international religious operation that seeks to win new converts in new regions and establish new religious communities in new cities and towns.[388] The early Christian mission was not a "rival mission,"[389] perhaps to a Jewish missionary activity, which in any case, as we have seen, did not exist. Contemporary scholarship often still proceeds on the assumption that the missionary activity of Paul, for example, should be understood in the context of Greco-Roman culture, for which religious propaganda was nothing unusual.[390] Such analyses usually paint with a very broad brush. Often the word "mission" goes undefined. If we define "mission" or "missionary activity" as the active endeavor to win people for a particular faith, with the goal to help people change their religious convictions, their behavior patterns in everyday life, and their loyalties—from family, city and country to the fellowship of the community of the followers of Jesus—then the parallels that scholars suggest for the early Christian mission lose their plausibility. We must not forget that the expansion of Greek and Egyptian cults did not follow a specific plan, nor was it the result of concrete and deliberate intentions.[391]

The opening sentences of a paper that Hans von Soden read in 1924 certainly were formulated from a Christian perspective: "Mission, propaganda, is an indispensable vital function of every genuine and healthy religion. Propaganda means procreation; procreation is a fundamental function of organic life, and religion is life. When there is no propaganda, this is always a symptom of an inner crisis of religion, which is constricted or weakened and therefore not able or not yet able to resume propagandistic action, or has

[387]Contra Beale 1997, 29.
[388]Thus Bowers (1980), who is too quick, however, to fade out other early Christian missionaries besides the apostle Paul (see ibid., 322-32). See more recently M. Goodman 1994; cf. C. Hezser, *JRS* 85 (1995): 316-17.
[389]Contra Wernle (1909, 3), who spoke of a "Konkurrenzmission." See also Aune 1991, 106.
[390]This was the older consensus; see Oepke 1920, 12-39; Clemen 1929.
[391]See Bowers 1980, 317-18.

to interrupt it temporarily. . . . The fact that Christianity still does missionary work today is a sure sign of its inexhaustible, procreative life and gives the lie to those who regard it as a dying entity and who have all sorts of misgivings about its missionary work."[392]

The French patristic scholar Gustave Bardy writes in his important study on conversion to the Christian faith, "The notion of a conversion in the sense in which we understand this word today remained totally alien to the Greco-Roman mentality for a long time, perhaps even until the rise of Christianity. It had never happened, indeed one could not conceive of a person who would renounce the religion of his *polis* and of his ancestors in order to pledge exclusive and personal allegiance to a very different religion. . . . Unlike Yahweh among the Jews, the pagan gods are not jealous gods. Far from obligating their devotees to an exclusive cult, they have no difficulties tolerating adjacent gods who can never be rivals."[393]

1. We have seen that Jews did not engage in an organized missionary outreach to Gentiles during the Second Temple period (§6). The center of the Jewish commonwealth in Jerusalem kept in contact with the Diaspora synagogues through authorized messengers (שְׁלוּחִים, *šĕlûhîm*, Gk., *apostoloi*). These *šĕlûhîm* can serve with some justification as a "personal model" for "global" communication.[394] But the institution of the *šaliah* was no model for the international missionary outreach of the early church, which sought to win Jews and pagans to faith in the good news of Jesus Christ. The *šĕlûhîm* maintained existing contacts, whereas the followers of Jesus in Jerusalem, in their mission, sought to win Jews to a new teaching and wanted to establish new contacts with people of other faiths.

2. There is no evidence for deliberate missionary endeavors of Hellenistic cults. Helmut Koester believes that an inscription found in the sanctuary of the Egyptian gods in Thessalonike that reports the introduction of the cult of Sarapis in the city of Opus in Locris in central Greece (*IG* X 2 225) belongs "to the propaganda narratives which are typical for the dissemination of the Hellenistic missionary religions."[395]

---

[392]Soden 1924, 18.

[393]Bardy 1988, 17.

[394]See Reck 1991, 157.

[395]H. Koester 1994, 402, with reference to Daniel Fraikin, "Introduction of Sarapis and Isis in Opus," *Numina Aegaea* 1 (1974); Philip Sellew, "Religious Propaganda in Antiquity: A Case from the Sarapeum at Thessaloniki," *Numina Aegaea* 3 (1980): 1520; R. Merkelbach, "Zwei Texte aus dem Sarapeum zu Thessalonike," *ZPE* 10 (1973): 45-54; Franciszek Sokolowski, "Propagation of the Cult of Sarapis and Isis in Greece," *GRBS* 15 (1974): 441-48. For the text and a translation see *NewDocs* 1:29-32 (no. 6). Brocke (2001), unfortunately, does not discuss the inscription. The quotation that follows above is from H. Koester 1994, 402. See also Clemen 1929.

The inscription dates to the first century A.D. and probably is a copy of an older inscription from Opus written in the second century B.C. Helmut Koester describes the content of the inscription as follows: "The inscription reports that Xenainetos of Opus, during a visit to Thessalonica, received in a dream from Sarapis the command to order Euronymos of Opus to introduce the god and his sister (i.e., Isis). Xenainetos awakens and remembers that this Euronymos is his political enemy, and falls asleep again. When he awakens for the second time, he finds under his pillow the letter that Sarapis had announced. He delivers the letter, and Euronymos decides, after he has read the letter and heard Xenaine-tos's story, to introduce Sarapis and Isis in Opus."

The claim that this story is a "close parallel" to the narrative in Acts 10 and that it belongs to "propaganda narratives" that are typical for the dissemination of "Hellenistic missionary religions" is neither proven nor plausible. We need to consider the following two facts. (a) The motif of "letters from heaven" (*Himmelsbriefe*) occurs in inscriptions, papyri and literary texts, and it played a certain role in later Christianity as well.[396] However, this motif plays no role whatsoever in the conversion narratives in the book of Acts: a dream or a vision, as, for example, reported for Paul at his conversion or before he set sail for Europe, cannot simply be identified with a "letter from heaven."[397] (b) The question of whether Euronymos was converted[398] depends on the definition of conversion that is presupposed. Without doubt Euronymos accepted the cult of Isis and Sarapis, which he initially rejected, and perhaps he even became a follower of the cult. It is unrealistic, however, to assume that he thereby abandoned the worship of any other gods: all he did was add Isis and Osiris to the group of gods that he worshiped. It was not an infrequent occurrence for a city or for individuals to include additional deities in the group of gods that were traditionally or individually worshiped. In the fundamentally polytheistic context of the Greco-Roman world it does not seem very meaningful to describe the addition of another deity to already existing cults as "conversion." If such an understanding of conversion is accepted, then many people were "converted" back and forth all the time!

There is no doubt that religious cults gained new adherents in the Greco-Roman world, and that priests and adherents played an important role in the dissemination of the particular cults. Lucian reports, for example, how a certain Alexander propagated the oracle of Abonuteichos, albeit with intent to defraud (*Alex.* 10, 15, 24, 36).[399]

---

[396]*IG* XI 4 1299; P.Cair.Zen. 59034; Pausanias 10.38.13; Palladius, *Hist. laus.* 32 (1099C); Herm. *Vis.* 2.1:3-4. See Nock 1933, 50-54; Speyer 1970; R. Merkelbach, *ZPE* 10 (1973): 53; Horsley, *NewDocs* 1:29-32; 5:136.
[397]Contra Merkelbach (*ZPE* 10 [1973]: 54), who sees the conversion of Saul/Paul as a parallel.
[398]Thus Horsley, *NewDocs* 1:31.
[399]See Robert 1980, 393-421; Lane Fox 1986, 241-50; M. Goodman 1994, 29-30.

Ramsay MacMullen mentions in this context a certain Julianus Euteknios, a merchant from Syria who lived in Laodikeia and whose epitaph in Lugdunum (mod. Lyon), dating probably to the third century, reads as follows: "If you desire to know what mortal lies here, this writing will not be silent, but will tell all. Euteknios is his surname, Julianos his name; Laodicea his city, Syria's remarkable ornament. His father's family was held in esteem, and his mother had a similar reputation. He was good and just, a man beloved by all. When he spoke to Kelts [οὗ Κελτοῖς λαλέοντος], persuasion flowed from his tongue [ἀπὸ γλώσσης ῥέε πειθώ]. He went about among diverse nations [ποικίλα μὲν περιῆλθεν ἔθνη], and knew many peoples; and he practised a virtuous life among them. He gave himself continually to the waves and to the sea, carrying to the Kelts and to the land of the West all gifts which God instructed the bountiful East to bear. For this reason the threefold tribes of the Kelts loved the man."[400] Julianos probably was not a Christian, as some scholars have assumed,[401] and thus not an itinerant missionary, but rather a merchant who traveled from one region to another by ship.[402] Nor was Julianos a pagan (philosophical) teacher: the formulation πολλοὺς δέ <τε> δήμους ἔγνω καὶ ψυχῆς ἀρετὴν ἤσκησεν ἐ<ν> αὐτοῖς in column 1, lines 8-9, should be translated not as "he knew many peoples and afforded training to the soul among them" (R. MacMullen), but as "he knew many peoples; and he practised a virtuous life among them" (G. Horsley).

The dissemination of the cult of a deity was deliberate, but it did not happen by imparting a set of beliefs. The divine nature of the propagated god could be presupposed. Ramsay MacMullen points out that the emphasis was on the attractions that the new cult, or some particular sanctuary, could boast of: healing miracles, knowledge of the future, festivals. One indeed could encounter representatives of Cybele or of some deity on the streets or at the agora, but they did not proclaim a message—they begged.[403] MacMullen concludes that "of any organized or conscious evangelizing in paganism there are very few signs indeed, though it is often alleged; of any god whose cult required or had anything ordinarily to say about evangelizing there is no sign at all." The cult of a deity was characterized by important identical uniform features in the various places to which it was exported; in the case of the cult of Cybele, for example, there were careful duplications of cult statues, fixed holy days in the calender, and sometimes identical hymns. On the other hand, the fact that there were significant differences in the way the same cult was practiced in different cities—for example, the cult of Dionysos—indicates that pagan cults were not disseminated according to a uniform plan. It is hardly possible to speak of *the* cult of Isis. MacMullen observes, "The sum was confusion.

---

[400]Editio princeps: Jean Pouilloux, *Journal des savants* (1975): 58-75. On the stele and on the Church of Saint-Just, where it was found, see, also in *Journal des savants* (1975), J.-F. Reynard, 47-56, and A. Audin, 56-58. The text is reprinted in *SEG* XXVI 1214; *NewDocs* 1:68-69 (no. 23). Thomas Corsten did not include the inscription in the corpus of *I. Laodikeia*.

[401]Pouilloux, *Journal des savants* (1975): 72-74; Margherita Guarducci, "Il missionario di Lione," *Mélanges de l'école française de Rome* 88 (1976): 843-52.

[402]C. P. Jones, "A Syrian in Lyons," *AJP* 99 (1978): 336-53, esp. 344, 351-53; Horsley, *NewDocs* 1:69; MacMullen 1981, 98, 192 n. 7.

[403]MacMullen 1981, 98; the quotation that follows above, ibid., 98-99.

No counterforce for order existed."[404] Not even the emperor cult was promoted (before A.D. 312) with the goal of achieving uniformity in religious beliefs or practice, not even in the army; the local forms and features were quite diverse. "The independence, not to say license and shapelessness, of paganism had suffered no disturbance from above." There is practically no evidence that the advantages of a cult were actively communicated to potential converts, perhaps by temple personnel or by adherents who were personally convinced of the superior truth or value of the cult. Evidently cults often disseminated within families whose members had settled in different cities. For example, the dissemination of the Egyptian cults was a function of the mobility of families and individuals, not the result of deliberate missionary activity.[405] Most polytheists did not understand themselves as members of a particular group defined by the worship of a particular deity.[406] Martin Goodman comments, "The adherents of no pagan cult claimed that the worship which they advocated superseded those practiced already."

3. The itinerant Cynic philosophers who are often cited as parallels for the early Christian missionaries (see §§10.2; 18.5)[407] hardly served as a model either. They did not attempt to disseminate their convictions from city to city or from province to province according to a plan, nor did they organize communities of sympathizers who shared their life. Paul Bowers encapsulates the differences between the itinerant philosophers and the missionary outreach of the early Christians in the observation that "they wandered, Paul progressed."[408]

In his influential study on religious propaganda in antiquity Dieter Georgi quotes the following passages from Epictetus: "But in such an order of things as the present, which is like that of a battlefield, it is a question, perhaps, if the Cynic ought not to be free from distraction, wholly devoted to the service of God [διακονία τοῦ θεοῦ], free to go about among men [ἐπιφοιτᾶν ἀνθρώποις], not tied down by the private duties of men, nor involved in relationships which he cannot violate and still maintain his role as a good and excellent man, whereas, on the other hand, if he observes them, he will destroy the messenger, the scout, the herald of the gods [τὸν ἄγγελον καὶ κατάσκοπον καὶ κήρυκα τῶν θεῶν] that he is" (*Diatr.* 3.22.69). "In the next place, the true Cynic, when he is thus prepared, cannot rest contented with this, but he must know that he has been sent by Zeus to men [ἄγγελος ἀπὸ Διὸς ἀπέσταλται], partly as a messenger, in order to show them that in questions of good and evil they have gone astray, and are seeking the true nature of the good and the evil where it is not, but where it is they never think" (*Diatr.* 3.22.23). "But what was the manner of his [Diogenes'] loving? As became a servant [διάκονος] of Zeus,

---

[404]MacMullen 1981, 102; cf. ibid., 107; for the observations that follow above see ibid., 102-12; quotation, 104. On the emperor cult see also Bardy 1988, 25-26.

[405]See Bowers 1980, 319-20; MacMullen 1981, 116-17.

[406]M. Goodman 1994, 27; the quotation that follows above, ibid., 22.

[407]See Goppelt 1959, 137; Georgi 1964, 32-34, 110-11, 187, 193-96 (ET, 28-30, 99-100, 151-52, 156-58); Hoffmann 1972, 318; Theissen 1973, 79-105 (ET, 33-59); Bardy 1988, 92-94; Marie-Odile Goulet-Cazé, "Le cynisme à l'époque impériale," *ANRW* II.36.4 (1990): 2720-2833; see also Liefeld 1967.

[408]Bowers 1980, 319.

caring for men indeed, but at the same time subject unto God. That is why for him alone the whole world, and no special place, was his fatherland" (*Diat.* 3.24.64).[409]

Similarities with the self-understanding of the early Christian missionaries in language and sense of mission must not obscure the following facts. (a) Epictetus's Cynics understand themselves as messengers and witnesses of god among the people. However, according to Margarethe Billerbeck, this religious concept of the calling of the Cynic "is Epictetus's own coinage, as he is the one Stoic who comes closest to a theistic concept of God,"[410] perhaps as a result of his personal religiosity. This means that Epictetus's description of a Cynic philosopher cannot automatically be presupposed for all itinerant Cynic philosophers. The older Cynics rejected the traditional religious cults without explicitly denying the existence of the gods. The neo-Cynic movement was influenced in terms of its religious ideas by Stoic philosophy.[411] But the Cynic philosophers never wanted to question or change the religious loyalties of their listeners, whereas such suasion was the primary intention of the early Christian missionaries when they preached to polytheists. (b) In view of the geographical scope of their activities, it is more than doubtful that the Cynics pursued "a mission in and to the entire world" and that they "executed" this function as "world missionaries."[412] The reference to the Cynics "going about among men" describes not geographical excursions but house visits, as Epictetus relates: "Where, pray, is this king, whose duty it is to oversee the rest of men; those who have married; those who have had children; who is treating his wife well, and who ill; who quarrels; what household is stable, and what not; making his rounds like a physician, and feeling pulses?" (*Diss.* 3.22.72). The Cynic Crates was called "door-opener" (Θυρεπανοίκτης) as a result of this kind of activity (Diogenes Laertius 6.86).[413] Lucian describes, not without sarcasm, that the Cynic market criers go from house to house, collecting money with threats (*Fug.* 14). Donald Dudley's comment, written in 1937, still represents the present state of research: "The aim of the [Cynic] system is not to produce little Cynics . . . the Cynic labours not on behalf of his movement but of mankind."[414] (c) The Cynics accepted the Socratic principle that people who act wrongly act out of ignorance and merely need to be informed about their errors.[415] The teaching of the Cynic philosophers, who understood ethical misdemeanors as intellectual error and enlightened their au-

---

[409]Georgi 1964, 32-33, 195 n. 1 (ET, 28-29); for a German translation see Billerbeck 1978.

[410]Billerbeck 1978, 8; for the observation that follows above see idem 1979, 40.

[411]Billerbeck 1979, 39-40, with reference to Diogenes, on the one hand, and to Epictetus, on the other.

[412]Georgi 1964, 33 (ET, 28); the quotation that follows above, ibid. (italics added).

[413]Billerbeck 1978, 133; for the remark that follows above see ibid., 133-34.

[414]Dudley 1937, 88; quoted in M. Goodman 1994, 35.

[415]On Socrates see Plato, *Soph.* 228c; cf. Billerbeck 1978, 79; Klauck 1995-1996, 2:110; for the remark that follows above see ibid., 2:112.

dience about mistakes, is too different from the early Christian missionary preaching, which presumed and announced the essential corruptness and lostness of all human beings, to warrant comparisons. (d) If the Cynic's moral self-consciousness has the final say as "quintessence of personal autonomy," and if the effect of the Cynic's speeches as "uncomfortable admonisher" depends on the speaker's ability to stand before an audience as a mature person, then the contrast to the personality of the early Christian missionaries is obvious: the authors of the New Testament do not hesitate to mention weaknesses and failures of the apostles and of other missionaries. The effect of their preaching does not depend upon their personality. (e) The example of the Cynic Demetrius, a friend of Seneca and a confidant of opposition Stoics at the time of Nero, demonstrates the intention of the Cynics' ethical instruction: they seek "to fortify the person engaged in moral progress for the struggle of life and to equip him so that he is able to walk the path of perfection independently."[416] The wise person is not forced by the laws of nature, "because since he sees through their causal relationships and grasps the will of the gods, he follows them out of his own volition." Demetrius complains to the gods only "that you did not earlier make known your will to me; for I should have reached sooner that condition in which, after being summoned, I now am."[417] The Cynic is willing to obey the gods "not as slave or under compulsion but with consent on the basis of his knowledge of the eternal laws." Again the contrast to the early Christian missionary and theologian is evident: the apostles understood themselves to be envoys of the Kyrios, as "slaves of Jesus Christ" who obeyed the divine "must." Their goal is not the demonstration of personal autarchy or the practice of moral independence but rather the "obedience of faith" (Rom 1:5). (f) The main themes of the neo-Cynic movement in the first century—the absence of wants, autarchy (which excludes friendship), tirades against wealth that seduces one to covetousness and greed—are not central themes of the early Christian missionary preaching, although the apostles do warn, of course, of covetousness and greed in their exhortations for the Christian communities. (g) The Cynics were consistently devoted to the authoritative example of philosophers who exemplified the proper way of life; they rejected book learning because they found "a small number of memorable aphorisms more effective than learned disputations."[418] Contrast with this ideal the apostles' respect for the sacred Scriptures as divine revelation, the significance of the apostolic letters, and the primacy of theological argumentation, particularly in Paul's epistles. (h) The Cynics' outspokenness or free-

---

[416]Billerbeck 1979, 35-36; the quotation that follows above, ibid., 38.
[417]Demetrius, according to Seneca, *Prov.* 5.5. For the explanation that follows above see Billerbeck 1979, 56.
[418]Billerbeck 1979, 31, with reference to Seneca, *Ben.* 7.1.3-2.1.

dom of speech (*parrēsia*)[419] refers to free speech, particularly before members of the upper classes and the powerful, in which they pointed out the moral lapses of their listeners and mercilessly denounced wealth and luxury. The Cynics defended the right to "free speech" with their moral perfection. In the early principate their *parrēsia* often was merely a pretense for lack of self-control or for simple impertinence. Even for the generally moderate Demetrius several shameless remarks are reported—for example, his comment "For me the talk of ignorant men is like the rumblings which issue from the belly. For what difference does it make to me whether such rumblings come from above or from below?" (in Seneca, *Ep.* 91.19). The early Christian missionaries were prepared to denounce human vices and sins, but they never scorned or mocked people, never denounced them with impertinent speeches in public, as they wanted to win them over to accept their beliefs and convictions.

Martin Goodman points to the significance of the fact that the two most popular philosophical systems during the early principate were not those of the Epicureans and the Cynics, who actively propagated their views, but rather those of the Stoics and the Platonists. It seems rather remarkable in this context that we never hear of attempts by Stoics or Platonists of a particular social group to win "adherents."[420]

The herald or public messenger (κῆρυξ, *kēryx*) of the Greco-Roman world does not provide a helpful background for the early Christian missionaries either, even though the Greek root, both as noun (*kēryx, kērygma*) and as verb (*kēryssein*), frequently is used in the New Testament to refer to proclamation (note *kēryx* in 1 Tim 2:7; 2 Tim 1:11). The Greek or Hellenistic *kēryx* was dependent upon (civil) institutions, whereas the early Christian heralds were primarily dependent upon a person, Jesus Christ.

4. The establishment of colonies in new regions by the Greeks and Romans might theoretically be a model for the early Christian mission. There were two waves of colonization emanating from Ephesus, reaching southern Gaul (France), among other areas. When the Phocians from Ionia established Massalia (mod. Marseille) around 600 B.C., they are said to have obeyed a Delphic oracle in bringing with them the cult of Artemis Ephesia from Ephesus, where they stopped on their way from Asia Minor to Gaul (Strabo 4.1.4). The Ionian colonists built a temple dedicated to Artemis Ephesia and celebrated the typical Ephesian festivals.[421] The reason for this initiative is not known. It seems to be unwarranted, however, to speak of "pagan missionaries in Greek Gaul":[422] the

---

[419]For the observations that follow above see Billerbeck 1979, 40-43.

[420]M. Goodman 1994, 37.

[421]Strabo 4.1.4 mentions an Ephesieion. See Malkin (1987, 69-72), who confirms the historical reliability of Strabo's report. For further evidence regarding the transfer of a cult from home city to colonies see Strabo 8.4.4; 8.7.2; 12.2.6; with regard to the cult of Artemis see Strabo 3.4.8; 4.1.4.

[422]Contra Malkin 1990, 42-52.

cult of Artemis Ephesia does not come from Phocis in central Greece, and the action of the Ionian colonists did not aim at the conversion of people of other faiths but rather served the transfer of a cult for the colonists themselves; Strabo (4.1.4) reports that this cult in Massalia was frequented by the colonists, in contrast to the pan-Ionian cult of Apollo Delphinios in Massalia.[423]

The military conquests of Alexander the Great that brought the Greek (Hellenistic) culture to Asia Minor, Syria, Persia and India did not represent a model for the small group of Jewish-Christian missionaries either—"fishers of people" who wanted to win individuals to faith in Jesus as messianic Savior.

5. Doron Mendels suggests that "culture heroes" may have served as models for the mission of the apostles, as Diodorus Siculus described them in his world history written in the first century B.C. Mendels defines "mission" in the Hellenistic world "before Paul" in terms of the activity of individuals who seek to communicate a message or convey some sort of progress to people within and/or outside of their political, religious or geographical area. Examples of such culture heroes are Osiris, Dionysos, Semiramis, Myrina and Heracles. Diodorus states that he recounts the deeds of those "most renowned heroes and demigods and, in general, about all who have performed any notable exploit in war, and likewise about such also as in time of peace have made useful discovery or enacted some good law contributing to man's social life" (4.1.5). Osiris "visited all the inhabited world in this way and advanced community life" (1.20.3).[424] Heracles traveled to Greece, sailed with the argonauts to Kolchi, and visited Crete, Libya, Egypt, Spain, Gaul, Liguria and Sicily before returning to Greece (4.17-19). His goal was to return the cattle of Geryones (4.17.1); at the same time he performed "civilizatory acts."[425]

The hypothesis of Mendels that "the various methods of mission which are to be found in Hellenistic culture heroes can be traced in Christian missionary activities as described by Luke" fails to convince for the following reasons. (a) The definition that Mendels gives for "mission" is much too vague, and missing are the elements of communication of a new way of life and integration into a new community. The early Christian mission was much more than the conveyance of a message across certain boundaries. A geographical round-trip by Heracles and courageous actions that defend (Greek!) civilization presented no "model" for the early Christian "itinerant" missionaries, no more than merchants who travel from place to place and carry "civilizational goods" across borders were "models" for the mission of the apostles. (b) The question regarding models of the early Christian mission is *not only* a question regarding literary or cultural

[423]See Malkin 1987, 72.
[424]Diodorus 1.20.3: τέλος δὲ τὸν Ὄσιριν πᾶσαν τὴν οἰκουμένην ἐπελθόντα τὸν κοινὸν βίον.
[425]Mendels 1996, 438; the quotation that follows above, ibid., 433. On Mendels see also J. M. Scott 2002, 62.

prototypes that Luke, the author of the book of Acts, may have had. The real question is whether Paul or any other missionary of the early church followed Hellenistic prototypes in missionary praxis. (c) Luke does not "mainly" focus on the mission of Paul:[426] in Acts 1—12 he describes the mission of Peter and Philip and anonymous Jewish-Christian missionaries from Jerusalem. In other words, one would need to demonstrate not only that Luke and Paul knew Hellenistic culture heroes and used them as models of communication, but also that the earliest missionaries of the Jerusalem church who initiated the early Christian mission knew and utilized the same model as well. (d) The fact that the culture heroes were accompanied by famous assistants—for example, Osiris is accompanied by Apollo as well as by his "sons" Anubis and Makedon, sometimes also by Pan, Maron and Triptolemos[427]—is hardly surprising for traveling benefactors, since people in antiquity rarely traveled alone. And the fact that Paul's travels are "cyclical," like those of the culture heroes, can easily be explained: Paul regularly returned to his starting point because he did not want to lose his connection with the church in Jerusalem. The proposed parallels with culture heroes are incidental. (e) Osiris and Heracles frequently overcome opposition with force. Mendels's point that Paul uses military metaphors that come from a non-Jewish background[428] cannot explain the rather obvious differences between the apostle and the alleged prototypes. (f) Whereas the culture heroes frequently "teach" technical progress—they build new roads and convey agricultural advances, they reveal new languages and present diverse inventions—the mission of the early church focuses on verbally communicated teaching and on existential and ethical integration into new communities. Mendels states that Paul "very wisely communicated with his gentile (and Jewish) audiences by presenting them with the socio-economic, religious, and even political reforms associated with his mission," but this does not adequately describe the mode, content or intention of Paul's missionary work. (g) If the fact that Paul cut his hair before his return to Jerusalem (Acts 18:18) is "one of the striking similarities to be found,"[429] then the similarities and parallels are weak indeed!

It seems impossible to avoid the conclusion that the active, expansive missionary work among Jews and Gentiles carried out by the early Christian was a shocking innovation in antiquity.[430]

The Variability of Religious Structures

A second barrier for the proclamation of the good news of Jesus Christ among

---

[426]Contra Mendels 1996, 433.

[427]Mendels 1996, 439; for the point that follows above see ibid., 448-49.

[428]Mendels 1996, 440 with n. 19; for the next point and quotation above see ibid., 441.

[429]Mendels 1996, 449.

[430]Correctly M. Goodman (1994, 105), whose comments on the origins of the early Christian mission (ibid., 90-105) are not very helpful, however.

polytheists was that basic beliefs and value judgments were in many ways fundamentally different. Jews found forgiveness of sins and meaning of life in the sacrificial rites prescribed by the Torah, in the temple cult, in the praxis of the revealed will of the one true God, and in the worship of Yahweh in the temple and in the synagogues. Gentiles found meaning, joy and comfort in religious rites performed personally or publicly, in private homes or in temples. The diverse pagan religions were alive and well in the first century and for quite some time after that, constantly introducing new, adapted forms of worshiping the divine.[431] The message of the early missionaries spoke of a Jewish Savior who had died on a cross and had been raised from the dead, a message that was incompatible with traditional Jewish or pagan notions about God and salvation (1 Cor 1:22-25). Luke emphasizes again and again, not least on account of this incompatibility, that it was the Holy Spirit of God who guided the missionary efforts of the early Christians and made them effective and fruitful.[432]

Social and Cultural Barriers

A third difficulty for the early Christian missionary activity was social and cultural barriers.

1. There were barriers between Jewish Christians and Jews, with differing convictions about Israel, the temple, the sacrifices stipulated by the Torah, forgiveness of sin, circumcision, food and purity, and last but not least, the Messiah. Both Luke and Paul indicate that the early missionaries attempted to take into account Jewish sensibilities whenever possible.[433]

2. There were barriers between Jewish Christians and polytheists. Traditionally the Jews had "built" these barriers as high as possible, which often brought ridicule and hostility from pagans.[434] This traditional Jewish divide was overcome, at least on a theological level, by the revelation that Peter received before his encounter with Cornelius, the Roman official (Acts 10:1—11:18). The leading apostle had to learn that he "should not call anyone profane or unclean" (Acts 10:28; see §21.2). The problem of hostility from Greeks and Romans toward Jews and their traditions is addressed in the exhortation of the early Christian missionaries to the believers to behave as exemplary citizens, to live in compliance with cultural conventions,[435] and to refrain from forcing Christian behavior upon non-Christians (1 Pet 4:15). Christians are exhorted not to repay evil that they may suffer from their neighbors with evil. Rather, they should overcome evil with good and pray for the unbelievers (Rom 12:17-21).

---

[431]See MacMullen 1981, 106; cf. Acts 14:11-15; 17:19-23.
[432]Acts 4:8, 31; 5:32; 6:5; 7:55; 8:29, 39; 10:10-20, 47; 13:4, 9; cf. 1 Thess 1:4-6; 1 Cor 2:5.
[433]See Acts 16:3; 18:18; 21:20-26; 1 Cor 9:19-23.
[434]See Let. Aris. 139, 142; Cicero, Flac. 28.67.
[435]See 1 Thess 4:12; 1 Cor 10:32-33; Col 4:5; 1 Tim 3:7; 1 Pet 2:12-14.

3. There were barriers between educated Christians in the cities and non-Hellenized barbarians, between poor missionaries and wealthy unbelievers—for example, owners of villas and patrons. The presence of poor freedmen and slaves in the new churches was a potential barrier for free citizens and members of the local aristocracy.

4. There was a potential conflict between Jewish-Christian missionaries and the officials of the synagogues in the Diaspora to whom they were legally responsible as Jews. And there was a potential conflict between the missionaries as noncitizens (*metoikoi*) and the local magistrates in the cities in which they engaged in missionary work. The New Testament describes the missionaries as fearless, unfazed by threats against their preaching activity. They are willing to be arrested and thrown into prison.[436] But they are also ready to defend themselves legally, if that is possible.[437] If the situation becomes too dangerous, they are willing to leave one city and move to another city.

5. We need to remember that the culture of the eastern regions of the Mediterranean world was relatively uniform. Neither Judea nor Galilee, neither Syria nor the Roman provinces in Asia Minor were "un-Hellenized." Klaus Haacker points out that the early church originated and expanded in a region whose degree of Hellenization differed from other regions only gradually; he observes that "for the early church the bridging of cultural barriers was not just a problem of evangelism in view of new target audiences, but a task of internal communication right from the beginning," as the difficulties between "Hebrew" and "Hellenistic" Jewish Christians in the Jerusalem church (Acts 6) demonstrate.[438]

Psychological Barriers

Fourth, there must have been psychological barriers that the early missionaries needed to overcome. They faced difficulties caused by at least the following factors: (1) the high level of self-assurance, perhaps arrogance, of the *archisynagōgoi* and the representatives of the local magistrates; (2) the anticipated derision in response to the message of the crucified and risen Jesus, the Savior from Nazareth; (3) the possibility of people confusing traveling missionaries with itinerant philosophers of the Cynics, who often were regarded as charlatans; (4) the scandal of conversion to the Jewish-Christian faith and its requirement of denying the existence of the traditional gods, with the potential accusation of atheism; (5) the politically dangerous situation of Christians, who could claim legal protection only in the context of the Jewish religion, and who rejected the veneration of the emperors.

---

[436]See Acts 4:1-31; 5:17-42.
[437]See Acts 18:12-17; 22:22-29.
[438]Haacker 1988a, 62.

Organizational Challenges

The early Christian mission did not follow a structured plan and did not have a carefully considered organization. This seems to have been true at least for six areas. (1) Finance: the missionaries could hope to be supported by existing churches that would finance their living and travel expenses. Or the missionaries would have to earn their own livelihood.[439] (2) Authority structures: some Christians in Jerusalem evidently claimed to have responsibility for the new churches in Syria, Asia Minor and Europe, whereas Paul defended his authority for the churches that he had established. (3) Headquarters: Paul's missionary activity initially was based in Damascus, then in Tarsus, later in Antioch, in Corinth and in Ephesus. Later he wanted to organize a mission to Spain, with the church in Rome as the new center. The Jerusalem church ceased to be a center of early Christian activity by A.D. 66, the beginning of the First Jewish Revolt. (4) Social networks: the missionaries traveled in pairs or in small groups and sought to engage strangers in cities that they had not visited before. In other words, they could not rely on the networks of social relationships that determined so much of life in the Greco-Roman cities. (5) Co-workers: the co-workers that churches made available to missionaries were responsible not only to the particular missionary but also to the sending church, which could lead to difficulties. (6) The eschatological situation: the conviction of living in the last days implied a tension between rapid dissemination of the gospel into new areas and consolidation of newly founded and existing churches.

Personal Difficulties

Finally, the early Christian missionaries faced personal difficulties that are scarcely addressed in the New Testament. These difficulties included, for example, the well-being of family members who were left behind or who came along on missionary travels (e.g., wives [1 Cor 9:5]); the cramped living conditions in the larger cities or in the modest houses of new believers; the dangers and the physical demands of travel on foot or by ship to other provinces or to other cities; the challenges of being in constant contact with numerous and diverse people and being confronted with their spiritual and personal needs.

Did the apostles reach "all nations to the end of the earth"? Perhaps not. Origen writes the following his commentary on Mt 24:14:

"Such being the position of affairs [i.e., at the end], the gospel, which formerly had not been preached in all the world—for many people, not only barbarians but even of our empire, have not yet heard the word of Christ—this gospel will then be proclaimed, so to that every race may hear the evangel, leaving none who fails to hear it. And thereafter the end will come. . . . For we are not told that the gospel has been preached among all

---

[439]See 1 Thess 2:9; 2 Thess 3:8; 1 Cor 4:12; Acts 18:3; 20:33-34.

the Ethiopians, particularly among those who are on the other side of the River; nor among the Serae, nor in Arice, has the tale of Christ been heard. But what shall we say of Britain or Germany, or the seaboard, or the barbarians, the Dacians, the Sarmatae, and the Scythians, most of whom have not yet heard the gospel, but are to hear it at the consummation of the ages? . . . If anyone would hastily affirm that the gospel of the kingdom had been already preached in all the world as a testimony to all nations, he would also be able to say, of course, 'then shall the end be,' the end is now here. Which would be an exceedingly rash assertion."[440]

Praeparatio evangelica?

Adolf von Harnack traces the success of the early Christian mission, the "mission and expansion of Christianity in the first three centuries," to external and internal conditions, arguing that social factors caused the rapid conversion of (Jews and) pagans and the multiplication of churches. Eusebius, the early proponent of the motif of the *praeparatio evangelica,* already attempted to specify social factors, apart from theological conditions, as the cause for the growth of the church.[441] In Harnack's description the external conditions include the missionary expansion of Judaism in the Diaspora,[442] then the Hellenization of the East with regard to language (Koine) and ideas, the political unity of the nations bordering on the Mediterranean that the Roman Empire had created, the intensive international traffic, the widespread conviction of the essential unity of humankind and of human rights and duties, the democratization of the old societies and the gradual equalizing of the social classes, the religious policy of the Romans with its tolerant attitude, the existence of associations and of municipal and provincial organizations, the expansion of oriental religions, the decline of the exact sciences and the rise of a mystical philosophy of religion that craved revelation and thirsted for miracles.[443] "The narrow world had become a wide world; the rent world had become a unity; the barbarian world had become Greek and Roman: *one* empire, *one* universal language, *one* civilization, a *common* development towards monotheism, and a *common yearning* for saviours!" The internal conditions that Harnack specifies include the religious needs of people, the development toward monotheism, the yearning for saviors: "*The soul, God, knowledge, expiation, asceticism, redemption, eternal life,* with *individualism* and with *humanity* substituted for nationality—these were the sub-

[440]Origen, *Comm. Matt.* 24:14; translation from Harnack 1924, ET, 2:13-14; for a modern German translation see H. Vogt, ed., *Origen: Der Kommentar zum Evangelium nach Mattäus* 3:111-12. Cf. Bardy 1948, 10.

[441]Eusebius, *Hist. eccl.* 8.1.5-9. See Kofsky 2002, 74-99; on the *Wirkungsgeschichte* of Eusebius concerning the *praeparatio evangelica* see White 1985-1986; Praet 1992-1993, 11-19.

[442]Harnack 1924, 1:5-23 (ET, 1:1-18). On Harnack's description of the early Christian mission see Jantsch 1990, esp. 108-13.

[443]Harnack 1924, 1:23-27 (ET, 1:19-23); the quotation that follows above, ibid., 1:22. See similarly Nock 1933, 187-212.

lime thoughts which were living and operative, partly as the precipitate of deep inward and outward movements, partly as the outcome of great souls and their toil, partly as one result of the sublimation of all cults which took place during the imperial age. Wherever vital religion existed, it was in this circle of thought and experience that it drew breath."[444] Harnack claims that because these yearnings could be satisfied most completely and most successfully by the Christian message, the mission of the early Christians was so successful.

Robert MacMullen criticizes Harnack not only with regard to his method but also concerning the fact that among the thousands of references to sources there is "not one to a pagan source and hardly a line indicating the least attempt to find out what non-Christians thought and believed."[445] In view of the huge amount of new *realia*—temples, theaters, marketplaces, forums, baths, not to mention thousands of inscriptions—Harnack's description also lacks differentiation of complex local situations.[446] An even more important objection from MacMullen concerns the fact, which he demonstrates with numerous specific pieces of evidence, that there was no "crisis" of pagan cults between the first and the third centuries. On the contrary, paganism was alive and dynamic: new temples were built, old temples were renovated.

Rudolf Brändle and Ekkehard Stegemann suggest that early Christianity was the product of "the 'diffusion' of Diaspora Jews within a society dominated by a non-Jewish majority," "a new, self-supporting, although somewhat unstable form of reaction to the encounter between Jews and pagans," and in terms of its substance, "a messianic-apocalyptic and charismatic movement in the gray area between Jews, proselytes, and God-fearers."[447] This hypothesis is historically untenable for at least three reasons. (1) The "diffusion" of Diaspora Judaism has hardly anything in common with the early Christian mission, in which men and women traveled to cities, regions and provinces in order to proclaim the gospel of Jesus Christ and establish communities of followers of Jesus. The Jewish "diffusion" brought individual Gentiles into the synagogues through attraction, while the early Christian missionaries were proactively engaged in a deliberate endeavor to win Jews and non-Jews. (2) The new Christian communities indeed existed in a "gray area" in terms of their legal status. With regard to their message, organization and missionary outreach, however, they became independent very quickly. As far as we know, there was no synagogue in any city between Jerusalem and Rome that became totally "messianic" or Christian or that tolerated a Christian "division." (3) The message and teaching that the early missionaries proclaimed and the ways of behavior that the Christian com-

---

[444]Harnack 1924, 1:36 (ET, 1:33). See earlier Wernle 1909, 2-4.
[445]MacMullen 1981, 206 n. 16; similarly, though not as harshly, White 1985-1986, 105 n. 39.
[446]See White 1985-1986.
[447]Brändle and Stegemann 1996, 4, 5 (ET, 121, 122).

munities practiced were much more than simply a "reaction to the encounter between Jews and pagans." The Christian faith and practice were the result of the conviction, propagated with energy and courage and the willingness to suffer, that Jesus of Nazareth was the promised Messiah, that he died on the cross for the sins of the world, that he was raised from the dead on the third day, that he was exalted at the right hand of God, and that he would return to establish the kingdom of God in a final and visible way. These convictions did not exist in a "gray area" but instead constituted a provocation, both for Jews and for Gentiles. For further discussion on the reasons for the success of the early Christian mission see §33.3.

17

SUMMARY

The historical origins of the early Christian mission are situated in Jesus' call of the Twelve to be trained as "fishers of people" (Mk 1:17), in their commission to a short-term tour through Galilee (Mt 10:1-15), and in Jesus' ministry with the geographically expansive proclamation of the kingdom of God and the miracles of healing and liberation in the towns and villages of Galilee. The effective origins of the early Christian mission are linked with the events of Easter, with the encounters of the disciples with the risen Jesus Christ, and with the events of Pentecost. The disciples realized that the crucified and risen Jesus, the Messiah, is the one mediator and Savior whom God had sent into the world for the salvation of Israel and of the world. As Jesus had trained the Twelve to be fishers of people, so now he sent them to the nations, beginning in Jerusalem and in Judea and reaching as far as the ends of the earth, to proclaim the good news of the crucified and risen Messiah, who would return in judgment of the world. Jerusalem was the center of the people of God, and now also of the community of the followers of Jesus the Messiah. The Twelve were directed, however, not to limit their proclamation of the arrival of the era of salvation to the Jews in Jerusalem and in Judea but to go also to the nations: in this way the promised restoration of Israel will become a reality (Acts 1:6-8).

The life of the Twelve is subordinate to the authority of the risen Christ and of the Holy Spirit of God, who is Lord of history and directs the (end) time as a time of missionary outreach among the nations. The Twelve are Jesus' "witnesses" (Acts 1:8) as witnesses of his life, ministry and resurrection (Acts 1:21-22). As witnesses they represent Jesus, the Messiah of Israel, in Jerusalem, in the towns of Judea and Samaria and in the towns outside of Palestine, to the ends of the earth. The disciples' missionary commission becomes a concrete reality for the first time at the Feast of Pentecost in A.D. 30. Peter and the other apostles proclaim in Jerusalem to thousands of (Jewish) pilgrims who have come to Zion from all over the world that the time of the last days has arrived, that the new time of salvation has dawned. They proclaim that Jesus of Nazareth, who died on the cross and was raised from the dead and exalted to the right hand of God, now pours out the Spirit of God, and therefore he is Lord, before whom all people must repent if they want to find salvation (Acts 2:1-41).

The first followers of Jesus gathered in Jerusalem, under the leadership of the Twelve, in a house on the southwestern hill in close proximity to the Essene quarter, in private houses and in the Royal Portico on the temple mount. According to passages such as Acts 2:42-47; 4:31-35; 5:12-16, a fundamental characteristic of this messianic community was the "teaching of the apostles": the Twelve taught and explained the tradition of Jesus as good news (gospel), as the message of God's intervention in the last days by the death and resurrection of his Son. They proclaimed and explained that salvation is now bound up with acceptance of and loyalty to Jesus as Messiah and Lord. Another characteristic of the Jerusalem church was the fellowship of the followers of Jesus as a community of learners who lived together, a community where God was worshiped, where people talked (and soon sang hymns) about Jesus, where they ate meals together and where the needy were cared for. A third characteristic was the daily proactive and courageous proclamation of the message of Jesus the Messiah, often accompanied by miracles, despite warnings and threats from the Jewish authorities. The Twelve, particularly Peter among them, challenged the people of Jerusalem and the surrounding areas to accept Jesus as the Messiah. As a result, the number of followers of Jesus grew dramatically: the small group of 120 disciples grew to three thousand, then to five thousand, among them many Pharisees and priests, probably Essenes.

All the members of the Jerusalem church were Jews: converted inhabitants of the Jewish capital; Hebrew- and Aramaic-speaking Jews whose families had lived in Jerusalem for decades or even centuries; Greek-speaking Jews who had moved from the Diaspora back to Jerusalem in more recent years. The community of the followers of Jesus was led by the Twelve, who soon had responsibilities that exceeded their energies so that seven presumably full-time co-workers were appointed to care for the needs of the widows in the church. Some of these co-workers soon were involved in the proclamation of the gospel as well. The leadership of the Jerusalem church seems to have been transferred in A.D. 41 from the Twelve to a council of Elders, with James the brother of Jesus as *primus inter pares,* evidently as a result of the persecution that Herod Agrippa I initiated against the church, particularly against the leaders, prompting the Twelve to embark on a missionary outreach that was no longer centered on Jerusalem.

The missionary vision of the disciples can be explained to a large degree by the ministry of Jesus: the Twelve learned from observing Jesus that the good news of the arrival of God's reign needed to be proclaimed in towns and villages, to poor and to wealthy people, to the educated and the uneducated, both in word and in deed. After Easter they were given the missionary commission to extend their ministry from the Jews in Jerusalem and in Judea to the Samari-

EARLY CHRISTIAN MISSION

tans and to all nations as far as the ends of the earth. For the early Christians, the geographical horizon of the phrases "all nations" and "to the ends of the earth" did not end at the borders of the Roman Empire. As Jews, they were used to thinking further afield, as thousands of Jews had lived since 722 B.C. in Babylonia, Persia and Parthia, regions that were not under Roman control. Nor did the geographical horizon end at the outer limits of the Jewish Diaspora. Luke mentions an Ethiopian who had come from the southern "end" of the earth to Jerusalem and been converted to faith in Jesus. Paul mentions the Scythians living toward the northern "end" of the earth, with a Scythian slave perhaps being a member of the church in Colossae. Paul plans a mission to Spain at the western "end" of the earth. And knowledge about India, the eastern "end" of the earth, was widespread in the first century, with travel opportunities rather common: the early traditions regarding Thomas in India seem to contain historically reliable information.

Strategic thinking and tactical considerations were not unknown in the ancient world; the military in particular operated in deliberate strategic and tactical terms. Evidence from these areas is relevant for the international mission of the Jerusalem Christians only in the most general form, however. The significance of geographical and ethnographical knowledge is clear: information in these areas could be obtained by Jesus' followers, theoretically, from libraries and archives. Much more relevant and practical were inquisitive contacts with Jews in synagogues who had information about local and regional matters, with people whom they met during preaching activities in the marketplaces of Greek and Roman cities, with captains in the harbors in which they embarked on sea voyages, with high-ranking officials who were sympathetic to their message.

There were no real parallels in the ancient world for the project of a group of people or organization operating in an international scope, neither in the religious nor in the philosophical or political realms. The impression that Luke's account in the book of Acts conveys is, at first glance, misleading: the apostles were not conservative men who were neither willing nor able to take missionary initiatives. Rather, they evidently were well aware of their responsibility to carry out Jesus' missionary commission, including the directive to take the gospel to the nations. The early tradition that the Twelve left Jerusalem twelve years after Easter (i.e., in A.D. 41/42), each one embarking on an international missionary work, could well be historical. The lack of useful models, the diversity of religious thought patterns, the social, cultural and psychological barriers, and the organizational and personal challenges did not keep the apostles from proclaiming the good news of Jesus Christ in Jerusalem, in Judea, in Samaria and among the nations. In the next section I will discuss the information that we have about the missionary work of the Twelve from Jerusalem to the ends of the earth.

PART IV

EXODUS

The Mission of the Twelve from Jerusalem to the Ends of the Earth

18

HISTORICAL, SOCIAL AND
RELIGIOUS REALITIES IN THE ROMAN EMPIRE

The twelve apostles were called by Jesus to be "fishers of people" among "all nations" between Jerusalem and the "ends of the earth." We have seen that Jesus' disciples evidently took this missionary commission seriously in the context of an international and universal geographical perspective. It is for this reason that my survey of the historical, social and religious realities in the Roman Empire will begin with the missionary outreach of the Jewish-Christian missionaries from Jerusalem rather than the mission of the apostle Paul. I begin with a quotation from Jochen Bleicken that illuminates the possibilities of personal development of people in the first century.

"In the long period of peace of nearly three hundred years that the Roman world empire bequeathed to the people before the chaos of the third century brought it to an end, politics and war disappeared so completely from the consciousness of the people that historiography and fiction had a hard time keeping the memory of both alive. Other areas of life became more important for people. What occupied people nearly exclusively was private life, with all its customs, needs and material or spiritual desires. The freedoms provided by the Roman Empire guaranteed that everybody could become acquainted with new things, or relativize or correct old things. There was essentially no barrier for the journey from one end of the empire to the other, apart from financial resources or the interest of the individual. Such unrestrained traffic in such a large area has never existed again until our time."[1]

The Mediterranean world witnesses fundamental changes between the second century B.C. and the second century A.D. It is difficult to characterize these changes in detail: there were no social or economic sciences in antiquity that described and analyzed social and economic processes. Still, a general synthesis of social reality particularly in the cities and to a certain degree even in the villages of the Roman Empire is possible when we analyze direct and indirect sources, literary texts and inscriptions as well as archaeological remains that in

---

[1]Bleicken 1978, 2:67.

many cases still have not been adequately researched. Since we are primarily interested in the activities of the early Christian missionaries, naturally it will not be our goal to describe all areas of Greco-Roman society with consistent differentiation of regional and local peculiarities. After a brief survey of important historical developments in the first century, we will focus on those aspects of Roman society that were particularly relevant, or potentially relevant, for the early Christian missionary activity: economy and trade, urban and rural areas, religious pluralism and realities of communication.

18.1 Historical Perspectives

Statistical Data

We begin with some numbers.[2] The population of the Roman Empire is estimated to have numbered between 50 and 80 million people, of whom about 7 million were free Roman citizens.

The last census whose figures are known was conducted under Claudius in A.D. 47. According to Tacitus, the census showed that 5,984,072 Roman citizens lived in the empire (Tacitus, *Ann.* 11.25). If we add the quotient of probable underregistration, the number of Roman citizens was about 7,000,000.[3] Elio Lo Cascio points out that it is impossible to arrive at reliable conclusions concerning population totals on the basis of philological arguments alone: we must not forget that the term *civium capita* referred to adult males only, perhaps only to specific groups of adult males.[4]

About 14 million people lived in Rome, Italy and the larger islands of the Mediterranean; 6 million lived in Spain, 5 million in Gaul, at least 2 million in the provinces on the Danube River, 3 million in Greece and the Aegean islands, between 11 and 13 million in Asia Minor, between 3 and 4 million in Syria, 2.5 million in Palestine, 5 million in Egypt, perhaps 5 million in the other North African provinces. Of the approximately 2,000 cities of the Roman Empire, most cities (or "central towns") had only between 2,000 and 15,000 inhabitants.[5] Medium-sized cities such as Pompeii had 20,000 inhabitants; larger cities such as Sardis had between 50,000 and 100,000 inhabitants. Most towns had between 2,000 and 3,000 inhabitants. The term "metropolis" can be applied only to Rome, Alexandria and Antioch on the Orontes. Rome had between 600,000 and

---

[2]See M. H. Crawford, *OCD* 1223; Levick 1967, 92-96; Duncan-Jones 1982, 259-87; Alföldy 1975; Christ 1992, 31, 99, 373; S. Mitchell 1995a, 1:199-201, 243-44; Ausbüttel 1998, 2. See also §8.1 in the present work.

[3]Scheidel 1996, 95; F. Vittinghoff, "Demographische Rahmenbedingungen," in Vittinghoff 1990, 20-24.

[4]Elio Lo Cascio, "The Size of the Roman Population: Beloch and the Meaning of the Augustan Census Figures," *JRS* 84 (1994): 23-40, discussing the assumptions of Beloch 1886.

[5]Ausbüttel 1998, 40.

1,000,000 inhabitants[6] (a figure that no other city of the Western world reached before London reached 1 million inhabitants in the eighteenth century); Alexandria had 500,000 inhabitants; Antioch in Syria had 250,000 inhabitants.

There were perhaps 130 cities (*poleis*) in Anatolia in Asia Minor: 13 in Bithynia, 11 in Pontus, 6 in Paphlagonia, 20 in Galatia and Lycaonia, 45 in Phrygia, 11 in Mysia, 20 in Lydia. Pergamon had probably about 180,000 inhabitants;[7] Nicomedia, Ancyra, Thyatira and Sardis[8] had over 25,000 inhabitants. Antiocheia in Pisidia (Phrygia) had probably less than 10,000 inhabitants. Some towns had hardly more inhabitants than large villages, between 2,000 and 3,000 people.

Most people, perhaps 80 or 90 percent of the population of the Roman Empire, worked in agriculture and lived in a rural setting. That most people lived in the countryside is demonstrated by the fact that even small towns controlled a large number of villages; for example, Oenoanda in Lycia controlled 35 dependent villages. A surface survey conducted between 1985 and 1990 on the territory of the city of Tarraco, the capital of the province Hispania Citerior, demonstrated that Tarraco had between 10,000 and 15,000 inhabitants in early Roman times, and that about 66,000 people lived in perhaps 3,300 villages that belonged to the territory of the city; in other words, about 80 to 87 percent of the people living in the territory controlled by Tarraco lived in rural villages.[9]

In regard to the number of Jews living in the Roman Empire, demographers provide the following estimates:[10] between 15,000 and 40,000 Jews lived in Rome (2 to 6 percent of the population there); about 150,000 to 200,000 Jews lived in Egypt (3 percent of the population there), approximately 100,000 in Alexandria alone; perhaps 18,000 Jews lived in Damascus (Josephus, *B.J.* 7.368). The Jewish population in the Diaspora is estimated at 5 to 10 percent of the total population, thus perhaps 5 million Jews; five times (some scholars think ten times) as many Jews as lived in Judea and in Galilee.[11] In regard to Asia Minor, some scholars estimate that less than 5 percent of the population were Jews.[12]

The life expectancy of a person born in the Roman Empire was fairly low: infant mortality rates were very high, and it is estimated that perhaps 25 per-

---

[6]Vittinghoff, "Demographische Rahmenbedingungen," 21.

[7]Galen (5.49) mentions 120,000 inhabitants: 40,000 males, plus women and slaves; if we add children under the age of eighteen, we have between 180,000 and 200,000 inhabitants. See S. Mitchell 1995a, 1:243-44.

[8]Hanfmann (1983, 146, 278 n. 92) estimates that Sardis had between 60,000 and 100,000 inhabitants; S. Mitchell (1995a, 1:244 n. 13) thinks that these figures are "generous."

[9]Josep-Maria Carreté, Simon Keay and Martin Millett, *A Roman Provincial Capital and Its Hinterland: The Survey of the Territory of Tarragona, Spain, 1985-1990* (JRASup 15; Ann Arbor, Mich.: Journal of Roman Archaeology, 1995); for the statistics on inhabitants see 277-78.

[10]See Solin 1983; Lampe 1987 (ET, 2003, 143 n.13); Horsley, *New Docs* 5:37.

[11]See Lichtenberger 1994, 93.

[12]Ameling 1996, 30.

cent of newborns did not survive the first year; only 43 percent reached the age of fifteen, and only 7.5 percent reached the age of sixty five. A fifteen-year-old could expect to reach the age of forty-five; a forty-five-year-old might reach sixty, and a sixty-year-old perhaps sixty-nine.[13] It is debated how many children an average family had. Newer estimates assume that an average household had at least 5.3 persons (i.e., 3 children), others assume 7 or 8 persons (i.e., 5 or 6 children).[14]

Historical Survey

The politics of Rome assumed a new dimension with the beginning of the principate, the rule of the emperors. The authority structures of the *res publica* had essentially served to establish and guarantee the power of the aristocratic families. Since Augustus, the power interests of the state needed to be reconciled with the interests of the emperor. For the provinces these developments had positive consequences indeed, as the politics of the empire became less subjective: the available instruments of power could be aligned in terms of method and scope with the objective necessities of the regions under the control of Rome, as they were no longer battlefields of Roman power struggles.

The term *provincia*[15] does not derive from *pro* + *vincere*, as Roman antiquarians have suggested. It originally described the material and spatial sphere in which a magistrate functioned. After the annexation of Sicily in the Second Punic War (218-201 B.C.) and the conquest of Spain (198/197 B.C.), the word *provincia* was used mainly for territories outside Italy under permanent Roman administration, governed by a praetor with *imperium,* supreme power. After the reorganization under Augustus in 27 B.C., the empire was divided into imperial and senatorial provinces. The imperial provinces were governed through a *legatus Augusti pro praetore,* a senator of consular rank. Egypt was governed by a *praefectus,* who came from equestrian ranks. Nearly all the legions were stationed in the imperial provinces. The senatorial provinces were governed through proconsuls from the senatorial class, without legions, but with *imperium* and assisted by quaestors and legates. In the first century, at the time of Claudius, thirteen imperial provinces were governed by procurators of equestrian rank, who in some provinces had to report to the imperial legate of a neighboring province—for example, the prefect (later procurator) of Judea, who had to report to the *legatus* of the province of Syria. The provinces were organized in administrative or assize districts (Gk., διοικήσεις, *dioikēseis,* "house-

---

[13]See Bruce W. Frier, "Roman Life Expectancy: Ulpian's Evidence," *HSCP* 86 (1982): 213-51; Ann Ellis Hanson, "Ancient Illiteracy," in Beard et al. 1991, 186 n. 99.

[14]See Bagnall and Frier 1994, 67-69.

[15]See H. Volkmann, *KP* 4:1199-1201; E. Badian, *OCD* 1265-67; on Asia Minor see Macro, 663-72; on administration see Ausbüttel 1998, 24-39, 58-61.

keeping, internal administration"; Lat., *conventus,* "assembly"). Each assize district had a fixed center (ἀγορὰ δικῶν, *agora dikōn;* Lat., *conventus iuridici*), a town or city that the governor visited regularly. The communication of the administration of the Roman Empire depended on the centers of these assize districts. "The annual assize-tour of the provincial governor constituted the practical framework within which he exercised all his routine administrative and jurisdictional duties."[16] The dates for the individual legal proceedings were noted in a calendar for the *conventus;* hearings and trials took place in public in the open air.[17] Financial dues and obligations, such as the cost for road construction, were divided among the administrative districts. The *koinon,* or organization, of the province represented the province before the Roman governor and took responsibility for the imperial cult, particularly through organizing imperial festivals. The annual assemblies of the *koinon* took place in different cities. The presence of the governors of the provinces of Asia, Galatia, Bithynia and Pontus was difficult to locate: given the size of their provinces, their staffs were quite small, and they traveled much of the time from one assize center to the next. It is still debated which city the governor of the province of Asia used as his base. The "capital" of the province of Asia possibly was Ephesus, but the excavations that have been ongoing for dozens of years have not yet uncovered buildings that can be identified with certainty as the seat of the Roman *legatus* and his staff or as the official residence of the governor; the same is true for Pergamon, Miletus and Sardis.[18]

Gaius Iulius Octavianus Caesar, "Augustus" for short, visited the provinces of Bithynia and Asia in the summer of the year 20 B.C.[19] In many cities he reorganized the finances: he improved the taxation procedures, especially through instituting a regular census that would allow more precise estimates of revenues. The economic situation of the provinces improved considerably during the following years and decades. Augustus founded several colonies: in Pisidia the colonies of Antiocheia, Cremna, Parlais, Comama, Olbasa; in Lycaonia the colony of Lystra. Augustus initiated the construction of new or improved roads and instituted an imperial postal system (Lat., *vehicula,* later *cursus publicus*) with horses, vehicles and road stations.

The available evidence does not permit us to write a *histoire evenementielle,* a detailed history of events that took place in the Roman provinces of the imperial period. The surviving literary texts report only sporadically and generally in a disconnected manner about events in the provinces.[20] The information that

---

[16]G. P. Burton, *OCD* 386; for the province of Asia see Engelmann and Knibbe 1989, 108.
[17]Ausbüttel 1998, 58, 60.
[18]S. Mitchell 1995a, 1:64-69; F. K. Yegül, in Fentress 2000, 136.
[19]On Augustus see now Kienast 1982; Southern 1998.
[20]See S. Mitchell, *RECAM* 14.

can be gleaned from inscriptions—our main source of information for the reconstruction of the society and history of the Roman province—is, of course, incomplete, and numerous sites have never been excavated.[21] Many questions remain open. It is not possible to write a quantitative economic history of the Roman provinces or a history of the mentality of their populations.[22] This is particularly true for the regions of Asia Minor (the term *Mikra Asia,* "Asia Minor," is used by Ptolemaios in the second century [*Tetrabiblos* 2.3.17]). What Theodor Mommsen, the great historian of the Roman Empire, wrote more than a hundred years ago about Asia Minor still rings true for those who attempt to write an integrated "history of Asia Minor" or who simply want to collect reliable information about the *status quaestionis* of facts and figures: "I do not like to proceed further in these matters related to Asia Minor, which are not much more than a woodworm in a tree. . . . And especially, I understand too little about these things, and I want to use as little as possible information that I would just repeat. Tarsus, for example: what shall I do with it?"[23]

The reality of the *pax Augustana* changed and dominated not only the economic sector but also most other areas of life. In the provinces arose new social groups (*equites,* the equestrian order, and senators), new economic entities (e.g., imperial domains), new legal structures (e.g., Roman colonies) and new administrative structures, including the legions that were stationed in the provinces.[24]

The establishment of colonies[25]—settlements outside of the homeland—originally was a measure used by both Greeks and Romans to consolidate a military conquest of foreign territories. Colonies were military outposts, army veterans were settled there, and trade interests in the area were maintained. The first Roman colony outside of Italy was Carthage (122 B.C.), but it was only under Caesar and Augustus that colonies were established more extensively. The establishment of a colony depended upon a decision by the senate; the settlers of the colony retained Roman citizenship. The eastern colonies used the standard constitution of *duoviri* and *ordo;* the Latin language was used for official purposes. Some colonies were like a "Rome abroad," divided into seven *vici* (local subdivisions), as was, for example, Pisidian Antiocheia. Since Claudius conferred the status of colony to several towns in Gaul, the establishment of new colonies served increasingly to enhance the status and the dignity of the town. Towns that were elevated from *municipium* to *colonia* are referred to as titular colonies; these new colonies probably did not receive a new constitution. Christa Frateantonio comments that a fundamental part of constituting a new colony "was the establishment of cults, that is, the designation of plots for

---

[21]See Brandt 1992, 4, with regard to Pisidia.

[22]Note Millar (1993, 15, 225), who comments that "a social and economic history of the Near East in the Roman period cannot be written."

[23]J. Malitz, "Nachlese zum Briefwechsel Mommsen-Wilamowitz," *Quaderni di storia* 17 (1983): 139, quoted in Ziegler 1985, 12 n. 5; S. Mitchell 1995a, 1:3 n. 3.

[24]Brandt 1992, 100. On the Roman colonies in Asia Minor, Levick 1967 is still basic.

[25]E. Kornemann, PW 4 (1901): 511-88; D. Medicus, *KP* 1:1248-50; A. N. Sherwin-White, *OCD* 364-65; Jones 1937; Vittinghoff 1952; Levick 1967; Macro 1980, 674-76; Frateantonio 1997, 85-97.

temples and altars, the selection of cults (Jupiter, Venus, *genius* of the town, etc.) and the organization of religious life (calendar, financing, priests, supply of sacrifices). . . . The colonists were autonomous insofar as they had their own cult organization and their own sanctuaries. What was Roman were the models for religious life."[26]

The Roman presence in Asia Minor has left hardly any traces apart from roads and bridges. Fergus Millar recently pointed out that from an archaeological viewpoint the Roman state is "nearly invisible."[27] Except for taxation and imperial edicts, Rome's influence was felt primarily in the emperor cult: the inhabitants of the larger cities worshiped the emperor and his statue. Cities competed for the privilege of being allowed to erect an imperial temple and to be called νεωκόρος (*neōkoros; neōkorein* means "to honor with a temple").

Before surveying the politics of the Roman emperors in the first century, I need to comment on the legal and social status of Jews in the Roman Empire. When Pompey conquered Jerusalem in the fall of 63 B.C. and entered the holy of holies in the temple, the independence of the Jewish Hasmonean state had come to an end.[28] Gabinius, the governor appointed by Pompey, continued to weaken the Jewish institutions. This was the reason why Julius Caesar could count on the sympathies of the Jews in his confrontation with Pompey.[29] Caesar was supported in his campaigns of 48/47 B.C. in Egypt by the Hasmonean Hyrcanus II and by Antipater, the governor of Idumea (the grandfather of Herod I). After his victory over Pompey, Caesar confirmed Hyrcanus II as high priest and appointed Antipater *epitropos* (i.e., *procurator*), thus separating the religious and the civic authorities. Caesar granted the Jews the best possible status that a client state could achieve.[30] He reversed many of Pompey's measures, but he did not grant Jerusalem the status of a free city (*civitas libera et immunis*), although he did permit the rebuilding of the city walls. The most important stipulation was the assurance that the Jews were allowed "to live in accordance with their customs" (ζῆν κατὰ τὰ αὐτῶν ἔθη [Josephus, *A.J.* 14.214]), a legal status that the Romans called *suis legibus uti*. This was an old, proven measure that previous rulers had used to keep the Jews quiet. Of particular importance in this context was the permission to keep the sabbath laws and to be exempt from military service in Roman legions (where one could not avoid contact with pagan deities).[31] The Roman document that was sent to Parion in the region of Troas

---

[26]Frateantonio 1997, 86.

[27]F. Millar, in the introduction to *Roman Architecture in the Greek World* (ed. S. Macready and F. H. Thompson; London: Society of Antiquaries, 1987), xi, quoted by F. K. Yegül, in Fentress 2000, 136.

[28]Josephus, *B.J.* 1.152-155; *A.J.* 14.71-73; Cicero, *Flac.* 28.67 (*GLAJJ* I 196-201). See Schürer 1:239; Smallwood 1976, 21-30; Gabba 1999, 95; Ball 2000, 10-12, and passim.

[29]For the account that follows above see Malitz 1996, esp. 377-86; Noethlichs 1996.

[30]Malitz 1996, 380; for the observations that follow above see ibid., 380-81.

[31]See Goldenberg 1979, 414-47.

(Josephus, *A.J.* 14.213-216) must be interpreted in the context of the decision of Caesar, who is explicitly mentioned in the document, about the *collegia* in the year 46 B.C. This text confirms that the Jews were granted the right to form *thiasoi* (i.e., assemblies in the synagogues), to collect money (i.e., tribute for the Jerusalem temple), and to come together for shared meals (i.e., Jewish festival banquets or the third meal before the end of the Sabbath). Jürgen Malitz observes that these stipulations "provided the Jews of the Diaspora with a precise definition of their status that was absolutely vital: it guaranteed the Jews the right to assemble and to engage in cultic activity in the synagogue. . . . The 'right of assembly' that Caesar and his successors granted the Jews largely protected them from all sorts of conflicts in their contacts with non-Jews."[32] Augustus adopted Caesar's politics concerning the Jews. He was regarded as a benefactor and friend of Jewish interests. He was the first Roman to send gifts to the Jerusalem temple (Philo, *Legat.* 157). Jews in Rome named synagogues after him, which could hardly have happened without prior permission from the imperial court.[33] However, a "Magna Carta" of Jewish rights under Emperor Claudius did not exist.[34]

According to Heikki Solin, autonomous Jewish communities were not allowed in the West: "Despite many individual privileges, such as exemption from military service, the Jews were never granted a publicly acknowledged privileged position or special courts in ancient Rome or in the Latin-speaking West. The privileges granted to the Jews were granted as a matter of principle in terms of constitutional law, that is, to the Jews who had citizenship rights of the city of Jerusalem."[35] Helga Botermann argues that the "tolerance edicts" of Claudius, which, according to Philo and Josephus, placed the Jewish religion under official protection, are a topos of Jewish apologetic for which the struggle to maintain freedom for the Jewish cult is a constant theme:[36] "There was no 'Magna Carta' of the Jews. . . . The information that we have about the imperial legislation, which generally was casuistic and reacted to initiatives from below, is reason enough to cast doubt on this ecumenical edict. It would be unique. The existence of the Diaspora is not sufficient to postulate such a global regulation—for the Jews of all people—as we are familiar with today but was totally foreign for the Romans. There were no attacks against Jews or empire-wide disturbances under Gaius. There was no general necessity to act."[37] Claudius "commands" the Jews of Alexandria in his famous letter of A.D. 41[38] "not to seek more rights than they already have. Specifically, they should refrain from sending two embassies and from pushing their way into games in the city—they already enjoy a large number

---

[32]Malitz 1996, 384.
[33]See Malitz 1996, 376-77.
[34]See Rajak 1984; Ameling 1996, 36; Botermann 1996, 107-32. On the Jews of Rome see Smallwood 1976, 210-16; Slingerland 1997.
[35]Solin 1983, 599-600; cf. ibid., 611-12.
[36]See Josephus, *A.J.* 14.194, 213, 216, 226-227; Philo, *Legat.* 157, 160-161.
[37]See Botermann 1996, 107-32; quotation, 110-11.
[38]P.Lond. 1912 = *CPJ* II 153; translation in Feldman and Reinhold 1996, 91-92 (no. 4.19); German translation in Barrett and Thornton, *Texte zur Umwelt des Neuen Testaments,* 55-57 (no. 52).

of privileges in a 'foreign' city. . . . He prohibits them from strengthening their colony by Jews from Syria and Egypt moving into the city. If they act contrary to his wishes, he will be forced to have grave suspicions and to proceed against them as against people who foment a common plague for the whole world. . . . This is not an emperor who is friendly to the Jews. He wants peace and quiet, that is all."[39]

Tiberius (A.D. 14-37) recognized that the military possibilities of the empire had reached their limits.[40] He therefore implemented a basically defensive policy for securing the borders of the empire. He abolished the large high command on the German front, recalled Germanicus, his adoptive son, and directed the legions to build legionary camps that served defensive functions. Germanicus, who received in A.D. 18 the *imperium proconsulare* over the eastern provinces, traveled in the same year to Asia Minor in order to bring "relief to provinces worn out by internecine feud or official tyranny" (Tacitus, *Ann.* 2.54). He organized Cappadocia and Commagene as procuratorial provinces, extending the territory of the empire in the east. Many cities of Asia Minor (e.g., Eumeneia, Myra, perhaps Pergamon) honored Germanicus as "savior and benefactor" (σωτήρ καὶ εὐεργέτης, *sōtēr kai euergetēs*).[41] In Cappadocia he stationed only auxiliary troops, who could not guarantee the defense of the border on the Euphrates River—a task he assigned to the Armenians. Tiberius allowed new military offensives only when they were unavoidable, as his campaigns against the Parthians show.

Tiberius promoted the norms of Augustan virtues of the ruler: *virtus, clementia, iustitia* and *pietas,* emphasizing particularly *clementia* and *iustitia* as well as *moderatio,* which often appears on the legend of his coins. The virtue of moderation corresponded both to the emphases of Stoic popular philosophy and to the norms of the Roman aristocracy. Tiberius rigorously tried to run the administration of the empire more economically. He did not initiate larger building projects, exceptions being several temples built to demonstrate his piety, and roads constructed in northern Africa, Spain, Gaul, Dalmatia and Moesia. He issued edicts against luxurious clothes (A.D. 16) and against sumptuous banquets (A.D. 22). His energetic policies against usury (A.D. 33) succeeded in stabilizing the capital market. At the same time, however, the principate of Tiberius

---

[39]Botermann 1996, 112-13.
[40]See S. T. Carroll, *ABD* 5:549-50; J. P. Balsdon and B. M. Levick, *OCD* 1523-24; Rémy 1986, 33; Christ 1992, 193-95; John P. Balsdon, "The Principates of Tiberius and Gaius," *ANRW* II.2 (1975): 86-94; Glanville Downey, "Tiberiana," *ANRW* II.2 (1975): 95-130; Robin Seager, *Tiberius* (London: Methuen, 1972); Barbara Levick, *Tiberius the Politician* (London: Thames & Hudson, 1976); Catherine Salles, *Tibère, le second César* (Paris: Laffont, 1985); Manfred Baar, *Das Bild des Kaisers Tiberius bei Tacitus, Sueton und Cassius Dio* (Beiträge zur Altertumskunde 7; Stuttgart: Teubner, 1990).
[41]Cf. *IGR* IV 723; *IGR* III 715, 716; *IGR* IV 326, 327. See Sencer Şahin, "Studien zu den Inschriften von Perge I: Germanicus in Perge," *EA* 24 (1995): 33.

manifested the phenomenon of dynasty, with its special privileges and the atmosphere of the imperial court and its intrigues and conflicts, a phenomenon that became fundamental for future developments. Karl Christ remarks, "It was only a question of personality, discipline and temperament when it came to how far a member of the family of the *princeps* would go in using his power and position."[42] For this reason, many believed that the traditional aspirations for magistrate positions and *honores* in the state were problematic. One could be deposed as quickly as one had risen through the ranks, without the former necessarily being justified by proof of guilt or unequivocal evidence—the fall of L. Aelius Sejanus is a case in point. The religious policies of Tiberius clearly were conservative. Even though he was a devotee of astrology, he evicted all astrologers and magicians from Italy in A.D. 16. In A.D. 19, after disturbances in Rome, he initiated strict measures against the cult of Isis and against the Jews (Tacitus, *Ann.* 2.85).[43] The measures that Tiberius initiated in the administration of the empire in general and of the provinces in particular cannot be reduced to a common denominator. In the last decade of his principate important decisions were deferred; there were no major initiatives but much insecurity, not least concerning appointments to administrative posts. The proconsular governors in the provinces, especially in the highly respected senatorial provinces of Africa and Asia, together with officials of high administrative positions in Rome, formerly occupied their posts for a relatively short period of time; now they often remained for many years, which, however, helped to consolidate the affairs of state. The last decade of Tiberius's principate also saw the ministry of Jesus of Nazareth in Galilee, his death in Jerusalem on April 7 in A.D. 30, and the beginnings of the Jerusalem church and its missionary outreach, including the missionary activities of Peter in Jerusalem, Judea and Caesarea, of Philip in Samaria, of Barnabas in Antioch and of Paul in Arabia, Syria and Cilicia.

Over the next thirty years, during the principates of the emperors who succeeded Tiberius—Gaius (Caligula), Claudius and Nero—little changed in Asia Minor. In Syria and in Judea the situation was much more volatile. When the principate was assumed by *Gaius* (A.D. 37-41)[44]—the nickname *Caligula* ("bootee") was used since A.D. 14—the provinces celebrated, even though he had neither military nor significant administrative experience, his major achievement being that he was the son of Germanicus. His civility was promising, and several early

---

[42]Christ 1992, 197.

[43]On the Jews in Rome during the principate of Tiberius see Smallwood 1976, 201-10.

[44]See S. T. Carroll, *ABD* 1:820-21; J. P. Balsdon and B. M. Levick, *OCD* 619-20; Rémy 1986, 34; Christ 1992, 209-14; Cineira 1999, 10-222; John P. Balsdon, *The Emperor Gaius (Caligula)* (Oxford: Clarendon, 1966); Daniel Nony, *Caligula* (Paris: Fayard, 1986); Anthony A. Barrett, *Caligula: The Corruption of Power* (London: Batsford, 1989); David Wardle, *An Historical Commentary on Suetonius' Life of Caligula* (Brussels: Latomus, 1994); Aloys Winterling, *Caligula: Eine Biographie* (Munich: Beck, 2003).

initiatives were popular—for example, the amnesty of political prisoners, the cancellation of the sales tax, the organization of games. After these measures had depleted the coffers of the state, and after the young emperor had survived a serious illness, disenchantment set in. Caligula's mood swings increased, and his moral instability allowed him to make the most of his view of the principate as absolutist ruler. He came to regard "people, provinces, the entire state as the property of the ruler."[45] Caligula was heavily influenced by Julius Agrippa, the grandson of Herod I, and by Antiochos IV, the son of the king of Commagene. When Caligula kept the king of Armenia as a prisoner in Rome, disturbances on the eastern border of the empire ensued: the Parthians took advantage of this situation and occupied Armenia. Caligula's desire to be worshiped—he identified himself with Sol and with other gods—provoked intense conflicts with the Jews. When Jewish envoys came to Rome to explain to him the background of attacks against the Jews of Alexandria, he declared that the Jews were hated by God because they refused to regard him as divine—this according to Philo, an eyewitness. When Jews in Jamnia destroyed an altar dedicated to Gaius Caligula, this, of course, did not help to raise his estimation of the Jewish religion. His plan to have a colossal statue of himself erected in the temple in Jerusalem provoked intense Jewish protests. It was only when Herod Agrippa I intervened that he desisted. In the course of the persecution that Herod Agrippa initiated in A.D. 41 against the Christians and their leaders, James the son of Zebedee, one of the Twelve, was killed. In that same year the other apostles seem to have left Jerusalem. Caligula was murdered by palace guards on January 24 in A.D. 41.

Tiberius Claudius (A.D. 41-54), the uncle of Gaius Caligula, was born at Lugdunum (mod. Lyons) in 10 B.C. and became emperor at the age of fifty-one.[46] Earlier scholarship relied almost exclusively on literary primary sources, particularly accounts by Tacitus (*Ann.* 11-12), Suetonius (*Claud.* 1-46) and Cassius Dio (*Hist.* 60). As a result, Claudius appeared as "a sickly, mentally imbalanced and morally corrupt ruler without real achievements of his own."[47] Many verdicts of the biographies written by the ancient authors can be explained by their resentments "as representatives of a senatorial and equestrian class that continued to lose power" against the emperor and his efficient administration.[48] New

---

[45]Christ 1992, 210.

[46]E. Groag, "Claudius," PW 6 (1899): 2778-36; B. W. Jones, *ABD* 1:1054-55; J. P. Balsdon and B. M. Levick, *OCD* 337-38; Eleanor G. Huzar, "Claudius—the Erudite Emperor," *ANRW* II.32.1 (1984): 611-50; Momigliano 1981 [1934]; Rémy 1986, 34-37; Levick 1990; Christ 1992, 215-29; Riesner 1994, 80-95; Volker M. Strocka, ed., *Die Regierungszeit des Kaisers Claudius (41-54 n.Chr.): Umbruch oder Episode?* (Mainz: Zabern, 1994).

[47]Riesner 1994, 80; the 1934 research work by Momigliano (repr., 1981; orig., 1932) and by Vincent M. Scramuzza, *The Emperor Claudius* (Cambridge, Mass.: Harvard University Press, 1940) provoked a reevaluation of research on Claudius.

[48]Riesner 1994, 82.

epigraphical discoveries and a stronger focus on social and economic history of this period have led to a new evaluation of Claudius. He obviously had serious historical, philological and antiquarian interests. Of his literary works written in Greek—for example, forty-one books on Augustus—none survives. His increased diplomatic and military activities often are explained as a response to pressure to prove himself: Claudius was constantly ill, stuttered and seems to have cut a somewhat ridiculous figure.[49] Military actions in Mauretania since A.D. 42 resulted in the division of the country into two provinces: Mauretania Tingitana in the west and Mauretania Caesariensis in the east. In A.D. 43 Claudius invaded Britain, which was annexed one year later as a province. In that same year—Paul was engaged in missionary work in Pisidian Antiocheia—several territories were organized as Roman provinces: Lycia, Lycaonia and Thrace become imperial provinces. In A.D. 44 Achaia and Macedonia were turned into senatorial provinces. When Herod Agrippa I died suddenly, in that same year, Judea again was made a Roman province, governed by a procurator of equestrian rank. In Armenia Claudius was able to install a Roman client king. In A.D. 46 Moesia and Thrace were separated from Macedonia and organized as separate imperial provinces. Since A.D. 47 the Roman bridgehead west of the Rhine River was expanded in the Taunus Mountains and in the Wetterau. Claudius consolidated Roman rule in many areas by establishing new colonies and elevating existing towns to the status of (privileged) colonies. The best-known example is the Colonia Claudia Ara Agrippinensium—Cologne in Germania.[50]

The influence of the freedmen in the administration of the empire grew under Claudius. Some freedmen rose to the highest positions. Claudius abolished the *maiestas* trials (diminution of Rome's majesty) that had been misused to eliminate personal enemies. He elevated the imperial court as a fixed institution besides the traditional *quaestiones* and Senate tribunals. He organized a new census in A.D. 47/48, which counted six million Roman citizens in the empire— the apostle Paul was engaged in missionary work in Galatia. He granted Roman citizenship to numerous Greeks, Spaniards, Gauls and Britons, and also to people of Asia Minor. He expanded the system of Roman roads. He reorganized the postal service. A basic feature of the principate of Claudius was his esteem for his great-uncle Augustus, as can be seen in his religious policies: he revived the old Roman cult, and he was tolerant toward the many diverse religions of the empire. As Augustus had been friendly to the Jews, the same basic attitude can be assumed for Claudius,[51] enhanced by the fact that Herod Agrippa I evidently

---

[49]Christ 1992, 217. Cf. Seneca, *Apokolokyntosis* ("Transformation into a Pumpkin"), a satire on Claudius. On the politics of Claudius in Asia Minor see Magie 1950, 1:540-53.

[50]Otto Doppelfeld, "Das römische Köln," *ANRW* II.4 (1975): 715-82; Polomé 1983, 512. Jews were attested in Cologne since A.D. 321.

[51]Riesner 1994, 85-86; cf. Huzar, *ANRW* II.32.1 (1984): 648-49. On the Jews in Rome under Claudius see Smallwood 1976, 210-16; Slingerland 1997; Cineira 1999, 160-216.

played an important role in his ascension to the throne.[52] He gave the province of Judea to Agrippa, restoring the entire territory that his grandfather Herod I had ruled; in addition he was given the kingdom of Lysanias, tetrarch of Abilene.[53] In the first year of his principate (Jan 25, A.D. 41 to Jan 25, A.D. 42) Claudius issued two edicts that expanded the freedoms that the Jews had, and he admonished people to be tolerant:

"It is right, therefore, that the Jews throughout the whole world under our sway should also observe the customs of their fathers without let or hindrance. I enjoin upon them also by these presents to avail themselves of this kindness in a more reasonable spirit, and not to set at nought the beliefs about the gods held by other people but to keep their own laws" (Josephus, *A.J.* 19.290).

Two specific measures against the Jews of the city of Rome probably resulted not from an anti-Jewish attitude on the part of Claudius[54] but from disturbance caused by the missionary activities of (Jewish) Christians among the Jews in Rome, prompting Claudius to intervene: in A.D. 41 by a prohibition of assembly (Cassius Dio 60.6.6), and in A.D. 49 by an edict of eviction (Suetonius, *Claud.* 25.3-4).[55] In his endeavors to restore the old Roman religion he celebrated on April 21, A.D. 47, the eight-hundreth anniversary of the foundation of Rome with *ludi saeculares.*[56] In that same year he introduced a law that reorganized the *haruspices,* the (ancient Etruscan) college of interpreters of prodigies and portents so that "the oldest art of Italy should not become extinct through their indolence" (Tacitus, *Ann.* 11.15). Claudius continues in his programmatic speech to complain about "the progress of alien superstitions" (*quia externae superstitiones valescant*), which is a reference to oriental cults. The contact with astrologers from the Orient became politically dangerous, one reason being that Claudius feared prophecies of doom.[57] In A.D. 48 he enlarged the *pomerium,* the line demarcating the augurally constituted city of Rome, beyond which the *auspicia urbana* could not be taken (*Ann.* 12.23-24). In the last year of the principate of Claudius, Paul was engaged in missionary work in Ephesus and kept in contact with the church in Corinth through letters and visits. Claudius was murdered on October 13 in A.D. 54 in the context of the political ambitions of his last wife, the younger Agrippina, who wanted to make her son Nero (L. Domitius Ahenobarbus), whom Claudius had adopted, emperor.

---

[52]The accounts in *B.J.* 2.206-213 and *A.J.* 19.236-266 are somewhat contradictory.

[53]Josephus, *B.J.* 2.215; *A.J.* 19.274-275.

[54]Contra Slingerland (1997), who has overlooked Riesner 1994, 139-80, and Botermann 1996.

[55]Botermann 1996; Riesner 1994, 139-80; Cineira 1999, 196-216. See more extensively §22.6 in the present work.

[56]Pliny, *Nat.* 7.159; Tacitus, *Ann.* 11.11; Suetonius, *Claud.* 21; *Nero* 7; *Vit.* 2.

[57]Riesner 1994, 94-95, with reference to Tacitus, *Ann.* 11.4.

Nero (A.D. 54-68)[58] become emperor at the age of seventeen. He wanted to be an artist more than anything else. He removed with brutal ruthlessness anyone who got in his way, and he was not interested in the administrative or military consolidation of the empire. The controversies with Vologaeses I, the king of the Parthians, regarding Armenia dragged on for years. The creation of the province Galatia-Cappadocia (from A.D. 54/55 to 64 or 66/67)[59] was intended to preserve Armenia. Eastern Pontus on the Black Sea was integrated into Galatia for the same reason. The dispute between King Agrippa II and Porcius Festus, the governor of the province of Judea, dating between A.D. 59/60 and 62, was solved by a Jewish delegation that included the high priests and the treasurer of the Jerusalem temple. Nero's wife, Poppaea Sabina, whom Josephus describes as "God-fearing"—she may have been a sympathizer with the Jewish faith[60]—was instrumental in securing a positive outcome. In A.D. 61 the Roman army quelled an uprising in Britannia. In A.D. 66 Vespasian went to Judea to put down the revolt of the Jewish population.

Trajan regarded the first five years of Nero's principate, A.D. 53-59, as no less than an ideal period of the principate.[61] The credit for this goes, however, not to Nero but to his leading advisers, especially Burrus and Seneca. When they left, the political climate changed noticeably. The new advisers at the imperial court "were only good for spreading terror, they had no capabilities for constructive politics. . . . The *maiestas* trials started up again, the number of executions and of confiscations of property increased when the budget of the state got into deep trouble." Whether the fire that burned Rome on September 18-19 in A.D. 64 was set by Nero, as rumors alleged, or not, the responsibility for the fire was laid at the door of the Christians, as Tacitus reports (*Ann.* 15.44):

"Therefore, to scotch the rumor, Nero substituted as culprits, and punished with the utmost refinements of cruelty, a class of men, loathed for their vices, whom the crowd styled Christians *[vulgus Christianos appellabat]*. Christus, the founder of the name, had undergone the death penalty in the reign of Tiberius, by sentence of the procurator Pontius Pilate and the pernicious superstition was checked for a moment, only to break out once more *[repressaque in praesens exitiabilis superstitio rursum erumpebat]*, not merely in Judaea, the home of the

[58]See M. T. Griffin, *ABD* 4:1076-81; M. P. Charlesworth, *OCD* 1037-38; Rémy 1986, 34-37; Christ 1992, 229-43; Griffin 2000; John P. Sullivan, *Literature and Politics in the Age of Nero* (Ithaca, N.Y.: Cornell University Press, 1985); David C. A. Shotter, *Nero* (London: Routledge, 1997).
[59]The names of the procurates of the province are not known; see Rémy 1986, 40.
[60]Josephus, *A.J.* 20.195. E. M. Smallwood ("The Alleged Jewish Tendencies of Poppaea Sabina," *JTS* 10 [1959]: 329-335; idem 1976, 278-79 n. 79) is skeptical regarding sympathies of Poppaea for the Jewish faith. See, however, Margaret H. Williams, "'θεοσεβὴς γὰρ ἦν'—The Jewish Tendencies of Poppaea Sabina," *JTS* 39 (1988): 97-111. Undecided are Kuhn and Stegemann 1962, 1250, 1264; Schürer 3:78.
[61]Christ 1992, 236; for the observations that follow above see ibid. 236-39; quotation, 237.

disease, but in the capital itself *[per urbem etiam]*, where all things horrible or shameful in the world collect and find a vogue. First, then, the confessed members of the sect were arrested *[igitur primum correpti qui fatebantur]*; next, on their disclosures, vast numbers were convicted *[multitudo ingens]*, not so much on the count of arson as for hatred of the human race. And derision accompanied their end: they were covered with wild beasts' skins and torn to death by dogs; or they were fastened on crosses *[aut crucibus adfixi]*, and, when daylight failed were burned to serve as lamps by night. Nero had offered his Gardens for the spectacle *[in usum nocturni luminis urerentur]*, and gave an exhibition in his Circus, mixing with the crowd in the habit of a charioteer, or mounted on his chariot. Hence, in spite of a guilt which had earned the most exemplary punishment, there arose a sentiment of pity, due to the impression that they were being sacrificed not for the welfare of the state but to the ferocity of a single man."

The opposition against Nero led to the conspiracy by C. Calpurnius Piso in A.D. 65, which involved senators, knights and officers of the praetorian guard. Several people were executed, and Seneca was forced to commit suicide. Resistance against the emperor soon spread to the provinces. Peter and Paul seem to have been executed during the last year of Nero's principate. The rule of the Julian-Claudian family ended with Nero's suicide on June 9 in A.D. 68.

The "year of the four emperors," A.D. 68/69, brought civil war that shook the whole empire, as different factions fought for the control. The emperors *Galba*, *Otho* and *Vitellius* were able to stay in power for only a few months each.[62] It was *Vespasian* (A.D. 69-79)[63] who managed to restore peace. He had been responsible, with his son Titus, for the victory over the Jewish revolt in Judea. He was proclaimed emperor on September 1 in A.D. 69; he entered Rome in the summer of A.D. 70. Vespasian's ruthless use of imperial power and the consistent concentration of administrative authority in his hands may have been an unavoidable consequence of the civil war. The purge of the senate and of the equestrian order, the reorganization of the army, the promotion of the emperor cult, and the rigorous collection of high taxes were intended to stabilize his rule. In A.D. 72 Vespasian created the province of Cilicia, and probably somewhat later the province Lycia-Pamphylia.

Titus (A.D. 79-81), co-regent for several years, continued the politics of his father.[64] Before he became emperor, he had brought the Jewish queen Berenike,

---

[62]See Herbert Grassl, *Untersuchungen zum Vierkaiserjahr 68/69 n.Chr.: Ein Beitrag zur Ideologie und Sozialstruktur des frühen Prinzipats* (Vienna: Wissenschaftliche Gesellschaft, 1973); Peter A. L. Greenhalgh, *The Year of the Four Emperors* (London: Weidenfeld & Nicholson, 1975); Kenneth Wellesley, *The Long Year: A.D. 69* (Bristol: Bristol Classical Press, 1976 [1989]).

[63]G. Chilver and B. Levick, *OCD* 1590-91; Rémy 1986, 49-64; Christ 1992, 247-61; H. Bengtson, *Die Flavier* (Munich: Beck, 1979); B. Levick, *Vespasian* (London: Routledge, 1999).

[64]See J. B. Campbell, *OCD* 1532-33; Bengtson, *Die Flavier;* Brian W. Jones, *The Emperor Titus* (London: Croom Helm, 1984).

the daughter of Agrippa I, to Rome in A.D. 75. She had been his lover since the Jewish revolt, but he did not dare marry her. Berenike was present with her brother, Agrippa II, when Porcius Festus, the new procurator of Judea, questioned the apostle Paul in A.D. 59. The principate of Titus saw the eruption of Mount Vesuvius on August 24 in A.D. 79, as well as a large fire and an epidemic of the plague in Rome.

Domitian (A.D. 81-96)[65] expanded the competences that Vespasian, his brother, and Titus had concentrated in the hands of the emperor. He was openly autocratic, and he initiated an expansion of new forms of court ceremony. Domitian sought to curb symptoms of decay; for example, he insisted on the consistent use of the law against pederasty, and he restored old Roman customs and norms. He allowed the use of the formula *dominus et deus* ("Lord and God"), referring to the emperor, in the administration of the empire (the formula has not yet been found on coins or in inscriptions, however). The "godlike superelevation"[66] reflected in this title was linked with the conviction that the salvation of humankind depended on the well-being of the emperor—at least this was believed in the circles of those who promoted the imperial cult. Domitian was, at the same time, a realistic ruler who secured and maintained a high level of quality in the administration of the empire—a fact that even Suetonius had to acknowledge (*Dom.* 8.2). Domitian made sure that the legal system functioned: he checked verdicts, he removed corrupt judges and he tried to maintain social justice, so that the effectiveness of the organs of administration would be guaranteed in times of crisis.

An inscription found in Pisidian Antiocheia honors L. Antistius Rusticus, Domitian's legate, as governor of Galatia-Cappadocia, who had prohibited profiteering by speculators during a crisis of wheat supply and who had made sure that the citizens were able to buy sufficient wheat at reasonable prices (*AE* [1925]: 126).

Domitian pursued a defensive strategy with regard to the borders of the empire. The campaigns in Germania (A.D. 83) and Britannia (A.D. 84) served defensive purposes, as did the campaign against invading Dacians on the lower Danube River (began A.D. 85/86). The sources report an intensive building activity under Domitian. The number of athletic contests increased. The high costs of the numerous initiatives, including the cost for the military campaigns, caused a huge deficit in the state budget, which led to an increase in taxation and to the misuse of the Jewish tax. The opposition of senators, irked by the arrogant style of

---

[65]J. B. Campbell, *OCD*, 491; B. Levick, "Domitian and the Provinces," *Latomus* 41 (1982) 51-96; Rémy 1986, 64-65; Christ 1992, 262-84; Brian W. Jones, *The Emperor Domitian* (London: Routledge, 1992); Pat Southern, *Domitian: Tragic Tyrant* (London: Routledge, 1997).

[66]Fritz Taeger, *Charisma. Studien zur Geschichte des antiken Herrscherkultes* (Stuttgart: Kohlhammer, 1960), 2:353 ("gottartige Überhöhung"); cf. Christ 1992, 276.

Domitian's rule, led to several waves of persecutions, beginning in A.D. 83, that climaxed ten years later in a rule of terror. Domitian hated not only the senators but also the Cynic itinerant philosophers and the Stoic moralists: he had them banned from Rome and from Italy in A.D. 88/89 and in 93/94. Christians also faced charges of "atheism": in the context of Domitian's actions against aristocrats and suspicious relatives, and in the context of the imperial cult in which the Christians refused to be involved, this caused the persecution of Christians. This persecution evidently was limited to Rome, Asia Minor and several other territories. Domitian was murdered on September 18 in A.D. 96.

18.2 Society, Economy and Culture

Social Realities

Ancient society[67] was characterized by the principle of inequality. Aristotle was convinced that "for the two parties to be on an equal footing or in the contrary positions is harmful in all cases" (*Pol.* 1254 b 9). If "the people" (Gk., *dēmos*) of Athens voted on a "democratic" decision, less than 10 percent of the population was allowed to participate in the decision.[68] The most important criterion for the social stratification in the Roman Empire was ownership of property, which defined one's legal status. The upper class consisted of wealthy landowners, while the huge mass of the lower classes worked as "producers" in agriculture; the small class in between the wealthy and the poor consisted of a minority of urban artisans and merchants. There was no real "middle class" whose existence would have required "its own economic functions, dealing with the care of a considerable technological machinery."[69] Since agricultural structures are relatively stable, the social structures had hardly changed since the time of the late republic, apart from the emergence and consolidation of the imperial monarchy, the new pinnacle of the social hierarchy. In theory the emperor did not possess unlimited power, but in reality he did. As Géza Alföldy comments, "There was no power in the Roman state which could be employed as an alternative to that of the emperor."

People who were wealthy, who occupied higher positions in the administration of the empire or the cities, who had prestige and who were members of an *ordo* (a corporately organized privileged order), belonged to the elite of the very

---

[67]See Rostovtzeff [1929] 1957; Duncan-Jones 1982; MacMullen 1974; Alföldy 1975, 85-132, 188-95; 1986; Bleicken 1978; Garnsey and Saller 1987, 107-59; Christ 1992, 350-433; Vittinghoff 1990, 161-369; Brandt 1992, 120-50; Feichtinger 1993; Gill 1994b; François Jacques and John Scheid, *Les structures de l'Empire romain* (vol. 1 of *Rome et l'intégration de l'empire [44 av. J.-C.-260 ap. J.-C.]*; Paris: Presses Universitaires de France, 1990 [6th ed., 2002]); German: *Die Struktur des Reiches* (vol. 1 of *Rom und das Reich in der Hohen Kaiserzeit 44 v. Chr.-260 n. Chr.;* Stuttgart and Leipzig: Teubner, 1998).

[68]M. Hansen 1991, 90-94.

[69]Alföldy 1975, 89 (ET, 99); the quotation that follows above, ibid.

small upper class. The possibility of acquiring social prestige on the basis of self-generated wealth alone is a modern notion that cannot simply be applied uncritically to Roman society.[70] Social status was controlled by access to the city magistrates (*honores*). According to Géza Alföldy's pyramid model,[71] four groups formed the top of Roman society. (1) Emperor (*imperator*) and the imperial family (*domus imperatoria*): this household also included the imperial slaves and freedmen. (2) Senatorial order (*ordo senatorius*): the senators (*consulares*) formed since the time of the republic the nobility, or aristocracy, of the empire. Augustus had fixed the number of senators at six hundred and introduced a new property qualification of one million sesterces. Senators followed a career path (*cursus honorum*), serving in legal, administrative and military posts. The members of the senatorial order, women and children included, numbered around A.D. 180 about five thousand people.[72] (3) Equestrian order (*ordo equester*): the military aspect of this order had disappeared by the time of the principate; the "knights" (*equites*) occupied positions in jurisdiction and administration as *praefecti* and *procurators,* and they could assume higher-level officer positions in the army. There were about twenty thousand knights at the time of Augustus. As provincials continued to be admitted, this number increased considerably. Many knights had positions as city magistrates. They belonged to the *ordo decurionum* as well, although membership was not formally required. (4) Municipal aristocracy (*ordo decurionum*): the number of *decuriones,* or councilors, who ran Roman local government in colonies and municipalities is estimated at between 100,000 and 150,000. Membership was not hereditary; members were recruited from wealthy citizens who had experience in municipal administration. The highest magistrates in the colonies since the *lex Iulia de municipium* (47 B.C.) were the *duoviri,* elected for one year; originally they were magistrates of the city of Rome without *imperium* who had particular functions such as prosecuting high treason, dedicating temples, commanding the fleet.[73]

The cities in the Roman provinces had diverse structures, due to the history of each city. Nevertheless, the following functions of the administration of free cities can be observed: jurisdiction, finances, food supply, building activities, maintenance of public order. The *decuriones* paid for most public expenses of the city out of their own pockets, including the costs of public buildings (temples, bouleuterion, odeion, theater, pavement) and the costs for honorary priestly offices.

---

[70]Botermann 1991, 300, with reference to Finley 1977 and Alföldy 1986. Becker (1992, 37 [ET, 36]) refers to socially advanced citizens of Corinth or of Tarsus as people who belonged to the upper classes on account of their profession. In view of the social realities of the Roman Empire, such language is meaningless.

[71]Alföldy 1975, 125 (ET, 146), summarizing 94-124 (ET, 106-46).

[72]T. D. Barnes, "Statistics and the Conversion of the Roman Aristocracy," *JRS* 85 (1995): 135-47, esp. 136.

[73]See W. Waldstein, *KP* 2:176-78; Ausbüttel 1998, 42-43, 56-57.

An inscription honoring a certain Quintus Pomponius Flaccus (first or second century A.D.) was erected by the *koinon* of the province of Asia, by the association of the Roman citizens in the province and by the people of Laodikeia. The inscription lists the beneficial work for the common good (δημωφελῶς, *dēmōphelōs*) of the honoree as follows: he was strategos (στρατηγός), administrator of public funds (γενόμενον ἐπὶ τῶν δημοσίων προσόδων), clerk of the market (ἀγορανόμος, *agoranomos*), who had to make sure that the price of food did not increase too steeply and who had to compensate for large price fluctuations with his own financial resources; he had been guardian of the laws (νομοφύλαξ, *nomophylax*), thus appointed to watch over the laws and their observance, recording decrees (ψηφίσματα, *psēphismata*) and punishing perpetrators, especially if they were members of the municipal administration; he had also been night-strategos (στρατηγὸς διὰ νυκτός), some type of police officer responsible for safety in the city during the night.[74]

Wealth or personal achievement (*meritum*) alone did not provide access to the privileged orders, which depended solely on lineage and on the legal status of full Roman citizenship. Admission into an *ordo* was granted by a formal act. Membership in the *ordines* could be recognized by articles of clothing that the members of the upper classes were wearing. The three "orders" of the upper classes, including women and children, probably constituted not even 1 percent of the total population of the Roman Empire.[75] The *honestiores* ("the more respectable ones") enjoyed both written and unwritten privileges, and they were treated by the state with particular respect. Whereas the *humiliores* could be punished with any punishment allowed by Roman law—flogging, forced labor, combat with gladiators or animals, death by crucifixion—the *honestiores* were spared some punishments; for example, *equites* were not placed into forced labor as a punishment but instead were sent into exile. Roman law, often praised in retrospect, was developed intentionally to guarantee the upper class its legal privileges. The courts worked according to this principle in their everyday practice of the law.[76] Lucian compares the life of a member of the lower classes with a rabbit that ducks before anybody whom it believes to be more powerful than itself.[77]

The elite of the urban societies, the full citizens (*cives Romani*), were not "organized" into a civic institution. The municipal aristocracy was an independent corporation in the city, consisting of members of the city council and magistrates. In the cities that were organized according to Roman law and custom the *ordo decurionum* had at least one hundred members. The council of elders (γερουσία, *gerousia*) in the larger cities of the eastern provinces had several hundred members in some cases. The career path in the city administrations does not seem to have been standardized. Hartwin Brandt concludes in a study on

---

[74]*IGR* IV 860 = *I. Laodikeia* 82 (commentary by T. Corsten); cf. Robert 1969-1990, I 265-77.
[75]See Alföldy 1975, 130.
[76]See Garnsey 1970; cf. B. Winter 2001, 44.
[77]Lucian, *Somn.* 9; cf. Kneppe 1994, 332-33.

Pamphylia and Pisidia that "citizens repeatedly appear in honorary inscriptions for benefactors and meritorious citizens as gymnasiarchs, demiourgoi, agonothete, agonothetai, imperial priests and holders of local priestly offices, but to hold these offices does not seem to have been an indispensable prerequisite for achieving a high level of prestige."[78]

The political significance of Roman citizenship declined during the principate. Generally speaking, Roman citizens were privileged with regard to real estate, taxation, civil law and criminal law. A Roman citizen could receive a death penalty only from the imperial court in Rome. A Roman citizen who became an officer in the army had prospects for social advancement. A Roman citizen received preferential treatment from Roman magistrates in commercial transactions, particularly outside of Italy.

A prerequisite for acquiring Roman citizenship had been knowledge of the Latin language,[79] but this requirement seems to have been dropped by the first century. Augustus provides the following figures for the number of Roman citizens in the empire: 4,063,000 (28 B.C.), 4,233,000 (8 B.C.), 4,937,000, including 836,100 provincials (A.D. 14). Tiberius was cautious about granting Roman citizenship, but under Claudius the number of Roman citizens increased: in A.D. 48 a census counted 5,984,072 Roman citizens (Tacitus, *Ann.* 11.25). Seneca accused Claudius of squandering Roman citizenship to "all" Greeks, Gauls, Spaniards and Britons (*Apocolocyntosis* 3.3). The politics of granting citizenship differed in the East from the situation in the West, where Rome had to subdue the backward tribes of Gaul and Spain by force. Bernard Holtheide writes in an important study on Roman citizenship, "The civilizational component that played a major role in the dissemination of the *civitas Romana* in the West was not decisive in the East. Collective grants of citizenship to members of the auxiliary troops, often found in the West since Marius, or the granting of citizenship to members of tribes, or the granting of certain forms of city rights which led to Roman citizenship did not exist in the Greek East. There was no need in Asia for a politics of urbanization, important for the territories in the west of the empire, due to the highly developed cities that existed there. Colonies were established only since Caesar, and only rarely."[80] The political and social changes of the early imperial period promoted a stronger integration of the provincial upper class: provincials who had become Roman citizens were recruited for the apparatus of the Roman state and its organs of administration.

The rule that Roman citizens can be recognized by their names (nomenclature) does not apply to the Roman provinces in Asia Minor. People living in the eastern territories of the Mediterranean world, but also in Greece, had only one name; details of origin may be indicated by the addition of an ethnicon (e.g., "Nicolaus from Antioch" [Acts 6:5]). A Roman citizen's name consisted of five elements, as is demonstrated by the name of M. Tullius M. f. Cor. Cicero.[81] (1) *Praenomen:* older names for individuals such as Marcus or Gaius, ab-

---

[78]Brandt 1992, 153.

[79]Cf. *Res Gestae Divi Augusti* 8. See Alföldy 1975, 92; Hans Volkmann, *Res Gestae Divi Augusti: Das Monumentum Ancyranum* (3rd ed.; Berlin: de Gruyter, 1969), 21.

[80]Holtheide 1983, 5-6; for the observation that follows above see ibid., 6. On Roman citizenship see E. Kornemann, "Civitas," PW 1 (1903): 304-17; M. H. Crawford, *OCD* 334-35; A. N. Sherwin-White, *The Roman Citizenship* (2nd ed.; Oxford: Clarendon, 1973 [1939]).

[81]See H. Rix, *KP* 4:659-60; H. Solin, *OCD* 1024-26.

breviated by sigla (*M.* for Marcus, *C.* for Gaius); people could choose from eleven praenomina, members of the aristocracy from six. (2) *Nomen* or *gentilicium:* family name passed from the father to the children, retained after marriage (Tullius). (3) *Filiation:* name of the father, either his praenomen or cognomen, noted in the genitive case before *filius,* "son," or *filia,* "daughter" (*M[arci] f[ilius]*). (4) *Tribus:* indication of the Roman voting tribe to which the citizen belonged (*Cor.* for *Cor[nelia tribu]*); there were four urban and thirty-one rustic tribes. (5) *Cognomen:* name of the individual; initially the cognomen supplemented the praenomen, but later it replaced it. The cognomen could be a Latin, Greek or "barbaric" name. The cognomen sometimes indicated personal characteristics, and sometimes it was derived from the names of gods. Apart from highly official contexts, only the *tria nomina,* the "three names," were used: praenomen, nomen and cognomen. This system was not used consistently in the province of Asia.[82] Of the 6,700 Roman citizens that have been identified for the province of Asia, only three hundred indicate the tribus in their name formula, usually members of the military. Many *peregrini* ("foreigners," the free citizens without Roman citizenship) who had received Roman citizenship omit in inscriptions the name of the father, which traditionally indicated both birth as a free citizen and legal status. Others omitted the praenomen or filiation. "The practice of the Roman nomenclature by the new citizens and their descendants in the province of Asia, as seen in the epigraphical sources, demonstrates that generally they were unselfconscious with respect to the Roman name formula."

When Jews received Roman citizenship and thereby accepted Roman names, they made use of several options, as examples from the sources indicate:[83] (1) Some used purely Roman names: P. Turronius Claudius in Akmonia.[84] (2) Some added a (Roman or Greek) patronymic to the Roman names: Aur. Phrygianos Menokritou in Akmonia.[85] (3) Some used Greek names followed by Roman names: Loukios Loukiou in Akmonia.[86] (4) Some used Roman or Greek names with or without a patronymic: Roupheina in Smyrna and Straton Tyrannou in Magnesia.[87] (5) Some used a Jewish name, a Greek patronymic and a toponymic: Aur. Eusanbatios Menandrou Korykiotes from the city of Korykos.[88] (6) Some used a Jewish name combined with a Roman or Greek supernomen: Beniames ho kai Dometios in Thessalonike and Iakob he ke Apellion in Aphrodisias.[89] (7) Some used a Greek cognomen followed by a Jewish supernomen: Cl. Tiberius Polycharmos ho kai Achyrios in Stoboi.[90] Jewish identity or descent often is indicated on funerary epitaphs by religious symbols (e.g., a menorah), titles (e.g., *archisynagōgos, archōn*) or an added ethnicon (*Ioudaios, Hebraios*).

Local or indigenous names continued to be used in Asia Minor by the second century. Many parents gave their children names from Greek tradition or other Greek names. Some names were inspired by religious loyalties. Some names carried meaning; many names were due to lallation. Descendants of Italic immigrants, not all of whom were Roman citizens, had Roman names. Some people had double names. The inscriptions of Anazarbos

---

[82]See Holtheide 1983, 16-17, 139; for the observation and quotation that follow above see ibid., 17.

[83]For the description that follows above, including the examples, see Nigdelis 1994, 302-3.

[84]*CIJ* II 767 (*IJudO* II, 347 n. 16,2); see also *CIJ* II 766 (*IJudO* II 168).

[85]*MAMA* VI 335 = *CIJ* II 760 (with erroneous localization); *IJudO* II 173.

[86]*CIJ* II 766 (*IJudO* II 168) line 4.

[87]*I. Smyrna* I 295 = *CIJ* II 741 (*IJudO* II 43); *I. MagnSip* 27 = *CIJ* II 753 (*IJudO* II 48).

[88]*MAMA* III 262 = *CIJ* II 788 (*IJudO* II 236).

[89]*CIJ* I² 693c (*IJudO* I Mac14); Reynolds and Tannenbaum 1987, 6 (*IJudO* II 14) line 20.

[90]*CIJ* I² 694 (*IJudO* Mac1).

in eastern Cilicia indicate that 12 percent of the population had indigenous names (140 examples), often derived from Hittite or Anatolian deities; 42 percent had Roman names (440 examples, of which thirty-six people were Roman citizens), and 46 percent had Greek names (over 500 examples).[91] The inscriptions of Aizanoi (mod. Çavdarhisar), which document many Phrygian names, are as good a source as any for examples of names that people used in Asia Minor.[92] Indigenous names of Phrygians include Ammios, Appas, Appe, Aphion, Babeis, Dades, Mateis, Nannas, Paparion, Papas, Papias, Tatakos, Tatas, Tatia. Some names refer to the fertility of the soil: Anthos, Euporia, Karpion, Karpon, Karpophorus, Klados, Kladaios, Staphylos, Thallos, Thallousa. Some names express the feelings of the parents upon the birth of the child: Auxanon, Auxanousa, Auxesis, Chrysion, Chrysotyches, Epictetus, Euche, Isochrysus, Philetus, Philoumenus, Pothus, Symphorus, Terpsis, Theodorus, Theodotus, Onesimus, Onesime, Onesiphorus. Some names indicate the hopes that parents link with the future of the child: Amerimnus, Andron, Andromenes, Chaereas, Dynamis, Elpis, Elpidephorus, Euboulus, Euphrosyne, Eupraxia, Euodia, Hilarion, Hygea, Itharus, Lampousa, Phaeinus, Philopappus, Philopator, Polychares, Tyche. Names expressing religious loyalties include Diogenes, Diogenikaue, Diodora, Diodoros, Diokles, Diomas, Diophantos (from Διο = Zeus); Metrobios, Metrogenes, Metrodoros, Metrophanes (from Μητηρ = Cybele); Menas, Menios, Menis, Menogenes, Menodotos, Monethemis, Menophas, Menophilus (from Μην, the moon god); Belos, Herodias, Mathias (Semitic cults); Nilus, Psamathe (Egyptian cults); Mithres (Iranian cult). Names that remember Greek tradition include Aeneas, Agathenor, Achilles, Atalanta, Demosthenes, Helen, Hylas, Menelaus, Diomedes, Pelops, Pericles, Phoenix, Pylades, Socrates, Solon, Troilus. Popular Greek names (often ending with -ās) include Achas, Agathas, Apellas, Apollas, Demas, Demosthas, Helicas, Heraclas, Heras, Hermas, Hermogas, Menas, Menophas, Menophoras, Mnaseas, Onesas, Philipas, Plotias, Praxias, Stephanas, Sotas, Teimas, Teuthras, Trophas, Trophimas, Zenonas. Roman names include Gargonius, Salius, Saturius, Sestullius, Steminius, Ulpius, Visedius. Some people had double names, imitating the Roman *tria nomina* or seeking to distinguish a person from other family members who had similar names. Examples from Aizanoi include Antiochos Trophimus, Apollonius Marcion, Asclepiades Charax, Dades Stephanas, Menophilus Bassus. Sometimes a Roman name was added to a Greek name, which probably indicates in many cases aspirations of social prestige. Examples in Aizanoi include Aeneas Lurius, Antiochos Gaius, Artemidorus Asclepiades, Asclepidorus Aulus, Asclepiades Menander, Menophilus Faustus, Metrodorus Menander, Teimotheus Gaius.

Below the Roman citizens who could hold office in the city magistrature or in the Roman administration we find the noncitizens, the *peregrini,* free people who did not hold Roman citizenship, "the former subjects of the Roman *Herrenvolk.*"[93] The *peregrini* lived in the provinces or had come from the provinces to Italy or to Rome, for which reason they also were called *provinciales.*

It is disputed whether it is legitimate to assume a "middle class" between the imperial aristocracy and the "mass basis." In his book on the apostle Paul, Jürgen Becker speaks of a middle-class "propertied class" that "achieved relative affluence through trade, produc-

---

[91]M. H. Sayar, in *I. Anazarbos,* 54.
[92]See B. Levick and S. Mitchell, *MAMA* IX, lix-lxiii, 200-204.
[93]Bleicken 1978, 1:318.

tion, or service" and was supported by specific imperial measures.[94] The imperial patronage that Becker refers to cannot be substantiated by hard evidence, and it is generally problematic whether the term "class" (*Schicht*), particularly the term "middle class," is helpful in describing the social reality of the ancient world.[95]

The legal status of the noncitizen varied. (1) First came the freeborn (πολῖται, *politai;* Lat., *ingenui*), who usually did not have Roman citizenship and therefore were ineligible to vote. The free noncitizens constituted the majority of the population. They included the peasants, artisans, businesspeople, merchants. (2) Next came the freedmen and freedwomen (*liberti*), the emancipated slaves. Their political and legal status was low, although some were able to compensate for this by personal wealth. Freed slaves worked in agriculture and other professions (see below). The next social level was occupied by the resident aliens (πάροικοι, *paroikoi,* or μέτοικοι, *metoikoi*), foreigners who had settled in the city or neighborhood. Generally they were agricultural workers who had no rights. (3) The lowest strata of Roman society was occupied by the slaves (Lat., *servi*), who in terms of legal status did not possess person (*persona*): they were objects (Lat., *res*), the property of the owner. The reality of slavery in classical antiquity needs to be described in a nuanced manner, as the situations that slaves found themselves in differed considerably. The situation of a slave who was in possession of a peculium[96] and was able to engage in profitable business ventures, or of a pedagogue who taught the children of an aristocratic family, cannot really be compared with the situation of slaves who worked in the mines or on warships. In Pergamon perhaps one-third of the 180,000 inhabitants were slaves. In other cities the figures were similar. Descent from slaves could tarnish the reputation of a family for centuries. Besides the slaves, women were another group that suffered discrimination. Aristotle argued that the inferiority of women was a function of the reality of nature (Pol. 1254 b 14). The conviction that women were less intelligent explains why women were subject to a male guardian for their entire life; their legal capacity was limited. Barbara Feichtinger notes that "the political, economic and social inequality of people was omnipresent in everyday life in the subtle language of symbols."[97] The social inequality could be seen in, for example, the seating arrangement in the theater or in the sequence in which a *patronus* received his *clientes* in his home during the morning hours.

The hierarchal structures of society were accepted as fundamental norms and

---

[94]Becker 1992, 255 (ET, 241).
[95]See Botermann 1991, 300.
[96]The term *peculium* designates assets that belonged to a person in power who could not own property, a business or animal flocks, but that could be administered by a son or a slave. "In practice, the assets were regarded as belonging to the son or slave, and a slave given his liberty on condition that he paid a sum of money (*statuliber*) could use his *peculium* to fulfil the condition" (A. F. Rodger, *OCD* 1130; see also E. Bund, *KP* 4:577-78).
[97]Feichtinger 1993, 6; for the discussion that follows above see ibid., 7-17.

traditions. One reason for this was the fact that the self-designation of the elites as *aristoi, boni, optimi* and *honestiores* not only expressed claims of political, social and moral leadership but also implied the voluntary obligation to care for the well-being of the city. In regard to building activities, the military and care for the poor, the Roman state was dependent nearly completely on private initiative. Words such as *dignitas* or *honor* therefore were not just propaganda terms but rather words that indeed reflected reality: the elites generally were engaged in practical, including financial, terms in the workings of the city and the empire. In the imperial period there were opportunities for social advancement for members of the nonprivileged segments of society. Funerary inscriptions sometimes record such "success stories." Both the elites and the members of the lower classes knew that one's personal existence depended on the support of the community. Thus the willingness to bring sacrifices for state, city and family was the highest virtue. Personal, private interests came second. It is not surprising, in this context, that the term *familias* not only described the nuclear family (parents, children) but also included the extended family with relatives (*gens*) as well as the economic community of the family (*domus*), which included slaves and freedmen and freedwomen. When the Jewish-Christian missionaries proclaimed the possibility, indeed the necessity, of a new relationship to God by faith in Jesus Christ, and when they sought to help people join the new community of the believers in Jesus, the salvation of the individual suddenly became more important than the solidarity of the family.

In a fundamental sense anyone might be referred to as an "alien" (*peregrinus;* Gk., *xenos*) who did not belong to the closely knit community of city, family or clan, not just the "foreigner," or *barbaros,* who spoke another language.[98] The Romans were long prejudiced against anyone who came from other regions of the empire, particularly Jews and Egyptians. Juvenal felt uneasy in Rome because so many Syrians lived there, as if "the Syrian Orontes has long since poured into the Tiber."[99]

Economic Realities

When the economic system of Rome[100] was exported to the provinces, two results followed: more profitable methods of production were introduced in underdeveloped regions, and Italy lost its economic predominance to northern Africa, Spain and Gaul. New forms of production were not developed in the first century. The Roman Empire remained an agricultural state, despite a unified currency, despite a developed banking system, despite technical know-how that

---

[98]Dagmar Stutzinger, "Das Fremde und das Eigene," in Dinzelbacher 1993, 400-415, esp. 401.

[99]Juvenal 3.62: "iam pridem Syrus in Tiberim defluxit Orontes."

[100]See Rostovtzeff [1929] 1957; Finley 1977; Pekáry 1980, 608-10; Duncan-Jones 1982; Garnsey and Saller 1987; Christ 1992, 481-506; Meijer and Nijf 1992.

was quite astounding in some areas, despite the upsurge in crafts and trade, and despite masses of cheap labor. Most people were in the agricultural sector, and the main resource for the gross national product was agriculture; most wealthy Romans owed their wealth to their estates, and the most important goods that were traded were agricultural products. Most farms were small, with only 2 to 2.5 ha of land (5 to 6 acres); when veterans settled in colonies, they received 7.5 ha (18.5 acres) on average. Small farms generally worked without slaves; the latter were found in greater numbers on the medium-sized and the large estates of the wealthy and on imperial estates. Medium-sized estates consisted of 25 to 75 ha (62 to 185 acres).

The agriculture of Asia Minor is a good illustration of the needs of the Roman Empire: crops included wheat, barley, wine, olives, almonds and pistachios. Sources also mention millet, sesame, raisins and cotton. Wheat production often was insufficient to supply what the cities needed. Bottlenecks in the supply of wheat often were the result not of bad harvests but of big landowners stockpiling their crops. It was not uncommon that wheat was confiscated and sold to the *sitōnia* (σιτωνία), a magistrate office set up for this purpose that would sell wheat at a fixed price. Inscriptions, which always represent accidental evidence, establish *sitōniai* for sixty-eight cities in Asia Minor alone during the imperial period.[101] The second pillar of agriculture was the cultivation of small livestock, particularly goats and sheep. Phrygia was famous for its horses.

Three factors changed traditional economic life in Syria and in Asia Minor. (1) Taxation was systematically organized and efficiently administered, in the early imperial period through tax collectors (*publicani*), later through the procurators and their staff. Taxes[102] that had to be paid in cash included the land tax (*tributum soli*) and the poll or capitation tax (*tributum capitis*). Additional dues that had to be paid included sales and auction taxes, the *vicesima libertatis* paid for the manumission of slaves, and special dues such as the *aurum coronarium* (contributions toward the golden crown offered to those to whom a "triumph" was given), contributions for the maintenance of roads (the repair of one mile of road cost 100,000 sesterces), compulsory labor and provision of wagons and draft animals (*angareia*). Additional indirect taxes included dues at toll stations (*portorium*), fees for roads, fees for passing bridges or fords. We have very little reliable information about the sum total of taxes and dues that an individual had to pay or about the consequences for the financial resources of the people.

---

[101]The material is collected in Johan H. M. Strubbe, "The Sitonia in the Cities of Asia Minor under the Principate," *EA* 10 (1987): 45-82; 13 (1989): 99-121. The inscription *AE* (1925): 126 provides evidence for this office in Pisidian Antiocheia at the time of the governor L. Antistius Rusticus under Domitian.

[102]See Howego 1992, esp. 18-22 on the provinces; cf. Ausbüttel 1998, 75-90 (on the cost of repairing roads, ibid., 97). See generally Hans-Ulrich von Freyberg, *Kapitalverkehr und Handel im römischen Kaiserreich (27 v.Chr.-235 n.Chr.)* (Freiberg: Haufe, 1988).

(2) The homogeneity of the Roman Empire prompted the development of regional and supraregional economic relations. The imperial and provincial minting of gold and silver coins was centrally controlled, which was the basis for a unified economic realm. Local mintages in Asia Minor produced only bronze coins. The majority of economic transactions were carried out with money. (3) The improvement of the infrastructure included in many regions the expansion of the road system. For example, under Augustus the new Roman colonies in Pisidia were linked with the Via Sebaste, built by the legate Cornutus Arruntius Aquila, with a southeastern and a southwestern trunk road in Pisidian Antiocheia.[103] The Augustan road network was further expanded in the second century. Trade relations were maintained not only with the provinces of the empire but also with southern Russia, India, China, Africa and northern Europe (as far as Iceland).

The local trade in the numerous small markets generally was carried on by the producers themselves, who sold their products or exchanged them for other goods. The transregional trade was controlled by Roman businessmen (*negotiatores*) who often functioned simultaneously as tax collectors (*publicani*) and as bankers.[104] Inscriptions and archaeological finds confirm numerous skilled trades that were important for the economy of city and province. In construction we encounter quarry workers, master builders, architects, stonecutters, stonemasons, sculptors, bronze casters, and in the textile industry dyers and weavers. Other professions included blacksmiths, tanners, shoemakers, bakers (for larger cities such as Side larger bakeries are attested, as are associations of flour sifters and bread formers), painters, mosaic layers, goldsmiths, silversmiths. Other people who sold their wares in the markets included linen dealers and sellers of vegetables, herbs, pastries, wine, olives, ointments, perfume and wood.

The supply needs of smaller cities were largely met by the hinterland. Larger cities were forced to import wheat, meat, oil, wine and textiles. A merchant usually specialized in a particular branch of business and had a fixed group of suppliers and buyers, as the merchant always traveled the same routes. These traveling merchants carried news from business partners or friends, or news that they picked up in the markets or in the guest houses, across huge distances. A frequently quoted inscription is the epitaph of the merchant Flavius Zeuxis, who sailed seventy-two times around Cape Malea, the southernmost point of mainland Greece, to Italy; he was familiar with many regions and knew many people and would regularly have "transported" information. Reinhold Reck comments that "he occupied the typical gatekeeper position as recipient, medium and communicator in one person."[105] Trade activities often required a change of residence: from a rural area to a city, from a small city to a metropolis, from a prov-

---

[103]See Radke 1973; French 1980.
[104]See Brandt 1992, 140.
[105]Reck 1991, 93.

ince to Rome, and vice versa. The lower classes in the cities were better off economically than the rural population.

Culture

Alongside agriculture and crafts/trade, the third pillar of the economy encompassed culture, education and sports (*agōnes*). The prosperity of urban culture in the provinces encouraged musical, theatrical and poetical productions as well as festivals and athletic contests.[106] The leading families required cultivated and exciting entertainment, a solid education for their children, and competent medical and legal services. Numerous honorary inscriptions and epitaphs document jurists, philologists, philosophers, teachers, actors, poets, dancers, singers, mimes, musicians, athletes and gladiators.

During the first and second centuries countless athletic and artistic contests (*agōn*, pl., *agōnes*) were instituted. Many artists and athletes participated in the contests of other cities, traveling "internationally" from tournament to tournament. The president of the games (*agōnothetēs*) sometimes was the *agoranomos*, and for the larger provincial games the high priest (*archiereus*) of the emperor cult. The festivals into which the *agōnes* were integrated proceeded in the following manner:[107] (1) Donning of garlands (*stephanēphoria*) by participants. (2) Procession (*pompē*) in which statues and pictures (painted on wooden boards) of the deity or the emperor are carried; the *agōnothetēs* leads, followed by the leading officials of the city in festive garb, and then the ephebes and the citizens. (3) Sacrifices (*thysia* for deities, *enagismos* for mortals); often it was predetermined who had to supply how many oxen. (4) Prayers (*euchē*). (5) Singing of a festival hymn, presented by hymnodes. (6) Banquet (*euōchia*). (7) Games (*agōnes*). (8) Speeches honoring the gods, presented by the *theologos*, and honoring the emperor, presented by the *sebastologos*. The majority of the citizens did not participate directly; essentially they served as staff for the festivities. The citizens, including the poor, profited indirectly through the special festival markets, or meals of foods were provided for free by a benefactor.

18.3 Cities and Rural Areas

The well-being of the community was a fundamental value of ancient society. Despite the greed and thirst for glory of the Roman nobility, this absolute value of aristocratic ethics was never abandoned.[108] The following description of cities and rural areas focuses on Asia Minor because the New Testament sources locate the activities of the early Christian missionaries particularly in

---

[106]See Brandt 1992, 144-45. On the Hellenistic culture of festivals see Köhler 1996.

[107]For the following description cf. Peter Herz, "Herrscherverehrung und lokaler Festkultus im Osten des römischen Reiches (Kaiser/Agone)," in Cancik and Rüpke 1997, 239-264.

[108]Dahlheim 1982, 33.

the Roman provinces of Syria-Cilicia, Galatia and Asia.

The Cities

According to the explicit information provided by the New Testament sources, the first missionaries concentrated on cities.[109] The definition of "city" (Gk., *polis;* Lat., *urbs*) in antiquity presents a well-known problem.[110] The criteria for the classification of a settlement as "city" are either symbolic or functional. Symbolic characteristics of a city are physical, political and religious structures (e.g., city walls, acropolis, palace, temple). Functional characteristics include administrative, economic and social institutions (e.g., *bouleuterion, agora, forum*). The Greeks defined a "polis" as an enclosed central town that had specific institutions (*boulē, agora, gymnasion*), specific rights, a particular way of life (baths) and cultural attractions (theater). In the Roman Empire facilities that characterized a city included expensively decorated public places, water supply (aqueduct), monumental temples, theater and amphitheater, features that dominated the polis by their sheer size. A village (κώμη, *kōmē;* Lat., *vicus*) was a politically dependent settlement, agrarian in nature, without walls (harbors and cult places dependent on cities may be exceptions). The size of large villages made it difficult to decide whether the settlement was a village or a town; this ambiguity is reflected in the term κωμόπολις (*kōmopolis* [Strabo 12.2.6; 12.6.1; 13.1.27; Mk 1:38]). The territory of a city (χώρα, *chōra;* Lat., *territorium*) often included dozens of villages that in turn controlled further hamlets and farmsteads.

Greek villages differed little from Roman villages. Roman cities, however—outside of Italy, the *coloniae*—were characterized by special features that embodied the Roman notion of the state.[111] In most Greek cities the *agora* was a political place independent of the main temple (or several main temples), spatially separated from the temple. The agora was a large empty area that had no major architectural characteristics; here the free (male) citizens met in order to guide the affairs of the city and make important decisions. The small altars and the small temples that belonged to the agora were dedicated to Zeus Agoraios or other deities connected with the institutions of the polis.

The lower agora of Pergamon, dating to the Hellenistic period, is a good example for the markets of the larger cities in Asia Minor (see fig. 19).[112] The lower agora (88 by 55 m)

---

[109]See Macro 1980; Pekáry 1980, 605-8; Dahlheim 1982; Kolb 1984; Lorenz 1987; Radt 1988, 106-30 (on Pergamon); Brödner 1989; Dräger 1993; Gesemann 1996; I. Barton 1996; Fear 1996, 6-30; Klaus Fittschen, "Stadt II: Neues Testament," *TRE* 32 (2001): 92-93.

[110]See Kolb 1984, 58-95; Sakellariou 1989; Lomas 1997; Schuler 1998, 18-21; A. K. Bowman, in Fentress 2000, 173-87.

[111]For the description that follows above see Zanker 2000. See also Tonio Hölscher, *Öffentliche Räume in frühen griechischen Städten* (Schriften der Philosophisch-historischen Klasse der Heidelberger Akademie der Wissenschaften 7; Heidelberg: Winter, 1998).

[112]Radt 1988, 112-14; on the upper market see ibid., 114-18.

was surrounded on all four sides by colonnaded halls and formed the business center of the city. The first story of the stoas was 3.16 m high, and the front of the stoas reached a height of 9 m. The agora probably had four entries. In contrast to a Roman forum, the agora of Pergamon had no monumental gate. The open plaza (64 by 34 m) was paved. A visitor would have seen numerous works of art and monuments, including inscriptions that informed readers about prominent citizens and the laws of the city.

The main temples of the Greek cities, dedicated to the worship of Zeus, Apollo, Aphrodite and other deities, were located on the acropolis above the city (e.g., the temple of Aphrodite in Greek Corinth) or outside of the city (e.g., the temple of Artemis in Ephesus). The Greek temples were accessible to all inhabitants regardless of social position or political influence, not only to the free citizens. Women and men, free citizens and slaves, adults and children visited the temples. The laws that had been decided in the agora were stored in the temple and often published as inscriptions. These two public spaces, the temple and the agora, provided the citizens of the polis a place where they could agree on political decisions irrespective of religious traditions and where they worshiped the deities as guarantors of safety and well-being.

The urban gestalt of a Roman city diverged from the Greek model considerably. The hierarchical structure of the Roman state was responsible for the same aristocratic families occupying both the political and the priestly offices. The political process was closely connected with religious traditions and rituals. For this reason, the forum and the temple belonged together. Soon after the kings had been driven out of the city of Rome, the new rulers erected on the Forum Romanum temples for Saturnus and for the Dioscuri (Castor and Pollux). Many cities that Rome founded, particularly in the western provinces, combined a forum with a *capitolium* (temple of Jupiter). Eventually the forum was separated from the street plan of the city, and the markets were relocated in neighboring streets or quarters. The forum became a place where the state could demonstrate its power and where the representatives of the state and the leading citizens of the city could exhibit their status and prestige. The public space of the forum became more and more crowded with the addition of temples and monuments. The city plan of Roman Corinth, refounded in 44 B.C. as a Roman colony, is a good example of this development (see fig. 36).

The colonies that Augustus established in Asia Minor, particularly in Phrygia and Pisidia, including Pisidian Antiocheia, represented the addition of a legally constituted group of army veterans to a fully developed Greek polis. In these cities the influence of Roman culture and architecture remained limited.[113]

The urban structures in the eastern Mediterranean regions usually retained the traditional Greek characteristics, which were much more varied than in the Ro-

---

[113]See Yegül 2000, 133-34.

man cities of the West. Karl Christ's description of Ephesus serves as a case in point: "A metropolis such as Ephesus still retained in the imperial period an assembly of the citizens (*ekklesia*) that met in the large theater, with the *grammateus* presiding. The city council, the *boule,* had (in this case) three hundred councilors, who met in the *bouleuterion.* In addition to the administrative offices (*stragegoi* and the *agoranomoi,* who were responsible for the supply of wheat and for the market), numerous municipal offices with supervising functions are attested for this ancient world city, for example, the *limenarchai,* who had to control the harbor, the *paraphylakes,* who were responsible for the safety of the citizenry, and the *eirenarchai,* who served as justices of the peace."[114]

Scholars often claim that one of the main characteristics of Roman rule in the provinces was urbanization: disadvantaged regions in the interior now received the blessings of urban civilization, and the difference between urban and rural areas was softened.[115] Frank Kolb assumes for the East "an accelerated development of large cities and, connected with this, the establishment or the development of true urban centers at the cost of numerous smaller *poleis* with their village-like settlements."[116] New epigraphical and archaeological discoveries and insights indicate, however, that such analyses are assumptions rather than reflections of historical reality: no fundamental variations, at least for Pamphylia and Pisidia, can be observed in the Roman period compared with the Hellenistic settlement structures.[117] The urban structure that had developed organically, adapted to local natural and geographical conditions, remained stable. The few new towns that were established during Roman rule remained in many cases relatively insignificant. The constant improvement of the settlements during the Roman period takes place on the basis of the Hellenistic urban structures, which usually are underestimated. Two developments can be clearly linked with Roman rule: first, the increased urbanization that can be assumed for a few settlements, or towns, that were located at important road junctions; second, the general tendency toward more ambitious facilities in the cities, which was a result of the increasing wealth of the local elites in regions such as Pamphylia. And we should note that some regions in the East received major economic impulses from the emperor.

The following cities are documented for the Roman period. In *Pamphylia:* Aspendos, Perge, Side, Attaleia, Sillyon, Seleukeia, Korakesion, Hamaxia, Laertes, Magydos, Kolybrassos, Karallia, Kasai. Four cities are new Roman foundations: Erymna, Kotenna, Lyrbe, Sennea.[118]

In *Pisidia* the following cities are known: Selge, Termessos, Sagalassos, Antiocheia,

---

[114]Christ 1992, 392. See also Macro 1980, 677-80.
[115]See Christ 1992, 445-57; Dahlheim 1982, 13-74.
[116]Kolb 1984, 174.
[117]For the observations that follow above see Brandt 1992, 100-120.
[118]See Brandt 1992, 101-7.

Cremna, Adada, Apollonia, Ariassos, Etenna, Anabura, Amblada, Isinda, Peduelissos, Timbriada, Kormasa, Phaselis, Kretopolis, Lysinia, Mistea, Olbasa, Pogla, Sibidunda, Prostanna, Seleukeia Sidera, Neapolis, Milyas, Andeda, Verbe, Komama, Parlais, Kolbasa, Malos, Keraitai, Konana, Baris, Pappa-Tiberiopolis, Tymandos. Three cities are Roman foundations: Andada, Verbe and Comama, cities for which magistrates, priestly offices, coinages and games have been confirmed. Four cities that minted coins have not been located yet: Kodrula, Palaiopolis, Panemoteichos, and Tityassos.[119]

Good examples for the continuity of the Anatolian cities are Selge, Termessos and Sagalassos, which dominated Pisidia in the Hellenistic and in the Roman periods. None of the new Roman colonies could compare with the level of their urban development.[120]

Selge (mod. Zerk),[121] about 65 km northwest of Attaleia (mod. Antalya), belonged to the province of Galatia. The city had superior urban facilities already in the third and second centuries B.C.: city walls with opulently decorated gates, a theater, an odeion; the agora was surrounded by colonnaded halls and had an *agoranomion*. The temple of Zeus stood on the acropolis above the city (called Κεσβέλιον). According to Strabo (12.7.3), twenty thousand inhabitants lived in the city. The styrax resin that was used for the production of ointments, aromata and perfumes was gathered near Selge, a fact reflected in the iconography of the coins minted in the city. The considerable increase of Selge's wealth during the first three centuries evidently was connected with a substantial expansion of economic activities that made it possible to construct a second (lower) agora (25,000 m^2). In the second century many new buildings were constructed: a street with colonnades, *nymphaeum,* theater, stadium, odeion, two *thermae* (baths), several new temples and two aqueducts.

Termessos,[122] in southwest Pisidia 34 km northwest of Attaleia, 1,000 m above sea level, about 7 km from the Via Sebaste connecting Attaleia and Perge with Pisidian Antiocheia, was founded probably in the eighth century B.C. Termessos successfully resisted Alexander the Great in 333 B.C. In the third/second century B.C. the city founded a colony in Oenoanda in Lycia (Τερμησσὸς ἡ μικρά, "Little Termessos"). The city enjoyed a great deal of freedom during the Roman period. The coins of the city record its autonomy. No temple has been identified that was dedicated to a Roman emperor. Termessos had fortified walls, a fortress, wells, an agora with a portico, a bouleuterion, a gymnasium, temples dedicated to Zeus and Artemis. We can observe an improved quality of many buildings in the Roman period in Termessos as well: new constructions include a second stoa, a new theater (with a capacity for over 4,000 spectators), an odeion and a gymnasium dating to the first century A.D., documenting the continued importance of Greek cultural traditions. In the second century the water supply was improved, and in the third century a

---

[119]Strabo 12.7.2 (quotation of Artemidoros of Ephesus [100 B.C.]); Ptolemaios 5.5.4-8. See Brandt 1992, 107-20.

[120]Brandt 1992, 109.

[121]See Levick 1967, 9, 16, 18-19, 30, 204; Brandt 1992, 51, 78, 107-8; McDonagh 2001, 456-56; S. Mitchell 1995a, 1:71-72, 152, 173, 225; 2:151; Alois Machatschek and Mario Schwarz, *Bauforschungen in Selge* (Vienna: Österreichische Akademie der Wissenschaften, 1981); Johannes Nollé and Friedel Schindler, *Die Inschriften von Selge* (Bonn: Habelt, 1981); J. Nollé, *EA* 12 (1988): 133-38.

[122]See R. Heberdey, "Termessos (2)," PW 9.A (1934): 732-75; Price 1984, 271; McDonagh 2001, 434-39; Brandt 1992, 51-52, 108; S. Mitchell 1995a, 1:71-72, 225; 2:13. Inscriptions: *TAM* III 1, 1941; see also Bülent Iplikçioğlu et al., *Epigraphische Forschungen in Termessos und seinem Territorium I* (Vienna: Österreichische Akademie der Wissenschaften, 1991); Bülent Iplikçioğlu, in Dobesch and Rehrenböck 1993, 255-63.

large new gymnasium was built. Inscriptions document several temples and magnificent tombs. Many of the nearly one thousand inscriptions of the city concern the agonistic games organized by Termessos, including foot races in the stadium and horse races in the hippodrome. A third-century inscription attests a pagan father who erected a tomb for a Jewish daughter named Aurelia Artemeis. She probably was one of "the very select band of upper class Graeco-Roman women who, instead of flirting with Judaism, fully embraced its tenets."[123] A recently discovered inscription is curiously connected with the burial of a dog: "This is the grave of the departed dog Stephanos. Rhodope has wept over him and buried him like a human being. I am the dog Stephanos, Rhodope has erected the grave for me." In the fourth century a bishop named Heuresios is documented for Termessos. It is not known when Christians came to Termessos for the first time.

Sagalassos,[124] about 7 km north of modern Ağlassun near Isparta, was the largest city in northern Pisidia. It had one of the most imposing urban structures of the region: fortified walls with towers protected the agora, the bouleuterion, temples, a heroon and the living quarters. The Doric temple from the Hellenistic period probably was dedicated to Kakasbos, a local deity. In the first and second century A.D. large temples were constructed for Apollo Clarios, Dionysios and for the emperor Pius Antoninus. During the time of Augustus new monumental buildings were erected in the Hellenistic upper city: colonnaded porticoes, triumphal arches dedicated to three emperors (among them Claudius) and a market hall were erected in the agora. The commercial center was northeast of the upper agora, whose pottery workshops produced for the regional markets of Pisidia and eastern Lycia but also exported their products to Italy and to the eastern Mediterranean regions. A new lower agora was systematically expanded. The construction of the Apollo temple was financed by members of the local elite. Sagalassos had an amphitheater, a library (dated to A.D. 120-125), which has been magnificently restored, and probably a stadium.

The cities presented better opportunities for commercial success than did the villages. The urban centers proved easier places to take up a new trade. The food supply was better, often guaranteed by members of the local aristocracy (in Rome by the emperor). Entertainment in the amphitheater, the stadium or the theater was a further advantage of life in the city, not to mention other opportunities for amusement, including visits to brothels, of which Pompeii alone had at least twenty-eight. However, an individual's industriousness did not guarantee economic success. Many people had to stay in miserable living quarters, suffered under unfavorable working conditions, had little to eat and hardly enough clothes. In many of the smaller provincial towns many inhabitants were peasants who worked on nearby farms and estates. Life in the city essentially

---

[123]Inscription: *TAM* III 612. See M. Williams 1997, 255, 259 (no. 15), 261-62 (appendix 2); the quotation above, 262. Williams corrects Ross S. Kraemer, "On the Meaning of the Term 'Jew' in Graeco-Roman Inscriptions," *HTR* 82 (1989): 35-53, esp. 44. For the inscription of Rhodope see Iplikçioğlu, in Dobesch and Rehrenböck 1993, 260-61.

[124]See S. Mitchell 1995a, 1:71-72, 157, 214-16, 242; 2:13, 151; on the ongoing excavations see Marc Waelkens et al., eds., *Sagalassos I-V* (5 vols.; Leuven: Leuven University Press, 1993-2000); M. Waelkens, "Die neuen Forschungen (1985-1989) und die belgischen Ausgrabungen (1990-1991) in Sagalassos," in Schwertheim 1992, 43-60; Brandt 1992, 52, 108, 138; Gates 1995, esp. 231-33. See also <www.esat.kuleuven.ac.be/sagalassos>.

was controlled by the *ordo decurionum,* the municipal aristocracy, the full citizens who usually were landowners and who "for generations competed for municipal offices and kept public life going with their munificence (donations, benefactions, building construction, assumption of embassies)."[125]

Streets and Roads

The streets of the cities in antiquity must be regarded as integrated living space of the citizens, in contrast to the streets of modern cities, which have little significance for the life of most inhabitants apart from offering the most expedient means of movement. The following description is based on a recent work by Björn Gesemann, who has studied the streets of ancient Pompeii.[126]

The main streets of Pompeii featured a traffic lane and sidewalks, and they had pavement and a drainage system. The traffic lane (Lat., *agger*) of most streets had a crown; they were lined with sidewalks (Lat., *margines, crepidines*) about 30 cm in height, irrespective of the width of the street or the existence of pavement. In some cities stepping stones were placed in the traffic lane to allow pedestrians to cross the street without having to step onto the traffic lane. The width of streets varied considerably. In Pompeii the streets were between 2.5 and 9.6 m wide, with the sidewalks using about half of the total width; only the traffic lane was paved. By no means were all streets paved. In Pompeii the streets of Regio II had no pavement, and the streets of Regio II and several *vici* of Regiones VI and VII had no sidewalks. The sidewalks sometimes were replaced by water channels serving as sewers. Maintenance of the sidewalks was the responsibility of the owners of the adjacent houses. The side streets and lanes were narrow, in Pergamon often just 2 m wide, sometimes even narrower, so that pack animals with bags could not pass each other. In some cities commercial traffic was prohibited during the night in order to maintain peace and quiet through the nighttime hours.[127] In Pompeii the magistrate attempted to keep commercial traffic away from specific streets and from entire city quarters: archaeologists have found steles erected in the middle of streets, stepping stones blocking traffic, narrowed lanes, even blockades. It is impossible, of course, to assume that the same situation applied in other cities in the Roman Empire. The fact that the streets of Athens and of Miletus were not paved demonstrates that generalizations are dangerous. Still, it remains a fact that the rectangular or gridiron type of layout for city streets, named after Hippodamus of Miletus (ca. 500 B.C.), which was developed in the early seventh century B.C. for the foundation of colonies of Greek cities, quickly became normative for the arrangement for new cities.

The streets were dominated by shops: not only the main streets but also many of the smaller streets in the city center were lined on both sides with shops and workshops. Artisans and their products, which often were offered for sale on the sidewalks, could be seen through the wide entrances of the workshops.

---

[125]Botermann 1991, 300.

[126]Gesemann 1996.

[127]See Suetonius, *Claud.* 25. It remains unclear whether the suspension of traffic in Italian cities prohibited traffic entirely or only for the main streets. See Gesemann 1996, 40-41.

Signs in the form of painted pictures, reliefs, linen curtains or awnings indicated what products were produced and sold in the workshops. It seems that the workshops of the various trades were scattered throughout the city. There were some merchants and street peddlers in the living quarters of the city as well, but the latter usually were much quieter than the city center. Vendors who sold their goods in stalls in the streets made the city center look like a warehouse. Martial's description of the colorful activity in the streets of Rome surely can be taken as a description for other large cities in the Roman world as well, notwithstanding differences in detail:

"The audacious retailers had appropriated the entire city; no threshold kept within its own bounds. You [Domitian] bade the narrow streets expand, Germanicus, and what had lately been a track became a road. No column is girt with chained flagons, and the praetor is not forced to walk through the mud. The razor is not drawn blindly in a dense crowd, nor does the grimy cook shop monopolize the whole street. The barber, the taverner, the cook, the butcher keep to their own thresholds. Now it is Rome; until recently it was a big shop" (Martial 7.61).

An important fact that touches the reality in which the early Christian mission was active is the function of the city streets as realm of religious life. The following religious activities took place in the street: (1) Some cults were "at home" in the streets, particularly the cult of the *lares compitales,* who were venerated in sanctuaries at street crossings as the guardians of crossways and of roads. The sanctuaries, called *compita,*[128] consisted of an altar placed against the wall of a house, or of a small niche in the wall; sometimes a religious painting replaced the altar. The *compita* usually depicted the *lares,* sometimes the sacrifice of the *vicomagistri,* or perhaps one or two *agathodaimones* (the good *genius*). At least in Pompeii the personification Fortuna Augusta was venerated in the streets as well. (2) The street was the realm of religious processions. Some processions were linked with public cults (e.g., the cult of Cybele), other processions with family events such as family celebrations, cultic activities, weddings and burial ceremonies; some processions were linked with lustrations, ceremonies of purification and of averting evil.[129] (3) Other religious activities in the streets included the offering of sacrifices for the *lares compitales,* the decoration of the entrances of houses on the occasion of particular festivals. For example, during the Vestialia the temples and the houses of the priests were decorated with fresh laurel.[130] Festive costumes that people wore in the streets often were linked with religious meaning as well: the participants in the *ludi Apollinares* wore garlands

---

[128]The Latin word *compitum* can designate both the sanctuary and the crossway. In Pompeii sixty-one *compita* have been identified, but certainly there were more than that. See Gesemann 1996, 82; for a description of the *compita* of Pompeii see ibid., 85-87.

[129]See W. Eisenhut, "Lustratio," *KP* 3:789-90; J. Linderski, "Lustration," *OCD* 893.

[130]See Pliny, *Nat.* 16.235; Ovid, *Fast.* 3.137.

of flowers; the women who participated in the Matronalia wore special costumes; the amusements of the Saturnalia, celebrated for seven days around December 17, included a masquerade in the streets. The political dimension of the street was seen in depictions of the imperial family and the acts of veneration performed in public. Since the reform of the cult under Augustus the omnipresence of the emperor, at least in the streets of Roman cities, was focused on the *compita* in the crossroads.

The streets were a "realm of encounter and conversation."[131] Two functions of the street are particularly important in this connection. (1) Edicts and election posters that were affixed to house walls demonstrate that the streets were important for the formation of public opinion. (2) Countless graffiti demonstrate that the street played an important role as a barometer of public opinion and as a "pressure relief valve" for the dissatisfaction of the citizenry that should not be underestimated. Suetonius's biographies of the emperors indicate that these spontaneous graffiti expressing agreement with or critique of the emperor and his family were taken seriously indeed. When Domitian "erected so many and such huge vaulted passageways and arches in the various regions of the city, adorned with chariots and triumphal emblems," the population reacted with criticism such "that on one of them someone wrote in Greek: 'It is enough'"(*ut cuidam Graece inscriptum sit: arci* [Suetonius, *Dom.* 13.2]).

The streets were places where people spent their free time. Most of the residents lived in cramped, uncomfortable lodgings that often had no daylight. In his third satire Juvenal graphically described the close living conditions in the city (3.227-250). The street thus constituted the expanded living space of the nonprivileged residents, a fact evidenced by the numerous taverns (*thermopolia,* Lat., *cauponae*) that had only limited seating and served their customers in the streets.

The streets of the cities were important places of information exchange, which functioned particularly well "when the information that needed to be communicated was directed at as many addressees as possible."[132] The street has retained this communicative function in the countries of the Mediterranean world and in the so-called two-thirds world until today. The following details are instructive.

1. Street names were not uncommon in the Greco-Roman world; they have been confirmed for many cities. In Ephesus the streets *Arkadiane* and *Embolos* are known, and in Alexandria the streets *Dromos tou megalou Sarapidou, Aspendia* and the *Via Mercurii*. In at least the large cities of the Roman Empire all important streets and many of the smaller streets had names, while smaller side streets or lanes presumably did not. We know, on the other hand, that even rela-

---

[131]Gesemann 1996, 46.
[132]See Gesemann 1996, 157-80; quotation, 157.

tively large provincial towns such as Oxyrhynchus in Egypt largely managed without street names. Only sixteen street names are known of this city of thirty thousand inhabitants—for example, the Street of Apollonios (the founder of the city), the main street (*plateia*), the Shepherds' Street, the Southern Broad Street.[133] Even some houses had names: not only villas of aristocrats but also commercial workshops and taverns. In order to locate a particular address, a person needed precise information or had to ask the locals for directions.

A papyrus found in Oxyrhynchus records the description of an address in Hermopolis (?) that had to be found by the person who took the letter to the recipient there: "Consignment of Rufus' letters: From the Moon gate walk as if towards the granaries and when you come to the first street turn left behind the thermae, where there is a shrine, and go westwards. Go down the steps and up the others and turn right and after the precinct of the temple on the right side there is a seven-story house and on top of the gatehouse a statue of Fortune and opposite a basket-weaving shop. Enquire there or from the concierge and you will be informed. And shout yourself; Lusius will answer you" (P.Oxy. 2719 [third century]). Some descriptions of addresses were shorter, especially if they were written on the verso of letters: "Consignment: At the Teumenout (quarter) in the lane opposite the well" (P.Oxy 1678).[134]

2. Shop signs informed passersby about which trade of craft the shop specialized in, or they provided specific information about that particular business.

3. Inscriptions in walls demonstrated as no other element to what degree the street was used as a medium of communication. The often large and sloganlike inscriptions (*dipinti*) were incised by professional writers and addressed the public at large: they published announcements of *munera,* of commercial shops and their goods, or election slogans for individual candidates or a combination of candidates.

Announcements of *munera* (e.g., of gladiator games) are customarily found at places that people frequented the most: near public institutions, in main streets, and particularly near the gates, where travelers could read them.[135] Announcements of gladiator games in neighboring cities found in Pompeii demonstrate the interest of the residents.

The city magistrates published administrative announcements on white wooden boards (Lat., *album*) that could be read by passersby. Besides these official bulletins there is evidence for wall newspapers in some cities. Caesar introduced the *acta urbis* (Suetonius, *Jul.* 20.1), which originally had a purely official char-

---

[133]Krüger 1990, 94-98, with reference to H. Rink, "Straßen- und Viertelnamen von Oxyrhynchus" (diss., University of Giessen, 1924).

[134]The translations follow S. R. Llewelyn, "The Sending of a Private Letter," in *NewDocs* 7:26-47, esp. 31-32, 37; for German translations see Krüger 1990, 99. See also E. J. Epp, "New Testament Papyrus Manuscripts and Letter Carrying in Greco-Roman Times," in *The Future of Early Christianity* (FS H. Koester; ed. B.A. Pearson; Minneapolis: Fortress, 1991), 35-56.

[135]Gesemann 1996, 176.

acter but with the passage of time became a means of more general information announcing and discussing rather diverse subjects.[136] Graffiti (i.e., "inscriptions") incised into walls by residents or passersby, often spontaneously, were addressed to either a very small or an arbitrary audience.[137]

We find private and commercial offers, including invitations from prostitutes on a bench in front of the suburban baths in Pompeii, notices of a loss, announcements of births, but also jokes (or scribblings, depending on taste) that satisfied primarily the "author." Some graffiti were even answered.

A *dipinto* on the facades of houses may have announced sales or rent opportunities or provided information about the owner of the house—potentially about the Christian community that met in the house. There is, however, no evidence that churches announced their presence in this manner in the first or the second century.

4. Tangible elements of communication included installations that were erected on order of the magistrates during festivals or that announced the birth of a child. On certain occasions rituals were performed on the doorsteps of houses that were intended to bring luck or avert harm; sometimes the door was decorated with flowers of garlands. The entrance was used for rituals during weddings and funerals as well. During festivals of the deities that the families worshiped, their temples or *compita* in front of the house were decorated. The decoration of streets during processions (Suetonius, *Nero* 25), which always included religious connotations, not only served the self-presentation of the participants but also defined and delineated the cultic realm.

Houses

Archaeological research has often neglected private houses of ancient cities.[138] There are only a few cities of the ancient world where private houses have been seriously investigated: Pompeii, Solunt, Ostia, Dura Europos, Priene, more recently Ephesus. Most of our knowledge is due to emergency excavations and accidental discoveries. This situation is largely explained by the non-public character of private houses, by the inconspicuous character of houses (compared with temples, palaces, aqueducts, baths), and by the continuity of settlement in many places that destroyed all evidence. At the same time we must recall that public buildings constituted only a relatively small portion of the layout of a city.

---

[136]See M. Fuhrmann, "Acta Nr. 2," *KP* 1:55; J. P. Balsdon and A. W. Lintott, *OCD* 10.
[137]See Karl-Wilhelm Weeber, *Decius war hier: Das Beste aus der römischen Graffiti-Szene* (Zürich: Artemis & Winkler, 1996).
[138]See W. H. Gross, *KP* 2:957-61; Etienne 1974; Bieritz and Kähler 1985; Radt 1988, 119-27; Weiser 1990; Gesemann 1996.

The masonry of private houses was often rather basic, as in the houses in Pergamon.[139] Smaller undressed stones were held together by a plaster that consisted of mud. The inner walls usually were plastered; scratched lines on the plaster imitated a rectangular pattern of the walls, which were painted simply in red and white. Floors consisted of beaten earth. In some houses remains of stucco ornaments have been found. The doors usually were made of wood, as was the stairway leading to the upper floor. The roofs that were not very steep were covered with clay tiles (70 by 50 cm). Many houses were not connected to the water conduits of the cities, even in imperial times. When more space was needed, the owners of houses divided rooms, added rooms or built additional structures in the courtyard. The peristyle courts often were paved and often contained a cistern in which rainwater from the roof was collected. Simpler houses, of course, did not have a central peristyle court.

In the larger cities we find the following types of private houses. (1) The Roman atrium house, in which the living and sleeping quarters, the kitchen and any other domestic rooms, usually closed by curtains, were built around the atrium. The atrium was a rectangular space open to the sky at the center (*compluvium*) so that sunlight and fresh air could enter, with columns at all four sides in the more elaborate houses. The atrium, a multipurpose room, was also the abode of the household deities. Access to the outside world was possible on one side of the atrium through a vestibule. (2) The Hellenistic peristyle house (Lat., *domus*) consisted of an atrium section and one or more atrium-like peristyle courtyards—that is, rectangular or square courtyards surrounded on all four sides with colonnaded corridors, behind which the living and sleeping quarters were found. In some cities a grand peristyle house could occupy an entire city block: in Priene, House 33 is some 35 m long.

Terrace House 2 in Ephesus (see fig. 39a)[140] occupied about 4,000 m² on three terraces with identical dimensions in the first phase of construction. In the first century A.D. two separate housing units were built in the form of peristyle houses. The entrance into housing unit 6 (see fig. 39b) was at the western end of Alytarch's Stoa on Curetes Street. A stairway led directly to the peristyle courtyard (31a), which was lined on all four sides by colonnaded corridors; the courtyard was paved and in the center open to the sky; the twelve marble columns surrounding the courtyard were 4.6 m high. An inscription on the narrow water basin made of marble, which was built at the southern side of the courtyard together with a semicircular fountain during the last building phase, identifies Caius Flavius Furius Aptus, priest of the Dionysos cult, as the owner of the house. Other inscriptions indicate that the owner also was active as a merchant and a shipowner. On the northern and western side of the courtyard were living quarters (31b-c, 42, 36c-e), which were accessed from the courtyard through wide doors. One of the rooms (31b) served the house cult; the bench-like socles probably supported cupboards made of wood. A room in the southeastern part

---

[139]For the description that follows above see Radt 1988, 166, 266; see also M. H. Jameson and N. Purcell, *OCD* 730-32.
[140]See Karwiese 1995, 111-12; Selahattin Erdemgil, *The Terrace Houses in Ephesus* (Istanbul: Hitit, 2000); cf. Brödner 1989, 167. For the description that follows above see <http://www.oeaw.ac.at/antike/homepage/ephesos/hh/hh2/hh2rundgang/04.html>.

of the unit housed a beautiful latrine (36b) whose walls were paneled with marble; it could be used by four or five persons simultaneously. On the south side of the courtyard was the entrance, through three doors, to the so-called marble room (31), a large room (180 m²) serving representative purposes. This room was decorated with expensive marble panels and other colorful stones; at the center of the southern wall there was a water basin with a fountain. The atrium (36) was equipped with a water basin in the center of the hall; it gave access to a second large banquet hall (12 by 7 m), the so-called basilica (8), a barrel-vaulted room about 11.5 m high and decorated with frescoes. This room was equipped with underfloor heating and a water basin on the northwest corner. The four steps that led from the atrium to the basilica were flanked by two statues of Aphrodite. The so-called stucco room (8a), to the west of the atrium, was decorated with murals depicting scenes from the Dionysos myth. A stairway behind the basilica led to the upper level, which had a living room, a kitchen and other work-related rooms.

The largest rooms in an atrium house or a peristyle house could accommodate thirty to forty people. This fact has led Jerome Murphy-O'Connor to the assumption that this limits, or rather indicates, the size of the early Christian houses churches.[141] (3) The vast majority of people in the cities did not have such spacious accommodations. The slaves and dependents of the wealthy lived in spaces in their houses: on street frontages, on upper floors, or even in small rooms under the floors of the main premises. Perhaps 90 percent of the free citizens and an even higher percentage of the rest of the population, slaves included, lived in apartment buildings.[142] The multistory tenement houses in the cities are called *insulae* (sg., *insula*) because one could go around them, at least originally, as they occupied an entire city block. Augustus determined for the *insulae* of Rome that they must not exceed 70 ft. (ca. 21 m) in height, which means that they had up to six stories. Often the *insulae* were named after the owner. The entrances generally were located at the center of the street frontage. Side entrances led to the domestic quarters or to a garden that belonged to the house. Separate entrances allowed access to the upper stories, which only rarely were connected with the ground floor. Most of the rooms in an *insula* served as apartments for families, some were used commercially, and some served semipublic purposes, being used by, for example, associations (*collegia*).[143] Families that could afford it had sufficiently large apartments (*cenacula*). Freedmen and their families and slaves had to make do with very small units, many families lived in one room measuring 10 m² (12 sq. yds.). These living arrangements explain the high population density of the large Roman cities: in Rome there were about 750 people per hectare (2.4 acres), nearly two and one-half

---

[141]Murphy-O'Connor 1983, 156.

[142]See James E. Packer, "Housing and Population in Imperial Ostia and Rome," *JRS* 57 (1967): 80-95; Bruce W. Frier, *Landlords and Tenants in Imperial Rome* (Princeton, N.J.: Princeton University Press, 1980).

[143]K. Ziegler, PW 18.3 (1949): 697-747; N. Purcell, *OCD* 731-32; Teixidor 1977; Bleicken 1978, 2:105-217.

times as many as in Calcutta and three times as many as in Manhattan.[144]

Erika Brödner provides a graphic description of life in the tenement blocks: "Renting space blossomed in every form: principal tenant, subtenants, lodgers, pensioners, larger and attractive apartments, lodgings, large rooms with a good view, perhaps with a balcony or a terrace, small rooms, tiny rooms, discounted wards. The closer one lived to the city center, the more opportunity one had to earn some money, and the more intensively the vitality of the *urbs* could be experienced. These simple lodgings in the big city had no kitchen and no latrine. Small portable charcoal burners were used for cooking and for boiling water and in the winter time for heating. A chamber-pot or a night-stool was always close at hand. Water ran day and night in fountains located in the courtyard of the tenement block or on street corners."[145] A good example for public latrines is the one for men in the Asclepius sanctuary in Pergamon, which could be used by forty persons simultaneously: people sat in a large room on marble benches along the walls and cleaned themselves with water that ran in a channel in front of the benches. An "inventory" of the city of Rome from the fourth century lists, besides 37 gates and 423 streets, exactly 46,602 *insulae* and 1,790 stately houses (*domus*), as well as 2,300 places for oil distribution, 1,352 fountains, 856 public baths, 290 warehouses, 254 baking ovens, 104 public latrines, 10 police stations of the praetorians, 7 fire stations with 14 squads, and 46 brothels.

The fronts of the tenement houses in the cities were connected so that the *insulae* were totally enclosed.[146] Entrances of (work)shops on the ground floor usually occupied the entire length of the shop: in Pompeii the entrances were 3 m long and between 2 and 5 m high. Most shops had a mezzanine floor that was used as storage, living space or showroom. Benches on the sidewalk served as waiting rooms for visitors to workshops and to medical doctors, or for clients of patrons. Sometimes there were benches at street altars as well.

There was no strict social discrimination with regard to living accommodations. In Pompeii, Regio VI was an elegant living quarter, but one could find commercial workshops there as well; Regio I can be characterized as the quarter of the artisans, but one also could find elegant houses there. In those sections of the city that were supplied with water one would find water towers: square towers (1.5 by 1.5 m, as high as 6 m) that helped to regulate the pressure in the pipes that distributed the water to baths, fountains and private houses.[147]

The "house" (οἶκος, *oikos;* Lat., *familia*) was the most fundamental and elementary social reality in the ancient world. The "house" included not only hus-

---

[144]Jewett (1994, 49), who refers to Stambaugh 1988, 337.
[145]Brödner 1989, 178; for the description that follows above see ibid.
[146]For the description that follows above see Gesemann 1996, 91-100.
[147]Gesemann 1996, 80. See Christoph P. J. Ohlig, *De aquis Pompeiorum: Das Castellum Aquae in Pompeji; Herkunft, Zuleitung und Verteilung des Wassers* (Circumvesuviana 4; Nijmegen: Books on Demand, Norderstedt, 2001); see the review by Renate Lafer in *Bryn Mawr Classical Review* (2002.11.13). On water supply in the cities see generally Brödner 1989, 99-106; Renate Tölle-Kastenbein, *Antike Wasserkultur* (Munich: Beck, 1990); A. Trevor Hodge, *Roman Aqueducts and Water Supply* (London: Duckworth, 1992 [2002]).

band and wife, parents and children, but also other dependents, relatives and friends, as well as slaves.[148] Since the "house" included not only people but also property, especially land, the authoritative position of the master of the house (*oikodespotēs;* Lat., *pater familias*) was the primary characteristic of the *oikos* as a self-supporting economic and social unit. Alfons Weiser characterizes the exercise of authority of the head of the family in a nuanced manner as follows:[149] "In the tradition of Aristotle, in Hellenistic popular philosophy and in the economic writings of the neo-Pythagoreans, the rule of the husband over his spouse is regarded as *political* because it serves common benefits, and the rule of the master over the slaves as *despotic* as it advances more his own benefit than that of the subordinates. In Roman civil law the *potestas* of the *pater familias* with regard to spouse and children is treated in terms of family law, the *potestas* with regard to the slaves as in terms of property law." This means that "the *pater familias* owns the *manus* ['hand'] over his wife, he exercises the *patria potestas* over the children, the *mancipium* over the semi-free and the *dominium* over objects and slaves; he is, in other words, the sole owner of all rights."[150]

Baths

Baths and bathing were among the most characteristic buildings and activities in the Greco-Roman world.[151] People who were wealthy enough to afford it in terms of time and money would visit the public baths (*thermae*) or private baths twice or three times a day. The public baths were among the most significant achievements of Roman architects and engineers, particularly the *hypocaustum,* the floor-heating system. In most baths the rooms were laid out in a straight line, or sometimes in a circle. The bathers moved from the changing room (*apodyterion*), where they disrobed, to an unheated room (*frigidarium*), which had a cold-water basin or a swimming pool (*piscina*) with lukewarm water; next came a heated warm room (*tepidarium*), which sometimes had a tepid pool; then the bathers moved into a strongly heated room (*caldarium*) that contained a hot plunge pool and a separate water basin for cold water applications.

Public baths had an open courtyard (*palaestra*), exercise grounds for sports and games, a swimming pool (*natatio*) and rooms for ball games, massages and

---

[148]Weiser 1990, 67, with reference to Wilhelm 1915, 161-71.
[149]Weiser 1990, 68.
[150]Bieritz and Kähler 1985, 480-81.
[151]W. H. Gross, *KP* 5:741-443; J. DeLaine, *OCD* 235-36; Brödner 1989, 106-11; Inge Nielsen, *Thermae et Balnea: The Architecture and Cultural History of Roman Public Baths* (Aarhus: Aarhus University Press, 1993 [1990]); Janet DeLaine and David E. Johnston, eds., *Roman Baths and Bathing* (JRASup 37; Portsmouth, R.I.: Journal of Roman Archaeology, 1999); Fikret K. Yegül, *Baths and Bathing in Classical Antiquity* (New York: Architectural History Foundation; Cambridge, Mass.: MIT Press, 1992).

application of ointments. The imperial baths had libraries and rooms for lectures and entertainment. Initially the baths had separate opening hours for women and men; since the middle first century A.D. there was mixed bathing as well (Pliny, *Nat.* 33.153). People usually had to pay nominal sums; frequently benefactions of rich patrons allowed free entrance. The baths not only served hygienic purposes but also fulfilled an important social and communicative function, as sports activities, educational and cultural events and philosophical and political discussions took place on a daily basis.

Statues

The sentiments and feelings of the people were expressed in the statues that were scattered by the thousands throughout the cities. Rhodes had seventy-three thousand statues.[152] In the theater of Ephesus alone stood 120 statues of Nike and Eros, besides numerous statues of other deities, emperors, poets, actors and influential citizens.

Besides statues of deities and emperors there were honorary statues of local benefactors, politicians and athletes, and statues of great figures from times past, of city founders and philosophers, of poets and orators, set up in public places. Some individuals could boast of having been honored with several statues: the actor Ti. Iulius Apolaustos was honored with twenty-three statues in Ephesus, Pergamon, Miletus, Sardis, Laodikeia and Thyatira. Many statues were washed regularly, anointed with oil, decorated with garlands during festivals, and carried through the city in processions.[153]

Rural Areas

It seems plausible to assume that the apostles engaged in missionary work not only in the cities but also in villages, despite the silence of Acts in this regard: Jesus had preached and healed in villages, and the majority of the people of any region lived in villages. New estimates for Roman Egypt assume that 20 to 37 percent of the population lived in cities, which means that about 60 to 80 percent of the population lived in villages.[154] I have already described what a village was in the ancient world:[155] a village (κώμη, *kōmē;* κατοικία, *katoikia;* Lat., *vicus*) was an unfortified settlement; it had no walls, and it was politically dependent on a larger entity such as a city or an imperial or large private estate, with villagers engaged in agriculture. As the village belonged to the territory (χώρα, *chōra*) of a city, so villages included outlying hamlets and farmsteads. Ownership of land was more widespread, and land was more parceled out than schol-

---

[152]Pliny, *Nat.* 34.36 (v.l.).
[153]See Thomas Pekáry, "Statuen in kleinasiatischen Inschriften," in Şahin et al. 1978, 727-44.
[154]See Rathbone 1990; Bagnall and Frier 1994, 56; A. K. Bowman, in Fentress 2000, 174.
[155]See again Schuler 1998, 17-32.

ars often have assumed—a fact supported by the large number of villages in Pisidia: for the surrounding territory of Antiocheia alone more than fifty villages have been confirmed. This evidence can be generalized in terms of the existence of smaller settlements and villages. Villages are rarely mentioned in literary sources, and they rarely can be studied on the basis of remains of buildings. The villagers worked the fields to satisfy their personal needs, for barter within the village and for trading products on small local markets. The small farmers, tenants and wage laborers in the villages that belonged to the territory of a city or to a private or imperial estate were subject to the magistrates of the city in terms of taxation and legal issues. Very seldom did slaves and freedmen live in villages, at least in western Anatolia. Some villages were able to manage their affairs on their own without discernible attachment to a polis, at least in southern Syria.[156]

Christof Schuler has summarized the available literary and archaeological evidence for the rural areas in the Greco-Roman world.[157] The traditional Greek terms for farmsteads are αὐλή (*aulē*), ἐπαύλις (*epaulis*) and ἐπαύλιον (*epaulion*). Sometimes an agricultural farm is also called "house" (οἰκία), but the formula "house and farmstead" (οἰκία καὶ αὐλή) is the traditional phrase for designating residential buildings in the village, even in the city. Since the term αὐλή was also used in the sense of "pen" or "fold" and also designated the buildings in the courtyard, we need additional information in order to ascertain whether we are dealing with a simple farmstead, a larger farm or the country estate of a big landowner. The traditional view that individual farmsteads were very rare in the eastern Mediterranean regions, as the scarcity of water sources excluded scattered settlements (*Streusiedlungen*), has been shown to be erroneous by more recent archaeological research. We know today that the lack of natural water sources could be remedied in the rural areas through cisterns, which allowed the existence of self-sufficient farmsteads. The farmsteads included storage buildings (ἀπόθεσις, *apothesis;* ἀποθήκη, *apothēkē;* παράθεσις, *parathesis*) with rooms or chambers (οἰκήματα, *oikēmata*), sunken earthenware vessels and cellars (πιθών, *pithōn*), and, depending on the crops, olive presses (ἐλαϊστήριον, *elaistērion*) and wine presses (πατητήριον, *patētērion*).

Inscriptions document the fact that ownership of land was widespread. In Asia Minor there were big landowners, Roman citizens who descended from Italic colonists, but also there were indigenous owners of private estates. Landowners usually were quite wealthy. In keeping with the traditional Greek aspirations for prestige, they donated public buildings such as temples, gymnasia or theaters, or they stipulated that the yields of real estate that they had donated should finance games and village festivals.

Roman rule changed the life of the rural population in the provinces very little. Erroneous is the older view according to which most of the available land that did not belong to the territory of a city was imperial land: in Pamphylia, for

---

[156]Millar 1993, 18.
[157]Schuler 1998, 57-100 (farmsteads), 101-36 (cultivated land), 217-72 (rural communities).

example, not a single imperial estate existed; in Pisidia there were only three or four *latifundia*.[158]

The connection between a village and a city often is recognized through the dating of inscriptions with reference to the eponymic offices of the polis or with reference to honorary dedications to a city magistrate.[159] Villages that belonged to imperial estates were followed by procurators or imperial agents; villages on private estates were administered by managers (οἰκονόμοι, *oikonomoi;* πραγματευταί, *pragmateutai*). Some villages were autonomous. Many villages in Asia Minor evidently borrowed the institutions of the Greek polis at an early stage. The village organization varied considerably, however. We find the following: (1) assemblies of the village community, often called δῆμος (*dēmos*), sometimes ἐκκλησία (*ekklēsia*); (2) associations of several villages (δικωμίαι, *dikōmiai;* τρικωμίαι, *trikōmiai*), and presidents of village associations (δήαρχοι, *dēarchoi*); (3) village councils (γερουσία, *gerousia*) with council members (*geraioi*); (4) chief leaders of the village (κωμάρχης, *kōmarchēs;* ἀρχών, *archōn;* later πρωτοκωμήτης, *prōtokōmētēs*) who supervised donations to, for example, sanctuaries or building projects; (5) magistrate officials with police functions in the rural areas (παραφύλακες, *paraphylakes*);[160] (6) organizers of festivals (βραβευτής, *brabeutēs*) who handed out garlands or announced winners of contests and who were responsible for providing room and board for guests and for the erection of steles; (7) village scribes (γραμματεῖς, *grammateis*) who supervised the financial resources of the village and kept the records; (8) in some villages an official who was responsible for the village archives (γραμματοφύλαξ, *grammatophylax*); (9) priests, the most documented officials in the villages on inscriptions. "Many communities are known only on account of their dedications to local deities, and donations which they receive usually fulfill cultic purposes."[161] Religious beliefs and activities presumably were even more important for the village people than for city residents. Village people found their identity in the common veneration of certain deities. For example, the people of the Motaleis (δῆμος Μοταλέων, *dēmos Motaleōn*), a village that belonged to the territory of Hierapolis in Phrygia, worshiped the "gods of [the people] of Motaleis" (θεοὶ Μοταλέων, *theoi Motaleōn*). A stele indicates that these were Zeus, Artemis, Men and a rider god with a double ax, probably Apollo.[162] The deities often were addressed as kings who were thought to control the village and from whom the villagers expected protection, fertility and good crops.

---

[158]Brandt 1992, 120-33; on *latifundia* see M. S. Spurr, *OCD* 816-17.
[159]For the description that follows above see Schuler 1998, 217-72.
[160]In Hierapolis a decree stipulated that *paraphylakes* had to take care of themselves when they stayed overnight in the villages; the villagers were responsible for providing wood for cooking meals, straw for the riding animals and a room (*OGIS* II 527).
[161]Schuler 1998, 247.
[162]*SEG* XXXIV 1298; see S. Mitchell 1995a, 2:14.

As far as public buildings in the villages are concerned, sanctuaries are most prominent. Some of the village temples are not without architectural elegance or decorations. We also find water installations, including ground-level channels and pipes, fountains, baths and statues. Only a few villages could boast of a colonnaded building (stoa, portico) with shops and workshops (ἐργαστήρια, *ergastēria*), as in, for example, a village in the territory of Philadelphia. Inscriptions document for many villages that local festivals played an important role in village life.

The villagers of Thiounta on the territory of Hierapolis in Phrygia celebrated a festival honoring Zeus that lasted eight days and took place mostly at night.[163] Several honorary inscriptions from the territory of Kyzikos in Mysia confirm the importance of festivals for the villages. Elmar Schwertheim comments, "During these festivals plays and musical presentations were performed, as the donations of masks or the compilation of scores demonstrate. In addition, these festivals were always linked with amusements of all kinds, as is indicated by the donation of kettles from which food or drink for the participants presumably was served. The Dionysian character of these festivals often is apparent."[164]

In the final analysis the conditions of life and work in the rural areas differed little from those in the city. Hartwin Brandt observes, "Economic contacts such as the exchange of goods between the market in the city and the rural areas as well as administrative, fiscal and legal affiliation of the two realms guaranteed numerous contacts."[165] The city and the countryside complemented each other in many ways, forming a social, economic and cultural union. Old prejudices against the level of education of the so-called simple rural population need to be revised. A surprisingly large number of personal names of villagers evidence cultural interests, which may have been encouraged by village teachers.[166] And we must remember that the difference between a city and a village is not always clearly defined.

The *astynomoi* inscription from Pergamon[167] reveals the situation concerning roads and paths in the vicinity of a city. The main roads (λεωφόροι, *leōphoroi*) were approximately 10 m wide, while the other roads had to be at least 4 m wide; private paths were not regularized. The list of streets of Erythrai (*I. Erythrai* 151) distinguishes main streets (ὁδοὶ δημόσιαι, *hodoi dēmosiai*) and private footpaths that were open to the public (ἀνδροβασμοί, *androbasmoi*). There were three types of roads in the rural areas: fortified roads for traffic with carriages

---

[163]Ramsay 1895-1897, 1.1:162-63; S. Mitchell 1995a, 1:187; Schuler 1998, 270.

[164]Elmar Schwertheim, "᾽Αΐδιος στέφανος: Zu vier Ehreninschriften aus dem Territorium von Kyzikos," in Schwertheim 1990, 97.

[165]Brandt 1992, 133.

[166]S. Mitchell 1995a, 2:86; Petzl 1995, 44-45. For the comment that follows above see Millar 1993, 18.

[167]See Günther Klaffenbach, *Die Astynomeninschrift von Pergamon* (Berlin: Akademie-Verlag, 1954).

(ὁδοὶ ἁμαξιτοί, *hodoi hamaxitoi;* ἁμαξήλατοι, *hamaxēlatoi;* λεωφόροι, *leōphoroi*), average roads that traversed mountains with the help of stairs (ὁδοὶ ἀτραποί, *hodoi atrapoi*),[168] and simple footpaths (ὁδοὶ ἀνδροβασμοί, *hodoi androbasmoi,* also ἀτραποί, *atrapoi*).

18.4 Religious Pluralism

The religiosity of the Greco-Roman world was characterized by an enormous diversity of deities and cults, views and ways of behavior, private and public piety.[169] This diverse plurality was the result not of religious tolerance defended on philosophical grounds, but of the fact that there were no political or religious authorities who proscribed what people had to believe or how they should express their spirituality. Because no Greek "state" existed, but instead numerous cities (*poleis*) that occasionally came together in alliances, there was no common religion that the Greeks shared. Nor did the Romans introduce a normative religion. When the Greeks encountered oriental religions with Alexander the Great, the foreign deities, such as Isis, were identified with traditional Greek gods, while the local population often continued to worship their traditional deities for a long time, as the worship of Men and Cybele in Asia Minor illustrates. As far as the Romans were concerned, loyalty to the gods (*pietas*) corresponded to a treaty that was maintained for the benefit of both partners: "The people acknowledged the leading role of the gods, documenting their allegiance through sacrifices and rituals, and thus obliged the gods to care for the state and for society."[170]

The deities that were worshiped in the cities and villages of the Roman Empire are known not only through the ancient authors but also through a wealth of epigraphical and numismatic material. Religious dedications on the bases of altars, together with funerary inscriptions, are the most important inscriptions in this regard. Coins depicting deities also inform about the gods that were worshiped in a particular city. Again, we must emphasize that the evidence that we have today is accidental and sparse.

Johannes Nollé reminds us, "We have no knowledge of the local epidemics and plagues that often provided the impetus for issuing coins depicting Asclepius; we do not know when extremely good or bad weather conditions prompted a city to issue coins honoring Demeter, Dionysos, Zeus and Helios. Even for the large cities we know only a few of the periodic festivals and *agones* connected with them, which emphasized for the cult of the city individual deities at particular dates. Even in cities where excavations have taken place we have very little information or data about the construction of new temples or

---

[168]See Amos Kloner, "Stepped Roads in Roman Palestine," *Aram* 8 (1996): 111-37.
[169]See Nilsson 1941-1950; MacMullen 1981; Grant 1986; Latte 1992; Muth 1988; Christ 1992, 562-77; Klauck 1995-1996; Cancik and Rüpke 1997; Beard, North and Price 1998; see also D. E. Aune, *DNTB* 917-26; N. C. Croy, *DNTB* 926-30; Bardy 1988, 17-54; Gill 1991; 1994a; Holger Sonnabend, "Religiosität," in Dinzelbacher 1993, 104-20.
[170]Sonnabend, "Religiosität," 115.

about the alteration of an existing temple, whose dedication would have been celebrated with issuings of coins honoring the divine residents in the temples."[171]

Temples

Greek and Roman temples[172] stood on demarcated sacred land called the *temenos,* often situated near a spring or a group of trees, subject to rules of purity, with a sanctuary (*hieron*) and an altar (*bōmos*). The temple building (*naos;* Lat., *cella*) proper consisted of an elongated rectangle, built on a platform (*krēpis;* Lat., *podium*), steps leading into the building (in Doric temples three steps, in Ionic temples more steps). The center of the temple building was a rectangular room whose elongated side walls formed on one end a porch with columns between the walls (*in antis*) or in a row across the front (*prostyle*); grander temples surrounded this structure with an external colonnade (*peripteral*). Important temples were "hundred footers" (*hekaktompeda*); exceptionally large temples, such as the temple of Artemis at Ephesus, were 85 m (300 ft.) long. The *cella* contained the statue of the deity, a table (τραπέζα, *trapeza*) for food offerings, a small incense altar and dedicatory gifts (e.g., further statues of the deity). Rooms that many temples had behind the *cella* were used by the temple personnel and for storage of the temple treasure. Anyone could enter the temple precinct and the temple building proper. Only a few temples had an *adyton,* an interior room that was off-limits for the public, as did, for example, the temple of Apollo in Delphi. The religious activity took place largely in front of the temple building in the open air, where the altar for the sacrifices stood. Worshipers first purified themselves with water. Then animals were slaughtered in front of the altar: bulls and cows, pigs and goats, sheep and poultry. Blood was sprinkled on the altar, and barley was thrown on the fire burning on the altar. The portion of the sacrifice that belonged to the deity was burned, particularly the bones. Then the worshipers ate the rest of the meat, portions of which were given to the temple or to the priest.

Other items used in the cult included wine, oil, honey, milk, bread, cakes and pastries in various forms and shapes. Lucian comments in his derisive treatise *De sacrificiis* that the gods receive hardly more than bones and fat and that the only thing they get to enjoy is the fatty vapors contained in the smoke of the fire on the altar (*Sacr.* 9).

Some cities stipulated on which days which deities had to receive offerings.

---

[171]Nollé 1992, 82.

[172]See W. H. Gross, *KP* 5:581-83; J. E. Stambaugh, "The Functions of Roman Temples," *ANRW* II.16.1 (1978): 554-608; Nanno Marinatos and Robin Hägg, eds., *Greek Sanctuaries* (London: Routledge, 1993); Klauck 1995-1996, vol. 1; Beard, North and Price 1998, 1:21-23, 87-91, 121-24, 197-201, 331-33; 2:78-103; Beate Dignas, *Economy of the Sacred in Hellenistic and Roman Asia Minor* (Oxford Classical Monographs; Oxford and New York: Oxford University Press, 2002).

In Mysian Miletopolis (mod. Melde, near Mustafakempalpaşa), for example, surviving fragments of a sacrificial calendar indicate that certain gods received sacrifices on different dates during the last two months of Thargelion and Skirophorion: Hermes, Eileithyia, Aphrodite, Zeus Polieus, Heracles, (Apollo or Heracles) Alexikakos, Zeus Olympos, Apollon Karneios, Eirene and Zeus Agoraios.[173]

Any free citizen, including women, could become a priest. Occupying a priestly office brought increased social prestige. Priestly offices were assigned by lot or upon a vote of the people of the city, or they could be bought with money. The priestly office was tied to the temple of a particular deity. The priests thus were not full-time professionals but volunteers. To be elected to life-long priestly office was a prerequisite for a successful career path. The priest was responsible for the organization of the activities in the temple precinct, for the maintenance of the temple buildings and for the correct performance of the sacrifices and other cultic activity. Priests presided over the cult and recited prayers.

Deities

The pantheon of Greek and Roman deities was large and diverse, with personal deities and abstract personifications, including gods with local significance and gods with supraregional significance. We should remember, however, that the divine powers were combined in larger complexes, especially in the first and second centuries. Martin Nilsson writes, "The content of the power that the individual god receives becomes blurred, even noncommittal, threatening to melt, together with the powers that are assigned to the other gods, into a uniform notion of the divine."[174] The *interpretatio Romana,* the replacement of the name of a foreign deity with that of a Roman deity, has to be seen in this context: both the traditional deity and the Roman deity faced the danger of losing their specific individuality. There were numerous gods, all of whom were acknowledged; it became more difficult, however, to comprehend and visualize the individual deity.

The pantheon of Greek and Roman and autochthonos deities was extremely diverse and complex. What is true for Lydia applies to other regions in Asia Minor as well: in earliest times the mother-goddess was the preeminent deity, appearing under different names, later generally venerated as Cybele. In the

---

[173]*I. Kyzikos* II 1. See the commentary by E. Schwertheim, *I. Kyzikos* 2:107-12. Christian Habicht ("Zu griechischen Inschriften aus Kleinasien," *EA* 31 [1999]: 19-29, esp. 26-29) believes that the inscription originally came from Athens or Attica and later was taken to Asia Minor.

[174]Nilsson 1941-1950, 664. See Josef Keil, "Die Kulte Lydiens," in *Anatolian Studies* (FS W. M. Ramsay; ed. W. H. Buckler and W. M. Calder; Manchester: Manchester University Press, 1923), 239-66, esp. 263; for the observations that follow above see ibid., 239-66; also Petzl 1995, 37-38.

younger, Phrygian stage of religious development a male deity was the main god, particularly the moon god Men (Μῆν, *Mēn;* also Μεῖς, *Meis*). Men served primarily as the "savior" of the community: he protected the family, children, adopted children and also graves; he was called upon for the punishment of evildoers.[175] During the Persian period the cult of Anahita became popular: she was close to the mother-goddess and was still worshiped during the Roman Empire, particularly in Hierokaisareia and Hypaipa. The influence of Greek religion can be seen in the fact that many localized (epichoric) deities were given the names of Greek deities. There were many local variations: inscriptions attest a "Zeus of Twin Oaks," a "Mountain Zeus," a "Zeus of (Fresh) Air" and a "Zeus of Good Weather." It was in this sense that Zeus, identified with ancient local deities, became the main god of the Mysians, the Lydians and the Carians.[176]

Examples are designations or "titles" such as Ζεὺς ἐκ Διδύμων Δρυῶν, Ζεὺς Ὀρείτης, Ζεὺς Ἀέριος, Ζεὺς Αἴθριος, as well as Ζεὺς Παρτομύσιος, Ζεὺς Λύδιος, Ζεὺς Κάριος. H. Schwabl points out that the phenomenon of syncretism was not a late development but rather can be observed at all stages of religious history: originally Zeus was the god of the "bright sky" and of the "day" before being depicted as the weather god in Greek mythology and iconography, comparable to the Semitic god Hadad.[177]

John North describes the religious pluralism of the Greco-Roman world with the phrase "supermarket of religions."[178] This was significant for the early Christian missionaries, as slaves often worshiped other deities than those worshiped by their masters. They took care of the cult of the *lares* and of the *genius,* and Tacitus knows Roman houses in which the servants belonged to tribes "with customs the reverse of our own, with foreign cults or with none" (*diversi ritus, externa sacra aut nulla [Ann.* 14.44.3]).

In addition to private cults there was the cult of the gods of the city (δημοτελεῖς, *dēmoteleis,* or πάτριοι θεοί, *patrioi theoi*). In every large city of (pre-) Hellenistic origins basically all the important deities of the Greco-Roman pantheon and of the oriental religions were worshiped along with the traditional local gods, both in private and in public cults. Personifications played an important role as well—for example, the (abstract) personification of the city (Τύχη τῆς πόλεως, *Tychē tēs poleōs*), as well as the loyalty cult honoring the city of Rome and the Roman emperors.[179] The cult of the πάντες θεοί (*pantes theoi,* "all

---

[175]Lane, *CMRDM,* vols. 1, 3.
[176]See Petzl 1995, 38, 40 with n. 18.
[177]On Zeus see Hans Schwabl, PW 10.A (1972): 253-376; PWSup 15 (1978): 993-1481; idem, *Zeus* (Munich: Druckenmüller, 1978); idem, "Zum Kult des Zeus in Kleinasien," in Dobesch and Rehrenböck 1993, 229-338; see also Fritz Graf, *OCD* 1636-38; Karim W. Arafat, *Classical Zeus: A Study in Art and Literature* (Oxford: Clarendon, 1990).
[178]J. North, "The Development of Religious Pluralism," in Rajak et al. 1992, 174-93.
[179]See Nollé 1992, 79-81.

gods"), which developed since the Hellenistic period, indicates the endeavor to pay homage to all divine beings. There is evidence for a priest of the pantheon of gods (πάντες θεοί) in Sillyon in Pamphylia during the Roman period.[180]

Cities enjoyed religious autonomy, meaning that they had their own cultic laws: "the organization, financing and administration of cult places, sacrifices and priestly offices was under the control of the individual city councils."[181] The lawyer Gaius Ateius Capito defined *religiosus* at the time of Augustus as "sociopolitical norms stipulated by the cities." He asserts, "Those are called religious who have made a choice with regard to the divine matters according to the customs of the city between those things that have to be done and those things that should not be done, and who do not get involved in superstitious practices."[182]

Cults often can be identified even for cities for which the literary and archaeological evidence is slim, particularly on the basis of inscriptions and coins. Isinda (mod. Alaeddin Mahallesi, near Korkuteli) in southern Pisidia serves as a good example. The city did not play a major role in the economic, historical or cultural development of Asia Minor, the archaeological evidence is limited, and yet we know that the following deities were worshiped in Isinda: Aphrodite, Apollo, Artemis, Athene, Dionysos, Dioscuri, Eubosia ("Good Pasture"), Helena, Helios, Heracles/Hercules, Hermes, Kakasbos, Cobulatus (river god), Cybele, Nemesis, Sarapis and Isis, Tyche, Zeus (Zeus Isindios, Olympian Zeus), the deity of the city, several additional goddesses (a goddess standing with a shield; a goddess with the Dioscuri), several male gods (three gods with dogs; Dodeka Theoi [Twelve Gods]).[183] Also venerated were various deities of justice and vengeance who played an important role in Phrygian religiosity: Apollo, Helios (the all-seeing sun)[184] and, particularly in Phrygia Epiktetos, the abstract personification *Hosios kai Dikaios* (Holy and Righteous), a deity that recently has been interpreted as a "messenger" (*angelos*, "angel") of Helios-Apollo,[185] who rides incognito across the land on behalf of the sun-god, and to whom Helios renders an account of the good and the evil deeds of the people so that the good receive their just rewards and the evil their punishment.[186]

Several hundred inscriptions throughout the Mediterranean world, particularly in Lydia and Phrygia, attest to the fact that Zeus Hypsistos or Theos Hyp-

---

[180] *IGR* III 801-802.

[181] Frateantonio 1997, 90; for the observation that follows above see ibid., 91.

[182] Ateius Capito, *De more et ritu* 13.

[183] See David French, "Isinda and Lagbe," in French 1994a, 53-92, esp. 71-73.

[184] Apollo: *RECAM* 44, 47, 54, 74, 154; Helios: *MAMA* I 399; V; *RECAM* 47, 110, 242.

[185] On Hosios and Dikaios see Marijana Ricl, "Hosios kai dikaios; Première partie: Catalogue des inscriptions," *EA* 18 (1991): 1-70, with the publication of 111 inscriptions. For an analysis see M. Ricl, "Hosios kai dikaios; Seconde partie: Analyse," *EA* 19 (1992): 71-102; on *angelos,* ibid., 95; Ricl (ibid., 100-101) does not see any Jewish or Jewish-Christian influence.

[186] R. Merkelbach, "Die Götter Hosios und Dikaios in Mäonien und Phrygien" [1993], in Merkelbach 1997a, 281-86, esp. 285.

sistos (Ζεὺς "Υψιστος, Θεὸς "Υψιστος) was worshiped—the "God Most High."[187] Franz Cumont, Martin Nilsson, Josef Keil and other scholars assumed that Theos Hypsistos is a reference to the God of the Jews and thus that these inscriptions are evidence for the influence of Judaism in these regions: the God of Israel was identified with the Zeus, the highest god of the Greeks.[188] Today most classical scholars assume that Theos Hypsistos may be taken as a reference to the Jewish God only when the presence of Jews in the area is independently attested.[189] In cases where this condition does not apply, Theos Hypsistos represents a pagan deity as the "most powerful god."[190] The pagan identity of Theos Hypsistos is particularly evident in those cases in which this deity is worshiped together with other pagan deities. For example, in Sattai a statue of Thea Larmene is dedicated both to Theos Hypsistos and to the deity Mega Theion Epiphanes; in another inscription Theos Hypsistos is worshiped together with Mega Theion. The female deity Thea Hypsiste, attested in several inscriptions, shows that the adjective "highest" was used for indigenous deities.[191] The epithet "the highest" ("Υψιστος) is repeatedly attested for Zeus in classical Greek literature.[192] In Egypt the same epithet is used for Isis.[193] The existence of the deity Theos Hypsistos often is explained with reference to the religious tendency that abstract deities were venerated as "highest," as, for example, the deity Hosios kai Dikaios or Mega Theion.[194] One inscription documents that the moon god Men could be worshiped as "The One God in Heaven."[195]

Stephen Mitchell, following the lead of Emil Schürer, suggests that the worshipers of "God Most High" or "Zeus Most High" (Θεὸς "Υψιστος, *Theos Hypsistos;* Ζεὺς "Υψιστος, *Zeus Hypsistos*) are identical with the "God-fearers" (θεοσε-

---

[187]H. Schwabl, PWSup 15 (1978): 1477-80; Trebilco 1989; 1991, 127-44; Drew-Bear and Naour 1990, 2032-36; C. Colpe and A. Löw, *RAC* 16:1035-56; C. Breytenbach, "Hypsistos," *DDD* 822-30; S. Mitchell 1995a, 2:49-51; 1998; 1999.

[188]Franz Cumont, " "Υψιστος," PW 9 (1914): 444-450; idem, "Les mystères de Sabazius et le Judaïsme," *CRAI* (1906): 63-79, esp. 73; Nilsson 1941-1950, 664; Josef Keil, "Die Kulte Lydiens," in Buckler and Calders, *Anatolian Studies,* 263.

[189]For example, the Jewish funerary inscription from Akmonia (*CIJ* II 769 = *IJudO* II 176), a dedication from Kalecik in northern Galatia (*SEG* XXXI 1080), and a dedicatory inscription from Sibidunda (*AnSt* 10 [1960]: no. 122 = *IJudO* II 215).

[190]Thus Robert 1969-1990, 1:417-18; Kraabel 1969; Trebilco 1989, 51-52; Horsley, *NewDocs* 1:25-29; Drew-Bear and Naour, *ANRW* II.18.3 (1990): 2032-33; Trebilco 1991, 128-29; S. Mitchell 1995a, 2:49; John Devreker, "Nouveaux monuments et inscriptions de Pessinonte (IV)," *EA* 23 (1993): 73-83 (regarding an inscription from Pessinonte; mod. Ballıhisar); Corsten 1997, 123 (on *I. Laodikeia* 61); Ricl 1997, 102 (on *I. AlexTroas* 76).

[191]See the evidence in Maria Paz de Hoz, "Theos Hypsistos in Hierokaisareia," *EA* 18 (1991): 75-77, esp. 76, with reference to *TAM* V 1, 186, 359; *SEG* XX 14.

[192]Pindar, *Nem.* 1.60; 11.2; Aeschylus, *Eum.* 28; Sophocles, *Phil.* 1289; Pausanias 9.8.5.

[193]Horsley, *NewDocs* 1:28, with reference to Ronchi, *Lexicon Theonymon,* 1120-22.

[194]For example, *SEG* XIV 759.

[195]*TAM* V 1, 75: Εἷς θεὸς ἐν οὐρανοῖς, μέγας Μὴν Οὐράνιος.

βεῖϲ, *theosebeis*) mentioned in the book of Acts, who appear in about a dozen inscriptions and were known in late antiquity as *Hypsistarii*. He states his conclusions as follows: "The cult of Theos Hypsistos, whose adherents called themselves God-fearers, was essentially a pagan monotheism that was strongly influenced and shaped by Jewish beliefs. It was practiced in nearly all areas of the eastern Mediterranean world, of Anatolia, of the Black Sea and of the Near East since late Hellenism, and it continued to flourish until late antiquity. When Paul was engaged in his mission in the Greek cities and the Roman colonies of Asia Minor and Greece, he encountered everywhere adherents of the cult who converted to faith in Christ. Without the God-fearers the transformation of the pagan world to Christian monotheism is hardly conceivable."[196] If this hypothesis is correct, it has crucial effects on the description of the early Christian mission, and so it must be discussed at some length.

Stephen Mitchell begins his study with an inscription from Oenoanda (mod. Ceylanköy) in northern Lycia, dating to the third century, that records an oracle of Clarian Apollo: "Born of itself, untaught, without a mother, unshakeable, not contained in a name, dwelling in fire, this is god [πολυώνυμοϲ, ἐν πυρὶ ναίων, τοῦτο θεόϲ]. We, his angels, are a small part of god [μεικρὰ δὲ θεοῦ μερὶϲ ἄγγελοι ἡμεῖϲ]. To you who ask this question about god, what his essential nature is, he has pronounced that Aether is god who sees all [Αἰ[θ]έ[ρ]α πανδερκ[ῆ θε]ὸν ἔννεπεν], on whom you should gaze and pray at dawn, looking towards the sunrise."[197] Lactantius (*Inst.* 1.7) and the *Theosophy of Tübingen* §13 (Erbse) provide a more extensive version of this oracle. The Oenoanda inscription is inscribed on the relief of an altar and placed in a section of the wall that was struck by the first rays of the sun at dawn. The semicircular open area in front of the oracle inscription seems to have been an open-air sanctuary. The god to be worshiped according to this oracle, who sees everything and lives in the fire, very probably is Theos Hypsistos: the only other inscription inscribed on a stone in the city walls of Oenoanda is the dedication of a lamp to Theos Hypsistos, who is identified in other inscriptions with Helios (light),[198] and lamps are mentioned several times in connection with the cult of Theos Hypsistos. In other words, the Oenoanda inscription clarifies that Theos Hypsistos was a god whose essence was beyond reach in the "aether," the upper air of heaven; he was a god to whom all other gods, such as Apollo, are subordinate, reduced to angels; a god who became visible in light and in fire, in the light of the sun or in the light of a lamp dedicated by devotees.

Mitchell adduces the following arguments for his identification of the God-fearers with

---

[196]S. Mitchell 1998, 63; see idem 1999, with a list of the documentary evidence for the 293 inscriptions that mention Theos Hypsistos and Zeus Hypsistos (appendix, 128-47). Cf. Schürer 1897. See the brief discussion in §6.2 in the present work.

[197]*SEG* XXVII 933; editio princeps: G. E. Bean, 1971; listed in S. Mitchell 1999 as no. 233; translation in S. Mitchell 1999, 86; for a German translation see R. Merkelbach and J. Stauber, "Die Orakel des Apollon von Klaros," *EA* 27 (1996): 1-53, esp. 41-42 (no. 25) = Merkelbach 1997a, 202-4 (no. 25). On this inscription see also Robert 1969-1990, 5:617-39; A. S. Hall, "The Klarian Oracle at Oenoanda," *ZPE* 32 (1978): 263-68; Lane Fox 1986, 168-71, 190-200; S. Mitchell 1999, 81-92.

[198]In an inscription from Alexandria (see A. D. Nock, *HTR* 29 [1936]: 61-69) and from Pergamon (*I. Pergamon* 330); see S. Mitchell 1999, nos. 186, 284.

the adherents of Theos Hypsistos. (1) Epiphanius, bishop of Salamis on Cyprus, describes in his book *Panarion,* written in A.D. 376, the religious practices of the Messaliani or Euphemitai, who worship Theos Hypsistos in places of prayer (*proseuchai*) in the open air: they light lamps and torches during their religious services, and they sing hymns and acclamations of god. Epiphanius compares these places of prayer with the extramural place of prayer that Paul visited in Philippi when he met the God-fearer Lydia.[199] (2) Gregory of Nazianzus delivered a funerary oration in A.D. 374 on the occasion of the death of his father. In this speech he describes the Hypsistarii (Ὑψιστάριοι) as Greeks who adopted Jewish beliefs and customs: they worship one single god (*pantokratōr*), they reject idols and sacrifices to idols, they worship the fire and the light of lamps, they acknowledge the sabbath and they refrain from certain food, but they are not circumcised.[200] Similar descriptions can be found in Gregory of Nyssa (fourth century).[201] (3) Josephus writes around A.D. 100 that Jewish customs are widespread in all Greek cities and in communities of the barbarians, specifically the acknowledgment of the sabbath, Jewish days of fasting, the lighting of lamps and abstinence from certain foods.[202] This descriptions agrees with the fact that "a large number of the dedications to Theos Hypsistos were very modest monuments, set up by ordinary people, and they are found indifferently in city and countryside. The god had an exceptionally wide appeal."[203] Juvenal (second century) mockingly describes in his fourteenth satire his God-fearing father (*metuentem sabbata patrem*), who worshiped no god but the clouds and the heavenly spirit, who abstained from pork and who did not work on the sabbath.[204] (4) Cyril of Alexandria writes at the beginning of the fifth century that the worshipers of Hypsistos in Palestine and in Phoenicia call themselves God-fearers (*theosebeis*).[205] (5) Four sanctuaries have been confirmed archaeologically in which Hypsistos was worshiped: on the Pnyx in Athens, on Delos, in Serdica (mod. Sofia, Bulgaria), and in Oenoanda. Inscriptions attest further sanctuaries of Hypsistos on Skiathos, in Odessos in Moesia and in Cotiaeum-Aezani in Phrygia. The 293 inscriptions that document the worship of Theos/Zeus Hypsistos that we know so far come from all regions of the Mediterranean: from Achaia and Macedonia, from Asia Minor, from the Aegean islands, from Phoenicia and Syria, from Thrace, Dacia and Moesia, from the northern coast of the Black Sea and from Egypt, and there is one inscription each from Italy and Spain.[206] (6) The fact that in Syria, for example, only a few inscriptions have been found can be explained by the relative infrequency of Greek inscriptions in Syria compared with Asia Minor. The Jewish associations with the cult of Theos Hypsistos and the descriptions of the Hypsistarii in Palestine and in Phoenicia by the church fathers allow the assumption that the cult was widespread in Syria as well.[207] (7) Some inscriptions indeed identify Theos Hypsistos with Zeus, and the iconographical symbolism of a relief that accompanies one inscription makes this connection as well. However, the god is hardly ever depicted in anthropomorphic form, and this tendency toward abstraction is striking. In contrast to other pagan deities, the god does not appear in human form. The only "tangible" indication of the presence of Theos Hypsistos is a footprint above an in-

---

[199]Epiphanius, *Pan.* 80.1-2.
[200]Gregory of Nazianzus, *Orationes* 18.5 (PG 35:990).
[201]Gregory of Nyssa, *Refutatio confessionis Eunomii* 38 (PG 45:482).
[202]Josephus, *C. Ap.* 2.39.
[203]S. Mitchell 1999, 105.
[204]Juvenal 14.96-106.
[205]Cyril, *De adoratione in spiritu et veritate* 3.92 (PG 68:281c).
[206]S. Mitchell 1999, 97-99.
[207]S. Mitchell 1999, 105.

scription from Pisidian Termessos.[208] (8) Both Theos Hypsistos and Zeus Hypsistos are linked with other divine beings that do not fit into the framework of Greek polytheism— in Anatolia, for example, with a divine "messenger" or angel (ἄγγελος, *angelos*), linked with the abstractions *Hosios* and *Dikaios,* which fits the veneration of angels in Judaism.[209] (9) The rare examples of religious acclamations, which occur in inscriptions only sporadically, come from Asia Minor and the Aegean islands and are connected with monotheistic worship. An inscription from Ephesus, for example, contains these lines: "Great is the name of God! Great is *Hosios* [the Holy One]! Great is *Agathos* [the Good]!"[210] Epiphanius reports that the Hypsistarii worshiped their deity with acclamations. (10) The inscriptions for Theos Hypsistos contain practically no references to rituals. Lydian reliefs connected with inscriptions that mention (divine) messengers depict people with their right hand raised in prayer. Sacrifices of animals have not been attested on these inscriptions as of yet, a fact that distinguishes this cult from most of the other pagan cults in the Mediterranean world. (11) Most of the inscriptions that document the cult of Theos Hypsistos date to the second and third centuries. We must remember, however, Mitchell argues, that in many regions of Asia Minor inscriptions are found with more regular frequency beginning only with the second century. Inscriptions clearly document the cult for the first century, and the veneration of Zeus Hypsistos is attested in inscriptions from the Hellenistic period.[211] (12) It is very difficult, if not impossible, to distinguish pagan and Jewish examples for the veneration of Theos Hypsistos on linguistic or on practical grounds. It is more convincing methodologically, therefore, to treat all the evidence together.[212] (13) The Theosebeis, the God-fearers, are identical with the worshipers of Theos Hypsistos. This conclusion is supported by evidence such as Acts 16:13-18, inscriptions from Tanais on the northern coast of the Black Sea,[213] and the description by Cyril of Alexandria quoted above. The evidence for the cult of Theos Hypsistos and the evidence for the Theosebeis is parallel both in terms of geography and in terms of chronology, and their religious convictions and practices are identical.

The evidence that Mitchell has compiled indicates that there was a widespread cult of a highest god. It seems probable that this cult adopted Jewish beliefs and traditions. However, Mitchell's hypothesis that the worshipers of Theos Hypsistos are identical with the Theosebeis who attended Jewish synagogues and thus with the God-fearers mentioned in the book of Acts seems problematic for the following reasons. (1) If the cult of Zeus Hypsistos in Greece and in Macedonia was not developed by pagans who sympathized with Judaism but rather represents local developments, and if the cult of Theos Hypsistos was an independent development in the non-Hellenized regions of Asia Minor and on the northern coast of the Black Sea,[214] three questions arise. (a) Is it methodologically justified to treat both cults together only because "at the practical level of the cult" there are close associations? It may indeed be "profitable" for a description of the religious mentality of people in the imperial period to concentrate on the "hypsistarian" nature of the cult of Zeus Hypsistos and Theos Hypsistos. However, if these were indeed two different cults,

---

[208]S. Mitchell 1999, 100-102, 107, with reference to *TAM* III 1, 32.

[209]S. Mitchell 1999, 102-4; cf. *I. Stratonikeia* 117, 118, 1307, 1308; *TAM* V 1, 159, 246.

[210]*I. Ephesos* 3100: Μέγα τὸ ὄνομα τοῦ θεοῦ | μέγα τὸ Ὅσιον | μέγα τὸ Ἀγαθόν. See also *TAM* V 1, 75; *IG* XII 8, 613.

[211]For the relevant evidence see S. Mitchell 1999, 109.

[212]S. Mitchell 1999, 112-13, 99-101.

[213]*CIRB* 1281, 1283, 1285, 1286.

[214]S. Mitchell 1999, 126; cf. ibid., 99: "Zeus Hypsistos and Theos Hypsistos are not two ways of denoting the same reality"; the quotation that follows above, ibid.

and if Theos Hypsistos is identified with Meter Theon (Beroea), with Meter Oreia (Nisa), with Nemesis (Thessalonike, Alexandria), with Helios (Gorgippia), with Larmene (Saittai) and with Men Ouranios,[215] we might be dealing with a series of different cults, all of which have monotheistic tendencies influenced by the Jewish faith and use similar or identical terminology. It is a different matter, however, to speak of "the" (one) cult of Theos Hypsistos, which should be identified with "the" God-fearers. (b) Is it methodologically justified to place evidence for the cult of Zeus Hypsistos next to evidence for the cult of Theos Hypsistos? Mitchell admits that "in a large number of cases the pagan credentials of the cult are unambiguously clear," noting the fact that the god is not named Theos "but precisely Zeus Hypsistos"—for example, in the cult on the Pnyx at Athens.[216] The dedication for Zeus Hypsistos that was found in Pydna in Macedonia, mentioning an *archisynagōgos*, confirms, according to Mitchell, that these worshipers of Zeus Hypsistos met in the synagogue. G. Horsley suggests that this inscription represents the rare example of the use of *archisynagōgos* in a pagan context.[217] Mitchell notes that an inscription from Miletupolis in Mysia, Zeus Hypsistos is represented with the thunderbolt traditionally linked with Zeus, who is called Zeus Brontaios (Thundering Zeus) in the inscription, and he points out that Zeus Brontaios must be distinguished from the strictly Phrygian deity Zeus Bronton.[218] If this indeed correct, it must be permitted methodologically to distinguish the worshipers of Zeus Hypsistos from the worshipers of Theos Hypsistos, and the latter from the worshipers of YHWH in the Jewish synagogues. (c) In view of the diversity of the concrete forms of the cult or cults of a "God Most High"—a diversity that is not rescinded by the similarity of beliefs and practices—it seems imperative, from a methodological point of view, for a *historical* investigation (e.g., of the God-fearers whom Paul encountered in Asia Minor and in Macedonia) to reckon with specific local developments. It seems that there is enough evidence to distinguish God-fearers who were connected with Jewish synagogues from God-fearers who were and remained purely pagan. It also seems that the worshipers of the Aether in Oenoanda in Lycia who acknowledged Apollo as a "messenger" of the Most High God and who worshiped at the sight of the sun at dawn must be distinguished from the worshipers of Theos Hypsistos in Amastris in Paphlagonia who set up an altar "at the behest of the One with unshorn hair [Apollo]" on which sacrifices presumably were offered[219] and from the worshipers of Men Ouranios in Sattai in Lydia who designate him as "the only god" but clearly speak of the ancient Anatolian deity of Men.[220] (2) Jewish texts that refer to Theos Hypsistos—there are more than one hundred

---

[215]Horsley, *NewDocs* 5:136 (Meter Theon); *TAM* II 3, 737 (Meter Oreia); *IG* X 2, 62 and *HTR* 29 (1936): 61-69 (Nemesis); *CIRB* 1123 (Helios); *TAM* V 1, 186 (Larmene); G. Bean, *AnSt* 10 (1960): 65, no. 115 (Men Ouranios).

[216]S. Mitchell 1999, 100, with reference to Pindar, *Nem.* 1.60; 11.1; Aeschylus, *Eum.* 28; Sophocles, *Phil.* 289; Theocritus 25.159. For the inscription mentioned in the observation that follows above see S. Mitchell 1999, 100.

[217]Horsley, *NewDocs* 1:27. Editio princeps of the Pydna inscription: J. M. R. Cormack, "Zeus Hypistos at Pydna," in *Mélanges helléniques offerts à Georges Daux* (Paris: Boccard, 1974), 51-55; the Greek text is found also in *NewDocs* 1:26-27 (no. 5); S. Mitchell 1999, 131 (no. 131).

[218]S. Mitchell 1999, 101 with n. 45, on *I. Kyzikos* II 5, with reference to, among others, C. Cox and A. Cameron, *MAMA* 5:xxxviii-xliv; Drew-Bear and Naour 1990, 1992-2013.

[219]C. Marek, *EA* 32 (2000): 135 (no. 2).

[220]*TAM* V 1, 75: Εἷς θεὸς ἐν οὐρανοῖς, μέγας Μὴν Οὐράνιος, μεγάλη δύναμις τοῦ ἀθανάτου θεοῦ ("One god in heaven, the great Men Ouranios, the great power of the immortal god").

references in the Septuagint alone—and describe the Jerusalem temple as "temple of God the Most High" (ὁ τοῦ ὑψίστου θεοῦ νεώς)[221] clearly and unambiguously refer to the YHWH, the God of Abraham, Isaac and Jacob. The difference between Theos Hypsistos mentioned in the sacred Scriptures of Israel and a highest god who was worshiped in Athens or in Ephesus was known in the Diaspora as well, where Jews read the Septuagint. When Jewish-Christian missionaries, historians and theologians such as Luke describe certain pagans as "God-fearers" who were present during religious services in the synagogues, they evidently use this designation because these pagans worshiped the God of Israel, not because they worshiped a highest god separate from YHWH. It seems implausible to assume that a Jew would refer to a pagan citizen of Oenoanda who worships a highest god in an open-air sanctuary at the sight of the sun, subordinating Apollo and perhaps other gods to this highest god as "messengers," as a "God-fearer" in the sense that the god whom such a person "fears" and worships is Yahweh, the God of Israel. In classical Greek literature the terms θεοσεβεία (*theosebeia*, "service of fear of god") and θεοσεβής (*theosebēs*, "fearing god") often mean "religiousness" and "religious" as a (non-Jewish) virtue or self-designation.[222] In view of this usage one cannot assume that all "God-fearing" worshipers of a Theos Hypsistos had links with synagogues or could be found in synagogue services. Of course, Mitchell accepts the classical literary meaning of *theosebēs* in the general sense of "religious" or "pious," but he argues that the "technical meaning"—the use of the term to designate worshipers of Theos Hypsistos—"became increasingly dominant."[223] This assertion has not been proven, however. (3) The argument that the beliefs and the practices of the worshipers of Theos Hypsistos and the beliefs and practices of the God-fearers "precisely coincided"[224] is an unproven hypothesis. The only feature that both groups unambiguously share is the veneration of a highest god. And even this common belief needs to be assessed in a nuanced manner: if a God-fearer attended a synagogue regularly or perhaps exclusively, then this person's "piety" was directed to Yahweh, the God of Israel as the only true God, whereas the worshipers of the Aether in Oenoanda worshiped a nameless abstraction in a separate sanctuary at sunrise while simultaneously acknowledging Apollo and perhaps Helios as well, thus clearly practicing a syncretistic faith. Since little is known about the ritual activities of both groups, it is difficult to speak of "agreement." (4) The role of angels (*angeloi*) in Jewish tradition may coincide in some specific details with the role of Apollo in the Oenoanda oracle or with the role of other "messengers" (*angeloi*) of gods that are mentioned in inscriptions from Asia Minor. This is not enough, however, to prove beyond doubt Jewish influence. We must not overlook structural differences: in Jewish tradition "angels" are regarded as heavenly beings created by God, while the Oenoanda oracle designates as *angelos* a traditional Greek deity that is being subordinated to the Highest God. And when the abstract deities *Hosios* and *Dikaios* are designated by *angelos,* this term refers to a messenger "who rides across the land on the behest of the sun-god and reports the good and the evil deeds of the people to Helios."[225] (5) Inscriptions that mention Zeus Hypsistos or Theos Hypsistos sometimes are

---

[221]Philo, *Legat.* 278.
[222]LSJ 791, s.v. "θεοσεβής," mentions Herodotus 1.86; 2.37; Xenophon, *Cyr.* 3.3.58; Plato, *Crat.* 394d etc.; Aristophanes, *Av.* 897. A search with *Thesaurus Linguae Graecae* yields twenty-three references for the fifth century, including passages in Euripides, Sophocles and Hippocrates.
[223]S. Mitchell 1999, 119 n. 126.
[224]S. Mitchell 1999, 120.
[225]Merkelbach 1997a, 285.

inscribed on altars on which sacrifices presumably were offered.[226] The possibility cannot be excluded that the people who were adherents of these cults simultaneously attended a synagogue. It is not certain, however, that they would have been labeled "God-fearers" by the Jews simply because they recognized a highest deity. (6) Traditional Greek conceptions of the divine could accept the notion of a god as an abstract deity.[227] This fact explains terminological and conceptual parallels between the Jewish notion of God and pagan notions of deity, but it stands, in my view, against a Jewish identification of all pagan adherents of a "Most High God" as "God-fearers" who adhered, in one sense or another, to Yahweh, the God of Israel. When the pagan veneration of Zeus Hypsistos takes places with altars or in connection, however indirect, with other gods such as Artemis and Apollo, as in, for example, Kyzikos,[228] it seems very unlikely that they would have been accepted by Jews as "God-fearers," as worshipers of Yahweh, in their synagogues. (7) The fact that it is difficult to distinguish Jewish examples and pagan examples of the worship of Theos Hypsistos, and the fact that the relevant inscriptions cannot formally be distinguished from each other,[229] hardly permit us to identify all adherents of Theos Hypsistos with the God-fearers in the Jewish synagogues. Jews who intimately knew and experienced the everyday reality of a city in Asia Minor or in Macedonia were well able to distinguish between the adherents of a highest god who was worshiped at the dawn of the sun in an independent cult of Zeus Hypsistos or Theos Hypsistos, and those who worshiped the God of Israel as the only true and living God. There is no evidence that the "God-fearers" mentioned in the book of Acts or in the Aphrodisias inscription had separate cult places that they frequented in addition to their attendance of synagogue services. It is possible that the God-fearers in the synagogues had their own organization,[230] but if they were indeed "regularly organized bodies of worshipers," they would hardly have been organized as adherents of Theos Hypsistos with their separate cult and sanctuary if they expected to be acknowledged and welcomed by the synagogue. (8) I do not think that Mitchell has successfully proven that the beliefs of the adherents of Theos Hypsistos and the beliefs of the God-fearers (Theosebeis) in the synagogues coincided "precisely."[231] The point is not whether the cult of Zeus Hypsistos and of Theos Hypsistos should be described as pagan monotheism influenced by Jewish ideas[232] or as henotheism. Whether the evidence presented by Mitchell represents "one of the most spectacular demonstrations of religious syncretism that the ancient world has to offer"[233] depends, from a Jewish (or Christian) perspective, on the answer to the question of whether the pagan adherents of Theos Hypsistos accepted other deities (such as Apollo or Helios) as having an influence on their life and worshiped in separate sanctuaries and sacrificed on separate altars. With regard to Diaspora Jews, one cannot use the label "syncretism" simply if they acknowledged that the influence of their monotheistic beliefs on pagans was a positive development, but only if they also accepted the simultaneous worship of Theos

---

[226]For Zeus Hypsistos see *I. Stratonikeia* 1306; LBW 2627 (near Palmyra); cf. the reference to two altars of Zeus Hypsistos in Pausanias 5.15.5; for Theos Hypsistos see *I. GBulg* IV 1941-1944 (sanctuary of Theos Hypsistos in Serdica in Thrace with included an altar and columns); *SEG* XL 1227 (Aezani); *MAMA* V 186 (Dorylaion); *MAMA* X 488 (Tembris valley).

[227]See S. Mitchell 1999, 107.

[228]S. Mitchell 1999, 139 (no. 182).

[229]S. Mitchell 1999, 112.

[230]S. Mitchell 1999, 116-17; the quotation that follows above, 117.

[231]S. Mitchell 1999, 120.

[232]Thus S. Mitchell 1998, 64; 1999, 121.

[233]S. Mitchell 1999, 121; similarly Ameling 1996, 45-46.

Hypsistos and the worship of Apollo, or of Men, or of Isis as a legitimate expression of their faith in the God of Abraham, Isaac and Jacob. It is problematic when Walter Ameling states in this regard that "precise distinctions" between pagans, Jews and Christians are sometimes difficult "because the ideas were very similar."[234] When we assess the Jewish faith in the context of the relationship between pagans and Jews, we must not take into consideration only the Theos Hypsistos inscriptions: the differences between Jewish and pagan religious ideas undoubtedly were much more potent than any similarities. And the central (Jewish) Christian message of Jesus, the crucified and risen Messiah, could always be distinguished from traditional Jewish beliefs, not to mention pagan conceptions.

Ameling attempts to confirm the hypothesis of Mitchell on the basis of a discussion of the inscription *I. Prusa* 39.[235] The relief that accompanies this inscription, depicting a sacrifice on an altar with flames visible, indeed indicates that neither Jews nor Christians could have set up this relief; he is also correct in pointing out that (later) Christian authors mention fire when they describe adherents of Theos Hypsistos. It seems questionable, however, that it is necessary to infer from the depiction of an altar on which a fire burns that the god of Epitherses, who is described as "God-fearing" (θεοσεβής, *theosebēs*), lives in this fire or that he is identical with Theos Hypsistos. Ameling himself points out that the Oenoanda oracle does not stipulate a sacrifice on an altar but only prayers recited in an easterly direction toward the rising sun.[236] The specific character of the cult that is represented by this inscription is in itself no proof for connections with the Jewish and Christian veneration of single "highest" God. Other scholars have not interpreted this as evidence for Jews living in the area or for pagan sympathizers of Judaism.[237] Thomas Corsten points out that the formula of the inscription is "typically pagan," and he argues on the basis of the name "Theoktistos" and on the basis of the description of Epitherses as "God-fearing" that it may be "crypto-Christian."[238] The fact that the same inscription can be variously interpreted as referring to Jews, or to pagans sympathizing with Judaism, or to Christians suggests that the inscription and its accompanying relief is ambiguous and certainly not evidence for an "impressive syncretism."

In summary: Obviously there was a widespread cult of a God Most High in many regions of the Mediterranean world. The assumption is plausible that this cult had adopted some Jewish traditions, possibly monotheistic, at least henotheistic convictions. For the reasons outlined above, however, it remains an unproven hypothesis that the adherents of Theos Hypsistos can be identified with the Theosebeis ("God-fearers") in the Jewish synagogues and thus with the God-fearers whom Paul encountered according to Luke's account in the book of Acts.[239] The position that has received support from a majority of scholars continues to be valid: the literary and archaeological context has to decide whether local adherents of Theos Hypsistos were henotheistic pagans whose syncretistic convictions allowed them to worship a Most High God along with other deities of the Greek pantheon, or monotheistic pagans who attended the synagogue services after having accepted the God of Israel as the only true God, or Jews who describe

---

[234]Ameling 1996, 46.

[235]Ameling 1999, 105-8.

[236]Ameling 1999, 107 n. 18; for the remark that follows above see ibid., 107-8, 105.

[237]Ameling (1999, 105 with nn. 4, 7) has misunderstood both Trebilco 1991, 146, and Levinskaya 1996, 67. Trebilco (1991, 246 n. 7) argues against L. Robert, who interpreted the inscription as evidence for the presence of Jews, and Levinskaya assumes a pagan context as well, although she does want to exclude the possibility that Epitherses had sympathies for Judaism.

[238]Corsten, *I. Prusa,* 110; idem, *EA* 16 (1990): 102.

[239]S. Mitchell (1998, 61) optimistically asserts that "nothing stands against this identification."

Yahweh as God Most High, or Christians who worship the Most High God.[240]

People in antiquity were interested in the origins of the gods they worshiped. Literary texts, local traditions and festivals described or acted out answers to the question of where the deity was born and where he or she was "at home." In nearly all cases there were conflicting answers: Delos, Ephesus and Lycia competed as "places of birth" of the twin pair of Apollo and Artemis.[241]

Javier Teixidor, in a study on popular religion in the Greco-Roman Near East, suggests that there was a tendency toward monotheism: people increasingly worshiped a single deity. This trend, he argues, facilitated or at least helped the dissemination of the Jewish and the Christian faiths, and later the Islamic faith.[242] However, the numerous diverse statues of deities that we find in the ancient world in this period, of deities that often do not belong to a particular mythological tradition and whose names often are unknown, indicate that one has to be very cautious about such assumptions.[243] Walter Burkert recently studied the expression "my God," which occurs in both the Old and the New Testaments (Ps 44:7; 20:1; Mt 27:46; Jn 20:28), and is similarly expressed in Mesopotamian sources, to investigate possible Greek parallels.[244] The expression "my" *daimōn* (δαίμων) could be used to express the conviction that a transcendent power governs every human being, and people could refer to the "beloved" (φίλε, *phile*) god Pan or speak of "the most beloved Apollo." However, according to Aristotle, "It would be an absurdity to profess a friend's affection for Zeus" (φιλεῖν τὸν Δία [*Mag. mor.* 1208 b 30]). The exclamation of Euripides' choir upon seeing the sculptures at the temple in Delphi, "I see Pallas, my own goddess" (Euripides, *Ion* 211), is one of the very few references in Greek literature that uses the phrase "my god." Burkert points out, however, that this exclamation must be understood as the "aesthetic wow-experience" of a collective. There is very little archaeological evidence for Greek cults of a "personal" god who was interested in or connected with the individual person. In the context of the Anatolian cult of Men, dedications refer to, for example, "the Men of Artemidoros" (*CMRDM* III 67-70), but such formulations do not imply a particular "pact" with the god. In a Greek polis the gods of the city were important, not the god worshiped by the individual. In everyday life people established contacts with gods only when needed. Burkert concludes that "insofar a person fulfills his religious obligations, there remained normally a realm of freedom, of the ὅσιον ["profane"], in which religious concerns vanished. This would be contradicted by a unique or com-

---

[240]See also Levinskaya 1996, 83-103.
[241]See Weiss 1995, 85-86.
[242]Teixidor 1977, 13-17.
[243]Millar 1993, 21; see now Bohak 2000.
[244]Burkert 1996, 3-14; the quotations that follow above, 11, 13.

prehensive obligation or affiliation. Resort to the gods becomes important in a time of need, however. . . . The pious person was prepared for being saved, but he does not have a revelation on a document and no treaty with 'his' god. Gods are not at his disposal."

Gods were worshiped not just in the large temples in the big cities. People worshiped in house shrines, cult niches and countless shrines scattered in the countryside.[245] In Apollonia in Lydia the police chief and eleven young mountain infantrymen (ὀροφύλακες, *salutarii*) dedicated a cult building to the Mother-Goddess of the Mountain (Μητρὶ Θεῶν᾽Ορείᾳ). In rural areas cattle were an important factor in religious activities.

A relief found in northeastern Lydia depicts a man in the posture of prayer; below him stands a man with a club holding the reins of two humpback cows, behind them another six oxen. The inscription that appears underneath the cows expresses the thankfulness of the two men, whose cattle are numerous and healthy: "After Philippkos together with his foster brother Bunion has made a vow to the Pereudenian gods concerning his cattle, he has dedicated with thankfulness [the stele]."[246] Some inscriptions attribute dead cattle to punishment by the gods: "The god demonstrated his own power and punished Hermogenes and caused him damage by killing his cattle: an ox and a donkey."[247]

An important feature of public and private religiosity were processions. The colorful atmosphere of a procession is vividly described by Xenophon from Ephesus in the second century:

"The local festival of Artemis was in progress, with its procession from the city to the temple nearly a mile away. All the local girls had to march in procession, richly dressed, as well as all the young men of Habrocomes' age—he was around sixteen, already a member of the Ephebes, and took first place in the procession. There was a great crowd of Ephesians and visitors alike to see the festival, for it was the custom at this festival to find husbands for the girls and wives for the young men. So the procession filed past—first the sacred objects, the torches, the baskets, and the incense; then horses, dogs, hunting equipment . . . some for war, most for peace. . . . And so when the procession was over, the whole crowd went into the temple for the sacrifice, and the files broke up; men and women and girls and boys came together" (Xenophon, *Ephesiaca* 1.2-5).

Cities encouraged residents to sacrifice on the altars in front of their houses during a procession.[248]

---

[245]S. Mitchell, *RECAM* 16; Petzl 1995, 39. Unfortunately, our knowledge of these shrines is limited because they cannot be documented through archaeological finds.
[246]*SEG* XXXIV 1214. See Petzl 1995, 40-41.
[247]*TAM* V 1, 464, lines 8-11: ὁ θεὸς ἀνέδιξεν τὰς εἰδίας δυνάμις καὶ ἐκόλασεν τὸν Ἑρμογένην καὶ ζημίας αὐτῷ ἐπόησεν ἀποκτίνας αὐτῷ τὰ κτή]νη βοῦν κὲ ὄνον. Cf. Petzl 1994, no. 34.
[248]Magie 1950, 1480 n. 31, with reference to Miletus.

The Emperor Cult

The significance of the emperor cult[249] must be assessed in a nuanced manner. The imperial cult was not exported from Rome, or by Rome, into the provinces, a fact that is not infrequently overlooked by New Testament scholars. At least in the first century many cites in the eastern part of the Roman Empire "demanded" the imperial cult, which was practiced in very diverse ways: *the* emperor cult never existed. The origins of the emperor cult go back as far as the third and fourth centuries B.C.; they are linked with the cult of hero and benefactor and with the consequences of the political upheavals of the time of Alexander the Great. The city-state had proven to be vulnerable, indeed impotent, and was replaced by a supraregional, international order controlled by "foreigners" who came from outside. The power of the ruler reached into all areas of everyday life and offered hope for order and stability, and it was assimilated by the traditional Olympian (or local Anatolian) gods. At the same time the emperor needed divine protection, which was sought through sacrifices offered to the gods for the emperor. Initially the power of the Roman state was honored in the personification of *Dea Roma,* and then individual representatives of Rome, such as governors and high officials, were honored. The Roman emperors received cultic veneration since Julius Caesar. After they died, the emperors were regarded as part of the state deities.

Ephesus provides a good example for the diverse forms of the veneration of the emperor and his family. At the end of the second century this metropolis of the province of Asia had several public places for the cultic veneration of the emperor.[250]

(1) Augustus allowed Ephesus in 30/29 B.C. to build a temple for *Dea Roma* and *Divus Caesar.* This temple was erected north of the upper ("state") agora ("Staatsaltar" [Dio 51.20.6]). (2) When Pergamon received the privilege of building a temple honoring Augustus, Ephesus was allowed to build a *Sebasteion (Augusteum)* on the precinct of the Artemis temple outside of the city; in 6/5 B.C. a wall was built around this sanctuary. (3) A magnificent stoa was erected between A.D. 11 and 13 near the state altar, dedicated to Artemis, Augustus, Caesar Tiberius and the Demos (*I. Ephesos* II 404). (4) Soon after Domitian's succession to the principate in A.D. 81, Ephesus was granted the status of *neōkoros* ("temple warden"), with the permission to build a separate temple for the emperor (*I. Ephesos* II 234). The imperial temple dedicated to Domitian was built on a newly

---

[249]See Latte 1992, 294-326; Wlosok 1978; Peter Herz, "Bibliographie zum römischen Kaiserkult (1955-1975)," *ANRW* II.16.2 (1980): 833-910; Price 1984 (with a catalogue of the imperial temples and sanctuaries in Asia Minor, 249-74); Pekáry 1985, esp. 116-29; A. V. Strom, W. Pöhlmann and A. Cameron, "Herrscherkult," *TRE* 15 (1986): 244-55; Fishwick 1993; Friesen 1993; B. Winter 1994; Klauck 1995-1996, 2:17-74; Bendlin 1997, 44-54; Beard, North and Price 1998, 1:206-10, 318, 348-63; 2:207-9, 222-26, 253-59; Cineira 1999, 55-97.

[250]See Price 1984, 254-56 (Ephesus nos. 27-36); Karwiese 1995, 78, 81, 89, 102-3, 110. The temple of Augustus that Price assumes for Ephesus for 27 B.C. represents a misinterpretation of the inscription *I. Ephesos* III 902. Ephesus attained the status of *neōkoros* only under Domitian.

constructed terrace west of the state altar. After Domitian had been murdered, Ephesus lost the status of *neōkoros* as a result of the *damnatio memoriae* of Domitian and was forced to dissolve the temple of Domitian and destroy the monumental statue of the emperor. An embassy to the Roman senate managed to obtain the right to rededicate the imperial temple to the honored *Divus Vespasianus*. (5) An imperial hall was erected on the north side of the palaestra of the harbor baths before A.D. 96, in which the official imperial cult was located. (6) Ephesus became "twice *neōkoros*" by A.D. 132/133 at the latest (*I. Ephesos* II 278): the Olympieion with the cult for the emperor Hadrian was erected at the foot of the acropolis, north of the harbor baths. Since A.D. 129 Ephesus honored Hadrian in inscriptions and on coins as Zeus Olympios. The building in Curetes Street that the architrave inscription dedicates "to Artemis, the emperor Hadrian and the once-*neōkoros* people of Ephesus" (*I. Ephesos* II 429) was not a second imperial temple ("temple of Hadrian"), as has been assumed.[251] (7) Around A.D. 166/167 a monumental altar ("Parthian monument") was erected, perhaps in the library square, which was dedicated to the emperors and their victorious armies, in particular to commemorate the emperor Lucius Verus, who had set up his headquarters in Ephesus during the Parthian wars. The altar was decorated with a frieze 70 m in length.

Augustus called himself "son of god" (*divi filius*), primarily, it seems, for political reasons: he was the nephew and adoptive son of Gaius Iulius Caesar, who had been honored by decree of the senate on January 1 in 42 B.C. as *Divus Iulius*. As son of the "god" Gaius Iulius, Gaius Iulius Octavianus Caesar (Augustus) was "the son of god." By 41 B.C. Augustus signed documents with *Caesar divi filius,* evidently to promote his political claims against the more experienced Mark Antony. The expression "son of god" (abbreviated as *divi f.*) became so strongly linked with his name that it was no longer thought of as a title.[252]

The inscription *CIL* XI 0367 (A.D. 21) attests the basic form of Augustus's titles: IMP CAESAR DIVI F AVGVSTVS. The inscription *ILS* 107 (A.D. 7/8) attests a fuller form of his titles: IMP CAESAR DIVI F AVGVSTO PONTIFIC MAXIMO PATRI PATRIAE AVG XV VIR S F VII VIR EPVLON COS XIII IMP XVII TRIBVNIC POTEST XXX, whose abbreviations are to be translated as follows: "Imperator Caesar, Son of God, Augustus, Pontifex Maximus, Pater Patriae (Father of the Fatherland), Augur, Quindecimviri sacris faciundis, Septemviri epulonum, Consul 13 times, Imperator 17 times, in the 30th year of his *tribunicia potestas.*" The office of the *pontifex maximus* was the highest priestly office; the office holder was the superior of the highest sacred college, which had sixteen priests (*pontifices*) since Caesar and was responsible for guaranteeing the strict observance of all ritual precepts. The second priestly office was the office of the *augures,* a college of sixteen "diviners of divine portents" who had to obtain divine sanction at important state functions. The third priestly office was the *quindecimviri sacris faciundis,* whose occupants were responsible for offering sacrifices (*sacris faciundis*), for non-Roman gods and especially for Apollo, as well as for guarding the Sibylline books and interpreting ritual precepts. The fourth office was the *septemviri epulonum,* whose occupants were responsible for the organization of particular games (*epulum Iovis, ludi plebei, ludi Romani*) and for other ceremonies. The *epu-*

---

[251]Karwiese 1995, 102.

[252]T. Kim 1998, 228; for the discussion that follows above see ibid., 230-38. See also Southern 1998, 27, 34, 61-62.

lum Iovis was a great feast at the games attended by the senate and the people.[253]

Tae Hun Kim suggests that it was especially Augustus who was called "son of god" (*divi filius;* Gk., υἱὸς θεοῦ), whereas Tiberius, Domitian and Nero were designated as DIVI F only rarely outside of the early years of their reign.[254] Robert Mowery has demonstrated that this interpretation of the evidence is erroneous: with the exception of Claudius, all emperors in the first century were called "son of god" on coins and in inscriptions: Augustus, Tiberius, Gaius Caligula, Nero, Vespasian, Titus and Domitian.[255]

Augustus was honored and venerated as "savior" (σωτήρ, *sōtēr*) of humankind and as peacemaker. An inscription from Halikarnassos in Asia Minor reads,

"[Beginning is lost] . . . since the eternal and immortal nature of everything has bestowed upon mankind the greatest good with extraordinary benefactions by bringing Caesar Augustus [Καίσαρα τὸν Σεβαστὸν] in our blessed time, the father of his own country, divine Rome, and ancestral Zeus, savior of the common race of men, whose providence has not only fulfilled but actually exceeded the prayers of all. For land and sea are at peace and the cities flourish with good order, concord and prosperity—it is the prime crop of all good, as mankind, filled with high hopes for the future and high spirits for the present, with festivals, dedications, sacrifices and hymns . . . [about 25 lines missing] . . . and that a copy of this decree be inscribed and placed in the precinct of Rome and Augustus by the high-priest, Gaius Julius . . . friend of Caesar, and in the other cities by the magistrates, and that the altars [?] be dedicated on 25th November by the priests and magistrates . . . while people keep festival. . . ."[256]

The people venerated as divine not the emperor as a person but his *genius*. The deified emperors occupied a middle position between gods and people. This becomes evident in the rituals as well as in the fact that the living emperors were the beneficiaries of the sacrifices, not their direct recipients. People, in other words, offered sacrifices not *to* the emperor but *for* the emperor. People continued to offer sacrifices for the well-being of the emperor, while the well-being of the gods was never an issue in the sacrifices that people offered. Also, the living emperor was never invoked in oaths, and he never received votive offerings (voluntary dedications to the gods). And vows were made to deified deceased emperors only in connection with other deities. People did not pray to the living emperor. The image or statue of an emperor was not a genuine statue of a god, some scholars argue, nor did it have the function of representing the emperor. Rather, the statue of the emperor was "a symbol of the unity of the

---

[253]K. Ziegler, *KP* 4:1047-48; W. Eisenhut, *KP* 1:734-36; G. Radke, *KP* 4:1304-6; H. Gärtner, *KP* 5:122; J. Linderski, *OCD* 214; J. A. North, *OCD* 1219-20, 1289, 1389.

[254]T. Kim 1998, 232-35 with n. 33-36. It seems that Kim analyzed only the coins of the American Numismatic Society.

[255]Mowery 2002, 102-6 with nn. 10-40.

[256]*IBM* IV 1, 894; Ehrenberg, Jones and Stockton 1976, no. 98a; English translation in Braund 1985, no. 123; for a German translation see Klauck 1995-1996, 2:50.

state in which many peoples lived, visible for all people, uniting the different people groups, communities and political and social organizations with the emperor and expressing their loyalty to him."[257]

The veneration of the emperor was promoted by the highest levels of the Roman state, but it remained generally voluntary throughout the first century. The emperor cult was never a rival for the traditional cults: people would sacrifice to Zeus, or Athene, or Dionysos, or Isis and participate at the same time in the emperor cult. Often an emperor was integrated into, for example, the cult of Zeus. There was no uniform cult of the emperor throughout the Roman Empire. The local manifestations of emperor worship were diverse, depending on whether the cult was practiced in the context of the province or the city, in rural areas or in the private home, in the East or in the West. And we must remember that the emperors of the first and second centuries did not demand emperor worship.

People in the Mediterranean world did not find it difficult to venerate the emperor. No one would have been embarrassed if asked to explain why he or she worshiped the emperor. Jochen Bleicken comments, "Apart from the fact that nobody wanted to dispute the monarchy, everybody could understand the religious content of the veneration of the emperor: notwithstanding the intensity of religious feeling that the individual brought to the gods that he preferred, he acknowledged the existence of other divine forces. He did not mind, therefore, pouring a bowl of wine or burning some incense seeds on one of the many altars dedicated to the living or the deceased emperors or to some deity connected with the emperor."[258] Exceptions were, of course, the Jews and particularly the Christians. The main problem for the Christians was not the act of honoring the emperor as such: passages such as 1 Tim 2:2 and 1 Pet 2:13, 17 encourage Christians to honor and pray for the emperor and for kings. The main problem was the attitude of Christians concerning sacrifices: while Jews could pray for the well-being of the emperor when they offered their sacrifices in the temple, Christians had no corresponding "cultic" act that was similar, at least in an external sense, to the pagan sacrifices.[259]

The ritual forms of the emperor cult corresponded essentially to the traditional religious practices of the Greco-Roman world. The imperial temples had their own festival calendars. Many individuals honored the emperor through regular sacrifices. For the people living in the cities, the emperor cult became concrete and tangible at least once a year—on the birth of the emperor, on the day of his accession, or on the anniversary of the day when the emperor cult had been granted—in sacrifices, processions, banquets, free meals and games.

---

[257]Pekáry 1985, 154; for the observation that follows above see ibid.
[258]Bleicken 1978, 1:101-2.
[259]See Price 1984, 123-25.

Many cities had several feast days that honored the emperor. As far as Asia Minor is concerned, no emperor visited the provinces of Asia, Galatia, Lycia-Pamphylia, Pontus-Bithynia or Cappadocia during the first century.[260]

Mentalities

Expressions of religious activity were manifold and diverse, but the fundamental religious mentality was the conviction that fortune and misfortune, happiness and calamity are gifts of the gods.[261] This was one of the main reasons why the cults of Tyche, the daughter of Zeus and goddess of fate who governs human affairs and grants each person a rightful share of fortune and misfortune, became increasingly significant. Many cities honored Tyche as a tutelary deity, a city goddess. She often was depicted with a rudder, carrying a cornucopia, and standing on a sphere. At the same time people were aware of the fact that somehow it was in the hands of individuals to experience fortune or misfortune. People who transgressed boundaries set by gods or by the community, who demonstrated *hybris,* attracted the vengeance of the gods. Poets and philosophers often reflected on the notion that fortune and calamity depend on one's moral and intellectual competence. Rational, knowledgeable behavior and learning from experience were ways by which one could attempt to influence one's fate.

Apart from poets and philosophers, the Greeks feared the gods as powers that could be influenced very little.[262] The Romans believed that one has cause to be afraid of the *numina*—the will of a deity and/or the manifestation of its power—but at the same time they were convinced that the correct performance of cultic actions gave less cause to fear the will of the gods. The Sophistic "enlightenment philosophers" of the fifth and fourth centuries B.C. among the Stoics[263] and Epicureans rejected not only fear of the gods but also angst as a *pathos* in general. For the majority of the people, however, fear of the gods remained a fundamental sentiment, demonstrated by the innumerable oracles and the magical practices, and corresponding with Greek and Roman authors who often provide an explicitly negative evaluation of hope (Gk., *elpis;* Lat., *spes*), arguing

---

[260]Price 1984, 1. This fact renders the observations in Klauck 1995-1996, 2:67 less relevant for the "context" of early Christianity.

[261]See Christian Böhme, "Freude, Leiden und Glück," in Dinzelbacher 1993, 302-7. On Tyche see G. Herzog-Hauser, PW 7.A (1943): 1643-89; N. Robertson and B. C. Dietrich, *OCD* 1566.

[262]Christian Böhme, "Ängste und Hoffnungen," in Dinzelbacher 1993, 275-85, esp. 276-77, with reference to A. Dihle, "Furcht," *RAC* 8:662-63; for the observations that follow above see Böhme, ibid.

[263]On Stoicism see Julia Anans, *OCD* 1446; Karl Bormann, "Stoa/Stoizismus I," *TRE* 32 (2001): 179-90; Max Pohlenz, *Stoicism* (New York: Garland, 1987; German original, 1940); John M. Rist, *Stoic Philosophy* (Cambridge: Cambridge University Press, 1969 [1977]); Brad Inwood, *Ethics and Human Action in Early Stoicism* (Oxford: Clarendon, 1985); Andrew Erskine, *The Hellenistic Stoa: Political Thought and Action* (London: Duckworth, 1990); Brad Inwood, *The Cambridge Companion to the Stoics* (Cambridge: Cambridge University Press, 2003).

that it has often proved to be groundless. Seneca believed that hope and fear belong to the illnesses of the soul, that hope is an uncertain good (*Ep.* 10.2). At the same time we find aspirations for material wealth, for fame, for glory, which indicates that people "hoped" in a "positive" sense after all.

The Greeks believed that after death people await a disconsolate existence in the shadow world of Hades.[264] According to Homer, the dead "are pathetic in their helplessness, inhabiting draughty, echoing halls, deprived of their wits [*phrenes*], and flitting purposelessly about uttering batlike noises" (*Od.* 24.5-6.). Other concepts about death and the afterlife included the transformation of the dead into stars (e.g., Castor and Pollux), the absorption of the dead into the upper atmosphere or aether, the Pythagorean and Platonic belief in transmigration (the immortal soul enters another body after death), and the "blessedness" that was promised to initiates in the Eleusinian mysteries. Since Greek eschatology generally does not posit a dualistic afterlife, as only gross sinners such as Tantalus and Sisyphus were thought to receive retributive punishment, "fear of the after-life was therefore largely absent." In the Roman tradition death was regarded "essentially as a blemish striking the family of the deceased, with the risk of affecting all with whom it had contact." The deceased joined the *di manes,* "an undifferentiated mass or (rather) a collective divinity" that lived outside towns on land set aside for this purpose (necropolis). The immortality of the *di manes* depended on the existence of descendants (or a funerary association). It is probably in the context of notions that sins in this world are punished in the afterlife[265] that even intellectual skeptics started to have doubts when death approached. The aged Kephalos says to Socrates,

"For let me tell you, Socrates," he said, "that when a man begins to realize that he is going to die, he is filled with apprehensions and concern about matters that before did not occur to him. The tales that are told of the world below and how the men who have done wrong here must pay the penalty there, though he may have laughed them down hitherto, then begin to torture his soul with the doubt that there may be some truth in them. And apart from that the man himself either from the weakness of old age or possibly as being now nearer to the things beyond has a somewhat clearer view of them. Be that as it may, he is filled with doubt, surmises, and alarms and begins to reckon up and consider whether he has ever wronged anyone" (Plato, *Pol.* 1.330 d-e).

Scholars traditionally argue that the hope for a blissful life after death was characteristic of the mysteries of Eleusis. Hans-Josef Klauck summarizes the aims of the Eleusinian mysteries as follows: "Human beings, threatened by transitoriness and death, are supposed to receive a share in the self-rejuvenating life-force of

---

[264]H. Sonnabend, "Religiosität," in Dinzelbacher 1993, 106. The quotation that follows above is from R. Garland and J. Scheid, *OCD* 433; for the observations and quotation that follow further see ibid.

[265]Werner Portmann, "Sterben/Tod," in Dinzelbacher 1993, 231-44, esp. 234.

nature. . . . The hope that they articulate is directed toward a better fate in the after-life."[266] Recent research into the mystery cults, particularly by the "School of Rome" since the 1960s (Ugo Bianchi), has shown that the mystery cults were not independent movements, let alone religions, but "merely an ingrained modality of (Greek, later Greco-Roman) polytheism. The Eleusinian mysteries, which were a regular part of the civic cult of Athens, institutionalized "collective purification, the dramatic representation of mythical narrative, the opportunity of awe, fear, wonder, scurrility, and humor, . . . explicit exegesis by the *mystagōgoi,* the privilege bestowed by an open secret 'that may not be divulged,' and public reaffirmation of a theodicy of moral desert linked to good fortune." In this interpretation "the offer of a blessed existence in the Elysian fields after death . . . received no special emphasis."

Specific suggestions in the rhetorical handbooks demonstrate that fears and hopes characterized the everyday life of people, giving advice on how orators may appeal to people's fears and hopes to achieve certain goals.[267] Seneca advises the rulers to maintain a certain measure of fear among the lower classes, as this helps to maintain discipline: "Fear in moderation restrains men's passions."[268]

The confession steles that have been found in Lydia, sporadically also in Phrygia, Caria, Cappadocia and Bithynia, dating to A.D. 50-260, provide insights in the religious sentiments and activities particularly of the rural population.[269] The inscriptions of the confession steles record a public confession of sin, nearly always caused by an illness that is interpreted as punishment from the god. The god demands a public confession of the sin(s) for atonement to become possible, a confession of the power of the god, and the erection of a stele. A healing is mentioned only rarely.[270] The following three examples illustrate the religious mentality that finds expression in these inscriptions.

"After Diogenes had made a vow to Zeus Peizenos for his ox and has not made good (on it), his daughter Tatiane was punished in her eyes. Now they have atoned (the god) and given (the stele) as dedication."[271]

"Tyche, Socrates, Ammianos and Trophimos, the children of Ammias, and Philete and

---

[266]Klauck 1995-1996, 1:94. On the Eleusian mysteries see George E. Mylonas, *Eleusis and the Eleusinian Mysteries* (Princeton, N.J.: Princeton University Press, 1961); Bianchi 1976; Cineira 1999, 117-24. For the observations and quotation that follow above see R. L. Gordon, *OCD* 1017-18.

[267]Böhme, "Ängste und Hoffnungen," in Dinzelbacher 1993, 282; cf. Kneppe 1994.

[268]Seneca, *Clem.* 1.12.4; see Kneppe 1994, 330.

[269]Most confession inscriptions have been found in rural areas; only three have been found in Sardis. Philostratus, *Vit. Apoll.* 1.6, attests confession steles for Cappadocia. For the confession inscriptions see Petzl 1994; 1995, 41-48; Ricl 1995; also Schnabel 2003.

[270]See *SEG* XXXV 94.

[271]*TAM* V 1, 509: Διεὶ Πειζηνῷ Διογένη[ς] εὐξάμενος ὑπὲρ τοῦ βοὸς κὲ μὴ ἀποδοὺς ἐκολάσθη αὐτοῦ ἡ θυγάτηρ Τατιανὴ ἰς τοὺς ὀφθαλμούς· νῦν οὖν εἱλασάμενοι ἀνέθηκαν. Petzl 1994, 54 (no. 54).

Socrat(e)ia, the daughters of Ammias, have propitiated the Mother Anatis as they have
brought the sacrifice and a written testimony to Thea Anaitis and Meis Tiamu for (their)
children and cattle. In the year 321, in the month Xandikos."²⁷²

"In the year 320, on the 12th day of the month Panemos. According to the enlightenment given by the gods, by Zeus and the great Men Artemidorou: 'I have punished
[ἐκολασόμην] Theodoros in respect to his eyes in consequences of the sins [κατὰ τὰς
ἁμαρτίας] which he committed.' 'In the *praetorium* I had sexual intercourse [συνεγενόμην]
with Trophime, the servant of Haplokomas, who is the wife of Eutyches.' He [Theodoros]
takes the first sin away [ἀπαίρι τὴν πρώτην ἁμαρτίαν] with a sheep, a partridge, a mole.
Second sin [δευτέρα ἁμαρτία]: 'Although I was a sacred servant of the gods in Nonou, I
had sexual intercourse [συνεγενόμην] with the unmarried Ariagne.' He [Theodoros] takes
(the sin) away with a piglet, a tuna fish. 'At the third sin [τῇ τρίτῃ ἁμαρτίᾳ] I had sexual
intercourse [συνεγενόμην] with the unmarried Arethousa.' He [Theodoros] takes (the sin)
away with a chicken (or a rooster), a sparrow, a pigeon, and with a *kypros* [14.6 l] of
wheat mixed with barley and with a *prochos* [6.6 l] of wine. Being pure (Theodoros gives)
to the sacred personnel a *kypros* of wheat and one *prochos* (of wine). 'As my legal adviser
I got Zeus [ἔσχα παράκλητον τὸν Δείαν].' (He says:) 'Behold, I had blinded him in consequence of his actions, but now he has made good his mistakes [ἀνερύσετον τὰς ἁμαρτί
ας] by propitiating the gods [εἰλαζομένου αὐτοῦ τοὺς θεούς] and by erecting an inscribed
stele.' (The god Men Artemidorou?) is asked by the council: 'I am merciful [εἴλεος εἶμαι],
because my stele gets set up the very day I have fixed. You may open the jail, I release
the condemned after one year and ten months have passed.'"²⁷³

The confession steles illustrate how people have transgressed a divine decree,
spoken arrogantly about the deity, ignored the god or expressed doubts about
the power of the god.

One inscription begins with the sentence "For Men Labana(s). (The woman) Elpis has disparaged [κατευτελίσασα] Men Labana(s) and ascended his podium without (prior) bathing
[ἀκατάλουστος] and examined his podium and his trays."²⁷⁴ Another stele was erected by
a woman who had resisted a deity for many years: "For Zeus from Twin Oaks. I, Claudia
Bassa, suffered for four years and (still) did not trust the god. After I was successful with
regard to my illness, I have gratefully dedicated the stele. In the year 338, on the 18th of
the month of Peritios."²⁷⁵ In another case a man refused to allow all his former slaves to
serve in a certain sanctuary: "Since I had caused the sacred slave Trophimus of Meter
Hipta and of Zeus Sabazios to be dragged away by the authorities, I was punished in my
eyes, and I have erected the stele."²⁷⁶

---

²⁷²*TAM* V 1, 322: Θεᾷ Ἀναείτι καὶ Μηνὶ Τιαμου Τύχη καὶ Σωκράτης καὶ Ἀμμιανὸς καὶ Τρόφι-
μος οἱ Ἀμμίου καὶ Φιλήτη καὶ Σωκρατία αἱ Ἀμμιάδος ποήσαντες τὸ ἱεροπόημα εἰλασάμενυ
Μητέραν Ἀναείτιν ὑπὲρ τέκνων καὶ θρεμμάτων ἔγγραφον ἔστησαν. Ἔτους τκα', μη(νὸς)
Ξανδικοῦ. See Petzl 1994, 90-92 (no. 70). Date: A.D. 236/237.
²⁷³Editio princeps: Hasan Malay, "New Confession-Inscriptions in the Manisa and Bergama Museums," *EA* 12 (1988): 147-52, esp. 151-52 (no. 5, table 12); for a German translation see Petz
1994, 7-11 (no. 5). Date: A.D. 235/236.
²⁷⁴*SEG* XXXV 1157; see Petzl 1994, 44-45 (no. 36). Date: A.D. 191/192.
²⁷⁵*SEG* XXXIII 1012; see Petzl 1994, 20-21 (no. 12). Date: A.D. 253/254.
²⁷⁶*TAM* V 1, 459; see Petzl 1994, 58 (no. 49).

Georg Petzl summarizes the religious mentality of the people of Lydia, and thus similarly of all the regions in Asia Minor, as follows: "The vast majority surely believed that weal and woe depend on higher powers. The δυνάμεις, the manifestations of divine power, were omnipresent. Countless gods and combinations of gods were everywhere at home. They were worshiped as individuals or in the cult collective, δοῦμος, φράτρα, συμβίωσις, etc. People not only prayed to the gods, but also sought their help with regard to very specific questions. They provided answers in dream-visions, through divine *angeloi* (ἀγγελοι), that is, messengers, signs and oracles spoken by prophets."[277] The atonement practices attested in the confession inscriptions show that the priests had a huge informal influence on the everyday life of villagers: "They are rarely mentioned in the texts because they depict the deity as acting subject, but they appear repeatedly on the reliefs that accompany the inscriptions. The visitors [to the sanctuaries] brought their worries to them; it depended on their ability to communicate whether they recognized the intervention of the god in their lives; they probably also assisted at the rites of atonement."[278] The fact that pagan religiosity in the first century and long afterwards was a fundamental reality of everyday life is confirmed by the conviction that a particular deity "rules" (βασιλεύειν, *basileuein;* κατέχειν, *katechein*) over a village as its property. An inscription stored in the Manisa Museum begins with the sentence "Great are the gods that own [the village] Nea Kome!"[279]

The early Christian missionaries encountered people who longed "for security in this life and in the afterlife, for consolation and affirmation, for meaning in a meaningless world."[280] Their offer of resurrection and salvation in the afterlife was particularly attractive, as was the life of the local Christian communities, in which the believers took care of each other in practical ways and people loved their neighbors. We will need to examine the issue of whether the early Christian missionaries used these "attractions" as "offers" in their missionary efforts in tactical ways, but we may note here that their work could easily lead to conflicts. (1) Personal level: the missionaries insisted that salvation is connected exclusively with the life, death and resurrection of Jesus, a Galilean Jew. A tolerant culture that integrates or at least accepts all gods as a matter of principle could be expected to react with rejection, ridicule and, depending on the circumstances, more severe measures. (2) Level of local associations: if several people agreed that the missionaries presented a threat to the peace of the community (e.g., of the synagogue) or to the prosperity of a trade guild (e.g., of the

---

[277]Petzl 1995, 46.
[278]Schuler 1998, 254.
[279]*EA* 12 (1988): 149 (no. 1): Μεγάλοι θεοὶ Νέαν Κώμην κατέχοντες. See further *CMRDM* 31-32, 39, 43.
[280]H. Sonnabend, "Religiosität," in Dinzelbacher 1993, 117, for the observation that follows above see ibid.

producers of statues of deities), then missionaries could expect personal threats and expulsion. (3) Municipal level: if members of the city council felt that the activities of the missionaries threatened to disturb order and peace in the city, they could react, quickly if necessary, with punishments or expulsion from the city. (4) Level of the ideology of the Roman state: the proclamation of the "kingdom of Jesus Christ" and the designation of Jesus as Kyrios could easily bring the missionaries into conflict with the local representative of the Roman state ideology because no power could be allowed to exist in the Roman Empire other than that of the emperor and his representatives.

18.5 Communication

Languages[281]

The writings of Herodotus, Strabo and Plutarch reveal that the Greeks did not learn other languages. The same is true for the Romans.[282] Anika Strobach suggests that the causes for this fact "surely lie in both a lack of necessity and a lack of interest."[283] Galen, born in A.D. 130 in Pergamon, was the personal physician of the emperor in Rome and was the most productive Greek author of medical texts. He comments in his book *De differentia plusuum* (8.586) that one could also write in a language other than Greek if need be, but the use of the Greek language is preferable: it is used everywhere, it is sweet-voiced (εὔγλωττον, *euglōtton*) and purely and simply "human" (ἀνθρωπική, *anthrōpikē*), while non-Greek languages can be compared to the sounds of pigs, frogs, ravens and jackdaws. There were, of course, some people who spoke two languages, as Galen knew: "There was formerly a bilingualist, this was a miracle: a person who understood and spoke two languages."[284] People who were multilingual could be found in mixed marriages where husband and wife spoke different languages, among educated and wealthy people, among merchants and traders whose knowledge of a second language was narrow and practical, and in regions in the eastern Mediterranean that were part of the world of Greek-Hellenistic culture since the campaigns of Alexander the Great.

Interpreters occasionally are mentioned by Herodotus, Polybius, Caesar, Cicero, Plutarch and other authors.[285] Plutarch describes many situations that pre-

---

[281]See Neumann and Untermann 1980; R. Schmitt 1983, 554-86; Brixhe 1987a; Reck 1991, 68-78.

[282]See Jürgen Werner, "Zur Fremdsprachenproblematik in der griechisch-römischen Antike," in Müller, Sier and Werner 1992, 1-20; Peter Robert Franke, "Dolmetschen in hellenistischer Zeit," in ibid., 85-96; Strobach 1997. There is no comprehensive study of this subject.

[283]Strobach 1997, 183.

[284]Galen 8.585: δίγλωττος γάρ τις ἐλέγετο πάλαι, καὶ θαῦμα τοῦτο ἦν.

[285]Strobach 1997, 171-74, with reference to Herodotus 1.86; 2.125, 154, 164; 3.38, 140; Polybius 1.67; 3.44; 5.83; 15.6; Caesar, *Bell. gall.* 1.19.3; 1.47.4; 5.36.1; Cicero, *Verr.* 2.3.37.84; *Fam.* 13.54; *Fin.* 5.29.89; *Balb.* 11.28; Plutarch, *Them.* 6, 28; *Art.* 13; *Alex.* 37; *Mulier. virt.* 249A; *Cat. Maj.* 12, 22; *Crass.* 28, 31; *Pomp.* 78-79; *Ant.* 27, 46; *Sull.* 27.

sume the presence of interpreters, although they are not mentioned. This could indicate that interpreters were taken for granted in the military and in negotiations.[286] Strobach comments, "If Plutarch mentions interpreters, we are never informed about their social background. Their name is only rarely recorded. Most of the time we do not know how they obtained their linguistic abilities, how far their language capabilities went, or which position they had." There is no evidence for schools where interpreters were trained. We know that there were people in the army of Alexander the Great, more or less accidentally, who knew local languages: people from mixed marriages, but also official interpreters. There is not sufficient evidence to answer the question of how the problem of communication between people who spoke different languages was "officially" solved. Only Grecized non-Greeks refer to their multilingual abilities—for example, Meleagros from Gadara in the first century B.C.[287] Greek ethnography was not interested in the languages of other nations, despite the fact that language is the most striking characteristic of a foreign people. We must recall, however, that for centuries Greeks spoke both the dialect of their region and Koine, which became widespread after the fifth century B.C.[288]

The Greek language played a significant role in the Roman Empire. Greek was the national language of the Greek people, it was the lingua franca of the eastern provinces and beyond, and it was the "language of culture" in the western provinces. For most people in the Roman Empire, Greek was the first or the second language.[289]

Rome, the capital, was bilingual in the first century. Latin was the official language; many if not most people spoke Greek. This was true for the members of the aristocracy: the leading families in the time of the republic and in the early imperial period spoke Latin as their mother tongue and Greek as a language of education. "The children of these families grew up bilingually, they were familiar with Greek poetry (Homer) and rhetoric (Demosthenes)."[290] Julius Caesar is said to have made the famous statement "The die is cast" (Lat., *iacta alea esto*) in Ἑλληνιστί (*Hellēnisti*), in Greek: Ἀνερρίφθω κύβος (*anerriphthō kybos*).[291] Many people of the lower class spoke Greek as well: the numerous slaves and voluntary immigrants (small merchants, artisans, jugglers, soldiers) as well as freedmen spoke Greek as a first language and Latin as a colloquial language.

Roman sources reveal little about the languages of other peoples, with the exception of Greek, of course. Iiro Kajanto observes, "The Romans were not in-

---

[286]Strobach 1997, 176; the quotation that follows above, ibid.

[287]See *Anthologia Graeca* 7.419.

[288]See W. Blümel, "Zum Verhältnis zwischen Gemeinsprache und Dialekt am Beispiel des Aiolischen der Troas," in Schwertheim and Wiegartz 1996, 9-14, esp. 12.

[289]See Zgusta 1980, 121-45.

[290]Strobach 1997, 142. On the Latin language see the survey by Robert G. Coleman, *OCD* 817-20.

[291]Plutarch, *Pomp.* 60. See Strobach 1997, 153.

terested in linguistic issues, and they had the least interest in languages that were spoken by the common people, let alone by the slaves."[292] Plutarch tells the story of a "barbarian" who was educated, good-looking, rather happy and spoke many languages; a dialogue partner wants to expose him as a Greek because his views about the number of existing worlds was neither Egyptian nor Indian, but Doric in origin.[293]

In Greece the different dialects had declined since the fourth century B.C. With the exception of some remote areas,[294] the people in the various regions spoke "common Greek" (κοινὴ διάλεκτος, koinē dialektos), a standard language that developed on the basis of Ionic-Attic (Strabo 12.4.6). Attic had been the dialect of Athens. The New Testament is one of the main sources for Koine Greek.[295] The language boundary between the Latin-speaking West and the Greek-speaking East coincided more or less with the administrative boundary between the provinces of Macedonia-Thrace and Dalmatia-Moesia.

In Spain the indigenous languages continued to be used during the imperial period: Iberian in the south on the Mediterranean coast, Celtiberian in the north and Lusitanian in the west. The population of the cities on the Mediterranean coast and in the highly urbanized south, where Latin was the official language, presumably was bilingual.[296] Sertorius had the boys of the noble families of the conquered city of Osca taught in Greek and in Latin (Plutarch, Sert. 14). In southern Gaul (France) Greek was the colloquial language of the population.[297]

In Asia Minor Greek had become the main language during the Hellenistic period, and it remained the lingua franca until the invasion of Turk tribes in the eleventh century.[298] The Greek language was συνήθεια (synētheia), the habitual or customary language. Coins with Latin legends during the imperial period do not suggest that the population spoke or understood Latin.[299] The vast majority of inscriptions of the Roman period in Asia Minor are written in Latin or in Greek.[300]

---

[292]Iiro Kajanto, "Minderheiten und ihre Sprachen in der Hauptstadt Rom," in Neumann and Untermann 1980, 83-101; quotation, ibid., 84.

[293]Plutarch, Def. orac. 421A-B: γλώσσαις δὲ πολλαῖς ἤσκητο χρῆσθαι; cf. 421A-B, 422D. See Strobach 1997, 159.

[294]See Strabo 8.1.2 on the Peloponnese.

[295]Zgusta 1980, 121-35; on the New Testament, ibid., 125. On the Greek language see the survey by Anna M. Davies, OCD 653-56. On the Greek of the New Testament see Stanley E. Porter, "The Greek Language of the New Testament," in A Handbook to the Exegesis of the New Testament (ed. S. E. Porter; NTTS 25; Leiden: Brill, 1997), 99-130.

[296]Jürgen Untermann, "Hispania," in Neumann and Untermann 1980, 1-17.

[297]Zgusta 1980, 138.

[298]See Günter Neumann, "Kleinasien," in Neumann and Untermann 1980, 167-85.

[299]See Levick 1967, 131; MacMullen 2000, 13, 142 n. 34.

[300]For the observations that follow above see S. Mitchell 1995a, 1:50-51, 171-75.

Exceptions are Hebrew inscriptions that the Jewish communities of Akmonia, Smyrna and Sardis have left behind.[301] There are inscriptions in Aramaic and in Phoenician as well as in the epichoric languages Carian, Lycian, Lydian and in several Pamphylian dialects dating to the classical and the Hellenistic periods.[302] Rosalinde Kearsley recently has published 171 bilingual, Latin-Greek inscriptions from Asia Minor, mostly funerary inscriptions (nos. 1-110) and honorary or dedicatory inscriptions (nos. 111-138, 147-171); only a few religious inscriptions were bilingual (nos. 139-146).[303] These inscriptions illustrate the significance particularly of freedmen who often belonged to the imperial family for the dissemination of Roman culture and of Latin in Asia Minor. "Imperial freedmen behaved towards the Greek communities more like civic benefactors than outsiders and, as such, they made an important contribution to the acculturation of Romans and Greeks in imperial Asia by their use of mixed language inscriptions in public context."

This does not mean, however, that the old indigenous languages of Asia Minor were dead or *in extremis*. The fact that, for example, the Galatian Celts even produced inscriptions is a result of their Hellenization: there are no indications that Celtic was a written language; the means of communication among the Galatian Celts was nearly exclusively oral. The diverse ethnic groups in Asia Minor continued to use their own languages besides using Greek.

Strabo (63 B.C.-A.D. 21) indicates that the Carian language was still spoken in the region around Kaunos and that in the region of Kibyra one could still hear the Lydian language (14.2.3; 14.2.8). When he comments on the progression of the Greek language to northwestern Asia Minor, he points out that now the Romans control the region "under whose reign most of the peoples have already lost both their dialects and their names."[304] In inner Anatolia and in the regions to the north and east the traditional languages were faring better: Mithradates VI Eupator of Pontus (120-63 B.C.) is said to have spoken all twenty-two languages that were in use in northern Anatolia; educated Cappadocians spoke Greek with a strong accent (Philostratus, *Vit. Soph.* 2.13); the common people spoke various Cappadocian languages. Iranian was still spoken in the fourth century A.D. in Iranian settlements in Cappadocia. When Hyacinthus, a slave from Amastris, was sentenced to death during the persecution under Valerius (A.D. 257-259), the judge apparently needed a translator in order to understand him. Strabo points out that four indigenous languages could be heard in the border areas of the provinces of Asia and Lycia: Pisidian, Solymian, Greek and Lydian (13.1.65). In the city territory of Selge two long texts have been found that have not yet been deciphered; they are written probably in Pisidian. In the rural areas of Galatia Celtic continued to be spoken for a long time; ethnic Galatians who consulted the oracle of Glykon in Abonuteichos in Paphlagonia needed a translator. Paul and Barnabas were addressed in Lystra in the Lycaonian language (Acts

---

[301]*MAMA* VI 334 (*IJudO* II 170); *CIG* 9897 = *CIJ* II 739 (*IJudO* II 41); for Sardis see Hanfmann 1983, 117.

[302]For documentation see S. Mitchell 1995a, 1:172 n. 66-67. On the Anatolian languages see A. M. Davies, *OCD* 81-82. On the Lydian language see Roberto Gusmani, "Zum Stand der Erforschung der lydischen Sprache," in Schwertheim 1995, 9-19.

[303]*I. GRIAsia* (ed. R. A. Kearsley, 2001); for the observations that follow above see ibid., 155-56; quotation, 156.

[304]Strabo 12.4.6: ἐφ᾽ ὧν ἤδη καὶ τὰς διαλέκτους καὶ τὰ ὀνόματα ἀποβεβλήκασιν οἱ πλεῖστοι.

14:11-12). When a certain Bendidianus visited the monk Auxentius in eastern Bithynia sometime in the fourth century, he was noted for speaking a "barbarian," meaning the Mysian, language (PG 114:1428b). The Lycaonian Christians who lived in two monasteries in Constantinople that were founded in the sixth century possibly still spoke the Lycaonian language. The miracle of the rescue of a Christian stonemason that happened in the sixth century was recounted in the Isaurian language by the citizens of his hometown upon his return. The church historian Socrates (A.D. 380-440) reports that the Arian bishop Selinus from Cotiaeum, who descended from Gothic and Phrygian families, used both of these languages in his sermons (Socrates, *Hist. eccl.* 5.23), despite the fact that Hellenistic culture and education had spread into the upper Tembris Valley and despite the fact that the mixed pagan-Christian population of the second, third and fourth centuries was able to speak Greek.

Despite the respectable evidence for the tenacity of the indigenous culture and language in the various regions of Asia Minor, it remains a fact that Greek was spoken in rural areas as well. This is attested not only for gravestones and other inscriptions but also for everyday life, a fact that can be inferred from the linguistic peculiarities of the language of the Greek inscriptions that have been found in rural areas.[305] A few people spoke no Greek at all, presumably mostly women who had only sporadic connections outside of the family. A few people spoke only Greek: the members of the elite who had abandoned their cultural roots and their linguistic heritage and were totally absorbed in the life of the big cities in Asia Minor. Between those two groups of people, small in number, was the great mass of people in the cities and in the rural areas who were bilingual, who spoke Greek but retained their traditional indigenous languages.[306] If bilingualism was indeed a commonplace and everyday phenomenon in the provinces of the Roman Empire, it is indeed correct to state that "the translation of important news was a rather normal and automatic process."[307]

In first-century Syria there were two linguae francae: Aramaic and Greek. Greek was the language of the educated class, and it was *the* trade language. In the old city states of Byblos, Sidon and Tyre the Phoenician language was still spoken in the Roman period. Outside the army, Latin was spoken only in Berytus (mod. Beirut), a colony founded by Augustus, in whose famous law school the professors taught Latin rhetoric.[308] After his conquest of Persia Alexander the Great arranged for thirty thousand boys to learn "Greek sciences" (γράμματα μανθάνειν Ἑλληνικά, *grammata manthanein Hellēnika*) under the tutelage of "supervisors" (ἐπιστάται, *epistatai*), a program that surely included learning the Greek language.[309]

---

[305]Günter Neumann, "Kleinasien," in Neumann and Untermann 1980, 173-80; Brixhe 1987a; 1987b, 45-80; S. Mitchell 1995a, 1:174-75.

[306]S. Mitchell 1995a, 1:175.

[307]Reck 1991, 77.

[308]R. Schmitt 1980, 198-205. On Berytus see §22.4 in vol. 1 of the present work.

[309]Plutarch, *Alex.* 47. See Strobach 1997, 178.

In Armenia the Armenian language was only spoken. The written languages were Greek and Aramaic. Written Armenian was introduced when the missionary Mesrop (ca. A.D. 407) translated the Bible into Armenian.[310] In Mesopotamia Aramaic was the main language; since the time of Alexander, Greek was the language of administration.[311]

In Egypt Ptolemy II Philadelphos promoted the dissemination of Greek culture and language. His measures included exemption from the salt tax for teachers. Greek was the official language until Diocletian. The indigenous population continued to speak Egyptian—that is, Demotic (from Gk., *dēmotikos*, "popular"), a native Egyptian cursive script in daily use from the seventh century B.C. until the adaptation of Coptic after the fourth century B.C. (developed from the cursive Third Intermediate Period hieratic; the traditional hieroglyphs continued to be used in the sacral language of the temples).[312] The story of the visit of Alexander the Great in the Temple of Ammon shows that Egyptians communicated with Greeks in the latter's mother tongue.[313] Cleopatra is said to have been able to converse without a translator with Ethiopians, Troglodyai (Nubians), Hebrews, Arabs, Syrians, Medes and Parthians. It can be presumed that she spoke Macedonian and Greek, as well as her native Egyptian. A papyrus from the early first century A.D. evidences that people living in the metropolises of Middle Egypt endeavored to learn Latin: a scribe repeated on a papyrus sheet two lines from Virgil's *Aeneid* (P.Oxy. 3554).

Someone who spoke Greek therefore had no problems whatsoever in communicating with practically all people in the eastern provinces (and beyond) of the Roman Empire. This was true for both non-Jews and Jews: Philo can describe Greek as "our language" (*Congr.* 8.44; cf. 129).

Reading and Writing

Some scholars estimate that between 20 and 30 percent of the inhabitants in Hellenized cities could read and write.[314] Among women, slaves and the lower social classes literacy generally was less common. Other scholars are more optimistic. Colin Roberts believes that literacy was widespread in the Near East in the first century on nearly all levels of society.[315] Nicholas Horsfall argues that

---

[310]Christianity was the state religion under King Trdat in A.D. 301 or 313.

[311]R. Schmitt 1980, 187-214.

[312]Dorothy J. Thompson, "Language and Literacy in Early Hellenistic Egypt," in Bilde et al. 1992, 39-52 (on the salt tax see 48); Erich Lüddeckens, "Ägypten," in Neumann and Untermann 1980, 241-65. The Egyptian texts of the second century A.D. written in Greek are called Old Coptic.

[313]Strobach 1997, 158, on Plutarch, *Alex.* 27; on Cleopatra (*Ant.* 27) see ibid., 160-61.

[314]See Harris 1989. In regard to the western provinces, Harris estimates that only 5 to 10 percent were literate (ibid., 272, 337).

[315]C. H. Roberts 1970, 48-66; cf. Roberts and Skeat 1983.

two facts suggest that the actual conditions of the Greco-Roman everyday world cannot be grasped by modern statistical methods: instruction in reading and writing in the home, among slaves, in the army and in connection with work, and the advantages provided by literacy. These factors suggest that elementary education, including the ability to read and write, was much more widespread, not only in the large cities but also in the smaller towns as well as in the rural areas.[316]

In some regions the percentage of people who could read and write was higher than in other regions of the Roman Empire. This is particularly true for Egypt and Judea.[317]

Travel

Travel was "*the* transmission belt for the gospel," as Reinhold Reck correctly points out.[318] The philosopher Aelius Aristides, who hailed from Hadrianuthera in Mysia and had traveled widely, including to the interior of Egypt, describes in his eulogy on Rome, given in A.D. 155, how easy travel was under the ideal conditions of the *pax Romana:*

> "Now it is possible for both Greek and barbarian, with his possessions or without them, to travel easily wherever he wishes [τὰ αὑτοῦ κομίζοντι καὶ χωρὶς τῶν αὑτοῦ βαδίζειν ὅποι βούλεται ῥᾳδίως], quite as if he were going from one country of his to another [ἀτεχνῶς ὡς ἐκ πατρίδος εἰς πατρίδα ἰόντι]. And he is frightened neither by the Cilician Gates, nor by the sandy, narrow passage through Arabia to Egypt, nor by inhospitable barbarian races. But it is enough for his safety [εἰς ἀφάλειαν] that he is a Roman, or rather one of those under you. And what was said by Homer, 'The earth was common to all' [*Il.* 15.193], you have made a reality, by surveying the whole inhabited world [καταμετρήσαντες μὲν πᾶσαν τὴν οἰκουμένην], by bridging the rivers in various ways, by cutting carriage roads through the mountains, by filling desert places with post stations, and by civilizing everything with your way of life and good order" (*Oration Regarding Rome, Or.* 26.100-101 [ed. C. A. Behr]).

> The phrase "narrow passage through Arabia to Egypt" (R. Klein: "Durchgangsstraße durch das Land der Araber nach Ägypten") refers to the road, built under Hadrian, from Antinoe to Berenike on the Red Sea "to enable his favorite foundation, participation in the transit trade with India."[319]

---

[316]Nicholas Horsfall, "Literacy in the Roman Empire: Mass and Mode," in Beard et al. 1991, 59-76. Horsfall describes William Harris as a "minimalist." See also Alan K. Bowman ("Literacy in the Roman Empire," in Beard et al. 1991, 119-31), who refers to, among other things, the phenomenon of multilingualism.

[317]On literacy in the first century in Judea and Galilee see Riesner 1988, 112-15, and passim.

[318]Reck 1991, 81; for the observations that follow above see ibid., 82 n. 85. See also F. F. Bruce, *ABD* 6:648-53; L. J. Kreitzer, *DPL* 945-46; N. Purcell, *OCD* 1547-48; Brödner 1989, 250-56; Meijer and Nijf 1992; 133-89; Casson 1994, esp. 115-329; Rapske 1994b; see earlier Zahn 1877.

[319]R. Klein, ed., *Aelius Aristides: Orationem ΕΙΣ ΡΩΜΗΝ,* in *Die Romrede des Aelius Aristides* (Texte zur Forschung 45; Darmstadt: Wissenschaftliche Buchgesellschaft, 1983), 116, with reference to *IGR* I 1142; Pliny, *Nat.* 6.26.102-103.

Aristides probably exaggerates somewhat, as travel still could prove dangerous in deserted regions and mountain areas, even in the second century. But there is no doubt that a traveler could reach any region or city, funds and weather permitting. Of course, only the larger cities were directly linked with transregional and international traffic. The people who traveled most frequently and most regularly "in the entire oikoumene included athletes, artists and gladiators as well as . . . soldiers, members of the imperial aristocracy and higher officials in the administration of the empire."[320] To this list should be added the early Christian missionaries, who came from humble backgrounds, for whom nobody erected a monument and who therefore are not attested in inscriptions. Traders and merchants traveled also, of course. The merchant Flavius Zeuxis of Hierapolis, who sailed seventy-two times around Cape Malea to Italy,[321] was mentioned earlier. A funerary stele found on the island Prokonnesos (mod. Marmara Island) in the Propontis, the Marmara Sea, commemorates a teenager who had left "land and mother" because he wanted "to get to know many cities by ship."[322]

Throughout antiquity the means of travel are by foot, carriage, horse or mule, and ship. Travel by litter (or sedan chair), "as a specialized form of the foot march, is suitable only for wealthy people for short distances."[323] A two-wheeled carriage (*carpentum*) could transport two or three people; the *birota,* the *carrus* and the *raeda* could transport between 200 and 1,000 pounds. Travel routes[324] were roads, rivers and seas. Travel by ship generally was the more comfortable mode of transportation, but also more dangerous.

David French, the foremost expert on the Roman roads in Asia Minor, distinguishes six types of roads: (1) *highway:* the paved Roman road built by engineers and maintained regularly, about 3.25 m wide and thus suitable for carriage traffic in both directions; (2) *roadway:* the paved Roman road built by engineers and maintained regularly, generally less than 3.25 m wide and suitable for travelers on foot and for traffic with animals; steeper ascents across mountains were managed with staircases, which made the road impassable for carriages; (3) *trackway:* a broad but unpaved road that was maintained regularly and could be used by carriages; (4) *pathway:* a narrow, unpaved road, impassible for carriages, that was maintained regularly; (5) *track:* a nonconstructed, unpaved line of communication that was known and regularly used and perhaps passable by vehicles; (6) *path:* a line of communication that was used irregularly and probably was impassable for vehicles.[325]

---

[320]Brandt 1992, 149.

[321]Robert 1969-1990, 1:543-44.

[322]M. H. Sayar, "Grabgedicht aus Prokonnesos für Alexandros," *EA* 32 (2000): 211: πλεύσε[ι]ν ἐθέλησα πολλὰς δὲ πόλεις ἰσαθρῆσαι.

[323]Reck 1991, 82 n. 85.

[324]See Radke 1973; French 1980; 1992; 1994b; Casson 1994, 147-75. No longer reliable is Levick 1967, 38-40.

[325]French 1981-1988, 2:520-21.

The road system of the Roman Empire in the first century could boast of roads about 90,000 km in length. If we add the secondary and tertiary roads, which were paved, there were perhaps 300,000 km of roads.[326] The quality of the large Roman roads was such that they were still in use in the Middle Ages and in early modern times. The expansion of the existing road system not only served military purposes but also intended to improve the infrastructure to facilitate the transport of wheat and other products, depending on the local situation. The network of roads in Pamphylia has been well documented (see figs. 26-27): the main artery was the Via Sebaste, many secondary roads branched off from main roads linked with the Via Sebaste, and smaller roads linked the smaller settlements with each other.[327]

Presumably the apostles did not use a carriage, as this would have necessitated ownership or rental of a vehicle and caused expenses for the accommodation and feeding of the animals; co-workers and wives who accompanied them would have required a second or even a third vehicle. And we must recall that the advantage of these carriages, which were not fitted with springs, "was not so much the comfort or the higher travel speed, but the possibility of transporting luggage."[328] A horse or mule for riding was hardly an option either, prohibited by the costs involved and by the fact that riding was not as advanced (lacking, e.g., horseshoe, saddle) for the nonmilitary traveler as in later times. The apostles covered the distances that they traveled by foot. This means of transport made it necessary to limit baggage to the absolute minimum.

In regard to travel by ship, there were no passenger ships as such, nor were there fixed shipping schedules. Nevertheless, we read of large numbers of passengers who traveled by ship. Josephus reports six hundred passengers for one particular sea voyage (*Vita* 15), a figure that scholars accept as a regular number of passengers.[329] Luke mentions 276 passengers for the ship that transported Paul to Rome (Acts 27:37). Passengers on ships had to bring their own food, and they had to take care of sleeping arrangements and protection against the elements by themselves. Cabins were scarce and expensive. Sea voyages over longer distances usually were booked in the offices of the shipping companies that regularly serviced particular routes. Shorter voyages along the coast could be booked on ships in the harbor. The largest ship known from antiquity could transport between 1,700 and 1,900 tons. The freight ships that transported wheat from Alexandria to Rome carried approximately 1,300 tons. There is no precise information about the costs of sea travel. Peter Lampe calculated the costs for

[326]Reck 1991, 82.
[327]See French 1992, 172.
[328]Reck 1991, 82-83; for the observation that follows above see ibid., 83.
[329]See Geoffrey Rickman, *The Corn Supply of Ancient Rome* (Oxford: Clarendon, 1980), 124. For the observations that follow above see Reck 1991, 83-84.

the four known sea voyages of Aquila and Priscilla (Pontus to Rome, Rome to Corinth, Corinth to Ephesus, Ephesus to Rome) and suggests that they cost less than 1,000 sesterces.[330]

Winter travel was avoided whenever possible. Shipping was closed between September or the beginning of November and March 5, the *ploiaphesia Isidis* (or *navigium Isidis*), not only because of the winter storms (cf. Acts 27:9-44) but also because navigation was possible only with clear skies.

In regard to the speed of travel, what Aelius Aristides wrote in the second century applied also during the first century:

"When were there so many cities on land or throughout the sea, or when have they been so thoroughly adorned? Who then ever made such a journey, numbering the cities by the days of his trip, or sometimes passing through two or three cities on the same day, as it were through avenues?" (*Oration Regarding Rome, Or.* 26.93).

An experienced traveler could journey on foot not much slower than people traveling on animals or in carriages. People who traveled to a court date were expected to travel 20 Roman miles (29 km or 18 mi.) per day.[331] Exceptionally fast travel times included a ride by Cato averaging 81 Roman miles (119 km or 74 mi.) per day for five days, and Caesar's voyage from Rome to the Rhone River in eight days, averaging 100 Roman miles (147 km or 91 mi.) per day. A typical pedestrian could travel between 15 and 20 Roman miles (22 to 29 km or 14 to 18 mi.) per day. Travel by mule-drawn carriage could cut the travel times in half. As far as sea voyages are concerned, the speed of travel depended on many factors. With fair winds, a ship could reach 4.5 to 6 knots, which means that the voyage from Puteoli, the harbor of Rome, to Corinth could be covered in four to five days, although usually it took one to two weeks. With headwinds, only 1.5 to 2.5 knots could be reached. In the Mediterranean the main wind direction during the shipping seasons was northwesterly. This means that the voyage from Rome to Alexandria lasted, with favorable winds, ten days, and the return voyage from Alexandria to Rome at least twenty days. William Ramsay was more cautious, estimating that one needed fifty days for the voyage from Alexandria to Rome.[332]

Wealthy travelers were accompanied by a large baggage train. Common people did not travel alone, however, especially on long overland voyages. They traveled with a companion or joined a group of travelers going in the same direction. Staying overnight in the same inn or sailing on the same ship made it easy to travel in groups.

---

[330]Lampe 1987, 162-64 (ET, 2003, 193-195); cf. Reck 1991, 84 n. 113.

[331]For the observations that follow above see Reck 1991, 86-87.

[332]W. M. Ramsay, "Roads and Travel in the New Testament," *Dictionary of the Bible* (extra vol.; ed. J. Hastings; Edinburgh: T & T Clark, 1909), 375-402, esp. 381; cf. Reck 1991, 87 n. 131.

There were two basic possibilities for accommodations: staying in a private
home of friends, acquaintances or acquaintances of acquaintances, or lodging
in a guest house. Wealthy travelers probably stayed mostly with friends or in
villas they owned. A traveler without connections had no choice but to stay in
commercial guest houses. The larger cities had "a broad range of hotels, restaurants and similar establishments."[333] Along the large overland routes *mansiones*
every 40 to 55 km (one day's journey with a carriage) provided hospitality, particularly to the more well-to-do travelers. Two smaller *mutationes* between the
mansiones allowed travelers to change animals and to buy something to eat. Pedestrians also could stay overnight in the *mutationes*. In other words, travelers
could expect to find an inn every 17 km (10.5 mi.) or so. If there was no room
in the *mutationes* or *mansions,* one had to stay in a *hospitium, deuersorium,
caupona* or *stabulum,* establishments that had a bad reputation. People who
worked in inns (*cauponae*), taverns (*popinae*) or restaurants occupied the bottom rung of the social ladder; we read of thieves and prostitutes, of bugs and
bad food. Hospitality played an important role for the travels of the early Christian missionaries, particularly at a period for which we can assume the existence
of a greater number of Christian communities, as indicated by, for example, the
comments in 3 John 5-8.[334]

Travel in the first century was safer than in previous times. Still, there were
dangers that we must not underestimate. Paul includes the following events in
the list of afflictions that he suffered (2 Cor 11:25-26):

2 Cor 11:25-26: "Three times I was beaten with rods. Once I received a stoning. Three
times I was shipwrecked; for a night and a day I was adrift at sea; [26]on frequent journeys,
in danger from rivers, danger from bandits, danger from my own people, danger from
Gentiles, danger in the city, danger in the wilderness, danger at sea."

Sea voyages could end in shipwreck. Travelers on land were in danger from
highwaymen, robbers and innkeepers. Greek sources document professional
robbers (*lēstēs*) and kidnappers (*andrapodistēs*) who robbed travelers not only
of their possessions but also sometimes of their freedom. Some people simply
disappeared—for example, into estates where they had to work as slaves, but
without the possibility of being released after seven years, which was granted

---

[333]Reck 1991, 89; on this subject see ibid., 88-89; see also A. Hug, PW 10.2 (1919): 2459-61; 18.3
(1949): 520-29; E. Badian and A. Spawforth, *OCD* 759-60; Tönnes Kleberg, *Hôtels, restaurants
et cabarets dans l`antiquité romaine: Études historiques et philologiques* (Bibliotheca Ekma-
niana 61; Uppsala, Almqvist & Wiksell, 1957). For a reevaluation of the view that all women
associated with hospitality businesses were prostitutes see John DeFelice, *Roman Hospitality:
The Professional Women of Pompeii* (Marco Polo Monographs 6; Warren Center, Pa.: Shangri-
La Publications, 2001; see the review by John R. Clarke in *Bryn Mawr Classical Review*
2002.06.33).
[334]See Di Berardino 1999, 240-44; Rapske 1994b, 15.

to house slaves.[335] Depending on the region (mountains, deserts, swamps) and the season (summer, winter), storms, heat and cold created dangerous situations for the traveler. Illness and accidents could not be ruled out either, of course, nor the problem of running out of money.

International Mobility

The *pax Romana* and the uniform political and administrative structures encouraged communication between the various regions and provinces.[336] The mobility of individual occupational groups demonstrates the numerous contacts in local, regional and supraregional frameworks. The travels of the following groups were not only characteristic but also a necessity of their profession: artists such as singers, musicians, poets, declaimers, companies of actors, puppet theaters, mimes, pantomimes, animal trainers, acrobats, prestidigitators, conjurers, rope dancers, knife throwers, fire eaters, snake charmers, ventriloquists, imitators of animal voices; athletes such as runners, wrestlers and gladiators; architects, stonemasons, fortune tellers, interpreters of dreams, faith healers, mendicants, and traders and merchants. Increased and regular communication is reflected in the epigraphical evidence for foreigners in many cities of the Mediterranean world. Syrian merchants from Apameia, Laodikeia ad Mare and Palmyra are attested on Rhodes and Delos, in Italy (Brundisium, Puteoli), Spain (Carthage Nova, Malaca, Corduba, Hispalis/Sevilla), Gaul (Lugdunum/Lyon) and Germania (Augusta Treverorum/Trier, Augusta Vindelicorum/Augsburg).[337] Pamphylians and Pisidians who are attested both in various Pamphylian and Pisidian cities and outside their home regions are a good illustration of intensive regional and supraregional communication. In Perge people from Side, Aspendos, Selge and Tarsus are attested as having made dedications to the temple of Artemis; foreigners from Termessos, Cremna, Klaudiopolis and Byzantion living in Perge are attested as well. In Side one could meet people from Aspendos, Perge and Aigeai (Cilicia), and in Aspendos people from Selge, Synnada, Apamea and Myra (Lycia). In Pisidian Antiocheia we find people from Synnada, Sagalassos, Adada and Dokimeion. In Athens one could meet citizens of Aspendos, Side, Perge, Oroandeis, Selge, Termessos, Pisidian Antiocheia and from other cities. Inscriptions found on the Greek islands of Syros and Nisyros attest residents from Perge and Pisidia. In an inscription found in Perge a runner boasts to have been victorious in games in Halikarnassos, Kleitor, Ilion, Corinth, Plataiai, Tralleis, Epidaurus and Lusoi.

---

[335]See B. Winter 2000, 287.

[336]For the observations that follow above see Brandt 1992, 138, 147-48.

[337]Glen W. Bowersock, "Social and Economic History of Syria under the Roman Empire," in Dentzer and Orthmann 1989, 64-80, esp. 75-76. On the runner in Perge mentioned in the discussion that follows above see *EA* 11 (1988): no. 56.

Tourism was a well-known phenomenon in antiquity. People traveled for pleasure, out of curiosity, for educational purposes; they traveled to vacation destinations, spas, pilgrimage sites, temples, games and festivals.[338] Pausanias of Magnesia ad Sipylum in Lydian Asia Minor wrote, around A.D. 150, *Description of Greece* (Περιήγησις τῆς Ἑλλάδος), in which he describes regions, cities and monuments, essentially in Achaia (Attica, Megara, Argolis, Laconia, Messenia, Elis, Olympia, Achaea, Arcadia, Boeotia, Phocis, Delphi).[339] Pausanias had visited not only Greece but also Rome, Syria and Palestine as well as Egypt, where he traveled as far as Thebes. Only the wealthy could travel to more distant places. The lower classes visited the numerous regional games, temples and baths.

The itinerant popular philosophers often are included among the traveling performers. They are mentioned separately here because their goals and communicative methods often are compared with those of the early Christian missionaries (see §§10.5; 16.2). The Stoic-Cynic popular philosophers were a well-known phenomenon in the Hellenistic period, with a second heyday in the first century.[340] They presented themselves on streets and plazas, in front of theaters and temples. They generally did not speak before a selected audience: they presented their teaching wherever people congregated. A Stoic-Cynic "sermon" is not documented, however. An important rhetorical element of their orations was the direct address in the second-person singular. The Cynics did not present systematic philosophical instruction: they took up contemporary subjects, pertinent questions of daily life that they presented using arguments, proverbs, anecdotes, witticisms, irony, rhetorical questions and fictitious dialogues.

The itinerant philosophers could easily be recognized by their appearance: they carried a pouch (*pēra*), a staff (*rabdos*) and a cloak (*tribōn*), and they let their hair grow long. The Cynic philosophers rarely enjoyed hospitality: they practiced the *kynikos bios,* which meant, among other things, that they did not own houses; they slept on the ground (at least that was the ideal), lived from charitable gifts and traveled by foot. They needed a robust voice, a certain measure of acting skills and some demagogic abilities. The Cynic philosophers had "a sense of mission as messengers of the gods and as educators of humankind."[341] They spoke with frankness: παρρησία (*parrēsia*) was one of the Cynic ideals.

---

[338]See Casson 1994, 229-99.

[339]Christian Habicht, *Pausanias und seine "Beschreibung Griechenlands"* (Munich: Beck, 1985; English: *Pausanias' Guide to Ancient Greece* [Sather Classical Lectures; Berkeley: University of California Press, 1985]); Karim W. Arafat, *Pausanias' Greece Ancient Artists and Roman Rulers* (New York: Cambridge University Press, 1996); Susan E. Alcock et al., *Pausanias Travel and Memory in Roman Greece* (New York: Oxford University Press, 2000). See also C. Auffarth, "'Verräter—Übersetzer'? Pausanias, das römische Patrai und die Identität der Griechen in der Achaea," in Cancik and Rüpke 1997, 219-38, esp. 220.

[340]On the ideal Cynic see Billerbeck 1978, 6-9; 1979; see also idem, ed., *Die Kyniker in der modernen Forschung* (Amsterdam: Grüner, 1991); Marie-Odile Goulet-Cazé, "Le cynisme à l'époque impériale," *ANRW* II.36.4 (1990): 2720-2833.

[341]Reck 1991, 136.

Their often blunt and direct presentations again and again caused conflicts with their audiences and the magistrates of the cities that they visited. They were banned from Rome repeatedly: under Nero, under Vespasian and twice under Domitian. For a discussion of the similarities with the early Christian missionaries see §§10.2; 16.5.

Another cause for travel were the wars and regional conflicts that displaced countless people. Caesar and Augustus promoted deliberate resettlement policies: they relocated hundreds of thousands of proletarians from Rome, Italic people and veterans, settling them in the provinces. These policies resulted in enormous migration flows from Rome to the provinces and from one province to another.

Other travelers included officials of the imperial administration and military personnel. High imperial officials often were transferred to new posts, cities and provinces: officials working in the finance departments, in the census bureaus, in taxation, in mints and in the postal service, in the grain administration, in the administration of the police and the military, in public works departments (building of temples, theaters, aqueducts, roads) and at the imperial court. The mid-level personnel in the bureaus of the prefects and procurators, who were recruited from among freedmen and slaves, were transferred less frequently. Soldiers who served in the legions of the Roman army, augmented by auxiliary troops recruited in the provinces, could be transferred on short notice to other cities within the empire.

A final group of travelers were the slaves. Slavery generally was connected with an enforced change of residence: there was the deportation at the beginning of enslavement and the transport after sale and resale. Wealthy people often were accompanied by slaves. The main flow of slaves was from east to west. A frequent problem was the escape of slaves, who would have used the roads to travel to other cities or back home.

If a philosopher of Perge in Pamphylia and a medical doctor of Side could work in Rome, if a woman of Pogla in Pisidia could accompany her husband on his travels, visiting Italy and many other countries, then clearly it was not a curious event when a Jewish legal scholar of Tarsus in Cilicia visited not only cities in his home province but also traveled to Cyprus, Pamphylia, Pisidia, Phrygia, Asia, Macedonia and Achaia.[342]

The mobility that was possible in the first century should not be overestimated as an "ideal situation" as far as the travels of the early Christian missionaries are concerned. It surely was relatively easy, albeit uncomfortable, to travel on the large paved Roman roads with their resthouses and inns—for example, from Jerusalem in Judea to Antioch in Syria, and from Antioch to Tarsus in Cilicia, and from there to Ephesus or Sardis or Pergamon in the province of Asia.

---

[342]See *IGUR* 371.626 (Perge); *CIL* VI 9580 (Side); *SEG* XIX 840 (Pogla).

But the early Christian missionaries were not dependent upon the system of the paved Roman roads. Similar to the merchants who traveled from city to city selling their goods, they would not have minded traveling by foot on unpaved roads from place to place. Unpaved roads often were solidly built and regularly used by the local population. And for pedestrians, the width of a road and the state of its maintenance are unimportant.

Communication Activities

Communication activities include all means of procuring, transmitting and disseminating information.[343] The most important means of transregional communication in antiquity was the letter. The oral message carried by messenger and the written letter were the main means of communicating with a specific group of recipients.[344] There was no general postal system (an invention of the sixteenth century) in the Roman Empire that the average citizen could have used to send letters to relatives or friends. Augustus introduced a postal system for the whole empire (Suetonius, *Aug.* 49.3) designed specifically for government purposes. The *vehicula,* later designated *cursus publicus,* was a well-organized and reliable government communication network that permitted long-distance communication for imperial officials who had the proper warrants (*diplomata*). The couriers (*tabellarii, speculatores*) could travel 70 km (43 mi.) per day for several days; one-day journeys of 100 km (or 62 mi.) were not unheard of. The *cursus publicus* generally could not be used for private purposes. The regular citizen had to use other means of communication: one could personally deliver information to relatives, friends or business partners, or send a reliable slave as a courier, or wait for a friend, a merchant acquaintance or even a stranger to travel to the destination of this "mail." For many people the last option was the only possibility. Despite these difficulties there was an intensive exchange of letters in Greek and especially Roman times, attested, for example, in the numerous letters that Cicero wrote and received.[345] Every traveler was a potential carrier of letters.

Municipal and imperial edicts were another means of communication. Official decrees by city magistrates were published in written form (inscriptions) at public places (e.g., in temples). In Greek cities heralds proclaimed decisions of the city council orally. Means of public communication by private individuals included, depending on interests, goals and financial resources, commercial advertisements, private ads, handbills, election posters and graffiti.

---

[343]For the observations that follow above see Riepl 1913; more recently Reck 1991, 106-18.
[344]Reck 1991, 108. On the postal service see O. Seeck, PW 4.2 (1901): 1846-62; W. H. Gross, *KP* 1:1346-47; N. Purcell, *OCD* 1233-34; Ausbüttel 1998, 104-14; Casson 1994, 182-90; see also S. Mitchell, "Requisitioned Transport in the Roman Empire," *JRS* 66 (1976): 106-31.
[345]J. Nicholson, "The Delivery and Confidentiality of Cicero's Letters," *CJ* 90 (1994): 33-63.

Since 59 B.C. Caesar published the *acta publica*, a gazette that recorded public events and ceremonies, lawsuits and public speeches, and the *acta senatus*, which recorded the proceedings in the senate, whose wider publication Augustus prohibited.[346] The *acta* was an officially edited instrument of imperial propaganda. They were published at public bulletin boards; copies, excerpts and oral dissemination made the relevant information known to the wider public. In Alexandria papyri document the existence of *acta Alexandrinorum*,[347] written for the Greek-speaking population of Egypt, informing about the new rulers. Julian Krüger observes, "Especially people in Alexandria were particularly interested in the events that took place at the imperial court. They received new information relatively quickly via the sea routes."[348]

Books and Libraries

The Greco-Roman world knew books, booksellers and book publishers.[349] Booksellers did not exist in every city: Pliny the Younger was surprised to learn of bookshops (*bibliopola*) in Lugdunum, and he expressed his joy about the fact that his works were popular outside of Rome as well (*Ep.* 9.11.2). The size of a book was limited by the capacity of the papyrus scroll: academic books generally had 1,100 to 4,500 lines of text, poetic books between 700 and 1,100 lines. The book trade played no role in the early Christian mission. The costs for the production, publication and dissemination of books that could convince Jews and Gentiles of the truth of the Christian message was prohibitive. However, the information that we possess about the production of books in the Greco-Roman period indicates that the level of education of the upper class was considerable and demonstrates the significance of supraregional contacts for information and educational purposes. People who were interested in certain books had contacts in other cities who bought and sent the books to them. The more than 1,400 papyri fragments of classical literary works that have been found in Oxyrhynchus, a city in Middle Egypt about 400 km (250 mi.) from Alexandria,[350] document the intensive grammatical, geographical and scientific interest of the educated class in the city. These books (or "scrolls") evidently belonged to the libraries of the gymnasia and to private libraries, and the pagan religious texts belonged to temples (and the Christian texts to churches).

---

[346]J. P. Balsdon and A. W. Lintott, *OCD* 10; cf. Riepl 1913, 387-429; Reck 1991, 118.

[347]See P.Oxy. 2177, 2264, 2435, 2690, 3021. The fragment P.Oxy. 2435 dates to the early first century, P.Oxy. 3021 dates to the first century as well.

[348]Krüger 1990, 212.

[349]See Reck 1991, 118-20; H. Maehler, *OCD* 252.

[350]See the lists in Krüger 1990, 162-87, 214-45 (referring to texts that were not published until 1989). The 169 fragments of Homer's *Iliad* should be augmented by the five *Iliad* texts published in *The Oxyrhynchus Papyri*, vol. 56.

About 32 percent of the literary papyri have text on the inside and the outside. It seems that civil servants took discarded administrative documents and reused them for copying literary texts.[351] These reused papyri probably came from private individuals or from schools. About 68 percent of the literary papyri have text only on one side and thus represent relatively expensive editions that probably belonged to the library of a gymnasium or to the library of a scholar. The postscript of the letter fragment P.Oxy. 2192 (second century) suggests that in Oxyrhynchus itself texts were copied and sold for commercial purposes. The literary papyri include fragments of texts of Homer (174 fragments of the *Iliad*), Hesiod, Pindar, Xenophon, Aristotle, Plato, Euripides, Thucydides, Demosthenes, Virgil, Cicero, Livy and Sallust. In the first century people in Oxyrhynchus read, at least, the works of Alkaios, Alkmanos, Anakreon, Apion, Apollonios of Rhodes, Archilochos, Bakchylides, Dionysios Skytobrachion, Euphorion, Eupolis, Euripides, Hesiod, Hippocrates, Homer, Isocrates, Kallimachos, Menander, Nikandros, Philodemos, Pindar, Sappho, Sophron, Stesichoros, Theocritus, Theon, Thucydides, Virgil and Xenophon.[352] This list indicates that nearly all literary genres were represented.

A cover letter for a book consignment sent to Oxyrhynchus in the first century illustrates how common it must have been to send books with advice on how to read them with profit (apart from documenting the significance of Stoic philosophy in Middle Egypt):

"Theon to Herakleides, his friend, Greetings. As I earnestly seek to procure useful books, as beneficial as possible for our way of living, thus I think you should also deign (and) not be negligent in (your) reading. Those who seriously seek to benefit, gain not only a general benefit. What has been sent through Achillas is listed (below). Farewell. I am doing well also. Greet everyone concerned. Written in Alexandreia. Of Boethos 'Exercise.' Of Diogenes 'On Marriage.' Of Diogenes 'On Mourning.' Of Chrysippos 'On the Usefulness of Parents.' Of Antipatros 'On the Usefulness of Slaves.' Of Poseidonios 'On Exorcism III.'"[353]

It is a realistic possibility that Christians sent copies of the Gospels to other churches at an early time and across larger distances.[354]

Several papyri from Oxyrhynchus document that literary works could be read in Middle Egypt not long after publication elsewhere. Virgil (70-19 B.C.) was read in Oxyrhynchus in the first century (P.Oxy. 3554). The glossaries on Homer that the grammarian Apion had written in the first half of the first century A.D. were read in the first century in Oxyrhynchus (P.Ryl. 26), the poet Babrios (around A.D. 100) in the second century (P.Oxy. 1249), the poet Pankrates (early second century) also in the second century (P.Oxy. 1085), as the Chronicle of Phlegon (P.Oxy. 2082).[355]

---

[351]Krüger 1990, 159, with reference to E. G. Turner, "Roman Oxyrhynchus," *JEA* 38 (1952): 78-93, esp. 90. For the observations that follow above see Krüger 1990, 161.

[352]For the evidence in detail see Krüger 1990, 228-29. The Latin texts include a number of anonymous texts.

[353]P.Mil.Vogl. 11 (ed. A. Vogliano, 1937). The text is available online in the Duke Databank of Documentary Papyri <http://www.perseus.tufts.edu/cache/perscoll_DDBDP.html>. German translation in Krüger 1990, 205-6.

[354]See Bauckham 1998.

[355]Krüger 1990, 224-25.

Oral Communication

The oral transmission of information is of fundamental importance for a society without mass media.[356] In the various situations of daily life oral communication is not only a necessity on a practical level but also a basic human need. Reinhold Reck comments, "The extensive and intensive dissemination of news, that is, the extent of the circle to which it spreads, and the degree of completeness with which it penetrates to the people it reaches depend on the strength of the inherent tendency to diffusion, on the degree of interest that the news causes."[357] The problem with oral communication, however, is that the dissemination of information is unregulated and the correctness of information cannot be confirmed, which means that it quickly can become rumor. A rumor "differs from information in that the path of information from its origins to the recipient can no longer be ascertained and therefore its content cannot be verified."[358] Rumors usually move within narrow social groups that they penetrate only slowly.

The function of rumor in antiquity (ἡ φήμη, *hē phēmē;* Lat., *fama, rumor,* "rumor, glory, prestige of a person"; *sermo,* "gossip"; *nuntium,* "news") can be summarized as follows. (1) Information is regarded as "rumor" if it cannot be traced back to a concrete and reliable source (Cicero, *Fam.* 12.4: *auctor erat nemo*). (2) Rumors are transmitted orally from neighbor to neighbor. People who wanted to get a rumor going organized helpers who spread the rumor simultaneously at different places (Tacitus, *Ann.* 2.39). (3) People were aware of the fact that a rumor could attain speeds that a courier service without exchange of couriers could reach only in exceptional cases (Livy 24.21.4-5). Plutarch (*Aem.* 24) relates that a rumor of a victory in Pydna in southern Macedonia, about 800 km from Rome as the crow flies, arrived in Rome after four days, which amounts to a speed of nearly 300 km per day. (4) The dissemination of a rumor depended on the interest that the news had for the population and on the topicality of the news. News that is of general interest can spread quickly in the entire city (Cicero, *Fam.* 8.1) or in the entire country (Tacitus, *Ann.* 2.40). News also can spread within a particular group (e.g., Jews) from province to province (Philo, *Flacc.* 45). (5) News with positive content, and particularly of negative content, is passed on from mouth to mouth. (6) Evidence for the reliability of a rumor was the firmness and the continuance of the oral news (Cicero, *Fam.* 12.9-10). However, tendencies to exaggerate, to elaborate and to mix truth and falsehood were strong (Tacitus, *Ann.* 4.12; Ovid, *Metam.* 9.137-139). (7) The reactions to rumors included the organization of victory celebrations (Livy 45.1.3), the destruction of a bridge over the Rhine River (Tacitus, *Ann.* 1.69), the cessation of commercial activities (Plutarch, *Pomp.* 15), and parlor games (Tacitus, *Hist.* 4.12). (8) Rumors were denied or refuted with arguments (Plutarch, *Alex.* 3; Tacitus, *Ann.* 4.11). Some rumors petered out by themselves (Plutarch,

---

[356]For the observations that follow above see Reck 1991, 120-29.
[357]Reck 1991, 121, with reference to John F. Kennedy on November 22, 1963: within one hour of the first radio broadcast at 12:30 in the afternoon, 82 percent of the citizens of Denver had heard of the shooting, mostly from other people through oral communication. In contrast to rumor, gossip is always "news" about people but may rest on true facts.
[358]Reck 1991, 121. On rumor see ibid., 124-29; also Hans-Joachim Neubauer, *The Rumor: A Cultural History* (London: Free Association Books, 1999); Allan J. Kimmel, *Rumors and Rumor Control* (Mahwah, N.J.: Lawrence Erlbaum, 2003).

Aem. 24-25). A Jewish sage compared the transience of a rumor with the transience of life (Wis 5:9).

The intentional use of rumors as a "method" of missionary work was entirely unsuitable. (1) The early Christian missionaries, at least the apostles, including Paul, understood themselves as eyewitnesses who heard Jesus teach and who saw the risen Jesus Christ, who could personally vouch for the reliability of their message of the crucified and risen Savior. (2) The miracles of Jesus and the miracles that happened in the ministry of the missionaries would provoke interest in the message of the Christians, even more so the report of Jesus' resurrection. However, since the Greek and Roman contemporaries of the apostles in the first century were accustomed to tales of supernatural and miraculous events from their traditional myths of their gods, and since many temples and oracles promised miracles and divine revelations, the interest in the Christian preachers was hardly so instantaneous and extraordinary that rumors of their activities would have spread like wildfire. The experience of Barnabas and Paul in Lystra in Lycaonia (Acts 14:8-20) may be regarded as an exception, with negative consequences, however: the refusal of the missionaries to act in conformity with local traditions caused the stoning of Paul. (3) The central message of the Christians is hardly news that is easily and dynamically transformed into rumor that people talk about and spread willingly and enthusiastically—the message that the Messiah had been rejected by the Jewish authorities in Jerusalem, condemned to crucifixion by the Roman governor, and died and risen from the dead on the third day, and that he is the only Savior in the world, who can rescue from all guilt and forgive all sins once and for all. (4) The good news of Jesus Christ does not consist of a single event or some basic truth or sentence that can easily and quickly be passed on by word of mouth: the message of God's eschatological revelation in Jesus, the crucified and risen Messiah, was a scandal for Jews and nonsense for Greeks. This was the actual experience of the early Christian missionaries, according to Luke's account in the book of Acts, and this was the inescapable consequence of the nature of the gospel, as Paul explains in 1 Cor 1:18-25. The gospel needs to be explained and elaborated; it cannot be condensed into a rumor.

Public Speech

Public speeches in important recurring social situations constituted the most important form for communicating information and influencing people: in the city council, before courts of law, before the troops in the legions, at victory celebrations, at funerals and in the ethical discourse of itinerant philosophers. It is no surprise that the Greeks reflected since earliest times on the most effective ways of preparing and delivering a speech. The subject matter of "rhetoric," as these endeavors were called, was all speech-acts that produce conviction. Aristotle writes, "Rhetoric then may be defined as the faculty of discovering the possible means of persuasion in reference to any subject whatever."[359]

The foundational method of argumentation in public speech is the proposition (λόγος, *logos*), which is formulated either deductively (enthymematic) or inductively (paradigmatic). A second method is the delineation of character (ἦθος, *ethos*), describing the credibility, erudition, moral integrity and friendly disposition of a person. A third method is emotional treatment (πάθος, *pathos*), with the goal of influencing the emotions on the basis of which people make decisions or that need to be known if one wants to influence others—for example, whether they are (or can be influenced to be) angry, friendly or forbearing. In antiquity rhetoric belonged to the basic sciences because a speech delivered to a live audience is unmatched in its ability to influence people immediately.[360] Jesus in Galilee, Peter in Jerusalem, Paul in Athens, Corinth, Ephesus and in many other cities seek to influence the thinking and the behavior of people by public speech. Luke's account in the book of Acts explicitly describes many such situations with regard to Peter and Paul. This feature of the early Christian missionary work will be discussed further (see §28.2).

Synagogues

The first missionaries, without exception, were Jews. The only Jewish institution outside Jerusalem in which speeches were given and discussions took place on questions of faith was the synagogue. It is not surprising that Paul, according to Luke's account in the book of Acts, first visited the synagogues and shared his message with Jewish audiences when he started a new missionary outreach in a city.

The synagogue was the central institution of Diaspora Judaism.[361] The assembly halls, usually called προσευχή (*proseuchē,* "place of prayer"), fulfilled a wide spectrum of functions: they could serve as a meeting place for religious services and community events or as a school, library, hostel or hospital. The leaders of the synagogue were the contacts of the Jewish community with the Gentile world, particularly with the city magistrates. Reinhold Reck comments, "The imperial edicts on associations evidently did not apply to the synagogues directly. In contrast to the associations, membership was not really voluntary but based on ethnicity; the by-laws were not arbitrary but stipulated by the Torah."[362] In Alexandria the various synagogues were combined in the *politeuma* with a coun-

[359]Aristotle, *Rhet.* 1355b: ἔστω δὴ ἡ ῥητορικὴ δύναμις περὶ ἕκαστον τοῦ θεωρῆσαι τὸ ἐνδεχόμενον πιθανόν. The literature on this topic is immense; see Lausberg 1960; G. Kennedy 1972; J. Martin 1974; Fuhrmann 1984.
[360]Reck 1991, 129.
[361]See §8.2. See also Kasher 1995, 205-15; Levinskaya 1996, 207-25; L. Levine 2000, 127-28; on the offices listed in the discussion that follows above see also Lichtenberger 1996a, 20-23.
[362]Reck 1991, 144-45. On the Diaspora synagogues see L. Levine 2000, 232-87.

cil (*gerousia*). However, the relationship between the individual synagogues and this governing body is not entirely clear.

Walter Ameling summarizes the extant knowledge about the Jewish communities in Asia Minor.[363] Jews arrived in Asia Minor during the Persian period as slaves, mercenaries or travelers. Larger groups of Jews settled in Asia Minor since the third century B.C. as a result of the military policies of the Seleucid king Antiochos III, who between 212 and 205 B.C. settled about two thousand Jewish families from Mesopotamia and Babylonia in Lydia and Phrygia as a safeguard in politically unstable regions. Another reason for the influx of Jews into Asia Minor was the growth of the Jewish population in Palestine. The Jewish communities had the legal status of an association. However, the structure of the relationship between the Jewish communities and the cities in which they lived as well as the organization of the Jewish communities themselves was not uniform: the authorizing procedures for an association of resident aliens (*metoikoi*) and the statutes for which authorization was sought may have varied from city to city. Nor were the (official) titles of the leaders and functionaries of the synagogues uniform. Recognition from the city magistrate allowed members of a synagogue to govern their own affairs. The Jewish communities did not have a supraregional organization. The only measure that linked the Jewish Diaspora communities with one another was the temple tax, which was collected in districts and taken to Jerusalem. The "center" was not the most important synagogue in the region, however, but rather the centers of the assize districts of the Roman governors.

Walter Ameling argues that this fact undermines the hypothesis of Gerd Theissen, who argues that the supraregional cooperation of the Christian communities was a result of their Jewish heritage.[364] Ameling believes that such federations are "Christian property" ("christliches Eigentum"), which "perhaps finds its explanation in the significance of itinerant charismatics, missionaries, etc."

The sources attest the following offices: leaders or presidents of the synagogues (*archisynagōgoi*), leaders, officials (*archontes*), council of elders (*gerousia*) and elders (*presbyteroi*), scribes (*grammateis*), readers (*anagnōstai*), servants (*diakonoi*), priests (*hiereis*), singers of psalms (*psalmologoi*), finance officials (*phrontistai*) and defenders or benefactors (*prostatai*).

The Jews were regarded as "aliens" who had brought their own cult, just as other foreigners had. This changed after the destruction of the temple in A.D. 70, when Vespasian abolished the temple tax that had been collected by the Diaspora Jews for the temple in Jerusalem, and when he diverted this tax to the temple of Jupiter Capitolinus in Rome: the *fiscus Iudaicus* received the poll tax

[363]Ameling 1996, 29-55.
[364]Theissen 1991, 346. For the observation that follows above see Ameling 1996, 37.

of two denarii a year, which all Jews had to pay. Loyalty to the Jewish faith and payment of the *fiscus Iudaicus* "defined" who was a "Jew"; those who left the synagogue community did not have to pay the tax. Gentiles who attended the synagogues as "God-fearers" did not have to pay the *fiscus Iudaicus,* as they were not official members of the Jewish community. It is therefore not surprising that the Aphrodisias inscriptions (see §6.2) record only three proselytes but fifty-four God-fearers, including God-fearers of the second and third generations.

Ancient authors repeatedly comment on the way of life of the Jews being different from that of other people, especially in the area of their food laws, marriage laws and festival calendar, and their refusal to participate in the cults of the city. Jewish life in the synagogues and with its institutions heightened the impression of separation. Josephus reports for the first century B.C. that Jews complained about their Gentile fellow citizens: they complained that "people stole their holy books from the synagogues. They were forced to appear before court on the sabbath and on holy days. They were hindered in sending the temple tax, these monies were even stolen; they forced the temple tax to be used for other purposes, as the Jews were coerced to liturgies [work for the state at their own expense] and military service."[365] Riots against the Jews caused by the Gentile population sometimes were accompanied by bureaucratic harassment. When the crisis caused by the turbulences of the civil war during the last decades of the Roman Republic had come to an end, peaceful coexistence between the Jewish communities and the Greek cities was reestablished in the first century A.D., as confirmed by Luke's account in the book of Acts.

The separation of the Jews from their Gentile surroundings was not absolute, however. The Jews living in Asia Minor could not be distinguished from their pagan neighbors in terms of appearance, dress, language and profession. Most Jews had Greek names. The prohibition of mixed marriages (i.e., marrying a non-Israelite) was not always followed, as the example of Timothy's parents demonstrates (Acts 16:3).[366] Members of the Jewish community had regular, fixed seats in the theater.[367] In cities one could find Jews among the ephebes and in the gymnasium.[368] Jews adopted local funerary traditions, and they buried their deceased in the necropolis of the city in which they lived. The Jewish associations imitated the organization of the Greek cities. The Diaspora Jews had to justify and integrate their participation in pagan institutions and traditions with regard to their religious convictions. It was not always easy to maintain a balance between their own Jewish traditions and pagan customs.

---

[365]Ameling 1996, 48-49; the observation that follows above, ibid., with reference to Josephus, *A.J.* 14.213-216, 223-230, 235-240, 256-258, 262-264; 16.27-65, 160-161, 167-168, 171-173, 235.

[366]See also *TAM* III 1, 448; *CPJ* 144; Josephus, *B.J.* 2.463.

[367]*CIG* II 748 = *IJudO* II 37 (Miletus); *SEG* XXXVII 846-487 = *IJudO* II 15-16 (Aphrodisias).

[368]*IK* 17.2 3822 = *IJudO* II 47 (Hypaipa); 28.2 284 = *IJudO* II 22 (Iasos); *SEG* XXXVI 970 = *IJudO* II 14 (Aphrodisias).

Tessa Rajak uses the phrase "the art of Diaspora living" when she describes the practical consequences of this challenge for the Jewish inscriptions concerning benefactions.[369] In contrast to their Gentile fellow citizens, Jews did not honor each other with statues, and many inscriptions leave the honors unmentioned that the donor had received. Rajak concludes, "To enter the Jewish world, as a sympathizer or proselyte, would have been to learn a new dialect of a familiar language."

Associations

The lowers classes in the Greek and Roman cities were allowed to organize themselves in associations or clubs (*collegia*).[370] These associations were controlled by the city magistrate, as there was no freedom of association in the Roman Empire.[371] Scholars usually distinguish religious associations, professional associations and burial associations. It seems, however, that few *collegia* were completely secular. The more obviously religious associations bridged the distance between the official state cult and the private cult practiced in the home. Since all ancient societies had a religious basis, cultic practices in a *collegium* are not automatically an indication of religious aims of the association. *Collegia* that were associated with trades and professions accepted as members mainly free citizens, although some accepted freedmen and sometimes even slaves, generally active practitioners of the particular trade. There is evidence for associations of shepherds, building trade workers, carpenters, potters, dyers, goldsmiths, bakers, traders, wholesalers, captains, sailors, artists, assistants at sacrifices, actors, flute players, civil servants, mercenaries, veterans. There is no evidence, however, that such trade associations aimed at improving their economic conditions: they were not guilds or unions. In most cases the real purpose was "to foster friendliness and social life among their members."[372] This included regular gatherings, common meals, festivities and common cultic activities. The by-laws often included stipulations for proper burials of club members. In cities the associations of carpenters, building trade workers and other professions capable of fighting fires functioned as a fire brigade.

The organizational framework of the associations was the city; supraregional associations were rare. The misuse of the by-laws of a *collegium* could lead to

---

[369]Rajak 1996, 318. Baruch Lifshitz had collected most of these inscriptions in *DF* (1967), a total of 102 inscriptions. For an analysis of 94 of these inscriptions see Rajak 1996, 310-18; the quotation that follows above, ibid., 319.

[370]The studies by Liebenam (1890) and Waltzing (1895-1900) are still basic; see also Kornemann, PW 4 (1900): 380-480; H. Hausmaninger, *KP* 1:1553-54; G. H. Stevenson and A. W. Lintott, *OCD* 352-53; Reck 1991, 130-33; Ascough 2002. See the *SEG* volumes, s.v. "Associations."

[371]See Alföldy 1975, 115.

[372]G. H. Stevenson and A. W. Lintott, *OCD* 352. For the observations that follow above see also Bleicken 1978, 2:89.

the dissolution of the association. If the by-laws stipulated assemblies of the members of the association, approval from the senate was required. The associations of the humbler population (*collegia tenuiorum*) that were regarded as not dangerous could organize with a general permission. The internal organization of the club was up to its members. Some associations had only a few members, while others had over one thousand people. Some associations had a building (*schola*), and others met in a temple or in the house of a member. The *collegia* financed themselves primarily through donations that the association officials were required to pay before assuming office, through admission fees of new members and through regular contributions from members (*stips menstrua*).

For Ostia, in the second century, forty religious and professional associations are attested. In Pergamon archaeologists discovered in 1980 a nearly complete cult room of the association of the *Bukoloi,* who devoted themselves to the worship of Dionysos.[373] This "Hall with the Podiums" (*Podiensaal*) is a rectangular building (24 by 10 m) with a paved court at the front. The walls of the cult room are lined by podiums (1 by 2 m). The small Dionysos altar on the eastern podium dates to the time of Augustus.

Wolfgang Radt describes the hall: "The cult community assembled in the hall, lying on the podiums with the feet toward the wall and the head toward the room. Calculations have shown that the hall could accommodate about seventy participants with this arrangement. On the forward edge of the podiums was a marble board on which the celebrants could place their drinking vessels, tableware and so on. . . . In the Hall with the Podiums much meat was eaten, as is indicated by the numerous remains of bones, found during the excavation, that had been trampled into the plaster of the floor. There were bones from oxen, pigs and poultry. The entire hall was plastered and painted, the walls and the cult niche as well as the front of the podiums and the small niches below the podiums. The walls of the hall were painted in rectangular areas. In the center of the rectangular areas small objects of scenes were depicted on a red background."

According to Reinhold Reck, the following features of the *collegia* are relevant for a discussion of the early Christian mission.[374] (1) The establishment of an association often was due to the initiative of an individual who then had a favorite position as *patronus*. Sometimes families were the basis of an association. (2) The main purpose of the associations was not economic, but social, political, cultural and religious. (3) The associations were locally constituted and organized. There were no tendencies toward regional or supraregional contacts or institutions, although there is some evidence for the establishment of associations on the basis of local unions of several clubs. (4) Associations generally were socially homogeneous: their members came from a similar religious, eth-

---

[373]Radt 1988, 224-28; the quotation that follows above, ibid., 225-26; cf. W. Radt, in H. Koester 1998, 28.
[374]Reck 1991, 130-33.

nic, professional or political background. Members were mostly men, which does not exclude the possibility, or likelihood, that women and children participated in the cultic and social activities of the *collegium*. (5) The associations had an organizational structure with by-laws and offices. (6) The members of the associations met regularly. There were business meetings and (cultic) festivals with meals. (7) The associations provided support to their members, according to stipulations in the by-laws, especially for burials. (8) The associations did not engage in propaganda for the club. (9) The associations were tolerated unless they were prohibited as *collegia illicita*. Associations that were regarded as dangerous were prohibited in the years 64 B.C. and 56 B.C., as well as under Caesar and Augustus. The status as a *collegium licitum* was applied for only in order to obtain the legal capacity of an incorporated body.

Schools

In regard to local structure and organization of community life, the early church had similarities with the *collegia*. In regard to universal orientation and substantial intentions, the early church had similarities with the philosophical schools. The philosophical schools wanted to provide "an evident explanation of human beings, of the gods and of the world" and to describe, on this basis, "a convincing and credible way of life."[375] It was not far-fetched when the Christian churches later were seen as philosophical schools.

Elementary education took place in the *gymnasion*, attested not only in the writings of Greek and Roman authors but also in inscriptions. In several cities in Asia Minor and Greece have been discovered lists of boys who excelled in competitions in various disciplines.[376]

The disciplines or classes of the gymnasiums can be categorized in four groups: (1) *Pedagogical classes:* reading and writing, reading out loud (ἀνάγνωσις, *anagnōsis*), calligraphy (καλλιγραφία, *kalligraphia*), arithmetic (ἀριθμητική, *arithmētikē*), orderly behavior (εὐταξία, *eutaxia*), industriousness (φιλοπονία, *philoponia*), general learning (πολυμαθία, *polymathia*). (2) *Sports:* running: long course (δόλιχος, *dolichos*) of a stadion (στάδιον, *stadion* [192 m; 210 yds. in Olympia]), double course of two stadia (δίαυλον, *diaulon*); wrestling (πάλη, *palē*), boxing (πυγμή, *pygmē*), combined boxing and wrestling match (παγκράτιον, *pankration*). (3) *Musical subjects:* singing to the harp (ψαλμῳδία, *psalmōdia*), playing on the cithara (κιθαρισμός, *kitharismos*), singing to the cithara (κιθαρῳδία, *kitharōdia*), recitation from comedies and tragedies (κωμῳδία, *kōmōdia;* τραγῳδία, *tragōdia*), recitation of epic poetry (ῥαψῳδία, *rapsōdia*). (4) *Military exercises:* throwing the javelin (ἀκόντιον, *akontion*), archery (τόξον, *toxon*), fighting with heavy weapons (ὁπλομαχία, *hoplomachia*), shooting with catapults (καταπάλτης, *katapaltēs*).

---

[375]Reck 1991, 134; for the observation that follows above see ibid.
[376]For the description that follows above see Wolfgang Blümel, "Inschriften aus Karien I," *EA* 25 (1995): 35-64, esp. 63.

The main communication process in the school consisted of the teacher sharing personal knowledge and experience with the students. In the Greco-Roman world people attended a school as children and teenagers for several years. In contrast, the early Christian missionaries knew the concept of lifelong learning from the synagogues, which were centers of spiritual and intellectual education for adult Jews as well teaching centers for children and youngsters.[377]

Mystery Cults

The early Christian churches and their religious services have been compared by some scholars with the mystery cults that were mentioned earlier.[378] The major communicative feature of the mystery cults were the cultic celebrations.[379] There were fixed liturgies, concrete representations of the sacred, exegesis, liturgical acclamations. The instruction took place during the preparation of the initiates, not during the celebrations proper. Significant characteristics were communal experience, ecstasy and visions, and the opportunity for awe, fear, wonder, hope and humor that the official cults did not provide.

There were no uniform organizational structures. We find local cults, such as the Eleusinian mysteries, that were organized as places of pilgrimage; we find small communities of some thirty people, such as the Mithras cult; we find large cult buildings, such as the Eleusinian Telesterion, and temples that were opened and closed daily, such as the temples of the Isis cult. The mystery cults were attractive: many people were prompted to join especially by the buildings, the secret and exotic ceremonies, public processions of the cult communities, common meals and reports of miracles. The common meals were celebrated in the sacramental "presence" of the god as "chief guest and host," who summons worshipers to the feast.[380] This conviction finds concrete expression in the wording of invitations to banquets, as illustrated by papyrus P.Köln 57, which contains an invitation to the *klinē* of the god Sarapis: "The god calls you to a banquet being held in the Thoereion tomorrow from the ninth hour."

The encounter with the God who offers salvation, whom the early missionaries proclaimed, was less concrete in terms of timing, but the claims on the believer were greater: decisive for membership in the Christian communities was not simply one's behavior during the assemblies of the community but

---

[377]See Reck 1991, 134.

[378]O. Kern and T. Hopfner, PW 16 (1935): 1209-1350; R. L. Gordon, *OCD* 1017-18; Bianchi 1976; Klauck 1986, 106-18; Burkert 1987; Klauck 1989, 313-58; Reck 1991, 136-42; D. Zeller, "Mysterien/Mysterienkulte," *TRE* 23 (1994): 503-26; Klauck 1995-1996, 1:77-128; see B. M. Metzger, *ANRW* II.17.3 (1984): 1259-1423 (bibliography).

[379]On questions of communication that had not been researched extensively with regard to the mystery cults see Reck 1991, 136-42.

[380]Aristides, *Or.* 45.27. On P.Köln 57 see Horsley, *NewDocs* 1:5-9 (text, translation and commentary); cf. Klauck 1995-1996, 1:119.

rather one's entire way of life as a follower of Jesus Christ. The missionaries expected, and preached and taught accordingly, that their basic religious and ethical convictions, attitudes and activities, and their specific behavior in daily life, were different from the convictions, attitudes and activities of their pagan contemporaries, and that they should be prepared to encounter ridicule and opposition, but also interest, conversion and integration into the community of believers in Jesus.

19

THE HELLENISTIC JEWISH CHRISTIANS IN JERUSALEM

The missionary work of the early Christians was significantly advanced by the theological position of Hellenistic, Greek-speaking Jewish Christians in Jerusalem during the first years of the existence of the Jerusalem church. Luke reports in Acts 6:1 of a group of Jewish Christians in Jerusalem whom he describes as "Hellenists."

The term "Hellenists" (Ἑλληνισταί, *Hellēnistai*) in Acts 6:1 refers to Jewish Christians, while the same term in Acts 9:29 refers to Jews in the synagogues of Jerusalem with whom Paul discussed the Christian message during his first visit to the Jewish capital after his conversion. Since studies by C. F. D. Moule and Martin Hengel, most scholars accept the view that the "Hellenists" refers to Greek-speaking Diaspora Jews who had returned to Jerusalem and lived there permanently.[1] Because many Jews of Judea spoke Greek since the second century B.C., the question arises of how and to what degree the "Hellenist" Jewish Christians of the Diaspora differed from the "Hebrew" Jewish Christians of Judea, apart from cultural characteristics that they may have brought back from their Diaspora communities. We must not exclude the possibility that the "Hellenist" Jewish Christians who lived in Jerusalem were able to communicate in Aramaic as well.[2] If the "Hellenists" of Acts 6:1; 9:29 were indeed former Diaspora Jews (which is not expressly stated by the text), then we can assume that they had returned to the "holy city" for religious reasons. The term "Hellenist" is derived from the verb ἑλληνίζειν (*hellēnizein*), "to use the Greek language."

---

[1] C. F. D. Moule, "Once More: Who Were the Hellenists?" *ExpT* 70 (1958-1959): 100-102; Hengel 1975; cf. J. Wanke, *EWNT* 1:1064-65 (*EDNT* 1:436-37). Previous suggestions identified the "Hellenists" as Gentile Christians (H. J. Cadbury), as Hellenistic proselytes (E. C. Blackman), or as Palestinian Jews of heterodox background who were open to syncretistic influences (O. Cullmann, M. Simon). See the survey of the history of research in Neudorfer 1983, 19-85.

[2] Contra Moule ("Who Were the Hellenists?" 100), who suggested that the Hellenists spoke *only* Greek; similarly Fiensy 1995, 235. For the observation that follows above see Fitzmyer, *Acts*, 347.

The negative nuance "to adopt a Greek (i.e., pagan) way of life" arose probably at a later date.[3] These "Hellenists" living in Jerusalem were organized in different synagogues, depending on origins (Acts 6:9): there were synagogues for Jews from Rome (the so-called *libertini* or freedmen), from Cyrenaica, from Alexandria, from Cilicia and from the province of Asia. The "Hellenists" of Acts 6:1 are Jewish Christians from these groups of Greek-speaking Diaspora Jews who had been converted to faith in Jesus Christ and were now members of the Jerusalem church. When we describe them as "Greek-speaking Jewish Christians from the Jerusalem church," we must remember that presumably the majority of Palestinian Jewish Christians were bilingual, speaking both Aramaic and Greek.

Some scholars maintain that the conflict between the "Hellenists" and the "Hebrews" that Luke reports in Acts 6:1-6 is evidence for a split in the Jerusalem church.

F. C. Baur argued that Luke plays down in Acts 6 a much deeper quarrel between Hellenistic and Hebraic Christians that caused a schism of the Jerusalem church in connection with the persecution after Stephen's death.[4] This view has been very influential. Many scholars suggested that this division existed already before the persecution. Ernst Haenchen argues that the primitive Jerusalem church split into two groups for theological reasons, as the Hellenists promoted a position critical of the Torah. This explains, he suggests, why the persecution after Stephen's death affected only the more radical Hellenists (Acts 8:1). He believes that the Hellenists formed "a community of their own under the leadership of the Seven."[5] Martin Hengel rejects this tradition-historical explanation. He interprets the split in the Jerusalem church, which he also assumes, as a result of the different languages that were spoken: language barriers between the Greek-speaking Hellenistic Jewish Christians and the Aramaic-speaking "Hebrews" led at an early date to separate services that soon occasioned an organizational separation, which eventually caused the problems in diaconal services as described in Acts 6.[6] Jürgen Roloff surmises that the schism was caused by "differences concerning the content and the agency of the proclamation," as the Aramaic-speaking Jewish-Christian church was governed by the Twelve while the Hellenistic Jewish-Christian church was guided by a group of seven who criticized the temple in powerful sermons inspired by the Spirit.[7]

The assumption of an early schism in the Jerusalem church is historically implausible. (1) It is improbable that the Diaspora Jews who resided in Jerusalem could not speak Aramaic. They hardly would have settled in the Jewish capital if they were unable or unwilling to communicate in Aramaic. It therefore is likely that the community of believers in Jesus in Jerusalem had common services with both "Hellenistic" and "Hebraic" Jewish Christians participating. (2) It is historically unlikely that the Jerusalem church consisted of groups that were organized separately and met separately already in the first years of the church's existence. Luke emphasizes repeatedly the unity of the Jerusalem church (Acts 1:14; 2:46; 4:24; 5:12). This characteristic may be due to the harmonizing "tendency"

---

[3]Wanke, *EWNT* 1:1064 (EDNT 1:436), following Hengel 1983a, 166-67.
[4]Baur 1853, 42-43.
[5]Haenchen, *Apg,* 262 (ET, 268); cf. Lüdemann 1987, 84 (ET, 78); Zmijewski, *Apg,* 281.
[6]Hengel 1975; cf. Fiensy 1995, 235.
[7]Roloff 1991, 117; similarly Ellis 1968, 118-19; B. Meyer 1987, 249-54.

of the author of the book of Acts, as critical scholars like to postulate, or it may be historically plausible, which seems more likely in view of the external dangers that the church faced and in view of the missionary activities and the growth of the church. In times of persecution internal unity and organizational solidarity seem to be a prerequisite for intensive missionary outreach that focuses on the essentials of the Christian message. Luke's picture of a united church is entirely plausible. (3) The fact that the solution of the conflict is both initiated and carried by the Twelve indicates that the Jerusalem church maintained its unity. (4) Craig Hill recently advanced cogent arguments against the view that early Christianity was divided into a conservative Jewish-Christian wing (the "Hebrews") and a progressive wing (the "Hellenists"). He argues that the position of Stephen, who criticized the temple, did not contradict the position of Peter. This means that the early church was much more homogeneous than the critical consensus allows.[8] Gerd Theissen also argues against the assumption of a divided early church with two communities that were separate from each other spatially and institutionally. He suggests that the formation of the group of seven was not the result of a division of the primitive church into two churches: the Seven represented "a first attempt to create local authorities for the church in Jerusalem beside the supraregional authority of the Twelve."[9]

We may assume, therefore, the basic unity of the Jerusalem church in the 30s and 40s. The events that resulted from the activities of Stephen demonstrate, however, that some leading Jewish Christians reflected more consistently on the practical consequences of God's revelation in the death and resurrection of Jesus the Messiah than did the Twelve. The theological position of Stephen that explicitly informed his preaching, a position that presumably was shared by other Jewish Christians in Jerusalem, had far-reaching consequences for the mission of the early church and therefore will be considered at some length.[10]

19.1 Stephen and His Friends

The seven men "of good standing, full of the Spirit and of wisdom" (Acts 6:3) who were appointed by the Jerusalem church for the task of providing for the widows in the church presumably belonged to the "Hellenists"; that is, they were Jews who grew up in Jewish communities in the Diaspora, who had returned to Jerusalem and settled there, and who had become believers in Jesus the Messiah as a result of the preaching of the apostles. All the names mentioned in the list in Acts 6:5 are common in the Greek world, although this does not prove by itself that these men were Hellenistic Diaspora Jews:[11] the description

---

[8]Hill 1992, 32-40, esp. 38-39; cf. idem 1996; 1997. Hill rejects the historicity of Acts 8:1, which reports that only the Hellenists were affected by the persecution. On the interpretation of this passage see §20.1 in the present work.

[9]Theissen 1996, esp. 326-31; quotation, 328; cf. Larsson 1987, 221-2l. See also also Fitzmyer (*Acts,* 345), who calls the theories of Haenchen and others "sheer speculation." See further §15.4 in the present work.

[10]Besides the commentaries see Hengel 1975; Neudorfer 1983; Schneider 1985b, 227-52; Larsson 1987; Löning 1987; Hill 1992; 1997; Theissen 1996. See also the literature on Stephen.

[11]See Barrett, *Acts,* 1:314; contra Zmijewski, *Apg,* 286.

of Nicolaus as a "proselyte of Antioch" could be interpreted as implying that his colleagues were of Palestinian origin,[12] and many Palestinian Jews had Greek names as well.

Stephen is not described with much detail, despite the fact that his speech in Acts 7 is the longest one in the book of Acts.[13] As a member of the Seven, he presumably was a "Hellenist": he was a Jewish Christian living in Jerusalem whose mother tongue was Greek. He is described as "a man full of faith and the Holy Spirit" (Acts 6:5). We learn that he was "full of grace and power," that he did "great wonders and signs among the people" (Acts 6:8), and that he had discussions about the gospel with Diaspora Jews who belonged to the synagogue of the Freedmen, the Cyrenians, the Alexandrians, the Cilicians and the Asians (Acts 6:9). This means that he was actively engaged in evangelistic missionary ministry.[14] Stephen evidently was "a particularly gifted member of the Seven."[15] The fact that he was buried by "devout men" who had "made loud lamentation over him" (Acts 8:2), probably in public, indicates that Stephen had a reputation that went beyond the Jerusalem church. His competent discussions in the Jerusalem synagogues about Jesus resulted in hostility from Hellenistic Jews who disparaged him publicly and in formal accusations before the Sanhedrin (Acts 6:11, 13-15; 7:1). Luke does not say how long Stephen was active as a member of the Seven and as an evangelist. The escalation of the antagonism that his activities caused presumably should be located in the Jerusalem synagogues in which Stephen presented, explained and defended the message of Jesus. Klaus Haacker suggests that "the cry for the law is but the reaction to the conspicuous intellectual superiority of Stephen in these disputations."[16] In the course of the legal proceedings Stephen gave a long speech (Acts 7:2-53). The ensuing tumult resulted in Stephen being stoned to death, an event that probably should be interpreted in terms of lynch law (Acts 7:54-60). Further biographical details are not available. The name *Stephanos* is a common Greek name; Josephus mentions a slave of Caesar by that name (*B.J.* 2.228). The fact that Stephen is mentioned first in the list in Acts 6:5 and the fact that Luke explicitly describes Stephen as fulfilling the conditions mentioned in Acts 6:3 surely prepare the reader for the following account of Stephen's arrest, defense and death. But

---

[12]Barrett, *Acts,* 1:315.

[13]On Stephen see, besides the commentaries, G. Schneider, *EWNT* 3:657-59 (*EDNT* 274-75); M.E. Boismard, *ABD* 6:207-10; Barnard 1960; Bihler 1963; Scharlemann 1968; Kilgallen 1976; J. J. Scott 1978; Légasse 1992; Haacker 1995a; Blackburn 1997; Hagner 1997, 580-81; Reinbold 2000, 242-45. The extreme position of H.-J. Schoeps (1949, 66, 440-48), who claims that the person of Stephen is an invention of Luke, is not shared by other scholars. On the history of research see Neudorfer 1983.

[14]This has been missed by Bolt (1998, 192-93, 202-3), who seeks to contrast Stephen with the Twelve and Paul as special "witnesses."

[15]Haacker 1995a, 1515, for the observation that follows above see ibid., 1516.

[16]Haacker 1995a, 1520.

these facts seem to indicate at the same time that Stephen, right from the beginning, occupied a leading role among the Seven and in the Jerusalem church.[17] According to Acts 6:10, Stephen was a gifted preacher who not only was able to convince others but also was willing and able to teach provocative convictions, conclusions from his understanding of the death, resurrection and exaltation of Jesus the Messiah, with personal courage.

Philip, the second person listed for the Seven (Acts 6:5), also has a common Greek name: this was the name of kings of Macedonia, of a son of Herod I (Lk 3:1), and of a disciple of Jesus (Acts 1:13). In Acts 21:8 Philip is described as "the evangelist" with regard to his later activity in Caesarea, and in Acts 8:4-25 Luke gives an account of his missionary activity in Samaria.

The assumption that Philip the "deacon" and evangelist is identical with Philip the apostle and disciple of Jesus[18] cannot be substantiated from the New Testament sources, nor is it plausible.[19] There is no reason to read the confusion in Eusebius (*Hist. eccl.* 3.39; 5.24.2) back into the first century.

The term "evangelist" (εὐαγγελιστής, *euangelistēs*) is used in the New Testament only in Acts 21:8 (Philip), Eph 4:11 (co-workers in the church) and 2 Tim 4:5 (Timothy).[20] It designates Christians who are prominently active in the proclamation of the *euangelion,* the good news of Jesus the Messiah and Savior. The term is rare in Greek. It is used in an inscription from Rhodes, where it possibly describes a "proclaimer of oracular messages,"[21] a meaning that is disputed by some scholars, however.[22] Some have suggested that Philip's activity as "evangelist" in Caesarea (and the surrounding region?) is identical with his missionary activity in Samaria, which theoretically is possible.[23] On Philip see §20.2; on the term "evangelist" see §28.6.

Prochorus is a rare name. Luke gives no details about him or about *Nicanor, Timon* and *Parmenas* (short form for "Parmenides" or "Parmenon"), whose names occur more frequently.

Nicolaus, the seventh Hellenistic Jewish Christian who is appointed to care

---

[17]Dobbeler (2000a, 250) has doubts and rejects the term "Stephanus-Kreis."

[18]See Räisänen 1995a, 1478; Theissen 1996, 331-31; Matthews 2002, 2-3, 33-34, 216; for Hengel (1975, 177 [ET, 14]) it is a possibility that cannot be excluded.

[19]See Zmijewski, *Apg,* 286; Kollmann 2000, 552.

[20]See A. Dieterich, "εὐαγγελιστής," *ZNW* 1 (1900): 336-38; G. Friedrich, *ThWNT* 2:735-36 (*TDNT* 2:736-37); G. Strecker, *EWNT* 2:176 (*EDNT* 2:70); U. Becker, *NIDNTT* 2:114; O. Betz, *ThBLNT* 1:441; Marshall, *PastEp,* 804 with n. 125; A. Campbell 1992; F. Spencer 1997a, 262-69.

[21]*IG* XII 1, 675 (line 6), published in 1895; cf. LSJ, s.v. "εὐαγγελιστής 705 (II)"; MM 259 ("proclaimer of oracular messages"); BAA 644 ("Titel heidnischer Priester"); BDAG 403 ("title of polytheistic priests"); Strecker, *EWNT* 2:176 (*EDNT* 2:70); G. Horsley, *NewDocs* 3:14. Alastair Campbell (1992, 117) has missed this piece of evidence.

[22]It is unclear whether one should read ὁ ἥρως or ὁ [ἱε]ρὸς εὐαγγελιστής; see *NewDocs* 3:14; cf. Spicq, *TLNT* 2:91-92; see also Marshall, *PastEp,* 804 n. 125. The inscription, not assigned a date in *IG,* perhaps was influenced by Christian usage, although Horsley (*NewDocs* 3:14) thinks that this is unlikely.

[23]A. Campbell 1992, 122-23.

for the widows, is described as a "proselyte of Antioch" (Acts 6:5). This implies
that his six colleagues were born as Jews, while Nicolaus was a Gentile who converted to Judaism before becoming a believer in Jesus. The fact that Luke specifically mentions his Gentile descent as a proselyte who had become a Jew was
perhaps "a deliberate act in order to emphasize the equation of the proselytes"
with the Jews.[24] Irenaeus asserted that this Nicolaus was the founder of the sect
of the Nicolaitans mentioned in Rev 2:6, 15: "The Nicolaitans are the followers of
that Nicolas who was one of the seven first ordained to the diaconate by the
apostles. They lead lives of unrestrained indulgence."[25] This description cannot
be substantiated and is rejected by most exegetes as highly unlikely.[26]

    Barnabas, whose original name was "Joseph," presumably belonged to the
group of people connected with Stephen, as the list in Acts 13:1 seems to suggest. This group probably was not limited to the Seven mentioned in Acts 6:5
but rather included "a fairly large number of outstanding personalities."[27] Barnabas was a Diaspora Jew from Cyprus whose family were Levites (Acts 4:36).
We do not know whether he was a resident of Jerusalem, as a Diaspora Jew,
who lived in Jerusalem and owned land in the region, or whether he had come
from Cyprus to Jerusalem as a pilgrim for one of the festivals, perhaps Pentecost,
where he came into contact with the followers of Jesus and was converted and
stayed, while owning land on Cyprus that he later sold for the needs of the Jerusalem church.[28] Barnabas sold a "field" and made the proceeds of the sale available to the church (Acts 4:37). When Paul returned to Jerusalem for the first time
after his conversion, it is Barnabas who attended to Paul and facilitated the contact with the apostles (Acts 9:27). When the Jerusalem church heard of the formidable success of the missionary work of the Jewish-Hellenistic believers from
Cyprus and Cyrene who had to flee from Jerusalem after Stephen's death and
who had reached Antioch, with numerous conversions of Greeks (Acts 11:20-
21), the leadership sends Barnabas to Antioch to coordinate and consolidate the
missionary work in the Syrian capital (Acts 11:22). Evidently, Barnabas was a
prudent believer with experience in the proclamation of the gospel and with
organizational gifts.

    The list of names in Acts 13:1 records the Jewish-Christian leaders of the new
church in Antioch. The leaders Simeon, Lucius and Manaen, who are listed be-

---

[24]Thus Theissen (1996, 337), who refers to the fact that in the Aphrodisias inscription two proselytes and two God-fearers belong to the leadership of the synagogue.

[25]Irenaeus, *Haer.* 1.26.3; also Eusebius, *Hist. eccl.* 3.29.1-3.

[26]See Haenchen, *Apg,* 257 (ET, 264); Barrett, *Acts,* 1:315; Zmijewski, *Apg,* 287. Räisänen (1995b)
believes that the connection between the Nicolaitans and the Nicolaus of Jerusalem is "not
implausible" but does not make Nicolaus responsible for the theological and ethical positions
of the Nicolaitans.

[27]Haenchen, *Apg,* 378 n. 1 (ET, 394 n. 1).

[28]See Pesch, *Apg,* 1:184.

tween Barnabas and Saul/Paul, may have belonged to the group connected with Stephen as well who came to Syria as a consequence of the persecution after Stephen's death.[29] It is not impossible, however, that they were among the first converts in Antioch.[30] The leading council of the church in Antioch is described with the phrase "prophets and teachers." A clear delineation between these two terms is not possible, as Jürgen Roloff argues: "The task of prophecy was to announce the will of the exalted Lord in the power of the Spirit for the specific situation (cf. Acts 11:28), while the teaching focused primarily on the cultivation and interpretation of the tradition. In actual reality both functions seem to have been fulfilled by the same persons, however. These prophets/teachers proclaimed the word and taught, they performed signs and wonders, but they were also leading the church services."[31]

Simeon was also called "Niger" (Συμεὼν ὁ καλούμενος Νίγερ [Acts 13:1]), a Grecized Latin name meaning "dark-complexioned" or "black," which may indicate African origin. Simeon may have come from a Proselyte family from Cyrenaica in North Africa, and he may have been dark-skinned. He probably belonged to the Hellenistic Jewish Christians from Jerusalem who originally came from Cyprus and from Cyrene and who came to Antioch after they had to flee from the Jewish capital.[32]

Lucius also hailed from Cyrene (Λούκιος ὁ Κυρηναῖος [Acts 13:1]). He may have belonged, together with Simeon, to the synagogue of the Cyrenians in Jerusalem (Acts 6:9), and he may have arrived in Antioch after fleeing from Jerusalem. He is not identical with the Lucius mentioned in Rom 16:21, nor with Luke, the author of the book of Acts.[33]

Manaen (for Heb., "Menahem") was an "intimate friend," "companion" or "foster-brother" (σύντροφος, *syntrophos*) of Herod Antipas (Acts 13:1).[34] Evidently Manaen belonged to a noble Jewish family and was brought up together with the later ruler of Galilee at the court of Herod I in Jerusalem.

---

[29]See Zmijewski, *Apg*, 479-80.

[30]See Pesch, *Apg*, 2:17.

[31]Roloff, *Apg*, 193; cf. idem 1993, 141-42; Schneider, *Apg*, 2:113; Zmijewski, *Apg*, 479; Jervell, *Apg*, 340; Pesch (*Apg*, 2:16) is more cautious. Alfred Zimmermann (1984, 118-40) argues that the teachers (*didaskaloi*) represented a separate office in the early church "concerning which Luke has no further information" (134); this view cannot be substantiated and is implausible.

[32]A. Zimmermann 1984, 129-30; Zmijewski, *Apg*, 480; Schneider, *Apg*, 2:113; similarly Pesch (*Apg*, 2:17), who suggests that Simeon's family may have resided in Antioch. Barrett (*Acts*, 1:603) is skeptical concerning a North African origin, as Josephus calls a man from Perea "Niger" (*B.J.* 2.520).

[33]Thus Ephraem in his commentary on Acts; for a Latin translation see F. Conybeare, in *Begs.* 3:373-453, on Acts 12:25—13:3. See also H. J. Cadbury, in *Begs.* 5:489-95.

[34]On Manaen see Hoehner 1972, 14, 121, 132, 184, 305-306; Hengel 1979, 63-64; A. Zimmermann 1984, 130-32; Riesner 1988, 66; Hemer 1989, 227; Hengel and Schwemer 1998, 334-35 (ET, 220, 450); also Pesch, *Apg*, 2:17; Schneider, *Apg*, 2:113; Zmijewski, *Apg*, 480. Herod Antipas is mentioned in Lk 3:1 and other places.

19.2 Theological Insights

The accusations against Stephen indicate that the conflict with the leaders of the synagogues in Jerusalem was connected with his views concerning the temple and the Torah.

Acts 6:9-14: "Then some of those who belonged to the synagogue of the Freedmen (as it was called), Cyrenians, Alexandrians, and others of those from Cilicia and Asia, stood up and argued with Stephen. [10]But they could not withstand the wisdom and the Spirit with which he spoke. [11]Then they secretly instigated some men to say, 'We have heard him speak blasphemous words against Moses and God.' [12]They stirred up the people as well as the elders and the scribes; then they suddenly confronted him, seized him, and brought him before the council. [13]They set up false witnesses who said, 'This man never stops saying things against this holy place and the law; [14] for we have heard him say that this Jesus of Nazareth will destroy this place and will change the customs that Moses handed on to us.'"

The Diaspora Jews who resided in Jerusalem, erstwhile discussion partners of Stephen, turned into hostile opponents. They presented to the Sanhedrin two accusations that were summarized in the charge of blasphemy (Acts 6:11, 14). They alleged that (1) Stephen attacks Moses, or more precisely, he proclaims that Jesus will change the traditions of Moses; (2) Stephen attacks the temple, or more precisely, he proclaims that Jesus will destroy the temple. Luke describes the witnesses whom Stephen's opponents bring forward as "false witnesses" (Acts 6:13). Their assertions are false for two reasons. First, Jesus never said that *he* would destroy the temple, but only that the temple *would be* destroyed. Second, Stephen argues in his speech that he neither criticized Moses nor wants to abolish the Torah.[35] At the same time, however, it is obvious that Stephen advanced and proclaimed positions in the course of his missionary activities that Jews could interpret as blasphemous.

The exegetical discussion about the connection between the accusations in Acts 6:12-14 and the speech in Acts 7:2-53 is complex, and not every detail can be addressed here. Both the authenticity of Jesus' saying about the temple (Mk 14:58) and the historicity of Stephen's speech are important. Many scholars have little confidence in the historicity of the speech, it being understood variously as an invention by the author of Acts,[36] an "aetiology of the Antiochene Gentile mission" composed with the help of written and oral sources,[37] a "salvation-historical credo" of the early church,[38] a Christian revision of a Hellenistic-Jewish synagogue sermon adopted by Hellenistic Jewish Christians.[39] The views concerning the extent of Lukan redaction vary widely.[40] There is no doubt, of course, that

---

[35]See S. Wilson 1983, 62-63; Haacker 1995a, 1521-30; Hill 1996, 140-41.
[36]See Schille, *Apg,* 178-92.
[37]See Rau 1994, 74-75, referring to Acts 6:8—8:4a; 11:19b-21.
[38]See Kliesch 1975, 11-47; followed by Zmijewski, *Apg,* 307-12.
[39]Schneider, *Apg,* 1:447-52; Weiser, *Apg,* 1:180-82; Barrett, *Acts,* 1:338-39; Dunn, *Acts,* 92.
[40]See Pesch, *Apg,* 1:246-47.

Stephen's speech in Acts 7 is written in Lukan style: it is not an "excerpt" of the actual speech. However, there is good reason to accept the historicity of the speech: if Luke understood the historical situation that the speech in Acts 7 presupposes correctly, Stephen's speech fits this situation very well.[41] The assumption that Luke freely composed Stephen's speech after the event is implausible: (1) The speech, longer than any other in the book of Acts, contains elements that occur at no other place in Acts. (2) The fact that circumcision plays no role whatsoever, even though Stephen is accused of attacking the law, points to the pre-Pauline period.[42] Recent attempts to explain Stephen's speech from a psychological point of view are less plausible.[43]

The central terms of the accusation against Stephen are Jesus, the temple and the Torah.[44] The main issue was the evaluation of the significance of the temple and the Torah in connection with faith in Jesus as the Messiah. The details that Luke provides concerning the accusation against Stephen can be integrated into a salvation-historical and christological position of the Hellenistic Jewish Christians in Jerusalem, with Stephen as their leading representative. Accepting and understanding Jesus' death on the cross as a death of atonement in which God forgave the sins of people, Stephen and his friends evidently arrived at the conclusion that the sin- and guilt-offerings that are sacrificed in the temple no longer have atoning efficacy, and therefore the cultic sections of the Torah that stipulate and regulate the process of the forgiveness of sin and the acquisition and maintenance of purity and holiness have lost their significance, and therefore the temple has lost its central significance and role for Israel and for the Jewish faith. The cult laws stand at the intersection of Torah and temple: the sacrifices that atone for sin and that guarantee both Israel's holiness and Israel's status as God's people are actions stipulated by the Torah that could be performed only in the temple. A person who declares redundant the fulfillment of the laws for sacrifice and of the holiness code attacks the Torah and the temple—unless one agrees that Jesus is the Messiah, who has the right, as Messiah, to redefine the function of Torah as God's revelation and to modify its stipulations.

Did Stephen and his Hellenistic Jewish-Christian friends develop these convictions independently, perhaps in distinction from, or even in contradiction to, the convictions of the "Hebrew" Christians Peter and James? Scholars who adopt or are influenced by the views of F. C. Baur answer this question positively, with varying degrees of nuanced differentiation. Craig Hill advises caution, however: (1) Luke does *not* assert in Acts 6—7 that Stephen was a "critic" of the temple or of the Torah, which does not eliminate the fact that Stephen emphasized in

---

[41]Marshall, *Acts,* 133; cf. Scharlemann 1968, 36-51; Larsson 1987, 217-18.
[42]See Dunn (*Acts,* 92), whose further arguments are less convincing.
[43]See Haacker (1995a, 1546-47), who cannot find any provocative heresy in Acts 6:8—7:60.
[44]Kilgallen 1976, 31-35, 119. Cf. Hengel 1975; Schenke 1990, 176-85; Rau 1994, 36-86; Räisänen 1995a, 1482-91; Theissen 1996; Kraus 1999, 38-55. Various scholars emphasize different details.

his preaching Jesus' prophecy of the destruction of the temple. (2) We must re-member that the "Hebrew" Jewish Christians also attracted the opposition of the Jerusalem authorities at an early date. Peter and the other apostles were repeat-edly arrested, James the disciple of Jesus was executed a few years later in A.D. 41 (Acts 12:2), and Peter came close to sharing his fate (Acts 12:4). (3) The ques-tion is not only whether Stephen advanced convictions that were provocative for Jews in Jerusalem, but also whether he advanced positions that would have been contradicted by the Hebrew-speaking Jewish Christians.[45] Scholars who operate on the assumption that there were diverse early Christian "parties," each with its own distinctive theology, fail to understand the diversity of the reality of the early church. Hill remarks, "The penchant of academics to think in terms of groups, parties, and schools has been, in the case of the early church, un-commonly unfortunate in its results. Jewish Christianity was too large and too varied an entity to fit neatly into Hellenist and Hebrew ideological pigeonholes. It appears that Christian theology did not develop along such straightforward or readily accessible lines." Hill argues that the Hellenistic *and* the Hebrew Jewish-Christian community in Jerusalem presented a united front to the opposing au-thorities. This still does not explain, however, why Stephen was the first believer in Jesus to die for his convictions, before the death of the apostle James (Acts 12:2, 4), and why the authorities or the synagogues in Jerusalem did not move more decisively against Peter, who was, after all, the most visible and the most vocal leader of the Christians. To say that his preaching was "more radical" than that of James or Peter is hardly satisfying. If Peter indeed said to the members of the Sanhedrin, "There is salvation in no one else, for there is no other name under heaven given among mortals by which we must be saved" (Acts 4:12), this was at least as "blasphemous" from a traditional Jewish point of view as Stephen's assertions concerning the temple or the Torah. Other scholars sug-gested that Stephen's message, with its emphasis on the universality of God not being bound to the Jerusalem temple, implied the later missionary work in the Diaspora.[46] This certainly is correct, but it does not answer the questions raised. We cannot escape the conclusion that the Hellenistic Jewish Christians in Jeru-salem evidently reflected more consistently about the consequences of Jesus' death and resurrection for the Torah and for the temple, and thus for Israel, than did the apostles.

How did the Hellenistic Jewish Christians, and how did Stephen, arrive at these convictions about the corollaries of Jesus' death and resurrection, convic-tions that prompted such a violent reaction against himself and against the church? First, tradition-historical insights probably played a major role. Stephen, his friends and, if Craig Hill is correct, perhaps Peter and the other apostles evi-

[45]Hill 1996, 139; the quotation that follows above, ibid., 153.
[46]Dollar 1993, 130.

dently adopted and emphasized elements of Jesus' proclamation, particularly Mk 7:15; 11:17; 13:2 and Jn 2:19, 21; 4:21-24.

Mk 7:15/Mt 15:11: "There is nothing outside a person that by going in can defile, but the things that come out are what defile."

Mk 11:17/Mt 21:13/Lk 19:46: "He was teaching and saying, 'Is it not written, "My house shall be called a house of prayer for all the nations" [Is 56:7]? But you have made it a den of robbers [Jer 7:11].'"

Mk 13:2/Mt 24:2/Lk 21:6: "Then Jesus asked him, 'Do you see these great buildings? Not one stone will be left here upon another; all will be thrown down.'"

Jn 2:19-21: "Jesus answered them, 'Destroy this temple, and in three days I will raise it up.' [20]The Jews then said, 'This temple has been under construction for forty-six years, and will you raise it up in three days?' [21]But he was speaking of the temple of his body."

Jn 4:21-24: "Jesus said to her, 'Woman, believe me, the hour is coming when you will worship the Father neither on this mountain nor in Jerusalem. [22]You worship what you do not know; we worship what we know, for salvation is from the Jews. [23]But the hour is coming, and is now here, when the true worshipers will worship the Father in spirit and truth, for the Father seeks such as these to worship him. [24]God is spirit, and those who worship him must worship in spirit and truth.'"

Stephen could interpret the statement of Mk 7:15 in the context of a cultic understanding of Jesus' death as implying that the purity laws of the Torah are no longer valid. He could interpret Jesus' action in the temple and his teaching on Jer 7:11 in this connection as indicating that Jesus proclaimed the opening up of the temple for the Gentiles.[47] He could interpret Mk 13:2 as implying that the temple to be destroyed soon no longer has a legitimate function in the last days of the messianic period that has arrived. He could interpret statements such as those recorded in Jn 2:19, 21 and Jn 4:21-24 not only in terms of a worship without sacrifices but also in terms of a spiritual worship in the presence of God that has become totally independent of geographical places.

Second, the specific personal experience of Stephen must be understood in the historical context of the first months and years of the early Christian community. Even though Luke reports few details about Stephen's biography, the following considerations surely are generally plausible.[48] (1) The personal conversion of Stephen. We do not know when and in what circumstances Stephen came to faith in Jesus as the Messiah and joined the community of the believers. Luke's account in the first chapters of the book of Acts suggests that Stephen probably heard a sermon in which one of the apostles presented the facts of

---

[47]See Theissen 1996, 334.
[48]For the analysis that follows above see Gooding, *Acts,* 119-24.

Jesus' life, including his death on the cross, his resurrection and his exaltation to the right hand of God. He would have heard the apostle argue for his conviction that Jesus of Nazareth was the Messiah and the "Lord," through whom people can receive the gift of the Holy Spirit, whom God has promised through the prophets for the "last days," if they repent and believe in the crucified and risen Jesus as Messiah and Savior from sin (cf. Acts 2:38; 3:19; 10:42-43; 13:38-39). When Stephen began to believe in Jesus as Messiah and Savior, surely in conscious opposition to the official position of the theological and spiritual leaders of Israel, he received the forgiveness of his sins, in the sense of an inner consciousness of having been accepted by God, as a result of his faith and trust in Jesus—without sacrifices and without the temple. Until now, Stephen's notions about forgiveness had been connected with the cultic-ritual stipulations of the Mosaic law and with his obedience to the these stipulations. His new experience of the forgiveness of his sins through faith in Jesus the Messiah and Savior must have been something entirely new and unprecedented. David Gooding comments, "Never before in all his days had forgiveness been offered him through believing in a man who had actually lived on this earth."[49] (2) The celebration of the Lord's Supper. Stephen would have experienced the presence of Jesus the Kyrios in the regular, often daily, celebrations of the Lord's Supper (Acts 2:42), reminding him of the "blood of the covenant, which is poured out for many" (Mk 14:24/Mt 26:28) that God had promised through the prophet Jeremiah (Jer 31:31-34). This constant reminder of the new messianic covenant and of the fact that it had become a reality in Jesus and his death on the cross made it impossible not to reflect, sooner or later, about the consequences for the old Sinaitic covenant. If God now forgives Israel's sins in connection with faith in Jesus the Messiah, God can hardly forgive sins simultaneously through the sacrifices in the temple. (3) The memory of Jesus' action in the temple. Stephen must have heard of Jesus' action in the temple and his teaching that accompanied this action from the apostles and other believers in Jerusalem. Jesus had taught at the end of his ministry that the temple would be destroyed and that the place of God's presence now, in the days of the Messiah in which the nations are expected to come to Mount Zion, is open for all nations—particularly now that Jesus died for the sins of the many. Does this teaching not imply that the locus of God's merciful, redemptive presence is no longer the temple but Jesus himself? Did this not prompt Stephen to see no need to go to the temple in order to be near to God, since he could be in God's presence by calling on Jesus the crucified and exalted Messiah? (4) Stephen evidently concluded from his understanding of Jesus' death as an eschatologically effective death of atonement and from his personal experience of the forgiveness of sins by faith in Jesus the Messiah that the sacrificial cult in the temple had been vacated as a

---

[49]Gooding, *Acts,* 119.

result of Jesus' death, resurrection and exaltation in a fundamental and ultimate manner. Stephen became aware that atonement of guilt, forgiveness and salvation no longer came through the sacrifice of animals and other cultic rituals but through the death of Jesus the Messiah. These convictions changed his view of the Torah and its validity. This must have been the reason why he was accused of speaking "against Moses."[50] This accusation amounted to a charge of blasphemy.[51] Stephen and other believers in Jesus became convinced that the foundation and focus of the concept and reality of "holiness"—a central term in both the Torah and the Jewish understanding of the law—shifted, as a result of Jesus' death of atonement, from the Torah to Jesus the Messiah and Kyrios. The path to obtaining holiness was no longer the path of obeying the relevant cultic and ritual stipulations of the Torah but the path of believing in Jesus the Messiah and experiencing the reality of the Holy Spirit of God, a reality that Jesus had initiated and inaugurated.

We do not know whether this is exactly what Stephen believed and concluded, and we can only speculate as to which specific areas of the Torah he regarded as eschatologically "abolished." He may have thought of the following areas of the Torah: laws that regulate (1) the removal of guilt and sin, thus all stipulations about sacrifices and cultic acts; (2) the maintenance of holiness, thus stipulations about the boundaries between clean and unclean, including the distinction of clean and unclean animals, and about purification from uncleanness; (3) the locus of holiness, thus all stipulations about the temple (or tabernacle) and priests and about clean and unclean animals; (4) membership in the people of God, thus stipulations about circumcision and about separation from non-Israelites or non-Jews.

The Cornelius narrative with the discussion in the Jerusalem church (Acts 10:1—11:18) and the apostolic council (Acts 15) demonstrate that such reflections about the consequences of the death, resurrection and exaltation of Jesus the Messiah were not automatic, and that such conclusions were not shared by all believers in the Jerusalem church. When Jewish Christians from the Jerusalem church insisted a few years later that the Torah continues to be valid, including the laws concerning circumcision and concerning food, and that the new Gentile believers must adhere to the laws of the Torah, a bitter dispute ensued in the churches established by the apostle Paul. There is no doubt, however, that the separation from the temple and from the cultic Torah that Stephen and other Jewish Christians from Jerusalem initiated was a prerequisite for effective mission among Gentiles.

Third, the content of Stephen's speech needs to be considered. This speech,

---

[50]See Wilckens 1982, 155; followed by Pesch, *Apg,* 1:239; cf. Stuhlmacher 1981, 116-17.
[51]O. Hofius, "βλασφημία," *EWNT* 1:531 (*EDNT* 1:221), with reference to *Sipre Num.* 112 on 15:30; CD V, 11-12.

the longest in the book of Acts, emphasizes two subjects that are connected with the twofold accusation against Stephen.[52]

1. God repeatedly called people in the course of Israel's history, which began with Abraham (Acts 7:2-8), who were commissioned to save his people: Joseph (Acts 7:9-16), Moses (Acts 7:17-43) and the prophets (Acts 7:52). Israel regularly rejected these messengers whom God had sent, however, and Israel also rejected the law that God had given. Israel's rejection of God's servants climaxed in the rejection of Jesus, the Righteous One (Acts 7:52). Stephen argues, implicitly, that it is not he who attacks the law; rather, the attackers have been the Israelites who rejected Moses and refused God: they worshiped the golden calf, the stars, the gods Moloch (Molech) and Rompha (Rephan); they killed the prophets and failed to keep God's commandments (Acts 7:39-43).

2. Israel had the tabernacle in the desert and later, under Solomon, the temple. But the Israelites fell into idolatry (Acts 7:39-43), as they believed that God indeed lives in the temple made by human hands (Acts 7:44-50). If the tabernacle moved from place to place with Israel, arriving from the desert in the promised land, and if God indeed says with respect to the temple that "the Most High does not dwell in houses made with human hands" (Acts 7:48), then it follows that it cannot be wrong to speak of a new "place" for the worship of God. If God indeed was with Israel even outside of the promised land (Acts 7:2-46)—with Abraham in Mesopotamia (Acts 7:2), with Joseph in Egypt (Acts 7:9), with Moses in Egypt (Acts 7:17-29), in Midian (Acts 7:30-35), in Egypt again (Acts 7:36), in the desert at Mount Sinai (Acts 7:36-38, 44)—and if God indeed spoke "living words" (λόγια ζῶντα, logia zōnta) to the "congregation" (ἐκκλησία, ekklēsia) of Israel in the wilderness far from the promised land (Acts 7:38), then it follows that God needs neither a promised land nor a fixed holy place in order to be present among his people. God's revelation in Israel was not static but progressive; the one true God has spoken at different times through different people. And the sacred Scriptures show that each new phase of God's self-revelation led to a more comprehensive divine provision for God's people: Abraham followed God's call and moved from Mesopotamia to Canaan (Acts 7:2-8); Jacob left Canaan and moved to Egypt, where God's people experienced the dramatic rescue by God (Acts 7:9-16); Moses left Egypt with a large group of people and moved to Canaan (Acts 7:19-22, 30-38). If the Messiah indeed has come in the present time, then God's people must allow for the possibility that again there is "movement" and change in the experience of God's presence and salvation.[53]

Stephen defends himself against the accusations recorded in Acts 6:11-14: he has not attacked the Torah; rather, the Israelites have disobeyed God's revela-

---

[52]For the analysis that follows above see Bruce, *Acts*, 161; Marshall, *Acts*, 131-32; Dunn, *Acts*, 90-91; Tyson 1992, 111-16.
[53]Gooding, *Acts*, 124-25. On the christology of Stephen's speech see Neudorfer 1998, 286-88.

tion and now have rejected the Messiah. His convictions about the temple agree with the presence of God in the history of Israel, who revealed himself in different times, ways and places.

Several scholars have suggested that Luke uses Stephen's speech to show that the Jews to whom the gospel had been preached rejected it and thus opened the way for the mission of the church to leave Jerusalem and the temple and move on to Samaria and the Gentiles.[54] This interpretation certainly connects with the general outline of the book of Acts. However, the content of Stephen's speech in Acts 7 and Luke's account of his ministry in Jerusalem in Acts 6 do not explicitly refer to this topic. When Stephen refers to the fact that Solomon built a "house" for God (οἰκοδόμησεν αὐτῷ οἶκον [Acts 7:47]), and when he follows this up with the comment that "the Most High does not dwell in houses made with human hands" (Acts 7:48), he does not want to denounce the Jerusalem temple as "fundamentally misconceived" or as the result of a false understanding of God.[55] Stephen's speech is not propaganda against Jewish Christians; his statements about the temple are not "sectarian" if we interpret them in the context of Second Temple Judaism, which knew a variety of positions concerning the temple. Stephen's convictions can be found already in the prophet Isaiah: the sacred Scriptures of Israel demonstrate that God's revelation always was progressive and would remain so until the coming of the Redeemer.[56]

Stephen did not attempt to use his speech to evade negative measures that the Jewish authorities or the agitated listeners might take. On the contrary, he articulated his theological position clearly and competently. His lucidity and his courage brought him death. He died as the first "witness" (*martys*) for faith in Jesus, the crucified Messiah and Savior in whom God had revealed himself.

Many scholars doubt that Stephen's death was a legal execution; they suggest that Stephen was the victim of a riotous act of lynch law.[57] Gerd Theissen maintains that the oddity of the proceedings can be explained in terms of an offense against the holiness of the temple, specifically the profanation of the temple by Gentiles: the Roman authorities are not alerted, the witnesses who appear suggest proper legal proceedings, but the execution by the furious crowd was not a legal one. The Jerusalem temple formed a "legal enclave" on whose grounds the Romans relinquished the *ius gladii*. Inscriptions warned Gentiles of a "legally tolerated law of the community." And if we take into consideration the tendency, prevalent in the first part of the first century, to expand the holiness of the temple,[58] we can conclude that Stephen evidently became the victim of fanatical defenders of the holiness of the temple who attempted "not only to punish Gentiles who entered the temple but also to punish every infraction of the holiness of the temple." The agreements between the fate of Stephen and the fate of Jesus, as told in the passion narrative of the Gospels,[59] provide no reliable evidence for critically distinguishing tradition and redaction in Acts 7.

---

[54]See Marshall, *Acts,* 132; similarly Neudorfer 1998, 280-81.

[55]Contra Dunn, *Acts,* 90; Weiser, *Apg,* 1:187; Pesch, *Apg,* 1:257.

[56]Gooding, *Acts,* 126-27; see also Zmijewski, *Apg,* 327-28; Barrett, *Acts,* 1:374.

[57]Pesch, *Apg,* 1:265. For the observations that follow above see Theissen 1996.

[58]Schwier 1989, 59-61, 102-17. For the quotation that follows above see Theissen 1996, 334.

[59]Fifteen agreements are listed in Schneider, *Apg,* 433, n. 6.

19.3 Implications for Missionary Work

The significance that the Hellenistic Jewish Christians from Jerusalem had for the history of missions is connected with the christological convictions concerning the meaning of Jesus and his death, resurrection and exaltation. On this basis Stephen drew conclusions concerning the temple and the Torah. The separation from the temple and from the cultic Torah that started to gain ground was one of the most important prerequisites for an effective Gentile mission. Rudolf Pesch argues that the Hellenistic Jewish Christians who shared Stephen's convictions were well equipped to initiate missionary work among Gentiles: the traditional Jewish ties to the temple were abandoned, as the temple was replaced by the community of believers in Jesus as the new locus of God's presence; the traditional ties to the Holy Land were relinquished, as the presence of the Holy Spirit in the community of believers is the new locus of God's holiness; and the traditional ties to the Torah are submitted to the revelation of God's will in Jesus and his death, resurrection and exaltation. With these convictions, the path to a universal and international mission was open.[60]

Stephen and his friends were convinced that the biblical notion that God does not live in temples made by human hands has consequences for the temple and for the cultic practiced in the temple, since the messianic days have arrived and since God had given a new revelation providing for the salvation of Israel. This conviction clearly implies a reference to the universality of God's act of salvation in Jesus Christ. From now on this universality will become a tangible reality in the Gentile mission.[61] The central place for the encounter with God is no longer the holy temple in the holy city as the one place of God's redemptive presence: salvation and holiness have became a reality as a result of Jesus the Messiah, through faith in the saving significance of his death, resurrection and exaltation. The normative center of the believers' relationship to God no longer is the sacred Scriptures of the Torah but is now Jesus the Messiah and the salvation and holiness that God has effected through Jesus' death, resurrection and exaltation. The fundamental home of the believers' relationship with God is no longer the holy land, since God's redemptive presence can be experienced in all places where people repent and believe in Jesus the Messiah and share their faith and lives in the community of the new covenant.[62]

It is no coincidence that Luke reports of the expansion of the gospel beyond the borders of Judea right after his account of Stephen's death and of the subsequent persecution of the believers in Jerusalem. Luke thus indicates that among the immediate results of the charitable and evangelistic ministry of Stephen, and probably his friends, was the missionary outreach in Samaria (Acts

---

[60]Pesch, *Apg,* 1:240.
[61]Zmijewski, *Apg,* 327.
[62]See Pesch, *Apg,* 1:240.

8:4-25), the conversion of a proselyte from Ethiopia (Acts 8:26-40) and the missionary work among Gentiles in Syria as far as Antioch, the provincial capital (Acts 11:19-20).

Manaen, brought up with Herod Antipas at the royal court in Jerusalem, indicates that individual members of the educated upper classes had become believers in Jesus. If the Twelve, who grew up in Galilee, had some education, then this would be true for the Hellenistic Jewish Christians who lived in Jerusalem and played a significant role in the first months and years of the early church. The ministry of these Greek-speaking Jewish Christians in the Jerusalem congregation and their evangelistic missionary involvement demonstrate the importance of linguistic competence in the mission of the early church.[63] Jewish Christians who spoke only Aramaic (if they existed) would have been limited to Palestine. Greek-speaking Jewish Christians could initiate missionary work both among Jewish communities in the Diaspora and among Gentiles. It therefore is not surprising that we find Philip, one of the Seven, in Samaria (Acts 8:5), in missionary dialogue with the finance minister of the Ethiopian queen (Acts 8:27-35), in Ashdod (Acts 8:40) and in Caesarea (Acts 21:8). Hellenistic Jewish Christians from Jerusalem carried the gospel to Phoenicia, Cyprus and Antioch (Acts 11:20). Hellenistic Jewish Christians thus were the first to preach the gospel of Jesus Christ in a large urban metropolis of the Roman Empire.

---

[63]See Pesch 1982, 47.

20

THE FIRST TRANSREGIONAL MISSION OF
JEWISH CHRISTIANS FROM JERUSALEM

After Stephen's defense and death the Jewish authorities forced many Jewish Christians to leave Jerusalem. Luke's account in Acts 8 and Acts 10—11 shows that these Christians did not wait for better times that would allow them to return to Jerusalem. Instead, Philip and many other Jewish Christians, whose names Luke does not mention, carried the gospel from Judea to Samaria and to regions in which Jesus' message of the arrival of God's kingdom had not yet been proclaimed. The discussion in §§12; 14.1; 16 has shown that the conceptual primer of the missionary outreach from Jerusalem was the commission of the risen Jesus Christ to make disciples and to establish communities of believers in Jerusalem, Judea, Samaria and to the ends of the earth. The foundation of the missionary program of these Jewish Christians was their faith in Jesus, who set in motion the arrival of God's reign, their conviction that Jesus' death atoned for the sins of the many, their conviction that Jesus' resurrection signified salvation and that his exaltation to the right hand of God provided the gift of the Holy Spirit of the last days, and their conviction that the messianic salvation of the last days can be obtained only through faith in and allegiance to Jesus the Messiah.

20.1 The Death of Stephen and Its Consequences

The death of Stephen (Acts 7:54-60) evidently was the signal for a general attack on the believers in Jesus in Jerusalem (Acts 8:1-3). These events took place probably in A.D. 31/32. Luke speaks of a "severe" or "great" persecution that affected the Jerusalem church (Acts 8:1). The term "persecution" (διωγμός, *diōgmos* [Acts 8:1]) is used here in the book of Acts for the first time, but not the last. The apostles had problems with the Jerusalem authorities before: they had been arrested repeatedly, and they had to defend themselves before the Sanhedrin. The persecution that followed Stephen's execution evidently was organized: Jews proactively moved against the believers in Jesus with the aim of compelling them to abandon their religious convictions or to "destroy" them

(Acts 8:3) by throwing them into prison and by forcing them to leave the city. Saul/Paul, a student of the eminent rabbi Gamaliel, was particularly active in the persecution (Acts 8:3). Luke's comments in Acts 9:1-2 show that Saul persecuted the believers in Jesus with the explicit authority of the high priests and with certain judicial powers.[1]

Many scholars assume on the basis of Acts 8:1 that the persecution affected only the more radical Hellenistic Jewish Christians, while the apostles, perhaps even all "Hebrew" Jewish Christians, were spared.[2] However, this text must be read carefully:

Acts 8:1: "And on that day a great persecution arose against the church in Jerusalem; and they were all scattered [πάντες δεδιεσπάρησαν] throughout the region of Judea and Samaria, except the apostles [πλὴν τῶν ἀποστόλων]" (RSV).

Luke does not say that the apostles were exempt from *the persecution,* nor does he say that they were not attacked or pressured by the Jewish authorities in Jerusalem.[3] Such an interpretation is rather improbable in light of the larger context of Luke's account, which repeatedly reports attacks by the Jewish authorities on the apostles (Acts 4:1-3; 5:17-18; 21:1-19). Also, the term "all" (πάντες, *pantes*) probably is hyperbolic, as the statement in Acts 8:3 indicates: Saul, one of the active agents in the persecution, enters "house after house," and "dragging off both men and women, he committed them to prison." This clearly shows that the Christians in Jerusalem did not flee Jerusalem immediately after Stephen's death or after the onset of the persecution. Luke speaks of a "great persecution" (Acts 8:1b) and of the fact that members of the Christian community in Jerusalem were "scattered" throughout the region of Judea and Samaria, which means that many prominent members of the Jerusalem church, particularly Greek-speaking believers, *permanently* settled in other regions of the country—for example, Philip, who went to Samaria and then settled in Caesarea (Acts 8:40), and other, anonymous Jewish Christians who settled in Phoenicia, Cyprus and Antioch (Acts 11:19-20)—while the apostles remained as leaders of the Jerusalem church. The formulation of Acts 8:1 leaves open the possibility that the apostles left Jerusalem for a short time and later returned, or that they were arrested just like other believers (Acts 8:3) but eventually were released. Richard Bauckham concludes, "All that Luke maintains is that the persecution did not bring their leadership of the Jerusalem church to an end."

---

[1]Pesch, *Apg,* 1:266. For a critique of the hypothesis that Paul persecuted Christians in Damascus, not Jerusalem, see Hengel and Schwemer 1998, 60-62 (ET, 35-37).
[2]See Cullmann 1952, 37, 45; Hengel 1975, 176 (ET, 25); Bruce 1985b, 649; Schneider, *Apg,* 1:479; Pesch, *Apg,* 1:265; Zmijewski, *Apg,* 341. Hill (1992, 7-15) doubts the historicity of the entire persecution mentioned in Acts 8:1-3.
[3]For the interpretation that follows above see Bauckham 1995b, 428-29; quotation, 429.

The Hellenistic Jewish Christians who were forced to flee from Jerusalem were significantly instrumental in taking the missionary outreach of the early church to new levels, in both theological and geographical terms.[4] The persecution of the believers led to the dissemination of the message of Jesus Christ in regions beyond Jerusalem and Judea. In his later account of the conversion of Cornelius in Acts 10:1—11:18, Luke emphasizes the role of Peter for the new initiative of the Gentile mission. But he has not suppressed the historical fact that the initial impetus for a genuine missionary outreach among Gentiles came not from Peter (or Paul) but from Hellenistic Jewish Christians from Cyprus and Cyrene whose names we do not even know.[5] After interrupting the account of the persecution in Jerusalem in Acts 8:4, Luke takes up his narrative thread again in Acts 11:19-21 (using the literary device of the prolepsis):

Acts 11:19-21: "Now those who were scattered because of the persecution that took place over Stephen traveled as far as Phoenicia, Cyprus, and Antioch, and they spoke the word to no one except Jews. [20]But among them were some men of Cyprus and Cyrene who, on coming to Antioch, spoke to the Hellenists also, proclaiming the Lord Jesus. [21]The hand of the Lord was with them, and a great number became believers and turned to the Lord."

Rainer Riesner observes, "This transition from a pure mission to the Jews to a mission to the Gentiles conducted by Hellenists should be understood not as a one-time event, but rather as a process. First, they turned their attention to Greek-speaking fellow Jews (Acts 6:9). The first more organized mission outside Judaism in the narrower sense occurred among the Samaritans (Acts 8:4-25), who could, however, still be viewed as members—albeit partially apostate—of the holy people Israel. From these Greek-speaking synagogues the Hellenists then reached the circles of 'God-fearers' (cf. Acts 8:26-39), that is, those Gentiles standing in variously intensive connections with Judaism. A special role in this transition to the Gentile mission was played by the Palestinian coastal plain— inhabited largely by Gentiles—with the cities Gaza (Acts 8:26), Azotus/Ashdod and Caesarea (Acts 8:40)."[6] Philip and other Jewish Christians from Jerusalem presumably transitioned to a "law-free" mission in this area—that is, missionary outreach among pagans without requiring that Gentile converts be circumcised or obey the ritual law.[7]

Luke emphasizes and implies several key factors that characterize the early Christian mission with the brief report in Acts 8:1-3 and Acts 11:19-21. (1) The fate of Jesus can be repeated in the fate of his witnesses. Luke indicates such a potential connection by depicting the martyrdom of Stephen along the same

---

[4]Hengel 1971-1972, 24-30 (ET, 54-58); 1979, 63-70; Hengel and Schwemer 1998, 43-60 (ET, 24-35).

[5]See Riesner 1994, 95 (ET, 108).

[6]Riesner 1994, 96-97 (ET, 109).

[7]Hengel 1983a, 164-69; Riesner 1994, 97 (ET, 107).

lines as the death of Jesus. (2) It is not necessarily an indication of cowardice when Christians flee in the face of danger and possible death. Jesus had done the same (Mt 14:13). (3) The impact of a persecution on the individual Christian may seem to be "unjust" from a human point of view. The dangers that the Greek-speaking Jewish Christians faced were so grave that they had to flee from Jerusalem, while Peter and the other apostles either were less affected or were able to return to Jerusalem. The apostles did not "practice solidarity" with the Hellenist Jewish Christians; they stayed in Jerusalem. (4) Courageous behavior is possible even in times of danger. Stephen's body was buried by "devout men" who "made loud" (i.e., public) lamentation: since Stephen had been executed as a criminal, this was risky behavior. If the rabbinic law that stipulates that there must be no lamentation for an executed criminal existed already in the first century, then Stephen's burial may have been a public protest by some people— Luke does not say whether they were Christians—against the Jewish authorities. (5) Not even danger to life and limb terminates Jesus' missionary commission. The forced exile of the Hellenistic Jewish Christians furthered the mission of the church decisively. Political oppression and social discrimination may be used by God in a sovereign plan to achieve the geographical expansion of the Christian message. Rudolf Pesch comments that the Christians "were driven into a corner but they were led to new expanses."[8] The history of the church in China in the extremely difficult decades after the takeover by Mao Ze-dong is a recent example for this possibility. We should not call the mission of the Hellenists "first tentative steps" ("erste tastende Versuche"):[9] their missionary outreach surely was not "attempts," since they had witnessed, observed and learned in Jerusalem what dynamic evangelistic outreach means. And since Luke gives only a summary account of the mission, with the exception of Philip's ministry in Samaria, without providing details, it is quite impossible to assess whether their missionary encounters—for example, with uncircumcised God-fearers—were "tentative" or whether they preached the message that the apostles and Stephen and others had proclaimed in Jerusalem with confidence, anticipating perhaps with eagerness that the good news of the arrival of God's reign now moves out to the nations that will accept it. (7) God remains sovereign even in a persecution; God's plans and ways are not contingent upon the initiative of the authorities who persecute the believers. This is demonstrated by the reference to Saul in the middle of the report about the persecution: this Pharisee with rabbinical training, who perhaps was the most active agent in the persecution of the believers, later was converted. (8) The success of missionary work is always and only due to God, whose "hand" was with the Jewish-Christian witnesses who carried the gospel to new, unreached regions.

---

[8]Pesch, *Apg*, 1:267.
[9]So Hengel and Schwemer 1998, 55 (ET, 32).

20.2 Missionary Work in Samaria by Philip

Missionary work in Samaria (see fig. 10) began relatively soon: according to
Luke's account, Philip, one of the Seven, fled Jerusalem with other Greek-speaking Jewish Christians and went to Samaria, presumably in A.D. 31/32. The distance from Jerusalem to Shechem at the foot of Mount Gerizim is only 60 km,
with a travel time of only two or three days. According to Jn 4:19-24, there were
already sympathizers of Jesus in some areas in Samaria. A second point of contact for Philip would have been the synagogues of the Sichemites, perhaps Samaritan disciples of John the Baptist as well.[10] We must keep in mind the plausible assumption that the believers of the church in Jerusalem had regular
contacts with sympathizers and supporters of Jesus in Galilee,[11] which means
that Christians would have traveled through Samaria on a frequent basis. However, we must also remember that Jesus and his disciples had not just positive
experiences in Samaria: on one occasion a town refused them hospitality.[12] The
mission in Samaria evidently was not a planned or deliberately organized action.
Luke connects the missionary outreach of Philip in Samaria with the persecution
of the church in Jerusalem and with the flight of Hellenistic Christians: "But Saul
was ravaging the church by entering house after house; dragging off both men
and women, he committed them to prison. Now those who were scattered went
from place to place, proclaiming the word. Philip went down to the city of Samaria and proclaimed the Messiah to them" (Acts 8:3-5).

The New Testament mentions a Philip in two different contexts.[13] The Gospels mention a disciple of Jesus called Philip who came from Bethsaida.[14] The
book of Acts mentions a Greek-speaking Jewish Christian in Jerusalem named
Philip who was a member of the Seven—mentioned in second place after
Stephen (Acts 6:5)—and who engaged in missionary work in Samaria and later
in Caesarea.[15]

The person and ministry of Philip, a Hellenistic Jewish Christian, has received
little attention in New Testament scholarship until recently, presumably a result
of the fact that Luke's narrative about Philip was excluded from the "Antiochene
source" postulated by Adolf von Harnack, who was followed by many scholars.[16] F. Scott Spencer's recent narrative analysis of the "portrait of Philip" in the
book of Acts is not interested in the "historical Philip" but investigates the liter-

---

[10]On the latter see Kraft 1981, 241; Pesch 1982, 56-57. John the Baptist probably baptized in
    Samaria or in the border region of Samaria, in Aenon near Salim, 12 km south of Scythopolis,
    according to Eusebius; see Riesner 2002, 143-54.
[11]Kraft 1981, 241; cf. Pesch 1982, 56.
[12]Lk 9:52-56, with the "fire and brimstone" suggestions made by the sons of Zebedee.
[13]Zahn 1900, 18-27, 158-75, 216-17; Hengel 1993, 82, 118, 303-4; Amsler 1999, 5-7, 441-68.
[14]Mt 10:2-4; Mk 3:16-19; Lk 6:14-16; Jn 1:43-48; 6:5, 7; 12:20-22; 14:8-9; cf. Acts 1:13.
[15]Acts 6:5; 8:5-13, 26-40; 21:8-9.
[16]See Dobbeler 2000a, 20-21; Kollmann 2000.

ary features that Luke uses to describe this "figure."[17] Spencer concludes that for the author of Acts, Philip is (1) the pioneer missionary who crossed social and religious boundaries in his mission among Samaritans and Gentiles; (2) the dynamic prophet whose ministry has similarities with Moses and Elijah; (3) the cooperative servant who serves as a deacon and provides hospitality. However, Luke's narrative in the book of Acts is hardly well served by the literary figure of a "Philip factor." The complexity and the multidimensional nature of the figure of Philip, who functions as a deacon, preacher, missionary and church leader, can indeed rest on historical reality.[18] Axel von Dobbeler analyzes in a recent study the role of Philip the evangelist in the history of early Christianity. He distinguishes four phases of his ministry: (1) his activity as a deacon and a member of the Seven in Jerusalem; (2) his missionary activity in Samaria and in the cities of the coastal plain; (3) his activity as the leader of a charismatic-prophetic center in Caesarea; (4) his activity during the last years of his life in Hierapolis in Phrygia. Dobbeler characterizes Philip as follows: "The notion of continuity with the ministry of Jesus evidently was important for Philip on all levels of his ministry: his ministry at tables, his proclamation of the kingdom of God, his mighty miraculous deeds, the exorcisms and healings of the lame, and his position in Caesarea and in Hierapolis should be understood, in terms of effective ministry, as a new realization of the powerful activity of Jesus. The fact that Philip presents himself, preaches and acts *like* Jesus, prompted by the same Spirit, and the fact that he consistently *points* to Jesus with his sermons and his actions indicates both the particularity (for example, with regard to Simon) and the legitimacy of his ministry." Christopher Matthews, in a new study on Philip, suggests that there was only one figure with the name "Philip," which was used in the early Christian tradition in different ways—in the Gospels, in the book of Acts and in gnostic and apocryphal texts. The significance of Philip in Christian texts of the second century was the impetus to reevaluate the canonical texts. Matthews concludes, "Philip emerges as an early Christian leader who is identified with a recognizable constellation of characteristics (apostle to the Greeks/ gentiles, advocate for the marginalized, apostolic guarantor, scribe of the words of Jesus, etc.)."[19] Philip was an important figure who was as well known in early Christian circles as the other apostles, a fact that is indicated not only by his as-

---

[17]F. Spencer 1992, 13-25; for the discussion that follows see ibid., 271-76; see also idem 1997b.

[18]Dobbeler 2000a, 27, formulated as a critique of Spencer. For the survey of Dobbeler's interpretation that follows above see ibid., 248, 305-13; quotation, 311.

[19]Matthews 2002, 216; the quotation that follows above, ibid., 217. Matthews explains Luke's identification of Philip as one of the Seven rather than as one of the Twelve with Luke's alleged "compositional freedom in relation to his traditional information" (ibid., 64). This view is predetermined by Matthews's decision to treat second-century sources, particularly Polycrates and Papias, as more reliable than Luke, a dubious procedure that is not necessitated by Acts 8.

sociation with Jerusalem, Samaria and Caesarea but also by his reputation as a "boundary-breaking missionary to non-Jewish groups in these areas."

The apocryphal *Acts of Philip* describes Philip as an apostle (*Acts Phil.* 1:1); he is assigned attributes of both Philip the disciple of Jesus and Philip the deacon and evangelist. Scholars generally assume that the author confused the two figures mentioned in the New Testament.[20] According to Frédéric Amsler, the Philip of *Acts of Philip* originally was a Christian from Hierapolis in Phrygia who was assimilated to Philip the deacon, who in turn was merged with Philip the apostle.[21]

The mission of Philip in Samaria (Acts 8:5-25) can be described as follows.[22] (1) Philip went "to a [the] city of Samaria" (εἰς [τὴν] πόλιν τῆς Σαμαρείας, *eis [tēn] polin tēs Samareias* [Acts 8:5]). There are two difficulties with this comment. First, it is unclear whether or not the original text included the definite article. The reading with the definite article ("the city of Samaria") probably would have to be interpreted in terms of a reference to Sebaste, the old city of Samaria that had been rebuilt by Herod I, who renamed it after Caesar Augustus. The reading without the definite article ("a city of Samaria") provides no specific information about the town in which Philip preached. Formal reasons make the second alternative, the reading without the article, more likely.[23] In other words, Luke provides (only) a general localization of Philip's ministry: Philip engaged in missionary work "in some city of Samaria." Second, the term "Samaria" can refer both to the region and to the (capital) city. Some scholars interpret the comment in terms of a reference to the city of Samaria-Sebaste.[24] This interpretation is seen to conflict with Luke's conception of the Gentile mission being initiated by Peter (Acts 10) rather than by Philip. Thus some scholars interpret the phrase "to a city of Samaria" as a reference to Shechem, the religious center of the Samaritans.[25] This is questionable, however, since Shechem does not seem to have been populated after its destruction in 128 B.C.[26] Justin suggested the city of Gitta, the birthplace of Simon Magus (*1 Apol.* 26); this identification cannot be confirmed, however. Since *Samareia* ("Samaria") can refer to the region, and since Luke does not specifically identify the city in which Philip preached, I con-

---

[20]See A. de Santos Otero, in Hennecke and Schneemelcher 1999, 2:425 (ET, 2:577); Hengel 1993, 118; Körtner 1998, 96 n. 23; Dobbeler 2000a, 233.

[21]Amsler 1999, 6-9, 441-68.

[22]Besides the commentaries and studies by F. Spencer (1992) and Dobbeler (2000a), see Böhm 1999, 279-308.

[23]See Böhm 1999, 281-89, with exhaustive detail.

[24]Barrett, *Acts,* 1:402-3; Fitzmyer, *Acts,* 402; Jervell, *Apg,* 259; Kollmann 2000, 555-56. For arguments against this interpretation see Hengel 1983b, 178-79 (ET, 123-25); 1995, 76-77.

[25]See Pesch, *Apg,* 1:272; Zmijewski, *Apg,* 349; cf. Roloff (*Apg,* 133), who argues that the pre-Lukan tradition refers to Shechem, while Luke thinks of the old capital, Samaria-Sebaste. Marshall (*Acts,* 154) and Dunn (*Acts,* 108) remain undecided.

[26]Zangenberg 1998, 29-30; cf. Hengel 1983b, 180 (ET, 125); 1995, 73-74.

clude that Luke had no interest in a precise geographical localization.[27] It should be noted at the same time that Luke's comment does *not* allow the conclusion that the tradition that Luke used implies "that Philip also engaged in missionary work among the Gentile population of Samaria."[28] In Acts 8:9 Luke refers to "the people of Samaria" (τὸ ἔθνος τῆς Σαμαρείας, *to ethnos tēs Samareias*) who had been under the spell of Simon Magus.[29] This phrase can have different meanings, as is indicated by the fact that in Sir 50:25-26 a similar phrase describes probably the population of the city of Samaria (identified polemically with the Gentiles), and as Josephus uses the phrase "the people of the Samaritans" for the members of the Gerizim community, probably with the connotation of "a foreign race" or "proselytes." In the context of parallel formulations and in the context of Acts 1:8, the phrase "the people of Samaria" in Acts 8:9 refers to "the population of the (geographical) region of Samaria . . . which belongs, in the perspective of Luke, evidently to the twelve tribes of Jacob or Israel."[30] According to Luke, Philip engaged in missionary work in Samaria in the cultic and legal community, "which belongs to Israel, but not to the Jewish cultic community focused upon the temple in Jerusalem. The passage describes these Samaritans as people who are open to faith in miracles and who have been excited by the magic tricks of Simon. They are not described as syncretistic, however, but only as people seduced by Simon. There are no traces of a general polemic or of religious defamation, and no influence of literary perspectives can be detected." (2) Philip "proclaimed the Messiah to them";[31] that is, he proclaimed "the good news about the kingdom of God and the name of Jesus Christ."[32] Since the missionary preaching of Philip focused on Jesus as Messiah, his listeners obviously were worshipers of Yahweh. He could presuppose faith in the one true God, and he does not preach repentance from idolatry and turning to the only true God. Philip is not engaged in missionary work among Gentiles.[33] This confirms that Philip's ministry probably was not located in the Hellenistic city of Samaria-Sebaste.[34] (3) The Samaritans listened attentively,[35] presumably to many sermons of the Jewish-Christian missionary from Jerusalem. (4) Miraculous signs (σημεῖα, *sēmeia* [Acts 8:6]) happened: people were liberated from unclean spirits and "many others who were paralyzed or lame were cured" (Acts 8:7). (5) The at-

---

[27]See Barrett, *Acts,* 1:403; Witherington, *Acts,* 282; cf. Hengel 1983b, 181-82 (ET, 126); Egger 1986, 198; Hengel 1995, 77-78.

[28]Kollmann 2000, 555.

[29]For the observations that follow above see Böhm 1999, 151-94, 296-97. On Simon Magus see also Klauck 1996, 25-28.

[30]Böhm 1999, 192; the quotation that follows above, ibid., 307.

[31]Acts 8:5: ἐκήρυσσεν αὐτοῖς τὸν Χριστόν.

[32]Acts 8:12: εὐαγγελιζομένῳ περὶ τῆς βασιλείας τοῦ θεοῦ καὶ τοῦ ὀνόματος Ἰησοῦ Χριστοῦ.

[33]Schneider, *Apg,* 1:487; Böhm 1999, 294; Kollmann 2000, 555.

[34]Böhm 1999, 288-89, 294.

[35]Acts 8:6: ἐν τῷ ἀκούειν αὐτοῦς.

mosphere in the town was characterized by "great joy" (πολλὴ χαρά, *pollē chara* [Acts 8:8]). (6) The citizens turned away from Simon the magician (Acts 8:9-12), who "for a long time had amazed them with his magic" (Acts 8:11). (7) The people "believed Philip."[36] (8) Men and women were baptized (Acts 8:12), among them Simon the magician (Acts 8:13). (9) The apostles in Jerusalem "heard that Samaria had accepted the word of God,"[37] and they sent Peter and John to Samaria (Acts 8:14). (10) When the apostles realized that the converted Samaritans had not yet received the Holy Spirit, they prayed for the new converts and laid their hands on them, with the result that the baptized Samaritans received the Spirit (Acts 8:15-17).

Axel von Dobbeler describes Philip's views of baptism as follows: "Baptism was an integral element in the missionary praxis of the evangelist, who evidently understood baptism as a baptism of repentance for the forgiveness of sins, following John the Baptist. The baptismal practice implies the exodus as a hermeneutical point of reference and refers thus to protection, to purification and to the binding of the people who are baptized to the baptizer. The baptism of Philip was plain water baptism without impartation of the Holy Spirit and thus close to forms of baptism that we have posited for Ephesus and for Damascus."[38] The hypothesis that Philip, one of the leaders of the Jerusalem church, had an understanding of baptism that was different from Peter's cannot be substantiated from New Testament texts, and it is hardly plausible. The situation with regard to Apollos was different (see below).

(11) Simon wanted to buy from the apostles the ability to convey the Holy Spirit, evidently misunderstanding the gift of the Spirit as the magical ability to induce pneumatic-ecstatic phenomena (Acts 8:18-19). Peter rejected Simon's request with a curse, asserting that Simon had no share in the fellowship of the Holy Spirit (Acts 8:20-23). Simon's response was ambiguous: "Pray for me to the Lord, that nothing of what you have said may happen to me" (Acts 8:24). Was his request honest, implying that he truly had been converted?[39] Or was his request egotistical, still "under the spell of magical thinking,"[40] implying that he had never really become a Christian? Or does Luke deliberately leave the answer to this question open?[41] Luke does not report specifically that Simon had received the Holy Spirit, but Simon indeed had "believed" and been baptized; and if all Samaritans who believed had received the Spirit once the apostles had prayed

---

[36]Acts 8:12: ἐπίστευσαν τῷ Φιλίππῳ.

[37]Acts 8:14: δέδεκται ἡ Σαμάρεια τὸν λόγον τοῦ θεοῦ.

[38]Dobbeler 2000a, 309; on Philip's view of baptism see ibid., 181-215; on Philip's missionary work in Samaria see ibid., 43-106.

[39]See Schneider, *Apg,* 1:495; Weiser, *Apg,* 1:205; Marshall, *Acts,* 159-60; Barrett, *Acts,* 1:418; Zmijewski, *Apg,* 348 (for the Lukan redaction); Berger 1994b (who wants to relate Acts 8:9, 10 to Simon as a Christian as well); Turner 1996a, 336-37.

[40]Pesch, *Apg,* 1:277. For the comment that follows above see Dunn 1970, 64-67.

[41]See Dunn, *Acts,* 112.

and laid hands upon them, this would have to be assumed for Simon as well. When Peter says of Simon that he is "in the gall of bitterness" and in "the chains of wickedness" (σύνδεσμον ἀδικίας, *syndesmon adikias* [Acts 8:23]), this does not prove that he cannot have been converted: in Acts 5:1-11 Luke had reported serious sin in the church in Jerusalem as well. The "gift of God" that Simon desired to purchase (Acts 8:21) is not the Spirit but rather the ability to convey the Spirit. Peter's threat in Acts 8:21 does not necessarily imply that Simon was not a Christian or could not have remained a Christian: Peter says that he has no "part" and "share" in conveying God's Spirit.[42] Luke does not refer to any connections between Simon and the gnostic movement that quoted him in support of their doctrines.[43] (12) The apostles proclaimed the word of the Lord in the city and "in many villages of the Samaritans" (Acts 8:25).[44] In other words, they engaged in missionary outreach in the entire region of Samaria. We know of 140 settlements in the Hellenistic period in Samaria and of 146 villages in the early Roman period.[45] The comment in Acts 8:25 could indicate "a broad and persistent success of the Christian mission in the region."[46]

Some scholars have argued that the Samaritans were not truly converted to the Christian faith before they received the Holy Spirit.

James Dunn argues this position forcefully.[47] (1) The Samaritans must have understood Philip's message of the messianic kingdom of God in terms of their expectation of the Taheb, the Samaritan messiah. (2) Philip's message was accepted, as it was accompanied by signs and miracles: the miracles that Simon had performed are now superseded by the miracles of Philip. (3) The Samaritans were baptized in terms of an initiation rite introducing them into the kingdom of Jesus as Taheb. (4) The reaction of the Samaritans was sincere but misguided due to their one-sided enthusiasm. (5) The Samaritans were superstitious, as is demonstrated by their rash reaction to Simon. Their reaction to Philip's preaching can be described as mass emotion. (6) The reaction of Simon is described by Luke in exactly the same words as their reaction to Philip, which means that their reaction to the proclamation of the gospel was as superficial and thoughtless as their reaction to Simon. (7) The faith of the Samaritans is not related to the gospel or to Jesus Christ: they "believed Philip." The dative construction of the Greek phrase, linking faith with a person other than God or Jesus Christ, is unique in the book of Acts. (8) Simon "believed" as well and was baptized, despite that fact that he understood little or nothing about the gospel, as his subsequent behavior demonstrates when he wanted to buy the "gift of conveying the Spirit." (9) In the New Testament possession of the Holy Spirit is *the* characteristic of being a Christian: without the Holy Spirit the Samaritans cannot be regarded as converted.

---

[42]See Turner 1996a, 366.

[43]On Simon Magus see Tamás Adamik, "The Image of Simon Magus in the Christian Tradition," in Bremmer 1998, 52-64.

[44]Acts 8:25: διαμαρτυράμενοι καὶ λαλήσαντες τὸν λόγον τοῦ κυρίου . . . πολλάς τε κώμας τῶν Σαμαριτῶν εὐηγγελίζοντο.

[45]Adam Zertal, "Mount Manasseh Survey," *NEAEHL* 4:1312; Böhm 1999, 102.

[46]Böhm 1999, 307; cf. Lindemann 1993, 65-66.

[47]Dunn 1970, 55-68; cf. Hoekema 1972, 36-37.

There is sufficient evidence, however, that supports the assumption that the Samaritans were converted to faith in Jesus Christ before they received the Spirit after the prayers and the laying on of hands by the Jerusalem apostles.

The following arguments suggest that Luke implied that the Samaritans had been genuinely converted when Philip baptized them.[48] (1) The description in Acts 8 must not be detached from Luke's terminology and theology in general: Luke clearly reports missionary success. Unclean spirits are driven out (Acts 8:7a), Samaritans are being healed (Acts 8:7b), people indeed "believe Philip"—the Philip "who was proclaiming the good news about the kingdom of God and the name of Jesus Christ" (Acts 8:12). (2) The crowd "with one accord listened eagerly to what was said by Philip" (Acts 8:6). (3) Luke does not describe the ministry of Philip in general or his preaching in particular as defective or as misunderstood by the Samaritans—for example, in the sense of the Samaritan expectations of the Taheb. When Peter and John arrive in Samaria, they do not correct, criticize or complement Philip's message, unlike Aquila and Priscilla in Ephesus when they encountered Apollos (Acts 18:26). Luke describes the ministry and message of Philip in Samaria in the same manner in which he describes the ministry and the message of the apostles.[49] (4) According to Luke, the apostles assess the events in Samaria as missionary success: "the apostles at Jerusalem heard that Samaria had accepted the word of God" (Acts 8:14). The phrase "accepted the word of God" in Acts 11:1, 18 (cf. Acts 2:41) describes genuine conversions. Luke does not distinguish between "believing a missionary" and "believing in God."

Luke explicitly marks the delay of the reception of the Holy Spirit as extraordinary: "For as yet the Spirit had not come upon any of them; they had only been baptized in the name of the Lord Jesus" (Acts 8:16). This explanation would be superfluous if Luke or his readers regarded an interval between baptism and the reception of the Spirit as normal.[50] Luke himself provides no explanation for the delay of the Spirit. Perhaps God sovereignly withheld the Spirit in order to establish a connection between the Samaritans and the Jewish-Christian church in Jerusalem through Peter and John and their mediation of the reception of the Spirit. Without this connection, demonstrated through the parallel reception of God's Spirit, the Samaritan Christians may have felt inferior, or they may have claimed an autonomy from the Jerusalem church that would have split the church right from the beginning, or the Jewish Christians may not have accepted the Samaritans as Christians of equal standing.[51]

It is plausible to assume that the Samaritan Christians spoke in foreign languages when they received the Holy Spirit: there must have been a visible or audible manifestation of the coming of the Spirit that prompted Simon to think

---

[48]E. A. Russell, "'They Believed Philip Preaching' (Acts 8.12)," *IBS* 1 (1979): 169-76; Carson 1988, 144; Menzies 1991, 252-57; F. Spencer 1992, 48-53; Turner 1996a, 362-67; Stenschke 1999a, 145-47.

[49]Turner 1996a, 364-65.

[50]Turner 1996a, 360-75, 451-53; 1996b, 92-93.

[51]See Carson 1988, 144; similarly Turner 1996a, 374.

that he might acquire with money the ability to convey the Spirit. When Luke links the reception of the Spirit with glossolalia, he always introduces a new group of people who accepted the gospel of Jesus Christ: Jews (Acts 2), Samaritans (Acts 8), Gentiles (Acts 10—11) and disciples of John the Baptist (Acts 19). These four events include all groups that would have to be distinguished from a salvation-historical perspective. The conversion of the Samaritans is particularly significant because the gospel for the first time reaches people who are not "unambiguous" Jews. In these four cases the manifestations linked with the reception of the Holy Spirit—whether it included speaking in tongues or the laying on of hands—constituted corporate rather than individual experiences. When Luke reports the conversion of individuals, such as Lydia (Acts 16) or the jailer in Philippi (Acts 16), he does not speak of a two-stage experience of conversion/baptism followed at a later date by the reception of the Spirit.[52] We must note also that Luke obviously is uninterested in the question of the normative sequence of faith, water baptism and reception of the Spirit.

Philip's mission in Samaria illustrates the following truths about the missionary work of the early church. (1) Missionaries are willing to go to and to live in areas where they can expect not sympathy, or at least neutrality, but hostility. According to Acts 8:1, the believers in Jesus who came to Samaria had fled Jerusalem because of the persecution. The fact that they stayed in Samaria is astonishing, given that Samaritans were no friends of the Jews. We must remember that the early Christians who came to Samaria may have made contact with previous Samaritan sympathizers of Jesus. (2) Missionary situations are not always the result of deliberate planning. They sometimes seem to be the result of accidental developments, sometimes even of external pressure and persecution. (3) Missionaries are not intimidated by magical practices or demonic phenomena: Philip had no qualms about contact with Simon, a locally prominent magician. At the same time we note that the Lukan report does not show any fascination with magic or with magical practices.[53] (4) Missionaries are not intimidated by local celebrities: Philip evidently was not afraid to acquaint Simon with the gospel of Jesus Christ, reckoning with the possibility that even this magician might be converted to faith in Jesus. (5) Missionaries are prepared for mass conversions, or are at least willing and able to handle mass conversions. The spectacular phenomena that Luke reports for the mass conversion of Samaritans may indicate that these remain an exception. (6) Not all confessions of faith are genuine, and converted celebrities do not automatically become the leaders of new communities of believers. Simon is a case in point. (7) Missionary work results in the reconciliation of hostile and resentful groups: Jewish and Samaritan believers have fellowship with each other.

---

[52]See Carson 1988, 145.
[53]See Wildhaber 1987, 52-53.

The question of which towns and villages of Samaria could have been reached with the gospel by Jewish-Christian missionaries from Jerusalem during these weeks will be discussed later (§22.3). I have already pointed out that the brief comment in Acts 8:25 about the missionary outreach of Peter and John in the Samaritan villages may indicate lasting successes of missionary work in Samaria.[54] Luke asserts in Acts 9:32 that Peter "traveled about the country" (TNIV; διερχόμενον διὰ πάντων, dierchomenon dia pantōn). This comment may refer to the regions mentioned in Acts 9:31 ("throughout Judea, Galilee, and Samaria"), or it may refer to all towns in which Christian communities existed.[55]

20.3 The Conversion of the Royal Official from Ethiopia

Luke reports in Acts 8:26-40 how the mission of the church reached a Gentile for the first time. Here again it is not Peter who takes the first step, but the Greek-speaking Jewish Christians from Jerusalem.

Philip walked on one of the arterial roads from Jerusalem[56] to Gaza and met a high official of the queen of Ethiopia. The queen of Ethiopia, who held the title "Candace," ruled the kingdom of Meroë (Nubia; mod. Sudan) in the middle Nile Valley south of the first cataract. Luke does not relate the name of the Ethiopian official, but he identifies him as being in charge of "the entire treasury" of the queen. He apparently was a dark-skinned Nubian who had visited Jerusalem on a pilgrimage and was on his way back to Ethiopia.[57]

Ethiopia (Αἰθιοπία, Aithiopia)[58] was regarded, according to old Greek traditions, as the region at the southeastern end of the world where the sun god arises and where, as a result, the skin of the inhabitants, called Aithiopes, is dark and burnt (Homer, Il. 1.423; 23.206; Od. 5.282). When the Greeks later encountered the dark Nubians living further to the west, they were given the name Aithiopes. Since Herodotus, the Greeks called the entire region south of Egypt "Ethiopia"—that is, the ancient cultures of Cush, Meroë and Aksum (Axumis), the modern states of Sudan and Ethiopia. Nubia became an independent kingdom in 1650 B.C. when Egypt's Thirteenth Dynasty collapsed, but it came again under

---

[54]See Böhm 1999, 307.

[55]Thus Pesch, Apg, 1:318 with n. 7.

[56]Pesch, Apg, 1:290.

[57]Bruce 1989, 379. Matthews (2002, 71-94) regards Acts 8:26-40 as a legend and is skeptical concerning the possibility of critically reconstructing an underlying historical event (75).

[58]See Wolfgang Helck, KP 1:201-3; idem, "Kandake," KP 3:106; R. G. Morkot, OCD 558. See also William Y. Adams, Nubia: Corridor to Africa (Princeton, N.J.: Princeton University Press, 1977 [1984]); Steffen Wenig, ed., Africa in Antiquity: The Arts of Ancient Nubia and the Sudan (Brooklyn, N.Y.: Brooklyn Museum, 1978); László Török, "Geschichte Meroes: Ein Beitrag über die Quellenlage und den Forschungsstand," ANRW II.10.1 (1988): 107-341; Inge Hofmann, "Die meroitische Religion: Staatskult und Volksfrömmigkeit," ANRW II.18.5 (1995): 2801-68; Steffen Wenig, ed., Studien zum antiken Sudan (Meroitica 15; Wiesbaden: Harrassowitz, 1999); Hölbl 2001, 2, 55-56, 161-62, 259-67; Edwin M. Yamauchi, ed., Africa and Africans in Antiquity (East Lansing: Michigan State University Press, 2001).

Egyptian rule a hundred years later. Such changes of self-government and foreign rule happened several times during the following centuries, until Nubia stopped dealing with Egyptian concerns after the seventh century. Ethiopians fought in the army of Xerxes when he invaded Greece (Herodotus 7.70). Greek explorers visited Ethiopia since the sixth century. Around 330 B.C. the capital was relocated from Napata to Meroë further south. King Ergamenes, who had a Greek education, resisted around 240 B.C. the influence of the Nubian priests. The queens of Nubia carried the title "Candace," often misunderstood by ancient authors as a personal name (see Strabo 17.1.54; Pliny, *Nat.* 6.11.29); they sometimes ruled for their sons. Petronius, the Roman prefect of Egypt, destroyed the old capital of Napata in a military campaign against Nubia in 23 B.C. (Strabo 17.1.54). In the first century A.D. regular contacts occurred between Ethiopia and Rome. Nero sent an expedition to Africa with the task of exploring Nubia (Pliny, *Nat.* 6.35.184); the 975 Roman miles (1,433 km or 890 mi.) that the expedition established for the length of Nubia corresponds rather exactly with the distance from Assuan (first cataract) to Meroë. Since the fourth century B.C. Aksum was the political center of Ethiopia.

Meroë (mod. Bagrawiya),[59] situated on the eastern bank of the Nile River between the fifth and sixth cataract south of the mouth of the Astaboras River (mod. Atbara), was the residence of the Ethiopian kings since about 300 B.C. Herodotus is the first Greek author to mention the city. He speaks of a temple of the Sun that had been erected by King Aspalta in the sixth century B.C. (2.29). Archaeological remains include a temple of Amun (135 m long), in which the state oracles were proclaimed, a temple of Isis and a temple dedicated to the lion god Apezemak. There were gold mines about 260 km south of Meroë on Marru, an island in the Nile River, and near modern Gebel Absol and Abu Hashim. There were twelve cities between Napata, the old capital, and Meroë, all on the eastern bank of the Nile with the exception of Alanan and Epis (listed from north to south): Alana (mod. Abidiya), Sakole (mod. Dangeil), Scammos (mod. Berber?), Gora (mod. Garrib?), Abale (mod. el Mogren?), Darou (mod. Sha'adinab?), Galim (mod. Hasaya), Seserem (mod. Zeidab?), Mallo (mod. Aliab?), Tadu (on the island of Shebeliya), Epis (opposite Meroë).

On which route did the Ethiopian official travel from Meroë to Jerusalem? There are several possibilities. (1) He was on a diplomatic mission to Egypt and had traveled on the Nile River from Meroë via the old capital of Memphis to Alexandria, the seat of the Roman imperial prefect. From there he traveled on the Via Maris via Gaza to Jerusalem. (2) If he wanted to go directly from Meroë to Jerusalem, he could travel on the Nile from Meroë via Syene (mod. Assuan) and Elephantine, the southernmost city of Egypt situated on an island at the first cataract, to Apollonopolis Magna (mod. Edfu, Idfu). From there he could travel on the caravan route through the desert east of the Nile in the course of a week to Berenike (mod. Bender el-Kebir, Medinet el-Haras), a port city on the Red Sea (about 135 km east behind Apollonopolis this route joined the *Hodos Berenikēs,* the caravan route from Koptos to Berenike).[60] From Berenike he could travel by ship to Aelana-Aila (mod. Aqaba in Jordan), and from there overland through

---

[59]See Helck, *KP* 3:1232-33; Morkot, *OCD* 963; L. Török, "Geschichte Meroes," *ANRW* II.10.1 (1988): 107-341. See *BAGRW,* map 82 (N. B. Miller).
[60]See J. Keenan et al., *BAGRW,* map 80 (1994).

Nabatea to Jerusalem. (3) He could have traveled from Meroë to Apollonopolis and, further north on the Nile River, to Koptos (mod. Qift). The shortest caravan route through the eastern desert, only 174 km, linked Koptos with Myos Hormos (mod. Quseir el-Qadim) on the Red Sea.[61]

In Koptos have been found two tablets made of black basalt with inscriptions that mention soldiers of two legions and several auxiliary units who dug wells along the northern and southern routes from Koptos to the Red Sea and who built a camp in Koptos (*CIL* III 6627, 14147). One of the soldiers originally came from Etenna in Pisidia. The inscription is dated to the time of Augustus or Tiberius.

(4) He also could have traveled about 100 km further north on the Nile to Abale (mod. el Mogren?), and from there via a caravan route to Sotērias limēn on the Red Sea; this was the shortest route from Meroë to the Red Sea.[62]

The Ethiopian is described as εὐνοῦχος (*eunouchos*), a term that literally means "a castrated male person."[63] Eunuchs were among the most ridiculed persons in ancient societies. Many eunuchs were slaves. In the Orient eunuchs often served as keepers of a harem. Eunuchs sometimes rose to high positions at the royal courts, which made the term *eunouchos* a virtual synonym for court officials. In some contexts men who had been physically castrated were described as *eunouchos*. According to Deut 23:1, castrates were not permitted to enter the sanctuary, and according to Deut 23:2-9, they could not be circumcised—that is, they could not become proselytes. Jewish eunuchs could not become members of the Sanhedrin or of a criminal court. However, some eunuchs managed to rise to high positions at the court of Herod I. Whether the *eunouchos* of Acts 8:26-40 was a castrate or whether the term is used as a title is contested.

The following arguments are important. (1) The literal meaning is supported by the fact that the term is repeated in the text several times and that it stands next to the term *dynastēs,* which can be used as the title for a "court official."[64] If the Ethiopian was a castrate,[65] Luke probably uses the account of Acts 8:26-40 to point out that the promise of Is 56:3-8 for eunuchs finds fulfillment in the mission of the early church.[66] (2) Luke uses

---

[61]For a discussion of the rest stations and garrisons along these routes see Valerie A. Maxfield, "The Eastern Desert Forts and the Army in Egypt during the Principate," in D. Bailey 1996, 9-19. For the observation that follows above see Nollé 1992, 108-9 (no. 2.11).

[62]For this route see P. Högemann, in *Tübingen Bible Atlas* [*TAVO*] B V 22 (Northeast Africa and Arabian Peninsula, 1987). N. B. Millet (*BAGRW,* map 82) does not record this route.

[63]See A. Hug, PWSup 3 (1918): 449-55; J. Schneider, *ThWNT* 2:763-67 (*TDNT* 2:765-68); B. Kedar-Kopfstein, *ThWAT* 5:948-54 (*TDOT* 10:344-50); G. Petzke, *EWNT* 2:202-4 (*EDNT* 2:80-81).

[64]Marshall, *Acts,* 163; cf. BDAG 409.

[65]Barrett, *Acts,* 1:424-25; Zmijewski, *Apg,* 362; Witherington, *Acts,* 296; Hengel 1994b, 250 n. 199; more recently Kraus 1999, 60; Kollmann 2000, 558-59. Undecided is Bruce 1989, 379; *Acts,* 175.

[66]Marshall, *Acts,* 163; Schneider, *Apg,* 1:498; Pao 2000, 140-42.

the term *eunouchos* to describe the Ethiopian as a court official,[67] since the repeated references to the man as "the castrated man" (Acts 8:34, 36, 38, 39) would be somewhat embarrassing. In this interpretation the phrase *eunouchos dynastēs* means "powerful high official"; that is, *dynastēs* is not the title proper but rather the attribute to the title *eunouchos* and its translation, as the phrase "queen of the Ethiopians" explains the title "Candace."

Was the Ethiopian a proselyte? The fact that he was on a pilgrimage to Jerusalem does not help to decide this question: not only proselytes visited Jerusalem as pilgrims but God-fearers as well, including God-fearers from Africa. If he was a castrate, he could not have been a proselyte: in this case he would have been a God-fearer who either maintained regular contacts with a Jewish community or was a sympathizer of the Jewish faith. If this is the correct scenario, then Acts 8:27 is the earliest piece of evidence for the presence of Jews in Nubia. Since Luke surely would note the conversion of a Gentile, it seems a plausible conclusion that the Ethiopian was a proselyte—that is, a circumcised Gentile.[68] Luke describes the dissemination of the gospel from Jerusalem to the Gentiles as an expansion that moved through all intermediate stages: from Jews to Samaritans to proselytes (the Ethiopian) to God-fearing Gentiles (Cornelius) to Gentiles (Antioch). However, the identity and background of the Ethiopian official remain uncertain.

The Ethiopian presumably did not speak or read Hebrew. We must assume, therefore, that the Isaiah scroll that he was reading on his journey back to Ethiopia was written in Greek. Martin Hengel comments, "The verses quoted from Is 53 in vv. 32-33 correspond exactly to the LXX version, which diverges in this passage significantly from the Masoretic Text."[69] He probably bought the scroll during his visit in Jerusalem.

Shmuel Safrai points out that pilgrims brought their own scrolls of Scripture texts to Jerusalem "in order to have them corrected in the temple with the help of the 'Book of the Forecourt,' which was in the custody of the temple scribes."[70] However, festival pilgrims also bought new scrolls in Jerusalem.

Luke's account of the Ethiopian official's conversion focuses on the fact that he came to faith as a result of the insight that the prophetic Scriptures have been fulfilled in Jesus. The following aspects of Luke's account in Acts 8:26-40 contribute to his description of the early Christian mission. (1) Luke makes the theological point that missionaries reckon with and follow divine guidance. Philip is ordered by an angel of the Lord to go to the street leading to Gaza. Luke repeatedly

[67]Pesch, *Apg,* 1:290; Jervell, *Apg,* 271; S. Wilson 1973, 171; cf. G. Petzke, *EWNT* 2:202-4 (*EDNT* 2:80-81).
[68]Jervell, *Apg,* 271. Pesch (*Apg,* 1:289) argues that the Ethiopian was a Gentile and that the account of his conversion was transposed to Acts 8.
[69]Hengel 1994b, 250.
[70]Safrai 1981, 262.

emphasizes God's initiative (Acts 8:26, 29, 39). (2) In terms of missionary strategy, the story illustrates that missionary outreach aims at encounters with individuals. Luke had reported mass conversions for Samaria; here he reports that the same missionary takes time to dialogue with an individual. (3) In geographical terms, the gospel moves to a new stage: the first African is converted. (4) In social terms, the conversion of the Ethiopian is the conversion of an educated and politically influential man to faith in Jesus Christ. (5) In hermeneutical terms, instruction from Scripture plays a central role in the conversion of the Ethiopian. The question "Do you understand what you are reading?" (Acts 8:30) is the most basic question of biblical hermeneutics.[71] Reading does not guarantee understanding— the private reading of Scripture does not guarantee proper understanding. The correct understanding of Scripture requires someone who can explain the meaning of Scripture. The Ethiopian official did not know whether Isaiah spoke about himself or about a contemporary: the correct interpretation of the text does not result from learned scribal discussion or from historical exegesis, "but only through insight into the history of Jesus of Nazareth as the climax of God's history with his people. The 'sensus plenior' of Scripture is grasped through salvation history in the interpretive realm of the assembly of God's people." (6) In terms of the theology of the mission of the early church, the baptism of the Ethiopian is significant. We can assume that the "good news about Jesus" (Acts 8:35) that Philip presented to the official included reference to water baptism, similar to Peter's description of the proper response to the gospel in Acts 2:38. Even though the encounter on the road between Jerusalem and Gaza was short, there was enough time for baptism. According to tradition, the baptism of the Ethiopian official took place in Beth Sur (Philip's well) north of Hebron.

Early traditions claim to know that Philip later traveled to Ethiopia, as did the apostle Matthew.

Acts of Philip includes a comment on a journey of Philip from Parthia (= Samaria?) to Ethiopia, and from there to Azotos (Ashdod; see §20.4) on the Mediterranean coast: "Then Philip came across the sea to the borders of the Candaces; there he found a ship that was about to sail to Azotos [καὶ ἦλθεν τότε ὁ Φίλιππος κατὰ θάλασσαν ὅροις τῶν Κανδάκων, καὶ εὗρεν πλοῖον μέλλον ἀπαίρειν εἰς Ἄξωτον]" (*Acts Phil.* 3.10). The context of *Acts Phil.* 3 possibly presupposes a journey from Palestine via the Sinai to Nubia.[72] Rufinus claims to know that the apostle Matthew went to Ethiopia as well (Rufinus, *Hist. eccl.* 1.9-10).

Irenaeus and Eusebius claim to know that the converted eunuch was the first missionary to Ethiopia.

Irenaeus, *Haer.* 4.23.2: "Immediately when [Philip] had baptized him, he departed from him. For nothing else [but baptism] was wanting to him who had been already instructed

---

[71] For the observations that follow above see Pesch, *Apg,* 1:295; quotation, ibid., 1:295-96.
[72] On this passage see Amsler 1999, 147-51; see also Matthews 2002, 166-67.

by the prophets: he was not ignorant of God the Father, nor of the rules as to the [proper] manner of life, but was merely ignorant of the advent of the Son of God, which, when he had become acquainted with, in a short space of time, he went on his way rejoicing, to be the herald in Ethiopia of Christ's advent [*praeco futurus in Aethiopia Christi adventus*]."

Eusebius, *Hist. eccl.* 2.1.13: "But as the preaching of the Savior's Gospel was daily advancing, a certain providence led from the land of the Ethiopians an officer of the queen of that country, for Ethiopia even to the present day is ruled, according to ancestral custom, by a woman. He, first among the Gentiles, received of the mysteries of the divine word from Philip in consequence of a revelation, and having become the first-fruits of believers throughout the world, he is said to have been the first on returning to his country to proclaim the knowledge of the God of the universe and the life-giving sojourn of our Savior among men; so that through him in truth the prophecy obtained its fulfillment, which declares that 'Ethiopia stretcheth out her hand unto God' [Ps 68:31; 67:32 LXX]."

These statements do not betray any detailed knowledge about churches in Ethiopia, which means that they could simply be assumptions of what might have or could have happened. With the exception of these two statements, the history of the church in Nubia can be traced back only to the fourth century.[73]

20.4 Missionary Work in the Cities of the Coastal Plain

The New Testament sources report Christian communities in areas outside of Judea and Samaria proper soon after these events: as a result of missionary outreach by Philip and by Peter churches are established in the coastal plain, at least in Lydda, Joppa, Caesarea and Ptolemais, and perhaps in Ashdod. Karl Löning plausibly suggests that the conversion of Paul on the road to Damascus may have been, at least as a matter of principle, "not an exception but an example for the first phase of an unsystematic missionary outreach from Jerusalem to more distant areas, using the existing roads between the more important cities of the Mediterranean world, mediated through the connections between the Diaspora Jews living in these cities and the temple in Jerusalem."[74]

Lydda (Λύδδα; Lod, later Diospolis; mod. Lud),[75] situated 44 km northwest of Jerusalem south of Naḥal Ayalon (mod. Wadi el-Kabir) in the coastal plain, was an old Canaanite city that was conquered by Tutmoses III in the fifteenth century B.C. Lod-Lydda came under Jewish control during the rule of the Seleucid king Demetrios II around 145 B.C. (1 Macc 11:34), which may indicate that the population was predominantly Jewish. Lydda became the capital of one of the eleven toparchies of Judea (Josephus, *B.J.* 2.567; 3.55). Josephus describes Lydda as "a village that was in size not inferior to a city" (*A.J.* 20.130),

[73]B. Metzger 1968b, 111-22.
[74]Löning 1987, 81.
[75]G. Hölscher, PW 13 (1927): 2120-22; M. Sharon, *EJ* 5:798-803; M. Hunt, "Lod," *ABD* 4:346; J. Kaplan, *NEAEHL* 3:917; J. Pahlitzsch, *DNP* 7:538; Schürer 1:142, 182; 2:190-93, 196; Hüttenmeister 1977, 284-99; Hengel 1983b, 170 (ET, 116); Kasher 1990, 297-99; Joshua J. Schwartz, *Lod (Lydda), Israel, from Its Origins through the Byzantine Period* (BAR International Series 571; Oxford: British Institute of Archaeology, 1991); idem 1995; Hengel 1995, 59-60.

which means that Lydda did not have city rights. Lydda was burned down by the Roman general Cestius in the initial phase of the First Jewish Revolt when Vespasian marched against Jerusalem; he settled loyal Jews in the city (*B.J.* 2.567; 4.445). Literary sources attest a rabbinic academy and a court of law in Lydda at the end of the first century, and a synagogue for the second century.[76] Since Lydda was located between Joppa and Jerusalem, it was a town in which Christians who had to flee from Jerusalem could stay and meet the other believers there.[77]

Joppa ('Ιόππη, *Ioppē;* Heb., יפו, Japho, Jaffa),[78] situated 18 km northwest of Lydda (5 km south of mod. Tel Aviv), was an old city of the Canaanites and the Philistines attested as early as 1500 B.C. in literary sources. Joppa was the port of entry for the timber from Lebanon that was used in building the first and second temples (2 Chron 2:16; Ezra 3:7). The prophet Jonah had traveled to Joppa-Japho, in his attempt to escape God's charge to preach repentance in Nineveh, by boarding a ship bound for Tarshish (Jon 1:3). During the Persian period Joppa was controlled by the city of Sidon. In the Hellenistic period Greeks settled in the city. During Seleucid rule Jonathan the Maccabean conquered the city in 147/146 B.C. (1 Macc 10:75-76; 13:11) and transformed it into a Jewish harbor on the Mediterranean. The city later fell to Pompey, Julius Caesar and Cleopatra. Joppa then belonged to the kingdom of Herod I and of his son Archelaus. When Judea became a Roman province, Joppa was controlled by the Roman procurator.[79] As a port city about 60 km west of Jerusalem, Joppa was the gateway to Judea. The city may have been the capital of one of the toparchies of Judea. Before A.D. 66 the population seems to have been predominantly Jewish: during the First Jewish Revolt, Joppa was an important center of the rebellion. When the Roman troops conquered the city under the command of the Syrian governor Cestius Gallus, 8,400 people were killed (Josephus, *B.J.* 2.507-509; 3.414-426). Remains of settlements of the Persian and Hellenistic periods have been discovered in the area of the Church of St. Peter (Area Y).

Caesarea (Καισάρεια, *Kaisareia;* Lat., Caesarea Maritima [see fig. 11]),[80] about 60 km north of Joppa, was built by Herod I between 22 and 10 B.C. (Josephus, *B.J.* 3.408-415; *A.J.* 15.331-341) at the site of the old Phoenician harbor that was called Straton's Tower

---

[76]See L. Levine 2000, 172, 190-91, 272.

[77]See Vidal Manzanares 1995, 136.

[78]See H. Donner, *KP* 2:1438-39; J. Kaplan and H. Ritter-Kaplan, *ABD* 2:946-49; idem, *NEAEHL* 2:655-59; R. Liwak, *DNP* 5:1085; Schürer 2:33-34, 110-14, 191-92; Hengel 1983b, 170 (ET, 116-17); Kasher 1990, 111-16, 224-27, 235-37; Hengel 1995, 60; Tsafrir, di Segni and Green, *Iudaea-Palaestina,* 152-53.

[79]Josephus, *A.J.* 14.76; 17.320.

[80]Benzinger, "Caesarea Nr. 10," PW 3 (1899): 1291-94; A. Negev, *PECS* 182; R. Riesner, *GBL* 1:224-25; R. L. Hohlfelder, *ABD* 1:798-803; K. G. Holum et al., *NEAEHL* 1:270-91; K. G. Holum, *OEANE* 1:399-404; T. Leisten, *DNP* 2:924-25; J. R. McRay, *DNTB* 176-77; Schürer 1:306-61; L. Levine 1975; Hüttenmeister 1977, 79-90; Hengel 1983, 167-69 (ET, 113-15); L. I. Levine and E. Netzer, *Excavations at Caesarea Maritima: 1975, 1976, 1979, Final Report* (Qedem 21; Jerusalem: Institute of Archaeology, Hebrew University of Jerusalem, 1986); Holum et al. 1988; Hopfe 1990; Kasher 1990, 240-46, 252-65, and passim; Vann et al. 1992-1999; Tsafrir, di Segni and Green, *Iudaea-Palaestina,* 94-96; Yosef Porath, "Herod's 'Ampitheatre' at Caesarea: A Multipurpose Entertainment Building," in Humphrey 1995-2002, 1:15-27; Raban and Holum 1996; Donaldson 2000 (with an annotated bibliography by Elaine A. Myers, 65-101); L. Levine 2000, 64-65, 69-71, and passim; D. Jacobson 2001. Inscriptions: Bradley H. McLean, "The Inscriptions of Caesarea and Their Relation to the Physical Remains of the City," *Ancient World* 28 (1997): 184-216; 30 (1999): 3-28. See <http://digcaesarea.org>.

(Στράτωνος Πύργος) in the Hellenistic period.[81] Straton's Tower seems to have had two ports around 150 B.C. The town was conquered around 100 B.C. by Alexander Jannaeus (Josephus, *A.J.* 13.334-335) and became Jewish in the following decades.[82] Pompey annexed the town into the new province of Syria; Augustus returned it to the Jewish state in 31 B.C. Herod I named the new city that he built at the site of Straton's Tower after Augustus, his patron, in order to demonstrate his loyalty to Roman traditions. The games that were organized every five years were dedicated to Augustus.[83] Caesarea was 1.5 km long from north to south. Herod constructed a large platform (100 by 90 m) on which he built a temple (28.6 by 46.4 m) dedicated to Augustus and Roma (Sebasteion).[84] Josephus praises the beauty and the size of the temple, which contained a statue of Julius Caesar that compared favorably with the statue of Zeus in Olympia, and the statue of Roma that stood in the temple could well be compared with the statue of Hera in Argos (*B.J.* 1.414). The temple could be seen from the approaching ships from afar (*A.J.* 15.339). This temple was positively identified by archaeologists in 1995. With the Sebasteion, the royal palace, the agora, the theater that could seat 3,500 spectators (*B.J.* 1.415; *A.J.* 15.341) and the amphitheater (265 by 50 m interior size), Caesarea had the infrastructure of a Roman provincial capital, a function that the city acquired in A.D. 6. The praetorium of the governor of the province of Judea initially was located in Herod's palace, the so-called Promontory Palace (110 by 55 m, with a water pond in the middle measuring 35 by 18 m) on the small peninsula south of the southern harbor, immediately east of the amphitheater.[85] Around A.D. 100 a governor's palace was built just north of the amphitheater, including a large warehouse complex; after A.D. 300 this palace was the praetorium of the Byzantine governor.[86] The amphitheater (60 by 95 m) was larger than the Colosseum in Rome. The marble for the sculptures was imported from Greece and Rome.[87] During Hadrian's principate a hippodrome was built in the southeast section of the city; it could accommodate over thirty thousand spectators. The city blocks of the rectangular city plan measured 80 by 120 m. The harbor complex Sebastos,[88] also called *Portus Augusti* on coins, consisted of four harbors that played an important role in international shipping. Numerous large warehouses (*horrea*) were used to store wheat, wine and other goods before they were loaded on the ships. The ships, entering the harbor from the northwest, passed by colossal statues of the imperial family standing on massive columns, showing the captains of

---

[81]See A. Raban, *NEAEHL* 1:286-87; idem, in Vann et al. 1992-1999, 1:7-22; D. W. Roller, in ibid., 1:23-25; T. W. Hillard, in ibid., 1:42-48.

[82]On the history of the Jewish community there see Murray 2000.

[83]Josephus, *B.J.* 1.415; *A.J.* 16.136-141; 19.343.

[84]See Kenneth G. Holum, "The Temple Platform: Progress Report on the Excavations," in Vann et al. 1992-1999, 2:13-34.

[85]See Ehud Netzer, "The Promontory Palace," in Raban and Holum 193-207; idem, "The Palaces Built by Herod—A Research Update," in Fittschen and Foerster 1996, 27-54, esp. 32-33; Burrell, "Palace to Praetorium: The Romanization of Caesarea," in ibid., 228-47; K. L. Gleason et al., "The Promontory Palace at Caesarea Maritima: Preliminary Evidence for Herod's *praetorium*," *JRA* 11 (1998): 23-52.

[86]Joseph Patrich, "The Warehouse Complex and Governor's Palace," in Vann et al. 1992-1999, 2:71-107.

[87]See Elise A. Friedland, "Graeco-Roman Sculpture in the Levant: The Marbles from the Sanctuary of Pan at Caesarea Philippi (Banias)," in Humphrey 1995-2002, 2:20. Friedland mentions Thasos, Pentelikon, Paros, Aphrodisias, Hymettus and Marmara as places of origin of the marble used in Caesarea.

[88]See Vann et al. 1992-1999, 1:49-78; 2:152-356.

the ships the way into the harbor. Caesarea had about thrity thousand inhabitants,[89] mostly Syrian Greeks, Roman soldiers and a large Jewish minority. There is archaeological and epigraphical evidence for Samaritan inhabitants as well.[90] The city territory extended from the brook Chorseos (mod. Nahal Daliyya) to the brook Bdellopotamos (mod. Nahal Poleg) 35 km further south. Caesarea controlled numerous farms, villas and small towns. When the Romans annexed Judea in A.D. 6, Caesarea became the seat of the provincial governor. An inscription discovered in 1961 confirms that Pilate, the governor, erected a temple dedicated to Tiberius.[91] The killing of twenty thousand Jews in the city was one of the causes of the Jewish revolt against Rome in A.D. 66.[92] At times ten thousand Roman soldiers were stationed in the city. After the fall of Jerusalem, Titus forced 2,500 Jewish prisoners of war to fight as gladiators in the amphitheater of Caesarea. Vespasian, who was proclaimed emperor in Caesarea in A.D. 69, granted the city the status of a Roman colony (Colonia Prima Flavia Augusta Caesarea). Most Greek and Roman cults are attested for Caesarea:[93] Aphrodite, Apollo, Artemis Ephesia, Asclepius, Astarte, Demeter, Dionysos, Horus, Isis, Sarapis, Tyche, Zeus, a river god (Nilus-Sarapis, or Euthenia-Isis-Tyche), and, of course, the imperial cult. A coin minted in A.D. 67/68 depicts Tyche, the goddess of fate: the population hoped for good fortune, protection and prosperity. The synagogue in the northwest section of the city dates to the fourth and fifth centuries; it was built on top of an older building that may have been a synagogue before A.D. 70.[94] Between A.D. 520 and 550 a church was built at the site of the old temple of Augustus (octagon, 39 m in diameter). An earlier church that must have existed for a long period of time, as Caesarea had become a Christian city long before, has not been found yet.[95]

  Ptolemais-Akko ('Ακκώ; Tell Akko, Tell el-Fukhar),[96] situated about 60 km north of Caesarea and 50 km south of Tyre, was an old Canaanite harbor on the Mediterranean coast. During the conquest Akko remained Canaanite (Judg 1:31); under David and during the first years of Solomon's reign the town was Jewish (see 2 Sam 24:7). In the eighth and seventh centuries B.C. Akko was Phoenician and later Assyrian. When the population rebelled against Assyrian rule, Sennacherib conquered and Ashurbanipal destroyed the city. In the fifth and fourth centuries Akko was a military and administrative center of the Persians. Trade contacts with Athens are attested for the fourth century. In 332 B.C. Akko surrendered to Alexander the Great. In the third century Ptolemy II Philadelphos refounded

---

[89]Reed (2000, 94) estimates between twenty thousand and forty thousand inhabitants.

[90]L. Levine 1975, 107-12; P. Richardson, in Donaldson 2000, 28; B. H. McLean, in ibid., 62.

[91]The inscription is housed in the Israel Museum in Jerusalem (IDAM Collection No. 61-529) and reads: "[. . .]S Tiberieum [.Po]ntius Pilatus [praeflectus Iuda[ea]e [dedit dedicavit]." See E. Weber, "Zur Inschrift des Pontius Pilatus," *Bonner Jahrbücher* 171 (1971): 194-200; K. G. Holum, in Holum et al. 1988, 109-11. Géza Alföldy ("Pontius Pilatus und das Tibériéum von Caesarea Maritima," *Scripta Classica Israelica* 18 [1998]: 85-108) reads the first word as *Nautis* and interprets the *Tiberieum* as a lighthouse in Caesarea's harbor.

[92]Josephus, *B.J.* 2.457. See Murray 2000, 136-37.

[93]See Hopfe 1990; R. Jackson Painter, "Greco-Roman Religion in Caesarea Maritima," in Donaldson 2000, 105-25.

[94]See B. H. McLean, "The Inscriptions of Caesarea," *Ancient World* 28 (1997): 184-216, nos. 8-13; Peter Richardson, in Donaldson 2000, 26-27; L. Levine 2000, 171, 204-5.

[95]K. G. Holum, in Vann et al. 1992-1999, 2:26; on the early Byzantine church see ibid., 2:27-31.

[96]Bertold Spuler, "Ptolemais Nr. 9," PW 23.2 (1959): 1883-86; J.-P. Rey-Coquais, *PECS* 742; M. Dothan and Z. Goldmann, *NEAEHL* 1:16-31; M. Aviam, *NEAEHL* 2:453; M. Dothan, *ABD* 1:50-53; Schürer 2:36, 121-25; Teixidor 1977, 52-59; Tsafrir, di Segni and Green, *Iudaea-Palaestina,* 204-5; Kasher 1990, 235, 238, and passim; Isaac 1993, 322-23.

the city and renamed it Ptolemais. After 200 B.C. the city came under Seleucid rule, and
in 83 B.C. the Armenian king Tigranes conquered it. The Roman general Pompey granted
Akko autonomy in 63 B.C. In 47 B.C. Julius Caesar visited Akko. Claudius refounded Ptolemais-Akko in A.D. 53/54 as a Roman colony (Colonia Claudia Felix Ptolemais Germanica
Stabilis), without full colony rights, however, and settled veterans in the city. The main
god of Ptolemais was the Syrian weather-god (Baal-)Hadad, who was worshiped together
with the Dea Syria Astargatis. The city had Jewish inhabitants: at the beginning of the Jewish revolt in A.D. 66, about two thousand Jews were killed in the city (Josephus, *B.J.*
2.477). Around A.D. 90 Rabban Gamaliel visited the baths of Aphrodite in Akko (*m. 'Abod.
Zar.* 3:4). Numerous pottery shards dating to the first century were found in the area of
the harbor, attesting to intensive trade activities.[97] The bishop Aeneas of Ptolemais was
present at the Council of Nicea in A.D. 325.

    Ashdod-Azotos (mod. Tel Ashdod),[98] about 50 km south of Joppa/Jaffo, situated about
4 km inland from the Mediterranean on the southern coast of Palestine, was the old capital
of the Philistines. The name of the city in the Roman period was Azotos Mesogeios
('Αζωτος μεσόγειος). Judas Maccabaeus had destroyed altars and idols in Ashdod; in
147 B.C. Jonathan burned the entire city to the ground, including the temple of Dagon (1
Macc 5:68; 10:83-84; 11:4). In the following decades the city, or what remained of it, belonged to Judea. Pompey granted the city autonomy, but it was the Roman governor Gabinius (57-55 B.C.) who rebuilt Ashdod-Azotos (Josephus, *A.J.* 13.395; 14.75; *B.J.* 1.166).
Ashdod belonged, like the other cities in the coastal plain, to the kingdom of Herod I,
who gave the city to his sister Salome (*A.J.* 18.31; *B.J.* 2.98), who in turn gave it to the
empress Livia. The size of the Jewish community in Ashdod in the first century probably
was considerable: Vespasian felt the need to station soldiers in Ashdod during the First
Jewish Revolt (*B.J.* 4.130). The bishop Silvanus of Azotos-Ashdod attended the Council of
Constantinople. The mosaic floor of the Byzantine church of Azotos was laid in A.D. 512.[99]

Luke indicates that Philip was the missionary who evangelized in Samaria and
in the cities of the coastal plain: "Philip found himself at Azotus, and as he was
passing through the region, he proclaimed the good news to all the towns until
he came to Caesarea" (Acts 8:40). It is quite possible that people were converted in Lydda and Joppa—the people whom Peter later met and stayed with
(Acts 9:32, 36, 38). Probably there also were conversions to the Christian faith
in Caesarea, where Philip was based as an evangelist and where Paul visited
him several years later (Acts 21:8). Luke does not say that Philip's missionary
outreach to the cities of the coastal plain presupposed or amounted to a mission to Gentiles: it is possible that he concentrated on the Jewish communities
that lived in these cities. However, his mission in Samaria and his encounter
with the Ethiopian official seem to make it unlikely that Philip limited his

---

[97] A. Raben, *NEAEHL* 1:30.
[98] A. Negev, "Azotos," *PECS* 133; M. Dothan, *NEAEHL* 1:92-102; M. Dothan, "Ashdod," *ABD*
    1:477-81; P. L. Redditt, "Azotus," *ABD* 1:541-42; M. Dothan et al., *Ashdod* (4 vols.; Jerusalem:
    Department of Antiquities and Museums in the Ministry of Education and Culture, 1962-1982);
    Schürer 2:32-33, 108-9; Hüttenmeister 1977, 19-21; Hengel 1983b, 166-67 (ET, 113); 1995, 53-
    55; Tsafrir, di Segni and Green, *Iudaea-Palaestina*, 72.
[99] *SEG* XXXVII 1469. See L. di Segni, in Humphrey 1995-2002, 2:167.

preaching activity to Jews. Some scholars comment favorably on the courageous missionary outreach of Philip across the borders of Judea in the largely
pagan cities of the coastal plain, while arguing that "the real, planned and also
revolutionary step to the Christian Gentile mission" took place in Antioch.[100]
However, Luke does not actually state in Acts 11:19-21 that the Hellenistic Jewish Christians from Cyprus and Cyrene who had fled from Jerusalem to Antioch
attempted to win Gentiles for faith in Jesus for the first time in Antioch. It is a
distinct possibility that Philip, and perhaps other members of the Seven,
preached the gospel to uncircumcised God-fearers whom they encountered in
synagogues, for example.

Martin Hengel underlines the reliability of Luke's account[101] and states "that
Hellenists such as Philip who carried on their missionary work particularly in
this mixed area, marked out by hatred between Gentiles and Jews, could be
connected with the 'pacifying' character of the gospel." This early missionary
work in the Greek cities of the coastal plain demonstrates the courage of the
missionaries from Jerusalem: they did not shrink back from preaching the message of Jesus the Messiah in areas that traditionally were difficult for Jews.

Did Philip engage in missionary work among the Jews in Caesarea, and perhaps among the Samaritan inhabitants, before Peter arrived in the city and led
the Roman officer Cornelius to faith in Jesus Christ (see §21.2-3)? This is possible,
but it cannot necessarily be deduced from the narrative sequence of Acts 8:40
and Acts 10:1-48. Luke ends his account of Philip's mission in Samaria and his
encounter with the Ethiopian official with the comment in Acts 8:40 and briefly
resurrects Philip as "evangelist" in Caesarea in Acts 21:8, which means that he
could have arrived in the city after the events described in Acts 10.[102] In other
words, Philip may have arrived in Caesarea after the conversion of Cornelius
through the ministry of Peter. It is not impossible, however, that a Jewish-Christian community had been established in Caesarea before Peter visited the city.
In any event, the Christian community in Caesarea dates to the 30s.

Philip is described in Acts 21:8 as εὐαγγελιστής (euangelistēs) living in Caesarea. This may imply that he is, at this later point in time, no longer an itinerant
missionary but rather a leader in the local church responsible for the proclamation
of the gospel.[103] Whether Philip can be called, on the basis of Eph 4:11 and 2 Tim
4:5, "the leader of the church responsible for proclamation"[104] is not clear, however.

---

[100]Stuhlmacher 1981, 117.

[101]Hengel 1983, 166 (ET, 112), the quotation that follows above, ibid., 167 (ET, 113).

[102]See Ascough 2000, 155-57. The hypothesis, based on Acts 21:16-18, of a rivalry between the
(Gentile-Christian) church in Caesarea and the (Jewish-Christian) church in Jerusalem (see
ibid., 158) is neither historically plausible nor alluded to in the text.

[103]See G. Strecker (EWNT 2:176 [EDNT 2:70]), who comments, correctly, that "a clearly demarcated church office is not apparent."

[104]Pesch, Apg, 2:213.

Axel von Dobbeler describes Philip in Caesarea as the leader of a house church whose home was "the spiritual center of a prophetic-charismatic Christianity."[105] Since there were Christian prophets in the congregations in Jerusalem, Antioch, Corinth and presumably in other churches as well, this description is not very helpful. At any rate, it should not be used to differentiate Philip from other early Christian missionaries.

Luke reports that not only Philip but also the apostle Peter engaged in missionary work in the cities of the coastal region. Philip "traveled about the country" (TNIV; διερχόμενον διὰ πάντων, *dierchomenon dia pantōn* [Acts 9:32a]), a phrase that refers in one respect to "Judea and Galilee and Samaria" (Acts 9:31).[106] He also journeys to Lydda-Lod in the coastal plain (Acts 9:32b). The churches in Lydda and Joppa were established perhaps as a result of missionary work by Peter: when Peter "found" the believer Aeneas in Lydda (Acts 9:33), this only means that he "met" him, not that he found Christians in Lydda whose existence had been unknown to him. The believers in Joppa know Peter before they ask him to come to Joppa when Tabitha had died (Acts 9:38), a fact that does not prove that Peter founded the church in Joppa but certainly leaves open the possibility. After Aeneas of Lydda is healed, "all the residents of Lydda and Sharon saw him and turned to the Lord" (Acts 9:35). And after the miracle of the resurrection of Tabitha of Joppa becomes common knowledge, "many believed in the Lord" (Acts 9:42). Luke continues his account with the comment that Peter "stayed in Joppa for some time with a certain Simon, a tanner" (Acts 9:43)— surely not as the leader of the church in Joppa but as an apostle who had been commissioned by Jesus to engage in missionary outreach among Jews and Gentiles. Peter was not simply the "inspector of the Jewish-Christian communities in the coastal plain,"[107] but also the pioneer missionary in this area.[108] Cities that the Jerusalem missionaries may have reached with the gospel besides Joppa, Lydda and Caesarea will be discussed below (§21.4).

Joshua Schwartz presents a revised version of the suggestion of B. Königsberger that the *mesit* (seducer) Ben Stada, mentioned in rabbinic sources of the second century as the man who seduced the masses in Lod to idolatry, might have been the apostle Peter.[109] In rabbinic literature Ben Stada is the only *mesit* identified by name. Any identification with Jesus is unconvincing.[110] The most prominent and influential believer in Jesus as the Messiah in Palestine whom the rabbis would have described as "seducer" presumably was Peter, the leader of the Twelve and of the Jerusalem church. Schwartz further points out that Peter performed miracles of healing and punishment (Acts 3:1-10; 5:1-11), that the

---

[105]Dobbeler 2000a, 221, 248.

[106]Acts 9:31: καθ᾽ ὅλης τῆς Ἰουδαίας καὶ Γαλιλαίας καὶ Σαμαρείας.

[107]Hengel 1983b, 171 (ET, 117); 1995, 59.

[108]See Pesch, *Apg,* 1:318-19; Barrett, *Acts,* 1:479.

[109]J. Schwartz 1995, with reference to *t. Sanh.* 10:11; *y. Yebam.* 16 (15d); *y. Sanh.* 7 (25c); *b. Sanh.* 67a; on the *mesit* see *m. Sanh.* 7.10.

[110]J. Maier 1978, 204-5; J. Schwartz 1995, 396-98.

Sanhedrin described Peter and John as "uneducated and ordinary men" (Acts 4:13), and that Peter was active in Lod-Lydda (Acts 9:32, 36, 38). This evidence indeed indicates that Peter perhaps was the Ben Stada of the rabbinic sources; the evidence is insufficient, however, to conclude that this is a historical certainty.

A comment in Acts 21:7 confirms that there was a Christian community in Ptolemais: Paul visits "the brothers" in Ptolemais during his return journey from Ephesus and Corinth, perhaps because the ship on which he and his companions sailed stayed in port overnight.[111]

Luke gives a detailed account of Paul's imprisonment in Caesarea about twenty years later in A.D. 57-59, but he provides no information about a local church. We do not know whether Cornelius was still stationed in Caesarea, nor do we know whether Philip was still in the city evangelizing in the region. If the hypothesis were valid that Paul's letter to the Christians in Philippi was written during the Caesarean imprisonment,[112] we would learn details about the church of Caesarea. This interpretation of the historical and geographical circumstances in which Paul wrote Philippians is implausible, however.

If the letter to the Philippians was written around 57/58 in Caesarea, we learn from Phil 1:14 that most of the believers in Caesarea were "made confident in the Lord by my imprisonment, dare to speak the word with greater boldness and without fear." According to Phil 1:15-18, a group of people within the church linked their proclamation of the gospel with their personal rivalry with the apostle Paul and attempted, somehow, to harm Paul. The causes of the rivalry are unknown, with regard both to Caesarea and to Rome. This passage does not allow for conclusions concerning the place of Paul's imprisonment.[113]

Benedict Viviano suggests that the Gospel of Matthew was written in Caesarea Maritima or received its final redactional form in the city.[114] This suggestions has found few supporters.[115] The traditional list of the bishops of the church of Caesarea—Zacchaeus the tax collector, Cornelius the Roman centurion, Theophilus, a second Zacchaeus (*Apos. Con.* 7.46)— is hardly reliable: Eusebius, who wrote his history of the church in Caesarea, does not list the bishops of the church of Caesarea. The first bishop that he knows is Theophilus, around A.D. 189 (*Hist. eccl.* 5.22), who presided over the Council of Caesarea in A.D. 195 with Narcissus, the bishop of Jerusalem. This information indicates that the church of Caesarea played a significant role at the end of the second century. Around A.D. 300 the church of Caesarea was the most important and most influential in Palestine, primarily due to the ministry of Origen (A.D. 185-254) and Eusebius (A.D. 263-339) in the city.[116] Jerome points out in the fourth century that Christian visitors to Caesarea are still shown the house of Philip.[117]

[111]See Barrett, *Acts,* 2:992.
[112]Lohmeyer, *Phil,* 3-4, 15-16, 40-41; Hawthorne, *Phil,* xli-xliv; J. Robinson 1976, 60-61; Krentz 1995, 263; as a possibility, Ascough 2000, 160-61.
[113]For a discussion of the various suggestions see O'Brien, *Phil,* 102-5.
[114]Viviano 1979, 533-46.
[115]Ascough (2000, 162-63) is cautiously optimistic without offering any new arguments.
[116]See Hopfe 1990, 2400; Krentz 1995; Ascough 2000, 164-79.
[117]Jerome, *Peregrinatio Sanctae Paulae* 31. See Hopfe 1990, 2399; Ascough 2000, 155.

The message about Jesus as Messiah and Savior reached Caesarea at the highest levels of the Roman administration of Judea in A.D. 57/58, when Paul defended himself in a trial that Jews from Jerusalem initiated against the apostle.

20.5 Christians in Damascus

The story of the conversion of Saul/Paul presupposes Christians in Damascus: Saul asks the high priest "for letters to the synagogues at Damascus, so that if he found any who belonged to the Way, men or women, he might bring them bound to Jerusalem" (Acts 9:2).

Luke mentions the name of one of the Christians in Damascus: Ananias (Acts 9:10-13, 17), "a devout man according to the law and well spoken of by all the Jews living there" (Acts 22:12). Some scholars have suggested that Ananias may have been an Essene: he calls Jesus "the Righteous One" (Acts 22:14), a messianic title that occurs in the book of Acts only in Stephen's speech (Acts 7:52) but is used in the Enoch literature (*1 En.* 38:2; 53:6), which is close to Essene theology.[118] Damascus is located 265 km north of Jerusalem; the journey from Jerusalem to Damascus led through Scythopolis, Hippos and Bethsaida on the Sea of Galilee, Caesarea Philippi and Suweida in the Decapolis (see fig. 24).

Damascus (Δαμασκός [see fig. 12])[119] was an old trading town situated in an oasis about 30 km east of the passage between Mount Hermon and the mountains of Anti-Lebanon at the western edge of the Syrian-Arabian desert. Damascus depended on the river (or

---

[118]See Riesner 1995a, 1863.

[119]I. Benzinger, PW 4.2 (1901): 2042-48; E. Kutch and K. Niederwimmer, *KP* 1:1371-73; J.-P. Rey-Coquais, *PECS* 256-57; D. J. Wiseman and R. Riesner, *GBL* 1:248-50; W. P. Pitard and J. McRay, *ABD* 2:5-8; A. H. M. Jones et al., *OCD* 427; T. Leisten, *DNP* 3:293-97; J. Murphy-O'Connor, *EDSS* 1:165-66; Carl Watzinger and Karl Wulzinger, *Damaskus I: Die Antike Stadt* (Wissenschaftliche Veröffentlichungen des deutsch-türkischen Denkmalschutz-Kommandos 4; Berlin: Vereinigung Wissenschaftlicher Verleger, 1922); idem, *Damaskus II: Die islamische Stadt* (Berlin: de Gruyter, 1924); Jean Sauvaget, "Esquisse d'une histoire de la ville de Damas," *REI* 8 (1937): 422-480; Schürer 2:127-30; Abd al-Qadir Rihawi, *Damascus: Its History, Development and Artistic Heritage* (Damascus, 1977); Dorothee Sack, "Damaskus, die Stadt *intra muros*," *Damaszener Mitteilungen* 2 (1985): 207-90; Kasher 1988, 101-3, 113-17, 158-61, 184-86; Sack 1989; Klaus S. Freyberger, "Untersuchungen zur Baugeschichte des Jupiter-Heiligtums in Damaskus," *Damaszener Mitteilungen* 4 (1989): 61-86; M. Sartre, in Dentzer and Orthmann 1989, 36; P. Leriche, in ibid., 276-78; Gawlikowski 1989, 334; Rey-Coquais 1989, 52-53; Will 1989, 228-29, 235-36; Kasher 1990, 283-86; Millar 1993, 36-37, 56-57, 310-19; Thomas Weber, "'Damaskòs Pólis Epísēmos': Hellenistische, römische und byzantinische Bauwerke in Damaskus aus der Sicht griechischer und lateinischer Schriftquellen," *Damaszener Mitteilungen* 7 (1993): 135-176; Riesner 1994, 70-79; Hengel and Schwemer 1998, 43-152 (ET, 24-90); Ball 2000, 184-87; Klaus S. Freyberger, "Das Heiligtum des Jupiter Damaszenus—Ein städtischer Kultbau lokaler Prägung," in Fansa et al. 2000, 212-17; D. Sack, "Die Topografie der historischen Stadt Damaskus," in ibid., 83-86; Jean-Marie Dentzer, "Damaskus in der hellenistischen und römischen Epoche," in ibid., 94-100; M. Braune and H. al-Zaym, "Stadttore und Stadtmauer von Damaskus," in ibid., 180-87.

brook) Chrysoroas (or Bardines; mod. Nahr Barada), whose water was distributed throughout a large territory by an elaborate system of canals. Strabo writes in the first century, "Above Massyas lies the Royal Valley, as it is called, and also the Damascene country, which is accorded exceptional praise. The city Damascus is also a noteworthy city, having been, I might almost say, even the most famous of the cities in that part of the world in the time of the Persian empire; and above it are situated two Trachones [rugged, strong tracts], as they are called" (16.2.20). According to Josephus, Damascus was founded by Uz, the great-grandson of Shem, probably together with Abraham's nephew mentioned in Gen 22:21 (Josephus, *A.J.* 1.145). Damascus is attested in Egyptian city lists dating from 1482 B.C. Abraham defeated a coalition of kings near Damascus (Gen 14:15). The Syrian kings who resided in Damascus used the names "Rab-Ramman" ("servant of the god Ramman" [= Hadad]) and "Ben Hadad."[120] Damascus was regarded as the center of the cult of the "Syrian gods." Hadad was venerated as weather-god in a sanctuary that had an oracle. It appears that the Aramaic temple site was already divided into an interior precinct with the *temenos* and an exterior precinct with a *peribolos* (enclosure). Damascus was the capital of an Aramaic state in the eleventh and tenth centuries B.C. David annexed the city (2 Sam 8:5-6), which, however, regained independence under Solomon (1 Kings 11:23-25). Damascus marked the northern boundary of the ideal Israelite or Jewish state (Ezek 47:16-18; 48:1; Zech 9:1). After the conquest by the Assyrians in 732 B.C., Damascus became the capital of an Assyrian province. When Alexander the Great conquered Syria in 332 B.C., Damascus fell to the Macedonians after an act of betrayal. The Macedonians founded a colony in the city, probably north of the Aramaic settlement between the temple/agora axis and the Barada River.[121] In the disputes between the Ptolemies and the Seleucids Damascus changed sides repeatedly; it belonged to the Seleucid Empire after 200 B.C. The Hellenistic Akra with the garrison was located probably in the western section of the city, at the site of the *castellum* of the time of Diocletian. Damascus was the capital of Coele-Syria and Phoenicia between 96 and 84 B.C. It then belonged to the Nabatean kingdom of Aretas III (85-72 B.C.), then to the Armenian kingdom of Tigranes (72-69 B.C.). Nabatean inhabitants probably settled in the third city quarter in the eastern section of Damascus.[122] The hippodrome (580 by 155 m), located about 500 m north of the Jupiter temple, existed by 88/87 B.C. (Josephus, *A.J.* 13.379); having a racetrack 70 m in width, which was used for horse, dromedary and camel races, the hippodrome was not much smaller than the Circus Maximus in Rome.[123] Damascus soon was surpassed by Antioch, a newly founded city on the Orontes River (Strabo 16.2.20), where Pompey maintained his capital even after the annexation of Damascus in 64 B.C. (Josephus, *A.J.* 14.29). After 64 B.C. the city was developed on the basis of Roman urban models: in the area of the southern quarters the connection between the eastern and the western parts of the oasis was expanded as *decumanus maximus* ("Straight Street" [Acts 9:11]; mod. Souk et-Tawil), which determines the layout of the city even today. The street between the temple and the agora was improved and built as a colonnaded street, and the *cardo* in the eastern section of the city as well (at the latest in the Severian period). Remains of two city gates survive: the north gate "to the gardens" (mod. Bab al-Faradis) and the east gate (mod. Bab Sharqi). The surviving remains of the east gate initially were dated to the third century A.D., whereas today

---

[120]R. Dussaud, "Hadad," PW 7 (1912): 2157-63.

[121]Sack 1989, 9. Sauvaget wanted to localize the Greek colony in the the eastern section of the city.

[122]Sack 1989, 11. In the Middle Ages the northeastern quarter was called Nabaṭiyin or Naybaṭun.

[123]Watzinger and Wulzinger, *Damaskus II,* 98; Weber, "'Damaskòs Pólis Epísēmos,'" 145.

a date during the time of Augustus is regarded as more likely.[124] The old temple was renovated in the early empire as a temple dedicated to Zeus or Jupiter, "with a temenos surrounding the cella, with colonnades on the inside at the front, and with a wide peribolos also lined with colonnades, and on the western side the 'gamma,' the street with shops."[125] The temple of Jupiter Damascenus is the largest known temple precinct in Syria in the Roman period: the *peribolos* (150 by 100 m) stood in a large temenos (385 by 305 m). Jupiter Damascenus was worshiped by merchants from Damascus in Puteoli (*CIL* X 1576).[126] Worshipers could exit the temple through a monumental gate leading to the agora east of the temple. The temple precinct was planned in the late first century B.C., according to building inscriptions found in Damascus, and built in the first century A.D. Structures of the northern side portal of the gate leading to the agora are dated to A.D. 16/17 or 46/47. Herod I built in Damascus a theater and a gymnasium (Josephus, *B.J.* 1.422), both situated probably in the southeastern quarter. Damascus had two theaters, with the easterly building probably representing an odeion.[127] Nicolaus, the non-Jewish adviser of Herod I, came from Damascus; besides tragedies, comedies and philosophical works he wrote a universal history in 144 volumes that was used by Strabo, Josephus and other authors.[128] Some scholars suggest that Gaius Caligula gave Damascus to the Nabatean king Aretas IV after the death of Tiberius in A.D. 37; this has not been confirmed, however. Damascus returned to direct Roman rule by A.D. 62 at the latest. The ethnarch serving under Aretas mentioned by Paul in 2 Cor 11:32-33 probably was "the head of the Nabatean colony of merchants in Damascus" who represented as "consul" the interests of the Nabatean state.[129] In the first and second centuries A.D. Damascus, at times, belonged to the Decapolis (Pliny, *Nat.* 5.16.74): like the cities of the Decapolis, Damascus was somewhat isolated geographically, separated from the other Greek cities in northern Syria by Semitic vassal kings. The territory controlled by Damascus was extensive: in the west it bordered on Abilene and, on the heights of Anti-Lebanon or in the Bekaa Valley, on the territory of Sidon; in the south it bordered on the territories of Paneas (Caesarea Philippi), Gaulanitis, Batanea, Trachonitis and Auranitis—areas that Augustus had granted to Herod I in 24 or 20 B.C. The influence of Damascus is seen not least in the fact that since A.D. 90 at the latest soldiers from Damascus were stationed in Germania (Mainz, Wiesbaden, Neckarburken). Damascus owed its wealth to the trade of figs, wine and wool, and since ancient times to the caravan trade. Damascene merchants are mentioned together with traders from Sidon and Tyre in inscriptions of Delos. The (few) inscriptions of the temples in the territory of Damascus were written in Greek (in contrast to the inscriptions of Palmyra, the city-state northeast of Damascus). This indicates that the population of Damascus evidently read and spoke Greek.

---

[124]See Watzinger and Wulzinger, *Damaskus I,* 77; now Freyberger, "Baugeschichte des Jupiter-Heiligtums," 86; Weber, "'Damaskòs Pólis Epísēmos,'" 152.

[125]Sack 1989, 11; see now Freyberger, "Baugeschichte des Jupiter-Heiligtums" and "Heiligtum des Jupiter Damaszenus."

[126]Freyberger, "Heiligtum des Jupiter Damaszenus," 216; on the building inscription on the market gate see ibid., 217.

[127]Watzinger and Wulzinger, *Damaskus I,* 27; Weber, "'Damaskòs Pólis Epísēmos,'" 160.

[128]*FGrH* 90 F 1-130, T 1-15; on his universal history see Josephus, *A.J.* 16.183-186. See B. Z. Wacholder, *Nicolaus of Damascus* (Berkeley: University of California Press, 1963); Schürer 1:28-32; L. H. Feldman, "Josephus," *CHJ* 3:901-21, esp. 910; Millar 1993, 314-15; Dueck 2000, 133-35.

[129]E. A. Knauf, "Zum *Ethnarchen* des Aretas: 2. Kor 11,32," *ZNW* 74 (1983): 145-47, esp. 147; Riesner 1994, 75.

Damascus had a substantial Jewish population.[130] The presence of Jews in Damascus can be traced back to the time of King Ahab and Ben-Hadad, when the Israelites maintained bazaars in Damascus (1 Kings 20:34). The fact that Saul asked the high priest for "letters to the synagogues at Damascus" (Acts 9:2) indicates that there were several synagogues in the city.[131] Josephus reports that in A.D. 66 locals killed 10,500 Jews in the gymnasium within a single hour (*B.J.* 2.561; the figure of eighteen thousand Jews that Josephus mentions in 7.368 possibly includes women and children). The Damascene population's trepidation about the Jews at the beginning of the war against Rome demonstrates the significance of the Jewish community in the city. Josephus reports that many Gentile women converted to Judaism (*B.J.* 7.368). The political and economic importance of the Jews who lived in southern Syria-Phoenicia "is confirmed by the fact that in the first century A.D. not only the south but also large parts of the former Ituraean territory west and northwest of the city was successively put under the rule of Jewish descendants of Herod."[132] Some scholars interpret several statements in the so-called Damascus Document as evidence for a group of Essenes living in the city (e.g., CD VI, 5, 19; VII, 15, 19);[133] other scholars interpret these references to "Damascus" in terms of the exile in Babylonia.[134] The connection between Damascus, Israel and Judea is demonstrated by the assertion of Nicolaus of Damascus that Abraham ruled over Damascus before he went to Canaan, that his name is still praised in Damascus, and that a village in the city territory is regarded as "Abram's abode" (Josephus, *A.J.* 1.159-160). Pompeius Trogus (around 10 B.C.), of southern Gaul, who wrote the first Roman universal history, believed that the Jews as a people came from Damascus, as Abraham and Israel were kings in that city.[135] The Jews of Damascus spoke Greek, as their situation was hardly different from that of the Jews in Antioch, Alexandria and Caesarea.[136]

We do not know when the first Christian missionaries came to Damascus, nor do we have information about the first Christians in the city. Julius Africanus comments in his letter to Aristides that the *desposynoi* ("those who belong to the Master"), meaning the relatives of Jesus, were active in two centers in Galilee: "the Jewish villages of Nazareth and Kokhaba."[137] If this is reliable information—that is, if indeed there were Galilean centers of early Christian missionary activity—it is possible to assume that Damascus may have been reached with the gospel of Jesus in the first months after Jesus' death and resurrection by missionaries from Galilee.[138]

---

[130]On the Jewish community in Damascus see Schürer 2:127-30; Hengel and Schwemer 1998, 80-101 (ET, 50-61); Binder 1999, 266-68.

[131]L. Levine (2000, 118) accepts this information from Acts 9:2 as historical evidence.

[132]Hengel and Schwemer 1998, 93 (ET, 58-59).

[133]F. M. Strickert, "Damascus Document VII,10-20 and Qumran Messianic Expectation," *RevQ* 12 (1986): 327-49, esp. 334-37; cf. Hartmut Stegemann, *Die Essener, Qumran, Johannes der Täufer und Jesus* (Freiburg: Herder, 1993), 207; Stegemann thinks that the references to Damascus should be understood in a literal sense.

[134]See recently J. Murphy-O'Connor, "Damascus Document (CD and QD)," *DNTB* 246-50, esp. 249; idem, *EDSS* 1:165-66.

[135]This comment is found in Justin, *Epitome Historiarum Philippicarum Pompeii Trogi* 3.2.1; see M. Stern 1974-1984, 1:335.

[136]Hengel and Schwemer 1998, 97 (ET, 61).

[137]In Eusebius, *Hist. eccl.* 1.7.14; see Harnack 1924, 2:635-36 (ET, 2:101-2).

[138]See Bauckham 1990, 57-68; Hertig 1997, 388.

The Jewish-Christian text *Pseudo-Clementine Recognitions* claims to know that Peter fled from Jerusalem to Damascus and that Paul went to Damascus in order to arrest him (*Clem. recogn.* 1.71.4-5). According to the Coptic *Acts of Matthew*, the region of Damascus was allotted to Peter as his region of missionary activity.[139] It is not very likely, however, that these late texts contain reliable historical recollections.

The information in Acts 8:36, 38 that Philip baptized the Ethiopian eunuch has prompted the suggestion that Jerusalem believers who came to Damascus baptized uncircumcised God-fearers.[140] It is possible, however, that Jewish Christians from Jerusalem, or from Galilee, engaged in missionary work in Damascus independently of the persecution after Stephen's death, establishing a community of believers in Jesus in the first weeks or months after the Easter events.[141] We cannot exclude the possibility that Jews from Damascus traveled to Galilee in order to see and hear Jesus, the messianic prophet and miracle-worker. The believer named Ananias whom Luke mentions (Acts 9:10, 12, 13, 17; 22:12) presumably was one of the leading Christians in Damascus. Luke reports in Acts 9:19, 25 that Paul joined "the disciples" (*hoi mathētai*) after his conversion. Martin Hengel suggests that Luke perhaps wants to indicate with this term "that the community had not been firmly consolidated and was still in no way an organization independent from the synagogue communities."[142] This must remain hypothetical. It is a fair assumption when Hengel states, "Presumably it met in one or more private houses as a kind of 'messianic conventicle,' but at the same time it presumably also attempted to exercise influence on those who went to the synagogues. That is precisely why Saul wanted to go to Damascus, in order to create order there, so that the followers of this 'tendency' could no longer confuse the Jewish synagogues there and lead their members astray." This scenario presupposes a community of believers in Jesus who actively sought to win others for faith in Jesus as Messiah and Savior.

When thousands of Jews were killed in Damascus in the anti-Jewish pogroms in A.D. 66, presumably many Christians were among the victims. Josephus writes, "Though believing that they had rid themselves of the Jews, still each city had its Judaizers [τοὺς ἰουδαΐζοντας εἶχον ἐν ὑποψίᾳ], who aroused suspicion; and while they shrunk from killing offhand this equivocal element in their midst [τὸ παρ᾽ ἑκάστοις ἀμφίβολον], they feared these neutrals as much as pronounced aliens [ὡς βεβαίως ἀλλόφυλον]" (*B.J.* 2.463). Josephus speaks probably about Christians and Gentile sympathizers with the Jewish faith.[143] Early Christian sources do not provide further information about the church in Damascus.

---

[139]Lipsius 1883-1890, 2.2:260; cf. Hengel and Schwemer 1998, 144-45 (ET, 84-85).
[140]See Hengel and Schwemer 1998, 85 (ET, 54).
[141]See Hofrichter 1993, 15; for the observation that follows above see Hengel and Schwemer 1998, 145.
[142]Hengel and Schwemer 1998, 141; the quotation that follows above, ibid. (ET, 81-82).
[143]Hengel and Schwemer 1998, 84 (ET, 53).

The Ananias Chapel is located in the former Nabatean quarter of Damascus, which is thought to have been in the modern quarter called en-Naibatûn, situated between the Roman East Gate (Bab Sharqi) and the Thomas Gate (Bab Touma). This chapel can be traced back to a Byzantine church of the fifth and sixth centuries; it was located probably right next to the Hellenistic-Roman city wall. If we take the local traditions of the early Byzantine period seriously (and there are good reasons to do so), this site might indeed have been the house of Ananias, from which Paul fled across the city wall according to 2 Cor 11:33.[144]

According to Symeon Metaphrates, Ananias died as a martyr when the prefect of Damascus commanded that he be stoned.[145] According to the *Chronicle of Arbela,* Ebed Meschichâ, who later became bishop in Arbela, was converted to the Christian faith in Damascus around A.D. 200.[146] A bishop of Damascus named Magnus was present at the Council of Nicea.

Walter Schmithals suggests that the "universalism" of Paul was the result of his conversion, in which he adopted the theological position of the Jewish Christians of Damascus, who, in contrast to the Jewish Christians in Jerusalem, already had abandoned the distinction between Jews and Gentiles entirely and had abolished the Torah for Jewish Christians as well.[147] This hypothesis has no basis in the New Testament texts. Peter Hofrichter suggests that "in the earliest phase of the mission the roots of different groups lie in Syria that did *not* interpret Jesus as 'Messiah.'"[148] This hypothesis cannot be proven with reference to the logia source Q or with the apocryphal *Gospel of Thomas,* nor with the assumption that there were early missionaries who did not believe that Jesus was the Messiah. If we accept the existence of Q as a plausible assumption, we must keep in mind the hypothetical nature of Q when formulating theories about the tradents of Q or about the "Q community." And if we accept the existence of a Q community, we must not postulate that the Christology of Q represents the full Christology of this Christian community: the logia source Q contains "only its collection of logia of Jesus."[149] The fact that Q does not contain the title "messiah" may be coincidental.[150] On the Q community and the itinerant missionaries that many scholars link with it see §22.2.

Some scholars have suggested that eschatological expectations linked with Damascus[151] played an important role for the motivation of the pioneer missionary outreach of the Hellenistic Jewish Christians in Jerusalem.[152] This is possible but seems unlikely. (1) Damascus did not have only an eschatological significance in the Jewish tradition: the city appears in many rabbinic texts as a stronghold of idolatry. According to *Lam. Rab.* proem 10 and *Esther Rab.* 3:4, Damascus had 365 temples, in which a different deity was worshiped daily. (2) The description of the early Christian mission in the book of Acts does not make this suggestion very plausible, at least not for Luke: when he reports the geographical locations of the missionary activity of the Jewish Christians in Jerusalem (Acts 8:1: Judea, Samaria; Acts 8:4-5, 25: Samaria; Acts 8:26: near Gaza; Acts 8:40: Ashdod and

---

[144]Riesner 1994, 76-77; Weber ("'Damaskòs Pólis Epísēmos,'" 158) seems skeptical.

[145]Symeon Metaphrastes, *Vita Ananiae* 10 (PG 114:1010).

[146]Harnack 1924, 2:657 n. 2 (note not included in ET).

[147]Schmithals 1989, 239-41, 250-51.

[148]Hofrichter 1993, 15 (italics added); cf. ibid., 18, 25-26.

[149]Hengel 1983a, 37; cf. Tuckett 1996, 213 with n. 14.

[150]Thus Tuckett 1996, 214.

[151]Cf. Zech 9:1; Amos 5:26; CD VI, 5-6; VII, 13; *b. Ber.* 19a; *Sipre Deut.* on Deut 1:1; Targum on Zech 9:1; *Pesiq. Rab Kah.* 20:7; *Gen. Rab.* 44:23; *y. Qidd.* 1:9 [61d].

[152]See Hengel and Schwemer 1998, 88 (ET, 55); for the observation that follows above see ibid.

coastal region, Caesarea; Acts 9:36: Joppa; Acts 10:1: Caesarea; Acts 11:19: Phoenicia, Cyprus, Antiochia), Damascus is not mentioned. And Luke never reports the establishment of the Christian community in Damascus. If eschatological motivations played a role in the missionary work of the Jerusalem missionaries, Luke does not need to mention them. The fact, however, that Damascus is never mention in connection with the activities of the Jerusalem missionaries means, at least, that the pioneer mission in Damascus evidently was not a significant event that would have forced him to report it. And Luke is not shy in other places to point out eschatological convictions of the apostles.

21

THE MISSIONARY WORK OF PETER

Simon Peter belonged to a family that had supported Jesus: his mother-in-law cared for Jesus and his disciples and was healed by Jesus,[1] his brother Andrew was also one of Jesus' disciples, and his wife accompanied him later on his missionary travels (1 Cor 9:5). Peter had been called by Jesus to be his student and follower and to be trained as a "fisher of people," and he had been commissioned after Jesus' resurrection to carry the message of Jesus to all nations "to the ends of the earth." As *primus inter pares* of the Twelve, Peter could not possibly delegate this task to others: his intense character ready for hard work, his impulsive courage to undertake dangerous tasks and his prompt willingness to fight makes this an implausible assumption. The central passage Acts 9:1—11:18 and other references to his missionary activities show, as O. Cullmann has observed, "that the apostle who later is regarded as the personification of organized church government in reality exercised such a function for only a short time at the beginning, and then exchanged it for missionary work."[2]

21.1 The Missionary Work in Judea, Galilee and the Cities of the Coastal Plain

Sermon in Solomon's Portico

When Peter healed a lame man in the Jerusalem temple on the occasion of a regular time of prayer in the temple,[3] crowds gathered in Solomon's Portico (Acts 3:11). Peter used this situation to give a speech in which he not only explained the miracle but also proclaimed the message of Jesus (Acts 3:12-26).

Acts 3:12-26: "When Peter saw it, he addressed the people, 'You Israelites, why do you

---

[1] Mt 8:14-15/Mk 1:29-31/Lk 4:38-39.
[2] Cullmann 1952, 39 (ET, 41). The literature on Peter is extensive; see particularly K. P. Donfried, *ABD* 5:251-63; R. Brown 1973; Pesch 1980; Thiede 1987; Dschulnigg 1989; Caragounis 1990; Grappe 1992, 139-308; 1995; Minnerath 1994; Perkins 1994; Böcher 1996; Dschulnigg 1996; Wehr 1996; Reinbold 2000, 43-79; Wiarda 2000; Meier 1991-2001, 3:221-45.
[3] Besides the commentaries see J. Schwartz 1995, 404-8.

wonder at this, or why do you stare at us, as though by our own power or piety we had made him walk? [13]The God of Abraham, the God of Isaac, and the God of Jacob, the God of our ancestors has glorified his servant Jesus, whom you handed over and rejected in the presence of Pilate, though he had decided to release him. [14]But you rejected the Holy and Righteous One and asked to have a murderer given to you, [15]and you killed the Author of life, whom God raised from the dead. To this we are witnesses. [16]And by faith in his name, his name itself has made this man strong, whom you see and know; and the faith that is through Jesus has given him this perfect health in the presence of all of you. [17]And now, friends, I know that you acted in ignorance, as did also your rulers. [18]In this way God fulfilled what he had foretold through all the prophets, that his Messiah would suffer. [19]Repent therefore [μετανοήσατε οὖν], and turn [ἐπιστρέψατε] to God so that your sins may be wiped out, [20]so that times of refreshing may come from the presence of the Lord, and that he may send the Messiah appointed for you, that is, Jesus, [21]who must remain in heaven until the time of universal restoration that God announced long ago through his holy prophets. [22]Moses said, 'The Lord your God will raise up for you from your own people a prophet like me. You must listen to whatever he tells you. [23]And it will be that everyone who does not listen to that prophet will be utterly rooted out of the people' [Deut 18:15, 19]. [24]And all the prophets, as many as have spoken, from Samuel and those after him, also predicted these days. [25]You are the descendants of the prophets and of the covenant that God gave to your ancestors, saying to Abraham, 'And in your descendants all the families of the earth shall be blessed' [Gen 22:18]. [26]When God raised up his servant, he sent him first to you, to bless you by turning each of you from your wicked ways."

Peter seeks to call the inhabitants of Jerusalem to repentance and to faith in Jesus as the crucified and risen Messiah, as in his sermon at Pentecost. The term "turn" (ἐπιστρέφειν, *epistrephein*) in Acts 3:19, used here for the first time in the book of Acts, later is used repeatedly for the conversion of Jews[4] and Gentiles.[5] The repentance and turning to God was, for Jews, an "insider conversion":[6] the Jews who reacted positively to Peter's preaching and who accepted Jesus as Messiah did not change their "religion"; that is, they neither abandoned their Jewish identity nor joined a new religious cult. For Jews, the call to repentance is a call to turn away from the insistence that temple and Torah are the exclusive and normative revelation of Yahweh and a call to accept and rely on Jesus as the promised Messiah and as the new locus of God's redemptive revelation.

When Peter preached in public for the first time during the Feast of Pentecost, fifty days after Easter, Luke emphasized the shock that his sermon caused among the listeners when he pointed out that Jesus, whom the Jerusalem authorities had rejected and crucified, had been vindicated as the Messiah chosen by God. In his account of Peter's second public sermon, Luke relates several supporting grounds:[7] the call to repentance is given not at the end of the sermon but in the

---

[4]Acts 3:19; 9:35; 26:20; cf. 2 Cor 3:16.
[5]Acts 11:21; 14:15; 15:19; 26:18, 20; cf. 1 Thess 1:9.
[6]See §9.1. See France 1993, 292, 294, 298.
[7]See Tannehill 1991, 405-6. On the historicity of the sermon see Hemer 1989, 418. Reinbold (2000, 45-46) remains skeptical.

middle (Acts 3:19a); the call to repentance is linked with the reference to the wiping out of sins by turning to God (Acts 3:19b), to the coming "times of refreshing" (καιροὶ ἀναψύξεως, *kairoi anapsyxeōs* [Acts 3:20a]), to the return of Jesus, the Messiah appointed by God (Acts 3:20b), and to the "times of universal restoration" (χρόνοι ἀποκαταστάσεως, *chronoi apokatastaseōs*) that had been promised by the prophets (Acts 3:21). The term *anapsyxis*, "refreshment," is used in the Greek translation of Symmachus of Is 32:15, where the prophet speaks of the provision of the Holy Spirit.[8] Peter emphasizes that the "times of refreshing," meaning the time of salvation characterized by the presence of the Spirit of prophecy, has become reality in "these days" (Acts 3:24)—that is, since the events of the Feast of Pentecost shortly after the death and resurrection of Jesus the Messiah.[9]

Peter does not say that the repentance of Israel hastens the return of Jesus the Messiah: he points out that the time of the last opportunity has come for Israel to obtain the salvation of the Messiah.[10] Peter emphasizes that "Israel's salvation is now at stake in view of the apostolic proclamation of what God has done through Jesus and what he will bring to completion through Jesus." The positive grounds for repentance are followed by the threat of being excluded from the people of God, a threat that will become a reality for all who will not listen to the "prophet like Moses" (Acts 3:22-23). Peter adds another reference to the messianic days that the prophets had promised and that now have become a reality (Acts 3:24): the listeners, who are all "the descendants of the prophets and of the covenant," must accept Jesus as the Messiah if the promise of the blessing given to Abraham is to become a reality for the nations of the earth (Acts 3:25). At the end of his sermon Peter points out that God raised his servant Jesus from the dead and "sent him first to you" (Acts 3:26), a statement that implies a subtle reference to the expansion of the proclamation of the gospel of Jesus the Messiah to the Gentiles.[11]

The reaction of the Jerusalem authorities to Peter's preaching in the temple follows promptly. The priests, the captain of the temple police, and the Sadducees have Peter and John arrested (Acts 4:1). Luke's comment about further conversions of Jews in Jerusalem that brought the number of believers to "about five thousand" (Acts 4:4) indicates that the process of Israel's restoration is making progress: more and more people turn to God and to his messianic revelation in the last days.[12]

---

[8]See W. Lane 1962, 163, quoted in Pao 2000, 132. BDAG 75, defines *anapsyxis* as "experience of relief from obligation or trouble, breathing space, relaxation, relief," and translates *kairoi anapsyxeōs* as "times of rest."
[9]See Pao 2000, 133-34.
[10]G. Lohfink 1969, 29; the quotation that follows above, Weiser, *Apg*, 1:118; Pesch, *Apg*, 1:155. Differently Wilckens 1974, 153; followed by Wasserberg 1998, 226.
[11]See Dumais 1993, 115.
[12]See Pao 2000, 139.

Speech Before the Sanhedrin I

After Peter and John had been arrested, they were brought before the Sanhedrin and asked to justify their activities in the temple in front of the "rulers, elders, and scribes" and "Annas the high priest, Caiaphas, John, and Alexander, and all who were of the high-priestly family" (Acts 4:5-6). Peter gives a speech in which he does not only address the legal issue that is being discussed (Acts 4:7): he proceeds to proclaim Jesus as Savior to Israel's leaders (Acts 4:8-12).

Acts 4:8-12: "Then Peter, filled with the Holy Spirit, said to them, 'Rulers of the people and elders, ⁹if we are questioned today because of a good deed done to someone who was sick and are asked how this man has been healed, ¹⁰let it be known to all of you, and to all the people of Israel, that this man is standing before you in good health by the name of Jesus Christ of Nazareth, whom you crucified, whom God raised from the dead. ¹¹This Jesus is "the stone that was rejected by you, the builders; it has become the cornerstone." ¹²There is salvation in no one else, for there is no other name under heaven given among mortals by which we must be saved.'"

Peter explains that the power by which the lame man had been healed (σέσωται, *sesōtai*) is the name of Jesus (Acts 4:9-10). And he points out that salvation can be found only in Jesus of Nazareth because he is the "cornerstone" (κεφαλὴ γωνίας, *kephalē gōnias*) that God himself had placed in Israel (Acts 4:11-12).

The movement from the miraculous healing—that is, from the specific event of salvation—to the proclamation of salvation as a general possibility for the entire people of Israel, including its leaders, provides the healing of the lame man a symbolic dimension. The healing represents a restoration that all people in Israel need, a restoration that is more than physical healing.[13] The reference to the "boldness" (*parrēsia*) of Peter and John (Acts 4:13) stands in stark contrast to the failure of the disciples described in the passion narrative.[14]

Speech Before the Sanhedrin II

The apostles were arrested again probably only a few months later: Luke mentions "jealously" as the motive of the high priests and the Sadducees (Acts 5:17-18). After being miraculously liberated from prison, the apostles followed the command of the angel who had told them to return to the temple and to tell the people "the whole message about this life" (Acts 5:19-20). The high priests and the Sadducees were dumbfounded when they heard that the apostles were free and had returned to the temple. They called another session of the Sanhedrin and asked that the apostles be brought to the chamber; the sympathies that the apostles enjoyed among the population made it impossible to use force against

[13]See Tannehill 1991, 407.
[14]See Tannehill 1986-1990, 1:262-74; 2:68-72. Reinbold (2000, 254) wants to eliminate the presence of John, which he sees as a redactional decoration ("Staffage"); this is as unnecessary as it is hypercritical.

them (Acts 5:25-26). After an interrogation (Acts 5:27b), they are commanded by the high priest to obey the previous injunction not to teach in the name of Jesus (Acts 5:28). In a short speech Peter summarizes the message that they proclaimed as believers and that they intend to continue to proclaim (Acts 5:29-32).

Acts 5:29-32: "But Peter and the apostles answered, 'We must obey God rather than any human authority. [30]The God of our ancestors raised up Jesus, whom you had killed by hanging him on a tree. [31]God exalted him at his right hand as Leader and Savior that he might give repentance to Israel and forgiveness of sins. [32]And we are witnesses to these things, and so is the Holy Spirit whom God has given to those who obey him.'"

This passage is the last public explanation of the message of the apostles in front of Jerusalem Jews in Luke's account. The speech emphasizes once again the contrast between God's action in the resurrection of Jesus and the action of the Jerusalem aristocrats who rejected Jesus and are responsible for his death (Acts 5:30). Peter refers to Jesus' exaltation at the right hand of God, an emphasis that already had characterized the sermon at Pentecost (Acts 5:31). And Peter ends his speech again with a reference to the Spirit of prophecy, who had been promised for the last days and is now granted by God to those who believe in Jesus (Acts 5:32). Peter emphasizes, more forcefully than in his previous speeches, that the repentance that they proclaim is God's gift for Israel and, at the same time, the purpose that God wanted to achieve with Jesus' exaltation. Peter points out that God's offer is still valid, even though Israel's leaders continue to reject Jesus and now even want to kill the apostles (Acts 5:33). The necessity of God's forgiveness becomes ever more apparent as opposition to God's offer increases.[15]

Missionary Travels

Peter's missionary activity in Samaria and in several cities of the coastal region, possibly also in Lydda and Joppa, was discussed earlier (§§20.2; 20.4).

21.2 The Vision of Peter in Joppa

The account of Peter's vision in Joppa, of the missionary encounter with the Roman centurion Cornelius, of the conversion of Cornelius and of Peter's explanation of his actions in Jerusalem (Acts 10:1—11:18) is a central episode in the book of Acts. This is confirmed not only by the length of the account but also by the threefold report of Peter's vision.[16] Rainer Riesner observes that "in the

---

[15]See Tannehill 1991, 409.

[16]On the Cornelius episode see, besides the commentaries, Dibelius 1947b; S. Wilson 1973, 171-78; Wall 1987; Lukasz 1993; Minnerath 1994, 72-77; Turner 1996a, 378-87; J. Green 1997. On Peter's speech see Stuhlmacher 1968, 266-82; Stanton 1974, 70-81; Wilckens 1974, 63-70; Schneider 1985a; Zmijewski 1995; Ascough 2000; Cotter 2000. Pesch (*Apg.* 1:330) believes that Acts 10 is "in reality" a narrative about Peter.

broad portrayal of the story of Cornelius, Luke emphasizes Peter's conversion of the Roman *centurio* in Caesarea as a special breakthrough for the mission to the Gentiles, underscoring in this way the fundamental unanimity of Peter and Paul in this question that was so decisive for primitive Christianity. Despite his theological agenda, however, Luke did not suppress the historical circumstance that the initiative for preaching to Gentiles did not come from Peter."[17]

The discussion about the historicity of Acts 10:1—11:18 is complex. Scholars interpret the so-called Cornelius tradition with the vision of Peter (Acts 10:9-16), and the sermon of Peter (Acts 10:34-43) and the Jerusalem scene (Acts 11:1-18) differently.[18] It must suffice at this point to indicate the main reasons for my view that a general skepticism concerning the historicity of the Cornelius episode is inappropriate. (1) It is highly unlikely that Luke simply invented the story. For example, the comment that the Holy Spirit fell upon Cornelius and his friends after they believed but before they were baptized can hardly have been invented: there is no parallel for this sequence of events anywhere in the book of Acts.[19] (2) In regard to Peter's vision, Rudolf Pesch argues that "it is a symbolic actualization of the central theme and thus was part of the narrative right from the beginning," and that "it is not a literary creation of Luke or a tradition from some other context that he adopted."[20] (3) In regard to Peter's sermon, Klaus Haacker emphasizes the details linked with the particular historical situation that point to the authenticity of the narrative.[21] (4) The statement in Acts 10:35-37 ("You know the message he sent to the people of Israel, preaching peace by Jesus Christ—he is Lord of all. That message spread throughout Judea, beginning in Galilee") is rejected as unhistorical by Martin Dibelius with the argument that there is no valid reason for the assumption that Cornelius knew these things.[22] This view cannot be substantiated with reference to Acts 10:1-4, however; on the contrary: a God-fearing Roman officer who has regular contact with Jews and synagogues must have heard details about Jesus and the movement that his public preaching and healing ministry initiated. On Acts 11:1-18 see below.

Wolfgang Reinbold argues that the Cornelius episode "took place in reality not before but after the Jerusalem conference (Acts 15; Gal 2:1-10)."[23] This hypothesis is not compelling. (1) The charge of the "circumcision faction" in Acts 11:2-3 does not have an explicit literary connection with Acts 10, but there are historical and cultural links: when Peter goes into the house of a pagan (Acts 10:22) and stays there for several days (Acts 10:48), it is not necessary to include an explicit reference to common meals; they can be presupposed. (2) If the "other place" to which Peter goes after his hasty departure from Jerusalem (Acts 12:17) is Antioch, and if Peter indeed stopped over in Caesarea and behaved

---

[17]Riesner 1994, 95 with n. 1 (ET, 108), arguing against P. Gaechter, who wants "to secure the theological and jurisdictional priority of Peter over against the Antiochene church as well." See also Dumais 1993, 116-17.

[18]See particularly Haenchen, *Apg,* 343-44 (ET, 355-57); Schneider 1985a; *Apg,* 2:61-64; Weiser, *Apg,* 1:249-62; Zmijewski, *Apg,* 410-15; 1995, 1595-97; Reinbold 2000, 52-65.

[19]Marshall, *Acts,* 183.

[20]Pesch, *Apg,* 1:333, with reference to F. Bovon, "Tradition et rédaction en Actes 10:1—11:18," *ThZ* 26 (1970): 22-45; Weiser, *Apg,* 1:254-56.

[21]Haacker 1980, 241-46; see also Pesch, *Apg,* 1:333.

[22]Dibelius 1947b, 98.

[23]See Reinbold 2000, 61-62; quotation, 62; similarly Wehnert 1997, 58-60.

there in the same way as later in Antioch, practicing table fellowship with God-fearing Gentiles, as Reinbold assumes, then he has to explain why Peter behaved in this very unorthodox, indeed "illegal" manner. Reinbold's reference to the position of James or to the decision of the apostolic council fails to convince because of Peter's report of Cornelius's conversion and the events connected with it (Acts 15:8-9), a report to which James refers in his statement during the council (Acts 15:14). (3) According to Reinbold, the acceptance of Cornelius into the church without him being circumcised would have been mentioned during the deliberations of the council. Reinbold does not seem to realize that this is exactly what happened (Acts 15:8-9, 14). Reinbold describes Luke's narrative in Acts 15 as "improved" ("geschönt") and claims to know that Peter could not have presented himself to the brothers as a Gentile missionary.[24] This kind of argumentation demonstrates that he only "proves" what he already claims.

A structural analysis of the Cornelius narrative shows that Luke's emphasis is on Peter's vision.[25] The encounter of Peter and Cornelius is prepared by two dreams: (1) The God-fearing Cornelius is directed by God in a dream to ask Peter to visit him. (2) In a dream God prepares Peter for accepting Cornelius's invitation. God shows Peter in three dream-visions that he must no longer distinguish between ritually clean and unclean food, allowing him to have table fellowship with Gentiles. The Cornelius narrative of Acts 10:1—11:18 consists of eight scenes connected with each other in various ways.

1. Cornelius and the angel (10:1-8)

2. Peter's vision (10:9-16)

3. Peter and the envoys of Cornelius (10:17-23a)

4. Peter and Cornelius (10:23b-29)

5. Cornelius's report (about 1; 10:30-33)

6. Peter's sermon (10:34-43)

7. Cornelius's reception of the Holy Spirit and baptism (10:44-48)

8. Peter's justification of his actions in Jerusalem (11:1-18)

Scenes 1-3 form a unit depicting the directive of the angel to Cornelius and the execution of the directive. Scenes 4-7 depict the conversion of Cornelius as well as Peter's discovery of the meaning of the dream-vision that he had received from God. Scene 8 repeats the events that had transpired in Caesarea, focusing on Peter's vision:

11:5-10   Scene 2: vision; precise repetition of the direct discourses
11:11-12a   Scene 3: mentioned briefly; focus is on the directive of the Spirit to Peter
11:12b   Scene 4: mentioned briefly; reference to six brothers as witnesses
11:13-14   Scene 5: mentioned briefly; extensive repetition of the angel's directive

---

[24]Reinbold 2000, 72.
[25]Pesch, *Apg,* 1:330-33. Tyson (1992, 120) combines scenes 3 and 4. Many exegetes combine scenes 4 and 5; see Witherington, *Acts,* 345.

11:15a	Scene 6: mentioned briefly
11:15b	Scene 7: brief report
11:16-17	Scene 8: extensive argument

The main focus is on Peter's vision, which means that the central subject of the passage is the fact that God had shown to the apostle Peter in a visionary revelation that Gentiles who have been converted to faith in Jesus and have received the Holy Spirit are members of the people of God in exactly the same manner as the apostles and the believers in Jerusalem.

Rudolf Pesch suggests that Peter was persuaded to cross the dividing barrier between Jews and Gentiles against his will.[26] In view of the previous discussion, this interpretation is hardly plausible: Peter's opposition was directed not against missionary outreach among Gentiles as such but against breaking down the barrier between Jews and Gentiles.[27] It was difficult and often impossible for devout Jews to eat with Gentiles at the same table with the same food. Gentiles did not follow the stipulations concerning food and the purity laws of the Torah and of Jewish halakah—neither in the market when they bought food nor in the kitchen when they prepared the food. One of the most impressive "self-definitions" of Jewish identity, found in *Letter of Aristeas,* illustrates this point:

Let. Arist. 139, 142: "In his wisdom the legislator [Moses], in a comprehensive survey of each particular part, and being endowed by God for the knowledge of universal truths, surrounded us with unbroken palisades and iron walls to prevent our mixing with any of the other peoples in any matter [μηδενὶ τῶν ἄλλων ἐθνῶν], being thus kept pure in body and soul, preserved from false beliefs, and worshiping the only God omnipotent over all creation. . . . So, to prevent our being perverted by contact with others or by mixing with bad influences, he hedged us in on all sides with strict observances connected with meat and drink and touch and hearing and sight, after the manner of the Law."

The limiting factor in encounters between Jews and Gentiles was, for devout Jews, the fear of idolatry and impurity. Table fellowship with Gentiles therefore was always problematic. In specific situations the contact with Gentiles depended on the question of whether one could assume, or negotiate with the Gentile host, to be served kosher food. As Markus Bockmuehl points out, devout Jews had essentially four options. (1) They could decline all table fellowship with Gentiles and refuse to enter the house of a Gentile. (2) They could invite Gentiles into their home and serve them a Jewish meal. (3) They could accept the invitation of a Gentile and bring their own food. (4) They could eat with Gentiles with the tacit agreement that the food to be served was neither prohibited by Torah nor made unclean through contact with idols; for example,

---

[26]Pesch (*Apg,* 1:333), who therefore does not want to describe the text as a "conversion narrative." See also Roloff, *Apg,* 164.
[27]See Pesch, *Apg,* 1:333.

they could ask for vegetarian food.[28] The Jewish positions concerning contact with Gentiles varied considerably. Not all Jews shared the view of Rabbi Eliezer b. Hyrcanus, a hard-liner, who taught that the Gentiles' intentions are always idolatrous (*m. Ḥul.* 2:7). The strict Essenes bathed after every contact with Gentiles (Josephus, *B.J.* 2.150). However, passages in the Mishnah assume as a matter of fact that Jews and Gentiles eat together (*m. Ber.* 7:1). Most Jews presumably did not think that the Gentiles were unclean as a matter of principle. If that were the case, it would be difficult to explain why Jewish halakah permits Gentile women to assist Jewish women as (wet) nurses (*m. 'Abod. Zar.* 2:1).

Peter thought and lived in accordance with the Jewish purity laws, until God showed him on the roof of the house of Simon the tanner in Joppa that he "should not call anyone profane or unclean" (Acts 10:28).[29] The vision concerned clean and unclean food. Peter interprets the vision in his sermon before Cornelius in terms of people. He recognized that God not only had canceled the food laws but also had directed him to abandon the Jewish practice of treating non-Jewish people as unclean.[30] He learned what it means that "God shows no partiality" (Acts 10:34). This formulation often was used in Old Testament and Jewish traditions to refer to God's activity as judge. Here this truth is applied to the mission of the church and its representatives. Peter learned that "God's ultimate standards are already being applied in the present."[31]

Luke's account emphasizes through its focus on the visions that the admission of Gentiles into the community of the covenant people that God was in the process of restoring was the result of God's initiative, and that the fact that the converted Gentiles were not forced to obey the stipulations of the Mosaic Torah was not a human decision but rather the result of God's intervention. With Peter's insight, the biggest obstacle that Jewish-Christian missionaries faced in evangelistic outreach to Gentiles had been removed: the problem of what should happen if devout and law-abiding Jews encounter ritually unclean Gentiles, if Gentiles turn to God and convert to faith in Jesus, and if Jewish Christians and Gentile Christians want to have fellowship as members of God's covenant people. Luke does not specify in Acts 10—11 the theological basis that accounts for the cancellation of the Mosaic cult law as a redemptive institution.

Luke emphasizes that God himself is responsible for the Gentile mission of the Jerusalem church. And he shows in a programmatic manner how an individual comes to faith in Jesus and thus obtains salvation.[32] (1) God takes the initiative: he prompts individuals to come to faith in Jesus, and he may use super-

---

[28]Bockmuehl 2000, 58; for the observations that follow above see ibid., 58-60.
[29]Acts 10:28: μηδένα κοινὸν ἢ ἀκάθαρτον λέγειν ἄνθρωπον.
[30]Schille, *Apg,* 248; Zmijewski, *Apg,* 324.
[31]K. Berger, *EWNT* 3:435 (*EDNT* 3:180).
[32]For the observations that follow above see Zmijewski 1995, 1597-99.

natural events in the process. (2) God uses missionaries as his instrument, people who proclaim the message of Jesus Christ as he directs them. (3) Salvation is not limited to particular groups of people: God seeks the salvation of all people, including Gentiles, polytheists and Romans, because "he is Lord of all" (Acts 10:36). (4) The proclamation of the word of God is of decisive significance in the communication of God's salvation: Peter speaks not about himself and his experiences but rather about God's revelation and action in and through Jesus. (5) The leaders of the church are challenged to be open for new developments. They must be ready, as Josef Zmijewski points out, "to comply obediently with the will of God and of his Spirit and to be prepared to undergo a perhaps long and painful learning process in which they surrender their own prejudices"; they must be willing to risk the encounter with people to whom God sends them, "even though this may mean under certain circumstances the 'loss of affiliation or friendship' or critical discussion (Acts 11:2)."[33]

21.3 Missionary Work in Caesarea

Luke characterizes Cornelius as follows. (1) He was a centurion (ἑκατόνταρχος, *hekatontarchos*) of the Italian Cohort in Caesarea Maritima, the seat of the Roman prefect or procurator in Judea (Acts 10:1).[34]

A Roman legion consisted of approximately five thousand soldiers. A legion consisted of sixty centuries organized in ten cohorts. A centurion commanded about eighty men; he was "the link between officers and the troops and the most significant representative of the professional military spirit."[35] The centurion carried a vine as a sign of his disciplinary authority and could be recognized by his greaves (until the end of the second century); he also wore a gold ring. Centurions were attracted by a high salary (five times that of the praetorian soldier) and good retirement benefits.

The Roman army included several *Cohortes Italicae.* The Italian Cohort of Acts 10:1 probably was the *Cohors II Italica Civium Romanorum,* a regiment attested by an inscription found in Carnuntum (mod. Bad Deutsch/Altenburg near Vienna, Austria).[36] (2) Cornelius was a Roman citizen and a Gentile, as is attested by his name, profession and position in the military. The Roman military camps have been described as a "religious microcosm."[37] The soldiers be-

---

[33]Zmijewski 1995, 1598-99, with a quotation from W. Ullrich.

[34]On the Italian Cohort see Schürer 1:362-67; Michael P. Speidel, "The Roman Army in Judea Under the Procurators: The Italian and the Augustan Cohort in the Acts of the Apostles," in idem, *Roman Army Studies II* (Stuttgart: Steiner, 1992), 224-32.

[35]Alfred Neumann, *KP* 1:1112; for the observation that follows above see ibid. See also H. Parker and G. R. Watson, *OCD* 310-11; Brian Dobson, "The Significance of the Centurion and 'Primipilaris' in the Roman Army and Administration," *ANRW* II.1 (1974): 392-434.

[36]*ILS* 9168 = *CIL* VI 3528; XI 6117. See Saddington 1996, 2415-16.

[37]John Helgeland, "Roman Army Religion," *ANRW* II.16.2 (1978): 1470-1505, esp. 1491; see also Cotter 2000, 286-300.

lieved that the camp was under the protection of the "military gods" (*dii militares*). They worshiped the *genius* of the centuria (*genius centuriae*) and of the legion (*genius legionis*), the spirit (*numen*) of the legionary standards and the eagle as symbol of Jupiter and of the power of Rome, the gods of Rome (Jupiter, Juno, Minerva), of course the gods Mars and Victoria (Venus), and frequently Salus, Janus, Dea Roma, Fides and Disciplina, also the emperor or the *genius* of the emperor, in many cases and depending on personal preferences the deities of the region or the city in which the cohort was stationed. (3) Cornelius was devout and God-fearing,[38] he practiced his piety "with all his household,"[39] he generously gave alms to the Jewish people and he prayed to God (Acts 10:2).[40] He was a righteous man, he had an excellent reputation among the Jewish people (Acts 10:22),[41] and he did "what is right" (Acts 10:35).[42] The suggestion that Cornelius made "progress" in terms of Stoic ideals of virtue[43] has no basis in the text: Cornelius would not have been different from other God-fearing Gentiles who attended the synagogue. As of yet, archaeologists have not confirmed the existence of a synagogue for Caesarea in the first century, but there is no doubt that Jews lived in the city.[44] (4) Cornelius took the initiative to get into contact with Peter (Acts 10:5, 8, 17, 29). Luke documents "the historically correct and irreversible gradient according to which Gentiles have to find their way to Judaism and take the initiative themselves."[45] Luke does not report a synagogue or obedience to Jewish laws on the part of Cornelius. He might have been a "hidden" God-fearer, and if so, for good reasons: as a leading military officer serving in a Roman city that was the seat of the prefect of a province, he would have found it difficult to demonstrate publicly his active sympathies for Jews and the Jewish faith. (5) Luke notes that when Peter arrived in the house of the Roman officer, he was welcomed not only by Cornelius but also by relatives and friends of the officer, who evidently was convinced that the divine message that he hoped to receive from Peter was relevant for everyone.[46] (6) Luke says that Cornelius fell at Peter's feet and worshiped him.[47] Peter's words of correction (Acts 10:26) demonstrate that the centurion evidently believes as a result of his vision that Peter

---

[38]Acts 10:2a: εὐσεβὴς καὶ φοβούμενος τὸν θεόν.

[39]Acts 10:2b: σὺν παντιτῷ οἴκῳ αὐτοῦ.

[40]Acts 10:2c: ποιῶν ἐλεημοσύνας πολλὰς τῷ λαῷ καὶ δεόμενος τοῦ θεοῦ.

[41]Acts 10:22: ἀνὴρ δίκαιος . . . μαρτυρούμενός τε ὑπὸ ὅλου τοῦ ἔθνους τῶν Ἰουδαίων.

[42]Acts 10:35: ἐργαζόμενος δικαιοσύνην.

[43]See Bassler 1985, 548-51.

[44]See Murray 2000.

[45]Wander 1998, 187; for the observation that follows above see ibid., 187-88.

[46]Acts 10:24: συγκαλεσάμενος τοὺς συγγενεῖς αὐτοῦ καὶ τοὺς ἀναγκαίους φίλους. See Barrett, *Acts*, 1:513; Stenschke 1999a, 151.

[47]Acts 10:25b: πεσὼν ἐπὶ τοὺς πόδας προσεκύνησεν. The TNIV translates "fell at his feet in reverence"; similarly Zmijewski, *Apg*, 407: "fiel ihm zu Füßen und huldigte ihm."

is more than an average human being.[48] The *proskynēsis* by Cornelius is a pagan element that Luke did not eliminate despite his otherwise positive description of the Roman officer.

In his sermon before Cornelius and his household (Acts 10:34-43) Peter takes into consideration "the specific listeners who stand between Judaism and paganism."[49] The sermon has three main parts.

1. *Introduction* (10:34b-35): comment related to the historical context
   God's nonpartiality (Deut 10:17; 2 Chron 19:7) applies now to Gentiles as well: God accepts all people who fear him and live accordingly
2. *Proclamation of Jesus* (10:36-38): survey of the life of Jesus
   (a) God, through Jesus, has fulfilled his promise to bring peace (i.e., salvation) to his people (Israel) (10:36ab)
   (b) God's salvation offered in Jesus is not limited to Jews: it is offered to all people, as Jesus, the bringer of peace, is the Lord of all people (10:36c)
   (c) The message of peace in the life of Jesus of Nazareth (10:37-38)
       (*i*) Beginning in Galilee (10:37a)
       (*ii*) Connection with John the Baptist (10:37b)
       (*iii*) Anointing with the Spirit, who conveys the power of God (10:38a)
       (*iv*) Healing of people who had been under the control of the devil (10:38b)
   Confirmation (10:39a): the apostles as eyewitnesses
   Proclamation of Jesus (10:39b-41): Jesus' death and resurrection
   (d) Jesus' death: reference to the crucifixion (10:39b; echo of Deut 21:22-23)
   (e) Jesus' resurrection on the third day (10:40a)
   (f) Jesus' appearances before witnesses in the midst of everyday life (10:41)
3. *Offer of salvation* (10:42-43)
   (a) Divine commission of the witnesses: the crucified Jesus is the one whom God appointed as judge of the living and the dead (10:42)
   (b) Exhortation to turn in faith to this judge in order to receive forgiveness of sins (10:43)

Peter's sermon before an audience of God-fearing Gentiles in Caesarea differs in two ways from sermons before Jewish audiences: first, there is no proof from Scripture but only a general reference to the testimony of the prophets (Acts 10:43a; interpretation of Ps 107:20 and Is 52:7); second, there is no reproach for the rejection of Jesus, and instead Peter provides a survey of Jesus' life and death. Compared with sermons before Gentile audiences, Peter's sermon before the God-fearers in Caesarea lacks, first, the typical proclamation of the one true God, the Creator of the world,[50] and, second, the exhortation to repent and turn to the one true God. Rudolf Pesch comments, "Peter instead describes in unique detail what these listeners who have already been heard by God (Acts 10:31)

---

[48]Barrett, *Acts,* 1:513-14; emphasized by Stenschke 1999a, 151-52; for the observation that follows above see ibid.
[49]Schneider, *Apg,* 2:63, quoted in Pesch, *Apg,* 1:333.
[50]See Acts 14:15-17; 17:24-31.

need to hear: he informs them about the sending, ministry, death and resurrection of Jesus, about his appearances, and about his witnesses and their commission (Acts 10:37-42)."[51]

As Peter spoke, the Holy Spirit fell upon Cornelius and the other listeners (Acts 10:44): they spoke "in tongues" and extolled God (Acts 10:46). Peter was reminded of his own experience at Pentecost: "And as I began to speak, the Holy Spirit fell upon them just as it had upon us at the beginning" (Acts 11:15). Peter compares the experience of the God-fearing Gentiles in Caesarea not with the experience of the Jews who were converted on Pentecost but with the experience of the apostles and disciples assembled in the upper room on Pentecost.[52]

The decisive event was the reception of the Holy Spirit, whose presence expressed itself in glossolalia, and not the speaking in tongues itself. Philip Esler suggests that the glossolalia of Gentiles such as Cornelius who belonged to Jewish-Christian churches was "infected" by the glossolalic speech of the Christians: glossolalia as an altered (disassociated) state of consciousness is contagious, a fact and an experience that the Jewish Christians in Jerusalem were forced to accept; this helped them to overcome the traditional Jewish barriers with regard to contacts with Gentiles.[53] This interpretation is problematic for three reasons. (1) Studies that explained glossolalia in terms of altered, trancelike states of consciousness have been disproved by more recent studies.[54] (2) Luke does not state in the Cornelius narrative that Peter or the "brothers from Joppa" (Acts 10:23) ever spoke in tongues: the scenario suggested by Esler would not have been initiated if they did not speak in tongues during the encounter with Cornelius. (3) If we assume, for the sake of the argument, that glossolalia was indeed a trancelike state of consciousness, it seems questionable to assume that this phenomenon would have been sufficient to convince both Peter and the believers from Joppa as well as the Jewish Christians in Jerusalem that the Holy Spirit had become a present reality in the life of Cornelius and his household. We must remember in this context that the apostles' "speaking in tongues" on Pentecost was xenolalia—that is, speaking in known languages that the speakers had not learned.

Peter recognized and acknowledged that God had accepted the God-fearing Gentiles who had responded with faith to his message of Jesus. And he recognized that he must be ready and willing to accept them into the church by baptism, which is what happened (Acts 10:47-48).

It is valid to ask why Peter did not apply Jesus' commission of universal and international missionary outreach (Mt 28:19/Acts 1:8) to this situation, where a Gentile asks him proactively to explain God's revelation and intervention. It is unnecessary to posit a contradiction between Peter's behavior and Jesus' missionary commission, however. A commission such as Acts 1:8 is not the same thing as initiating outreach to Gentiles and applying the commission in a particu-

---

[51]Pesch, *Apg,* 1:334 (who mistakenly refers to 4:31 instead of 10:31).
[52]Marshall, *Acts,* 197. On Cornelius's reception of the Spirit see Turner 1996a, 378-87.
[53]Esler (1992), who refers for his interpretation of glossolalia to F. Goodman 1972.
[54]Samarin 1972; G. Palmer 1966; Spanos and Hewitt 1979; Malony and Lovekin 1985; Forbes 1995, 44-181; Turner 1996b, 305-7.

lar situation.[55] We may also ask why Peter would not have been reminded of Jesus' statement that food that enters people does not make them unclean (Mk 7:15-19).[56] Perhaps Peter had not understood Jesus' statement, or perhaps he had not grasped the scope of its significance—before Easter he had not understood Jesus' announcements of his suffering and death either.

Luke reports the conversion of Cornelius, relatives and friends (Acts 10:44-48, cf. 10:24) and continues with a report of the discussion that ensued in Jerusalem after Peter had returned from Caesarea: Jewish believers questioned him concerning the baptism of Gentiles (Acts 11:1-18). Luke does not report what happened in Caesarea itself: whether a church was established or whether Cornelius and his converted friends joined a Jewish-Christian community that had been previously established by Philip.[57]

We do not know to what degree Peter was able to win the Jerusalem believers to his new convictions. Luke reports in Acts 11:18 that "they"—that is, "the apostles and the brothers who were in Judea" (Acts 11:1)—were silenced by Peter's account and they praised God that he had "given even to the Gentiles the repentance that leads to life."[58] Jacob Jervell observes, "New is not only the salvation of the Gentiles but also the fact that it is granted without circumcision and that the non-Jews become members of the people of God in this manner."[59] This conviction certainly applies to Peter, who reports the events of Caesarea in Jerusalem, as well as for Luke as the author of the book of Acts, but it does not necessarily apply to all the Jewish Christians present at the meeting in Jerusalem at which Peter gave his report. This means that the congregational meeting in Acts 11:1-18 does not make the apostolic council of Acts 15 necessarily superfluous, apart from the fact that there might have been new developments between the two "conferences" that could have made another discussion about these questions necessary. And we must recall that the two meetings deal with different questions: Acts 11:1-18 answers the question of whether Gentiles may be admitted into the people of God, and if so, under what circumstances; Acts 15 answers the question of how Jewish Christians and Gentile Christians should behave when in fellowship together in a local congregation, presupposing that non-Jews have been admitted to the church.[60] It is also true that the results of the Jerusalem conference in Acts 11:18 did not mean that from now on the entire

---

[55]See Best 1984, 12.

[56]Barrett, *Acts,* 1:493.

[57]See Hopfe 1990, 2400; Ascough 2000, 162.

[58]On repentance (*metanoia*) as salvation and as gift of God see Stenschke (1999a, 156-64), who argues against the interpretation of Conzelmann (1962, 92, 214; *Apg,* 47 [ET, 42]), who asserted that the author speaks of the "opportunity for repentance" and not of repentance as a gift.

[59]Jervell, *Apg,* 316.

[60]See Barrett, *Acts,* 1:494.

Jerusalem church supported wholeheartedly the missionary outreach to the Gentiles.[61] The assumption that the Jerusalem church kept its distance from the Gentile mission and as a result lost significance over time cannot be substantiated from the available sources.

Some scholars regard Acts 11:1-18 as "a scene that Luke created freely and without direct basis in tradition" with the intention of "integrating the previous story of the conversion and baptism of Cornelius into the general thematic ductus of the book and thus to help the reader understand its meaning."[62] This view is implausible. (1) Jewish readers would have readily understood the significance of Peter's vision on the basis of the narrative in Acts 10. (2) Peter gives a report in Acts 11:1-18 that makes perfect sense in the context of the Semitic law of the messenger (*Botenrecht*).[63] (3) If the story of the establishment of the church in Caesarea goes back to the Caesarean church, as C. K. Barrett assumes, then the ending of the Caesarea narrative makes good sense, reporting the acknowledgment of the legitimacy of the Caesarean Christians by the Jerusalem church.[64] If Jewish Christians had table fellowship with Gentile Christians for the first time in Caesarea, and if Gentile Christians were admitted into the church in Caesarea for the first time, then it is credible that some believers in Jerusalem protested—believers who are distinguished in Acts 11:2 from the "apostles and brothers" of Acts 11:1.

Meals and thus implicitly a house or a household and a family play a central role in the account of Acts 10:1—11:18. Hospitality in a home and the common meals served there presented a problem that made the elaborate report of the events in Caesarea necessary in the first place. This is confirmed by the inquisitive and critical statement of the "apostles and brothers in Judea" who confront Peter after his return to Jerusalem: "Why did you go to uncircumcised men and eat with them?" (Acts 11:3). Even though Luke does not explicitly refer to a meal, he repeatedly uses several terms that are relevant in this regard: the "house" of Cornelius, the house of Simon, eating, animals as food.[65] Luke had referred to houses as places where the believers were meeting and to common meals when he described the life of the Jerusalem Christians (see §15.3). But the Cornelius episode is the first reference to the role that houses played in the mission of the early church.[66] The divine revelation that canceled the Mosaic food and purity laws did not occur in the temple in Jerusalem or in a synagogue but in the house of Simon in Joppa. And Peter understood the significance of this divine revelation in the house of Cornelius in Caesarea. Simon is the host of Peter (Acts 9:36;

---

[61]Marshall, *Acts,* 198.

[62]Roloff 1991, 118-19; cf. Schneider, *Apg,* 2:64; Roloff, *Apg,* 167.

[63]Haacker 1980, 234-51. The critique by Roloff (1991, 119 n. 21) fails to convince: all apostles are "envoys" who give an account of their activities at least to their fellow envoys. For the "law of the messenger" see K.-H. Rengstorf, *TDNT* 1:416.

[64]Barrett, *Acts,* 1:496-97, 535.

[65]House of Cornelius: Acts 10:2, 22, 30; 11:7, 12, 13, 14; implicitly 10:24, 25, 28, 48; 11:3, 8; house of Simon: 10:9, 17; eating 10:10, 13, 14, 23; 11:3; animals as food: 10:12; 11:6.

[66]For the observations that follow above see J. H. Elliott 1991, esp. 105.

10:6, 17-18, 32; 11:11), Peter and Simon are the hosts of Cornelius's emissaries
(Acts 10:17-23a), Cornelius and his family are the hosts of Peter and the brothers
from Joppa (Acts 10:24-25, 48; 11:3, 12-17). Peter preaches in the house of Cornelius (Acts 10:34-43; 11:15a), the Roman centurion and his family receive the
Holy Spirit and speak in tongues in his house (Acts 10:44-47; 11:15), Cornelius
and his "house" or "household" are baptized because they experienced God's
salvation (Acts 10:48; 11:14-17). In his account of the mission of the early church
Luke repeatedly refers to houses and households as bases for missionary outreach and as meeting places of local congregations (Acts 16:14-15; 17:5-7; 18:2-
3; 21:8).

Walter Wilson argues that Luke tells the story of Peter and Cornelius to provide Gentile
Christians with a "foundation myth" that he created in order to help them better understand and defend their identity.[67] He suggests that foundation myths of Greek colonies
such as Messene, Rhegium, Massalia and Pallanteum provide the cultural context whose
phenomena and literary traditions show how Luke Hellenized in Acts 10:1—11:18 the traditions of the origins of the group to which he belonged. This hypothesis is not cogent
for the following reasons. (1) Wilson admits that the similarities between Greek foundation legends and the Peter/Cornelius story neither constitute "parallels" nor establish direct influence but he nevertheless uses them as the "cultural context" for a proper understanding of Acts 10:1—11:18. This "comparison" is methodologically unconvincing. (2)
Existing parallels between the foundation of a polis and the foundation of an *ekklēsia* of
believers in Jesus Christ must not be used to gloss over significant differences. The question of whether the visions that often play an important role in many Greek foundation
legends of colonies actually occured may be left aside at this point. There is no doubt,
however, that the foundation of colonies always served economic interests, and also military purposes in the Seleucid and particularly in the Roman period in many if not most
cases. Neither of these two purposes plays even a remote role in the "story" of the conversion of Cornelius and of his family. Luke notes that Cornelius generously gave alms to
the Jewish people before his conversion (Acts 10:2) but omits any reference to Cornelius
as a "patron" of the church in Caesarea or the church in Jerusalem, which soon is dependent upon alms, as Luke will report (Acts 11:28-30). A Christian "foundation myth" that
seeks to strengthen the self-consciousness of the Gentile Christians and a myth that is
ready to "play" with historical facts as it suits its author surely would have presented Cornelius at least as a patron of the church in Caesarea and presumably as a benefactor of
the Jerusalem church. If Luke indeed wanted to compose an effective "foundation legend"
in Acts 10:1—11:18, he failed. (3) Luke reports in Acts 10:1—11:18 the conversion of Gentiles in Caesarea, but he never explicitly mentions the establishment of an *ekklēsia*. He
mentions "disciples from Caesarea" only in Acts 21:16. It therefore is highly questionable
whether Luke could have evoked in his Greek readers connotations of foundation legends when he wrote Acts 10:1—11:18, even if he wanted to do so. The text portrays not
the "foundation" of a body politic but the conversion of Gentiles to faith in Jesus the Savior in one of the most important port cities of Palestine.

Luke regarded Peter as the first missionary among Gentiles. This is demon-

---

[67]W. Wilson 2001; on foundation myths of Greek colonies see ibid., 81-87.

strated by three facts: (1) The conversion of Cornelius, a Roman officer in Caesarea, is described comprehensively as the result of the missionary work of Peter. (2) Paul and Barnabas apparently played only a minor role at the apostolic council, whereas the contribution of Peter is highlighted as he relates again the conversion of Cornelius (Acts 15:7-11, 14). (3) Paul became active as a missionary among Gentiles only after Peter's mission in Caesarea (Acts 11:25-26; 13:2; the only early reference to a missionary activity of Paul, in Acts 9:27-29, presumably is limited to Jews).[68]

21.4 Missionary Work After A.D. 41

Peter left Jerusalem in connection with the persecution that Herod Agrippa I organized against the Jerusalem church, after his apostolic colleague James had been executed. Herod Agrippa I had been appointed king of Judea on January 25 of the year A.D. 41 by Claudius, the new emperor. When Agrippa returned from Rome to Jerusalem, presumably immediately after the reopening of ship traffic on March 10, Judea was in a state of religious-revolutionary ferment resulting from the temple sacrilege that the late emperor Caligula had ordered.[69] Caligula had ordered that a statue of himself be erected in the temple, accompanied by the usual religious-civic cult. The protest movement that formed in Judea evidently was led by priests and scribes of the temple. The resistance movement in Galilee had strong eschatological overtones and not only sought contact with the representative of the emperor but also promoted the abandonment of agricultural activity.[70] The execution of James the son of Zebedee (Acts 12:2), one of the Twelve, took place "for the pleasure of the Jews" on the Feast of Passover (Acts 12:3), probably the Passover of A.D. 41, which fell on April 5 that year.

If the papyri P.Oxy. 3021 and P.Berl. 8877 (*CPJ* II 156c) are to be interpreted in connection with the negotiations of spring A.D. 41, Agrippa still would have been in Rome at the time of the Passover in A.D. 41.[71] Wolfgang Reinbold believes that the action of Agrippa was directed only against James and Peter and that there was no general persecution of Christians.[72] It is true that Luke does not describe a general persecution of Christians in Acts 12. It is difficult to see, however, why the use of the term "persecution" should be anachronistic: since the Jews had executed one prominent Christian leader and intended to execute another, the assumption that this was a singular event seems to be naïve. The elimination of the leaders of the church surely was but a prelude to the intended termination

---

[68]See Best 1984, 12.
[69]See Riesner 1994, 105 (ET, 118).
[70]Philo, *Legat.* 197-337; Josephus, *B.J.* 2.184-203; *A.J.* 18.256-309. See N. H. Taylor, "Popular Opposition to Caligula in Jewish Palestine," *JSJ* 32 (2001): 54-70.
[71]See D. Hennig, "Zu neuveröffentlichten Bruchstücken der 'Acta Alexandrinorum,'" *Chiron* 5 (1975): 317-35; cf. Reinbold 2000, 66 n. 93.
[72]Reinbold 2000, 68, following D. Schwartz 1990, 122-23.

of the entire Jesus movement. Gerd Lüdemann maintains that Agrippa realized that the execution of James was unpopular and therefore decided to set Peter free.[73] This view is creative but not in any way related to the New Testament sources. Equally imaginative and indefensible is the assertion by Wolfgang Reinbold that the relationship between Jews and (Jewish) Christians in Jerusalem was amicable and peaceful. Reinbold labels the references about repeated arrests of the apostles in Acts 3—5 "redactional" and thus historically worthless and contends that we should disregard the events connected with the death of the "untypical Stephen" and the events connected with the arrest of the "thoroughly atypical Paul"—a methodological procedure that does violence to the only sources we have for this period and accepts only what harmonizes with a preconceived picture of the history of the church in Jerusalem. Reinbold seems to accept "information" from the book of Acts as trustworthy only if and when scholars whom he regards as reliable do so.

Herod Agrippa had just witnessed in Rome how Claudius dealt with unrest provoked by Jews who proclaimed Jesus as Messiah: Claudius had issued an edict in A.D. 41 nullifying their right of assembly. Being the loyal vassal of the emperor that he was, Herod Agrippa would have found it easy to move against Jewish believers in Jesus as the Messiah in Jerusalem, his capital city.[74]

Luke reported that Jesus' disciples replaced Judas Iscariot after his suicide so that the group of the Twelve would be complete again (Acts 1:15-26); he does not report the replacement of James. Rainer Riesner describes the situation as follows: "Jesus had already brought to expression with this number twelve his own eschatological claim and his mission to Israel, the people of twelve tribes (cf. Mt 19:28/Lk 22:29f). When Peter, as the leader among the twelve, now left the holy city and the holy land itself, now completely under the rule of Agrippa I, this marked a clear break in the activity on behalf of Israel itself. This absence of any reestablishment of the circle of twelve in its entirety betrays a consciousness of living in a new age, one in which missionary efforts on behalf of the older people of God in Jerusalem and in the holy land no longer constituted the only task."[75]

After Peter had escaped from prison with divine help (Acts 12:3-11), he left Jerusalem (Acts 12:17), probably in A.D. 41.

Jürgen Roloff believes that Peter left Jerusalem not because his life was in danger but because of disputes concerning his person that resulted from his openness toward Gentiles (Acts 10), prompting the church "to replace him with James, whose Jewish attitude was above suspicion"; and Peter's arrest by Herod Agrippa may have been connected with these controversies.[76] Christian Grappe argues that Peter's disappearance from Jerusalem can be

---

[73]Lüdemann 1987, 151-52 (ET, 145-46), referring to Baur 1866, 1:184-85. Lüdemann is followed by Reinbold 2000, 69-70; the quotation that follows above, 70.
[74]D. Schwartz 1990, 123; Wander 1994, 226-29; Botermann 1996, 133-34. The critique by Reinbold (2000, 69) is unconvincing.
[75]Riesner 1994, 107-8 (ET, 120-21).
[76]Roloff (1991, 124), who describes the narrative of Peter's escape from prison (Acts 12:6-17) as an "impressive legend."

explained by two factors: first, the increasing influence of radical, Torah-observant Jews who put the Jerusalem church progressively under pressure, particularly with regard to its support of the Gentile mission; second, the vision in Acts 10:9-16 (which Luke allegedly backdated), which caused Peter to abandon his traditional exclusivist position and accept table fellowship with Gentile Christians, a practice that meant that Peter suddenly found himself on the side of the Hellenists. These developments caused conflict with the Jerusalem church, which was undergoing a progressive "Qumranization" and which soon turned to James the brother of Jesus, whose charisma was established by hereditary succession.[77]

These theories do not hold up under close historical scrutiny. (1) Luke depicts Peter's imprisonment as the cause for James taking over the leadership of the Jerusalem church, while Roloff regards the former as the consequence of the latter. It is doubtful that Roloff, who writes nearly 2000 years after Luke, has better insights into the historical reality of events that transpired in Jerusalem and in the Jerusalem church. (2) Roloff and Grappe transform the old assumption of a conflict between Paul and James into a conflict between Peter and James. This is unconvincing because Acts 12 gives no hint of any differences between Peter and James. (3) The points of contact that may have existed between the Essenes and the Jerusalem church can hardly be integrated into a hypothesis of a Qumranization of the church in Jerusalem. And it must be pointed out, against Grappe, that Peter evidently adopted an "open" attitude concerning Gentiles and Gentile Christians at an early date.[78] (4) The suggestion that Herod Agrippa arrested Peter because of his friendly attitude concerning Gentiles[79] but tolerated the (allegedly) conservative James is an audacious construction that is historically implausible: according to Acts 12:1-3, Herod Agrippa arrested and mistreated Christians at this time, he had James, one of the Twelve, executed by the sword, and now he intended to eliminate Peter. This indicates that he organized comprehensive measures against the church and its leadership. The assumption that he was concerned about and took sides in (alleged) internal disputes among the Christians about their leadership is absurd. (5) There indeed were differences of opinion concerning the question of how to integrate converted Gentiles into the church as the people of God. Luke's account indicates that the believers in Jerusalem neither immediately nor permanently agreed on the best course of action. But Luke's account also shows that the people who argued differing positions continued to confer and tried to reach an agreement. We must not underestimate the significance of the difficulties of the long journeys that, for example, the apostolic council (Acts 15) presupposes for Peter, Paul and Barnabas. The geographical challenges presented by conferences should help us understand the energy and expense that the early Christians invested in their quest to maintain unity of theology and practice. (6) The assumption that the Jerusalem church dismissed Peter because he was regarded as too liberal seems preposterous. A dismissal of Peter presumably could have been engineered only by the Twelve, or rather by the ten remaining apostles (James had been killed, Peter allegedly was disputed). The Twelve (or Ten) are not mentioned or hinted at in Acts 12, however. (7) It is historically implausible to assume that the Jerusalem church would have sent its effective and proven leader into the wilderness in the turbulent political situation of the year A.D. 41. And we must keep in mind that the question regarding the integration of Gentile Christians was not directly relevant for the Jerusalem church, as presumably there were few if any Gentile Christians in Jerusalem.

---

[77]Grappe 1992, esp. 253-308. See the critical reviews by J. A. Crampsey, *JTS* 44 (1993): 263-66, J. Roloff, *BZ* 38 (1994): 142-46.
[78]Thus correctly Roloff, *BZ* 38 (1994): 145.
[79]Thus also Bruce 1985b, 651-52.

Where did Peter go when he left Jerusalem? Luke says only that he went "to another place" (εἰς ἕτερον τόπον, *eis heteron topon* [Acts 12:17]). Did Peter go to Rome? Since the middle of the second century A.D. Christian authors unanimously relate that Peter visited Rome and that he died in Rome.[80] Most scholars assume that Peter arrived in Rome shortly before his death, thus not long before A.D. 67. In his letter to the church in Rome, written around A.D. 106, Ignatius already assumes that Peter ministered in Rome.[81] According to the apocryphal *Apocalypse of Peter,* written around A.D. 135, Peter preached the gospel in the entire world before his martyr's death in Rome (*Apoc. Pet.* 14:5).[82] Dionysius, bishop of Corinth, wrote in a letter to the Christians in Rome around A.D. 170 that the church there is a "planting" of Peter and Paul and that the two apostles died in Rome at the same time as martyrs.[83] Gaius, a presbyter of the church in Rome at the time of the bishop Zephyrinus (ca. A.D. 199-217), states that the "trophies" of the apostles Peter and Paul, "who laid the foundations of this church," can be seen in Rome.[84] Irenaeus writes in connection with his debate against the gnostics around A.D. 180 that the church in Rome had been established and organized by Peter and Paul, implying a longer stay in Rome of at least Peter.

"Matthew also issued a written Gospel among the Hebrews in their own dialect, while Peter and Paul were preaching at Rome, and laying the foundations of the church *[cum Peter et Paulus Romae evangelizarent et fundarent ecclesiam]"* (Irenaeus, *Haer.* 3.1.1).

"Since, however, it would be very tedious, in such a volume as this, to reckon up the successions of all the churches, we do put to confusion all those who, in whatever manner, whether by an evil self-pleasing, by vainglory, or by blindness and perverse opinion, assemble in unauthorized meetings; [we do this, I say,] by indicating that tradition derived from the apostles, of the very great, the very ancient, and universally known church founded and organized at Rome by the two most glorious apostles, Peter and Paul *[maximae et antiquissimae et omnibus cognitae, a gloriosissimus duobus apostolis Petro et Paulo Romae fundatae et constitutae ecclesiae];* as also [by pointing out] the faith preached to men, which comes down to our time by means of the successions of the bishops. For it is a matter of necessity that every church should agree with this church, on account of its pre-eminent authority *[propter potentiorem principalitatem],* that is, the faithful everywhere, inasmuch as the apostolical tradition has been preserved continuously by those [faithful men] who exist everywhere. The blessed apostles, then, having founded and built up the church *[fundantes igitur et instruentes beati apostoli ecclesiam],* committed into the hands of Linus the office of the episcopate. Of this Linus, Paul makes mention in the Epistles to Timothy [2 Tim 4:21]. To him succeeded Anacletus; and after him, in the third place from the apostles, Clement was allotted the bishopric. This man, as he had seen the blessed apostles, and had been conversant with them, might be said

---

[80]See Froehlich 1996, 275.

[81]Thus the implication of his comment in Ign. *Rom.* 4:3: "I do not, as Peter and Paul, issue commandments unto you." See Bauckham 1992, 587-89; Elliott, *1 Pet,* 885.

[82]For this passage see Bauckham 1992, 575-77.

[83]Eusebius, *Hist. eccl.* 2.25.8.

[84]Eusebius, *Hist. eccl.* 2.25.7.

to have the preaching of the apostles still echoing [in his ears], and their traditions before his eyes *[qui et vidit apostolos ipsos, et contulit cum eis et cum adhuc insonantem praedicationem apostolorum et traditionem ante oculis haberet]*. Nor was he alone [in this], for there were many still remaining who had received instructions from the apostles" (Irenaeus, *Haer.* 3.3.2-3).

Irenaeus's statements about succession and his list of bishops of the church in Rome seem to accord the Roman church precedence over all other churches. This impression is unwarranted, however, as Norbert Brox argues: "The opposite is the case. He is concerned with the large number of churches with apostolic status everywhere in the world (3:1; 4:1) with their provable possession of the truth. It is this proof that Irenaeus wants to demonstrate in this passage, but he begins by stating explicitly (3:2) that he has to limit himself for pragmatic reasons . . . to a single example, namely, the church in Rome (3:3)."[85] Irenaeus writes in Lugdunum (mod. Lyon) in Gaul, and the only church in the western part of the Roman Empire that has been established by an apostle, according to Irenaeus, is the church in Rome, which explains why he praises this church in the highest terms.

Eusebius and Jerome know the tradition, uncontested for many centuries, that Peter came to Rome after his escape from prison in Jerusalem in A.D. 41 and that he worked in Rome as a missionary, pastor and bishop for twenty-five years (until his death during the principate of Nero in A.D. 67).[86]

Eusebius claims to know that the dispute between Simon Magus and Peter that had taken place in Samaria (Acts 8:18-23) continued in Rome at the time of Claudius (who was emperor in A.D. 41-54): "And coming to the city of Rome, by the mighty co-operation of that power which was lying in wait there, he [Simon Magus] was in a short time so successful in his undertaking that those who dwelt there honored him as a god by the erection of a statue. But this did not last long. For immediately, during the reign of Claudius, the all-good and gracious Providence, which watches over all things, led Peter, that strongest and greatest of the apostles, and the one who on account of his virtue was the speaker for all the others, to Rome against this great corrupter of life" (*Hist. eccl.* 2.14.5-6). After Peter arrived in Rome, the word of God spread in the city, and the "power of Simon was quenched and immediately destroyed, together with the man himself." Eusebius continues: "And so greatly did the splendor of piety illumine the minds of Peter's hearers that they were not satisfied with hearing once only, and were not content with the unwritten teaching of the divine Gospel, but with all sorts of entreaties they besought Mark, a follower of Peter, and the one whose Gospel is extant, that he would leave them a written

---

[85]Brox 1993-2001, 3:8; for the observation that follows above see ibid., 3:8-9.

[86]Eusebius, *Chronicorum liber prior* 153 (ed. A. Schoene); cf. *Eusebii Pamphili Chronici Canones* 261 (ed. J. Fotheringham). The Latin text of Jerome states, *Petrus apostolus cum primum Antiochenam ecclesiam fondasset Romam mittitur. Ubi evangelium praedicans XXV annis eiusdem urbis episcopus perseverat.* See Cullmann 1952, 73-169 (ET, 70-152); Smallwood 1976, 211 n. 31; J. Wenham 1972; 1991a, 275-76 n. 1; Bauckham 1992; Perkins 1994, 131-50. On Peter's grave in Rome see J. Fink, "Das Peter grab—Glaube und Grabung," *VigChr* 32 (1978): 255-75. Margherita Guarducci ("La data del martirio di San Pietro," *La parola del passato* 23 [1968]: 81-117) argues on the basis of *Ascen. Isa.* 4:12, 14 for October 13, A.D. 64, as the date of Peter's death; for a critique see Bauckham 1992, 569-70. According to Bauckhaum, the sources of the first and second centuries only allow the conclusion that Peter died as a martyr in Rome under Nero.

monument of the doctrine which had been orally communicated to them. Nor did they cease until they had prevailed with the man, and had thus become the occasion of the written Gospel which bears the name of Mark" (*Hist. eccl.* 2.15.1).

The apocryphal *Acts of Peter,* written around A.D. 180-190, also contains the information that Peter came to Rome in order to fight against the heresy of Simon Magus: "Now the rumor flew about the city to the brethren who were scattered that Peter at the Lord's command had come because of Simon, in order to show that he was a deceiver and a persecutor of good men. So the whole multitude collected to see the Lord's apostle establishing (the church) in Christ. And on the first day of the week, when the multitude came together to see Peter . . . " (*Acts Pet.* 7). As a result of Peter's ministry, which is not described in detail—miracles are reported only in later sections of the text—"many more were added as believers in the Lord" (9). The decisive encounter with Simon Magus, who lives in the house of a certain senator Marcellus (8), took place in the presence of senators, prefects and officials on the Forum (23-29). After the author recounts several miracles and further debates with Simon Magus, who flies along the Via Sacra and eventually dies as a result of an operation performed by a sorcerer (32), further missionary successes of Peter are reported: "But Peter stayed in Rome and rejoiced with the brethren in the Lord and gave thanks night and day for the mass of people who were daily added to the holy name by the grace of the Lord" (33).

The early tradition that Peter established the church in Rome does not necessarily assert that the church in Rome claimed that Peter was the first Christian to preach the gospel in Rome. One problem in the evaluation of the early Christian tradition is the meaning of the term "church": since Paul's letter to the Roman Christians and other evidence attest several house churches in Rome in the first century, it is unclear which *ekklēsia* Peter is supposed to have established. There is no doubt that Peter *could* have traveled to Rome after escaping from the dangerous situation that Luke describes in Acts 12:1-19. Sea voyages from Caesarea to Rome, for example, in April or May were only a question of financial resources; there would have been many ships in the ports of the Mediterranean waiting for Jewish pilgrims who needed transportation back to the cities from which they had come to Jerusalem to celebrate the Feast of Passover, which had just concluded. Peter's main concern in the spring of A.D. 41 was to leave the jurisdiction of Herod Agrippa I and stay in areas outside of Judea, Galilee and Samaria.

Luke's comment in Acts 12:17 indicates in the context of 1 Cor 9:5 and Gal 2:11-15 that Peter was engaged in intensive and extensive missionary work after his escape from the Jerusalem prison.[87] As a missionary, Peter had several options.

1. He could go to Caesarea, where he had already engaged in missionary work and where he knew other believers.[88] The New Testament and the later

---

[87]Cullmann 1952, 40 (ET, 41-42); Dschulnigg 1996, 109, following Walter Radl, "Befreiung aus dem Gefängnis: Die Darstellung eines biblischen Grundthemas in Acts 12," *BZ* 27 (1983): 81-96, esp. 87; see also Barrett, *Acts,* 1:587.

[88]Thus Ellis 1999, 372-74.

early Christian sources do not mention a prolonged missionary work or sojourn of Peter in Caesarea, however.

2. He could travel to some remote region and engage in missionary work in cities with large or small Jewish Diaspora communities: in Babylonia,[89] northern Africa, Spain or Asia Minor. Early traditions point to the northern regions of Asia Minor, particularly Pontus and Bithynia: the areas mentioned in 1 Pet 1:1 possibly represent not only areas with Christian churches that are the recipients of Peter's letter but also regions in which Peter engaged in missionary work—Pontus, Galatia, Cappadocia, Asia and Bithynia.

The authenticity of 1 Peter has been intensively discussed.[90] Jens Herzer reckons "with some influence of Petrine activity in these areas," as 1 Peter presupposes the acknowledgment of Peter's authority in churches that existed in these regions.[91] Andreas Lindemann believes that 1 Peter is "a witness to the attempt at self-definition of non-Pauline Christianity in Asia Minor."[92] The common assumption that 1 Peter is a pseudonymous text does not hold up under close scrutiny. At least the following three arguments need to be considered. (a) The churches and the Christians that 1 Peter mentions as recipients largely lived in the sphere of influence of Paul's missionary work: why would an anonymous author not identify Paul as the author of his pseudonymous letter? Otto Knoch argues that the author knew Peter as the "highest ecclesial authority" and was better able to relate to those Christians who had not been influenced by Paul by appealing to Peter.[93] This hypothesis is less than convincing. It is questionable, for example, whether Christians in Asia Minor would have been impressed by "highest ecclesial authorities" who did not even bother to visit their churches. (b) The fact that there are no clear "Petrine elements" in 1 Peter prompts some scholars to look for connections with Peter (a good forger intersperses the text with appropriate hints), as otherwise there would be no plausible explanation why the letter was sent in the name of Peter.[94] (c) If 1 Peter was written between A.D. 80 and 100,[95] then we have to assume either that the Christians in Asia Minor did not know that Peter had been dead for some fifteen to thirty years or that the pseudepigraphical form did not bother them. Armin Baum demonstrates that it is historically implausible to think that the early Christians would have readily accepted pseudonymous letters.[96] The traditional view that 1 Peter was written by Peter in Rome, perhaps in A.D. 63/64, continues to be a plausible working hypothesis.[97]

Most scholars interpret the geographical terms in 1 Pet 1:1 not as regions but as provincial names.[98] Some have suggested that the provinces mentioned in 1 Pet

---

[89]Foakes-Jackson (1927, 177) suggests Mesopotamia; R. Osborne (1968) suggests Edessa.
[90]See recently Achtemeier, *1 Pet,* 1-43; Elliott, *1 Pet,* 118-30.
[91]Herzer 1998, 264.
[92]Lindemann 1979, 259; cf. Herzer 1998, 261.
[93]Knoch 1991, 116. Knoch surmises that Silvanus may have been the author of 1 Peter.
[94]See Achtemeier, *1 Pet,* 43.
[95]See Achtemeier, *1 Pet,* 50. Elliott (*1 Pet,* 138) suggests A.D. 73-92.
[96]A. Baum 2001.
[97]See Ellis 1999, 303-6.
[98]See Herzer 1998, 36 n. 66, with a list of authors.

1:1 encompass practically the entire area of Asia Minor[99] and thus large parts of the region in which Paul had engaged in missionary work. Philipp Vielhauer links this suggestion with the hypothesis that the author of 1 Peter wanted to establish Peter's authority in the territory of Paul's missionary work.[100] At least three reasons render this interpretation unlikely. (a) The list does not mention Cilicia, Lycia and Pamphylia, a fact that can hardly be explained with the "orientation toward Syria and Cyprus" of these provinces:[101] both Cilicia *and* Syria belong to the areas in which Paul did missionary work. (b) Paul did not evangelize in Pontus, nor in Cappadocia or Bithynia. The view that 1 Pet 1:1 lays claim to the "territory of Paul's missionary work" therefore is implausible.[102] (c) The fact that Pontus and Bithynia are mentioned separately in 1 Pet 1:1 is striking, since these two regions had been combined into one province in 25 B.C. The sequence of the names of the provinces may indicate the route of the person who carried the letter to the churches in these areas,[103] but also it may indicate that the letter is addressed to churches in the northern regions of Asia Minor that know Peter. According to my reconstruction of Paul's missionary work in Galatia (see §27.1), Paul did not evangelize in northern Galatia, and there are no indications that he worked in the northwestern regions of the province of Asia. This means that 1 Peter may well be addressed to churches in regions in which Paul had not evangelized—areas in which Peter may have engaged in missionary work some time after A.D. 41.[104] Stephen Mitchell accepts the notice in 1 Pet 1:1 as historical, assuming that Peter evangelized the areas in northern Galatia: "In so far as the gospel was taken here in the early years of the Church, the evangelist was surely Peter, who addressed the Jews of Pontus, Galatia, Cappadocia, Asia, and Bithynia in his first epistle."[105]

3. Peter could have traveled to larger centers of Jewish life: Antioch in Syria,[106] Alexandria in Egypt, Ephesus in Ionia in the province of Asia or to Rome in Italy. In the early Christian traditions only Rome is mentioned as a place where Peter engaged in sustained missionary activity, a fact that supports the authenticity of an early visit by Peter in the capital of the empire.[107]

---

[99]Brox, *1 Petr,* 25.
[100]Vielhauer 1981, 589; cf. Brox, *1 Petr,* 26.
[101]Brox, *1 Petr,* 25 n. 39.
[102]See Elliott, *1 Pet,* 316; Herzer 1998, 35-38, 263-64.
[103]See Elliott, *1 Pet,* 90-93, 317.
[104]See Witherington (2001, 221, 350), who wants to restrict Peter to missionary work among Jews, however.
[105]S. Mitchell 1995a, 2:3; see Klaus Belkle, *Galatien und Lykaonien,* 84, with reference to 1 Pet 1:1; Eusebius, *Hist. eccl.* 3.1.2; 3.4.2; see also Harnack 1924, 1:86-87 (ET, 1:80-81); Witherington 2001, 350.
[106]Wellhausen 1907, 9; recently Reinbold 2000, 60-61, 65.
[107]See Minnerath 1994, 135-47. Ellis (1999, 267-68) rejects these traditions as unreliable.

Most scholars reject the identification of the *heteros topos* in Acts 12:17 with Rome, particularly Protestant exegetes, whether liberal or conservative.[108] The argument that the assumption of a missionary activity of Peter in Rome soon after A.D. 41 contradicts the New Testament sources or well-known facts is simply wrong. It is indeed correct that Paul does not mention Peter as either present in Rome or as the founder of the church in Rome in his letter to the Roman Christians, written in the winter of A.D. 56/57. However, this silence cannot be turned, without further ado, into an argument against early Christian traditions that report a sustained early missionary activity of Peter in Rome.[109] Paul does not discuss the origins of the church in Rome, which means that there is no need to mention Peter. Paul's motivation to go to Rome is connected not with a "lack of apostles" in Rome but with the project of his future mission to Spain.

The view that Luke uses the phrase *heteros topos* in Acts 12:17 to indicate that Peter was able to leave safely[110] surely is correct but is rather minimalist. The view that there is no need to answer the question where Peter went because his fate is "of no interest"[111] is hardly insightful in light of the historical nature of the book of Acts and the significance of Peter for the history of the early church. The view that Luke had no information about Peter's whereabouts is unlikely: Luke had accompanied Paul to Jerusalem, Caesarea and Rome, places where the local Christians must have known as much about the missionary work of Peter as they did about the activities of Paul.

Numerous scholars assume that Peter came to Rome in A.D. 41/42.[112] If this view is correct, then the question arises as to why Luke did not mention Peter's move to Rome. One possible answer is that a reference to Rome in Acts 12:17 would have raised questions about the origins of the church in Rome, which Luke does not want to discuss at this point in the book of Acts, where he transitions from his account of the missionary work of Peter in Jerusalem, Samaria and the cities of the coastal plain to an account of Paul's missionary work in Asia Minor and Europe.[113] We should keep in mind that Luke never provides an account of the establishment of the church in Rome. John Wenham argues that Rom 15:20 ("Thus I make it my ambition to proclaim the good news, not where Christ has already been named, so that I do not build on someone else's foundation") supports the foundation of the church in Rome by the missionary work of a particular individual,[114] a position that is untenable in view of the context in Rom 15 and the sentence structure of that particular verse.

It is generally accepted that Peter was executed under Nero. *Acts of Peter* claims to know that Peter was crucified upside down (*Acts Pet.* 38). Tertullian knows that both Peter and Paul died as martyrs in Rome during Nero's reign: Peter was crucified, and Paul was

---

[108]Wellhausen 1907, 9; E. G. Selwyn, *1 Pet,* 61; Bruce, *Acts,* 238-39 with n. 22; Marshall, *Acts,* 211; Schille, *Apg,* 274; Barrett, *Acts,* 1:587; Witherington, *Acts,* 388-89. Fitzmyer (*Acts,* 489-90), a Roman Catholic scholar, is cautious.

[109]Contra Witherington, *Acts,* 388-89, and others.

[110]Thus Conzelmann, *Apg,* 79 (ET, 95); Barrett, *Acts,* 1:587, and others.

[111]Recently Jervell, *Apg,* 335.

[112]Harnack 1893-1904, 2.1:243-44; 1924, 1:49-50 (ET, 44-45); J. Wenham 1972; Sordi 1986, 29 with n. 16; further authors are mentioned in Riesner 1994, 106 n. 78 (ET, 119 n. 78). See Hengel and Schwemer (1998, 388-89 [ET, 257-58]), who are unconvinced, however. See also the discussion in Hemer 1989, 359-62.

[113]J. Wenham 1972, 99; for an (unconvincing) defense of an apologetic purpose of Luke in writing Acts see ibid.

[114]J. Wenham 1972, 100.

executed by the sword.[115] Peter's death as a martyr took place in A.D. 64 at the earliest, the year of the great fire in Rome, or in A.D. 68 at the latest, the year of Nero's death.

The fact that Paul mentions Peter and his missionary activity in his letters as a matter of course indicates that Gentile Christians in Galatia and in Corinth knew Peter as a leading disciple of Jesus and as a leading apostle, even though they may not have met him personally.[116] Paul's comment in 1 Cor 9:5 ("Do we not have the right to be accompanied by a believing wife, as do the other apostles and the brothers of the Lord and Cephas?") implies that the Corinthian Christians know that Peter is engaged in missionary travels with his wife.[117] These comments possibly indicate that Peter may have visited some of the churches that Paul had founded.[118] The references to Cephas-Peter in 1 Cor 1:12; 3:22 suggest that he may have visited the church in Corinth.[119]

There can be no certainty concerning the geographical movements of Peter and his missionary activity after he left Jerusalem in A.D. 41. The comment of Eusebius that the Gospel of Mark was written in connection with the ministry of Peter[120] is of no help in clarifying these issues.

Oscar Cullmann describes the mission of Peter after he left Jerusalem as a mission among Jews "in the service of the Jewish Christian primitive church"[121] in Jerusalem in which James "was the authoritative leader." The protest by Lucien Cerfaux against this historical reconstruction[122] seems to stem from confessional prejudices. We must remember that in neither the Gospels nor the book of Acts is Peter portrayed as a follower of Jesus who differed from the other apostles in any fundamental sense. Luke portrays the change of leadership in the Jerusalem church as a result of a persecution in which God remained sovereign.[123] The history of the church is guided, in the final analysis, not by people and certainly not by Peter making authoritative decisions, but rather by the almighty God, the Lord of history and of the church.

Wolfgang Reinbold suggests that "the common view of Peter as a great missionary preacher and 'leader of the Jewish mission' who engaged in missionary travels seeking to convert female and male Jews" needs to be critically evaluated: "As far as we know, it

---

[115]Tertullian, *Praescr.* 36. For a historical evaluation of the early patristic traditions see, for Peter, Bauckham 1992, 587-89; for Paul, Tajra 1989, 198-200. See also Prior 1989, 85-89.
[116]See Perkins 1994, 118.
[117]See Wolff, *1 Kor,* 22; Schrage, *1 Kor,* 1:145; 2:292-93.
[118]Ellis 1999, 366-68, with reference to 1 Cor 1:12; 3:22—4:1, 9; 9:5; Gal 2:11-14; 2 Pet 3:15.
[119]See Barrett 1964, 271, 273.
[120]See Ellis (1999, 293, 357-76), who suggests that the Gospel of Mark was written in Caesarea.
[121]Thus the heading of the second section of the chapter "Peter the Apostle"; see Cullmann 1952, 39 (ET, 40); for the observation that follows above see ibid., 42 (ET, 43).
[122]Cerfaux 1953 (ET, 1960 [1957]).
[123]See Perkins 1994, 103.

does not correspond with historical reality."[124] Reinbold states, "We possess no clear evidence for the view that the apostle engaged in deliberate propaganda [i.e., missionary work] among his compatriots before or after the Jerusalem conference." This assessment rests on Reinbold having eliminated relevant evidence in the book of Acts as redactional, legendary or historically worthless for other reasons (see below). Reinbold plays with the New Testament sources using rather arbitrary rules: that which fits his basic hypothesis he accepts as historical; that which does not fit he rejects as redactional or legendary. He refers to differing opinions, usually in footnotes, but he hardly gives them a fair hearing. He does not seem to believe that it is the task of a historian first to attempt a synthesis of the information provided by all extant sources before engaging in source criticism and form-historical analyses. If Peter indeed visited only already existing churches that he did not establish himself, then Reinbold must explain who was responsible for the establishment of these churches. It is correct that according to Acts 11:20-21, anonymous Jewish Christians established churches. There is no valid reason, however, to eliminate as "redactional" the evangelistic activity of Peter that is repeatedly mentioned in the first chapters of the book of Acts. Perhaps Reinbold does not know any church leaders today who have served as pioneer missionaries or who combine their responsibilities as bishops with evangelistic outreach. He fails to treat the New Testament sources with the meticulous care that classical scholars extend to primary sources as a matter of course, and he seems to have little knowledge about dynamic churches that grow as a result of mission and evangelism.

---

[124]Reinbold 2000, 43-79; quotations from the conclusion, 78; the quotation that follows above, ibid.

22

THE JEWISH-CHRISTIAN MISSIONARY WORK
FROM JERUSALEM TO ROME

J ewish-Christian missionaries from Jerusalem carried the gospel of Jesus Christ to Judea, Samaria, Syria and Rome. They evidently engaged in missionary work not only among Jews but also among Samaritans, God-fearers and polytheists.

22.1 Missionary Work in Jerusalem and Judea

The missionary sermons of Peter in Acts 1—5 may be interpreted as reflecting the proclamation of the early Jewish-Christian missionaries before Jewish audiences. They emphasize five main convictions.[1] (1) Jesus is the Messiah sent by Yahweh to the Jewish people.[2] The titles and epithets used for Jesus vary, but the *cantus firmus* is the proclamation that Jesus is the promised Messiah who was expected to come and save his people. It is possible that the early missionary indicated, before Jewish audiences, that Jesus was significant for the Gentiles also (see Acts 3:25-26). (2) The leaders of the Jewish people share the responsibility for Jesus' death.[3] This charge sometimes is softened with reference to their ignorance (Acts 3:17). (3) God has raised Jesus from the dead.[4] (4) The sacred Scriptures predicted the death and resurrection of Jesus,[5] events that thus are part of God's plan of salvation. (5) Jews need to repent in order to receive forgiveness.[6] The reception of forgiveness is connected with the reception of the Holy Spirit and baptism.

Jerusalem

Luke's account in the book of Acts reports the numerical growth of the Jerusalem church.

---

[1]See Tyson 1992, 100-129, esp. 105-9.
[2]Acts 2:36; 3:13, 15, 18, 20, 22-23; 4:10; 5:31.
[3]Acts 2:23, 36; 3:13, 14; 4:10; 5:30.
[4]Acts 2:24, 31-32; 3:15; 4:10; 5:30.
[5]Acts 2:16-21, 25-28, 30-31, 34-35; 3:22-23; 4:11.
[6]Acts 2:38; 3:19-20; implicit in 4:12; 5:21.

1. The followers of Jesus who had assembled in Jerusalem before the Feast of Pentecost were a "crowd" (ὄχλος, *ochlos*) numbering "about one hundred twenty persons" (Acts 1:15). This figure is meant to be understood in a literal sense, which means that besides the eleven remaining disciples of Jesus there were about one hundred people who probably had heard and seen Jesus teach and heal in Galilee, possibly in Jerusalem, who presumably had seen him after the crucifixion as the Risen One, who believed that he was the Messiah, and who now waited for the next phase of the movement that Jesus had initiated.

Rudolf Pesch interprets the figure given in Acts 1:15 as a reference to the Twelve (10 times 12) and suggests that the number 120 symbolically describes "the constitution of eschatological Israel."[7] Since ten people could constitute a group engaging in official worship,[8] the number 120 constitutes, according to Pesch, "the full number of the people necessary for the 'rebirth' of Israel" and thus establishes the possibility and the necessity of replacing Judas Iscariot with a twelfth apostle. Since Luke no longer fully understood these connections, he relativized the exact figure by adding the term "about." Jürgen Roloff also interprets the number 120 in the context of the symbolic reconstitution of eschatological Israel by Jesus and thus as an expression of the conviction "that the claims and the promise of Jesus are in the process of being fulfilled."[9] A symbolic meaning of the number 120 cannot be excluded a priori. However, the terms that Luke uses in Acts 1:15 indicate clearly that he describes a specific situation, a singular moment in the history of the first congregation of the followers of Jesus in Jerusalem (ἐν μέσῳ, *en mesō*, "among"; ἀδελφοί, *adelphoi*, "brothers"; ὄχλος, *ochlos*, "crowd"; ἐπὶ τὸ αὐτό, *epi to auto*, "together" [i.e., at the same place];[10] ὀνόματα, *onomata*, "names" [i.e., people]; ὡσεί, *hōsei*, "about"). The symbolic significance may be present in the event, but this is not indicated in the terms and phrases that Luke uses: Luke does not refer to "saints" (ἅγιοι, *hagioi*) or to the "assembly" (ἐκκλησία, *ekklēsia*). Hans Weder is correct: "The reference in Acts 1:15 to 120 persons probably has no metaphorical meaning."[11]

2. The events of Pentecost and the preaching of Peter resulted in "about three thousand persons" being added to the church (Acts 2:41). Rudolf Pesch correctly observes that "the figure indicates that the 25-fold number of persons was added to the initial congregation of 120 people. Since the figure has no apparent symbolic significance, and since clearly we are not dealing with a Lukan fiction that wanted to express the blessing that rested on the mission of the primitive church, we need to consider the possibility that the pre-Lukan tradition knew about large-scale initial successes of the early Christian mission at the Feast of Pentecost (among inhabitants of Jerusalem and among pilgrims,

---

[7]Pesch, *Apg*, 1:87; for the observation that follows above see ibid.
[8]See 1QS VI, 2-3; 1QSa II, 22; CD XIII, 1-2; *m. Sanh.* 1:6; *m. 'Abot* 3:6.
[9]Roloff, *Apg*, 31.
[10]Schneider (*Apg*, 1:216 n. 28) sees a "possible" reinterpretation in the sense of "in total"; cf. NRSV. For the meaning "together" see BDAG 363 s.v. "ἐπί 1cβ"; BDF §233.2.
[11]H. Weder, *EWNT* 1:982 (*EDNT* 1:404).

perhaps from Galilee, who had already come into contact with Jesus' proclamation)."[12]

Jürgen Roloff states, categorically, "This is, of course, an unreal figure that is impossible to reconcile with the actual conditions: Jerusalem had hardly more than thirty thousand inhabitants at the time of Jesus."[13] Ernst Haenchen remarks, "People should realize how hard it is—without a microphone!—to make one's voice carry to three thousand people."[14] He believes it to be far more probable "that the little flock of Christians led 'a quiet, even in the Jewish sense "devout" life in Jerusalem. It was a model existence, and nothing but the triumphant conviction of the faithful betrayed that from this flock was to go forth as a movement that would transform the world.'" Haenchen asserts that as Luke speaks of multitudes here and in later passages, he is guided by the conviction expressed in Acts 26:26 that "this was not done in a corner." This concept controlled his account of the early Christian mission. And "the crowds streaming into the fold of Christ are for him the visible expression of the divine blessing resting on the church."

These and similar interpretations are not only entirely hypothetical but also unwarranted from both historical and literary perspectives. (a) Neither Dibelius nor Haenchen explains his criteria for what "probably" could or could not have happened in reality. One wonders whether it is the modest conditions of their own ecclesial existence in *Landeskirchen* (state churches) that have not known real, let alone rapid, growth for centuries but only decline. (b) The assumption of a "quiet" existence of the church is contradicted by the repeated attacks, unrelenting opposition and arrests on the part of the Jewish authorities. People who are "quiet" and live a "model existence" do not come to the attention of authorities, nor are they put under pressure or persecuted. (c) If Luke indeed understood his numbers as expressions of divine blessing, then he easily could have found ones that carry greater symbolism—for example, 12,000 (12 times 1,000) or 144,000 (12 times 12 times 1,000). (d) Jerusalem had more than 30,000 inhabitants in the mid-first century A.D. Most scholars today estimate between 100,000 and 120,000 inhabitants. If we assume 100,000 inhabitants, 3,000 converts constitute but 3 percent of the population. And Jürgen Roloff seems to neglect entirely the pilgrims who were in Jerusalem for the Feast of Pentecost. Some scholars estimate that 1,000,000 pilgrims visited Jerusalem for Pentecost. The 3,000 converts to faith in Jesus as the Messiah probably included a large number of festival pilgrims.[15] (e) The argument about the microphone is somewhat embarrassing: when issuing verdicts on the basis of comparisons, one should use as the standard not professors whose voices are amplified even in small auditoriums but rather the powerful voices of evangelists such as George Whitefield who preached in the open air. Whitefield wrote the following entry in his diary on Friday, June 1, 1739: "Gave a short exhortation to a few people in a field, and preached in the evening, at a place called Mayfair, near Hyde Park Corner. The congregation, I believe, consisted of nearly eighty thousand people. It was by far the largest I ever preached to yet [Whitefield was twenty-four years old]. In the time of my prayer there was a little noise, but they kept a deep silence during my whole discourse. A high and

---

[12]Pesch, *Apg,* 1:126.

[13]Roloff, *Apg,* 63-64; similarly Söding 1990b, 140 n. 14.

[14]Haenchen, *Apg,* 190 (ET, 188). The argument about the microphone is used also in Siegert 1993, 46. For the quotation that follows above see Haenchen (*Apg,* 19 [ET, 189]), who quotes Dibelius 1968, 109 [ET, 124]).

[15]See Reinhardt 1995b, 261.

very commodious scaffold was erected for me to stand upon, and though I was weak in myself, yet God strengthened me to speak so loud, that most could hear, and so powerfully, that most, I believe, could feel. All love, all glory, be to God through Christ!"[16] Arnold Dallimore, Whitefield's biographer, concludes on the basis of various calculations[17] that the figures mentioned by George Whitefield (and John Wesley) need to be halved, which still leaves forty thousand people—a colossal achievement.

Luke's reference to the making of three thousand converts and their "addition" to the church leaves open the question of whether they were baptized on the same day. Some scholars concluded from the approximately 150 ritual baths (*miqvaot*) that have been found in Jerusalem dating to between 100 B.C. and A.D. 70 that the apostles would have had no difficulty baptizing three thousand people on Pentecost.[18]

3. Several weeks or months after Pentecost, after a lame man had been healed and after the apostles had continued to preach, particularly Peter and John, "many of those who heard the word believed; and the number of the men [ὁ ἀριθμὸς τῶν ἀνδρῶν, *ho arithmos tōn andrōn*] came to about[19] five thousand" (Acts 4:4 RSV). Evidently the congregation had grown considerably so that only the men were counted. Considering the population of Jerusalem, the number of over five thousand believers is not impossible.[20]

4. When Paul visited Jerusalem after the conclusion of his missionary work in Ephesus, he was informed by the local leaders of the church that "many thousands" (μυριάδες, *myriades*) of Jews have come to faith who "are all zealous for the law" (Acts 21:20). This figure presumably refers not just to believers in Jerusalem[21] but to all Jewish Christians in Judea and perhaps also in Galilee. The term *myriads,* which means literally "tens of thousands," is a general expression indicating a large number, although it is not impossible that Luke uses the term to indicate literally how many people in Jerusalem and Judea had come to faith. It is also possible that Luke, or rather the leadership of the Jerusalem church,

---

[16]Arnold Dallimore, *George Whitefield: The Life and Times of the Great Evangelist of the Eighteenth-Century Revival* (2 vols.; Edinburgh: Banner of Truth Trust, 1970-1980), 1:292.

[17]When Whitefield preached in North America in 1740, Benjamin Franklin measured the area that Whitefield's voice reached: "I computed that he might well be heard by more than thirty thousand." A further piece of evidence are the collections that Whitefield received: on one occasion "above £20 in half pence," thus nearly ten thousand coins. Dallimore (*George Whitefield,* 296) comments, "It is highly probable that these crowds, which were the largest of Whitefield's whole career, were also the largest ever reached by the unamplified human voice in the whole history of mankind."

[18]See recently B. Grasham, "Archaeology and Christian Baptism," *RestQ* 43 (2001): 113-16.

[19]Some manuscripts read ὡς (B D 0165 33 pc), while others read ὡσει (E 044 𝔐). Some manuscripts omit the term (𝔓[74] ℵ A 81 1175 pc vg), a reading that is less likely to be original because the omission is easier to explain than the addition.

[20]See Reinhardt 1995b, 264.

[21]Contra Roloff (*Apg,* 314), who regards this figure to be "as unrealistic as the earlier information about the converts in Jerusalem."

uses the term in a hyperbolic sense[22] to indicate in a general manner that many people in Judea had come to faith in Jesus Christ.

These relatively sparse and general statistical data that Luke provides for the growth of the church in Jerusalem and in Judea indicate two points. (1) The early Christians evidently were not very interested in precise statistical data for the size of the church(es). Luke is the only New Testament author to provide any figures, and he limits himself to these three passages in Acts and to approximate figures for the believers in Jerusalem (Acts 2:41; 4:4; 19:7). Luke normally refers to the growth of the church only with general formulations.[23] Since Luke imitates the style of the Septuagint and surely knew the Old Testament books of Numbers, Ezra and Nehemiah, he had several models and precedents for exact statistical information. But clearly he is not interested in precise statistics. We should also recall that he repeatedly notes that people did *not* believe. These facts correspond to the overall picture in the New Testament, including the Gospels. The New Testament authors record positive reactions to the preaching of Jesus and the apostles, they rejoice when people respond to the message of the gospel with faith, they are not surprised about rejection and opposition, and they recognize that faith and unbelief are not simply the result of good or bad methods of preaching or witnessing but are, in the final analysis, a mystery of the sovereign grace of God and of the willful reception or rejection of the gospel message by people.[24] (2) The growth of the church is not a vague, mysterious or merely "spiritual" process but rather a visible event that can be described with numbers. Luke includes statistical information about the growth of the church indeed to show "how God's blessing accompanies his work and asserts itself even against hostile forces."[25] However, clearly Luke is also interested to provide specific historical information to describe the quantitative and extensive growth of the Jerusalem church.[26] The view that Luke wanted to paint an "ideal picture" of an ideal church that grows continuously seems to apply more to some interpreters[27] than to Luke himself. The repeated persecutions resulting in Jewish Christians fleeing from Jerusalem demonstrate that Luke has indeed a differentiated view of the growth of the Jerusalem church.

The information that Luke provides in the book of Acts about the growth of the church has been ably studied by Wolfgang Reinhardt; it can be summarized as follows.[28] (1) The Greek terms that Luke uses to present the growth of the

---

[22]See Pesch, *Apg,* 2:219.

[23]Acts 5:14; 6:1, 7; 8:6, 12; 9:31, 35, 42; 11:21, 24; 13:43; 14:1, 21; 16:5; 18:8, 10; 21:20.

[24]See Taber 1986, 392; for the observation that follows above see ibid.

[25]Zingg 1974, 296, in the conclusion.

[26]See Reinhardt 1995a, 200.

[27]Note, for example, the caveat in Noordegraaf 1983, 14, contra Zingg 1974.

[28]Reinhardt 1995a; summary, 308-40. Older studies of the subject include Zingg 1974; G. Lohfink 1975, 51-61; Taeger 1982, esp. 164-82; Noordegraaf 1983; Taber 1986; Trites 1988.

church[29] describe the latter against the background of the history of Israel as the effect of God's intervention in the history of his people, corresponding to and fulfilling Old Testament promises, expectations and experiences. The "growth of the word" (see Acts 6:7; 12:24) is the spreading of the communities of the believers. The growth of the church, the messianic people of God who believe in Jesus the Messiah and Savior, is the eschatological realization of the promises of the prophets concerning the restoration of Israel. (2) Seen from the perspective of the missionaries who have been commissioned by the risen and exalted Lord, the proclamation of the gospel of Jesus Christ is the basic cause of the growth of the church. This clearly is what Luke wants to communicate with the phrase "the word spread" in the context of information about the growth of the church[30] and in his references to the cause of this growth.[31] The sermons of the apostles are significant for the growth of the church: they take into account the situation of the various audiences but also include elements of contradiction. Luke reports that the missionary proclamation was carried out not only by the apostles but also by many other Christians whose names he supplies or in many more cases does not supply—Jewish Christians who preached in synagogues, private homes and marketplaces. (3) The growth of the church is connected with repentance of individual people who "received the word" (Acts 2:41), who became "obedient to the faith" (Acts 6:7), who became "persuaded" (Acts 17:4) and joined "the Way." (4) The unanimity of the believers, their ability to deal with conflict, and the manner in which the churches mastered crisis situations promoted the growth of the church, with prayer playing a significant role.[32] Praise to God and the joy of the believers, often the result of reports of missionary advances, are "characteristics of the early church and its attractiveness."[33] (5) Signs and miracles had a certain missionary function in preparing the ground for and supporting evangelistic proclamation. In some cases they lead to faith,[34] in other cases they lead to divisions among the people and to misunderstandings,[35] and they certainly do not protect the missionaries from suffering.[36] (6) The growth of the church is primarily the work of God and the effect of the Holy Spirit.[37] This is the reason why growth cannot be organized or planned:

---

[29]Particularly the terms αὐξάνειν (auxanein), πληθύνειν (plēthynein), προστίθημι (prostithēmi); see Reinhardt 1995a, 56-102; Noordegraaf 1983, 20-25, 112-25.

[30]See Acts 2:41 in the context of 2:14-36, 38-40; cf. 4:4; 5:28; 11:24; 13:49.

[31]Acts 5:14 (cf. 4:31, 33; 5:42); 6:7 (cf. 6:2, 4); 9:31 (cf. 8:4; 9:20, 22, 27-29); 19:20 (cf. 19:8-10).

[32]Acts 6:1-7; 15:30-31, 36-41; 16:5, cf. the summaries in Acts 1—4. On prayer: 2:42, 47; 4:24-31, 33; 5:14; 6:4, 7.

[33]Reinhardt 1995a, 323. Joy: 2:46; 8:8; 13:52; 15:3; praise: 2:47; 3:8-9; 4:21; 11:18; 13:48; 19:17; 21:20; reports: 14:27; 15:3.

[34]See Acts 8:6-13; 9:35, 42; 13:12; 14:3.

[35]See Acts 14:3, 8-18.

[36]See Acts 5:18-42; 13:4-12; 16:23-40.

[37]See, e.g., Acts 1:8; 5:31; 11:18; 18:10. See Reinhardt 1995a, 318-19, contra Taeger 1982, 225-26.

"The missionary work which often causes growth is a combination of guidance by God's Spirit and methodical planning that cannot be put into a mathematical formula."[38] This is a point that Albert Noordegraaf emphasizes: "Luke portrays for us the growth of the construction (development) of the church as a part of the continuing work of God."[39] (7) Opposition and persecution cannot stop the growth of the church. On the contrary, they sometimes create new opportunities for further growth. (8) Internal and external growth are connected.[40] Although Luke's notices about the growth of the church always have a quantitative meaning,[41] he displays "great interest in the 'internal' life of the congregations and between the congregations. Strengthening, building up, encouragement, consolidation, *koinōnia* [fellowship] . . . also enhance the attractiveness of the congregations and contribute to further external growth." Luke's account asserts that the early church grew rapidly during the first years (Acts 2:41, 47; 4:4; 5:14; 6:1). Rainer Riesner comments that this development "provided a decisive motivation for at least an oral formulation of the Jesus tradition."[42] And the growth of the church immediately resulted in the necessity of translating the Aramaic Jesus tradition into Greek.[43]

The Successors of James

James the brother of Jesus was succeeded by Symeon bar Cleopas as leader of the church in Jerusalem. According to Hegesippus, Symeon bar Cleopas was a member of Jesus' family.[44] Cleopas (or Clopas) was a brother of Joseph, Jesus' father (i.e., he was Jesus' uncle). Symeon the son of Cleopas therefore was a cousin of Jesus[45] and a cousin of James the brother of Jesus. According to Jn 19:25, Mary, Cleopas's wife, was present during Jesus' crucifixion. Some scholars have suggested that this Symeon was the unnamed companion of Cleopas on the road to Emmaus (Lk 24:13, 19), an assumption that must remain hypothetical.[46] If Symeon became James's successor immediately after James died as a martyr in A.D. 62, then he would have been between forty and fifty years of age when he assumed leadership of the Jerusalem church. Symeon died during

---

[38]Reinhardt 1995a, 333, with reference to Taber 1986, 392-93.

[39]Noordegraaf 1983, 201.

[40]See Zingg 1974, 300-301; Noordegraaf 1983, 202-3; Reinhardt 1995a, 333-35; the quotation that follows above, 334.

[41]Noordegraaf 1983, 203. Exceptions might be Acts 9:31; 16:5.

[42]Riesner 1988, 68.

[43]See J. Wanke, *EWNT* 1:1065 (*EDNT* 1:436).

[44]Hegesippus, in Eusebius *Hist. eccl.* 3.11; 3.22; 3.32.1-6; 4.5.3; 4.22.4. See Zahn 1900, 245-43, 282, 352; Bauckham 1990, 79-94; Pixner 1994, 358-64.

[45]Eusebius, *Hist. eccl.* 3.11; 3.32.6; 4.22.4. See Bauckham 1990, 16-17.

[46]Zahn, *Lk,* 710-13; 1900, 282, 350-52; R. Riesner, "Kleopas," *GBL* 2:794; 1995, 1844. Bauckham (1990, 17-18, 87) remains skeptical. On Mary the wife of Cleopas see now Bauckham 2002, 203-23.

the principate of Trajan (A.D. 98-117) as a martyr.[47] This means that Symeon was one of the most influential leading Jewish Christians for about forty years. According to a presumably reliable tradition, he built a church in Jerusalem after the Jerusalem Christians had returned from exile in Pella in A.D. 72/73, evidently at the site of the upper room in pre-70 A.D. Jerusalem where the followers of Jesus had gathered after Easter.

Eutychius, the bishop of Alexandria in the tenth century, writes on the basis of older sources, perhaps using the Jewish-Christian historian Hegesippus, who wrote around A.D. 180, "When the Christians who had fled in those days from the Jews to near and distant regions heard that Titus had destroyed the holy city and killed the Jews they returned to the ruins of the holy city and lived there. They built a church and appointed a second [i.e., new] bishop with the name of Simeon, son of Cleopas. He [Cleopas] was a brother of Joseph who had reared our Lord Jesus Christ. This happened in the fourth year of Uspasian [Vespasian]. He [Simeon] remained 26 years and then he was killed."[48] Epiphanius, bishop of Salamis (A.D. 315-403), knows Jewish-Christian traditions deriving from Hegesippus that state that the church built by Simeon/Symeon stood at the site of the upper room: "And Hadrian found the temple of God trodden down and the whole city devastated, save for a few houses and the very small church of God [ἡ τοῦ θεοῦ ἐκκλησία μικρά], where the disciples, when they had returned after the Savior had ascended from the Mount of Olives, went to the Upper Room [ὑπερῷον]. For there it had been built, that is, in that portion of Zion that escaped destruction, together with blocks of houses in the neighborhood of Zion and the seven synagogues that alone remained standing in Zion, like solitary huts, one of which remained until the time of Maximinus, the bishop and the emperor Constantine, like a booth in a vineyard."[49] It is important to remember that leading Gentile Christians of the church in the second and third centuries were interested in local traditions in Palestine in general and in Jerusalem in particular. Eusebius comments on such interests of Melito of Sardis, who visited the Holy Land around A.D. 160 (Eusebius, *Hist. eccl.* 4.26.13-14). And he reports of Alexander, a friend of Origen who later became bishop in Cappadocia, that he visited Palestine in A.D. 212 "in consequence of a vow and for the sake of information in regard to its places" (εὐχῆς καὶ τῶν τόπων ἱστορίας ἕνεκεν [*Hist. eccl.* 6.11.2]).

If this tradition is historically reliable, then the Jewish Christians who returned from exile in Pella built a place of assembly between A.D. 73/74 and the end of the first century in Jerusalem, at the site of the so-called David's Tomb on Mount Zion.[50] Eudocia, wife of the emperor Theodosius II, built the Gerontocomion of St. George (A.D. 457-460) and St. Stephen (A.D. 460; at the traditional place of Stephen's martyrdom, now the famous Do-

[47]Hegesippus, in Eusebius *Hist. eccl.* 3.32.1-6, asserting that Symeon was 120 years old, which can hardly be correct; see Bauckham 1990, 72, 87, 91-92, with reference to Gen 6:3 and Deut 34:7.
[48]Breydy, CSCO 472.47; see Riesner 1995a, 1842-43 n. 323.
[49]Epiphanius, *De mensuris et ponderibus* 14 (PG 43:260); translation by J. E. Dean; see Riesner 1995a, 1843 n. 327.
[50]On the apostolic synagogue on Mount Zion see Pixner 1994, 287-334; Riesner 1995a, 1845; J. Murphy-O'Connor, "The Cenacle—Topographical Setting for Acts 2:44-45," in Bauckham 1995a, 303-22; Capper 1995, 345-49.

minican convent and École Biblique). Other early churches in Jerusalem are St. Thomas (A.D. 524-552) and Nea Church (ca. A.D. 549/550).[51]

Eusebius records a list of bishops of the Jerusalem church. He asserts that the church in Jerusalem was a Jewish-Christian church until the Second Jewish Revolt, led by Bar Kokhba, and that this changed after the catastrophic defeat in the war against Rome:

"The chronology of the bishops of Jerusalem I have nowhere found preserved in writing; for tradition says that they were all short-lived. But I have learned this much from writings, that until the siege of the Jews, which took place under Hadrian, there were fifteen bishops in succession there all of whom are said to have been of Hebrew descent, and to have received the knowledge of Christ in purity, so that they were approved by those who were able to judge of such matters, and were deemed worthy of the episcopate. For their whole church consisted then of believing Hebrews who continued from the days of the apostles until the siege which took place at this time; in which siege the Jews, having again rebelled against the Romans, were conquered after severe battles. But since the bishops of the circumcision ceased at this time, it is proper to give here a list of their names from the beginning. The first, then, was James, the so-called brother of the Lord; the second, Symeon; the third, Justus; the fourth, Zacchaeus; the fifth, Tobias; the sixth, Benjamin; the seventh, John; the eighth, Matthias; the ninth, Philip; the tenth, Seneca; the eleventh, Justus; the twelfth, Levi; the thirteenth, Ephres; the fourteenth, Joseph; and finally, the fifteenth, Judas. These are the bishops of Jerusalem that lived between the age of the apostles and the time referred to, all of them belonging to the circumcision. . . . At this time Narcissus was the bishop of the church at Jerusalem, and he is celebrated by many to this day. He was the fifteenth in succession from the siege of the Jews under Hadrian. We have shown that from that time first the church in Jerusalem was composed of Gentiles, after those of the circumcision, and that Marcus was the first Gentile bishop that presided over them" (*Hist. eccl.* 4.5.1-4; 5.12.1).[52]

This list of names of fifteen bishops between James and Judas, "the fifteenth in succession . . . under Hadrian," has one problem: it is impossible to accommodate thirteen bishops of the Jerusalem church between Symeon, the successor of James who died under Trajan (i.e., between A.D. 98 and 117), and the year A.D. 138. Eusebius's explanation that each of these thirteen men were "short-lived"—that is, that every one of them died after just one or two years in office (*Hist. eccl.* 4.5.1)—is not very satisfactory. Equally hypothetical is the suggestion of Theodor Zahn, who assumed that the list included the bishops of other Jewish-Christian churches in Palestine, perhaps the bishops of Caesarea, as well as the suggestion of Hans-Joachim Schoeps that the list records the bishops of the church in Pella.[53]

Roelof van den Broek argues more recently that Eusebius's list can be inter-

---

[51]L. di Segni, in Humphrey 1995-2002, 2:166-69.
[52]On the list of bishops from Jerusalem see Zahn 1900, 281-301; Bauckham 1990, 70-79.
[53]Zahn 1900, 300-301; Schoeps 1949, 286-87.

preted with the help of the apocryphal letter of James to Quadratus, which belongs to the Jewish-Christian milieu and provides a list of six names: Philip, Senicus, Justus, Levi, Aphre, Judas. These six men are described as Jewish scribes who converted to the Christian faith and sought to lead Jews in Jerusalem to faith in Jesus Christ using scriptural arguments; that is, they were contemporaries of James who engaged in missionary work in Jerusalem.[54] What is striking is the fact that these six names are identical with the last names of Eusebius's list of bishops.[55] If we assume that Justus, the third bishop in Eusebius's list, was the last Jewish-Christian *episkopos* of the Jerusalem church after the death of Symeon before the Bar Kokhba Revolt, then we are left with twelve names. These twelve men can be interpreted as a council of twelve elders who assisted James in leading the Jerusalem church. If such a council of elders existed in the Jerusalem church after the departure of the Twelve, we may expect their names to crop up somewhere in the early Christian traditions: the elders of the Jerusalem church after A.D. 42 surely were remembered as significant Christian leaders. Richard Bauckham assumes that apostles from the group of the Twelve who never left Jerusalem belonged to this council of elders, together with other disciples of Jesus. Interpreted in this context, the names that Eusebius lists become plausible: John, Matthew and Philip could be members of the Twelve. Levi and Zacchaeus could be disciples of Jesus who are mentioned in the Gospel tradition. Justus might be identical with the Justus Barsabbas, a prominent member of the Jerusalem church mentioned in Acts 1:23. Joseph/Josis and Judas, the last two names, could be identical with the brothers of Jesus with these names (Mk 6:3); we should note, however, that Mark mentions another Joses who evidently was a known figure in the early church (Mk 15:40, 47), and Luke mentions a Judas Barsabbas who was a prominent member of the Jerusalem church (Acts 15:23, 27, 32).[56]

Judea

The missionary work of the apostles in Jerusalem[57] impacted the surrounding areas: "The people also gathered from the towns around Jerusalem, bringing the sick and those afflicted with unclean spirits, and they were all healed" (Acts 5:16). Members of the church came from Bethany, Emmaus and Jericho. Jesus had commissioned the Twelve to proclaim the good news in Judea, beginning in Jerusalem (Acts 1:8): I assume that the twelve apostles fulfilled this commission. In connection with the persecution after Stephen's death Christians from

---

[54]Broek 1988, 56-65, esp. 58.
[55]For the argument that follows above see Bauckham 1990, 73-76; Bauckham relies on Broek 1988.
[56]See Bauckham 1990, 76-77.
[57]See Pesch 1982, 48-49.

Jerusalem reached regions in Judea and in Samaria (Acts 8:1).

Paul mentions, in passing, that there were "churches in Christ in Judea" (Gal 1:22; 1 Thess 2:14). We do not know in which towns and villages these churches had been established. Luke focuses nearly exclusively on Jerusalem in the first half of the book of Acts; he uses the term *ekklēsia* for a local congregation other than the Jerusalem church only in Acts 13:1, where he describes the church in Antioch, the capital of Syria.[58] Karl Pieper had no explicit evidence but assumed correctly that there were "numerous small Christian congregations scattered in the villages and towns of the Judea" that owed their existence to "the missionary activity of the first apostles and other members of the primitive church."[59]

The apostles and other Jewish-Christian missionaries could have proclaimed the gospel and established churches in the following towns and villages within a radius of 25 km (15 mi.) from Jerusalem (listed from north to south and from west to east; see fig. 13):[60]

Modiin: town in the Shephelah, 30 km northwest of Jerusalem and 10 km east of Lod; place of origin of the Hasmonean family.

Bethel (mod. Beitin):[61] village in Ephraim 17 km north of Jerusalem; mentioned in connection with Abraham and Jacob (Gen 12:8; 13:3; 28:10-22; 31:13). During the monarchy the town was the center of the new cult established by Jeroboam (1 Kings 12:28—13:32). Bethel was destroyed in 721 B.C. when the Assyrians conquered Samaria. Jews who had returned from the Babylonian exile settled in Bethel (Neh 11:31). The Syrian general Bakchides fortified the town in 160 B.C. (1 Macc 9:50). Vespasian conquered the town in A.D. 69 and rebuilt it as a Roman town.

Beeroth (Berea): village on the road to Neapolis.

Khirbet Khudria: village about 2 km east of Deir Dibwan in northern Judea, 4 km southeast of Bethel; remains of a church.

Caphar Ruta: village in northwestern Judea.

Aialon: 5 km east of Bethel; olive presses, cisterns, tombs.

Bethasan (mod. Khirbet Deir Hassan): 24 km northwest of Jerusalem.

Bethoron (mod. Beit ʿUr):[62] double village at the seventh milestone on the Jerusalem-Nicopolis road through the Aialon Valley about 16 km northwest of Jerusalem. The town was rebuilt by Solomon (2 Chron 8:5). Jews returning from the Babylonian exile settled in Bethoron (Jdt 4:4-5). The town was fortified by the Syrian general Bakchides (1 Macc 9:50).

Khirbet es Sibiya: settlement in northern Judea, 2 km east of Upper Bethoron; remains of buildings.

---

[58]See Bruce 1985b, 641.

[59]Pieper 1929, 3.

[60]See the map in Tsafrir, di Segni and Green, *Iudaea-Palaestina*. For the information provided for the towns and villages, which in most cases have been investigated by archaeologists only superficially, see the gazetter in Tsafrir, di Segni and Green, *Iudaea-Palaestina* (with further references to primary sources and secondary literature).

[61]A. R. Millard, *IBD* 1:186-87; J. L. Kelso, *NEAEHL* 1:192-94; M. Köckert, *DNP* 2:594; W. F. Albright and J. L. Kelso, *The Excavation of Bethel 1934-1960* (Cambridge: American Schools of Oriental Research, 1968).

[62]J. A. Thompson, *IBD* 1:189.

Masepha (Tell en-Naṣbeh):[63] 12 km northwest of Jerusalem; probably the Old Testament town of Mizpeh in Benjamin, which Samuel visited regularly (1 Sam 7:15-17). After the destruction of Jerusalem in 587 B.C. Gedaliah, the governor of Judea appointed by the Babylonians, ruled from Mizpeh, where Jeremiah and surviving Jewish officers joined him (2 Kings 25:23; Jer 40:6). Judas Maccabaeus was based in the town when he prepared for a battle against the Seleucid army (1 Macc 3:46). Roman remains of a watchtower and coins have been found.

Khirbet el Chadatha (Chorvat Chadat): settlement in the Shephelah 5 km northeast of Emmaus; remains of buildings and tombs have been discovered. A church from the fifth century was discovered in 1962.[64]

Khirbet el Machme: village 3 km southeast of Upper Bethoron; remains of buildings.

Ataroth: double village about 10 km north of Jerusalem; olive and wine presses, bath house, quarry, tombs have been found.

Machmas (Mukhmas): seat of Jonathan Maccabaeus until 152 B.C.; remains of a church from the sixth century.[65]

Kefar Tabi: perhaps identical with Enetaba, where the new moon was announced after A.D. 70 (*y. Sukkah* 53a; *b. Roš Haš.* 25a).

Selebi: village in the Shephelah.

Rafat: village about 2 km southwest of Ataroth; remains of buildings, wine presses and cisterns are preserved.

Gazara (Tell Jezer, the Gezer of the Old Testament):[66] 8 km south-southeast of Ramleh; a town attested already in the fifteenth century B.C., mentioned in connection with the conquest (Josh 10:33): the Israelites were not able to drive out all Canaanite inhabitants of the town (Judg 1:29). Solomon received Gezer as a dowry from Pharaoh (1 Kings 9:15-17) and fortified the town. In the Seleucid period, Bakchides fortified the city (1 Macc 9:52). Simon Maccabaeus conquered Gezer in 142 B.C. and built a residence there (1 Macc 13:43-48). His son John Hyrcanus had his headquarters in Gezer (1 Macc 13:53). At the time of the Herodian dynasty Gezer was no longer an independent city but seemed to have belonged to a large private estate whose owner, or manager, is identified on inscriptions as Alkios.

Betoannaba (mod. Beit Nuba): 18 km southeast of Lod.

Caphar Salama: village northwest of Jerusalem where Judas Maccabaeus won a battle against Nicanor.

Khirbet Bir el Biyar: village about 1 km north of Anablata; remains of buildings, mosaic pavements.

Rama (mod. er-Ram):[67] town about 8 km north of Jerusalem, a station on the road leading north (Judg 19:13). After the destruction of Jerusalem in 578 B.C. Nebusaradan assembled the Jewish prisoners here (Jer 10:1). The town was resettled by Jews returning from the exile (Ezra 2:26; Neh 11:33).

Gabalda: village in the tribal territory of Benjamin (Judg 19:12—20:44).

Adasa: village where Judas Maccabaeus defeated Nicanor (1 Macc 7:40, 45).

Anablata (mod. Bir Nabala): village about 9 km northwest of Jerusalem.

Gabaon (mod. el Jib): The Roman Cestius Gallus had his camp here in A.D. 66.

---

[63]J. R. Zorn, *NEAEHL* 3:1098-1102.

[64]M. Avi-Yonah et al., *NEAEHL* 1:310.

[65]M. Avi-Yonah, *NEAEHL* 1:311.

[66]W. G. Dever, *NEAEHL* 1:496-506; E. A. Knauf, *DNP* 4:1063.

[67]J. A. Thomson, *IBD* 3:1318.

Carnaea: village 10 km northeast of Jerusalem; identical with Beth Qarnayim (?).

Hizmah: village 4 km west of Carnaea; evidence for stone-vessel industry.

Emmaus (Ἐμμαοῦς; later Nicopolis; mod. ʿImwas, near Latrun):[68] about 30 km west of Jerusalem in the Aialon Valley; an important town in the Shephelah on the main road to Joppa. The town is mentioned for the first time in 1 Macc 3:40, 57; 4:3 as the place where the Syrian army suffered a devastating defeat by Judas Maccabaeus. In the first century B.C. Emmaus was the headquarters of a Jewish toparchy. The Roman general Cassius sold the inhabitants into slavery. After the death of Herod I, Emmaus was the center of a rebellion led by the shepherd Anthronges in 4 B.C. Varus, the proconsul of the province of Syria, punished the city by burning it down. Emmaus had a famous market. Remains of baths, an aqueduct and Roman villas have been discovered. This town is probably the Emmaus mentioned in Lk 24:13. It is not impossible that the basilica built in the fifth century (46.4 by 24.4 m) was erected on top of the house of Cleopas, who hailed from Emmaus:[69] remains of a Roman villa (18 by 17 m) from the second century have been discovered underneath the basilica, erected on the foundation walls of a structure dated to the second and first centuries B.C. During the First Jewish Revolt, Vespasian fortified Emmaus as a Roman military colony and stationed soldiers of the Fifth Legion in town. Emmaus is mentioned in the Talmud as a large town in the Shephelah (*y. Šeb.* 8:9 [38d]) and as a center of the Samaritans (*y. ʿAbod. Zar.* 85 [44d]). In the third century Emmaus was granted city rights by Emperor Elagabal and renamed Nicopolis. We do not know when the church of Emmaus was established. The view that Lk 24:13-32 represents the "foundation legend" (*Gründungslegende*) of the church in Emmaus is unconvincing, since the text does not mention a community of believers.[70] From A.D. 230 the Christian historian, military strategist and theologian Julius Africanus lived in Emmaus. He also investigated the traditions of Jesus' relatives (Eusebius, *Hist. eccl.* 1.7) and wrote the first Christian chronicle of the world. Emmaus was the seat of a bishop by A.D. 325 (Nicea).

Khirbet el ʿAqd: village about 1 km west of Emmaus; remains of structures from the Hellenistic and Roman periods.

Aialon: olive presses, cisterns, tombs.

Beth Thamar: small village 5 km north of Jerusalem; mentioned in the Essene (?) Copper Scroll (3Q15).

Pharan (ʿEin Fara): village 8 km northeast of Jerusalem; fortress of Bakchides, who fought against Judas Maccabaeus (2 Macc 8:30).

Gedrus: large village in western Judea.

Chorvat Chirsha: village about 1.5 km southeast of Aialon; remains of buildings, mosaic, tombs.

Ailamon: village 6.5 km northeast of Jerusalem.

Gabath Saulis: village 5 km north of Jerusalem; last camp of the army of Titus before reaching Jerusalem.

Cariath Iarim: about 13 km east of Jerusalem; remains of buildings, mosaic pavements.

---

[68]A. Negev, *PECS* 302; R. Riesner, *GBL* 1:313-14; M. Avi-Yonah and M. Gichon, *NEAEHL* 2:386-89; M. Gichon, *OEANE* 2:240-41; J. Pahlitzsch, *DNP* 3:1009; Tsafrir, di Segni and Green, *Iudaea-Palaestina,* 119-20; Isaac 1993, 318, 428-29; Markschies 1997, 279-85; Freeman-Grenville 2003, 148.

[69]A. Negev, *PECS* 302; R. Riesner, *GBL* 1:314.

[70]Contra Wilckens 2002, 1.2:146, and others. On Julius Africanus see Harnack 1893-1904, 1:507-13.

Anathoth: village 5 km northeast of Jerusalem; birthplace of Jeremiah; ritual bath.

Moza (near mod. Qalonije): 7 km west of Jerusalem, on the road to Cariath Iarim and Emmaus in the Sorek Valley; mentioned in Josh 18:26, it still existed in late rabbinic times as a Jewish village (Str-B 2:217). A Roman road passed nearby. Vespasian is reported to have established a military colony for veterans in the town (Josephus, *B.J.* 7.217). The village is identified by some scholars with the Emmaus of Lk 24:13, which is unlikely, however.[71]

Arath: village 8 km west of Jerusalem.

Iasonis Pagus (mod. Deir Yassin): 5 km west of Jerusalem.

Sorech: village in the Shephelah; remains of buildings.

Zorʿah: village in the Shephelah; caves, cisterns, tombs.

Eshthaol: remains of buildings, cisterns, wine presses, tombs.

Chasalon (Kesalon): large village.

Bethphage (Βηθφαγή):[72] a small village on the Mount of Olives (Mt 21:1), reckoned by the rabbis as the most distant of Jerusalem's living quarters.

Bethania-Bethany (Βηθανία; Heb., ʿAnanya; mod. el ʿAzariye):[73] village 3 km southeast of Jerusalem, according to Mk 11:1 (Lk 19:29) situated on the eastern slopes of the Mount of Olives near the Roman road to Jericho. This is perhaps the town Ananja of Neh 11:32, where returning Jews from the Babylonian exile settled, and perhaps one of the places where lepers lived (1QT XLVI, 16-18). Bethany was the home town of Martha, Mary and Lazarus (Jn 11:1). Jesus was anointed in Bethany in the house of Simon the leper (Mt 26:6-13/Mk 14:3-9) before his death, and he stayed here during the last days before his death (Mk 11:11). The rock-hewn tomb that is linked with Lazarus is mentioned before A.D. 313 (Eusebius, *Onom.* 58).

Beth Abudison: village 1 km southeast of Bethany.

En-Kerem (ʿAin Karim):[74] 7 km west of Jerusalem; the birthplace of John the Baptist, according to a tradition that dates to the sixth century (which would fit Lk 1:39). A statue of Venus was found here. Possible evidence for Jewish-Christian inhabitants.

Iarimuth: village in the Shephelah; walls, cisterns, wine presses.

Beera: village in western Judea.

Beth Shemesh (Tel Beth-Shemesh):[75] about 20 km west of Jerusalem in the Shephelah; mentioned repeatedly in the Old Testament. According to *y. Meg.* 1:70a, Beth Shemesh was the smallest village between Gabatha and Antipatris; remains of buildings, cisterns, tombs.

Chorvat Saʿadim: village about 4 km southwest of Beth ha-Kerem; remains of buildings, olive presses.

Thamna (mod. Kh. et Tibbane): fortress of the Syrian general Bakchides in the Shephelah; walls, remains of buildings, olive presses.

Enadab: village 18 km southwest of Jerusalem; remains of a fortress.

Kephar Gamala: village in the western hill country; tradition has it that the bones of Stephen were found here in A.D. 415.

---

[71]See R. Riesner, *GBL* 1:313-14; J. Pahlitzsch, *DNP* 3:1010.

[72]R. Riesner, *GBL* 1:196; Str-B 1:839-40; Tsafrir, di Segni and Green, *Iudaea-Palaestina,* 85; Freeman-Grenville 2003, 121-22.

[73]R. Riesner, *GBL* 1:193; K. Bieberstein, *DNP* 2:593-94; Tsafrir, di Segni and Green, *Iudaea-Palaestina,* 80.

[74]R. Riesner, *GBL* 2:776.

[75]S. Bunimovitz and Z. Lederman, *NEAEHL* 1:249-53.

Zanoach (Zanoua; Kh. Zanuʿ): village in the Shephelah; remains of village, public building.

Kobi: village 13 km southwest of Jerusalem; aqueduct, cisterns.

Beth Ther (mod. Battir):[76] town 12 km southwest of Jerusalem; fortified by Bar Kokhba.

Khirbet Abu Shawan: village 2 km east of Beth Ther; remains of a fortified settlement. EDNT.

Beth ha-Kerem (Karem; mod. Kibbuz Ramat Rachel):[77] about 3 km south of Jerusalem, on the road to Bethlehem; in Israelite times a royal estate, in the Persian period an administrative center (Neh 3:14). The old citadel was abandoned in the Hellenistic period. No district with the capital in Beth ha-Kerem is known from Herodian times. The town is mentioned in the Essene Copper Scroll (3Q15). According to an old tradition, a church was built in the town around A.D. 450 to commemorate the place where Mary rested.

Metopa: village 6 km south of Jerusalem.

Caphar Tob: village in western Judea; conquered by Vespasian.

Azekah (mod. Tell Zakariya):[78] village in the western hill country above the valley of Elah, mentioned in connection with a victory of Joshua (Josh 10:10-11). David killed Goliath in the vicinity. King Rehoboam fortified the city (2 Chron 11:9). Azekah is mentioned in Jer 34:7 together with Lachish as the two last cities that resisted the Babylonian army. It was conquered by Nebuchadnezzar in 588 B.C. After the return from the exile, Jews settled here (Neh 11:30). Remains of buildings.

Iermucha (mod. Khirbet Yarmuk): remains of buildings from the Roman period.

Wadi Fukhin (Phichola or Pequiʿin): about 5 km southwest of Beth Ther; remains of buildings.

Khirbet Umm el Qalʿa: village 3 km southwest of Beth Ther; fortress, remains of buildings.

Bethlehem (Βηθλέεμ; Arab., Bet Lahm):[79] 9 km south-southwest of Jerusalem; a city in Judah (Josh 19:59 LXX) that also was called Bethlehem-Ephrata (e.g., Mic 5:1). David came from Bethlehem (1 Sam 16:18) and was anointed king here (1 Sam 16:4-13). After the return from the Babylonian exile, 123 or 188 Jews settled here (Ezra 2:21; Neh 7:26). It is possible that Joseph, the (step)father of Jesus, came from Bethlehem: he seemed to have owned property here (Lk 2:1-5; Mt 2:11). Emperor Hadrian ordered in A.D. 135 that a temple of Adonis be built over the grotto where the birthplace of Jesus was thought to have been. The modern Church of the Nativity can be traced back to a five-aisled basilica built during the time of Constantine (built in A.D. 333, renovated ca. A.D. 560).

Betholetepha: headquarters of a Jewish toparchy; remains of buildings, columns, mosaic.

Bethbassi: village 2 km southeast of Bethlehem; Maccabean fortress.

Khirbet el Khawkh (Etam?): about 3 km south of Bethlehem; remains of buildings, cisterns.

Socho: two villages in the Shephelah; remains of buildings, mosaic, tombs.

Chorvat Malka: village 3 km east of Socho; remains of buildings, olive press.

Gabatha: village in the Shephelah; tomb of the prophet Habakkuk (tradition).

---

[76] Hüttenmeister 1977, 73-76.

[77] R. Riesner, *GBL* 2:776; Y. Aharoni, *NEAEHL* 4:1261-67.

[78] E. Stern, *NEAEHL* 1:123-24; Tsafrir, di Segni and Green, *Iudaea-Palaestina,* 72.

[79] A. M. Schneider, *RAC* 1:224-28; W. L. MacDonald, *PECS* 153; A. Strobel, *EWNT* 1:513-15 (*EDNT* 1:214-15); R. Riesner, *GBL* 1:196-97; M. Avi-Yonah *NEAEHL* 1:204-8; M. Köckert and J. Pahlitzsch, *DNP* 2:595-96; Pixner 1994, 24-39; Kay Prag, "Bethlehem: A Site Assessment," *PEQ* 132 (2000): 169-81.

Phaora: village about 7 km southwest of Bethlehem.

Drusias: town in western Judea; remains of a watchtower and a synagogue.

Robbo: remains of buildings, olive press, cisterns.

Odollam: large village in the Shephelah; remains of buildings.

Beth Zacharia: mountain pass 20 km south of Jerusalem; remains of buildings.

Caphetra: small town in Idumea in the Judean hills; remains of buildings.

Gedora (Tel Gedor; mod. Beit Ummar):[80] village 11 km north of Hebron in Judea (Josh 15:58).

Chorvat Berakhot (Kh. Bureikut):[81] village in southern Judea 9 km south of Bethlehem; remains of a church from the fourth century.

Thekoa (Kh. Taqua):[82] 8 km southeast of Bethlehem, birthplace of the prophet Amos; built into a fortress by Rehoboam (2 Chron 11:6); resettled after the exile (Neh 3:5, 27). The town is attested for the Maccabean and the Roman periods.

Jericho (Ἰεριχώ; Arab., ar-Riha),[83] 10 km north of the Dead Sea, 8 km west of the Jordan River; known for its palms, dates and balsam. The site was settled since 9000 B.C. Jericho played an important role in the time of the conquest (Josh 2—6). During the Persian period an unfortified settlement was located on the northern slope of the Tell (see Ezra 2:34; Neh 3:2; 7:36). By the Hasmonean period there was a palace southwest of the oasis that was enlarged by Herod I with gardens and bath installations. His son Archelaus enlarged the palace further (Josephus, *B.J.* 1.407; *A.J.* 17.340). A hippodrome and an amphitheater were located near the Herodian palace (*B.J.* 1.659, 666). There must have been a settlement on the site of the oasis since the Hellenistic period, although archaeologists have not been able to confirm this. Three churches and a synagogue date to the Byzantine period.

If the disciples visited about 150 towns and villages in a short-term missionary trip through Galilee during Jesus' earthly ministry, they would have had neither theoretical nor practical difficulties in systematically reaching eighty towns and villages of Judea with the message of Jesus the crucified and risen Messiah.[84] If the Twelve would have decided, for example, that six of their group should preach in the Jewish towns outside of Jerusalem, three teams with two disciples each would have had to visit twenty-six towns—a task that could have been accomplished in half a year if they spent six days in each town. Luke reports in Acts 21:20 that there were *myriades* of Jewish-Christian believers in Jerusalem and possibly Judea. This comment either makes a literal statistical statement ("tens of thousands" [cf. Acts 19:19]) or describes the number of believers as "very large" ("countless thousands" [cf. Heb 12:22; Jude 14; Rev 5:11]).

Some scholars interpret the comment in Acts 21:20 as an emphasis of the Lukan composition that needs to be understood in the context of Lk 12:1, where Luke referred to *myriades* of people who wanted to hear and see Jesus. Against this background Gerhard Lohfink interprets Acts 21:20 in terms of "the countless multitudes who once pressed around Jesus in Judea and who are now assembled in the post-Easter church."[85]

---

[80]S. Ben-Arieh, *NEAEHL* 2:468.

[81]Y. Hirschfeld and Y. Tsafrir, *NEAEHL* 1:188-90.

[82]J. A. Thompson, *GBL* 3:1532.

[83]See K. M. Kenyon, *NEAEHL* 2:674-97; K. Bieberstein, *DNP* 5:900-901, with bibliography on the excavations.

[84]A. Offer (*NEAEHL* 3:816) states that there were eighty-seven settlements in the Herodian period.

[85]G. Lohfink 1975, 54, quoted in Reinhardt 1995a, 281.

The comment in Acts 21:20 might indeed reflect historical reality.[86] The figure probably includes not only the Jewish Christians in Jerusalem but also all believers in Judea and Galilee,[87] possibly even the Jewish Christians in the Diaspora.[88] The events described in Acts 21 took place during the Feast of Pentecost of May 29, A.D. 57, when thousands of Diaspora Jews would have come to Jerusalem as pilgrims (cf. 22:27). In Acts 9:31 Luke had spoken of the quantitative growth of the church "throughout all Judea and Galilee and Samaria."

Form-critical research has assumed for a long time that the earliest collections of sayings and stories of Jesus must be seen in the context of the early Christian mission. Helmut Koester summarized the position linked with scholars such as Martin Dibelius and Rudolf Bultmann as follows: "As miracles stories linked with Jesus were used very early in Christian propaganda and mission, the first collection of these narratives belong to the context of early Christian propaganda as well. . . . Such written collections were used a short time later by the authors of the 'Gospel of Mark' and the 'Gospel of John.'"[89] Koester asserts that the passion narrative and the resurrection stories also arose in the context of preaching and instruction: "Different appearance stories arose in different congregations which ultimately derive from the missionary of the first generation who had established that particular church." Koester claims to know that "none of the forms of narrative material" has anything to do with historical memory, as they belong "to the context of the early Christian mission, religious practices and theology." Bultmann was certain that the literary form of the gospel was created by the Hellenistic church, which adopted the Palestinian tradition.[90]

Certainly the first Jewish-Christian missionaries referred to Jesus' miracles and death in their preaching, because why would they have otherwise engaged in missionary work? The claim that "historical memory" played no role in their proclamation is historically totally implausible. If the Jewish-Christian missionaries based in Jerusalem wanted to convince Jews living in the area of the claims made by Jesus concerning the significance of his person and his ministry, they could not simply invent stories whose fictitious character or accuracy could easily be checked. The fact that Helmut Koester and other New Testament scholars use the terms "mission" and "propaganda" interchangeably may reveal the root of the problem inherent in their approach: the apostles did not engage in a "propaganda campaign" for which they needed exciting stories in order to guarantee a favorable reception among the population. On the contrary, their message of the crucified and risen Messiah depended entirely upon the historical accuracy and reliability of their convictions; otherwise, they ran the risk of being rejected out of hand by their Jewish contemporaries as illusionary dreamers or dangerous seducers of the people. Furthermore, the "kerygma of faith" and the history of the life and ministry of Jesus are not mutually exclusive. Julius Schniewind correctly emphasized that the early Christian missionaries "proclaimed as Messiah whose presence and ministry supports the church a human being, Jesus of Nazareth."[91] Paul and surely all early Christian missionaries connected the mes-

---

[86]Contra scholars who regard Acts 21:20 as an unrealistic exaggeration; see Haenchen, *Apg,* 539 (ET, 608-9); Weiser, *Apg,* 2:597; Roloff, *Apg,* 314; Zingg 1974, 39; Lüdemann 1987, 240 (ET, 232: "tendency to increase numbers").

[87]See Pesch, *Apg,* 2:220.

[88]See Reinhardt 1995a, 281.

[89]Helmut Koester, "Überlieferung und Geschichte der frühchristlichen Evangelienliteratur," *ANRW* II.25.2 (1984): 1463-1542, esp. 1509; the quotations that follow above, ibid., 1525, 1508.

[90]R. Bultmann 1995, 394 (ET, 369).

[91]Julius Schniewind, "Zur Synoptiker-Exegese," *ThR* 2 (1930): 129-189, esp. 184-85; see also Hengel 1979, 39-47, on the unity of kerygma and historical narrative.

sage of reconciliation that they preached "with a fact of the past: the cross of the Christ, which is significant for world history, drawing its power and its truth from this event."[92] The conviction of the form critics that the early Christian missionary activity played an important role in the origins of the Synoptic Gospels is important and correct, however, as probably all the leaders of the early church were engaged in missionary work. Luke refers to "eyewitnesses and ministers of the word" (αὐτόπται καὶ ὑπηρέται, *autoptai kai hypēretai*) as informants of his Gospel (Lk 1:2). Form-historical studies have shown that many pericopes have typical structures and that certain forms and genres are used regularly. Bo Reicke comments, "The eyewitnesses and co-workers who had been involved in proclaiming the word from the earliest days, mentioned by Luke as informants, and generally the tradents who stand behind the Gospels communicated to Luke and the other evangelists the reports about the actions and the quotations of the words of Jesus not as immediate, informal reminiscences but as fixed pieces of tradition that were frequently recounted. . . . The first eyewitnesses and their co-workers played a part in this process because they had to present their reports repeatedly already in Jerusalem and later on the mission field."[93] David Tiede argues that pre- or semi-literary collections of traditions, particularly the eschatological discourses, miracles stories and sapiental sayings, had precursors in the missionary literature of Judaism.[94] This view founders on account of the fact that there was no Jewish "mission" that aimed at convincing people of other faiths of the exclusive validity of the Jewish faith (see §6).

Hubert Frankemölle and other scholars argue that both the literary genre of the Gospels and the concept of "gospel" were developed in connection with the early Christian mission. He states, "Hellenistic missionaries as tradents of the pre-Markan and pre-Pauline tradition . . . formed the noun [i.e., *euangelion*] in analogy to the verb in order to describe the basic statement of the Christ event (death and resurrection, cf. 1 Cor 15:3ff.), the sum of the Christian missionary proclamation (1 Thess 1:5—2:9), the faith in the fulfillment of Old Testament promises and in the exaltation of Jesus (Rom 1:1-4), the sum of Jesus' proclamation (Mk 1:15; 8:35; 10:29; 13:10) or of an individual aspect of their verbal or nonverbal actions (Mk 14:9)."[95] Peter Stuhlmacher emphasizes critically and correctly that it is more plausible, from a historical point of view, "to think *with* the texts rather than to oppose the texts and follow one's own subjective suppositions."[96] According to the account of the evangelists, Jesus himself used the term *euangelion* ("gospel") with reference to passages such as Is 52:7 and Is 61:1-2. In his sermon in Nazareth Jesus interpreted Is 61:1-2 as the program of his (messianic) ministry, which is now, before the eyes of the listeners, "fulfilled," as the "acceptable year of the Lord" has begun, as the promised salvation becomes a reality in the present, as "good news" is preached to the poor—a message that is confirmed by the miracles that Jesus performs (Lk 4:16-21). When Jesus was asked by the emissaries of John the Baptist if he is "the coming one," the Messiah, Jesus referred them to his healing miracles, which had been promised for the last days by Isaiah (see Is 29:18; 35:5-6), and to his proclamation of the "good news" to the poor (Mt 11:2-5). Otto Betz remarks, "In the gospel completed facts are proclaimed or realized together with the message; the Savior can proclaim the gospel on the basis of such miracles performed in

---

[92]Otto Betz, "Evangelium," *ThBLNT* 1:438.
[93]Reicke 1984, 1776, with reference to Acts 2:42; 1 Cor 11:23; 15:3.
[94]Tiede 1984.
[95]Hubert Frankemölle, "Evangelium als literarische Gattung und als theologischer Begriff," *ANRW* II.25.2 (1984): 1543-1704; quotation, 1690.
[96]Stuhlmacher 1992-1999, 1:xi, with reference to Martin Hengel.

the power of the Spirit and announce the beginning of the kingdom of God (Mt 4:23)."[97]

The available sources provide only limited information about details of the development and expansion of the churches in Judea. The bishops' list of the Council of Nicea (A.D. 325)[98] includes nineteen bishops for *Syria Palaestina:* Makarios in Jerusalem, Germanos in Shechem-Neapolis, Marinos in Sebastenis, Gaianos in Sebaste, Eusebios in Caesarea, Sabinos in Gadara, Logginos in Askalon, Petros in Emmaus-Nikopolis, Makrinos in Jamnia, Maximos in Beth Guvrin-Eleutheropolis, Paulos in Legio-Maximianopolis, Ianuarius in Jericho, Heliodoros in Chabulon, Aetios in Lydda, Silvanos in Ashdod-Azotos, Patrophilos in Beth Shean-Scythopolis, Asklepas in Gaza, Petros in Elat-Aila, Antiochos in Capitolias-Jerusalem. Christoph Markschies comments that this evidence is "as arbitrary as the presence or absence of bishops on synods in distant cities tends to be." The Nicean list demonstrates, however, that the bishops and churches of the economically significant port cities on the Mediterranean coast and the traditional urban centers in the interior were dominant.[99] The sparse literary information about Christians in Jewish villages indicates "that an exclusive focus on the bishops and on their connection with the urban structure would indeed distort the evidence considerably. Eusebius describes not only one particular village near Madaba in Transjordan, but also two other villages in Judea as 'completely Christianized.'"[100]

22.2 Missionary Work in Galilee and in Gaulanitis

The missionary commission in Acts 1:8 mentions Jerusalem, Judea and Samaria as regions where the apostles will proclaim the gospel. It is striking that Galilee is not mentioned, as Rudolf Pesch observes: "Galilee as the main region of Jesus' ministry, of his own and of the disciples' mission during his lifetime, is no longer mentioned."[101] Luke does not report any missionary activity in Galilee. However, a comment in Acts 9:31 abruptly and without explanation mentions Jewish-Christian churches in Galilee.[102]

Acts 9:31: "So the church throughout all Judea and Galilee and Samaria had peace and was built up; and walking in the fear of the Lord and in the comfort of the Holy Spirit it was multiplied." (RSV)

---

[97]O. Betz, "Evangelium," *ThBLNT* 1:435.
[98]See Gelzer, Hilgenfeld and Cuntz 1898, lx-lxi; on the Council of Nicea see Markschies 1997, 267-91.
[99]Markschies 1997, 272; for the observation that follows above see ibid., 276.
[100]Eusebius, *Onom.* 112 (Kiriathaeim); 26 (Anaea; Aneim; mod. Khirbet ʿAnim); 108 (Ietheira; Iether; mod. Khirbet ʿAttir; cf. 88: Ether), each village described as ὅλη Χριστιανῶν (*holē Christianōn*) "wholly (composed) of Christians."
[101]Pesch, *Apg,* 1:70 n. 17.
[102]See Kasting 1969, 89-90; Pesch, *Apg,* 1:51.

Missionary Churches

Ernst Lohmeyer argues on the basis of Luke's silence concerning missionary activity in Galilee that the real centers of the early church must have been located in Galilee; according to 1 Cor 9:5, Jesus' brothers engaged in missionary work based in Galilee.[103] Several factors may account both for the early establishment of churches in Galilee and for Luke's silence concerning Galilean churches.

1. Matthew and John report appearances of the risen Jesus in Galilee; Mark appears to presuppose them.[104] This evidence may imply that soon after Jesus' resurrection assemblies of Jewish followers of Jesus formed in Galilee (Acts 9:31),[105] perhaps in Capernaum, where Peter and Andrew had families (Mk 1:29), and in Bethsaida, where Peter and Andrew grew up and where Philip had lived (Jn 1:44; 12:21). The appearance of Jesus before five hundred brothers (1 Cor 15:6) may have taken place in Galilee.[106]

2. There were so many followers of Jesus in Galilee from the time before Easter that this "earliest home of Christianity" did not need to be evangelized from Jerusalem: Galilee was already *terra Christiana*. This is the reason, suggests Ernst Lohmeyer, that no tradition about a mission in Galilee developed.[107] This explanation must remain hypothetical as well. A major objection is related to the fact that we have hardly any news about Christians in Galilee before A.D. 325.[108] Some scholars speak of a "conspiracy of silence" concerning Galilee in the church of the third and fourth centuries. Many scholars acknowledge the possibility, however, that the early Christian missionaries may have had more success in the time before the outbreak of the First Jewish Revolt in A.D. 66.[109]

3. The missionary preaching of the apostles in Jerusalem might have reached Galileans as early as Pentecost in A.D. 30, resulting in the establishment of churches in Galilee during the first months after Easter.[110] This is possible but remains hypothetical; also, this view does not explain why Galilee is not mentioned in Acts 1:8.

4. The Twelve came from Galilee and presumably maintained their connections with Galilee even while they resided in Jerusalem after Easter. Eric Meyers suggests that not all Jewish Christians from Jerusalem fled to Pella in A.D. 66 at

---

[103]E. Lohmeyer 1936, 54-56; followed by Schoeps 1949, 270.
[104]Mt 28:16-20; Jn 21; Mk 14:28; 16:7.
[105]Thus R. Riesner, *DJG* 253.
[106]Thus Schlatter, *Kor,* 99; Kasting 1969, 89-90; E. F. F. Bishop, "The Risen Christ and the Five Hundred Brethren (1Cor 15.6)," *CBQ* 18 (1956): 341-44. Gordon Fee (*1 Cor,* 730) regards assumptions about time and place as entirely hypothetical.
[107]E. Lohmeyer 1936, 51-52; cf. Kasting 1969, 89-90; Roloff, *Apg,* 157. See, however, Pesch (1982, 51-52), who points to the opposition and rejection that Jesus encountered in Galilee as well.
[108]See Harnack 1924, 2:639-55 (ET, 2:106-20).
[109]See Barrett, *Acts,* 1:473.
[110]See Pesch 1982, 51.

the beginning of the First Jewish Revolt, but rather some escaped to Galilee, together with citizens of Jerusalem, and settled there.[111] This attractive hypothesis cannot be proven because of the lack of explicit evidence.

5. The sympathizers of Jesus in Galilee who had heard him preach, who saw him perform miracles and who accepted him, at least as a powerful prophet, presumably continued to have an active interest in the Jesus movement. And it is plausible to assume that at least some of them believed the reports about Jesus' resurrection. Possibly some of them formed local assemblies.

6. Julius Africanus reports in the early third century in his letter to Aristides that the *desposynoi* (lit., "those who belong to the master," i.e., the relatives of Jesus) were active in two centers in Galilee: "the Jewish villages of Nazareth and Kokhaba."[112] Kokhaba is only 16 km (10 mi.) from Nazareth. The genealogy that the *desposynoi* explain and interpret during their travels "around the rest of the land" presumably played an important role in their missionary proclamation, in which they would have argued that Jesus was the Messiah. Paul mentions in 1 Cor 9:5, besides James (and Cephas-Peter), other brothers of Jesus who engage in missionary travels and are accompanied by their wives: this may be a reference to the missionary activity of the *desposynoi* based in Nazareth and in Kokhaba in Galilee, who easily could have reached towns in southern Syria: Phoenicia, Damascus, the Decapolis and other regions east of the Jordan River.[113] Richard Bauckham offers a bold but quite plausible interpretation of Paul's comment in 1 Cor 9:5 and of the testimony of Julius Africanus about the missionary travels of the relatives of Jesus who were based in Nazareth and Kokhaba, asserting that these two texts significantly modify the picture of the history of the early Christian mission provided by Luke in the book of Acts. He argues that the evidence "reveals an extensive Jewish Christian missionary activity which did not result from developments in Jerusalem, but could be regarded by Paul, writing to Corinth in the 50s, as a matter of common Christian knowledge." We may plausibly assume that there were no major differences in emphasis between the church in Jerusalem and its missionary efforts and successes—first coordinated by the Twelve with Peter as *primus inter pares,* after A.D. 42/43 by a council of Elders with James the brother of Jesus as leader, and since A.D. 62 by Symeon the cousin of Jesus as leader of the Jerusalem church—and the churches in Galilee and their missionary efforts under the leadership of other relatives of Jesus. Bauckham describes the most likely scenario as follows: "James and Symeon in Jerusalem were the acknowledged heads of the churches founded and supervised by their relatives based at Nazareth and Kokhaba in Galilee. These Galilean homes of the *despo-*

---

[111]Meyers 1979, 687.

[112]Julius Africanus, in Eusebius, *Hist. eccl.* 1.7.14. See Harnack 1924, 2:635-36 (ET, 101-2); Bauckham 1990, 60-62.

[113]See Bauckham 1990, 57-68; the quotation that follows above, 67.

synoi were given special messianic-theological significance along with the central eschatological role inevitably attributed to Jerusalem. From the beginning the Jewish Christian mission was not only to pilgrims in Jerusalem, but also extended throughout Palestine through the travels of missionaries among whom the younger brothers of Jesus and other members of the family were prominent. It is as missionaries engaged in preaching Jesus the Messiah to their fellow-Jews that the relatives of Jesus are primarily to be envisaged."[114]

7. If Jude the brother of Jesus engaged in missionary work based in Galilee, and if the canonical Epistle of Jude was written by him, then we possess an important, albeit short, document of this Jewish-Christian mission.[115] Evidently Jude was a knowledgeable interpreter of the sacred Scriptures who used formal scriptural exegesis resembling the style of the Qumran pesharim to argue for and explain faith in Jesus as Messiah. Jude interacts with traveling charismatics who seemed to have derived from the effective revelation of God's grace in Jesus Christ a libertinistic ethic rejecting moral standards. Jude argues that Jesus is the Messiah, who has brought God's eschatological salvation and judgment: as Messiah he is *kyrios* (Jude 14), as God himself is *kyrios* (Jude 5, 9), and he possesses divine authority both in the church and in the world.

8. We do not know in which Galilean towns and villages early Jewish-Christian missionaries or local sympathizers established churches in the months and years after Easter. Assemblies of believers in Jesus may have existed in any of the towns and villages that the Twelve had visited during their evangelistic tours through Galilee (see §10.4; cf. fig. 5). We possess some evidence for Christian churches in the following Galilean towns.

Capernaum

It is a plausible assumption that soon after Easter believers in Jesus established a congregation in Capernaum, the base of Jesus' Galilean ministry and the hometown of Peter and John. The church (octagon) that was built in the fifth century, located directly on the main street (*cardo maximus*) about 30 m (33 yds.) south of the synagogue, was erected above a house church (*domus ecclesia*) of the fourth century that had been built above a complex of private houses dating to the first century A.D.[116] The Franciscan archaeologists are convinced that this was the house of Peter, in which a house church had been meeting.[117] For more details see §8.4.

---

[114]Bauckham 1990, 375; cf. Paget 1999, 748.
[115]Bauckham 1990, 134-78; for the observations that follow above see ibid., 162-68 (the opponents), 179-234 (Jude's exegesis), 281-314 (Christology).
[116]See Corbo 1972, 16-18; Brenk 1991a.
[117]V. Corbo, *Cafarnao I: Gli Edifici della Città* (Jerusalem: Franciscan Printing Press, 1975), 26-58; Corbo 1993, 71-76; Stanislao Loffreda, "La tradizionale casa di Simon Pietro a Cafarnao a 25 anni dalla sua scoperta," in Manns and Alliata 1993, 37-67; Freyne 1997b, 305. For the presence of Christians in Capernaum in later periods see Brenk 1991a.

Bethsaida

The reference to Bethsaida in the Gospel of John (Jn 1:44; 12:21) is striking because John mentions relatively few Galilean towns. He does not mention Caesarea Philippi as the largest city of the tetrarchy of Herod Philip, and he mentions Bethsaida only in passing. Mark Appold interprets these references to Bethsaida as evidence that this town played a role in the history of the early church and that a house church existed there.[118] The discovery of markings in the form of a cross on the fragment of a jar found in a private house in Bethsaida have led some scholars to suggest that this may be evidence for a Christian house church.

The fragment (20.7 by 19 cm), incomplete at the top, was discovered on May 13, 1994, in the so-called House of the Vintner in the northern section of Bethsaida (see fig. 14).[119] The cross scratched on the jar measures 10.7 cm from right to left and 10.6 cm from top to bottom. The cross has four arms and a circle in the center: the arms are between 1.8 and 2.8 cm wide; the circle measures 4.2 by 3.6 cm. The circle probably was scratched first; several lines of the arms were scratched several times. Heinz-Wolfgang Kuhn interprets the "Bethsaida cross" in the context of similar drawings that combine a cross with a circle, symbolizing the Assyrian sun god Shamash—for example, on a stele of King Ashurnasirpal II (883-859 B.C.).[120] However, Kuhn cannot explain how a neo-Assyrian symbol of the ninth century B.C. is found in an archaeological context that is consistently Hellenistic. Mark Appold interprets the cross as Christian, arguing that there are no Jewish or Hellenistic parallels.[121] He argues that the Bethsaida cross does not refer to an instrument of execution and does not constitute a reference for the providence and the protection of God (as in Ezek 9:4); the circle in the center of the cross indicates that we are dealing with a "reflection on the meaning of the crucifixion" in the sense of the "high Christology" of the Gospel of John, which emphasizes the exaltation and the glory of the crucified Jesus Christ.

If the House of the Vintner in Bethsaida was indeed the site of an early Christian house church, then it would constitute a second piece of evidence, besides Peter's House in Capernaum, for the external conditions under which the early Christians met.[122] The house, including the central courtyard, measures 16 by 18 m. The size suggests that the house might have belonged to a well-to-do family. The oldest wall (W209) is dated to the Iron Age. The large central courtyard (L911) measured about 12 by 12.8 m; it had a roof in the southeastern corner (along wall W201). The entrance to the house was located in the southern wall of the courtyard. The kitchen (L900), measuring about 10 by 4.5 m, was accessible from the courtyard; its floor appears to have been paved. There was an oven near the entrance, and remains of kitchenware was found along the southern wall of the kitchen (W209); a hand-operated mill was found in the southeast corner. The northern

---

[118]Appold 1995a, 238-39; 1995b, 383-84; cf. earlier Vogler 1982, 787.

[119]R. Arav, "Bethsaida Excavations: Preliminary Report, 1994-1996," in Arav and Freund 1995-1999, 2:3-113, esp. 97-102, 105-6.

[120]H.-W. Kuhn, "An Introduction to the Excavations of Bethsaida (= et-Tell) from a New Testament Perspective," in Arav and Freund 1995-1999, 2:283-94, esp. 286-87.

[121]Appold 1995b, 373-96; the quotation that follows above, 384.

[122]For the description that follows above see Arav, in Arav and Freund 1995-1999, 2:97-98; Appold 1995b, 378-81. In the case of differing measurements I follow Arav.

end of the courtyard provided access to a relatively large room (4.5 by 5.4 m) that possibly served as a dining room (*triclinium*): the wall on the west side (W211) has a bench. A door led to another, smaller room (3.5 by 2.1 m, with wall W214 on the eastern side). The function of the room to the west of wall W206 that has no recognizable entrance has not been determined. East of the kitchen a subterranean room (L948; 4.5 by 2.8 m) was discovered under a ceiling consisting of ten basalt stones. Due to the presence of four large jars (and a cooking utensil), this room is identified as a wine cellar. Certainty concerning the existence of a house church in Bethsaida depends on further discoveries.

Cana

Jesus performed his first miracle at Cana (see §9.2). Nathanael, a disciple of Jesus, came from Cana. Jesus' family was acquainted with a well-to-do family in Cana, as the story of the miracle of the water turned into wine indicates. And Jesus visited Cana several times, as the Gospel of John indicates.[123] Since John the evangelist focuses his narrative of Jesus' ministry on Jerusalem, the references to Cana are striking. Seán Freyne interprets the evidence as indicating that there must have been an early Christian church in Cana.[124] This is quite possible but must remain hypothetical, as must the suggestion that Jesus' promise to Nathanael in Jn 1:50 ("You will see greater things than these") has a significance in this context.

Nazareth and Kokhaba

If the testimony of Julius Africanus[125] that we saw earlier is historically reliable, then Nazareth and Kokhaba were bases of early Christian missionary work, with relatives of Jesus having a leading role. According to Mk 6:3, Jesus had four brothers: James (the leader of the church in Jerusalem), Joseph, Simon and Jude. It is possible that the early missionary outreach to southern Syria—to towns in Phoenicia, in Decapolis and to Damascus—might have been coordinated from Nazareth and Kokhaba.

Shikhin

A comment in the Tosefta, a rabbinic document redacted in the second century, attests a Jewish-Christian in the town of Kefar Sekanyah (Shikhin [see §10.4]), located about 6 km north-northeast of Sepphoris. According to *t. Ḥul.* 2:24, a certain Jacob from Kefar Sekanyah was a *talmid* (student) of Jeshua ben Panthera.[126] This comment is to be regarded as authentic, as Origen knew that rumors circulated among the Jews that Jesus was the illegitimate child of his

---

[123]See Jn 2:1-11; 4:45-51; cf. 21:2.
[124]Freyne 1997b, 300.
[125]Eusebius, *Hist. eccl.* 1.7.14.
[126]The parallel passage in *b. 'Abod. Zar.* 16b-17a reads "Jeshua ha-nozri" (i.e., Jesus the Nazorean). Johann Maier (1978, 144-81) believes that these traditions are not historical. See the discussion in Bauckham 1990, 106-21.

mother and a Roman soldier named Panthera (*Cels.* 1.32).[127] This Jacob is the only Jewish Christian whom Jewish literature identifies for the time between Jesus' disciples and the end of the third century. He possibly is identical with James the grandson of Jude the brother of Jesus, a prominent leader of churches in Galilee.[128] Shikhin was only 6 km from Kokhaba, one of the two bases of the *desposynoi,* the relatives of Jesus.[129] It is impossible to know whether there was a Christian church in Shikhin, however.

Sepphoris and Tiberias

Rabbinic sources also indicate that there was a church in Sepphoris. It was possibly Jacob of Kefar Sekanyah, who was just mentioned above (the sources speak of Kefar Sama), who healed in the name of Jeshua and who had an encounter with Rabbi Eliezer in Sepphoris in the "Upper Street" when the famous rabbi had to defend himself because he had agreed with a *minut* (an unorthodox legal decision) of "Jeshua ben Jacob."[130] However, the presence of Jacob of Kefar Sekanyah in Sepphoris constitutes no unequivocal evidence for the existence of a church in Sepphoris in the second century.[131]

There are late references to Jewish Christians in Tiberias that might indicate but do not prove the existence of a church in Tiberias.[132]

The People of the Q Tradition

Some scholars believe that the Galilean churches were responsible for the sayings source Q, which supplied most of the sayings of Jesus recorded by Matthew and Luke. The people more particularly responsible for Q are identified as itinerant Christian missionaries who are assumed to have preached in Syria.[133] Since Q contains a missionary discourse of Jesus (Lk 10:1-16)—viewed as the result of redaction and composition of a Christian church—some scholars assume that there were "Q missionaries."

Paul Hoffmann understands the Q missionaries as peace activists who were influenced by the conviction that the eschatological kingdom of God was offered particularly to the poor and the oppressed, a fact that they emphasized with the frugality of their appearance. He believes that this prophetic-charismatic movement was active in Palestine, as

---

[127]See Pritz 1988, 96-97, 101-2; Freyne 1997b, 301; Bauckham 1990, 114-15.

[128]Bauckham 1990, 115-16; for the observation that follows above see ibid., 116.

[129]Eusebius, *Hist. eccl.* 1.7.14; see Bauckham 1990, 116.

[130]See *t. Hul.* 2:22-23; *y. Šabb.* 1:14b; *b. 'Abod. Zar.* 27b. See Freyne 1997b, 301-2.

[131]See S. Miller, "The *minim* of Sepphoris Reconsidered," *HTR* 86 (1993): 377-402.

[132]See *y. Sanh.* 25d; *y. Šabb.* 14d. See J. F. Strange, *ABD* 6:548.

[133]See Hoffmann 1972, 312-34; Theissen 1973; 1974-1975; Zeller 1977, 195-98; Aune 1983, 211-17; Wegner 1985, 305-32; Uro 1987, 126-61, 210-23; Braun 1991, 284-85; Feldtkeller 1993, 152-255; Hartin 1993; Mack 1993, 51-68; Reed 2000, 170-96; Reinbold 2000, 226-35. For a discussion of the social localization of Q see Kloppenborg Verbin 2000, 166-96.

confirmed by the minimal equipment that these activists carried with them.[134] Rudolf Pesch
suggests that the structure and the content of Q (or of the earliest layer of Q) yield information about the missionary work and program of the Palestinian mission of the early
church. He maintains that "we should think of the 'envoys of the Son of Man' as engaged
in repeated missionary advances, like the disciples before Easter, returning to Jerusalem
after each outreach. It is remarkable that the sayings source included material about John
the Baptist and about Jesus' views concerning the Baptist, a fact that suggests that the
early mission among Jews sought to win adherents particularly among John's disciples."[135]
Heinrich Kasting asserts that the sayings source "probably was once used in the mission
of the early church and might have been originally written down as a tool and a memory
aid for their missionaries. Considering the large number of missionaries, it is not surprising
why Q did not assume, or maintain, a fixed form. The kerygma of the death and resurrection of Jesus did not need such a memory aid, but Jesus' message did."[136] Gerd Theissen, in a frequently quoted article about the early Christian "wandering radicals," describes the ethos of the Q missionaries as follows: "The ethical radicalism of the sayings
transmitted to us is the radicalism of itinerants. It can be practiced and passed on only
under extreme living conditions. It is only the person who has severed his everyday ties
with the world—the person who has left home and possessions, wife and child, who lets
the dead bury their dead, and takes the birds and the lilies of the field as his model—it is
only a person like this who can consistently preach renunciation of a settled home, a family, possessions, the protection of the law, and his own defense. It is only in this context
that the ethical precepts which match this way of life can be passed on without being
unconvincing. This ethic only has a chance on the fringes of society; this is the only real-
life situation it can have. Or to be more exact: it does not have a situation *in* real life at
all. It has to put up with an existence *on the fringes* of normal life, an existence that from
the outsider's point of view is undoubtedly questionable. It is only here that Jesus' words
were saved from being reduced to allegory, from reinterpretation, from softening or repression—simply because they were taken seriously and put into practice. And that was
possible only for homeless charismatics."[137] Theissen argues that "behind Q is a renewal
movement within Judaism that, with prophetic radicalism, demands the conversion of every individual in Israel," a movement that can be dated to the 40s, that had an ambivalent
relationship with non-Jews, and that was persecuted by the Pharisees.[138] Wendy Cotter
interprets the parables of the mustard seed and of the yeast (Lk 13:18-19, 20-21) as evidence for the methods of the Q missionaries, who were directed to travel and work in a
concealed manner, as the directives of the missionary discourse of Q in Lk 10:2, 4 confirm.[139] It remains Cotter's secret how missionaries would have been able to keep their
efforts a secret from public scrutiny in Galilee, a region that is not large and whose villages
surely did not provide any "cover." Paul Meyer thinks that the Q community accepted the
Gentile mission as a fait accompli and used the fact that God now "fills" his kingdom with
Gentiles in its Jewish mission as a summons to Israel to repent and submit to the kingdom
of God, accepting the same conditions as the Gentiles, since their past refusal to repent

---

[134]Hoffmann 1972, 312-34; for a critique see Kloppenborg Verbin 2000, 179-81.

[135]Pesch 1982, 49.

[136]Kasting 1969, 97,

[137]Theissen 1973, 86 (ET, 40); cf. idem 1974-1975, 202-9 (ET, 28-35); for a friendly critique see
Kloppenborg 2000, 179-83.

[138]Theissen 1993, 232-45; quotation, 233 (ET, 221-34; quotation, 222).

[139]Cotter 1992; for the observation that follows above see ibid., 47.

otherwise would become irreversible.[140] Dieter Zeller believes that the churches that collected and assembled the material of the sayings source were itinerant missionaries. He argues on the basis of Lk 10:2 that these itinerant missionaries are not to be identified with the Q communities, since the missionary discourse of Q is addressed to those responsible for the sending out of the "workers."[141] Risto Uro believes that the Q community not only accepted missionary outreach to Gentiles but also actively supported such a mission. The autonomous wandering radicals had become representatives of their home churches at the time of the final redaction of Q.[142] In contrast, David Catchpole is convinced that even though the Q community knew of the Gentile mission, it focused exclusively on a mission to Israel, in accordance with the practice of Jesus to preach only to Jews.[143] In a study motivated by a sociopolitical view critical of missionary work, Myungsoo Kim characterizes the Q community as an anonymous group of followers of Jesus in the hinterland of northern Palestine and southern Syria near the rural towns of Capernaum, Chorazin and Bethsaida, who operated between A.D. 30 and 70 as a *basileia* movement of the socially oppressed. Kim suggests that the Q community consisted of three groupings: itinerant prophets as charismatic leaders, the "sons of peace" as solitary sympathizers, and the socially oppressed who represented the absolute majority of the church members and who were both the main addressees and "a subject" of the mission of the Q community. The mission of the Q community can be described, according to Kim, as a "gathering of the sons of peace (sympathizers), passing on of the message of liberation, and praxis of liberation for the benefit of the socially oppressed."[144] Gerhard Dautzenberg believes that the Q community initiated a early Christian "missionary movement" outside of Palestine that continued to proclaim Jesus' message of the kingdom of God and that decided, on the basis of a progressive understanding of the universal significance of Jesus' proclamation of the kingdom of God, to engage in missionary outreach to the nations. These developments are attested by the Markan sayings tradition, as, for example, Mk 1:14-15 shows.[145] Wolfgang Reinbold characterizes the "Q group" as a Jewish renewal movement that sent out itinerant charismatic preachers who were active in Galilee and in Jewish regions in order to confront their Jewish compatriots with the message of the imminent kingdom of God that decides their salvation or their judgment.[146]

There is no consensus concerning these questions: many assumptions are purely speculative, including the view that the (hypothetical) Galilean churches were responsible for the (hypothetical) sayings source.[147] For example, Gerd Theissen's theory of early Christian itinerant radicals has been criticized by scholars with the argument that he overestimates the role of itinerant charismatics with regard to the preservation of sayings of Jesus.[148] Richard Horsley points

---

[140]P. Meyer 1970, with reference to Lk 11:29-32; 13:28-29; 14:15-24; 13:34-35; and parallels; similarly A. Jacobson 1992, 110, 256.

[141]Zeller 1977, 93; 1982b.

[142]Uro 1987, 205-23.

[143]Catchpole 1991; cf. more recently Reinbold 2000, 229.

[144]M. Kim 1990; summary, 361-65.

[145]Dautzenberg 1979.

[146]Reinbold 2000, 226-35.

[147]See the trenchant critique by Hengel and Schwemer 1998, 52-53 (ET, 30-31).

[148]Aune 1983, 214; Uro 1987, 18-19, 127-29; Horsley 1989; Kloppenborg Verbin 2000, 166-213; Arnal 2001, 67-95.

out that the texts that are adduced for the existence of these itinerants (Lk 10:4) must be interpreted in a metaphorical sense in many cases (Lk 9:59-60; 14:26-27), or they do not refer *exclusively* to "itinerant" followers of Jesus (Lk 6:20-23; 12:11-12, 22-31, 33-34; 16:13).[149] Athanasius Polag argues that it is highly unlikely "that missionary activity as such was the real locus of the tradition of sayings of Jesus, that the sayings material was not only applied here but also preserved and developed."[150] Seán Freyne points out that the "prophets of the Q gospel" were rejected in several Galilean towns and that therefore it is rather implausible that they established churches in Galilee.[151] Mark Appold argues that the "woe" spoken against Chorazin and Bethsaida, a saying that originally was independent, was included in a second revision of Q when the Q community incorporated specific experiences of their missionaries.[152] John Kloppenborg Verbin believes that "churches" with fixed membership and identifiable rituals are hardly conceivable in the Galilean villages, in which between eighty and a hundred families lived, representing two, three or four clans. Instead of speaking of a "Q community" or "Q communities," one should simply reckon with "Q people." He argues that the leaders of the Q people were village scribes (*kōmogrammateis*) who formulated an answer to the social pressure brought by the urbanization and capitalization of the economy and by the actions of the new urban elites in the first century. Their instructions, collected in the sayings Gospel Q, proposed "a model of local cooperation based on strategies of tension reduction, debt release, and forgiveness, and appealing to an image of God as a generous patron and parent who could be depended upon for sustenance."[153] Martin Hengel argues that the influence that these scholars accord itinerant charismatics is totally exaggerated, a result of contemporary popular social romanticism. He points out that there is no evidence whatsoever for the assumption that Galilean churches and their alleged theologies had a special role in missionary outreach in Syria.[154] Hengel traces the sayings (or logia) source to the Greek-speaking Jewish Christians of Jerusalem who fixed "the Jesus tradition in writing in their own language, because of the break in the linguistic tradition . . . first perhaps in the form of a notebook."

The existence, extent, origin and setting of the sayings source Q remain hy-

---

[149]Horsley 1989, 43-46, 117; cf. Kloppenborg Verbin 2000, 189.
[150]Polag 1977, 19.
[151]Freyne 1997b, 299.
[152]Appold 1995a, 233.
[153]Kloppenborg Verbin 2000, 171-72, 200-201, 214-61; quotation, 261; similarly Arnal 2001, 97-203 (a student of Kloppenborg). See also Crossan 1998; for a critique of Crossan see N. T. Wright, *SJT* 53 (2000): 72-91.
[154]Hengel and Schwemer 1998, 52-53, 359 (ET, 30-31, 235); the quotation that follows above, ibid., 59 (ET, 35). Kloppenborg Verbin (2000, 432-44) believes that most of the criticism of hypotheses about Q is theologically motivated; similarly Arnal 2001, 7; see also Wegner 1985, 305-32.

pothetical. It is especially German scholars who often ignore arguments against the existence of Q (while arguments against even the existence of Jesus are taken more seriously!).[155] In North America William Farmer has renewed the Griesbach hypothesis, arguing for the priority of the Gospel of Matthew and for the assumption that Luke used Matthew and that Mark used Matthew and Luke, thus making the assumption of a sayings source superfluous. In the United Kingdom Austin Farrer, Michael Goulder and Mark Goodacre have marshaled arguments against the existence of Q, arguing for the priority of Mark and for the assumption that Matthew used Mark and that Luke knew Mark and Matthew. It is methodologically problematic to attempt to describe the early history of the early Christian mission on the basis of various interdependent hypotheses concerning the tradition history of a hypothetical document and a hypothetical Christian community. Rudolf Pesch correctly acknowledges that many details of this tradition history can no longer be elucidated.[156]

Gottfried Schille defends in several studies the theory that early Christian communities existed in Galilee that had not been influenced by the "Easter experience," that were established on "non-apostolic tradition" and engaged in an early mission that included outreach to Gentiles right from the beginning.[157] Schille bases his reconstruction on local traditions in Galilee, on call narratives and on miracle stories in the Gospels. Rudolf Pesch criticizes Schille for indulging in "cheerful speculation":[158] (1) Schille overlooks the fundamental role of the "Galileans" in the Jerusalem church, the most important witnesses of the life of Jesus, as mediators of the Galilean Jesus tradition: rather than arriving in Jerusalem at a late date, they established and formed right at the beginning the messianic community of the believers in Jesus. (2) There is no evidence supporting the hypothesis that the disciples relocated the center of the church from Galilee to Jerusalem only after some time had passed, bringing with them the program of a Gentile mission.

Jens Schröter presents a revised version of a reconstruction by Helmut Koester, who argued that the tradition-historical trajectory from Jerusalem via Samaria to Antioch and via Paul to Asia Minor was independent of the second early Christian trajectory of the Jesus traditions represented by the canonical Gospels.[159] Schröter argues that Koester did not take sufficient account of the common ground of the early Christian traditions and convictions. He further argues that there was a "Galilean tradition," represented by the sayings source Q, that preserved the proclamation of Jesus and was independent of the conviction of the Jerusalem Christians that Jesus' death had redemptive significance in terms of the atonement for sins.

These and similar theories operate nearly exclusively on a literary level, without seriously raising the historical question of whether and how the suggested developments actually

---

[155]Note the complaint in Goodacre 2002, 11-12. For the comment that follows above see Farmer 1976; 1983; also McNicol et al. 1996; Farrer 1955; Goulder 1989; Goodacre 2002; similarly E. P. Sanders and M. Davies 1989; see also Stoldt 1977.

[156]Pesch, *Apg,* 1:295.

[157]Schille 1966, 175; cf. idem 1967; 1969.

[158]Pesch 1982, 53.

[159]Schröter 2000; cf. H. Koester 1982. For the comments that follow above see Schröter 2000, 157.

could have taken place. Richard Bauckham and others argue on the basis that the early churches had regular and intensive contacts with each other that the Gospels were written not for separate churches or communities or circles but in principle for all early Christian churches.[160] If this assumption is correct, applying also to the sayings source (if it did indeed exist as an independent literary document), then both Koester's trajectories and Schröter's revised model are implausible. Reconstructions of early Christian history positing diverse churches, groups, circles, theologians, missionaries, editors and redactors with differing and in part contradicting theologies need to be thoroughly revised. Peter and John, Stephen and Barnabas, James and Jude, and Paul and his co-workers all held the common and fundamental conviction that Jesus' death on the cross atoned the sins of all people and that his resurrection and exaltation vindicate him as Messiah, Lord and Savior. This conviction constituted both the center of their faith and the center of their missionary proclamation—a fact that renders Schröter's reconstructed Galilean Christianity "without confession of Christ"[161] a lifeless entity without church leaders, without theologians and without missionaries whose names have not been preserved, and thus an entity without recognizable shape and form.

According to Mk 10:29-30, Jesus told his disciples who had left "house or brothers or sisters or mother or father or children or fields, for my sake and for the sake of the good news" that they would be rewarded "in this age" with "houses, brothers and sisters, mothers and children, and fields," albeit accompanied by "persecutions." This perhaps is a reference to house churches that would be established in the course of the ministry of the disciples or that had been established as a result of the apostles' ministry. The house churches, using all their resources, provided the missionaries with "a new home, familial fellowship and material security."[162]

Some scholars suggest that the readers of the Gospel of John should be localized in Galilee and/or Gaulanitis. Markus Barth, who dates the Fourth Gospel between A.D. 45 and 65, suggests that John wrote his Gospel "for rural Jewish Christian churches in Samaria, Galilee and/or beyond the Jordan."[163] Klaus Wengst dates the Gospel of John to the end of the first century and locates the readers in the Jewish regions beyond the Upper Jordan, which were governed by Agrippa II (i.e., in Trachonitis and Batanea).[164] These and similar suggestions must remain hypothetical. It is equally uncertain whether the churches that produced the pseudo-Clementine literature, whose *Grundschrift* is dated to the third century,[165] were located in Galilee.[166]

---

[160]See Bauckham 1998, with contributions by Bauckham, M. B. Thompson, L. Alexander, R. A. Burridge, S. C. Barton and F. Watson.
[161]Schröter 2000, 155 ("ohne Christusbekenntnis"). He argues that the focus of these Galilean Christians was "the proclamation of the imminent kingdom of God and the identification of Jesus the Son of Man as its decisive representative."
[162]Klauck 1981, 58-59; cf. Weiser 1990, 73.
[163]M. Barth 1990, 45; on the early date for John's Gospel see ibid., 53-83.
[164]Wengst 1992, 160-70; see idem 1990.
[165]J. K. Elliott 1993, 391; text: 431-38; for a German translation see Hennecke and Schneemelcher 1987-1989, 2:63-80 (G. Strecker), 2:373-99 (J. Irmscher).
[166]Thus A. Baumgarten 1992.

The list of signatories of the Council of Nicea (A.D. 325) does not include representatives of churches from Galilee, with the exception of Chabulon in western Galilee on the road to Acco-Ptolemais.[167] The earliest Galilean bishops mentioned in the ecclesiastical tradition are the bishop of Tiberius who attended the Council of Ephesus (A.D. 449) and the bishop of Diocaesarea (Sepphoris) who attended the Council of Jerusalem (A.D. 519). The nearly complete silence of the sources about Christian churches in Galilee after the second century probably has robust historical reasons. Justin reports that Jewish Christians were persecuted during the Second Jewish Revolt, led by Bar Kokhba (*1 Apol.* 31.6-7). Some Jewish Christians were executed, presumably because they refused to participate in the "messianic war" against Rome.[168] Johann Maier observes, "After Jerome had some difficulties at a later date finding Jewish Christian churches, and since the rabbinic tradition does not contain information that can be reliably connected with Christians, it is conceivable that the regional withdrawal of Jewish Christians during the first Jewish-Roman war was followed by a further emigration during the Second Revolt, perhaps due to violence which they suffered." References in Eusebius to the Gentile-Christian character of the Jerusalem church after the Bar Kokhba Revolt may indeed reflect historical reality (*Hist. eccl.* 4.5.1-2; 5.12.1; see also §21.4 in the present work).

The Minim

Rabbinic literature mentions a group of people called *minim,* who are consistently rejected in the synagogues and by devout Jews, as is confirmed by the condemnation of the *minim* in the Twelfth Benediction in the Amidah. This obligatory prayer, spoken three times a day,[169] probably was added "in the course of the Pharisaic-rabbinic reorganization of prayer practices and of liturgy after A.D. 70 to the existing *Shema Yisrael* (and its benedictions) that had been connected with the two times of sacrifice, with individual benedictions or whole portions going back to an earlier date."[170] The Twelfth Benediction, usually known as the *birkat ha-minim* ("blessing of the heretics," although it is actually a curse) in rabbinic texts, contains an imprecation of the *minim.*[171] Two questions are debated: First, what does the term *minim* mean? Second, when was the Twelfth Benediction introduced? (1) The talmudic tradition has not pre-

---

[167]Markschies 1997, 272; overlooked by J. Maier (1982, 134-35).

[168]J. Maier 1982, 134; the quotation that follows above, ibid., 135.

[169]See *m. Ber.* 4:3; *y. Ber.* 4:2 (7d).

[170]J. Maier 1982, 136; for the observations that follow above see ibid., 136-41.

[171]On the *birkat ha-minim* see K. Kuhn 1950; J. Maier 1982, 28-74, 136-41; Kimelman 1981; Urbach 1981, 288-93; Pritz 1988, 102-107; Horbury 1998, 8-11, 67-110; Schiffman 1985, esp. 53-61; P. Alexander 1992, 6-16; Horst 1994; S. Stern 1994; Wander 1994, 272-75; M. Goodman 1996; Paget 1999, 772-73; Gniesmer 2000, 394-424; see also Theissen 1991; J. Sanders 1996 is not very helpful.

served a full text of the Eighteen Benedictions. According to *y. Ber.* 4:3-4 (8a)
and *b. Ber.* 28b-29a, a "benediction of the *minim*" was added to the existing
prayer under Rabbi Gamaliel II. This would mean that the imprecation was officially recognized during the time of Gamaliel II, who taught around A.D. 90 in
Yavneh/Jamnia. (2) Several textual variants read instead of *minim* the terms
zaduqim (Sadducees), *zedim* ("the presumptuous ones") or *qamenu* ("our opponents"),[172] terms that describe in specific contexts external enemies, Roman-
Hellenistic culture or the hostile world power, or internal opponents from a
Pharisaic-rabbinic viewpoint. Other terms used in references to the Twelfth
Benediction are *perushim* (Pharisees) and *poshʿim* ("the sinners") and *reshaʿim*
("the transgressors").[173] The version of the Eighteen Benedictions found in the
Cairo Geniza lists in the Twelfth Benediction, besides the *minim,* the *nozrim,* a
term that many scholars interpret in terms of Jewish Christians. This does not
mean that the *minim* are identical with Jewish Christians: in rabbinic lists of dis-
sidents other groups are also called opponents, apostates and heretics.[174] For
this reason some scholars argue that the Twelfth Benediction was not directed
against Christians at all.[175] The third group, the heretics, varies in the (late) textual tradition depending on place and time. Johann Maier argues that it therefore
makes no sense to try to reconstruct an "original text." It is very probably correct
that the *nozrim* mentioned in the tradition refers to Jewish Christians: both Jerome and Epiphanius report that the *Nazareni* (or *Nazaraei*) are cursed three
times a day in the synagogues, which points to corresponding formulations in
the *birkat ha-minim.* William Horbury argues on the basis of evidence in rabbinic and early patristic sources that the imprecations uttered against the heretics were directed primarily against Christians at the time of the official acknowledgment of the curses.[176]

Scholars often assume that the *birkat ha-minim,* part of the Eighteen Benedictions, sought
to make the participation of heretics in synagogue services impossible. They could hardly
recite a prayer in which they express hope for their own imprecation. Scholars who interpret the *minim* in terms of Jewish Christians often assert that the Twelfth Benediction
was introduced after A.D. 70 with the intention of excluding the Jewish Christians from
the synagogues.[177] In view of my earlier comments on the *minim,* however, this is not
very likely. Nor is it clear how the exclusion of the Jewish Christians would have been
effected by the *birkat ha-minim,* unless we assume that it aimed at making it impossible
for one of the *minim* to act as precentor in the synagogue, leading the prayers, who

---

[172]See *b. Ber.* 28b; *y. Ber.* 2:4-5 (8a); *y. Ber.* 1:4-5 (4d).

[173]See *t. Ber.* 3:25; *y. Ber.* 4:3-4 (8a/j); *b. Meg.* 17b.

[174]J. Maier (1982, 137) refers to *'Abot R. Nat.* A 16; *t. B. Meṣiʿa* 2:33; *b. ʿAbod. Zar.* 26a-b.

[175]Schäfer 1978, 45-55; Stemberger 1977; Kimelman 1981, 226-444. For the comment that follows above see J. Maier 1982, 137.

[176]Horbury 1998, 67-110 (originally *JTS* 33 [1982]: 19-61); for Horbury's response to his critics
see ibid., 8-11.

[177]See Klauck 1985, 197-99.

would have to exclude himself if he was a Christian.[178] Johann Maier formulates the most plausible historical scenario as follows: "The original purpose of the *birkat ha-minim* was not the exclusion of *minim* from religious services, as the imprecations against Rome aimed at excluding Romans. Rather, it was a basic imprecation, and the addressees were not so much *minim* who were potentially present but the participants in the service themselves. . . . The Twelfth Benediction sought to strengthen the salvation-historical self-confidence vis-à-vis the hostile world power that was destined to ruin anyway, and to express the boundaries of the community controlled by the rabbis over against any opposing or centrifugal elements—for the benefit of the community itself. . . . It is possible that the rabbis included Jewish Christians among the *minim,* but the majority of the passages about the *minim* refer to non-Christian people, particularly Jews opposing the rabbis and those oriented toward syncretistic-assimilatory lifestyles."[179] New Testament scholars who use the *birkat ha-minim* as criterion for dating material in the Gospels or the Gospels themselves need to remember that this is historically problematic no matter what date is assumed for such a decision of "the synagogue." Reinhart Hummel argues that "sectarian Judaism also had its own assemblies that did not lead to a final, formal excommunication from official Judaism."[180]

James Dunn argues with customary forcefulness and brilliance that the paths of Judaism and Christianity separated finally and irreversibly between the First Jewish Revolt in A.D. 66-70 and the Second Jewish Revolt in A.D. 132-135.[181] The beginnings of this parting of ways are to be sought in Jesus' proclamation, in the Easter message and in the Gentile mission of the apostle Paul. Dunn argues that the acceptance and admission of Gentiles constituted an irreversible break for Jews, whose identity was focused on the Torah and who described their ethnic identity in terms of their religious identity. On the other hand, many Christian Jews were involved on both sides of this debate—Paul, for example, never abandoned the basic conviction of Israel's election. The ultimate break between Christianity and synagogue was the result of developments that occurred after the destruction of Jerusalem in A.D. 70. Dunn refers to the alleged revision of the *birkat ha-minim,* which indicated the beginning of orthodox, normative Judaism, and he refers to the fact that the destruction of Jerusalem meant that Jewish Christians had lost the symbolic power that represented the continuity between the older Judaisms and the more recent Jesus movement. Further factors that advanced the parting of the ways between Judaism and Christianity included, according to Dunn, the following developments: the work of the Christian theologians of the second century increasingly focused on christological questions; the more prominent writings of Christian authors became more controversial; the Christians took over the Septuagint; the Christians and the Jews adopted a different Old Testament canon of authoritative writings; Greek and Roman authors recognized the Christians increasingly as an independent group; between A.D. 132 and 135 many Jews saw Bar Kokhba as an acceptable alternative to Jesus as Messiah.

This reconstruction of the parting of the ways of Judaism and Christianity in the second century is not consistently plausible in all details. (1) What does it mean, specifi-

---

[178]Thus Dunn (1991, 320 n. 44), who (implausibly) assumes that the *birkat ha-minim* was revised (!) between A.D. 70 and 100 (ibid., 222).

[179]J. Maier 1982, 140-41.

[180]Hummel 1966, 30. For the argument that Lk 6:22 and Jn 9:22 might well reflect the *early* stages of the conflict between "the synagogue" and Jewish Christians see Lincoln 2000, 266-78, esp. 277.

[181]Dunn 1991, 230-59. On this subject see also Evans 1997.

cally, that Jewish Christians were "involved on both sides"? It is correct, of course, that the early Christian missionaries attended synagogue services and explained their convictions about Jesus the Messiah in their contributions during the services, as long as they were allowed to attend and to speak. The New Testament sources indicate, however, that the time period in which such an "involvement" was possible was generally rather short. The Jewish-Christian preachers and missionaries, in most if not in all cases, soon were barred from participating. Can we say that Jewish Christians such as Paul continued to be "involved" in "Judaism" if they preached and gathered new converts outside of the synagogue in a particular city after having been prohibited to work within the infrastructure of the synagogue, while they continued to speak of Israel's election? There is not a single piece of evidence that Jewish Christians were allowed over a longer period of time to be "involved members" of local synagogues. This is not entirely an argument from silence: there is ample evidence for the expulsion of Jewish Christians from synagogues. (2) The rabbinic passages that Dunn adduces in support of continuing contacts between Jews and Christians are problematic for chronological and exegetical reasons. He links two famous passages in the Tosefta with the New Testament Gospels: *t. Šabb.* 13:5 ("The *gilyonim* and the books of the *minim:* they are not saved from a fire, but they are burnt in their place, they and their sacred names") and *t. Yad.* 2:13 ("The *gilyonim* and the books of the *minim* do not defile the hands. The book of Ben Sira and all books which have been written from that time onward do not defile the hands"). Dunn interprets (and translates) the term *gilyonim* as Hebraicized form of the Greek *euangelion,* "gospel."[182] However, this interpretation is far from certain. The term *gilyonim* might refer to (blank) margins of scroll leaves,[183] to book scrolls or to biblical texts in the form of single folios instead of scrolls that were deemed to be the only reliable form of authoritative exemplars of Scripture that needed to be rescued in a fire.[184] At any rate, the context of the Tosefta passage and its interpretation in the rabbinic tradition makes it clear that the *gilyonim* are scrolls of biblical Scripture and not other religious texts. (3) The limited knowledge that we possess about Jewish realities in the second century does not allow certainty with regard to tendencies, developments and majorities in the synagogues. The same applies to the Christian churches of the second century. This is the reason why we cannot be totally sure about the meaning of the *minim* clause in the Twelfth Benediction or about its historical origins. The evidence of the rabbinic sources seems to favor a "parting of ways" of (rabbinic) Judaism and Christianity at a later date.[185] The parting of ways was final and irreversible only when Jewish Christianity disappeared. As long as there were Jewish Christians, there was hope that Judaism, or "Israel," might become Christian.[186] (4) It is a curious argument to assert that the theologians of the second century were absorbed with christological questions: the same can be easily argued with regard to Matthew, Mark, Luke and John as authors in the first century, who wrote entire books about Jesus the Messiah, and Paul asserts that he preached nothing but "Christ crucified." Martin Hengel has repeatedly pointed out that the decisive christological developments

---

[182]Dunn 1991, 235-36. For *t. Yad.* 2:13 see J. Maier 1982, 28.

[183]Karl Georg Kuhn, "Giljonim und Sifre Minim," in *Judentum, Urchristentum, Kirche* (FS J. Jeremias; ed. W. Eltester; 2nd ed., BZNT 26; Berlin: de Gruyter, 1964), 24-61.

[184]J. Maier 1982, 30-69; for the observation that follows above see ibid., 69. See also Paget 1999, 773 n. 172.

[185]See P. Alexander 1992, 1-25; M. Goodman 1992b, 27-38.

[186]See P. Alexander 1992, 24.

occurred in the period A.D. 30-45[187] and derive from the messianic self-understanding of Jesus and from his death and resurrection.[188] The message of the justification of sinners by faith in Jesus Christ played an important role.[189] (5) The Jewish-Christian segment of the church surely viewed Jerusalem as the center. However, if the Twelve indeed left Jerusalem around A.D. 41 and traveled to more distant missionary regions, the question arises as to how important Jerusalem as a symbolic center really was. We do not know whether Jewish Christians lamented the loss of Jerusalem as a symbolic center after the destruction of A.D. 70. (6) It probably is fair to say that the Christian texts of the second century were not more "controversial" than, for example, the Epistle to the Galatians or the Epistle to the Hebrews in the first century. I do not detect evolutionary tendencies promoting the "parting of ways" in *Barnabas* or in the writings of Justin. Several scholars have pointed out that the tensions within Christian texts or within rabbinic texts are at least as great as the divergence between Jewish faith and practice and Christian faith and practice.[190] (7) The question of whether Matthew and "his" community, for example, were outside or inside Judaism implies a false set of alternatives because both "options" are true at the same time,[191] especially if we think not just in terms of Jewish institutions but also include Jewish self-definitions.

The parting of the ways between the growing (Jewish) Christian church and the Jewish synagogue is ultimately independent of the question of the *birkat ha-minim* and the consequences of the destruction of Jerusalem in A.D. 70. The process of separation began with (1) Jesus and his claim to messianic identity and authority, (2) the acceptance of this claim by an increasing number of Jews, and (3) the believers in Jesus the Messiah meeting in separate gatherings immediately after Jesus' resurrection, guided and nurtured by leaders and teachers who were independent of the Sanhedrin or the synagogues. The process of separation was intensified as a result of the conviction of the early Christians that the new movement of believers in Jesus the Messiah represents and constitutes the eschatological people of God. This conviction was articulated particularly by Paul, but it can be traced back to the office of the Twelve and to the early conviction that the *ekklēsia* of believers in Jesus represents the new eschatological temple built on Jesus the Messiah as the "cornerstone." The process of separation was also intensified as a result of the Jewish polemic against the "sect of the Nazarenes" (Acts 24:5). Jewish authorities accused Jesus of seducing the people and of practicing magic in the name of Beelzebul. They arranged for the arrest of Jesus and for his trial, which led to his execution. Jewish opposition to Stephen and his preaching caused his death. Jewish opposition to Paul's missionary ministry resulted in repeated punishments in synagogues, in legal pro-

---

[187]Hengel 1975; 1983a; 1990; idem, in Dunn 1992, 368; Hengel and Schwemer 1998, 153-73 (ET, 91-105).
[188]Cf. P. Stuhlmacher, "Das Christusbild der Paulus-Schule," in Dunn 1992, 159-75.
[189]See N. Cohen 1992, 409-19.
[190]See Chester 1992, 239-313.
[191]See Luz, *Mt*, 3:392-93.

ceedings in Corinth and in Jerusalem eventually leading to his arrest and imprisonment in Caesarea. And the process of separation was intensified by the
growing number of Gentiles Christians. Martin Hengel observes, "The 'sympathizers' who had been won over to the new message will not have had such a
strong personal tie to particular communities as old-established Jewish families;
certainly sympathy and curiosity had driven them into the synagogue, but legally they never had the opportunity there really to gain completely equal rights.
Even proselytes were initially still always second-class Jews in comparison to
those who appealed proudly to their 'circumcision on the eighth day,' their origin 'from the people of Israel, the tribe of Benjamin, as a Hebrew of the Hebrews,' or even to their origin from 'the descendants of Abraham.' In the new,
small, and therefore narrow community, which awaited the imminent coming
of the Lord and in possession of the eschatological Spirit celebrated its prophetically inspired and sometimes also rather chaotic worship, all these differences
fell aside, such as national, sociological and biological differences. What remained was the difference in the knowledge of Scripture, the wealth of traditions and competence to teach."[192] The parting of the ways was "already in full
swing or even presupposed" at the time of Paul's major theological writing in
the 50s of the first century.[193] The separation becomes clearly visible in A.D. 36/
37 or in 39/40 when the believers in Jesus the Messiah (Gk., *christos*) were
called "Christians" (*christianoi*) for the first time.[194] The view that history may
have taken a different course without the ministry of Paul, who argued for a mission without circumcision,[195] is a serious misjudgment.

Why did rabbinic Judaism triumph in Palestine in the third and fourth centuries, and not the Christian faith? There is no easy answer to this question. Philip
Alexander points to two factors that presumably were decisive.[196]

(1) Jewish Christians would hardly have felt at home in the historical and social context of Jewish nationalism, which was very strong in the first and second
centuries, provoking two wars of liberation and various revolts in the Diaspora
(e.g., in Cyrene) with catastrophic consequences. The Jewish Christians must
have become increasingly estranged from their patriotic compatriots who championed the Torah, the temple and the Holy Land, as they preached the presence
of a kingdom of God in which the Torah did not occupy a central position and
in which the temple and the promised land had lost their significance. (2) The
Gentile mission of churches in which Jewish Christians were actively involved
led to the conversion of more Gentiles than Jews before long. Even though Gen-

---

[192]Hengel and Schwemer 1998, 307 (ET, 200 [the last sentence is only in the German version]).
[193]Frey 1994, 232. See R. Bauckham, "The Parting of the Ways: What Happened and Why," *StTh*
    47 (1993): 135-51; Wander 1994; Horbury 1998, 11-14, and passim.
[194]See §22.5. Cf. Judge 1994, 362-66.
[195]Luz 1993, 170-71.
[196]See P. Alexander 1992, 22-24; cf. Chester 1992, 305.

tile Christians called Abraham their "father," and even though they understood themselves as (the new) Israel, they certainly did not live like Jews in their daily routines. Jewish-Christian congregations increasingly faced the difficulty of not being seen as a *Jewish* movement by their Jewish compatriots.

22.3 Missionary Work in Samaria

In Luke's account Samaria is mentioned on two further occasions after his report of the Samaria mission of Philip (Acts 8:4-25). In the summary statement in Acts 9:31 Luke states that "the church throughout Judea, Galilee, and Samaria had peace and was built up." And in Acts 15:3 he presupposes churches in "both Phoenicia and Samaria" that Paul and Barnabas visited on their return from missionary work in Galatia, bringing "great joy to all the believers" when they reported the conversion of the Gentiles.

Acts 9:31: "Meanwhile the church throughout Judea, Galilee, and Samaria had peace and was built up. Living in the fear of the Lord and in the comfort of the Holy Spirit, it increased in numbers."

Acts 15:3: "So they were sent on their way by the church, and as they passed through both Phoenicia and Samaria, they reported the conversion of the Gentiles, and brought great joy to all the believers."

Since the missionary work of Philip (Acts 8:4-14) and Peter and John (Acts 8:25), churches may have been established in the following towns and villages (from north to south and from west to east [see fig. 10]):[197]

Betoanea (Bethannaba): village 25 km east of Caesarea; the town was known for its medicinal baths.
Umm Richan:[198] small town in northwestern Samaria; in the Roman period the village consisted of about one hundred houses closely clustered together; remains of shops, public bath, olive and wine presses, fortifications are extant.
Ianua: village in northern Samaria.
Paquʿa: settlement in northern Samaria, on the road to Scythopolis.
Burqin: village in northern Samaria.
Ginae: village on the northern border of Samaria.
Bethacath: village in northern Samaria; remains of a pottery workshop, reservoirs, a Byzantine church.
Meṣer: village in northwestern Samaria; remains of mosaic pavements, bath house, wine presses, quarries, tombs.
Quaffin: village in western Samaria; remains of settlement, cisterns, tombs.
Khirbet Masʿud: village in western Samaria; remains of buildings.
Belemoth (Ibleam): Jewish village in northern Samaria; traditional birthplace of the

---

[197]For the information that follows above see the maps and gazetteer in Tsafrir, di Segni and Green, *Iudaea-Palaestina,* as well as *NEAEHL.*
[198]See Dar, *NEAEHL* 4:1314-15.

prophet Hosea; remains of settlement.

'En Kushi: village on the territory of Caesarea in which Jews and Samaritans lived; known for its wine production.

Kefar Parshai: village in western Samaria; remains of settlement.

Chorvat Ner: village in eastern Samaria; remains of buildings, wine presses, cisterns.

Geth (Gitta): village about 10 km northwest of Sebaste; birthplace of Simon Magus.

Narbata (Khirbet el-Chammam):[199] probably the headquarters of Solomon's third district, called Arubbot (1 Kings 4:10); center of a Jewish toparchy and most important town in northwestern Samaria. During the heyday of the city in the first centuries B.C. and A.D., Narbata probably had three thousand inhabitants. In the beginning of the First Jewish Revolt in A.D. 66, the Jews of Caesarea moved to Narbata (Josephus, *B.J.* 2.291). Remains of houses, cisterns, ritual bath, city walls.

Dothaim (Tel Dothan):[200] 20 km north of Sebaste, in a wide valley on the road from the hills of Samaria to the Jezreel Valley; first mentioned in connection with Joseph (Gen 37:17), later as a place in which the king of Aram wanted to have the prophet Elisha arrested (2 Kings 6:13-14). Dothan was destroyed in the eighth century B.C. and resettled only in Hellenistic times.

Merrus: village in northern Samaria, 20 km north of Sebaste.

Sephirin: village in eastern Samaria.

Bardala: village in eastern Samaria; remains of settlements, wine press, tombs.

Bezek: double village in northeastern Samaria, on the road to Scythopolis.

Zir: Jewish village on the territory of Sebaste.

Khirbet Jabaris: village in eastern Samaria; remains of settlement, wine and olive presses, rock-hewn caves, mausoleums.

Salaba (Shelaf): Jewish village in northeastern Samaria in the territory of Sebaste.

Aser: village between Neapolis and Scythopolis.

Socho (Shuweika): village in northwestern Samaria.

Khirbet Bajura: village in northwestern Samaria; remains of settlement.

Pardesliya: Jewish village in the territory of Sebaste.

Ataroth: village in Samaria, 6 km north of Sebaste.

Leviya: village in the territory of Sebaste.

Gaba: village north of Sebaste, known for its vegetables.

Thebes: village in northeastern Samaria, 21 km north of Neapolis.

Abelmea: village in eastern Samaria; spring.

'Anabtah: village 7 km northwest of Sebaste.

Shiltha: village 4 km north of Sebaste.

Pentakomia: village 4.5 km north of Sebaste.

Kefar Kasdaya: village in eastern Samaria, belonging to Sebaste.

Khirbet Yarza: village in eastern Samaria; columns of a monumental building, pond.

Tur Kerem: Samaritan village in the eastern plain of Sharon.

Iezeth: village in the territory of Sebaste.

Deir Serur (Khirbet Samara): 5 km east of Sebaste; Samaritan synagogue.

Samaria (Sebaste): see §9.5.

Kefar Yudith: village in the territory of Sebaste.

Tur Loza: village in eastern Samaria.

---

[199]See Adam Zertal, *NEAEHL* 2:563-65; idem, "The Roman Siege-System at Khirbet al-Hamam (Narbata)," in Humphrey 1995-2002, 1:71-94.

[200]D. Ussishkin, *NEAEHL* 1:372-73.

Baddan: village 7 km northeast of Neapolis; famous for its pomegranates.

Enbeteba: village 6 km south of Sebaste.

ʿEin Beit el Ma: village 3 km northwest of Neapolis; one of the sources of the aqueduct of Sebaste; possibly Samaritan synagogue; inscriptions.

Khirbet Mufiyye: village in eastern Samaria; remains of settlement.

Tel Miske: village in eastern Samaria; remains of settlement.

Sychar (mod. ʿAskar):[201] village near Mabartha-Neapolis, on the lower slopes of Mount Ebal; numerous pottery remains attest a settlement in Hellenistic-Roman times. When Samaria was placed, as an independent district, under the control of the Roman province of Syria at the end of the Hasmonean kingdom, Sychar was perhaps the capital of the Samaritans, located in the vicinity of Mount Gerizim. The village mentioned in Jn 4:5 was close to Jacob's well. The episode of Jn 4:5-42 presumably took place in Sychar. Scholars who reject the historical authenticity of the account in Jn 4 sometimes assume that there was an early Christian community in Sychar, with Jn 4 representing a "missionary aetiology"—that is, a "foundation legend of Gentile-Christian nuclei of churches."[202]

Kiriath Chagga: village 8 km west of Neapolis.

Qedumim:[203] 4 km west of Neapolis; Samaritan *miqvaot;* remains from the first century.

Shechem:[204] about 1.5 km south of Neapolis; one of the oldest cities in Palestine. Shechem was abandoned after the fall of the northern kingdom, rebuilt around 330 B.C., destroyed by John Hyrcanus in 107 B.C. Life in the valley seems to have recovered quickly, however, as most villages in the immediate vicinity of the destroyed city were settled in the early Roman period.[205] Shechem sometimes is identified with Sychar or Neapolis.

Mabartha-Flavia Neapolis:[206] Neapolis was founded by Vespasian in A.D. 72/73 after the destruction of Jerusalem, apparently on the site of a town called Mabartha (Josephus, *B.J.* 4.449) or Mamortha (cf. Pliny, *Nat.* 5.69). Public buildings, a theater and a hippodrome were built in the second century. Around A.D. 100 Justin, one of the apostolic fathers, was born in Neapolis to pagan parents; his father was Priscus, his grandfather was Bacchus; Justin was converted to faith in Jesus Christ via Platonic philosophy; he defended the Christian faith in his teaching and writing; he was martyred in A.D. 165 in Rome.

Platanus: near Shechem; Samaritan place of worship, with a holy tree; a Samaritan synagogue was discovered nearby.

Salem (Salem Rabatha): village in eastern Samaria; Samaritan synagogue.

Luza: village 2 km south of Neapolis.

Garizim (Jebel et Tur):[207] mountain above Shechem and Mabartha-Neapolis; on the

---

[201]See Zangenberg 1998, 96-106; Böhm 1999, 90-101.

[202]Zeller 1991, 84; cf. Zangenberg (1998, 192-96), who remarks that "the evangelist stylizes the argument for the acceptance of the Samaritan-Christian church in Sychar as an event in the life of Jesus" (195).

[203]I. Magen, *NEAEHL* 4:1225-27.

[204]Edward F. Campbell, "Shechem (Tell Balata)," *NEAEHL* 4:1345-54; Itzhak Magen, "Shechem (Neapolis)," *NEAEHL* 4:1354-59; Lawrence E. Toombs, *ABD* 5:1174-86; Zangenberg 1998, 27-30; Böhm 1999, 54-68. Excavations: Edward F. Campbell, *Shechem II: Portrait of a Hill Country Vale; The Shechem Regional Survey* (ed. K. I. Summers; Archaeological Reports 2; Atlanta: Scholars Press, 1991); idem, *Shechem III: The Stratigraphy and Architecture of Shechem/Tell Balâttah* (2 vols.; Archaeological Reports 6; Boston: American Schools of Oriental Research, 2002).

[205]Böhm 1999, 55.

[206]I. Magen, *NEAEHL* 4:1355; Zangenberg 1998, 30-35; Böhm 1999, 86-90.

[207]I. Magen, *NEAEHL* 2:485-92; Zangenberg 1998, 35-47; Böhm 1999, 68-86.

main peak (881 m) there was a Samaritan town (about 30 ha) since about 200 B.C., built around a sacred precinct, with substantial fortifications added later. The four quarters of the town had two-story houses. The sanctuary and the cult practiced on Mount Gerizim by Israelites following the Torah was reached via a staircase (8.5 m wide) and imposing gates. John Hyrcanus completely destroyed the city and the temple in 107 B.C. In the fourth century A.D. a church (the Theotokos Church) was built at the site of the old Samaritan sanctuary.

Beth Dagon: village 10 km east of Neapolis; Samaritan synagogue (?).

Khirbet Basasliyye: village in eastern Samaria.

Tirat Namara: village on Mount Gerizim.

Khirbet ʿUskur: village in southwestern Samaria; remains of settlement.

Addara: village in southwestern Samaria.

Khirbet et Tira (Tirath Ana?): village 6 km south of Neapolis.

ʿAwartha: village 6 km south of Neapolis; remains of a synagogue (?).

Perekh: village 8 km southeast of Neapolis; famous for its nut trees; burial caves.

Thena: village 16 km southeast of Neapolis, on the road to the Jordan River.

Iano: village in eastern Samaria.

Coreae: station on the road to the Jordan Valley; on the border with Judea.

Acraba: town in eastern Samaria, headquarters of a toparchy, a day's journey from Jerusalem; on the border with Judea.

Arus: village in southwestern Samaria.

Beth Sarisa: village in southwestern Samaria.

Khirbet el Buraq:[208] village in southwestern Samaria; remains of settlement.

Kefar Iathma: village 12 km south of Neapolis.

Gerasa: village in eastern Samaria, probably the birthplace of the leader of the Zealot movement Simon Bar Giora; destroyed by Vespasian.

Anathu Borcaeus: village on the border of Samaria and Judea, 16 km south of Neapolis, on the road to Jerusalem.

Galod: village in southeastern Samaria.

Shiloh (Arab., Sailun):[209] 30 km north of Jerusalem. During the conquest of the promised land the ark of the covenant was kept here (Josh 18:1). During the time of the judges Shiloh was the main sanctuary of the Israelites (Judg 18:31). For the time of the priest Eli a temple is attested here (1 Sam 1:9). In Hellenistic times Shiloh was a village that belonged to Samaria. Remains of buildings from the Roman period; synagogue (?).

Eduma: village in southeastern Samaria.

Beth Laban: village in southwestern Samaria, famous for its wine.

Sereda: village in southwestern Samaria, mentioned in 1 Kings 11:26; home town of Rabbi Yose ben Ioezer.

Aruir: village in southern Samaria, 32 km north of Jerusalem.

Arimathea (Ramathaim; near mod. Rentis):[210] a village mostly inhabited by Jews (Lk 23:51), located in the Shephelah about 15 km northeast of Lydda and 25 km east of Jaffa. Arimathea probably is identical with Ramatajim-Zofim in Ephraim (1 Sam 1:19) and with the Samaritan capital of a toparchy in southwestern Samaria. The town became Jewish under the Maccabean ruler Jonathan around 145 B.C. (1 Macc 11:34; Josephus, *A.J.*

[208]I. Magen, *NEAEHL* 4:1317.

[209]A. Kempinksi and I. Finkelstein, *NEAEHL* 4:1364-70.

[210]See R. Riesner, *GBL* 1:114-15; Jerry A. Pattengale, *ABD* 1:378; see also the commentaries on the biblical passages mentioned.

13.127). Birthplace of Joseph, a member of the Sanhedrin, who buried Jesus (Mt 27:57/ Mk 15:43/Lk 23:50/Jn 19:38). According to the apocryphal *Gospel of Nicodemus*, this Joseph established the church in Lydda (*Gos. Nic.* 12, 15); later legends describe Joseph as a missionary in France and in England.[211]

Beth Rima: village in southwestern Samaria, famous for its wine.

Gaba: village in southern Samaria, on the road to Jerusalem.

Thamna: headquarters of a toparchy in Samaria; belonged to Judea during the rule of the Maccabean ruler Jonathan.

Tarfin: village in southern Samaria; remains of settlement.

Isana: village in southern Samaria between Neapolis and Jerusalem.

Khirbet Siya: village in southwestern Samaria; remains of buildings.

Khirbet Marjame:[212] in southern Samaria on the eastern slopes of Mount Baal-Hazor; destroyed in 722 B.C.; remains of settlement in the Roman period; church.

Khirbet Samiyeh: village in southeastern Samaria; remains of settlement.

Aialon (mod. Beit Illu): village in southern Samaria, on the road from Gophna to Thamna.

Beth Zaith: village in southern Samaria.

Gophna: about 25 km north of Jerusalem; headquarters of a toparchy in southern Samaria; in Herodian times a village; remains of buildings, tombs.

Apharaema (mod. et Tayyibe): headquarters of a toparchy in southern Samaria; belonged to Judea after 145 B.C.

Deir Shabab: village in southern Samaria; remains of settlement, olive press.

We have no information about the development of the Samaritan churches. In the second century Samaritan gnostics adopted the teachings of Simon Magus, interpreting him in terms of their myth of salvation.[213] The church fathers saw in Simon Magus the author of the "Simonian" heresy—that is, Gnosticism. The verdicts of Justin and Irenaeus about the Samaritans, formulated in the context of their struggles against gnosticism, often are polemical and exaggerated and thus not always historically reliable.[214]

22.4 Missionary Work in the Cities of the Syrian Coast

The missionary work of Philip, Peter and other early missionaries led to the establishment of churches at least in Lydda (Lod), Joppa, Caesarea, Ptolemais-Acco and probably also in Azotos (Ashdod [see §19.2]). The available evidence seems to allow the conclusion that the churches in Lydda, Joppa and Caesarea

---

[211]See Hennecke and Schneemelcher 1987-1989, 1:407, 410-11; E. von Dobschütz, "Joseph von Arimathia," *Zeitschrift für Kirchengeschichte* 23 (1902): 1-17, esp. 1-4; Harnack 1924, 2:648 (ET, 2:114).

[212]A. Mazar, *NEAEHL* 3:965-66.

[213]Roloff, *Apg*, 137-38; Pesch, *Apg*, 1:279. On Simon Magus see Tamás Adamik, "The Image of Simon Magus in the Christian Tradition," in Bremmer 1998, 52-64.

[214]For this we reason we should exercise caution with regard to the assertion of Gijs Bouwman (*EWNT* 3:542 [*EDNT* 3:227]), who argues that "one should not overestimate the success of Christian mission activity in Samaria," because, according to Justin (*1 Apol.* 26.3; *Dial.* 120.6), almost all Samaritans still venerated Simon as the highest god in the mid-second century.

were centers of missionary outreach in the coastal regions: Peter stayed in Joppa "for some time" (ἡμέρας ἱκανάς, *hēmeras hikanas* [Acts 9:43]), and Philip was an evangelist based in Caesarea for many years (Acts 21:8). Philip could have evangelized among the population of the sixteen towns and villages that belonged to the territory of Caesarea, from Me'arath Telimon in the north to Tibetha and Zora in the south.

Evangelism on the Southern Coast

Peter, Philip, and other missionaries could also have visited the following towns and villages in the coastal plain, including the settlements in the Shephelah, the hill country of western Judea (listed from south to north [see fig. 15]):[215]

Gaza (Γάζα; Tell Charube; Tell 'Azza; mod. Gaza):[216] the old city of the Philistines in the southern coastal plain, about 5 km from the Mediterranean, was rebuilt in the Persian period as an important royal fortress. It was the only city that dared to resist Alexander the Great; after being conquered, it was destroyed in September of 332 B.C. Members of tribes in the vicinity resettled the site (Arrian 2.27.2). Gaza was controlled by the Ptolemies in the second century B.C. It became famous as a center of the trade with Arabia that extended as far east as India. Gaza was a center of Hellenistic culture; there was, for example, a famous school of rhetoric in the city. Alexander Jannaeus annexed Gaza in 99 B.C., and in 61 B.C. the city became a Roman colony. Herod I controlled Gaza after 37 B.C. After his death, Gaza was a semiautonomous polis under the "care" of the Roman governor in Syria. At the time of Claudius Gaza is again described as an important city (Pomponius Mela 1.11): it boasted of numerous temples, dedicated to Marnus Zeus Helios, Aphrodite, Apollo, Athene, Hekate and Tyche. In A.D. 295 the bishop Sylvanus died as the first martyr of Gaza.

Anthedon (Agrippias; mod. Khirbet Teda):[217] seaport about 3 km north of Gaza; conquered by Alexander Jannaeus; controlled by the Romans after the conquest by Pompey in 64 B.C. The city was enlarged by Herod I and renamed Agrippias (as competition for Gaza).

Buriron: village 20 km northeast of Gaza, on the road to Jerusalem.

Agla: village 8 km east of Buriron, on the road to Jerusalem.

Beth Zedek: village 16 km east of Agla, on the road to Jerusalem.

Beth Guvrin (Bēgabris; mod. Beit Jibrin):[218] village in the Shephelah, 6 km north of Beth Zedek, on the road from Jerusalem (Ptolemaios 5.16.6); several well-known rabbis came from Beth Guvrin. The town was renamed Eleutheropolis by Septimius Severus in 200 A.D. Remains of the amphitheater are preserved.

---

[215]For the information that follows above see the maps and gazetteer in Tsafrir, di Segni and Green, *Iudaea-Palaestina,* as well as *NEAEHL.*
[216]C. Colpe, *KP* 2:705-6; A. Negev, *PECS* 345-46; H. J. Katzenstein, *ABD* 2:912-17; A. Ovadiah, *NEAEHL* 2:464-67; E. A. Knauf and T. Leisten, *DNP* 4:815-16; Jones 1937, 231, 252, 271-73, 280-82; Schürer 2:98-103; Hüttenmeister 1977, 130-37; Martin A. Meyer, *History of the City of Gaza* (New York: AMS Press, 1966 [1907]); Carol A. M. Glucker, *The City of Gaza in the Roman and Byzantine Periods* (Oxford: British Institute of Archaeology, 1987).
[217]A. Negev, *PECS* 59; Schürer 2:104.
[218]Hüttenmeister 1977, 51-53; A. Kloner, *NEAEHL* 1:195-97, 201.

Saraphia: village 5 km south of Askalon (later Diocletianopolis?).

Barbarith: village 5 km northwest of Saraphia; famous for figs (*y. Mo'ed Qat.* 81d).

Ascalon (mod. Ashkelon):[219] the old capital of the Philistines on the Mediterranean, 16 km north of Gaza and about 70 km southwest of Jerusalem. Ascalon was the only seaport to be spared by Alexander Jannaeus. The city was independent since 104 B.C. and seems not to have been integrated into the Roman province of Syria, nor into the kingdom of Herod I, who had baths built in Ascalon; he also had a palace in the city (Josephus, *A.J.* 17.321; *B.J.* 2.98). According to Julius Africanus, Ascalon was the birthplace of Herod I (see Eusebius, *Hist. eccl.* 1.6.2). At the beginning of the First Jewish Revolt, the Gentile population of Ascalon massacred the 2,500 Jews who lived in the city (*B.J.* 2.460; 2.477). Ascalon was a center of trans-shipment for the wheat trade. Dates, vegetables and onions that were cultivated here were exported into many Roman cities of the Mediterranean world (Strabo 16.2.29; Pliny, *Nat.* 19.32.101-107). Remains from the Roman period have been discovered. Attested are temples of Apollo, Atargatis, Derketo, Heracles and Isis. In A.D. 493 a church was built in Ascalon Barnea.[220]

'Ozem (mod. Khirbet Beit Mamin):[221] village 15 km east of Ascalon in the southern Shephelah, on the road to Jerusalem; remains of buildings and a church.

Saalim (mod. Khirbet Umm Kalkha): 11 km west of *'Ozem* (Josephus, *B.J.* 3.20).

Caphar Zacharia (mod. Khirbet Zikhrin/Dikhrin): 16 km northwest of *'Ozem;* according to tradition, the burial place of the prophet Zechariah (*Lives of the Prophets* 36).

Saphir: village 17 km northeast of Ascalon; remains of settlement.

Azotos (Ashdod): see §19.2.

Bareca: village about 5 km northeast of Azotos; remains of buildings, cisterns.

Asor: village 5 km west of Bareca; remains of settlement from the Roman period.

Galaia: village in the Shephelah, 11 km west of Asor.

Accaron (Ecron; mod. Tel Miqne):[222] old Philistine city 17 km northwest of Azotos on the border with Judea, about 35 km southwest of Jerusalem. Jonathan Maccabaeus Judaized the city (1 Macc 10:88-89; Josephus, *A.J.* 13.102). Headquarters of a toparchy.

Cariathmaus (**Mizpe Yonah**): situated on the Mediterranean about 7 km northwest of Azotos; birthplace of the prophet Jonah (*Lives of the Prophets* 18); Hellenistic and Roman remains of buildings.

Iamnia (Ιαμνεῖα; Yavneh; mod. Yibna):[223] an important town in the coastal plain, 22 km south of Joppa. Evidently there was a small rabbinic court in the city even before A.D. 70. In the second century Iamnia/Yavneh was a center for rabbinical scholars.[224] Philip could well have preached in Iamnia in the course of his missionary activity between Azotos and Caesarea (Acts 8:39-40).[225]

Jamnia Paralios (Maoza; mod. Minet Rubin):[226] seaport about 9 km from Iamnia (2 Macc 12:9; Josephus, *A.J.* 13.395).

---

[219]C. Colpe, *KP* 1:641; A. Negev, *PECS* 98-99; L. E. Stager, *NEAEHL* 1:103-12; M. Köckert, *DNP* 2:86; Schürer 1:308; 2:105-8; Hüttenmeister 1977, 21-22; Kasher 1990, 180-83, and passim.

[220]*SEG* XXXVII 1517. See L. di Segni, in Humphrey 1995-2002, 2:167.

[221]M. Avi-Yonah et al., *NEAEHL* 1:311.

[222]T. Dothan and S. Gitin, *NEAEHL* 3:1051-59.

[223]1 Macc 4:15; 5:58; 10:69; 15:40; 2 Macc 12:8-9, 40; Philo, *Legat.* 200-203; Josephus, *A.J.* 5.87; 12.308, 350-351; *B.J.* 1.50, 156, 166.; Strabo 16.2.28-29; Pliny, *Nat.* 5.14.68; Ptolemaios 5.16.6.

[224]A. Negev, *PECS* 424-25; Hüttenmeister 1977, 483-513.

[225]See also Kollmann 2000, 560.

[226]J. Kaplan, *NEAEHL* 4:1504-1506. See B. Isaac, "A Seleucid Inscription from Jamnia-on-the-Sea," *IEJ* 41 (1991): 132-44.

Gazara (mod. Tell Jezer): village on the coast, 12 km south of Joppa; a Seleucid fortress conquered by the Maccabean ruler Simon, subsequently settled by Jews (1 Macc 13:43-48).

Şeriphin (Zeriphin; mod. Sarafend el ʿAmar): village 5 km west of Lydda; famous for its gardens (*m. Menaḥ.* 10:2).

Lydda (Lod): see §20.4

Sapharea (mod. Saferiye): village 6 km northwest of Lydda, on the road to Joppa.

Beth Dagon (mod. Beth Dagan): large village 8 km northwest of Lydda, on the road to Joppa; a temple dedicated to Dagon is attested (1 Macc 10:83).

Joppa (Japho): see §20.4

Ono (mod. Kafr ʾAna): town about 12 km southeast of Joppa; often mentioned in rabbinic literature.

Bene Beraq (mod. Ibn-Ibraq; Khiriyyeh):[227] 7 km east of Joppa; the village was known as the home of Rabbi Aqiba.

Khirbet Zikhrin: village 20 km northeast of Joppa; belonged to Samaria.

Antipatris (Aphek; Arethusa; Pegae; mod. Ras el ʿAin):[228] situated near the springs of the Yarkon River, about 20 km northeast of Joppa (between Jerusalem and Caesarea); identical with the Old Testament Aphek (Josh 12:18). In the Hellenistic period the city was called Pegae. It was conquered by John Hyrcanus and reestablished by Pompey under the name Arethusa, and refounded by Herod I as Antipatris (Ἀντιπατρίς [Josephus, *A.J.* 14.75; 16.142-143; *B.J.* 1.417]). The main street of the Herodian town has been attested by the discovery of pavement and shops. When Philip visited "every city" between Azotos and Caesarea (Acts 8:39-40) during his missionary travels, he presumably preached in Antipatris as well.[229] Paul visited the city as a prisoner when he was taken from Jerusalem to Caesarea (Acts 23:31). A synagogue of the second century is attested.

Kefar Kesem: village about 5 km east of Antipatris; it belonged to Samaria and was famous for a sacred (pagan) tree (*t. ʿAbod. Zar.* 6:8).

Kapparetaia (mod. Khirbet Kafr Hatta): village 4 km northeast of Antipatris; belonged to Samaria; birthplace of the gnostic Menander mentioned by Justin (*1 Apol.* 26).

Galgulis: 6 km north of Antipatris.

Kaphar Saba (mod. Khirbet Sabiye): village 10 km north of Antipatris; remains of buildings, mosaic, Roman baths, cisterns.

Apollonia (Rishpon; mod. Arsuf):[230] seaport between Joppa and Caesarea; an old trading center of Sidon; in Canaanite and Phoenician times known as the "town of the god Resheph." The city was established as a seaport by the Persians. The city became Jewish under Alexander Jannaeus (Josephus, *A.J.* 13.395). It was conquered in 64 B.C. by Pompey and rebuilt by Gabinus. The town is mentioned by Pliny (*Nat.* 5.69) and Ptolemaios (5.15.2).

Beth Ther (Betthar; mod. et Tire): 33 km south of Caesarea, on the road to Antipatris.

Theraspis: village 3 km north of Beth Ther; remains of buildings, mosaic pavement.

Tibetha (mod. et Tayyibe): 6 km northeast of Theraspis, on the border of the territory of Caesarea, in the eastern plain of Sharon (see *y. Demai* 22c).

---

[227]J. Kaplan, *NEAEHL* 1:186-87.
[228]See Schürer 2:167-68; A. Negev, *PECS* 64; Hüttenmeister 1977, 2-4; M. Kochavi, *ABD* 1:272-74; A. Eitan et al., *NEAEHL* 1:62-72.
[229]Kollmann 2000, 560.
[230]A. Negev, *PECS* 72; I. Roll, *ABD* 1:298-99; I. Roll and E. Ayalon, *NEAEHL* 1:72-75; Schürer 2:114-15.

Zoran (mod. Umm Ṣur): 23 km south of Caesarea, a village on the border of the territory of Caesarea (see *y. Demai* 22c).

Natania (mod. Umm Khalid): 20 km south of Caesarea, on the coastal road.

Bir el ʿAbd: 15 km southeast of Caesarea; Roman and Byzantine settlement; estate of Antipas (?).

Kefar Shalem (mod. Kh. el Jelleme): 17 km southeast of Caesarea; the village had Jewish and Samaritan inhabitants; famous for its wine production (*t. Šeb.* 4:4; *y. ʿAbod. Zar.* 44d; *b. ʿAbod. Zar.* 31a).

Mikhmoret:[231] seaport 12 km south of Caesarea; Persian and Hellenistic remains.

Minet Abu Zabura (Gidra shel Qisrin? [*t. Šeb.* 7:10-11]): village on the coast about 11 km south of Caesarea; remains of buildings.

Khirbet Zalafa: 13 km southeast of Caesarea in the plain of Sharon.

ʿEn Kushi (Kh. Kusiya): 16 km southeast of Caesarea, a village that belonged to the territory of Caesarea; inhabited by Jews and Samaritans; wine production.

Tel Gador: coastal village 8 km south of Caesarea.

Burgatha (mod. Khirbet Ibreiktas): coastal village 8 km south of Caesarea; remains of buildings (see *y. ʿAbod. Zar.* 44d; *b. ʿAbod. Zar.* 31a).

Givʿat Olga: coastal village 7 km south of Caesarea; Roman and Byzantine remains of buildings.

Caesarea: see §19.2.

Krokodilonpolis (mod. Tel Tanninim): coastal town 4.5 km north of Caesarea; remains of buildings, mosaic; mentioned by Ps.-Scylax 104; Strabo 16.2.27; Pliny, *Nat.* 5.17.75.

Kefar Shuni (mod. Shuni): about 6 km northeast of Caesarea; aqueduct, Roman theater.

Ramat ha-Nadiv (mod. **Chorvat ʿEleq; Kh. Manṣur** el-ʿAqab):[232] a fortified village with a fortress in the center of town, about 6 km northeast of Caesarea. This probably was one of the "fortified towns" that Alexander Jannaeus built in connection with his conquest of Judea (Josephus, *A.J.* 13.422). Herod I fortified the Hasmonean fortresses further, probably also Ramat ha-Nadiv. The village was settled until A.D. 73/135 (and again after A.D. 400). The complex of buildings measured 59 by 58 m and was surrounded by a wall. Remains of the wall, tower (13.2 by 11.5 m), bath house (16.5 by 5.5 m), living quarters, storage rooms, stables, a ritual bath (*miqveh*), a rock-hewn sitz bath (for personal hygiene), wine and olive presses, threshing floor, oil lamps, pottery, coins.

Meʿarath Telimon (mod. Kh. es Suleimaniya): 12 km northeast of Caesarea, on the border of the territory of Caesarea (see *y. Demai* 22c).

Dora (Δῶρα; Dor; mod. Khirbet el-Burj):[233] an old Phoenician seaport 15 km north of Caesarea; problems with silting in the first century (Josephus, *A.J.* 15.333). Dor is mentioned in connection with the Israelite conquest as an ally of Jabin, the king of Hazor (Josh 12:23). After the fall of the northern kingdom in 732 B.C. Dor became the capital of an

---

[231]Z. Porath et al., *NEAEHL* 13:1043-46.

[232]See Y. Hirschfeld and R. Birger-Calderon, "Early Roman and Byzantine Estates near Caesarea," *IEJ* 41 (1991): 81-111; Y. Hirschfeld, *NEAEHL* 4:1257-60; idem, "The Early Roman Bath and Fortress at Ramat Hanadiv near Caesarea," in Humphrey 1995-2002, 1:28-56; Y. Hirschfeld, "Jewish Rural Settlement in Judaea in the Early Roman Period," in Alcock 1997, 72-88, esp. 74.

[233]A. Negev, *PECS* 281-82; Ephraim Stern, *ABD* 2:223-35; idem, "Dor," *NEAEHL* 1:357-68; idem, *OEANE* 2:168-70; K. Raveh and S. A. Kingsley, "Maritime Dor," *NEAEHL* 1:368-72; M. Köckert, *DNP* 3:776; Schürer 2:118-21; Hüttenmeister 1977, 105-6; Millar 1993, 267; Binder 1999, 268-69. Between 1980 and 1991 there were excavations directed by E. Stern.

Assyrian province. During the Persian period the city was controlled by Sidon. In the Hellenistic period Dor was a mighty fortress (Josephus, *A.J.* 13.223). The city was conquered by Alexander Jannaeus in the late second century B.C. Pompey granted Dor autonomy (Josephus, *A.J.* 13.334-335; 14.76). Dor was not large, but it was an important fortress due to its location. In the Hellenistic and Roman periods Dor was a Gentile city. Coins attest cults of Zeus (or Dorus), Aphrodite (Astarte) and perhaps Hermes. Literary sources attest Jewish inhabitants and a synagogue for the time of Herod Agrippa I (A.D. 41-44). Josephus reports that the Jewish population had to fight for their religious freedom (*A.J.* 19.300-311). At the site of a temple that had been dedicated to Apollo and then to Asclepius (25 by 45 m), a large church in the basilica style (14.5 by 25 m) was built toward the end of the third or the beginning of the fourth century.[234] Between A.D. 340 and 366 Acaciua built a church in Dor.[235]

> *Gaba Philippi* (mod. Tel Shosh): 27 km north of Caesarea; remains of buildings, mosaic.
>
> *Migdal Malcha:* 22 km north of Caesarea; tombs, wine presses (see *y. Demai* 22c).
>
> *Bukolonpolis* ('Atlit?): coastal town 25 km north of Caesarea; perhaps deserted in the first century (Strabo 16.2.27).
>
> *Magdiel* (mod. Khirbet Mitilya): large village 30 km north of Caesarea.
>
> *Sycamina* (mod. Shiqmona): village about 40 km north of Caesarea; remained Jewish into the seventh century (see Josephus, *A.J.* 13.332; Strabo 16.2.27).
>
> *Hefa:* village 45 km north of Caesarea, on the slopes of Mount Carmel.
>
> *Kefar 'Ako* (mod. Tell el Fukhkhar?): 2 km south of Ptolemais (see *t. Kil.* 1:12).
>
> *Ptolemais-Acco:* see §19.4.
>
> *Lochame* (mod. Lochame ha-Getaot): about 5 km north of Ptolemais; wine presses from the Hellenistic and Roman periods.
>
> *er Ras*: about 6 km north of Ptolemais; remains of settlement.
>
> *Nea Kome* (mod. Nahariya): 13 km north of Ptolemais, belonged to western Galilee; Latin inscription honoring Nero (*AE* [1948]: 142). Marble slabs of a church displaying the monogram of John, the archbishop of Tyre, dating to A.D. 555.[236]
>
> *et Tuweiri:* 4 km northeast of Nea Kome; remains of settlement.
>
> *Kabritha:* 5 km northeast of Nea Kome in western Galilee; springs for the aqueduct to Ptolemais; tombs.
>
> *Kadasa* (Tel Qedesh):[237] village between Ptolemais and Caesarea Panias, belonged to Tyre. The village was attacked in A.D. 66 by a Jewish army (Josephus, *B.J.* 4.2.3). The temenos of the temple (80 by 55 m) dates perhaps to the beginning of the second century. Greek inscriptions mention "Theos Hagios Ouranios" (the "sacred god of heaven"), probably Baalshamin, a deity worshiped in the village.

Evangelism on the Phoenician Coast

Luke reports missionary activity on the part of the Hellenistic Jewish Christians who left Jerusalem after Stephen's death and went to Antioch, leading to the conversion of many people and presumably to the establishment of local churches (Acts 11:20-21). Luke locates their evangelistic activity in Antioch. The

---

[234]See Claudine Dauphin, "From Apollo and Asclepius to Christ: Pilgrimage and Healing at the Temple and Episcopal Basilica of Dor," *SBFLA* 49 (1999): 397-430.

[235]*SEG* XXXVII 1478. See L. di Segni, in Humphrey 1995-2002, 2:166.

[236]See L. di Segni, in Humphrey 1995-2002, 2:169.

[237]Millar 1993, 293.

fact, however, that he also mentions Phoenicia and Cyprus in Acts 11:19 leads to the assumption that these Jewish Christians from Jerusalem engaged in missionary work along the entire Mediterranean coast between Caesarea and Antioch,[238] presumably mainly in towns in which Jews lived, at least in Byblos, Berytus, Dora, Ptolemais, Sidon and Tyre. The following towns and villages would have been good candidates for missionary work (listed from south to north):

Bibra (mod. Chorvat Sugar?): 6 km northeast of Nea Kome belonging to the territory of Tyre; remains of buildings, columns, mosaic pavements, cisterns (see *t. Šeb.* 4:9).

Ecdippa (mod. Achzib; ez-Zib):[239] village on the coast, about 10 km north of Acco, on the road to Tyre; an independent town during the Persian period.

Giv'at Hamudot (mod. Khirbet Chumṣin): about 3 km east of Ecdippa; Hellenistic and Roman remains.

Bezeth (mod. el Bassa): Jewish village about 4 km northeast of Ecdippa; belonged to the territory of Tyre (see *t. Šeb.* 4:9).

Mazi: Jewish village on the coast, 22 km south of Tyre, to whose territory it belonged.

Tyre (Τύρος; mod. Soûr):[240] already attested in the thirteenth century B.C., Tyre was the most important town on the southern Phoenician coast. The city was situated 45 km north of Acco and 40 km south of Sidon on a peninsula, with some living quarters on the mainland. The city had two harbors. Tyre came under Seleucid control in 200 B.C. and received autonomy in 126 B.C., which it managed to maintain after 63 B.C. as the result of a treaty with Rome. Strabo (16.2.22) and Pliny (*Nat.* 5.17.76-77) describe the city extensively. Tyre owed its wealth to crafts, purple production and trade. The city goddess was Melqart/Heracles. The games that were organized every five years were renowned (2 Macc 4:18-20). The population of Tyre participated repeatedly in anti-Jewish actions (1 Macc 5:15). Herod I built colonnade halls and an agora in Tyre (Josephus, *B.J.* 1.422). There was a Jewish colony in Tyre (*CIJ* II 879, 880, 991 = *IJudO* III Syr1-2, 5). Ulpianus (ca. A.D. 200), the most famous Roman jurist of the classical period, came from Tyre. Septimius Severus (A.D. 193-211) made Tyre a Roman colony (Septimia Turus Metropolis Colonia) and the capital of the province Syria Phoenice. In A.D. 254 Origen was buried in Tyre. The bishop Zenon represented Tyre at the Council of Nicea in A.D. 325.

Sarepta (Makra Kome; mod. Sarafend):[241] an old Phoenician coastal town 22 km north of Tyre; mentioned already in thirteenth century Egyptian sources, described by Sennach-

---

[238]See Hengel and Schwemer (1998, 148 [ET, 87]), who do not mention any towns that this missionary work could have reached.

[239]See A. Negev, *PECS* 292. Mentioned by Josephus, *B.J.* 1.257; *A.J.* 5.85; 14.343; *m. Šeb.* 6:1; *t. Ter.* 2:12; Pliny *Nat.* 5.17.75; Ptolemaios 5.15.5.

[240]See W. Röllig, *KP* 5:1027-29; D. J. Wiseman, *IBD* 3:1603-5; W. L. MacDonald, *PECS* 944; William A. Ward, *OEANE* 5:247-50; A. H. M. Jones et al., *OCD* 1568; Schürer 1:308; 2:44, 123; 3:14-15; Millar 1993, 118, 123-24, 264-66, 287-95; H. Jacob Katzenstein, *The History of Tyre, From the Beginning of the Second Millenium B.C.E. until the Fall of the Neo-Babylonian Empire in 538 B.C.E.* (Jerusalem: Schocken, 1973); Patricia M. Bikai, William J. Fulco, and Jeannie Marchand, *Tyre: The Shrine of Apollo* (Amman, Jordan, 1996).

[241]See Ray L. Roth, "Zarephath," *ABD* 6:1041. Excavations: J. B. Pritchard, *Recovering Sarepta, a Phoenician City: Excavations at Sarafand, Lebanon, 1969-1974, by the University Museum of the University of Pennsylvania* (Princeton, N.J.: Princeton University Press, 1978); R. B. Koehl et al., *Sarepta* (4 vols.; Publications de l'Université libanaise, section des études archéologiques 2; Beirut: Université libanaise, 1985-1988).

erib as a town with city walls (*ANET* 287). In the seventh century Sarepta came under the control of Tyre. In 1 Kings 17 Sarepta is mentioned as the town in which the prophet Elijah lived during a famine in Israel and where he restored to life the son of the widow in whose house he stayed. The prophet Obadiah described Sarepta as a village at the northern border of restored Israel (Obad 20). The town was a traditional center for the manufacture and trade of pottery and textiles; wheat, olive oil, wine and the purple dye that gave both Phoenicia and Sarepta their names were exported. Remains from Roman harbor facilities are preserved. A temple dedicated to the goddess Tanit stood on a hill overlooking the harbor.

Sidon (Σιδών; Σειδών; mod. Saïda):[242] 37 km north of Tyre, was an ancient seaport that owed its wealth to its glass and purple industry and to the significance of its harbor. The existence of close ties with Athens is seen in the temple of Eshmun/Asclepius (Alsos Asklepiou; mod. Bostan esh-Shaikh [see Strabo, 16.2.2]), situated 4 km north of the city. Unfortunately, the sources provide little information about local traditions and cults. The city was under Seleucid rule before achieving autonomy in 111 B.C. Herod I had several buildings erected in Sidon. An inscription attests an *archisynagōgos* in Sidon (*CIJ* II 991 = *IJudO* III Syr5). The philosophers Boethos and Diodotos as well as the Epicurean Zenon came from Sidon. According to Josephus (*A.J.* 18.6.3), the territory of Sidon bordered on the territory of Damascus; that is, it extended east across the Leontes River and the southern end of the Bekaa Valley, perhaps as far as Mount Hermon. Many of the numerous rural temples in the Lebanon Mountains (Lebanon and Anti-Lebanon) presumably belonged to the territory controlled by Sidon—for example, the temples of Kasr Nimrud and Der el Ashair.[243] The superior architecture of these temples, the complex administrative structures that can be partly reconstructed, and the use of the Greek language (for inscriptions) attest the vitality and independence of life in the villages.[244] Between A.D. 14 and 37 there were border disputes with Damascus (Josephus, *A.J.* 18.6.3). The bishop Theodoros from Sidon attended the Council of Nicea in the fourth century.

Berytus (Βηρυτός; mod. Beirut):[245] an important harbor in Phoenician times; known during the Seleucid period as *Laodikeia en tē Phoinikē*. Berytus was the only colony that Augustus founded in the East (in 15 B.C., as Colonia Iulia Augusta Felix Berytus [Pliny, *Nat.* 5.17.78]). Berytus represented in the region the strongest influence of Roman-Latin culture and thus was described as an "island of Romanization."[246] At least two of Rome's senators came from Berytus. The territory of the city extended as far as the sources of the Orontes River in the Bekaa Valley. Marcus Agrippa stationed veterans of two legions in Berytus

---

[242]See W. Röllig, *KP* 5:175-76; D. J. Wiseman, *IBD* 3:1449-50; K. Günther, *GBL* 3:1437-38; J.-P. Rey-Coquais, *PECS* 837; Issam Ali Khalifeh, *OEANE* 5:38-41; A. H. M. Jones and J.-F. Salles, *OCD* 1404; Schürer 1:308; 2:91, 103, 123; 3:14-15, 88-89; Millar 1993, 285-88, 310-11; Josette Elayi, *Sidon, cité autonome de l'Empire perse* (Paris: Idéaphane, 1989).

[243]On Kasr Nimrud see Daniel Krencker and Willy Zschietzschmann, *Römische Tempel in Syrien* (2 vols.; Denkmäler antiker Architektur 5; Berlin: de Gruyter, 1938), 178-81, 275 (dating to the first century A.D.); on Deir el Ashair see ibid., 256-64; the large temple measured 25 by 40 m.

[244]Millar 1993, 287.

[245]H. Treidler, *KP* 1:872; J.-P. Rey-Coquais, *PECS* 152; A. H. J. Jones et al., *OCD* 240; T. Leisten, *DNP* 2:584; Schürer 1:308, 323-24, 451; 2:47, 91, 96; Millar 1996, 36, 279-81, 527-28; Isaac 1993, 60-61, 318-21, 342-43; Tracey 1994, 239-43; Ball 2000, 173-74; D. Jacobson 2001, esp. 23. Excavations: René Mouterde and Jean Laufray, *Beyrouth, ville romaine: Histoire et monuments* (Beirut: Publications de la Direction des antiquités du Liban, 1952).

[246]MacMullen 2000, 13.

(Strabo 16.2.19). Herod I visited Berytus in 7/6 B.C. and erected colonnaded halls, temples and a forum. His grandson Agrippa I built an expensive theater, an amphitheater, baths and further stoas. During the games that celebrated the inauguration of the amphitheater, 1,400 prisoners died in gladiator fights (Josephus, *A.J.* 19.335-337). Agrippa II restored a building erected by Herod I, placed statues in the city and financed games and the free distribution of wheat and olive oil (*A.J.* 20.211). Inscriptions attest Jewish citizens (*CIJ* II 869-872 = *IJudO* III Syr28-31). As a *colonia*, Berytus was governed by the traditional Roman administration with city council and magistrates. The influence of Roman culture can be seen in the use of the Latin language. Valerius Probus, the most significant Latin grammarian in the first century A.D., was able to read older Latin texts in Berytus that were no longer read in Rome (Suetonius, *Gramm.* 24). After the destruction of Jerusalem in A.D. 70 Titus paraded his Jewish prisoners in the city (Josephus, *B.J.* 7.20.36-40, 96). There was an academy for legal scholars in Berytus since the mid-second century with an archive, which attracted students from all regions of the eastern Mediterranean. The bishop Gregorius from Berytus attended the Council of Nicea. David Parker suggested in a study of Codex Bezae, a biblical manuscript, that this important witness for the so-called Western Text was written about A.D. 400 in Berytus.[247] Berytus was destroyed in the earthquake of A.D. 551.

Byblos (Βύβλος; mod. Jbaïl):[248] 38 km north of Berytus, was also an old Phoenician seaport that owed its wealth to trade, in this case particularly to the export of wood. Byblos had early contacts with Egypt, Crete, Greece and Mesopotamia. The city lost some of its influence during the Hellenistic period. Herod I erected buildings in Byblos, as he did in other Phoenician cities. The main god of Byblos was the cult of Baalshamin; in the Hellenistic period particularly Cronos was worshiped. In the Roman period Byblos was dedicated to the god Adonis (ἱερά ἐστι τοῦ ᾿Αδώνιδος [Strabo 16.2.18]), but Zeus, Aphrodite and other deities were worshiped as well. West of the city, high in the Lebanon Mountains, was a sanctuary dedicated to Aphrodite; the sacred prostitution that was practiced there prompted Constantine in the fourth century to have the temple destroyed. In Byblos remains of a colonnaded street, the theater, a nymphaeum, a temple and the city walls can still be seen. Greek funerary inscriptions from Byblos (*IJudO* III Syr28-31) and Beth Shearim confirm Jewish citizens in Byblos (*IJudO* III Syr32).

Botrys (mod. Batrun):[249] an old Phoenician port, was involved in 218 B.C. in the struggle of the Seleucid king Antiochos III against Egypt (Polybius 5.68). Botrys was part of the Roman road system and is mentioned by Josephus and Pliny (Josephus, *A.J.* 8.13.2; Pliny, *Nat.* 5.17.78).

Trieres (mod. el Heri): 10 km north of Botrys, north of Cape Lithoprosopon (mod. Ras Shaqqa); attested in the Hellenistic and Roman periods.

Kalamos (mod. Qara): 13 km north of Trieres, attested in the Hellenistic (Polybius 5.68.8) and Roman periods.

Tripolis (Τρίπολις; mod. el-Mîna):[250] a seaport about 65 km north of Berytus. Accord-

---

[247]Parker 1992, 269-78; for the critique of L. Holtz and J. Irigoin see Parker, "The Palaeographical Debate," in *Codex Bezae: Studies from the Lunel Colloquium, June 1994* (ed. D. C. Parker and C.-B. Amphoux; NTTS 22; Leiden: Brill, 1996), 329-36, esp. 332-34.

[248]H. Treidler, *KP* 1:977-78; J.-P. Rey-Coquais, *PECS* 176; J. Boardman and J.-F. Salles, *OCD* 266; U. Finkbeiner, *DNP* 2:864-65; Schürer 1:308; 3:14-15; Teixidor 1977, 46-48; Millar 1996, 274-78; Ball 2000, 172-73; Brigitte Servais-Soyez, *Byblos et la fête des Adonies* (Leiden: Brill, 1977). Excavations: Maurice Dunand, *Fouilles des Byblos* (Paris: Geuthner/Maisonneuve, 1939-1982).

[249]See H. Treidler, *KP* 1:936; H. Klengel, *DNP* 2:757.

[250]W. Röllig, *KP* 5:964; Schürer 1:308; J.-P. Rey-Coquais, *PECS* 935; A. H. M. Jones et al., *OCD* 1552-53.

ing to Diodoros and Strabo, Tripolis was founded by the Phoenician cities Arados, Sidon and Tyre and had, as a result of this history, three quarters. Pompey liberated the city in 64 B.C. from a tyrant. Herod I erected buildings in Tripolis as well. The presence of Jews among the population has not been confirmed as of yet. Coins show that Tripolis was the capital of a Roman *conventus*. In the third century the city had an imperial temple. In A.D. 325 the bishop Hellanikos from Tripolis attended the Council of Nicea.

Orthosia (mod. Khan ard Artusi):[251] a coastal town 17 km north of Tripolis. The city received its name from the goddess Artemis Orthosia; the coins of the city depict Astarte. The autonomous city was an important center on the Syrian coast from the Hellenistic period far into the Middle Ages.

Arka (Arkea; Caesarea ad Libanum; mod. Arqa):[252] about 30 km northeast of Tripolis on the northern slopes of the Lebanon Mountains; mentioned in Gen 10:17; during the Seleucid period also known as *Herakleia en Phoinikē*. In the first century Arka belonged, at times, to the territory controlled by Agrippa II (Josephus, *B.J.* 7.5.1). Remains date as far back as the Bronze Age. It is not known whether Jews lived in the city. Emperor Severus Alexander came from Arka (*IJudO* III Syr33).

Arados (mod. Arwad; Rouad):[253] an old town in northern Phoenicia, situated on an island, mentioned in Gen 10:18 and Ezek 27:8, 11. Arados boasted of famous seafarers and warriors. In the Phoenician period Arados controlled Antarados, Gabala, Marathus (Amrith) and Simyra. The city was the capital of a kingdom. King Gerostratus surrendered to Alexander the Great (Arrian, *Anab.* 2.13.8); it preserved its autonomy during the Seleucid period. Strabo (16.2.13) reports that the city had multistoried houses. An important sanctuary of Melqart/Heracles was in the territory of the city. The ancient sources attest a large agora that was lined by colonnaded halls. About 30 km west of the city, on Jebel Ansariyeh (1,000 m high), in the village Baetokaeke, there was a large temple of Zeus since the third century B.C., with a huge temenos (135 by 85 m). The letter that the Roman senate wrote in 139/138 B.C. to the kings and countries in the east instructing "that they should not seek their [the Jews'] harm or make war against them and their cities and their country, or make alliance with those who war against them" (1 Macc 15:19) was also sent to Arados (1 Macc 15:23). This brief notice is not sufficient grounds for assuming the existence of a Jewish community in Arados. In the first century the significance of Arados was diminished. Inscriptions and coins confirm cults of Zeus (Cronos), Poseidon and Astarte.

Balaneae (Claudia Leucas; mod. Baniyas):[254] situated at the southern end of a fertile plain; a less important town that, however, occasionally minted its own coins. An inscription attests offices typical for a large city: a man is honored who had occupied the offices of *stratēgos, agoranomos, dekaprōtos* and *archōn,* who had accompanied an embassy to the emperor and who had financed the distribution of wheat in the city. Coins seem to indicate a special interest on the part of Emperor Claudius for Balaneae. For the fourth century the bishop Euphration from Balaneae is attested.

---

[251]E. Honigman, "Orthosia 3," PW 18.2 (1942): 1494-95; C. Colpe, "Orthosia 2," *KP* 4:366; A. Plontke-Lüning, "Orthosia 2," *DNP* 9:78.

[252]Jones 1937, 281-82; Schürer 1:478; Millar 1996, 91, 304.

[253]H. Treidler, *KP* 1:486-87; M. Köckert, "Arados 1," *DNP* 1:951; Schürer 3:4; Teixidor 1977, 48-52; J.-P. Rey-Coquais, *PECS* 82; idem, *Arados et sa pérée aux époques grecque, romaine et byzantine* (Paris: Geuthner, 1974); idem 1989, 47, 50-51; M. Sartre, in Dentzer and Orthmann 1989, 39; Millar 1993, 239, 270-73; Ball 2000, 171-72.

[254]See Rey-Coquais 1989, 49, 52; Grainger 1990, 101, 117, 131; Millar 1993, 240, 260.

Paltos (mod. Arab al Moulk):[255] a coastal town 10 km north of Balaneae, situated in the same fertile plain.

Gabala (mod. Jableh; Jebele):[256] an old Phoenician port north of Paltos; belonged to Arados. The city gained autonomy in the first century B.C., attested by the coins of the city. The *cavea* of the theater was 90 m in diameter. Pausanias mentions a temple of Nereid; coins attest the worship of Zeus, Aphrodite/Astarte and Helios. The bishop Zoilos from Gabala attended the Council of Nicea. Bishop Severianus led the church in the early fifth century (Socrates, *Hist. eccl.* 6.11.3).

Laodikeia (Λαοδίκεια; Laodiceia ad Mare; mod. Latakia):[257] about 20 km north of Gabala and 60 km south of the mouth of the Orontes River, originally a Phoenician town (Ramitha), is described by Strabo (16.2.9) as a beautiful city that has a good (artificial) harbor, situated in a fertile region. In the mountains (Jebel Ansariyeh) east of the city wine was cultivated that was exported to Alexandria in Egypt and to other towns of the Mediterranean world. The old Phoenician city was reestablished by Seleukos I Nikator and renamed in honor of his mother, Laodike. During the Seleucid period Laodikeia was hardly inferior to Antioch; the two cities were linked with a road across the northern Bargylos Mountains.[258] The magistrates of the city were called *peliganes*. Laodikeia was able to preserve its autonomy after the Roman province of Syria was established (Pliny, *Nat.* 5.18.79). The city minted its own coins at times and controlled a large territory with numerous villages. Laodikeia became a *metropolis* in A.D. 194 and was made a colony with the *ius Italicum* in 198. Seleukos I built a temple for Zeus Bottiaios. Strabo reports (16.2.5) that Zeus of Antioch was worshiped on Mount Kasios (mod. Jebel al Akra, 65 km southwest of Antioch, at 1,728 m the highest mountain in northern Syria; Mount Kasios falls steeply into the Mediterranean south of the Orontes River);[259] this cult was the ancient cult of Baal Saphon (Baalshamin).[260] The city had a temple of Sarapis and Isis, built by Egyptians. The huge theater (the *cavea* was 39 m in diameter) could compare with any of the theaters of Rome or southern France. Syrian traders from Laodikeia are attested in Rhodos and Delos as well as in Brundisium and Lugdunum (Lyon).[261] A road from Laodikeia in a northeasterly direction ran across Mount Kasios to Seleukeia. The bishop Theodotos from Laodikeia attended the Council of Nicea.

---

[255]Grainger 1990, 101, 117, 145.

[256]J.-P. Rey-Coquais, *PECS* 340; Jones 1937, 232, 252, 261; Teixidor 1977, 49; E. Frézouls, in Dentzer and Orthmann 1989, 389-90; Grainger 1990, 101, 117, 129, 145-46, 166, 183.

[257]H. Treidler, "Laodikeia 1," *KP* 3:482-83; J. Gippert, "Laodikeia 1," *DNP* 6:1131-31; Rey-Coquais 1989, 47, 51; idem, *PECS* 482; J. Teixidor, in Dentzer and Orthmann 1989, 91-92; G. Bowersock, in ibid., 75-77; E. Frézouls, in ibid., 388-89; Will 1989, 228-29; Grainger 1990, 48-50, 71-72, 127-28, 152-53, 166-69, 171-76, 199; Millar 1993, 123, 239-40, 258-59; Ball 2000, 157-58.

[258]Grainger 1990, 105.

[259]The temple of Zeus on Mount Kasios possibly was located at the site of the Church of St. Barlaam on the eastern peak (1,316 m). Barlaam (Bar-laha or bar Aloho; Gk., Theoteknos), who lived in the fourth century and performed miracles, is said to have destroyed the statue of Zeus on Mount Kasios. See Wachtang Djobadze, *Archeological Investigations in the Region West of Antioch on-the-Orontes* (Stuttgart: Steiner, 1986), 4-5; for a description of the monastery see ibid., 7-54.

[260]Teixidor 1977, 32-34; for the information that the later emperors Hadrian and Julian offered sacrifices at sunrise on Mount Kasios (Ammianus Marcellinus 22.14.4) see ibid.

[261]C. P. Jones, "A Syrian in Lyons," *AJP* 99 (1978): 336-353. On this inscription see §16.5 in the present work.

Seleukeia (Σελεύκεια; Seleukia Piera; mod. Suweydiyah):[262] founded around 300 B.C. by Seleukos I Nikator, about 10 km north of the mouth of the river Orontes, on the southwestern slopes of Mount Koryphaios (mod. Musa Dağ), a ridge of the Amanos Mountains. The old name of the city was Hydatos Potamoi (Strabo 16.2.8). The city was surrounded by a wall 12 km in length, extending as far as the acropolis that was situated on a hill about 4 km inland. The quarter closest to the harbor was called *emporion* (Polybius 5.58.3-11). Seleukeia was one of the most important seaports on the Syrian coast, with an artificial inner and outer harbor: as Alexandria was the most important port of the Ptolemaic Empire, Seleukeia was the most important seaport for the Seleucid kings. Polybius knows that in 219 B.C. about six thousand free citizens lived in the city (5.61.1); this number would have been higher in later periods.[263] Seleukos I was buried in the city; the temple built on this occasion was called Nikatoreion. The large Doric temple (37 by 19 m) dominated the city. Pompey granted Seleukeia autonomy. The city remained an important naval base for the imperial fleet. The tunnel (1,300 m long) that Vespasian's soldiers dug to divert a brook was meant to prevent the silting of the harbor. Polybius (5.59-61) describes suburbs, the downtown business center, temple and public buildings. Coins mention Zeus Kasios. When Paul traveled from Antioch to Cyprus in A.D. 45, he sailed from Seleukeia (Acts 13:4). In the fourth century the bishop Zenobios was active in Seleukeia.

22.5 Missionary Work in Syria and on Cyprus

The Hellenistic Jewish Christians from Jerusalem brought the gospel of Jesus to Syria, at least to Damascus (Acts 9:2, 10, 19 [see §20.5]) and to Antioch (11:20-21).

Syria (Συρία)[264] extended from the Mediterranean coast between Tyre in the south and Antioch in the north westward across the mountain chains of Lebanon and Anti-Lebanon and into the northern regions of the Syrian desert as far as the Euphrates River. The northern part of this area became a Roman province in 64 B.C. after Pompey's victory over the Seleucid kingdom. The province was enlarged in subsequent years in the east and southeast by the annexation of several client states, such as Commagene and Palmyra (under Tiberius). Several Roman legions were stationed in Syria in the first century A.D.: Legiones III Gallica, III Scythica, VI Ferrata, X Fretensis and XII Fulminata.[265] By this time the ethnica had only historical significance; that is, they provide no information about the geographical origins of the soldiers. The sources mention several bases in which these legions were stationed: near Laodikeia (perhaps in Apamea), Kyrrhos, Raphaneai and perhaps in Zeugma. A Roman legionary earned 225 denarii per year[266] and was (at times) given sub-

---

[262]W. Röllig, "Seleukeia 2," *KP* 5:85; J.-P. Rey-Coquais, *PECS* 822; A. H. M. Jones et al., *OCD* 1380; J. Teixidor in Dentzer and Orthmann 1989, 83; Will 1989, 228-29; Grainger 1990, 48-49, 56-58, 68-71, 122-23, 152, 159-61, 198-99; Millar 1993, 87-88, 103-4, 257-58; Ball 2000, 156-57; Pollard 2000, 56-60, 279-83; Hölbl 2001, 51.

[263]Grainger 1990, 95-97.

[264]See E. Honigmann, PW 4.A2 (1932): 1549-1727; W. Röllig, *KP* 5:469-73; A. H. M. Jones et al., *OCD* 1464-65; Millar 1993; John D. Grainger, *The Cities of Seleucid Syria* (Oxford: Clarendon, 1990); Feldtkeller 1994; idem, "Syrien II. Zeit des Neuen Testaments," *TRE* 32 (2001) 587-89. On the roads in Syria see Thomas Bauzou, in Dentzer and Orthmann 1989, 204-22; Pollard 2000.

[265]Josephus, *A.J.* 17.286; *B.J.* 2.40; Tacitus, *Ann.* 4.5. See Pollard 2000, 22; A. Comfort, "Legio III Scythica," *ZPE* 138 (2002): 275-76.

[266]Pollard 2000, 179. M. A. Speidel ("Roman Army Pay Scales," *JRS* 83 [1992]: 87-106) suggests 300 denarii. Cf. Tacitus, *Ann.* 1.17; Suetonius, *Dom.* 7.3.

stantial financial compensation upon retirement (under Augustus, 3,000 denarii). The soldier of an auxiliary division earned five-sixths of the yearly wages of a legionary.

The largest cities of the central regions of the Seleucid Empire included Seleukeia, Laodikeia, Antioch and Apamea, all founded by Seleukos Nikator (358-281 B.C.); it appears that there had been no larger cities in this area during the Persian period. The old city of Damascus, located south of the mountains of Anti-Lebanon (2,700 m), was isolated from central Syria. According to Ptolemaios (5.7.1), the border between Cilicia and Syria ran along the Kilikiai Pylai; the towns of Platanoi and Alexandreia kat'Isson north of Antioch still belonged to Syria.[267] In the south both Ptolemais-Acco and Dora on the Mediterranean coast belonged to the province of Syria. In the east at least some of the cities of the Decapolis belonged to Syria. The Roman census conducted in A.D. 6 in Apamea provides general clues concerning the density of the population: the figure of 117,000 inhabitants, which possibly includes only the men, suggests that several hundred thousand inhabitants lived in the city of Apamea and in the villages that belonged to the territory of the city.[268] Similar figures can be assumed for Damascus, Gadara and Palmyra and the territories controlled by these cities.[269] The numerous villages that existed in Syria have left hardly any traces. The many temples in the mountains of Hermon, Lebanon and Anti-Lebanon suggest high population densities for the mountainous regions as well. Fifteen temples are attested for the Mount Lebanon and the northern Bekaa Valley, eleven temples in Anti-Lebanon and in the southern Bekaa Valley, and eight temples on Mount Hermon. One of the largest temples in the Mount Hermon region, a building 40 m long, was located in Hine, about 38 km southwest of Damascus.[270] The inhabitants of northern Syria, the central region of the Roman province of Syria, spoke Greek. It is unclear whether the inhabitants of the villages in the rural areas or in the steppe spoke a Semitic language, as no inscription or coin has survived from pre-Constantinian times that uses "Syrian."[271] In eastern Syria (Edessa, Palmyra) people spoke both Greek and Aramaic dialects, in southwestern Syria people spoke Phoenician and Aramaic, and in southeastern Syria people spoke Aramaic and Nabatean. The main crops in many areas were olives and wine, cultivated not only for local consumption but also for export. Other agricultural products included nuts, plums, dates and onions. Main industries included textile weaving (linen and wool), particularly in Laodikeia and in the cities along the Phoenician coast, with Damascus being famous for its wool weavers, as well as purple dyeing (Mediterranean coast) and glass blowing (Sidon).[272]

Evangelism in Antioch

The origins of Jewish-Christian missionary activity in Antioch perhaps date back

---

[267]Hierocles (795.6-7) includes Alexandreia and Rhosos in Cilicia, which reflects the situation after A.D. 72. See Hild and Hellenkemper 1990, 17.

[268]See Millar 1993, 250.

[269]See Tracey 1994, 230.

[270]Daniel Krencker and Willy Zschietzschmann (*Römische Tempel in Syrien* [2 vols.; Berlin and Leipzig: de Gruyter, 1938], 256) conclude with regard to the temple in Deir el Ashair on Mount Hermon, "The remains that have been preserved indicate that this would have been no insignificant place. The ruins of the building, originally planned as a peripteros, make a truly great and huge impression. The structures that are preserved to the southeast of the building were very extensive."

[271]See Millar 1993, 233-34, 241-42.

[272]See E. M. Stern, "Roman Glassblowing in a Cultural Context," *AJA* 103 (1999): 441-84.

to A.D. 31/32, when Hellenistic Jewish Christians left Jerusalem after the death of Stephen in the context of the subsequent persecution, some of whom reached Antioch.[273] Antioch (see fig. 16) was the capital of the province of Syria, and it was the third largest city of the Roman Empire after Rome and Alexandria.

Antioch (Ἀντιόχεια; mod. Hatay; Antakya)[274] was founded by Seleukos I Nikator (311-281 B.C.), a general of Alexander the Great, in honor of his father, Antiochos, around 300 B.C. on the south banks of the navigable Orontes River (mod. Nahr el-Asi), which divided at this site into two branches forming an island, at the foot of Mount Silpius, about 24 km from the Mediterranean. His successor, Seleukos II, integrated the island into the city, and Antiochos IV Epiphanes expanded the city further by adding the quarter Epiphania; Cossutius, his Roman architect, built not only aqueducts but also a temple of Zeus. Pompey annexed the city in 64 B.C. and proclaimed it the capital of the newly established province of Syria. Antioch thus was the seat of the Roman proconsul of the province. The *libertas* that Pompey granted to Antioch included the right to mint its own bronze coins, the right of having its own constitution (which corresponded to the traditional "democratic" model of Hellenistic *poleis*), and exemption from paying tribute.[275] Early building activities after 64 B.C. included the circus (hippodrome), a palace for the Roman governor on the Orontes island, and a bouleuterion for the city council. Caesar spent some time in Antioch in 47 B.C.; it appears that he wanted to be regarded as the new founder (*ktistēs*) of the city. Antioch used the Caesarean era (beginning on October 1 in 49 B.C.) until the Arabian conquest. Caesar initiated the building of a new theater, an amphitheater, baths, an aqueduct and a Kaisareion dedicated to the veneration of the emperor with the cult of Divus Iulius (located near the temple of Ares). It appears that during the reign of Augustus only baths and another theater were built, although one of the city quarters was named after his architect (*geitnia Agrippiton*). Major building activities took place during the principate of Tiberius, who also was remembered as *ktistēs*. Tiberius rebuilt the quarter called Epiphania, which had been destroyed in the fire of A.D. 23/24, surrounding it with a city wall. He restored (or completed) the temple of Zeus and built a temple of Dionysos. German-

---

[273]I use the traditional English spelling for Antioch on the Orontes River, the Syrian capital, while using the Greek form Antiocheia for Pisidian Antioch, the Roman colony in southern Galatia.

[274]I. Benzinger, "Antiocheia 1," *PW* 2 (1894): 2442-45; J. Kollwitz, *RAC* 1:461-69; H. Treidler, "Antiocheia 1," *KP* 1:386; J. Lassus, *PECS* 61-63; F. W. Norris, "Antiochien I. Neutestamentlich," *TRE* 3 (1978): 99-103; F. W. Norris, "Antioch," *ABD* 1:265-69; A. H. M. Jones, "Antioch 1," *OCD* 107; Georges Tate, "Antioch on Orontes," *OEANE* 1:144-45; A.-M. Wittke, "Antiocheia 1," *DNP* 1:762-63; D. J. Williams, *DLNTD* 53-55; L. M. McDonald, "Antioch (Syria)," *DNTB* 34-37; Magie 1950, 1:296-97, 368, 468, 498; Downey 1961; J. H. W. G. Liebeschuetz, *Antioch: City and Imperial Administration in the Later Roman Empire* (Oxford: Oxford University Press, 1972); Schürer 1:308; 2:45, 47; 3:13, 121, 126-27, 141; Lassus 1978; Fatih Cimok, *Antioch on the Orontes* (Istanbul: Turizm Yayinlari, 1980 [1994]); M. Sartre, in Dentzer and Orthmann 1989, 35; Rey-Coquais 1989, 51; Canivet 1989, 118-21; Will 1989, 228-29, 232-32; Grainger 1990; Norris 1990; Longenecker, *Gal,* 65-71; Millar 1993, 159-60; Tracey 1994, 236-39; Kolb 1996; Hengel and Schwemer 1998, 274-99, 404-23 (ET, 178-204, 268-79); Schwemer 1998, 162-66; Ball 2000, 150-56, and passim; Kondoleon 2000; Pollard 2000, 30, 60, 245-46, 277-79. Excavations: G. W. Elderkin, R. Stillwell and W. A. Campbell, *Antioch on-the-Orontes: The Excavations* (5 vols.; Princeton, N.J.: Princeton University Press, 1932-1972).

[275]Kolb 1996, 106.

icus, Tiberius's son, visited Antioch in the context of the planned annexation of Commagene and Amanus; when he died in Antioch on October 10 in A.D. 19, he was buried in a monumental tomb on the forum. Tiberius built a gate on the northeastern end of the large colonnaded street, decorated with the statue of the Roman She Wolf with Romulus and Remus (Antioch officially became a Roman colony only at the beginning of the third century). Herod I visited Antioch several times; he financed the expansion of the main street of the city (3 km long) to 16 m in width; Tiberius added colonnaded halls (with 3,200 columns of polished marble), which widened the main artery of the city to 30-40 m.[276] The center of the city (*omphalos*), where the colonnaded street crossed the Parmenios River, was marked by a plazalike expansion with a nymphaeum and a column with a bronze statue of Tiberius. The earthquake of A.D. 37 caused considerable damage in the city;[277] reconstruction efforts are reported for the principates of Caligula and Claudius. A fire in A.D. 70 destroyed the old agora, the city archives and the basilicas. The Flavian emperors contributed to the reconstruction. Vespasian and Titus donated objects that they had taken from Jerusalem to the city; for example, they erected bronze statues of the cherubim from the Jerusalem temple along the street to Daphne, close to or even inside the Jewish quarter. The building inscription dating to A.D. 73/74 that was erected on the occasion of the digging of a canal between Antioch and a lake 7 km to the north (and perhaps on the occasion of the cutting through of the canal between Antioch and Seleukeia Piera mentioned by Pausanias)[278] provides information not only about forced labor (rarely attested outside of Egypt) but also about the infrastructure of the city: Antioch consisted of 1,100 city blocks measuring on average 126 by 56 m. Most of the city blocks were named after specific persons, and some were named after deities—for example, one block was named after Zeus Soter, suggesting that a sanctuary dedicated to this deity was located in this area. Other city blocks were named after associations—for example, the Stephanites (victorious athletes and musicians) or the Keraunistes (devotees of Zeus Keraunios). The Roman army in the eastern Mediterranean was stationed in Antioch, but the city was militarized only during the wars against the Parthians and Persians during the second and third centuries.[279]

As a result of earthquakes and fires that seriously damaged Antioch, particularly in the sixth century, and due to the continuous occupation of the site, hardly any inscriptions of the early Roman period survive. Frank Kolb compares the available inscriptional evidence of Antioch with that of a North African village. The numerous coins inform mostly about the pagan cults of the city. The available knowledge about Antioch derives from literary sources: Strabo 16.2.4-7; Ptolemaios 5.14.12; Pliny, *Nat.* 5.18.79; Josephus, *B.J.* 7.43-62, 110-111; the world history written in the sixth century by Malalas, a citizen of Antioch, includes a survey of the history of Antioch that seems to have been composed on the basis of local city chronicles, but the information often is unreliable.[280] Gladiator and animal fights in the amphitheater are attested since the mid-second cen-

---

[276]Malalas (232.1-235.7) probably is more reliable than Josephus, who states that Herod I built the colonnaded halls (*B.J.* 1.425; *A.J.* 16.148). See Kolb 1996, 111. On the visits of Herod I in 38, 20, 15 and 10 B.C. see D. Jacobson 2001, 23.

[277]See D. H. K. Amiran et al., "Earthquakes in Israel and Adjacent Areas: Macroseismic Observations since 100 B.C.E.," *IEJ* 44 (1994): 260-305, esp. 287.

[278]*SEG* XXXV 1985 1483; Pausanias 8.29.3. See D. Feissel, "Deux listes de quartiers d'Antioche astreints au creusement d'un canal (73-74 J.C.)," *Syria* 62 (1985): 77-103; Kolb 1996, 113-15.

[279]See Isaac 1993, 270-77, 436-38.

[280]Alexander Schenk von Stauffenberg, *Die römische Kaisergeschichte bei Malalas: Griechischer Text der Bücher 9-12 und Untersuchungen* (Stuttgart: Kohlhammer, 1931).

tury B.C. Literary evidence reports a museion, including a library and a theater, for 100 B.C.[281] Since A.D. 43/44 Olympieia were regularly organized, with athletic contests, drama and chariot races in the circus. Daphne, a suburb south of Antioch, boasted luxurious villas (the mosaics that have survived can be viewed in the archaeological museum of Antakyas), waterfalls, a theater, a stadium and several temples, including a temple of Apollo. The inhabitants of Antioch worshiped Zeus Bottiaios, Zeus Olympios, Apollo, Poseidon, the city goddess Tyche, Artemis, Aphrodite, Ares, Athene, Dionysos and Hermes. The worship of Syrian deities has not been confirmed so far, possibly because the sources for Antioch are scarce, although it may indicate that the Syrian element was less visible in Greco-Roman Antioch.[282] In regard to archaeological remains, only a section of an aqueduct and remains of the circus and of the city wall have been discovered. It therefore is difficult to paint an accurate picture of Antioch in the first century, unless one is prepared to risk the danger of reading conditions of late antiquity back into Antioch during the early imperial period.[283]

Antioch, capital of the province of Syria, was the third largest city of the Roman Empire after Rome and Alexandria (see Josephus, *B.J.* 3.29; Libanius, *Orationes* 20), although there is the possibility that Seleukeia on the Tigris River was larger. The estimates for the population of Antioch in the first century differ widely. According to Strabo, Antioch was hardly smaller than Seleukeia on the Tigris or Alexandria. Diodoros reports that Alexandria had 300,000 inhabitants (excluding resident aliens and slaves?), and according to Pliny, Seleukeia on the Tigris had 600,000 inhabitants.[284] Many scholars suggest 250,000 inhabitants for Antioch.[285] The city certainly owed its wealth to its location on the road from Asia Minor into the East; the production of wine and olive oil also played a major role. However, there are no primary sources that confirm an extensive transit trade. Cicero praised Antioch for its culture (*Arch.* 4), but this comment may be hyperbole due to its literary context. In regard to cultural life in Antioch, Christian and pagan authors after A.D. 180 provide more reliable information, indicating, according to Frank Kolb, "that Greek philosophical and rhetorical traditions were alive in Antioch during the first and second century A.D., although the city is not particularly praised for these traditions. On the contrary . . . Apollonios [of Tyana] criticized the Antiochenes publicly, apparently for their decline into barbarism; he believed that their cultural and intellectual life did not correspond to the standards of other larger urban centers in the eastern Mediterranean world."[286]

It is unclear whether the inhabitants always were of mixed origin. The Syrian quarter that many scholars postulate has not yet been confirmed. Most of the inhabitants spoke Aramaic; after the annexation by Pompey in 64 B.C. many Romans lived in the city as well. After A.D. 16 the deposed Armenian king Vonones lived in Antioch. In the second century a person with the Persian name "Artabanios" was priest of the imperial cult and organizer of the Olympic games.[287] Antioch had a large Jewish com-

---

[281]Philostratus, *Vit. Apoll.* 1.16; 6.38; Pausanias 8.29.3; Malalas 264.6—266.11; 282.11-12.

[282]See Kolb 1996, 104; Schwemer 1998, 164. Contra Gnilka (1996, 59), who believes that Antioch lacked "the character of genuine Greek culture" and that "the mixture of Greek and Syrian elements" resulted in a "fickle citizenry."

[283]See Kolb 1996, 97, 99-101.

[284]Strabo 16.2.5; Diodoros 17.52; Pliny, *Nat.* 6.122; John Chrysostom, *Ign.* 4 (PG 50:591). See Kolb 1996, 100.

[285]Jones et al., *OCD* 107; Kolb 1996, 101; Schwemer 1998, 162.

[286]Kolb 1996, 102.

[287]Tacitus, *Ann.* 2.4; Josephus, *A.J.* 18.52. On Artabanios see Malalas 285.17-19.

munity.[288] Jews settled in Antioch when the city was founded: Josephus reports that Seleukos Nikator invited Jews to come to Antioch and that he granted them the same citizenship rights as he did to 5,300 Greeks from Athens and Macedonia (*A.J.* 12.119). Carl Kraeling thinks that there were 45,000 Jews in Antioch in the first century, Richard Longenecker suggests 65,000, and Martin Hengel and Anna Maria Schwemer suggest between 20,000 and 35,000;[289] Wayne Meeks and Robert Wilken think that these figures are too high and suggest 22,000.[290] If we assume that Antioch had approximately 250,000 inhabitants and that the Jewish community numbered about 25,000, then they constituted still 10 percent of the inhabitants (if 40,000 Jews lived in Antioch, they would have constituted 16 percent of the total population). Josephus reports that some Jews of Antioch had become very wealthy (*A.J.* 17.24). According to 2 Macc 4:33-38, the former high priest Onias II lived around 170 B.C. in Daphne. When Antiochos IV Epiphanes plundered the Jerusalem temple, he took part of the temple treasure to Antioch. Josephus reports that the Jews of Antioch supplied the temple with richly decorated and expensive gifts (*B.J.* 7.45). Some Antiochene Jews of the second century were still wealthy: they were visited by the rabbis Eliezer, Joshua and Aqiba, who asked them to support the poor Torah teacher in Palestine financially.[291] Josephus reports that a large number of Gentiles were attracted by the Jewish faith (*B.J.* 7.45), presumably attending the synagogues. It is a fair assumption that many of the Gentiles who accepted the Christian message came from the group of these God-fearers.[292] Malalas claims to know that a fight between fan groups of the circus resulted in attacks on the Jews, causing numerous deaths and the burning of synagogues. His assertion that the high priest Phineas marched with thirty thousand men from Jerusalem to Antioch and massacred a large number of Antiochenes probably is fictitious.[293] The inhabitants of Antioch (and Alexandria) attempted, unsuccessfully, to have the Jews stripped of their citizen rights after the Jewish revolt (Josephus, *A.J.* 12.121-122).

Luke was a native of Antioch, according to an old tradition asserted by Eusebius (*Hist. eccl.* 3.4.6) and Jerome (*Vir. ill.* 7). Codex Bezae Cantabrigienses (Codex D), from the fifth century, and several Latin manuscripts presuppose the presence of Luke in the church in Antioch in Acts 11:28 (the first "We-Passage" in the Western Text). Some scholars accept this tradition as probably reliable.[294] Anna Maria Schwemer argues that the sparse information about the origins of the church in Antioch in the book of Acts indicates "that Luke cannot have been a native of Antioch, nor could he have been identical with the Lukios of Cyrene mentioned in Acts 13:1."[295] This argument is unconvincing. (1) There is no other church in the first century, with the exception of Jerusalem and perhaps Corinth, for

---

[288]See C. H. Kraeling, "The Jewish Community at Antioch," *JBL* 51 (1932): 130-60; Smallwood 1976, 176, 358-64; M. Stern, in Safrai and Stern 1987, 1:137-42; Meeks and Wilken 1978, 2-13; Brown and Meier 1983, 30-32; Longenecker, *Gal,* 68-70; Levinskaya 1996, 127-35; Binder 1999, 264-66; Smallwood 1999, 187-90; Bockmuehl 2000, 52-56.

[289]Hengel and Schwemer 1998, 300 (ET, 1997, 189): 30,000 to 50,000 Jews; followed by Bockmuehl 2000, 54. Schwemer (1998, 165) mentions between 20,000 and 30,000 Jews.

[290]Kraeling, *JBL* 51 (1932): 136; Longenecker, *Gal,* 68; Meeks and Wilken 1978, 8; followed by Levinskaya 1996, 134.

[291]See *y. Hor.* 3:7 (48a); *Lev. Rab.* 5:4; *Deut. Rab.* 4:8. See Bockmuehl 2000, 55.

[292]See Riesner 1994, 98 (ET, 111).

[293]Malalas 244,14-16. See Kolb 1996, 116.

[294]See Zahn, *Lk,* 10-11; Fitzmyer, *Lk,* 1:41-47; Barrett, *Acts,* 1:564; Riesner 1988, 25.

[295]Schwemer 1998, 167.

which we have as much information as we have for the church in Antioch. (2) The implied assumption that an eyewitness of the beginnings of the Christian mission in a city would give an extensive report about this missionary activity is a premise that is not necessarily true. Later sources report that around A.D. 200 Bishop Serapion of Antioch ordained a bishop in Edessa, where the ruler Abgar VIII (A.D. 179-214) had been converted. The bishop Eustathios attended the Council of Nicea.

The establishment of the church in Antioch was one of the most significant events in the history of the early church.[296] Luke reports this event Acts 11:19-26, somewhat understating its significance.

Walter Schmithals's skepticism concerning the historical value of the book of Acts can be observed in this context again: he states that we have no reliable information about the origins of the church in Antioch and about the early phase of the Christian mission in Antioch.[297] Anton Dauer concludes on the basis of the current state of research that the report of the establishment of the church in Antioch has traces of Lukan redaction; it is not fictitious, however, but based "without doubt" on the use of traditional material.[298] The question of whether Luke used "a continuous, comprehensive (written Antiochene) source" or whether he relied on oral "individual traditions" can be reformulated as follows: was there a "history of the church in Antioch" written by a Christian from Antioch or perhaps from Jerusalem that Luke was able to use, or was there only oral tradition that Luke would have had to obtain through interviews? If the author of the book of Acts was indeed a companion of Paul, repeatedly visiting Antioch between A.D. 44 and 57, where he would have been able to interview eyewitnesses who were present when the church was established between A.D. 32 and 35, then the difference between these two options is not all that great. Scholars who reject such an early date for "Luke" are in no position to voice convincing doubts concerning the information that the book of Acts provides for the establishment of the church in Antioch: to reject the information provided by Luke—information that can hardly be described as "suspicious" on historical or theological grounds—as materially false or one-sided is to say that the book of Acts is unsuitable as a historical source altogether, an implication that should prompt these scholars to admit that we can know practically nothing about the establishment of any church in the first century.

Luke provides the following information in Acts 11:19-26 about the church in Antioch and its prehistory:[299] (1) Greek-speaking Jews from Jerusalem engaged in missionary outreach on Cyprus and in Phoenician cities (i.e., between Ptolemais and Laodikeia) among the Jewish population (Acts 11:19). (2) Greek-speaking Jewish Christians from Jerusalem who originally hailed from Cyprus and Cyrene came to Antioch and engaged in missionary outreach among the Jewish population and soon among the "Greeks" as well (Acts 11:20), likely among the pagan sympathizers of Judaism first whom the missionaries encoun-

---

[296]Pesch, *Acts,* 1:354; see also Dieckmann 1920.
[297]Schmithals 1963, 242.
[298]Dauer 1996, 14; the quotations that follow above, ibid.
[299]For the description that follows above see Schenke 1990, 318; Dauer 1996, 14-21; Hengel and Schwemer 1998, 274-313 (ET, 178-204); Schwemer 1998, 167-69.

tered in the synagogues in Antioch. (3) The missionary work of the Jerusalem missionaries was successful, as large numbers of the inhabitants of Antioch were converted to Jesus Christ: "The hand of the Lord was with them, and a great number became believers and turned to the Lord" (Acts 11:21). (4) When the Jerusalem church heard about the conversion of Jews and Gentiles in Antioch, they sent Barnabas to the Syrian capital. Barnabas clearly was not just "inspector": he was sent as coordinator, missionary leader and theological teacher. The young church continued to grow as a result of Barnabas's work (Acts 11:22-25).

The first point above can hardly be fictitious, resulting from a conclusion based on Acts 13:4 and Acts 15:39 that according to Luke, Cyprus was evangelized by Paul and Barnabas. The comments in Acts 15:3; 21:3-4, 7; 27:3, made in passing, show that there were churches at least in Tyre, Ptolemais and Sidon, without Luke reporting when and how they were established. In regard to the second point, there is no reason to doubt its historicity: the information is concise and to the point, without any hint concerning special interests controlling the report. Some scholars argue that the fact that Acts 11:20b has no "internal connection" with Acts 10:1—11:18 indicates that we are dealing here with "independent" (i.e., reliable) information.[300] This argument is hardly convincing: the comment in Acts 11:20b describes not the "beginning" of the Gentile mission in general terms but specifically the beginning of the Gentile mission among the Hellenistic Jewish Christians from Jerusalem. The third point can be questioned only on the basis of the premise that successful missionary work in one of the large urban centers of the Roman Empire was impossible, or on the basis of the premise that Luke always exaggerates.[301]

The information that Luke provides for the foundational months and years of the church in Antioch can be analyzed as follows.

1. The establishment of the church in Antioch goes back to Hellenistic Jewish Christians from Jerusalem who had to flee the Jewish capital. They were Diaspora Jews who originally came from Cyprus and from Cyrene in North Africa. They reached both Jews and Gentiles with the message of Jesus (Acts 11:20). It is a plausible assumption that they attended the synagogues of Antioch and proclaimed the message of Jesus the Messiah to the Jews, proselytes and God-fearers who attended the synagogue services. Before long they also reached the polytheistic inhabitants of the city with the gospel. According to Acts 13:1, Lucius of Cyrene played an important role in this initial missionary outreach, as probably did Simeon-Niger and Manaen. Rainer Riesner plausibly comments, "After their expulsion from Jerusalem, some Hellenists probably settled immediately in the metropolis, whose prosperous economy offered various opportunities for newcomers. It is equally possible, however, that other Jewish Christians (more faithful to the law) were already there even before the expelled Hellenists (cf. Gal

---

[300]Weiser, *Apg*, 1:274, and other commentators; cf. Schenke 1990, 318; Dauer 1996, 15.

[301]Even Hengel and Schwemer (1998, 337 [ET, 222]), suggest that "the missionary success, as almost always, may have been heavily exaggerated by Luke." There are no objective reasons to doubt the information that Luke provides.

2:11-14)."[302] We do not know for certain whether Nicolaus, a Hellenistic Jewish Christian mentioned in Acts 6:5 who was a proselyte from Antioch, who lived in Jerusalem and who was a member of the Seven, also played a role in the missionary outreach to Jerusalem. It is quite possible that he was among the Hellenistic Jewish Christians who left Jerusalem and settled in Antioch.[303]

It is unclear whether there is a connection between this Nicolaus of Acts 6:5 and the Nicolaitans mentioned in Rev 2:6, 15. Andreas Feldtkeller suggests that the Nicolaitans were a Christian group that was active in Antioch or in the surrounding areas that rejected the decisions of the apostolic council (Acts 15) and whose theological position influenced Paul.[304]

2. The Jerusalem apostles knew themselves to be responsible for the consolidation of the group of new believers in Antioch: they sent Barnabas, a wealthy Christian from Cyprus who lived in Jerusalem, to the Syrian capital to coordinate the ministry (Acts 11:22-23; cf. 13:1). Usually Luke uses the term *apostolos* for the Twelve (six times in his Gospel, twenty-six times in the book of Acts); he diverges from this customary use and applies the term *apostolos* in the sense of "messenger, envoy" to Paul and Barnabas in Acts 14:4, 14.[305]

Joseph-Barnabas (Ἰωσὴφ ὁ ἐπικληθεὶς Βαρναβᾶς)[306] came from a Levitical family that lived on Cyprus. The formulation Κύπριος τῷ γένει (*Kyprios tō genei* [Acts 4:36]) suggests that he was born on Cyprus. He lived in Jerusalem, where apparently he had been converted to faith in Jesus the Messiah at an early date. The patristic tradition since the end of the second century assumes that he was among the Seventy or Seventy-Two whom Jesus sent on a missionary tour through Galilee (Lk 10:1).[307] If Joseph had resided in Jerusalem for several years before he became a believer in Jesus, "there is the possibility that he may at least have had an encounter with Jesus." Bernd Kollmann argues that Joseph-Barnabas joined the followers of Jesus only after Easter as the result of an epiphany: Paul recognizes him as an apostle (1 Cor 9:4-6), a fact that presupposes a "vision of Christ by Barnabas"

---

[302]Riesner 1994, 98 (ET, 110).
[303]See Brown and Meier 1983, 33; Riesner 1994, 97-98 (ET, 110). This possibility is not discussed by Hengel and Schwemer.
[304]Feldtkeller 1993, 185-87; for a critique see Hengel and Schwemer 1998, 335 with n. 1378 (ET, 220 with n. 1139). On the Nicolaitans see, besides the commentaries, Räisänen 1995b.
[305]Lindemann 1979, 61-62; Haacker 1988b, 11-12, 38. Reinbold (2000, 38-39) follows Haenchen, *Apg,* 404 n. 5 (ET, 420 n. 10) and other commentators who argue that Acts 14:4, 14 is traditional material. It is unlikely that Luke would not have recognized the "tension" that this (allegedly) created with his own understanding of apostleship. On Acts 14:4, 14 see also Hengel and Schwemer 1998, 45, 333 (ET, 25 with n. 25, 219).
[306]See J. Schmid, *RAC* 1:1207-17; J. B. Daniels, *ABD* 1:610-11; Gary M. Burge, *DPL* 66-67; Richard J. Bauckham, "Barnabas in Galatians," *JSNT* 2 (1979): 61-70; Bruce 1979, 49-85; C. W. Roberts 1993; Bruce 1995, 15-22; Hengel and Schwemer 1998, 314-36 (ET, 205-21); Kollmann 1998; Maness 1998, 7-16, 76-80, 111-16, 141-42; Reinbold 2000, 84-106; Cara 2001; Öhler 2003.
[307]Clement of Alexandria, *Strom.* 2.20.112; Eusebius, *Hist. eccl.* 1.12.1; 2.1.4; *Clem. hom.* 1.9.1; *Clem. recogn.* 1.7.7. See Hengel and Schwemer 1998, 314, 333 (ET, 205, 218); Kollmann 1998, 19 (with reference to Schermann 1907, 292-321); the quotation that follows above, ibid.

because Paul's concept of apostleship is decisively linked with an epiphany of the risen Lord (1 Cor 9:1; 15:8-9).[308] This argument is not compelling, however: a post-Easter encounter with the risen Jesus Christ does not eliminate the possibility of a pre-Easter encounter. The apostles called Joseph "Barnabas," a surname that Luke translates as "son of encouragement" (Acts 4:36). The name "Barnabas" is connected not with the Babylonian deity of oracles Nabu or Nebo, as some have suggested,[309] but rather with the Aramaic expression *bar nebiya* ("son of prophecy") that was smoothed down to *bar naba,* which can be translated as "the one with prophetic gifts." If this is correct, then "Luke's translation would be a periphrasis for the 'man of the (prophetically inspired) admonition' or 'the one gifted with inspired speech.'"[310] The Aramaic surname suggests, perhaps, that Joseph-Barnabas did not belong to the group of Jewish-Christian "Hellenists" but to the Hebrew- or Aramaic-speaking Jewish Christians in Jerusalem. The identification of Joseph Barsabbas, the candidate for the position of the twelfth apostle, with Barnabas, presupposed by the Western Text (Codex D, minuscule 6 suppl.) in a variant reading in Acts 1:23, is secondary and historically unreliable.

Luke mentions Barnabas for the first time in connection with the sacrificial giving of Jerusalem believers: he sold a piece of land that he owned and gave the proceeds to the church (Acts 4:36-37). It remains unclear whether the real estate that he sold was in the vicinity of Jerusalem or on Cyprus.[311] Scholars who regard both the Levitical descent of Barnabas and his activity in the church in Jerusalem as Lukan fiction in effect separate Barnabas from Jerusalem. Martin Hengel and A. M. Schwemer observe, "The questionable separation of Barnabas from Jerusalem, in analogy to that of Paul, is caused by the ahistorical tendency, in the footsteps of F. C. Baur, to make the gulf between Jerusalem and Antioch as wide as possible from the beginning. Behind this lies a latent aversion to the Judaism of the mother country."[312] Barnabas was "a disciple of the very early period in Jerusalem who won esteem in the earliest community and among its leaders through the gift of a substantial piece of land and who, although born in Cyprus, as a Levite speaking Greek and Aramaic and with family ties to the Holy City, belonged to the 'Hebrews,' but was a 'link man' with the Hellenists."[313] Barnabas introduced Saul/Paul to the Jerusalem apostles when he returned after his conversion from Arabia to Damascus and visited the Jerusalem church for the first time (Acts 9:27), probably in A.D. 33/34. It is possible that "the Hellenists who had fled to Damascus drew Paul's attention to Barnabas" as a liaison with the Twelve. A short time later, perhaps in A.D. 35, Barnabas traveled to Antioch, commissioned by the Jerusalem apostles to consolidate the missionary successes of the Hellenistic Jewish Christians from Jerusalem. "If Barnabas remains in Antioch, according to 11:2ff. he does so because he is needed more in this new growing but still unconsolidated community than in Jerusalem and the surrounding areas; he may well have enjoyed the open milieu and the broad mission field."

[308]Kollmann 1998, 20, with reference to Wolff, *1 Kor* 2:21.

[309]Most recently Kollmann 1998, 23.

[310]Hengel and Schwemer 1998, 323-24 (ET, 211), following a suggestion by Hugo Grotius; for the observation that follows above see ibid., 326 (ET, 213).

[311]Schneider, *Apg,* 1:367 (in Jerusalem); Pesch, *Apg,* 1:183 (on Cyprus).

[312]Hengel and Schwemer 1998, 328 (ET, 214); on the criticism of Luke by Haenchen, Loisy, Schille and Schmithals, whom Reinbold (2000, 85-88) still follows, see ibid., 324-28 (ET, 214-14).

[313]Hengel and Schwemer 1998, 330-31 (ET, 216); the quotations that follow above, ibid., 313, 332 (ET, 216, 217). A better translation for *Verbindungsmann* ("link man") is "liaison." The arguments in Kollmann 1998, 27-28, against this reconstruction are unconvincing. See Öhler 2003.

Barnabas engaged in missionary outreach in A.D. 45-47, along with Paul and with his cousin John Mark, on Cyprus and in southern Galatia (Acts 13:1—14:28). After his separation from Paul he returned with John Mark to Cyprus, presumably to consolidate the newly founded churches on the island and to continue their missionary outreach (Acts 15:39).[314] The later history of effects (*Wirkungsgeschichte*) is indicative of "the leading role and the high prestige of Barnabas in early Christianity."[315] Because Tertullian mentions a "Letter of Barnabas to the Hebrews" (*Pud.* 20), Barnabas often has been identified as author of the canonical Epistle to the Hebrews, which is unlikely, however.[316] The apocryphal *Letter of Barnabas* (second century), the *Acts of Barnabas* (fifth century), the *Laudatio Barnabae* of Alexander Monachus (sixth century) and *Acta Bartholomaei et Barnabae* (eleventh century) contain no historically relevant information about Barnabas. The prologue of the Spanish version of the late medieval *Gospel of Barnabas* (written between the fourteenth and sixteenth centuries) contains a comment to the effect that Irenaeus knew a "Gospel of Barnabas"; if this is correct, it must have existed already in the second century, although links with the historical Barnabas cannot be established.[317]

3. The church in Antioch grew rapidly. Luke reports that "a great many people (ὄχλος ἱκανός, *ochlos hikanos*) were brought to the Lord" (Acts 11:24), including many Greeks (Acts 11:20-21). These "Greeks" ('Ελληνισταί, *Hellēnistai*) are neither Greek-speaking Jewish Christians (as in Acts 6:1) nor Greek-speaking Jews (as in Acts 9:29), but Greek-speaking Gentiles; in other words, not necessarily "the Greek or Grecized middle and upper class," for whom the designation ''Ελληνας (*Hellēnas*) would be more appropriate,[318] but the Gentile population of Antioch that was Greek-speaking. Some scholars suggest that the early Christian prophetic-ecstatic phenomena, "with predictions, prophetic paraclesis, hymn-singing, glossolalia and its charismatic interpretation, exorcisms and other spontaneous healings," might have been particularly attractive for the Syrian and Arab population: several local cults of Syria—for example, the cult of *Dea Syria* in Hierapolis (Bambyke) described by Lucian— were linked with oracles and other ecstatic phenomena.[319]

4. Joseph-Barnabas located Paul in Tarsus, probably in A.D. 42/43, and invited him to come to Antioch and help in the consolidation and expansion of

---

[314]On Acts 15:36-41 see Cara 2001.

[315]Kollmann 1998, 63; for the early Christian *Wirkungsgeschichte* for Barnabas see ibid., 63-71.

[316]Spicq (*Heb*, 1:199 n. 8) mentions A. Ritschl, B. Weiss, F. Blass, E. Riggenbach, A. F. Loisy, K. Bornhäuser, H. H. Hobbs. For a critical discussion of the relevant arguments see Weiss, *Heb*, 63; Ellingworth, *Heb*, 14-15.

[317]See Kollmann 1998, 69-71.

[318]Schwemer 1998, 167, follows 𝔓[74] ℵ[c] A D* and reads ''Ελληνας (against B D[c] E Ψ 𝔐), which is unlikely, however; see Metzger, *Textual Commentary*, 388; Barrett, *Acts*, 1:550-51.

[319]Hengel and Schwemer 1998, 301 (cf. ET, 197), cf. ibid., 357-63 (ET, 234-39); Feldtkeller 1993, 150-51. On the text *De Dea Syria,* attributed to Lucian, see now J. L. Lightfoot, *Lucian on the Syrian Goddess* (Oxford: Oxford Univesity Press, 2003); cf. also Jaś Elsner, "Describing Self in the Language of the Other: Pseudo (?) Lucian at the Temple of Hierapolis," in Goldhill 2001, 123-53.

the church in the Syrian capital. Barnabas had met Paul ten or eleven years before (A.D. 33/34) in Jerusalem for the first time after the converted rabbi and student of Gamaliel had returned from Arabia and Damascus, where he had engaged in missionary work for one or two years (see §26.1), to visit the church in Jerusalem. After his departure from Jerusalem, Paul had been involved in pioneer missionary work in Syria and Cilicia between A.D. 33 and 43, thus for about ten years (see §26.2). Several factors played a role in Barnabas's missionary cooperation with Paul. (a) Barnabas knew that Paul had preached fearlessly and openly ten years earlier in Damascus (Acts 9:27b). (b) Barnabas had introduced Paul after his conversion and after his return from Arabia to the apostles in Jerusalem (Acts 9:27a). (c) Barnabas had seen how Paul spoke boldly in the name of the Lord Jesus (Acts 9:28) and how he "talked and debated" with the Greek-speaking Jews of Jerusalem (Acts 9:29). (d) Barnabas surely was informed about the missionary activity of Paul in Syria and Cilicia (Gal 1:21). (e) The fact that Paul understood his calling at his conversion in terms of pioneer missionary work, and the fact that the missionary activity of the Hellenistic Jewish Christians from Jerusalem had led to the establishment of a church in Antioch, means that Barnabas and Paul intended both to consolidate the young congregation in the Syrian capital and to engage in continued missionary work in the city and the surrounding region.

Luke reports that Barnabas and Paul worked together in Antioch for an entire year: "so it was that for an entire year they met with the church" (Acts 11:26b).[320] They taught "great numbers of people" (διδάξαι ὄχλον ἱκανόν, *didaxai ochlon hikanon* [Acts 11:26c]). This teaching activity of the new converts took place in house churches: presumably several house churches had come into existence in the city. Rudolf Pesch suggests that the teaching of Barnabas and Paul focused on the "translation of the gospel for the Gentiles who had received no instruction in the synagogue."[321] The main topics of their teaching included at least the following subjects: the life of Jesus of Nazareth, his messianic dignity, the atoning efficacy and the universal significance of his death, the possibility of salvation for Gentiles and their admission into the eschatological people of God, God's plan of salvation in the context of the scheme of promise and fulfillment of Israel's sacred Scriptures, the interpretation of Scripture as God's word for the renewed people of God, including the explanation of Israel's law as the eschatologically and salvation-historically modified word of God for the church.

---

[320]Hengel and Schwemer (1998, 336-37 [ET, 221]) translate συναχθῆναι (*synachthēnai*) as "come together" and reproduce the Western Text as follows: "Now it happened that they came together for a whole year in the community and taught a considerable crowd of people."
[321]Pesch, *Apg*, 1:354.

Martin Hengel and Anna Maria Schwemer comment, "Not only the living preaching of the person of Jesus as heavenly redeemer and judge—a contemporary who had lived around ten years previously and was now expected again soon as the Lord of the community and of the world and the one who had been exalted to God—but also the man Jesus must have played a key role here. Paul and Barnabas could certainly not have preached the new and amazing message without telling of this man, his death on the cross and his resurrection, but also his actions and his life."[322]

Whether the assemblies in the house churches, to which interested persons and acquaintances were invited, constituted "the real place of the earliest Christian 'mission'"[323] is not certain. While it should not be doubted that everyone who was interested could attend the gatherings of the Christians and could hear the message of Jesus in these house assemblies, it is equally obvious that the Twelve had learned from their time with Jesus that the message of the arrival of the kingdom and of Jesus the Messiah was not like the treasure in the field, waiting to be discovered, but like the seed of the sower or the net of the fisherman. They had been called to proactively go to people of all kinds, whether interested or not, and to meet them where they live and work. This experience and this calling of the Twelve had been communicated to other Jewish-Christian missionaries from Jerusalem, as the ministry of Stephen and Philip demonstrates. Paul had worked as a missionary for ten years, and surely he continued to actively and aggressively proclaim the gospel in Antioch.

Luke's comment about the duration of the ministry of Barnabas and Paul may indicate that they concentrated for an entire year exclusively on the city of Antioch before visiting other cities in (northern) Syria and establishing churches there.[324]

5. The believers in Jesus the Messiah were called "Christians" for the first time in Antioch: "It was in Antioch that the disciples were first called 'Christians'" (χρηματίσαι τε πρώτως ἐν Ἀντιοχείᾳ τοὺς μαθητὰς Χριστιανούς, *chrēmatisai te prōtōs en Antiocheia tous mathētas Christianous* [Acts 11:26c]).[325] This information is generally accepted as authentic. Rainer Riesner comments, "The development of a larger church composed of Jews and Gentiles would itself already make it comprehensible that outsiders would coin this new, distinguishing name Χριστιανοί. At the same time this does not exclude the possibility that Christians themselves also soon adopted this particular appellation, since it would have corresponded to their own new self-consciousness as a third entity over against

---

[322]Hengel and Schwemer 1998, 339 (ET, 223-24).

[323]Hengel and Schwemer 1998, 337 (ET, 222).

[324]See Hengel and Schwemer 1998, 338 (ET, 222-23).

[325]See G. Schneider, *EWNT* 3:1145-47 (*EDNT* 3:477-78); Barrett, *Acts,* 1:556-57; Judge 1994, 362-66; J. Taylor 1994; Hengel and Schwemer 1998, 340-51 (ET, 225-30); Botermann 1996, 141-88 (with a history of research); K. Haacker, *ThBLNT* 2:1088-89; Reinbold 2000, 20-21; Trebilco 2002, 241-48; Barrett, *Acts,* 1:556-57; Elliott, *1 Pet,* 789-91.

Jews and Gentiles; especially in the social environment of the metropolis Antioch, this self-consciousness probably acquired clear contours."[326]

The term *Christianoi* occurs only three times in the New Testament: here in Acts 11:26, in Acts 26:28 on the lips of Herod Agrippa II during the legal proceedings involving the apostle Paul ("Do you think that is such a short time you can persuade me to be a Christian?" [TNIV]), and in 1 Pet 4:16 in the context of Christians in Asia Minor who face the possibility of having to give an account of their beliefs before the magistrates in the cities in which they lived ("Yet if any of you suffers as a Christian, do not consider it a disgrace, but glorify God because you bear this name").

Tacitus reports in connection with the fire in Rome in A.D. 64 that Nero brutally executed "Christians" (*chrestiani*).[327] In a graffito discovered in Pompeii (*CIL* IV 679; dated before A.D. 79) the term seems to be used as well. Ignatius, the bishop of Antioch, is the only apostolic father who speaks (between A.D. 110-113) of "Christians." He writes in his letter to the Christians in Rome, "For me, ask only that I have power both inside and out, that I not only speak but also have the desire, that I not only be called a Christian [μὴ ἵνα μόνον λέγωμαι Χριστιανός] but also be found one. For if I be found a Christian, I can also be called one and then be faithful—when I am no longer visible in the world" (Ign. *Rom.* 3:2; cf. Ign. *Eph.* 11:2; Ign. *Magn.* 10:3; Ign. *Pol.* 7:3).[328] The term "Christians" also occurs in the *Didache:* "Everyone who comes in the name of the Lord should be welcomed. . . . If he does not have a trade, use your foresight to determine how he as a Christian may live among you without being idle [πῶς μὴ ἀργὸς μεθ' ὑμῶν ζήσεται Χριστιανός]" (*Did.* 12:1, 4).

Two questions need to be answered. First, is the term *christianoi* (sg., *christianos*) in Acts 11:26 a self-designation of the believers in Jesus the Messiah, or was the appellation coined by another party? Second, was this designation used already during the earliest phase of the establishment of the church in Antioch between A.D. 32 and 41, or perhaps in the context of the activity of Paul in Antioch in A.D. 42/43? Since the term *christianos* is used by Ignatius of Antioch for the first time explicitly as a self-designation, it is unlikely that *christianos* was a self-designation of the followers of Jesus as early as the 30s. The verbal form χρηματίσαι (*chrēmatisai*) in Acts 11:26 does not need to be translated as a reflexive ("they called themselves [Christians]"). The followers of Jesus called themselves "disciples," "believers," "brothers," "slaves" or "servants of Jesus Christ," perhaps also "those who are in Christ Jesus." The ending *-iani* (sg., *-ianus*) also refers to origins outside of the church, specifically to Latin-speaking circles, because a Greek-speaking context would suggest formulations such as *Christeioi* or *Christikoi*.[329] Jews called the followers of Jesus usually *Naṣrayya* or

---

[326]Riesner 1994, 98-99 (ET, 111-12).

[327]Tacitus, *Ann.* 15.44.2: "vulgus chrestianos appellabat"; Suetonius, *Nero* 16.2; Pliny, *Ep.* 10.96; Lucian, *Alex.* 25, 38.

[328]On Ignatius and the city of Antioch see Meeks and Wilken 1978, 19-20.

[329]Hengel and Schwemer 1998, 346 n. 1413 (ET, 453 n. 1171), with reference to C. Spicq.

Noṣrim (Gk., *Nazoraioi*)—that is, "Nazarenes."[330] Orthodox Jews would hardly have called the believers in Jesus "followers of the Messiah" (*Christeioi* or *Christianoi*), because they refused to acknowledge Jesus as Messiah. Erik Peterson suggests that the term Χριστιανοί (*Christianoi*) was an official designation coined by the Roman authorities in Antioch for the new religious group, based on the following evidence.[331] In Rome we hear of the *Caesariani* and *Augustiani,* and in Judea we encounter the *Herodiani,* who were the relatives, clients and the supporters of the Herodian court, who are also mentioned in the New Testament (Mk 3:6; 12:13) and who must have been a known entity in Antioch, as Herod I had financed substantial building activities in the city. The verb *chrēmatisai* occurs "in official contexts just as does πρώτως . . . in legal documents, and, finally, the construction Χριστιανός corresponds to other party names with a Latin ending."[332] If the believers in Jesus the Messiah coined this term themselves, we would expect a more frequent use at least in the book of Acts, where, however, it is used only once more—by Herod Agrippa II (Acts 26:28)! Numerous scholars accept the assumption as plausible that the Roman authorities in Antioch coined this term in order to describe the new movement as a political group. "The designation probably was applied to the Christians by outsiders . . . when, not least as a result of their missionary activity to the Greeks, they began to separate themselves from the synagogue congregations and acquire an identity as a separate group."[333] Martin Hengel suggests that "perhaps the new church had to register in the provincial capital with the magistrates of the city or of the province of Syria as a Jewish 'special synagogue' or 'religious association,' i.e., as *collegium,* συναγωγή or ἔρανος."[334] Perhaps the believers in Jesus the Messiah who engaged in missionary activity in Antioch had come to the attention of the authorities in connection with the unrest of A.D. 39 provoked by Caligula's directive to have his statue erected in the Jerusalem temple—as a very active group of people who believed in a Jew named Jesus as the Messiah (*christos*), who grew numerically and had to be watched but who were politically harmless.

Some scholars suggest that the unrest that broke out between Jews and the native popu-

---

[330]Cf. Acts 24:5, where Tertullus uses this term in accusing Paul to Felix; also 26:9 (Paul before his conversion). See also Tertullian, *Marc.* 4.8.1; Epiphanius, *Pan.* 29; Jerome, *Vir. Ill.* 3; *Comm. Isa.* 5.18; *Comm. Matt.* 13.53-54. On the Nazarenes or Ebionites see Pritz 1988; J. E. Taylor 1990.

[331]Erik Peterson, "Christianos," in *Frühkirche, Judentum und Gnosis: Studien und Untersuchungen* (Rome: Herder, 1959), 269-277; cf. Downey 1961, 275-76; Sordi 1986, 15; Riesner 1994, 99-100 (ET, 112-13); Brown and Meier 1983, 35 n. 81; Hengel and Schwemer 1998, 345-47 (ET, 225-30).

[332]Riesner 1994, 99 (ET, 112).

[333]Schneider, *EWNT* 3:1146 (*EDNT* 3:478).

[334]Hengel and Schwemer 1998, 348 (expansion of ET, 226).

lation of Antioch, according to Malalas, in the third year of Caligula's reign (i.e., A.D. 39/40), provides the historical occasion for this novel appellation of the believers in Jesus the Messiah.[335] Caligula had ordered in the winter of A.D. 39/40 that his statue be erected in the temple in Jerusalem (Philo, *Legat.* 185-190). The anti-Semitic unrest that this directive provoked in Alexandria in Egypt in A.D. 40/41 prompted Herod Agrippa I to ask Claudius to send an edict to Antioch confirming the privileges of the Jewish community in the city (Josephus, *A.J.* 19.279). Rainer Riesner suggests that "in connection with this newly emerging anti-Semitism, especially the Gentile Christians in Antioch probably saw the value in not being viewed as a Jewish group, a circumstance which then might have led to their special designation as Χριστιανοί."[336] Martin Hengel and Anna Maria Schwemer refer to the Piso inscription as a possible background for the appellation *Christianoi:* Cn. Calpurnius Piso was the Roman governor in Syria when the revered Germanicus died in Antioch after a violent altercation; Piso was accused in a decree of the senate in Rome, passed on December 10 in A.D. 20, that he had distributed money from the imperial coffers in his own name among the soldiers in order to win their favor, and that he was proud when they called themselves *Pisoniani,* while the supporters of Germanicus called themselves *Caesariani.*[337] The decree stipulated that the *senatus consultum* was to be "engraved on a bronze plaque and displayed publicly in the most visited city of every province and on the most frequented square of that city" (lines 170-171); in other words, the text was displayed in public when the first believers in Jesus the Messiah were active in Antioch.

Helga Botermann argues that the new appellation for the Christians was connected with the arrest of Paul and with his trial in Caesarea. She suggests that Agrippa, who could speak Latin and who knew the Jewish tradition, may have coined the term *Christiani,* and that the term was used in the letter that Festus, the Roman governor, sent to Rome.[338] This hypothesis is unconvincing. If historians are allowed to formulate hypothetical scenarios in connection with Paul's arrest that "catapulted Christianity into world history," then the same allowance must be granted with regard to Acts 11:26: Antioch was the first "world city" in which the gospel gained a foothold. If indeed a "great number of people" were converted to faith in Jesus Christ in Antioch (Acts 11:24, 26), it is rather plausible that the magistrates of the capital of the province of Syria became aware of the followers of Jesus and that they coined a term that summarized their beliefs: these Jews, proselytes, God-fearers and Gentiles believed in a messiah (*christos*) and worked hard to convince others to join their group. If Luke had mentioned in connection with Acts 26:28 that the believers in Jesus Christ were called *Christiani* for the first time during the trial of Paul in Caesarea, then Botermann's argument would be plausible and valid. However, since Luke includes such a comment with regard to events that took place in Antioch seventeen years earlier, I see no reason why Acts 11:26b should be "lifted from its narrative context" and why we should "look for a chronological and material context" independently of the context of Acts 11:26.[339] Wolfgang Reinbold correctly points out that Botermann's theory destroys the

[335]Malalas, 244.15-245.20. See Downey 1961, 194-95; F. W. Norris, *TRE* 3 (1978): 102; Riesner 1994, 100-101 (ET, 113-14).
[336]Riesner 1994, 101 (ET, 114).
[337]Hengel and Schwemer 1998, 350-51 (expansion of ET), with reference to W. Eck, "Das s.c. de Cn. Pisone patre und seine Publikation in der Baetica," *Cahiers du Centre G. Gotz* 4 (1993): 189-208, esp. 196-201; Werner Eck, Antonio Caballos and Fernando Fernández, *Das Senatus consultum de Cn. Pisone patre* (Vestigia 48; Munich: Beck, 1996), esp. 42-43, 175-76.
[338]Botermann 1996, 171-76; for the observation that follows above see 172.
[339]Botermann 1996, 146.

context of the comment in Acts 11:26 and that she cannot explain why the designation *christianoi,* which Luke evidently wants to date, at least implicitly, arose in Caesarea and not in Rome.[340]

Botermann asserts, "There were initially no Christians. They were Jews and did not want to be anything else. They separated from Judaism only in the course of a longer development."[341] The problem is, of course, how we define "Christians" and "Jews." Barnabas, Paul and other early Christian missionaries in Antioch were Jews in terms of their ethnic descent, a "link" that cannot possibly be "severed," even if one wanted to do so. They understood themselves as "Jews" or "Israelites" in a religious-theological sense as well, as descendants of Abraham and as members of God's covenant people *precisely* as people who believed that Jesus of Nazareth is the promised Messiah. Since the leaders of the Jewish people in Jerusalem had rejected Jesus, and since some of them attempted to suppress believers in Jesus the Messiah by force, the latter assembled in gatherings distinct from the services in the temple and in the synagogue, thus forming a group within Judaism that was clearly identifiable right from the beginning. The fact that being a Christian and being a Jew came to be understood as an irreconcilable contrast is indeed the result of a long development, with the well-known tragic consequences for the Jews—but also, sometimes, with deplorable consequences for Jews who convert to faith in Jesus the Messiah.

In any event, the appellation ***Christianoi*** clearly is evidence for the visible profile and for the effective missionary outreach of the believers in Antioch. Paul Zingg observes, "The unbelievably strong growth of the Antiochene church (vv. 21, 24, 26!) told their contemporaries that these were no longer Jews only but an independent group of its own kind."[342]

6. The authors of several recent studies of the early Christian history of theology accord Antioch a central role, generally the result of hypothetical reconstructions of the place and time of composition of New Testament documents and of the influence of the church in Antioch.

In his comprehensive work published in 1994, *Theologiegeschichte des Urchristentums* ("History of Theology of Early Christianity"), Klaus Berger uses "Antioch" as the heading for his description of the (uncontested and contested) letters of Paul, the Synoptic tradition, the Johannine writings, the letters of Peter and the letter to the Hebrews—in other words, nearly the entire New Testament; the letter of James is treated under the heading "Off Antioch," as are Samaritan Christianity and the Christians in Rome before Paul.[343] Since Berger does not offer chronological surveys or diachronic historical discussions, it is difficult to follow his argument. Also in 1994 Eckhard Rau published his study *Von Jesus zu Paulus: Entwicklung und Rezeption der antiochenischen Theologie im Urchristentum* ("From Jesus to Paul: Developments and Reception of Antiochene Theology in Early Christianity").[344] He focuses on the Hellenistic Jewish Christians from Jerusalem and on

---

[340]Reinbold 2000, 20 n. 47.

[341]Botermann 1996, 141.

[342]Zingg 1974, 218; cf. Reinhardt 1995a, 234.

[343]Berger 1994a, parts 4, 5-11, 15-16.

[344]Rau 1994; for his discussion of "aspects of Antiochene theology," which he bases on Acts 6:8—8:4; 11:19b-21, see ibid., 78-86.

the church in Antioch, but he is also unable to answer the question of how much we really know about the church in Antioch and about its theology. It is questionable whether one can infer "aspects of Antiochene theology" from Acts 6:8—8:4 and Acts 11:19b-21. Walter Schmithals describes in his study *Theologiegeschichte des Urchristentums* (ET, *The Theology of the First Christians* [1997]), likewise published in 1994, an Antiochene "theology of suffering" that Paul supposedly adopted, and an Antiochene adoptionist Christology with an Antiochene soteriology focused on Jesus' passion that Paul developed into his theology of the cross on the basis of his antinomian and universalistic Damascene theology inspired by Gnosticism.[345] Martin Hengel describes Schmithals's study as a consequence of the radical critique of Luke and of the book of Acts that allows uncontrolled and fantastic reconstructions. It is somewhat surprising that Antioch plays hardly any role in Andreas Feldtkeller's study of the religious-historical development of Syrian Christianity, as he mostly describes pan-Syrian matters.[346] Feldtkeller's studies are, of course, also dependent upon decisions concerning date, place and authorship of New Testament documents, decisions for which there is no consensus. For example, it is misleading to maintain that "the origin of the Gospel of Matthew from Syria is supported in New Testament scholarship largely unanimously."[347] Other suggestions for the place of origin of the Gospel of Matthew include Caesarea Maritima,[348] and Sepphoris or Tiberias,[349] while Jack Kingsbury, after surveying these and other suggestions, concludes that the Gospel of Matthew was "situated in an urban environment, perhaps in Galilee or perhaps more toward the north in Syria but, in any case, not necessarily Antioch."[350] The argument of "internal constellations of interests"[351] would allow us to situate all New Testament documents in cities whose population spoke Greek and that had a Jewish community with a synagogue. Andreas Lindemann argues in his study *Paulus im ältesten Christentum* ("Paul in Earliest Christianity") that the Christian texts written in Syria in the first century—the Gospels, *Didache, 2 Clement*—show no traces of influence from the Pauline tradition, "which seems to demonstrate that this tradition was not known there."[352] This argument from silence not only is a non sequitur but also betrays a lack of knowledge of the intensive contacts of the early churches in the first century in general that make the assumption of independent Christian trajectories of traditions impossible,[353] and a lack of knowledge of the numerous points of contact of Paul's letters with the Gospels.[354]

Evangelism on Cyprus

Paul, Barnabas and his cousin John Mark had engaged in missionary work on Cyprus in A.D. 45 (Acts 13:4-12 [see §27.1]). After separating from Paul in A.D. 49,

---

[345]Schmithals 1994, 77-80, 90-94, 94-104, 116-17, 139 (ET, 69-71, 88-99, 109-12, 161-65, 221-23). For Martin Hengel's critique of Schmithals see Hengel and Schwemer 1998, 33 n. 119 (cf. ET, 328 n. 70), 43 n. 151, 325 (ET, 212), 433 n. 1781.

[346]Feldtkeller 1994; for a critique see Hengel and Schwemer 1998, 421-22 (ET, 277-78).

[347]Feldtkeller 1993, 17. One need see only the discussions in Luz, *Mt,* 1:73-75 (ET, 1:90-92); Davies and Allison, *Mt,* 1:138-47.

[348]Viviano 1979, 533-46.

[349]Overman 1996, 16-19.

[350]Jack D. Kingsbury, in Balch 1991, 259-69, 264.

[351]Feldtkeller 1993, 19.

[352]Lindemann 1979, 397.

[353]See recently Bauckham 1998.

[354]See recently D. Wenham 1995.

Barnabas and John Mark returned to Cyprus (Acts 15:39 [see fig. 28]). Luke provides no information about their missionary outreach on Cyprus or about further activities by Barnabas.

The apocryphal *Acts of Barnabas* claims to know that Barnabas and John Mark arrived at Cape Kormakiti and that they proclaimed the gospel in the following cities: Lapethos, Lampadistos, Tamassos, Palai-Paphos (Old Paphos), Kourion, Amathus, Kition and Salamis (*Acts Barn.* 11—26). Barnabas is reported to have died as a martyr in Salamis (23) after Barjesus had instigated local Jews to drag him on a rope from the hippodrome into the synagogue (18—20). The historical value of this information is probably nil: *Acts of Barnabas* must be interpreted in the fifth century in connection with the Council of Ephesus (A.D. 431), where demands were voiced that the church of Cyprus should be made subject to the bishop of Antioch. The text was written by an author who was familiar with the geography of Cyprus and who wanted to demonstrate the apostolicity of the Cypriot church.[355]

Evangelism on the Aegean Islands?

Jewish communities existed on several islands in the Aegean that could have been the targets of missionary outreach of Jewish Christians. The early Christian tradition contains some hints regarding the establishment of churches in the first century, which cannot be verified, however.

On the island of *Aegina* (Αἴγινα), 25 km southwest of Athens, there possibly was a Jewish community in the city of Aegina. The synagogue (13.5 by 7.6 m, with a mosaic floor), discovered in 1829, dates to the fourth century; the earlier building on which this structure was erected dates to the second century and may also have been a synagogue.[356] In the Hellenistic period Aegina had special links with Pergamon; in the city there was a heroon for King Attalos II, who may have built the theater and the stadium. The *Apostolic Constitutions* suggest that there was a Jewish community in Aegina in the first century; Crispus (the Crispus of 1 Cor 1:14?) is supposed to have been the first bishop of the church (*Apos. Con.* 4.146).[357]

Delos (Δῆλος)[358] was regarded in antiquity as a sacred island because of the temple of

---

[355]Kollmann 1998, 66-68; cf. B. B. Thurston, "Christian Cyprus I: Beginnings through the Old Catholic Period (from Barnabas to Constantine)," *ANRW* II.24 (forthcoming).

[356]Mazur 1935, 26-27; Stavroulakis and DeVinney 1992, 27; L. Levine 2000, 250; Runesson 2001, 175-76 with n. 24.

[357]McDonald 1992, 961; cf. R. Scheer, in Lauffer 1989, 84-85: before A.D. 350.

[358]R. Catling, *OCD* 442-44; H. Kalcyk, *DNP* 3:394-400; H. Kaletsch, in Lauffer 1989, 181-85; Philippe Bruneau, *Recherches sur les cultes de Délos à l'époque hellénistique et à l'époque impériale* (Bibliothèque des écoles françaises d'Athènes et de Rome 217; Paris: Boccard, 1970); Philippe Bruneau and Jean Ducat, *Guide de Délos* (3rd ed.; Paris: Boccard, 1983 [1965]); Philippe Bruneau et al., *Délos, île sacrée et ville cosmopolite* (Paris: CNRS, 1996). Excavations: *Fouilles de Delos* (L'École française d'Athènes; Paris: Fontemoing, 1909-); see the series *Exploration archéologique de Délos* (L'École française d'Athènes; Paris, 1909-). Inscriptions: *I. Délos*. See also <http://www.efa.gr/frame/sites.htm>.

Apollo. The city of Delos was located in the west of the island. In the Hellenistic period Delos was a trading center and a meeting place for many foreigners who erected their own temples to, for example, Sarapis, Atargatis and Hadad. The sanctuary of Apollo was expanded by the addition of several colonnaded halls. In the Hellenistic period Delos had about twenty-five thousand inhabitants. In 166 B.C. the Roman senate declared Delos a free port (intended to undermine Rhodes). In the following decades colonists from Athens and Italy as well as Egyptians, Syrians, Phoenicians (from Berytus) and Jews settled in the city. The merchants built imposing houses of their associations. After the destruction of Corinth in 146 B.C. Delos served as the most important center for the trade between Rome and the eastern Mediterranean; the Apollo festival became an international trade fair, with ten thousand slaves sold on a single day. Delos never recovered from the destruction wrought by the pirate Athenodoros in 69 B.C. The new center for the trade between Italy and the eastern Mediterranean was the newly refounded city of Corinth. The existence of a Jewish community, attested by 1 Macc 15:23, was confirmed by excavations in the year 1913: about 60 m east of the southern end of the stadium, on the northeastern coast of the island, archaeologists discovered the remains of a building (15.5 by 28.16 m) that evidently served as a synagogue. Four Greek inscriptions mention *Theos Hypsistos;* the context of these inscriptions—benches were found along the western wall of the building, together with a marble chair that possibly was a Seat of Moses—indicates that they are Jewish and that the building was a synagogue.[359] Some scholars regard this building as the oldest Diaspora synagogue discovered so far.[360] The synagogue was in use from the first century B.C. to the second century A.D. Two inscriptions were set up by the "Israelites of Delos,"[361] evidently a reference to a synagogue of Samaritans.[362] Josephus reports a decision of the Delians to exempt the Jews from military service (*A.J.* 14.231-232). On the island of Rheneia, where the Delians buried their dead, two Jewish inscriptions have been found dating to the second and first centuries B.C. in which *ho Theos ho Hypsistos* is implored to avenge the murder of two Jewish girls.[363] A Christian community existed on Delos around A.D. 300 at the latest.

Chalkis (Χαλκίς)[364] on Euboea, about 75 km northeast of Athens, controlled by Macedonians, was an important fortress during the Hellenistic period. According to Philo,

---

[359]*I. Délos* 2330, 2331, 2332, 2333, 2328; *CIJ* I 726, 727, 728, 729, 730; *IJudO* I Ach60-65; Building 80 in Bruneau and Ducat, *Guide de Délos;* cf. André Plassart, "La synagogue juive de Délos," *RB* 23 (1914): 523-34; Hengel 1969, 83 with n. 327, 146 with n. 160 (cf. ET, 1:43; 2:54 n. 165); Bruneau, *Recherches sur les cultes de Délos,* 480-93; Kraabel 1979, 491-94; Bruneau, "'Les Israélites de Délos' et la juiverie délienne," *BCH* 106 (1982): 465-504; Schürer 3:70-71; M. L. White, "The Delos Synagogue Revisited: Recent Field-work in the Graeco-Roman Diaspora," *HTR* 80 (1987): 133-60; Trebilco 1991, 133-34; Binder 1999, 299-317; L. Levine 2000, 100-105, and passim; A. Panayotov, in *IJudO* I, 2004, 210-19.

[360]Bruneau, *Recherches sur les cultes de Délos,* 486-91; idem, "'Les Israélites de Délos' et la juiverie délienne," *BCH* 106 (1982): 465-504; Stavroulakis and DeVinney 1992, 69-72; Binder 1999, 297-317; L. Levine 2000, 100; Runesson 2001, 185.

[361]*SEG* XXXII 809, 810 = *IJudO* I Ach66, 67. See Bruneau, "Les Israélites de Délos."

[362]According to A. T. Kraabel (*BA* 47 [1984]: 44-46), the Samaritans called themselves Ἰσραηλῖται (*Israēlitai*) in order to document their descent from the population of the northern kingdom (i.e., Israel). On these inscriptions see L. Levine 2000, 102-3; Panayotov, in *IJudO* I, 2004, 228-33.

[363]*CIJ* I 725a.b. See A. Deissmann 1923, 351-62 (ET, 413-24); Schürer 3:70; *NewDocs* 1:29; Trebilco 1991, 133; *IJudO* I, 2004, 235-42 (Ach70-72).

[364]E. Meyer, "Chalkis 1," *KP* 1:1125-26; H. Kalcyk, "Chaliks 1," *DNP* 2:1090-91; E. Freund, in Lauffer 1989, 164-66.

there was a Jewish community on Chalkis.[365]

Cos (Κῶς)[366] initially was settled by colonists from Crete and Mycenae; in the fifth and fourth centuries B.C. it was controlled by either Athens or Sparta. In 366 B.C. the new capital city of Cos was built on the northern coast of the island, replacing the old Cos Meropis. The island owed its wealth to the export of wine and olive oil, fine weaving products and the production of ointments. Cos was famous for its medical school, which traced back to Hippocrates (460-370 B.C.). The most important site on Cos was the temple of Asclepius, located about 4 km southwest of the city, which was expanded during the Roman period by the addition of several temples and baths. In 333 B.C. Cos came under Macedonian rule; in 32 B.C. the island was annexed to the Roman province of Asia. Claudius granted Cos tax-exempt status. According to 1 Macc 15:23 and Josephus (*A.J.* 14.112-113), a Jewish community existed on Cos, which is confirmed by four inscriptions.[367] Remains of the agora, colonnaded halls, gymnasia, baths, stadium, theater, temples (of Aphrodite, Pandemos, Heracles, Dionysos) and of the city walls survive. A bishop of Cos attended the Council of Ephesus in A.D. 431.

Rhodes (Ῥόδος)[368] was a flourishing commercial center after 300 B.C. for the trade in the entire Mediterranean, not least because of its five harbors. The island managed to remain neutral in the Diadochi wars. After Rhodes successfully survived the year-long siege by Demetrius I Poliorcetes in 305 B.C., the Rhodians sold his siege equipment to finance the Colossus, a towering (33 m or 110 ft.) bronze statue of the sun-god Helios, regarded as one of the seven wonders of the world.[369] Pompeii, Caesar, Cicero, Tiberius and many other Romans eager to improve their education visited Rhodes. According to 1 Macc 15:23, there was a Jewish community on Rhodes in the second century B.C. Poseidonios and Apolloios Molon, two Stoic philosophers of the first century B.C. who lived on Rhodes, wrote about the Jews and their alleged intolerance. Suetonius mentions a grammarian named Diogenes who lectured on Rhodes on the sabbath (*Tib.* 32.2). A Christian community is attested for Rhodes in the second century.

22.6 Missionary Work in Rome and in Italy

The message of Jesus Christ apparently was preached at an early date in Italy. There is a near consensus that the church in Rome must have been established very early and that the early history of the church happened without the involvement of an apostle. The first assertion most likely is correct; the second needs to be evaluated more closely.

Evangelism in Rome

The Christian church in Rome originated with Jews living in Rome being con-

---

[365]Philo, *Legat.* 282. A funerary inscription from the second century A.D. (see L. Roberts, *CRAI* [1978]: 245) contains a formulation that sounds Jewish. See Schürer 3:69.

[366]H. Sonnabend, *DNP* 6:762-65; P. W. Haider, in Lauffer 1989, 348-51; S. M. Sherwin-White, *Ancient Cos: An Historical Study from the Dorian Settlement to the Imperial Period* (Hypomnemata 51; Göttingen: Vandenhoeck & Ruprecht, 1978). Inscriptions: *I. CosPH*.

[367]*I. CosPH* 63, 278, 303, 323 (*IJudO* II 6-7). See Sherwin-White, *Ancient Cos,* 187-88; Trebilco 1991, 134-35; Stavroulakis and DeVinney 1992, 129; Ameling, in *IJudO* II, 2004, 52-53.

[368]E. Meyer, *KP* 4:1421-22; C. M. Bowra and E. E. Rice, *OCD* 1315-16; Stavroulakis and DeVinney 1992, 143-44; A. Wittenburg, in Lauffer 1989, 588-93; Ameling, in *IJudO* II, 2004, 57-63.

[369]See W. Hoepfner, "Der Koloss von Rhodos," *AA* (2000): 129-53.

verted to faith in Jesus as the Messiah.[370] We do not know when and where Roman Jews came into contact with the gospel of Jesus for the first time. Scholars have suggested the following possibilities. (1) Jews of Rome who visited Jerusalem on the occasion of the Feast of Pentecost in A.D. 30 may have met Peter and the other apostles, heard the message of Jesus the crucified and risen Messiah, were converted to faith in Jesus and took the message of Jesus back to Rome. (2) Jews of Rome may have come into contact with (Jewish) Christians in other cities in the eastern Mediterranean,[371] perhaps at an early date in Antioch in Syria, where Barnabas and other Jewish Christians from Jerusalem engaged in missionary work, or in Tarsus in Cilicia, where Paul preached the gospel. (3) Peter may have gone to Rome when he left Jerusalem in A.D. 42 to preach the message of Jesus the Messiah in the synagogues of Rome. (4) Sergius Paullus, the Roman governor of Cyprus who was converted through the ministry of Paul and Barnabas in A.D. 45, may have helped to start a Christian community as a patron after his return to Rome.[372]

Rome (Ῥώμη; Lat. *urbs Roma* [see fig. 17])[373] was the capital of the empire that we call the Roman Empire. The topography of Rome was determined by the location of the city in the Tiber Valley, which was 3 km wide in places, and by the seven hills around and on which it was built: the Caelian, Esquiline, Viminal, Quirinal, Capitoline, Palatine and the Aventine. Rome had grown enormously during the late republic and by the early imperial period, both with regard to the population, estimated for the first century at one million people, and with regard to the urban infrastructure. Numerous public buildings and temples had been erected in a relatively short time. The aristocrats lived mostly on the Palatine, the overcrowded living quarters of the majority of the population; for example, the Subura at the foot of the Viminal consisted of a maze of high apartment blocks and narrow lanes. The Campus Martius, the flood plain between the Pincian, Quirinal and Capitoline hills, originally used for military exercises and assemblies, was built up with housing. The numerous new trading relationships caused the expansion of the Emporium south of the Aventine, of the Horrea on Mons Testaceus and of the Navalia on Campus Martius. Pompeii built the first theater made of stone in 55 B.C. Caesar rebuilt the Forum; gardens and parks were built. Augustus restored twenty-eight temples that had become dilapidated or had been destroyed in the civil war; he built new temples (for Jupiter Tonans and for Apollo, including a library) on the Capitol and

---

[370]On the early history of the church in Rome see, besides the commentaries on Paul's letter to the church in Rome, particularly Lampe 1987 (ET, 2003); also Caragounis 1998; Lampe 2001.

[371]See Wilckens, *Rom,* 1:35-36.

[372]See Judge and Thomas 1966; cf. Nobbs 1994, 289 n. 44. On Sergius Paulus see §27.1.

[373]The literature on the city and the history of Rome is immense. See H. Volkmann, *KP* 4:1441-44; Rudolf Gross, *KP* 4:1444-51; I. A. Richmond, *OCD* 1334-35; Platner and Ashby 1965; Donald R. Dudley, *Urbs Roma: A Source Book of Classical Texts on the City and Its Monuments* (London: Phaidon, 1967); Filippo Coarelli, *Guida archeologica di Roma* (Milano: Mondadori, 1975 [1989]); W. MacDonald 1982; Brödner 1989, 171-85; L. Richardson, *A New Topographical Dictionary of Ancient Rome* (Baltimore: John Hopkins University Press, 1992); Clarke 1994; Kolb 1996.

on the Palatium, and he built the first imperial forum, the Forum Augusti. The buildings that the emperors of the first century erected on Greek models were characterized more by their huge dimensions and bombastic decoration than by artistic creativity. Tiberius built the Castra Praetoria, the camp of the Praetorian guard, Claudius completed two aqueducts, and Nero built the Macellum Magnum and the temple of Divus Claudius on the Caelian hill and his imperial palace (*domus aurea*) between the Palatine and the Esquiline. Vespasian erected the Amphitheatrum Flavium, the Colosseum, near Nero's imperial palace; the Forum Pacis, which he built, was the second imperial forum. Buildings erected in the last decades of the first century include the Titus baths, the arch of Titus, and under Domitian the stadium on the Campus Martius and palace buildings on the Palatine.

Rome was already an international city during the late republic. Cicero describes Rome as *civitas ex nationum conventu constituta* (*Comm. pet.* 54). The orator Aelius Aristides (A.D. 117-181),[374] who hailed from Mysia and lived in Smyrna, a representative of the Second Sophistic, visited Greece and Egypt and knew Rome very well. He vividly describes cosmopolitan Rome in his *Oration Regarding Rome* (*Or.* 26):

"About the sea the continents lie 'vast and vastly spread' [Homer, *Il.* 16.776], ever supplying you with products from those regions. Here is brought from every land and sea all the crops of the seasons and the produce of each land, river, lake, as well as of the arts of the Greeks and barbarians, so that if someone should wish to view all these things, he must either see them by traveling over the whole world or be in this city. It cannot be otherwise than that there always be here an abundance of all that grows and is manufactured among each people. So many merchant ships arrive here, conveying every kind of goods from every people every hour and every day, so that the city is like a factory common to the whole earth. It is possible to see so many cargoes from India and even from Arabia Felix, if you wish, that one imagines that for the future the trees are left bare for the people there and that they must come here to beg for their own produce if they need anything. Again there can be seen clothing from Babylon and ornaments from the barbarian world beyond,[375] which arrive in much larger quantity and more easily than if merchantmen bringing goods from Naxus or Cythnus had only to put into Athens. Your farmlands are Egypt, Sicily, and all of Africa which is cultivated. The arrivals and departures of the ships never stop, so that one would express admiration not only for the harbor [i.e., Ostia], but even for the sea. Hesiod said about the limits of the Ocean, that it is a place where everything has been channeled into one beginning and end [Hesiod, *Theog.* 738-741]. So everything comes together here, trade, seafaring, farming, the scourings of the mines, all the crafts that exist or have existed, all that is produced and grown. Whatever one does not see here, is not a thing which has existed or exists [ὅτι δ᾽ ἂν μὴ ἐνταῦθα ἴδῃ τις, οὐκ ἔστι τῶν γενομένων, ἢ γιγνομένων]" (*Or.* 26.11-13).

Of the 1,000,000 inhabitants of Rome, between 40,000 and 50,000 were

---

[374]On Aelius Aristides see R. Klein 1981, 71-108; on his oration on Rome see ibid., 113-72.
[375]It is unclear whether this comment refers to the Roman trade with China; see R. Klein, *P. Aelii Aristidis Orationem ΕΙΣ ΡΩΜΗΝ*, 72.

Jews.[376] They lived mostly in Trastavere, the large quarter beyond the Tiber (Philo, *Legat.* 155), but also in the Subura, at the edge of the Campus Martius and near the Porta Capena.

When Pompeii conquered Jerusalem in 63 B.C., he brought thousands of Jewish prisoners to Rome.[377] Cicero's speech *Pro Flacco* of 59 B.C., in which he speaks of the large number of Jews living in Rome and of their influence in the assemblies (*GLAJJ* 68), indicates that Jews settled at an early date in the capital of the Roman Republic. Because of their support for Julius Caesar they were exempt from the prohibition of the associations (*collegia*). When Caesar was murdered, Jews visited his tomb for several nights (Suetonius, *Jul.* 84). There is literary evidence for the presence of Jews in the area of the grove of the nymph Egeria southeast of the Porta Capena, on the Campus Martius, and in the Subura.[378] The Jews of Rome spoke Greek: of the 534 inscriptions in the catacombs, which constitute practically the only direct source for information about the language of the Jews of Rome, 405 (76%) are in Greek and 123 (23%) in Latin, and only one inscription is written in Aramaic. The tendency to use Latin names (46%, while only 13% are Semitic) is striking, probably to be explained by the fact that Greek names were associated with slavery.[379]

We know specifically of eleven or twelve synagogues in Rome, at least four of which existed in the first century.[380] (1) The synagogue of the Augustesians (Συναγωγὴ τῶν Ἀυγουστησίων, *synagōgē tōn Augoustēsiōn*), in which Jewish freedmen of the imperial household met.[381] (2) The synagogue of the Agrippesians (Σ. Ἀγριπησίων, *Synagōgē Agripēsiōn*), named after Marcus Vipsanius Agrippa, Augustus's son-in-law; Marcus Agrippa had received, in 29 B.C., the house of Marcus Antionius on the Palatine. He journeyed to the eastern provinces at the end of the 20s as the general governor, and he maintained a close friendship with Herod I since 15 B.C. Josephus reports that he was favorably disposed to the Jews. His household employed Jewish slaves and freedmen who formed a synagogue in the first century, as inscriptions confirm.[382] (3) The synagogue of the Hebrews (Σ. Ἑβραίων), perhaps the oldest of the Roman synagogues. (4) The synagogue of the Calcaresians (Σ. Καλκαρησίων), perhaps named after a street or a region in which limekiln workers lived. (5) The synagogue of the Campesians (Σ. Καμπησίων), on the Campus Martius on the east bank of the Tiber. (6) The synagogue of Elaia, perhaps named

---

[376]Leon 1960, 135; Clarke 1994, 466; Juster 1914, 1:209-10; and Riesner 1994, 177: between 15,000 and 50,000 Jews; Solin 1983, 700: 15,000 Jews. On the Jews of Rome see Leon 1960; Smallwood 1976, 201-19; Penna 1982; Solin 1983, 587-789 (cf. ibid., 698-99 n. 240, for bibliography); Wiefel 1991; Clarke 1994, 466-68; Westenholz 1995; Levinskaya 1996, 167-93; Lichtenberger 1996a, 2155-61; M. Williams 1998; Binder 1999, 317-22; Smallwood 1999, 172-77; L. Levine 2000, 97-99, and passim; for the later evidence see Rutgers 1992; 1995.

[377]See Schürer 1:240-41.

[378]See Juvenal, *Sat.* 3.10-18; *CIJ* I 210; *GLAJJ* no. 296. See Lichtenberger 1996a; 1996b, esp. 16-17; for the information that follows above see ibid., 17-18.

[379]See Polomé 1983, 515.

[380]L. Levine 2000, 97: the synagogues named after Augustus, Agrippa and Volumnius, and the synagogue of the Hebrews. For the discussion that follows above see Lichtenberger (1996b), 19), who lists the first eleven synagogues; Westenholz 1995, 23-27 (nos. 3-9, 25-27, 31, 48, 65-66); Levinskaya 1996, 182-85; P. Richardson, "Augustan-Era Synagogues in Rome," in Donfried and Richardson 1998, 17-29; L. Levine 2000, 97-99, 263-66, and passim.

[381]*CIJ* I 284, 301, 338, 368, 416, 496. See Lampe 2001, 125.

[382]*CIJ* I 503, 425, 365; cf. Josephus, *A.J.* 15.350-351; 16.12-16, 21-62. See Lampe 2001, 125.

after Elaia in Mysia, the harbor of Pergamon. (7) The synagogue of the Secenians (Σ. Σεκηνῶν), perhaps named after the North African seaport of Scina. (8) The synagogue of the Siburesians (Σ. Σιβουρησίων), named after the Subura, the Roman quarter. (9) The synagogue of the Tripolitans (Σ. Τριπολαιτῶν), perhaps founded by Jews who came from Tripolis. (10) The synagogue of the Vernaclesians (Σ. Βερνακλησώρων [there are other spellings]), in which Roman house slaves or autochthonous Jews of Rome met.[383] (11) The synagogue of the Volumnesians (Σ. Βολουμνησίων), probably the Jewish freedmen and slaves of the Roman legate Volumnius, who lived in Syria in 8 B.C. and was a friend of Herod.[384] (12) A later inscription attests a synagogue of the Herodians ([Ἡρῳδιῶν); the name might indicate that the synagogue was established at the time of Augustus. Members of this synagogue would have been Jewish freedmen and slaves of the Herodian royal house in Rome.[385]

Each synagogue evidently had its own offices and officers. There is evidence for the following officers: *archisynagōgos* (president/ruler, or patron/benefactor), *gerousiarchēs* (chairman of the elders' council), *archōn* (member of the executive committee), *grammateus* (secretary), *hyperetēs* (assistant of the president, perhaps responsible for meting out synagogal punishments), *phrontistēs* (manager), *patēr/mētēr synagōgēs* (patron/benefactor, and benefactress, or person responsible for charities), *hiereus* ("priests," descendants of Aaron, who may have played a role in the recitation of the blessings).

In regard to the possibility that Roman Jews converted to faith in Jesus the Messiah during the Feast of Pentecost in Jerusalem in A.D. 30, Luke mentions "visitors from Rome" among the pilgrims (Acts 2:10). Luke does not state that some of these "visitors from Rome" were among those who heard Peter preach, accepted his message and were baptized. We should note, however, the following facts. (1) Luke first lists three names of peoples (Parthians, Medes, Elamites), then nine names of regions that are grouped in pairs, with the exception of the first country, Mesopotamia: Judea and Cappadocia, Pontus and Asia, Phrygia and Pamphylia, Egypt and Libya Cyrenaica. The Jews visiting from Rome are mentioned separately.[386] (2) The reference to the city of Rome follows the listing of twelve nations.[387] (3) The reference to Rome does not fit the geographical framework of the previous names, listed from east to west and then from north to south.[388] (4) The visitors from Rome are the only European contingent of pilgrims that Luke mentions explicitly.[389] It is striking that neither Italy nor Macedonia nor Achaia is mentioned.[390]

---

[383]*CIJ* I 318, 383, 398, 494. See Lampe 2001, 126.

[384]*CIJ* I 343, 402, 417, 523; cf. Josephus, *B.J.* 1.535-536, 538, 542; *A.J.* 16.277, 332, 335, 351, 354. See Lampe 2001, 125.

[385]*CIJ* I 173. See Lampe 2001, 125.

[386]The reference to the "visitors from Rome" is followed by the "religious-legal distinction" (Pesch, *Apg,* 1:106) of Jews and proselytes and the reference to Cretans and Arabs at the end of the list, perhaps a summary reference to "people from islands and the mainland" or "people from west and east"; cf. Schneider, *Apg,* 1:253; Pesch, *Apg,* 1:106.

[387]See Schneider, *Apg,* 1:253 n. 88.

[388]Schneider, *Apg,* 1:254 n. 93; Pesch, *Apg,* 1:106.

[389]See Bruce, *Acts,* 63.

[390]Pesch and Schneider infer from this fact that the list is pre-Lukan.

These factors that render the reference to Rome unique might be due to Luke's interest in Rome as the goal of his account in the book of Acts.[391] They may, however, also be significant for the question of the origins of the church in Rome, which perhaps goes back to the conversion of Jews from Rome during the Feast of Pentecost in Jerusalem.[392] However, there can be no certainty.

Several factors suggest that the first Christians in Rome had adopted theological positions similar to those of the Hellenistic Jewish Christians connected with Stephen in Jerusalem. And it seems that the Jewish Christians in Rome engaged in missionary activities in the capital of the Roman Empire by A.D. 40.

1. The Greek-speaking Jewish Christians connected with Stephen had contact with a synagogue in Jerusalem in which *libertini* ("freedmen") were members (Acts 6:9).

Libertini (or *liberi*) were, according to classical Roman law, the *ex iusta causa manumissi*—that is, those who had been freed from slavery for adequate legal reasons and had become Roman citizens on account of their manumission.[393] Jewish *liberti* were descendants of those Jews whom Pompeii had taken to Rome as prisoners after his conquest of Judea in 63 B.C.[394] and who had settled after their emancipation on the left bank of the Tiber. Some of these Jewish *liberti* had returned to Jerusalem and attended one of the synagogues there.[395] Besides these *liberti,* Jews from Cyrene and Alexandria also belonged to this synagogue (Acts 6:9).

It is possible that the *liberti* who had returned to Jerusalem and converted to faith in Jesus the Messiah left Jerusalem after the persecution that followed the execution of Stephen in A.D. 32/33 and returned to Rome. Since Stephen and his friends engaged in active evangelistic work, it is fair to assume that *liberti* from Jerusalem who had become believers in Jesus and who returned to Rome would have proclaimed the message of Jesus the Messiah in the capital of the empire.[396] It can also be assumed that such a missionary activity of Jerusalem *liberti* in Rome led to the conversion of other Jewish *liberti* and generally of Jews and God-fearers in the Roman synagogues. If this possibility corresponds to historical reality, then there may have been Jewish Christians in Rome as early as A.D. 32/33, just two or three years after Jesus' death and resurrection. Peter Lampe recently pointed out that there were Jewish *servi* and *liberti* (slaves and freedmen) in pagan households in the city of Rome: they are attested for the *gens Valeria,* for the *gens Volumnia,* for the *gens* of Marcus Agrippa and for the

---

[391]Thus Barrett, *Acts,* 1:123-24, and other exegetes.

[392]As a possibility: Bruce, *Acts,* 57; more recently Fitzmyer, *Rom,* 29; Witherington, *Acts,* 137.

[393]F. Raber, "Libertini," *KP* 3:624-25; W. Schrage, "συναγωγή," *ThWNT* 7:835-36 (*TDNT* 7:835-36).

[394]See Josephus, *A.J.* 14.54-91; *B.J.* 1.155-157; on Jewish prisoners *A.J.* 14.79.

[395]Cf. Acts 24:12. See Conzelmann, *Apg,* 51 (ET, 47); Schneider, *Apg,* 2:435 with n. 19.

[396]See Wilckens, *Röm,* 1:38; Botermann 1996, 131 with n. 411; Hengel and Schwemer 1998, 389-91 (ET, 257-58); Cineira 1999, 373.

imperial household. Such Jewish slaves and freedmen, once they had converted to faith in Jesus the Messiah, would have been natural "bridgeheads" for the expansion of the Christian faith from the East into the capital of the Roman Empire, an expansion that soon would have reached non-Jews as well.[397]

2. The edict of Claudius of A.D. 41 that the Roman historian Cassius Dio mentions probably presupposes missionary activity of Jewish Christians in synagogues in the city of Rome. Cassius Dio reports with regard to the first year of Claudius's principate that the emperor commanded the Jews to adhere to their ancestral way of life and to refrain from conducting meetings:

"As for the Jews, who had again increased so greatly that by reason of their multitude it would have been hard without raising a tumult to bar them from the city, he did not drive them out, but ordered them, while continuing their traditional mode of life [τῷ δὲ δὴ πατρίῳ βίῳ χρωμένους ἐκέλευσε], not to hold meetings [μὴ συναθροίζεσθαι]" (Cassius Dio 60.6.6).[398]

Recent analyses conclude that the edict mentioned by Cassius Dio (60.6.6) must be distinguished from the edict mentioned by Suetonius (*Claud.* 25.4 [see below, point 4]), and that the unrest in the Jewish community in Rome in A.D. 41 may be explained by the missionary activity of Jewish Christians in the capital of the empire.[399] Helga Botermann asserts, "The conclusion is thus justified that the emperor's order that the Jews should adhere to πάτριος βίος was a reaction to the Christian mission, which had provoked the disturbances among the Jews. Jews from Palestine could have come to Rome within a few years after Easter with the message that Jesus is the Messiah. This caused quarrels in the synagogues."[400] Leading representatives of the synagogues may have complained at the imperial court about the Jewish-Christian missionaries, hoping to get rid of them as the result of official charges before the Roman authorities. The Jews of Corinth attempted a similar procedure ten years later in order to silence Paul (Acts 18:13). Or aristocratic women in Rome who sympathized with the Jewish faith may have used their influence informally to suppress the Jewish-Christian missionaries, provoking unrest, as happened four years later in Pisidian Antiocheia (Acts 13:50). Or king Herod Agrippa I, a friend of Claudius, or one of his advisors, perhaps played a role: "Any member of the Jewish upper class who knew both the Jews and the Romans and who was interested in the maintenance of a good relationship with the emperor could easily foresee serious po-

---

[397]Lampe 2001, 123-27.

[398]See Conzelmann 1969, 146 (ET, 164); Riesner 1994, 139 (ET, 157); Botermann 1996, 103; Feldman and Reinhold 1996, 332 no. 10, 32.

[399]Riesner 1994, 148-59 (ET, 167-79); Botermann 1996, 103-40; Cineira 1999, 260-90; Hengel and Schwemer 1998, 389-91 (ET, 257-58); similarly F. Watson 1986, 88-90; Otto Wittstock, *Suetons Kaiserbiographien* (Berlin: Akademie-Verlag, 1993), 549.

[400]Botermann 1996, 131, with reference to Acts 2:10; 6:9; 8:1; for the observations that follow above see ibid., 131-32; quotation, 132. On Agrippa see also D. Schwartz 1990, 123.

litical conflicts if the supporters of Jesus, who had been executed ten years earlier as 'king of the Jews,' assembled and spoke of him as Messiah."

3. If the early tradition that Peter left Jerusalem in the context of Herod Agrippa I's persecution of the believers in the Jewish capital and traveled to Rome (see §21.4) is historically correct, then he would have preached the message of Jesus the Messiah in Rome in A.D. 41/42, presumably among Jews, at least initially. There is, however, no evidence for the supposition that the unrest in the Jewish community in Rome in A.D. 41 was caused by missionary activities of the apostle Peter, as an early visit of Peter to Rome cannot be fully ascertained from our available sources.[401]

4. Tacitus reports that Pomponia Graecina, the wife of Aulus Plautius, who had conquered Britannia between A.D. 43 and 47, was accused in A.D. 57 of adhering to a *superstitio externa,* an "alien superstition," since A.D. 43 (*Ann.* 13.32).

"Pomponia Graecina, a woman of high family, married to Aulus Plautius—whose ovation after the British campaign I recorded earlier—and now arraigned for alien superstition [*superstitio externa*], was left to the jurisdiction of her husband. Following the ancient custom, he held the inquiry, which was to determine the fate and fame of his wife, before a family council, and announced her innocent. Pomponia was a woman destined to long life, and to continuous grief: for after Julia, the daughter of Drusus, had been done to death by the treachery of Messalina, she survived for forty years, dressed in perpetual mourning and lost in perpetual sorrow; and a constancy unpunished under the empire of Claudius became later a title to glory" (Tacitus, *Ann.* 13.32).

Since Tacitus (*Ann.* 12.43), Suetonius (*Nero* 16.2) and Pliny the Younger (*Ep.* 10.96.9) describe the beliefs of the Christians as *superstitio externa,* it can be assumed that Pomponia Graecina was a Christian woman.[402]

Marta Sordi links the conversion of Pomponia Graecina with the arrival of Peter in Rome in A.D. 42: the changed way of life of Pomponia is connected with the death of Julia, the daughter of Drusus (and granddaughter of Tiberius), which is to be dated to A.D. 42. Giuseppe Scarpat believes that she recanted her Christian faith before she was exonerated, a suggestion that Sordi thinks unlikely: Tacitus only states that her husband, Aulus Plautius,[403] established her innocence.

5. The existence of a Jewish-Christian church in Rome probably is the background for Claudius's edict of A.D. 49 ordering the expulsion of the Jews from

---

[401]See Hengel and Schwemer (1998, 392), who assert, "Es bleibt bei einem non liquet" (ET, 259: "That remains 'not proven'").

[402]See Sontheimer, ed., *Tacitus: Annalen,* 266 n. 97; Giuseppe Scarpat, *Il pensiero religioso di seneca e l'ambiente ebraico e cristiano* (Antichità classica e cristiana 14; Brescia: Paideia, 1977), 130-32; Sordi 1986, 26-27, 29, 36 with n. 9; Riesner 1994, 177 with n. 246 (ET, 198 n. 246: "worth considering"); overlooked in Beard, North and Price 1998, 1:225-26, 229.

[403]R. Hanslik, "Plautius II.1," *KP* 4:910; C. E. Stevens and B. M. Levick, *OCD* 1194; Levick 1990, 141-42.

Rome.[404] The texts in question are Suetonius, *Claud.* 25.3-4, and Acts 18:2.

Both Suetonius, *Claud.* 25.3-4, and Acts 18:2 report restrictive measures by Claudius against the Jews in Rome for the end of the 40s. (a) Suetonius mentions, in connection with measures that Claudius initiated against "men of foreign birth" (*peregrinae condicionis* [25.3]), that "since the Jews constantly made disturbances at the instigation of Chrestus, he expelled them from Rome" (*"Judaeos impulsore Chresto assidue tumultuantes Roma expulit"* [25.4]). (b) Luke reports in Acts 18:2 that Paul met in Corinth the Jewish couple Aquila and Priscilla, "who had recently come from Italy" because "Claudius had ordered all Jews to leave Rome" (χωρίζεσθαι πάντας τοὺς Ἰουδαίους ἀπὸ τῆς Ῥώμης). Paul arrived in Corinth in A.D. 50, so the expulsion of the Jews from Rome must have been a very recent event. (c) A third text, which is dependent upon Suetonius, is a statement by the later church historian Paulus Orosius, who dates in his work *Historiae adversus paganos* (published ca. A.D. 417) this edict in the ninth year of Claudius (i.e., between January 25 in A.D. 49 and January 24 in A.D. 50: "In the ninth year of the same reign, Josephus reports that the Jews were expelled from the city by Claudius. But Suetonius impresses me more, who speaks in the following manner: 'Claudius expelled the Jews from Rome, who at the instigation of Christ were continually causing disturbances.' But it is by no means discernible whether he ordered that [only] the Jews causing disturbances against Christ were to be checked and repressed, or whether he simultaneously wanted to expel the Christians as well, as adherents of a related religion" (7.6.15-16).[405] The date given by Orosius is disputed: some assume the first year of Claudius (i.e., A.D. 41), since an edict prohibiting the Jews' right of assembly is attested for that year.[406]

There is no need at this point to review the discussion of the question of whether Suetonius and Cassius Dio describe the same edict or two different edicts. The arguments of Rainer Riesner and Helga Botermann are convincing; they conclude that two measures of Claudius are in view: in A.D. 41 Claudius ordered a prohibition of assembly of the Jews, while in A.D. 49 he ordered the expulsion of the Jews. Botermann describes the relationship of these two edicts as an "intensification of Claudius's restrictive Jewish policies."[407] Riesner points out that the year A.D. 49 was a particularly critical time for the Jews in Rome: Seneca, the anti-Jewish adviser of the imperial court, returned from exile, and Claudius intensified his program of restoring the ancient Roman religion, extending the *pomerium* to the Aventine in A.D. 49.[408]

The emperor evidently reacted to severe disturbances among the Jewish com-

---

[404]See Momigliano 1981, 33; Riesner 1994, 139-80 (ET, 157-201); Smallwood 1976, 210-16; Murphy-O'Connor 1996, 9-15; Botermann 1996 (with a history of research); Brändle and Stegemann 1996, 9; Cineira 1999, 187-216; see also Cranfield, *Rom,* 1:16-17; Wilckens, *Röm,* 1:35-36; Dunn, *Rom,* 1:xlviii-xlix; Stuhlmacher, *Röm,* 12-13; Fitzmyer, *Rom,* 31; Moo, *Rom,* 4-5. Clarke (1994, 471) remains undecided. Several scholars argue against this position; see Judge 1994, 361-62; Solin 1983, 659; Slingerland 1997, 179-217.

[405]See Pesch, *Apg,* 2:252, with reference to Jewett 1979, 85-86.

[406]See Lüdemann 1980, 183-85 (ET, 186-87); idem, "Das Judenedikt des Claudius (Acts 18,2)," in Bussmann and Radl 1991, 289-98; Slingerland 1992; 1997, 111-50. On this discussion see Riesner 1994, 159-67 (ET, 180-87).

[407]Botermann 1996, 114 ("Verschärfung der restriktiven Judenpolitik des Claudius"); cf. ibid., 117 n. 365.

[408]Riesner 1994, 173 (ET, 194).

munity in the capital, provoked on account of a certain *Chrestus*. Most scholars interpret the name *Chrestus* as a misunderstanding on the part of Suetonius and understand the text as referring to Jesus Christ: the disturbances were provoked by the missionary outreach of Jewish Christians who preached Jesus as the Messiah in the synagogues of Rome.[409]

Orosius, who does not preserve independent traditions, was the first to interpret the phrase *impulsore Chresto* as a reference to Jesus Christ, a fact reflected in the (Christian) manuscripts of Suetonius's text in variant readings.[410] This means that since all Suetonius manuscripts were written by Christian copyists who do not consistently distinguish between *Chrestus* and *Christus* or *Chrestiani* and *Christiani* in other texts either,[411] we cannot be certain what the original reading was. Perhaps Suetonius wanted to say that the citizens called the Christians *Chrestiani,* even though the name of their founder was *Christus,* and the Christian copyists of Suetonius did not change *Chrestus* to *Christus,* since they assumed that Jesus Christ neither visited Rome nor was an *impulsor*—that is, someone other than Jesus is in view here. This means that the texts do not permit a definitive conclusion concerning the identity of the person named *Chrestus.* However, the identification with an unknown Jewish troublemaker is less plausible than the identification with Jesus Christ or, rather, with the Jewish-Christian missionary message about Christ, the Messiah.[412]

It appears, therefore, that Jews of Rome who believed that Jesus of Nazareth was the Messiah, the *Christos,* and who wanted to convince their fellow Jews of the messianic dignity and ministry of Jesus provoked unrest in the Jewish community. These disturbances may be linked with outreach to Gentiles in Roman synagogues, particularly perhaps the God-fearers. The Gentile mission of the Hellenistic Jewish Christians in Jerusalem was linked with the conviction that Jesus' atoning death on the cross rendered both the temple and the cultic Torah irrelevant (Acts 6:13), as faith in Jesus procures full and complete salvation. Thus Gentiles could obtain salvation from Israel's God without circumcision and without obedience to the purity and food laws of the Torah. The traditional differentiation between proselytes and God-fearers, indeed between Jews and Gentiles, was canceled: everyone who confesses faith in the crucified and risen Jesus as Messiah, Lord and Savior belonged to the people of God of the last days.

Friedrich Horn has proposed the plausible hypothesis that three formula-type state-

---

[409]See especially H. Janne, "Impulsore Chresto," in *Mélanges Bidez* (Annuaire de l'Institut de philologie et d'histoire orientales 2; Bruxelles: Secrétariat de l'Institut, 1934), 531-53.

[410]See Botermann 1996, 72-73; Levinskaya 1996, 179-81; Slingerland 1997, 203, 243.

[411]The original copyist of Codex Sinaiticus wrote Χρηστιανός (*Chrēstianos*) in Acts 11:26; 26:28; 1 Pet 4:16. Cf. Levinskaya 1996, 178, with reference to F. Blass, "ΧΡΗΣΤΙΑΝΟΙ—ΧΡΙΣΤΙΑΝΟΙ," *Hermes* 30 (1895): 465-70. The earliest Suetonius manuscript is Codex Memmianus from the ninth century, with corrections from the eleventh and twelfth centuries. For the observation that follows above see Levinskaya 1996, 179-80.

[412]Levinskaya 1996, 181.

ments in Paul's letters represent a tradition that can be traced back to the position of the Antiochene mission concerning the circumcision of converted Gentiles.[413] These statements contain the oldest Christian statement on the question of circumcision. 1 Cor 7:19: "Circumcision is nothing, and uncircumcision is nothing; but obeying the commandments of God is everything." Gal 5:6: "For in Christ Jesus neither circumcision nor uncircumcision counts for anything; the only thing that counts is faith working through love." Gal 6:15: "For neither circumcision nor uncircumcision is anything; but a new creation is everything!"

The missionary outreach of the Jewish Christians in Rome presumably concentrated, initially, on the numerous God-fearers who attended the synagogue services. They would have left, or been forced to leave, the synagogue after converting to faith in Jesus the Messiah and claiming full membership in the people of God without circumcision and full obedience to the Torah. If the Jewish Christians in Rome formulated and preached convictions similar to the beliefs of Hellenistic Jewish Christians in Jerusalem such as Stephen, then violent reactions on the part of the Diaspora Jews of Rome become understandable. The synagogues must have regarded both the beliefs and the practices of the Jewish Christians as a provocation: as they lost the God-fearers who had sympathized with Judaism to the new movement, they lost important contacts with the non-Jewish population. They lost part of their reputation in the society of Rome. They lost, perhaps, important financial supporters. And since Jews accepted the new faith as well, they were confronted, often in their own families, with righteous "sons of the covenant" (בני הברית) who had faithfully obeyed the law but who now identified with "Gentile sinners" (Gal 2:15).

Claudius's edict of A.D. 49 that ordered the expulsion of the Jews presumably remained in force until his death in A.D. 54. Helga Botermann believes that Claudius's action was "essentially not an expulsion of Jews but of Christians": the edict of Claudius was prompted by those in Jewish circles who officially or through informal channels pointed the police or the magistrates of the city of Rome to the (Jewish-Christian) preachers who proclaimed that the crucified Jesus of Nazareth was the Messiah, the King of the Jews, and who provoked disturbances in several synagogues.[414] There is no evidence, however, for the suggestion that the imperial order was limited to Jewish Christians. The comment of Suetonius is general and suggests that everybody connected with the disturbances was evicted from Rome. The fact that the disturbances in the city of Rome required an imperial edict for order and control to be restored suggests that a large number of people were expelled, not just the leading figures of the provocation.[415]

Luke states in Acts 18:2 that Claudius ordered "all Jews" to leave Rome. Even Rudolf Pesch believes that this assertion is "grossly" exaggerated, as the Jewish community in Rome was fifty thousand strong.[416] Pesch and many other scholars argue that a mass evic-

---

[413]Horn 1996, 484-86.
[414]Botermann 1993, 77; similarly Brändle and Stegemann 1996, 9.
[415]See Pesch, *Apg,* 2:152.
[416]Pesch, *Apg,* 2:152.

tion of such proportions is unthinkable. At least two considerations are important in this context, however. (a) The imperial edict may indeed have been formulated with a general stipulation that is reflected in Luke's formulation, without a radical or fully resolute execution of the measure. (b) A general expulsion from the city of Rome could have affected only those Jews in Rome who were not Roman citizens, as Jews with Roman citizenship may not have been regarded as "Jews" in Rome and in the West.[417]

If this reconstruction of the development of the church in the city of Rome is correct, it corresponds to the early history of the church in Jerusalem: the missionary activities of members of a "Hellenistic" synagogue in Jerusalem to convert their fellow Jews to faith in Jesus as the Messiah provoked strong reactions by the majority of Jews against these "apostates," reactions that included the use of force against the believers in Jesus (Acts 6—8). Luke repeatedly reports similar incidents in the course of his account of Paul's missionary activities in the synagogues of the cities of Asia Minor and of Greece.[418]

6. When Paul came to Corinth in A.D. 50, he met "a Jew named Aquila, a native of Pontus, who had recently come from Italy with his wife Priscilla, because Claudius had ordered all Jews to leave Rome" (Acts 18:2). It is generally assumed that Aquila and Priscilla had become believers in Jesus the Messiah already in Rome: Luke sometimes specifies the first converts in a city (as, for example, Lydia in Philippi [Acts 16:14-15]), which is not the case here, however. Paul explicitly describes the household of Stephanas as "first fruits," meaning "first converts," of Achaia (1 Cor 16:15).[419] When Aquila is described as a "Jew" (Acts 18:2), Luke comments not on his religious convictions but on his ethnic affiliation (cf. Acts 16:1, 20; 21:39; 22:3, 12). Aquila was already a Christian when he moved from Rome to Corinth. The Gentile Christians in the church in Rome that Paul's letter to the Roman Christians presupposes must have been converted through an early Jewish-Christian missionary outreach among Gentiles in the city of Rome.[420] This explains why Aquila and Priscilla became Paul's missionary co-workers immediately after their initial encounter in Corinth: they knew, and had perhaps experienced, what missionary outreach among Gentiles entailed.

7. Paul arrives in Rome in A.D. 60 as a prisoner, eleven years after the expulsion of the Jews under Claudius and about twenty-seven years after the establishment of the church in the city of Rome, if the first believers indeed came to Rome in A.D. 32. Paul clearly had no influence on the early history of the church in the city of Rome.

---

[417]Thus Bruce 1979, 368.

[418]Acts 13:45, 50-51; 14:2, 4-5, 19; 17:5, 13; 18:6, 12-17; 19:9; 20:3; 21:27-36; 28:24.

[419]E. Meyer 1921-1923, 3:111; F. Watson 1986, 89; Lampe 1987, 5 (ET 2003, 11); Becker 1992, 353-54 (ET, 335-36); Riesner 1994, 169-70; Botermann 1996, 46-47; Haenchen, *Apg*, 517 (538-39); Roloff, *Apg*, 270. Differently Zahn, *Apg*, 2:632-33; Judge and Thomas 1966, 81-94; Lüdemann 1987, 209 (ET, 201).

[420]See Wilckens, *Röm*, 1:36-39.

8. After Claudius expelled the Jews from Rome in A.D. 49, and with them the Jewish Christians, the Roman church survived only as there were Gentile Christians in the city who stayed in the capital. As Gentiles, they presumably had no part in the disturbances in the synagogues. Paul writes in Rom 1:8, "I thank my God through Jesus Christ for all of you, because your faith is proclaimed throughout the world." This statement is not just a *captatio benevolentiae*. Paul evidently refers to the excellent reputation that the church in the city of Rome had among the believers in the eastern Mediterranean. The church seemed to have been growing continuously during the time that the Jewish Christians had been forced to leave Rome. When the Jewish Christians were allowed to return five years later in A.D. 54, they encountered a Gentile-Christian church into which they had to be (re)integrated. When Paul wrote his letter to the Christians in the city of Rome three years later, in the winter of A.D. 56/57, he addressed the Roman church as a Gentile-Christian church.

The list of greetings in Rom 16:3-16 allows us to reconstruct the existence of seven house churches in the city of Rome for the time around A.D. 50-55.[421] And there is also evidence for other house churches.

1. The house church of Priscilla and Aquila (16:3-5a): τὴν κατ᾽ οἶκον αὐτῶν ἐκκλησίαν (*tēn kat᾽ oikon autōn ekklēsian,* "the church in their house" [16:5a]). A church met in the house that Aquila and Priscilla, Jewish businesspeople, had in Rome.

2. The church in the house of Aristobulus (16:10b): τοὺς ἐκ τῶν Ἀριστοβούλου (*tous ek tōn Aristoboulou,* "those who belong to the household of Aristobulus"). Aristobulus, the patron of this house church, was not a Christian, as he is not greeted himself. Since "Aristobulus" was a rare name in Rome, he could have resided in the East, with only a part of his household living in Rome.[422]

3. The church in the house of Narcissus (16:11b): τοὺς ἐκ τῶν Ναρκίσσου (*tous ek tōn Narkissou,* "those in the household of Narcissus" who are in the Lord). Narcissus, the patron of this house church, also seems not to have been a Christian.

4. The church of Asyncritus, Phlegon, Hermes, Patrobas and Hermas (16:14): τοὺς σὺν αὐτοῖς ἀδελφούς (*tous syn autois adelphous,* "the brothers [and sisters] with them").

5. The church of Philologus, Julia, Nereus, and the latter's sister Olympas (16:15): τοὺς σὺν αὐτοῖς πάντας ἁγίους (*tous syn autois pantas hagious,* "and all the saints who are with them").

If we assume that the fourteen additional people whom Paul greets did not belong to these five house churches that are explicitly pointed out, we may reconstruct two additional house churches ("between" 16:5a/10b and 16:11b/14):

6. The church with Epaenetus, Maria, Andronicus, Junia, Ampliatus, Urbanus, Stachys and Apelles (16:5b-10a).

7. The church with Tryphaena and Tryphosa, Persis, Rufus and his mother (16:12-13).

The existence of two more churches can be inferred from Phil 4:22 and from inscriptions in the city of Rome:

A house church may have met in the imperial household. Paul states in Phil 4:22 that

---

[421]Lampe 2001, 126; cf. Klauck 1981, 26-30.
[422]See Lampe 2001, 126.

there were Christians in the "household of Caesar" (οἱ ἐκ τῆς Καίσαρος οἰκίας, *hoi ek tēs Kaisaros oikias*). The Jewish Christians who belonged to this church presumably had been members of the synagogue of the Augustesians (Σ. Αὐγουστησίων), in which Jewish freedmen of the imperial household were meeting.[423]

The "association in the house of Sergius Paullus" (*collegium quod est in domo Sergiae Paullinae*), who is mentioned in twenty-three Roman inscriptions (*CIL* VI 9148-9149), could have been a Christian house church founded by L. Sergius L. f. Paullus, the procurator of Cyprus in A.D. 45 and consul in A.D. 70, who probably was converted in the course of the missionary activities of Paul and Barnabas on Cyprus (see §27.1). This *collegium* continued to be led by the daughter of this Sergius Paullus, named Sergia Paulla, who was married to Cornelius Severus, who was consul in A.D. 112. A daughter of this Sergia Paulla married M. Acilius Glabrio, consul in A.D. 124, the son of Acilius Glabrio, who had been executed under Domitian (A.D. 81-96) possibly because of Christian convictions (see Cassius Dio 67.14.1-3).[424]

Clement mentions Valerius Biton (*1 Clem.* 63:3; 65:1), an old Christian living in Rome, who was a member of the delegation that took Clement's first letter from Rome to Corinth after A.D. 90. If Valerius Biton was born in the 30s or 40s, he could have belonged to one of the churches in the city of Rome since his youth.[425] A pagan tombstone from the first century A.D. (*CIL* VI 27948) lists freedmen of the *gens Valeria,* including a woman named Valeria Maria, one of the slaves freed by a certain Lucius Valerius Diogenes, who possibly is identical with the senator Lucius Valerius, who lived in the first century B.C. and is mentioned by Josephus (*A.J.* 14.145). Valeria's Semitic cognomen "Maria," rare in Rome, indicates that she very probably was a Jew or a Jewish Christian. It seems probable that Valerius Biton "came into contact with the Christian message through Valerian Jewish freedmen, perhaps the Jew or Jewish Christian Valeria Maria was his mother or a close relative."

Paul advises the Christians in the city of Rome with regard to the behavior toward people who persecute them (Rom 12:14: "Bless those who persecute you; bless and do not curse them" [cf. Rom 12:17-21]). If this advice is connected with local situations,[426] Paul may be referring to reprisal attacks by Jews who returned from the exile forced upon them by Claudius's edict, which resulted from the activities of (Jewish) Christians in Rome. "Revenge by the Christians directed against their Jewish persecutors would have escalated the violence and provoked a deterioration of the situation that pertained between Jews and Christians, which means that the situation of the year A.D. 49 might be repeated. . . . A confrontation with the Jews and a violation of the Roman peace would have endangered both Paul's desire to visit Rome and the survival of Christianity in the capital of the empire. This is the reason why Paul insisted on avoiding disputes in Rome. Paul knew that the political and social situation played an important role for the expansion of Christianity."

---

[423]See Lampe 2001, 127.
[424]Sordi 1986, 28, 185-86; Riesner 1994, 124-25 (ET, 140-41), with caution.
[425]Lampe 1987, 123 (ET, 2003, 184); the quotation that follows above, idem 2001, 127. On Valeria Maria see Lampe 2001, 123-24.
[426]Thus Cineira 1999, 390-95, 425-29; the quotation that follows above, 427.

The precise geographical location of these churches in the city of Rome cannot be established. Peter Lampe remarks, "There is no evidence for a special center of the Christian circles scattered throughout the city, neither during this time nor in the first two centuries."[427] Lampe, from local Roman traditions, from the living quarters of the Jewish community and from the density of the titular churches in the city of Rome, draws this conclusion: "(a) Trastevere, Augustus' region XIV, was very probably a quarter where Christians lived. (b) The same applies to the area on the left and on the right side of the Via Appia within the city, i.e., the low plain from the Porta Capena to the Almone River. (c) With less certainty, left of the Via Appia, the Aventine Hill and the little Aventine (Augustus' regions XII and XIII). (d) Perhaps on the Campus Martius on both sides of the Via Lata/Flaminia."[428] The members of the house churches, which included freedmen and slaves, would have spoken Greek. Latin certainly would have been heard in the Christian assemblies; we do not know, however, whether there was a Latin-speaking house church in the first century.[429]

Many scholars assume that there was a "Petrine school" in Rome. This suggestion is based on the widely held view that the Gospel of Mark, in which Peter's role is particularly emphasized, was written in Rome, and on the fact that 1 Peter was written in Rome. Otto Knoch argues that the church in Rome believed itself to be, after Peter and Paul had died in Rome as martyrs, the new "advocate of the apostolic tradition of faith, of the unity and of the life of the church in its struggle against persecution and heresy."[430] This and similar views remain hypothetical. It appears, in any event, that the church in Ephesus was the center of the Christian movement after the destruction of Jerusalem in A.D. 70.

9. Between A.D. 90 and 100 a Christian leader named Clement was active in the church(es) in the city of Rome. The anonymous letter known as *1 Clement* is generally attributed to him. Following the lead of J. B. Lightfoot, most scholars assume that Clement probably was a freedman of the family of Titus Flavius Clemens, a cousin of the emperor Domitian, who was consul in Rome in A.D. 95.[431] Flavius Clemens was ordered to be executed "suddenly and on a very slight suspicion" (*tenuissima suspicione* [Suetonius, *Dom.* 15.1]), while his wife, Flavia Domitilla, the niece of Domitian, was sent into exile. Cassius Dio notes that Flavius Clemens and his wife, Domitilla, were accused of atheism or impiety (ἔγκλημα ἀθεότητος [67.14.2]). Eusebius suspected that Flavius Clemens and Flavia Domitilla were Christians (*Hist. eccl.* 3.18.4), an assumption that many scholars regard as plausible.[432]

---

[427]Lampe 2001, 126; 1987, 301-45 (ET, 2003, 359-408).

[428]Lampe 1987, 30-31 (ET, 2003, 42-43); for a description of the quarters of Rome see ibid., 36-52 (ET, 48-65); cf. Cineira 1999, 375.

[429]Bardy (1948, 10) is skeptical.

[430]Knoch 1991, 126.

[431]See Caragounis 1998, 266. Lampe (1987, 173; ET, 2003, 203-204) is skeptical.

[432]Lightfoot, *Apostolic Fathers* 1.1:34-35; Brown and Meier 1983, 161-62; cf. Caragounis 1998, 266-67; R. Syme and B. M. Levick, "Flavius Clemens," *OCD* 600-601.

10. Around A.D. 250 the Roman churches supported 150 full-time Christian workers, who were responsible for, among other matters, the care of 1,500 widows and poor people.

"This avenger of the Gospel [i.e., Novatus] then did not know that there should be one bishop in a catholic church [i.e., in the Roman church]; yet he was not ignorant—for how could he be?—that in it there were forty-six presbyters, seven deacons, seven subdeacons, forty-two acolytes, fifty-two exorcists, readers, and janitors, and over fifteen hundred widows and persons in distress, all of whom the grace and kindness of the Master nourish" (Eusebius, *Hist. eccl.* 6.43.11).

These figures suggest that there were thousands of Christians in Rome at this time. Some scholars estimate on the basis of this comment by Eusebius that between 10,000 and 50,000 Christians lived in Rome in the mid-third century. If so, the church formed the largest "association" in the city of Rome at this time.[433]

The earliest church building in the city of Rome that can be dated is S. Crisogono in Trastevere, measuring 33.8 by 19.8 m, built around A.D. 300. The church SS. Giovanni e Paolo, which dates to the third century, was erected on the site of a complex of shops dating from the first century A.D. Whether the one room that was used by Christians before the fourth century was an early house church cannot be established with certainty.[434]

There may have been a Christian community in Ostia, the port of Rome, in the first century. The synagogue that dates to the fourth century may have roots in a Jewish community of the first century.

Ostia (mod. Ostia Antica):[435] the port city of Rome was located south of the mouth of the Tiber River; the port itself (*Portus,* near mod. Fiumicino)[436] was 3 km to the north. The oldest remains date to about 350 B.C. Because of the continuously increasing import trade of Rome, the city grew considerably in the second century B.C. Emperor Claudius built a large artificial harbor north of the mouth of the Tiber; two canals linked the port with the river. The harbor could not provide safety: in A.D. 62 about two hundred ships sank in a storm. The problem was solved only under Trajan, with the result that Ostia flourished in the second century, with the number of inhabitants doubling. There is ample evidence in Ostia for guilds (*collegia*) and their economic and political significance. Traditional gods that were worshiped in Ostia include Hercules, Bona Dea and especially Vulcanus. Buildings that were erected in the early imperial period include the

---

[433]Beard, North and Price 1998, 267 with n. 66; Kraft, *Eusebius: Kirchengeschichte,* 314 n. 76: 50,000; Lane Fox 1986, 268-69, believes that 50,000 is too high and does not want to speculate.

[434]See G. F. Snyder, *ABD* 5:834-35.

[435]G. Radke, *KP* 4:374; N. Purcell, *OCD* 1081-82; G. Uggeri and V. Kockel, *DNP* 9:96-97 (cf. 99-102, for a map); R. Meiggs, *PECS* 658-61; idem *Roman Ostia* (Oxford: Clarendon, 1985 [1973]); R. Chevallier, *Ostie antique: Ville et port* (Paris: Les Belles Lettres, 1986); A. Gallina Zevi and A. Claridge, eds., *Roman Ostia Revisited* (London: British School at Rome, 1996). The excavations of 1938-1942 uncovered nearly the entire city of Ostia. Inscriptions: *CIL* XIV.

[436]Vanni Mannucci, ed., *Il parco archeologico naturalistico del Porto di Traiano* (Rome: Gangemi, 1992).

theater (for three thousand spectators), the forum in the south and a temple of Roma and Augustus. The synagogue that was discovered in 1961 at the edge of modern Ostia (24.9 by 12.5 m; the hall, including the apse, measures 15 by 12 m)[437] dates to the fourth century A.D. but apparently is at the site of a building dating to about A.D. 50, probably connected with the building activities under Claudius and used from the beginning as a synagogue.[438]

Evangelism in Puteoli, Herculaneum and Pompeii

When Paul the prisoner was taken via Syracuse and Rhegium to Rome, the ship docked in Puteoli, where he met "brothers," meaning Christians (Acts 28:13-14).

Acts 28:13-14: "Then we weighed anchor and came to Rhegium. After one day there a south wind sprang up, and on the second day we came to Puteoli. [14]There we found believers [Gk., ἀδελφοί, "brothers"] and were invited to stay with them for seven days. And so we came to Rome."

The term "brothers" (ἀδελφοί, *adelphoi*) clearly refers to Christians, not to fellow Jews. We do not know when or through whom the gospel was preached for the first time in Puteoli. Perhaps Jews living in Puteoli came into contact with Christians during travels in the East, perhaps during pilgrimages to Jerusalem. It is also possible that Christians of Rome engaged in missionary outreach in Puteoli. Or perhaps Jewish-Christian missionaries from Jerusalem were the first to preach the gospel in the city. Paul's seven-day visit in Puteoli

---

[437]There is still no final report on the excavations; see the scattered preliminary reports of the archaeologist, Maria Floriani Squarciapino: "La sinagoga recentamente scoperta ad Ostia," *Rendiconti della pontificia accademia romana di archeologia* 34 (1961-62): 119-32; idem, "The Synagogue at Ostia," *Archaeology* (1963): 193-203; idem, "La sinagoga di Ostia: seconda campagna di scavo," in *Atti del VI Congresso Internazionale di Archeologia Cristiana* (Rome: Vatican, 1965), 299-315. See also L. Michael White, "Synagoge and Society in Imperial Ostia: Archaeological and Epigraphic Evidence," *HTR* 90 (1977): 23-58; Kraabel 1979, 497-500; H. Shanks, *Judaism in Stone: The Archaeology of Ancient Synagogues* (New York: Harper & Row, 1979), 162-99; Johannes S. Boersma, *Amoenissima Civitas: Block V.ii at Ostia; Description and Analysis of Its Visible Remains* (Assen: Van Gorcum, 1985); Steven Fine and Miriam Della Pergola, "The Synagogue of Ostia and Its Torah Shrine," in Westenholz 1995, 42-57; White 1996-1997, 2:379-391; Beard, North and Price 1998, 2:107-8; Binder 1999, 322-36; Anders Runesson, "The Oldest Original Synagogue Building in the Diaspora: A Response to L. Michael White," *HTR* 92 (1999): 409-33, esp. 410 n. 3; L. Levine 2000, 97, 255-58, and passim; Runesson 2001, 187-89, and passim. Inscription: *SEG* XLV 916; Guarducci 3:115-17; *NewDocs* 4:112; *I. WEuropeJud* I 13.

[438]Thus Squarciapino, "La sinagoga di Ostia," 310-15; Boersma, *Amoenissima Civitas,* 15-16, 25-26, 160-66; cf. Runesson ("Oldest Original Synagogue"), who seeks to show that this synagogue was erected *as* a synagogue, which would make it the oldest synagogue building in the Diaspora. Still unconvinced is L. M. White, "Reading the Ostia Synagogue: A Reply to A. Runesson," *HTR* 92 (1999): 435-64. On the discussion concerning White's views see Binder 1999, 332-33 with n. 207; see L. M. White, "Synagogue and Society in Imperial Ostia: Archaeological and Epigraphic Evidence," in Donfried and Richardson 1998, 30-68, esp. 46-47.

may be connected with the schedule of the ship, which might have needed a week to unload its freight, although Luke notes that the transport of the prisoners took the overland route to Rome. This leads some scholars to the assumption that the soldiers needed time to replenish their equipment before continuing on their journey to Rome, a need that arose as a result of the shipwreck before Malta.[439]

Puteoli (Gk., Δικαιάρχεια; mod. Pozzuoli),[440] 230 km southeast of Rome, was reached via Capua and on the Via Appia via Casilinum, Urbana, Minturnae, Formiae, Fundi, Tarracinae, Forum Apii, Tres Tabernae, Ad Sponsas, Aricia and Bovillae. Puteoli was founded by Samian refugees around 520 B.C. on the northern coast of the gulf between Misenum and Pausilypon. The city was long dependent upon Cumae. In the second century B.C. the port of Puteoli was preferred to the port of Naples because of its proximity to the Via Appia. The Augustan harbor facilities consisted of a breakwater (16 by 372 m), at least one triumphal arch, columns with statues, and a light house. Puteoli continued to flourish after Claudius expanded the port of Ostia, so much so that Nero connected the city with the Tiber River by a canal. Puteoli had about sixty-five thousand citizens, including numerous foreigners (e.g., Tyrians). Besides the usual Greek and Roman deities and the emperor cult, the veneration of Sarapis, Cybele, Bellona and Dusares is attested for Puteoli. The city had a forum, a market, two amphitheaters (130 by 95 m, and 149 by 116 m; the latter was built by Vespasian), baths and a temple of Augustus. Worshipers of Jupiter Damascenus are attested in Puteoli, which suggests that merchants from Damascus lived in the city who venerated their ancestral deity.[441] There was a Jewish community in Puteoli since 4 B.C. at the latest.

There are references to Christians in Herculaneum and Pompeii, two cities that were destroyed in the eruption of Mount Vesuvius in A.D. 79. The evidence is not conclusive, however.

Herculaneum (mod. Resina),[442] 23 km southeast of Puteoli on the southwestern side of Mount Vesuvius, was founded, according to legend, by Heracles. The city occupied an area 370 by 320 m and had a rectangular street plan. Traffic was not allowed on the wide *decumanus maximus* in the center of the city, fulfilling the function of a forum. Herculaneum had about five thousand inhabitants. The city was destroyed in A.D. 79 when Mount Vesuvius erupted.

---

[439]Pesch, *Apg,* 2:303; Barrett, *Acts,* 2:1230.

[440]H. Comfort, *PECS* 743-44; G. Radke, *KP* 4:1244-45; Hemer 1989, 154-55.

[441] *CIL* X 1576: *sacerdotes Iovis optimi maximi Damasceni.* See Klaus S. Freyberger, "Das Heiligtum des Jupiter Damaszenus—ein städtischer Kultbau lokaler Prägung," in Fansa et al. 2000, 212-17, esp. 216. For the observation that follows above see Josephus, *B.J.* 2.101-110; *A.J.* 17.324-338.

[442]G. Radke, *KP* 2:1053-54; A. de Franciscis, *PECS* 386-88; N. Purcell, *OCD* 688; F. U. Pappalardo, *DNP* 5:400-402; Amedeo Maiuri, *Ercolano: I nuovi scavi (1927-1958)* (Rome: Istituto poligrafico dello Stato, Libreria dello Stato, 1958); A. and M. De Vos, *Pompei, Ercolano, Stabia* (Guide archeologiche Laterza 11; Rome: Laterza, 1982), 260-306; Luisa Franchi Dell'Orto, *Ercolano, 1738-1988: 250 anni di ricerca archeologica* (Rome: Bretschneider, 1993).

Pompeii (mod. Pompei Scavi),[443] about 13 km southeast of Herculaneum south of Mount Vesuvius, was settled by Greeks in the sixth century B.C. Strabo called the city Pompaia; the Roman colony at the site during the time of Sulla was named Colonia Veneria Cornelia Pompeianorum. Pompeii had about twenty thousand inhabitants. The city formed an oval (1200 by 720 m) and was surrounded by a wall since the third/second centuries B.C. In the eastern part of the city stood the oldest known amphitheater (80-70 B.C.). The earthquake in February A.D. 62 caused major destruction (Tacitus, *Ann.* 15.22.4). The city was destroyed in late August A.D. 79 when Mount Vesuvius, inactive for hundreds of years, suddenly erupted and buried the city under a thick layer of lava and ash (Pliny the Younger, *Ep.* 6.16).

An imprint in the Casa Bicentenario in Herculaneum has been interpreted as a cross and thus as evidence for Christians in the city.[444] The archaeological evidence is not unambiguous, however. The imprint is interpreted by some archaeologists as related to the support of a shelf.

In Pompeii two inscriptions with the "Sator square" were found, which was used later by Christians. These inscriptions represent the earliest occurrence of this formula.[445]

The Sator square consists of five words: SATOR/AREPO/TENET/OPERA/ROTAS, which can be read forward and backward (palindrome). Read in this sequence, the words mean: "The sower (sator) Arepo (personal name) holds (tenet) with effort (opera) the cart (rotas

---

[443]The literature on Pompeii is immense; see G. Radke, *KP* 4:1020-22; L. Richardson, *PECS* 724-26; N. Purcell, *OCD* 1214-15; Hans Eschebach, *Die städtebauliche Entwicklung des antiken Pompeji* (Mitteilungen des Deutschen Archaeologischen Instituts, Römische Abteilung 17; Heidelberg: Kerle, 1970); De Vos, *Pompei, Ercolano, Stabia,* 2-258; Lawrence Richarson, *Pompeii: An Architectural History* (Baltimore: Johns Hopkins University Press, 1988); Paul Zanker, *Pompeji Stadtbild und Wohngeschmack* (Kulturgeschichte der antiken Welt 61; Mainz: Zabern, 1995; English: *Pompeii: Public and Private Life* [Revealing antiquity 11; Cambridge, Mass.: Harvard University Press, 1998); Gesemann 1996; Felix Pirson, *Mietwohnungen in Pompeji und Herkulaneum Untersuchungen zur Architektur, zum Wohnen und zur Sozial- und Wirtschaftsgeschichte der Vesuvstädte* (Studien zur antiken Stadt 5; Munich: Pfeil, 1999).

[444]Amedeo Maiuri, "La Croce di Ercolano," *Rendiconti della Pontificia Accademia romana di Archeologia* 15 (1939): 193-218; cf. Lorenzo Falanga, *La croce di Ercolano: Cronistoria di una scoperta* (Quaderni dell' Associazione per lo studio e la divulgazione dell'archeologia biblica 2; Naples: D'Auria, 1981). For arguments against a Christian interpretation see Luciano de Bruyne, "La 'crux interpretum' di Ercolano," *Rivista di Archeologia Cristiana* 21 (1945): 281-95; E. Dinkler, "Zur Geschichte des Kreuzsymbols," *ZThK* 48 (1951): 148-72, esp. 159.

[445]*CIL* IV Suppl. 8623, 8123. See Heinz Hofmann, "Satorquadrat," *PWSup* 15 (1978): 477-565; F. V. Filson, "Were There Christians at Pompeii?" *BA* 2 (1939): 13-16; D. Atkinson, "The Sator-Formula and the Beginnings of Christanity," *BJRL* 22 (1938): 419-34; idem, "The Origin and Date of the 'Sator' Word-Square," *Journal of Ecclesiatical History* 2 (1951): 1-18; D. Fishwick, "On the Origin of the Rotas-Sator Square," *HTR* 57 (1964): 39-53; Walter O. Moeller, *The Mithraic Origin and Meanings of the Rotas-Sator Square* (Leiden: Brill, 1973); Margherita Guarducci, "Dal gioco letterale alla crittografia mistica," *ANRW* II.16.2 (1978): 1736-173; William Baines, "The Rotas-Sator Square: A New Investigation," *NTS* 33 (1987): 469-76; Kurt Aland, "Noch einmal: Der ROTAS/SATOR-Rebus," in *Text and Testimony: Essays on New Testament and Apocryphal Literature* (FS A. F. J. Klijn; ed. T. Baarda; Kampen: Kok, 1988), 9-23.

[the wheels])." Felix Grosser interpreted the formula in 1926 as an anagram: he connected the letters symmetrically and read the sentence PATER NOSTER AO, PATER NOSTER AO, with A and O standing for Alpha and Omega ("Our Father, Alpha and Omega"); the letters can be combined to form a "Paternoster cross," with the letters alpha and omega in the upper and in the lower squares. In this interpretation the Sator square is seen as an early Christian cryptogram that Christians used as a secret sign of recognition. This once widely held interpretation is questioned by many scholars today. Walter Moeller argued in 1973 that the square originated in the Mithras cult. And if one selects geometrically relevant positions in the square and interprets the letters in these positions as representing figures (on the basis of the Greek or the Aramaic alphabet, depending on the approach), it is possible to deduce the astronomical precession period—that is, the so-called Platonic year (25,850 years).

Many scholars accept the conclusion that the Sator square does not have Christian origins. Colin Hemer did not want to dismiss the Christian interpretation for the squares found in Pompeii, and argues that the Christian faith developed and expanded much more quickly than our fragmentary sources indicate.[446] A fragmentary graffito found in Pompeii is read by some scholars as "Christiraii" and interpreted as a reference to Christians. However, this is uncertain.[447]

Paul Berry recently revived the discussion about the inscription discovered in 1862 by Alfred Kiessling in Pompeii and attempts to demonstrate that the inscription is of Christian origin, which would prove that there was a Christian community in Pompeii before A.D. 79. He also argues, against the traditional consensus, that the Christians living in Italy spoke Latin in their religious services, as early as the first communities that were formed after the first early Christian missionaries arrived in Italy.[448]

22.7 Missionary Work in the Province of Asia

The dissemination of the Christian faith in Asia Minor (see fig. 18) seems to have happened with general success. In the last decades of the first century, at the latest, churches existed in many of the larger cities of the province of Asia: in Smyrna, Pergamon, Thyatira, Sardis, Philadelphia and Ephesus. With the exception of Ephesus, we do not possess reliable information about the establishment of these Christian communities. Early traditions suggest that the apostle John was active in at least some of these churches. It is impossible to know, however, whether he was the founder of the churches in any of these cities.

The following sources attest churches in these cities for the first century: (1) The so-called letters to the seven churches in Rev 2—3, in the context of the assumption that the traditional ascription of John's Revelation to the apostle John and the traditional date of the composition of John's Revelation in the first century are reliable. (2) Irenaeus writes, "John, the disciple of the Lord, who also had leaned upon his breast, did himself publish

---

[446]Hemer 1989, 155-56.
[447]*CIL* IV 679. See Hemer 1989, 156 n. 156.
[448]Paul Berry, *The Christian Inscription at Pompeii* (Lewiston, N.Y.: Mellen, 1995).

a Gospel during his residence at Ephesus in Asia" (*Ephesi Asiae commorans* [*Haer.* 3.1.1]).
In *Haer.* 3.3.4 Irenaeus writes explicitly that "the church in Ephesus, founded by Paul, and
having John remaining among them permanently until the times of Trajan, is a true witness of the tradition of the apostles." (3) Clement of Alexandria reports in his treatise *Quis
dives salvetur* ("What Rich Man Can Be Saved?" in Eusebius, *Hist. eccl.* 3.23.6) of old traditions according to which the apostle John lived in Ephesus after his return from exile
on Patmos: "He went away upon their invitation to the neighboring territories of the Gentiles [ἐπὶ τὰ πλησιόχωρα τῶν ἐθνῶν], to appoint bishops in some places, in other places
to set in order whole churches, elsewhere to choose to the ministry some one of those
that were pointed out by the Spirit." Helmut Koester argues that this tradition may indeed
go back to earliest times, when Polycarp was not yet bishop of Smyrna.[449] (4) The newly
published *Fragments of Polycarp* 63r refer to John appointing Polycarp as bishop of
Smyrna.[450] (5) Irenaeus states that Polycarp "also was not only instructed by apostles, and
conversed with many who had seen Christ, but was also, by apostles in Asia, appointed
bishop of the Church in Smyrna" (*Haer.* 3.3.4).[451] (6) Tertullian also states that Polycarp
was appointed bishop of Smyrna by John (*Praescr.* 32.2).[452] (7) The apocryphal *Acts of
John* (A.D. 125-150?)[453] describes the ministry of the apostle John in Miletus (*Acts John* 18),
Ephesus, including the alleged destruction of the temple of Artemis as a result of his ministry (18-54, 62-86), Smyrna (56-57) and Laodikeia (58-59). Some scholars suspect that an
account of a journey of John to Pergamon, Thyatira, Sardis and Philadelphia is missing
between *Acts of John* 57 and 58.[454] M. Oberweis argues that John died early as a martyr,
like his brother James;[455] if he is correct, all of these traditions are legendary. This interpretation is not a consensus, however.

Evangelism in Smyrna

We do not know when the first Christian missionaries reached Smyrna. By A.D.
90 a Christian community existed in the city, and John communicates with the
church in Smyrna in Rev 2:8-11 as a church established for quite some time.

---

[449]H. Koester 1995b, 138; cf. Weidmann 1999, 131.

[450]Weidmann 1999, 43; commentary, ibid., 76-79.

[451]See Eusebius, *Hist. eccl.* 4.14.3. Brox, ed., *Epideixis: Adversus Haereses*, translates *Haer.* 3.3.4
as follows: "Auch Polykarp wurde von den Aposteln nicht nur unterrichtet und hatte nicht
nur mit vielen Umgang, die den Herrn noch gesehen hatten, sondern er ist auch von den
Aposteln in der Kirche von Smyrna als Bischof für Asien eingesetzt worden."

[452]Hengel (1993, 71 n. 218) suggests that this statement is a tendentious development of information provided by Irenaeus (Eusebius, *Hist. eccl.* 5.20.6). Weidmann (1999, 131) argues,
however, that Tertullian's description of John agrees with the reports of Irenaeus and with
the traditions about John in general.

[453]See Junod and Kaestli 1983; Knut Schäferdiek, "Johannesakten," in Hennecke and
Schneemelcher 1990-1997, 2:138-90 (ET, 2:188-259). On *Acts of John* see also Bremmer 1995;
Lalleman 1998, with a discussion on the dating of *Acts of John* around A.D. 125-150 (268-70).

[454]K. Schäferdiek, in Hennecke and Schneemelcher 1990-1997, 2:151, 177 (ET, 2:211), following
T. Zahn, "Die Wanderungen des Apostels Johannes," *Neue kirchliche Zeitschrift* 10 (1899):
191-218, esp. 198. This is rejected by Junod and Kaestli (1983, 1:93-94), who maintain that
the identity of the λοιπαὶ πόλεις that John is said to have visited remains unknown.

[455]Michael Oberweis, "Das Papias-Zeugnis vom Tode des Johannes Zebedäi," *NovT* 38 (1996):
277-95, discussing Papias *Fragment* 10.17. See also Reinbold (2000, 254-56), who is generally
skeptical regarding the patristic traditions about John.

Smyrna (Σμύρνα; mod. Izmir),[456] situated about 73 km north of Ephesus on the mouth of the Hermos River at the end of the Hermaic Gulf (mod. Izmir Körfezi), was one of the great Ionian port cities along with Miletus and Ephesus. Smyrna was founded in the tenth century as a Greek colony, which was expanded in the ninth century. Homer probably was born in Smyrna in the eighth century, where he wrote the *Iliad*. The temple of Athene that was built in the seventh century was destroyed in 545 B.C. by the Persians. The growth of the city prompted in the third century the foundation of New Smyrna on the slopes of Mount Pagos (mod. Kadife Kale). David Magie estimates that Smyrna had at least two hundred thousand inhabitants.[457] Cicero praised Smyrna as the oldest and most faithful of Rome's allies in Asia Minor (*Phil.* 11.5). A statue of Tiberius was erected in Smyrna even before he became emperor in A.D. 14.[458] When Smyrna and Sardis competed for the honor of being allowed to erect a second imperial temple in the province of Asia, Smyrna was victorious (Tacitus, *Ann.* 4.15.55-56): Tiberius granted Smyrna in A.D. 26 the right to build a temple for the provincial imperial cult, dedicated to Tiberius, to his mother, Livia, and to the Senate. Smyrna thus became "temple warden" (νεωκόρος, *neōkoros*). Between A.D. 54 and 59 the famous astrologer Tiberius Claudius Balbillus erected a bilingual inscription with a dedication for Nero.[459] Hadrian granted Smyrna a second imperial temple, dedicated to Zeus, probably during the emperor's stay in the city.[460] Aelius Aristides reports that there was a Zeus altar in the middle of the agora since 150 B.C. Other deities that were worshiped in Smyrna include Apollo, Artemis, Asclepius, Aphrodite, Demeter, Dionysos, Hermes, Heracles, Isis, Kore, Nemesis, Nike, Sarapis, Theos Hypsistos and (Agathe) Tyche. Demeter and Dionysos had the attribute πρὸ πόλεως (*pro poleōs*, "before the city"), which does not necessarily point to a sanctuary outside the city walls but presumably designates these deities as patron gods of the city.[461] The fish of a pond that belonged either to the Syrian goddess Atargatis or to Artemis (Ephesia?) were regarded as sacred.[462]

---

[456]L. Bürchner, "Smyrna 2," PW 3.A1 (1927): 730-64; E. Olshausen, *KP* 5:244; E. Akurgal, *PECS* 847-48; W. M. Calder et al., *OCD* 1417; Cecil John Cadoux, *Ancient Smyrna: A History of the City from the Earliest Times to 324 A.D.* (Oxford: Blackwell, 1938); Magie 1950, 1:76-77, 99-100, 448, 450, 543, 584-85; 2:888-90 (nn. 91-95); Akurgal Ekrem, (Ankara: Türk Tarih Kurumu Bas Mevi, 1983); Price 1984, 64-67, 185, 258 (nos. 45-47); Hemer 1986, 57-75; S. Mitchell 1995a, 1:57, 65, 206, 244; J. M. Cook et al., *Old Smyrna Excavations: The Temples of Athena* (Annual of the British School at Athens Supplementary Volume 30; London: British School at Athens, 1998). Inscriptions: Georg Petzl, *Die Inschriften von Smyrna* (2 vols.; IK 23-24; Bonn: Habelt, 1982-1990); Donald F. McCabe, Tad Brennan and R. Neil Elliott, *Smyrna Inscriptions: Texts and List* (Princeton, N.J.: Institute for Advanced Study, 1988); Dräger 1993, 180-88; G. Cohen 1995, 180-83.

[457]Magie 1950, 585.

[458]See *I. Smyrna* 618, an honorary inscription that probably belonged to the base of a statue.

[459]*I. Smyrna* 619.

[460]*I. Smyrna* 697 (= *IGR* IV 1431). The inscription *I. Smyrna* 594 (= *IGR* IV 1398) lists the personnel of the cult who were appointed when Smyrna became "twice *neōkoros*," including hymnodes, or choral singers, and θεολόγοι (*theologoi*), who were orators at the feasts who praised the ruler with prose discourses. See Price 1984, 258; Robert 1969-1990, 2:837; Petzl, *Die Inschriften von Smyrna,* 2:75-76.

[461]Cf. *I. Smyrna* 639, 655, 730.

[462]Cf. *I. Smyrna* 735: "It is prohibited to misappropriate the sacred fish, to damage any equipment of the goddess or to remove it, in order to steal it. He who does any of this shall perish as transgressor, he shall end as feed of the fish" (dated to the first century B.C.; see the commentary by Petzl, *Die Inschriften von Smyrna,* 2:239).

The family of a certain C. Iulius Mithres occupied a hereditary priestly office of the Dionysos cult in the first century A.D.[463] A certain Apolloios Sparos was priest of Helios Apollo Kisauloddenos, whose temple had been donated by Apolloios's father, including the equipment used in the cult.[464] The council and the people of Smyrna, together with the association of the mysteries of Demeter, honored the two sisters Claudia Antonia Sabina Prokliane and Claudia Antonia Iuliane in the first or second century A.D., who were *theologoi,* orators who entertained with religious discourses during the feast of the cult mysteries.[465]

Smyrna was known for its wealth, great buildings and involvement in the sciences and in medicine. Strabo describes New Smyrna as the most beautiful city of Ionia (νῦν ἐστὶ καλλίστη τῶν πασῶν [14.1.37]). He describes the regular layout of the city, the straight and paved streets, the large two-storied colonnaded halls,[466] the library, the Homerium (a square stoa with a shrine and a wooden statue of Homer) and the harbor, which could be closed.[467] The marble that Smyrna imported for its statues came from quarries in, for example, Chemtou in Numidia (Tunesia) and Mons Porphyrites in Egypt.[468] Neither the theater on the northwestern slope of Mount Pagos nor the stadium located in the west of the city has been preserved. The state agora (120 by 80 m) survives; the two-storied stoas on the east and the west side of the agora are 17.5 m wide. A relief (2.2 m high) that was found in the agora depicts Poseidon, flanked by Artemis and Demeter, presumably a reference to Smyrna's claim to control both the land trade and the sea trade.[469]

Smyrna, along with Pergamon and Ephesus, was an important center of the Second Sophistic since the mid-first century A.D. Niketes of Smyrna, who taught at the time of Nero, is regarded as the founder of the Second Sophistic.[470] Studies at the academy of the Sophist Antonius Polemon (A.D. 90-145) were, for many students, the climax of their literary and rhetorical education, comparable with modern university studies.[471] Polemon's student Aelius Aristides, who had traveled and lectured in the entire Greek world, including Egypt and Rome, lived and taught at the end of his life in Smyrna. The members of the association of the initiates (*mystēs*) and artisans (*technitēs*) of Dionysios honored in the first century a certain C. Iulius Cheirisophos, the son of C. Iulius Mousonios, a teacher

---

[463]Cf. *I. Smyrna* 731, lines 7-9 (Records of the Dionysian Synodos, dated to A.D. 80-83).

[464]See *I. Smyrna* 753.

[465]See *I. Smyrna* 653. See L. Ziehen, "θεολόγος," PW 5.A2 (1934): 2033.

[466]For epigraphical evidence for stoas in Smyrna see *I. Smyrna* 424, 683.

[467]See *I. Smyrna* 696, an inscription dated between A.D. 26 and 123, which listed the names of those "who promised to contribute and who contributed to the renovation of the harbor"; the list of names is not preserved. There is epigraphical evidence for ferry services across the Hermaic Gulf or across the Hermos River; see *I. Smyrna* 712, recording an edict against the cartel of ferry operators from the first or second century A.D.

[468]*I. Smyrna* 697, lines 40-42 (dated shortly after A.D. 124; see the commentary by Petzl, *Die Inschriften von Smyrna,* 2:196-97).

[469]For a picture see Jale Dedeoğlu, *Izmir Archaeological Museum* (Istanbul: Turizim Yayinlari, 1993), 74. The relief dates to the second century.

[470]Philostratus, *Vit. soph.* 1.19; probably together with Niketes Sacerdos, a teacher of Pliny the Younger (*Ep.* 6.6.3); see L. Radermacher, "Niketes 6," PW 17.1 (1936): 319-21; O. Dreyer, *KP* 4:103. Claudia Niketes, who is mentioned in an inscription from Smyrna (*I. Smyrna* 697, line 22), perhaps is the daughter of this Niketes (see the commentary by Petzl, *Die Inschriften von Smyrna,* 2:194).

[471]R. Klein 1981, 74 n. 10. On Polemon see Reader 1996, 7-22 (critical text and translation, ibid., 87-183; notes and commentary, ibid., 185-409).

of grammar.[472] Under Hadrian the philosopher and mathematician Theon taught in Smyrna; he also wrote commentaries on Plato's writings.[473] Among the important magistrates of Smyrna in the first century was T. Flavius Onesimos Paternianos. He was *stratēgos,* high priest in the temple of Nemesis, in charge of the archive, president of the *prytaneis,* supervisor of the market and treasurer.[474] Another famous son of the city was Tiberius Claudius Rufus, who had been victorious in many athletic games (ἄνδρα πλειστο-νείκην) and was a member of the association (σύνοδος) of athletes; he was known to several emperors and was honored with the citizenship of Olympia and with a statue erected "by the people of the Smyrneans."[475] An inscription that was erected not long after A.D. 124, honoring the donors of buildings and of finances, documents the existence of Jews in Smyrna who participated in the public life of the city.[476] It therefore is a fair assumption that Jews lived in Smyrna in the first century. There is inscriptional evidence for the beautification of a synagogue in the fourth or fifth century.[477]

The apocryphal *Acts of John* claims that the citizens of Smyrna sent a delegation to Ephesus to ask the apostle John to come to Smyrna:

"While performing these deeds at Ephesus, the people in Smyrna sent messengers to him [Σμυρναῖοι διεπέμψαντο πρὸς αὐτόν] saying, 'We hear that God whom you preach is an unenvious God, and has bidden you not to show partiality and remain in one place [ἀκούομεν ὃν κηρύσσεις Θεὸν ὅτι ἄφθονός ἐστι καὶ διετάξατό σοι μὴ ἐμφιλοχωρεῖν ἐν ἑνὶ τόπῳ]. Being the preacher of such a God, come to Smyrna and the other cities [ἐλθὲ εἰς τὴν Σμύρναν καὶ εἰς τὰς λοιπὰς πόλεις], that we may know your God and, knowing him, put our hope in him'" (*Acts John* 55).

At the beginning of the second century Polycarp (A.D. 69-155) was bishop in Smyrna.[478] Tertullian states, as has been pointed out, that Polycarp was appointed bishop by the apostle John (*Praescr.* 32.2).

Evangelism in Pergamon

The church in Pergamon was established some time before A.D. 90, as John sends a message to the Christian community there (Rev 2:12-17). Since neither John nor any other early Christian source reports the history of the church in

---

[472]See *I. Smyrna* 652.

[473]Theon's son erected a bust of his father in Smyrna, which was discovered in the seventeenth century; see *I. Smyrna* 648.

[474]See *I. Smyrna* 641. Other treasurers in the first and second century were Nikomedes, Ti. Claudius Zenon, M. Vibius Theodoros; see *I. Smyrna* 683, 653.

[475]See *I. Smyrna* 657 (this inscription is found in Olympia [*Inv* 358]).

[476]See *I. Smyrna* 697 (*IJudO* II, 40), line 30; see Petzl, *Die Inschriften von Smyrna,* 2:195, with reference to A. T. Kraabel, *JJS* 33 (1982): 455. See also Ameling, in *IJudO* II, 2004, 177-79.

[477]See *I. Smyrna* 844 = *CIJ* II, 739-740 = *IJudO* II, 41-42.

[478]On Polycarp see William R. Schoedel, *ABD* 5:390-95; M. W. Holmes, "Polycarp of Smyrna," *DLNTD* 934-38; A. Lindemann and H. Paulsen, eds., *Die Apostolischen Väter: Griechisch-deutsche Parallelausgabe* (Tübingen: Mohr-Siebeck, 1992), 242-57; Johannes B. Bauer, *Die Polykarpbriefe* (Kommentar zu den Apostolischen Vätern 5; Göttingen: Vandenhoeck & Ruprecht, 1995); Weidmann 1999.

Pergamon, we do not know the identity of the first missionaries or the exact date when they arrived there.

Pergamon (Πέργαμον; mod. Bergama)[479] was 110 km north of Smyrna on the Selinos River (mod. Bergama Çay) at the northern edge of the plain of Kaykos in Mysia. The road from Ephesus to Pergamon was repaired in A.D. 75, during the principate of Vespasian.[480] Since the Kaykos valley (mod. Bakir Çayi) did not allow a direct route to the Anatolian highland, the main traffic moved through the Hermos Valley in the south. Pergamon did not control one of the major trade routes. North of the city was Mount Pindasos (mod. Madra Dağ, Kozak [1243 m]), and to the south Mount Aspordenos (mod. Yund Dağ [782 m]) with a sanctuary of Cybele built in the third century B.C. (Meter Theon; mod. Mamurt Kale, about 32 km from Pergamon as the crow flies). The acropolis of Pergamon is 330 m high, linked with Mount Pindasos by a low ridge and flanked by the gorgelike valleys of the rivers Selinos and Keteios. Pergamon was 26 km from the coast (near mod. Dikili) and 28 km from the mouth of the Kaykos River. Cities in the vicinity of Pergamon included the ports Elaia (mod. Kazıkbağarı, at the mouth of the Kaykos), Pitane (Çandarli) and Atarneus (near Dikili), where Aristotle had lived for a time. About 28 km northwest of Pergamon was Perperene (Aşagı Beyköy), the most important town in the Pindasos Mountains, whose wine was praised by Galen.[481] About 30 km south of Pergamon was Aigai (Aegae; mod. Nemrut Kale) in the Aspordenos Mountains. Several smaller towns in the Kaykos Valley included (from west to east): Teuthrania (mod. Kalerga), Halisarna (Eğrigöltepe), Gambreion (Poyraçık), Parthenion (Eski Bergama), Apolloia (Duvurlar) and Gergitha (Germe; mod. Yirce). Further east, on the upper Kaykos, on the road toward the southeast into the Hermos Valley and on the road toward the north into the Makestos Valley, before reaching the territory of Thyatira, other towns were controlled by Pergamon: Nakrasos (mod. Maltepe?

---

[479]W. Zschietzschmann, PW 19.1 (1937): 1235-63; E. Meyer, *KP* 4:626-31; J. Schäfer, *PECS* 688-92; M. Rudwick and C. H. Hemer, *GBL* 3:1154-56; D. S. Potter, *ABD* 5:228-30; W. Röllig and W. Eder, *DNP* 9:543-44; A. Spawforth and C. Roueché, *OCD* 1138-39; Jones 1937, 45-48, 82-83; Magie 1950, 1:3-4, 134, 232-33, 403, 422, 482, 594-95; 2:725, 771, 1258; Hemer 1989, 78-103; Radt 1988; S. Mitchell 1995a, 1:45-46, 100, 114 (fig. 18e), 177, 219, 243-44; 2:33, 43; Gates 1995, 240-45; Köhler 1996, 54-60; H. Koester 1998, especially the essay there by W. Radt, "Recent Research in and about Pergamon," 1-40; Radt 1999. Excavations: *Altertümer von Pergamon I-XI* (Berlin: Deutsches Archäologisches Institut, 1885-1975); see also *Pergamenische Forschungen* (Berlin: Deutsches Archäologisches Institut, 1972-). See also the CD-ROM *Pergamon: Geschichte und Monumente der antiken Stadt* (Stuttgart: Theiss, 2001). Inscriptions: *I. Pergamon* (M. Fränkel, ed., *Die Inschriften von Pergamon* [2 vols.; Altertümer von Pergamon 8; Berlin: Spemann,1890-1895]; C. Habicht 1969); the inscriptions that were discovered during the campaigns of 1896-1909 will by published by Helmut Müller; many inscriptions are included in the CD-ROM by the Packard Humanities Institute (PHI # 8). On the history of the Attalids see Esther V. Hansen, *The Attalids of Pergamon* (Ithaca, N.Y.: Cornell University Press, 1971); Reginald E. Allen, *The Attalid Kingdom: A Constitutional History* (Oxford: Clarendon, 1983); Dräger 1993, 176-80, and passim; G. Cohen 1995, 168-70.

[480]See *I. Smyrna* 823, 824 (= *CIL* III Suppl. 7203, 7204 = *IGR* IV 1486) and the nearly identical inscription from Thyatira (*CIL* III 470 = *IGR* IV 1193). A milestone from the Ephesus-Smyrna-Pergamon road that is dated in the year A.D. 51 was found several kilometers north of ancient Smyrna (in mod. Bornova): *I. Smyrna* 825 (= *CIL* III 476).

[481]See Frank-Michael Kaufmann and Joseph Stauber, "Perperene—Theodosiupolis," *EA* 23 (1994): 41-57. Perperene is attested by Pliny, *Nat.* 5.122.3; 5.126.9; 31.29.1-4; Ptolemaios 5.2.16; Galen, *De victu attenuante* 102.

Ilyaslar?), Attaleia (Selçikli) and Stratonikeia (Hadrianopolis; mod. Siledik; Yağmurlu).[482]

The significance of Pergamon was linked with its mighty fortress and its powerful rulers who extended their influence beyond the Kaykos Valley. Greeks settled in the area at the beginning of the first millennium B.C. According to legend, Telephos founded Pergamon. The first historical information reports the Greek mercenary army of the "Ten Thousand" under Xenophon coming to Pergamon in 399 B.C., when the city belonged to the Persian Empire, ruled by the local princes of the Gongylides, who were of Greek descent. In the fourth century the cult of Asclepius was introduced, upon which the later fame of Pergamon was based.[483] When Alexander the Great defeated the Persian army in 334 B.C. at the Granikos River, Pergamon came under Macedonian rule. Philetairos, one of Alexander's officers, became governor of Pergamon; he expanded the territory of the city considerably and financed several temples. After Attalos I (241-197 B.C.) defeated the Gauls at the sources of the Kaykos River in 280 B.C., he became king of Pergamon. The bronze figure of a dying Gaul, made by Epigonus, was placed on a victory column in the temple of Athene (a copy made of marble survives). After successful disputes with the Seleucid rulers about hegemony in Asia Minor, Pergamon became a major power in the region. Attalos's son and successor, Eumenes II (197-159 B.C.), continued to support Rome as his father had done. In the peace of Apamea (188 B.C.) he received Lydia, Phrygia, Pisidia and large parts of Lycaonia; several years later he also received western Pamphylia and Galatia. Eumenes instituted games in 180 B.C. to commemorate this victory (Nikephoria) that were to be held every three years. In the second century B.C. Krates of Mallos (Cilicia) was the most significant scholar at the royal court: he was the head of the grammatical school of Pergamon, presumably the director of the library and evidently the first scholar to build a globe of the earth. His student Panaitios (of Rhodes) was the first philosopher who acquainted a larger audience in Rome with Greek philosophy.[484] Attalos III mistrusted relatives and friends and had many of them killed. When he died in 133 B.C., he left Pergamon to the Romans and granted the inhabitants of the villages citizenship (*OGIS* I 338). After the rebellion of Aristonikos had been crushed in 129 B.C., larger areas of the kingdom of Pergamon were given to the Gauls and to the rulers of Cappadocia, Bithynia and Pontos, while the central areas were transformed into the province of Asia. Despite the significance of Pergamon, the Roman governor chose Ephesus as the capital of the new province because of its more favorable location. When all of Asia Minor was under Roman control after 64 B.C., Pergamon was only one of many provincial cities. After 29 B.C. Pergamon was the seat of the assembly of the *koinon* of the province of Asia. When Octavian had been proclaimed Emperor Augustus in 27 B.C., the Greeks of Asia were given permission to erect in Pergamon a temple for the veneration of Augustus and Roma, the divine personification of the state (Cassius Dio 51.20.6; Suetonius, *Aug.* 52). This temple was depicted on several series of coins minted in Pergamon. The imperial cult in Pergamon served as a model for many provinces. Tacitus reports that "about the same time, Further Spain sent a deputation to the senate, asking leave to follow the example of Asia by erecting a shrine to Tiberius and his mother. On this occasion, the Caesar, sturdily disdainful of compliments at any time, and now convinced that an answer was due to the gossip charging him with a declension into vanity, began his speech in the following vein: 'I know, Conscript Fathers, that many deplored my want of consistency because, when a

---

[482]See W. Ruge, PWSup 7 (1940): 1244-50; H. Volkmann, "Stratonikeia 2," *KP* 5:394-95; G. Cohen 1995, 232-38. For newly discovered inscriptions in this area see Malay 1999, 25-30 (nos. 5-13).

[483]See Wolfgang Fauth, *KP* 1:644-48; Debord 1982, 33-40; Radt 1999, 220-42.

[484]See Radt 1999, 279.

little while ago the cities of Asia made this identical request, I offered no opposition. I shall therefore state both the case for my previous silence and the rule I have settled upon for the future. Since the deified Augustus had not forbidden the construction of a temple at Pergamon to himself and the city of Rome, observing as I do his every action and word as law, I followed the precedent already sealed by his approval, with all the more readiness that with worship of myself was associated veneration of the senate. But, though once to have accepted may be pardonable, yet to be consecrated in the image of deity through all the provinces would be vanity and arrogance'" (*Ann.* 4.37). Augustus also authorized imperial games in Pergamon (*Romaia Sebasta*). The office of the high priest was shared with the cities of the province of Asia.[485] Pergamon thus was an important center of the imperial cult in the province. When Augustus visited Pergamon in the summer of 20 B.C., he erected a monument in the temple of Athene. In A.D. 113/114 a second imperial temple was built on the highest point of the acropolis in honor of Trajan. The emperor was worshiped in the Traianeum as Zeus Philios.[486] Pergamon was proud to be "twice *neōkoros*" (νεωκόρος). One of the famous sons of Pergamon in the early first century A.D. was Menippos, who wrote a "Periplus of the Interior Sea" (Περίπλους τῆς ἐντὸς θαλάσσης [i.e., the Mediterranean]), in which he described in three books Europe, Asia and Africa. One of the first citizens from Asia Minor who achieved high office in Rome came from Pergamon: Aulius Julius Quadratus was consul in A.D. 94.

We do not possess detailed information about the history of Pergamon in the first century. The city evidently participated in the thriving economy of Asia Minor that resulted from the financial and administrative reforms of the empire under Augustus and Tiberius. The earthquake of A.D. 17 caused some destruction in the city, but less so than in other cities in the region.[487] During the principates of Caligula, Claudius and Nero (i.e., A.D. 37-68) the situation in Asia Minor did not change significantly. When Nero began to remove works of art from cities in Greece and Asia Minor for his new palace (the *domus aurea*) in Rome around A.D. 64, his initially positive reputation declined rapidly. In Pergamon the monuments that remembered the victories against the Gauls were "exported." According to Galen, Pergamon had about 160,000 inhabitants, at least in the second century, including women and slaves and probably including the inhabitants of the villages that belonged to the territory of the city. If we include children under eighteen years of age, Pergamon had a total population of between 180,000 and 200,000 inhabitants.[488] A traditional source of Pergamon's wealth was the wood industry as well as the copper, silver and probably also gold mined in the area. Further sources of income were the cultivation of wheat, barley, wine and olives and the raising of poultry. Pergamon was known for breeding superior horses. The so-called Hellenistic Pergamene (Eastern Sigillata), red-slipped pottery used for luxury items, comparable to modern-day china, flourished between 50 B.C. and A.D. 50; in the subsequent period the forms became more crude, the vessels thicker and the finish inferior. The metal industry of Pergamon was advanced. Writing material produced from animal skins, the so-called parchment, even received its name from the city of Pergamon (*membrana Pergamena*, "Pergamene skin").

Zeus, the supreme deity, and Athene, the deity bringing victory (νικηφόρος), were re-

---

[485]Radt 1999, 44, for the observation that follows above see ibid., 45.

[486]See Daniel N. Schowalter, "The Zeus Philios and Trajan Temple," in H. Koester 1998, 233-49; Radt 1999, 209-20.

[487]See Radt 1988, 47, 282; 1999, 45.

[488]Galen, *De cognoscendis curandisque animi morbis* ch. 9 (Kühn 5.49). See Radt 1988, 175; Magie 1950, 1:585; S. Mitchell 1995a, 1:244.

garded as the patrons of Pergamon.[489] The temple of Athene (peripteros, with 6 times 10 columns), built in 330-325 B.C. and expanded in 197 B.C., was the oldest sanctuary of Pergamon; the temple precinct was surrounded by colonnaded halls that were two stories high; the northern hall (72 by 12 m) had two naves. The temple and the theater, built directly beneath the temple into the steep slope of the acropolis, provided a sweeping view across the valley below. The theater provided seating for ten thousand spectators. Around 220 B.C. a new temple of Athene was built below the acropolis, the Nikephorion, which has not yet been located. Numerous dedications were made to Athene and Zeus simultaneously. There is a general consensus that the royal library donated (or expanded) by Eumenes II was housed in the temple of Athene.[490] Marcus Antonius donated 200,000 books (scrolls) from this library to the Egyptian queen Cleopatra in 41/40 B.C. Numerous inscriptions as well as the royal art collection were exhibited in the temple of Athene, including the victory monuments commemorating the victories of the Pergamene kings over the Gauls. A colossal statue of Athene Promachos stood originally on the round base in the sanctuary of Athene, probably replaced in 20 B.C. by a statue of Augustus. Between the temple of Athene and the temple of Zeus to the south stood the so-called Great Altar, the most famous piece of art in Pergamon, dedicated to Athene and Zeus Soter, perhaps also to the θεοῖς πᾶσι καὶ πάσαις (*theois pasi kai pasais,* "all deities")[491] (it can be seen in the Pergamon Museum in Berlin, Germany). The altar was built probably after 170 B.C.; its size of 35.6 by 33.4 m made it larger than the Athene temple. The altar was flanked on three sides by halls 10 m high. The precinct was entered via a monumental staircase 20 m wide. The interior walls of the halls were decorated with the Telephos frieze, a chronicle of the life of Telephos, the legendary founder of Pergamon, in thirty illustrations.[492] The term "Pergamon altar," as it is generally used, refers to the socle construction and the flanking halls that surrounded the altar proper. Klaus Stähler describes the Pergamon altar as follows: "Above the staircase rests the nearly rectangular socle . . . the basis of the gigantomachy frieze. A broad flight of stairs cuts into this socle on one side, leading to its upper side, a rectangular platform on the larger square of the socle. This platform was understood as a public square and was thus surrounded by a colonnaded hall. . . . In the interior court was the goal and the center of the structure, the sacrificial altar proper. The upper cornice of the altar is known, whereas the shape of the altar is obscure."[493] It

---

[489]For the most important temples and sanctuaries of Pergamon see Radt 1988, 179-274; 1999, 159-244. The "Red Hall" (60 by 26 m), which stood in the center of a large temple precinct (270 by 100 m), evidently dedicated to the veneration of Egyptian deities, was built around A.D. 100-150 at the west side of the Roman forum; see Radt 1999, 200-209; Klaus Nohlen, "The 'Red Hall' (Kızıl Avlu) in Pergamon," in H. Koester 1998, 77-110.

[490]See Radt 1999, 165-68; Gregory Nagy, "The Library of Pergamon as a Classical Model," in H. Koester 1998, 185-232. H. Mielsch ("Die Bibliothek und die Kunstsammlungen der Könige von Pergamon," *AA* [1995]: 765-79) argues that the library was housed in the gymnasium.

[491]See Gioia De Luca and Wolfgang Radt, *Sondagen im Fundament des grossen Altars* (Pergamenische Forschungen 12; Berlin: de Gruyter, 1999), 125. They point to the many diverse epiphanies of gods in the large frieze and in the round sculptures on the roof.

[492]For a full description see Radt 1999, 174-78. See also <http://cobweb.cc.oberlin.edu/~jromano/images/grkscuprg.html>.

[493]See Klaus Stähler, "Überlegungen zur architektonischen Gestalt des Pergamonaltares," in Şahin et al. 1978, 838-67; quotation, 838-39. Stähler interprets the altar as a place for hero worship. On the history of research and on newer theories see Radt, in H. Koester 1998, 19-24. See also De Luca and Radt, *Sondagen,* 1999; on the hypothesis of W. Hoepfner (*AA* 1996) see ibid., 121-23; for the remark that follows above see ibid., 125.

is also unclear whether the altar on the platform was used for sacrifices or for libations. Wolfgang Radt comments, "The sacrificial ceremony resembled those in more or less all sanctuaries of antiquity: only the priestess of Athene and probably a priest of Zeus had, together with the king, the highest officials and the envoys from other cities, access to the sacrificial altar proper. . . . Cattle, sheep and pigs were offered as sacrifices; that is, they were killed at the altar and some of the best pieces were burnt on the altar for the gods. The rest of the meat was distributed among the participants in the feast."[494] The large temple of Demeter stood west of the gymnasium; in the first century statues of members of the imperial family were erected in the temple, which thus served the cult of the emperor. The temple of Hera stood above the upper gymnasium. The fact that Dionysos was the deity of the royal dynasty of Pergamon explains why there were several sanctuaries dedicated to Dionysos in the city. A temple of Dionysos (21 by 12 m) of Ionian style stood near the theater, accessible via a flight of twenty-five stairs, forming the northern end of the theater terrace, which was 250 m long, the longest promenade on the acropolis. Directly south of the theater was the "Nischenbau," as it is called, a structure built on three terraces; the size of the main hall was 10.3 by 8.7 m. This building is identified as the Attaleion—that is, the meeting place of the association of the Attalists, a branch of the artisans of Dionysos whose feasts lasted for days and included wild carousals. The so-called Podium Hall (24 by 10 m), another place for the worship of Dionysos, was located in the residential quarters of the city and probably served also as the location of the imperial cult. The podiums on the right and left sides of the entrance and of the cult niche provided space for about seventy participants reclining on the marble surface. The temple of Augustus has not been located yet, although the (later) Traianeum can be excluded as a location; it may have stood in the Lower City. Southwest of the acropolis, between the Old City and the temple of Asclepius, was the "amusement park" of Pergamon, with theater, amphitheater and stadium.[495] The Christians in Pergamon who were tortured and executed because of their faith, according to early traditions, should be located here in the (Roman) amphitheater, where gladiator games and fights with animals took place.

The *Via Tecta*, a street covered with cross vaulting, 1 km long, led to the temple of Asclepius, a sacred precinct measuring 120 by 90 m that was surrounded on three sides by colonnaded halls. The Doric stoa on the north side was just over 100 m long. The precinct was the site of three smaller temples of Asclepius, Apollo and Hygieia, incubation buildings that served therapies involving healing sleep with the interpretation of dreams,[496] dormitories, a sacred spring, a gymnasium, a library, a caravanserai and a theater that seated 3,500 spectators. The Roman temple that was erected in the first century in the southwest corner may have been linked with festivals honoring the emperors, attested by inscriptions for the time after A.D. 50. The new temple dedicated to Asclepius Soter, which was supported by Hadrian, quickly became the most significant of all the Asclepius temples in the Roman Empire, which more resembled an academy than a sanatorium.

The affair involving monies connected with the temple tax that the Jews of western

---

[494]Radt 1988, 199. See Volker Kästner, "The Architecture of the Great Altar of Pergamon," in H. Koester 1998, 137-61. On the temple of Demeter see C. M. Thomas, "The Sanctuary of Demeter at Pergamon," in H. Koester 1998, 277-98; Radt 1999, 180-86; on the temple of Hera see ibid., 186-88; on the various sanctuaries of Dionysos see ibid., 188-99.

[495]See Radt 1999, 262-66.

[496]Radt 1999, 222. On the Asclepieion see O. Ziegenaus and G. De Luca, *Das Asklepieion* (2 vols.; Altertümer von Pergamon 11; Berlin: Deutschen Archäologischen Institut, 1975); C. Jones, "Aelius Aristides and the Asklepieion," in H. Koester 1998, 63-76; Radt 1999, 220-42.

Asia Minor had collected, which the proconsul Lucius Valerius Flaccius allegedly channeled to Rome in 62 B.C., confirms that there was a Jewish community in Pergamon. Cicero states, however, in his defense of Flaccius, that the Jews of Pergamon did not collect
large sums of money (*Flac.* 69), a comment that may indicate that the Jewish community
in the city was not very large. An inscription from the second century A.D. was erected by
a certain Zopyros, who worshiped "God the Lord" and who placed lanterns on a *bomos;*[497]
some scholars interpret the *bomos* as an altar and interpret Zopyros as a God-fearer, while
other scholars believe that he was a Jew.[498] One of the most famous sons of Pergamon
was Galen (A.D. 130-199), who was the personal physician of several emperors and was
the most versatile medical author of antiquity; he presumably was active in the Asclepieion as well. According to the Arab tradition of his writings preserved by Abulfeda, Galen
criticized the Christians for being easily convinced by parables and miracles. In his book
De differentia pulsuum he asserts that Jews and Christians follow unproven laws (2.4),
but he also knew that the "followers of Moses and Christ" can be more easily taught new
information than physicians and philosophers, who generally keep to the traditions of the
schools to which they belong (3.3).[499]

We do not know when and how the gospel arrived in Pergamon.[500] Epigraphical
and archaeological evidence confirms that the Greek, Roman and Egyptian cults
continued to enjoy the uninterrupted support of the population in the second century. The traditional emphasis of the ruler cult since the time of the Attalids, with
its incarnation in the emperor cult in the first century A.D., seems to be the background of the persecution that Rev 2:13 alludes to: Antipas "the faithful witness"
was killed in Pergamon, "where Satan's throne is" (ὅπου ὁ θρόνος τοῦ Σατανᾶ)
and "where Satan lives" (ὅπου ὁ Σατανᾶς κατοικεῖ). The phrase "throne of Satan"
has been variously interpreted:[501] (1) as a reference to the city of Pergamon as the
center of pagan religiosity in the province of Asia; (2) as an allusion to the soaring
acropolis of Pergamon with its numerous temples, which might appear to a traveler approaching the city from Smyrna as the "throne" of the gods;[502] (3) as a reference to the Great Altar of Zeus Soter ("Zeus the Savior"), who often was depicted with the symbol of the serpent and whose epithet *Sōtēr* implied a

---

[497]Gerhard Delling, "Die Altarinschrift eines Gottesfürchtigen in Pergamon," (1964), in Delling
1970, 32-38. Delling dates the inscription to the third/fourth century A.D. following the advice
of W. Peek. E. J. Bickerman ("The Altars of the Gentiles: A Note on the Jewish 'ius sacrum,'"
Revue Internationale des Droits de l'Antiquité 5 [1958]: 137-164, esp. 158) dates the inscription to the second century A.D.; thus also Trebilco 1991, 163; S. Mitchell 1999, 140, no. 188.

[498]Bickermann and Delling think that he was a God-fearer, while Trebilco (1991, 163) argues
that he was a Jew. Ameling, in *IJudO* II, 2004, 305-6 n. 5, argues that Zopyros was a pagan
God-fearer.

[499]Text in R. Walzer, *Galen on Jews and Christians* (London: Oxford University Press, 1949), 15-
16, 90. J. G. Cook (1993) overlooked this passage in *De differentia pulsuum;* cf. Lührmann
1994, 194.

[500]Most commentaries on Rev 2 do not discuss this question; see Beale, *Rev,* 245-56; also Hemer
1986, 78-105.

[501]See, besides the commentaries, Hemer 1986, 84-87.

[502]See Yarbro Collins 1998, 171.

blasphemous claim, both for Jews and for Gentiles; (4) as a reference to the complex of temples consisting of the temple of Zeus, the Great Altar and the temple of Athene;[503] (5) as a reference to the cult of Asclepius, a god who was also represented by a snake, who was also designated as *Sōtēr* and who was regarded purely and simply as the god of Pergamon; (6) as a reference to the imperial cult, of which Pergamon was an important center and which presented a genuine danger for the Christian community. The last explanation seems the most plausible: the risen Lord identifies himself in the introduction to the message for the church in Pergamon as "he who has the sharp two-edged sword" (Rev 2:12),[504] very probably an allusion to the *ius gladii*, the right to wield the sword (i.e., to punish and to execute), reserved, in Asia Minor, for the governors of the Roman provinces.[505] The twofold reference to Satan not only underlines how dangerous the situation was for the church in Pergamon but also directs the church to remain faithful to Jesus and to continue to be a faithful witness precisely in this city: the risen Lord knows where the church lives, continuously (οἶδα ποῦ κατοικεῖς): in the same city where Satan "lives."[506] We do not know for certain whether Antipas was a member of the church in Pergamon. The formulation that he was killed "among you" (παρ᾽ ὑμῖν, [Rev 2:13]) possibly indicates that he had been brought from another city to Pergamon to stand trial or for execution.

A letter that the churches of Lugdunum (mod. Lyon) and Vienne in Gaul (Eusebius, *Hist. eccl.* 5.1.3-2.8) wrote to the churches in the province of Asia and in Phrygia describes the martyrdom of Christians in A.D. 177 during the principate of Marcus Aurelius (A.D. 161-180) and of Lucius Verus. One of the Christians who was killed was a certain "Attalos, a native of Pergamon, where he had always been a pillar and foundation" (5.1.17). He is described as "a person of distinction" (ἦν ὀνομαστός, *ēn onomastos*) who was "called for loudly by the people" to be tortured in the amphitheater precisely because of his nobility (5.1.43). We do not know whether it was coincidence that he had the name of the three kings of Pergamon in the Hellenistic period. This Attalos "entered the contest readily on account of a good conscience and his genuine practice in Christian discipline, and as he had always been a witness for the truth among us" (5.1.43). When he was brought into the amphitheater, "a tablet being carried before him on which was written in the Roman language 'This is Attalos the Christian' [οὗτός ἐστιν Ἄτταλος ὁ Χριστιανός, *houtos estin Attalos ho Christianos*], the people were filled with indignation against him" (5.1.44). Because he was a Roman citizen, he was taken back to the prison to wait for the decision of the emperor, who ordered that everyone who denied that he was a Christian should be released, while everybody else should be decapitated. Because the governor wanted to please the people, however, he had Attalos fight against animals a second time and tortured: "But when Attalos was placed in the iron seat, and the fumes arose from his burning body, he said to the people in the Roman language: 'Lo! this which you do is devouring men; but we do not devour men; nor do any other wicked thing.' And being

---

[503]See Yarbro Collins 1998, 171-76.
[504]Rev 2:12: ὁ ἔχων τὴν ῥομφαίαν τὴν δίστομον τὴν ὀξεῖαν.
[505]See Hemer 1986, 87, and most interpreters.
[506]See Hemer 1986, 85; for the comment that follows above see ibid., 86.

asked, what name God has, he replied, 'God has not a name as man has'" (5.1.52). The apocryphal *Acts of Carpus, Papylus and Agathonike* speak of three Christians, two men and a woman, who were executed for the faith in Pergamon; Papylus, one of the Christian men, came from Thyatira. Some scholars date these events (and the *Acts of Carpus*) to the time of Emperor Marcus Aurelius,[507] including Eusebius, who writes, "And there are also records extant of others that suffered martyrdom in Pergamus, a city of Asia, of Carpus and Papylus, and a woman named Agathonike, who, after many and illustrious testimonies, gloriously ended their lives" (*Hist. eccl.* 4.15.48). The Latin version (B) transfers these events to the time of Emperor Decius (A.D. 249-251) and describes Carpus as the bishop of Gordos. Some scholars argue that this date is more likely.[508]

Some scholars observe a decline of the temples of Pergamon in the third century, due, according to Wolfgang Radt, "both to the economic conditions of the late imperial period and to the competition with Christianity. The salvation cults of the late Roman Empire, the cults of Isis and of Asclepius, had to give way to the new religion of salvation which had a greater inner strength, Christianity."[509] In the fifth century the Red Hall was converted into a Christian church. In the sixth century a Christian church, of which remains survive, was erected in the precinct of the old Asclepieion, which had been severely damaged in A.D. 262 in an earthquake.

Evangelism in Thyatira

The city of Thyatira is mentioned in the New Testament for the first time in Acts 16:14-15 in connection with Paul's initial missionary outreach in Europe: Lydia, a dealer in purple cloth, whom Paul met in Philippi in Macedonia, originally came from Thyatira. The message to the Christians in Thyatira in Rev 2:18-29 presupposes a Christian community in Thyatira at the latest in the last few decades of the first century.

Thyatira (τὰ Θυάτειρα; mod. Akhisar),[510] about 75 km southeast of Pergamon and 60 km northwest of Sardis in northern Lydia on the Lykos River (Gördük Çay), was founded as the sanctuary of the sun-god Tyrimnus, according to local legend. Strabo asserts that the city was a Macedonian foundation (Strabo 13.4.4). During the reign of Seleukos I, Thyatira was refounded in 281 B.C. as a Seleucid military colony. After 190 B.C. Thyatira was under the control of Attalos I, and after 133 B.C. under the control of the Romans. The city belonged to the province of Asia and to the assize district of Pergamon. Thyatira was one of the larger cities of Asia Minor, with a population estimated at 25,000 inhabitants.[511] Since Livia, Augustus's wife, had acquired land in the vicinity of Thyatira, administrators

---

[507]Adolf von Harnack, *Die Akten des Karpus, Papylus und der Agathonike* (TU 3.2; Leipzig: Teubner, 1888), esp. 433-38; Musurillo, *The Acts of the Christian Martyrs,* xv.

[508]Yarbo Collins 1998, 165 n. 5, referring to B. Aubé, J. de Guibert, H. Delehaye, P. Franchi de'Cavalieri, and C. P. Jones; Yarbro Collins herself is undecided.

[509]Radt 1988, 271.

[510]J. Keil, PW 6.A1 (1936): 657-59; E. Olshausen, *KP* 5:804; U. Serdaroğlou, *PECS* 919; Ramsay 1904, 231-39; Magie 1950, 1:48, 123, 232, 469; 2:776, 972-73, 977-78 (nos. 10-11); Robert 1962, 252-60; Price 1984, 142, 260 (no. 59); Hemer 1986, 106-126; S. Mitchell 1995a, 1:17, 20, 102, 161, 180, 183, 244, 257; see also Trebilco 1991, 120-22; G. Cohen 1995, 238-42; Aune, *Rev,* 1:201. Inscriptions: *TAM* V.2; Malay 1999, nos. 16-35.

[511]See S. Mitchell 1995a, 1:244.

of the imperial estates lived in the city.[512] Thyatira was famous for its processes for dying wool.[513] Guilds of bakers, dyers, tanners, textile workers, potters, wool merchants, slave traders, shoemakers and coppersmiths had a long tradition in Thyatira. Between 27 B.C. and A.D. 154 four citizens of Thyatira, originally colonists (κάτοικοι, *katoikoi*) who had been settled by the Seleucids or by the Attalids in the vicinity the city, donated a colonnaded hall for Artemis, Heracles Kallinikos and Apollo (described as *sōtēr*, "savior") intended for prayers for the health of the emperor Augustus.[514] Further cults attested in inscriptions were dedicated to Apollo Tyrimnos, Theos Hypsistos and Hestia; in villages in the territory of Thyatira we find the worship of Artemis Persike and Zeus Sabazios.[515] In early summer of the year A.D. 76 the city honored Emperor Titus with the erection of a monument.[516] In the early first century A.D. eight communities (or guilds) honored a certain Nemerius Terentius Primus.[517] An inscription from the imperial period (date uncertain) honors a certain C. Valerius Menogenes Annianus, who had occupied the following offices: gymnasiarch, strategos, agoranomos, seitones, dekaprotos (for three years), secretary of the youth (γραμματέα τῶν νέων), director of the archive (*grammatophylax*); and he had been "useful for his home town in other services as well" (καὶ ἐν ἄλλαις ὑπηρεσίαις τῇ πατρίδι χρήσιμον γεγονότα).[518] Apart from some inscriptions and coins, only a few remains of ancient Thyatira survive.

An inscription from Thyatira that dates to the early second century A.D. mentions a *sabbateion*, probably a reference to a synagogue.[519] In A.D. 325 the bishop Seras of Thyatira attended the Council of Nicea.

In Rev 2:19 the Christian community in Thyatira is complimented: "I know your works: your love, faith, service, and patient endurance. I know that your last works are greater than the first." The "works" (τὰ ἔργα, *ta erga*) do not describe "services" generally but seem to stand particularly for missionary activity in the pagan world. When John uses the terms "love," "faith" and "patience," particularly "faith" and "patience," he nearly always describes continuous witness for Jesus Christ.[520] The prophetess Jezebel, whom the church tolerated, according to the censure in Rev 2:20-22, was a member of the church, a woman who had the gift of prophecy or claimed to be a prophet and who had seduced other Christians to live immoral lives and to eat meat sacrificed to idols. Both sins probably are connected with membership in or the activities of the trade guilds of Thyatira at their banquets.[521]

---

[512]Two inscriptions attest the presence of *procuratores arcae Livianae* in Thyatira: *TAM* V.2 913, 935.
[513]*CIG* 3496-3498 (= *IGR* IV 1250, 1213, 1265).
[514]Malay 1999, no. 24. Price (1984, 260) lists only the "royal room" (*basilikos oikos*) in the Hadrianeion mentioned in *IGR* IV 1290.
[515]Malay 1999, nos. 25, 26, 27, 29, as well as no. 51 (dedication for Stratoneike, priestess of Artemis Persike, from Akselendi) and no. 55 (dedication for Zeus Sabazios of Tiyenlim, the site of a village named Kidoukome [?]).
[516]See Malay 1999, no. 18.
[517]*TAM* V.2 1133 (= *I. GRIAsia* 52); the inscription possibly dates to the late first century B.C.
[518]Malay 1999, no. 22.
[519]*CIJ* II 752; *IJudO* II 146; L. Levine 2000, 107 n. 176.
[520]See Rev 1:19; 2:4, 13; 3:10; 13:10; 14:12; cf. 1:5; 2:10; 3:14; 17:14. See Beale, *Rev*, 260.
[521]See Ramsay 1904, 254-56; Hemer 1989, 117-20.

Evangelism in Sardis

The reference to Sardis in Rev 3:1-6 presupposes the existence of the Christian community in the last decades of the first century.

Sardis (Σάρδεις; mod. Sart),[522] about 85 km east of Smyrna and 135 km southeast of Pergamon on the middle Hermos River (mod. Gediz Çay), had been the capital of the Lydian empire whose most famous and last king was Croesus (560-546 B.C.?). The acropolis of the city was located on a narrow ledge of the northern ridge of Mount Tmolos. The center of ancient Sardis, which was a temple of Artemis, was located on the western section of the acropolis on the slopes leading down to the Pactolus River, the "gold carrying" river to which the legendary wealth of the Lydian kings was traced. Pliny reports that the process of dyeing was invented in Sardis (Pliny, *Nat.* 7.196), a tradition that indicates the reputation of the city in antiquity. The finely woven carpets produced in Sardis could be found in the palaces of the Persian kings. Sardian sofa covers were known in Athens around 400 B.C. The wealth of the city was also a function of its location: Sardis was situated at the crossroads of the major routes leading to Ephesus, Smyrna, Pergamon and into the interior regions of Anatolia. After the conquest by Cyrus in 547 B.C., Sardis was the capital of a Persian satrapy and the center of the Lydian royal dynasty. Ionians destroyed the city in 498 B.C. Xerxes assembled his troops in Sardis before crossing the Hellespont. After the death of Alexander the Great, Sardis initially was controlled by Antigonos, and after 282 B.C. by the Seleucid kings, who converted Sardis as one of their royal cities. During this period Sardis became a Greek polis with an agora and a theater. Antiochos I stayed in Sardis between 276 and 274 B.C. during the campaigns against the Celts (Galatians), who had invaded Asia Minor. After 188 B.C. the city was controlled by the Attalid dynasty of Pergamon. When Eumenes II of Pergamon defeated the Galatians near Synnada in 167 B.C., the citizens of Sardis honored him by instituting games that were to be celebrated every five years (*OGIS* II 763). When the Romans took over control in 133 B.C., Sardis became the capital of a *conventus* in the new province of Asia. Just before their Macedonian campaign, Cassius and Brutus met in Sardis in 42 B.C. For the subsequent years inscriptions and a temple for Augustus document the enthusiasm of the citizens of Sardis for Augustus as the new ruler of the world.[523]

---

[522]E. Olshausen, *KP* 4:1551-52; J. A. Scott and G. Hanfmann, *PECS* 808-10; John G. Pedley, *ABD* 5:982-84; W. M. Calder et al., *OCD* 1356-57; Magie 1950, 1:47-48, 121-22, 426, 448, 482, 500; 2:974-76, 1358; George Hanfmann, *Letters from Sardis* (Cambridge, Mass.: Harvard University Press, 1972); idem 1983 (bibliography on Sardis, xviii-xxvi); G. Hanfmann, F. K. Yegül and J. S. Crawford, "The Roman and Late Antique Period," in ibid., 139-67; Price 1984, 66, 151-52, 187, 214, 259-60 (nos. 56-58); Hemer 1986, 129-50; Guralnick 1987; Sherwin-White and Kuhrt 1993, 135, 180-84; S. Mitchell 1995a, 1:18, 25-26, 110, 172, 244; 2:32-33, 36-37, 49; Peter Herrmann, "Sardeis zur Zeit der julisch-claudischen Kaiser," in Schwertheim 1995, 21-36; Peter Weiss, "Götter, Städte und Gelehrte: Lydiaka und 'Patria' um Sardes und den Tmolos," in Schwertheim 1995, 85-109; Gates 1995, 240. Excavations: *Sardis I-IX* (Publications of the American Society for the Excavation of Sardis; ed. H. C. Butler et al.; Leiden: Brill, 1922-); see also Robert L. Vann, *The Unexcavated Buildings of Sardis* (Oxford: British Institute of Archaeology, 1989). Inscriptions: William H. Buckler and David M. Robinson, eds., *Sardis VII, 1: Greek and Latin Inscriptions* (Leiden: Brill, 1932); Robert 1964; Philippe Gauthier, ed., *Nouvelles inscriptions de Sardes II* (Genf: Droz, 1989); G. Cohen 1995, 230-31; Malay 1999, nos. 131-33.

[523]*IGR* IV 1756 (= *ISardBR* 8, lines 13-14); Herrmann, "Sardeis," 23-24; Price 1984, 259, no. 56.

Pliny calls the severe earthquake of A.D. 17 in western Asia Minor the greatest earthquake in human history ("maximus terrae memoria mortalium motus").[524] Tiberius granted Sardis 10 million sesterces for the reconstruction of the city, which had been nearly entirely destroyed, as well as exemption from all financial obligations for five years (Tacitus, *Ann.* 2.47.3-4). The citizens of the destroyed cities expressed their gratitude by erecting a monumental statue (*colossos*) of the emperor and further statues in many cities in Asia Minor as well as in the Forum in Rome (*FGrH* 257 F 36.13). Sardis assumed the name Καισάρεια (*Kaisareia*). In Sardis we find an entire series of inscriptions and monuments dedicated to Tiberius and to Claudius and their relatives.[525] The reconstruction of Sardis was directed by the Roman Marcus Ateius (Tacitus, *Ann.* 2.47). Tiberius Claudius Apollophanes played an important role in A.D. 53/54, perhaps as member of the planning commission or as building technician.[526] A new colonnaded street running from east to west (the so-called Marble Street) was constructed as the main artery of the city. The crossing of the main north-south street formed the center of the city, where a huge gymnasium with baths (120 by 170 m) was built in the first century. Adjacent on the eastern side of this complex was a large public square with diverse buildings of the city magistrate. South of Marble Street were living quarters on the slope extending upward to the acropolis, with one- and two-storied houses. Also in this area were the theater, the stadium, temples (dedicated to Zeus, Men, Men Askenos, Attis and Augustus), clubhouses, meeting halls and gardens. On the slope underneath the acropolis was the so-called North Palace as well as a large building that could be identical with the legendary palace of Croesus. The aqueduct was completed during the principate of Claudius. The reconstruction of the temple of Artemis was completed only in the second century. Emperor Antoninus Pius (A.D. 138-161) granted Sardis the status of temple warden (*neōkoros*); the temple dedicated to Antoninus and Faustina was erected in the Artemision. The city had between 60,000 and 100,000 inhabitants in the second century.[527] When the emperor Diocletian (A.D. 284-305) organized the province of Lydia, Sardis became the capital.

Myths extending back into the classical period and robustly flourishing in the imperial period linked Sardis and Mount Tmolos (mod. Boz Daği [2,100 m]) south of the city with Zeus and his birth from the loins of the Great Mother Goddess, as well as with Dionysos, whose home was thought to be on Mount Tmolos.[528] A cave on Mount Tmolos west of Sardis was regarded as the birthplace of Zeus. Several issues of coins displayed the words *Zeus Lydios* (Ζεὺς Λύδιος). The significance of the cultivation of wine in Lydia—Mount Tmolos and the volcanic region of the Katakekaumene and Maionia produced excellent wines in the imperial period—explains why Lydia was "the land of Dionysos par excellence."[529] Euripides claims to know that the triumphal march of Dionysos through the

---

[524]Pliny, *Nat.* 2.86.200; cf. Strabo 12.8.18; 13.4.10; Tacitus, *Ann.* 2.47.3-4; Cassius Dio 57.17.8; Velleius Paterculus 2.126.4; Suetonius, *Tib.* 48.2. According to Tacitus, the following cities were affected: Sardis, Magnesia ad Sipylum, Temnus, Philadelphia, Aegae, Apollonis, Mostene, Hyrcanis, Hierocaesareia, Myrina, Cyme and Tmolus. See Phlegon of Tralles, *FGrH* 257 F 36.

[525]See Herrmann, "Sardeis," 28-29, 33-34; *I. GRIAsia* 164.

[526]Herrmann, "Sardeis," 35; for the observation that follows above see Firket K. Yegül, "Roman Architecture at Sardis," in Guralnick 1987, 46-61.

[527]See Hanfmann, Yegül and Crawford, "The Roman and Late Antique Period," 146.

[528]For the observation that follows above see Weiss, "Götter, Städte und Gelehrte," in Schwertheim 1995, 85-109.

[529]Weiss, "Götter, Städte und Gelehrte," 94; see Ovid, *Metam.* 11.86; Seneca, *Phoen.* 602; Statius, *Theb.* 7.685-87; Arrian, *Anab.* 5.1.2; Euripides, *Bacch.* 13-14, 460-464; Himerios, *Or.* 46.47-53; 47.42-64; 48.66-69 (fourth century).

world began in Lydia and Phrygia: the question "Who is your family?" can be answered "easily without boasting: I suppose you are familiar with flowery Tmolus." When Pentheus answers, "I know of it; it surrounds the city of Sardis," Dionysos responds, "I am from there, and Lydia is my fatherland" (*Bacch.* 460-464). Nonnos tells the story of Dionysos in the fifth century A.D. in his work *Dionysiaka,* published in forty-eight books, three of which are devoted to the sojourn of Dionysos on Mount Tmolos, particularly at the rivers Hermos and Paktolos, thus in the vicinity of Sardis (10.139-147). It is here that the god has invented wine and where he taught, for the first time, his "sleepless feast" (ἐδίδαξεν ἑήν ἄγρυπνον ἑορτήν [12.397]). Joannes Lydus from Philadelphia (sixth century A.D.) relates the tradition that people believe that the Lydians invented the wine and that the Romans call wine *mustum,* "like a *mystes;* the Sardians were the first to use the designation *mysterion*" (*Mens* 1.3-4). The late Hellenistic, early Roman Orphic Hymns also link the birth of Dionysos with Mount Tmolos (*Orph. hym.* 48-49). On Lydian inscriptions Dionysos is a prominent cult object. The coins of many Lydian cities depict Dionysos; since the second century coins of Sardis also depict Tmolos (as a bearded man with grapes and vines or ivy in his hair). For the city of Sardis, Dionysos and Mount Tmolos were only one theme among many: Kore and Demeter, the gods of the cultivation of wheat, dominated.

Jews lived in Sardis since the Hellenistic period at the latest.[530] Obadiah 20 states that Jews who fled from Jerusalem in the sixth century B.C. settled in the city of Sefarad, identified with Sardis by some scholars. When Antiochos III settled two thousand loyal Jewish families from Babylonia in Lydia and Phrygia (Josephus, *A.J.* 12.147-153), some families presumably came to Sardis, as the city was the center of the governor, who was responsible for the immigrants.[531] The influence of the Jews in Sardis in the first century is seen in the fact that both a Roman official and the city council of Sardis confirmed their considerable autonomy rights. The Jewish inhabitants of Sardis regularly sent the yearly temple tax to Jerusalem, and they insisted on their own diet.[532] In the third century, when Sardis had three imperial temples, the southern wing of the palaestra of the bath-gymnasium complex was remodeled as a monumental synagogue (85 by 20 m), the largest synagogue found in the Roman Empire. The main hall could accommodate one thousand people.

We do not know who founded the Christian community in Sardis. The message to the church in Sardis in Rev 3:1-6 reflects information about the history of the city, but we do not learn much about the history of the church. Allusions to the Jesus tradition, particularly to material in the Gospel of Matthew, and

---

[530]See A. T. Kraabel, "The Synagogue at Sardis: Jews and Christians," in Guralnick 1987, 62-73; Seager and Kraabel 1983; Smallwood 1976, 139-40, and passim; Kraabel 1979, 483-88; M. P. Bonz, "The Jewish Community of Ancient Sardis: A Reassessment of its Rise to Prominence," *HSCP* 93 (1990): 343-59; Trebilco 1991, 37-54; Kraabel 1994; Binder 1999, 283-84; L. Levine 2000, 242-49, and passim; Ameling, in *IJudO* II, 2004, 209-97. The majority of the eighty inscriptions of the synagogue are in Greek. A bilingual Latin-Greek inscription of a "Hebrew woman" ('Εβρέα) called Getiores dates to the third or the fourth century (*CIJ* II 750; *I. GRI-Asia* 107; *IJudO* II 54).

[531]See Robert 1964, 9-21; Seager and Kraabel 1983, 178-79.

[532]Josephus, *A.J.* 14.261; 16.171, 235, 259-261. See John G. Pedley, *Ancient Literary Sources on Sardis* (Cambridge: Harvard University Press, 1972) nos. 212, 275. For the comments that follow above see Fikret K. Yegül, ed., *The Bath-Gymnasium Complex at Sardis* (Archaeological Excavations of Sardis 3; Cambridge, Mass.: Harvard University Press, 1986).

parallels with the message to Ephesus in Rev 2[533] do not seem to provide information about the foundation of the church. The main problem of the church was spiritual lethargy, reflected in the fact that believers had assimilated to pagan lifestyles (Rev 3:3-4). John does not refer to attacks on the church. The believers are reproached for their "works," which are not as they should be: "You have a name of being alive, but you are dead. Wake up, and strengthen what remains and is on the point of death, for I have not found your works perfect in the sight of my God" (Rev 3:1b-2). Greg Beale interprets this exhortation to reflect the basic problem of the church of Sardis as being spiritual lethargy, shown in the fact that the Sardian Christians do not give witness to their faith in the city: they have no missionary impact on their pagan fellow citizens.[534] The "seven stars" (= angels) in Rev 3:1 can be understood as provision of divine help for the Christians in Sardis, if and when they regain their Christian identity and their evangelistic zeal toward their contemporaries. The believers who had "not soiled their clothes" are commended (Rev 3:4): they have not compromised their faith in the numerous and diverse situations of everyday life in Sardis with its pagan gods, temples and feasts.[535] In other words, they were faithful witnesses of the gospel in Sardis. The promise in Rev 3:5 for those who "conquer" states, "You will be clothed like them in white robes, and I will not blot your name out of the book of life; I will confess your name [ὁμολογήσω τὸ ὄνομα αὐτοῦ] before my Father and before his angels." This confirms the interpretation in terms of a lack of missionary zeal of the church in Sardis and the significance of this attitude: the believers who confess the name of Jesus in Sardis by a lifestyle in tune with the gospel, rather than with pagan society, will find their name in the book of life and "confessed" by Jesus Christ before God the Father.

Around A.D. 160 Melito was bishop of the church in Sardis.[536] The bishop Artemidoros attended the Council of Nicea in A.D. 325.

Evangelism in Philadelphia

The message for the church in Philadelphia in Rev 3:7-13 attests a Christian community in the city for the first century.

Philadelphia (Φιλαδέλφεια; mod. Alaşehir),[537] about 45 km east of Sardis, was founded by

---

[533]Besides the commentaries, see Hemer 1996, 143-44.
[534]Beale, *Rev,* 273-80; for the comments that follows above see ibid.
[535]See Rev 14:4, 6-9; cf. 2:14, 20-21; 1 Cor 8:7; 2 Cor 7:1. See Beale, *Rev,* 276.
[536]See Seager and Kraabel 1983, 186-88.
[537]J. Keil, "Philadelphia Nr. 1," PW 19.2 (1938): 2091-93; E. Olshausen, *KP* 4:733-34; idem, "Philadelphia 1," *DNP* 9:777-78; T. S. Mackay, *PECS* 703; W. W. Gasque, *ABD* 5:304-5; Ramsay 1904, 286-93; Magie 1950, 1:124-25, 448, 499-500; Hemer 1986, 153-74; G. Cohen 1995, 227-30; S. Mitchell 1995a, 100, 161, 221, 258. Recent inscriptions: Malay 1999, nos. 182-197.

Antiochos I around 281 B.C.[538] Philadelphia was situated on the southwestern edge of the fertile plain of Kogamos (mod. Gediz Nehri) at the foot of Mount Tmolos (Boz Daği) and controlled the shortest route from Pergamon to the northeastern cities of Kotiaeum and Dorylaium and to the southwestern city of Laodikeia in the upper Maeander Valley. Only one year after Augustus had assumed the epithet *Sebastos,* a priest of Dea Roma and of Augustus is attested in Philadelphia (*SEG* XXXV 1985 1169, dated 27/26 B.C.). Philadelphia was the center of the imperial estates in the region, which were administered by their own procurator and assistants (*IGR* IV 1651). The games of the city, called the *Philadelphia,* were instituted as a result of the peaceful cooperation of Eumenes II and Attalos II. The city suffered from numerous earthquakes. Strabo relates that the citizens adapted the construction of their houses to the earthquakes (ἀρχιτεκτονοῦντες πρὸς αὐτα [12.8.18]). The earthquake of A.D. 17 (see the section on Sardis above) destroyed large parts of the city. Tiberius helped finance the reconstruction; the citizens expressed their gratitude by renaming the city Neokaisareia. In Sarıgöl, 21 km southeast of Philadelphia, the citizens erected an honorary inscription for Claudius.[539] A certain Fl. Praxeas presided over five cults for life at the time of Domitian.[540] In A.D. 214 the emperor Caracalla granted Philadelphia the honor of being *neōkoros.*[541] Among the few surviving remains of ancient Philadelphia are the theater, a city gate of the second century and a city wall of late antiquity. The presence of Jews is attested in literary texts and in inscriptions.[542] A newly published funerary inscription from the vicinity of Philadelphia attests a Jew named Joseph for the fourth century (*I. ManMus* 432; *IJudO* II 51).

The "works" for which the risen Lord commends the church in Philadelphia are the continuous missionary witness of the believers in view of the "synagogue of Satan" (Rev 3:9): "I know your works. Look, I have set before you an open door, which no one is able to shut. I know that you have but little power, and yet you have kept my word and have not denied my name" (Rev 3:8). The "little power" that the church has (μικρὰν ἔχεις δύναμιν, *mikran echeis dynamin*) probably is related to the effectiveness of its witness, which has not reached larger segments of the people living in the city, perhaps because the church is small. The church is promised that unbelieving Jews will be converted in the future (Rev 3:9).[543] The faithfulness of the Christians in Philadelphia—that is, their witness to Jesus—guarantees that Christ will be faithful to them in the immediate future when trials and persecution come (Rev 3:10).

Ignatius's *Letter to the Philadelphians,* written in the early second century,

[538]See Mitchell 1995a, 1:181, on the basis of *SEG* XXXV 1170, an inscription discovered in 1985. Attalus II Philadelphus traditionally was regarded as the founder of the city.
[539]Malay 1999, no. 183.
[540]Peter Weiss, "Ein Priester im lydischen Philadelphia: Noch einmal zu einer Münzlegende," *EA* 26 (1996): 145-48; the cults are not named in the inscription.
[541]On the imperial letter that was inscribed on a large stele (*IGR* IV 1619) see Jens Bartels and Georg Petzl, "Caracallas Brief zur Neokorie des lydischen Philadelphia—eine Revision," *EA* 32 (2000): 183-88.
[542]Rev 3:9; Ign. *Phld.* 6:1-2; *CIJ* II 754; *DF* 31; *IJudO* II 49). See Trebilco 1991, 27-29; L. Levine 2000, 98, 272, 308-9; Ameling, in *IJudO* II, 202-8.
[543]Beale, *Rev,* 286; cf. ibid., 289, on Rev 3:10; see also Hemer 1986, 172.

provides some information about the history of the church in the city.[544] The
church evidently had lost its unity (Ign. *Phld.* 2:1; 3:1-3; 6:2; 7:2; 8:1-2), a group
within the church refused to submit to the church leaders (Ign. *Phld.* 3:2), and
some Christians were in danger of being lured to the synagogue (Ign. *Phld.* 6:1).
The Jews of Philadelphia evidently attacked the validity of the gospel message,
or of the written Gospels, as divine revelation. The controversy provoked by
Montanus seems to have been a reaction to these problems: his claim to and
emphasis on continuous prophetic revelation was one possible answer to the
kind of attacks that the church in Philadelphia faced. It is perhaps no coincidence that the Montanist movement started in Phrygia, a region in which the
inscriptions "Christians for Christians" (ca. A.D. 300)[545] attest courageous believers: to confess faith in Jesus Christ in the Tembris Valley, for example, was indeed dangerous in view of massive resistance of the population and of the local
magistrates.

In A.D. 325 the bishop Hetoimasios attended the Council of Nicea. The city
of Philadelphia, described as "little Athens" in the fifth century, was "the last
bridgehead of Christianity in Asia Minor," which was overpowered not before
A.D. 1391, when Sultan Bajesid I conquered the city.[546]

Evangelism in Ephesus?

It is possible that Jewish-Christian missionaries reached the province of Asia and
proclaimed the gospel in Ephesus before the arrival of the apostle Paul. The
Jewish believer Apollos, a native of Alexandria, whom Luke mentions in Acts
18:24-26, may not have been a well-informed Christian, but "he spoke with
burning enthusiasm and taught accurately the things concerning Jesus" in the
synagogue(s) of Ephesus. Apollos clearly sought to acquaint Jews in Ephesus
with the message of Jesus. It therefore is possible that there was an ongoing
Jewish-Christian missionary outreach in Ephesus before the arrival of Paul in the
city.[547]

22.8 Missionary Work in Cappadocia, Pontus and Bithynia

Luke's account of the events of the Feast of Pentecost in A.D. 30 mentions Jewish
pilgrims from Cappadocia and from Pontus (Acts 2:9). It is possible that some

---

[544]For the observations that follow above see Hemer 1986, 168-70; on Montanism, see ibid.,
170-74; cf. W. M. Calder, "Philadelphia and Montanism," *BJRL* 7 (1923): 309-54. On Montanism see Gottlieb N. Bonwetsch, *Die Geschichte des Montanismus* (Erlangen: Deichert, 1881);
Christine Trevett, *Montanism* (Cambridge: Cambridge University Press, 1996); William Tab-
bernee, *Montanist Inscriptions and Testimonia* (Patristic Monograph Series 15; Macon, Ga.:
Mercer University Press, 1997).
[545]See E. Gibson 1978.
[546]Olshausen, *KP* 4:734.
[547]Riesner 1994, 253 (ET, 285).

of these Diaspora Jews heard Peter explain the life, death and resurrection of Jesus and were converted to faith in Jesus and brought the gospel to the northern areas of Asia Minor. Paul planned missionary outreach in Bithynia after his initial plans to reach the province of Asia in A.D. 49 had to be canceled (Acts 16:7), a project, however, that could not be realized either. Luke explicitly points out that Aquila, a Jewish Christian from Rome whom Paul met in Corinth, was a native of Pontus (Acts 18:2). It is possible that Aquila became a Christian in Pontus before he moved to Rome and later to Corinth, although this cannot be proven, of course. The First Epistle of Peter is addressed to Christians in "Pontus, Galatia, Cappadocia, Asia, and Bithynia" (1 Pet 1:1), which attests the existence of churches in these areas around A.D. 60, assuming that the letter is authentic (see §21.4).

Evangelism in Cappadocia

The First Epistle of Peter is the earliest piece of evidence for Christians in Cappadocia (1 Pet 1:1). We do not know, however, in which Cappadocian cities these Christians lived.

Cappadocia (Καππαδοκία)[548] extends from the Taurus Mountains in the south to the coast of the Black Sea in the north; the Halys River marked the western boundary with Paphlagonia and Phrygia and the Roman province of Galatia, while the Kolchis River, Armenia Minor and the upper Euphrates River formed the eastern boundary. During the Seleucid period Cappadocia was part of a strategy in Asia Minor. After 280 B.C. Cappadocia became a kingdom ruled by the dynasty of the Ariarathides, which flourished in the second century B.C. Internal disturbances and external threats were brought to an end by the Romans. In A.D. 18/19 Tiberius combined Cappadocia and Commagene into a Roman province. The former royal estates were transformed into imperial domains. The fact that Cappadocia was not ruled via cities but through domains and estates indicates that this province did not have a network of cities, unlike its neighbors to the north and to the west.[549] Strabo notes in the twelfth book of his *Geography,* written probably in A.D. 18 or 19, that there were only two cities in all of Cappadocia: Tyana and Mazaca (later called Kaisareia). He passes over Ariaratheia and Hanisa, and in another passage he describes Cappadocia Comana as a city (12.2.7; 12.2.3). These geopolitical realities did not make travel in or through Cappadocia impossible or difficult: Kaisareia was located at the crossroads of four major routes. Since the rhythm of life was not determined by cities and their culture, and since the old feudal structures persisted for centuries, Greeks and Romans had their doubts whether this region was a part of the Greco-Roman word: "Cappadocia was, for them, a region at the fringe of the civilized world."[550] It is no coincidence that the Council of Nicea was attended by five bishops of Cappadocian cities—Leontios of Kaisareia, Euthychios of Tyana, Erythrios of Koloneia, Timotheos of Kybistra, Elpidios of Co-

---

[548]H. Treidler, *KP* 3:114-15; Pekáry 1980, 655-56; R. D. Sullivan, *ABD* 1:870-72; T. Broughton and A. Spawforth, *OCD* 288-89; K. Strobel, *DNP* 6:262-64; Teja 1980; Berges and Nollé 2000, 479-92, and passim; D. Jacobson 2001.

[549]See Jones 1937, 182-83; Mitchell 1995a, 1:98.

[550]J. Nollé, in Berges and Nollé 2000, 490.

mana—and by five "country-bishops" (χωρεπίσκοποι, *chōrepiskopoi;* later suffragan bishops) in rural areas:[551] Gorgonios, Stephanos, Eudromios, Rodon and Theophanes. This indicates that there were Christian communities around A.D. 300 among the non-Hellenized population in rural Cappadocia. Around A.D. 258 the Goths kidnapped Christians, among them the parents of Wulfila, the later bishop, who lived in the village Sadagolthina near Parnassos.

The following cities would have been candidates for missionary outreach in Cappadocia.

Tyana (Τύανα; mod. Kemerhisar),[552] about 75 km north of the Cilician Gates in the Taurus Mountains, only 120 km north of Tarsus, had already been settled by the Hittites. Xenophon knew the city as Dana, which he described as large and wealthy (*Anab.* 1.2.20). Tyana was refounded in the second century B.C. by the Cappadocian king Ariarathes V Eusebes Philopator, who demonstrated his love for Greek culture by promoting games in Cappadocia itself as well as in Athens. Tyana was also called Eusebeia in his honor. Tyana was, next to Kaisareia, the only "real" city in the sense of a Hellenized urban center in the Cappadocian kingdom. The territory that belonged to Tyana extended as far as the Cilician Gates (Strabo 12.2.7), which means that Tyana controlled the traffic in the northern Taurus Mountains. Strabo describes the strategic location of the city, the fertility of the region and the beauty of the city walls (12.2.7). About four km south of Tyana, beside a spring, stood a temple dedicated to Zeus Asbamaeus. The neo-Pythagorean "holy man" (θεῖος ἀνήρ) Apollonius of Tyana was born there in the first century; Philostratus wrote his biography in the third century.[553] Apollonius advised cities such as Sparta, prophesied the death of Nero and Domitian, and was an ascetic itinerant philosopher who reached India. During the principate of Caracalla, Tyana was promoted as Colonia Aurelia Antoniniana. In the course of the reorganization of the administration of the Roman Empire in the fourth century Tyana became the capital of the province Cappadocia Secunda. The Mithras cult survived in Tyana for centuries. The main sanctuary was dedicated to Astarte. Apart from the aqueduct only a few remains survive. The bishop Eupsychios (or Euthychios) attended the Council of Nicea in A.D. 325.[554]

Kaisareia (Καισάρεια, Mazaka, Caesarea; mod. Kayseri)[555] was situated about 130 km northeast of Tyana, east of the bend of the Halys River south of the Melas River (mod.

---

[551]Cf. Harnack 1924, 1:477 n. 1 (ET, 1:471); W. Jannasch, *RGG* 1:1678; cf. Harnack 1924, 2:743 (ET, 2:192), for the following observation, with reference to Philostorgos, *Hist. eccl.* 2.5.

[552]W. Ruge, PW 7.A2 (1948): 1630-35; Magie 1950, 2:1095; E. Olshausen, *KP* 5:1015; R. P. Harper, *PECS* 942; S. Mitchell 1995a, 2:29, 86; Berges and Nollé 2000.

[553]On Apollonius as a citizen of Tyana see Berges and Nollé 2000, 414-19 (Testimonia nos. 100-109). See generally Maria Dzielska, *Apollonius of Tyana in Legend and History* (Rome: Bretschneider, 1986); Swain 1998, 380-400.

[554]I Tyana 77; *IJudO* II 258. According to a late version of the *Acts of Andrew,* the apostle Andrew is said to have stayed with a Jew in Tyana (*Epiphanii monachi et presgbyteri edita et inedita* [ed. A. Dressel; Paris: Brockhaus et Avenarius, 1843], 47). For the following comment see Berges and Nollé 2000, 386-87 (Testimonia no. 60); cf. Gelzer 1898, LXII, 25.

[555]W. Ruge, "Caesarea 5," PW 3.1 (1897): 1289-90; H. Treidler, *KP* 3:48-49; R. P. Harper, *PECS* 182; A. H. M. J. Jones et al., *OCD* 272; K. Strobel, *DNP* 6:1139; Jones 1937, 183-91; Ramsay 1890, 28, 39, 50; Hild and Restle 1981, 193-96; S. Mitchell 1995a, 1:81, 97-98, 132, 218-21; 2:29, 76, 86; Berges and Nollé 2000, 310, 323-24, 483-84, 507, 515.

Karasu) on the northern slopes of Mt Argaeus (mod. Erciyes Dağım [3,916 m]). The old Hittite name of the city was Mazaka (Pliny, *Nat.* 6.3.8). Kaisareia was the capital of the Cappadocian kingdom. King Ariarathes V refounded Kaisareia as a city which he also called Eusebeia (Strabo 12.2.7). The city was destroyed by the Armenian king Tigranes, and later rebuilt by Pompey. When Tiberius organized the new Province of Cappadocia in A.D. 17, Kaisareia became the capital. The city minted her own coins; the metal for the silver coins presumably came from the silver mines of Bulgar Maden. Strabo reports that the few people who climb the peak of Mt Argaeus, which is always covered with snow, can see the Black Sea when the weather allows, that the region around Kaisareia is relatively unfertile but centrally located, and that the journey to the Cilician Gates lasts six days (12.2.7-9). Hardly any remains of the ancient city survive; in recent years tombs of wealthy Romans were discovered.

The church of Kaisareia had close ties with the churches in Antioch and Jerusalem in the second and third centuries:[556] Alexander, a young bishop of Kaisareia around A.D. 200, was a friend of Clement and Origen and became bishop of Jerusalem, where he founded a library. Firmilian of Kaisareia (third century) had contacts with all the important theologians of his time, including Cyprian in Carthage in North Africa; he made Kaisareia into a center of theological learning.

Archelais (Colonia Claudia Archelais; mod. Aksaray),[557] about 85 km northwest of Tyana on the road to Ankara, originally was called Garsaura, a fortress on the border to Lycaonia (Strabo 12.2.6). Strabo describes Garsaura as a "small city" (πολίχνιον, *polichnion* [14.2.6]) and a "village-town" (κωμόπολις, *kōmopolis* [12.6.2]). Claudius founded a colony in the town (Pliny, *Nat.* 6.3.8), and further west in Iconium, Laodikeia Katakekaumene and Derbe. Archelais probably did not have a developed urban constitution.

Comana (Κόμανα; Hierapolis; Chryse; mod. Şar)[558] was situated about 160 km north of Anazarbus (eastern Cilicia) and 150 km southeast of Kaisareia-Mazaka on the western branch of the upper Saros River (mod. Göksu) in a deep valley of the Anti-Taurus Mountains. This probably was the site of the Hittite village of Kummani, the religious center of the goddess Hepat. Strabo describes Comana as a "considerable city" (πόλις ἀξιόλογος). In the Hellenistic period Comana was a temple state, together with Pontic Comana, one of the two cult centers of the goddess Ma, whom Strabo identifies with Enyo. The high priest who ruled Comana and who had connections with the Roman aristocracy occupied the second position in the Cappadocian kingdom, after the king. Strabo states that the temple of Ma had six thousand servants (hierodules), including women (12.2.3). Another deity that was worshiped in Comana was Apollo Archegetes, who was honored all over Cappadocia (12.2.6). The city controlled the plain of Kataonia. An inscription honors King Archelaos. During the Roman period Comana was the only town in central Cappadocia that had the status of a city and that minted coins. During the principate of Vespasian inscriptions call the city Hieropolis (Tacitus, *Ann.* 2.42). Remains of a temple (second century) and of a theater as well as inscriptions survive (Archaeological Museum of Adana).

---

[556]Harnack 1924, 2:744-45 (ET, 2:193-94); S. Mitchell 1995a, 2:67-68.

[557]G. Hirschfeld, "Archelais 2," PW 2.1 (1895): 445; K. Strobel, *DNP* 1:984; Magie 1950, 2:1353; Hild and Restle 1981, 207; S. Mitchell 1995a, 1:84, 89, 95-97; Berges and Nollé 2000, 314, 491.

[558]W. Ruge, PW 11.1 (1921): 1127-28; K. Ziegler, "Komana 1," *KP* 3:277; R. P. Harper, *PECS* 233-34; idem, "Tituli Comanorum Cappadociae," *AnSt* 18 (1968): 93-147, 149-58; K. Strobel, *DNP* 6:672; Hild and Restle 1981, 208-9; Mitchell 1995a, 1:32, 81-82, 98, 136; Berges and Nollé 2000, 330-31, 339, 375, 439-40.

Ariaratheia ('Αριαράθεια; mod. Pınarbaşi; former Azizie),[559] about 55 km north of Comana, was founded by the father of King Ariarates V. Strabo omits the city in his description of Cappadocia. The sculptor who made the statue that was erected in the agora of Samos around 100 B.C. seems to have been a citizen of Ariaratheia.

Rainer Riesner suggests that it is theoretically conceivable that Paul engaged in missionary outreach to Cappadocia during the ten years of missionary work in Syria and Cilicia between A.D. 33 and 42.[560] Even though this possibility must remain hypothetical for lack of hard evidence, the certainty displayed by Ramon Teja is hardly appropriate when he asserts, "Paul never visited Cappadocia during his travels; surely a region such as this with only a sparse population and with few cities was not attractive enough."[561] The criterion of "attractiveness" seems inappropriate with regard to the missionary strategy of Paul or of the other early Christian apostles. The next comment by Teja is historically correct, however: "Nevertheless, the Christian faith entered the province already in the apostolic period, presumably initially in the Jewish communities."

Evangelism in Pontus-Bithynia

We have already noted Luke's account of the Feast of Pentecost in A.D. 30, in which he mentions Jewish visitors from Pontus (Acts 2:9), and Paul's project of missionary outreach in Bithynia in A.D. 49, which could not be carried out, however. Peter mentions Christians in Pontus and Bithynia in his first letter (1 Pet 1:1). These facts indicate that the province of Pontus-Bithynia clearly was within the purview of Paul, Peter and Luke.

Pontus (Πόντος)[562] has the southern coast of the Black Sea between the Halys River (mod. Kızıl Irmak) in the west and the Ophis River (Istala Dere) in the east as a northern boundary; in the south Pontus bordered on Cappadocia, on a ridge of hills running parallel to the Taurus Mountains. The main routes in Pontus run from west to east. This fact, emphasized by Stephen Mitchell,[563] relates specifically to the movement of troops—for example, of Mithradates and Pompey. Of course, there also existed north-south connections, particularly the old route from Sinope to Tarsus, a route that could be covered in five days,

[559]G. Hirschfeld, PW 2.1 (1895): 815; K. Strobel, *DNP* 1:1079; Hild and Restle 1981, 151; G. Cohen 1995, 375-77; S. Mitchell 1995a, 1:82-83, 98.
[560]Riesner 1994, 237 (ET, 267); for Riesner's "admonition to be cautious" see ibid., 238 (ET, 268).
[561]Teja 1980, 1120; the quotation that follows above, ibid; cited also in Reinhardt 1995, 238 n. 198. Similarly, earlier, Harnack 1924, 2:743.
[562]E. Olshausen, PWSup 15 (1978): 396-442; T. Broughton and S. Mitchell, *OCD* 1220; J. Biller and E. Olshausen, "Notizen zur historischen Geographie von Pontos," in Şahin et al. 1978, 163-77; Pekáry 1980, 638-41; E. Olshausen, "Götter, Heroen und ihre Kulte in Pontos," *ANRW* II.18.3 (1990): 1865-1906; E. Olshausen and Joseph Biller, *Historisch-geographische Aspekte der Geschichte des Pontischen und Armenischen Reiches I* (BTAVO B 29/1; Wiesbaden: Reichert, 1984).
[563]S. Mitchell 1995a, 1:32.

according to Herodotos (1.72; 2.34.2), which may be somewhat optimistic.[564] If Peter or other early Christian missionaries indeed preached the gospel in Pontus, they would have traveled from Syrian Antioch to Tarsus (210 km) via Tyana (120 km) and Kaisareia-Mazaka (130 km) to Zela (300 km) and Amaseia (80 km). From Amaseia one could reach, in a southerly direction, Sebasteia-Megalopolis (130 km), and in a southeasterly direction along the Iris Valley, Comana Pontica (100 km). From Comana one could travel in an easterly direction to Nikopolis (140 km), Satala (140 km) and to the port city Trapezus (125 km). From Amaseia one could travel in a northwesterly direction, through the Iris Valley and the Amnias Valley, to Neoklaudiopolis (70 km) and Pompeiopolis-Sebaste (135 km), and in a northerly direction to the port Amisos (110 km), and along the coastal road in a westerly direction to Sinope (145 km), Amastris (240 km) and Herakleia (105 km).

Bithynia (Βιθυνία)[565] was the name for the peninsula in the northwestern tip of Asia Minor, originally inhabited by Thracian tribes. Greeks from Megara established colonies in the Bithynian heartland: Chalcedon on the Bosporus (opposite mod. Istanbul/Constantinople) and Astakos on the eastern end of the Astacenian Gulf. Zipoites (356-280 B.C.) was the first king of the Bithynian kingdom, which had been founded in the aftermath of the death of Alexander the Great. His successors Nikomedes I (280-255 B.C.), Ziaëles (244-235 B.C.) and Prusias I (235-183 B.C.) managed to expand the kingdom: Bithynia extended in the west as far as the lower Rhyndakos River (mod. Orhaneli, Koca Dere), in the east to the Parthenios (mod. Bartin Su, entering the Black Sea near Amastris), and in the south as far as the upper Sangarios (mod. Sakarya) and the Bithynian Mount Olympus (mod. Ulu Dağ). The capital of the Bithynian kingdom was Nikomedia. When King Nikomedes IV died in 74 B.C., he bequeathed Bithynia to the Romans. Pompey organized the province *Pontus et Bithynia* by integrating Pontic regions in the new province, which was administered after 27 B.C. as a senatorial province. Jewish communities are attested in several Bithynian cities: Gangra, Chalcedon, Klaudiou Polis, Nikaia, Nikomedia and Geyve (?), in part in later periods.[566] When Paul planned missionary outreach in Bithynia, these cities would have been natural stations. Dio Chrysostom, one of the most prominent representatives of the Second Sophistic, came from Prusa in Bithynia. Dio, born in A.D. 40, became a celebrated orator and philosopher; he was persecuted by Domitian, but later he was a friend of the emperors Nerva and Trajan. He was known for speeches in which he gave advice to Greek cities, including Tarsus (*Or.* 33; 34).[567]

The following cities would have been natural goals for missionary outreach in Pontus-Bithynia:

Zela (Ζῆλα; mod. Zile),[568] on the important north-south route from Tarsus via Kaisareia

---

[564]See Seibert 1985, 21.
[565]E. Meyer and W. Ruge, PW 3.1 (1897) 507-24; A. M. Schneider, *RAC* 2:417-422; F. K. Dörner, *KP* 1:908-11; K. Strobel, *DNP* 2:698-702; T. Broughton and S. Mitchell, *OCD* 244-45; Pekáry 1980, 638-41; C. Marek, *Stadt, Ära und Territorium in Pontus-Bithynia und Nord Galatia* (Istanbuler Forschungen 39; Tübingen: Wasmuth, 1993).
[566]See Walter Ameling, "Ein Verehrer des Θεὸς Ὕψιστος in Prusa ad Olympum (IK 39, 115)," *EA* 31 (1999): 105.
[567]On Dio see Swain 1998, 197-241.
[568]Magie 1950, 1:182; 2:1073 n. 14; K. Abel, PWSup 14 (1974): 984-86; E. Olshausen, *KP* 5:1489; D. R. Wilson, *PECS* 999; T. Broughton and S. Mitchell, *OCD* 1634; S. Mitchell 1995a, 1:32, 36, 82, 91-94.

to Amisos on a side branch of the Iris River, was an Assyrian foundation at the site of the cult place of the goddess Anahita. When Pompey reorganized Pontus, the territory was considerably enlarged. The temple state of Zela possibly was the goal of the campaign of the Roman general Licinius Murena in 82 B.C.[569] The battle in which Caesar defeated the king of Pontus Pharnakes II in 47 B.C., a victory that he announced to Rome with the famous words "Veni, vidi, vici" ("I came, I saw, I conquered"), took place at Zela. The city was annexed by Rome in A.D. 64/65. The theater was located northeast of the site that marks the ancient city. In A.D. 325 the bishop Herakleios of Zela attended the Council of Nicea.

Amaseia ('Αμάσεια; mod. Amasya),[570] situated in a basin of the Iris River at the crossroads of important trade routes, was the capital of the kingdom of Pontus until 183 B.C. and the birthplace of Mithradates VI Eupator. The Pontic kings were buried in Amaseia. Strabo the geographer, who had traveled throughout the Mediterranean world from Armenia to Sardinia and from the Black Sea to Ethiopia, was born in Amaseia in 64 B.C. His work *Geography* (Γεωγραφία), published in seventeen books and based on his own investigations (which he rarely refers to, but see 2.5.11) as well as on older literature, relates a wealth of geographical, historical, mythological and literary details and information related to natural history; it is the most significant source for ancient geography. He provides a detailed description of his hometown (12.3.39). In 64 B.C. Pompey made Amaseia the center of a large area, including the Chiliokomon, the "plain of a thousand villages." In 3/2 B.C. Amaseia became part of Galatia and became the district capital of Pontus Galaticus. Remains from the Hellenistic period, including burial monuments of the kings of Pontus, survive.

According to the apocryphal *Acts of Andrew,* the apostle Andrew performed miracles in Amaseia and proclaimed the gospel in the city over a longer period of time before he traveled to Macedonia and Achaia, where the proconsul and his family convert to the Christian faith (*Acts Andr.* 3—4).[571] The tombstone dated A.D. 201/202, erected by Iulia Faustina and Kapiton, Eutykhes and Pistikos for Kyrilios, probably is Christian, an assumption based on the names "Pistikos" and "Kyrilios."[572] If so, this is the oldest dated Christian tombstone found in Asia Minor (the tombstone found in the territory of Lystra that may be Christian and from the first century is not dated [see §27.1]). The bishop Eutychianos of Amaseia attended the Council of Nicea.

Sebasteia (Σεβάστεια; Megalopolis; mod. Sivas),[573] situated on the Halys River, probably is identical with Megalopolis, which Pompey founded in 64 B.C. in the most southerly region of the former kingdom of Mithradates. The name "Sebasteia" probably is connected with the refoundation of the city when it was annexed by the province of Galatia between 2 B.C. and 2 A.D.

Comana (Κόμανα; Comana Pontica; Hierocaesarea; mod. Kılıçlı; former Gümenek),[574] on the Iris River, founded by settlers from Cappadocian Comana, was a cult cen-

[569]Dennis G. Glew, "400 Villages? A Note on Appian, *Mith.* 65, 271," *EA* 32 (2000): 155-61.

[570]C. Danoff, *KP* 1:288-89; D. R. Wilson, *PECS* 47; S. Mitchell, *OCD* 69; E. Olshausen, *DNP* 1:571-72; S. Mitchell 1995a, 1:31, 39, 82, 84, 88, 92, 132, 178; D. H. French, "Amasian Notes 3: Dated Inscriptions from Amasia and Its Territory," *EA* 26 (1996): 71-85; idem, "Amasian Notes 4: Cult and Divinities; The Epigraphic Evidence," *EA* 26 (1996): 87-98.

[571]Prieur 1989, I:47-49, 444-47; idem, in Hennecke and Schneemelcher 1990-1997, 2:99, 109.

[572]See S. Reinach, "Inscriptions d'Amasie et autres lieux," *REG* 8 (1895): 77-87, esp. 78, no. 6 = *I. Pont* III 1.161 (F. Cumont); see recently French, *EA* 26 (1996): 73, 78 (no. ΣΔ).

[573]W. Ruge, PW 2.A1 (1921): 952-53; E. Olshausen, "Sebasteia 2," *KP* 5:58; D. R. Wilson, *PECS* 816; Jones 1937, 167-68, 170-71; S. Mitchell 1995a, 1:94, 98.

[574]W. Ruge, PW 11.1 (1921): 1126-27; K. Ziegler, *KP* 3:277; D. R. Wilson, *PECS* 234; E. Olshausen, *DNP* 6:672-73; S. Mitchell 1995a, 1:30-31, 63, 82, 93-94, 176-77.

ter of the goddess Ma-Enyo as well. When Pompey reorganized Pontus in 64 B.C., Comana became independent; between A.D. 33 and 35 it was annexed by Pontus Galaticus. The name "Hierokaisareia," used since the time of Tiberius, underlines the significance of Comana as a religious center. Comana was the seat of a bishop during the Severian emperors in the second and third centuries; the bishop Elpidios attended the Council of Nicea.

Nikopolis (Νικόπολις; mod. Yeşilyayla; former Pürk)[575] was founded by Seleukos I. In 66 B.C. Pompey settled veterans, wounded soldiers, and local people here after his defeat of Mithradates VI. It later received the *ius Italicum*. In the Byzantine period Nikopolis was the seat of the bishop of the eparchy Armenia I.

Satala (Σάταλα; mod. Sadak),[576] at the intersection of several important roads, was the base of the Legio XV Apollinaris since the time of Trajan. The city was founded perhaps as late as the second century. A bishop Euethios is attested for the fourth century.

Trapezus (Τραπεζοῦς; mod. Trabzon),[577] a colony founded by settlers from Miletus[578] on the coast of the Black Sea east of Cape Hieron, was refounded in 630 B.C. by Sinope. Mithradates VI annexed the city into the kingdom of Pontus; under king Polemon II Trapezus became the base of the royal fleet. During the Roman period Trapezus became important for the military because of its proximity to the border with Armenia. In A.D. 64 Trapezus became independent. Hadrian built new harbor facilities. Arrian describes Trapezus in the second century as still culturally backward (*Peripl. M. Eux.* 1.2). A bishop Domnos is attested for the fourth century.

Neoklaudiopolis (Νεοκλαυδιόπολις; mod. Vezirköprü),[579] on the Halys River, was founded by Pompey in 64 B.C. as Neapolis at the site of an earlier settlement called Andrapa. Under Claudius the name of the city changed again, to Neoklaudiopolis. About 6 km northwest of the city, in the village of Bahcekonak, a funerary inscription dating to A.D. 237/238 recently was discovered in which the "Lord the Almighty" (Κύριε Παν–τοκράτωρ, *Kyrie Pantokratōr*) is invoked to avenge the murder of the boy Argyrion, since he created him (σὺ μὲ ἔκτισες). The editor surmises that the stele belongs to a Jewish family or to people sympathizing with the Jewish faith.[580]

Pompeiopolis (mod. Taşköprü),[581] founded by Pompey on the occasion of the organization of the province of Pontus-Bithynia in 64 B.C. on the trade route in the Amnias Valley, became the seat of the assembly (*koinon*) of the province of Paphlagonia under Antonius.

---

[575]E. Honigmann, "Nikopolis 7," PW 17.1 (1936): 535-36; J. Sturm, "Nikopolis 8," PW 17.1 (1936): 536-38; Magie 1950, 2:1085, 1233, 1262; E. Olshausen, "Nikopolis 6," KP 4:126; idem, "Nikopolis 6," DNP 8:938; R. P. Harper, PECS 626; S. Mitchell et al., "Nicopolis (1)," OCD 1043; S. Mitchell 1995a, 1:32, 34, 36, 94.

[576]W. Ruge, "Satala 2," PW 2.A1 (1921): 59; E. Olshausen, KP 4:1562; R. P. Harper, PECS 810; G. Cohen 1995, 232.

[577]W. Ruge, PW 6.A2 (1937): 2114; C. Danoff, PWSup 9 (1962): 1062; idem, KP 5:928; D. R. Wilson, PECS 932; T. Broughton and S. Mitchell, OCD 1547; S. Mitchell 1995a, 1:33-34, 93-94, 124, 135.

[578]See N. Ehrhardt, *Milet und seine Kolonien: Vergleichende Untersuchung der kultischen und politischen Einrichtungen* (EHS 3.206; Frankfurt: Lang, 1988 [1983]).

[579]W. Ruge, PW 16.2 (1935): 2394; Jones 1937, 159; E. Olshausen, KP 4:53-54; idem, DNP 8:826; S. Mitchell 1995a, 1:92-94, 151; 2:151-52.

[580]Christian Marek, "Der Höchste, Beste, Grösste, Allmächtige Gott: Inschriften aus Nordkleinasien," EA 32 (2000): 129-146, esp. 137-45.

[581]A. M. Schneider, PW 21.2 (1952): 2044; Magie 1950, 2:1232; E. Olshausen, KP 4:1022; Belke 1996, 260-62; S. Mitchell 1995a, 1:32, 88, 91, 93, 116.

Amisos (᾽Αμισός; mod. Samsun)[582] was an old Greek city founded by colonists from Miletus (or Phocaia[583]) on the coast of the Black Sea between the mouths of the Halys and the Iris, without a natural harbor. Strabo provides an extensive description of the city (12.3.14). Amisos was a flourishing center of trade whose significance increased when the city became the residence of the kings of Pontus, when Mithradates VI established his residence Eupatoria. The Roman general Licinius Lucullus conquered Amisos, which was granted autonomy and an expansion of its territory. An important source of the city's wealth was the trade in olives and olive oil. The coins of Amisos and inscriptions of its citizens in many parts of the Greek world confirm the significance of the city. Remains of city walls and towers, of a temple and of sculptures survived until the nineteenth century. Today a military installation is at the site.

Sinope (Σινώπη; mod. Sinop),[584] located on a peninsula on the Black Sea with two excellent natural harbors, was founded by colonists from Miletus in the seventh century B.C. Sinope was one of the most important cities on the northern coast of Asia Minor. After the Pontic king Pharnakes II had caused much destruction, Caesar assisted Sinope and founded a colony in the city (Colonia Iulia Felix Sinope). Coins and inscriptions that mention Sinope are found as far away as the Aegean and in Athens. Strabo describes Sinope as a city with impressive buildings, an agora, colonnaded halls, a gymnasium, city walls, the oracle of Autolykus and famous sons of the city such as the Cynic Diogenes and the historian Baton, who wrote a book about the Persians (12.3.11). Inscriptions attest the veneration of Zeus (as Zeus Helios Sarapis and as Zeus Dikaiosynos), Athene Polias and Athene Sotira, Asclepius (as Asclepius Soter and Hygeia), Isis, Mercurius, Meter Theon (Cybele), Sarapis, Theos Heracles, Theos Megalos Hypsistos, as well as the imperial cult. According to *Acts of Andrew,* the apostle Andrew preached the gospel in Sinope (*Acts Andr.* 5).[585]

Amastris (῎Αμαστρις; mod. Amasra),[586] another coastal city in Paphlagonia, with two harbors, was founded in the fourth century B.C. by the princess of Heracleia Pontica via the combination of four small Ionian colonies (Tios, Sesamos, Kromna, Kytoros). During the imperial period Amastris was a flourishing city. Remains of a temple and of a three-storied warehouse (115 m long) survive.

Herakleia (῾Ηράκλεια; mod. Ereğli),[587] another port city on the Black Sea, was founded

---

[582]C. Danoff, *KP* 1:300-301; D. R. Wilson, *PECS* 49; E. Olshausen, *DNP* 1:592; S. Mitchell, *OCD* 72; Jones 1937, 155-60, 167-68; Magie 1950, 1213; E. Olshausen and Joseph Biller, *Historisch-geographische Aspekte der Geschichte des Pontischen und Armenischen Reiches* (BTAVO B 29/1; Wiesbaden: Reichert, 1984), 81ff.; G. Cohen 1995, 384; S. Mitchell 1995a, 1:36-41, 81-82, 88. Inscriptions: J. G. C. Anderson, *Studia Pontica* 3 (1910): 1-32.
[583]A synagogue is attested for Phocaia: *CIJ* II 738 (*IJudO* II 36; cf. *NewDocs* 1:111-12 no. 69). See Trebilco 1991, 230; Rajak 1996, 314-15.
[584]W. Ruge, PW 3.A (1927): 252-55; Magie 1950, 1:183-85; 2:1074-77; E. Olshausen, *KP* 5:209; E. Akurgal, *PECS* 842; T. Broughton and S. Mitchell, *OCD* 1412; D. French, "Sinopean Notes 4: Cults and Divinities; The Epigraphic Evidence," *EA* 23 (1994): 99-108; S. Mitchell 1995a, 1:31, 81-82, 91, 235; Askold I. Ivantchik, "Die Gründung von Sinope und die Probleme der Anfangsphase der griechischen Kolonisation des Schwarzmeergebietes," in Tsetskhladze 1998, 297-330.
[585]See Prieur 1989, I:82-83; idem, in Hennecke and Schneemelcher 1990-1997, 2:99, 109.
[586]C. Danoff, "Amastris 5," *KP* 1:290; D. R. Wilson, *PECS* 47; C. Marek, "Amastris 4," *DNP* 1:574; Jones 1937; 150-54, 156-57; Magie 1950, 1193-94; Belke 1996, 161-70; G. Cohen 1995, 383-84; S. Mitchell 1995a, 1:31, 88, 212.
[587]Magie 1950, 1:307; F. K. Dörner, "Herakleia 7," *KP* 2:1035; D. R. Wilson, *PECS* 383; Belke 1996, 208-16; T. Broughton and S. Mitchell, *OCD* 684; K. Strobel, "Herakleia 7," *DNP* 5:366-

in the sixth century b.c. by colonists from Megara and Boeotia. Around 300 b.c. Herakleia was a flourishing trade city. In the course of the third Mithradatic war Herakleia was destroyed by a Roman army. The colony that Caesar founded in Herakleia did not result in the growth that was expected. Herakleia was overshadowed by the neighboring cities of Prusias and Amastris.

Nicea (Νίκαια; Nikaia; İznik),[588] the most southerly of the great Bithynian cities, was located on the Ascania Lake (mod. İznik Gölü), on one of the major routes into the interior of Asia Minor, linked with Dorylaion by a direct route. According to myth Nicea was founded by Dionysos, while according to the historical record settlers from a small village near the Thermopylae established the city, which was named in honor of the first wife of Lysimachos around 300 B.C. From 280 B.C. Nicea belonged to Bithynia and was a main rival of the capital, Nicomedia. Augustus erected a temple for Roma and Caesar in 29 B.C. Pliny, the Roman governor, enlarged Nicea in the second century; Hadrian fortified the city walls. Literary texts and inscriptions attest the temple of Roma and Caesar, a theater, a temple of Apollo, a market (second century) and an aqueduct. An inscription documents a Jewish community possibly for the second century A.D. (*IJudO* II 153). The apocryphal *Acts of Andrew* claims to know that the apostle Andrew was the first to preach the gospel in Nicea; he is said to have freed the city from dangerous demons (*Acts Andr.* 6).[589] The first synod of bishops from the entire empire was opened by Emperor Constantine on May 20 in A.D. 325 in Nicea. The bishop Theognios represented Nicea at the council.

Nicomedia (Νικομέδεια; mod. İzmit),[590] about 60 km north of Nicea on the Astacenian Gulf, was founded by Nikomedes I in 265 B.C. to become the capital of the Bithynian kingdom. The miraculous signs that allegedly helped to determine the precise location for the establishment of the city were still depicted on coins five hundred years later. Nicomedia was the capital of the Roman province of Bithynia since 74 B.C. Augustus built an imperial temple for Roma and Augustus in 29 B.C. The games of the assembly (*koinon*) of the province of Bithynia were held in Nicomedia, which had over twenty-five thousand inhabitants. Remains of a large nymphaeum (second century) and of several aqueducts survive; texts and inscriptions attest a temple of Demeter, a temple of Isis, a theater, an agora and a colonnaded hall. The royal palace has not yet been located. Inscriptions document a Jewish community for the third century A.D. (*IJudO* II 154-158). The bishop Eusebios represented the city at the Council of Nicea in A.D. 325.

Chalcedon (Καλχηδών, Kadıköy),[591] about 80 km northwest of Nicomedia, was founded in 685 B.C. as a colony of Megara on the southwestern side of the entrance into

---

67; Jones 1937, 149-54; S. Mitchell 1995a, 1:16, 31, 37, 81, 88, 212; John Hind, "Megarian Colonisation in the Western Half of the Black Sea (Sister- and Daughter-Cities of Herakleia)," in Tsetskhladze 1998, 131-52.

[588]W. Ruge, "Nicaea 7," PW 17.1 (1936): 226-43; F. K. Dörner, "Nikaia 5," *KP* 5:94-95; N. Bonacasa, *PECS* 622-23; O. Dilke and S. Mitchell, "Nicaea (1)," *OCD* 1040; K. Strobel, "Nikaia 5," *DNP* 8:895; S. Mitchell 1995a, 1:64, 89, 160, 181, 207, 212-13, 219-21. Inschriften: S. Şahin, *Katalog der antiken Inschriften des Museums von İznik* (2 vols.; IK 9-10; Bonn: Habelt, 1979-1987).

[589]See J.-M. Prieur, in Hennecke and Schneemelcher 1990-1997, 2:99, 109.

[590]W. Ruge, PW 17.1 (1936): 468-92; F. K. Dörner, *KP* 4:116-18; W. L. MacDonald, *PECS* 623-24; T. Broughton and S. Mitchell, *OCD* 1043; K. Strobel, *DNP* 8:927-28; S. Mitchell 1995a, 1:88, 100, 111, 203, 212-13, 214, 244.

[591]W. Ruge, PW 10.2 (1919): 1555-59; F. K. Dörner, *KP* 3:55-56; G. E. Bean, *PECS* 216; K. Strobel, *DNP* 6:153-54; S. Mitchell 1995a, 1:16. Inscriptions: R. Merkelbach, *Die Inschriften von Kalchedon* (IK 20; Bonn: Habelt, 1980).

the Bosporus, at the site of a Phoenician and Thracian settlement. Chalcedon was able to preserve its independence during the time of the Diadochi. The city maintained contact with Rome at an early date. We have almost no information for the history of the city during the imperial period. Coins of Chalcedon date from the fifth century B.C. to the third century A.D. The bishop Maris represented the city in the Council of Nicea.

We do not know when the first missionaries preached the gospel in Pontus and Bithynia. If Peter writes his first letter to churches that he established himself (which is not certain), then he could have engaged in missionary work in northern Asia Minor after his departure from Jerusalem in A.D. 42.

The apocryphal *Acts of Andrew,* written between A.D. 150 and 200, assert that the apostle Andrew preached the gospel in Pontus, in the cities of Amaseia and Sinope (*Acts Andr.* 3-5). It is difficult to assess the historical value of this early Christian tradition. Most scholars regard this information as inauthentic,[592] a decision that seems based more on presupposition than on specific arguments. Some regard these early traditions at least as being worthy of consideration.[593]

How many Christians were there in Asia Minor around A.D. 60, a few years before the deaths of Peter and Paul? Bo Reicke suggests 5,000, which grew to about 80,000 after A.D. 100.[594] He refers to the comment of Pliny the Younger that the Christian "superstition" had penetrated not only the cities but also the villages and the rural areas (*Ep.* 10.96.9-10), and he argues that the number of Christians around A.D. 100 "could have hardly been less than 1/50 of the total population in Asia Minor." John Elliott believes that these estimates are conservative, since Reicke assumes only 4.5 million inhabitants for Asia Minor, a figure that some scholars double.[595] Does this mean that there could have been 150,000 Christians in Asia Minor around A.D. 100? Such figures always remain hypothetical. We have no details for any church in the first century, with the exception of the church in Jerusalem, allowing somewhat reliable estimates of the number of Christians. The exchange of letters between Pliny the Younger, the imperial legate in the province of Bithynia between A.D. 110 and 112, and Emperor Trajan confirms, in any event, the growth of churches and the increase in the number of Christians in the cities and villages of northern Asia Minor at the end of the century (*Ep.* 10.96-97).

Fifteen bishops from Pontus and Bithynia attended the Council of Nicea in A.D. 325: Herakleios of Zela, Eutychianos of Amaseia, Elpidios of Comana, Eusebios of Nicomedia, Theognios of Nicea, Maris of Chalcedon, Kyrillos of Kios, Hesychios of Prusa, Gorgonios of Apolloia, Georgios of Prusias, Euethios of Adriani, Rufus of Kaisareia and the two country-bishops Theophanes and Eulalios.[596]

---

[592]Peterson 1958, 6-13, 24-31, 47-48; Prieur 1989; recently Reinbold 2000, 256.
[593]See McDonald 1992, 961.
[594]Reicke 1982, 302-3; quotation, 303.
[595]Elliott, *1 Pet,* 89.
[596]Gelzer, Hilgenfeld and Cuntz 1898, lxiv.

22.9 Missionary Work in Macedonia and Achaia

The apocryphal *Acts of Andrew* also claims to know that the apostle Andrew preached the gospel in Achaia and Macedonia.[597] The apostle is said to have traveled from Pontus via Amaseia, Sinope, Nicea and Nicomedia to Byzantion, through Thrace and via Perinth, Philippi and Thessalonike to Patras (*Acts Andr.* 2-21), to have worked in Patras (22-24) and in Achaia—Corinth, Megara and perhaps Lakedaimon (25-29)—before continuing his ministry in Patras (30-35), where eventually he died as a martyr (36).

The historical value of this tradition remains uncertain.[598] We do not know which missionaries preached when in regions of Macedonia and Achaia that had not been reached by Paul and his co-workers.

22.10 Missionary Work in Thrace

Acts of Andrew claims to know that the apostle Andrew engaged in missionary work in Thrace (*Acts Andr.* 9). Early traditions attest Christians in Thrace in the second century. We do not know, however, when the first churches were established.

Thrace (Θρᾴκη),[599] the eastern half of the Balkans between the rivers Timacus (mod. Timok) and Strymon (mod. Struma, Bulgaria) in the west and the Black Sea in the east, with the Danube forming the northern border and the Propontis and the Aegean (called the *Thrace Thracium*) as a southern border, was inhabited by numerous tribes that were known to the Greeks as their neighbors in the north since the seventh century B.C. Greek authors mention at least eighteen Thracian tribes, including the Odrysiae, Mysiae, Serdiae, Dentheletiae and Madoi. Many Aegean islands were settled by Thracians (e.g., Samothrake), and many Macedonian cities were established by Thracians. Thracians also lived in northwestern Asia Minor (e.g., Bithynia). Herodotus states that the Thracians were the most populous people after the Indians. The last ruler of the Odrysiae was Cotys I (383-360 B.C.). Since 341 B.C. much of Thrace was ruled by the Macedonian king Philipp II. Alexander the Great also defeated Thracian tribes, but his successors were unable to subjugate the region. In the third century B.C. the Galatians, a Celtic tribe, invaded Thrace. The empire that the Celts established in Thrace collapsed some time after 220 B.C. when the population rebelled. In the second century B.C. Thrace was politically torn. The Thracian population in the Aegean and in Macedonia had largely assimilated to Hellenistic cul-

---

[597]Peterson (1958, 47-48) rejects this tradition.

[598]Prieur (1989, 1:68-89) remains skeptical. The collection of essays in Bremmer 2000 does not discuss historical questions.

[599]C. Danoff, *KP* 5:777-81; J. M. R. Cormack, *OCD* 1514-15; Stanley Casson, *Macedonia, Thrace and Illyria: Their Relations to Greece from the Earliest Times Down to the Time of Philip Son of Amyntas* (London: Oxford University Press, 1926); Jones 1937, 1-27; Aleksandur Fol and Ivan Marazov, *Thrace and the Thracians* (London: Cassell, 1977); Christo M. Danoff, "Die Thraker auf dem Ostbalkan von der hellenistischen Zeit bis zur Gründung Konstantinopels," *ANRW* II.7.1 (1979): 21-185; Boris Gerov, *Beiträge zur Geschichte der römischen Provinzen Moesien und Thrakien: Gesammelte Aufsätze* (Amsterdam: Hakkert, 1980); Basilike D. Papoulia, *Thrace* (Athens: General Secretariat of the Region of East Macedonia-Thrace, 1994).

ture and language. The rural population in Thrace maintained its traditional culture, especially the cult of the rider-god. After the Romans established the province of Macedonia, which included the coastal area between Thessalonike and the Thracian Bosporus, Roman armies repeatedly fought against Thracian tribes, particularly the Madoi. Under Augustus Thrace became a client state ruled by King Rhoimetalkes I and his successors. Around 15 B.C. the Romans organized the province of Moesia in northern Thrace, later divided into Upper and Lower Moesia by Domitian. Thrace was divided into southern Thrace, ruled by Cotys VIII (A.D. 13-19), and *Ripa Thraciae,* ruled by Rhascuporis III (A.D. 13-19). After A.D. 19 the two Thracian kingdoms continued to exist. Despite the efforts of Tiberius to act prudently, the Thracians revolted. When King Rhoimetalkes III, who had been installed by Caligula, was murdered, Claudius annexed Thrace in A.D. 45 and organized the imperial province of Thrace, with Perinthos as the capital.

Christian missionaries would have focused on the following cities: along the Via Egnatia, coming from Nicomedia and Chalcedon in Mysia and Bithynia and traveling to Neapolis and Philippi in Macedonia, on Byzantion, Selymbria, Perinthos, Bisanthe, Aproi; along the road through the Hebros Valley into the interior regions of Thrace, on Beroia, Parembole, Philippopolis, Pautalia and Stobi (160 km north of Thessalonike).

Byzantion (Βυζάντιον; later Constantinopolis; mod. Istanbul)[600] was founded by settlers from Megara (668 B.C.) at the southeastern corner of Thrace on the European side, at the southern end of the Bosporus. The city had extensive harbor facilities and was an important center of trade because of its strategic location. The Romans granted Byzantion autonomy. *Acts of Andrew* claims to know that the apostle Andrew engaged in missionary work in the city (*Acts Andr.* 8) but mentions no details.[601] The Eastern churches regard Stachys, mentioned in Rom 16:9, as the successor of Andrew, the first bishop of Byzantion.[602] Emperor Constantine I refounded Byzantion as "New Rome" on May 11 in A.D. 330.

Selymbria (Σηλυμβρία; mod. Silivri, Turkey),[603] about 70 km east of Chalcedon on the northern coast of the Propontis (Sea of Marmara), was a colony founded by settlers from Megara at the site of a Thracian settlement. Both Strabo (7.6.1) and Ptolemaios (3.11.6) mention Selymbria, which also is mentioned in bishop lists of the Byzantine period.

Perinthos (Πέρινθος; mod. Ereğli),[604] a Thracian port 30 km west of Selybria, was founded by colonists from Samos around 600 B.C. In the fourth century B.C. Perinthos was the most important trade center of the region. During Macedonian rule Perinthos man-

[600]C. Danoff, *KP* 1:981-82; W. L. Macdonald, *PECS* 177-79; A. J. Graham and S. Mitchell, *OCD* 266; I. von Bredow, *DNP* 2:866-67; Jones 1937, 13-14, 164-65.
[601]Prieur 1989, 1:87-88.
[602]See H. Delehaye, ed., *Synaxarium Ecclesiae Constantinopolitanae e codice Sirmondiano,* 177. The Stachys mentioned in *Acts Phil.* 14:1, who was converted by Philip in Hierapolis in Phrygia, is to be distintuished from this Stachys. See Bovon, Bouvier and Amsler 1999, 318 n. 1.
[603]C. Danoff, *KP* 5:93; Jones 1937, 3, 25.
[604]E. Oberhummer, PW 19.1 (1937): 802-13; C. Danoff, *KP* 4:638; E. N. Borza, *OCD* 1140; I. von Bredow, *DNP* 4:574-75; Jones 1937, 13-15, 24-25; M. H. Sayar, *Perinthos-Herakleia (Marmara Ereglisi) und Umgebung: Geschichte, Testimonien, griechische und lateinische Inschriften* (Veröffentlichungen der Kleinasiatischen Kommission 9; Vienna: Österreichische Akademie der Wissenschaften, 1998).

aged to preserve its independence and the right to mint coins. After 129 B.C. the city belonged to Roman Macedonia; after A.D. 46 Perinthos was the capital of the province of Thrace. In the late third century the city was renamed Herakleia, the capital of Domitian's province of Europe.

Bisanthe (Βισάνθη; later Resisthon; mod. Tekirdağ),[605] about 40 km west of Perinthos, was founded by Samians as well. Alcibiades (450-404 B.C.) built his palace in Bisanthe.

Apros (mod. Germeyan),[606] about 40 km west of Bisanthe, later became Colonia Claudia Aprensis. The city was the seat of a bishop in A.D. 312 at the latest.

Kypsela (Κύψελα; mod. İpsala, Turkey),[607] about 60 km west of Apros on the lower Hebros River (mod. Evros; Meriç), is mentioned by Strabo as a city on the Via Egnatia (7.7.4).[608] In the second century a Christian woman named Glyceria died as a martyr in Traianopolis, about 35 km west of Kypsela.[609] The road in a northerly direction through the Hebros Valley reached, after 230 km, Beroia, a city on the important east-west route from Apolloia Pontica (Sozopol) on the Black Sea[610] to Serdica and Naissus on the Margus River (mod. Morava), a branch of the Danube leading to Dacia.

Beroia (Βέροια; mod. Stara Zagora),[611] about 75 km west of Kabyle on the upper Hebros River, was situated in a fertile plain that is the breadbasket of Bulgaria even today. The city was founded probably in the Hellenistic period. In the second century A.D. the city was called Augusta Traiana. According to a later tradition Karpos, the coworker of Paul, was bishop in Beroia.[612]

Parembole (mod. Belozem?), 56 km west of Beroia, may have already existed in the early Roman period. A Christian named Alexandros died as a martyr here in the second century.[613]

Philippopolis (Φιλιππόπολις; Trimontium; mod. Plovdiv),[614] 34 km west of Parembole, was founded by Philip II of Macedonia in 342 B.C. on the south bank of the Hebros River. It was the most important city in the interior of Thrace, situated on the most important crossroads in the region. During Roman rule the city was called Trimontium because of the three rocky hills on which the city was founded. The inhabitants included Hellenized Thracians, Greeks, Macedonians and Romans. Coins attest a temple of Artemis and a temple of Apollo. The main deity of the city was Apollo Kendresenos. Under Septimius Severus, Trimontium was the capital of the province of Thracia; Domitian granted the city the right to mint coins. Remains of temples, baths, the stadium and the aqueduct survive. An inscription attests the existence of a Jewish community (*I. GBulg* III.1 937); in 1981 a

---

[605]Danoff, *KP* 1:908; I. von Bredow, *DNP* 2:694; Jones 1937, 3.
[606]Jones 1937, 17-19; I. von Bredow, *DNP* 1:916.
[607]E. Oberhummer, PW 12.1 (1924): 117-18; Danoff, *KP* 3:408; Bredow, *DNP* 6:995-96.
[608]On the Via Egnatia see Radke 1973, 1666-67. The term *via Egnatia* applies with certainty only to the stretch from Dyrrhachion or Apollonia to Thessalonike.
[609]See Soustal 1991, 125, 203-4, 482. Source: Delehaye, *Synaxarium,* 679.
[610]Benjamin Isaac, *The Greek Settlements in Thrace until the Macedonian Conquest* (Leiden: Brill, 1986), 241-47; Kristina Panayotova, "Apollonia Pontica," in Tsetskhladze 1998, 97-113.
[611]C. Danoff, "Beroia 2," *KP* 1:869; von Bredow, *DNP* 2:578.
[612]See Delehaye, *Synaxarium,* 4, 681, 709, 878, 927.
[613]See Soustal 1991, 125, 203-4, 482. Cf. Delehaye, *Synaxarium,* 681.
[614]Jones 1937, 5, 12, 15; C. Danoff, PW 19.2 (1938): 2244-63; idem, *KP* 4:743-44; idem, "Philippopolis, Serdica, Odessos: Zur Geschichte und Kultur der bedeutendsten Städte Thrakiens von Alexander d. Gr. bis Justinian," *ANRW* II.7.1 (1979): 241-300, esp. 245-67; N. Hammond, *OCD* 1163; I. von Bredow, *DNP* 9:796-97; Panayotov, in *IJudO* I, 2004, 38-48.

synagogue was discovered (13.5 by 14.2 m, with two rows of columns), which appears to date into the third century.[615] A Christian community evidently existed in the city by A.D. 200 at the latest.[616]

Pautalia (Παυταλία; mod. Kjustendil),[617] about 175 km west of Philippopolis (on the direct route via Germania), was situated in a fertile plain on the upper Styrmon River. The city had warm mineral springs, and mines in the vicinity produced lead, iron, copper, silver and gold. Pautalia was an important administrative and economic center.

Stobi (mod. Pustogradsko, in mod. Macedonia),[618] 120 km southwest of Pautalia on the confluence of the Axios River (Vardar; Axios) and the Erigon River (mod. Crna), was an important center of trade. Stobi was a fortified Macedonian city in the second century B.C., and a *municipium* and eventually a *colonia* in the Roman period. The city minted its own coins at least since the time of Titus. An inscription attests the existence of a synagogue for the second century A.D. at the latest (*SEG* XXXIV 679; *IJudO* I Mac1). Structures from the Hellenistic period and 500 Roman silver drachmas were discovered underneath the third century synagogue (in 1971). An inscription honors Claudius Tiberius Polycharmus as the "father of the synagogue" and mentions a *triclinium,* probably a room for common meals that also served as a hostel.[619] A bishop Budius of Stobi attended the Council of Nicea in A.D. 325. Remains of the theater (second century), which could seat 7,600 spectators, and of the church of a bishop Philip (sixth century) survive. Tombs dating to the first century A.D. were found outside the Heraklea gate.

22.11 Missionary Work in Egypt and North Africa

There is evidence that Egypt and regions in North Africa were reached by Christian missionaries in the first century A.D.

Evangelism in Egypt

The origins of the church in Egypt are unknown, and there is no explicit or reliable information for the first century. It is plausible to assume, however, that there were Christian communities in Egypt in the first century, probably at least in Alexandria.

---

[615]L. Levine 2000, 251-52; Panayotov, in *IJudO* I BS39-48.

[616]C. Danoff, PW 19.2 (1938): 2259.

[617]Jones 1937, 20-21; Danoff, PWSup 9 (1962): 800-824; *KP* 4:574-75; Bredow, *DNP* 9:451-52; Alexandrov 1976, 98.

[618]B. Saria, PW 4.A1 (1931): 47-54; J. Szilágyi, *KP* 5:379; J. Wiseman, *PECS* 859; J. J. Wilkes, *OCD* 1445-46. Excavations: James Wiseman, ed., *Studies in the Antiquities of Stobi* (Beograd: National Museum of Titov Veles; Austin: University of Texas, 1973); idem, *Stobi: A Guide to the Excavations* (Beograd: National Museum of Titov Veles; Austin: University of Texas, 1973); Panayotov, in *IJudO* I, 2004, 56-57.

[619]See M. Hengel, "Die Synagogeninschrift von Stobi," *ZNW* 57 (1966) 145-183; Kraabel 1979, 494-97; Rajak 1996, 316; Lichtenberger 1996b, 24-26; Levine 2000, 252-55; Runesson 2001, 175, 181 and passim. The inscription contains the earliest reference to the "patriarch," i.e., the head of the all Jews in the Roman Empire with its seat in Galilee; the first patriarch was Jehuda I. ha-Nasi (since A.D. 170).

Egypt (Αἴγυπτος)[620] was a Roman province since 30 B.C., after having been governed by the successors of Ptolemy, one of Alexander the Great's generals. Augustus annexed Egypt after his victory over Marcus Antonius, converting it into a province administered by a *praefecti Aegypti* as the personal property of the emperor. Between A.D. 30 and 70 the following prefects governed Egypt:[621] Ti. Iulius Severus (31/32), A. Avillius Flaccus (32-37/38), C. Vitrasius Pollio (39-41), L. Aemilius Rectus (41/42), C. Iulius Postumus (47), Cn. Vergilius Capito (47/48), M. Mettius Modestus (under Claudius), Ti. Claudius Balbillus (56), L. Iulius Vestinus (59/60-61/62), Caecina Tuscus (during Nero's late reign), Ti. Iulius Alexander (67-69). The Egyptian temples and priests had been allowed to retain most of their privileges, but they had to accept the dissemination of the imperial cult. The status of the cities was strengthened; the *mētropolis* ("mother city") of each administrative district (*nomos*) enjoyed a certain measure of autonomy. The urbanization that resulted from the new structures prompted the construction of public buildings. The strict social order privileged the Roman citizens in Egypt and the Alexandrinians, who were exempted from, for example, certain taxes that the "Egyptians" had to pay. The majority of the population was engaged in agriculture despite the Roman urbanization. Egypt was the most populous province in the Roman Empire. Ancient sources mention specific figures: Diodorus Siculus mentions 7 million people (1.31.8), while Josephus mentions 7.5 million without Alexandria (*B.J.* 2.385). Diodorus writes around 50 B.C., "In density of population it far surpassed of old all known regions of the inhabited world, and even in our own day is thought to be second to none other; for in ancient times it had over eighteen thousand important villages and cities, as can be seen entered in their sacred records, while under Ptolemy son of Lagus these were reckoned at over thirty thousand, this great number continuing down to our own time. The total population, they say, was of old about seven million and the number has remained no less down to our day"(1.31.6-9). Modern estimates range between four and eight million inhabitants.[622]

Jews possibly settled in Egypt during the time of Alexander the Great in order to escape the political upheavals in Syria, according to the contemporary observer Hekataios of Abdera.[623] Under the rule of Ptolemy I Soter (king since 304 B.C.), who conquered Jerusalem probably in the spring of 311 B.C., thousands of Jewish prisoners were brought to Egypt, who were forced to do guard duty in various fortresses (*Let.*

---

[620]H. W. Helck, *KP* 1:166-71; D. J. Thompson and D. W. Rathbone, *OCD* 510-12; S. Seidlmayer and K. Jansen-Winkeln, *DNP* 1:156-66; Alan K. Bowman, *The Town Councils of Roman Egypt* (American Studies in Papyrology 11; Toronto: Hakkert, 1971); Édouard Will, *Histoire politique du monde hellénistique (323-30 av. J.C.)* (Annales de l'Est 30; Nancy: Presses Universitaires de Nancy, 1979); Maehler Herwig and Volker M. Strocka, *Das Ptolemäische Ägypten* (Mainz: Zabern, 1978); A. K. Bowman, *Egypt after the Pharaohs 332 B.C.—A.D. 642: From Alexander to the Arab Conquest* (Berkeley: University of California Press, 1986); idem, *Agriculture in Egypt from Pharaonic to Modern Times* (Oxford: Oxford University Press, 1999); idem, "Urbanization in Roman Egypt," in Fentress 2000, 173-87; Hölbl 2001.

[621]See Paul M. Meyer, *Das Heerwesen der Ptolemäer und Römer in Ägypten* (Aalen: Scientia, 1966 [1900]), 145.

[622]Bagnall and Frier (1994, 53-57) assume 4 to 4.5 million; Bowman ("Urbanization in Roman Egypt," 177) assumes 7.5 million.

[623]Hekataios's information is recorded by Josephus, *C. Ap.* 1.186-194. Cf. *GLAJJ* I 12. See Schürer (3:41 with nn. 38, 44, 46), who accepts this information as reliable.

Arist. 14; Josephus, *A.J.* 12.4-9).[624] Inscriptions attest synagogues already for the time of Ptolemy III Euergetes (246-221 B.C.).[625] Philo perhaps exaggerates when he writes that a million Jews lived in Egypt "from Katabathmos near Libya to the Ethiopian border" (*Flacc.* 6 [43]). There is no doubt that several hundred thousand Jews lived in Egypt in the first century A.D. The geographical distribution from Lower to Upper Egypt can be evaluated on the basis of papyri and inscriptions.[626] Jewish authors from the Second Temple period who were active in Alexandria include Artapanus, Ezekiel the tragician, Aristobulos, Philo, and the authors who wrote Wisdom of Solomon, the novel *Joseph and Aseneth* and 3 Maccabees. The Greek translation of the Old Testament, the Septuagint, possibly was published in Alexandria as well. On the Jews in Egypt see also §6.

Most historians assume that the gospel was brought to Egypt, specifically to Alexandria, at an early date from Palestine, probably from Jerusalem.[627] The large Jewish population in Egypt, particularly in Alexandria, is generally regarded as to have been too attractive for the early Christian missionaries to ignore.[628] Alexandria, in the Greco-Roman period the capital of Egypt, was about 560 km from Jerusalem and could be reached on foot within twenty-two days. The Jewish communities of Alexandria and Rome were the largest outside of Palestine. The Jews of Alexandria would have been a natural destination for the Christian missionaries.

Alexandria (᾿Αλεξάνδρεια; Alexandria ad Aegyptum [see fig. 20]),[629] a port city on the northwestern corner of the Nile Delta, was founded by Alexander the Great in 332/331 B.C. It was the first ancient city that we know whose foundation was not ascribed to a god or to a mythical hero but rather was named after its founder right from the beginning. The city plan is traced back to Deinokrates, the Macedonian architect who built the new tem-

---

[624]J. G. Griffiths, "Egypt and the Rise of the Synagogue," *JTS* 38 (1987): 1-15; J. K. Winnicki, "Militäroperationen von Ptolemaios I. und Seleukos I. in Syrien in den Jahren 312-311 v.Chr," *Ancient Society* 22 (1991): 147-227, esp. 147-64; A. Kasher, "The Civic Status of the Jews in Ptolemaic Egypt," in Bilde et al. 1992, 100-21; Hölbl 2001, 189-90.

[625]*I. EgJud* 22, 117. See J. Gwyn Griffiths, "Egypt and the Rise of the Synagogue," in Urman and Flesher 1995, 1:3-16, esp. 4-5; Kasher 1995, 205; L. Levine 2000, 75-76.

[626]See Schürer 46-59. On the Jews in Egypt see Smallwood 1976, 220-55; Kasher 1985; Barclay 1996, 19-228; Binder 1999, 233-54; Smallwood 1999, 179-187; L. Levine 2000, 75-84, and passim.

[627]H. Bell 1944, 190; Goppelt 1954, 211; Plumley 1957; Kasser 1962, 13; Molland 1962, 52; Barnard 1963, 439; Roncaglia 1966, 53-60, 126; C. H. Roberts 1949, 161; 1979, 71; Gunther 1982, 221; H. Koester 1982, 2:222; T. Robinson 1988, 66-67; Griggs 1991, 14-15; cf. H. Green 1986, 110-12; Klijn 1986, 163-65; Pearson 1992, 959; Hornschuh 1959. Frankfurter (1998, 31-33, and passim) discusses only the fourth and fifth centuries. On the Christian witnesses of the second, third and fourth centuries see Naldini 1998; on Christian architecture in Egypt see Grossmann 2002.

[628]See Gunther 1982, 219-20.

[629]S. Shenouda, *PECS* 36-38; B. A. Pearson, *ABD* 1:152-57; E. Schwertheim, *DNP* 1:463-66; D. W. Rathbone, *OCD* 61-62; A. D. Clarke, *DNTB* 23-25; Jones 1937, 303-6, 311-12; Fraser 1972; E. G. Huzar, "Alexandria ad Aegyptum in the Julio-Claudian Age," *ANRW* II.10.1 (1988): 619-68; Isaac 1993, 277-79; Sly 1996; Bernand 1998. On the Ptolemaieia see Köhler 1996, 35-45.

ple of Artemis in Ephesus. The construction of the *heptastadion*—a jetty 1,500 m long between the island of Pharos and the village of Ra-kedet at the western end of the narrow isthmus between Lake Mareotis and the Mediterranean—created two harbors. The original inhabitants were resettled in Kanopus, a village northeast of Alexandria. After Alexander's death, his general Ptolemy, the son of Lagus and Arsinoë, became ruler over Egypt. He was crowned king in 304 B.C. and established the dynasty of the Lagides, which ruled Egypt until 30 B.C. Important institutions and buildings were established and erected during the reign of Ptolemy I Soter ("Savior"): the library and the museion—both a temple and an academic research institute with emphasis on the philological disciplines[630] and a medical "faculty"[631]—as well as temples for Alexander, the dynasty of the Lagides and Sarapis.[632] The cult of Sarapis, originally the Egyptian Osiris-Apis, seems to have been developed under Ptolemy I as a unifying force for Greek Egypt. Cleopatra erected a Kaisareion for Marcus Antonius in 34 B.C., which was completed by Octavius (Augustus) and renamed Sebasteion; the sanctuary complex consisted of a temple dedicated to the imperial cult, two colonnaded halls (300 m long), a library, open courtyards, monumental gates, gardens and terraces. When Strabo visited the city in 25 B.C., he saw the lighthouse Pharos, the two harbors, palaces, the museion, two libraries (the main library housed about 700,000 papyrus and parchment scrolls in the first century B.C.), the theater, the Kaisareion, the Timonium, a gymnasium, a stadium, the Paneion, the Sarapeion (the west side of the building was 77 m long), a large park and the necropolis with gardens. The significance of Alexandria is seen in the rumors among the population of Rome, noted by Suetonius (*Iul.* 79.3), that Julius Caesar wanted to plunder the city of Rome and all of Italy and to move the capital to Alexandria or to Ilium (the later Constantinople). Augustus expanded the city toward the east (Nikopolis). Claudius granted the philosophers of the museion tax-exempt status in 38 B.C. (P.Ryl. 143). Vespasian was proclaimed emperor in Alexandria in A.D. 69. Several scholars moved from Alexandria to Rome in the first century, particularly teachers of rhetoric such as Aristonikos, Philoxenos and Chairemon. A letter, written in the second half of the first century, laments the thinning out of the intellectual life of the city, the "brain drain" to Rome (P.Oxy. 2190). Young Neilos from Oxyrhynchus complains in a letter to his father, Theon, about the difficulty of finding a "decent teacher" and states, "Knowing as I do that apart from paying useless and excessive fees there is no good to be had from a tutor, I am depending on myself."[633] Aelius Aristides visited Alexandria probably in May of A.D. 141, and he describes the city as sparkling, on account of it treasures, like the diadem that a wealthy woman wears around her neck.[634] Alexandria had between 300,000 and 500,000 inhabitants in the first century.[635] Heron, a mathematician and technician who taught and wrote in Alexandria around A.D. 60, is our

---

[630]W. H. Gross, *KP* 3:1482-85; Fraser 1972, 1:633-34; Bernand 1998, 127-38.

[631]Fraser 1972, 1:338-76; R. J. Littman, "Medicine in Alexandria," *ANRW* II.37.3 (1996): 2678-2708. On the museion and the library see Fraser 1972, 1:305-35; A. D. Clarke, *DNTB* 25-26.

[632]On the cults and temples of Alexandria see Fraser 1972, 1:189-301, on the cult and temple of Sarapis (in Rhacotis) see Fraser 1972, 1:246-70; 2:83-90; cf. Bernand 1998, 139-155. For the following comment cf. D. J. Thompson, *OCD* 1272.

[633]For the text and an English translation of P.Oxy. 2190 see B. Winter 1997, 245-49; for a German translation see Krüger 1990, 210-11.

[634]Aelius Aristides, *To the Rhodians: Concerning Concord* 56 (*Or.* 24; see C. A. Behr, ed., *Aristides*, 45-58).

[635]See Bagnall and Frier 1994, 54. Opting for the higher figures are D. Delia, "The Population of Roman Alexandria," *TAPA* 118 (1989): 275-92; Dominic W. Rathbone, "Villages, Land and Population in Graeco-Roman Egypt," *PCPS* 36 (1990): 103-42.

main source for applied mathematics in the Greco-Roman world. Another mathematician active in Alexandria in the first century was Menelaos, who wrote a book about spheric trigonometry.

There is epigraphical evidence for a Jewish place of payer in the second century B.C. in Alexandria.[636] It is estimated that about 100,000 Jews lived in Alexandria in the first century A.D.[637] The Jewish community of Alexandria lived mostly in the "Delta" quarter (i.e., the fourth district of the city).[638] The earliest evidence of anti-Jewish literature comes from Alexandria (see §6), represented by Manetho of Sebennytos, an Egyptian priest of the third century B.C.[639] According to the *Letter of Aristeas,* the writing of the Greek translation of the Hebrew Bible, the so-called Septuagint, took place under Ptolemy II Philadelphos (282-246 B.C.) in Alexandria. The most famous Jew of Alexandria is Philo, born around 20 B.C. In A.D. 38 Emperor Caligula and Flaccus, his governor in Egypt, provoked a bloody pogrom among the Jewish population of Alexandria that could have been put down within an hour by the two Roman legions stationed in the city (Philo, *Flacc.* 11.86-91; cf. Josephus, *B.J.* 2.385). In his famous letters to the citizens of Alexandria, specifically to the Roman prefect Aemilius Rectus (P.Lond. 1912 = *CPJ* II 153),[640] Claudius speaks in the fourth section (lines 73-104) about the Jews. He refrains from a legal investigation of the causes of the conflict, but he threatens the Alexandrians with his wrath if they do not end the hostilities. He implores them (line 82) to be friendly to the Jews because they have been living in the city for a long time (τὴν αὐτὴν πόλειν ἐκ πολλῶν χρόνων οἰκοῦσει). He warns the Alexandrians not to interfere with "the rites observed by them in the worship of their god [μηδὲν τῶν πρὸς θρησκείαν αὐτοῖς νενομισμένων τοῦ θεοῦ λοιμένωνται], but allow them to observe their customs [ἐῶσιν αὐτοὺς τοῖς ἔθεσιν χρῆσθαι] as in the time of the Deified Augustus, which customs I also, after hearing both sides, have sanctioned." He directs the Jews "not to agitate for more privileges than they formerly possessed" (line 89); they must not send two embassies to Rome, they must not force their way into the games of the city, and they must not "bring in or admit Jews who come down the river from Egypt or from Syria, a proceeding which will compel me to conceive serious suspicions." If they refuse to obey these directives, he will "by all means take vengeance on them as fomenters of which is a general plague infecting the whole world" (τῆς οἰκουμένης νόσον ἐξεγείροντας [line 100]). Claudius knows that the Alexandrians are to be blamed for the disturbances, not the Jews. "Nevertheless, he 'conjures' the former, while he 'orders' the Jews. If we take into account the obliging phrases of the introduction, then it is clear who enjoys the greater sympathies of the emperor. The formulation of the threat with the hateful undertone seems to have been prompted by the Alexandrian delegation. Not even King Agrippa, who was present during the negotiations and who surely supported the Jews, was able to influence the emperor. Claudius clearly was not an emperor who was a friend

---

[636] *CPJ* III 1432, 1433 = *I. EgJud* 9, 13. See Trebilco 1991, 133; Binder 1999, 246-52; L. Levine 2000, 76-77.

[637] Horsley, *NewDocs* 5:37, with reference to Mélèze-Modrzejewski 1981, 20-21; see also Smallwood 1976, 224-42; Bernand 1998, 262-64.

[638] See Fraser 1972, 1:35, 54-58, 281-85, 298-300, 687-716; Hassoun 1981; Kasher 1985; Bernand 1998, 261-79; Mélèze-Modrzejewski 1991; Hölbl 2001, 190-91.

[639] Manetho, *FGrH* 609 F 10 = Josephus, *C. Ap.* 1.223-253.

[640] For the text and an English translation see Hunt and Edgar, eds., *Select Papyri* 2:78-89; German translation in Barrett and Thornton, *Texte zur Umwelt des Neuen Testaments,* no. 52. For a discussion of the letter see the commentary and bibliography in *CPJ* II 153 (Tcherikover and Fuks); Kasher 1985, 310-26; Riesner 1994, 88-89 (ET, 99-100); Bernand 1998, 275-76; Botermann 1996, 107-14; for the comments that follow above see ibid., 111-12.

of the Jews. He wants to have peace and order, period."[641] The Jews of Alexandria had a synagogue of monumental dimensions in the first century, if the rabbinic tradition describes the same building that Philo escribes: the main hall was a *dyplastoon*—a stoa within a stoa—with two rows of columns on two, three or four sides; the hall was so large that people used handkerchiefs to signal to the assembled congregation when to start singing.[642]

The fact that Luke is silent about a mission of the early Christians to Egypt or to Alexandria does not prove that the gospel came to Egypt at a later date. We have observed repeatedly that Luke reports the history of the mission of the early church selectively: he does not tell everything that he knows. Luke's account of the missionary activity of the church after A.D. 42, after Peter and evidently most if not all of the other apostles left Jerusalem, focuses nearly exclusively on the missionary work of Paul. This consistent focus in the second half of the book of Acts suggests that we should not expect a report about missionary outreach in Egypt. At least six pieces of evidence indicate that the Christian message very probably had already come to Egypt and to Alexandria in the 30s.

Two late apocryphal Infancy Gospels, written after the fourth or the fifth century—the *Arabic Infancy Gospel* translated from a Syriac original, and the *Gospel of Pseudo-Matthew*[643]—mention miracles performed by the infant Jesus during the sojourn of Joseph and Mary in Egypt mentioned in Mt 2:14-15. According to Ps.-Mt. 22-24, the population of the city Sotinen, located perhaps in the region of Hermopolis, was converted after Mary entered the temple with the infant Jesus, which resulted in the 365 idols of the temple falling to the ground and bursting into pieces. Raymond Brown calls these "charming tales" a Christian midrash.[644] They have no historical value. Origen claims to know that Joseph and Mary settled in Panopolis (*Comm. Matt.* 2:7).[645]

1. Claudius's directive to the Alexandrian Jews to stop the immigration of Syrian

---

[641]Botermann 1996, 112-13, in connection with her argument that the edicts of Claudius reported by Josephus (*A.J.* 19.278-291) that are friendly to the Jews are not authentic (see ibid., 103-14).

[642]Philo, *Legat.* 311; *Flacc.* 48; *Spec.* 3.171; *t. Sukkah* 4:6; *y. Sukkah* 5:1 (55a-b); *b. Sukkah* 51b. On the historicity of these traditions see L. Levine 2000, 84-89.

[643]O. Cullmann, in Hennecke and Schneemelcher 1990-1997, 1:363-70 (ET, 1:408-13).

[644]R. Brown 1993, 203-4.

[645]See Harnack 1924, 2:722 n. 4 (addition to ET, 2:173 n.3). On Panopolis see A. Egberts, B. P. Muhs and J. van der Vliet, eds., *Perspectives on Panopolis: An Egyptian Town from Alexander the Great to the Arab Conquest* (Papyrologica Lugduno-Batava 31; Leiden: Brill, 2002). On Panopolis in the Roman period see R. S. Bagnall, "Public Administration and the Documentation of Roman Panopolis," in ibid., 1-12. Nonnos, who wrote a large epic on the adventures of Dionysos and converted to Christianity, was a native of Panopolis in the fifth century, as was the famous Christian ascetic Shenoute, who ransacked the area in an effort to eradicate the last traces of paganism and headed the impressive monastery across the Nile from Panopolis after A.D. 385. On Shenoute see S. Emmel, "From the Other Side of the Nile: Shenute and Panopolis," in ibid., 95-113.

Jews is interpreted by some scholars as a reference to Christian missionaries.[646] If this interpretation were correct, it would constitute evidence for Christian missionary activity in Alexandria around A.D. 40/41 at the latest. However, several factors indicate that this interpretation is incorrect. The reference to the contagious plague affecting the world is found also in Acts 24:5, where this formulation is mentioned in Tertullus's charge against Paul and his missionary activity before Felix, as well in Greek texts that speak in general terms of political unrest (see Plato, *Prot.* 322D). Also, Claudius's letter implies the arrival of larger groups of Jews rather than the activity of a few people. And Claudius's letter does not refer to or hint at Christians. Most scholars therefore do not interpret the letter as evidence for the activity of early Christian missionaries,[647] even though "it is entirely possible that Christian missionaries had already come to Alexandria in A.D. 41."

2. When Luke mentions the opponents of Stephen in Acts 6:9, he implies that he was at home and active in synagogues in which Jews of Cyrene and Alexandria were meeting. Lucius of Cyrene, a teacher of the church in Antioch mentioned in Acts 13:1, also came from North Africa. And the tradition of Jesus' passion mentions Simon of Cyrene (Mt 27:32; Mk 15:21; Lk 23:26), the father of Alexander and Rufus (Mk 15:21), who probably belonged to the Hellenistic Jewish Christians in Jerusalem.[648] These references do not prove missionary outreach at an early date, but it can be assumed "that the missionary work among the festival pilgrims of the African Diaspora in Jerusalem which the Stephen tradition presupposes affected their synagogues at home in the Diaspora, especially if we take into account the fact that the pilgrims traveled to the temple in Jerusalem in groups and they stayed together in synagogue communities organized on the basis of their geographical origin. We also have to reckon with the possibility that some Hellenists returned to their home countries as missionaries after they were driven out from Jerusalem."[649] It is perhaps no coincidence that the later Egyptian gnostics regarded Nicolaus and Prochorus, two members of the Seven, as authorities.

3. Luke reports in Acts 18:24-26 that Apollos, a Jew from Alexandria, knew the sacred Scriptures and had received the baptism of John. Luke introduces Apollos abruptly, with little explanation, when he came to Ephesus and taught in the synagogue about Jesus.

---

[646]P.Lond. 1912 = *CPJ* II 153 (line 96). See especially Reinach 1924; followed by F. Cumont, "La lettre de Claude aux Alexandrins," *RHR* 91 (1925): 3-6; more recently Lüdemann 1980, 191; J. Taylor 1994; G. M. Lee, "Eusebius on St. Mark and the Beginnings of Christianity in Egypt," *Studie Patristica* 12 (1975): 422- 431, here 431 ("attractive possibility"); also Pearson 1986, 134-35. See the critique in Griggs 1991, 18-19.

[647]Bruce 1974, 196-98; Riesner 1994, 89 (ET, 100); Botermann 1996, 112 n. 350; the quotation that follows above, ibid.

[648]Pesch, *Mk,* 2:477; cf. Davies and Allison, *Mt,* 2:611.

[649]Löning 1987, 85-86.

Acts 18:24-26a: "Now there came to Ephesus a Jew named Apollos, a native of Alexandria. He was an eloquent man, well-versed in the scriptures. [25]He had been instructed in the Way of the Lord; and he spoke with burning enthusiasm and taught accurately the things concerning Jesus, though he knew only the baptism of John. [26]He began to speak boldly in the synagogue."

The New Testament manuscript Codex Bezae (fifth century) includes the additional statement that Apollos had been taught in the word of the Lord ἐν τῇ πατρίδι (*en tē patridi*)—that is, in Alexandria. If this comment were authentic, it would imply that there was a Christian community in Alexandria in A.D. 50 at the latest.[650] It cannot be demonstrated, however, that this notice is historical.[651] Nevertheless, the assumption is not impossible that Christians were active in the capital of the Roman province of Egypt twenty years after Easter. The Jewish community in Alexandria was large, it maintained regular contacts with Jerusalem, and it was easy to travel from Jerusalem to Alexandria. In Jerusalem there was a synagogue of Alexandrian Jews (Acts 6:9). If followers of Jesus from Jerusalem founded a church in Antioch, the capital of the province of Syria in the 30s, it is plausible to assume that Christian missionaries preached the gospel in Alexandria and established a Christian community. And it is not impossible that Jewish pilgrims from Egypt came to Jerusalem to attend the Feast of Pentecost in A.D. 30, heard Peter preach (Acts 2:10), and were converted to faith in Jesus as the Messiah.[652]

Apollos is mentioned by Luke in Acts 18:24—19:1 and by Paul in 1 Cor 1:12; 3:4-6.22; 4:6; 16:12; Tit 3:13.[653] Some manuscripts write Ἀπελλῆς (*Apellēs*) instead of Ἀπολλῶς (*Apollōs*): Apelles is a typical Egyptian name. Probably the same person is meant.[654] In Acts 18:24-25 Luke mentions the following details: Apollos was a Jew and came from Alexandria; that is, he was born in the Egyptian capital and he grew up there. He was an "eloquent man" (ἀνὴρ λόγιος, *anēr logios*) and "well-versed in the Scriptures" (δυνατὸς ὢν ἐν ταῖς γραφαῖς, *dynatos ōn en tais graphais*); that is, he had studied the sacred Scriptures and was able to interpret them. It is not impossible that he studied in the academy of Philo, the Jewish exegete and philosopher who taught in Alexandria in the first century.[655] He had been "instructed in the Way of the Lord" (ἦν κατηχημένος τὴν ὁδὸν τοῦ κυρίου, *ēn*

---

[650]Metzger, *Textual Commentary*, 413: "The implication of the statement no doubt accords with historical fact"; cf. Hengel 1994b, 185 n. 7.

[651]Positive are Metzger, *Textual Commentary*, 413; Hunter 1976, 148; Gunther 1982, 220; H. Green 1986, 110; Griggs 1991, 16-17; A. F. Segal 1992b, 337-38; Maness 1998, 35 n. 114; as a possibility: Bruce 1995, 53; Barrett, *Acts*, 2:888; Pearson 1986, 136; undecided is Klijn 1986, 163-64.

[652]See Arnold 1997, 149.

[653]On Apollos see H. Merkel, *EWNT* 1:328-29 (*EDNT* 1:136-37); L. D. Hurst, *ABD* 1:301; B. B. Blue, *DPL* 37-39; Schumacher 1916; Ollrog 1979, 37-41, 215-19; L. D. Hurst, "Apollos, Hebrews and Corinth," *SJT* 38 (1985): 505-13; Wolter 1987; Beatrice 1995 (bibliography); see also the commentaries.

[654]See Horsley, *NewDocs* 1:88; Beatrice 1995, 1235 n. 2.

[655]This is often assumed; see Beatrice 1995, 1236.

katēchēmenos tēn hodon tou kyriou); he "spoke with burning enthusiasm" (ζέων τῷ πνεύματι ἐλάλει, *zeōn tō pneumati elalei*), meaning that he had a fiery temperament;[656] and he "taught accurately the things concerning Jesus" (ἐδίδασκεν ἀκριβῶς τὰ περὶ τοῦ Ἰησοῦ, *edidasken akribōs ta peri tou Iēsou*), meaning that he was a Christian. Luke does not report whether Apollos was converted in Alexandria or in another city (unless the comment in Codex Bezae is authentic). Pier Beatrice argues on the basis of Apollos's understanding of baptism that he was converted in Palestine, probably at an early date during the baptismal activity of Jesus and his disciples (cf. Jn 4:1-3), although he does not exclude a conversion in connection with the activity of early Christian missionaries in Alexandria.[657] Francesco Pericoli-Ridolfini infers from Acts 18:24-28 that Apollos became acquainted with the content of Jesus' teaching during Jesus' lifetime while living in Alexandria.[658] It is not impossible that Jews in Alexandria who had regular contact with Jews in Judea received news at a very early date of the rabbi and "prophet" Jesus who performed miracles and proclaimed the arrival of God's kingdom. This possibility does not prove, however, that there were sympathizers of Jesus in Alexandria before A.D. 30 and that there were believers in Jesus soon after Easter. According to the *Chronicon Paschale* (PG 92:521c), a text written in the seventh century, Apollos belonged to the seventy disciples whom Jesus sent out (he is mentioned as the thirty-second disciple), an assertion that seems rather unlikely. It is also possible that Apollos had contacts with the synagogue of Alexandrian Jews in Jerusalem (Acts 6:9; 9:29).

4. According to early church tradition, Mark was the first missionary in Alexandria and in Egypt. This is asserted by Clement of Alexandria, Eusebius, Epiphanius, the *Apostolic Constitutions,* the *Acts of Mark,* the *Acts of Barnabas,* Jerome and John Chrysostom.[659] The New Testament links John Mark with Jerusalem, Antioch, Cyprus, Asia Minor and Rome, but not with Egypt.[660]

Eusebius writes, "And they say that this Mark was the first that was sent to Egypt, and that he proclaimed the Gospel which he had written, and first established churches in Alexandria. And the multitude of believers, both men and women, that were collected there at the very outset, and lived lives of the most philosophical and excessive asceticism, was so great that Philo thought it worthwhile to describe their pursuits, their meetings, their entertainments, and their whole manner of life" (*Hist. eccl.* 2.16.1-2). Eusebius refers to Philo's description of the Therapeutae, who often are linked with the Essenes; the differences between the two groups suggest, however, that the Therapeutae and the Essenes represented different movements.[661] Eusebius writes in his *Chronicle* that Mark came to

---

[656]See the commentaries of Zahn, Bruce, Marshall. Less plausible is the interpretation in terms of glossolalia (see the commentaries of Roloff, Pesch, Schille, Zmijewski; also Beatrice 1995, 1236).

[657]See Beatrice 1995, 1240.

[658]See Pericoli-Ridolfini 1962, 313-16.

[659]Eusebius, *Hist. eccl.* 2.16.1; 2.16.24; *Theoph.* 4.6; Epiphanius, *Pan.* 29.5.4; 51.6.10; *Apos. Con.* 7.46; *Acts Mk.* (PG 115:164-66); *Acts Barn.* 26; Jerome, *Vir. ill.* 8; *Comm. Matt.* Praef. 6; John Chrysostom, *Hom. Matt.* 1.3.

[660]Acts 12:12, 25; 13:5, 13; 15:37-40; Col 4:10; Philem 24; 2 Tim 4:11; 1 Pet 5:13.

[661]C. T. R. Hayward, "Therapeutae," *EDSS* 2:943-46. On Philo's text *De vita contemplativa* see F. Daumas and P. Miquel, *De vita contemplativa* (Les œuvres de Philon d'Alexandrie 29; Paris: Cerf, 1960); Schürer 2:591-97.

Alexandria in the third year of the reign of the emperor Claudius (i.e., A.D. 43). The *Chronicon Paschale* dates Mark's arrival in Alexandria two years before Claudius's acension to the throne (i.e., A.D. 39). Severus, the bishop of al-Ashmunein in the tenth century, claims to know that Peter sent Mark to Alexandria fifteen years after Christ's ascension, (i.e., in A.D. 45). And Eutychius, Severus's rival in Alexandria, mentions the ninth year of Claudius's reign (i.e., A.D. 49/50).[662]

The apocryphal *Acts of Mark* and the text *Martyrdom of Mark*[663] claim to know that Mark came via Cyrene to Alexandria, that he preached there, performed miracles, founded a church, appointed a bishop (Ananias/Annianus) and three presbyters (Milaius, Sabinus, Cerdo), seven deacons and eleven further co-workers, and that he then returned to Cyrene (Pentapolis). Two years later he returned to Alexandria, where he encountered a church in the quarter Boukolou near the coast. Mark was arrested during Passover, which the Jews celebrated on the same day as the Feast of Sarapis, the twenty-ninth of Pharmouthi (April 24), by angry Gentiles, and he died the next day. According to the apocryphal Acts of Barnabas (fifth or sixth century), John Mark came from Cyprus to Alexandria after Barnabas had died as a martyr in Salamis: "And having come to the shore, we found an Egyptian ship; and having embarked in it, we landed at Alexandria. And there I remained, teaching the brethren who came the word of the Lord, enlightening them, and preaching what I had been taught by the apostles of Christ."[664] The historical value is unclear, and the text probably refers not to John Mark as pioneer missionary in Alexandria but to later events.

Francesco Pericoli-Ridolfini wants to combine all available traditions into a coherent picture of the early history of the church in Alexandria: Mark visited Alexandria for the first time in A.D. 43, he engaged in missionary work together with Barnabas, Paul and Peter in other regions of the Mediterranean world, and he died as a martyr in Rome in connection with the pogrom that the Roman prefect Tiberius Alexander organized against the Alexandrian Jews in A.D. 66. The "bishops" of the Alexandrian church in the first century were Annianus (A.D. 62-85), Abilius (A.D. 85-97/98) and Cerdo (A.D. 98-109).[665] The traditions about Mark's missionary activity in Egypt go back to the second century, but they may be older. Their historicity cannot be proven, but there is no hard evidence that

---

[662]Schoene, ed., *Eusebi Chronicorum libri duo*, 2.152; *Chronicon Paschale* (PG 92:560a). On Severus see Basil Evetts, *History of the Patriarchs of the Coptic Church of Alexandria* (PO 1:2; Paris: Firmin-Didot, 1948), 140; cf. Pearson 1986, 142 n. 47. On Eutychus see PG 145:792c; cf. Pearson 1986, 139 n. 30.

[663]See A. de Santos Otero, in Hennecke and Schneemelcher 1990-1997, 2:417-21.

[664]A. Walker, *Apocryphal Gospels, Acts and Revelations* (Ante-Nicene Christian Library 16; Edinburgh: T & T Clark, 1870), 293-300; Hennecke and Schneemelcher (1990-1997) offer only a summary.

[665]Pericoli-Ridolfini 1962, esp. 317-29; on the bishops of the first century see ibid., 329-31. Pearson (1986, 142) does not reject this reconstruction in principle, but he refers to the problematic tradition history of the martyrdom of Mark.

would render this reconstruction impossible.[666]

5. An important piece of evidence for an early presence of Christians in Middle Egypt, about 300 km south of Alexandria, around A.D. 100 is represented by the earliest fragment of a New Testament manuscript that has survived, the so-called Papyrus Rylands Greek 457 ($\mathfrak{P}^{52}$), with the text Jn 18:31-33, 37-38. This papyrus is dated between A.D. 100 and 125 and was found probably in the Fayum (in Oxyrhynchus?). Several papyri found in Oxyrhynchus that contain portions of the New Testament are private copies—that is, copies of New Testament texts that belonged not to churches but to private individuals. If we assume that copies of New Testament books were initially in the possession of churches and used in the worship services and in teaching believers and new converts, and if we assume that copies of New Testament books were copied by private individuals only at a later date, then the existence of private copies of New Testament books around A.D. 100 in geographical areas far from Alexandria suggests that the first churches in Middle Egypt must have been established at a fairly early date and that they expanded rather rapidly.[667]

6. There is evidence that church buildings were destroyed in Alexandria in connection with the persecution under Diocletian. The earliest church that is documented in Alexandria, St. Theonas—Theonas was bishop between A.D. 282 and 300—was located in the northwestern section of Alexandria in the quarter "Delta," where many Jews lived in the first century. This fact allows for the possibility that there was a Jewish-Christian community in Delta at an earlier date, perhaps already in the first century.[668] The famous Catechetical School, the center of Christian life in Alexandria since the second century, was located in the quarter "Brouchion" (*Pyroucheion*).[669]

Justin refers in his *First Apology*, around A.D. 155, to a Christian who wanted to remain unmarried and sought to be castrated; the doctors of Alexandria declined to perform the operation because Felix, the governor of Alexandria, refused permission for the procedure, with the result that the young man "remained single, and was satisfied with his own approving conscience, and the approval of those who thought as he did [τῶν ὁμο– γνωμόνων]" (*1 Apol.* 29.2-3). This episode clearly implies that there was a Christian community in the early second century. Irenaeus knows of churches in Egypt and Libya at the end of the second century: "As I have already observed, the Church, having received this preaching and this faith, although scattered throughout the whole world [ἡ ἐκκλησία, καί περ ἐν ὅλῳ τῷ κόσμῳ διεσπαρμένη], yet, as if occupying but one house, carefully preserves it. . . . For the churches [ἐκκλησίαι] which have been planted in Germany do not believe

---

[666]Pearson 1986, 137-45; Petersen 1992, 966. Griggs (1991, 19-22) remains skeptical, but he accepts the possibility of a Christian presence in Alexandria in the mid-first century.

[667]Thus Epp 1993, 279. This scenario presupposes, of course, that the fragments of New Testament books that were found in Egypt were copied in Egypt and not imported from, for example, Jerusalem. See also Griggs 1991, 23-28.

[668]Pearson 1986, 151-52. On St. Theonas see Grossmann 2002, 16-17.

[669]See Andresen 1979, 428-52; Pearson 1986, 151.

or hand down anything different, nor do those in Spain, nor those in Gaul, nor those in the East, nor those in Egypt, nor those in Libya, nor those which have been established in the central regions of the world [i.e., Palestine with Jerusalem]" (*Haer.* 1.10.2).

The apocryphal *Acts of John* and *Acts of Andrew* (ca. A.D. 150-200) often are linked with Alexandria as the place of origin,[670] which would presuppose the existence of a church in Egypt in the early or middle second century. This connection between these apocryphal Acts and Alexandria has been disputed by some scholars, however.[671] Fourteen bishops from Egypt and the Thebais attended the Council of Nicea in A.D. 325: Alexandros from Alexandria, Harpokration from Alphokranon, Adamantnios from Kynon, Arbetion from Pharbaetus, Philippos from Panephysis, Potamon from Heraklia, Secundus from Ptolemais, Dorotheos from Pelusion, Gaius from Thmuis, Antiochos from Memphis, Tiberius from Tauthe, Atthas from Schedia, Tyrannos from Antinou, and Plousianos from Lykopolis.[672] Some of the most renowned theologians of the early church came from Alexandria: Clement, Origen, Athanasius.

The question of when the first missionaries came to Alexandria and established the first church in Egypt cannot be answered with certainty. Speculations concerning the travels of Apollos, Barnabas and John Mark do not help to answer this question, since even a creative combination of hints from the book of Acts and from Paul's letters can only demonstrate "gaps."[673] The possibility that early Christians missionaries came to Alexandria in the 30s of the first century could be confirmed only as the result of new discoveries.

Martin Hengel and Anna Marie Schwemer are perhaps unnecessarily skeptical regarding missionary outreach in Egypt in the first century.[674] True, the silence of Luke and of the early Christian literature concerning Alexandria and Egypt is striking. We have seen, however, that there are more than "two—scanty—exceptions" regarding this silence: the New Testament provides more evidence than the Ethiopian eunuch, who, strictly speaking, did not come from Egypt, and the Jewish Christian Apollos, who came from Alexandria. Hengel and Schwemer point to two reasons why the Jerusalem church and other Jewish Christians deliberately refrained for a long time from missionary outreach to Egypt: (1) In the Old Testament we find not only an aversion against Egypt as the "house of slavery" but also specific prohibitions of returning to Egypt.[675] (2) Egypt (Mizraim) is the son of Ham, the son of Noah who had been cursed, and the brother of Canaan.[676] Hengel and Schwemer conclude, "The 'Gentile mission' of the Hellenists and also of Paul focused initially

---

[670]Junod and Kaestli 1983, 2:689-94; idem, in Bovon and Geoltrain, *Écrits apocryphes chrétiens,* 983 (*Acts John*); Prieur 1989, 1:414-16; idem, in Bovon and Geoltrain, *Écrits apocryphes chrétiens,* 881 (*Acts of Andrew*).

[671]See Attila Jakab, "Les Actres d'André et le christianisme alexandrin," in Bremmer 2000, 127-39, esp. 128-29, with regard to the *Acts of Andrew.*

[672]See Gelzer 1898, lx.

[673]See Gunther (1982, 225-30), who describes Barnabas and John Mark as missionaries in Egypt; or Mounce (*PastEp,* 458), who suggests that Zenas and Apollos traveled to Alexandria.

[674]For the remarks that follow above see Hengel and Schwemer 1998, 392-93; quotation, 393 (cf. ET, 259-60, which is expanded in the German version).

[675]Ex 14:13; Deut 17:16; 28:68; Jer 42:7-22.

[676]Gen 9:22-25; 10:13-20; cf. *Jub.* 7:10, 13; 9:1; *T. Sim.* 6:46.

and primarily on the regions of Shem and continued in 'Japheth.' As indeed Paul and Luke show clearly that plans for traveling and mission were connected with 'instructions by the Spirit' and sometimes also with the exegesis of particular scriptural texts, we can assume that these Old Testament prohibitions were for a long time combined with warnings from early Christian prophets and at first prevented any plans of extending mission to Egypt." This interpretation of the evidence is implausible for the following reasons. (1) If we can accept the flight of Jesus' parents to Egypt (Mt 2:13-15), then we can also accept that followers of Jesus would hardly have had qualms about going there. (2) The Old Testament and Second Temple traditions have an "aversion" not just against Egypt but against all Gentiles, non-Jews, pagans, polytheists, an aversion that was annulled as a result of Jesus' ministry, message and commission: Jesus sent his disciples to *all nations*. (3) If Peter did not mind contacting a Roman officer in Caesarea, albeit only after a divine revelation, it is difficult to argue that Jewish Christians would have refused to interact with Egyptians. The presence of North African Christians (from Cyrene, see below) in Jerusalem makes this view highly unlikely. (4) The view that the Jewish Christians from Jerusalem and Paul deliberately focused on "Shem" and "Japheth" in accordance with the geographical-ethnic tradition of the table of nations in Gen 10 has been defended by James Scott. As we have seen (§16.2), there are serious objections to this suggestion. (5) The early Christian prophets who supposedly warned the Jerusalem church against missionary activities in Egypt are purely fictitious. We simply do not know whether Paul was warned by prophets not to travel to the province of Asia (Ephesus) or the province of Bithynia, or whether other circumstances brought about the change of plans that Luke reports. There is no evidence whatsoever that early Christian prophets ever played a role in the missionary strategy and tactics of the church. (6) We must remember that the New Testament authors, including Luke, are silent about the foundation of the church in Rome; since scholars generally distrust the assertions of early church traditions about, for example, early missionary activities of Peter in Rome, they are content with reconstructions on the basis of the available evidence. It admittedly remains a fact that the evidence for an early foundation of the church in Rome is better than the evidence for similar assumptions concerning Alexandria or Egypt.

The following Egyptian cities would have served as natural targets for missionary work outside of Alexandria at an early date, as each had a Jewish community (with the one exception of Pelusion).

In Lower Egypt:

Schedia (Σχεδία; Chaireon; mod. Kom el-Gizah?), 30 km southeast of Alexandria, had a Jewish "house of prayer" (*proseuchē*) during the time of Ptolemy III Euergetes (247-221 B.C.).[677] The bishop Atthas attended the Council of Nicea.

Xenephyris (near mod. Damanhur), 55 km southeast of Alexandria on a branch of the Nile River; a synagogue is attested for 143 B.C. at the latest.[678]

Nitriai (Νιτρίαι; mod. Kom el-Barnugi),[679] about 60 km southeast of Alexandria on the

---

[677] *CIJ* II 1440 = *I. EgJud* I 22. See Kasher 1985, 107-10; Binder 1999, 230-31; L. Levine 2000, 80.
[678] *CIJ* II 1441 = *I. EgJud* I 24. See Schürer 2:426 n. 5(g); 3:49; Kasher 1985, 111-14; Binder 1999, 242-43; L. Levine 2000, 80, 363.
[679] K. Jansen-Winkeln, *DNP* 8:965; Schürer 2:426 n. 5(f); 3:49; Kasher 1985, 114-16; L. Levine 2000, 76, 80; Grossmann 2002, 247 with n. 190.

western edge of the Nile Delta, was a production center of sodium. A synagogue is attested for 143 B.C. at the latest. After A.D. 315 Nitriai was the site of an important Christian settlement of hermits.[680]

Pelusion (Πηλούσιον; Pelusium; mod. Tell el-Farama)[681] was situated on the mouth of the eastern arm of the Nile called Pelousiakos, 200 km west of Gaza. The coastal road from Gaza to Pelusion ran along the so-called Via Maris via Raphia ('Ραφία; mod. Tell es Sheikh Suleiman [32 km]),[682] Bitylion (mod. Sheikh Zuweid? [15 km])[683] and Rhinocolura (mod. el Arish [32 km]).[684] The city, which is already attested in Egyptian sources and whose name is connected with the veneration of the god Amun, was fortified by Alexander the Great and served the Ptolemies as a customs station. In 48 B.C. Pompey was murdered in Pelusion. During the Roman period Pelusion/Pelusium was an assize town of the Roman prefect. The population celebrated the feast of a drowned fertility god on March 20th; Zeus Kassios also was worshiped, as was Isis, who was venerated as the patron of seafarers. Flax was cultivated in the area, and salt was produced. Pelusion was the natural port of entry into Egypt from the northeast. In a papyrus dated A.D. 107 a Roman soldier stationed in Bostra mentions that "every day merchants from Pelusium" come into the city. It is not known whether Jews lived in Pelusion. In the Byzantine period the city was the seat of a bishop; in A.D. 325 the bishop Dorotheos of Pelusion attended the Council in Nicea. Recently, remains of a large basilica were discovered on the hill Tall al-Maḥzan, which evidently was dedicated to St. Epimachos; the foundations of the church seem to date to the time of A.D. 324-331.[685]

Magdolos (mod. Tell el-Heir?), 15 km southwest of Pelusion, probably is identical with the settlement Migdal, where Jews lived, according to Jer 44:1; 46:14; Ezek 29:10. A papyrus dated 310 B.C. mentions Jews in Migdal.[686]

Tanis (Τάνις; mod. San el-Hagar),[687] situated on a branch of the Nile (Tanitikos) about 57 km west of Pelusion, on the canal Boutikos, was the Old Testament Zoan.[688] During the time of the Twenty-first Dynasty (1176-931 B.C.), established by Pharaoh Smendes, Tanis was the new capital of Egypt, transferred here from Pi-Ramesses, which was 30 km to the south. When the last king of the Twenty-second Dynasty died around 725 B.C., Tanis ceased to be the capital of Egypt, but it remained a flourishing city during the Roman period.

Thmouis (Θμοῦϊς; mod. Tell Timai el-Amdid),[689] 35 km west of Tanis, was the cap-

---

[680]On the synagogue see *CIJ* II 1442 = *I. EgJud* I 25. See Binder 1999, 245. On the settlements of the Anachorete monks see Grossmann 2002, 247, 491-92.

[681]H. Kees, PW 19.1 (1937): 407-15; W. Helck, *KP* 4:610; D. J. Thompson, *OCD* 1134-35; K. Jansen-Winkeln, *DNP* 9:513-14; Kasher 1985, 12-14; S. Snape and S. White, "Rescue Excavation at Pelusium," in D. Bailey 1996, 107-12; Hölbl 2001, 9, 12, 145-46, 209, 236-37; Grossmann 2002, 361-64.

[682]See C. Burchard, *KP* 4:1339; E. D. Oren, "Sinai: Northern Sinai," *NEAEHL* 4:1396.

[683]See R. Reich, *NEAEHL* 1:15.

[684]See E. D. Oren, *NEAEHL* 4:1395-96; Joan M. Frayn, "Aspects of Trade on the Judean Coast in the Hellenistic and Romand Periods," *Aram* 8 (1996): 101-9, esp. 104-5.

[685]On the Roman soldier stationed in Bostra see Michigan Papyrus 5903: ἀπὸ Πηλουσίου γὰρ καθ᾽ ἡμέραν ἔρχονται πρὸς ἡμᾶς ἔμποροι; see Frayn, "Aspects of Trade," 105. On the basilica see Grossmann 2002, 106, 129, 194, 471-75 with fig. 89; on the circular church, ibid., 133-35, 145, 232, 470-71 with fig. 88; on the southern church, ibid., 121, 131, 475-76 with fig. 90.

[686]Schürer 3:40; Kasher 1985, 44, 149-50.

[687]Helck, *KP* 5:511; D. B. Redford, *ABD* 6:1106-7; Kasher 1985, 66, 178.

[688]See Num 13:22; Ps 78:12; Is 19:11, 13; 30:4; Ezek 30:14.

[689]Helck, *KP* 5:770; Schürer 3:40.

ital of the sixteenth district (*nomos*). A papyrus dated 310 B.C. mentions Jews in Thmouis.

Athribis (mod. Tell Atrib),[690] 65 km south of Sebennytos (175 km southeast of Alexandria) on the branch of the Nile called Damietta in the delta, was the capital of the tenth district of Lower Egypt. The temple of Horus was donated by Ptolemy IX (143-80 B.C.) and renovated under Tiberius. The main god of the city was Chentechthai, worshiped initially as a crocodile, later as a falcon. Two inscriptions mention King Ptolemy, who helped the local Jewish community (οἱ ἐν ᾽Αθρίβει ᾽Ιουδαῖοι) erect a house of prayer in the first century B.C. The reference probably is to Ptolemy VI Philometor (king since 170 B.C.), who was friendly to the Jews. In the Byzantine period there was a church dedicated to Mary in Athribis.[691]

Leontopolis (Λεοντόπολις; "Lion City"; Tell el-Yahoudiyeh),[692] 22 km southeast of Athribis on an eastern branch of the Nile called Pelousiakos in the thirteenth district, had a large Jewish community in the second century B.C. Around 160 B.C. Ptolemy VI permitted Onias the high priest to build a Jewish temple in Leontopolis; it was destroyed in A.D. 71 on orders from Vespasian.[693] The "district of Onias," as the settlement was called (Josephus, *A.J.* 14.131; *B.J.* 1.190), possibly had its origins in a military settlement.

Babylon (Fostat; Cairo), 27 km south of Leontopolis in the district of Heliopolis on the Nile, had a Jewish community in the first century. An inscription dated A.D. 59 states that a Roman soldier gave credit to a certain Petos and his sons Helkias and Dor[. . .]koas, "all three Jews" (οἱ τρῖς ᾽Ιουδαῖοι [*CPJ* II 417]).[694]

Serapeum (mod. N Saqqara) probably had a Jewish community as well; papyri of the Persian period mention a Jew named Yehoram and a Jewish slave named Yehomori.[695]

In Middle Egypt:

Memphis (Μέμφις; mod. Mit Rahina),[696] about 220 km north of Pelusion, was the old

---

[690]Helck, *KP* 1:707-8; S. Shenouda, *PECS* 110; K. Jansen-Winkeln, *DNP* 2:209; Schürer 2:426 n. 5(e); 3:49; Kasher 1985, 116-19; Hölbl 2001, 271; see also K. Mysliwiec, "Polish Excavations at Tell Atrib in 1985," *Annales du service des antiquités de l'Égypte* 72 (1992-1993): 53-77.

[691]*CIJ* II 1443, 1444 = *I. EgJud* I 27, 28; see Binder 1999, 243-44; L. Levine 2000, 80, 363. On the Church of Mary see Grossmann 2002, 3 n. 8, 17, 414.

[692]Helck, *KP* 3:574-75; Jansen-Winkeln, *DNP* 7:67-68; Schürer 3:47-48, 145-47; Kasher 1985, 119-35; L. Levine 2000, 2, 76, 78; Hölbl 2001, 190.

[693]Josephus, *A.J.* 12.388; 13.62-73; 13.285; 20.236; *B.J.* 7.421-425. See *GLAJJ* 1:99; *CIG* II 1451-1530 (= Horbury and Noy 1992, 29-105); L. Levine 2000, 75-76, 78, 88.

[694]It is unclear whether the Roman fortress of the third century A.D. that survives in the old city of Cairo goes back to the legionary camp that Strabo mentions (17.1.30). See Kasher 1985, 44; Peter Sheehan, "The Roman Fortress of Babylon in Old Cairo," in D. Bailey 1996, 95-97; Grossmann 2002, 66, 159, 351. On the Christian churches in Babylon—the churches of St. Sergios and of St. Barbara—see Grossmann 2002, 10, 77, 112, 150, 192, 414-17 with figs. 33-34.

[695]J. B. Segal, *Aramaic Texts from North Saqqâra, with Some Fragments in Phoenician* (Texts from Excavations 6; London: Egypt Exploration Society, 1983), nos. 47, 54. See Schürer 3:39. On the Jeremiah Monastery of Saqqara see Grossmann 2002, 69-70, 105-6, 151, 166-67, 249, 321, 507-11 with figs. 125-126.

[696]H. Kees, *PW* 15.1 (1931): 660-88; Helck, *KP* 3:1192-94; S. Shenouda, *PECS* 571; Jansen-Winkeln, *DNP* 7:1208-9; Dorothy J. Thompson, *Memphis under the Ptolemies* (Princeton, N.J.: Princeton University Press, 1988); idem, *OCD* 955; Hölbl 2001, 9, 12, 25-26, 77-78, 80.

royal city of the Egyptian kings, replaced as the capital by Alexandria under the Ptolemies. The Ptolemaic kings were crowned in the old temple of Ptah, the god of creation and patron of the artisans. The temple of Ptah was connected with the cult of Apis, one of the sources of the cult of Sarapis that made the city into a tourist center. For the Greeks Memphis was the center of Egyptian wisdom. A Jewish community is attested already for the sixth century B.C. (Jer 44:1). Alexander the Great was buried in Memphis. In the Roman period Memphis continued to be an important city, although details of its history remain unknown. The bishop Antiochos of Memphis attended the Council of Nicea.

Arsinoë ('Αρσινοΐ; mod. Fayum),[697] 70 km southwest of Memphis as the crow flies, was the capital of the district of Arsinoë, with about fifty thousand inhabitants.[698] The city was originally called Crocodilopolis, later Ptolemais Euergetis (mod. Medinet el-Fayūm). The Fayum, a region on the left bank of the Nile between several lakes, was developed during the Twelfth Dynasty (nineteenth/eighteenth century B.C.) and continued to be culturally important in the Ptolemaic and Roman periods.[699] Strabo describes the region and a sacred lake where the cultically venerated crocodile Souchos was a tourist attraction (17.1.38). The Roman elite of Arsinoë comprised 6,475 persons. Arsinoë was the fourth assize town of the Roman prefect along with Alexandria, Pelusion and Memphis. There was a Jewish community in Arsinoë in the third century B.C., which owned a synagogue (*proseuchē*).[700] A papyrus dated A.D. 73 contains a list with the names of the people who had to pay the 'Ιουδαϊκὸν τέλεσμα (*Ioudaikon telesma*), the Jewish tax of two drachmas that was imposed on the Jews after the destruction of the temple in A.D. 70 (*CPJ* II 421). Significant remains of ancient Arsinoë survive. Several inscriptions confirm that many Jews lived in the district of Arsinoë. In the town of *Psenyris* (mod. Sinuris), 13 km north of Arsinoë, the Jewish and the Greek inhabitants formed two clearly identifiable groups in the third century B.C. (*CPJ* I 33). In *Tebtynis* (mod. Tell Umm el-Buregat), about 25 km southwest of Arsinoë, a loan contract between two Jews from the third century B.C. survives (*CPJ* I 20). An inscription from the second century B.C. confirms the existence of a synagogue (προσευχὴ 'Ιουδαίων, *proseuchē Ioudaiōn*) that owned real estate (ἱερὰ παράδεισος, *hiera paradeisos*, lit., "sacred garden" [*CPJ* I 134]). In the early middle ages four churches are attested for Tebtynis. In *Philadelphia* (mod. Kom el-Khara-ba el-Kebir), 27 km northeast of Arsinoë, a papyrus dated to the second century B.C. mentions a Jewish farmer with the name "Jude son of Dositheos" (*CPJ* I 43); another papyrus dated A.D. 25 mentions the Jewish taxpayers Iosephos and Sambathion (*CPJ* I 416). *Apolloias* is mentioned in a papyrus that reports a theft committed by three Jews (*CPJ* I 21). *Alexandrou Nesos* (mod. Komm el-Nihas), 40 km southwest of Arsinoë, had a Jewish house of prayer in 218 B.C.[701] *Ankyronpolis* (mod. el-Hiba),[702] on the right bank of the Nile, belonged to the district of

---

[697]Helck, "Arsinoë III. Städte 2," *KP* 1:612; D. J. Thompson, *OCD* 178; Jansen-Winkeln, "Arsinoë III.2," *DNP* 2:40. On the Jewish presence see Schürer 3:51-54; Kasher 1985, 138-144; Levine 2000, 79-81.

[698]See Bowmann, in Fentress 2000, 179.

[699]See Mary-Ellen Lane, *A Guide to the Antiquities of the Fayyum* (Cairo: American University in Cairo Press, 1985); Dominic Rathbone, "Towards a Historical Topography of the Fayum," in D. Bailey 1996, 50-56. Inscriptions: Étienne Bernard, *Recueil des inscriptions grecques du Fayoum I-III* (3 vols.; Leiden: Brill, 1975-1981).

[700]*CPJ* III 1532A = *I. EgJud* I 117. See Binder 1999, 112-13. This *proseuchē* probably is mentioned also in *CPJ* I 134; see Binder 1999, 236-38.

[701]*CPJ* I 129. See Kasher 1985, 146-48; Binder 1999, 238-40; L. Levine 2000, 79.

[702]Schürer 3:50. R. Müller-Wollermann (*BAGRW* 1126) identifies el-Hiba with Ankyronpolis, with reference to M. Rosaria Falivene, *The Herakleopolite Nome: A Catalogue of the Toponyms*

Herakleopolis; in the third century B.C. Jews lived in the city (*CPJ* I 18). In *Herakleopolis,* the capital of the district, and in *Tebetnu,* a village in the district, both Jews and a Jewish administrative council are attested for the second century B.C. (*NewDocs* 9:24).

Oxyrhynchus (mod. el-Bahnasa),[703] about 80 km south of Arsinoë,[704] was the capital of the nineteenth district and the crossroads of the routes leading to the Fayum. The rise of the city began in the late Egyptian period when it was conquered by the Ethiopian king Pianchi around 715 B.C. During the Ptolemies Greek settlers came into the city since the fourth century B.C., but the Egyptian population dominated until the Byzantine period. The Greek inhabitants named the town after the "sharp-nosed" fish of the Nile River (Mormyrus) that was venerated as the incarnation of the god Seth.[705] During the Roman imperial period Oxyrhynchus was an important city of possibly 30,000 thousand inhabitants.[706] The district comprised about 900 km² (348 sq. mi.), with 300,000 people living in several hundred towns and villages, 613 of which are mentioned in the approximately 9,000 papyri that have been discovered[707] by British and Italian archaeologists since 1897 and 1910, respectively. The papyri reveal that Oxyrhynchus had forty-five quarters (ἡ λαύρα, *hē laura;* τὸ ἄμφοδον, *to amphodon*), including the Apolloios Quarter, the Gymnasium Square Quarter, the Locust Quarter, the Warm Baths Quarter, the Quarter of Abraham the Doctor [SB 8987 [seventh century]). The papyri document the following temples and cults for the city: Sarapis, Thoeris (Athene), Ibis, Isis, Osiris, as well as Apollo, Ares, Atargatis, Bethennynis, Cleopatra sanctuary, Cybele, Demeter, Dioscuri, Dionysos, Hera, Hermes, heroes, imperial cult (Sebasteion, Kaisareion), Kore, Muses, Nemesis, Sabazios, Tyche, Zeus, Zeus capitolium (Jupiter, Juno, Minerva).[708] The over 1,400 classical literary texts that have been discovered (mostly in fragmentary form) are an impressive testimony to the standard of education and intellectual life in Oxyrhynchus. In the first century A.D. Oxyrhynchus had close contacts with Alexandrian philology: Tryphon, Teon, Aristonikos, Philoxenos and Apion are either mentioned in papyri or taught in the city.[709] Jews lived in Oxyrhynchus since the Ptolemaic period. A papyrus dating to the first century refers to the Jews living in the city: τῶν ἀπ᾽ Ὀξ(υρύγχων) πόλ(εως) ᾽Ιουδαίων (*tōn ap᾽ Oxyrynchōn poleōs Ioudaiōn* [P.Oxy. 335 = *CPJ* II 423]). A fragmentary papyrus from the first century contains verses from Job 40 (P.Oxy. 3522), and a papyri from the late first century contains verses from the book of Esther (P.Oxy. 4443). A papyrus of the third century mentions a synagogue (P.Oxy. 1205).

Christians lived in the city at least by the second century. Among the papyri dating to the second century are a fragment with verses from Mt 12 (P.Oxy. 4404 = 𝔓¹⁰⁴), a fragment

with Introduction and Commentary (American Studies in Papyrology 37; Atlanta: Scholars Press, 1998), 39-43.

[703]Helck, *KP* 4:390-91; Shenouda, *PECS* 663; J. Quack, *DNP* 4:122-23; Jones 1937, 320-21, 327-31, 333-36; E. G. Turner, "Roman Oxyrhynchus," *JEA* 38 (1952): 78-93; Schürer 3:53-57, 91; Kasher 1985, 150-57; Krüger 1990; L. Levine 2000, 556; see the exhibition volume *Oxyrhynchus: A City and Its Texts* (Oxford: Ashmolean Museum, 1999).

[704]About 200 km south of Cairo, and 400 km south of Alexandria by rail.

[705]J. Whitehorne, "The Pagan Cults of Roman Oxyrhynchus," *ANRW* II.18.5 (1995): 3050-91.

[706]I. F. Fichman, "Die Bevölkerungszahl von Oxyrhynchos in byzantinischer Zeit," *APF* 21 (1971): 111-20; Krüger 1990, 8, 68-69; Bowman, in Fentress 2000, 179.

[707]Krüger 1990, 38, 41-42, 144. Note the (so far) sixty-six volumes of the series *Oxyrhynchus Papyri* (P.Oxy.), which appears since 1898, as well as the series *Papiri della Societa Italiana* (PSI).

[708]Krüger 1990, 101-5.

[709]Krüger 1990, 199-200, 204.

with Jn 18:36—19:7 (P.Oxy. 3523 = $\mathfrak{P}^{90}$), the fragment of a noncanonical Gospel (P.Oxy. 840)[710] and a fragment of the apocryphal *Gospel of Peter* (P.Oxy. 4009). From the second or third century date a papyrus with sayings of Jesus (P.Oxy. 1), a fragment with verses from Mt 13—14; 23 (P.Oxy. 2683, 4403, 4405 = $\mathfrak{P}^{77}$, $\mathfrak{P}^{103}$), a fragment of the Epistle of Jude (P.Oxy. 2684) and an apocryphal Gospel (P.Oxy. 2949). From the third century date fragments with verses from the Gospel of Matthew,[711] two fragments with verses from Lk 17; 22 (P.Oxy. 4495, 2383 = $\mathfrak{P}^{111}$, $\mathfrak{P}^{69}$), fragments with verses from the Gospel of John,[712] a fragment with verses from Acts 26 (P.Oxy. 1597 = $\mathfrak{P}^{29}$), a fragment with verses from Rom 2; 8—9 (P.Oxy. 4497, 1355 = $\mathfrak{P}^{113}$, $\mathfrak{P}^{27}$), a fragment with verses from 1 Cor 7—8 (P.Oxy. 1008 = $\mathfrak{P}^{15}$), a fragment with verses from 1 Thess 4—5 and 2 Thess 1 (P.Oxy. 1598 = $\mathfrak{P}^{30}$), a fragment with Heb 1:7-12 (P.Oxy. 4498), two fragments with verses from Jas 1—3 (P.Oxy. 1229, 1171 = $\mathfrak{P}^{23}$, $\mathfrak{P}^{20}$), the fragment of a Gospel of Mary (P.Oxy. 3525), P.Oxy. 3035 (February 28, A.D. 256), a Christian prayer (P.Oxy. 407), a theological work (P.Oxy. 210) and P.Oxy. 3119. A papyrus dated to the end of the third century, P.Oxy. 43, which lists guards in the streets and in front of public buildings, mentions two churches: ῥ[ύμῃ] τῇ βοριν[ῇ] ἐκκλησία (*rumē tē borinē ekklēsia* [verso I.10]); ῥ[ύμῃ] τῇ νοτινῇ ἐκκλησία (*rymē tē notinē ekklēsia* [verso III.19]). At the beginning of the fourth century Oxyrhynchus was the seat of a bishop; in the fourth century the city was an important center of the monastic movement in Egypt. At the beginning of the fifth century Oxyrhynchus had 12 churches, and around A.D. 535 at least 37 churches and 20 monasteries; Rufinus states that 10,000 monks and 20,000 nuns lived in the city.[713] Remains that have survived include ruins of the Roman theater (with a capacity for 12,500 spectators [second century]), colonnaded halls, a pedestal and the necropolis.

In Upper Egypt:

Thebes (Θῆβαι; Diospolis Magna; mod. Luxor),[714] about 500 km south of Oxyrhynchus, was the old capital of the Pharaohs. At the time of the Macedonian conquest Thebes was still an important city, although it had lost its eminent position after repeated revolts against the Ptolemaic rulers in 207 and 88 B.C. and against the Romans in 30 B.C. According to Strabo, Thebes was "only a collection of villages" during his time (17.1.46). The buildings of Thebes, particularly the colossi of Memnon (20 m high)—two seated statues of Amenophis III on the west bank of the Nile below the mortuary temples—and the Pharaohs' tombs were visited by numerous Roman tourists. It seems that Jews lived in or near Thebes in the second century B.C. (*CPJ* I, 200-202). A papyrus dated A.D. 113 indicates that the Jews from Thebes who lived in Arsinoë were so numerous that they had their own synagogue (*CPJ* II 432). The church in front of the Pylon dates to the sixth century; the churches at the Avenue of Sphinxes and in the former palace of Rameses II date to the seventh century.

---

[710]The fragment itself dates to the fourth or fifth century.

[711]Mt 2; 11—12; 24: P.Oxy. 2, 2384, 4401 = $\mathfrak{P}^{1}$, $\mathfrak{P}^{70}$, $\mathfrak{P}^{101}$.

[712]Jn 1; 6; 8; 12—13; 15—16; 20—21: P.Oxy. 208, 1228, 1596, 1780, 1781, 4445, 4446, 4447, 4448 = $\mathfrak{P}^{5}$, $\mathfrak{P}^{28}$, $\mathfrak{P}^{39}$, $\mathfrak{P}^{22}$, $\mathfrak{P}^{106}$, $\mathfrak{P}^{107}$, $\mathfrak{P}^{108}$, $\mathfrak{P}^{109}$.

[713]See Stefan Timm, *Das christlich-koptische Ägypten in arabischer Zeit* (4 vols.; TAVO B 41; Wiesbaden: Reichert, 1984-1988), 1:284 (with a list of bishops), 287 (list of churches). See also Grossmann 2002, 12, 337-39.

[714]Helck, "Thebai 2," *KP* 5:670-72; Shenouda, *PECS* 904; J. G. Milne and A. Spawforth, *OCD* 1496; Schürer 3:55, 57-58; Kasher 1985, 158-60; L. Levine 2000, 81; Hölbl 2001, 155-57, 268-71. On the remains of Christian churches see Grossmann 2002, 31, 33-35, 39, 103-4, 115, 146, 448-54 with figs. 68-71.

Apollonopolis Magna (Edfu; mod. Idfu),[715] about 110 km north of Thebes on the river Nile, was the capital of the second district of Upper Egypt. Edfu was the starting point of a caravan route to the gold mines of the eastern desert and to Berenike on the Red Sea, which could be reached within a week.[716] Remains of the temple of Horus from the Ptolemaic period survive. A papyrus attests Jews in Apollonopolis in the first century B.C. (*CPJ* I 139). Ostraca confirm Jews living in the city who paid the tax of two drachmas imposed by Vespasian between A.D. 71/72 and 116 (*CPJ* II 160.227-229).

Syene (Συήνη; mod. Assuan),[717] about 110 km north of Apollonopolis Magna on the east bank of the Nile below the first cataract, was an important emporium. During the Ptolemaic period the goddess Isis was the patron of the army in the city. The Romans stationed three cohorts in Syene; the Roman satirist Juvenal, born in A.D. 67, was the commander of the troops in Syene for a period of time. Eratosthenes used the well of Syene, located on the Tropic of Cancer, which did not cast a shadow on the day of the solstice, to calculate the circumference of the earth. The quarries near Syene produced red granite. Jews living in Syene are mentioned in Ezek 29:10 and in a papyrus dated 310 B.C.

Elephantine (Ἐλεφαντίνη; mod. Geziret Aswan),[718] an island in the Nile, probably owes its name to the ivory trade. Strabo mentions Chnum as the main deity of the city (17.1.48); remains of the temple from the third century A.D. survive. During the Persian period a Jewish military colony was established on Elephantine (since the sixth century B.C.), documented for the period 410-398 B.C. The Jewish community of Elephantine had a temple dedicated to "Yaho."[719] The earliest version of the story of Ahiqar was discovered in Elephantine, found on a fragmentary papyrus scroll.[720] When Aelius Aristides traveled to Egypt in A.D. 141, he reached Syene and Elephantine.[721]

We have evidence for Christian communities in sixty-six Egyptian cities for the time before the Council of Nicea in A.D. 325.[722] It is fair to assume that these

---

[715]S. J. Seidlmayer, *DNP* 3:876; Kasher 1985, 161-67; L. Levine 2000, 129.
[716]Thus Strabo (17.1.45), who, however, seems to confuse Koptos (mod. Qift), situated north of Thebes, with Apollonopolis. The journey from Koptos to Berenike was twice as long as the journey from Apollonopolis to Berenike.
[717]Helck, *KP* 5:440; D. J. Blackman, *PECS* 871; Schürer 3:40; W. Cockle, *OCD* 1459; Schürer 3:40; Kasher 1985, 38, 174; Hölbl 2001, 87, 156. On the (late) church of St. Pšoti see Grossmann 2002, 88.
[718]Helck, *KP* 2:242-43; Cockle, *OCD* 519-20; Seidlmayer, *DNP* 3:981-82; Schürer 3:38-40, 174-75; Kasher 1985, 1-2, 38-41; Hölbl 2001, 86, 167-68, 205-6, 271. Publication of papyri and ostraca: Sachau (1911); Kraeling (1969); Cowley (1967); Grelot (1972); Zauzich (1978). See Bezalel Porten, *Archives from Elephantine: The Life of an Ancient Jewish Military Colony* (Berkeley: University of California Press, 1968); Yochanan Muffs, *Studies in Aramaic Legal Papyri from Elephantine* (New York: Ktav, 1973); Michael H. Silverman, *Religious Values in the Jewish Proper Names at Elephantine* (Kevelaer: Butzon and Bercker, 1985); B. Porten, *The Elephantine Papyri in English: Three Millennia of Cross-Cultural Continuity and Change* (Leiden: Brill, 1996). On the church in the pronaos of the temple of Chnum see Grossmann 2002, 38, 78, 460-61 with fig. 77.
[719]Sachau, nos. 30-31; Grelot, no. 102.
[720]Sachau, 147-82. Cf. Schürer 3:232-39.
[721]R. Klein 1981, 75.
[722]See Mullen 2001 (I am grateful to Dr. Mullen for providing me with a copy of his manuscript). On the Christian papyri from the second, third and fourth centuries see Naldini 1998.

churches already existed in the third century, and some may have existed in the second century, if not already in the first century. Peter Grossmann observes with regard to early Christian architecture in Egypt that all the Christian buildings that we know so far are located in the smaller towns, where their remains survived only by accident or have become known only on account of archaeological discoveries.[723] Important centers of Christian life, some of which are attested only in literary sources, include (in alphabetical order): Alexandria, Alphokranon, Antinoe, Apollonopolis Magna,[724] Arsinoë,[725] Athribis, Bubastos, Diospolis, Esneh (Latopolis), Herakleopolis Magna, Herakleopolis Parva (Sethron), Hermethes, Hermopolis Magna,[726] Karanis,[727] Kellis,[728] Kleopatris, Koptos, Kusae, Kynopolis, Kynos, Lenaios,[729] Leontopolis, Letopolis, Lykopolis, Memphis, Metelis, Narmuthis,[730] Nikiopolis, Nilus (Nilopolis), Oxyrhynchus, Panephysis, Panopolis,[731] Parembole,[732] Pelusion, Phakusa, Pharbaitos, Phthenegys, Sebennytos, Tanis, Tentyra, Thmuis, Schedia. The existence of Christians in, for example, the oasis of Dakhleh (Kellis) around A.D. 280 indicates that the Christian faith spread rapidly in the third century, at the latest, in the Egyptian hinterland outside of the Nile valley. The question of whether Christian communities existed in some of these cities in the first century cannot be answered without new discoveries.

Evangelism in North Africa

It seems that Christian communities were established in North Africa at an early

---

[723]Grossmann 2002, 18. On the pre-Constantinian history of Christianity in Egypt see Harnack 1924, 2:628, 705-27; Judge and Pickering 1977; Mullen 2001.

[724]Modern Edfu. Mullen (2001) points to a scroll that was discovered recently in Edfu with a copy of Irenaeus, *Adversus Haereses;* the back of the scroll contains a Christian polemic against Isis, Horus and Osiris. The papyrus, which dates to the third or fourth century, evidently was not written in Apollonopolis Magna itself.

[725]See P.Vindob. G 32016; P.Kiseleff 3.

[726]Eusebius, *Hist. eccl.* 6.46.2; P.Ryl. 616-651; P.Berl. 11863; P.Giss.Univ. 17 P.Würzb. 3 (Van Haelst, nos. 356, 694, 1036). See Judge and Pickering 1977, 61-63; Mullen 2001.

[727]P.Coll.Youtie 77. See Judge and Pickering 1977, 62.

[728]Modern Ismant el-Kharab, in the oasis Dakhleh. In regard to the Christians papyri and the remains of a church dating to the fourth century see Bowen 1998; idem, "The Christian Monuments," in *Dakhleh Oasis Project: Preliminary Reports on the 1995-1996 to 1998-1999 Field Seasons* (ed. C. A. Hope and G. E. Bowen; Oxford: Oxbow, 1999). See <http://www.arts.monash.edu.au/archaeology/ismant>.

[729]P.Duke 438, published by P. Van Minnen, *Analecta Bollandiana* 113 (1995): 13-38; cf. Mullen 2001. This is the oldest extant Coptic martyrological text (fourth century), reporting the martyrdom of a presbyter named Stephanos.

[730]P.Narmuthis 69 29a.229a (= $\mathfrak{P}^{92}$ [Eph 1:11-13, 19-21; 2 Thess 1:4-5, 11-12]).

[731]P.Gen 108; P.Berl.Bork. (Zbigniew Borkowski, *Une description topographique des immeubles à Panopolis* [Warsaw: University of Warsaw, 1975]); P.Stras. *Inv* 1017. See Judge and Pickering 1977, 61; Mullen 2001.

[732]P.Lond. 1914 (lines 13-15). See Mullen 2001. Parembole is not north of Syene (contra Harnack), but rather near Alexandria.

date. The New Testament repeatedly mentions Jews and Christians from the city of Cyrene or the Cyrenaica (Pentapolis), about 800 km east of Alexandria between modern Tobruk and Benghasi.

A certain "Simon of Cyrene, father of Alexander and Rufus" was forced by Roman soldiers to carry Jesus' cross to Golgotha (Mk 15:21/Mt 27:32/Lk 23:26). He may have been a pilgrim who had come to Jerusalem to celebrate Passover. It is perhaps more likely that he was a Diaspora Jew from Cyrene or from the Pentapolis who lived in Jerusalem.

In 1962 Nahman Avigad published an ossuary inscription from the necropolis in the Kidron Valley[733] that mentions, in Greek, "Alexandros, son of Simon" and describes him in Hebrew letters as "Alexandros QRNYT." The expression "QRNYT" may be a reference to Kyrēnē/Cyrene as the hometown of Alexandros/Alexander. It is a distinct possibility that this is the son of Simon of Cyrene mentioned in Mk 15:21/Mt 27:32/Lk 23:26 and that the ossuary contained his bones. It is impossible to prove that this is a historical certainty. However, this inscription is the only evidence for the combination "Alexander, son of Simon," and if the reference to Cyrene could be regarded as certain, the likelihood of a reference to the Simon mentioned in Mk 15:21 increases.[734]

Luke reports that Jews from Cyrene heard Peter and the other followers of Jesus explain the events of the Feast of Pentecost in A.D. 30 when they received the Holy Spirit (Acts 2:10). Luke reports that Jews from Cyrene who lived in Jerusalem and who had their own synagogue engaged in robust discussions with Stephen (Acts 6:9). Some of these Cyrenaic Jews were converted: when the Greek-speaking Jewish Christians were forced to leave Jerusalem, and when some of them reached Antioch in Syria, where they preached the message of Jesus the Messiah, believers from Cyrene were among the missionaries (Acts 11:20). One of the leading prophets and teachers of the church in Antioch was a certain Lucius from Cyrene (Acts 13:1). Ward Gasque rightly asserts that "with so many Jews moving back and forth between Jerusalem and Cyrene, and between Antioch and Cyrene, it is likely that there was a church established there at a very early date."[735] All five cities of the so-called Pentapolis—Cyrene, Apolloia, Ptolemais, Teucheira, Berenike—had Jewish communities.[736] Hellenistic

---

[733]See Nahman Avigad, "A Depository of Inscribed Ossuaries in the Kidron Valley," IEJ 12 (1962): 9-12.

[734]See Pieter W. van der Horst, "Das Neue Testament und die jüdischen Grabinschriften aus hellenistisch-römischer Zeit," BZ 36 (1992): 161-78, esp. 174-75.

[735]W. W. Gasque, "Cyrene," ABD 1:1231. Joel Williams (1995, 182-83) does not elaborate the implications for the "implicit reader" of the Gospels regarding the reference to Cyrene.

[736]See Y. Le Bohec, "Inscriptions juives et judaïsants de l'Afrique romaine," Antiquités Africaines 17 (1981): 165-207; idem, "Juifs et judaïsantes dans l'Afrique romaine," Antiquités Africaines 17 (1981): 209-29; cf. Joachim W. Hirschberg, A History of the Jews in North Africa from Antiquity to Our Time (Jerusalem: Mosad Byalik, 1965 [Hebrew]); André Chouraqui, Histoire des juifs en Afrique du Nord (Monaco: Roucher, 1998). On the Pentapolis see J. M. Reynolds, OCD 1135-36.

Jewish Christians from Jerusalem certainly would have targeted these cities as primary goals.

Cyrene (Κυρήνη; mod. Ain Shahat, Grennah; Libya),[737] 800 km west of Alexandria, 13 km from the Mediterranean coast, was the most important of the Greek colonies in Africa. The city was founded around 630 B.C. by settlers from Thera who followed a directive of the oracle of Delphi (Herodotus 4.150-158). The name of the city became the name of the entire region, extending from Paliouros (mod. Wadi et-Tmimi) in the east to Cape Arae Philaenorum (Ras el-Aali) in the west, marking the boundary with the Latin-speaking world. Cyrene's founder, Aristoteles Battus, and his successor ruled as kings until 440 B.C. The city was annexed into the Ptolemaic kingdom after 322 B.C. The Ptolemies' development of other cities and the influx of Jews reduced the prestige of the old royal city of Cyrene. When Ptolemy Apion died in 96 B.C., Cyrene became Roman. Under Augustus, Cyrene together with Crete formed the senatorial province *Creta et Cyrenae*. Vespasian, who became emperor in A.D. 69, was quaestor of the province probably in A.D. 35/36.[738] Cyrene's wealth was based on the export of wheat[739] and silphium, which was derived from a now-extinct plant whose latex was used to produce a cure-all,[740] as well as on the breeding of horses, sheep and cows. The infrastructure of Cyrene was that of a typical Greek city, with agora (105 by 125 m), colonnaded halls, prytaneion, baths, theater, hippodrome and sculptures. There was a temple of Apollo on the acropolis, a monumental temple of Zeus in the city, a temple dedicated to Augustus and, on the Roman forum (150 m from the old agora) a large temple dedicated to Caesar. Outside the city walls was a temple of Demeter. Famous sons of Cyrene included the mathematician Theodoros (ca. 450 B.C.; Plato was one of his students), the poet Kallimachos (ca. 300 B.C.; his œuvre comprised eight hundred scrolls), and the geographer Eratosthenes (275-194 B.C.).

A large number of Jews lived in and near Cyrene since Ptolemy I at the latest.[741] The "golden age" of the Jews in Cyrene began in 145 B.C. The Jewish historian Jason, the author of 2 Maccabees, who wrote a history of the Jewish war of liberation in five volumes (see 2 Macc 2:19-23), came from Cyrene, as did Ezekiel, a Jewish tragic poet. A list of ephebes dating to A.D. 3/4 and found in Cyrene contains several Jewish names (Julius son of Jesus, Elazar, Chaireas son of Jude);[742] a list of city officials (*nomophylakes*) dating to

---

[737]H. C. Broholm, "Kyrene 2," PW 12.1 (1924): 156-69; H. Volkmann, *KP* 3:410-11; D. White, *PECS* 253-55; J. M. Reynolds, *OCD* 421-22; W. Huss, *DNP* 6:1002-4; Jones 1937, 351-63; R. G. Goodchild, *Cyrene and Apollonia: An Historical Guide* (Tripoli: Department of Antiquities, Libyan Arab Republic, 1970); Schürer 1:512, 529-32; 3:60-63, 94; Applebaum 1979; on the Roman period, 63-73; Lüderitz 1983, 9-42; Kasher 1985, 10-12, 288-89, 335-37; A. Laronde, "La Cyrénaique romaine, des origines à la fin des Sévères (96 av. J.-C.-235 ap. J.-C.)," *ANRW* II.10.1 (1988): 1006-64; Barclay 1996, 232-42; L. Levine 2000, 89-96, 124-29; Hölbl 2001, 10, 14-15, 59-60, 288; D. J. Mattingly, *BAGRW*, map 38 (1996).

[738]B. Levick, *Vespasian* (London: Routledge, 1999), 9.

[739]See Geoffrey Rickman, *The Corn Supply of Ancient Rome* (Oxford: Clarendon, 1980), 109-10.

[740]See K. Ziegler, "Silphion," *KP* 5:197; J. Scarborough, "Pharmacology," *OCD* 1154; Else Schranz, *Zur Silphionfrage* (Berlin: Friedlander, 1909); C. L. Gemill, "Silphium," *Bulletin of the History of Medicine* 40 (1966): 295-313; F. Michelon, "Le Silphium plante médicinale de l'antiquité," *Histoire des sciences médicales* 18 (1984): 343-56.

[741]Josephus, *C. Ap.* 2.4; *A.J.* 14.114; cf. 1 Macc 15:23; 2 Macc 2:23. See Applebaum 1979, 130-200; on the Jewish revolt, ibid., 201-344; Schürer 3:60-61. Sources: *I. KyrenJud* 6-29.

[742]*SEG* XX 741 = *I. KyrenJud* 7.

A.D. 60/61 mentions a certain "Eleazar son of Jason";[743] several tomb inscriptions contain Jewish names or names frequently used by Jews.[744] After the destruction of Jerusalem in A.D. 70 a weaver named Jonathan came from Judea to Cyrene and initiated a revolt of the Jewish lower classes against the Romans in A.D. 73 that was crushed by the Roman governor Catullus, resulting in the death of three thousand Jews (Josephus, *B.J.* 7.477-450). A generation later a second Jewish revolt broke out in A.D. 115/116, organized by a certain Loukuas, who evidently made messianic claims (Eusebius, *Hist. eccl.* 4.2). The insurgent Jews are said to have killed 220,000 residents of the Cyrenaica (Cassius Dio 68.32). It seems that few Jews survived the reactions of the Romans under Marcius Turbo.

Apollonia (mod. Marsa Susa)[745] was the port of Cyrene, 13 km north of the city. Remains of the theater, a temple and baths survive. Several funerary inscriptions document the existence of a Jewish community.[746] The city was called Sozousa in the Byzantine period.

Ptolemais (mod. Tolmeta; Tulmeitia),[747] about 100 km west of Cyrene, was an old city on the Mediterranean coast founded by Greek settlers in the seventh century. Ptolemy III refounded the city and named it Ptolemais. In the course of the reorganization of the Roman Empire that took place under Diocletian, Ptolemais became the capital of the province Libya Pentapolis. The city had three theaters, an amphitheater, a hippodrome and baths; villas with mosaics also have been excavated. Funerary inscriptions document a Jewish community.[748] The port city of Barke, 25 km north of Ptolemais, was founded as a colony of Cyrene; there was a Christian community in Barke at least by A.D. 300; the bishop Zopyros of Barke attended the Council of Nicea.

Teucheira (Arsinoë; mod. Tocra),[749] a coastal city 45 km west of Ptolemais, was also called Arsinoë since the reign of Ptolemy III. The deities worshiped in the city included Demeter, Kore and Cybele. Funerary inscriptions document a large Jewish community.[750] The bishop Secundus of Teucheira attended the Council of Nicea in A.D. 325.

Berenike (mod. Benghazi),[751] the westernmost city in the Cyrenaica, was originally called Euesperides; under Ptolemy III it was refounded around 250 B.C. southwest of the old seaport, whose harbor had silted up. A stele that was discovered in 1972 mentions unrest among the population and attacks by pirates in the first century B.C. Two inscriptions that date between 8 B.C. and A.D. 55 document a large Jewish community whose members financed repairs of their synagogue (*amphitheatron, synagōgē*)[752] and honored the services of a Roman official (ἔπαρχος) during the Feast of Tabernacles in the first half of the first century A.D. by erecting an inscribed stele in the *amphithea-*

---

[743]*SEG* XX 737 = *I. KyrenJud* 8.

[744]*I. KyrenJud* 10-16.

[745]D. White, *PECS* 71-72; R. G. Goodchild, ed., *Apollonia, the Port of Cyrene: Excavations by the University of Michigan, 1965-1967* (Tripoli: Department of Antiquities, 1980).

[746]*I. KyrenJud* 1-2, perhaps also nos. 3-5.

[747]See O. Brogan, *PECS* 742; Applebaum 1979, 167-70.

[748]*I. KyrenJud* 31-34.

[749]W. Helck, *KP* 5:536; O. Brogan, *PECS* 886.

[750]*I. KyrenJud* 41-69. See Applebaum 1979, 144-60; Schürer 3:61; Barclay 1996, 235-36.

[751]Cf. O. Brogan, *PECS* 320; J. M. Reynolds, "Berenice (a)," *OCD* 2399; J. Pahlitzsch, "Berenike 8," *DNP* 2:567; Applebaum 1979, 160-67.

[752]First inscription: *SEG* XVI 931 = *I. KyrenJud* 70 (*amphitheatron* [8-6 B.C.]); see Binder 1999, 140-145, 257-58; second inscription: *SEG* XVI 823 = *I. KyrenJud* 72 (*synagōgē* [A.D. 55]); see Binder 1999, 109-10, 260-62. See also Schürer 3:94-95; Applebaum 1979, 148-51, 162; J. Gwyn Griffiths, "Egypt and the Rise of the Synagogue," in Urman and Flesher 1995, 1:3-16, esp. 5-6; L. Levine 2000, 79-81. On the synagogue in Berenice see L. Levine 2000, 89-96.

tron.[753] A Christian community is attested in Berenike around A.D. 300; the bishop Dakes attended the Council of Nicea.

Jewish Christian missionaries surely would have been active in synagogues of these cities of the Pentapolis. Other towns in the Cyrenaica that had Jewish communities included Balagrae, ʿAin Targunya,[754] Boreion, Marmarika, Magdalis and Katabathmos.[755]

The province Africa Proconsularis, west of the Cyrenaica, had at least six cities with synagogues that would have been used by Jewish Christian missionaries as initial points of contact.

Leptis Magna (mod. Lebda, Tunisia),[756] the easternmost of the three cities of the Tripolitana on the mouth of Wadi Lebdah (120 km east of Tripoli), originally called Neapolis (Strabo 17.3.16), was renamed Leptis Magna (Pliny, *Nat.* 5.4.27; Ptolemaios 1.8.1), in inscriptions often called Lepcis Magna. The city was founded shortly before 600 B.C. and was one of the most important Punic emporiums. The main source of income was the production of olive oil; Julius Caesar demanded an annual tribute of three million pounds of olive oil. The city expanded rapidly during the early empire. The Forum Vetus, paved in A.D. 53, was adorned with six temples, including a temple dedicated to Roma and Augustus. Close to the theater (first century) stood a temple of Ceres (A.D. 35/36), a temple of the Di Augusti (A.D. 43) and a temple of Venus Chalcidia (A.D. 11/12). The amphitheater dates to A.D. 56. Under Trajan, Leptis became a Roman colony (Colonia Ulpia Traiana Fidelis). Septimius Severus, a native of Leptis Magna, built a new harbor, a triumphal arch and a circus. There seems to have been a Jewish community in the city: an inscription mentions a Jew named Ioses Theodoros.[757] Leptis was the seat of a bishop in the third century.

Oea (ʿΕὡα; mod. Tripoli),[758] 115 km west of Leptis Magna, was founded probably by the Phoenicians; the earliest archaeological evidence dates to the fifth century B.C. The Sophist Apuleius, born in A.D. 125 in Madaurus and educated in Carthage, Athens and Rome, reports that the population of Oea spoke mostly Punic (*Apol.* 98). A temple dedicated to the *genius coloniae* and a triumphal arch (A.D. 163/164) survive. Tombstones attest the presence of Jews in the city, among them a tombstone discovered in a catacomb and decorated with a menorah.[759] Augustine reports that a bishop consulted the Jews of

---

[753]*IGR* I 1024 = *I. KyrenJud* 71; new edition: J. M. Reynolds, in *Excavations at Sidi Khrebish, Benghazi (Berenice) I* (Supplements to Libya Antiqua 6; Tripoli: Department of Antiquities, 1981), 242-47; cf. Applebaum 1979, 161; *NewDocs* 4:202-9; Rajak 1996, 313; Binder 1999, 109-10, 258-60; L. Levine 2000, 89-93. Some scholars date the inscriptions to the first century B.C.

[754]Applebaum 1979, 170-74.

[755]See Lüderitz 1983, 43-47, 161-82.

[756]M. Leglay, *KP* 3:581-82; J. B. Ward-Perkins, *PECS* 499-500; O. Brogan and R. Wilson, *OCD* 844-45; W. Huss and H. G. Niemeyer, *DNP* 7:75-78; Ernesto V. Caffarelli et al., *Leptis Magna* (Rome: Astaldi, 1964); Ranuccio B. Bandinelli et al., *The Buried City: Excavations at Leptis Magna* (London: Weidenfeld & Nicolson, 1966); Schürer 3:63; L. Levine 2000, 233 n. 3; Mac-Mullen 2000, 35-42; D. J. Mattingly, *BAGRW,* map 35.

[757]See Schürer 3:63.

[758]M. Leglay, *KP* 4:244; Ward-Perkins, *PECS* 639; O. Brogan and R. J. A. Wilson, *OCD* 1061; W. Huss, *DNP* 8:1116; Schürer 3:63.

[759]Schürer 3:63.

Oea with regard to the new Bible translation of Jerome (*Epist.* 71.3.5). Oea was the seat of a bishop by A.D. 256 at the latest.

Sabratha (Ζάβραθα; mod. Sabrata; Zuaga),[760] the westernmost city of the Tripolitana, has not yielded evidence for a Jewish community. The citizens worshiped Hercules, Isis and Liber Pater (Shadrapha). The *statio Sabratensium* in Ostia documents trade with Italy, including the sale of elephants. An important caravan route through the Sahara desert ended in Sabratha. There was a Christian community with a bishop in the city by A.D. 253 at the latest.

Thaenae (mod. Henchir-Thina),[761] a port city about 320 km south of Carthage, had a Jewish community. A funerary inscription written in Hebrew and decorated with a menorah mentions a boy named Abedo.[762]

Sullectum (mod. Salakta),[763] a port city north of Thaenae, also had Jewish inhabitants, documented by a tombstone decorated with a menorah.

Henchir el-Faouara,[764] between Biia (Ain Batria) and Segermes (Henchir Harat) about 60 km south of Carthage, seems to have had Jewish inhabitants as well: a Latin inscription decorated with a menorah includes the words "D[eus Abr]aham, Deus Isa(a)c" (*CIL* VIII 16701).

Naro (Aquae Persianae; mod. Hammam-Lif, Tunisia),[765] a port city 32 km south of Carthage, had a Jewish community with a synagogue (discovered in 1883). A Latin inscription in the anteroom of the synagogue reads: "Asterius filius Rustici arcosinagogi M(a)rgarita Riddei [?] partem portici tesselavit" (*CIL* VIII 12457).

Carthage (Καρχηδών, *Karchēdōn;* north of Tunis),[766] about 600 km south of Rome on the North African coast, was founded by Phoenician settlers from Tyre in the ninth century (Timaeus, *FGrH* 566 frg. 60) as a center for trade with gold, silver and tin in the western Mediterranean. After Carthage was completely destroyed at the end of the Punic Wars in 146 B.C., Augustus colonized the site in fulfillment of Caesar's wishes and founded the Colonia Concordia Iulia Carthago, which became the capital of the province Africa Proconsularis. Augustan Carthage had an amphitheater, a theater, an odeion and a circus. Strabo estimated that the city had 700,000 inhabitants (17.3.15); modern estimates assume that Carthage had about 150,000 inhabitants around 200 B.C. The forum that was constructed in the second century A.D. had the largest basilica outside of Rome. The large Jewish necropolis of Carthage revealed over one hundred tombs with sixteen graves each. Tertullian's book *Adversus Judaeos* (*Against the Jews*) is not necessarily evidence for a Jewish community in Carthage, but an anecdote that he relates about an

---

[760]M. Leglay, *KP* 4:1485; P. Orlandini, *PECS* 779-80; Brogan and Wilson, *OCD* 1342.

[761]R. B. Hitchner, *BAGRW,* map 33, directory 513.

[762]Schürer 3:63.

[763]R. B. Hitchner, *BAGRW,* map 33, directory 513; Schürer 3:63.

[764]R. B. Hitchner, *BAGRW,* map 32, directory 497. Schürer (3:64) localizes Henchir Fouara near Tebessa (Theveste), which is about 220 km to the southwest.

[765]R. B. Hitchner, *BAGRW,* map 32, directory 499; Schürer 2:434; 3:63.

[766]G. Schrot, *KP* 3:135-38; A. Ennabli, *PECS* 201-202; B. H. Warmington and R. J. A. Wilson, *OCD* 295-96; W. Huss, *DNP* 6:295-97; W. Huss, *Karthago* (WF 654; Darmstadt: Wissenschaftliche Buchgesellschaft, 1992); Muhammad H. Fanttar, *Carthage: Approche d'une civilisation* (2 vols.; Tunis: Alif, les Éditions de la Méditerranée, 1993); idem, *Carthage: La cité punique* (Patrimoine de la Méditerranée; Tunis: Alif, les Éditions de la Méditerranée; Paris: CNRS Editions, 1995); Friedrich Rakob, "The Making of Augustan Carthage," in Fentress 2000, 73-82. Excavations: F. Rakob, ed., *Karthago I-II: Die deutschen Ausgrabungen in Karthago* (2 vols.; Mainz: Zabern, 1991-1997).

apostate Jew who evidently lived in Carthage certainly is (*Nat.* 1.14.2).[767] Carthage was one of the most important centers of Latin-speaking Christianity in the third century, with Tertullian and Cyprian among its outstanding theologians. The bishop Kaikilianos attended the Council of Nicea.

Thagura (mod. Taoura, Algeria), 210 km southwest of Carthage in the hinterland of the province, evidently had Jewish inhabitants as well, indicated by an inscription decorated with a menorah.[768]

There is evidence for Jewish communities in several cities of Numidia, although it is not always clear whether they existed in the first century A.D.[769]

Numidia (Νομαδία)[770] is the region west of Carthage between the rivers Tusca and Ampsaga (mod. Rhummel). Originally inhabited by nomadic Berber herders, the population became largely settled under King Masinissa (238-148 B.C.). Town life developed, the elite adopted Punic as their language, and the worship of Baal-Hammon was added to the native cults. The tribal confederacies were always difficult allies. The last Numidian king was Juba (69-46 B.C.). Pompey established eastern Numidia as the province of Africa Nova, and the area west of Cirta was made the client kingdom of Mauretania under Juba II. Under Augustus, Africa Nova was united with the old province of Africa Proconsularis; as a separate military district, Numidia was essentially autonomous.

Hippo Regius (mod. Annaba, formerly Bône, Algeria),[771] about 230 km west of Carthage, was a port of the Carthaginians probably since the sixth century B.C. The name of the city indicates that Hippo was the residence of Numidian kings for a certain period. During the Second Punic War Scipio's legate C. Laelius landed in Hippo in 205 B.C. In 46 B.C. Hippo became Roman, and under Augustus the city was granted the status of a *municipium*. In the second century Hippo became a Roman colony. Hippo played an important role in the trade between Ostia, Rome's harbor (700 km to the north), and North Africa, a fact confirmed by the remains of large warehouses in the harbor. By the time of

---

[767]Schürer 3:62-63. On Tertullian see Timothy D. Barnes, *Tertullian: A Historical and Literary Study* (Oxford: Clarendon, 1985). On the church in Carthage in the second and third centuries see J. B. Rives, *Religion and Authority in Roman Carthage from Augustus to Constantine* (Oxford: Oxford University Press, 1995); also Hayes 2002, 136-42.

[768]See Schürer 3:63.

[769]For the comments that follow above see Schürer 3:63-64.

[770]F. Windberg, PW 17.2 (1937): 1343-97; B. E. Thomasson, PWSup 13 (1973): 315-22; W. Huss, *DNP* 8:1056-58; R. J. A. Wilson, *OCD* 1054-55; Charles Saumagne, *La Numidie et Rome: Masinissa et Jugurtha* (Paris: Presses universitaires de France, 1966); Elizabeth W. B. Fentress, *Numidia and the Roman Army: Social, Military and Economic Aspects of the Frontier Zone* (BAR International Series 53; Oxford: British Archaeological Reports, 1979); André Berthier, *La Numidie Rome et le Maghreb* (Paris: Picard, 1981); Hans Werner Ritter, *Rom und Numidien: Untersuchungen zur rechtlichen Stellung abhängiger Könige* (Lüneburg: Albech, 1987).

[771]M. Leglay, "Hippo 6," *KP* 2:1160; J. Lassus, *PECS* 394-96; E. H. Warmington and R. Wilson, *OCD* 709-10; W. Huss, "Hippo 6," *DNP* 5:579-80; Holmes Van Mater Dennis, *Hippo Regius: From the Earliest Times to the Arab Conquest.* (Amsterdam: Hakkert, 1970 [1924]); Said Dahmani, *Hippo Regius* (Algiers: Ministère de l'information et de la culture, 1973); E. W. B. Fentress, *BAGRW,* map 31.

Augustine, at the latest, a Jewish community existed in Hippo (*Serm.* 196.4).[772] Remains of the agora, theater (100 m in diameter, the largest in Africa), forum (76 by 42 m), temples, baths and villas with mosaics survive. Hippo Regius was the seat of a bishop by A.D. 259. Augustine, one of the most significant Latin theologians of the church, was bishop of Hippo Regius in A.D. 395-430. Augustine noted that the rural population still spoke Punic (*Ep.* 209).

Cirta (Cirta Regia; mod. Constantine),[773] about 130 km southwest of Hippo Regius, on a hilltop above the gorges of the Ampsaga (mod. Oued el Kebir), was the capital of the Numidian princes Syphax and Masinissa, who encouraged Italian merchants to settle in Cirta. Rusicade (mod. Ras Skikda) and Chullu (mod. Collo) were developed as seaports of Cirtas. The temple of Baal-Hammon dates to this period (third century B.C.). King Jugurtha conquered Cirta in 112 B.C. and murdered the Italian citizens. Publius Sittius, who had supported Julius Caesar during the civil war, was granted Cirta and the surrounding region in 46 B.C., and he established the colony Colonia Cirta Sittianorum, later renamed Colonia Iulia Iuvenalis Honoris et Virtutis Cirta. The territory of Cirta included three further colonies: the seaports Chullu and Rusicade as well as Milev (mod. Mila). Under Diocletian, Cirta became the capital of the new province Numidia Cirtensis; when Cirta became the capital of all of Numidia, it was renamed Constantia. Three inscriptions document a Jewish community in Cirta.[774] In the third century Cirta was an important center of the Christian churches in the region.

Several cities of Mauretania had Jewish communities as well. It is not known, however, when Jews settled in this area.

Mauretania (Μαυρουσία)[775] stretched from the Ampsaga River to the Atlantic and comprised the area of modern Morocco and western Algeria. Most of the region is at a high elevation, the western half of the Atlas range. Exports included wine, ebony, precious woods and purple dyes; corn and olives were cultivated on the coast, in the Mulucha Valley and on the plains of Volubilis and Sala (see Strabo 17.3.11).

Sitifis (mod. Sétif, Algeria),[776] 115 km west of Numidian Cirta and 55 km south of the seaport Choba (mod. Ziama) in East Mauretania. In A.D. 96 Nerva settled veterans in the city (Colonia Nerviana Augusta Martialis Veteranorum Sitifensium); under Domitian it became the capital of the new province Mauretania Sitifensis. Two inscriptions document a Jewish community (*CIL* VIII 8423) and a synagogue: "Avilia Aster Iudea, M. Avilius Ianuarius pater sinagogae fil(iae) dulcissimae" ("Avilia Aster, a Jewess, Marcus Avilius Ianuarius, Father of the Community [Synagogue], to his sweetest daughter" [*CIL* VIII 8499]). An inscription that dates to the second century (or perhaps later) mentions a Jew who had

---

[772]See Helmut Castritius, "The Jews in North Africa at the Time of Augustine of Hippo: Their Social and Legal Position," in *Proceedings of the Ninth World Congress of Jewish Studies* (7 vols.; Division B/1; Jerusalem: World Union of Jewish Studies, 1986), 2:31-37.

[773]M. Leglay, *KP* 1:1196; P. A. Février, *PECS* 224-25; R. Wilson et al., *OCD* 333; W. Huss, *DNP* 2:1221.

[774]*CIL* VIII 7150, 7155, 7530, Suppl. I-II 19468. See Schürer 3:63-64; M. Williams 1997, 260, nos. 27-29.

[775]B. E. Thomasson, PWSup 13 (1973): 2344-86; W. Huss and H. G. Niemeyer, *DNP* 7:1048-52; R. J. A. Wilson, *OCD* 939; Maurice Euzennat and Jean Marion, *Inscriptions antiques des Maroc 2: Inscriptions latines* (Paris: Centre National de la Recherche Scientifique, 1982).

[776]M. Leglay, *KP* 5:216; P. A. Février, *PECS* 844-45; Schürer 64; Fentress, *BAGRW* 484, map 31.

converted to the Christian faith: "Memoria innocenti[um] Istablici qui et Donati. P(osuit) frater ips[i]us Peregriniu(s) q(ui et) Mosattes de Iudeus" (*CIL* VIII 8640); the inscription is decorated with the Christogram.[777] Remains of temples (for Magna Mater and other deities), amphitheater, hippodrome, aqueduct and houses survive; most structures were erected after the first century.

Auzia (Αὐζία; mod. Sour-Ghozlan; former Aumale),[778] 80 km south of the seaport Cissi (near mod. Cape Dijnet), on the west-east route through inner Mauretania running from Siga (Takembrit) via Tigava Municipium (mod. el Kherba; Ksar Solane) and Auzia to Saldae (Béjaja). The town was situated at an important crossroads. Josephus claims to know that Auzia was founded by Phoenician settlers from Tyre (*A.J.* 8.324). In A.D. 24 the Numidian Tacfarinas, who had provoked a revolt against the Romans (in A.D. 17), was executed in Auzia (Tacitus, *Ann.* 4.25).[779] An inscription dated to the second/third century attests the presence of Jews (*CIL* VIII 20759: "Furfanius Honoratus Iudeus").

Tipasa (mod. Tipasa),[780] a Punic seaport between Icosium (mod. Algiers) and Iol Caesarea (mod. Cherchel), later belonged to the Mauretanian kingdom; it was granted Latin rights in A.D. 46 by Claudius when Mauretania was annexed (Pliny, *Nat.* 5.2.20). A synagogue is attested for the late Roman period;[781] it is unknown whether Jews lived in the city in the first century. Remains of city walls (2.3 km long in the second century), forum, theater, amphitheater, nymphaeum, temples and basilicas survive.

Iol Caesarea (Καισάρεια; Punic Iol; mod. Cherchel),[782] 96 km west of Algiers, an ancient Punic seaport, was the capital of the kingdom of Mauretania, whose last king, Bocchus, died in 33 B.C. The Romans gave the city to C. Iulius Juba II (25 B.C. to A.D. 23), a Berber prince educated in Rome, who renamed the city Caesarea (Strabo 17.3.12).[783] He expanded the harbor facilities and transformed the city into a center of Hellenistic culture: it had a theater, an amphitheater (120 by 70 m), a circus, baths, temples, villas

---

[777]On *CIL* VIII 8423, 8499 (= Le Bohec 73-74) see Williams 1997, 260, nos. 30-31. On the Christogram see K. Aland, "Bemerkungen zum Alter und zur Entstehung des Christogrammes anhand von Beobachtungen bei 𝔓[66] und 𝔓[75]," in Aland 1967, 173-75; E. Dinkler, "Zur Geschichte des Kreuzsymbols," *ZThK* 48 (1951): 148-72; M. Black, "The Chi-Rho Sign—Christogram and/or Staurogram?" in Gasque and Martin 1970, 319-27.

[778]M. Leglay, *KP* 1:784; W. Nuss, *DNP* 2:365-66; T. W. Potter, *BAGRW* 476, map 30. Inscriptions: *CIL* VIIII.2 9014-9177, Suppl. III 20735-20815.

[779]R. Syme and B. L. Levick, *OCD* 1468. On *CIL* VIII 20759 (= Le Bohec 76) see Williams 1997, 260, no. 32.

[780]M. Leglay, "Tipasa 2," *KP* 5:859; Février, *PECS* 925-26; Warmington and Wilson, *OCD* 1530; S. Lancel, "Tipasa de Maurétanie: histoire et archéologie I. État des questions des origines préromaines à la fin du IIIe siècle," *ANRW* II.10.2 (1982): 739-86.

[781]See Schürer 3:64.

[782]M. Leglay, "Caesarea 1," *KP* 1:1003-4; J. Lassus, *PECS* 413-14; S. Lancel et al., *DCPP* 104-105; T. W. Potter, "Caesarea (3)," *OCD* 272; W. Huss, "Casearea 1," *DNP* 2:924; Nacéra Benseddik, *Cherchel* (Algiers: Direction des musées, de l'archéologie et des monuments et sites historiques, 1983); Philippe Leveau, *Caesarea de Maurétanie, une ville romaine d'Afrique et ses campagnes* (Paris: Boccard, 1984); T. W. Potter, *Towns in Late Antiquity: Iol Caesarea and Its Context* (Oxford: Ian Sanders Memorial Committee, 1995). Excavations: Nacéra Benseddik, *Fouilles du forum de Cherchel: 1977-1981* (Bulletin d'archéologie algérienne supplément 6; Algier: Ministère de la Culture et du Tourisme, 1993).

[783]Klaus Fittschen, "Juba II. und seine Residenz Jol/Caesarea (Cherchel)," in *Die Numider: Reiter und Könige nördlich der Sahara* (ed. H. G. Horn and C. B. Rüger; Köln: Rheinland-Verlag, 1979), 227-42; MacMullen 2000, 42-46; D. Jacobson 2001, esp. 31-32.

with impressive mosaics and an aqueduct (in some places 35 m high). After the murder of the Mauretanian king Ptolemy in A.D. 40, Caesarea became the capital of the new province Mauretania Caesariensis. The city became a Roman colony under Claudius (Pliny, *Nat.* 5.2.20). Caesarea had about twenty thousand inhabitants and was one of the largest cities in North Africa (with a circumference of 7 km). The apocryphal *Acta Marcianae* mentioned the president of a synagogue in the city (*Acts Mark* 4).[784] Christians in Iol Caesarea are attested for the second century, many of whom died as martyrs under Diocletian.

Volubilis (mod. Ksar Pharaoun, Morocco),[785] 225 km south of Tingi (mod. Tangier) in Western Mauretania, a Punic town in the fourth century, became Roman in 34 B.C. Claudius granted the city the status of a *municipium*. The population is estimated at ten thousand people, who worshiped Jupiter, Iuno, Minerva, Baal, Bacchus, Mithras, Isis and Anubis, the emperor and local gods. A Greek inscription documents a synagogue.[786] The fifty-five oil presses that have been discovered underline the significance of the cultivation of olives in the area. Christians are attested for the third century.

Sala (mod. Chellah, near Rabat, Morocco),[787] 120 km west of Volubilis in the Wadi Bou Regreg on the Atlantic (88 km northeast of Casablanca), was visited by Phoenicians since the seventh century B.C. The city minted its own coins in the first century. Sala engaged in traded with Gades (mod. Cadiz) and with other cities in southern Spain. Many of the public buildings, such as the agora, several temples and the capitolium (with a large Jupiter statue), date into the reign of Juba II (25 B.C.—A.D. 23). Some statues were made of Greek marble. After Mauretania was annexed by Rome, the center of the city was remodeled, particularly along the road that linked Sala with the Atlantic, a distance of 4 km. The approximately five hundred tombs of the necropolis were in use from the first century B.C. until the end of the second century A.D. An inscription attests a certain "Mareinos Ptolemaios, a Jew."[788] An inscription that was discovered in the forum was dedicated to Emperor Constantine. After the fourth century Sala was only a large village.

22.12 Missionary Work in India and Parthia

Written sources of the Syrian church and the oral tradition of the so-called Thomas Christians in South India assert that the apostle Thomas engaged in missionary work in India (see fig. 21). The following discussion seeks to clarify whether these traditions are reliable.

Thomas is mentioned in the Synoptic Gospels and in the book of Acts only in the lists of disciples (Mt 10:3; Mk 3:18; Lk 6:15; Acts 1:13). He is more prominent in the Gospel of John, where he attracts attention as a disciple who is both pessimistic and impulsive, a strange mixture that nonetheless is rather plausible for the contexts in which he is mentioned (Jn 11:16; 14:5; 20:24-29; 21:2). He is portrayed in Jn 11:16 as a leading apostle who is courageous and

[784]See Schürer 3:64.
[785]M. Leglay, *KP* 5:1328-29; M. Euzennat, *PECS* 988-89; Warmington and Wilson, *OCD* 1612; M. Euzennat, *BAGRW* 462, map 28.
[786]*AE* (1969-1970): 748: ὧδε κοιμᾶτε Καικιλιανὸς ὁ πρωτοπολίτες, πατὴρ τῆς συναγωγῆς τῶν Ἰουδέον.
[787]M. Leglay, "Sala 2," *KP* 4:1503; M. Euzennat, *PECS* 793-94; idem, *BAGRW* 461, map 28.
[788]Le Bohec 78 = *AE* (1949): 142. See Schürer 64; Williams 1997, 259, no. 13.

prepared to go with Jesus to his death.[789]

James Charlesworth has suggested that the apostle Thomas is the Beloved Disciple mentioned in the Gospel of John, and thus that he is the witness who testifies to the truth of the traditions recorded in the Fourth Gospel.[790] This suggestion is hardly more plausible than the identification of the Beloved Disciple with the apostle John in the early tradition of the church.

According to *Acts of Thomas,* the apostle Thomas engaged in missionary work in northwestern India (i.e., the region of modern Pakistan) at the royal court of "Gondophares." The tradition of the Christians in southern India asserts that Thomas reached the coast of southwest India coming from the island of Sokotra, that he engaged in missionary work in Travancore, and that later he traveled to the east coast of India at Malabar, where he was also able to win many people to faith in Jesus Christ before he died as a martyr, killed by a spear. These traditions raise two questions: (1) Is the report of Thomas traveling to the court of Gondophares in northern India historically reliable? (2) Is the tradition of missionary activity by Thomas in southern India historically reliable?

The "Acts of Thomas"

The earliest written source that mentions a journey of Thomas to India is the apocryphal *Acts of Thomas,* redacted around A.D. 200-240 in Edessa.[791] The narrative of *Acts of Thomas* at least indicates that there were Christian communities in India in the second century.[792]

The narrative begins in Jerusalem: the apostles met in order to divide the world into regions of missionary responsibility. The lot to go to India fell on Thomas, who initially refused to go: "By lot India fell to Judas Thomas, also called Didymus. And he did not wish to go, saying that he was not able to travel on account of the weakness of his body. He

---

[789]Dodd 1963, 317; R. F. Collins, "Thomas," *ABD* 6:528-29. Barrett (*John,* 571-72) describes Thomas's characterization in the Gospel of John as "a loyal but obtuse, rather than a doubtful and hesitating character." It is striking that the major commentaries on the Gospel of John do not discuss and often do not even mention the tradition of a missionary activity of Thomas in India as reported in the *Acts of Thomas;* the brief comment in Schnackenburg, *Joh,* 2:411 (ET, 2:327) in the context of Jn 11:16 is an exception.

[790]See Charlesworth 1995.

[791]For the text of *Acts of Thomas* see H. J. W. Drijvers, in Hennecke and Schneemelcher 1990-1997, 2:289-367 (ET, 2:425-531 [G. Bornkamm, translated by R. McL. Wilson]); A. F. J. Klijn, *The Acts of Thomas;* J. K. Elliott 1993, 439-511; Paul-Hubert Poirier and Yves Tissot, in Bovon and Geoltrain, eds., *Écrits apocryphes chrétiens,* 1323-1470. Brock (1992, 225-26) questions the origins of *Acts of Thomas* in Edessa. The tradition that the apostle Bartholomew also traveled to India is mentioned only rarely (Eusebius, *Hist. eccl.* 5.10.3; Gelasius) and cannot be confirmed by independent sources; other traditions link Bartholomew with Armenia, Phrygia, Lycaonia, Mesopotamia and Persia.

[792]See Amjad-Ali 1988, 39. The quotations from *Acts of Thomas* that follow above are taken from the translation by J. K. Elliott (1993).

said, 'How can I, being a Hebrew, go among the Indians to proclaim the truth?' And while he was considering this and speaking, the Savior appeared to him during the night and said to him, 'Fear not, Thomas, go away to India and preach the word there, for my grace is with you.' But he would not obey saying, 'Wherever you wish to send me, send me, but elsewhere. For I am not going to the Indians.'" (*Acts Thom.* 1). However, Jesus his master sold him as a slave to the merchant Habban, "who had come from India, sent from King Gundaphorus, having received an order from him to buy a carpenter and bring him to him" (2). Habban and Thomas traveled to India by ship. After a stopover in Andrapolis (3-16) they arrived at the court of Gundaphorus. The king directed Thomas to build him a palace, and he accepted the assignment: "Yes, I shall build it and finish it; for because of this I have come, to build and to do carpenter's work" (17). After initial preparations worthy of an architect, Thomas took the money and distributed it among the poor: "And the apostle took everything and divided it, going about in the cities and surrounding villages, distributing to the poor and needy, and bestowing alms, and gave them relief" (19). When the king came to see the finished palace, his friends in the city informed him, "He has neither built a palace, nor did he do anything of that which he promised to do, but he goes about in the cities and villages, and if he has anything he gives it to the poor, and teaches a new God, heals the sick, drives out demons, and performs many miracles. And we believe that he is a magician. But his acts of compassion and the cures done by him as a free gift, still more his simplicity and gentleness and fidelity, show that he is a just man, or an apostle of the new God, whom he preaches" (20). When the king challenged Thomas directly, Thomas informed him that he indeed built a palace, albeit a palace that he cannot see now: "But you shall see it when you depart this life" (20); in other words, he built him a palace in heaven. The king decided to flog Thomas and have him burned with fire. On the very night in which he wanted to kill Thomas and Habban, Gad, the brother of the king, became ill and died (21). When Gad's soul arrived in heaven, he saw the palace that Thomas had built for the king; he is granted his wish to return to earth and inform the king that he indeed has a palace in heaven (22-23). As a result of this news the king released Thomas from prison and said, "I entreat you, as a man entreating the servant of God, pray for me, and ask him, whose servant you are, to pardon me and to overlook what I have done to you or intended to do, and that I may become worthy to be an inhabitant of that house for which indeed I have done nothing, but which you, labouring alone, have built for me with the help of the grace of your God, and that I may also become a servant and serve this God, whom you preach" (24). Both the king and Gad, his brother, accepted faith in Jesus, which Thomas confirms (25-27). Thomas continued to preach in the city and lead many to faith (28-29). He performed many miracles and continued to lead many Indians to faith in Jesus (30-61). Some time later a captain of King Misdaeus (Mizdaios) came to Thomas while he "was preaching the word of God in India" and asked him to come to him in order to heal two women (62-64). Thomas agreed, entrusted the believers in the city into the care of a certain Xenophon (Xanthippus), and traveled to the land of Mizdaios (66-68). As a result of Thomas' ministry several members of the royal family were converted and baptized (82-158). Some time later Thomas and other believes were imprisoned (159). Thomas prepared himself to die and eventually was killed: "The four (soldiers) came and pierced him with their spears, and he fell down and died" (168). The book ends by pointing out that King Mizdaios was converted too (170).

The numerous and sometimes bizarre miracle stories in *Acts of Thomas* provide no encouragement for scholars to accept the narrative of a mission to India by the apostle Thomas as historically authentic.[793] Scholars sometimes point to casual details in the narrative that refer to or imply an Indian context, suggesting that these details confirm a historical core for the sometimes legendary stories (e.g., at one point a donkey speaks). Such details include repeated references to bathing, demonstrations of homage and the means of transportation.[794] However, it cannot be demonstrated that these details are unambiguously or typically Indian.[795] Many scholars therefore reject the tradition of *Acts of Thomas* as historically worthless.[796]

One detail that clearly refers to an Indian context is the reference to Gondophernes (Gondophares), the Indo-Parthian ruler in Taxila between A.D. 20 and 46. Gondophernes was accepted as a historical figure only when archaeologists discovered coins whose legend included his name. For today's classical scholars Gondophernes is a ruler whose reign is as securely dated as that of any ruler in central Asia in the first century.[797] The section of *Acts of Thomas* that narrates the encounter between Thomas and Gondophernes in Taxila (*Acts Thom.* 17-29) is one of the few stories in the narrative that does not concentrate on sexual abstinence. This fact may indicate that we are dealing with historical recollection.

Taxila (τὰ Τάξιλα; mod. Sirkap; Saraikhala),[798] about 30 km northeast of Rawalpindi, was founded in the sixth century B.C. and was the largest city between the rivers Indus and Hydaspes (mod. Jhelum), according to Arrian. Taxila had been occupied by Alexander the Great and was known since then to the Western world as a large, superbly administered and magnificent city (Arrian, *Anab.* 5.3.6; Strabo 15.1.28). At the beginning of the second century B.C. Taxila was refounded as Taxila-Sirkap, whose streets were built according to the Hippodamian model. In the period 200-100 B.C. the city belonged to Indo-Greek Bactria, before being conquered by the Sacae from central Asia and by the Parthians. Taxila at the time of the Sacae and the Parthians was surrounded by a city wall 5 km in length. Excavations unearthed at least two temples and a palace. The ruins of the royal residence in the western section of the city (94 by 73 m) date to the first century

---

[793]For arguments against the authenticity of *Acts of Thomas* see Vadakkekara 1995, 184-250. On the miracles in *Acts of Thomas* see Kelhoffer 2000, 303-10.

[794]See Medlycott 1905, 277-89; Rooney 1984, 49-51; Vadakkekara 1995, 168.

[795]See Amjad-Ali 1988, 38.

[796]A very influential study was Garbe 1914; see, before Garbe, Dahlmann 1912. See more recently G. Bornkamm, in Hennecke and Schneemelcher 1959-1964, 2:297-372 (ET, 2:425-42); Dihle 1963, 54-70; J. K. Elliott 1993, 440-41; H. J. W. Drijvers, in Hennecke and Schneemelcher 1990-1997, 2:292 ("entirely legendary"); Reinbold 2000, 258-60 (superficial); Meier 1991-2001, 3:255-56 n. 17.

[797]Posch 1995, 109. A. D. H. Bivar (1983, 197) states that the Gondophares in *Acts of Thomas* is chronologically acceptable and confirms with this information the proposed date for the inscription of Takht-i-Bahī; see also R. M. Smith 1997, 114; Posch 1995, 109, n. 39.

[798]F. F. Schwarz, *KP* 5:549-50; M. Mirabella Roberti, *PECS* 843; John H. Marshall, *Taxila: An Illustrated Account of Archaeological Excavations* (3 vols.; Cambridge: Cambridge University Press, 1951; repr., New Delhi, 1975); Dar Saifur Rahman, *Taxila and the Western World* (Lahore: al-Waqar, 1984); Ahmad Hasan Dani, *The Historic City of Taxila* (rev. ed.; Paris: Unesco, 1998 [1986]); Chakrabarti 1998, 174-81. On Alexander the Great's campaign to India see Seibert 1985, 156.

A.D. Around A.D. 59 the Kushan, under their ruler Kujala Kadphises, conquered Taxila and founded a new city at the end of the first century in Sirsukh, about 2 km north of Sirkap. There was no national religion in Bactria or in Kushan; the ethnic groups practiced, and sometimes mixed, a complex diversity of different religions.[799] The fusion and the coexistence of Greek Hellenism, Indian Hinduism, the Western cult of Mithras and early Buddhism had been cultivated by the Indo-Greek rulers: we have already noted the conversion of the Bactrian king Menander to Buddhism around 100 B.C. (see §16.2). The Parthians, the Sacae and the Kushan continued to be tolerant toward all religions. Evidence for the occasional promotion of Buddhism and for a process of Hinduization in Kushan can be explained in the context of the historical and political situation.

The neo-Pythagorean itinerant philosopher Apollonius of Tyana visited Taxila in A.D. 43, according to his biographer Philostratus (A.D. 200), who compared Taxila in terms of its size with Nineveh (*Vit. Apoll.* 2.20).

"Taxila, they tell us, is about as big as Nineveh, and was fortified fairly well after the manner of Greek cities; and here was the royal residence of the personage who then ruled the empire of Porus. And they saw a temple, they say, in front of the wall, which was not far short of 100 feet in size, made of porphyry, and there was constructed within it a shrine, somewhat small as compared with the great size of the temple which is also surrounded with columns, but deserving of notice. For bronze tablets were nailed into each of its walls on which were engraved the exploits of Porus and Alexander. . . . I have already described the way in which the city is walled, but they say that it was divided up into narrow streets in the same irregular manner as is Athens, and that the houses were built in such a way that if you look at them from outside they had only one story, while if you went into one of them you at once found subterranean chambers extending as far below the level of the earth as did the chambers above. And they say that they saw a Temple of the Sun in which was kept loose a sacred elephant called Ajax, and there were images of Alexander made of gold, and others of Porus, though the latter were of black bronze. . . . Then he [King Phraotes] took Apollonius by the hand, and having bidden the interpreter [ἑρμηνέα] to depart, he said: 'You will then, I hope, choose me for your boon companion.' And he asked the question of him in the Greek tongue [φωνῇ ʽΕλλάδι]" (*Vit. Apoll.* 2.20, 23-24, 27). When Apollonius expresses his surprise that the king is able to converse in Greek, the king states that he had not wanted to be presumptuous but "that I am quite competent in the Greek speech I will show you amply" (27). When Apollonius asks the king how he "acquired such a command of the Greek tongue" (29), the king explains that "philosophy is highly esteemed in this country, and it is held in honour by the Indians" (30).

Since Philostratus's description of Taxila has been confirmed by excavations, his reference to a journey of Apollonius of Tyana to Babylonia and to Taxila is regarded as reliable.[800] Carsten Colpe is convinced that Apollonius would have felt at home in Taxila when he saw the Greek temples and when he discussed his

---

[799]C. Colpe, "Development of Religious Thought," *CHI* 3:847-51; cf. R. E. Emmerick, "Buddhism among Iranians," *CHI* 3:949-64, esp. 952-53.

[800]See Tarn 1984, 360; Bivar 1983, 76. Excavations were conducted by Alexander Cunningham between 1863 and 1864, and by John Marshall between 1902 and 1931.

philosophy, in Greek, with the king and the Brahmin who were present.[801] If scholars accept as historical a visit to India by Apollonius of Tyana in A.D. 43, recorded about 150 years later by Philostratus, then we should accept the *possibility* that Thomas could have come to India and preached the gospel in Greek there. This means that *Acts of Thomas* could indeed preserve authentic information about such a missionary visit. If both the philosopher and the missionary indeed met with King Gondophernes in Taxila, then they would have visited India only a few years apart.

Clearly, the notion of an early Christian missionary who preached the gospel in India in Greek is historically possible. And it is not impossible to assume that such a missionary could have had success: both the population and the ruling dynasty were open to new religious teachings; and a change of religious loyalties was not unheard of. It is historically possible that the Indo-Parthian king Gondophernes welcomed the apostle Thomas at his court.[802]

There is no doubt that *Acts of Thomas* contains unreliable information. For example, the author states that the Egyptian city of Andropolis had its own king—at that time, however, Claudius was emperor in Rome, and Egypt was a Roman province. Equally problematic is the suggestion that king Gondophernes could find no architect in Taxila to build him a palace.

There are two possible answers to the question of how the tradition of a missionary journey of Thomas to India arose. First, Thomas indeed engaged in missionary work in "India"—that is, in Parthia and in the Punjab in northwestern India.[803] Second, the churches in India were established by a missionary from the church in Edessa for whom the apostle Thomas was an important person.[804] The following arguments suggest that the first answer is historically more plausible.

1. If the missionary journey of Thomas to India is an entirely fictitious story written to establish a belated apostolic origin for the churches in this region, then the author would have had to remember Gondophernes about 130 to 180 years after the breakup of his Indo-Parthian empire in A.D. 45 or 55—and this at a distance of over 3,000 km. And he would have had to remember Gondophernes's reign in a relatively reliable manner (on Gondophernes see §16.2). Both prerequisites are not impossible, but the fact that Gondophernes is mentioned only in *Acts of Thomas* and in Philostratus's *Life of Apollonius* suggests that the narrative is not purely fictitious. And the argument that the author of *Acts of Thomas* could have relied on local traditions for his knowledge about

---

[801]See Colpe, "Development of Religious Thought," 3:849.

[802]See Emmerick, "Buddhism among Iranians," 3:953.

[803]Farquhar 1926; Waldmann 1996, 9-57; as a plausible possibility: V. Smith 1924, 245-49; Grafe 1981, 65-71, esp. 66; Dar 1988, 19; Amjad-Ali 1988, 39; Moffett 1992, 25-44, esp. 35-36.

[804]See Amjad-Ali 1988, 39, as a possibility.

Gondophernes can with equal justification be used as evidence for the view that the tradition of an encounter between Thomas and Gondophernes is historically authentic. John Farquhar concluded from this evidence that the author of *Acts of Thomas* must have had a document that was written more or less contemporaneously with these events in the first century.[805] This assumption is hypothetical but essentially plausible.

2. The churches in Edessa and in Adiabene that claim a close connection with the apostle Thomas never claim that Thomas visited Edessa. This indicates that the narrative of a mission to India by Thomas can hardly be fictitious: what would be the purpose for such a creation? The connection that the Christians of Edessa claim to have with Thomas consists in the telling of information that Thomas sent Addai as a missionary to their city.[806]

3. The creation of a fictitious mission to India by Thomas would not have promoted the general argument of the author of *Acts of Thomas*. He presupposes such a mission as common knowledge and uses it for his purposes, which are totally unrelated to India or to missionary activity.[807]

4. The initial refusal of the apostle to travel into the region that was allotted to him for missionary work suggests that the narrative has a historical core in view of the fact that the author of *Acts of Thomas* generally parallels the life of Thomas with the life of Jesus—and Jesus never refused to do God's will.[808]

5. Later church authorities also know of a missionary activity of Thomas in India: Ephraem the Syrian, Gregory of Nazianzus, Ambrose and Jerome.[809] Eusebius reports that Origen knew that Thomas engaged in missionary work in Parthia:

"Such was the condition of the Jews. Meanwhile the holy apostles and disciples of our Savior were dispersed throughout the world. Parthia, according to tradition, was allotted to Thomas as his field of labor. . . . These facts are related by Origen in the third volume of his Commentary on Genesis" (Eusebius, *Hist. eccl.* 3.1-2; cf. *Clem. recogn.* 9.29; Rufinus, *Hist. eccl.* 2.5; Socrates, *Hist. eccl.* 1.19).

If the author of *Acts of Thomas* locates Thomas's missionary activity in India, this does not contradict the statement of Origen, nor is it necessary to connect these pieces of information and assume that Thomas evangelized in both areas (thus

---

[805]Farquhar 1926, 106; he assumes that Thomas wrote a report in Taxila that he sent to Edessa; Syrian sources claim to know that Thomas wrote letters from India (ibid., 102-5). Vadakkekara (1995, 165-66) accepts this argument as convincing.

[806]Eusebius, *Hist. eccl.* 1.13.4; 2.1.6; cf. *Doctrina Addai* 11-21 (Howard, ed., *The Teaching of Addai*).

[807]See Vadakkekara 1995, 172-76.

[808]See Waldmann 1996, 43.

[809]See G. Bickell, *St Ephraemi Syri Carmina Nisibena* (Leipzig: Brockhaus, 1866), 163-64; Gregory of Nazianzius, *Hom.* 33; Jerome (PL 22:588).

the harmonization by Pseudo-Hippolytus, Dorotheus of Beirut and Bar-Hebraeus).[810] Origen and the author of *Acts of Thomas* both knew a part of historical reality: Gondophernes was a Parthian king whose independent kingdom comprised Parthian regions as well as parts of northwestern India.

John Farquhar suggests that Origen received his information from the church in Alexandria, which knew the merchant Habban. He surmises that Habban, whose name is Semitic, was a Jew from Parthia who was the "merchant of king Gūdnaphar," the authorized agent of the king (*rājavaidehaka*); every four or five years Habban traveled to Alexandria, from where he could easily reach Jerusalem. Farquhar suggests that Habban might have been converted at the Feast of Pentecost (Luke's first reference is to pilgrims of Parthia [Acts 2:9]), and that Habban later was able to convince Thomas, who was already involved in missionary work in Alexandria, to accompany him to India.[811] There is no evidence that Thomas was a carpenter.[812] There is ample evidence, however, for artisans who traveled great distances in antiquity. Farquhar's reconstruction is historically possible but must remain hypothetical.

Eusebius relates that the Alexandrian teacher Pantaenus traveled to India at the end of the second century and encountered Christians who had the Gospel of Matthew written in Hebrew, given to them by the apostle Bartholomew (*Hist. eccl.* 5.10). This information is used by Albertus Klijn as an argument against a mission to India by Thomas: the assertions of the church fathers about India are too contradictory to warrant any certainty about what happened. However, if Pantaenus heard "Bar Thoma" instead of "Mar Thoma"—*Mar* being an oriental honorific title—then the confusion of Thomas with Bartholomew would become understandable and the tradition of a mission to India by the apostle Bartholomew would find an explanation.[813]

6. If the historical probability of a mission by Thomas to India and particularly to Gondophernes and Taxila, as attested in *Acts of Thomas*, has to be regarded as high, the same applies perhaps to the reference in the same document that Thomas preached the gospel in a second region in India. *Acts of Thomas* provides no description of the "land of Mizdaios," and the reason that is given for Thomas's journey to this region—to heal two sick women—is not particularly plausible. There may have been another reason for a relocation of his missionary activity from the kingdom of Gondophernes into another region: Gondophernes died around A.D. 55, and in A.D. 59 the Kushan from central Asia, under the leadership of Kujala Kadphises, conquered Taxila after having put pressure on the Punjab for some time. These political events may have prompted the missionary to leave northwestern India and travel to another region. The possibility that Thomas worked as a missionary in a second region in India leads us to consider the tradition of the Christians of South India who call themselves Thomas Christians.

---

[810]Dorotheus (PG 92:1071); Bar-Hebraeus, *Chron. eccl.* 1.34.
[811]See Farquhar 1926, 86-94, 106, generally followed by Waldmann 1996, 33-35, 43-50.
[812]Waldmann (1996, 45-47) tries to argue this, with reference to Ephraem.
[813]See Cheriyan 1973, 61; Waldmann 1996, 16-17, contra Klijn, *Acts of Thomas,* 1962, 27.

The Travancore Tradition

The tradition of the church of South India in Travancore (in Kerala) is found in songs and ballads. The most well-known ballad has the title *Thōmā Parvam,* a work that was written, according to a colophon, in 1601 by Maliekel Thoma Ramban, the forty-eighth descendant of a certain Thōmā, who is said to have been baptized by the apostle Thomas himself. It is assumed that the ballad is a summary of a longer work that the nephew of this Thōmā had written.[814] The fact that the tradition of the Thomas Christians is not supported by written documents is not surprising: until the recent past none of the Indian people groups had a history that was documented by written sources. There are hardly any written historical documents for the first three thousand years of Indian history: the numerous and enormous Indian works on metaphysics, cosmography, astrology and poetry, written in Sanskrit, include essentially no historical information. In India, oral tradition *is* history.[815]

The demand of Western historians for written sources does not get us anywhere in India. The Indian scholar Benedict Vadakkekara asserts that the oral tradition of the Thomas Christians is reliable and that the dividing line between the "physical possibility" of a mission to India by the apostle Thomas and the "historical factuality" of such a mission should be dissolved. He argues that *Acts of Thomas* is less specific than the oral tradition in terms of details that are provided, and he points out that there are no Christian churches in North India that claim to have been founded by Thomas—a fact, however, that could be explained by the turbulent political events in northwestern India at the end of the first century, as he acknowledges. Vadakkekara does not exclude the possibility that Thomas was involved in missionary work in the kingdom of Gondophernes, but he sees such a mission only as a "physical possibility."

The South Indian tradition includes the following details about the missionary work of the apostle Thomas.[816]

The apostle Thomas sailed by ship from the island of Sokotra to the Indian coast in Malabar near Muziris in A.D. 52, accompanied by the merchant Aban. He first preached in the kingdom of the Chola, where many people were converted. Thomas founded seven churches and ordained two presbyters. He then went to the east coast,[817] where he preached with much success. The king of this region and many of his subjects accepted Christian baptism. Then Thomas visited Malacca and China and led many people to faith in Jesus Christ. When he returned to the east coast of India, he was so successful in his missionary work that the Brahmin of the district were filled with envy and resentment. In a sudden commotion one of them pierced him with a spear, with the result that Thomas won the crown of a martyr. He died in A.D. 72. The ballad *Thōmā Parvam* mentions six stages of Thomas's missionary work: (1) mission in the kingdom of the Chola on the east

---

[814]See Thoma 1924, 214. On the history of the Thomas Christians see Vadakkekara 1995, 13-121.

[815]Vadakkekara 1995, 4, 322-55; for the observations that follow above see ibid., 458-70,

[816]See Thoma 1924; Farquhar 1927, 20-50; Vadakkekara 1995, 47-77.

[817]For the summary that follows above see Farquhar 1927, 20-50.

coast; (2) mission in Malacca and China; (3) mission in Malabar on the southwest coast, establishment of seven churches; (4) return to Chola; (5) return to Malabar; (6) return to the east coast, where he dies as a martyr on July 3 in A.D. 72.[818]

If Thomas left northwestern India in connection with the advance of the Kushan warriors and sailed south on the Indus River, then he may have arrived in the region called "Scythia" or *Indoscythia*,[819] with the capital Minnagar and the large seaport of Barbarikon. The possibility that Thomas traveled from the kingdom of Gondophernes in northwestern India on the Indus River to Patala-Minnagar (mod. Bahmanabad?) and Barbarikon[820] in southern India is historically plausible, considering the well-documented trade relations between the Indus Delta and the Punjab in the first century A.D. We should note, however, that the Travancore tradition mentions Sokotra and Muziris as the first stations of Thomas's missionary journey. Sokotra is an island in the Gulf of Aden, a frequent stopover of the ships that plied the trade routes between India, southern Arabia and Roman Egypt (Ptolemaios, Periplus 31.10.21-22).[821] Muziris (mod. Cranganore), about 2,000 km south of the Indus Delta (about 250 km north of the southern tip of India), was the most important seaport of the kingdom of the Chera. The Peutinger Table (a medieval copy of an original Roman map) indicates that Muziris had a temple of Augustus,[822] a fact that documents extensive trade relations with the West.

John Farquhar suggests the following harmonization of *Acts of Thomas* with the Travancore tradition: Thomas left northwestern India with the goal of preaching the gospel in another region of India. Habban, the authorized agent of King Gondophernes, had contacts with the most important seaports in the south and suggested that he could travel to the kingdoms of the Chera, Panya and Chola, beginning in Muziris in the ports of South India, where he could reach many Greeks with the gospel as well. Since the journey from Barbarikon to Muziris in the south was not immediately possible due to the winds of the northeast monsoon (assuming that Thomas arrived in Barbarikon during the winter), he embarked on a ship headed to Sokotra, where he waited for the southwest monsoon (in early summer).

This scenario is not impossible, but it seems rather contrived. The journey from Sokotra to Muziris in the Travancore tradition suggests the traditional route from Alexandria to India via the Red Sea and the Gulf of Aden. The reference to Sokotra in the Travancore tradition makes a straightforward harmonization of Thomas's travels to and in India in *Acts of Thomas* with those in the Travancore tradition difficult.

---

[818]See Thoma 1924.

[819]See Ptolemaios 7.1.55; *Periplus* 38.12.

[820]The localization of Barbarikon is not secured. M. U. Erdosy (*BAGRW*, map 6 [1997]) marks the city to the east of the Chrysoun Stoma River (a former branch of the Indus River) with a question mark.

[821]See Casson 1989, 164-69.

[822]See Cimino 1994, 10; Ball 2000, 123.

According to the Travancore tradition, Thomas engaged in missionary work in all three kingdoms of southern India: in the kingdom of the Chera in the cities Palur, Muziris, Parur, Gokkamaṅgalam and Chayal; in the kingdom of the Panya or Pandya in the cities Nelkyanda (mod. Nirkunnam)[823] and Quilon; in the kingdom of the Chola in the cities Kavirippaṭṭinam, Poduke-Arikamedu (mod. Virampatnam near Pondicherry) and Sopatma (Marakanam near Madras).[824] Thomas was killed and buried in the vicinity of Mylapore near Madras.

We need to remember at this point that the "urban centers" in which the elites lived were located in the interior of India, not on the coast. In antiquity the Indian seaports were mostly only transit points for the transshipment of goods for the trade networks that were concentrated in the interior.[825] Since the archaeological investigation of India has made little progress in many regions of India, we cannot expect soon a confirmation of the Travancore tradition from archaeology. For example, in Madura and Korkai, two important centers of the kingdom of the Panya, no large-scale excavations have ever been attempted.[826] We must not forget, however, that the ministry of Jesus and of the apostles in the first century cannot be confirmed by archaeological discoveries either (with the exception, perhaps, of the recent discovery of Peter's house in Capernaum).

John Farquhar suggests that the reference to China in the South Indian tradition might be due to a loose use of the word "China." There was no direct sea link between India and China in the first century. Thomas could have reached, by ship, ports in the mouth of the Irrawaddy River as well as the Malayan peninsula. In other words, the term "China" could refer to Malaya.[827] Several cities engaged in trade with Ceylon and with Southeast Asia: Barygaza, Kalliena, Muziris and Nelkyanda on the west coast of India, and Arikamedu and other cities on the east coast.[828]

The following considerations suggest that the Travancore tradition of the Christians in South India is essentially reliable.[829] (1) The churches that Thomas is said to have established in cities in southern India in the kingdom of the Chera and of the Panya fit the general historical context of sea trade in the first century. (2) The tradition does not claim that Thomas erected church buildings or appointed bishops. (3) The tradition mentions neither Edessa nor Persia, whose churches controlled the churches in South India in a later period. (4) The tradition does not mention any miracles that Thomas is said to have performed. (5) The details of the tradition are not dependent upon *Acts of Thomas*. (6) Local traditions that

---

[823]On the possible identification of Nelkyanda with Niranom see Casson 1989, 298 with n. 11. On the tradition that Thomas preached the gospel in Niranom see Thoma 1924, 216-17, 219.

[824]Vadakkekara (1995, 133, 137) notes the following seven cities, which are mentioned in the tradition of the Thomas Christians (from north to south): Palayūr, Cranagore, Kokkamangalam, Parûr, Niranam, Nilakkel, Quilon.

[825]See Himanshu Prabha Ray, "A Resurvey of 'Roman' Contacts with the East," in Boussac and Salles 1995, 97-114, esp. 98.

[826]See Chakrabarti 1998, 232.

[827]Farquhar 1927, 32.

[828]See Chakrabarti 1998, 217, 227.

[829]See Thoma 1924; Farquhar 1927, 36, 43-49.

are not Christian seem to confirm Christian traditions. The Thomas Christians claim that the apostle baptized many Brahmin in Pâlayur, while other Brahmin rejected his message, solemnly cursed the city and swore to leave Pâlayur never to return—Brahmin do not drink water and do not eat betel nuts on the city territory of Pālayur. (7) The fact that there is no unequivocal evidence for churches in South India before the fourth century established by Thomas does not prove that the tradition is fictitious: the church of South India did not produce theological writings for centuries (at least, no historical theological works are preserved), and even the church of Edessa produced only a few texts in the second and third centuries (or rather, only a few texts have been preserved, and they all show an interest in Thomas). (8) The view that the churches of South India were established by Persian Christians who emigrated to India between A.D. 300 and 350 in connection with the persecution that the Sasanid rulers initiated against the Christians in Persia/Iran[830] is unconvincing. First, there is no evidence whatsoever for the alleged emigration of Persian Christians. Second, a bishop John of Persia, who attended the Council of Nicea in A.D. 325, was responsible for the "churches in all Persia and greater India," a fact that proves that there were Christian communities in India by A.D. 300. Third, there is evidence from the third century that Christians from the West traveled to India and met Indian Christians, and that Indian Christians visited churches in the West: the Alexandrian teacher Pantaenus traveled to India around A.D. 190,[831] as did bishop Dudi of Basra;[832] the *Chronicle of Arbela* lists seventeen bishoprics east of the Tigris River by A.D. 225; Philostorgius relates that the Indian Christian, Theophilus of Diu, led an embassy to Emperor Constantius.[833] (9) Several customs of the Thomas Christians could derive from Jewish customs and might constitute evidence that the early churches in South India included converted Jews. For example, Thomas Christians regard mothers after childbirth as unclean.[834]

Bendict Vadakkekara argues that the tradition of the Thomas Christians is unique, specific, consistent, unified, straightforward and independent.[835] It is unique because no other Christian community traces its origins to the apostle Thomas. It is specific because it links the arrival, mission and death of Thomas with specific places and situations. It is consistent because the Thomas Christians maintained for centuries the tradition of the apostle Thomas and his mis-

---

[830]See Garbe 1914, 153.

[831]Eusebius, *Hist. eccl.* 5.10.2-3. Lane Fox (1988, 278) accepts the mission of Pantaenus to India as historical.

[832]See *Chronicle of Se'ert* (PO 4:236, 292).

[833]Philostorgius, *Hist. eccl.* 3.4-6.

[834]Vadakkekara 1995, 130, with reference to Placid J. Podipara, *The Thomas Christians* (London and Bombay: Darton, Longman & Todd, 1970), 225. On the presence of Jews in India see below.

[835]See Vadakkekara 1995, 134-48, 255-75.

sionary work in India with a plethora of details. It is unified because the tradition is accepted by all Thomas Christians as well as by Hindu authorities. It is straightforward because the core of the tradition is the simple story of the successful missionary work of the apostle. It is independent because there are no recognizable links with *Acts of Thomas*.

Conclusion: The written and oral tradition that report and describe a mission to India by the apostle Thomas is very likely historical. Whether this "likelihood" is probable or certain is a matter of scholarly discretion.[836] General skepticism is no longer warranted today. The historical context confirms that people living in the Mediterranean world could easily obtain both general and specific knowledge about India, that there was a robust sea trade between Egypt and India, that the overland route from Syria to India was frequently traveled, and that Gondophernes was an Indo-Parthian king and a historical person. In other words, the historical context demonstrates the historical plausibility of a mission to India by the apostle Thomas. The literary and the oral sources, many of which are independent of each other and come from different geographical regions—*Acts of Thomas* from Edessa, Travancore tradition from India, Origen from Alexandria—suggest that the apostle Thomas indeed engaged in missionary work in India. The lack of historical documents from India represents no cogent objection: in India tradition functions as history.[837] And the character of Thomas, the disciple of Jesus, who is impulsive and courageous and who confesses Jesus as Lord and divine Savior after the resurrection (Jn 11:16; 14:5; 20:24-29; 21:2), fits the tradition of a mission to India as well.

A traveler to India could choose among several possible routes in the first century (see fig. 22).[838] (1) The overland route via Damascus and Palmyra in a southeasterly direction to Dura-Europos and Seleukeia (Kutal-Imara), in a northeasterly direction via Artemita and Ecbatana (Hamadan) through the Caspian Gates to Hekatompylos (Damghan, capital of Parthia), from there in an easterly and a southeasterly direction via Marv (Antiochia Margiana) to Balkh, the capital of Bactria, and from there through Kushan and on mountain roads through the Hindukush via Begram to Taxila-Sirkap, and from there to the Indus Delta. (2) The route via Damas-

---

[836]Some scholars accept the possibility of a mission to India by Thomas but are uncertain about its historicity: Kawerau (1983, 17) acknowledges the "purely theoretical possibility" that an apostle could have traveled in the mid-first century from Palestine to India, and that he could have established a church there; similarly Hough 1839-1860, 1:46; Keay 1960, 2; Firth 1976, 17. Neill (1984, 49) acknowledges that the tradition is ancient but warns of optimistic conclusions because we have no historical documents that might prove the reliability of the tradition; similarly undecided are Richter 1924, 31; Forrester 1980, 13-14; Scott Sunquist, "Syria, Syrian Christianity," *DLNTD* 1151. Authors who accept the tradition of *Acts of Thomas* as being very probably historical were mentioned earlier.

[837]See Vadakkekara 1995, 457.

[838]See "Contacts with India" in §16.2. See also *Tübingen Bible Atlas* [*TAVO*] B V 22: "Northeast Africa and Arabian Peninsula: States and Peoples" (fourth-first centuries B.C.).

cus and Palmyra to Hit on the Euphrates River, from there via Teredon and Apamea (Mesene) to Spasinou Charax in the kingdom of Charakene, frequented by Jewish merchants (Josephus, *A.J.* 20.34), and from there by ship to India.[839]

An inscription from Palmyra dated to A.D. 157 mentions "the merchants who returned in the fleet of Honainu, son of Haddudan, from Scythia [i.e., India]."[840] Indian products (e.g., Indian red-polished ware) and Indian coins (e.g., a bronze coin from central India [!] found on the coast of the Persian Gulf in ed-Dur [United Arabian Emirates])[841] confirm the trade with India on this route.

(3) The route via Petra east of the Jordan River to the oasis Domata (Gabba, al-Ğauf) in central Arabia, in a southeasterly direction along the main trade route via Phigea (Tağ) to the port Hē Polis Gerrhaioi (al-Hufuf) on the Persian Gulf (*Persikos kolpos*), and from there by ship via Portus Macedonum (on the Anamis River in Karmania, Persia) to India. (4) The sea route through the Red Sea (*Arabios kolpos*), either from Berenike (Tall al-Hulaifa, Eilat) or Aila (al-Aqaba) in the Gulf of Aqaba (*Kolpos Laianitēs*) along the east coast of the Red Sea via Chermutas (*Leukē komē*) and Akila into the Erythraean Sea, or from Arsinoë at the northern end of the Red Sea along the west coast via Myos Hormos, Philotera, Berenike, Elaia, Saba, Arsinoë and Deirē into the Erythraean Sea.[842] From the southern end of the Red Sea, where the Erythraean Sea (*Hē Erythrē thalatta*, or *Indicus oceanus*) begins, there was a northern route to the mouth of the Indus River via Eudaimōn Polis (Sokotra) and Qana', with a secondary route to the coast of (mod.) Gujurat, and a southern route to the Malabar coast in (mod.) Kerala. The last, direct route was by far the most important route to India in the first century.[843]

It is unclear whether a Jewish traveler could have relied on Jewish communities on the way to India.

C. V. Cheriyan suggests that there were Jewish trading posts in South India,[844] a suggestion

---

[839]See D. T. Potts, "The Roman Relationship with the *Persicus sinus* from the Rise of Spasinou Charax (127 B.C.) to the Reign of Shapur II (A.D. 309-379)," in Alcock 1997, 89-107, esp. 94-95. Potts calls the route from the Persian Gulf to India "the Characene Corridor."

[840]*Inv* 96 = *SEG* VII 156. See S. A. Nodelman, "A Preliminary History of Characene," *Berytus* 13 (1959-1960): 111-19, esp. 114-15; Tubach 1986, 37; John F. Healey, "Palmyra and the Arabian Gulf Trade," *Aram* 8 (1996): 33-37, esp. 37; Potts, "Roman Relationship," 97.

[841]See E. Haerinck, "Ed-Dur, Umm al-Qaiwain (U.A.E.)," in *Materialien zur Archäologie der Seleukiden- und Partherzeit im südlichen Babylonien und Golfgebiet* (ed. U. Finkbeiner; Deutsches Archäologiches Institut Abteilung Baghdad; Tübingen: Wasmuth, 1993), 186-87; Potts, "Roman Relationship," 99-101.

[842]Warmington 1928, 83, as the most plausible route of the Thomas tradition.

[843]Pliny, *Nat.* 6.100-101; *Periplus Maris Rubri* 57. See Dihle 1974, 112; 1978, 121.

[844]Cheriyan 1973, 28-34, 62; cf. Mundadan 1984, 19-20; Waldmann 1996, 17-20. Surjit Mansingh (*Historical Dictionary of India* [Asian Historical Dictionaries 20; Lanham, Md.: Scarecrow Press, 1996], 204-5) asserts that the first Jews settled in India in the first century A.D. on the west coast in the districts of Konkan and Malabar, but does not cite any evidence.

based on inferences from Eusebius's comment on Pantaenus's mission to India and on oral traditions. Benedict Vadakkekara agrees that there was a Jewish presence in India, arguing that South India was "one of the greatest emporiums" in antiquity.[845] Neither Greek nor Roman texts mention Jewish communities in India, nor do the early Christian texts that mention missionaries who traveled to India contain any direct evidence for the presence of Jews there. Early Jewish and rabbinic texts confirm that Palestinian Jews had information about India but do not mention Jewish colonies in India. Rabbinic texts that mention Rabbi Juda "the Indian" and his son describe him as a proselyte; the relevant passages contain vocabulary that may have its origins in Sanskrit, Tamil or Dravidian (*b. Qidd.* 22b; *b. B. Bat.* 74b).[846] The earliest text that mentions Jewish merchants who live in India is a Jewish-Arabic document from the Cairo Genizah dating from the tenth to the twelfth century. Travelers such as al-Idrisi (ca. A.D. 1156) and Benjamin of Tudela (ca. A.D. 1167) report of Jewish communities on the Malabar coast.[847] The two copper plates that mention a Jew named Rabban who had been granted the area Anjuvannam (about 30 km north of Cochin), probably on account of services rendered to the raja of the region, date to A.D. 970-1035.[848] The question of whether Jews lived in India in the first century can be answered with certainty only on the basis of new archaeological discoveries.

Travelers on the overland routes to India stopped in cities, many of which had been founded or refounded by Alexander the Great or by the Seleucid rulers in the east, and whose population preserved a Hellenistic identity.

The Hellenistic identity of these cities even 150 years or more after they were established was connected with the gymnasium, the theater, the library and the temples. The excavations in Ai Khānum in northern Afghanistan show that people who lived in Bactria, some 5,000 km away from their ancestral homes, were interested in astronomy, philosophy and poetry, and they worshiped Greek and locals gods and heroes and were devoted to mystery cults.[849] A papyrus fragment discovered in the library of the palace in Ai Khānum attests to the interest of the population in Greek philosophy: the document contains parts of a Platonic or Aristotelian dialogue on Plato's doctrine of "Ideas." The Asoka inscriptions in Kandahar in Arachosia presuppose translators who translated Prākrit texts into Greek. This confirms that "as late as the third century it was commonplace for people in the distant East to have solid knowledge of linguistic and conceptual details of Platonic and Ar-

---

[845]Vadakkekara 1995, 133; he relies on William Logan, *Malabar* (2 vols.; New Delhi: Asian Educational Services, 1989 [1887]), 1:8; Väth 1925, 22; Puthiakunnel 1970, 187-88; Daniel 1986, 1:8. Väth refers to the "Black Jews" of Cochin in South Malabar, who trace their ancestry to Jews who emigrated during the reign of Kyros in the sixth century B.C. from Babylonia to India.

[846]See Walter J. Fischel, "India," *EncJud* 8:1349-50.

[847]See Walter J. Fischel, "The Present State of Research on the History of the Jews in India from the 16th Century On," in Caspi 1981, 23-33, esp. 24-25; idem, "Cochin in Jewish History," *PAAJR* 30 (1962): 37-59; idem, "The Exploration of the Jewish Antiquities of Cochin on the Malabar Coast," *JAOS* 87 (1967): 230-48; Tarn 1984, 434; David G. Mandelbaum, "A Case History of Judaism: The Jews of Cochin in India and Israel," in Caspi 1981, 211-30. Meir Bar-Ilan ("The Discovery of *The Words of Gad the Seer*," *JSP* 11 [1993]: 95-107, esp. 97 n. 5) dates the emigration of Jemenite Jews to India, who, according to the "Chronicle of the Jews of Cochin (Malabar)," brought with them books mentioned in the Old Testament, to the twelfth century.

[848]Fischel, "India," *EncJud* 8:1352-53.

[849]See Posch 1995, 23-44.

istotelian philosophy."[850] It is impossible to provide generalizing information about the religious situation in these cities. More recent excavations have shown some evidence for syncretistic tendencies. A monument found in Ai Khanum exhibits Greek iconographical forms; the inscription is in Greek (εὐχὴν ἀνέθηκεν Ἀτροσώκης Ὄζωι; "Atrosokes erected this as dedication to [the god] Oxos"), and the dedication involves the Iranian-Bactrian god Oxos, a local deity.[851]

The apostle Thomas could have communicated with the population living in the cities of northwest and southwest India in Greek, and in North India also in Aramaic. The Mauryan king Asoka (273-236 B.C.) published several of his edicts (e.g., in Kandahar) in a bilingual form, Greek and Aramaic.[852]

According to a tradition mentioned by Eusebius (*Hist. eccl.* 5.10.3) and in the Latin text *Passion of Bartholomew* (in *Acts Andr.* 2.1, 128-150), the apostle Bartholomew also preached in India. The late date of the tradition and the diverse details provided speak against the reliability of this tradition.[853]

Missionary Work in Babylonia and in Parthia?

Tens of thousands of Jews lived in Babylonia since the exile that began in 587 B.C., thus for over six hundred years by the first century. The Jewish communities were concentrated in the north on Adiabene with the capital Arbela, and on Osrhoene with the capital Edessa, an area that was ruled by the kings of Adiabene for a certain time. As was mentioned earlier, the royal house of Adiabene had converted to the Jewish faith in the first century at the time of Queen Helena. In the south the Jews lived predominantly in Seleukeia, Ctesiphon and Neardea. Josephus knows that tens of thousands of Jews lived in Parthia east of the Euphrates River (*A.J.* 11.133). There is some evidence for missionary outreach to Parthia at an early date, but the available information does not allow us to tell the full story of these missionary efforts.

1. Luke mentions in Acts 2:9 Jews from Parthia as among the first group of Diaspora Jews who witnessed the events of the Feast of Pentecost in A.D. 30 and who heard Peter preach the message of Jesus the Messiah. The origins of the Christian communities in Babylonia and in Parthia/Persia could have been connected with the Jewish festival pilgrims from Parthia, Media, Elam and Mesopotamia mentioned in Acts 2:9, as some of them may have been converted to faith in Jesus on the day of Pentecost.[854]

---

[850]Posch 1995, 30. On the Asoka inscriptions see §16.2 in the present work.

[851]See Posch 1995, 38.

[852]*I. Asoka.* See R. Schmitt, "Ex Occidente Lux: Griechen und griechische Sprache im hellenistischen Fernen Osten," *Palingenesia* 28 (1990): 41-58. See Lerner (1999, 77), who points out that Aramaic was the lingua franca in Bactria in the third century B.C.

[853]A. de Santos Otero, in Hennecke and Schneemelcher 1990-1997, 2:404-8; differently Dihle 1963, 61-62.

[854]Thus J. P. Asmussen, "Christians in Iran," *CHI* 3:924-48, esp. 924.

2. The Jewish Christian prophet Elchasai was active in Mesopotamia between
A.D. 100 and 120. Elchasai likely was a native of the area east of the Jordan River.
He wrote a book "in the third year of Trajan"[855] (i.e., A.D. 116/117) that contained, among other material, an apocalyptic vision, and he propagated a second baptism that would forgive all sins.[856] We have no information about Christian communities in Mesopotamia during this period whose origins go back to
the first century.

3. Eusebius informs his readers that Thaddaeus, one of the seventy disciples
of Jesus, proclaimed the gospel in Edessa (*Hist. eccl.* 1.13.4,11)—that is, in Osrhoene, a vassal state of the Parthians east of the Euphrates River. This late information cannot be confirmed in terms of its historical value for events in the
first century.

The apocryphal *Acts of Philip*, written in the fourth century, claims to know
that Peter, John and Philip all preached the gospel in Parthia: "When Philip, the
apostle of Christ, came to the empire of the Parthia, behold he met in a city Peter, the apostle of Christ. . . . The blessed John was there as well" (ἡνίκα δὲ Φίλιππος ὁ τοῦ Χριστοῦ ἀπόστολος κατῆλθεν εἰς τὴν ἀρχὴν τῆς Παρθίας, καὶ ἰδοὺ
εὗρεν κατά τινα πόλιν τὸν τοῦ Χριστοῦ ἀπόστολον Πέτρον . . . ἦν δὲ ἐκεῖ καὶ ὁ
μακάριος ᾽Ιωάννης [*Acts Phil.* 3:1, 2]).[857] According to Origen, Thomas was a
missionary in Parthia and in India (cf. Eusebius, *Hist. eccl.* 3.1.1; *Acts Phil.* 8:1).
François Bovon and Frédéric Amsler argue, therefore, that the statement in *Acts
Phil.* 3:1-2 is secondary: in the later Philip tradition Samaria seems to have been
replaced by Parthia.[858]

Parthia (Παρθία)[859] extended southeast of the Caspian Sea from the Elbruz Mountains in
the north to the Persian Gulf in the south. Parthia bordered in the north on Hyrcania, in
the east on Margiane, Areia and Drangiane, and in the west on Media. The political center
of Parthia was located in the western part, which was more populous and more wealthy.

---

[855]Hippolytus, *Haer.* 9.16.4.

[856]The *Book of Elchasai* is extant only in fragments, found in Hippolytus, *Haer.* 9.13-17, 10.29;
Epiphanius, *Haer.* 19; 30; Origen, in Eusebius, *Hist. eccl.* 6.38; see J. Irmscher, in Hennecke
and Schneemelcher 1990-1997, 2:619-23 (ET, 2:745-50). See Schoeps 1949, 325-34; idem, *RGG*
2:435; G. Strecker, *RAC* 5:1171-86; Luttikhuizen 1985; J. K. Elliott 1993, 685-86; R. Merkelbach,
"Mani," in Merkelbach 1997a, 401-30. On the Ebionites see G. Strecker, *RAC* 4:487-500; D. F.
Wright, *DLNTD* 313-17; Klijn and Reinink 1973; Pritz 1988.

[857]Bovon, Bouvier and Amsler 1999, 76-77, 78-79.

[858]F. Bovon, "Les Actes de Philippe," *ANRW* II.25.6 (1988): 4431-27, esp. 4451, 4479; cf. Amsler
1999, 144 n. 4, 147-48.

[859]H. Volkmann, *KP* 4:532-37; J. Whatmough, *OCD* 1117-18; J. Wiesehöfer, *DNP* 9:377-78; Karl-
Heinz Ziegler, *Die Beziehungen zwischen Rom und dem Partherreich* (Wiesbaden: Steiner,
1964); Malcom A. R. Colledge, *The Parthians* (New York: Praeger, 1967); Ehsan Yarshater,
CHI 3 (1983); D. Kennedy, "Parthia and Rome," in D. Kennedy 1996, 67-90; Josef Wiesehöfer,
ed., *Das Partherreich und seine Zeugnisse* (Historia: Einzelschriften 122; Stuttgart: Steiner,
1998); Lerner 1999.

In the Persian period Parthava was a satrapy that included Hyrcania. Alexander the Great did not change this arrangement, nor did the Seleucid kings. In the third century B.C. the Parni invaded Persia; they belonged to the nomadic Dahae, who lived in the region east of the Caspian Sea. The Parni settled in the satrapy of Parthava, which explains their name. The Arsacid dynasty dates the independence of Parthia to 247 B.C. The territorial gains of Mithradates I (176-138/137 B.C.) included Elymais, Babylonia and Media and secured independence from the Seleucid Empire. Mithradates invaded India as far as the Indus River and established Parthia as a major power. The summer capital was Ecbatana in the Zagros Mountains; during the winter the king moved to Seleukeia on the Tigris River, which used to be the second capital of the Seleucid Empire after Antioch on the Orontes. After the destruction of Seleukeia at the end of the second century B.C., the winter residence was moved to nearby Ctesiphon. In 66 B.C. the Parthian ruler Phraates III negotiated with Pompey the Euphrates River as the boundary between Parthia and Rome. In the first century B.C., Lucullus, Pompey, Gabinius and Crassus repeatedly attacked Parthia, and Parthian armies invaded the Roman province of Syria several times (Josephus, *A.J.*13.371, 384-385; *B.J.* 1.180-182). Eventually Phrates IV was forced to relinquish Armenia and agree to a peace treaty with Augustus in 20 B.C. that confirmed the Euphrates as the boundary. In the first century A.D. Gotarzes (A.D. 38-51) and Vardanes (A.D. 39-47) fought each other. At the time of Nero, Parthian and Roman armies fought each other again, mostly on Armenian soil. In the second century Trajan adopted aggressive politics directed against Parthia, attacking the Parthian heartland. In regard to economy and trade, Parthia had an important role in the trade between China, India and Syria. Recent discoveries in the area (e.g., coins) show that the Parthian kings were open to Greek culture. The Parthians seem to have adopted the Zoroastrian cult of fire, but they tolerated all religions.

The following description of regions and cities in which early Christian missionaries might have preached the gospel begins with areas in northern Mesopotamia (i.e., Osrhoene and Adiabene), before describing southern regions and cities.

Evangelism in Osrhoene?

The kingdom of Osrhoene, situated in the west of Parthia's sphere of influence, could be reached by early Christian missionaries via two routes: they could travel from Jerusalem via Damascus and Palmyra[860] to Nikephorion on the Euphrates River, and from there in a northerly direction to Edessa or in an easterly direction to Resaina. If missionary outreach to Mesopotamia and Parthia was or-

---

[860]See Daniel Schlumberger and Henri Seyrig, *Palmyre, bilan et perspectives* (Strasbourg: AECR, 1976); Jean Starcky and Michal Gawlikowski, *Palmyre* (Édition revue et augmentée des nouvelles découvertes; Paris: Librairie d'Amérique et d'Orient, 1985); Iain Browning, *Palmyra* (London: Chatto & Windus, 1979); Richard Stoneman, *Palmyra and Its Empire: Zenobia's Revolt Against Rome* (Ann Arbor: University of Michigan Press, 1992); Ball 2000, 74-87; Gérard Degeorge, *Palmyre: Métropole caravanière* (Paris: Imprimerie nationale, 2001). On more recent excavations see A. Schmidt-Colinet, "Kurzbericht über die Arbeiten in Palmyra 2001," *Forum Archaeologiae* 20.9 (2001): <http://farch.net>. The bishop Marinos of Palmyra attended the Council of Nicea.

ganized in Antioch in Syria, then the missionaries would have traveled via Imma, Gindaros and Kyrrhos to Zeugma on the Euphrates River, and from there to Edessa. Han Drijvers believes that Edessa probably had contact with Christians in the first century.[861]

Osrhoene (᾽Οσροηνή)[862] was a region in the northeastern corner of Mesopotamia; it bordered on the Euphrates River in the west and in the south; the eastern boundary was the Aborras River (mod. Habur; Khabur), and the northern boundary was Mount Masius (mod. Karaca Dağ). The local dynasty, whose rulers were called Abgar, achieved independence from the Seleucid Empire in 132 B.C. The capital of the kingdom was Edessa. Osrhoene was a vassal state of the Parthians in the first centuries B.C. and A.D. Since the kingdom was the border area between the Roman and the Parthian Empires, the political situation was difficult. After the campaigns of L. Verus in the second century A.D., Osrhoene came under direct Roman rule and later became a Roman province. The kings of Osrhoene in the first century were Abgar V Ukhama (4 B.C.—A.D. 7; Tacitus calls him Rex Arabum Acharus [*Ann* 12.12.2]), Manu IV bar Manu (A.D. 7-13), Abgar V Ukhama (A.D. 13-50), Manu V bar Abgar (A.D. 50-57), and Manu VI bar Abgar (A.D. 71-91). Pliny describes the population of Osrhoene as Arab (*Nat.* 6.9.25).

The journey from Jerusalem via Damascus (265 km), Palmyra (230 km), Nikephorion (210 km) and Carrhae (35 km) to Edessa (40 km) is 780 km; the journey from Antioch via Imma (40 km), Gindaros (60 km), Kyrrhos (50 km) and Zeugma (110 km) to Edessa (90 km) is about 300 km. East of Edessa were the cities Antiochia Arabis and Resaina.

Zeugma (Ζεῦγμα; mod. Kavunlu, former Belkis, Turkey)[863] was located at the most important crossing of the Euphrates River and belonged to Syria. Seleukos I founded two colonies in 300 B.C.: Seleukeia on the west bank and Apamea on the east bank of the Euphrates River, known together by the generic name Zeugma ("junction"). It is possible that the Romans stationed the Legio X Fretensis since A.D. 18 in Zeugma; in the second century Zeugma was home to the Legio III Scythica. In the summer of the year 2000 the ruins of ancient Zeugma were flooded after the completion of the Birecik Dam.

Edessa (῎Εδεσσα; former Urhai; mod. Şanliurfaı; Urfa)[864] was situated on the Skirtos

---

[861]Han J. W. Drijvers, "Die Götter Edessas," in Şahin et al. 1978, 262-83, esp. 263; he thinks that the second century is a more likely setting for a mission to Edessa, however.

[862]W. Röllig, *KP* 4:370-71; M. S. Drower et al., *OCD* 1081; K. Kessler, *DNP* 9:88; Angeli Bertinelli, "I Romani oltre l'Eufrate nel II secolo d. C. (le province di Assiria, di Mesopotamia e de Osroene)," *ANRW* II.9.1 (1979): 3-45; Ross 2001.

[863]B. Spuler, PW 10.A (1972): 251-52; E. Olshausen, *KP* 5:1516; J.-P. Rey-Coquais, *PECS* 1000; M. S. Drower, *OCD* 1636; J. Wagner, *Seleukeia am Euphrat/Zeugma* (BTAVO B 10; Wiesbaden: Reichert, 1976); David Kennedy, *The Twin Towns of Zeugma on the Euphrates: Rescue Work and Historical Studies* (JRASup 27; Portsmouth, R.I.: Journal of Roman Archaeology, 1998); Pollard 2000, 257-61, and passim; on Apamea on the Orontes see ibid., 262-66. See <http://www.zeugma2000.com>.

[864]E. Meyer, PW 5.2 (1905): 1933-38; H. Treidler, "Edessa 2," *KP* 2:197-98; J. B. Segal, "Antioch by the Callirhoe," *PECS* 61; E. W. Gray et al., *OCD* 505; T. Leisten, "Edessa 2," *DNP* 3:875; Jones 1937, 217, 221-23; Tubach 1986, 52-56, 63-125; J. Segal 1970; Han J. W. Drijvers, "Die Götter Edessas," in Şahin et al. 1978, 263-83; idem, *Cults and Beliefs at Edessa* (Leiden: Brill, 1980); Tubach 1986; Millar 1993, 456-67, 472-88, 553-62; Ball 2000, 87-96; Ross 2001. Inscriptions: Han J. W. Drijvers and John F. Healey, *The Old Syriac Inscriptions of Edessa and Osrhoene: Texts, Translations and Commentary* (Handbuch der Orientalistik 1.42; Leiden: Brill, 1999).

River (mod. Kara Koyun), a tributary of the Euphrates, as was the Balihi River (mod. Balikh). Edessa was the cult center of the moon-god during the neo-Assyrian period. Seleukos I refounded the city in 303/302 B.C. as a military colony, which sometimes was called Antiocheia Kallirhoë. When Osrhoene became independent in 132 B.C., Edessa became capital of the kingdom. The city was damaged during the Parthian campaign of L. Varus in the second century; it later became a Roman colony. Literary and archaeological sources document the worship of Bel, Nebo, Atargatis, Bath Nikkal, Hadad, the goddesses Gadlat and Tarata, Tyche, the sun accompanied by Azizos (Ares) and Monimos (Hermes), the moon (Sin) worshiped as Marālahe (Lord of the Gods), and the eagle-god. The inhabitants of Edessa were Arameans and Greeks, and there was a Jewish community, as three funerary inscriptions written in Hebrew attest.[865] Bardesanes (Bar Daisān), a member of the court of King Abgar VIII (A.D. 179-214), became a Christian around A.D. 180. Subsequently the Christian faith became the state religion. Bardesanes later was regarded as a heretic.[866] The bishops of Edessa were the most important leaders of the church in Syria since the fourth century. The bishop Aïthalas of Edessa attended the Council of Nicea. Ephraem was one of the most significant theologians of the Syrian church.

Antiochia Arabis (mod. Viranşehir)[867] was situated on the road from Edessa to Nisibis in the east; it later was called Antoninopolis.

Carrhae (Κάρραι; mod. Altınbaşak; Harran),[868] about 40 km southwest of Edessa on the crossroads of several important trade routes, is mentioned in the Old Testament and in the Mari Letters as Haran. Carrhae was a provincial capital in the Assyrian Empire; the Seleucid kings stationed Macedonian troops in the city. The Roman general M. Licinius Crassus lost an important battle against the Parthians in 53 B.C. in the vicinity. Carrhae remained Parthian even under the rule of the kings of Osrhoene.

Resaina (mod. Tell-Fakhariya, near Ras al-Ain; Syria)[869] was located on the route from Hierapolis (Bambyke) via Batnae and Carrhae to Thannuris and Shadikanni into the valley of the Aborras (mod. Habur), a tributary of the Euphrates River. Remains of the Assyrian and the Hellenistic periods survive. The history of the city during the early Roman Empire is unknown. Resaina became a Roman colony in the second century.

The origins of the Christian community in Edessa are unclear. The only solid date is provided in the *Chronicle of Edessa* (written ca. A.D. 550), which begins with the account of a flood in Edessa in the month of November in A.D. 201 that damaged "the sanctuary (*baykla*) of the church of the Christians."[870] The tombstone of Bishop Aberkios of Hierapolis in inner Phrygia, discovered in Phry-

[865]See Schürer 3:9.
[866]On Bardesanes see S. Brock and S. Zamponi, *DNP* 2:446; Han J. W. Drijvers, *Bardaisan of Edessa* (Assen: Van Gorcum, 1965); Ball 2000, 94-95; Ross 2001, 119-23. Downing (1992, 271-72) suggests that Bardesanes was a Christian-Cynic preacher.
[867]M. Roaf, *BAGRW* 1270, map 89.
[868]F. H. Weissbach, PW 10 (1919): 2009-21; W. Röllig, *KP* 3:129-30; W. Kramer, *RAC* 15:634-50; J. B. Segal, *PECS* 200-201; S. Sherwin-White, *OCD* 294; K. Kessler, "Harran," *DNP* 5:166-67.
[869]Pollard 2000, 58-59, 273-74; M. Roaf, *BAGRW* 1278, map 89.
[870]See Ludwig Hallier, *Untersuchungen über die Edessenische Chronik: Mit dem syrischen Text und einer Übersetzung* (Leipzig: Hinrichs, 1892); J. Segal 1970, 24-25; Brock 1992, 221-22.

gia,[871] who visited Syria and Nisibis east of the Euphrates River on his extensive travels, documents Christians in this area for A.D. 150-200.[872] According to Eusebius, Jesus sent Thaddaeus, one of the Seventy, "in the 340th year" (i.e., A.D. 28/ 29) to Edessa, who healed the king and led him to faith in Jesus.[873] This Thaddaeus probably is to be identified with the Jewish-Christian missionary Addai, who engaged in missionary work in Edessa and in Adiabene, according to *Apocr. Jas.* 36:15-24 and the *Doctrina Addai*. Several scholars accept that these references to a missionary with the name "Addai" are historically authentic, dating his mission to Edessa around A.D. 100.[874] Helmut Waldmann suggests that the mission of Thaddaeus to Edessa should be dated to A.D. 33/34, pointing to the exchange of letters between Abgar and the emperor Tiberius mentioned in the *Doctrina Addai*.[875] Other scholars regard this tradition as a legend of the third century.[876] But even such skeptics generally reckon with Christians in Edessa in the early second century.[877]

The general outline of Eusebius's account corresponds to the description in the work *Doctrina Addai*.[878] This text states that Addai, "one of the seventy-two apostles" (cf. Lk 10:17), was sent to Edessa by the apostle Judas Thomas, and that a Jew named Tobias ben Tobias facilitated an encounter with King Akbar Ukāmā (Abgar V, "the Black One," A.D. 13-50)—who had already exchanged letters with Jesus[879]—who subsequently was converted through the preaching of Addai. A disciple of Addai named Aggai continued the missionary work "in all of Mesopotamia." *Doctrina Addai* was written around A.D. 300 (the oldest extant copy on which the modern editions are based dates to ca. A.D. 500; it seems that the text was redacted ca. A.D. 400-450) and cannot be used uncritically as a source for events in the first century. The story of King Abgar, who supposedly

---

[871]Editio princeps: T. Preger (1901). The tombstone is stored in the Vatican Museum; see Guarducci 4:377-86 (photo, ibid., 4:378-79 [fig. 111 a-b]); W. Wischmeyer 1980, 22-47; G. Filippi, in *Le iscrizioni dei cristiani in Vaticano,* ed. I. Di Stefano Manzella (Rome: Quasar, 1997), 220-22; Merkelbach 1997b, 381-99.

[872]Ross 2001, 117-18; cf. Bundy 1992, 971; Merkelbach 1997b.

[873]Eusebius, *Hist. eccl.* 1.13; *Doctrina Addai* 11-21 (Howard, ed., *The Teaching of Addai*).

[874]Harnack 1924, 2:680-81, 684-85, 689 (cf. ET, 2:143-44); Lietzmann 1935, 95; Barnard 1968, 162. Ball (2000, 94-95) is undecided, perhaps on account of Western or Roman-Catholic prejudices concerning Eastern traditions.

[875]Waldmann 1996, 23. He argues that the emphasis on the humility of Christ and the reference to his descent to Hades (later deemphasized) are evidence for the authenticity of Eusebius's information about the ministry of Thaddaeus. Cf. M. Black 1967, 281-86; see the critique in Brock 1992, 234 n. 57. The exchange of letters between Abgar and Tiberius is mentioned also by Moses of Khoren in his *History of Greater Armenia,* written in the fifth century; see Sordi 1986, 17.

[876]See Brock 1992, 221-29; Bundy 1992, 971; Beskow 1970, 105; Desreumaux 1993, 25-29 ("une figure apocryphe").

[877]See Lane Fox 1986, 279-80; Tubach 1986, 49; Chaumont 1988; Brock 1992, 221-24, 228.

[878]See Brock 1992, 213-21. The edition by G. Howard (1981) reproduces the text of G. Phillips (1876) and provides a new translation. Cf. J. K. Elliott 1993, 541-42.

[879]See H. J. W. Drijvers, in Hennecke and Schneemelcher 1987-1989, 1:389-95 (ET, 1:492-500); cf. J. K. Elliott 1993, 538-40.

wrote a letter to Jesus—the best-known version comes from Eusebius (*Hist. eccl.* 1.13)—says probably more about the churches in Edessa in the third and fourth centuries than about the history of the Christian community in Edessa in the first century.[880] Walter Bauer interpreted the narrative of the *Doctrina Addai* as a fictitious story created around A.D. 300,[881] while F. C. Burkitt interpreted the text as a reminiscence of the historical conversion of King Abgar VIII (A.D. 179-214) that was read back to Abgar V (A.D. 13-50).[882] Han Drijvers has demonstrated that the *Doctrina Addai* should be interpreted against the background of Manicheism.[883] It seems probable, however, that the text contains some historical recollection—for example, the notice that after his arrival in Edessa, Addai lived in the house of Tobias, who was the son of a Tobias from Palestine (*Doctrina Addai* 5-6). Even though the text paints a somewhat negative picture of the Palestinian Jews as people who are responsible for Jesus' crucifixion, the Jews of Edessa are described as being friendly toward the Jewish Christian missionaries.[884]

The inscription of Aberkios of Hierapolis, which attests Christians in Nisibis for the second century, and the *Chronicle of Edessa*, which attests Christians in Edessa for the time around A.D. 200, have already been mentioned as reliable sources for Christianity in eastern Syria. Further sources include the *Demonstrationes* of Afrahat, written between A.D. 337 and 345, and the writings of Ephraem, who was active as pastor and theologian in Nisibis (until A.D. 363) and in Edessa (until his death in A.D. 373).[885] The bishops Aïthalas of Edessa and Iakobos of Nisibis attended the Council in Nicea in A.D. 325.

Evangelism in Adiabene?

We do not know when the first missionaries reached Adiabene. According to the Chronicle of Arbela, a Syrian text written in the sixth century by a Christian with the name "Meschīhā-Zekā,"[886] a certain Mār Peqīdā was appointed bishop of the church in Adiabene by his teacher Addai around A.D. 100. It is striking that his successors also have Jewish names: Shemshōn, Ishāq, Abraham, Nōch, Hābēl. This seems to suggest, plausibly, that the first Christians in this region were converted Jews, as in other young churches in other regions. Even though

---

[880]Ross 2001, 117, 131-32; on the Abgar legend see also Abrahamsen 1995, 179-91.

[881]Bauer 1934, 7-45; followed by, for example, H. Koester, "ΓΝΩΜΑΙ ΔΙΑΦΟΡΟΙ," *HTR* 58 (1965): 279-318; H. J. W. Drijvers, in Hennecke and Schneemelcher 1987, 1:389-95 (ET, 1:492-500).

[882]Burkitt 1904; cf. Barnard 1968; J. Segal 1980. The suggestion by F. C. Burkitt ("Syriac-Speaking Christianity," *CAH* 12:492-96) that the apostle Addai should be equated with Tatian is unconvincing; see Emily J. Hunt, *Christianity in the Second Century: The Case of Tatian* (Routledge Early Church Monographs; New York: Routledge, 2003), 144-45.

[883]Drijvers 1970; idem, "Mani und Bardaisan: Ein Beitrag zur Vorgeschichte des Manichäismus," in *Mélanges d'histoire des religions offerts à Henri-Charles Puech* (Paris: Presses Universitaires de France, 1974), 124-46; idem, "Addai und Mani, Christentum und Manichäismus im dritten Jahrhundert in Syrien," *Oriens Christiana Analecta* 221 (1983): 171-85; idem, "Syrian Christianity and Judaism," in Rajak et al. 1992; cf. Ross (2001, 135-36), who relies on Drijvers and does not seem to know the study by Waldmann.

[884]See Barnard 1968, 162-63.

[885]See Brock 1992, 221.

[886]See Peter Kawerau, *Die Chronik von Arbela* (2 vols.; CSCO 467-468; Leuven: Peeters, 1985).

this "chronicle" is not entirely without value,[887] it cannot be used as a reliable source for events in the first century.[888]

Adiabene (᾿Αδιαβηνή)[889] was the region of the two Zab rivers in the mountains east of the upper Tigris River in northern Mesopotamia; today it is the Kurdish region in northeastern Iraq and northern Iran. Adiabene, with its capital, Arbela, seems to have been an administrative district in the Seleucid Empire, later to become a satrapy in the Parthian Empire. In the first century A.D. Adiabene was ruled by kings who were dependent upon the Parthians and were repeatedly drawn into the military controversies between Rome and the Parthians. Josephus reports that the dynasty of King Izates II (A.D. 30-54) converted to Judaism (*A.J.* 20.17-53; *B.J.* 5.474-475; see §16.2 in the present work).[890] Izates supported in A.D. 38/39 the Parthian king Artabanos III and was rewarded with the city Nisibis. In A.D. 116 Trajan conquered Adiabene and organized the region as the Roman province of Assyria.

Nisibis (Νίσιβις; mod. Nusaybin),[891] about 240 km east of Edessa on the upper Hirmas (or Mygdonios) River (mod. Jaghjagh), a tributary of the Euphrates, today a Turkish-Syrian border town, was located on the royal road leading to the West.[892] Nisibis was an important trade center, and after 886 B.C. it was the capital of a province in the Assyrian Empire. Nisibis was the center of the towns ("in Halah, on the Habor, the river of Gozan, and in the cities of the Medes") in which the ten tribes of Israel's northern kingdom were exiled after 722 B.C., according to 2 Kings 17:6; 18:11.[893] In the Seleucid period the city was called Antiocheia Mygdonia. After 129 B.C. Nisibis belonged to the Parthian Empire, prior to being occupied in 80 B.C. by Tigranes of Armenia, who fortified the city. Artabanos III retook the city for the Parthians and gave it in A.D. 38/39 to his vassal Izates of Adiabene (Josephus, *A.J.* 20.68). Nisibis became Roman in the second century. The population consisted of Arameans, Arabs, Greeks and Parthians. Josephus (*A.J.* 20.3.3) and the Talmud (*b. Qidd.* 72a) attest the existence of a Jewish community. Nisibis had a Christian community by the second century; the first documented bishop was Babu (ca. A.D. 300). His successor, James, who died in A.D. 338, attended the Council of Nicea. The Syrian church father Ephraem was active until A.D. 363 in Nisibis, which later became the intellectual center of the Nestorians (who sent the first missionaries to China).

Nineveh/Ninos (Νίνος; mod. Kuyunjik, Iraq),[894] about 190 km southeast of Nisibis on the east bank of the Tigris River (near mod. Mosul), was the capital of Assyria in the seventh century B.C. After being destroyed by Cyrus II in 612 B.C., the city was rebuilt. Strabo mentions only Ninos, who was the founder, the city's destruction and the plain of Aturia,

---

[887]See Kawerau, *Die Chronik von Arbela;* J. Neusner, "The Conversion of Adiabene to Christianity," *Numen* 14 (1966): 144-50; Chaumont 1988; Bundy 1992, 973.

[888]See J. P. Asmussen, "Christians in Iran," *CHI* 3:924-48, esp. 926-27.

[889]W. Sontheimer, *KP* 1:64-65; J. Oelsner and B. Ego, *DNP* 2:112; M. S. Drower, *OCD* 12. See *Tübingen Bible Atlas* [*TAVO*] B V 4.

[890]See J. Neusner, "The Conversion of Adiabene to Judaism," *JBL* 83 (1964): 60-66; Schiffman 1987; Broer 1994; see also Schürer 3:9-10, 163-65; S. Cohen 1987; Gilbert 1991; Wander 1998, 62-64, 224.

[891]J. Sturm, PW 17.1 (1936): 714-57; W. Röllig, *KP* 4:138-39; J. Whatmough, *OCD* 1046; K. Kessler, *DNP* 8:962-63; Fiey 1977; Pollard 2000, 63, 272-73, 286-87.

[892]See Seibert 1985, 23.

[893]See Schürer 3:8 n. 18.

[894]S. M. Dalley, *OCD* 1045; E. Frahm, *DNP* 8:951-52.

in which Nineveh was located (2.1.31; 16.1.1-3).

Arbela (Ἄρβελα; mod. Erbil),[895] about 80 km southeast of Edessa in the east of the Adiabene, is mentioned in connection with the victory of Alexander the Great against the Persians at Gaugamela in 331 B.C. Strabo describes the city as Babylonian (16.1.3). Arbela was the capital of the Adiabene in the Parthian period.

Jewish communities are also attested in Nikephorion and Dura-Europos, two cities in northern Babylonia.

Nikephorion (Νικηφόριον, later Kallinikos; mod. Raqqa, Syria),[896] 210 km northeast of Palmyra on the road from Ctesiphon and Babylon on the Euphrates in northwestern Babylonia, was founded by Alexander the Great or by Seleukos I. A synagogue is attested for the fourth century (Ambrose, *Ep.* 40-41), although a Jewish community may have existed much earlier.[897]

Dura-Europos (mod. Salihiya; Syria),[898] on the middle Euphrates about 210 km southeast of Nikephorion and 420 km northwest of Seleukeia on the Tigris, on the main road from Syria to the Euphrates River, was founded around 312 B.C. as a military colony by the Seleucids. After 150 B.C. the city had a Hippodamian layout; attested are an agora, a temple of Zeus Megistos, of Artemis, of Mithras and of other gods, a palace, and houses built according to the Greek model. After 100 B.C. Dura was a Parthian border town for 250 years, but the inhabitants continued to speak Greek. There was a Palmyrene colony of merchants in Dura in the first century who had their own temple.[899] The excavations (since 1928) brought to light a synagogue with colorful frescoes from the third century.[900] The synagogue was located in the second block north of the main gate; a temple of Tyche was in the first block, a temple of Mithras in the second block, on the northwest corner of the block was the temple of the Palmyrene gods, and in the block to the east was a temple of Adonis. A dozen inscriptions, papyri and graffiti were found in connection with the synagogue.[901] One of the houses in Dura was transformed

---

[895]H. Treidler, "Arbela 1," *KP* 1:495; K. Kessler, *DNP* 1:973.

[896]E. F. Weidner, "Nikephorion 2," PW 17.1 (1936): 309-10; E. Olshausen, *KP* 4:102; K. Kessler, *DNP* 8:908-9; J. P. Brown, *BAGRW* 1046, map 68; *Tübingen Bible Atlas* [*TAVO*] B V 4.

[897]See Schürer 3:9.

[898]Kroll, PWSup 5 (1931): 183-86; H. Treidler, "Dura 2," *KP* 2:179-80; C. Hopkins, *PECS* 286-87; M. S. Drower et al., *OCD* 574-75; T. Leisten, *DNP* 3:846-47; Millar 1993, 445-50; Nigel Pollard, "The Roman Army as 'Total Institution' in the Near East? Dura-Europos as a Case Study," in D. Kennedy 1996, 211-28; S. B. Downey, "The Transformation of Seleukcid Dura-Europos," in Fentress 2000, 155-72; Ball 2000, 166-70, and passim; Pollard 2000, 25-26, 44-67, 143-44, 243-44. Excavations: M. I. Rostovtzeff et al., eds., *The Excavations at Dura-Europos: Final Report* (8 vols.; New Haven: Yale University Press, 1929-1977).

[899]Lucida Dirven, "The Nature of the Trade between Palmyra and Dura-Europos," *Aram* 8 (1996): 39-54, esp. 51.

[900]See Carl H. Kraeling, *The Excavations at Dura-Europos: Final Report VIII, Part 1, The Synagogue* (New Haven: Yale University Press, 1957); J. Gutmann, ed., *The Dura-Europos Synagogue: A Reevaluation (1932-1972)* (SFSHJ 25; Atlanta: Scholars Press, 1992 [1973]); Kraabel 1979, 481-83; Dan Urman and Paul V. M. Flesher, eds., *Ancient Synagogues: Historical Analysis and Archaeological Discovery* (2 vols.; StPB 47.1-2; Leiden: Brill, 1995), vol. 2; Beard, North and Price 1998, 2:108-10; L. Levine 2000, 234-39.

[901]See Schürer 3:10-13.

into a Christian house church between A.D. 240 and 250.[902]

Jewish communities are attested in southern Babylonia (the southern part of modern Iraq) as well: Josephus reports that a Jewish merchant named Ananias visited the small kingdom of Charakene (Mesene) and conversed with Izates, later the king of Adiabene, about the Jewish faith (A.J. 20.34). Josephus informs his readers that the Jews of Babylonia lived mainly in Nehardea in the south as well as in Nisibis (A.J. 18.310-313, 379). Jews are also attested for the important cities Ctesiphon and Seleukeia on the Tigris. We do not know when the first missionaries brought the gospel to this region. Churches with bishops are attested for the third century; probably there were Christian communities already in the second century.[903]

The comment of Josephus has been understood as evidence for a second Nisibis, located in southern Babylonia,[904] which is questioned by other scholars.[905]

  Spasinou Charax (Σπασίνου Χάραξ, Charax Spasini; Mesene, Arab., Maysan; Jebel Khayabi),[906] situated in the delta of the Tigris and Euphrates rivers, was founded as Alexandria in 324 B.C. and refounded as Antiocheia in 166 B.C. Since 140 B.C. the city was the capital of the small kingdom of Charakene, which became independent, two years after the death of the Seleucid king Antiochos VII in 127 B.C., under King Hyspaosines. Many of the rulers of the kingdom of Charakene came from the royal families of the Parthian Empire. The kingdom lost its independence only in A.D. 224, when it was absorbed by the Sasanid Empire. According to Pliny (*Nat.* 6.31.136) and Ptolemaios (6.3.3), Spasinou Charax was a flourishing city because of its location on the northern end of the Persian Gulf and its role in the trade with India. Inscriptions found in Palmyra attest an influential Palmyrene trade colony in Spasinou Charax.[907] The city had a Jewish community. A Jewish woman named Sarah, who came from Mesene, was buried in Beth Shearim in the third or the fourth century (*CIJ* II 1124). Later rabbis discuss the problem of the ritual purity of Jews from Mesene (*b. Qidd.* 71b).[908] A Christian community is attested for A.D. 310, when a bishop of Mesene is mentioned.[909] In the fourth century a Christian missionary from Me-

---

[902]Carl H. Kraeling, *The Excavations at Dura-Europos: Final Report VIII, Part 2, The Christian Building* (New Haven: Yale University Press, 1967); White 1996-1997, 2:123-34; Beard, North and Price 1998, 2:110-11.

[903]See Bin Seray 1996, 318.

[904]See Schürer 3:8 with nn. 18-20.

[905]See J. Neusner, "The Jews East of the Euphates and the Roman Empire I: 1st-3rd Centuries A.D.," *ANRW* II.9.1 (1979): 46-69, esp. 47.

[906]A. Dietrich, *KP* 1:1130-31; D. N. Wilber, *PECS* 60; J. Oelsner, *DNP* 2:1097; S. A. Nodelman, "A Preliminary History of Characene," *Berytus* 13 (1959-1960): 111-19; Oppenheimer 1983, 433-36; Hamad M. Bin Seray, "Spasinou Charax and Its Commercial Relations with the East through the Arabian Gulf," *Aram* 8 (1996): 15-23; D. T. Potts, "The Roman Relationship with the *Persicus sinus* from the Rise of Spasinou Charax (127 B.C.) to the Reign of Shapur II (A.D. 309-379)," in Alcock 1997, 89-107. A. Hausleiter et al. (*BAGRW* 1328, s.v. "Jebel Khayabir" [map 93]) localize, though with a question mark, Spasinou Charax 4 km east of the Tigris River.

[907]See Bin Seray, "Spasinou Charax," 18-21; Potts, "Roman Relationship," 94-97.

[908]See Schürer 3:9.

[909]Fiey 1965-1968, 3:263-66.

sene named ʿAwdischoʿ was active in eastern Arabia and in the region of Bahrain.[910]

Seleukeia on the Tigris (Σελεύκεια ἡ ἐπὶ τῷ Τίγρει; Tell Omar, Iraq),[911] on the west bank of the Tigris River about 95 km northeast of Babylon (32 km south of Baghdad), about 500 km north of the Persian Gulf, was founded by Seleukos I in 305 B.C. as the royal residence of the Seleucid Empire, on the river crossing of the important route to Ecbatana and Media to the East (in 293 B.C. Antioch on the Orontes became the capital of the Seleucid Empire). Seleukeia was linked with the Euphrates River by a canal. It was planned as a much larger city than Antioch on the Orontes: the city wall was 6.7 km long. Seleukeia was an important center of the Asian trade. The city had about 600,000 inhabitants, mostly Babylonians, Macedonians, Greeks and also Jews (Pliny, *Nat.* 6.30.122). Since 141 B.C. the Parthians controlled the region; they permitted the city to retain its Greek institutions. The Parthian troops and officials lived in Ctesiphon on the opposite bank of the Tigris. During the reign of Artabanos III the city supported the opposing king Tiridates; it was occupied seven years later in A.D. 43 by Vardanes and severely punished (Tacitus, *Ann.* 11.8-9). In the first century A.D. Seleukeia was still an important center of trade in the region. Famous sons of the city included the Stoic philosopher Diogenes (240-150 B.C.) and the Epicurean Diogenes (d. 144 B.C.). According to Josephus, there was a Jewish community in Seleukeia (*A.J.* 18.372-377). The limited excavations partially unearthed an "administrative block," which might have been a palace, and a heroon.

Ctesiphon (Κτησιθῶν; mod. Qatusif; al-Maʾaridh)[912] was founded probably by Macedonians. Strabo calls it a "large village" (i.e., an unfortified city) with a large population; Ctesiphon served as the winter residence of the Parthian kings and displayed Parthian works of art (16.1.16). The city was destroyed in the Parthian campaign of L. Verus in A.D. 165, but it was rebuilt in the subsequent years. Josephus reports that Ctesiphon had a Jewish community (*A.J.* 18.377-378). The later tradition that Mari, a disciple of Addai the Christian missionary in Edessa, brought the gospel to Ctesiphon at the end of the first or the beginning of the second century could well be historical.[913] The Jewish Christians Abraham and Yaʿqub (James) who are mentioned in the tradition may indeed have been leading Christians and missionaries in the region in the second century; the assertion that they were relatives of Jesus should not be rejected out of hand, since such claims are made very rarely in the Christian tradition for individual persons.[914]

Neardea (Nehardea; about 12 km northwest of Tell al-Hargawi),[915] on the Euphrates River, about 40 km west of Seleukeia, had a Jewish community that was the center of a quasi-independent "state" between A.D. 20 and 35 under the leadership of the brothers Hasinai and Hanilai (Josephus, *A.J.* 18.310-313, 379).[916] The most famous synagogue of the Jews in Babylonia was located in Shaf-yateb, a quarter of Neardea.[917] Palmyrenes destroyed Neardea in A.D. 259.

---

[910]See Bin Seray 1996, 320.

[911]W. Röllig, "Seleukia 1," *KP* 5:83-85; D. N. Wilber, *PECS* 822; M. S. Drower and S. Sherwin-White, *OCD* 1380; Oppenheimer 1983, 207-23.

[912]E. Honigmann, PWSup 4 (1924): 1102-19; K. Ziegler, "Ktesiphon 2," *KP* 3:370; M. Colledge, *OCD* 412; S. R. Hauser, *DNP* 6:879; Oppenheimer 1983, 198-207.

[913]See Fiey (1970, 39-43), who mentions a date of A.D. 79-116.

[914]See Bauckham 1990, 68-70.

[915]See Oppenheimer 1983, 276-93; M. Road and S. J. Simpson, *BAGRW* 1305, map 91.

[916]See Schürer 3:7 n. 13, 8; Oppenheimer 1983, 276-93.

[917]Cf. *b. Roš. Haš.* 24b; *b. ʾAbod. Zar.* 43b; *b. Nid.* 13a; *b. Meg.* 29a. See Aharon Oppenheimer, "Babylonian Synagogues with Historical Associations," in Urman and Flesher 1995, 1:40-48, esp. 40-43; L. Levine 2000, 270-71.

Missionary Work in Scythia?

Origen states that the apostle Andrew went to Scythia after A.D. 70—that is, to the Bosporan kingdom on the north coast of the Black Sea: "The holy apostles and disciples of our Savior were scattered throughout the whole world. Thomas, as tradition relates, obtained by lot Parthia, Andrew Scythia" (in Eusebius, *Hist. eccl.* 3.1.1). This tradition agrees with the assertion of the apocryphal *Acts of Andrew and Matthias,* written in the fourth century, whose author asserts that the apostle Andrew engaged in missionary work among the "man-eaters" (ἀνθρω-ποφάγοι, *anthrōpophagoi*).[918] The Greeks localized the cannibals on the north coast of the Black Sea (Herodotus 4.106). The apocryphal *Acts of Andrew* does not mention a mission of Andrew to Scythia; the author describes only his ministry in Pontus, Thrace, Macedonia and particularly in Achaia. The view that *Acts of Andrew and Matthias* was originally a part of *Acts of Andrew* is disputed by Jean-Marc Prieur.[919] Francis Dvornik suggested that Andrew may have traveled from Pontic Sinope to Scythia,[920] from where he could have traveled via Thrace and Macedonia to Achaia. The historical value of the tradition of a mission to Scythia by Andrew that repeatedly surfaces in (late) church traditions is generally regarded as negligible.[921]

Scythia (Σκυθία),[922] the region between the Danube River in the west and the Don River in the east, between the Caucasus Mountains and the Volga River, was known by the Greeks and Romans as the territory to the north and to the east of the world that they knew. The Scythians consisted of numerous tribal confederations: the Sacae in the east, the Callipidae (Hellenoscythai) in the hinterland of Olbia, the Alazonae to the north and the Aroteres. The war against the Persian king Darius I in 514/513 B.C. fostered the political unification of the Scythian tribes. They formed a kingdom in the fourth century B.C.

---

[918]See A. de Santos Otero, in Hennecke and Schneemelcher 1997, 2:400 (ET, 2:576); J. K. Elliott 1993, 240-42; for a new English translation see ibid., 283-99. On the date of *Acts of Andrew and Matthias* see also A. Hilhorst and P. J. Lalleman, in Bremmer 2000, 12.

[919]See A. Santos Otero, in Hennecke and Schneemelcher 1997, 2:400 (ET, 2:397); Prieur, in ibid., 2:99; idem 1989, 1:32-35; cf. the discussion between Prieur and D. R. MacDonald in *Semeia* 38 (1986): 9-39.

[920]F. Dvornik, *The Idea of Apostolicity in Byzantium and the Legend of the Apostle Andrew* (Cambridge, Mass.: Harvard University Press, 1958), 199-200.

[921]Prieur 1989, 1:68-72; J. K. Elliott 1993, 236. Lipsius (1883-1890, 1:609-10) believed that Andrew could have made a missionary journey to the regions bordering on the Black Sea.

[922]P. Kretschmer, PW 2.A (1921): 923-42; C. Danoff, *KP* 5:241-42; D. C. Braund, *OCD* 1374-75; Renate Rolle, *Die Welt der Skythen* (Lucerne: Bucher, 1980; English: *The World of the Scythians* [Berkeley: University of California Press, 1989]); Gocha Tsetskhladze, ed., *Greek and Roman Settlements on the Black Sea Coast* (Colloquenda Pontica 1; Bradford: Loid, 1994); Heinen 2001. On the region of the Black Sea see also John M. Fossey, ed., *Antiquitates Propontiacae, Circumponticae et Caucasicae II* (McGill University Monographs in Classical Archaeology and History 19; Amsterdam: Gieben, 1997). Inscriptions: Dionisie M. Pippidi and Iorgu Stoian, *Inscripţiile din Scythia Minor Greceşti şi Latine* (2 vols.; Bucharest: Academiei Republicii Socialiste Romania, 1983-1987).

whose center was near modern Nikopol. In the second century B.C. Neapolis was the capital of Scythia, which flourished economically, politically and culturally, only to collapse in the third century A.D. under the pressure of the Goths. The Greeks and Romans regarded Scythia as a barren steppe in which nomadic cattle herders and archers lived, wild and uncivilized people who scalped foreigners and drank wine without diluting it with water. The Scythians were a popular theme for many Sophists in the early imperial period: since they were regarded as a people who had no cities of their own, the philosophers could discuss the advantages and the disadvantages of the Greek city with rhetorical effectiveness with reference to the Scythians.[923]

The possibility that Jewish Christians engaged in missionary work in Scythia in the first century should not be discounted. Jewish communities are attested in the Greek colonies on the north coast of the Black Sea, which the Greeks called *Pontos Euxeinos* (Lat., *Pontus Euxinus*). We do not know exactly how far Greek influence and the Greek language had penetrated into inner Scythia. We do know, however, that many Scythians appreciated Greek culture: tombs discovered in Chertomlyk (the region Dnepropetrovsk, far from the Black Sea) contained depictions of scenes from Homer's *Iliad*.[924] The following Scythian cities could have been easily reached by early Christian missionaries who were determined to reach the northern "end" of the earth.

Chersonesos (Χερρόνησος; near mod. Sevastopol),[925] on the southwestern cape of the Crimean, probably would have been the base for missionary work in Scythia, as Neapolis, the Scythian capital, was only 65 km northeast of Chersonesos. Strabo relates that Chersonesos was a colony of Herakleia in Pontus (7.4.2). Recent finds confirm that the city was founded in 422 B.C. and that it was engaged in regular trade with the cities on the south coast of the Black Sea. In the second century Chersonesos was forced to ask Mithradates VI for help against attacks of the Scythians under King Palak. When Pontus became Roman in 63 B.C., Chersonesos continued to be controlled by the Pontic dynasty, which formed a vassal state in East Pontus under Deiotaros. Since the time of Nero a Roman garrison was stationed in the city, but its Greek character was maintained. Numerous remains survive: city walls, the mint (fourth century B.C.), place of wine production, pottery workshops, cisterns for the salting of fish, baths, a theater (ca. 200 B.C.), an odeion, houses and an inscription with the oath of the citizens (third century B.C.).

Neapolis (mod. Keremenchik, Ukraine),[926] in the south of the Crimean peninsula, was

---

[923]Philostratus, *Vit. soph.* 572-573, 620; Dio Chrysostom, *Or.* 13.32. See David C. Braund, "The Black Sea Region and Hellenism under the Early Empire," in Alcock 1997, 121-36, esp. 127.

[924]See Heinen 2001, 10-15.

[925]C. Danoff, "Chersonesos 3," *KP* 1:1145; M. L. Bernhard and Z. Sztetyllo, "Neapolis Scythica," *PECS* 221-22; D. C. Braund, "Chersonesos 3," *OCD* 321; I. von Bredow and S. R. Tokhtas'ev, "Chersonesos 3," *DNP* 2:1118; John Hind, "Megarian Colonisation in the Western Half of the Black Sea (Sister- and Daughter-Cities of Herakleia)," in Tsetskhladze 1998, 131-52, esp. 141-51; Sergei Y. Saprykin, "The Foundation of Tauric Chersonesus," in ibid., 227-48; S. Y. Vnukov, "The North-Western Crimea: An Historical-Archaeological Essay," in Tsetskhladze 2001, 149-75; on the first century see ibid., 171-73.

[926]Bernhard and Sztetyllo, "Neapolis Scythica," *PECS* 615-16; D. Braund, *BAGRW* 337, map 23.

the capital of the Scythians since the third century B.C. (Strabo 7.4.7). The city comprised an area of 20 ha and was surrounded by city walls 2.5 m wide (in some places 11-12 m wide). The main gate of the city was flanked by two towers. The monumental tomb (8.5 by 8.1 m) with seventy-two graves perhaps was the burial site of the Scythian kings, who might have been buried here from the second century B.C. to the second century A.D. The graves contained frescoes that depict scenes from the daily life of the Scythians. Inscriptions and graffiti leave open the possibility that there was a permanent Greek settlement in the city.

   Olbia (ʿ Ολβία; mod. Parutino, Ukraine),[927] to the west of Crimea on the mouth of the Hypanis River (mod. Bug) near the mouth of the Borysthenes (mod. Dnieper), was founded in 550 B.C. The agora and a temple date to the sixth century B.C. Olbia was one of the most important cities of the northern coast of the Black Sea, a trading post for the export of wheat, fish and slaves to Greece. Olbia, with five thousand Greek citizens, flourished in the fourth century B.C. Olbia was attacked by the Sarmatae and by Scythians in the second century B.C., and it was burned down in the catastrophic attack of the Getae in the first century B.C. Herodotus visited Olbia (4.78.79), as did the philosopher Dio Chrysostom (perhaps in the summer of A.D. 97, on his travels through Scythia to the Getae in northern Thrace [*Or.* 36.1]). Dio describes a city in decline that maintains its Greek traditions—for this philosopher, whom Domitian had banned from Rome, perhaps it was the end of the world to which the god Apollo had sent him through the oracle in Delphi (*Or.* 36.1-9).[928] During the imperial period Olbia was a small town. Dio mentions that Homer's *Iliad* was popular and that the philosophy of Plato was known in Olbia, but he deplores the influence of the barbarian world on the manner in which Greek was spoken (*Or.* 36.9). At the beginning of the second century A.D. a certain M. Ulpos Pyrrhos was the president of the *stratēgoi* of the city: his name and his function indicate that he was a Greek aristocrat who was a Roman citizen; he had an Iranian (Sarmatian) father and dedicated a statue to the gods Apollon Prostates and Nike.[929] The surviving ruins include the city wall, a large city gate, a temple of Zeus (14 by 7 m), a temple of Apollo Delphinios (30-35 by 16 m), the agora with a colonnaded hall (45 by 17 m), and nearly two thousand graves. Olbia had a Jewish community: an inscription documents the renovation of a synagogue (*CIJ* I² 682; *IJudO* I BS1).[930]

   Borysthenes (Βορυσθένης; mod. Berezan),[931] about 40 km from Olbia, with which the city used to be identified, was a small island at the mouth of the Bug River in the Black Sea. The site was visited as early as the seventh century B.C. by Greek merchants, partic-

---

[927]C. Danoff, "Olbia 1," *KP* 4:273; Bernhard and Sztetyllo, *PECS* 642-43; I. von Bredow, "Olbia 1," *DNP* 8:1569-70; N. Ehrhardt, *Milet und seine Kolonien* (Frankfurt: Lang, 1988), 74-79; David C. Braund, *OCD* 1063; idem, "The Black Sea Region," 126-31; idem, *BAGRW* 354, map 23, s.v. "Borysthenes/Olbia"); J. G. Vinogradov and S. D. Kryziskij, *Olbia: Eine altgriechische Stadt im nordwestlichen Schwarzmeerraum* (Mnemosyne, bibliotheca classica Batava, Suppl. 149; Leiden: Brill, 1995); cf. Tsetskhladze 2001.

[928]See Braund, "The Black Sea Region," 127.

[929]*I. PontEux* I² 93. See Heinen 2001, 21-22.

[930]See L. Levine 2000, 112, 403, 590.

[931]C. Danoff, *KP* 1:931; I. von Bredow, *DNP* 2:750; Sergei L. Solovyov, *Ancient Berezan: The Architecture, History and Culture of the First Greek Colony in the Northern Black Sea* (Colloquia Pontica 4; Brill: Leiden, 1999); idem, "Archaic Berezan: Historical-Archaeological Essay," in Tsetskhladze 1998, 205-25; idem, "The Archaeological Excavation on the Berezan Settlement (1987-1991)," in Tsetskhladze 2001, 117-41; also G. R. Tsetskhladze, "Greek Colonisation of the Black Sea Area," in Tsetskhladze 1998, 19-22.

ularly from Miletus, who looked for fish, wood, metal and wheat. Borysthenes generally is regarded as the oldest Greek colony on the northern coast of the Black Sea. In the first century A.D. the island was the state sanctuary of Achilles Pontarches controlled by Olbia.[932] There is no evidence for a Jewish presence in Borysthenes.

Pantikapaion (Παντικάπαιον; Bosp[h]orus; mod. Kerch, Ukraine),[933] on the eastern side of the Crimean peninsula on the western Cimmerian Bosporus, was founded by colonists from Miletus. The city minted its own coins since the sixth century B.C. The unification of the Greek cities on both sides of the Bosporus led to the foundation of the Bosporan kingdom in the fifth century B.C. Pantikapaion had a good harbor and a fertile hinterland; the city was a center of the fish export and of the cultivation of wheat and wine. Between the fourth and the second centuries B.C. the city was the largest trans-shipment port in the area. The kings promoted Greek culture; the main god of the city was Apollo Ietros, and temples dedicated to Demeter, Cybele and Dionysos stood on the acropolis and the agora. The city was severely damaged in an earthquake in 63 B.C. and was rebuilt in the first century A.D. The surviving ruins include the city walls, an Ionic temple (20 by 40 m), the votive inscription of a temple dedicated to the cult of the Bosporan king Aspurgos (dated A.D. 23) and monumental tombs. An inscription dated to A.D. 81 confirms the existence of a Jewish community: "[Date, Name] I release in the synagogue: Elpis (a?), my slave brought up in my house. She shall be left unmolested and unchallenged (in her freedom) by any (of my) heirs, but she shall adhere to the synagogue [χωρὶς τοῦ προσκαρτερεῖν τῇ προσευχῇ]. The protection (of her freedom) is vouched for by the community (synagogue) of the Jews and the God-fearers [ἐπιτροπευούσης τῆς συναγωγῆς τῶν Ἰουδαίων καὶ θεὸν σέβων]."[934] This means that there was a Jewish community in Pantikapaion in whose synagogue God-fearers had an important role, as indicated by the fact that they are mentioned right next to the Jews.[935] The owner of the slave girl evidently was a wealthy woman who was a rather self-confident member of the Jewish community and wanted to have this documented in writing. "This inscription is thus an impressive testimony to the fact that the Jewish communities may even have offered the status of 'God-fearers' to a Gentile public in order to preserve their prestige and existence."[936] An inscription of the third century documents the construction of a synagogue (*CIJ* I[2] 682; *IJudO* I BS1).

Gorgippia (Γοργιππία; Sindikos Limēn; mod. Anapa, Ukraine),[937] on the north coast of the Pontus Euxinus, was a port city on the eastern side of the Cimmerian Bosporus in the

---

[932]Solovyov, *Ancient Berezan,* 117-18 (fig. 106); idem, "Archaeological Excavation on the Berezan Settlement," 137-38 (figs. 12-13).

[933]C. Danoff, PWSup 9 (1962): 1118-24; idem, *KP* 4:477-78; M. L. Bernhard and Z. Sztetyllo, "Neapolis Scythica," *PECS* 672-73; D. C. Braund, *OCD* 1107; I. von Bredow, *DNP* 9:273; Schürer 3:36-38. See Braund, *BAGRW* 1246, map 87.

[934]*CIJ* I[2] 683a N.6 (= *CIRB* 71; *IJudO* I BS7); see H. Bellen, *JAC* 8/9 (1965-1966): 171-76; Wander 1998, 111-12. The expression θεὸν σέβων (*theon sebōn*) in the last line evidently is a mistake: the stonemason probably misread the rare word θεοσεβής (*theosebēs*) in the text that was given to him. See also the inscriptions *CIRB* 70 = *CIJ* I[2] 683; *CIRB* 72 = *CIJ* I[2] 683b; *CIRB* 73 = *CIJ* I[2] 684, as well as the fragmentary funerary inscriptions *CIRB* 735 = *CIJ* I[2] 685, 686, 687, 689. A bilingual tombstone with a Hebrew and a Greek inscription dates to the fourth century (*CIRB* 736 = *CIJ* I[2] 688). The tombstone of a certain Saul is decorated with the menorah (*CIRB* 743 = *CIJ* I[2] 689a).

[935]See Figueras 1990, 202-3; L. Levine 2000, 112 n. 195, 115, 590; Noy, in *IJudO* I, 2004, 264-94.

[936]Wander 1998, 113-14.

[937]Danoff, *KP* 2:851-52; Bernhard and Sztetyllo, "Neapolis Scythica," *PECS* 360-61; A. Plontke-Lüning, *DNP* 4:1153; Schürer 3:37-38; cf. D. Braund, *BAGRW* 1205, map 84.

territory of the Sindae, situated on the Taman peninsula (Strabo 11.2.10). Gorgippia was founded by colonists from Miletus and had the usual infrastructure of a Greek polis. Inscriptions document games dedicated to Hermes. After flourishing in the fourth and third centuries B.C. and subsequent decline, Gorgippia prospered again in the first and second centuries A.D. The trade in wheat was particularly important. Two inscriptions dated A.D. 41 evidently are Jewish,[938] and certainly so is an inscription dated A.D. 59.[939]

People in the first century knew the region that today we call China, but the views about the Seres people were rather vague, and there were no direct travel routes. Even later traditions of the church do not indicate that any of the apostles traveled to China to preach the gospel.

The earliest presence of Christians in China is connected with the establishment of churches in Bactria, Persia and central Asia in the third and fourth centuries.[940] The earliest archaeological evidence for Christians in China is a Syrian-Chinese inscription from Siangfu, discovered in 1625, that confirms the mission of the Nestorians to China. A recent discovery 80 km southwest of Xi'an, the old capital of China, confirms the presence of Christians in this region for the year A.D. 638.[941]

---

[938]*CIRB* 1123 = *CIJ* I² 690 = *IJudO* I BS20; *CIRB* 1126 = *CIJ* I² 690a = *IJudO* I BS22. See Schürer 3:37; Trebilco 1991, 136; Levinskaya 1996, 239-40; Binder 1999, 274-76 (with a discussion of the objections against the Jewish character of these inscriptions); L. Levine 2000, 114-15.

[939]*CIRB* 1127 = *IJudO* I BS24 (manumission of a slave).

[940]See A. Mingana, "The Early Spread of Christianity in Central Asia and the Far East," *BJRL* 9 (1925): 297-371; Kenneth S. Latourette, *A History of Christian Missions in China* (New York: Macmillan, 1929), 46-48; Frend 1968/70, 48-49.

[941]Bay Fang, "Did Christianity Thrive in China? Digging for Evidence in an Ancient Church," *U.S. News & World Report,* March 5, 2001, 51.

23

SUMMARY

The Hellenistic, Greek-speaking Jewish Christians of Jerusalem seem to have been the first followers of Jesus who understood and proclaimed the consequences of the death and resurrection of Jesus the Messiah for the identity of Israel the people of God. Stephen and his friends understood that the biblical conviction that YHWH does not dwell in temples made by human hands has consequences—now, in the days of the Messiah, in the time of the arrival of the kingdom of God—for the temple in Jerusalem and for the sacrificial cult practiced there. They understood that God had revealed himself for the salvation of Israel and of the world in Jesus of Nazareth, the Messiah from Galilee, who died on the cross and rose from the dead on the third day. They understood that this means that salvation—forgiveness of sins, atonement of guilt, fellowship with YHWH—is possible now, in the last days, only in connection with Jesus the Messiah. They understood that the temple is no longer the place of God's atoning presence. They understood that the sacrifices that the Mosaic law prescribed no longer forgave sins. Thus they proclaimed that forgiveness of sins and obedience to Israel's God are irrevocably tied to the name of Jesus the Messiah.

If the Torah is no longer the normative center of Israel's relationship with Yahweh, if the temple is no longer the central place of Yahweh's atoning presence, if Judea is no longer holier than any other land, if God's salvation is no longer concentrated exclusively on Israel and its traditional institutions of salvation, if God's merciful presence can now be experienced wherever people repent and depend on Jesus the Messiah for salvation—if these convictions are held deeply and consistently and joyfully, then the path to world mission has been opened up. Jesus' surprising directive to go to all nations as far as the ends of the world, rather than to wait for the nations to come as repentant pilgrims to Jerusalem, can now be fulfilled in an equally surprising way: non-Jews, whether sympathizers, God-fearers or polytheists, no longer have to become Jews and join Israel through circumcision and submission to the Torah in order to receive forgiveness of sins and enjoy life in submission to and fellowship with the only true and living God; rather, they can join and be integrated into the messianic people of God as *ethnē,* as Gentiles. This new, revolutionary mode of realizing God's promise to Abraham, in whose name all families of the earth were to be blessed, was a theologically consistent corollary of the redefinition of the significance and the role of the temple and the Torah in the messianic era that had dawned.

This new view of temple and Torah, initiated by Stephen and other Jewish Christians from Jerusalem, proved a major precondition for an effective outreach to the Gentiles. When the Hellenistic Jewish Christians had to leave Jerusalem after Stephen's death in A.D. 31/32, they immediately and matter-of-factly proclaimed the message of Jesus the Messiah in non-Jewish regions and cities: in Samaria, to an Ethiopian; in the Greek cities of the coastal plain, at least in Lydda, Joppa, Caesarea, Ptolemais and perhaps in Ashdod; and also in Syria, at least in Damascus and in Antioch the capital of the Roman province. And it is possible that some preached the message of Jesus the Messiah in Italy and in Rome at a very early date.

The earliest missionaries may have been the Hellenistic Jewish Christians from Jerusalem, Stephen and his friends and like-minded believers. However, the apostles preached the good news of Jesus the Messiah both in Jerusalem and in regions outside of Judea at an early date as well. We know that Peter preached, with immense success—if Luke's account gives any indication of what happened after Easter—the message of Jesus the Messiah in Jerusalem, both publicly in Solomon's Portico on the temple mount and privately in the homes of followers of Jesus who regularly met to learn and to fellowship. Soon we find Peter in Samaria and in the cities of the coastal plain, then in Caesarea, the Gentile capital of the Roman province of Judea, where Cornelius, a soldier in the Roman army, and his family are converted to faith in Jesus. Peter understood, as the result of a divine revelation, that the Mosaic food laws have been revoked by God when Gentiles grasp and accept God's revelation in Jesus and when they repent and become members of the messianic people of God.

Luke describes Peter as the first Gentile missionary. The first conversion of a Gentile that he narrates in the book of Acts is the conversion of the Roman Cornelius, who responds both to God's initiating revelation and to Peter's explanation of the good news of Jesus the Messiah. Luke emphasizes the missionary activity of Peter among Gentiles when he provides an account of the apostolic council, with Paul and Barnabas seemingly playing a more minor role at the council. Luke begins his report of the missionary work of Paul, who focuses on both Jews and Gentiles only after Peter's activity in Caesarea. It is unclear whether Luke's literary intentions precisely reflect historical reality, since he reports selectively, omitting Paul's early outreach in Arabia, Syria and Cilicia. It cannot be ruled out that Peter's mission in Caesarea coincided with Paul's mission in Arabia or Syria-Cilicia, or took place at a slightly later date: Paul initiated missionary work immediately after his conversion in A.D. 32/33, preaching in Damascus, Arabia, Syria and Cilicia among Jews and evidently also among Gentiles (see §26), while Peter's mission in Samaria and in the coastal plain probably should be dated around A.D. 34, and the mission to Caesarea perhaps to A.D. 37.

Peter left Jerusalem in A.D. 41 at a time of revolutionary ferment in Judea and particularly in Jerusalem, resulting from the intended sacrilege to be committed by Emperor Caligula in the temple in Jerusalem. Herod Agrippa I had increased the pressure on the followers of Jesus: he executed the apostle James, and he arrested Peter with the intention of executing him too. Agrippa's motives probably were connected with his desire to consolidate his acceptance as the new Jewish king. He seems to have believed that this could be achieved by suppressing the Christians, who did not honor the holiness of the temple as law and custom prescribed, using the furor in the population about Caligula's disrespect for Israel's traditions. Peter left Jerusalem in A.D. 41 for an unknown destination. He may have gone to Antioch in Syria, or to Rome, or to northern Asia Minor. It is clear, however, that Peter remained active as a missionary, evidently until his death in A.D. 67 (?) in Rome. Paul attests to the continued, long-term missionary work of the "first" apostle: he mentions the missionary travels of Peter and his wife in his first letter to the Corinthian Christians, written in A.D. 54.

When Peter left Jerusalem in A.D. 41, most if not all of the other apostles seem to have left the Jewish capital as well. The early tradition of a strategic "missionary conference" of the Twelve, who decided in which regions they should engage in missionary work, may contain a historical core. When Luke refers to the Jerusalem church after the year A.D. 41, we encounter elders as leaders of the Jerusalem church, no longer the apostles. If this reconstruction is correct, then the striking fact emerges that the Twelve understood themselves not primarily as organizers or coordinators of the work of the church but rather as missionaries. After the churches in Jerusalem and in Judea, and presumably in Galilee and also in Samaria, with thousands of believers as members, had been consolidated, they were willing to hand over all leadership responsibilities to other leading Christians. Another early tradition that may be historically authentic states that relatives of Jesus assumed leading roles in the Jerusalem church: first James, and after James's death in A.D. 63, Symeon bar Cleopas.

Jewish Christians from Jerusalem, and soon probably believers from Judea and Galilee, proclaimed the gospel in their home areas and "abroad": they established communities of believers in Jesus in Syria and on Cyprus; in Rome and in Puteoli, and perhaps in Herculaneum and in Pompeii; in the province of Asia in Smyrna, Pergamon, Thyatira, Sardis and Philadelphia; in cities in the provinces of Cappadocia, Pontus and Bithynia; perhaps in Macedonia and in Achaia; probably in Egypt, in India and perhaps even in Scythia. The information that we have about the early Christian missionaries who preached in these regions is sparse, and the historical value of the available literary sources often is doubtful. There is no doubt, however, that the missionary work of the early believers in Jesus the Messiah in the first century led to the establishment of Christian communities in dozens of cities of the Roman Empire.